UNDERSTANDING
ART

10TH EDITION
LOIS FICHNER-RATHUS
THE COLLEGE OF NEW JERSEY

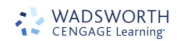
WADSWORTH
CENGAGE Learning·

Australia · Brazil · Japan · Korea · Mexico · Singapore · Spain · United Kingdom · United States

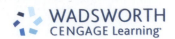

Understanding Art, Tenth Edition
Lois Fichner-Rathus

Publisher: Clark Baxter

Senior Development Editor: Sharon Adams Poore

Assistant Editor: Ashley Bargende

Editorial Assistant: Elizabeth Newell

Associate Media Editor: Kimberly Apfelbaum

Marketing Manager: Jeanne M. Heston

Marketing Coordinator: Klaira Markenzon

Senior Marketing Communications Manager: Heather Baxley

Senior Content Project Manager: Lianne Ames

Senior Art Director: Cate Rickard Barr

Print Buyer: Mary Beth Hennebury

Rights Acquisition Specialist: Mandy Groszko

Production Service: Lachina Publishing Services

Text and Cover Designer: Lisa Kuhn

Cover Image: Anish Kapoor, *Tall Tree and the Eye*, 2009, The Royal Academy, London. Photograph: Peter Macdiarmid/Getty Images.

Compositor: Lachina Publishing Services

> For product information and technology assistance, contact us at
> **Cengage Learning Customer & Sales Support, 1-800-354-9706**
> For permission to use material from this text or product,
> submit all requests online at **www.cengage.com/permissions**.
> Further permissions questions can be emailed to
> **permissionrequest@cengage.com**.

Library of Congress Control Number: 2011936463

ISBN-13: 978-1-111-83695-5

ISBN-10: 1-111-83695-7

Wadsworth
20 Channel Center Street
Boston, MA 02210
USA

Cengage Learning is a leading provider of customized learning solutions with office locations around the globe, including Singapore, the United Kingdom, Australia, Mexico, Brazil and Japan. Locate your local office at **international.cengage.com/region**

Cengage Learning products are represented in Canada by Nelson Education, Ltd.

For your course and learning solutions, visit **www.cengage.com**.

Purchase any of our products at your local college store or at our preferred online store **www.cengagebrain.com**.
Instructors: Please visit **login.cengage.com** and log in to access instructor-specific resources.

Printed in the United States of America
2 3 4 5 15 14 13 12

The tenth edition of *Understanding Art* is dedicated to my husband, Spence, and our daughters, Allyn, Jordan, and Taylor.

ABOUT THE COVER

As each edition of your textbook has gotten underway, I've challenged myself to choose a cover image that symbolizes, in a visually compelling way, the concept of *Understanding Art* and the essence of my perspective as an author. Sometimes, the idiom "you can't judge a book by its cover," just doesn't apply. I believe that the cover of a textbook can communicate a great deal.

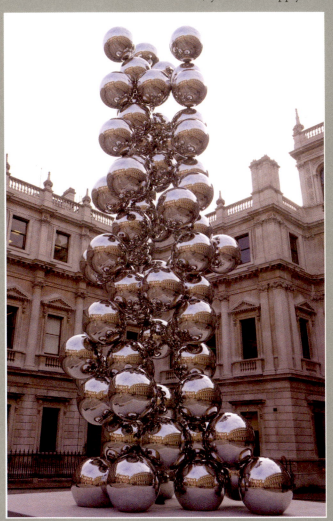

ANISH KAPOOR (2009). *Tall Tree and the Eye.* Stainless steel over carbon. Approx. 42'8" x 16'5" x 16'5". Installation view, Royal Academy Courtyard, London, England.

My approach to *Understanding Art* emphasizes equally the visual elements and history of art; it balances the historical and the contemporary; and it represents the diversity of art and culture. The cover of the tenth edition encompasses in a single, dynamic image, all of the things that Understanding Art aims to do.

What you see on the cover is a detail of Anish Kapoor's monumental steel sculpture, *Tall Tree and the Eye*, exhibited in the courtyard of the Royal Academy of Arts in London in 2009. Seventy-six shiny and seemingly weightless spheres nest and rise to form a tower that reaches more than 40 feet into the air—as tall as the walls of the building that embraces it. Reflected a myriad of times in the highly polished surfaces of this contemporary work—designed by an artist raised in Mumbai and educated in British schools of art and design—is The Royal Academy of Arts, one of the oldest and most venerable art institutions in London. Established by King George III in 1758, it has counted more than a few artists featured in this book among its members: the celebrated eighteenth-century portrait painter Thomas Gainsborough (page 407); the innovative architect Richard Rogers (page 473); David Hockney (page 129), a contemporary English artist whose vast range of mediums include everything from painting to stage design; Tracey Emin (page 545), one of the controversial YBAs (Young British Artists); and Kapoor himself (page 207).

All of its members are practicing artists who, in all of their diversity, have committed to a common goal of the Academy's founders: "to promote the arts of design."

Regardless of how tenuous the connections may sometimes appear between the art of our times and the art of the past, or the art of one's culture and that of the rest of the world, the frame of art history expands to fit the picture.

CONTENTS

PART V. ART THROUGH THE AGES

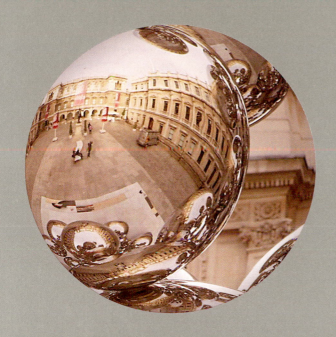

Everyone wants to understand art. Why not try to understand the song of a bird? Why does one love the night, flowers, everything around one without trying to understand them? But in the case of a painting, people have to understand.

—Pablo Picasso

PREFACE

There is a note of frustration in Picasso's statement, reflecting perhaps the burden of having to explain his paintings to viewers who were trying desperately to understand them. Perhaps he was concerned that some of the "indescribable" in art—that which mesmerizes, enchants, frightens, and delights—would be, quite literally, lost in translation. Maybe he was guarding against affixing meaning to his work that he as the artist never intended. Picasso seems to suggest, in this quote, that mystery enhances experience and that too much knowledge will compromise the authenticity of the relationship between art and the viewer. Do you think Picasso was right?

Here we are, embarking together on the study of art and art history between the covers of a book called *Understanding Art*. Maybe we can declare Picasso's view half right, and it can serve as our cue for how to confront what we are about to see. A textbook on art is not like a textbook in other academic disciplines. Yes, there is a special vocabulary of art. Yes, this vocabulary is woven into a language that, once learned, enables us to better verbalize the visual. But the most important aspect of an art book is its images, because a student's journey toward understanding art ought always to begin with looking.

Think of this art appreciation textbook as your "*i*-book"—it begins with looking at *i*mages. Having said that, *learning to look* is equally important for art appreciation, and that's where some other "*i*-words" play an important role: *i*nformation, *i*nsight, and *i*nterpretation. We gather information about how a work of art is conceived and constructed using elements, design principles, composition, content, style, and symbolism. We explore the motives of artists and the historical, social, political, and even personal contexts in which a work of art came into existence. These investigations will lend insight into the complex factors contributing to the creation of works of art. And as we gather confidence in our knowledge and insights, we will turn more comfortably to the dimension of interpretation—your dimension. It is here where the "I" really counts, for we all bring the weight of our own experience to our interpretations, our unique perceptions to our likes or dislikes of a work of art.

Picasso said, in the same interview, "People who try to explain pictures are usually barking up the wrong tree." The words *explain* and *understand*, though, have very different meanings. One can argue that only artists can *explain* their work, can make intelligible something that is not known or not understood. But *understanding* is defined as full awareness or knowledge that is achieved through an intellectual or emotional process—including the ability to extract meaning or to interpret. The ability to *appreciate*, or to perceive the value or worth of something from a discriminating perspective, then, is the consummate reward of understanding.

WHAT'S NEW IN THIS EDITION

In the spirit of the conviction that "understanding art ought always to begin with looking," the tenth edition features more than 100 new works and a new design that has allowed for the enlarging of key works and monuments that comprise the core of the text's art program. Two examples: half of the works in the chapter on drawing are new; the last chapter—**Art in the Twenty-First Century: A Global Perspective**—reflects the fluid nature of the contemporary art scene with 24 new works. In many instances, superior photographs of key monuments have been acquired and we have been as diligent as possible regarding color accuracy.

In this new edition, Chapter 15, now **The Age of Faith**, has been revised to integrate discussions of the world's Abrahamic religions—Judaism, Christianity, and Islam. Many topics and art historical periods include new sections: Chapter 11, **Architecture**, features a timely discussion of "Green Buildings"; Chapter 13, **Art of the Ancients**, now includes the "Art of Ancient China and India"; Chapter 21, **The Twentieth Century: Post-War to Postmodern**, has a new section on "Conceptual Art."

We are all aware that slides in the classroom are poor substitutes for real-life encounters with paintings and sculpture, or for the perception of form and space that comes with physically standing in a building. There are new Art Tours on Los Angeles and Chicago, which, along with the text's already familiar tours, will encourage students to visit cities and their art collections in the United States and abroad, and to be aware of the ubiquity of art and design in their lives.

THE APPROACH OF UNDERSTANDING ART

The tenth edition of *Understanding Art,* as earlier editions, is intended to work for both students and professors. *Understanding Art* continues to serve as a tool to help organize and enlighten this demanding, often whirlwind-like course. My goal has been to write a book that would do it all: edify and inform students and, at the same time, keep them engaged, animated, and inspired—while at the same time meeting instructors' desire for comprehensive exposition. All in all, *Understanding Art* contains a fully balanced approach to appreciating art. The understanding and appreciation of art are enhanced by familiarity with three areas of art: the language of art (visual elements, principles of design, and style), the nature of the mediums used in art, and the history of art.

FEATURES

The tenth edition of *Understanding Art* contains unique features that stimulate student interest, emphasize key points in art fundamentals and art history, highlight contemporary events in art, and reflect the ways in which professors teach.

Compare + Contrast   These features show two or more works of art side by side and phrase questions that help students focus on stylistic and technical similarities and differences. They parallel the time-honored pedagogical technique of presenting works in class for comparison and contrast. For example, "Compare and Contrast Wood's *American Gothic* with Rosenthal's *He Said . . . She Said*" in Chapter 4 shows how artists may use different styles to illustrate themes about similar subjects.

CourseMate includes interactive quizzes directly linked to all the Compare + Contrast features.

A Closer Look   These features offer insights into artists' personalities and delve into various topics in greater depth. In Chapter 5, "Life, Death, and Dwelling in the Deep South" highlights an African American artist's portrayal of the organic relationship between a woman and her home in South Carolina. Chapter 19's "Why Did van Gogh Cut Off His Ear?" offers a number of possible explanations, including psychodynamic hypotheses, for why the Postimpressionist mutilated himself. In Chapter 9, visit the Storm King Art Center, a 500-acre sculpture garden in New York State.

A Closer Look features are expanded upon through the use of related web links on CourseMate.

ArtTour The tenth edition includes ArtTours on the cities of New York, Washington D.C., Jerusalem, Rome, Dallas/Fort Worth, Florence, London, Chicago, Paris, and Los Angeles. Each ArtTour is rich in photographs and works of art. The ArtTours are no mere lists of works and sites and museums in these cities. Instead, the tours literally walk students through the cities, providing them with routes they can take to benefit from the cultural riches that are available. The ArtTours in New York, Washington, D.C., Chicago, Dallas/Fort Worth, and Los Angeles will help many students appreciate the art and architecture that are situated close to home.

The companion CourseMate expands on the ArtTours with helpful "travel-guide" information, such as additional photos, maps, restaurant guides, and links to useful web pages. The tours are meant to encourage students to travel as well as to guide them once they have reached their destinations.

Quotations Quotations at the top of pages by artists, critics, and others allow students to "get into the minds" of those people closest to the art world. For example, Chapter 22, **Art in the Twenty-First Century**, includes quotations by Damien Hirst, Shelly Silver, Wangechi Mutu, and Kara Walker.

Glossary Key terms are boldfaced in the text and defined in a glossary at the end of the textbook. An "Audio Glossary" also appears in CourseMate.

THE CONTENTS OF THE TENTH EDITION OF UNDERSTANDING ART

The book is organized into the following parts:

I. Introduction The first chapter of the text, **What Is Art?**, helps the student arrive at a definition of art by discussing the things that art does, from enhancing our environment to protesting injustice and raising social consciousness.

II. The Language of Art Chapters 2–4 provide comprehensive discussion of the visual elements of art, principles of design, and style, form, and content. The language of art is then applied throughout the remainder of the text in discussions of mediums and surveys of art through the ages and throughout the world.

III. Two-Dimensional Mediums Chapters 5–8, on drawing, painting, printmaking, and imaging, explain how artists combine the visual elements of art to create two-dimensional compositions. The mediums discussed are as traditional as drawing a pencil across a sheet of paper and as innovative as spray painting color fields and clicking a mouse to access a menu of electronic techniques and design elements.

IV. Three-Dimensional Mediums Chapters 9–12 discuss the opportunities and issues provided by three-dimensional art forms, including sculpture, site-specific art, architecture, and craft and design.

V. Art through the Ages Chapters 13–18 contain a solid core of art history on the development of art from ancient times to the dawn of the modern era. Chapter 15, **The Age of Faith**, includes new material on Islamic Art. Chapter 18, **Non-Western Perspectives**, introduces students to art forms beyond the Western tradition, including the art of Africa, the South Pacific, and the Americas; the Islamic art of the Near, Middle, and Far East; Indian art; and the art of China and Japan. The chapter offers a broadening experience, as students learn that much of this art cannot be appreciated by means of the same concepts and standards that are applied to Western Art.

VI. Art in Modern and Postmodern Times Chapters 19–21 examine the great changes that have occurred in the world of art since the late eighteenth century. These chapters attempt to answer the question, "Just what is modern about modern art?" Whereas some artists have rejected the flatness of the canvas and moved art into innumerable new directions, others have maintained traditional paths. Controversy and conflict are part of the modern history of art. But movements such as Postmodern art and Deconstructivist architecture also make it possible to speak of the "modern world and beyond." Although nobody can say exactly where art is going, these chapters discuss the movements and works that appear to be vital at the current moment.

VII. Art in the Twenty-First Century: A Global Perspective Chapter 22 shows how the phenomenon of globalization has created a new art world in which cultures are no longer distant from one another and people and places are no longer as separate as they once were. As a result, we have trends such as hybridity, appropriation, high art and low culture, and post-colonialism in the arts. We see how these trends are expressed today within—and without—various cultural traditions around the world.

STUDENT RESOURCES

CourseMate with eBook   provides an ebook for interactive and portable reading, as well as many study aids to help make studying more efficient. Zoomable image flashcards provide the easiest way to study for exams, and to learn more about each work through links to quizzing, downloadable student guides to studying, related video, audio, websites, interactive tutorials and exercises, and ArtTours. Videos include demonstrations of various studio art techniques, YouTube clips, topical video podcasts, and three-dimensional panoramic views of architecture.

Thinking and Writing about Art   *Thinking and Writing about Art,* also written by Lois Fichner-Rathus, enhances students' critical thinking and interpretive skills.

INSTRUCTOR RESOURCES

PowerLecture with Digital Image Library   Bring digital images into the classroom with this class presentation tool that makes it easy to assemble, edit, and present customized lectures for your course using Microsoft® PowerPoint® or your preferred presentation software. Available on a flash drive, PowerLecture with Digital Image Library provides high-resolution images (maps, diagrams, and the fine art images from the text) for lecture presentations, either in an easy-to-use PowerPoint presentation format, or in individual file formats compatible with other image-viewing software. A zoom feature allows you to magnify selected portions of an image for more detailed display in class or you can display images side by side for comparison and contrast. You can easily customize your classroom presentation by adding your own images to those from the text.

The PowerLecture also includes an electronic Instructor's Manual, and a Test Bank with multiple-choice, matching, short-answer, and essay questions in ExamView® computerized format.

WebTutor™ on Blackboard and WebCT   With the WebTutor text-specific, preformatted content and total flexibility, you can easily create and manage your own custom course website. Instructors can provide virtual office hours, post syllabi, set up threaded discussions, track student progress with the quizzing material, and much more.

ACKNOWLEDGMENTS

I consider myself fortunate to have studied with a fine group of artists, art historians, and art professionals who helped shape my love of art and my thinking about art throughout my career. *Understanding Art* would not have taken its present form and might not have come into being without the broad knowledge, skills, and dedication of James S. Ackerman, Stanford Anderson, Wayne V. Anderson, Whitney Chadwick, Michael Graves, George Heard Hamilton, Ann Sutherland Harris, Julius S. Held, Sam Hunter, Henry A. Millon, Konrad Oberhuber, John C. Overbeck, Michael Rinehart, Andrew C. Ritchie, Mark W. Roskill, Theodore Roszak, Miriam Schapiro, Bernice Steinbaum, and Jack Tworkov.

I wish to thank those reviewers who helped to revise this edition: Joy Bertinuson, American River College; Don Bevirt, Southwestern Illinois College; Sandra Bird, Kennesaw State University; Suzaan Boettger, Bergen Community College; Melanie Eubanks, Jones County Junior College; Stephen Henderson, Quinnipiac University; Aditi Samarth, Richland College; Clarence Talley, Prairie View A&M University; Paul Valadez, University of Texas-Pan American; and the nearly one hundred instructors who responded to our survey regarding online teaching and online resources.

The tenth edition of *Understanding Art* is also indebted to the support and expertise of a fine group of Wadsworth publishing professionals. Let me begin by acknowledging the support of Sean Wakely, executive vice president, Cengage Learning Arts and Sciences; Clark Baxter, publisher; Sharon Adams Poore, senior development editor; Lianne Ames, senior content project manager; Kimberly Apfelbaum, media editor; Ashley Bargende, assistant editor; Elizabeth Newell, editorial assistant; Cate Rikard Barr, senior art director; and Jeanne Heston, senior marketing manager. I would also like to thank Pam Connell of Lachina Publishing Services for doing the impossible—and in a timely manner.

LOIS FICHNER-RATHUS

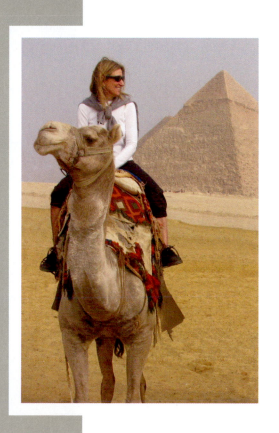

ABOUT THE AUTHOR

Lois Fichner-Rathus is Professor of Art in the Art Department of The College of New Jersey. She holds a combined undergraduate degree in fine arts and art history, an M.A. from the Williams College Graduate Program in the History of Art, and a Ph.D. in the History, Theory, and Criticism of Art from the Massachusetts Institute of Technology. Her areas of specialization include contemporary art, feminist art history and criticism, and modern art and architecture. She has contributed to books, curated exhibitions, published articles in professional journals, and exhibited her large-format photographic prints. She is also the author of *Foundations of Art and Design*. She resides in New York.

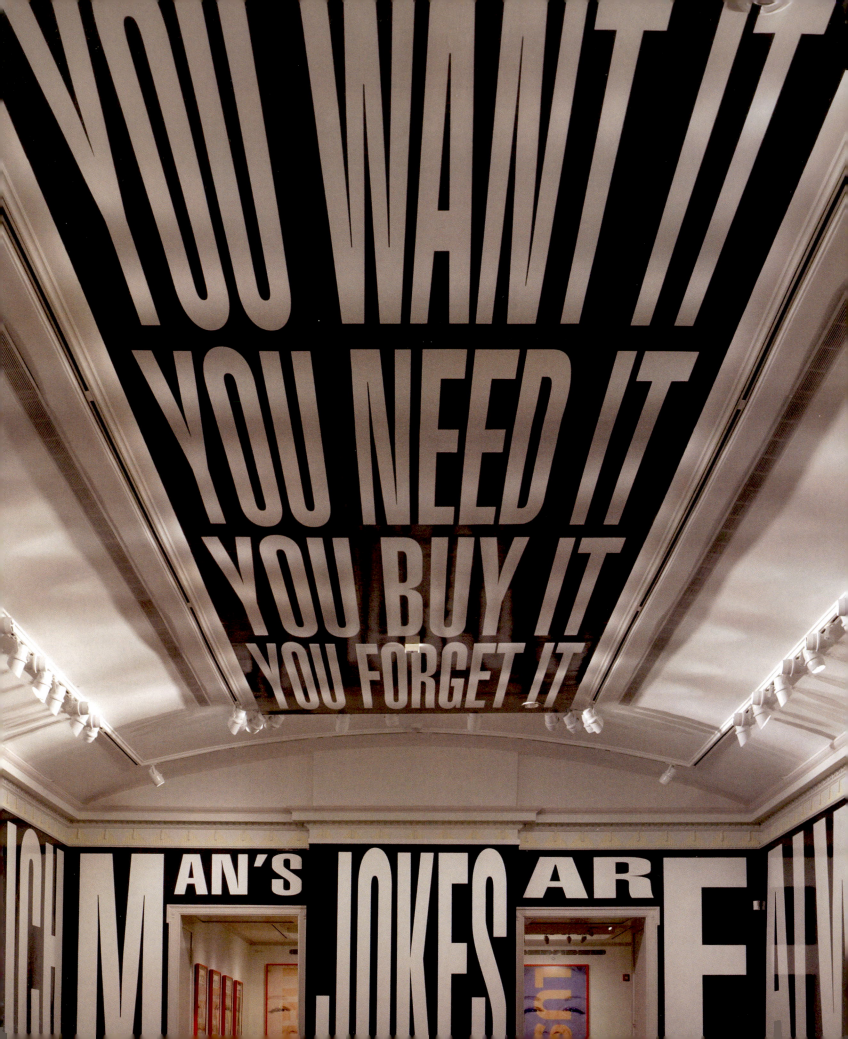

WHAT IS ART?

1

Beauty, truth, immortality, order, harmony—these concepts and ideals have occupied us since the dawn of history. They enrich our lives and encourage us to extend ourselves beyond the limits of flesh and blood. Without them, life would be but a mean struggle for survival, and the value of survival would be unclear.

In the sciences and the arts, we strive to weave our experiences into coherent bodies of knowledge and to communicate them. Many of us are more comfortable with the sciences than with the arts. Science teaches us that the universe is not ruled purely by chance. The sciences provide ways of observing the world and experimenting so that we can learn what forces determine the courses of atoms and galaxies. Even those of us who do not consider ourselves "scientific" recognize that the scientific method permits us to predict and control many important events on a grand scale.

The arts are more elusive to define, more difficult to gather into a conceptual net. We would probably all agree that the arts enhance daily experience; some of us would contend that they are linked to the very quality of life. Art has touched everyone, and art is all around us. Crayon drawings, paper cutouts, and the like are part of the daily lives of our children—an integral function of both magnet and refrigerator door. We all look for art to brighten our dormitory rooms, enhance our interior decor, beautify our cities, and embellish our places of worship. We are certain that we do not want to be without the arts, yet we are hard-pressed to define them and sometimes even to understand them.

BARBARA KRUGER. *Money Makes Money and a Rich Man's Jokes Are Always Funny, and You Want It. You Need It. You Buy It. You Forget It.* (2010). Guild Hall, East Hampton, NY.

In fact, the very word *art* encompasses many meanings, including ability, process, and product. As ability, art is the human capacity to make things of beauty and things that stir us; it is creativity. As process, art encompasses acts such as drawing, painting, sculpting, designing buildings, and using the camera to create memorable works. This definition is ever expanding, as materials and methods are employed in innovative ways to bring forth a creative product. As product, art is the completed work—an etching, a sculpture, a structure, a tapestry. If as individuals we do not understand science, we are at least comforted by the thought that others do. With art, however, the experience of a work is unique. Reactions to a work will vary according to the nature of the individual, time period, place, and culture. And although we may find ourselves standing before a work of art that has us befuddled, saying, "I hate it! I don't understand it!," we suspect that something about the nature of art transcends understanding.

This book is about the visual arts. Despite their often enigmatic nature, we shall try to share something of what is known about them so that understanding may begin. We do not aim to force our aesthetic preferences on you; if in the end you dislike a work as much as you did to start, that is completely acceptable. But we will aim to heighten awareness of what we respond to in a work of art and try to communicate why what an artist has done is important. In this way, you can counter with, "I hate it, but at least I understand it."

As in many areas of study—languages, computers, the sciences—amassing a basic vocabulary is intrinsic to understanding the material. You will want to be able to describe the attributes of a work of art and be able to express your reactions to it. The language or vocabulary of art includes the visual elements, principles of design, style, form, and content. We shall see how the visual elements of art, such as line, shape, and color, are composed according to principles of design into works of art with certain styles and content.

We shall examine many mediums, including drawing, painting, printmaking, the camera and computer arts, sculpture, architecture, ceramics, and fiber arts.

When asked why we should study history, the historian answers that we must know about the past in order to have a sense of where we are and where we may be going. This

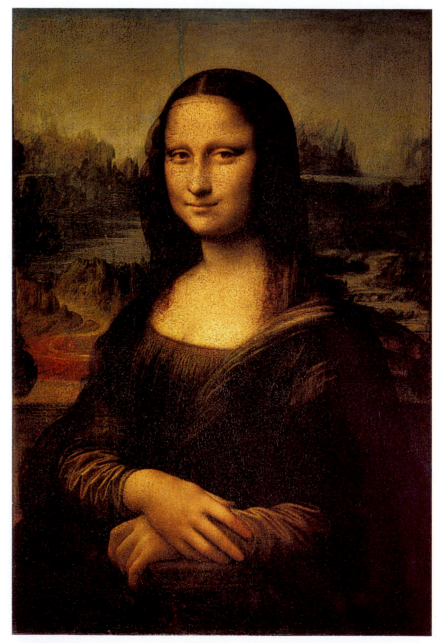

1 in.

1-1 LEONARDO DA VINCI. *Mona Lisa* (c. 1503–1505). Oil on wood panel. 30¼" × 21". Louvre, Paris, France.

argument also holds true for the arts; there is more to art history than memorizing dates! Examining a work in its historical, social, and political context will enable you to have a more meaningful dialogue with that work. You will be amazed and entertained by the ways in which the creative process has been intertwined with world events and individual personalities. We shall follow the journey of art, therefore, from the wall paintings of our Stone Age ancestors through the graffiti art of today's subway station. The mediums, the forms, the styles, and the subjects may evolve and change from millennium to millennium, from day to day, but uniting threads lie in the persistent quest for beauty, or for truth, or for self-expression.

Many philosophers have argued that art serves no function, that it exists for its own sake. Some have asserted that the essence of art transcends the human occupation with usefulness. Others have held that in trying to analyze art too closely, one loses sight of its beauty and wonderment.

These may be valid points of view. Nevertheless, our understanding and appreciation of art often can be enhanced by asking the questions "Why was this created?" and "What is its purpose?" In this section, we shall see that works of art come into existence for a host of reasons that are as varied as the human condition. Perhaps we will not arrive at a single definition of art, but we can come to understand art by considering our relationship to it.

1-2 Kenyan woman, Masai tribe.
Standards for beauty can differ from culture to culture.

ART AND BEAUTY

Art and beauty have been long intertwined. At times, the artist has looked to nature as the standard of beauty and has thus imitated it. At other times, the artist has thought to improve upon nature, developing an alternative standard—an idealized form. Standards of beauty in and of themselves are by no means universal. The Classical Greeks were obsessed with their idea of beauty and fashioned mathematical formulas for rendering the human body in sculpture so that it would achieve a majesty and perfection unknown in nature. The sixteenth-century artist Leonardo da Vinci, in what is perhaps the most famous painting in the history of Western art, enchants generations of viewers with the eternal beauty and mysteriousness of the smiling *Mona Lisa* (Fig. **1-1**). But appreciation of the stately repose and refined features of this Italian woman is tied to a Western concept of beauty. Elsewhere in the world, these features may seem alien, unattractive, or undesirable. On the other hand, the standard of beauty in some non-Western societies that hold scarification, body painting, tattooing, and adornment (Fig. **1-2**) both beautiful and sacred may seem odd and unattractive to someone from the Western world. One art form need not be seen as intrinsically superior to the other; in these works, quite simply, beauty is in the eye of the society's beholder.

ART AND UGLINESS

The images of the Mona Lisa and the Masai woman challenge our fixed notions of classical beauty, but they nonetheless reflect someone's, some era's, some culture's standard of beauty. But need art be equated with beauty? Since the nineteenth century, grotesque images have been an inextricable part of art. They reflect the dark or comical side of human experience, provide a vehicle for artistic expression that is not limited to replicating visual reality, and challenge preconceived notions and standards of beauty.

Much in the modern era provided impetus for the development of the grotesque in art—world wars with their mass destruction and genocide, theories of human psychology, uses and misuses of technology, the birth of science fiction, and more. Characteristics of the grotesque in art are, like imagination, almost limitless. Grotesque art has in common, however, a deviation from and distortion of what is considered by most to be ideal form. Artists typically combine a variety of components in unpredictable ways to create deformities that signify their individual styles. Their images can be, on balance, humorous, as in *The Apparition* by George Condo (Fig. **1-3**), or nightmarish, as in Otto Dix's *The Skat Players* (Fig. **1-4**). The result is typically defined as ugly—a subversion of the long-standing association of art with beauty and a challenge to conventional theories of aesthetics.

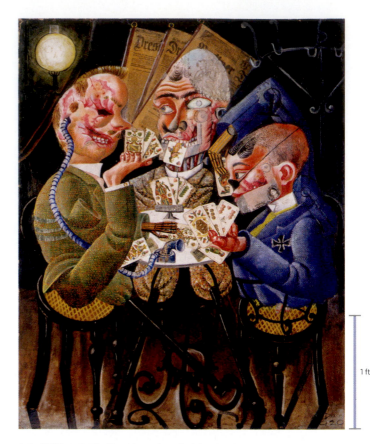

1 ft.

1-4 OTTO DIX. *The Skat Players* (1920). Oil and collage on canvas. 43 5/16" × 34 1/4". Galerie der Stadt Stuttgart, Stuttgart, Germany.

ART AND TRUTH

What does it mean for art to "speak a truth"? The concept of truth in art is subjective; it can mean many and different things to each viewer. Does it mean true to nature, true to human experience, true to materials? The answer is yes to all of these and more. Art can be used to replicate nature, or reality, in the finest detail. Renaissance painters came up with techniques and devices to create a convincing illusion of three-dimensionality on two-dimensional surfaces. Artists throughout history have used their rendering skills to trick the eye into perceiving truth in imitation. Sometimes the tales of their virtuosic exploits survive the work, as in anecdotes recorded on the subject of the ancient Greek painter Apelles. In one such story, we are told that the artist, fearful that other painters might be judged more superior at realistic representation, demanded that real horses be brought before paintings of horses that were entered into a competition. When the horses began to neigh in front of Apelles' work, he received the recognition he deserved.

Artists have sought to extract universal truths by expressing their own experiences. Sometimes their pursuit has led them to beauty, at other times to shame and outrage. The

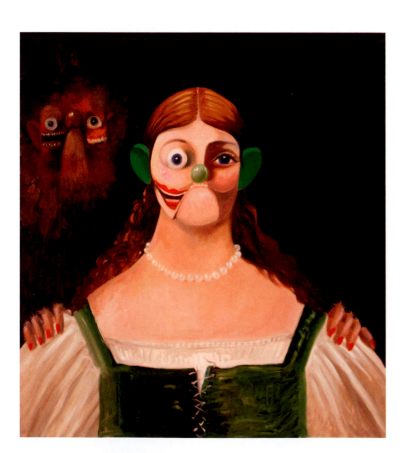

1-3 GEORGE CONDO. *The Apparition* (2009). Oil on canvas. 40" × 36". The Living and the Dead, Gavin Brown's enterprise, NY.

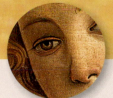
FOR CENTURIES, ARTISTS have devoted their full resources, their lives, to their work. Orlan has also offered her pound of flesh—to the surgeon's scalpel. Orlan (Fig. 1-5) is a French multimedia performance artist who has been undergoing a series of cosmetic operations to create, in herself, a composite sketch of what Western art has long set forth as the pinnacle of human beauty: the facial features that we find in classic works such as Botticelli's *The Birth of Venus* (Fig. 1-6), Leonardo's *Mona Lisa* (Fig. 1-1), and Boucher's *Europa*, or, more specifically, Venus's chin, the Mona Lisa's forehead, and Europa's mouth.

Most people undergo cosmetic surgery in private, but not Orlan. Several of her operations have been performances or media events. Her first series of operations were carried out in France and Belgium. The operating rooms were filled with symbols of flowering womanhood in a form compatible with medicine: sterilized plastic fruit. There were huge photos of Orlan, and the surgeons and their assistants were decked out not in surgical greens but in costumes created by celebrated couturiers. A recent operation was performed in the New York office of a cosmetic surgeon and transmitted via satellite to the Sandra Gering Gallery in the city's famed SoHo district. Orlan did not lie unconscious in a hospital gown. Rather, she lay awake in a long, black dress and read from a work on psychoanalysis while the surgeon implanted silicone in her face to imitate the protruding forehead of *Mona Lisa*.

When will it all end? Orlan says that "I will stop my work when it is as close as possible to the computer composite,"* as the lips of Europa split into a smile. ●

---

* Margalit Fox, "A Portrait in Skin and Bone," *New York Times*, November 21, 1993, V8.

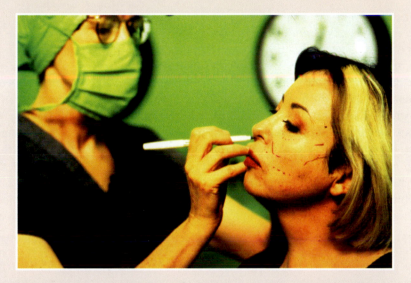

1-5 French performance artist Orlan, who has dedicated herself to embodying Western classic beauty as found in the works of Leonardo, Botticelli, and Boucher through multiple plastic surgeries. Here Orlan is being "prepped" for one in a series of operations. © 2011 Artists Rights Society (ARS), NY/ADAGP, Paris.

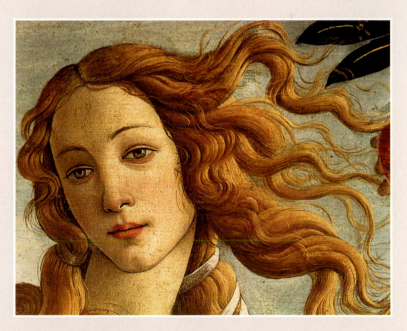

1-6 SANDRO BOTTICELLI. *The Birth of Venus* (1486). Detail. Tempera on canvas. 5' 8⅞" × 9' 1⅞". Galleria degli Uffizi, Florence, Italy.

"ugly truth," just like the beautiful truth, provides a valid commentary on the human condition.

In her self-portraits, the Mexican painter Frida Kahlo used her tragic life as an emblem for human suffering. At age 18, she was injured when a streetcar slammed into a bus on which she was a passenger. The accident left her with many serious wounds, including a fractured pelvis and vertebrae, and chronic pain. Kahlo's marriage to the painter Diego Rivera was also painful. She once told a friend, "I have suffered two serious accidents in my life, one in which a streetcar ran over me. . . . The other accident was Diego."[2] As in *Diego in My Thoughts* (Fig. **1-7**), her face is always painted with extreme realism and set within a compressed space, requiring the viewer to confront the "true" Frida. When asked why she painted herself so often, she replied, "*Porque estoy muy sola*" ("Because I am all alone"). Those who knew Kahlo conjecture that she painted self-portraits in order to "survive, to endure, to conquer death."

Zhang Xiaogang's (b. 1958) *Big Family* (Fig. **1-8**) features a passage of bright red in a sea of monotonous beige and gray tones. For this Chinese artist, the uniformity of a drab palette reflects the appearance—indeed the lives—of what he calls a typical revolutionary family: "asexual, dressed in Mao suits, their gaze glassy and dismal. . . . They could be clones."[3] Red as a signifier of Chinese Communist culture creates points of narrative and visual emphasis, but there is more to the print than its design elements. The work addresses a truth of contemporary Chinese life: this "big" family is as big as a family is permitted to get in this overpopulated country, given its one-child policy. And because of sexism, abortion is not uncommon when an early sonogram reveals that the fetus is female. Chinese social critics worry that the country seems to be headed toward a surplus of males and a resultant era of social instability.

Modern artists who discarded the practice of manipulating materials and techniques to create illusionistic surfaces built their compositions instead on the principle of "truth to materials." Paint retained its identity as paint, rather than pretending that it was cloth or glass or leaves. Modern architects also championed truth to materials by making visible the raw, structural elements of a building and arguing their aesthetic validity.

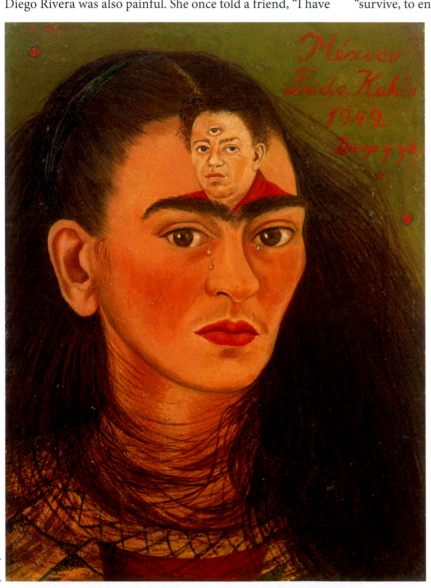

1 in.

1-7 FRIDA KAHLO. *Diego in My Thoughts (Diego y yo)* (1949). Oil on canvas, mounted on Masonite. 24" × 36". Collection of Mary-Anne Martin/Fine Arts, NY. © 2011 Banco de México Diego Rivera Frida Kahlo Museums Trust, Mexico, D.F./Artists Rights Society (ARS), NY.

---

[2] Martha Zamora, *Frida Kahlo: The Brush of Anguish* (San Francisco: Chronicle Books, 1990), 37.

[3] M. Nuridsany, *China Art Now* (Paris: Flammarion, 2004), 114.

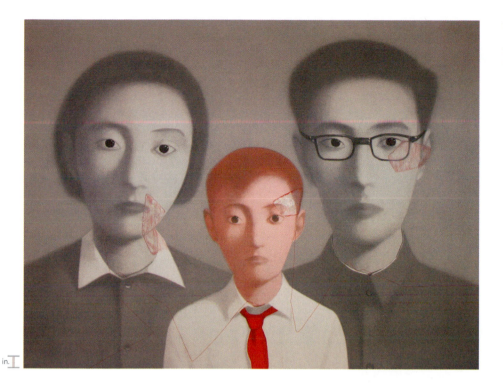

1 in.

1-9 ANDY WARHOL. *Four Marilyns* (1962). Synthetic polymer paint and silkscreen ink on canvas. 30" × 23⅞". © 2011 The Andy Warhol Foundation for the Visual Arts/ Artists Rights Society (ARS), NY.

ART, IMMORTALITY, AND GLORY

In the face of certain death, an artist such as Robert Mapplethorpe can defy mortality by creating a work that will keep his talents and his tragedy in the public's consciousness for decades. Human beings are the only species conscious of death, and for millennia they have used art to overleap the limits of this life.

In *Four Marilyns* (Fig. **1-9**), Pop artist Andy Warhol participated in the cultural immortalization of a film icon of the 1960s by reproducing a well-known photograph of Monroe on canvas. Proclaimed a "sex symbol" of the silver screen, she rapidly rose to fame and shocked her fans by taking her own life at an early age. In the decades since Monroe's death, her image is still found on posters and calendars, books and songs are still written about her, and the public's appetite for information about her early years and romances remains insatiable. In other renderings, Warhol arranged multiple images of the star as if lined up on supermarket shelves, commenting, perhaps, on the ways in which contemporary flesh peddlers have packaged and sold her—in death as well as in life.

The lines between life and death, between place and time, are temporarily dissolved in the renowned

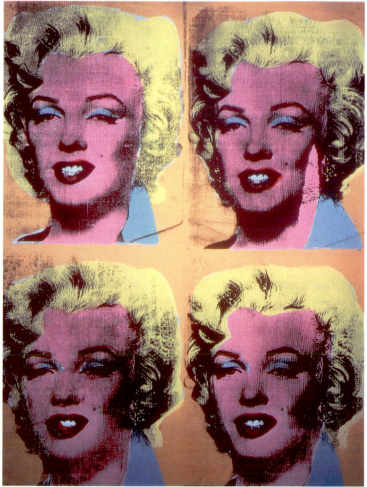

1 in.

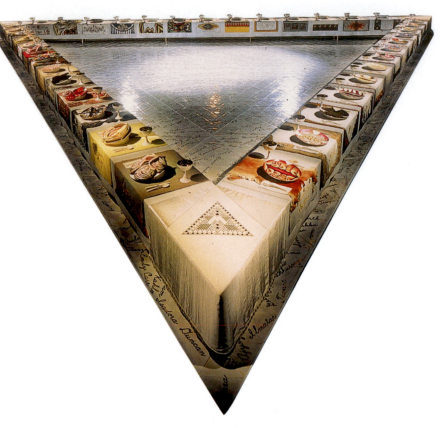

1-10 JUDY CHICAGO. *The Dinner Party* (1974–1979). Painted porcelain and needlework. 48' × 48' × 48' × 3'. Brooklyn Museum, Brooklyn, NY. © 2011 Judy Chicago/Artists Rights Society (ARS), NY.

installation *The Dinner Party* (Fig. **1-10**) by feminist artist Judy Chicago. The idea for this multimedia work, which was constructed to honor and immortalize history's notable women, revolves around a fantastic dinner party, where the guests of honor meet before place settings designed to reflect their personalities and accomplishments. Chicago and numerous other women artists have invested much energy in alerting the public to the significant role of women in the arts and society.

The desire to immortalize often goes hand in hand with the desire to glorify. Some of art history's wealthiest patrons, from the Caesars of ancient Rome and the Vatican's popes to emperors around the world, commissioned artists to create works that glorified their reigns and accomplishments. The Roman emperor Trajan's tomb (Fig. **1-11**), 128 feet high, is covered with a continuous spiral relief that recounts his victories in military campaigns in great detail. Centuries later, the French would adapt this design for a column erected to glorify the victories of the emperor Napoleon Bonaparte.

In China during the early third century BCE, the first emperor of Qin prepared a tomb (Fig. **1-12**) for himself that was filled not only with treasure, but also with facsimiles of more than 6,000 soldiers and horses, along with bronze chariots. The site, which is still being excavated, was probably

1-11 Column of Trajan, Forum of Trajan, dedicated 112 CE. 128' high. Rome, Italy.

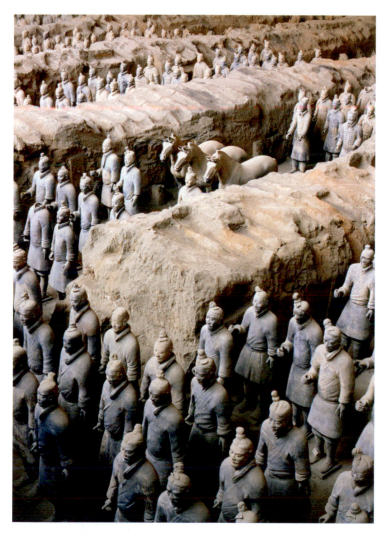

1-12 Terra-cotta warriors. Pit No. 1 (Han Dynasty c. 210 BCE). Museum of the First Emperor Qin, Shaanxi Province, China.

intended to recreate the emperor's lavish palace. The sheer manpower that was necessary to create the imperial funerary monument—literally thousands of workers and artists—is a testament to the emperor's wealth, power, and ambition.

ART AND RELIGION

The quest for immortality is the bedrock of organized religion. From the cradle of civilization to the contemporary era, from Asia to the Americas, and from the Crimea to the Cameroon, human beings across time and cultures have sought answers to the unanswerable and have saved their souls with belief in life after death. In the absence of physical embodiments for the deities they fashioned, humans developed art forms to visually render the unseen. Often the physical attributes granted to their

gods were a reflection of humans. It has been said, for example, that the Greeks made their men into gods and their gods into men. In other societies, deities were often represented as powerful and mysterious animals, or composite men-beasts. Ritual and ceremony grew alongside the establishment of religions and the representation of deities, in actual or symbolic form. Until modern times, one could probably study the history of art in terms of works expressing religious values alone.

The *North Wind Mask* (*Negakfok*) (Fig. **1-13**), is one of a series of masks from the Yup'ik speaking Inuit of western Alaska, worn during rituals designed to mediate the spirit world—in this case the spirits of the north, east, and south winds—and the human and animal worlds. Dancers, adorned with such masks and elaborate costumes, were believed to be transformed into spirits. The spirit of the north wind is associated with snowstorms and frigid cold temperatures. White spots painted on the mask may allude to snowflakes; the sound created by the clanking of the wood pieces that hang from the mask suggests the whooshing of cold winds.

Another artist of color, Aaron Douglas, translated a biblical story into a work that speaks to the African American

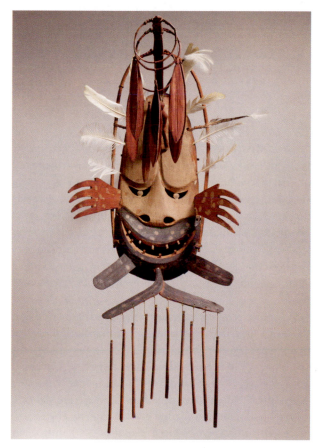

1-13 *North Wind Mask* (*Negakfok*) (early 20th century). Wood, paint, and feathers. 45¼" × 21⅜" × 17⅞". The Michael C. Rockefeller Memorial Collection, Purchase, Nelson A. Rockefeller Gift, 1961 (1978.412.76a, b). The Metropolitan Museum of Art, NY. © The Metropolitan Museum of Art.

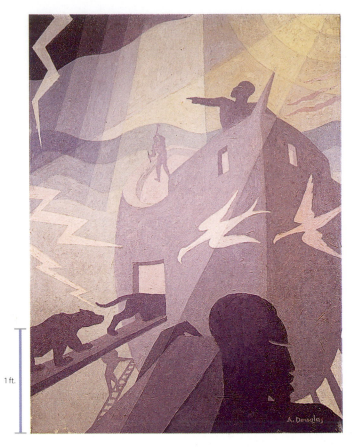

1-14 AARON DOUGLAS. *Noah's Ark* (c. 1927). Oil on Masonite. 48" × 36".

sensibility. In his *Noah's Ark* (Fig. **1-14**), one of seven paintings based on James Weldon Johnson's book *God's Trombones: Seven Negro Sermons in Verse*, Douglas expressed a powerful vision of the great flood. Animals enter the ark in pairs as lightning flashes about them, and the sky turns a hazy gray purple with the impending storm. African men, rendered in rough-hewn profile, ready the ark and direct the action in a dynamically choreographed composition that takes possession of and personalizes the biblical event for Douglas's race and culture.

Traditions in Islamic art vary, reflecting regional styles, different eras, and the embracing or prohibition of representational imagery. For the Islamic artist, expression of religious beliefs can be seen in simple yet elegant calligraphic renderings of sacred text or, as in the miniature depicting Muhammad with Moses and the angel Gabriel (Fig. **1-15**), a narrative of significance in the life of the Prophet. The exquisitely painted miniature depicts a vision of Muhammad in which he is led through seven heavens by Gabriel. On this journey he meets Moses, who asks Muhammad about his prayer obligations to God. It is written in the Qur'an—the Muslim holy book—that, upon Moses' recommendation,

Muhammad petitioned God to reduce the number of obligatory daily prayers from fifty to five. Gabriel is the central figure, identified by his wings and intricate apparel. Moses is shown on the left, standing next to a throne, and Muhammad stands to the right in a green tunic. His face, in compliance with proscriptions for representing the Prophet, appears blocked out in white. Muslims believe that Abraham was the first prophet, that Jesus was also a prophet, and that Muhammad was the last prophet, completing God's revelation.

ART AND IDEOLOGY

Throughout history, works of art have been used to create or reinforce ideology. Defined as an organized collection of ideas, ideologies articulate the way societies look at things. These ideas spring from commonly held beliefs or are imposed on members of society by ruling or dominant classes. The degree

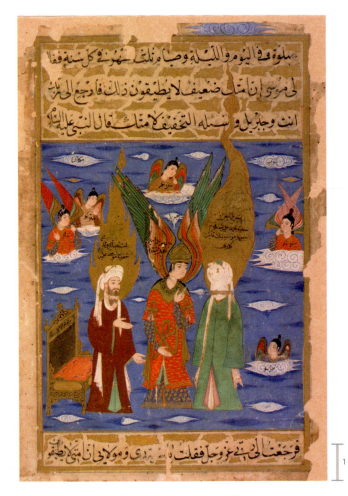

1-15 *Prophets Moses and Muhammad with the Angel Gabriel.* Miniature. 12¼" × 8¹⁄₁₆". Museum of Islamic Art, Berlin, Germany.

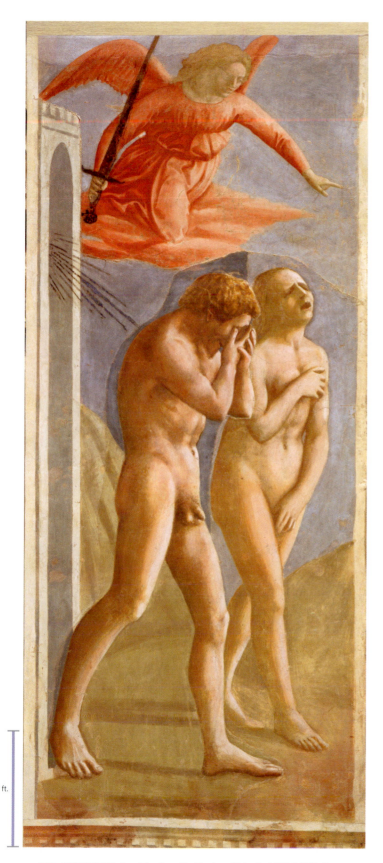

1 ft.

1-16 MASACCIO. *Expulsion from the Garden of Eden* (c. 1424–1428). Fresco. 7' × 2' 11". Brancacci Chapel, Santa Maria del Carmine, Florence, Italy.

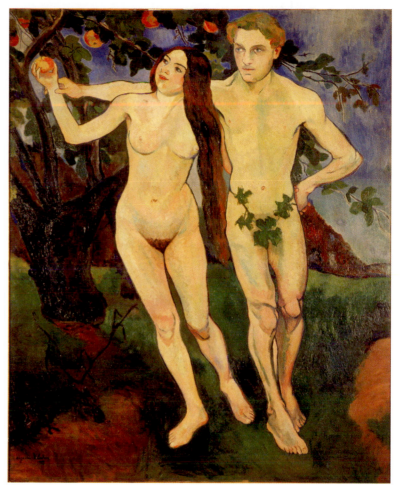

1-17 SUZANNE VALADON. *Adam and Eve* (1909). Oil on canvas. 6⅓" × 5⅛". Musee National d'Art Moderne, Centre Georges Pompidou, Paris, France.

to which an ideology is perpetuated depends on the degree to which members of a society subscribe to it.

When it comes to ideology, sometimes images speak louder than words. Think of representations of Adam and Eve. Every time you see Eve tempting Adam with an apple, you are witnessing the representation of an ideology in art, in this case that Eve (and, by extension, women in general) was responsible for humankind's fall from grace and loss of paradise. For hundreds of years, Christianity perpetuated a negative view of women based on this ideological position. Masaccio's fifteenth-century version of the expulsion from the Garden of Eden (Fig. **1-16**) illustrates the distraught first couple being forcibly cast into the wilderness at swordpoint. Adam holds his head in his hands, shielding his eyes while Eve, her head thrown back in desperate weeping, covers her body in shame. It is as if the artist is suggesting, in these gestures, that Adam's was a sin of the mind (he made a decision to succumb to temptation) whereas Eve's was a sin of the flesh (her uncontrolled passion and weakness led to their predicament). In the twentieth century, Suzanne Valadon subverted the traditional assignment of blame and guilt in a new version of the story of Eden in which Adam appears to lead Eve's hand toward the apple (Fig. 1-17). His body parts, not hers, are covered in shame by a strategically placed vine.

ART AND FANTASY

Art also serves as a vehicle by which artists can express their innermost fantasies. Whereas some have labored to reconstruct reality and commemorate actual experiences, others have used art to give vent to their imaginary inner lives. There are many types of fantasies, such as those found in dreams and daydreams or simply the objects and landscapes that are conceived in the imagination. The French painter Odilon Redon once said that there is "a kind of drawing which the imagination has liberated from any concern with the details of reality in order to allow it to serve freely for the representation of things conceived" in the mind. In an attempt to cap-

ture the inner self, many twentieth-century artists looked to the psychoanalytic writings of Sigmund Freud and Carl Jung, who suggested that primeval forces are at work in the unconscious reaches of the mind. These artists sought to use their art as an outlet for these unconscious forces, as we shall see in Chapters 20 and 21.

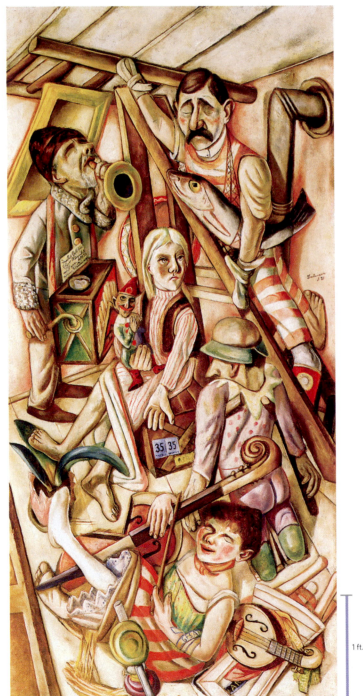

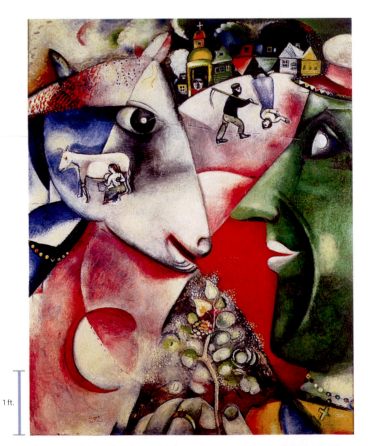

1-18 MARC CHAGALL. *I and the Village* (1911). Oil on canvas. 6'3⅝" × 4'11⅝". The Museum of Modern Art, NY.

1-19 MAX BECKMANN. *The Dream* (1921). Oil on canvas. 73⅛" × 35". The Saint Louis Art Museum, Saint Louis, MO.

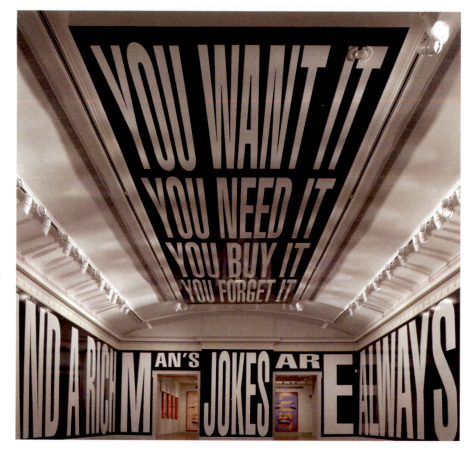

Marc Chagall's self-portrait *I and the Village* (Fig. 1-18) provides a fragmented image of the artist among fantasized objects that seem to float in and out of one another. Fleeting memories of life in his Russian village are assembled like so many pieces of a dream-like puzzle, reflecting the fragmentary nature of memory. Chagall's world is a happy, though private, one; the strange juxtaposition of images is reconciled only in the artist's own mind.

A similar process of fragmentation and juxtaposition was employed by German artist Max Beckmann in *The Dream* (Fig. 1-19), but with a very different effect. The suggestion of space and atmosphere in Chagall's painting has given way to a claustrophobic room in which figures are compressed into a zigzag group. The soft, rolling hills and curving lines that gave the village painting its pleasant, dreamy quality have been forfeited for harsh, angular shapes and deformations. Horror hides in every nook and cranny, from the amputated and bandaged hands of the man in red stripes to the blinded street musician and maimed harlequin. Are these marionettes from some dark comedy or human puppets locked in a world of manipulation and hopelessness?

ART, INTELLECT, AND EMOTION

Art has the power to make us think profoundly, to make us feel deeply. Beautiful or controversial works in all mediums can trigger many associations for us: gazing at a landscape painting may remind us of a vacation past, puzzling over a work of geometric abstraction may bring back memories of tenth-grade math, or a quilt may have the power to evoke family ties and traditions. It is almost impossible to truly confront a work and remain unaffected. Art can ask us to consider our definitions of self and the world. Art can demand us to consider and reconsider our preconceived notions of the definition and parameters of art. Art and idea, it seems, are inseparable. Yet sometimes they are purposefully separated to great effect.

Consider Barbara Kruger's installation of graphic text on the walls and ceiling of East Hampton's Guild Hall in the summer of 2010 (Fig. 1-20). As an example of **conceptual art**, it prioritizes the *idea* of the work over the object, emphasizing the artist's thinking and often de-emphasizing traditional artistic techniques. The visual aspect of Kruger's text relates to the billboards, magazines, and commercial advertising that saturate our cultural landscape and remind us of the constant media bombardment in our lives. The work forces us to think about the impersonal information systems of our era and the degree to which we are affected by their subliminal messages. In this piece, Kruger asks the viewer to think about the cult of materialism and the adage "Money talks." The scale of the type and almost claustrophobic installation make confronting ourselves, our morals, and our way of life inescapable.

ART, ORDER, AND HARMONY

Artists and scientists have been intrigued by, and have ventured to discover and describe, the underlying order of nature. The Classical Greeks fine-polished the rough edges of nature by applying mathematical formulas to the human figure to perfect it; the nineteenth-century painter Paul Cézanne once remarked that all of nature could be reduced to the cylinder, the sphere, and the cone.

One of the most perfect expressions of order and harmony is found in the fragile Japanese rock garden (Fig. **1-21**). Also known as "dry landscape," they are frequently part of a pavilion complex and are tended by the practitioners of **Zen**, a Buddhist sect that seeks inner harmony through introspection and meditation. The gentle, raked pattern of the stones symbolizes water and rocks, with mountains reaching heavenward. Such gardens do not invite the observer to mill about; their perfection precludes walking. They are microcosms, really—universes unto themselves.

When can order pose a threat to harmony and psychological well-being? Perhaps this is the question that Laurie Simmons set out to answer in her color photograph called *Red Library #2* (Fig. **1-22**). Here, in a compulsively organized library, where nothing is a hair out of place, a robotlike woman assesses her job well done. She has become one with her task; even her dress, hair, and skin match the decor.

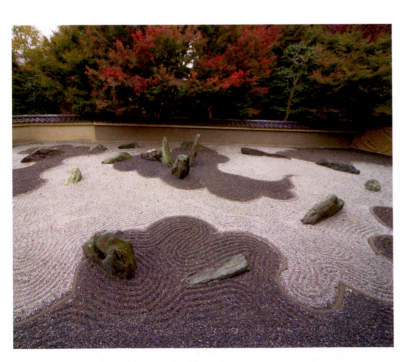

1-21 Ryogintel Rock Garden, Kyoto, Japan.

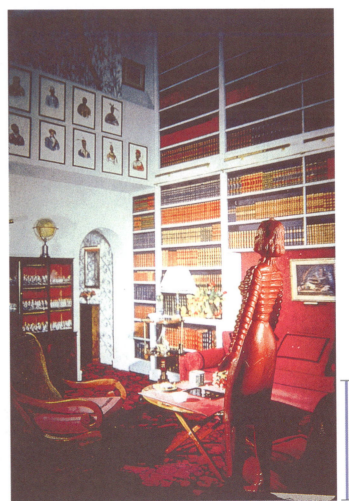

1-22 LAURIE SIMMONS. *Red Library #2* (1983). Color photograph. 48½" × 38¼".

THE *PIANO LESSON(S)* BY MATISSE AND BEARDEN

FREQUENTLY AN ARTIST WILL USE COMPOSITION, or the arrangement of elements, to impose order. In Henri Matisse's *Piano Lesson* (Fig. **1-23**), every object, every color, every line seems to be placed to lead the eye around the canvas. The pea green wedge of drapery at the window is repeated in the shape of the metronome atop the piano, the wrought-iron grillwork at the window is complemented by the curvilinear lines of the music desk, and the enigmatic figure in the upper-right background finds her counterpart in a small sculpture placed diagonally across the canvas. Through contrast and repetition, unity within the diversity is achieved. The painting exudes solitude, resulting from the regularity of the compositional elements more than the atmosphere in the room. The boy's face appears quite tense, in fact, under the watchful eye of the seated woman behind him.

With Matisse's painting in mind, does Romare Bearden's *Piano Lesson* (Fig. **1-24**) appear then to be an example of disharmony, of disorder? Certainly it is a cacophony of shapes, lines, and unpredictable vantage points. But as in Matisse's painting, color repetition draws the composition's disparate

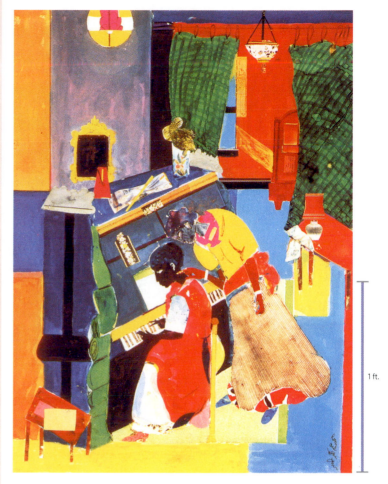

1-24 ROMARE BEARDEN. *Piano Lesson* (1983). Oil with collage. 29" × 22". The Walter O. Evans Collections of African American Art, SCAD Museum of Art, Savannah, GA. Art © Romare Bearden Foundation/Licensed by VAGA, NY.

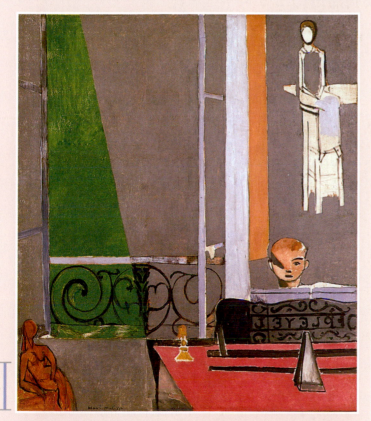

1-23 HENRI MATISSE. *Piano Lesson* (1916). Oil on canvas. 8'½" × 6'11¾". The Museum of Modern Art, NY. © 2011 Succession H. Matisse/Artists Rights Society (ARS), NY.

parts together—the red of the background is balanced by the touches of red in the costumes of the figures up front; an undulating green strip on the piano is echoed in the billowing green drapes beyond. Ironically, there seems to be a more genuine feeling of serenity, despite the jumbled atmosphere. Is it because Matisse's seated woman—not touching? not feeling?—has a more flesh-and-blood counterpart in Bearden's work—a teacher? a mother?—who guides the young girl with the loving placement of a hand on her shoulder? When seen side by side, these paintings convey two different experiences. Matisse's piano student seems a product of his surroundings, a child of privilege partaking in an obligatory cultural ritual. Bearden's student, an African American girl in an apartment decorated catch-as-catch-can, seems to be breaking the bonds of her surroundings through the transcendence of music. ●

Art is not a handicraft; it is the transmission of feeling the artist has experienced.
—Leo Tolstoy

ART AND CHAOS

Just as beauty has its dark side and the intellect is balanced by the emotion, so, too, do order and harmony presume the existence of chaos. Artists have portrayed chaos in many ways throughout the history of art, seeking analogies in apocalyptic events such as war, famine, or natural catastrophe. But chaos can be suggested even in the absence of specific content. In *Eclipse* (Fig. **1-25**), without reference to nature or reality, Native American artist Jaune Quick-to-See Smith creates an agitated, chaotic atmosphere of color, line, shape, and movement. The artist grew up on the Flathead Indian reservation in Montana and uses a full vocabulary of Native American geometric motifs and organic images from the rich pictorial culture of her ancestors.

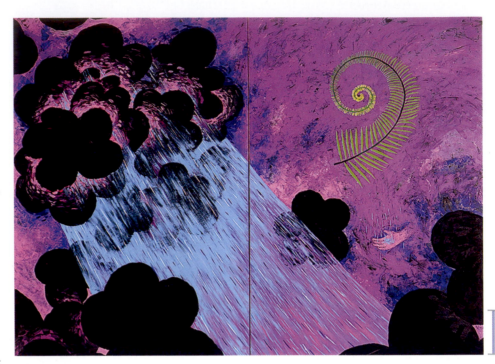

1 ft.

1-26 LOUISA CHASE. *Storm* (1981). Oil on canvas. 90" × 120". Denver Art Museum, Denver, CO.

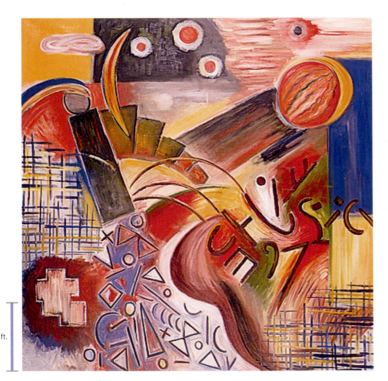

1 ft.

1-25 JAUNE QUICK-TO-SEE SMITH. *Eclipse* (1987). Oil on canvas. 60" × 60". Flomenhaft Gallery, NY.

ART, EXPERIENCE, AND MEMORY

From humanity's earliest days, art has been used to record and communicate experiences and events. From prehistoric cave paintings, thought to record significant events in the history of Paleolithic societies, to a work such as the Vietnam Memorial in Washington, D.C.—installed in honor of American service personnel who died during this country's involvement in that war—art has been used to inform future generations of what and who have gone before them. Art also conveys the personal experiences of an artist in ways that words cannot.

American painter Louisa Chase was inspired to paint nature's unbridled power as revealed in waves, waterfalls, and thunderstorms, although the intensity of her subjects is often tempered by her own presence in the piece. In *Storm* (Fig. **1-26**), a cluster of thick, black clouds lets go a torrent of rain, which, in league with the decorative **palette** of pinks and purples, turns an artificial blue. The highly charged images on the left side of the canvas are balanced on the right by the most delicate of ferns, spiraling upward, nourished by the downpour. Beneath the sprig, the artist's hand cups the raindrops, becoming part of the painting and part of nature's event as well. Chase said of a similar storm painting, "During the [marking] process I do become the storm—lost—yet not lost. An amazing feeling of losing myself yet remaining totally conscious."[4]

The photographer Alfred Stieglitz, who recognized the medium as a fine art as well as a tool for recording events, happened upon the striking composition of *The Steerage* (Fig. **1-27**) on an Atlantic crossing aboard the *Kaiser Wilhelm II*. He rushed to his cabin for his camera, hoping that the upper and lower masses of humanity would maintain their balanced relationships to one another, to the drawbridge that divides the scene, to the stairway, the funnel, and the horizontal beam of the mast. The "steerage" of a ship

was the least expensive accommodation. Here the "huddled masses" seem suspended in limbo by machinery and by symbolic as well as actual bridges. Yet the tenacious human spirit may best be symbolized by the jaunty patch of light that strikes the straw hat of one passenger on the upper deck. Stieglitz was utterly fascinated and moved by what he saw.

More than 80 years after Stieglitz captured the great hope of immigrants entering New York harbor, African American artist Faith Ringgold tells the story of life and dreams on a tar-covered rooftop. *Tar Beach* (Fig. **1-28**) is a painted patchwork quilt that stitches together the artist's memories of family, friends, and feelings while growing up in Harlem. Ringgold is noted for her use of materials and techniques associated

[4] Louisa Chase, journal entry for February 20, 1984, in *Louisa Chase* (New York: Robert Miller Gallery, 1984).

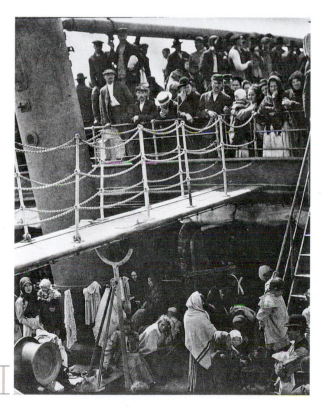

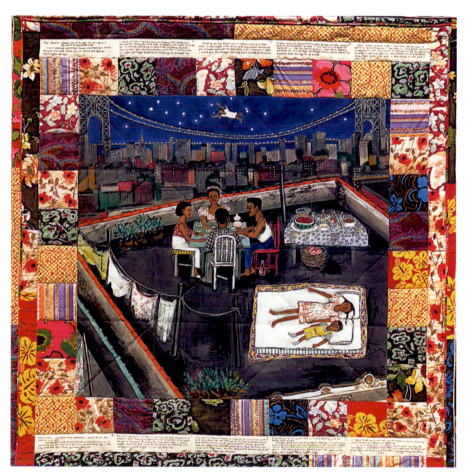

1 in.

1-27 ALFRED STIEGLITZ. *The Steerage* (1907). Photograph. 12¹¹⁄₁₆" × 10³⁄₁₆".

1-28 FAITH RINGGOLD. *Tar Beach* (1988). Acrylic paint on canvas and pieced fabric. 74" × 68½". Solomon R. Guggenheim Museum, NY.

with women's traditions as well as her use of narrative or storytelling, a strong tradition in African American families. A large, painted square with images of Faith, her brother, her parents, and her neighbors dominates the quilt and is framed with brightly patterned pieces of fabric. Along the top and bottom are inserts crowded with Ringgold's written description of her experiences. This wonderfully innocent and joyful monologue begins:

> I will always remember when the stars fell down around me and lifted me up above the George Washington Bridge . . .

ART AND THE SOCIAL AND CULTURAL CONTEXT

Faith Ringgold's *Tar Beach* tells us the story of a young girl growing up in Harlem. Her experiences take place within a specific social and cultural context. In recording experi-

ence, artists frequently record the activities and objects of their times and places, reflecting contemporary fashions and beliefs, as well as the states of the crafts and sciences.

The architecture, hairstyles, hats, and shoulder pads, and even the price of cigars (only five cents), all set Edward Hopper's *Nighthawks* (Fig. **1-29**) in an unmistakably American city during the late 1930s or 1940s. The subject is commonplace and uneventful, though somewhat eerie. There is a tension between the desolate spaces of the vacant street and the corner diner. Familiar objects become distant. The warm patch of artificial light seems precious, even precarious, as if night and all its troubled symbols are threatening to break in on disordered lives. Hopper uses a specific sociocultural context to communicate an unsettling, introspective mood of aloneness, of being outside the mainstream of experience.

In Richard Hamilton's *Just What Is It That Makes Today's Homes So Different, So Appealing?* (Fig. **1-30**), the aims are identical, but the result is self-mocking, upbeat, and altogether fun. This little collage functions as a veritable time capsule for the 1950s, a decade during which the speedy advance

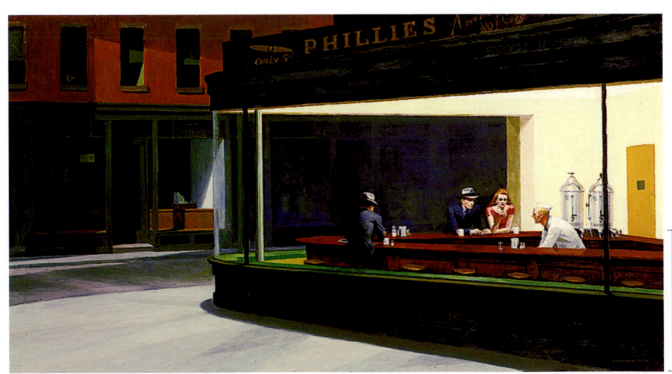

1-29 EDWARD HOPPER. *Nighthawks* (1942). Oil on canvas. 30" × 60". The Art Institute of Chicago, Chicago, IL.

of technology finds everyone buying pieces of the American dream. What is that dream? Comic books, TVs, movies, and tape recorders; canned hams and TV dinners; enviable physiques, Tootsie Pops, vacuum cleaners that finally let the "lady of the house" clean all the stairs at once. Hamilton's piece serves as a memento of the time and the place and the values of the decade for future generations.

We more commonly think of visual art (painting and sculpture, for example) when we consider the connection between art and social or cultural context, but art history is full of examples of architecture that reflect or embody the ideas or beliefs of a people at a point in time. Think of the Parthenon in Classical Athens or Chartres Cathedral in the Middle Ages. Symbolism is often disguised in architecture, but sometimes it is the essence of its design. Zaha Hadid's Sheikh Zayed Bridge (Fig. **1-31**), connecting Abu Dhabi island to the mainland, is composed of sweeping, irregular rhythms of arches. Hadid has acknowledged the influence of Arabic calligraphy on the flowing forms of her structures, but in this work, the arches—

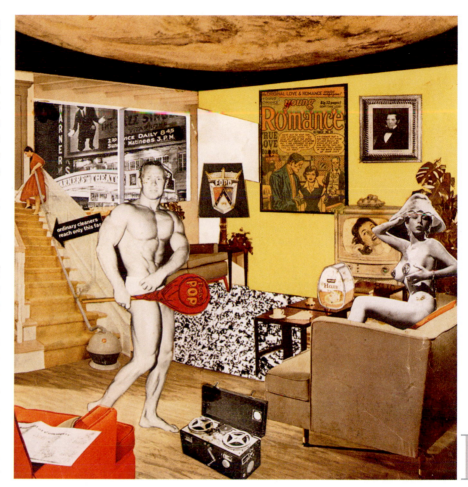

1 in.

1-30 RICHARD HAMILTON. *Just What Is It That Makes Today's Homes So Different, So Appealing?* (1956). Collage. 10¼" × 9¾". Kunsthalle Tübingen, Tübingen, Germany.

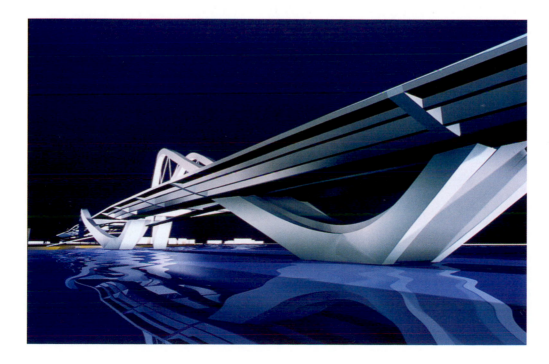

1-31 ZAHA HADID. Sheikh Zayed Bridge, 2006. Abu Dhabi, United Arab Emirates.

each different from one another in height and span—reflect the dunes of the nearby topography, thus connecting it (metaphorically and literally) to a specific place and time.

ART AND SOCIAL CONSCIOUSNESS

As other people have, artists have taken on bitter struggles against the injustices of their times and have tried to persuade others to join them in their causes, and it has been natural for them to use their creative skills to do so.

The nineteenth-century Spanish painter Francisco Goya used his art to satirize the political foibles of his day and to condemn the horrors of war (see Fig. 19-6). In the twentieth century another Spanish painter, Pablo Picasso, would condemn war in his masterpiece *Guernica* (see Fig. 20-9).

Goya's French contemporary Eugène Delacroix painted the familiar image of *Liberty Leading the People* (Fig. **1-32**) in order to keep the spirit of the French Revolution alive in 1830. In this painting, people of all classes are united in rising up against injustice, led onward by an allegorical figure of liberty. Rifles, swords, a flag—even pistols—join in an upward rhythm, underscoring the pyramid shape of the composition.

Suzanne Lacy and Leslie Labowitz's performance *In Mourning and in Rage* (Fig. **1-33**) was a carefully orchestrated media

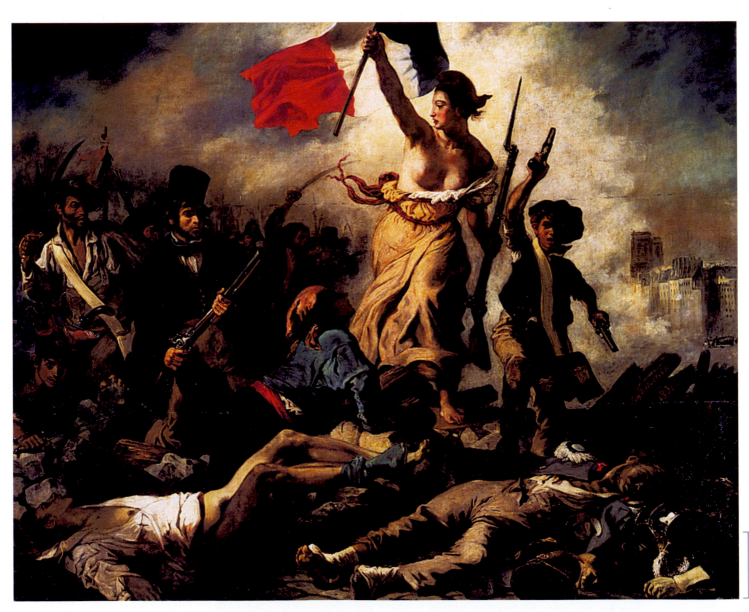

1 ft.

1-32 EUGÈNE DELACROIX. *Liberty Leading the People* (1830). Oil on canvas. 8'6" × 10'10". Louvre, Paris, France.

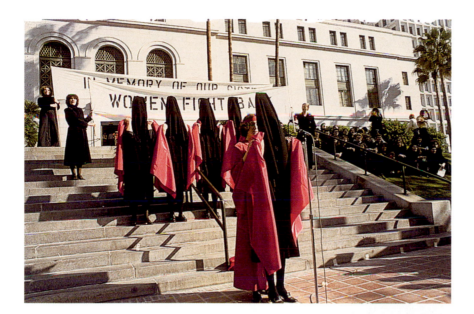

1-33 SUZANNE LACY AND LESLIE LABOWITZ. *In Mourning and in Rage* (1977). Performance at Los Angeles City Hall, Los Angeles, CA.

1-34 BETYE SAAR. *The Liberation of Aunt Jemima* (1972). Mixed media. 11¾" × 8" × 2¾". University of California, Berkeley Art Museum, Berkeley, CA.

event reminiscent of ancient public rituals. Members of feminist groups donned black robes to commemorate women who had been victims of rape-murders and to protest the shoddy media coverage usually given to such tragedies.

Millions of us have grown up with a benevolent, maternal Aunt Jemima. She has graced packages of pancake mix and bottles of maple syrup for generations. How many of us have really thought about what she symbolizes? Artists such as African American artist Betye Saar have been doubly offended by Aunt Jemima's state of servitude, which harks not only to the days of slavery but also to the suffocating traditional domestic role of the female. Sharon F. Patton notes:

> *The Liberation of Aunt Jemima* subverts the black mammy stereotype of the black American woman: a heavy, dark-skinned maternal figure, of smiling demeanor. This stereotype, started in the nineteenth century, was still popular culture's favorite representation of the African-American woman. She features in Hollywood films and notably as the advertising and packaging image for Pillsbury's "Aunt Jemima's Pancake Mix."[5]

The Aunt Jemima in Betye Saar's *The Liberation of Aunt Jemima* (Fig. **1-34**) is revised to reflect the quest for liberation from servitude and the stereotype. She holds a broomstick in one hand but a rifle in the other. Before her stands a portrait with a small white child violated by a clenched black fist representing the symbol of Black

[5] Sharon F. Patton, *African-American Art* (New York: Oxford University Press, 1998), 201.

1 in.

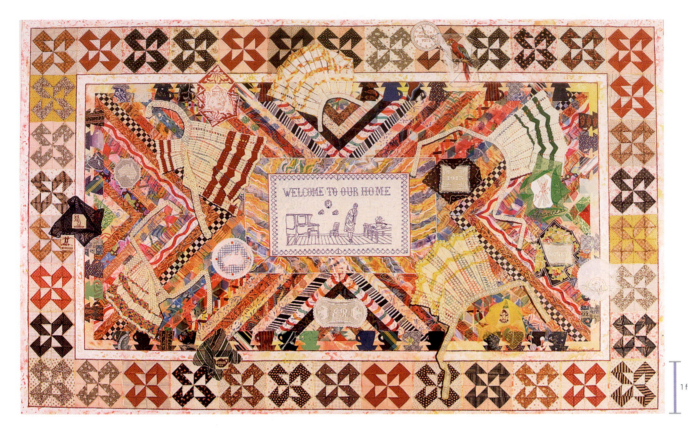

1 ft.

1-35 MIRIAM SCHAPIRO. *Wonderland* (1983). Acrylic and fabric collage on canvas. 90" × 144". Smithsonian American Art Museum, Washington, D.C.

Power. The image of the liberated Aunt Jemima confronts viewers and compels them to cast off the stereotypes that lead to intolerance.

ART AND POPULAR CULTURE

Have you come across embroidered dish towels or aprons with the words *God Bless Our Happy Home* or *I Hate Housework*? Miriam Schapiro's *Wonderland* (Fig. **1-35**) is a collage that reflects her "femmage" aesthetic—her interest in depicting women's domestic culture. The work contains ordinary doilies, needlework, crocheted aprons, handkerchiefs, and quilt blocks, all anchored to a geometric patterned background that is augmented with brushstrokes of paint. In the center is the most commonplace of the commonplace: an embroidered image of a housewife who curtsies beneath the legend "Welcome to Our Home."

Some of the more interesting elevations of the commonplace to the realm of art are found in the **readymades** and **assemblages** of twentieth-century artists. Marcel Duchamp's

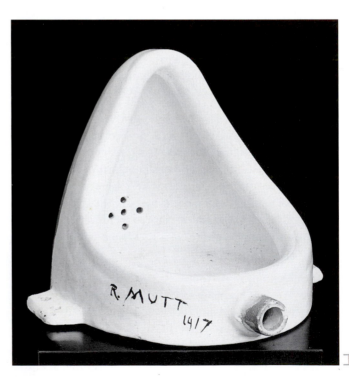

1 in.

1-36 MARCEL DUCHAMP. *Fountain* (1917). 1951 version after lost original. Porcelain urinal. 24" high. © 2011 Artists Rights Society (ARS), NY/ADAGP, Paris/Succession Marcel Duchamp.

Fountain (Fig. **1-36**) is a urinal, turned upside down and labeled. Pablo Picasso's *Bull's Head* (see Fig. 9-15) is fashioned from the seat and handlebars of an old bicycle. In **Pop Art**, the dependence on commonplace objects and visual clichés reaches a peak. Prepared foods, soup and beer cans, and media images of beautiful women and automobile accidents became the subject matter of Pop Art. As we saw in Figures 1-9 and 1-30, Pop Art impels us to cast a more critical eye on the symbols and objects with which we surround ourselves.

ART AND DECORATION

We have all decided at one time or another to change the color of our bedrooms. We have hung a poster or painting here rather than there, and we have arranged a vase of flow-ers or placed a potted plant in just the right spot in the room. We may not have created works of art, but we did manage to delight our senses and turn our otherwise ordinary environments into more pleasurable havens.

Works of art have been used to create pleasing environments for centuries. From tapestries that adorned and insulated the cold stone walls of medieval castles to elaborate sculpted fountains that provided focal points for manicured, palatial gardens, whatever other functions they may serve, many works of art are also decorative. Joyce Kozloff's *Galla Placidia in Philadelphia* (Fig. **1-37**), a mosaic for the Penn Center Suburban Station in that city, elevates decorative patterns to the level of fine art and raises the art-historical consciousness of the casual commuter. The original Mausoleum of Galla Placidia is the fifth-century chapel and burial place of a Byzantine empress, a landmark monument known for its complex and colorful mosaics. Kozloff's own intricate and diverse designs dazzle the eye and stimulate

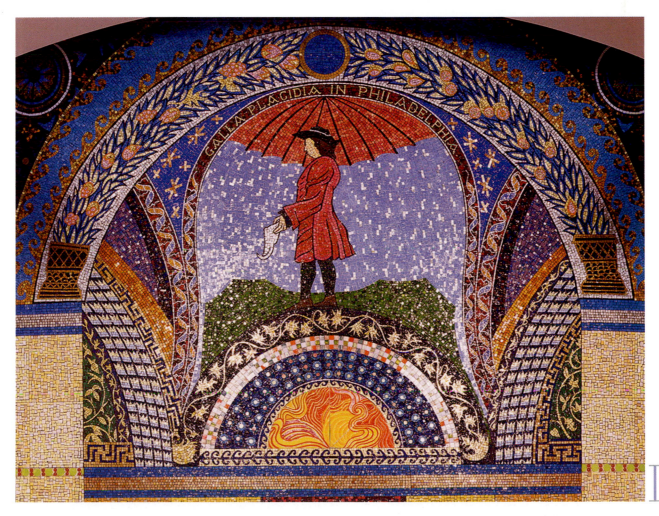

1 ft.

1-37 JOYCE KOZLOFF. *Galla Placidia in Philadelphia* (1985). Mosaic installation. 13' × 16'. Penn Center Suburban Station, Philadelphia, PA.

the intellect, providing an oasis of color in an otherwise humdrum city scene.

Glass sculptor Dale Chihuly's *Fiori di Como* (Fig. **1-38**) is a 70-foot-long ceiling installation suspended above the reception area of the Bellagio Hotel in Las Vegas. Even in a city of neon and assorted trappings of excess, Chihuly's piece dazzles with its colors and textures. Reminiscent of the undulating shapes and brilliant palette of Venice's renowned Murano glass, it is another set piece in the hotel's interior decor that is intended to transport its guests to that famed small town of Bellagio on the shore of Italy's spectacular Lake Como.

ART AND THE NEEDS OF THE ARTIST

Artists may have special talents and perceptive qualities, but they are also people with needs and the motivation to meet those needs. Psychologists speak of the need for *self-actualization*—that is, the need to fulfill one's unique potential. Self-actualizing people have needs for novelty, exploration, and understanding; they also have aesthetic needs for art, beauty, and order. Under perfect circumstances, art permits the individual to meet needs for achievement or self-actualization and, at the same time, to earn a living.

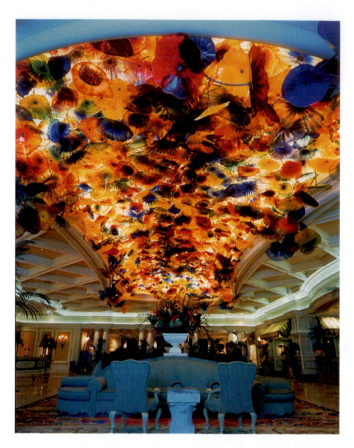

1-38 DALE CHIHULY. *Fiori di Como* (1998). 70' × 30' × 12'. Bellagio Resort, Las Vegas, NV.

1-39 JOSÉ CLEMENTE OROZCO. *Epic of American Civilization: Hispano-America* (c. 1932–1934). Fresco. 10' × 9'11". Hood Museum of Art, Hanover, NH. © 2011 Artists Rights Society (ARS), NY/SOMAAP, Mexico City.

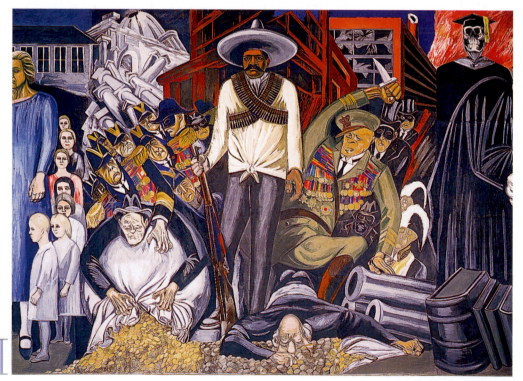

1 ft.

Murals such as José Clemente Orozco's *Epic of American Civilization: Hispano-America* (Fig. **1-39**) were created for a branch of the Works Progress Administration (WPA), a federal work-relief program intended to help people in the United States, including artists, survive the Great Depression. The WPA made it possible for many artists to meet basic survival needs while continuing to work, and be paid, as artists. Scores of public buildings were decorated with murals or canvas paintings by artists in the Fine Arts Program (FAP) of the WPA. Some of them were among the best known of their generation. Orozco's epic also met another, personal need—the need to call attention to and express his outrage at what he believed to be financial and military injustices imposed on Mexican peasants.

Creating works of art that are accepted by one's audience can lead to an artist's social acceptance and recognition. But sometimes art really is created only to meet the needs of the artist and nothing beyond—with no thought to sale, exhibition, review, or recognition. Such is the story of *outsider art*, a catchall category that has been used for works by untrained artists; self-taught artists who have been incarcerated for committing crimes and who use the circumstances of their isolation as a motive for creating; and people who are psychologically compromised and sometimes institutionalized. Works of art by these individuals and others like them are often *not* intended to be seen. Thus, in the purest sense, they come into existence to meet some essential emotional or psychological need of the artist and the artist alone.

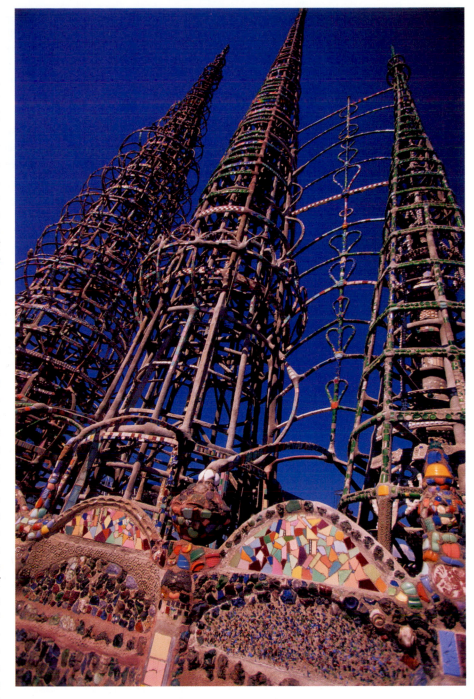

1-40 SIMON RODIA. *Simon Rodia Towers in Watts* (1921–1954). Cement with various objects. 98' high. Cultural Affairs Department, Los Angeles, CA.

The sculptural environment known as the *Simon Rodia Towers in Watts* (Fig. **1-40**) was constructed by an Italian-born tile setter who immigrated to Watts, a poor neighborhood in Los Angeles. Rodia's whimsical towers of cement on steel frames rise to nearly 100 feet and are encrusted with debris such as mirror fragments, broken dishes, shards of glass and ceramic tile, and shells. The result is a lacy forest of spires that glisten with magical patterns of contrasting and harmonious colors. The towers took 33 years to erect and were built by Rodia's own hands. He knew nearly nothing of the world of art and, when asked why he undertook the endeavor, said "I wanted to do something big and I did it."

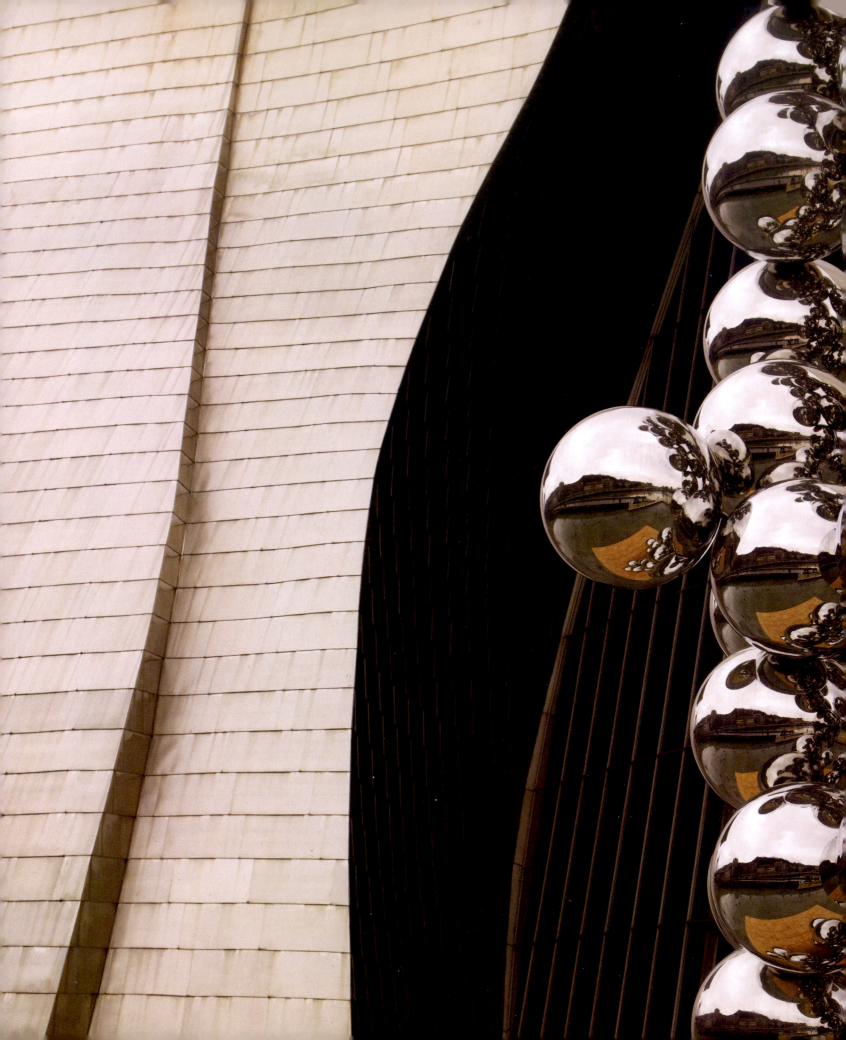

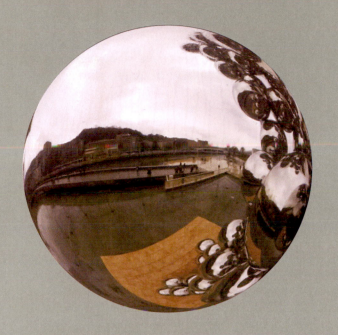

I found I could say things with color and shapes that I couldn't say in any other way—things I had no words for.

—Georgia O'Keeffe

VISUAL ELEMENTS OF ART

The language of art is the language of our visual and tactile experiences in the world, and the words or vocabulary of this language consist of the visual elements of *line, shape, light, value, color, texture, space, time,* and *motion.* Line can define shape; light can reveal it. Color can describe the world we see around us and reveal the psychological worlds within us; we are blue with sorrow, red with rage. Texture is linked with all the emotion of touching, with the cold sharpness of rock or the yielding sensations of flesh. We exist in space; we occupy space and space envelops us. Time allows us to develop into what we are capable of being; time ultimately takes from us what we have been. We are all in motion through space, in a solar system that is traversing the rim of our galaxy at thousands of miles per second, or rotating on the surface of our own globe at a thousand miles per hour. Yet it is the smaller motion—the motion of lifting an arm or of riding through a field—that we are more likely to sense and hence to represent in art.

This vocabulary—*line, shape, light, value, color, texture, space, time,* and *motion*—comprises what we call the **visual elements** or **plastic elements** of art. Artists select from a variety of mediums, including, but by no means limited to, drawing, painting, sculpture, architecture, photography, textiles, and ceramics. They then employ the visual elements of art to express themselves in the chosen medium. In their self-expression, they use these elements to design compositions of a certain style, form, and content.

View of *Tall Tree and the Eye* by Anish Kapoor at the Guggenheim Museum, Bilbao, Spain.

Visual elements, design, style, form, and content—these make up the language of art. Languages such as English and French have symbols—words—that are combined according to rules of grammar to create a message. The visual arts have a "vocabulary" of visual elements that are combined according to the "grammar" of art, or principles of design. These principles include unity, balance, rhythm, scale, and proportion, among others. The composition of the elements creates the style, form, and content of the work—even if this content is an abstract image and not a natural subject, such as a human figure or a landscape. In this chapter, we explore the basic vocabulary or visual elements in the language of art.

LINE

Line is at once the simplest and most complex of the elements of art. It serves as a basic building block around which an art form is constructed and, by itself, has the capacity to evoke thought and emotion. In geometry, we learn that line is made up of an infinite number of points and that the shortest distance between two points is a straight line. In art, a line is more commonly defined as a moving dot.

Characteristics of Line

MEASURE OF LINE The **measure** of a line is its length and its width. If we conceptualize line as a moving dot, the dots that compose it can be of any size, creating a line of lesser or greater width, and of any number, creating a shorter or a longer line.

Sol LeWitt's *Lines from Four Corners to Points on a Grid* (Fig. **2-1**) consists of lines whose measures are precise and carefully plotted. Both the concept of their placement and the act of measuring to create exact mathematical relationships are intrinsic to the work and define it. LeWitt's installations are temporary and can be reproduced by permission of the owner of the instructions, in this case The Whitney Museum of American Art. Because the artist's relationship to his work begins and ends in a set of instructions, the actual implementation of the work can vary from one embodiment to another. Much Conceptual Art, of which this is an exam-

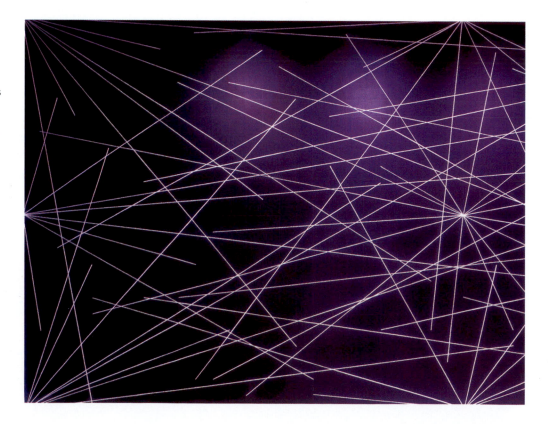

2-1 SOL LEWITT. *Lines from Four Corners to Points on a Grid* (1976), detail. A 6-inch grid covering each of four black walls. White lines to points on grids. First wall: 24 lines from the center; second wall: 12 lines from the midpoint of each of the sides; third wall: 12 lines from each corner; fourth wall: 24 lines from the center; 12 lines from the midpoint of each of the sides, 12 lines from each corner. White crayon lines and black crayon grid on black walls. Dimensions variable. Whitney Museum of American Art, NY.

ple, challenges our notions of whether an artist is obligated to create the physical work of art to be its author or whether the idea of the work is sufficient.

By contrast, the notion of measuring the lengths of line that are both the subject and the process of Jackson Pollock's *Number 14: Gray* (Fig. **2-2**) seems ludicrous and incomprehensible. Pollock's lines weave and overlap and swell and pinch, creating a sense of infinite flow and freedom from constraint (where *constraint* is defined as logical and mathematical measurement). LeWitt's lines are precise; Pollock's are gestural, fluid, and loose. The effects of the LeWitt and the Pollock are very different. The LeWitt is static; the Pollock expands and contracts, shoots forward and recedes.

EXPRESSIVE QUALITIES OF LINE The works by LeWitt and Pollock also reveal the expressive characteristics of line. Lines may be perceived as delicate, tentative, elegant, assertive, forceful, or even brutal. The lines in the LeWitt installation are assertive but cold. The emotional human element is missing. The work seems to express the human capacity to detach the intellect from emotional response, and perhaps to program computers (and other people) to carry out pre-

cise instructions. The lines in the Pollock work combine the apparently incongruous expressive qualities of delicacy and force. They are well rounded and human, combining intellect with passion. The LeWitt suggests the presence of a plan. The Pollock suggests the presence of a human being weaving elegantly through the complexities of thought and life.

TYPES OF LINE The variety of line would seem to be as infinite as the number of points that, we are told, determine it. Lines can be straight or curved. They can be vertical, horizontal, or diagonal. A curved line can be circular or oval. It can run full circle to join itself where it began, thereby creating a complete shape. Curved lines can also be segments or arcs— parts of circles or ovals. As a line proceeds, it can change direction abruptly: A straight line that stops and changes course becomes a zigzag. A curved line that forms an arc and then reverses direction becomes wavy. Circular and oval lines that turn ever inward on themselves create vertiginous spirals. Art's most basic element is a tool of infinite variety.

Contour lines are created by the edges of things. They are perceived when three-dimensional shapes curve back into space. Edges are perceived because the objects differ from

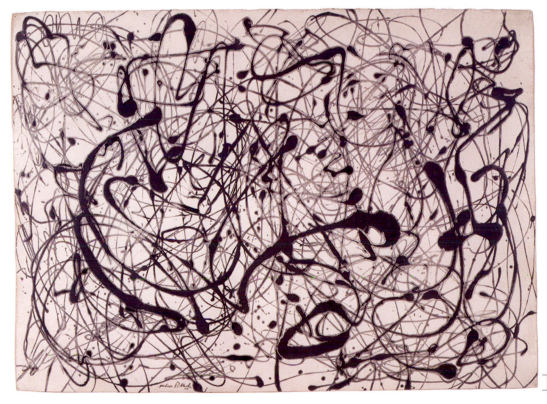

2-2 JACKSON POLLOCK. *Number 14: Gray* (1948). Enamel and gesso on paper. 22¾" × 31". Yale University Art Gallery, New Haven, CT. © 2011 Pollock-Krasner Foundation/Artists Rights Society (ARS), NY.

1 in.

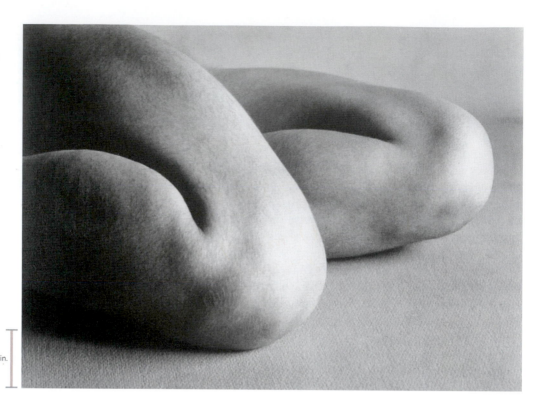

2-3 EDWARD WESTON. *Knees* (1927). Gelatin silver print. 6¼" × 9³⁄₁₆". San Francisco Museum of Modern Art, San Francisco, CA.

1 in.

the backgrounds in value (lighter versus darker), texture, or color. If you hold up your arm so that you perceive it against the wall (or, if you are outside, the sky), you will discriminate its edge—its contour line—because the wall is lighter or darker, because it differs from the wall in color, and because the texture of flesh differs from the wallboard or plaster or wood or brick of the wall.

Edward Weston's photograph *Knees* (Fig. **2-3**) highlights the aesthetic possibilities of contour lines. Weston was drawn to the sculptural forms of the human figure, plant life, and natural inanimate objects such as rocks. In *Knees*, the contour lines (edges) of the legs are created by the subtle differences in value (light and dark) and texture between the legs and the wall and the floor. The legs take on the abstract quality of an exercise to demonstrate how contour lines define the human form and how shading creates or *models* roundness.

Actual line can be distinguished from *implied line*. The points in **actual line** are connected and continuous. The LeWitt (Fig. 2-1) and Pollock (Fig. 2-2) are examples of works with actual line. Works with **implied line** are completed by

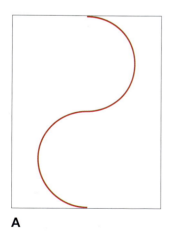

A

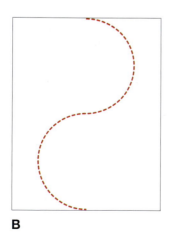

B

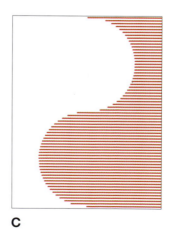

C

2-4 A, B, and C Actual line (A) versus two kinds of implied lines, one formed by dots (B) and the other formed by psychologically connecting the edges of a series of straight lines (C).

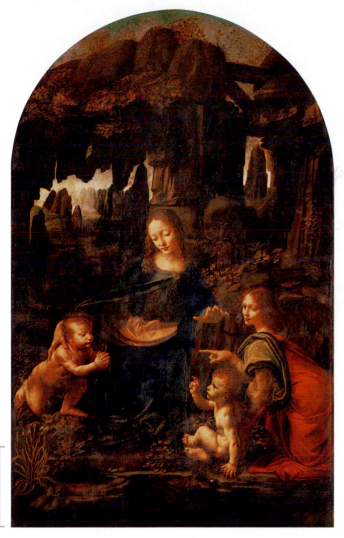

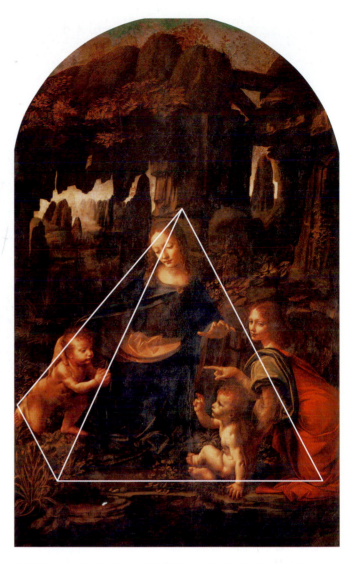

1 ft.

2-5 LEONARDO DA VINCI. *Madonna of the Rocks* (1483). Oil on panel, transferred to canvas. 78½" × 48". Louvre, Paris, France.

2-6 The pyramidal structure of the *Madonna of the Rocks*. Oil on panel, transferred to canvas. 78½" × 48". Louvre, Paris, France.

the viewer. An implied line can be a discontinuous line that the viewer reads as continuous because of the overall context of the image. Implied lines can be suggested by a series of points or dots, as in Part B of Figure 2-4. They can be suggested by the nearby endpoints of series of parallel or nearly parallel lines of different lengths, as in Part C of Figure 2-4. The movements and glances of the figures in a composition also imply lines.

One of the hallmarks of Renaissance paintings is the use of implied lines to create or echo the structure of the composition. Geometric shapes such as triangles and circles are suggested through the use of linear patterns created by the position and physical gestures of the participants and, often,

glances between them. These shapes often serve as the central focus and the main organizational device of the compositions. In the *Madonna of the Rocks* (Fig. **2-5**), Leonardo da Vinci places the head of the Virgin Mary at the apex of a rather broad, stable pyramid formed not by actual lines but by the extension of her arms and the direction of her glance. The base of the pyramid is suggested by an implied line that joins the "endpoints" of the baby Jesus and the infant John the Baptist. Figure **2-6** highlights the pyramidal structure of the composition.

A mental or perceptual connection can create a **psychological line**. If a character in a painting points to an object, or if one figure gazes directly toward another—as in Emily

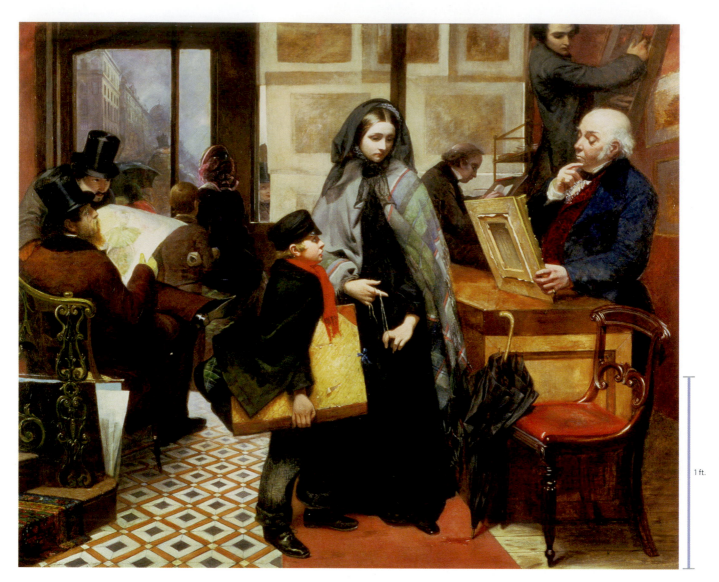

1 ft.

2-7 EMILY MARY OSBORN. *Nameless and Friendless* (1834–?). Oil on canvas. 34" × 44". Private Collection.

Mary Osborn's *Nameless and Friendless* (Fig. **2-7**)—we perceive the connection between the two as a psychological line, even though the artist has not created an actual or implied line. In Osborn's painting, which represents the plight of the woman artist, a small boy (her brother?) stares directly at the condescending art dealer as he feigns serious consideration of her work. The boy's unflinching glance and the dealer's face are visually connected with a psychological line. Another psychological line connects the downward face of the impoverished woman with the tip of her shoe, which emerges from the bottom of her long black skirt. She stands in judgment, fidgeting with the fringe of her shawl, not quite knowing where to look. Gestures and glances such as those in Osborn's work lead the viewer's eye around the composition. Therefore, psychological lines are also called compositional lines.

Functions of Line

The line, as an element of art, is alive with possibilities. Artists use line to outline shapes, to evoke forms and movement, to imply solid mass, or for its own sake. In groupings, lines can create shadows and even visual illusions.

TO OUTLINE AND SHAPE When you make or observe an outline, you are describing or suggesting the edge of a form or a shape. Line defines a shape or form as separate from its surrounding space; line gives birth to shape or form. Line grants them substance.

In addition to defining shape, line can also function as form itself. *Madonna and Child* (Fig. **2-8**) by Rimma Gerlovina and Valeriy Gerlovin is a revision of one of the most popular religious themes of the Renaissance. Taking their cue from works by artists such as Raphael, the Gerlovins use their signature combination of the body and braided hair to embroider a contemporary image of the Virgin Mary and the infant Jesus. The Gerlovins are the principal subjects of their work, and in this piece Gerlovina serves as the model for the Virgin. Braid extensions of her own sandy brown hair cascade from a sculptural head whose three-dimensionality stands in marked contrast to the flatness of the rippling braids. These braids flow into the contours of the Christ-child's body, nested in the palm of a sculpted hand.

TO CREATE DEPTH AND TEXTURE The face of Elizabeth Catlett's sturdy *Sharecropper* (Fig. **2-9**) is etched by a series of short, vigorous lines that are echoed in the atmosphere that surrounds her. The lines give the woman's features a gaunt, hollowed-out look and are also used to create a harsh texture in a turbulent environment. The textures of her garment, hair, and hat are also represented by series of lines.

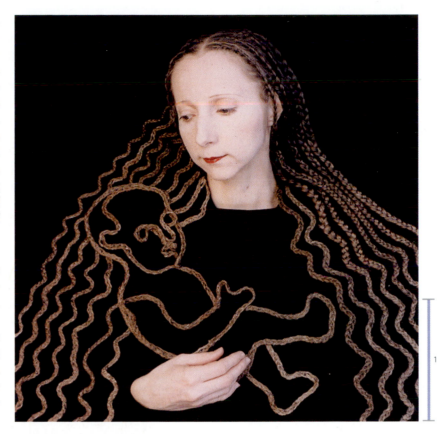

1 ft.

2-8 RIMMA GERLOVINA AND VALERIY GERLOVIN. *Madonna and Child* (1992). 40" × 40". Chromogenic print. Collection of DZ Bank, Germany.

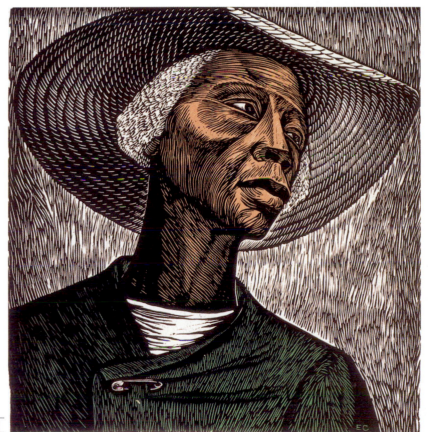

1 in.

2-9 ELIZABETH CATLETT. *Sharecropper* (1968). Color linocut. 26" × 22". Hampton University Museum, Hampton, VA. Art © Elizabeth Catlett/ Licensed by VAGA, NY.

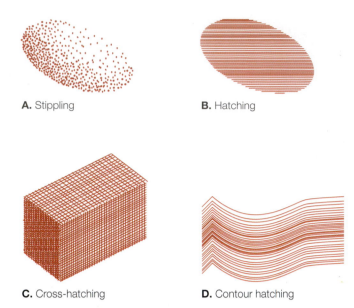

A. Stippling   **B.** Hatching

C. Cross-hatching   **D.** Contour hatching

2-10 Illusion of three-dimensionality.

Dots and lines can be used to create the illusion of three-dimensionality through shading. Part A shows the method of stippling, in which shading is represented by a pattern of dots that thickens and thins. Part B represents shading by means of hatching—that is, using a series of closely spaced parallel lines. Part C shows the method of cross-hatching, in which the series of lines intersects another series of lines. Part D shows how directional changes in hatching can define contours.

Modeling on a two-dimensional surface is the creation of the illusion of roundness or three dimensions through the use of light and shadow. As shown in Figure **2-10**, shadows can be created by the use of dots and lines. Part A shows the method of **stippling**, of using a pattern of dots that thickens and thins. Areas where the dots are thicker are darker and create the illusion of being more shaded. Part B shows the technique of **hatching**, or using a series of closely spaced parallel lines to achieve a similar effect. Areas in which lines are closer together appear to be more shaded. **Cross-hatching**, shown in Part C, is similar to hatching, but as the name implies, a series of lines run in different directions and cross one another.

Contours can be created when hatching changes direction, as in Part D. Notice how the sharecropper's face is carved by hatching that alters direction to give shape to the wells of the eyes, the nose, the lips, and the chin. Directional changes in hatching also define the prominent anatomic features of the sharecropper's neck.

TO SUGGEST DIRECTION AND MOVEMENT Renaissance artist Sandro Botticelli's *The Birth of Venus* (Fig. **2-11**) shows how line can be used to outline forms and evoke movement. In this painting, firm lines carve out the figures

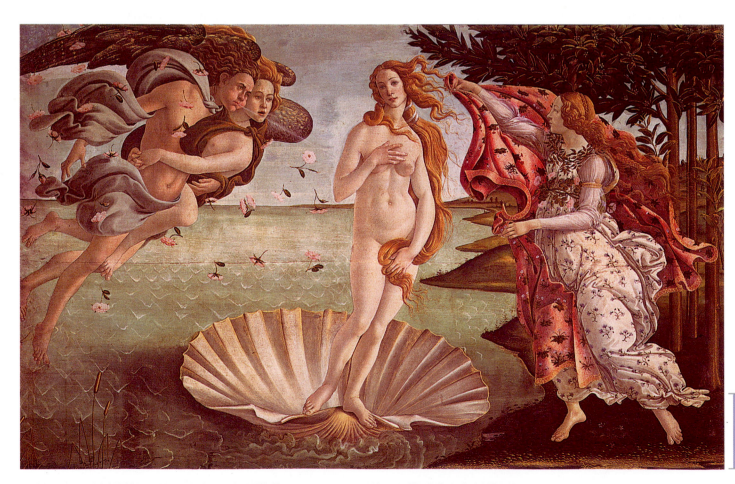

2-11 SANDRO BOTTICELLI. *The Birth of Venus* (c. 1482). Tempera on canvas. 5'8⅞" × 9'1⅞". Galleria degli Uffizi, Florence, Italy.

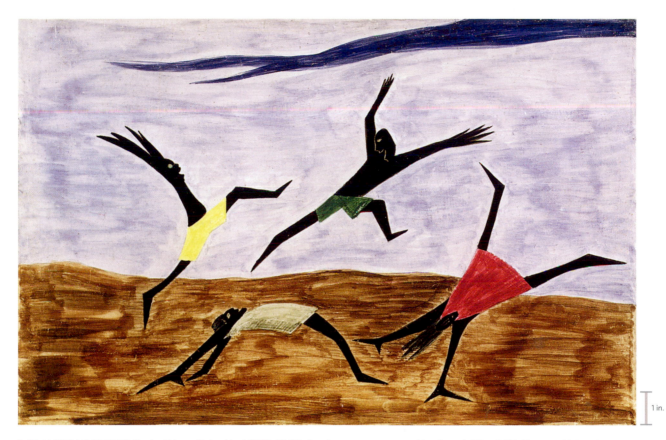

1 in.

2-12 JACOB LAWRENCE. *Harriet Tubman Series, No. 4* (1939–1940). Casein tempera on gessoed hardboard. 12" × 17⅞". Hampton University Museum, Hampton, VA.

from the rigid horizontal of the horizon and the verticals of the trees. Straight lines carry the breath of the Zephyr from the left, and the curved lines of the drapery imply the movement of the Zephyrs and of the nymph to the right. Implied compositional lines give this work an overall triangular structure.

Horizontal lines, like horizon lines, suggest stability. Vertical lines, like the sweeping verticals in skyscrapers, defy gravity and suggest assertiveness. Diagonal lines are often used to imply movement and directionality, as in the directionality and movement of the breath of the Zephyr in *The Birth of Venus*. African American artist Jacob Lawrence used assertive sticklike diagonals to give the slave children in his painting *Harriet Tubman Series, No. 4* (Fig. **2-12**) a powerful sense of movement and directionality. While the horizon line provides a somewhat stable world, the brightly clad children perform acrobatic leaps, their branchlike limbs akin to the wood above. The enduring world implied by the horizon is shattered by the agitated back-and-forth of the brushed lines that define ground and sky. Such turmoil presumably awaits the children once they mature and realize their lot in life.

SHAPE, VOLUME, AND MASS

The word *shape* has many meanings. Parents or teachers may tell you to "shape up" when they are concerned about your behavior. When you started arranging things in your dorm room or apartment, you may have had thoughts as things began to "take shape." Such expressions suggest *definition*—that is, pulling things together within defined boundaries to distinguish them from what surrounds them. We say our bodies are "out of shape" when they violate our preferred physical contours. In works of art, **shapes** are defined as the areas within a composition that have boundaries that separate them from what surrounds them; shapes make these areas distinct.

Shapes are formed when intersecting or connected lines enclose space. In Botticelli's *The Birth of Venus* and in the Lawrence painting, for example, shape is clearly communicated by lines that enclose specific areas of the painting. Shape can also be communicated through patches of color or texture. In three-dimensional works, such as sculpture and architecture, shape is discerned when the work is viewed against its environment. The edges, colors, and textures of the work give it shape against the background. Theo van Doesburg's

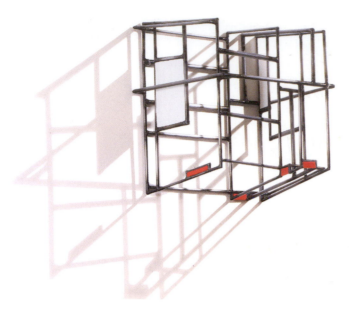

2-13 HELENE BRANDT. *Mondrian Variations, Construction No. 3B with Four Red Squares and Two Planes* (1996). Welded steel, wood, paint. 22" × 19" × 17".

Mass

Like volume, the term *mass* also has a specific meaning in science. In physics, the mass of an object reflects the amount of force required to move it. Objects that have more mass are harder to budge. In three-dimensional art, the **mass** of an object refers to its bulk. A solid work made of steel with the same dimensions as Helene Brandt's sculpture would have more mass.

We would be hard-pressed to conjure a better exemplar of mass than Rachel Whiteread's Holocaust Memorial in Vienna (Fig. **2-15**). It possesses the gravity of a stone pyramid and evokes the simplicity and serenity of a mausoleum. Built of concrete and weighing 250 tons, the memorial is designed as an inverted library—the "books" protrude on the outside—in recognition of the significance of study to the Jewish people, "the people of the book." But the doors to this "library" are bolted, making the books inaccessible. In the wake of the destruction of the Austrian Jewish community, there is no longer any use for them. The names of the places to which the country's Jews were deported for annihilation are inscribed in alphabetical order around the exterior. There is murder, death, and loss here, and the massiveness of the memorial shapes a sense of gloom that cannot be lifted.

ACTUAL MASS VERSUS IMPLIED MASS The Whiteread Memorial has **actual mass**. It occupies three-dimensional space and has measurable volume and weight. Objects that are depicted as three-dimensional on a two-dimensional surface (such as a drawing or a painting) have what we call **implied**

Composition (Fig. 20-17) features colorful geometric shapes of various dimensions that are created when vertical and horizontal black lines slice through the canvas space and intersect to define areas distinct from the rest of the surface.

The word **form** is often used to speak about shape in sculpture or architecture—three-dimensional works of art. Helene Brandt's *Mondrian Variations, Construction No. 3B with Four Red Squares and Two Planes* (Fig. **2-13**) is a translation into three dimensions of a composition by painter, Piet Mondrian—a contemporary of van Doesburg. Therefore, some artists and people who write about art may prefer to speak of the *form* of the Brandt sculpture rather than its shape. Others use the word *shape* to apply to both two-dimensional and three-dimensional works of art. We will use the terms interchangeably.

The word **volume** refers to the mass or bulk of a three-dimensional work. The volume of a work is the amount of space it contains. In geometry, the volume of a rectangular solid is computed as its length times its width times its height. But one may use the concept more loosely to say that a structure has a great *volume* as a way of generally describing its enormity. Gerrit Rietveldt's Schroeder House in Utrecht (Fig. **2-14**) seems to be a volumetric translation of Mondrian's geometric shapes. Here is an example of the usefulness of the term *volume* as it conveys a sense of containment.

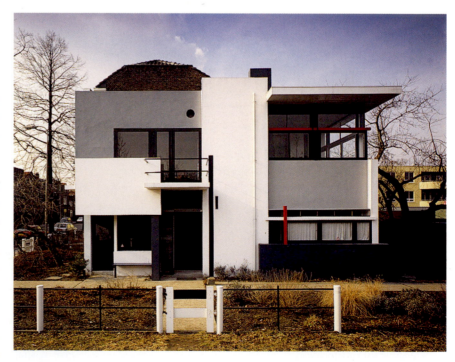

2-14 GERRIT RIETVELDT. Schroeder House (1924). Utrecht, Netherlands.

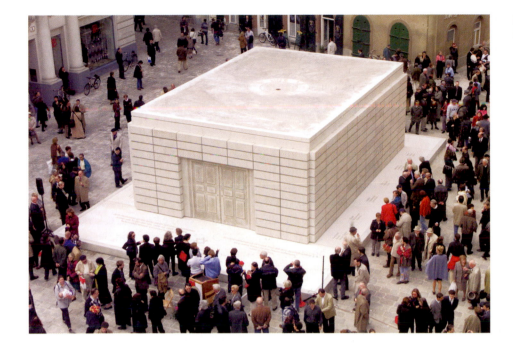

mass. That is, they create the illusion of possessing volume, having weight, and occupying three-dimensional space. Consider a two-dimensional work of art that features massive shapes, broken and fragmented and piled in a pyramidal shape, like so much fuel for a funeral pyre of art's historical icons. In *Landscape* (Fig. **2-16**), Mark Tansey meticulously portrays the remnants of colossal sculptures amid the unending sands of a bleak desert. His realistic style gives the illusion of three dimensions on the two-dimensional canvas surface and implies the extraordinary mass of the oversized stone figures. In the painting, the shapes have implied mass, whereas the sculptures they reference, in reality, have actual mass.

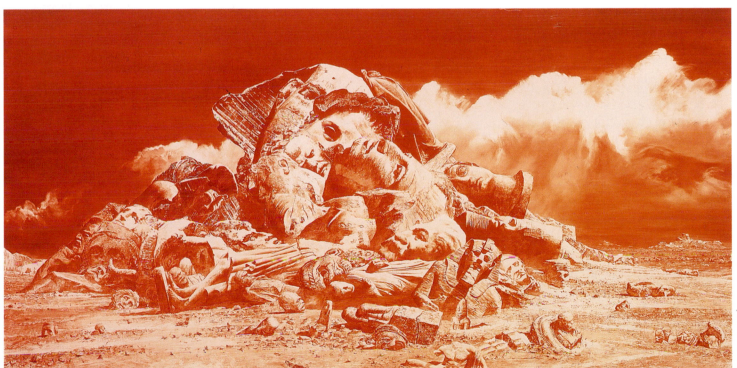

1 ft.

2-16 MARK TANSEY. *Landscape* (1994). Oil on canvas. 71½" × 144".

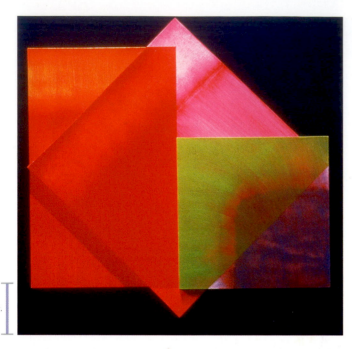

1 ft.

2-17 DOROTHEA ROCKBURNE. *Pascal's Provincial Letters* (1987). Oil on linen. 67" × 67" × 8". © 2011 Dorothea Rockburne/Artists Rights Society (ARS), NY.

Types of Shape

Shapes that are found in geometric figures such as rectangles and circles are called **geometric shapes**. Geometric shapes are regular and precise. They may be made up of straight (rectilinear) or curved (curvilinear) lines, but they have an unnatural, mathematical appearance. Shapes that resemble organisms found in nature—the forms of animals and plant life—are called **organic shapes** and have a natural appearance. Most of the organic shapes found in art are soft, curvilinear, and irregular, although some natural shapes, such as those found in the structure of crystals, are harsh and angular. Artists also work with **biomorphic** and **amorphous** shapes.

Geometric shapes can be **rectilinear** when straight lines intersect to form them. Geometric shapes can also be **curvilinear** when curving lines intersect to form them or when they circle back to join themselves and make up closed geometric figures. Geometric shapes frequently look crisp, or hard-edged, as in painter Dorothea Rockburne's *Pascal's Provincial Letters* (Fig. **2-17**). Rockburne's work has frequently been guided by her interest in mathematics, where we find a purity of form that is rare in the real world. *Pascal's Provincial Letters* is a shaped canvas constructed of overlapping geometric shapes—a rectangle and two squares. Blaise Pascal was a seventeenth-century French mathematician who made many discoveries in geometry, including the fact that the sum of the angles of a triangle equals two right angles (180 degrees). Rockburne rotates the center square, forming triangles in the overlapping shapes, parts of which are obscured. The artist redraws the hidden edges of the shapes, visually fusing the layers. The fusion is enhanced by the softness of the colors and the fluid way in which the pigment is absorbed by the linen.

Frank Gehry, the architect of the Guggenheim Museum in Bilbao, Spain (Fig. **2-18**), refers to his work as a "metallic flower." Others have found the billowing, curvilinear shapes to be reminiscent of ships, linking the machine-tooled

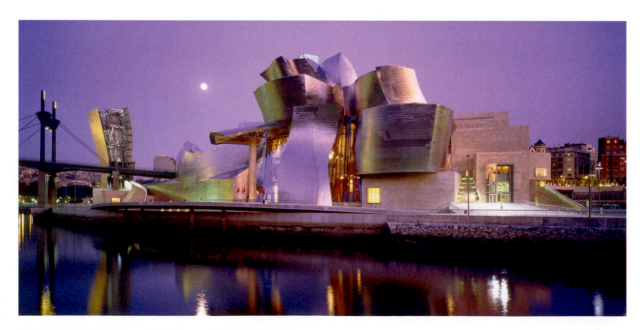

2-18 FRANK GEHRY. Guggenheim Museum (1997). Bilbao, Spain.

PICASSO'S *LES DEMOISELLES D'AVIGNON* WITH COLESCOTT'S *LES DEMOISELLES D'ALABAMA: VESTIDAS*

IN THE YEAR 1907, A YOUNG PABLO PICASSO unveiled a painting that he had been secretly working on for a couple of years. A culmination of what was known as his Rose Period, this new work—*Les Demoiselles d'Avignon* (Fig. **2-19**)—would turn the tide of modern painting. Picasso had studied the work of African and Iberian artists in Parisian museums and galleries. He was struck by the universality of the masks, believing that their rough-hewn, simplified, and angular features crossed time and culture. This painting launched the movement called Cubism, which geometricizes organic forms. The contours of the body in *Demoiselles* are harsh and rectilinear, forming straighter lines than are found in nature. The women in the painting are expressionless and lack identity; some of them even have rectilinear masks in lieu of faces. The intellectual exercise of transforming the human form into geometric shapes takes precedence over any interest in expressing the plight of these women, who are prostitutes in the French underworld. The "figures" in the work transcend the period and culture in which the women lived and worked.

You have probably heard the expression "Clothing makes the man." In Robert Colescott's *Les Demoiselles d'Alabama: Vestidas* (Fig. **2-20**), it could be argued that clothing makes

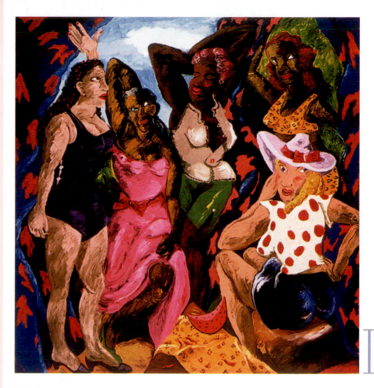

2-20 ROBERT COLESCOTT. *Les Demoiselles d'Alabama: Vestidas* (1985). Acrylic on canvas. 96" × 92".

the woman. The women in Picasso's painting are dehumanized in part by their nudity. The subjects of Colescott's painting, executed some 80 years later, are given strong individuality by their choice of costume. Colescott's painting is one of the thousands of instances in which one artist transforms the work of another in a certain way to make a certain point. Picasso's nudes have a harsh and jagged quality that gives an overall splintered effect to his work; the movement of the women seems to be abrupt and choppy. By contrast, Colescott's women are well rounded (in the literal sense) and fleshy—they are natural, organic, "real" counterparts to Picasso's geometry. The flowing, curvilinear lines of the women cause them to undulate across the canvas with fluid movement.

Whereas Picasso's rectilinear women are timeless (and "placeless"), the curvilinear, clothed women of Colescott are very much tied to their time and place—an American South full of life and spontaneity and emotional expression. Whereas Picasso seemed to relish the intellectual transformation of the prostitutes into timeless figures, Colescott seems to revel in the tangibility and sensuality of his sexy subjects. ●

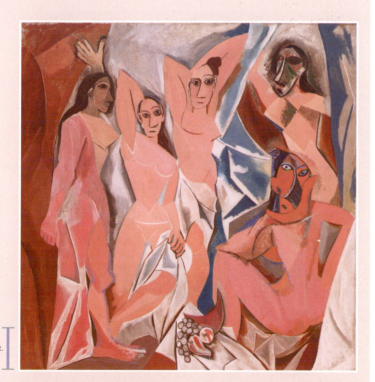

2-19 PABLO PICASSO. *Les Demoiselles d'Avignon* (1907). Oil on canvas. 8' × 7'8". The Museum of Modern Art, NY. © 2011 Estate of Pablo Picasso/ Artists Rights Society (ARS), NY.

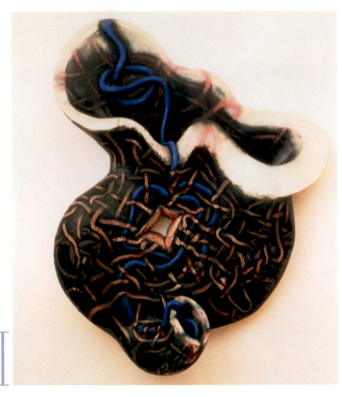

1 ft.

2-21 ELIZABETH MURRAY. *Tangled Fall* (1989–1990). Oil on canvas. 83½" × 66" × 19". © 2011 The Murray-Holman Family Trust/Artists Rights Society (ARS), NY.

2-22 HELEN FRANKENTHALER. *Bay Side* (1967). Acrylic on canvas. 6'2" × 6'9". Private Collection, NY. © 2011 Helen Frankenthaler/ Artists Rights Society (ARS), NY.

structure that is perched on the water's edge to the history of Bilbao as an international seaport. It is as if free-floating geometric shapes have collided on this site, and on another day, they might have assumed a different configuration.

Elizabeth Murray's *Tangled Fall* (Fig. **2-21**) is reminiscent of any number of bodily organs or underwater life—although no medical student or botanist could ever quite place it according to kingdom, phylum, and so on. The shape looks rawly excised from some creature. The interlacing tubes are reminiscent of veins and capillaries carrying who knows what (or who wants to know what). Such imagery is said to have a bio-morphic shape—that is, it has the form (the Greek *morphē*) of biological entities. Rather than have strictly defined shapes, whose boundaries are unyielding, biomorphic shapes seem to ebb and flow, expand and contract, or metamorphose as directed by some inner life force.

Shapes need not be clearly defined or derived from nature or the laws of geometry. Many artists, such as the contemporary painter Helen Frankenthaler, create **amorphous** shapes. In *Bay Side* (Fig. **2-22**), Frankenthaler literally poured paint onto her canvas, creating a nebulous work that is dense in form and rich in texture. The "contents" of the loosely defined shapes spill beyond their boundaries, filling the canvas with irregularly shaped pools of poured paint.

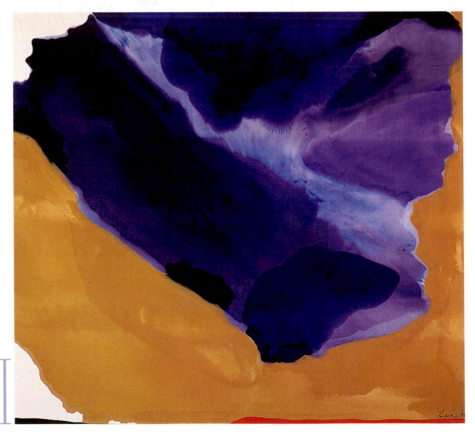

1 ft.

My lordship My lancelot My crusader for peace with dignity My ... hairman of the ... M... guardian of culture My p... ... in the ... ... My d... ... My P... ... My ... forte... My provider My lawye... ... lan... ... My better half My wunderkind My quarterback My to... the charts My great artist My baby mogul My sugar daddy My ticket to ride My jack of all trades My ... eader of the pack My c... ... a... ... at... ... ddy My l... ... ader ... nity My C... M... ... ... an ...lture My professor of desire My host with the most My Dagwood My Rambo My Popeye My pimp My doctor My banker M... lawyer My landlord My so... er of fortune My provider ch... ... My ab... ... ddy My ti... to ... My jack of ... ll ... ... le... ... ck ... capo My pope My stickman My ayatollah My daddy

What big muscles you have!

1 ft.

POSITIVE AND NEGATIVE SHAPES Viewers usually focus on the objects or figures represented in works of art. These are referred to as the **positive shapes**. Whatever is left over in the composition, whether empty space or space filled with other imagery, is termed the **negative shape** or shapes of the composition.

Positive and negative shapes in a work of art have a **figure–ground relationship**. The part or parts of the work that are seen as what the artist intended to depict are the figure, and the other parts are seen as the ground, or background. Barbara Kruger's *Untitled (What Big Muscles You Have!)* (Fig. **2-23**) illustrates that the figure and ground can be distinct even when the relationship between the two is not so clear-cut. Against a satirical running text of the mindless mantra of a hero-worshiper, Kruger sums up the litany with the proclamation "What big muscles you have!" The viewer identifies the larger type as figure and the smaller type of the running text as ground. Notice the visual tension between the large and small type. As we read the larger type, our eye shifts to the pattern and flow of the words behind, and vice versa. The smaller type serves as a kind of psychological wallpaper, signifying one of the horrors of an age of male supremacy that Kruger hopes we left behind in the last millennium.

For many sculptors, negative shapes, or open spaces, are part and parcel of their compositions. The positive shapes in Nancy Holt's *Sun Tunnels* (Fig. **2-24**) consist of the huge

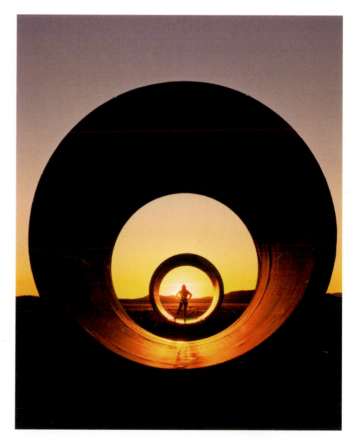

2-24 NANCY HOLT. *Sun Tunnels* (1973–1976). Concrete. Great Basin Desert, UT.

Shape, Volume, and Mass   **41**

concrete pipes she placed in the Utah desert. But the views framed by looking through the interiors of these massive structures—the voids, or negative shapes—have as much meaning as the solids, or more. The flow of air and light through the pipes—the "sun tunnels"—lends them a lightness of being that contrasts with their actual mass. The artist has, in effect, enlisted the sun as an element in her composition.

Gestalt psychologists have noted that shapes can be ambiguous, so as to encourage **figure–ground reversals** with viewers. Figure **2-25** shows a Rubin vase, which is a classic illustration of figure–ground reversals found in psychology textbooks. The central shape is that of a vase, and when the viewer focuses on it, it is the figure. But "carved" into the sides of the vase are the shapes of human profiles; when the viewer focuses on them, they become the figure and the vase becomes the ground. The point of the Gestalt psychologists is that we tend to perceive things *in context*. When we are focusing on the profiles, the vase is perceived as ground, not figure.

The Rubin vase and other psychological illusions were favorite subjects for the contemporary artist Jasper Johns. His painting *Spring* (Fig. **2-26**) shows Rubin vases on a flat canvas with muted colors, among human figures and other fragments of the psychological mind. The askew vases are ambiguous, encouraging figure–ground reversals. The shad-

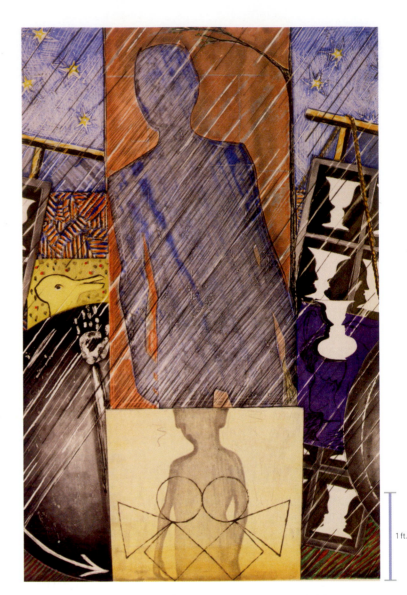

2-26 JASPER JOHNS. *Spring* (1986). Encaustic on canvas. 75" × 50". The Museum of Modern Art, NY. Digital Image ©The Museum of Modern Art, NY/Art Resource, NY. Art © Jasper Johns/Licensed by VAGA, NY.

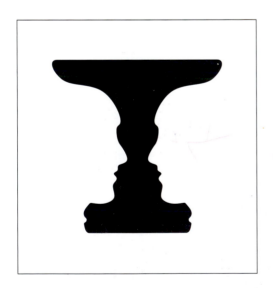

2-25 A Rubin vase.
Gestalt psychologists use this drawing to illustrate the fact that humans tend to perceive objects within their context. When we focus on the vase, it is the figure, and the white shapes to the sides are part of the ground. But when we focus on the "profiles of heads" suggested by the white shapes where they intersect with the sides of the vase, the vase becomes the ground. The drawing is ambiguous; that is, it can be perceived in different ways. As a result, the viewer may experience figure–ground reversals.

owed vase beneath them in the center right is given more prominence by its implied three-dimensionality, and therefore the viewer is not as encouraged to perceive profiles in the negative shapes to its sides. Psychology buffs will also find a well-known drawing of a younger/older woman in the purple space just below the shadowed vase. Can you see why this drawing is ambiguous and allows the viewer's perceptions to shift back and forth so that now one sees a younger woman and now an older woman?

Edward Steichen's photograph of the sculptor Auguste Rodin silhouetted against his sculpted portrait of Victor Hugo (Fig. **2-27**) creates a visual limbo between figure and ground.

EDWARD STEICHEN. *Rodin with His Sculptures "Victor Hugo" and "The Thinker"* (1902). Carbon print, toned. Musée d'Orsay, Paris, France.

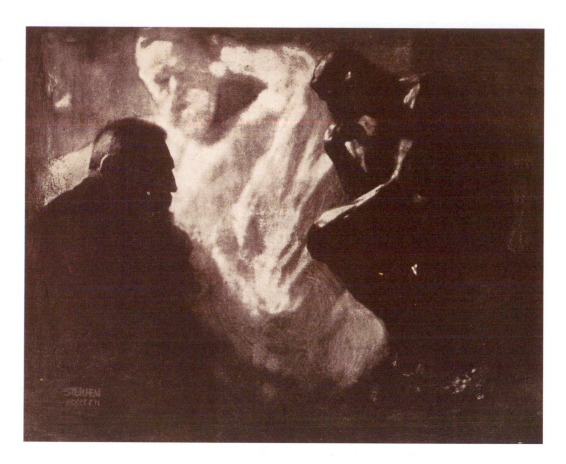

The eye readily perceives the contours of the face of Rodin sitting opposite his bronze sculpture of *The Thinker*, also set against the Hugo sculpture. The viewer's sense of what is a positive shape and what is a negative shape undergoes reversals, as the white-clouded image of the background work seems to float toward the viewer. The spectrelike image of Hugo hovers between and above the dark images, filling the space between them and pushing them visually into the background.

Shape as Icon

Some shapes have entered our consciousness in such a way as to carry with them immediate associations. They are never mistaken for anything else. We could say that they have become cultural icons in the same way that an icon of an opening folder in the toolbar of a word-processing program signifies "Click here to view a list of your files." Some of these images have symbolic resonance that raises them above their actual configuration. Consider the Christian cross, the Jewish Star of David, or the Chinese symbol of yin and yang.

Based on what has been called the most famous photograph in the world, the stylized shape of the social activist and revolutionary, Che Guevara (Fig. **2-28**), has become an icon associated with class struggle, guerilla warfare, and, in

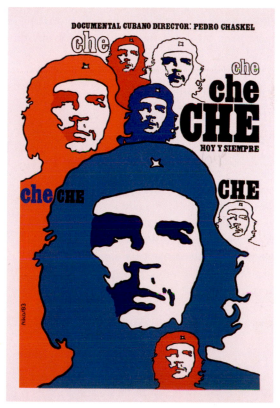

2-28 *Che, Hoy y Siempre* Movie Poster by Niko.

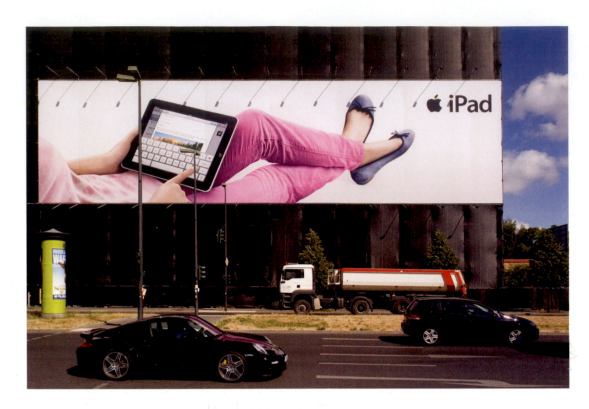

general, counterculture. Although many young people wear merchandise such as wristwatches and T-shirts emblazoned with the bearded, beret-sporting Che, it is not necessarily because they are familiar with who he was and what he did (an Argentinian physician-turned-Marxist revolutionary who joined Fidel Castro's efforts to depose the U.S.-backed dictator Fulgencio Batista). From Cuba, Che went on to inspire (or incite) revolutions in Africa and Latin America, where he was captured with the help of the U.S. Central Intelligence Agency (CIA) and executed. For most young people, Che's instantly recognizable image is simply synonymous with rebellion against authority and idealistic struggle.

Similarly, the ad campaigns for iPod MP3 players, iPhones, and the iPad from Apple, Inc. have capitalized on shape—from the minimalist design of the objects themselves to the print and TV ads featuring consumers using the products (Fig. 2-29). The shapes of Apple products—iPods, Mac computers, iPhones, and the iPad—have been so intrinsic to their appeal that financial commentators link the company's success to consumer identification with the products' shapes. Shape is a powerful visual element, and the representation of shape is a powerful design tool.

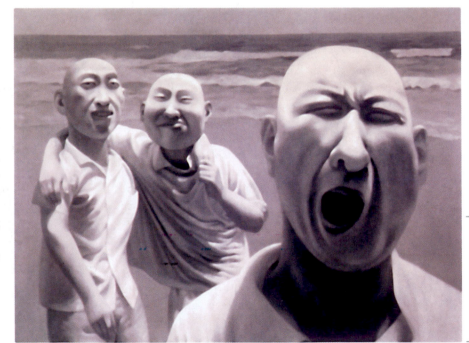

1 ft.

2-30 FANG LIJUN. *No. 2* (1990–1991). Oil on canvas. 31½" × 39⅓". Rheinisches Bildarchiv, Colonge, Germany.

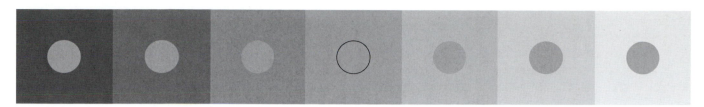

2-31 A value scale of grays.

Do the circles become darker as they move to the right, or do they only appear to do so? How does this value scale support the view of Gestalt psychologists that people make judgments about the objects they perceive that are based on the context of those objects?

LIGHT AND VALUE

Light is fascinating stuff. It radiates. It illuminates. It dazzles. It glows. It beckons like a beacon. We speak of the "light of reason." We speak of genius as "brilliance." **Visible light** is part of the spectrum of electromagnetic energy that also includes radio waves and cosmic rays. It undulates wavelike throughout the universe. It bounces off objects and excites cells in our eyes, enabling us to see. Light is at the very core of the visual arts. Without light there is no art. Without light there is no life.

One of the lobes of the brain contains a theater for light. Somehow it distinguishes light from dark. Somehow it translates wavelengths of energy into colors. We perceive the colors of the visible spectrum, ranging from violet to red. Although red has the longest wavelength of the colors of the visible spectrum, these waves are measured in terms of *billionths* of a meter. And if our eyes were sensitive to light of a slightly longer wavelength, we would perceive infrared light waves. Sources of heat, such as our mates, would then literally glow in the dark. And our perceptions, and our visible arts, would be quite different.

Light makes it possible for us to see points, lines, shapes, and textures. All of these can be perceived as light against dark or, in the case of a pencil line on a sheet of paper, as dark against light. Light against dark, dark against light—in the language of art, these are said to be differences in *value*.

The value of a color of a surface is its lightness or darkness. The value is determined by the amount of light reflected by the surface: the greater the amount of light reflected, the lighter the surface. More light is reflected by a white surface than by a gray surface, and gray reflects more than black. White, therefore, is lighter than gray, and gray is lighter than black.

Infinite shades of gray lie between black and white. Consider the variations in Fang Lijun's *No. 2* (Fig. **2-30**). Figure **2-31** is a value scale of gray that contains seven shades of gray, varying between a gray that is almost black to the left and one that is slightly off-white to the right. When we describe works of art in terms of value, not only do we distinguish their range of grays, but we also characterize their *relative* lightness and darkness, that is, their value contrast. **Value contrast** refers to the degrees of difference between shades of gray. Look again at Figure 2-31. Note that there are circles within the squares. Each of them is exactly the same value (they are all equally dark). However, their value contrast with the squares that contain them differs. The circle and square in the center are of the same value, and therefore they have no value contrast. The circles at either end of the scale have high value contrast with the squares that contain them.

Drawing objects or figures with high value contrast makes them easy to see, or makes them "pop." Consider Figure **2-32**. Part A shows a gray sentence typed on gray paper that is nearly as dark; it is difficult to read. Part B shows nearly black type on off-white paper; it is easy to read. Part C shows light

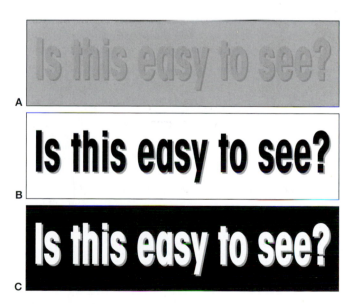

2-32 Value contrast.

Artists and designers know that figures with high value contrast are easier to see. They tend to "pop" out at the viewer. Why is Part A of this figure relatively difficult to read? Why are Parts B and C easier to read?

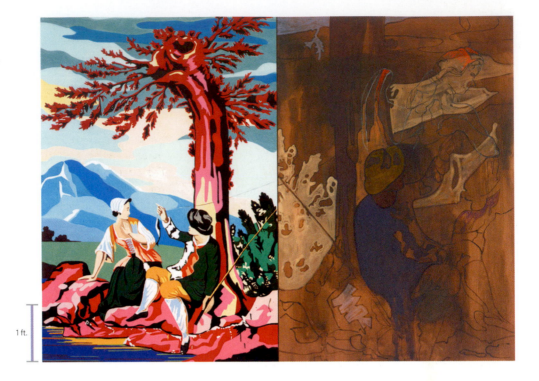

2-33 DAVID SALLE. *Angel* (2000). Oil and acrylic on canvas and linen (two panels). 72" × 96". Art © David Salle/Licensed by VAGA, NY. Courtesy of Mary Boone Gallery.

1 ft.

type that is "dropped out" of dark gray—it, too, pops out at the reader because of high value contrast.

We can discuss the relative lightness and darkness in a work regardless of whether it is a black-and-white or full-color composition. The term *value pattern* describes the variation in light and dark within a work of art and the ways in which they are arranged within a composition. Value patterns can be low-contrast or high-contrast. A high-contrast value pattern can be seen on the left side of David Salle's *Angel* (Fig. **2-33**), and a low-contrast value pattern can be seen on the right side.

Chiaroscuro

Artists use many methods to create the illusion of three dimensions in two-dimensional media, such as painting, drawing, or printmaking. They frequently rely on a pattern of values termed **chiaroscuro**, or the gradual shifting from light to dark through a successive gradation of tones across a curved surface. By use of many gradations of value, artists can give objects portrayed on a flat surface a rounded, three-dimensional appearance.

In *La Source* (Fig. **2-34**), Pierre-Paul Prud'hon creates the illusion of rounded surfaces on blue gray paper by using black and white chalk to portray light gradually dissolving into shade. His subtle modeling of the nude is facilitated by the middle value of the paper and the gradation of tones from light to dark through a series of changing grays. Prud'hon's light source is not raking and harsh, but diffuse and natural. The forms are not sharply outlined; we must work to find out-

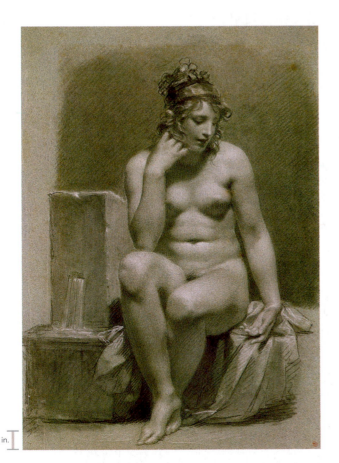

1 in.

2-34 PIERRE-PAUL PRUD'HON. *La Source* (c. 1801). Black and white chalk on blue gray paper. 21³⁄₁₆" × 15⁵⁄₁₆". Sterling and Francine Clark Art Institute, Williamstown, MA.

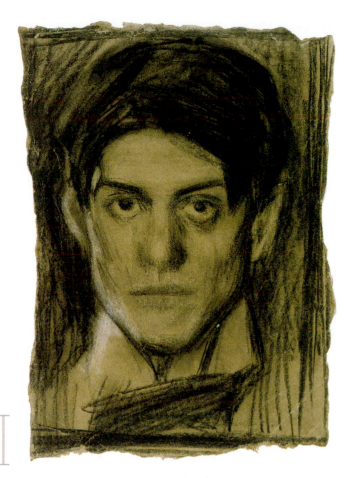

2-35 PABLO PICASSO. *Self-Portrait* (1900). Charcoal on paper. 8⅞" × 6½". Museu Picasso, Barcelona, Spain. © 2011 Estate of Pablo Picasso/Artists Rights Society (ARS), NY.

1 in.

lining anywhere but in the drapery and in the hair. The softly brushed edges of the figure lead your eye to perceive three-dimensional form (continuing around into space) rather than flat, two-dimensional shape.

Picasso used chiaroscuro in his *Self-Portrait* (Fig. **2-35**), sketched at age 19. Although he restricted himself to the use of charcoal, he managed to effect a more subtle gradation of tone through shading that softly delineates his facial features. Sharp contrasts are eliminated by the choice of a buff-colored paper that provides a uniform flesh tone. In effect, the sides of the nose and cheek are built up through the use of soft shadows. The chin and jaw jut out above the neck through the use of sharper shadowing. The eyes achieve their intensity because they are a dark counterpoint to the evenly modeled flesh. There is a tension between the angularity of the lines in the drawing and the modeling. If you focus on the lines, the drawing may seem to be more angular and geometric than organic, but the use of chiaroscuro creates a more subtle and human rounding of the face.

Descriptive and Expressive Properties of Value

Values—black, grays, white—may be used purely to describe objects, or they can be used to evoke emotional responses in the viewer.

Black and white may have expressive properties or symbolic associations. Consider the photograph of a performance piece by Lorraine O'Grady (Fig. **2-36**) staged in protest of the opening of an exhibit titled "Personae," which featured the work of nine white artists and *no* artists of color. Labeling herself "Mlle Bourgeoisie Noire" (or Miss Middle-Class Black), O'Grady appeared in an evening gown constructed of 180 pairs of white gloves and shouted poems that lashed out against the racial politics of the art establishment. Clearly, the white gloves were both evocative and provocative. They were at once a symbol of high society and servitude, of the elegant attire of the exclusive dinner party and the vaudevillian costume of blackface and white-gloved hands.

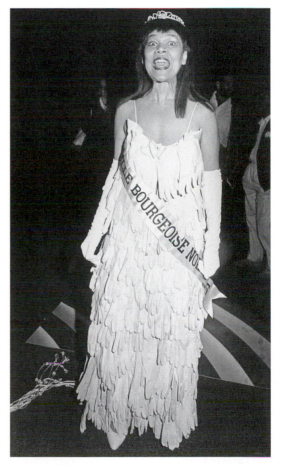

2-36 LORRAINE O'GRADY. *Mlle Bourgeoise Noire Goes to the New Museum* (1981).

ROTHKO'S *NUMBER 22* WITH ROTHKO'S *BLACK ON GREY*

THE AMERICAN ARTIST MARK ROTHKO (1903–1970) worked in many styles during his lifetime. His early work, like that of many twentieth-century artists, was largely in a realistic vein. By the time he was 40 years old, he showed an interest in **Surrealism**, which was imported from Europe. But within a few years, he was painting the **Abstract Expressionist** color-field paintings with which he is mainly associated.

He painted *Number 22* (Fig. **2-37**) in 1949, at about the time a critic remarked that his work tended to evoke the color patterns of French Impressionists and to create "lovely moods." The realistic images of his early days and the symbols of his Surrealistic days were replaced with large, abstract fields of color, which were more or less vertically stacked. Here Rothko uses a high key palette with intensely saturated color. The values in *Number 22* are bold, jaunty, hot, and abrasive. We observe the work of an innovative 46-year-old painter coming into his own—creating his mature style, being invited to teach in academies across the country, and receiving some critical acclaim. The light values seem to imbue the work with boisterous emotion and life. Rothko was developing his signature image of "floating" rectangles that continued to be his model throughout his life's work. The canvases consisted solely of these shapes, stacked one atop the other, varied in width and height and hue, edges softened with feathered strokes that created the illusion of subtle vibration. By not referring to any specific visual experience, the high key values of these nonobjective works seem to suggest a divine, spiritual presence. The luminosity of *Number 22* is perhaps suggestive of the birth of the universe. The red band in the middle is reminiscent of a horizon line, but all is aglow and alive.

Compare *Number 22* to a work Rothko painted some 20 years later: *Black on Grey* (Fig. **2-38**). The painting reveals one of the most dramatic and resonant uses of black in the history of abstract painting. Toward the end of the 1960s, Rothko began to simplify his color fields, stretching his rectangles out to the very edges of the canvas and effectively dividing the surface into two simple fields. He also reduced his palette to low key values—particularly grays, browns, and black. In Rothko's last painting, *Black on Grey*, created just before he took his own life in his studio on February 25, 1970, black and gray merge at a horizon punctuated by a dull light. Darkness falls heavily on the mottled gray field; note that the title, *Black on Grey*, underscores the symbolism of the encroaching of death. It is as if he has brought his life, and his life's work, to a close. The spiritual presence has flickered out.

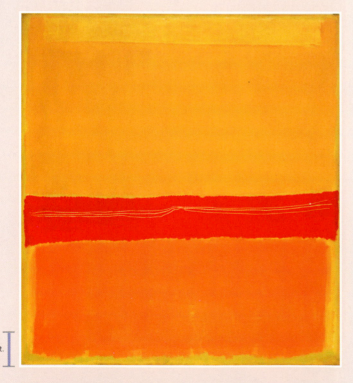

1 ft.

2-37 MARK ROTHKO. *Number 22* (1949). Oil on canvas. 117" × 107⅛". The Museum of Modern Art, NY.

1 ft.

2-38 MARK ROTHKO. *Black on Grey* (1970). Acrylic on canvas, 80¼" × 69". The Solomon R. Guggenheim Museum, NY.

COLOR

Color is a central element in our spoken language as well as in the language of art. The language connects emotion with color: we speak of being blue with sorrow, red with anger, green with envy.

The color in works of art can also trigger strong emotional responses in the observer, working hand in hand with line and shape to enrich the viewing experience. The Postimpressionist Vincent van Gogh often chose color more for its emotive qualities than for its fidelity to nature. Likewise in some amorphous abstract works, such as *Bay Side* (Fig. 2-22), color seems to be much of the message being communicated by the artist.

What is color? You have no doubt seen a rainbow or observed how light sometimes separates into several colors when it is filtered through a window. Sir Isaac Newton discovered that sunlight, or white light, can be broken down into different colors by a triangular glass solid called a **prism** (Fig. **2-39**).

Psychological Dimensions of Color: Hue, Value, and Saturation

The wavelength of light determines its color, or **hue**. The visible spectrum consists of the colors red, orange, yellow, green, blue, indigo, and violet. The wavelength for red is longer than that for orange, and so on through violet.

The value of a color, like the value of any light, is its degree of lightness or darkness. If we wrap the colors of the spectrum around into a circle, we create a color wheel such as that shown in Figure **2-40**. (We must add some purples not found in the spectrum to complete the circle.) Yellow is the

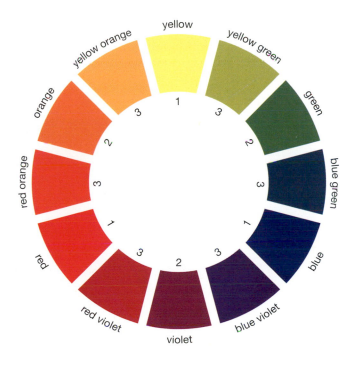

2-39 Prism.
A prism breaks down white light into the colors of the visible spectrum.

2-40 A color wheel.
The color wheel bends the colors of the visible spectrum into a circle and adds a few missing hues to complete the circle.

lightest of the colors on the wheel, and violet is the darkest. As we work our way around from yellow to violet, we encounter progressively darker colors. Blue-green is about equal in value to red-orange, but green is lighter than red.

The colors on the green-blue side of the color wheel are considered **cool** in "temperature," whereas the colors on the yellow-orange-red side are considered **warm**. Perhaps greens and blues suggest the coolness of the ocean or the sky, and hot things tend to burn red or orange. A room decorated in green or blue may appear more appealing on a hot day in July than a room decorated in red or orange. On a canvas, warm colors seem to advance toward the picture plane. Cool colors, on the other hand, seem to recede.

The **saturation** of a color is its pureness. Pure hues have the greatest intensity, or brightness. The saturation, and hence the intensity, decrease when another hue or black, gray, or white is added. Artists produce **shades** of a given hue by adding black, and **tints** by adding white.

Additive and Subtractive Colors

When all those years as a child you were mixing fingerpaints together, or rubbing crayons across already colored surfaces, you probably thought you were adding colors to other colors. In a piece of irony in which science contradicts common sense, it turns out that you were actually subtracting colors from one another. **Additive colors** have to do with mixing *lights*, and **subtractive colors** have to do with mixing *pigments*.

Additive colors are rays of colored light, which, when overlapped or "mixed" with other rays of color, produce lighter colors and white (Fig. **2-41**). White light can be rec-

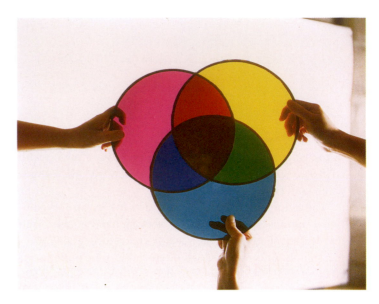

2-42 Subtractive color mixtures.
One subtracts colors by mixing pigments.

reated by overlapping orange-red, blue-violet, and green. Because these colors cannot be derived from the mixing of other colored light, they are called **primary colors**. When they are overlapped, they form lighter colors known as **secondary colors**: the overlap of orange-red and green create yellow; the overlap of blue-violet and green create indigo (or cyan); and lights of blue-violet and orange-red "mix" to form magenta. White is at the center of the three-way overlap of these primary colors.

Subtractive color refers to the mixing of pigment rather than light and is actually more relevant to the experience of the artist (Fig. **2-42**). When you apply a pigment to a surface, as in applying paint to a canvas, you are applying a substance that causes that surface to reflect every color of the visible spectrum *except for the color you see on the surface*.

Complementary versus Analogous Colors

With pigments, red, blue, and yellow are the primary colors, the ones that we cannot produce by mixing other hues. Mixing pigments of the primary colors creates secondary colors. The three secondary colors are orange (derived from mixing red and yellow), green (blue and yellow), and violet (red and blue), and they are denoted by the number 2 on the color wheel. **Tertiary colors** are created by mixing pigments of primary and adjoining secondary colors and are denoted by a 3 on the color wheel.

Hues that lie next to one another on the color wheel are **analogous**. They form families of color, such as yellow and

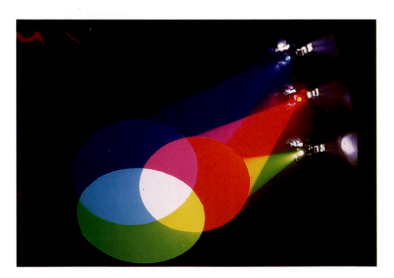

2-41 Additive color mixtures.
One adds colors by mixing lights.

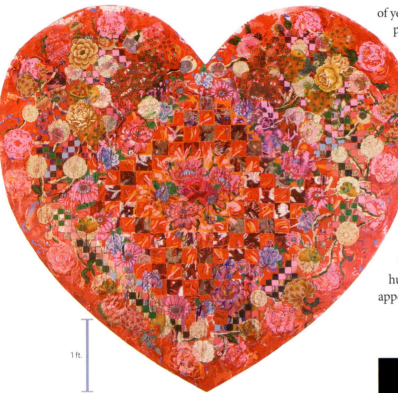

2-43 MIRIAM SCHAPIRO. *Atrium of Flowers* (1980). Acrylic and fabric on canvas. 64" × 60". Flomenhaft Gallery, NY.

of yellow—again, complementary colors—complete the vibrant palette. The painting serves as homage to Tintoretto, a seventeenth-century Venetian artist known as a colorist whose intense palette and dramatic lighting gave a theatrical feeling to his work.

Local versus Optical Color

Have you ever driven at night and wondered whether vague, wavy lines in the distance outlined the peaks of hills or the bases of clouds? Objects may take on different hues as a function of distance or lighting conditions. The greenness of the trees on a mountain may make a strong impression from the base of the mountain, but from a distant vantage point, the atmospheric scattering of light rays may dissolve the hue into a blue haze. Light-colored objects take on a dark appearance when lit strongly from behind. Hues fade as late

orange, orange and red, and green and blue. As we work our way around the wheel, the families intermarry, such as blue with violet and violet with red. Works that use closely related families of color seem harmonious. Miriam Schapiro's *Atrium of Flowers* (Fig. **2-43**) reveals how neighboring colors can be harmoniously augmented by incorporating an array of values of each. Here a palette of reds, pinks, mauve, and peach lends an overall unity to a complicated patchwork design of flowers and quiltlike squares. The color unity that we see in Shapiro's painting is sometimes referred to as the *tonality* of a work of art. *Atrium of Flowers* has a red tonality; red dominates the composition even though other colors are evident in the work.

The dramatic contrasts found in complementary color schemes can heighten the expressive or emotional quality of a work. Italian Neo-Expressionist painter Sandro Chia confined his palette to the complementary scheme of orange and blue in his explosive painting *Incident at the Tintoretto Café* (Fig. **2-44**). An oversized orange-draped figure leaps away from the viewer toward the tumultuous blue drapery of the background. In the confusion, the candles of a swinging chandelier spew their flames and tables tip and fly. Shadows of purple and highlights

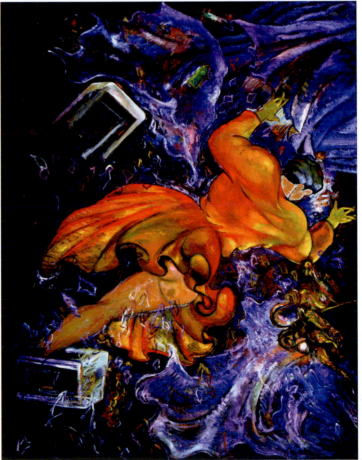

2-44 SANDRO CHIA. *Incident at the Tintoretto Café* (1982). Oil on canvas. 88⅝" × 130". Collection Galerie Bruno Bischofberger, Zurich, Switzerland.

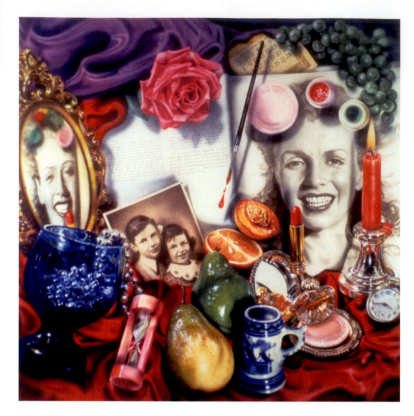

2-45 AUDREY FLACK. *Marilyn (Vanitas)* (1977). Oil over acrylic on canvas. 96" × 96". University of Arizona Museum, Tucson, AZ.

rate than others (faces really do turn red when angry or white when frightened), but they have in common their use of symbolism: feelings and behavior are symbolized with color.

Abstract notions and ideas also have their symbolic color coordinates. For example, what does it mean if one is true to the red, white, and blue? If you are an American citizen, it means that you are loyal to your country—the United States of America—as symbolized by the red, white, and blue colors of the flag. But this would also be true if you were, say, a British student or a French student, because their national flags (the Union Jack or the tricolor) bear the same color combination, albeit with different designs.

In a subtle but chilling commentary on issues of equality, oppression, and difference, contemporary Nigerian British artist Yinka Shonibare reworked typical Victorian costume in fabrics expressing African identity, both constructed and adopted. In *Victorian Couple* (Fig. **2-46**) the profiles of the coat and bustle may seem familiar, but the colorful textiles and printed designs create a cultural disconnect with symbolic ramifications. Shonibare was born in London to Nigerian parents and spent most of his childhood in Nigeria. He returned to England to study at the University of London and

afternoon wends its way to dusk and dusk to night. **Local color** is defined as the hue of an object as created by the colors its surface reflects under normal lighting conditions. **Optical color** is defined as our perceptions of color, which can vary markedly with lighting conditions.

Audrey Flack's oversized photorealist still life paintings—such as *Marilyn (Vanitas)* (Fig. **2-45**)—take advantage of local color to underscore the familiarity of her everyday objects. An orange is orange; grapes are green. Even our "concept" of lipstick is confirmed as a pillar of creamy red. The type of still life that Flack presents here is one in a long tradition of what are called *vanitas* paintings, the contents of which include objects pertaining to vanity—cosmetics, mirrors, jewelry. They are juxtaposed with objects that reference the eventuality of death: an hourglass, a pocket watch, a candle burning down. Between the objective colors and the enormous scale of the work (this painting is eight feet square), the viewer cannot escape the reality of the commonplace objects and the inevitability of fate.

Color as Symbol

The connectedness between emotion and color often explains an artist's palette choices. We all link mood with color—we are green with envy, red with anger, blue with sorrow, white with fright. Some of these descriptions may be more accu-

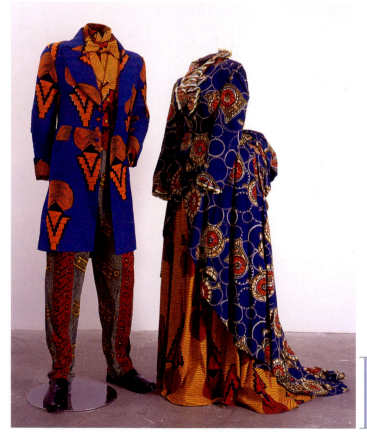

2-46 YINKA SHONIBARE. *Victorian Couple* (1999). Wax-printed cotton textile. Approx. 60" × 36" × 36" and 60" × 24" × 24".

has focused his art on issues of African identity and authenticity, in which the symbolism of color plays a central role.

This brings us to an important fact concerning color and symbolism: The symbols of colors, their meanings, are culture-specific. You may associate white with a bride in American culture, but in China, brides wear red. If you happen to spot a young Chinese American newlywed couple posing for their wedding portraits in a city park, you will likely notice that even though the bride is dressed in white, she wears a prominent red ribbon on her bodice—East meets West.

Texture is another element of art that can evoke a strong emotional response.

TEXTURE

The softness of skin and silk, the coarseness of rawhide and homespun cloth, the coolness of stone and tile, the warmth of wood—these are but a few of the **textures** that artists capture in their works. The word *texture* derives from the Latin for "weaving," and it is used to describe the surface character of woven fabrics and other materials as experienced primarily through the sense of touch.

The element of texture adds a significant dimension to art beyond representation. An artist may distort or exaggerate textures used to define a subject in order to communicate a feeling about it or an emotional state the artist was in when the work was in process. These textures can produce an empathetic response in the viewer. Consider the contrasting use of texture—and the differing emotional impact—of Leon Kossoff's *Portrait of Mrs. Peto No. 2* (Fig. **2-47**) and Marie Laurencin's *Mother and Child* (Fig. **2-48**). The first contains thickly brushed lines and the harsh, gouged textures of impasto—that is, the thick buildup of paint on the surface

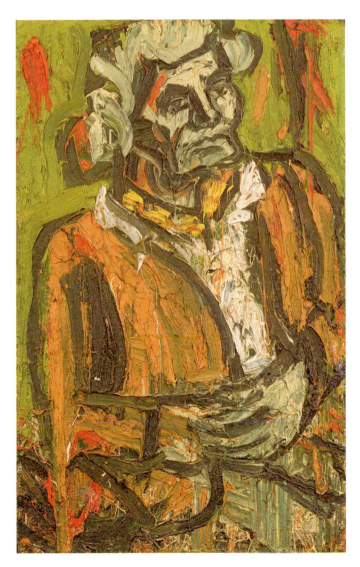

2-47 LEON KOSSOFF. *Portrait of Mrs. Peto No. 2* (c. 1972–73). Oil on board. Private collection. The Bridgeman Art Library International.

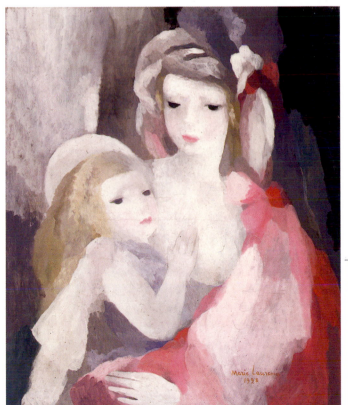

2-48 MARIE LAURENCIN. *Mother and Child* (1928). Oil on canvas. 32" × 25½". The Detroit Institute of Arts, Detroit, MI. © 2011 Artists Rights Society (ARS), NY/ADAGP, Paris.

1 ft.

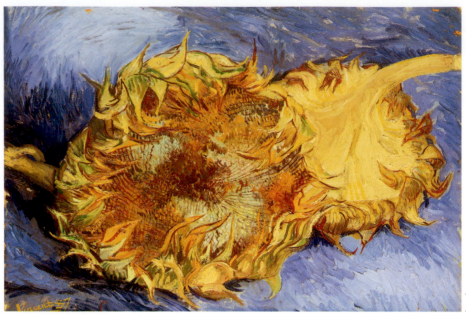

 1 in.

2-49 VINCENT VAN GOGH. *Sunflowers*
(1887). Oil on canvas. 1'5" × 2'.
The Metropolitan Museum of Art, NY.

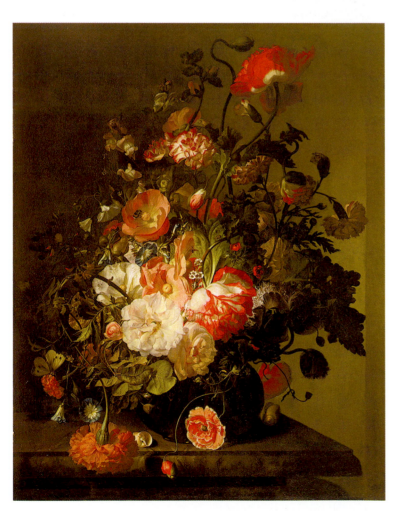

2-50 RACHEL RUYSCH. *Flower Still Life* (after 1700). Oil on canvas.
29¾" × 23⅞". The Toledo Museum of Art, Toledo, OH.

of the canvas. The overall feeling is one of anxiety or somberness. The agitated textural brushwork and the drab palette drag the emotion down.

Laurencin's *Mother and Child*, like Kossoff's *Portrait of Mrs. Peto No. 2*, is an oil painting. But here the brushstrokes are shorter and flatter, and they gradually build up the imagery rather than "carve" it. The overall texture of *Mother and Child* is soft and seems comforting, reinforcing the feeling of tenderness between mother and child. In these contrasting portraits, the role of texture surpasses the literal content of the works—that is, they are both portraits of people—to add an emotional dimension for the viewer.

Types of Texture

In three-dimensional media such as sculpture, crafts, and architecture, the materials have definable textures or *actual texture*. In a two-dimensional medium such as painting, we discuss texture in other terms. For example, the surface of a painting has an *actual* texture—it can be rough, smooth, or something in between. But we typically discuss the surface only when the texture is palpable or unusual, as when thick impasto is used or when an unusual material is added to the surface.

ACTUAL TEXTURE **Actual texture** is *tactile*. When you touch an object, your fingertips register sensations of its actual texture—rough, smooth, sharp, hard, soft. Any work of art has actual texture—whether it is the hard, cold texture of marble or the rough texture of pigment on canvas. Vincent van

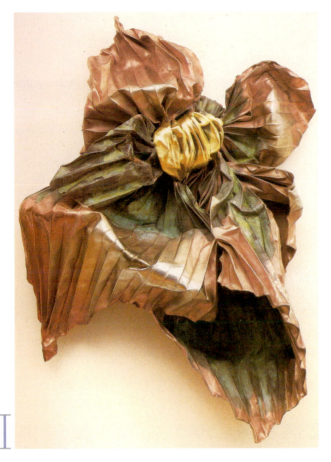

2-51 LYNDA BENGLIS. *Morisse* (1985–1987). Copper, nickel, chrome, and gold leaf. 148" × 43" × 14". Art © Lynda Benglis/Licensed by VAGA, NY.

Gogh's *Sunflowers* (Fig. **2-49**) is rendered with a great deal of surface texture. Van Gogh used impasto—the most common painting technique that yields actual texture—to define his forms, and he often deviated from realistic colors and textures to heighten the emotional impact of his work. The surface texture of the painting goes beyond the real texture of the blossom to communicate an emotional intensity and passion for painting that is independent of the subject matter and more linked to the artistic process—that is, to the artist's method of using gestural brushstrokes to express his sensibilities.

VISUAL TEXTURE Simulated texture in a work of art is referred to as **visual texture**. Artists use line, color, and other elements of art to create the illusion of various textures in flat drawings and paintings. The surface of Rachel Ruysch's *Flower Still Life* (Fig. **2-50**) is smooth and glasslike; however, an abundance of textures is *simulated* by the painstaking detail of the flowers and leaves.

Artists employ a variety of materials to create visual texture, or the illusion of surfaces or textures far removed from their actual texture. In *Morisse* (Fig. **2-51**), for example, sculp-

tor Lynda Benglis creates the illusion of soft, pleated, billowing fabric tied in a knot. It is hard to imagine how the artist can create the impression of silk with materials such as copper, nickel, and chrome. The observer is tempted to reach out and touch the work to reconcile what the eyes are witnessing with what the museum label says. Here the visual texture is vastly different from the actual texture.

In *Gift Wrapped Doll #19* (Fig. **2-52**), Pop artist James Rosenquist uses a common medium—oil on canvas—to simulate the texture of cellophane wrapped around the head of a wide-eyed porcelain doll. The folds of the transparent wrap reflect light, tearing across the innocent face like white-hot rods. We feel, as observers, that were we to poke at the cellophane, we would hear a crackling sound and the pattern of lightning-like stripes would change direction. The image of a doll is usually that of a cuddly companion, but Rosenquist's specimen is haunting and sinister. Perhaps it is a commentary on the ways in which the Western ideal of beauty—blue eyes, blond hair, and a "Cupid's bow" mouth—can suffocate the little girls who grow into women.

The success of *Gift Wrapped Doll* is dependent on the artist's ability to fool the eye. Artists call this **trompe l'oeil**—the French phrase that literally means "trick the eye." Trompe l'oeil has made its appearance throughout the history of art, from first-century-BCE Roman wall painting to contemporary Photorealism.

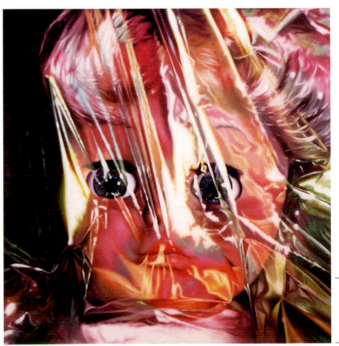

2-52 JAMES ROSENQUIST. *Gift Wrapped Doll #19* (1992). Oil on canvas. 60" × 60". Art © James Rosenquist/Licensed by VAGA, NY.

GÉRICAULT'S *THE RAFT OF THE MEDUSA* WITH STELLA'S *RAFT OF THE MEDUSA*

IN THE YEAR 1816, off the coast of West Africa, a makeshift raft laden with Algerian immigrants was set adrift by the captain and crew of the crippled French ship *Medusa*. Two years later, the artist Théodore Géricault began what was to be his most controversial and political painting, *The Raft of the Medusa* (Fig. **2-53**). Like many of his liberal contemporaries, Géricault opposed the French monarchy and used the tragedy of the *Medusa* to call attention to the mismanagement and ineffectual policies of the French government. The plight of the survivors and victims of the *Medusa* became a national scandal, and Géricault's authentic documentation—based on interviews with the rescued—was construed as a direct attack on the government. Géricault's powerful composition is full of realistic detail and explores the full gamut of human emotion under extreme hardship and duress. The drama of Géricault's composition rests on the diagonal placement of the figures, from the corpse in the lower left that will soon slip into the dark abyss of the ocean, upward along a crescendo that culminates in the muscular torso of a black man waving a flag toward a rescue ship barely visible on the horizon. The fractured raft is tossed about mercilessly by the winds and waves; humans battle against nature, and their own, for sheer survival.

Nearly two centuries later, Frank Stella revisited the subject of the tragedy of the raft of the *Medusa* (Fig. **2-54**) in his aluminum and steel sculpture of the same title. While the heroic drama of "man against the elements" in Gericault's version is conveyed through dramatic lighting, linear forces, and realistic detail, the sense of the event is captured in Stella's work primarily through texture. The structure of the raft, parts of it turned to twisted steel by the forces of the ocean, is overrun by the coarse textures of aluminum fashioned to suggest the frothing of assaulting waves. These textures convey the uneven match between the ill-fated castaways and the unleashed power of nature. ●

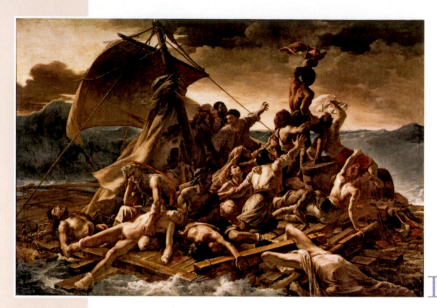

1 ft.

2-53 THÉODORE GÉRICAULT. *The Raft of the Medusa* (1818–1819). Oil on canvas. 16'1" × 23'6". Louvre, Paris, France.

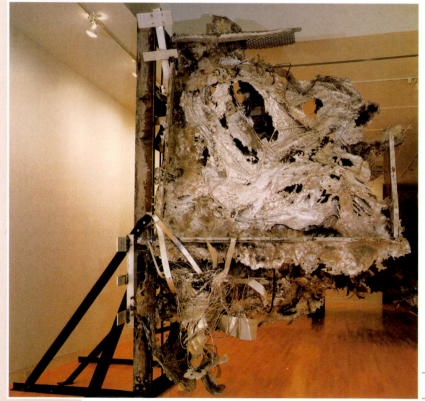

1 ft.

2-54 FRANK STELLA. *Raft of the Medusa, Part 1* (1990). Aluminum and steel. 167½" × 163" × 159". © 2011 Frank Stella/Artists Rights Society (ARS), NY.

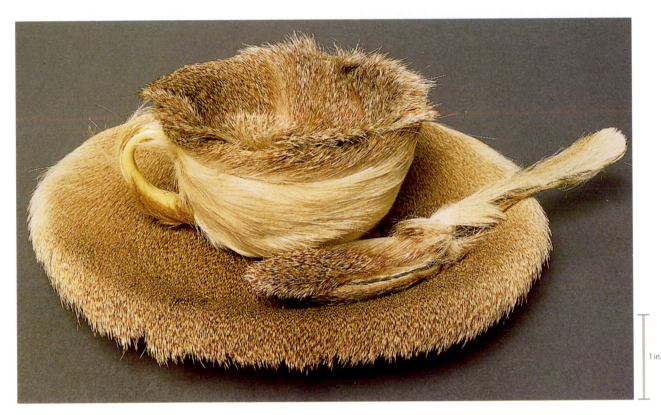

1 in.

2-55 MERET OPPENHEIM. *Object* (1936). Fur-covered cup, saucer, and spoon. Overall height: 2⅞". The Museum of Modern Art, NY.

SUBVERSIVE TEXTURE Textures are sometimes chosen or created by the artist to subvert or undermine our ideas about the objects they depict. **Subversive texture** compels the viewer to look again at an object and to think about it more deeply.

You may take objects such as a cup, saucer, and spoon for granted, but not after viewing Meret Oppenheim's *Object* (Fig. **2-55**). Oppenheim uses subversive texture in lining a cup, saucer, and spoon with fur. Teacups are usually connected with civilized and refined settings and occasions. The coarse primal fur completely subverts these associations, rendering the thought of drinking from this particular cup repugnant. *Object* also shows how textures can simultaneously attract and repel us. Does Oppenheim want the viewer to ponder the violence that has enabled civilization to grow and endure?

SPACE

"Space, the final frontier." Every die-hard Trekker is familiar with the opening mantra of the hit TV and film series *Star Trek*. But it just as well describes the "mission impossible" of millennia of artists seeking to recreate three-dimensional space on a two-dimensional surface. The space explored by the starship *Enterprise* was that beyond the earth's atmosphere—the space between celestial spheres and galaxies. Artists are less ambitious. They seek to explore ways to visually and psychologically extend the space of a finite rectangle—a canvas, let's say—into nothing less than a vast universe.

If pulling three dimensions out of a two-dimensional hat seems a trick, it is. Artists have had to develop a variety of tricks over the centuries in order to create the much-sought illusion of space on a two-dimensional surface. The history of the pursuit of this illusion is long and it has taken winding turns, but we hear about it in the art of ancient Greece, we see it in ancient Rome, and we follow its path to perfection in the Renaissance. The value placed on achieving this goal is illustrated in an anecdote about the famed Greek painter Apelles. In bringing before a panel of judges an example of his painting, Apelles was admonished by the judges for setting nothing on the easel for review. Of course he had. Apelles's work was so realistic, was so remarkable in its illusionism, that it went unseen in its surroundings. The painted image blended imperceptibly with that which surrounded it in actual space. Or so we've been told. What we do know for certain is that artists, like ordinary people, have been surrounded by the reaches of space as they look into the heavens, out over

First study science, and then follow with practice based on science. . . . The painter who draws by practice and judgment of the eye without the use of reason is like the mirror that reproduces within itself all the objects which are set opposite to it without knowledge of the same. . . . The youth ought first to learn perspective, then the proportions of everything, then he should learn from the hand of a good master.
—Leonardo da Vinci

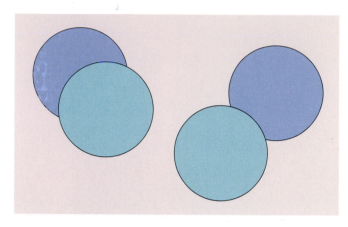

2-56 Overlapping circles and arcs.

mountains, or into the seas. They have seen fog collide with distant hills. They have seen sunlight burn at its edges. They have seen objects appear and disappear—lost in the distance, emerging from it. How can this be captured, communicated, shared? What's the trick?

However numerous and varied they are, the tricks took millennia to develop. From simple methods such as overlapping and relative size to complex systems of linear perspective, the goal of entire eras of artists was to transcend the space at their fingertips, to defy its limitations. In Chapters 9 and 11, which discuss the three-dimensional art forms of sculpture and architecture, we explore ways in which artists situate their objects in space and envelop space. In Chapter 11, we chronicle the age-old attempt to enclose vast reaches of

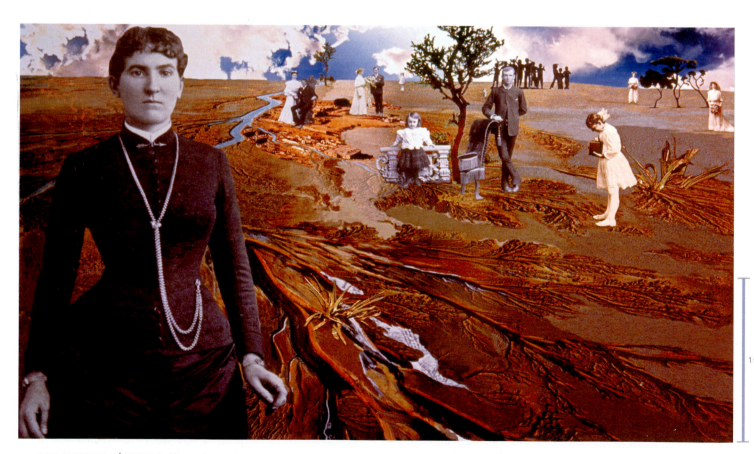

1 ft.

2-57 MARTINA LÓPEZ. *Heirs Come to Pass, 3* (1991). Silver dye bleach print made from digitally assisted montage. 2'6" × 4'2". Smithsonian American Art Museum, Washington, D.C.

space that began with massive support systems and currently focuses on lightweight steel-cage and shell-like structures. In this section, we examine ways in which artists who work in two dimensions create the illusion of depth—that is, the third dimension.

Overlapping

When nearby objects are placed in front of more distant objects, they obscure part or all of the distant objects. Figure **2-56** shows two circles and two arcs, but our perceptual experiences encourage us to interpret the drawing as showing four circles, two in the foreground and two in back. Likewise, this perceptual phenomenon allows an artist to create the illusion of depth by overlapping objects, or apparently placing one in front of another. Many of the works in your textbook illustrate the technique of overlapping and its effect in suggesting space—whether deep, as in Church's *The Andes of Ecuador* (Fig. 2-68), or shallow, as in Orozco's *Epic of American Civilization* (see Fig. 1-39).

Relative Size and Linear Perspective

The farther objects are from us, the smaller they appear to the eye. To recreate this visual phenomenon and to create the illusion of three-dimensionality on a two-dimensional surface, such as a canvas, artists employ a variety of techniques, among them **relative size** and **linear perspective**. For example, things that are supposed to be closer to the viewer are larger, whereas things that are supposed to be more distant are smaller. This simple principle of relative size can do wonders to suggest spatial complexity in works such as *Heirs Come to Pass, 3* (Fig. **2-57**) by Martina López.

The space in the composition is divided into three principal areas—foreground, middle ground, and background. The stagelike setting consists of a broad and minimally defined landscape that fills most of the area of the piece, leaving just a small strip for a cloud-soaked sky. With no apparent design, figures (from old family photographs) are digitally patched into the print. They range from looming to barely visible, and their size relative to one another creates whatever illusion of space there is. For López, this "visual terrain" is open, not only to her own memories, but also to those of the viewer.

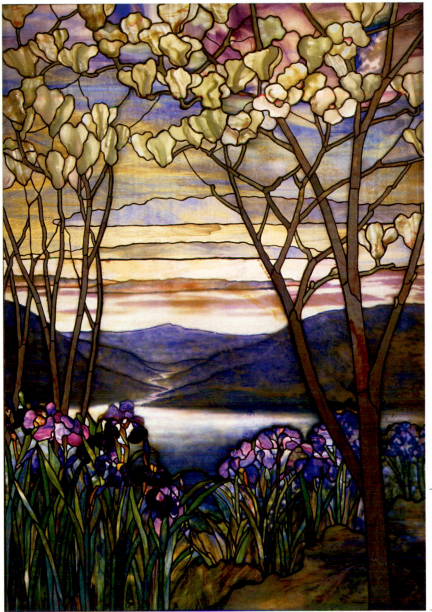

2-58 LOUIS COMFORT TIFFANY. *Magnolias and Irises* (c. 1908). Leaded Favrile glass. 60¼" × 42". Anonymous Gift, in memory of Mr. and Mrs. A. B. Frank, 1981 (1981.159). The Metropolitan Museum of Art, NY. Image copyright © The Metropolitan Museum of Art / Art Resource, NY.

1 ft.

In the Tiffany Studios' *Magnolias and Irises* (Fig. **2-58**) there are a few different cues for perceiving depth. The flowering trees and purple irises along the edge of the water are large, brightly colored, and clearly defined. Situated in the extreme foreground as they are, the plants not only seem close to us but also frame our view of the distant hills. Their relative size accounts for our perception that the space between us and the horizon is deep. In the valley between the hills, a serpentine line—a river—leads our eyes from the reflective surface of the water in the middle ground to the hills and sunset of the extreme background. As we move from foreground to background, the imagery becomes less distinct. The vastness of space is reinforced by the use of cool blues and purples—colors which, as we have learned, tend to recede into the distance.

We see this again in Figure **2-59**. Note how the cylinders appear to grow larger toward the top of the composition. Why? For at least two reasons: (1) Objects at the bottom of a composition are usually perceived as being closer to the picture plane; and (2) the converging lines are perceived as being parallel, even when they are not. However, if they were parallel, then space would have to recede toward the center right of the composition, and the cylinder in that region would have to be farthest from the viewer. According to rules of perspective, a distant object that appears to be equal in size to a nearby object would have to be larger, so we perceive the cylinder to the right as the largest, although it is equal in size to the others.

Figures **2-60** through **2-63** show that the illusion of depth can be created in art by making parallel lines come together, or converge, at one or more **vanishing points** on an actual or implied **horizon**. The height of the horizon in the composition corresponds to the apparent location of the viewer's eyes, that is, the **vantage point** of the viewer. As we shall see in later chapters, the Greeks and Romans had some notion of linear perspective, but Renaissance artists such as Leonardo da Vinci refined perspective.

In **one-point perspective** (Fig. **2-60**), parallel lines converge at a single vanishing point on the horizon. Raphael's (1483–1520) Renaissance masterpiece *School of Athens* (Fig. **2-64**) is a monumental example of one-point perspective. Representing Philosophy, it was one of four match-

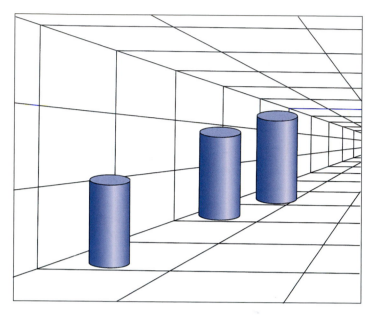

2-59 A visual illusion.

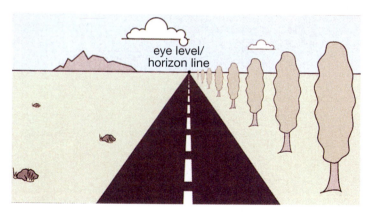

2-60 One-point perspective.

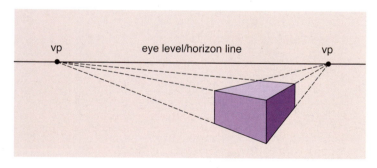

2-61 Two-point perspective.

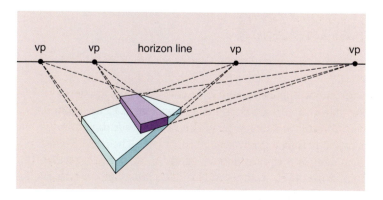

2-62 Perspective drawing of objects set at different angles.

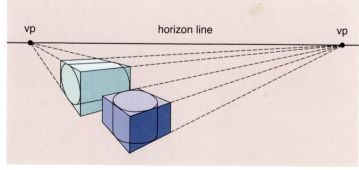

2-63 Curved objects drawn in perspective.

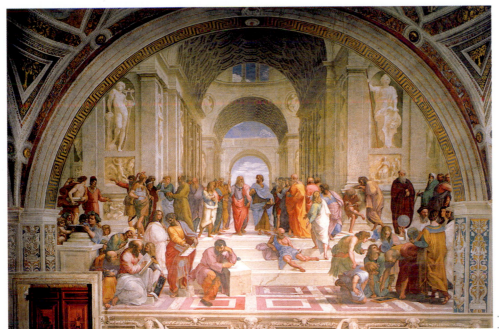

2-64 RAFFAELLO SANZIO (CALLED RAPHAEL). *Philosophy, or School of Athens* (1509–1511). Fresco. 26' × 18'. Stanza della Segnatura, Vatican, Rome, Italy.

 1 ft.

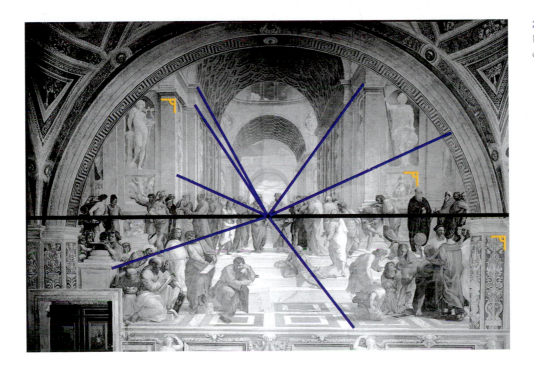

2-65 Perspective in *School of Athens*. Raphael's painting is a powerful example of one-point perspective.

ing frescoes depicting the most valuable aspects of a pope's education. The painting is a virtual *Who's Who* of intellectual movers and shakers from antiquity to the Renaissance. Plato (left) and Aristotle (right) occupy the center of the congregation, sharing the spotlight and representing divergent philosophical perspectives. The horizon line cuts through the center of their bodies, and the vanishing point sits squarely between them (Fig. **2-65**). Converging on this point are orthogonals that can be traced from the patterns of the marble flooring below the horizon line and the horizontal entablatures sitting atop the piers that recede dramatically toward the rear of the arcade.

In **two-point perspective** (Fig. **2-61**), two sets of parallel lines converge at separate vanishing points on the horizon. You would be hard-pressed to find a clearer use of two-point perspective than in Gustave Caillebotte's *Paris Street: Rainy*

Space **61**

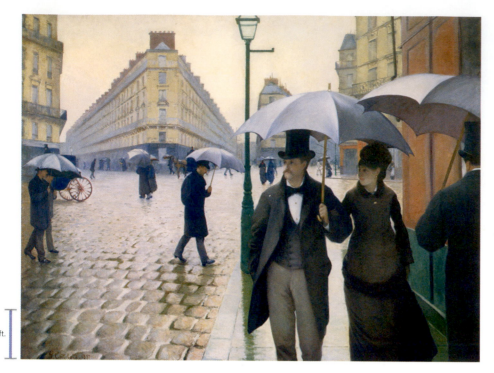

2-66 GUSTAVE CAILLEBOTTE. *Paris Street: Rainy Day* (1877). Oil on canvas. 83½" × 108¼". The Art Institute of Chicago, Chicago, IL.

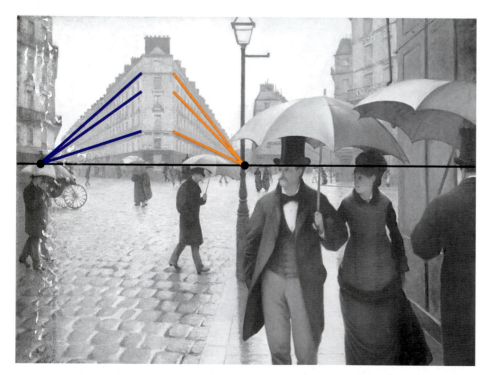

2-67 Perspective in Caillebotte's *Paris Street: Rainy Day.*

The use of two-point perspective in the Caillebotte painting is powerful and obvious. It draws our attention upward from the prominent figures in the foreground.

Day (Fig. **2-66**). We see the building in the background from the eye level of the figures in the foreground. The sight lines follow the receding dual facades of the building toward two distinct vanishing points (Fig. **2-67**).

We can use additional sets of parallel lines to depict objects that are set at different angles, as shown in Figure **2-62**. Figure **2-63** shows how curved objects may be "carved out" of rectangular solids.

Atmospheric Perspective

In **atmospheric perspective** (also called *aerial perspective*), the illusion of depth is created by techniques such as texture gradients, brightness gradients, color saturation, and the manipulation of warm and cool colors. A gradient is a progressive change. The effect of a **texture gradient** relies on the fact that closer objects are perceived as having rougher or more detailed surfaces. The effect of a **brightness gradient** is due to the lesser intensity of distant objects.

Frederic Edwin Church's masterpiece, *Andes of Ecuador* (Fig. **2-68**), relies in part on atmospheric perspective to create the illusion of deep vistas. The foreground of the picture contains great botanical detail. As the vista recedes into the distance, the plants and hills become less textured and the colors become less saturated. Church belonged to the Hudson River School of nineteenth-century American painting. The group's members used landscape as a vehicle for communicating the feeling of awe they experienced when they encountered the romantic, scientific, and religious ideas of the era—a world without limits.

The haunting painting *Schunnemunk Mountain* (Fig. **2-69**) reveals Sylvia Plimack Mangold's fascination with the transitional moments of the day. Here in the evening of the Hudson River Valley, brightness gradients employing purple, navy, and cobalt set the hills beneath the sky. The dark foreground is rendered more vacant by twinkling lights that suggest habitation in the valley beyond.

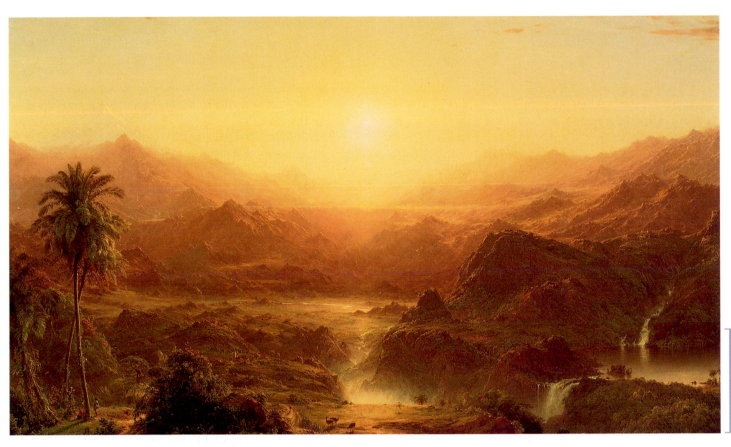

1 ft.

2-68 FREDERIC EDWIN CHURCH. *Andes of Ecuador* (1855). Oil on canvas. 48" × 75". Museum of American Art, Winston-Salem, NC.

1 ft.

2-69 SYLVIA PLIMACK MANGOLD. *Schunnemunk Mountain* (1979). Oil on canvas. 60" × 80⅛". Dallas Museum of Art, Dallas, TX.

I paint with shapes.
—Alexander Calder

TIME AND MOTION

Objects and figures exist and move not only through space but also through the dimension of time. In its inexorable forward flow, time provides us with the chance to develop and grasp the visions of our dreams. Time also creates the stark limits beyond which none of us may extend.

Artists through the ages have sought to represent three-dimensional space in two-dimensional art forms as well as to represent, or imply, movement and the passage of time. Only in modern times have art forms such as cinematography and video been developed that involve *actual* movement and *actual* time.

Actual Motion

Artists create or capture **actual motion** in various ways. **Kinetic art** (from the Greek *kinesis*, meaning "movement")

and photography are two of them. Most works of art sit quietly on the wall or, perhaps, on a pedestal, but kinetic art is designed to move.

The **mobiles** of Alexander Calder are among the most popular examples of kinetic art in the twentieth century. *The Star* (Fig. **2-70**) is composed of petal-like discs of different sizes and colors that are cantilevered from metal rods in such a way that they can rotate horizontally—in orbits—in the breeze. However, the center of gravity remains stable, so that the entire sculpture is hung from a single point. The composition changes according to air currents and the perspective of the observer. The combinations of movements are for all practical purposes infinite, so that the observer will never see the work in quite the same way.

With Liz Magic Laser's *The Thing #25* (Fig. **2-71**), the work of art is the record of a moment in time choreographed for the purposes of the photograph. Many of Laser's works examine the relationship between people and liquid; her

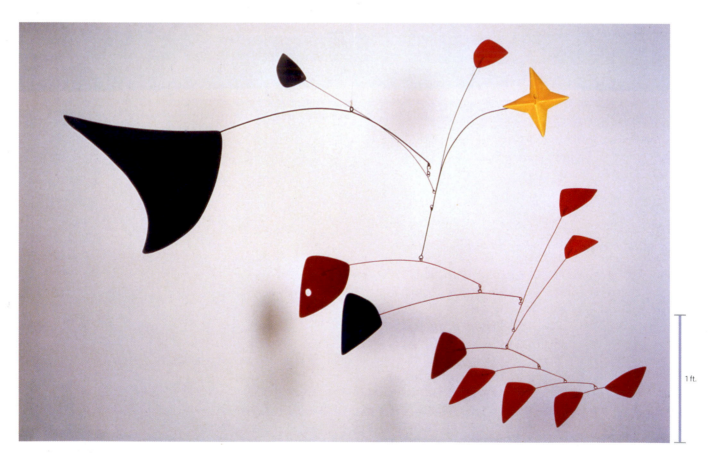

2-70 ALEXANDER CALDER. *The Star* (1960). Polychrome sheet metal and steel wire. 35¾" × 53¾" × 17⅝". University of Kentucky Art Museum, Lexington, KY. © 2011 Calder Foundation, NY/Artists Rights Society (ARS), NY.

1 ft.

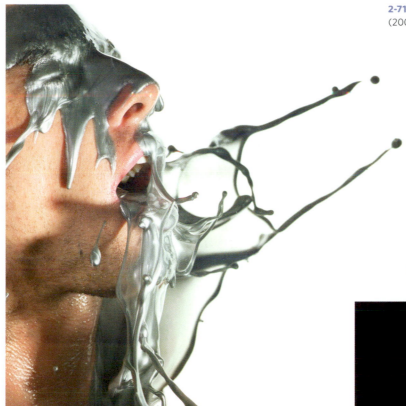

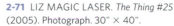
2-71 LIZ MAGIC LASER. *The Thing #25* (2005). Photograph. 30" × 40".

2-72 GIANLORENZO BERNINI. *Apollo and Daphne* (1622–1624). Marble. 7'6". Galleria Borghese, Rome, Italy.

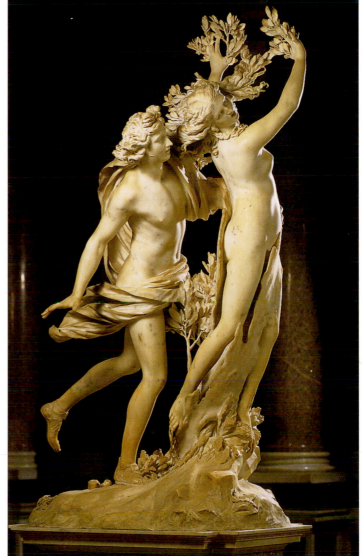

subjects are typically immersed in it, spattered by it, or projecting it. What captivates the viewer, however, is the way in which time has stopped in this work, exaggerating the impact and ejection of a mysterious green goo.

Implied Motion and Time

The Thing #25 captured motion through the use of **stopped time**. Other works of art imply motion; that is, the viewer infers that motion is occurring or has occurred. **Implied motion** and **implied time** are found in Baroque sculptor Gianlorenzo Bernini's *Apollo and Daphne* (Fig. **2-72**) through the use of diagonal lines of force that help simulate movement from left to right. In the Greek myth, the wood nymph Daphne beseeches the gods to help her escape the overtures of Apollo. As Apollo gains on her, her prayer is answered in a most ironic manner because the gods choose to facilitate her "escape" by transforming her into a tree. In Bernini's sculpture, we see Daphne just at the point when bark begins to enfold her body, her toes begin to take root, and her fingertips are transformed into the branches of a laurel. The passage of time is implied as she is caught in the midst of her transformation.

The Illusion of Motion

There is a difference between implied motion and the illusion of motion. Works such as *Apollo and Daphne* imply that motion has occurred or that time has passed. In other works, artists use techniques to suggest that motion is *in the process of occurring* rather than that motion has occurred. We say that these works contain the illusion of motion.

Early experiments with photography provided an illusion of the figure in motion through the method of rapid multiple exposures. In his *Man Pole Vaulting* (Fig. **2-73**), Thomas Eakins—better known for his paintings—used photo sequences to study the movement of the human body. In the wake of these experiments, several artists created the illusion of motion by applying the visual results of multiple-exposure photography to their paintings.

Marcel Duchamp's *Nude Descending a Staircase #2* (Fig. **2-74**) in effect creates multiple exposures of a machine-tooled figure walking down a flight of stairs. The overlapping of shapes and the repetition of linear patterns blur the contours of the figure. Even though an unkind critic labeled the Duchamp painting "an explosion in a shingle factory," it symbolized the dynamism of the modern machine era.

The movement of the 1960s and 1970s known as **Op Art** was based on creating optical sensations of movement through the repetition and manipulation of color, shape, and line. In kinetic sculpture, movement is real, whether activated by currents of air or motors. In Op Art, bold and apparently vibrating lines and colors create the illusion of movement. Bridget Riley's *Gala* (Fig. **2-75**) is composed of a series of curved lines that change in thickness and proximity to one another. These changes seem to suggest waves, but they also create a powerful illusion of rip-

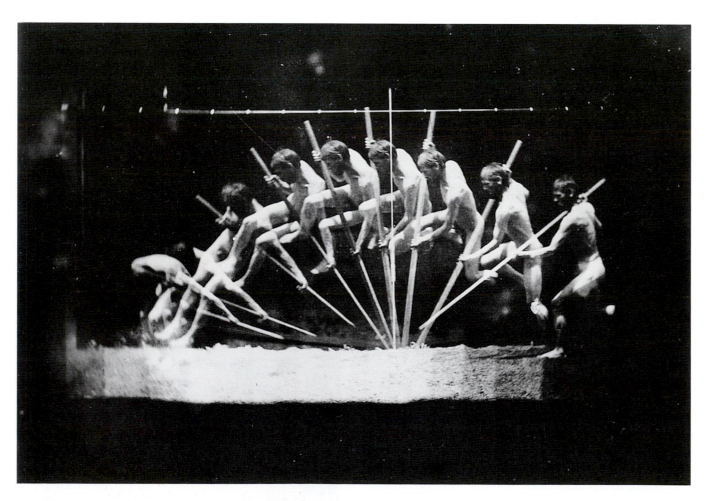

2-73 THOMAS EAKINS. *Man Pole Vaulting* (c. 1884). Photograph. The Metropolitan Museum of Art, NY.

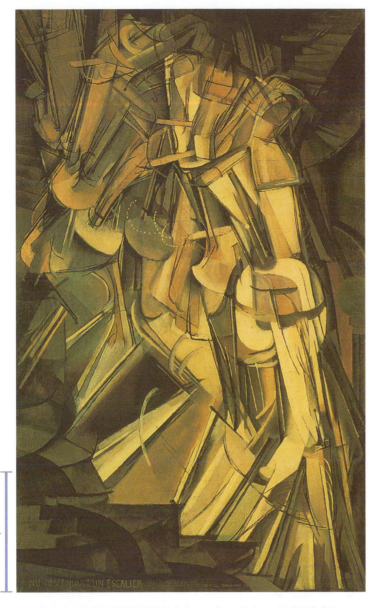

1 ft.

2-74 MARCEL DUCHAMP. *Nude Descending a Staircase #2* (1912). Oil on canvas. 58" × 35". The Philadelphia Museum of Art, Philadelphia, PA. © 2011 Artists Rights Society (ARS), NY/ADAGP, Paris/Succession Marcel Duchamp.

pling movement. Complementary red and green colors also contribute to the illusion of vibration. When we look at a color for an extended period of time, we tend to perceive its **afterimage**. Red is the afterimage of green, and vice versa. Therefore, there seems to be a pulsating in Riley's selection of color as well as in the tendency of the eye to perceive the lines as rippling.

If the visual elements are considered the basic vocabulary of art, principles of design may be viewed as the grammar of art. Artists use principles of design to combine the visual elements into compositions. In art, as in life, this "language" is idiosyncratic to the individual.

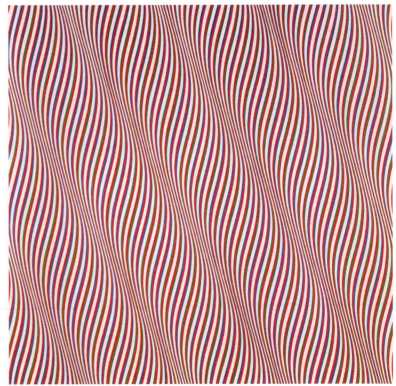

2-75 BRIDGET RILEY. *Gala* (1974). Acrylic on canvas. 5'2¾" square.

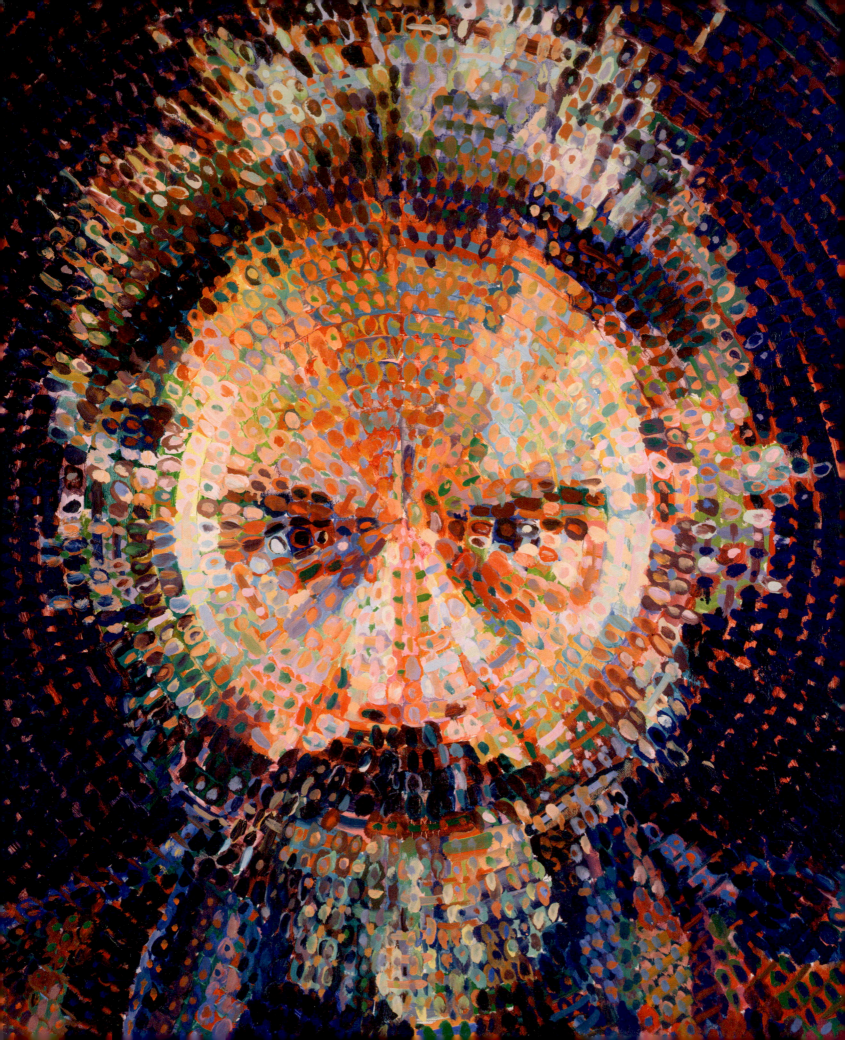

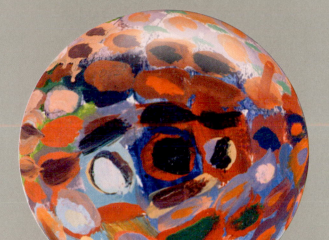

PRINCIPLES OF DESIGN

3

Unity is one of the principles of design, which, like visual elements, are part of the basic language of art. Just as people use principles of grammar to combine words into sentences, artists use principles of design to combine the visual elements of art into compositions that have a certain style, form, and content.

Design or **composition** is a process—the act of organizing the visual elements to effect a desired aesthetic in a work of art. Designs can occur at random, as exemplified by the old mathematical saw that an infinite number of monkeys pecking away at an infinite number of typewriters would eventually (though mindlessly) produce *Hamlet*. But when artists create compositions, they consciously draw upon design principles such as unity and variety, balance, emphasis and focal point, rhythm, scale, and proportion. This is not to say that all artists necessarily apply these principles, or even always recognize the extent of their presence in their work. In fact, some artists prefer to purposefully violate them.

CHUCK CLOSE. *Lucas II* (1987). Oil on canvas. 36" × 30". Collection of John and Mary Shirley, NY.

UNITY AND VARIETY

Unity is oneness or wholeness. A work of art achieves unity when its parts seem necessary to the composition as a whole. Artists generally prefer to place some variety within a unified composition to add visual interest, but the principle of variety is most often subservient to the sense of oneness or overall unity in a work.

Ways to Achieve Unity and Variety within Unity

Andy Warhol built *Ethel Scull Thirty-Six Times* (Fig. **3-1**) on the principle of a grid—an extreme example of unity—drawing attention to the ubiquity of mass-produced consumables of any and all types, including human beings of celebrity. Reflecting his signature compositional arrangement, the work consists of the repetition of silk-screened photo-booth-type images, in this case of Ethel Scull, an important patron of the arts in the 1960s. An overall unity abides within the nine-by-four grid and repetitive color scheme, but the wide variety of expressions create a multidimensional view of Scull's appearance and personality. Warhol's multiportrait serves as an excellent illustration of variety within unity. The more you look at works of art, the better you will become at sensing the unity of compositions and at pinpointing the ways that artists achieve it. Sometimes the techniques will be obvious, and at other times they will be subtler.

Archibald Motley Jr.'s *Saturday Night* (Fig. **3-2**) offers the viewer a captivating array of characters—from the dining and drinking patrons and the waiters balancing their orders on tottering trays to one particularly flamboyant woman in a flame red costume who seems lost in the expressive rhythms of her solo dance. Yet this cacophony of sights and sounds and movements achieves a sense of oneness through a unified color field. To be sure, there is also some variety in the color scheme: the eye leaps from patches of black to black and from white to white, mimicking the riot of movement

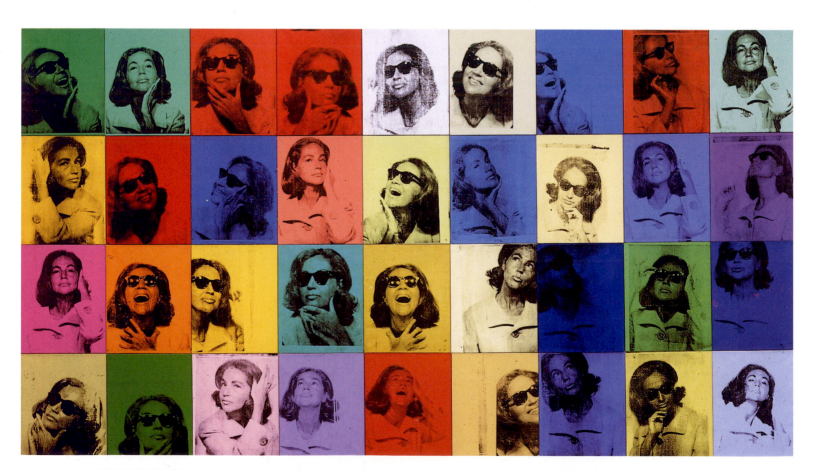

3-1 ANDY WARHOL. *Ethel Scull Thirty-Six Times* (1963). Synthetic polymer paint silkscreened on canvas. 79¾" × 143¼". Whitney Museum of American Art, NY. © 2011 The Andy Warhol Foundation for the Visual Arts/Artists Rights Society (ARS), NY.

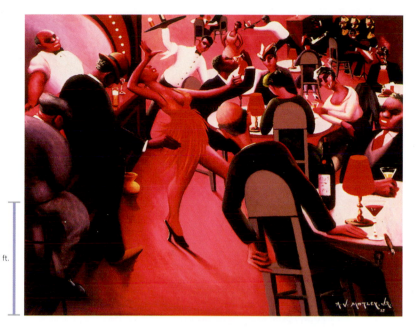

1 ft.

in the nightclub. However, the overall composition is unified by the pulsating reds that seem to emanate from the center of the dance floor and bathe the atmosphere with emotion, energy, and an almost mystical glow.

Although color harmonies also contribute to a sense of oneness in Thomas Hart Benton's *Palisades* (Fig. **3-3**), the curvilinear rhythms of shape and line are the strongest purveyors of unity in this work. Here the diversity of the players in this mythologized narrative of American history—the Spanish conquistador, the European colonizer, the Native American—are joined symbolically and pictorially by the echoing shapes and lines and rhythms that define and distinguish the figures and landscape elements. The emergence of a visual pattern of similar elements dominates the individual parts.

When working with the principles of variety and unity, an artist will often keep one or more aspects of the work constant so that despite the multiplicity of images or elements, the composition's overall unity will not be compromised. The device of continuity to effect unity is also seen in a

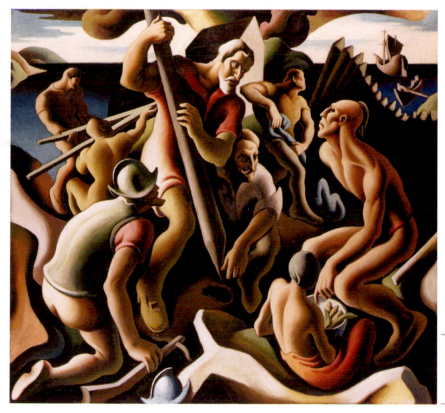

1 ft.

work that is, literally, a world apart—Delilah Montoya's *Los Jovenes* (Youth) (Fig. **3-4**). It too features eight figures (and here a hovering image of the Virgin of Guadalupe), some interacting, some not; some confronting the viewer, some not the least bit interested in doing so. Continuity is reflected in the ages of the youths, their ethnicity, and a suggested bond of friendship. As in *Palisades*, our eye can travel from one side of the photograph to the other, picking out lights and darks, shifts in foreground and background, and the prominence of hand gestures and positions. The visual flow is effortless.

All of the works we have discussed have **visual unity**; most embrace the principle of variety within unity. There is, however, a way to achieve unity in a composition that does not rely on the consistency or repetition of the elements of art. Sometimes artists pursue, instead, a unity of ideas and impose a **conceptual unity** on their work. They will recognize that the strength of a composition lies in the diversity of elements and their juxtaposition. They reject visual harmonies in favor of discordant punctuations and focus on the relationships between the meanings and functions of the images. Emma Amos's *Measuring Measuring* (Fig. **3-5**) offers an example of conceptual unity. The "ideal" human form is represented by works of art from the Western canon flanking the seminude figure of an African woman. "Measuring" has at least a double meaning—the measure of the African standard of beauty against that of the Western tradition and the measure of black against white. The images are physically incongruous, and the elements of the composition do not

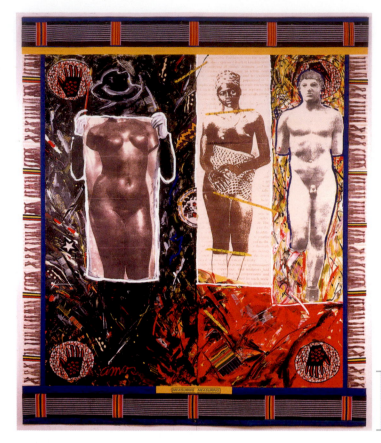

3-5 EMMA AMOS. *Measuring Measuring* (1995). Acrylic on linen canvas, African fabric, laser-transfer photographs. 84" × 70". Flomenhaft Gallery, NY.

encourage visual unity. What unites this composition is the concept behind the work: the challenge to address the standard and the canon.

Emphasis on Variety

When artists emphasize variety, they are usually exaggerating differences rather than similarities among their images. Palmer Hayden's painting called *The Subway* (Fig. **3-6**) is a demographic and ethnic cross section of the strap-hanging population of 1930s New York City. Even though they are unified by the common need to move efficiently from place to place beneath the streets of the metropolis, this fact is not the main theme of the work. Rather, the artist builds his painting around the individuality and diversity of the riders. Hayden's emphasis on variety is signified in the juxtaposition of the light and dark hands at the center of the painting. This snapshot of subway life hasn't changed much in three-quarters of a century. The underground in New York City remains a great equalizer, and as one surveys the contemporary scene, one finds an even greater human diversity, with even more emphasis on variety.

3-4 DELILAH MONTOYA. *Los Jovenes* (Youth) (1993). Collotype. 9 3/16" × 10". Smithsonian American Art Museum, Washington, D.C.

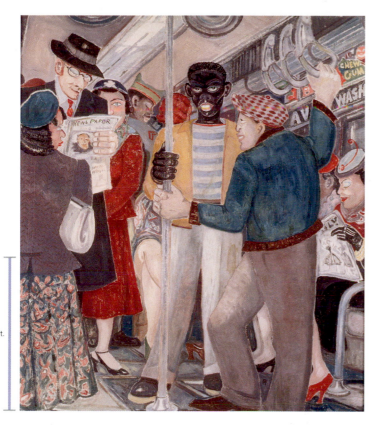

1 ft.

3-6 PALMER HAYDEN. *The Subway* (c. 1930). Oil on canvas. 31" × 26½". New York State Office of General Services, Adam Clayton Powell, Jr., State Office Building, NY.

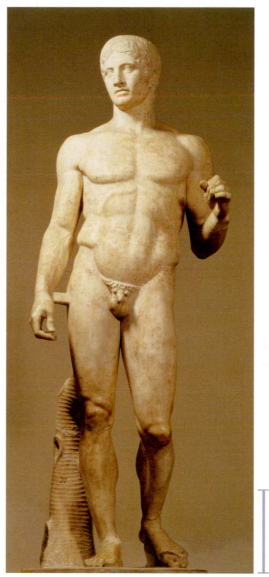

1 ft.

3-7 POLYKLEITOS. *Doryphoros* (c. 450–440 BCE). Roman copy after bronze Greek original. Marble. 6'6". Museo Archeologico Nazionale, Naples, Italy.

BALANCE

Most people prefer to have some stability in their lives, to have their lives on a "firm footing." In the same way, most people respond positively to some degree of balance in the visual arts. When we walk, run, or perform an athletic feat, balance refers to the way in which our weight is distributed, or shifts, so that we remain in control of our movements. **Balance** in art also refers to the distribution of the weight— of the actual or apparent weight of the elements of a composition. As the athlete uses balance to control movement, so might the artist choose to use balance to control the distribution or emphasis of elements such as line or shape or color in a composition.

The Classical Greek artist Polykleitos was perhaps the first artist to observe the body's shifting of weight in order to achieve balance and to develop a set of rules to apply this observation to representations of the figure. In his *Doryphoros* (Fig. **3-7**), or Spear Bearer, Polykleitos featured his weight-shift principle. He observed that when the body is at rest, one leg bears the weight of the body and the other is relaxed. Further,

in order for the body to balance itself, the upper torso shifts, as if corresponding to an S curve, so that the arm opposite the tensed leg is tensed, and the one opposite the relaxed leg is relaxed. Thus, with the weight-shift principle, tension and tension and relaxation and relaxation are read diagonally across the body. Overall figural balance is achieved.

Actual Balance and Pictorial Balance

Sculptures such as *Doryphoros* have *actual weight* and may thus also have actual balance. Even though actual weight and **actual balance** are not typically at issue in two-dimensional works such as drawings, paintings, and prints, we nonetheless do speak of balance in these compositions. **Pictorial balance** refers to the distribution of the apparent or *visual weight* of the elements in works that are basically two-dimensional, and there are many ways to achieve it.

Symmetrical Balance

You can divide the human body in half vertically, and in the ideal, as in Leonardo da Vinci's most famous drawing, *Proportion of the Human Figure* (Fig. **3-8**), there will be an exact correspondence between the left and right sides. **Symmetry** refers to similarity of form or arrangement on either side of a dividing line or plane, or to correspondence of parts in size, shape, and position. When the correspondence is exact, as in Leonardo's drawing, we refer to it as *pure* or *formal symmetry*. In reality, nature is not as perfect as Leonardo would have had it.

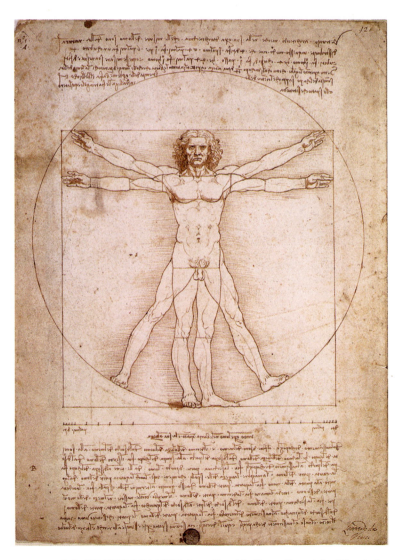

3-8 LEONARDO DA VINCI. *Proportion of the Human Figure* (after Vitruvius) (c. 1485–1490). Pen and ink. 13½" × 9¾". Accademia, Venice, Italy.

Examples of pure or formal symmetry appear no more frequently in art than in nature. More typically, **symmetrical balance** is created through *approximate* symmetry, in which the whole of the work has a symmetrical feeling, but slight variations provide more visual interest than would a mirror image. When the variations to the right and left side of the composition are *more* than slight, yet there remains an overall sense of balance, there is said to be **asymmetrical balance**.

In *pure* or *formal symmetry*, also known as **bilateral symmetry**, everything in a composition to either side of an actual or imaginary line is the same. The regularity and predictability of symmetry cannot help but conjure a sense of peace, calm, comfort, and order. The effect of repetition can be mesmerizing. In architectural works like the U.S. Capitol Building (Fig. **3-9**)—the house in which the laws of the land are created—repetition and symmetry can imply rationality and decorum, tying the structure of the building to a certain symbolic ideal. The design of the Capitol consists of a solid rectangular structure flanked by identical wings that extend from the central part of the building, project forward at right angles, and culminate in "temple fronts" that echo the main entrance beneath a hemispherical dome. An ordinary citizen of the republic takes pride in the architectural grandeur, feels secure in the balance of all of the parts, and—with the obvious references to Greek architecture of the Golden Age—feels a part of the history of democracy. It is no coincidence that, for the nation's Capitol, our founders adapted structures such as the Parthenon of Athens in the hope of associating the new republic with the ancient birthplace of democracy.

In many works of art, the symmetry is *approximate* rather than exact. For example, the overall impression of William Wegman's *Ethiopia* (Fig. **3-10**) is that of symmetry, primarily attributable to the echoing shapes of the Weimaraners' heads and the firm vertical line that bisects the composition. Yet there are elements that break the monotony of the symmetry, such as the juxtaposition of near-complementary shades of red and green, and the contrast of the clear, detailed face of the dog on the right with ghostlike iteration on the left.

Asymmetrical Balance

When your eyes are telling you that the elements of a composition are skewed but your brain is registering overall balance, chances are you are witnessing asymmetrical balance. There is probably a human tendency to effect balance at any cost. Sometimes the right and left sides of a composition bear visibly different shapes, colors, textures, or other elements, yet they are arranged or "weighted" in such a way that the impression, in total, is one of balance. In such cases, the artist has employed the design principle of *asymmetrical* or *informal balance*.

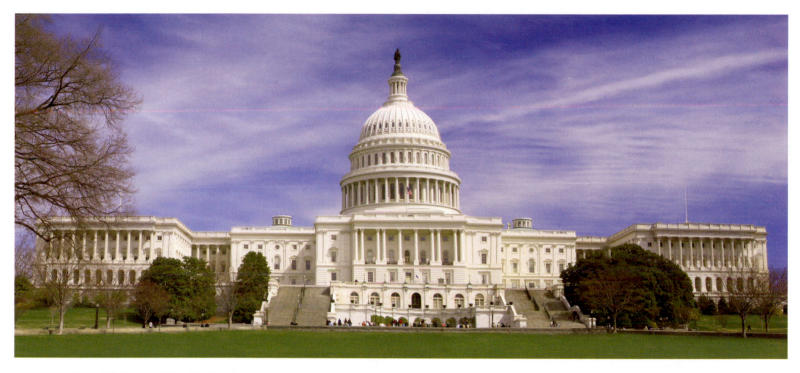

3-9 The U.S. Capitol Building, Washington, D.C.

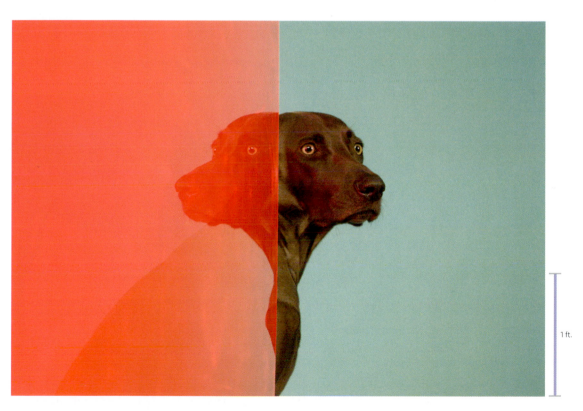

1 ft.

3-10 WILLIAM WEGMAN. *Ethiopia* (2006). Pigment print. 36" × 44".

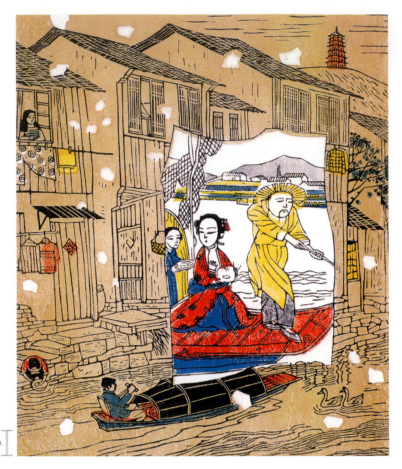

1 in.

3-11 WU JIDE. *River Dwellers* (1998). Multiblock woodcut printed with water-soluble ink. 16⅞" × 13⅝". Muban Foundation, London, England.

In Wu Jide's *River Dwellers* (Fig. **3-11**), patches of white and well-placed touches of color are responsible for the overall visual balance in an asymmetrical and essentially monochromatic composition. Like a movie within a movie, the large, square canvas sail of a small boat is printed with a scene of another boating party. The bright colors of the sail dominate the ocher atmosphere of the woodcut, as does the scale of the figures therein. Asymmetrical balance is achieved as the artist picks up the reds and yellows and blues of the sail and adds them as almost random touches to other parts of the composition. The stark white of the sail, which provides a luminous backdrop for the boating group, is echoed in scattered bits and pieces that float like large snowflakes or a torn love note and tie the entire work together.

In Deborah Butterfield's *Verde* (Fig. **3-12**), the mane and head of the horse are defined by greenish strips of steel that enframe void space. (The title *Verde* calls our attention to the finish of the steel, a greenish coating referred to as *verdigris*.) The *actual weight* of this upper part of the horse is negligible. The body, on the other hand, is composed of heavy molded sheets of steel, approximating the volume of the animal's torso. Overall visual balance is achieved in this work because the outlines of the head and neck, silhouetted

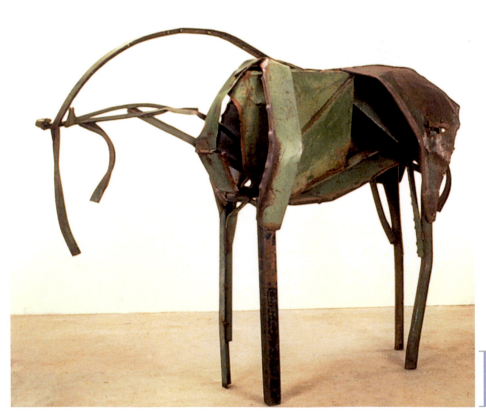

3-12 DEBORAH BUTTERFIELD. *Verde* (1990). Found steel. 79" × 108" × 31". Collection of the artist. Art © Deborah Butterfield/Licensed by VAGA, NY.

1 ft.

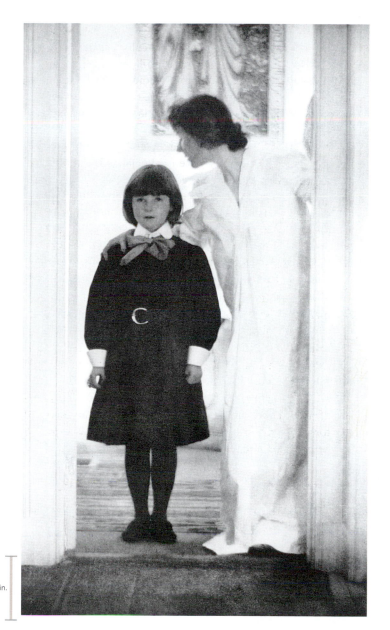

1 in.

3-13 GERTRUDE KÄSEBIER. *Blessed Art Thou among Women* (c. 1898). Photograph. 9¼" × 5½".

Käsebier's delicately textured photograph *Blessed Art Thou among Women* (Fig. **3-13**). Notice how the dark value of the girl's dress is balanced both by the dark wall to the left and by the woman's hair. Similarly, the stark light value of the vertical shaft of the doorway to the left and the light values of the right side of the composition are in equilibrium.

With **vertical balance**, the elements at the top and bottom of the composition are in balance. In Kay Sage's *I Saw Three Cities* (Fig. **3-14**), a firm horizon line separates a bleak landscape from a bleaker sky. Most of the visual weight in the composition occurs in the lower half, where geometric shapes casting long shadows lead your eye from the picture plane toward a kind of desolate futuristic city. The hard-edged structures that litter the landscape, however, are balanced in the upper reaches of the sky by a flowing column of drapery that billows up from the ground and across to the left, floating toward the source of the light on a strange breeze that breaks the stagnant gray air.

Artists employ **diagonal balance** by establishing equal visual weight to either side of a pictorial space that is divided

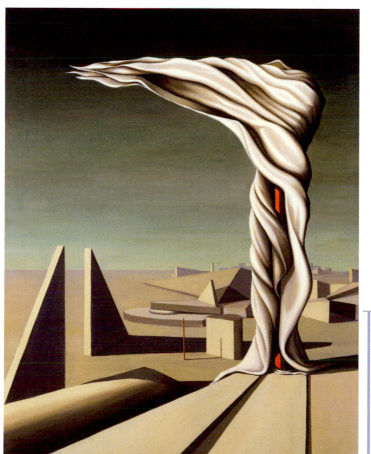

1 ft.

3-14 KAY SAGE. *I Saw Three Cities* (1944). Oil on canvas. 36" × 27⅞". Princeton University Art Museum. Princeton, NJ.

against the white wall, pop out at the viewer. They become so prominent that they carry enough *visual weight* to balance the more densely compacted sheet metal of the animal's body.

Horizontal, Vertical, Diagonal, and Radial Balance

In works of art with **horizontal balance**, the elements at the left and right sides of the composition seem to be about equal in number or visual emphasis. The U.S. Capitol Building (Fig. 3-9) has horizontal balance. So too does Gertrude

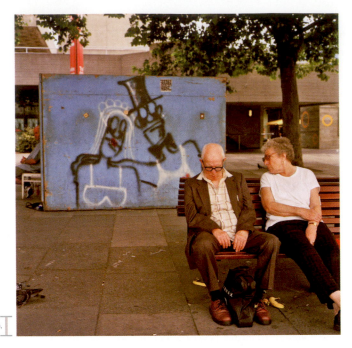

1 in.

3-15 ADIL JAIN. *Two Heads* from the series *London Portraits*. (c. August 2004). Color C-Print. 16" × 16".

by means of a perceived diagonal. In Adil Jain's *Two Heads* (Fig. **3-15**), the photographer captures the juxtaposition of evocative images and, in the process, creates a striking compositional equilibrium. The elderly couple on a bench in the lower right are partially cut off by the frame of the camera's viewfinder. Yet they are pulled back into the work along an implied diagonal that visually connects them to the large blue square of the trash receptacle behind them. The diagonal positioning of the woman and her backward glance facilitate the connection. The spray-painted image of a bride and groom echoes their figures, balancing the composition and creating a symbolic connection. The viewer's eye moves from the couple to their graffiti counterparts and back along the perceived diagonal.

In the case of **radial balance**, the design elements radiate from a center point. Radial balance is familiar to us because nature offers us so many examples. From the petals of a daisy and the filaments of a spider's web to the sun's powerful rays, lines or shapes radiate from a central point and lead the viewer's eye in a circular pattern around the source.

Radial balance is frequently a major principle of design in art forms such as ceramics, jewelry, basketry, stained glass, and other crafts. The decorative tabletop from nineteenth-century Iran (Fig. **3-16**) is a classic example of radial balance. At the center of the piece is a large, round, intricately painted tile surrounded by a circular garland of flowers, birds, and clusters of grapes. Both the central tile and the garland are framed by narrow, decorative bands; diagonals fan outward from these bands toward the perimeter, dividing the remaining space into eight separate pictorial segments. Like the spokes of a wheel, the narrow framing device directs the gaze of the

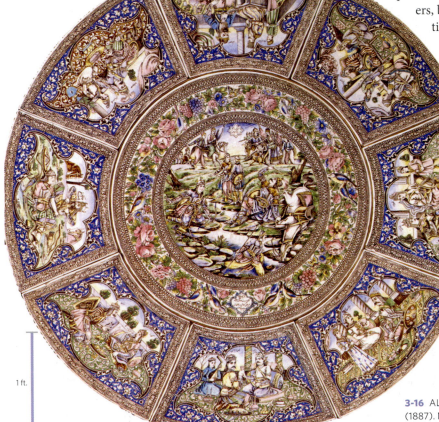

1 ft.

3-16 ALI MUHAMMAD KASHIGAR ISFAHANI. Iranian tabletop (1887). Nine separate tiles. Table diameter 54½". Victoria and Albert Museum, London, England.

viewer both outward and inward and provides order to the content. The tiles are decorated with scenes inspired by the *Book of Kings*, an Iranian epic.

Imbalance

Balance affords a certain level of comfort. The viewer will usually try to impose balance on a work, even when there is asymmetry. But not all art is about comfort; not all art aims to be aesthetically pleasing. Some artists aim to shock the viewer or to play into a viewer's discomfort by creating works with **imbalance**.

Consider Robert Capa's photograph *Death of a Loyalist Soldier* (Fig. 3-17), which was taken during the Spanish Civil War. The photographer has captured the soldier just as an enemy rifleman shot him. By allowing the composition to remain unbalanced, or weighted on the left, the drama of the moment is intensified. The long black shadow behind the soldier seems to pull the figure toward the ground, as he stumbles from the impact of the bullet. The photographer no doubt maintained the visual imbalance in the composition to correspond with the physical imbalance of the victim.

In Capa's photograph, there is a clear sense of movement. The soldier has been running down a grassy hill and suddenly falls backward. Imbalance in a work of art can be used to capture a sense of movement—the fourth dimension—in a two-dimensional or a three-dimensional work. Niki de Saint-Phalle's *Black Venus* (Fig. 3-18) is a larger-than-life figure of a woman in a psychedelic bathing suit who is catching a beach ball. The placement of the legs and feet at the very least suggests a precariously balanced body. She seems to leap into the air to catch the ball, defying gravity and her own ponderousness. Despite, or because of, her mountainous appearance, the

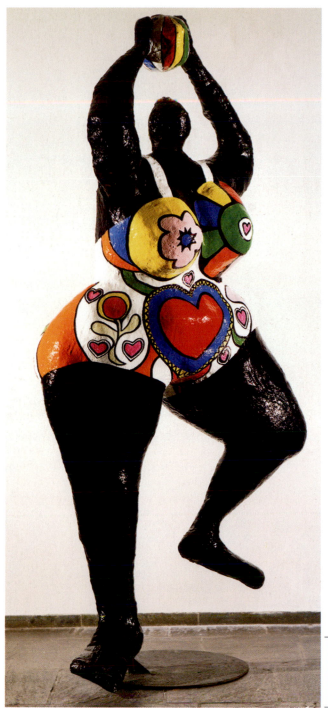

3-18 NIKI DE SAINT-PHALLE. *Black Venus* (1967). Painted polyester. 110" × 35" × 24". Whitney Museum of American Art, NY. © 2011 Artists Rights Society (ARS), NY/ADAGP, Paris.

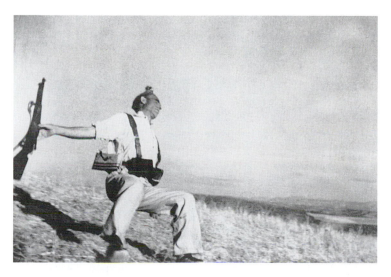

3-17 ROBERT CAPA. *Death of a Loyalist Soldier* (September 5, 1936). Gelatin silver print.

unbalanced position of her lower body gives the figure a contradictory sense of weightlessness. Niki de Saint-Phalle challenges the ideal of feminine beauty in the Western tradition with figures such as *Black Venus*. How does this spirited form stand apart from traditional Western nudes such as the *Venus of Urbino* (see Fig. 16-27)?

EMPHASIS AND FOCAL POINT

For the most part, we do not view a work of art as we read a page of text. The eye does not start in the upper left corner and then systematically work its way to the right in rows. Rather, some feature of the work usually commands our attention. Artists use the design principle of **emphasis** to focus the viewer's attention on one or more parts of a composition by accentuating certain shapes, intensifying value or color, featuring directional lines, or strategically placing the objects and images. Emphasis can be used to create **focal points** or specific parts of the work that seize and hold the viewer's interest.

As if the overwhelming presence of the face—that is, the *content*—in Chuck Close's *Lucas II* (Fig. **3-19**) is not enough to focus the viewer's attention on the center of the composition, the artist emphasizes or draws our eye to a single point—the focal point—between the subject's eyes by creating a target-like pattern of concentric circles around it. The circles are intersected by broken lines of color that radiate from the center, causing a sense of simultaneous movement outward from the center point and back inward.

Emphasis on a particular area or image in a composition can be effected when several of its components direct the viewer's gaze toward a focal point. *Welcome the World*

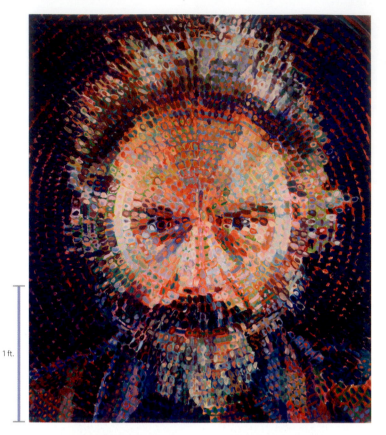

3-19 CHUCK CLOSE. *Lucas II* (1987). Oil on canvas. 36" × 30". Collection of John and Mary Shirley, NY.

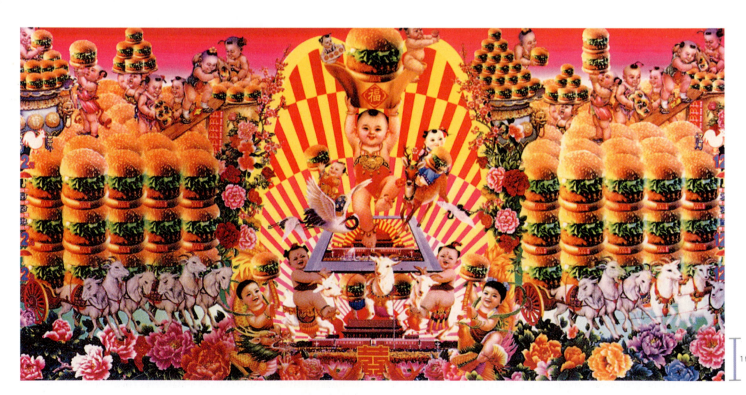

3-20 THE LUO BROTHERS. *Welcome the World Famous Brand* (2000). Collage and lacquer on wood. 96⅞" × 49⅝" × 1³⁄₁₆". Ray Hughes Gallery, Sydney, Australia.

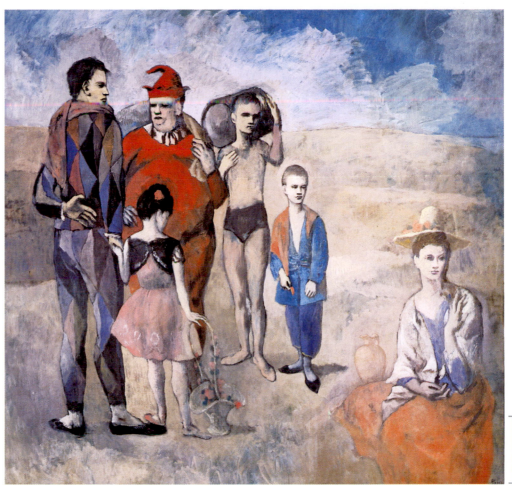

1 ft.

Famous Brand (Fig. 3-20) by the Luo Brothers features their signature emphasis on the convergence of consumerism and globalism. Mimicking the garish packaging of Chinese merchandise, their compositions are often overcrowded, intensely colored, and exuberant in mood. There is so much energy bound up in the imagery that it is almost impossible for the eyes to stop and focus. Emphasis through placement is an important device in this work, and to achieve it, once again, the Luo Brothers use mimicry. The "enthroned" baby raising a McDonald's sandwich in the center of the piece becomes the focal point. It is emphasized by the red and yellow bands of lines that look like divine rays emanating from behind the baby, who, in turn is bolstered on a floating rectangle by lesser, though no less jubilant, little ones. To the left and right are regimented stacks of burgers riding on chariots pulled by teams of lambs. Brightly colored peonies add to the outrageously festive atmosphere. This formula—enthroned central figure buoyed by devoted onlookers and flanked by symmetrical groups of regimented figures—is standard in religious altarpieces over centuries of art history. The Luo

Brothers appropriate this formula to sharpen their statement about what we "worship" in contemporary society.

In Pablo Picasso's *Family of Saltimbanques* (Fig. 3-21), we see how artists use the principle of emphasis by isolation, in which they separate one object or figure from the many. Amidst a rather desolate landscape, figures of circus performers stand silent, seemingly frozen in their sculptural poses. The patterns, colors, and costume variety of the main figural group are, interestingly, less visually significant than the more delicately rendered figure of the woman seated apart from them in the lower right. Picasso has emphasized her aloneness by pulling her from the group. Her solitude draws us into her private musings; her inner world becomes the focus of our attention.

In *Bauhaus Stairway* (Fig. 3-22), Oskar Schlemmer used powerful directional lines and a bright area of color to create the focal point in his composition. The diagonal thrusts of the staircase railing would meet in the center of the composition and would by themselves create the focal point. However, the focal point is further reinforced by the orange-red of

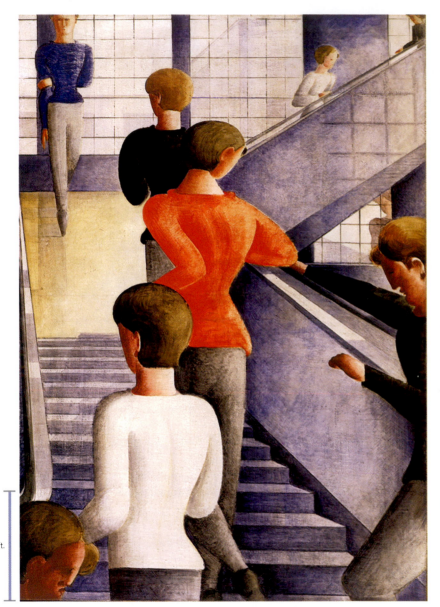

1 ft.

3-22 OSKAR SCHLEMMER. *Bauhaus Stairway* (1932). Oil on canvas. 63⅞" × 45". The Museum of Modern Art, NY.

point that despite other devices used to create focal points, the image will have the tendency to negate or override them. In Edgar Degas's *Woman Leaning near a Vase of Flowers* (Fig. **3-23**), the centerpiece—quite literally—of the composition is an enormous bouquet of chrysanthemums. It has almost everything one could ask of a focal point—central position, brilliant color, dominant texture. And yet our eyes are drawn to the woman who sits off to the side of the vase, daydreaming, gazing beyond the borders of the canvas. A viewer's gaze is seduced by the sight of a human face.

If you look at Francisco Goya's *The Third of May, 1808* (see Figure 19-6), you will see one of the best historical examples of the design principle of emphasis. Goya uses multiple strategies to focus the viewer's eyes and sympathies on a Spanish peasant who is about to be executed by riflemen under the authority of the French emperor Napoleon. The doomed man's bright white shirt, spotlighted by a cube-shaped lantern, immediately fixes our gaze. The bayonets read as strong, repeated, horizontal lines pointing directly at the victim; the soldiers lean determinedly into action along diagonals that also direct our eyes toward the group. Can you name other ways in which Goya has used emphasis in this painting?

RHYTHM

The world would be a jumble of sights and sounds were it not for the **regular repetition** of sensory impressions. Natural **rhythms**, or orderly progressions, regulate events ranging from the orbits of the planets to the unfolding of the genetic code into flesh and blood. Artists can enhance or exaggerate individual elements in their compositions through minor and major variations in rhythm. And rhythm can move a viewer visually as well as emotionally. Repetitive patterns can be used to lead the eye over the landscape of the work and to evoke a psychological response in the viewer.

Rhythm can be present in a work of art even if there is a slight variation in repetition. Magdalena Abakanowicz's *Backs* (Fig. **3-24**), from a series of body works called *Alterations*, consists of 80 fiber sculptures representing human

a woman's sweater, while it partially obscures the meeting of the diagonals and leaps out against a backdrop of quiet blues and off-whites. Content helps too. The people in the foreground are in the act of climbing the stairs and, in so doing, ascending toward the focal point of the composition.

The power of content can sometimes overwhelm the power of shape, texture, and other elements of art to the

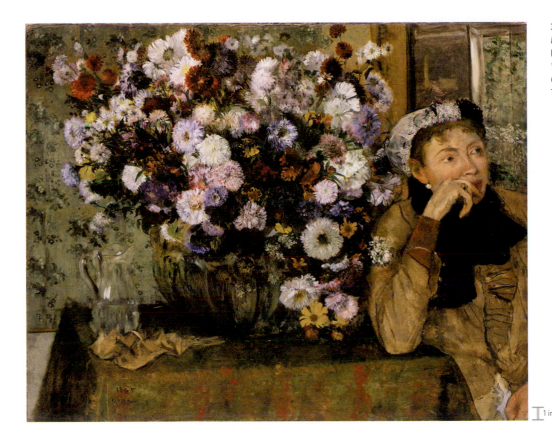

3-23 EDGAR DEGAS. *Woman Leaning near a Vase of Flowers* (Mme Paul Valpinçon; erroneously called *Woman with Chrysanthemums*) (1865). Oil on canvas. 29" × 36½". The Metropolitan Museum of Art, NY.

1 in.

backs. Although the individual forms look like hunched-over figures, they are without heads, legs, or arms. Even the fronts of the torsos have been hollowed out, leaving an actual and symbolic human shell. In this work, the artist, whose mother was mutilated by the Nazis in World War II, seems to bring to her work the memory of the dehumanization she witnessed. The potency of this message is largely attributable to the repetition of forms that have lost their individuality.

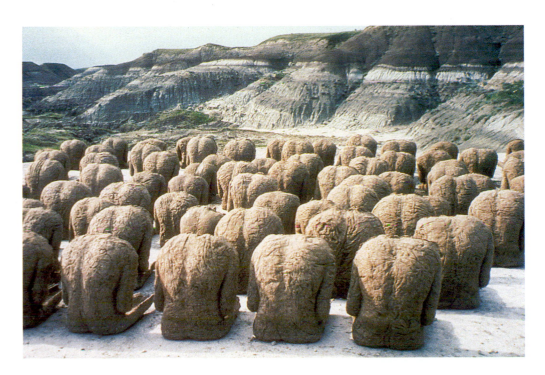

3-24 MAGDALENA ABAKANOWICZ. *Backs* (1976–1982). Burlap and glue. 80 pieces, 3 sizes: 24" × 19 ¹¹⁄₁₆" × 21 ¹¹⁄₁₆"; 27 ³⁄₁₆" × 22" × 26"; 28 ³⁄₈" × 23 ¼" × 27 ³⁄₁₆". Marlborough Gallery, NY.

Making art is about objectifying your experience of the world, transforming the flow of moments into something visual, or textual, or musical. Art creates a kind of commentary.
—Barbara Kruger

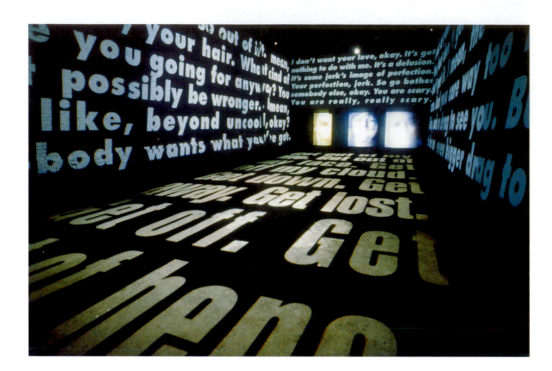

3-25 BARBARA KRUGER. *Power Pleasure Desire Disgust* (1997). Multimedia installation. © Barbara Kruger, Courtesy Mary Boone Gallery, NY.

SCALE

Scale refers to size—small, big, or in between. Scale is the relative size of an object compared with others of its kind, its setting, or human dimensions. The Great Pyramids at Gizeh (see Fig. 13-12) and the skyscrapers of New York are imposing because of their scale; that is, their size compared with the size of other buildings, their sites, and people. Their overall size is essential to their impact.

Barbara Kruger's multimedia installation *Power Pleasure Desire Disgust* (Fig. **3-25**) combines steadily changing video images of talking heads and projections of the artist's signature phrases and text all over the gallery floors and walls. The overwhelming scale of the work envelops us so completely and the slogans bombard us so relentlessly that it may seem as though the thoughts expressed in the environment have somehow originated in our own minds—phrases we may have once used to hurt others or that have been used to hurt us, comments that may have cut to the quick. But interspersed with the bitter are flashes of wit, even flirtatiousness, as the work touches on communication across boundaries of gender and social definition. Thoughts are compelling and haunting things, made all the more inescapable by the sheer size of their verbal and written articulation.

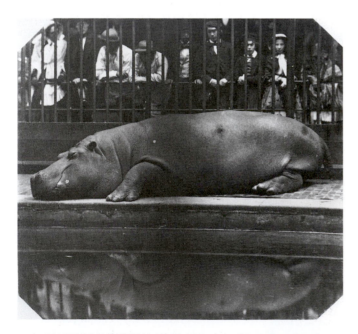

3-26 COUNT DE MONTIZON. *The Hippopotamus at the Zoological Gardens, Regent's Park* (1852). Salted-paper print.

In the Count de Montizon's photograph *The Hippopotamus at the Zoological Gardens, Regent's Park* (Fig. **3-26**), we see how artists communicate the scale of objects in their works by comparing them with other objects. In this photograph, a specimen record of the zoo's prized tenant, the photographer used *relative* size to communicate size. We see that it takes nine people standing shoulder to shoulder to match the length of one animal lazing in the sun. The photographer used the relationship between the familiar (the observers) and the unfamiliar (the hippopotamus) to communicate the size of the hippo to those who weren't there to witness it firsthand. At the time the picture was taken, 1852, the hippopotamus was not yet a familiar denizen of zoos in Europe and the United States. A gift from the pasha of Egypt to Queen Victoria, this hippo was the main attraction at the London Zoo.

Nineteenth-century London's hippopotamus was exotic, its size dramatic. In relation to the scale of ordinary human beings, it was extraordinary. In viewing the photograph, a person could pretty much grasp the magnitude of the animal. By contrast, in Magritte's *Personal Values* (Fig. **3-27**), it is impossible for the viewer to comprehend the dimensions of any of the objects within the work because their familiar size relationships are subverted. We don't know whether the objects—the comb and matchstick and glass—are blown out of proportion or whether the bed has shrunk. We cannot rely

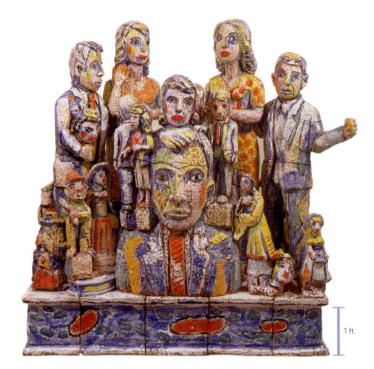

3-28 VIOLA FREY. *Family Portrait* (1995). Glazed ceramic. 84" × 82⅝" × 34⅝". Collection of the Hirshhorn Museum and Sculpture Garden, Smithsonian Institution, Washington, D.C. Art © Artists' Legacy Foundation/Licensed by VAGA, NY.

on our experience of actual dimension to make sense of the content of the work, so our tendency to understand size in relation to other things fails us.

Hierarchical Scaling

Standing "ten feet tall" is a familiar idiom. We use it to describe heroes or to communicate a certain pride we feel in our own accomplishments. It describes our feelings about a deed that sets others or ourselves above the rest, even if for one fleeting moment. In the visual arts, this metaphor, this idiom, finds its analogy in **hierarchical scaling**, or the use of relative size to indicate the relative importance of the objects or people being depicted. The method has been used for thousands of years. In ancient Egyptian art, members of royalty and nobility are sized consistently larger than the underlings surrounding them, making very clear their social positions. In medieval manuscript illumination, artists often had their celestial figures, such as angels and saints, tower over humans.

In Viola Frey's *Family Portrait* (Fig. **3-28**), we interpret the positioning and relatively large scale of the central male figure as an

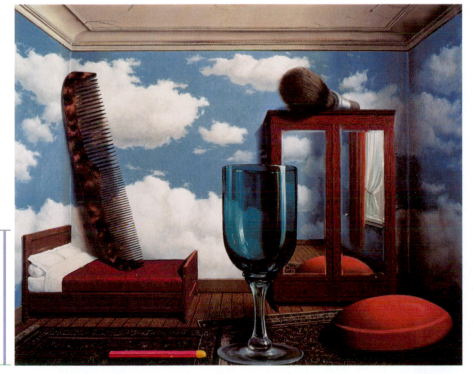

3-27 RENÉ MAGRITTE. *Personal Values* (1952). Oil on canvas. 31⅝" × 39½". San Francisco Museum of Modern Art, San Francisco, CA.

VAN EYCK'S *MADONNA IN THE CHURCH* WITH PANNINI'S *INTERIOR OF THE PANTHEON*

ARTISTS OVER THE GENERATIONS have used hierarchical scaling to assign relative importance to the subjects of their work. The Flemish artist Jan van Eyck dramatically increased the size or scale of his Madonna, depicted in a jewel-studded crown befitting her status as the Queen of Heaven, within the interior of a typical Gothic cathedral (Fig. **3-29**). He relies on the viewer's understanding of the vastness of such an interior to convey, through her relative size, her importance in Christian belief.

Van Eyck set himself the task of attempting to convey the notion of the Queen of Heaven. How can he signify such status within the realm of human experience? In order to

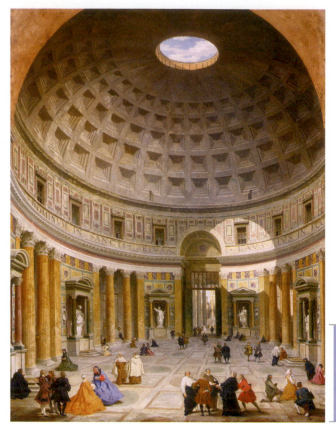

3-30 GIOVANNI PAOLO PANNINI. *Interior of the Pantheon* (c. 1740). Oil on canvas. 50½" × 39". National Gallery of Art, Washington, D.C.

find some measure of the vastness of the heavens relative to human experience, van Eyck went to the interior of a Gothic cathedral—the very height of which is intended to replicate the unreachable dome of heaven. By rendering the Madonna in such a large scale relative to the seemingly infinite height of the vaulted ceilings, the ordinary earthbound worshiper begins to comprehend her majesty.

Pannini's goal was quite different. The Pantheon is one of Rome's most awesome monuments. How to describe the feeling of overwhelming space that one experiences within the realm of the *Interior of the Pantheon* (Fig. **3-30**)? Pannini sprinkles his interior with figures rendered in a realistic scale relative to the architecture. They seem insectlike compared to the reaches of the dome and thus we get some idea of what it must feel like to stand beneath it. The relationship between these humans and the grandeur of this architecture makes it seem as if it must have been the work of giants.

What is the focus of each of these paintings? What is each of them about? Are they about architecture or about the figures within? In the van Eyck, the architecture is used to suggest the importance of the Madonna. In the Pannini, the people are used to show the grandeur of the architecture. ●

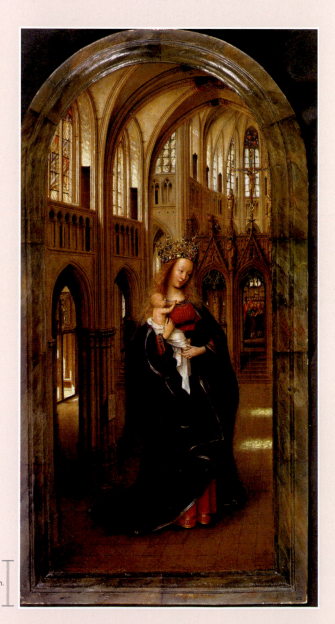

3-29 JAN VAN EYCK. *Madonna in the Church* (c. 1437–1438). Oil on oak panel. 12¼" × 5½". Gemäldegalerie, Staatliche Museum, Berlin, Germany.

indicator of his status within the family. Frey includes only his head and shoulders, against which are measured the full-bodied figures of the other family members. The influence of the patriarch is sensed not only in his relative size, but also in the crowding of the group.

Distortion of Scale

Some artists distort or even subvert the realistic scale of objects to challenge the viewer to look at the familiar in a new way.

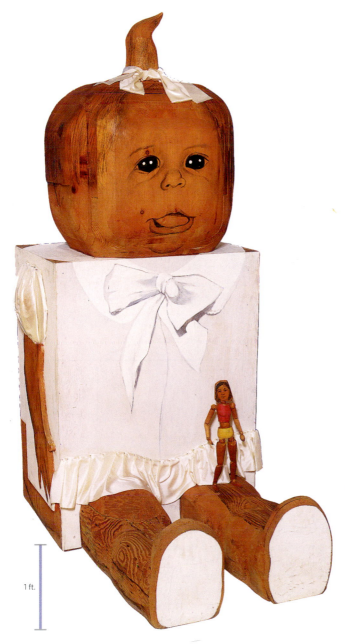

3-31 MARISOL. *Baby Girl* (1963). Wood and mixed media. 74" × 35" × 47". Albright-Knox Art Gallery, Buffalo, NY. Art © Marisol Escobar/Licensed by VAGA, NY.

Sometimes they are interested in providing a new perspective on the forms of things; sometimes on the relationships between things.

Altering the viewer's sense of scale partly creates the visual shock and sheer humor of Marisol's *Baby Girl* (Fig. **3-31**). A wooden doll with adjustable limbs and torso—the sort used for drawing exercises in art classes—sports a portrait of Marisol herself. It is perched on the stocky thigh of the baby, who neither looks at nor touches the "toy." The baby girl—by any other definition a subject that suggests delicacy and softness—is transformed into a cumbersome hunk of a figure. Only the shirring of her puffy sleeves and frilly gathers of her white dress soften the harshness of the overall form. Marisol's manipulation of scale and our perception of it are confirmed by the fact that in looking at the illustration of this work in your book (without sneaking a peek at the dimensions), you would have no real sense of how large or small the work actually is.

PROPORTION

"Everything is relative." That is, we tend to think of objects or of works of art as large or small according to their relationships to other things—often to ourselves. However, the objects depicted within works of art can also be large or small in relationship to one another and to the work as a whole. **Proportion**, then, is the comparative relationship, or ratio, of things to one another.

Artists through the ages have sought to determine the proper or most appealing ratios of parts of works to one another and the whole. They have used proportion to represent what they believed to be the ideal or the beautiful. They also have disregarded or subverted proportion to achieve special effects—often to compel viewers to take a new look at the familiar.

The Canon of Proportions

The ancient Greeks tied their vision of ideal beauty to what they considered the "proper" proportions of the human body. Polykleitos is credited with the derivation of a **canon of proportions**—a set of rules about body parts and their dimensions relative to one another that became the standard for creating the ideal figure. The physical manifestation of his canon was his *Doryphoros* (Fig. 3-7). Every part of the body is either a specific fraction or multiple of every other part. Ideally, for Polykleitos, the head is one-eighth of the total height of the body, and the width from shoulder to shoulder should not exceed one-fourth of the body's height.

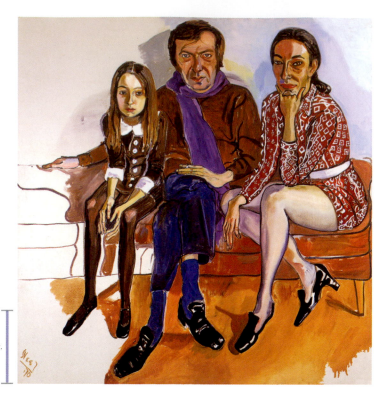

3-32 ALICE NEEL. *The Family* (John Gruen, Jane Wilson, and Julia) (1970). Oil on canvas. 4'11⅞" × 5'. The Museum of Fine Arts, Houston, TX.

1 ft.

Violating the Canon for Expressive Purposes

If the *Doryphoros* represents ideal form, Alice Neel's *The Family* (Fig. **3-32**) leaves the canon behind in what appears to be the pursuit of unidealized form. The enlarged heads, elongated fingers and calves, and outsized feet are glaring obstacles to realistic representation. And yet, somehow, there is an overarching realism despite these artistic liberties that emanates from the relationships among the family members.

The Golden Mean

Just as the Greeks developed a canon of proportions for representing the human figure in the ideal, they developed the concept of the **golden mean** or the **golden section** in order to create ideal proportions in architecture. The golden mean requires that a small part of a work should relate to a larger part of the work as the larger part relates to the whole. The line in Figure **3-33** is divided, or *sectioned*, at point B so that the ratio of the shorter segment (AB) is to the larger segment (BC) as the larger segment (BC) is to the whole line (AC). Segment BC is the golden mean.

The rectangle in Figure **3-34** is based on the golden mean and is termed a **golden rectangle**. Its width is 1.618 times its height. The golden rectangle was thought by the Greeks to be the most pleasing rectangle, and it became the basis for many temple designs.

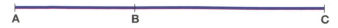

3-33 The golden mean.
To create the golden mean, a line is divided ("sectioned") so that the ratio of the shorter segment (AB) is to the larger segment (BC) as the larger segment (BC) is to the whole (AC). Line segment BC is 1.618 times the length of segment AB. Segment BC is the "mean" in the sense that its length lies between the smaller segment (AB) and the entire line (AC). The Greeks considered segment BC to be "golden" in that its use created what they considered to be ideal proportions in architecture.

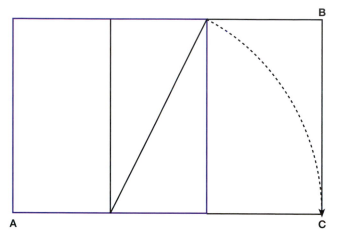

3-34 The golden rectangle.
The width of this rectangle is exactly 1.618 times its height. The triangle can be created by rotating the diagonal of the half square on the left (outlined in red) to the base on the right (point C). This "ideal" rectangle became the basis for the floor plans of Greek temples and represented the artistic embodiment of the Greek maxim "Moderation in all things."

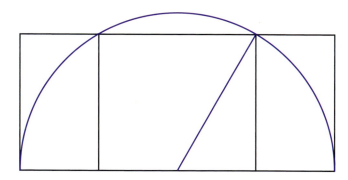

3-35 The root five rectangle.
One obtains a root five rectangle by rotating the diagonal of the square in Figure 3-34 in both directions. The rectangle obtains its name from the fact that its length is 2.236 (the square root of the number 5) times its width. The root five rectangle has frequently been used to define the frame for works of art, including buildings (Figure 3-36) and paintings (Figure 3.37).

A golden rectangle can be made either by measuring the lengths of the lines or by rotating the diagonal of the half square, as shown in Figure 3-34. We can also rotate the diagonal of the square in both directions, sort of like a windshield

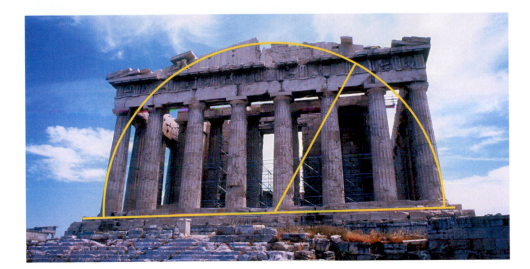

3-36 The east facade of the Parthenon, superimposed with a root five rectangle. When we do not consider the gable (which is absent in this photograph), the facade of the Parthenon is a root five rectangle.

wiper. If we add the second smaller rectangle, we obtain a rectangle that is made up of a central square and two smaller rectangles (Fig. **3-35**). The entire rectangle is called a root five rectangle, because its length is 2.236 (the square root of 5) times its width.

The proportions of the root five rectangle have also served as the frame for various works of art and architecture. If you superimpose a diagram of a **root five rectangle** over a photograph of the east facade of the Parthenon (Fig. **3-36**), you can see the almost compulsive adherence to geometric order that the Greeks visited on their places of worship. The facade is constructed of eight columns. The four in the center fit within the central square of the root five rectangle. The portions of the facade occupying the flanking rectangles include the two end columns to either side as well as the outermost points defined by the steps leading to the temple platform.

Most viewers are unaware of the mathematical basis for the Parthenon's design, but they come away with an overall impression of harmony and order. The root five rectangle is also the foundation of some paintings that have harmonious compositions. Michelangelo's *The Fall of Man and the Expulsion from the Garden of Eden* (Fig. **3-37**), from the Sistine Chapel ceiling (see Figs. 16-21 and 16-22), maximizes the components of the root five rectangle. The central square contains the Tree of Knowledge from the book of Genesis, that all-important symbol of the temptation and fall of man. The Tree connects the imagery in the outer parts of the root five rectangle—the repetitive figures of Adam and Eve as separated by time and the serpent.

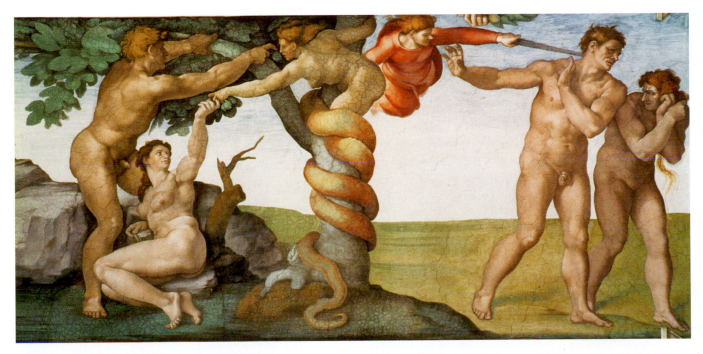

3-37 MICHELANGELO. *The Fall of Man and the Expulsion from the Garden of Eden* (1508–1512). Portion of the Sistine Chapel ceiling. Fresco. Vatican, Rome, Italy.

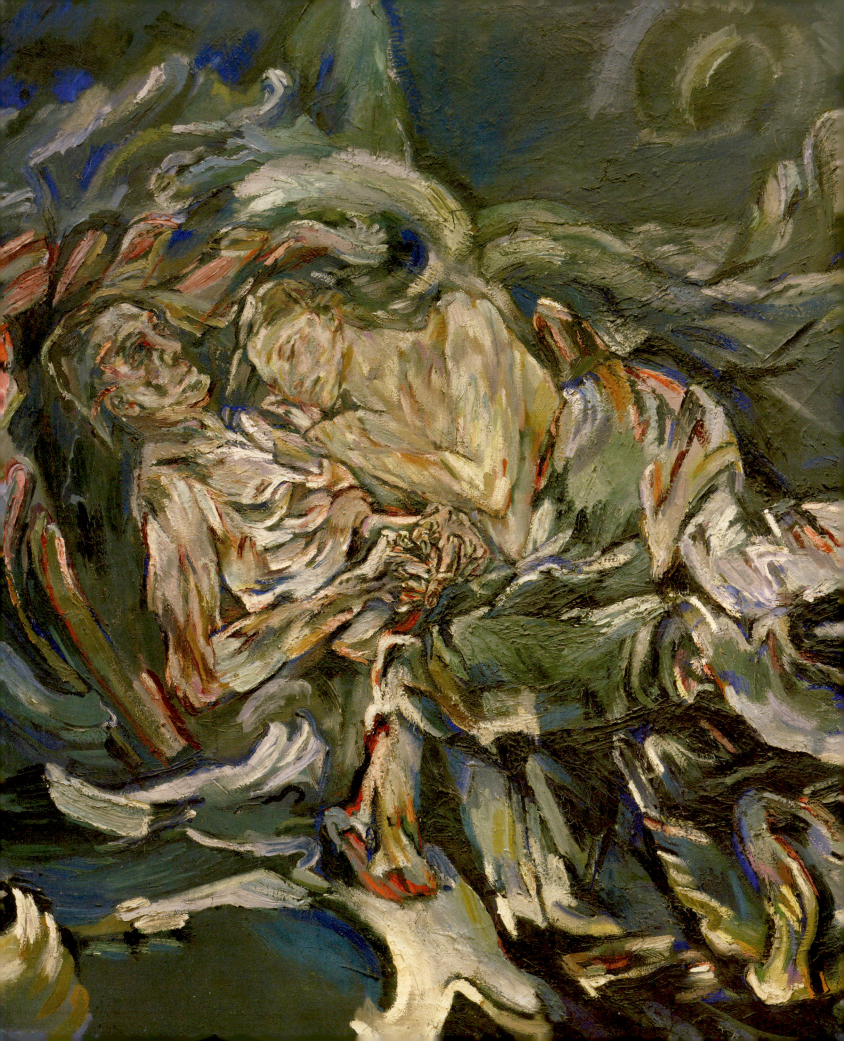

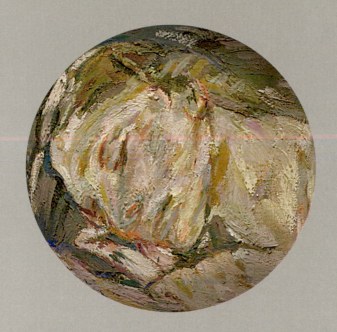

The duty of an artist is to strain against the bonds of the existing style.

—Philip Johnson

STYLE, FORM, AND CONTENT

4

Human languages combine words according to rules of grammar to express and communicate emotions and meanings. Artists use the language of art to combine the visual elements of art according to principles of design. The resultant works of art are said to have style and form and to express and communicate a certain content.

Despite individual differences—and despite wholesale revolutions!—through the ages several characteristic methods of expression have developed that we refer to as *style*. Works of art can also be said to have a certain *form*, which is the totality of what we see—the product of the composition of the visual elements according to (or in total violation of) principles of design. The *content* of a work includes not only its form but also its subject matter and its underlying meanings or themes. Some works of art can seem to be devoid of content other than the pencil marks or, perhaps, the swaths of paint we find on a sheet of paper or on a canvas. But many are filled with levels of content, more of which are perceived by some viewers than by others. The content of a work varies with the amount of information available to the viewer. For example, viewers who are aware of the symbolism of a particular work of art will find more content in it. Awareness of style, form, and content helps viewers understand and appreciate the visual arts more fully.

OSKAR KOKOSCHKA. *The Tempest* (1914). Oil on canvas. 71½" × 86½". Kunstmuseum, Basel, Switzerland.

STYLE

In the visual arts, **style** refers to a distinctive handling of elements and media associated with the work of an individual artist, a school or movement, or a specific culture or time period. Familiar subjects may come and go, but creativity, originality, and authenticity dwell in the style or unique handling of the artist.

One of the best ways to illustrate stylistic differences is to choose a group of works with a common theme (such as those illustrated in Figures 4-1 through 4-10) and challenge ourselves to articulate the similarities and differences among them. The first and seemingly obvious connection is that all of the works represent couples. Yet immediately we are struck by the differences among them, in terms of both the stories they imply and the styles in which they are rendered.

To begin with, the images demand that we get beyond the conventional definition of *couple*, for not all couples are composed of a male and a female. What is really striking, however, are the variations in *style*, sometimes linked to the use of different media and sometimes connected to diverse cultural contexts, but always indicative of the characteristic approach of the artist to the subject.

Art, Culture, and Context

The Mayan ceramic couple (Fig. **4-1**), for example, is an eighth- to tenth-century pre-Columbian sculpture, whose garments, hairstyles, and facial features link it to the life and times of the Yucatecan people before the onslaught of the Europeans. Similar telltale attributes connect Roy Lichtenstein's *Forget It! Forget Me!* (Fig. **4-2**) to the United States in the decade of the 1960s. Henri de Toulouse-Lautrec's *The Two Girlfriends* (Fig. **4-3**) transports us to the demimonde of

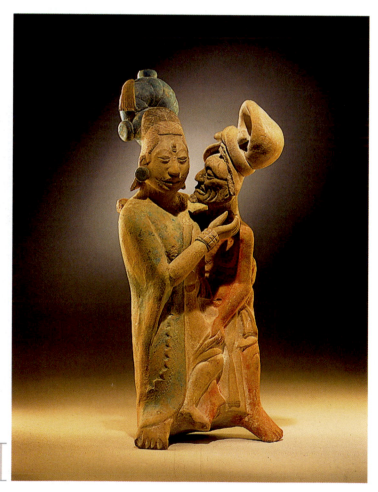

4-1 *Amorous Couple* (Mayan, Late Classic, 700–900 CE). Polychromed ceramic. H: 9¾". Detroit Institute of the Arts, Detroit, MI.

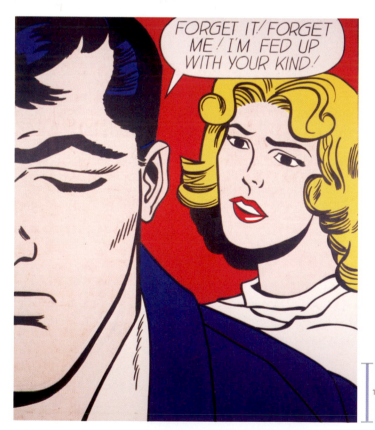

4-2 ROY LICHTENSTEIN. *Forget It! Forget Me!* (1962). Magna and oil on canvas. 79⅞" × 68". Rose Art Museum, Brandeis University, Waltham, MA.

How can you say one style is better than another? You ought to be able to be an Abstract-Expressionist next week, or a Pop artist, or a realist, without feeling you've given up something.
—Andy Warhol

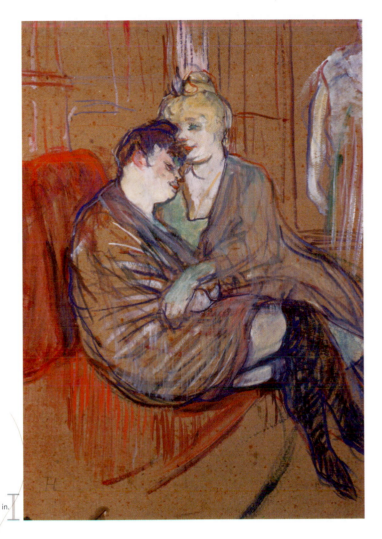

1 in.

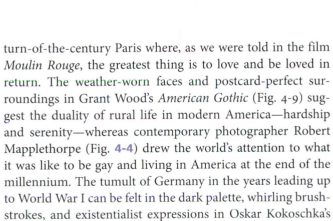

4-3 HENRI DE TOULOUSE-LAUTREC. *The Two Girlfriends* (1894). Oil on cardboard. 18 7⁄8" × 34 5⁄8". Musée Toulouse-Lautrec, Albi, France.

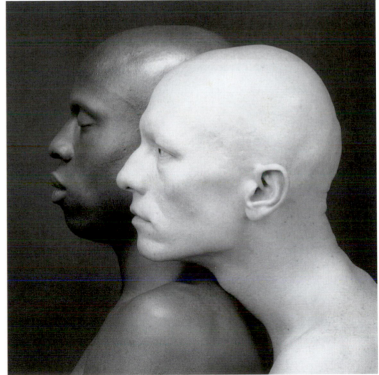

4-4 ROBERT MAPPLETHORPE. *Ken Moody and Robert Sherman* (1984). Photograph. 19 1⁄2" × 19 5⁄8". Solomon R. Guggenheim Museum, NY.

turn-of-the-century Paris where, as we were told in the film *Moulin Rouge*, the greatest thing is to love and be loved in return. The weather-worn faces and postcard-perfect surroundings in Grant Wood's *American Gothic* (Fig. 4-9) suggest the duality of rural life in modern America—hardship and serenity—whereas contemporary photographer Robert Mapplethorpe (Fig. **4-4**) drew the world's attention to what it was like to be gay and living in America at the end of the millennium. The tumult of Germany in the years leading up to World War I can be felt in the dark palette, whirling brushstrokes, and existentialist expressions in Oskar Kokoschka's

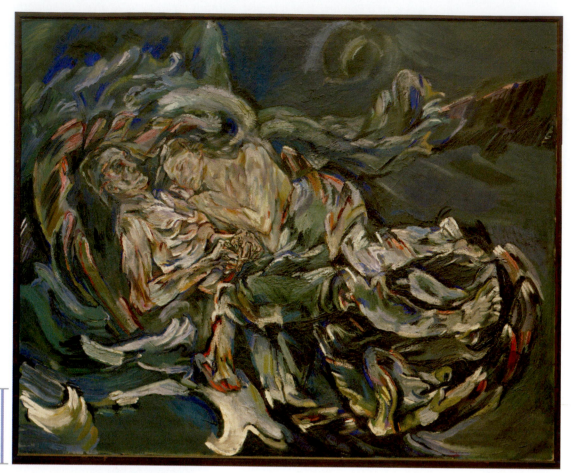

1 ft.

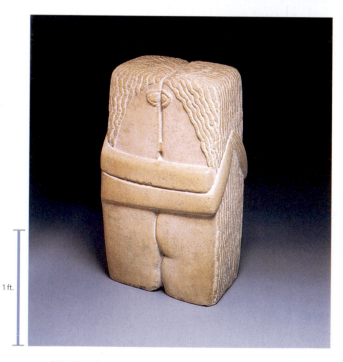

1 ft.

The Tempest (Fig. **4-5**). Donna Rosenthal's *He Said . . . She Said* (Fig. 4-10) seems to tap into some sort of collective unconscious ballroom in its unique yet universal ruminations. Constantin Brancusi's *The Kiss* (Fig. **4-6**) could be said to transcend context in the simple accessibility or readability of its subject.

In their abstraction, Jackson Pollock's *Male and Female* (Fig. **4-7**) and Barbara Hepworth's *Two Figures* (Fig. **4-8**) are more difficult to decipher. Pollock's painting was created while he was undergoing psychoanalytic therapy and ought to be read in that context. It reveals a complex scheme of images that he believed were derived from his collective unconscious mind. Hepworth, by contrast, aims to disconnect her work from context by reducing her figures to their most common denominators—organic vertical shapes punctuated by softly modeled voids. Yet curiously, when we view *Two Figures* in the context of this grouping of "couples," it seems to belong, even if eyes may resist making a connection.

Context has a profound influence on style. We can see this in the similarities among artists of a specific era, regardless of their individual "signature." Claude Monet and Auguste Renoir, for example—both Impressionist artists working in

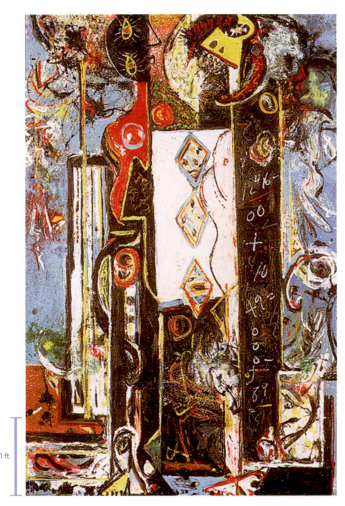

4-7 JACKSON POLLOCK. *Male and Female* (1942). Oil on canvas. 73⅓" × 49". The Philadelphia Museum of Art, Philadelphia, PA. © 2011 Pollock-Krasner Foundation/Artists Rights Society (ARS), NY.

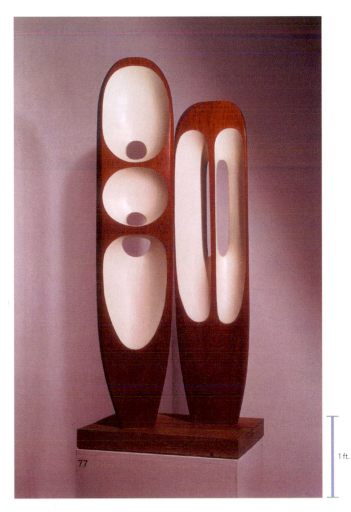

4-8 BARBARA HEPWORTH. *Two Figures (Menhirs)* (1954–1955). Teak. H: 54". The Art Institute of Chicago, Chicago, IL.

nineteenth-century France—are recognized for their distinct styles, but they have more in common with each other than they do with, say, Rembrandt. And although you probably wouldn't mistake one for the other, the works of both artists are very much a product of their culture at a moment in time.

Styles in art are numerous, ever changing, and ever new. The vocabulary we use to discuss style, on the other hand, has been fairly standard for a long time.

Realistic Art

Realism refers to the portrayal of people and things as they are seen by the eye or really thought to be, without ideal-

ization, without distortion. Wood's painting (Fig. 4-9) is described as realistic in terms of style. The term, with a capital *R*, also defines a specific school of art that flowered during the mid-nineteenth century in France. Realism featured subjects culled from daily life and experience and developed a new respect for the real substance of the artist's materials.

Grant Wood's renowned *American Gothic* is a painstakingly realistic portrait of the staid virtues of the rural life in America. It is also one of our more commercialized works of art; images derived from it have adorned boxes of breakfast cereal, greeting cards, and numerous other products. Note the repetition of the pitchfork pattern in the man's shirtfront, the upper-story window of the house, and the plant on the porch.

*I observe the effects of traditional and societal influences on the lives of women. . . .
I use text, repetition, and the cultural symbolism of clothing to expose the struggles between
the internal and external self. The manner in which I compose my work gives clues to age-old
personal and collective realities, the longings, presumptions, and predicaments of women.*
—Donna Rosenthal

He is very much tied to his environment. Were it not for the incongruously spry curl falling from the mistress's otherwise tucked-tight hairdo, we might view this composition—as well as the sitters therein—as solid, stolid, and monotonous.

We think of most photographs as realistic. The very nature of the technique—shooting, capturing, documenting—suggests candid truth, unadulterated reality. Although photographers in the twentieth century and beyond have pursued photography as an art form and strained against the bonds of representation, the impact of Mapplethorpe's photographs is largely a result of his unflinching realism (Fig. 4-4).

REALISTIC VERSUS REPRESENTATIONAL ART The Lichtenstein couple (Fig. 4-2) is portrayed in a style that departs from strict Realism, yet the observer clearly identifies the caricature-like renderings of the figures as that of a man and woman. This is **representational art**. It presents natural objects in recognizable, though not realistic, form. *Forget It! Forget Me!* is an example of Pop Art, which adopts the visual clichés of the comic strip. Donna Rosenthal's *He Said . . . She Said* (Fig. 4-10) also clearly depicts an interaction between a man and a woman, in this case capturing the verbal clichés of the human comedy. Both works can be described as representational.

The term *representational art*, often used synonymously with figurative art, is defined as art that portrays, however altered or distorted, things perceived in the visible world. The people in the Lichtenstein work may not be realistic, but they are clearly recognizable. The Mayan couple (Fig. 4-1) and Toulouse-Lautrec's *The Two Girlfriends* (Fig. 4-3) are similarly representational but not realistic.

Expressionistic Art

In expressionistic art, form and color are freely distorted by the artist in order to achieve a heightened emotional impact. Expressionism also refers to a modern art movement, but many earlier works are **expressionistic** in the broader sense of the term.

In *The Burial of Count Orgaz* (see Fig. 16-29), El Greco's expressionistic elongation of the heavenly figures seems to emphasize their ethereal spirituality. Postimpressionist Vincent van Gogh relied on both an expressionistic palette and brushwork to transfer emotion to his canvases. Kokoschka's expressionistic painting *The Tempest* (Fig. 4-5) is marked by frenzied brushstrokes that mirror the torment of his inner life as well as the impending darkness of war in Germany. Reclining figures occupy the center of a dark, imaginary landscape. Images of earth, water, and flesh merge in a common palette and bevy of strokes; little distinguishes one from another. All seem caught up in a churning sky, very much in danger of being swept away.

Abstract Art

The term **abstract** applies to art that departs significantly from the actual appearance of things. Such art may be completely **nonobjective**; that is, it may make no reference whatsoever to nature or reality. On the other hand, abstract art may be rooted in nature, even though the finished product bears little resemblance to the source that inspired it. Several aspects of the Brancusi sculpture (Fig. 4-6) are recognizable: One can discern an upper torso, arms, eyes, and hair. Yet the artist seems to have been more interested in the independent relationships of the shapes than in being true to the human form. For this reason, we would more likely characterize *The Kiss* as abstract rather than representational.

In *The Kiss*, the human torso is reduced to a simple block form. Twentieth-century proponents of **Cubism**, such as Pablo Picasso and Georges Braque (see Figs. 20-6 and 20-7) also transcribed natural forms into largely angular geometric equivalents. To some degree, despite their reduction to essential geometric components and line–shape relationships, the figures of Picasso and Braque remain somewhat decipherable. In any event, both artists—despite some brief dabbling in nonobjectivity—abstracted from reality.

Jackson Pollock's *Male and Female* (Fig. 4-7) "figures" are a great deal more difficult to discern than Brancusi's, but the totemic shapes bear some visual cues that suggest gender differences. At the time of the painting, Pollock was undergoing psychoanalysis, and he was quite convinced that the unconscious played a major role in his art. Using a method called **psychic automatism**, Pollock attempted to clear his mind of purpose and concerns so that inner conflicts and ideas could find expression through his work. The result in *Male and Female* is abstraction.

Although much of Barbara Hepworth's sculpture has been inspired by nature, it is not always derived from nature. That

WOOD'S *AMERICAN GOTHIC* WITH ROSENTHAL'S *HE SAID . . . SHE SAID*

THE STYLE OF A WORK OF ART refers to the characteristic ways in which artists express themselves and the times in which they live. In our consideration of the theme of couples, we were able to assess the way in which a full range of media, methods, and styles contributes to the uniqueness of each work. If we add to these the historical and cultural contexts of the works, we gain insight into the ways in which art reflects its place and time.

Consider Grant Wood's *American Gothic* and Donna Rosenthal's *He Said . . . She Said.* On a trip to Europe in the 1920s, Wood was influenced by the realistic works of fifteenth-century German and Flemish painters. His initial goal in *American Gothic* (Fig. **4-9**) was to render realistically the rural Iowan house in the background of the painting. He enlisted a local dentist along with his own sister to pose as models for the farmer and his wife. The realism of

their faces is so exacting and their expressions so intent that the viewer cannot but wonder what thoughts lie buried in their minds.

And then there is the expression "to wear one's heart on one's sleeve." In Rosenthal's *He Said . . . She Said* (Fig. **4-10**), thoughts and feelings are broadcast plainly, as the (implied) individuals quite literally wear their thoughts on their clothes—a suit and party dress made from the pages of discarded books and newspapers. We know exactly what's on their minds, verbalized through cultural stereotypes of the conflicting definitions of males and females perpetuated from childhood onward. A nursery rhyme that dates back to the nineteenth-century poses the questions "What are little girls made of?" ("Sugar and spice and all things nice") and "What are little boys made of?" ("Snips and snails and puppy-dogs' tails"). Rosenthal calls attention to the tendency for childhood gender expectations to frame gender discourse in adult relationships. Other works by the artist express man's desire for sex and woman's desire for security. Stereotypes are by definition extreme; they represent conventional notions and not individual conceptions. Yet Rosenthal succeeds in her communication with the viewer in large part because of the ubiquity of these phrases.

As the physical couple is absent from the work, we are left with the notion that the clothes make the individual. This is conceptual art; that is, the ideas being expressed by the artist have greater meaning than their physical expression. ●

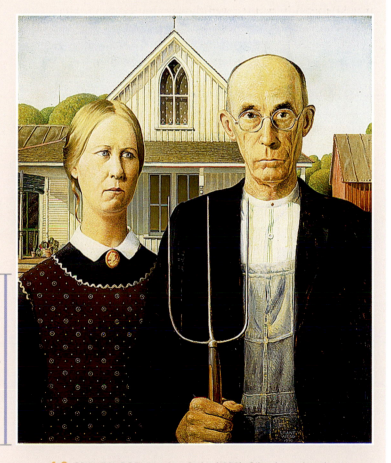

1 ft.

4-9 GRANT WOOD. *American Gothic* (1930). Oil on beaverboard. 29 ⅞" × 24 ⅞". The Art Institute of Chicago, Chicago, IL.

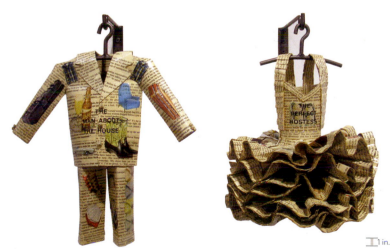

1 in.

4-10 DONNA ROSENTHAL. *He Said . . . She Said (Romance Comics)* (2007). Paper and mixed media. 25" × 16" × 10" each set.

is why we characterize work such as *Two Figures* (Fig. 4-8) as nonobjective; that is, it is not intended to make any reference to reality. On the other hand, titling the piece *Two Figures* places viewers in a quandary. It sends us searching for details that might represent the human form, even gender differences. Is the taller "figure" the male? Could the concave

4-11 JUDY PFAFF. *Voodoo* (1981). Contact paper collage on Mylar. 98" × 60" (framed). Albright-Knox Art Gallery, Buffalo, NY.

shapes in the shorter figure suggest femininity? Here the connection to reality may be fully in the eye of the beholder. Nonobjective artists do this type of thing quite a lot. Sometimes they label their paintings and sculptures *Untitled* partially as a way to discourage Rorschach-like readings of their work. At other times, they assign titles to their nonobjective works based on some association that is triggered by the work itself.

A case in point is Judy Pfaff's *Voodoo* (Fig. **4-11**), a nonobjective painting in which highly saturated colors and jagged shapes comprise the content and spirit of the work. Though the elements and technique are the "subject" of the work, the title suggests the presence of mysterious figures undulating in a Caribbean jungle undergrowth. One of the issues that many viewers have with nonobjective art is that they want it to make sense. They want to connect it with something familiar—even if the familiar in this case is as abstruse as the title, *Voodoo*. But nonobjective art is just that—nonobjective—and viewers may come closer to the intention of the artist by allowing themselves to focus on what's there rather than to go on scavenger hunts for what probably isn't.

FORM

The **form** of a work refers to its totality as a work of art. Form includes the elements, design principles, and composition of a work of art. A work's *form* may include, for example, the colors that are used, the textures and shapes, the illusion of three dimensions, the balance, rhythm, or unity of design. **Formalist criticism**, by extension, is an approach to art criticism that concentrates primarily on the elements and design of works of art rather than on historical factors or the biography of the artist.

CONTENT

The **content** of a work of art is everything that is contained in it. The content of a work refers not only to its lines or forms but also to its subject matter and its underlying meanings or themes.

The Levels of Content

We may think of works of art as containing three levels of content: (1) subject matter, (2) elements and composition, and (3) underlying or symbolic meanings or themes.

To give a body and a perfect form to your thought, this alone is what it is to be an artist.
—Jacques-Louis David

Consider a comparison between the subject matter of two visually similar paintings as a way of exploring these levels. In 1793, just a few years after the taking of the Bastille and the start of the French Revolution, Jacques-Louis David painted *Death of Marat* (Fig. **4-12**), a memorial to a political martyr. Almost 200 years later, Sandow Birk appropriated David's image for *Death of Manuel* (Fig. **4-13**), his graphic deposition on urban violence.

There is a macabre similarity between the two paintings in their elements and composition. David's Marat is found dead in his bath—murdered by a counterrevolutionary fanatic named Charlotte Corday. The artist brings the viewer face-to-face with the slaughtered hero, whose arm drops lifeless and whose sympathetic facial expression leans toward us yearningly. Birk's *Manuel* is rendered in the same pose, although

Marat's bath has been replaced with a Chevy Impala, riddled with bullets. Marat's left hand holds a false letter requesting a visit from the would-be murderer; Manuel's left hand grasps the steering wheel of his car. Marat's head is wrapped in a turban; Manuel's, in a brightly printed bandana. In both paintings, the figure is set in the extreme foreground, and the backgrounds are monochromatic and nondescript. The spatial depth is severely limited. This dramatic silhouette effect, coupled with the strong linear style used to render the figures, creates the feeling of a sculptural frieze.

The underlying themes or symbolism in these works may not bear the same relationship as do the elements and composition. Yet the choice of the David prototype suggests ideas of revolution, heroism as it is defined within a group or culture, and the cold-blooded murder of the unsuspecting victim. The

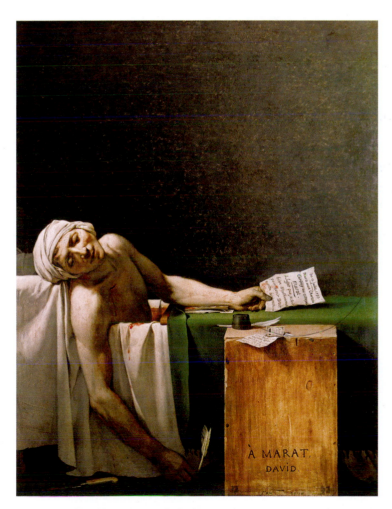

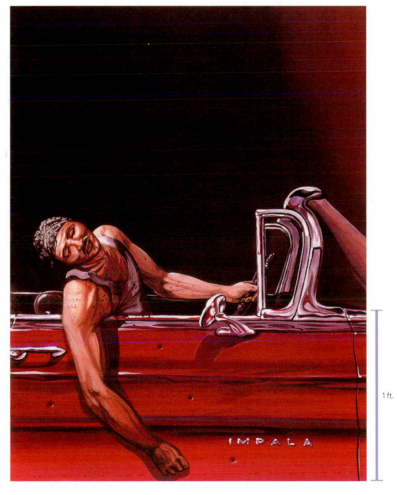

4-12 JACQUES-LOUIS DAVID. *Death of Marat* (1793). Oil on canvas. 63¾" × 49⅛". Musées Royaux des Beaux-Arts de Belgique, Brussels, Belgium.

4-13 SANDOW BIRK. *Death of Manuel* (1992). Oil on canvas. 33" × 25". Koplin Del Rio Gallery, Culver City, CA.

1 ft.

DAVID'S *THE OATH OF THE HORATII* WITH KRUGER'S *UNTITLED (WE DON'T NEED ANOTHER HERO)*

THE OATH OF THE HORATII (Fig. **4-14**), by Jacques-Louis David, is one of the most readily recognizable works of the nineteenth century—indeed, the whole of the history of art. It is a landmark composition—symbolically and pictorially. David worked for the king of France in the days before the French Revolution. Ironically, although the *Oath* was painted for Louis XVI, who along with his wife, Marie Antoinette, would lose his head to the guillotine, the painting became an almost instant symbol of the Revolution. The loyalty, courage, and sacrifice it portrayed were an inspiration to the downtrodden masses in their uprising against the French monarchy. David, because of his position, was imprisoned along with the members of the court and other French aristocracy, only to be—as it were—"bailed out" by another who could use his services

as a painter. Thus David, court painter to the French king, would become painter to Napoleon Bonaparte, who would eventually crown himself emperor.

Pictorially, the work is also groundbreaking. It compresses space and forces us to concentrate on the meticulously rendered figures in the foreground. This treatment of space would open the door to the flattening of space in Modernist paintings. The tradition of treating the picture frame as a window frame through which one peers into the infinite distance would be abandoned by many artists in favor of the two-dimensionality of the canvas.

Knowing something of the historical circumstances under which *The Oath of the Horatii* was created, and understanding what is new about it in terms of style and composition, helps us appreciate its significance. But our

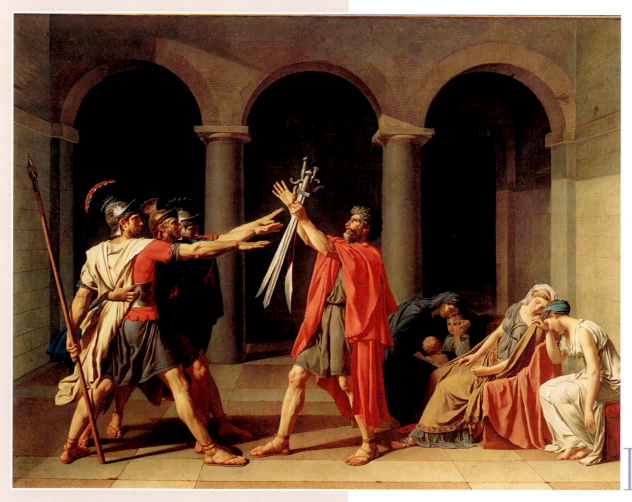

1 ft.

4-14 JACQUES-LOUIS DAVID. *The Oath of the Horatii* (1784). Oil on canvas. 11' × 14'. Louvre, Paris, France.

full comprehension and appreciation of the work can occur only with our consideration and interpretation of the subject matter. The subject of David's *The Oath of the Horatii* is, on the face of things, fairly easy to read. Three brothers—the Horatii—swear their allegiance to Rome on swords held high by their father. They pledge to come back victorious or not come back at all. Their forward-thrusting and stable stances convey strength, commitment, and bravery. And there is something else—something that has been referred to by feminist critics and scholars as a *subtext*, or an additional level of content in the work. David's *Oath* is also a painting about the ideology of gender differences. The women in the painting collapse in the background, terrified at the prospect of the death of the brothers. To make matters worse, one of the Horatii sisters is engaged to be married to one of the enemy. She might lose her brother to the hands of her fiancé, or vice versa. The women's posture, in opposition to the men's, represents, according to historian Linda Nochlin, "the clear-cut opposition between masculine strength and feminine weakness offered by the ideological discourse of the period." Whatever else the content of this painting is about, it is also about the relationship of the sexes and gender-role stereotypes.

Several contemporary feminist artists have challenged the traditional discourse of gender ideology as damaging both to men and women. Barbara Kruger's *Untitled (We Don't Need Another Hero)* (Fig. **4-15**) can be interpreted as an "answer" to David's *Oath*. In appropriating a Norman Rockwell illustration to depict the "innocence" of gender ideology—in this case, the requisite fawning of a little girl over the budding muscles of her male counterpart—Kruger violates the innocuous vignette with a cautionary band blazing the words *We don't need another hero*. The representation of the opposition between strength and weakness—male and female—is confronted and replaced with the gender discourse of a more socially aware era.

The subject matter of these works is strangely related, oddly linked. Visually, the works could not be more dissimilar. In David's composition, the subtext of gender ideology exists simultaneously with the main narrative—that of the soldiers preparing for battle. In Kruger's work, by contrast, the main narrative *is* gender ideology—and how to counteract it. In both, however, the essential nature of evaluating the content, or subject matter of the works we view, is underscored. They are, after all, really about the same thing, aren't they? ●

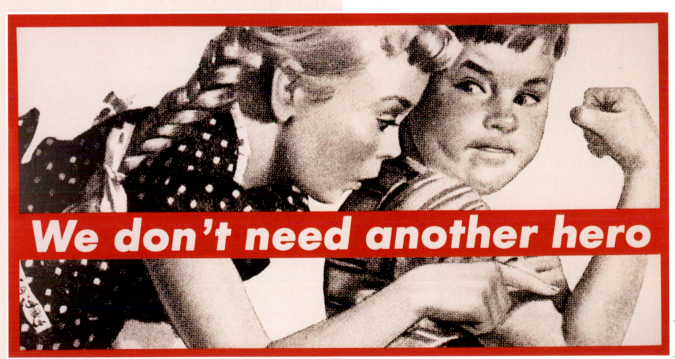

1 ft.

4-15 BARBARA KRUGER. *Untitled (We Don't Need Another Hero)* (1987). Photographic silkscreen, vinyl. 109" × 210". Mary Boone Gallery, NY.

appropriation of the David image by Birk validates the historic significance of the eighteenth-century painting. Understanding the relationship between the two makes each more meaningful to the viewer.

Iconography

I prefer winter and fall, when you feel the bone structure in the landscape—the loneliness of it—the dread feeling of winter. Something waits beneath it—the whole story doesn't show.
—Andrew Wyeth

Winter is a perennial symbol of death and aloneness in the arts, and fall is a common symbol of either harvest or decline. Yet artists who paint the winter or the fall, or who write of them, may not directly speak of death or of the harvest. "The whole story" does not always show, but rather may lie beneath a work of art.

Iconography is the study of the themes and symbols in the visual arts—the figures and images that lend works their underlying meanings. Bronzino's sixteenth-century masterpiece *Venus, Cupid, Folly, and Time (The Exposure of Luxury)* (Fig. **4-16**) is a classic example of works in which there is much more than meets the eye. The painting weaves an intricate **allegory**, with many actors, many symbols. Venus, undraped by Time and spread in a languorous diagonal across the front plane, is fondled by her son Cupid. Folly prepares to cast roses on the couple, while Hatred and Inconstancy (with two left hands) lurk in the background. Masks, symbolizing falseness, and other objects, meanings known or unknown, complete the scene.

Works such as these offer an intricate iconographic puzzle. Is Bronzino saying that love in an environment of hatred and inconstancy is foolish or doomed? Is something being suggested about incest? self-love? Can one fully appreciate Bronzino's painting without being aware of its iconography? Is it sufficient to respond to the elements and composition, to the figure of a woman being openly fondled before an unlikely array of onlookers? No simple answer is possible, and a Mannerist artist such as Bronzino would have intended this ambiguity. Certainly one could appreciate the composition and the subject matter for their own sake, but awareness of the symbolism enriches the viewing experience.

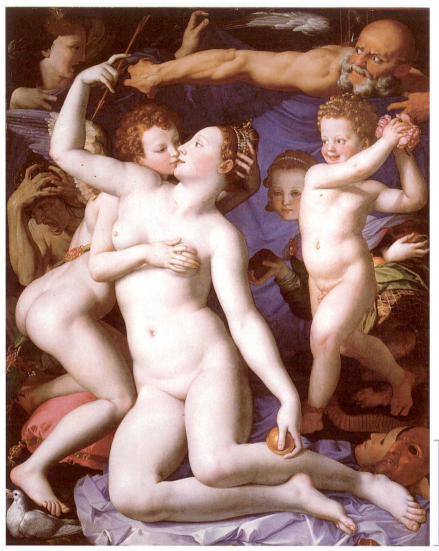

1 ft.

4-16 BRONZINO. *Venus, Cupid, Folly, and Time (The Exposure of Luxury)* (c. 1546). Oil on wood. Approx. 61" × 56¾". National Gallery, London, England.

Whereas Bronzino's painting illustrates a complex allegory, the symbolism of which would seem relevant only to the initiated, Willie Bester's *Semekazi (Migrant Miseries)* (Fig. **4-17**) uses images and objects to communicate a tragic story to anyone who will listen. Bester is an artist who was classified as "colored" under South African apartheid rule and thus, as with most nonwhite artists, was deprived of opportunities for formal training in art. Collages such as *Semekazi* combine painting with found objects in a densely covered surface that seems, in its lack of space and air, to reflect the squalid living conditions among black Africans. The many images and objects serve as symbols of rampant oppression and deprivation affecting a whole people, while a single portrait of a worker in the center of the composition—peering from under bedsprings—serves as a single case study.

The paintings by Bronzino and Bester, as far apart in time, tenor, and experience as can be imagined, both supply the viewer with clear, familiar images intended to communicate certain underlying themes. But in some cases, the underlying themes may be at least in part the invention of the viewer. In Helen Frankenthaler's *Bay Side* (see Fig. 2-22), for example, we may interpret the juncture of the blue and tan fields as surf meeting sand. Did the artist intend this symbolism, however, or is it our own invention? Many of us love a puzzle and are willing to spend a great deal of time attempting to decipher the possible iconography of a work of art. In other cases, the subject matter of a work may be in the eye of the beholder.

Our exposition of the language of art is now complete. We have seen that artists use the visual elements of art in compositions that employ various principles of design. Their compositions are usually created within certain traditional and contemporary styles. The totality of the form of their works—everything that we see in them—also has certain subject matter or content, which may exist on several levels. Our understanding of these various levels of content helps us appreciate the works.

Several chapters follow that show how artists apply the language of art to works in two dimensions and three dimensions. Then we survey the history of art, where we see how artists through the ages and around the globe have spoken a similar language. Although it may take us adults years to become fluent in the spoken languages of other peoples in other times and other places, we may find ourselves capable of more readily understanding the language in their visual works.

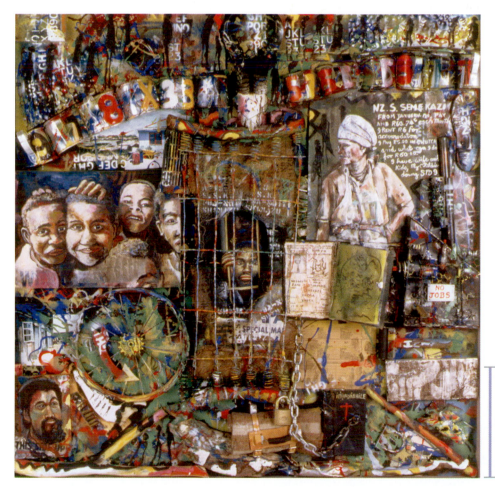

4-17 WILLIE BESTER. *Semekazi (Migrant Miseries)* (1993). Oil, enamel paint, and mixed media on board. 49¼" × 49¼".

1 ft.

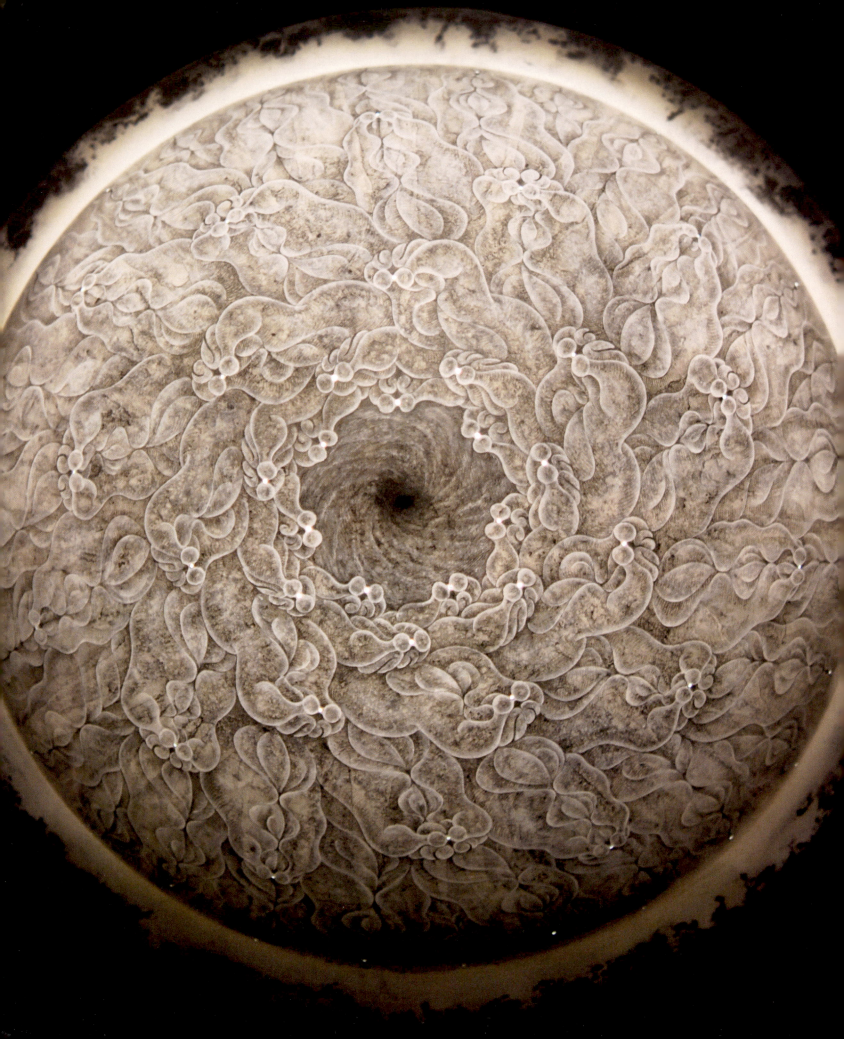

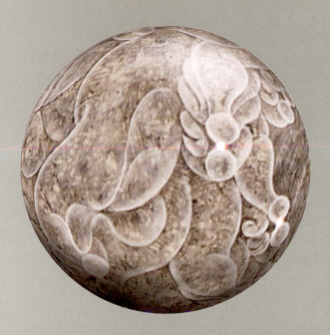

DRAWING

5

The first sketch was probably an accident. Perhaps some Stone Age human idly ran a twig through soft clay and was astounded to find an impression of this gesture in the ground. Perhaps this individual then made such impressions as signs for family members (as in an arrow pointing "that way") and to record experiences, such as the hunt for a beast or a gathering around a fire. Similarly, children may learn to trace a shell fragment through damp sand at the shore's edge and soon expand their shape vocabulary to include circles, triangles, animals, toys, and people. Artists engage in an essentially similar act when they sketch from life, from memory, from their imaginations.

Drawing is the most basic of two-dimensional art forms. In its broadest definition, **drawing** is the result of an implement running over a surface and leaving some trace of the gesture. But the art of drawing goes far beyond this simple description and its materials, forms, and functions vary widely.

The surface, or **support**, of a drawing is usually, although not always, two-dimensional. Most often the support is **monochromatic** paper or parchment, although drawings can be made on any number of surfaces. The implements and mediums can range from burned wood (charcoal) to burned paper, from bristle brushes dipped in ink to gunpowder ignited by a fuse. Most drawings, by virtue of the implements, consist of black and tones of gray. But many full-color drawings have also been created with colored chalks, pastels, and wax crayons.

CAROL PRUSA. *Whirl* (2010). Silverpoint, graphite, titanium white pigment with acrylic binder on acrylic hemisphere with fiber optics. 12" × 12" × 6". Bernice Steinbaum Gallery, Miami, FL.

Some drawings are predominantly **linear**; others are constructed solely by tonal contrasts. The quality of line and the nature of shading are affected by the texture of the support. Artists often capitalize on the idiosyncratic characteristics of the implements and support to create a specific effect in a drawing.

CATEGORIES OF DRAWING

Drawing is basic to the visual arts. For centuries, painters and sculptors have made countless preparatory sketches for their major projects, working out difficulties on paper before approaching the more permanent medium of paint or bronze. Architects proceed in the same fashion, outlining buildings in detail before breaking ground. Drawing has also served artists as a kind of shorthand method for recording ideas.

Artists carry sketchbooks everywhere, and perhaps no one is better known for his "little book of leaves" than Leonardo da Vinci (see the sketch by Leonardo on page 74), who advised artists to note everything, and when the book was "full, [to] keep it to serve [their] future plans, and take another and carry on with it." Leonardo's own work also served as inspiration for generations of artists who copied his masterpieces. Imitation has been said to be the sincerest form of flattery, and art-world luminaries and students alike have "gone to

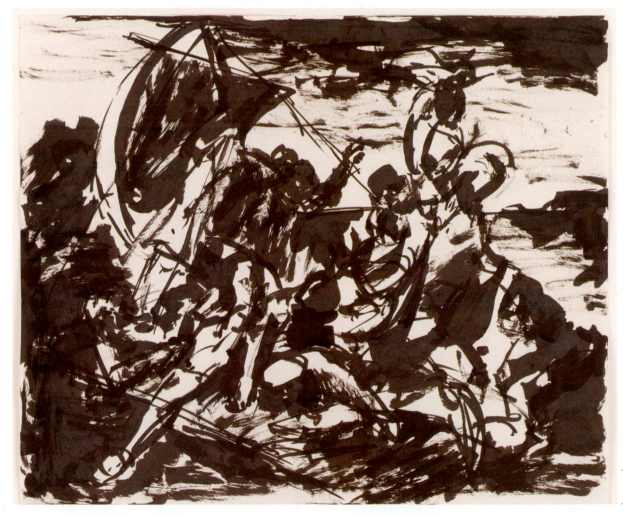

1 in.

5-1 CHEYNEY THOMPSON. *Untitled* (2003). Ink on paper. 14" × 17". The Museum of Modern Art, NY.

school on" the works of the masters. As in Cheyney Thompson's untitled study (Fig. **5-1**), after Theodore Gericault's *The Raft of the Medusa* (see page 56), copying permits the artist to, in a sense, retrace another artist's steps—from conception to completion. Far from being an exercise in mere duplication, the effort can lead to an understanding and feeling of form, rhythm, and design. Many artists, over many generations, have traveled well beyond their cities of origin to meet the works of the masters and to unlock their secrets through the scrutiny of copying.

But drawing does not serve only a utilitarian purpose. Drawing can be the most direct way of bringing what is in the artist's mind to the artist's surface. Many artists enjoy the sheer spontaneity of drawing, tracing a pencil or piece of chalk across a sheet of paper to capture directly their thoughts or to record the slightest movement of their hand.

Yet a drawing can stand as complete work of art, an entity unto itself. Gary Kelley's sensual and rhythmic pastel drawing (Fig. **5-2**) possesses all of the detail, all of the finish of a work of art in a medium that might be considered more permanent. Its powerful zigzag composition contributes to the sense of life and movement, as do the contrasts between the harsh angularity of the male singer's zoot suit and the sinuous curves of the woman who writhes in response to his music. Kelley's drawing was commissioned as a promotional piece for the Mississippi Delta Blues Festival and was no doubt purposefully reminiscent of the Harlem jazz age as depicted by 1930s African American artists such as Archibald J. Motley Jr. (see Fig. 3-2).

Drawings may thus be said to fall into at least three categories:

1. Sketches that record an idea or provide information about something the artist has seen
2. Plans or preparatory studies for other projects, such as buildings, sculptures, crafts, paintings, plays, and films
3. Fully developed and autonomous works of art

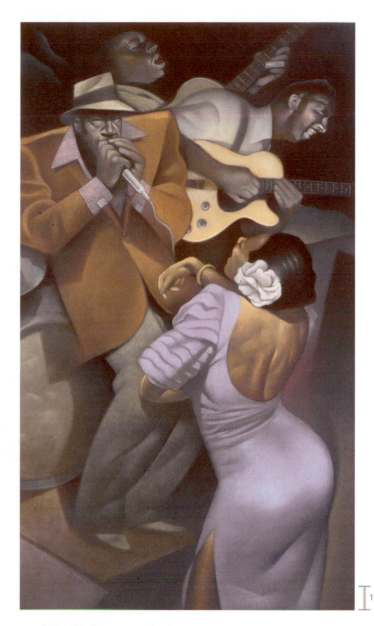

1 in.

5-2 GARY KELLEY. Promotion for the Mississippi Delta Blues Festival (c. 1989). Pastel. 24" × 14".

DRAWING MATERIALS

Over the millennia, methods of drawing have become increasingly sophisticated and materials more varied and standardized. It would seem that we have come a long way from our prehistoric ancestors' use of twigs, hollow reeds, and lumps of clay. Conventional drawing materials are typically divided into two major groups: *dry mediums* and *fluid mediums*. But almost anything can be used to make a drawing, as we shall see.

Dry Mediums

The **dry mediums** used in drawing include silverpoint, pencil, charcoal, chalk, pastel, and wax crayon.

SILVERPOINT **Silverpoint** is one of the oldest drawing mediums and was used widely from the late Middle Ages to the early 1500s. Silverpoint drawings are created by dragging a silver-tipped implement over a surface that has been coated with a **ground**—a sort of base layer—of bone dust or chalk mixed with **gum**, water, and **pigment**. This ground is sufficiently coarse to allow small flecks of silver from the instrument to adhere to the prepared surface as it is drawn across. These bits of metal form the lines of the drawing; they are barely visible at the start but eventually oxidize, becoming tarnished or darkened. Each silverpoint line, a soft gray to begin with, mellows and darkens to a grayish brown hue.

If the artist desires to make one area of the drawing appear darker than others, it is necessary to build up a series of close, parallel, or cross-hatched lines in that area to give the impression of deepened tone. Because they lack sharp tonal contrasts, the resultant drawings are often extremely delicate in appearance.

The technique of working in silverpoint is itself delicate. The medium allows for little or no correction. Thus, the artist is not in a position to experiment while working. The artist must have a fairly concrete notion of what the final product will look like, and the lines must be accurate and confidently drawn. Although this challenging medium is most closely associated with drawings of the past, its signature effect has been explored by contemporary artist Carol Prusa in works such as *Whirl* (Fig. **5-3**). Complex, intertwining and repetitive patterns of silverpoint, graphite, and white acrylic paint pulse across its acrylic domed surface.

The bright spots of light that coalesce at the work's center are emitted through pinpoint holes in the dome and illuminated from within using fiber optics. Her works, painstakingly rendered, are flawless in execution, their finish exquisite and polished. This technique is not for the fainthearted. Anyone working in silverpoint is likely to create detailed preliminary sketches before launching into this more permanent and less forgiving medium.

PENCIL Silverpoint was largely replaced by the lead **pencil**, which came into use during the 1500s. Medieval monks, like the ancient Egyptians, ruled lines with metallic lead but pencils, as we know them, began to be mass-produced only in the late eighteenth century. A pencil consists of a thin rod of **graphite** encased within wood or paper. The graphite is composed of ground dust mixed with clay that is baked until hardened. The relative hardness or softness of a pencil's lead depends on the quantity of clay in the mixture. The more clay, the harder the pencil.

Pencil produces a wide range of effects. Lines drawn with hard pencil can be thin and light in tone; those rendered in soft lead can be thick and dark. The sharp point of the pencil will create a firm, fine line suitable for meticulous detail. Softer areas of tone or shading can be achieved through a buildup of parallel lines, smudging, or dragging the side of a lead tip across a surface.

As seen in the contrasting works of George Condo and Marc Brandenburg, pencil can be manipulated to achieve dramatically different effects that complement the subject. The juxtaposition of fine cross-hatching, compact wavy and curly lines, and quick, zigzag scribbles work in tandem with the multiple perspectives that comprise the facial features in Condo's *Study for The Jester* (Fig. **5-4**).

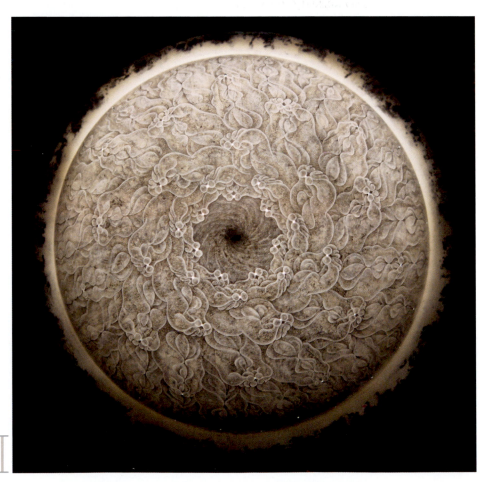

1 in.

5-3 CAROL PRUSA. *Whirl* (2010). Silverpoint, graphite, titanium white pigment with acrylic binder on acrylic hemisphere with fiber optics. 12" × 12" × 6". Bernice Steinbaum Gallery, Miami, FL.

Brandenburg's drawing (Fig. **5-5**), on the other hand, emulates a photographic negative in its meticulous execution and sharp tonal contrasts. The artist creates a visual correlate to paparazzi's candid photos of unsuspecting celebrities. In this drawing, Brandenburg highlights the instantly recognizable attributes of the pop star Michael Jackson, reduced to binary lights and darks. The convincing suggestion of another medium altogether is a consequence of the exacting detail that is possible with a tightly controlled use of pencil.

The exercise of drawing from life has been integral to the art academy experience for hundreds of years, a method by which the human form might be painstakingly analyzed and recorded. Perhaps this is why, in part, Adrian Piper chose the medium of drawing to render her dramatic *Self-Portrait Exaggerating My Negroid Features* (Fig. **5-6**). With it, Piper invites the spectator to focus on those aspects of her physical genetic composition that reveal her mixed black and white parentage. The portrait gives us an unflinching record of Piper's countenance, but perhaps more important, the image challenges us to confront our prejudices about the physical differences between the races.

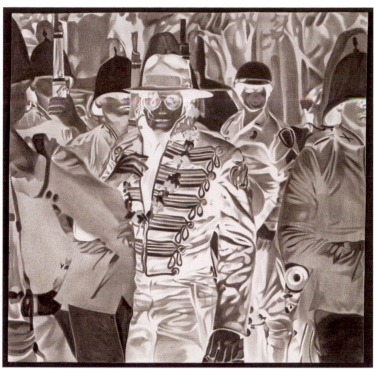

1 in.

5-5 MARC BRANDENBURG. *Untitled* (2004). Pencil on paper. 8¼" × 8⅜". The Museum of Modern Art, NY.

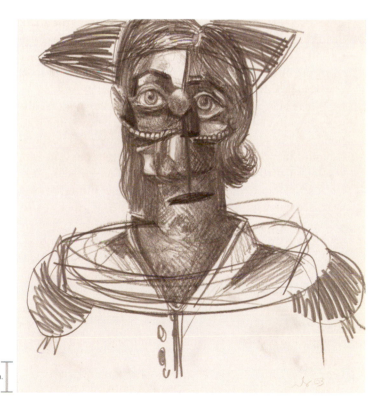

1 in.

5-4 GEORGE CONDO. *Study for The Jester* (2003). Pencil on paper. 11¾" × 10⅞". The Museum of Modern Art, NY.

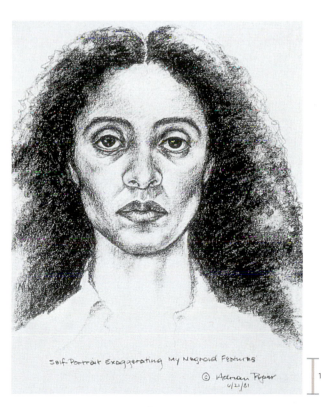

1 in.

5-6 ADRIAN PIPER. *Self-Portrait Exaggerating My Negroid Features* (1981). Pencil on paper. 10" × 8".

Drawing Materials   **109**

Adrian Piper has authored "calling cards" to hand out to people whom she overhears making racist remarks: "I regret any discomfort my presence is causing you, just as I am sure you regret the discomfort your racism is causing me."

COLORED PENCIL Colored pencils consist of waxlike cores mixed with pigment and other substances surrounded, as with graphite pencils, by wood or paper. Like graphite pencils, which can be sharpened to a point, colored pencils can render fine lines, as in Elizabeth Peyton's drawing *Marc* (*April*) (Fig. **5-7**). The young man's hair is composed of myriad nesting lines that create an expressive counterpoint to the more tightly controlled, finely modeled, and realistic drawing of his face. The movement suggested in his wispy, tousled locks is echoed in the sketchy rendering of his tailored shirt.

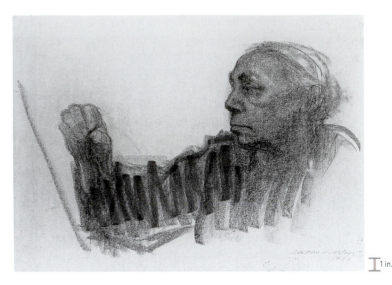

1 in.

5-8 KÄTHE KOLLWITZ. *Self-Portrait* (1924). Charcoal. 18¾" × 25". National Gallery of Art, Washington, D.C. © 2011 Artists Rights Society (ARS), NY/VG Bild-Kunst, Bonn.

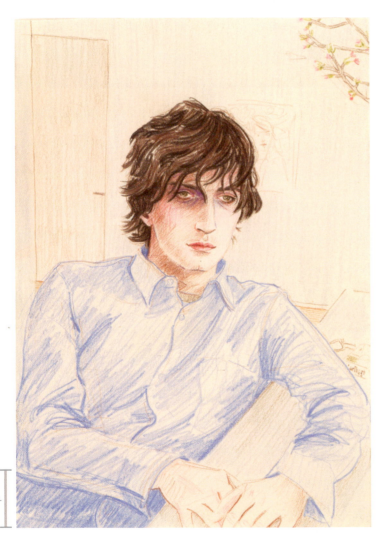

1 in.

5-7 ELIZABETH PEYTON. *Marc* (*April*) (2003). Colored pencil on paper. 8⅝" × 6". The Judith Rothschild Foundation Contemporary Drawings Collection Gift. Digital Image © The Museum of Modern Art/Licensed by SCALA/Art Resource, NY/The Museum of Modern Art, NY.

CHARCOAL **Charcoal**, like pencil, has a long history as a drawing implement. Used by our primitive ancestors to create images on cave walls, these initially crumbly pieces of burnt wood or bone now take the form of prepared sticks that are formed by the controlled charring of special hardwoods. Charcoal sticks are available in textures that vary from hard to soft. The sticks may be sharpened with sandpaper to form fine and clear lines or may be dragged flat across the surface to form diffuse areas of varied tone. Like pencil, charcoal may also be smudged or rubbed to create a hazy effect.

When charcoal is dragged across a surface, bits of the material adhere to that surface, just as in the case of silverpoint and pencil. But charcoal particles rub off more easily, and thus the completed drawings must be sprayed with a solution of thinned varnish to keep them affixed. Also, because of the way in which the charcoal is dispersed over a surface, the nature of the support is evident in each stroke. Coarsely textured paper will yield a grainy image, whereas smooth paper will provide a clear, almost pencil-like line.

A self-portrait of the German Expressionist Käthe Kollwitz (Fig. **5-8**) reveals one aspect of the character of the charcoal medium. Delicate lines of sharpened charcoal drawn over broader areas of subtle shading enunciate the two main points of interest: the artist's face and her hand. Between these two points—that of intellect and that of skill—runs a surge of energy described by aggressive, jagged strokes overlaying the lightly sketched contour of her forearm.

Values in the drawing range from hints of white at the artist's knuckles, cheekbone, and hair to the deepest blacks of the palm of her hand, eyes, and mouth. The finer lines override the texture of the paper, whereas the shaded areas,

Chalks are available in many colors, some of which occur in nature. **Ocher**, for example, derives its dark yellow tint from iron oxide in some clay. **Umber** acquires its characteristic yellowish or reddish brown color from earth containing oxides of manganese and iron. Other popular "organic" or "earth" colors include white, black, and a red called **sanguine**.

Michelangelo used red chalk in a sketch for the Sistine Chapel (see Chapter 16), in which he attempted to work out certain aspects of the figure of the Libyan Sibyl (Fig. **5-10**). Quick, sketchy notations of the model's profile, feet, and toes lead to a detailed torso rendered with confident lines and precisely defined tonal areas built up from hatching. The exactness of muscular detail and emphasis on the edges of the body provide insight into the concerns of an artist whose forte was sculpture.

Pastels consist of ground chalk mixed with powdered pigments and a binder. Whereas chalk drawings can be traced to prehistoric times, pastels did not come into wide use until the 1400s. They were introduced to France only in the 1700s,

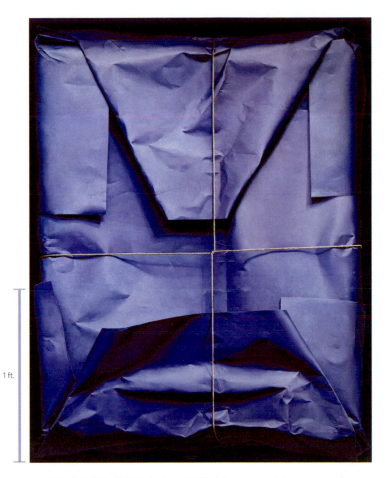

5-9 CLAUDIO BRAVO. *Package* (1969). Charcoal, pastel, and sanguine. 30⅞" × 22½".

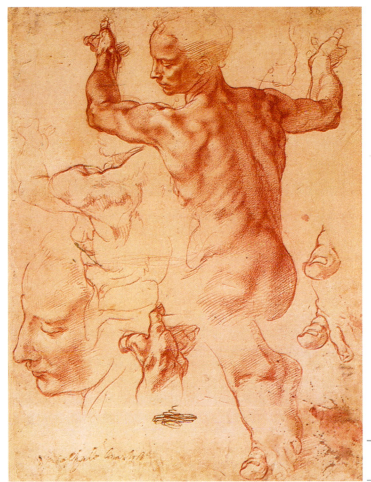

5-10 MICHELANGELO. *Studies for The Libyan Sybil* (1510–1511). Red chalk. 11⅜" × 8⅜". The Metropolitan Museum of Art, NY.

particularly around the neck and chest area, reveal the faint white lines and tiny flecks of pulp that are visual remnants of the papermaking process.

Charcoal can be expressive or descriptive, depending on its method of application. Claudio Bravo's *Package* (Fig. **5-9**) is a finely rendered, trompe l'oeil drawing that bears almost no trace of the artist's gesture and almost no indication of the "dusty" quality of the media—primarily charcoal and pastel. The illusion of the smooth sheen and crinkled indentations of the wrapping paper, attributed to painstaking gradations in value, is so convincing that the implied texture of the package completely overrides the actual texture of the drawing materials. The viewer is enticed to touch the forbidden surfaces, just to test whether they are real.

CHALK AND PASTEL The effects of charcoal, **chalk**, and **pastel** as they are dragged across a surface are very similar, although the mediums differ in terms of their composition. Chalk and pastel consist of pigment and a **binder**, such as **gum arabic**, shaped into workable sticks.

create a glowing, almost iridescent effect, whereas Severini's rigorous technique and more reserved palette mirror the cool and exacting movements of his dancer.

CRAYON Strictly defined, the term **crayon** includes any drawing material in stick form. Thus, charcoal, chalk, and pastels are crayons, as are the familiar Crayolas you used on walls, floors, and occasionally coloring books when you were a child. Wax crayons, like pastels, combine ground pigment with a binder—in this case, wax. Wax crayon moves easily over a surface, creating lines that have a characteristic sheen. These lines are less apt to smudge than charcoal, chalk, and pastels.

One of the most popular commercially manufactured crayons for artists is the **conté crayon**, a square stick of

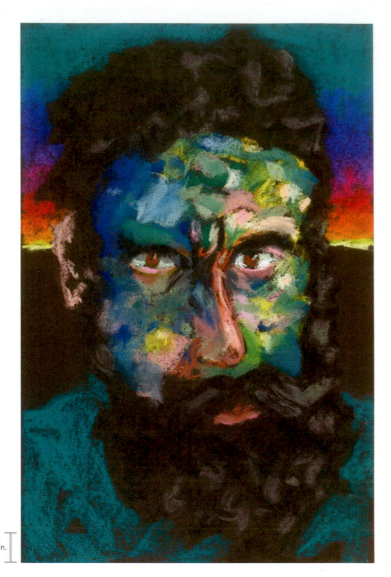

1 in.

5-11 LUCAS SAMARAS. *Head #12* (1981). Pastel on black paper. 17¾" × 11½". The Museum of Modern Art, NY.

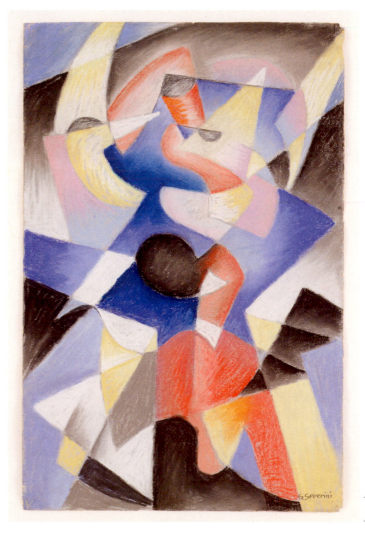

1 in.

5-12 GINO SEVERINI. *Dancer* (1912). Pastel on paper. 19¼" × 12½". The Riklis Collection of McCrory Corporation.

but within a century, pastels captured the imagination of many important painters. Their wide range of brilliant colors offered a painter's palette for use in the more spontaneous medium of drawing.

Pastels are manipulated in countless ways to create different effects. At times, colors are left pure and intense, as in *Head #12* (Fig. **5-11**) by Lucas Samaras. At other times subtle harmonies can be created through blending or smudging. As with pencil and other dry mediums, pastel can be used to render precise drawings like Gino Severini's *Dancer* (Fig. **5-12**), in which clean contours and discreet shapes evoke fragmented glimpses of a dancer whirling in space. Samaras's coarse splotches of vibrant color contrast with black paper to

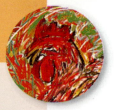

A CLOSER LOOK

LIFE, DEATH, AND DWELLING IN THE DEEP SOUTH

SOME YEARS AGO, AFRICAN AMERICAN SCULPTOR Beverly Buchanan came to know Ms. Mary Lou Furcron. They were both artists, one might say. Both the builders of structures. Both nurturing, creative, and colorful. Ever since this meeting, Buchanan's life and art have revolved around the art and life of the Southern shack dweller.

This way of living is an existence unto itself, as the photographs indicate (Fig. **5-13**). Ms. Furcron's shack reflects her life, and her life reflects the shack in which she lived. She devoted a part of each day to maintaining the structure, replacing rotted posts with new logs; using bark, lathing, and other odd materials to repair the siding. The shack stood as an organic and ever-evolving structure—an extension of Ms. Furcron herself. Because the shack required her constant attention for its survival, her move to a nursing home brought its rapid disrepair. Just one month after Ms. Furcron's departure, the shack was unrecognizable as its former self.

Buchanan's art, in sculpture, and especially in drawing, reflects a structural approach to the creation of the shack image. As Ms. Furcron built with the recycled remnants of nature and human existence, so does Beverly Buchanan. Her mixed-media shacks are created from old pieces of wood, metal, and found objects, such as in *Hometown—Shotgun Shack* (Fig. **5-14**). Her oil pastel drawing *Henriette's Yard* (Fig. **5-15**) is vigorously and lovingly constructed of a myriad of vibrant strokes. These strokes at once serve as the building blocks of the shack image and the very stuff that reduces the structure to an almost indecipherable explosion of color. The precarious balance of the shacks in relation to one another and the uncertain ground on which they stand further symbolize the precious and fragile nature of the shack dwelling, and human existence. ●

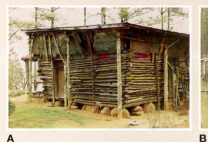
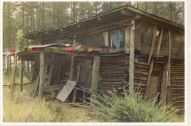

A   B

5-13 Photographs of Ms. Mary Lou Furcron's home.
Photo A shows the shack while Ms. Furcron was living in it and tending to it. Photo B shows the shack just one month after her placement in a nursing home.

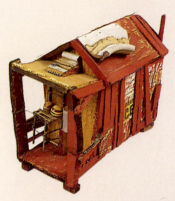

5-14 BEVERLY BUCHANAN. *Hometown—Shotgun Shack* (1992). Wood, mixed media. 12" × 9¼" × 15".

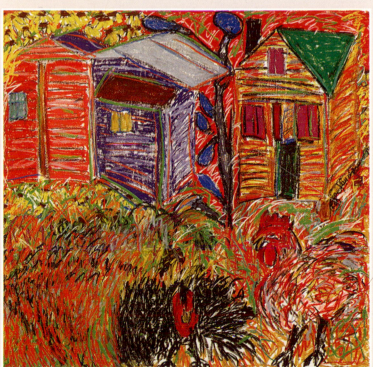

1 ft.

5-15 BEVERLY BUCHANAN. *Henriette's Yard* (1995). Oil pastel on paper. 60" × 60".

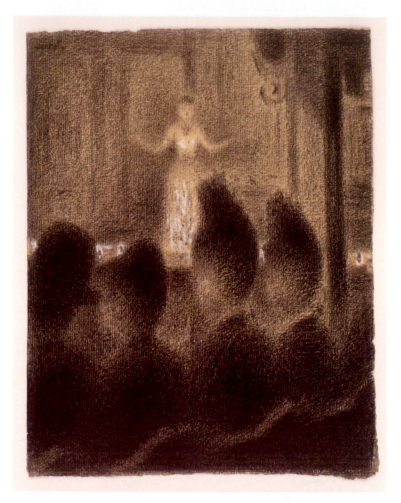

5-16 GEORGES PIERRE-SEURAT. *At the Concert Européen (Au Concert Européen)* (c. 1886-88). Conté crayon and gouache on paper. 12¼" × 9⅜". Lillie P. Bliss Collection. The Museum of Modern Art, NY.

compressed graphite or charcoal mixed with wax or clay. Like pencils, conté crayons are available in different degrees of hardness and can be manipulated to create different effects. Artists working with conté crayons often use rough paper so that bits of crayon will adhere to the surface as it is dragged across, creating an overall texture that can be a prominent feature of the drawing.

The conté crayon was invented in the late eighteenth century by Nicola-Jacques Conté out of necessity: there was a shortage of graphite in France due to a blockade during the Napoleonic Wars with England. A century or so later, conté crayon became one of the favorite mediums of the French painter Georges Seurat. *At the Concert Européen* (Fig. **5-16**) is built up almost solely through contrasts of tone. Deep, velvety blacks absorb the almost invisible heads of the musicians in the orchestra pit, while a glaring strip of untouched white paper seems to illuminate the stage. The even appli-

cation of crayon to coarse paper creates a diffuse light that accurately conveys the atmosphere of a small café. By working the crayon over a highly textured surface he was able to emulate the fine points of paint that comprised his signature technique in his large canvas works (see Fig. 19-25).

Fluid Mediums

The primary **fluid medium** used to make a drawing is ink. The traditional instruments used to carry ink are pen and brush, but, as evident in Rosemary Trockel's untitled drawing (Fig. **5-17**) or Gabriel Orozco's handprint piece (Fig. **5-18**), ink can be applied to paper or any other surface in any number of ways. Ink has a history that stretches back thousands of years, appearing in Egyptian **papyrus** drawings and ancient Chinese scrolls. Some ancient peoples made ink from the dyes of plants, squid, and octopus. By the second century CE, blue-black inks were being derived from galls—growths found on oak trees that are rich in resin and tannic acid. The oldest-known ink is India or China ink, composed of a solution of carbon black (tar mixed with oil) and water. It is a permanent, rich, black ink that is used in Asian **calligraphy** to this day.

As with the dry mediums, dramatically different effects can be achieved with fluid mediums through a variety of tech-

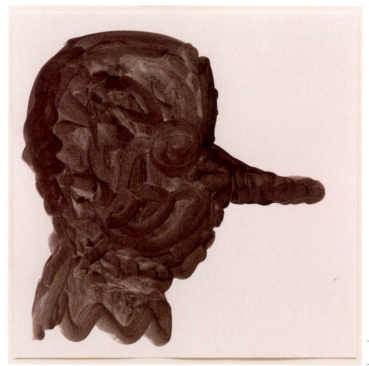

1 in.

5-17 ROSEMARIE TROCKEL. *Untitled* (1992). Ink on paper. 13¾" × 13¾" The Museum of Modern Art, NY.

Drawing is like making an expressive gesture with the advantage of permanence.
—Henri Matisse

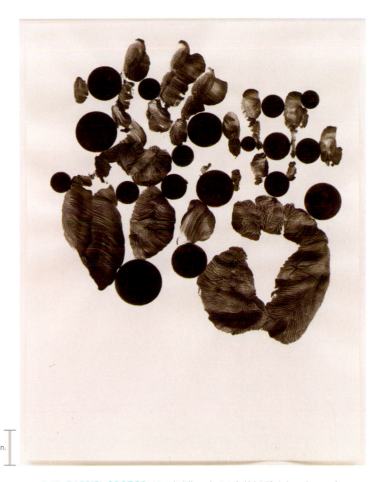

1 in.

5-18 GABRIEL OROZCO. *Untitled* (handprints) (2000). Ink and gouache on paper. 12" × 9". The Museum of Modern Art, NY. © 2011 Artists Rights Society (ARS), NY/SOMAAP, Mexico City.

niques. The ratios of water to ink can be altered to achieve lighter or darker tones, and a wide variety of brushes and pen points can be used to render lines of different character.

PEN AND INK Pens also have been used since ancient times. The earliest ones were hollow reeds that were slit at the ends to allow a controlled flow of ink. **Quills** plucked from live birds became popular writing instruments during the Middle Ages. These were replaced in the nineteenth century by the mass-produced metal **nib**, which is slipped into a wooden **stylus**.

Pen and ink are used to create drawings that are essentially linear, although the nature of the line can vary considerably according to the type of instrument employed. A fine, rigid nib will provide a clear, precise line that is uniform in thickness. Lines created by a more flexible quill tip, by contrast,

will vary in width according to the amount of downward pressure exerted on the tip.

Jean Dubuffet all but filled his *Garden* (Fig. 5-19) with pen-and-ink scribbles of varying thicknesses outlining mostly organic shapes. Just as a garden's plant life may give the eye a variegated experience of texture as well as color, Dubuffet's lines vary in length and thickness, sometimes culminating in little pools of ink. Here and there more angular, even craggy shapes suggest a path or an outcropping of rock, but realism was not the artist's aim. Rather, the high horizon line and the endless intertwining of lines and shapes convey the feeling or memory of a lush bed of flowers and plants in which the eye can wander and get lost.

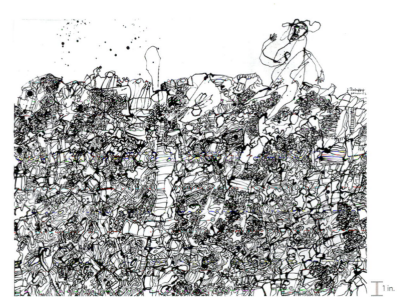

1 in.

5-19 JEAN DUBUFFET. *Garden* (1952). Pen and carbon ink on glazed white wove paper. 18¾" × 23¾". Harriott A. Fox Fund, 1952.1144, The Art Institute of Chicago, Chicago, IL. © 2011 Artists Rights Society (ARS), NY/ADAGP, Paris.

BRUSH AND INK Brushes are extremely versatile drawing implements. They are available in a wide variety of materials, textures, widths, and shapes that produce many different effects. The quality of line in brush and ink drawing will depend on whether the brush is bristle or nylon, thin or thick, pointed or flat tipped. Likewise, characteristics of the drawing surface, such as texture or absorbency, will affect the character of the completed drawing. Brush and ink touched to silk leaves an impression quite different from that produced by brush and ink touched to paper.

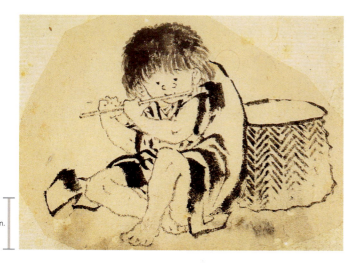

5-20 KATSUSHIKA HOKUSAI. *Boy Playing Flute* (c. 1800). Ink and brush on paper. 4½" × 6¼". Freer Gallery of Art, Smithsonian Institution, Washington, D.C.

Japanese artists are masters of the brush-and-ink medium. They have used it for centuries for every type of calligraphy, ranging from works of art to everyday writing. Their facility with the technique is most evident in seemingly casual sketches, such as those done in the late eighteenth and early nineteenth centuries by Japanese artist Katsushika Hokusai (Fig. **5-20**). Longer, flowing lines range from thick and dark to thin and faint, capturing, respectively, the heavy folds of the boy's clothing and the pale flesh of his youthful limbs. Short, brisk strokes define the youngster's disheveled hair and are echoed in the pattern of the woven hemp basket. There is an extraordinary simplicity to the drawing attributable to the surety and ease with which Hokusai handles his medium.

WASH Wash is diluted ink that typically is applied with a brush. It can be used exclusively or can be combined, as in Giovanni Tiepolo's eighteenth-century drawing (Fig. **5-21**), with fine, clear, pen-and-ink lines. If you compare this drawing with Dubuffet's *Garden*, you will see what a difference it makes to add areas of subtly washed tone. The contours of the biblical figures of Hagar, Ishmael, and the angel are described in pen and ink, but their volume derives from the application of wash. The gestural vitality of the pen lines and the generous swaths of watery ink surrounding areas of untouched white paper combine to create an illusion of three-dimensionality and a sense of dynamic movement.

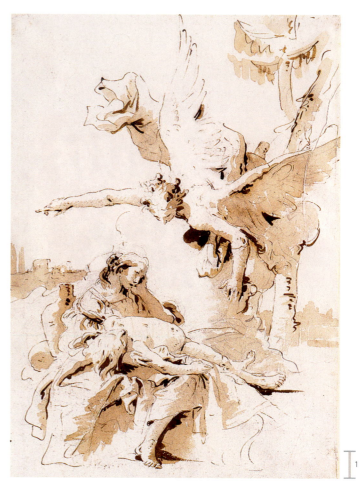

5-21 GIOVANNI BATTISTA TIEPOLO. *Hagar and Ishmael in the Wilderness* (c. 1725–1735). Pen, brush and brown ink, and wash, over sketch in black chalk. 16½" × 11⅛". Sterling and Francine Clark Art Institute, Williamstown, MA.

The medium of brush and wash is even more versatile. It can duplicate the linearity of brush-and-ink drawings or be used to create images solely through tonal contrasts. The remarkable illusion of deep space in Fang Lijun's drawing (Fig. **5-22**) is achieved through the distribution of zones of grey wash rendered in a variety of grayscale tones. They originate at the feet of an old man on a bluff and meander, like irregular stepping-stones, toward a large sun disk on the horizon. The glowing sphere, ringed in light (unwashed areas of paper), creates a halo effect at the edges of the man's clothing and encircles the pebblelike concentrations of wash. The detail in the drawing—from fine to fluid—is a result of the artist's control of his brush as well as the ratio of ink to water. The ink can be diluted to varying degrees to provide a wide tonal range. Different effects can be achieved either by adding water directly to the ink or by moistening the surface before drawing.

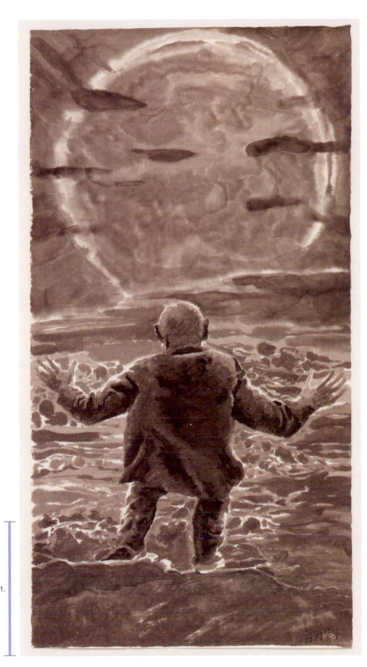

1 ft.

5-22 FANG LIJUN. *Ink-and-Wash-Painting No. 3* (2004). Ink on paper, 54½" × 28½". The Museum of Modern Art, NY.

CARTOONS

The word **cartoon** derives from the Italian *cartone*, meaning "paper." Originally, cartoons were full-scale preliminary drawings done on paper for projects such as fresco paintings, stained glass, or tapestries. The meaning of *cartoon* was expanded to include humorous and satirical drawings when a parody of fresco cartoons submitted for decoration of the Houses of Parliament appeared in an English magazine in 1843. Modern cartoons rely on *caricature*, the gross exaggeration and distortion of natural features. While students today may be more familiar with cartoons created for animated films (see Fig. 8-28), video games, action comics, anime (Japanese animation), or manga (Japanese print cartoons, Fig. **5-23**), the art of the cartoon has deep historical roots.

Honoré Daumier is perhaps the only famous painter to devote so great a part of his production—some 4,000 works—to cartoons. Known for his riveting images of social and moral

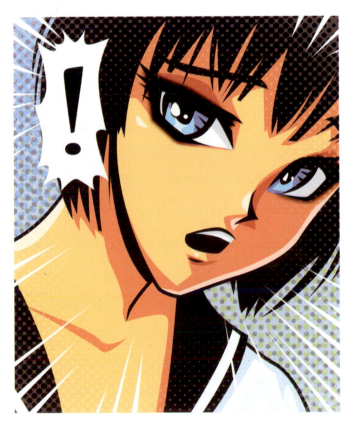

5-23 Example of manga artwork.

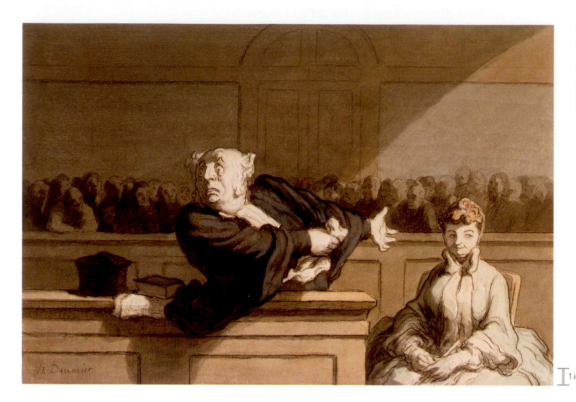

5-24 HONORÉ DAUMIER. *Counsel for the Defense (the Advocate)* (1862–1865). Pen and ink, charcoal, crayon, gouache, and watercolor. 20⅜" × 23¾". The Corcoran Gallery of Art, Washington, D.C.

I— 1 in.

injustices in nineteenth-century France, he also created caricatures in which he displayed a sharp, sardonic wit. Daumier's *Counsel for the Defense (the Advocate)* (Fig. **5-24**) is a taunting illustration of the theatrics employed by a defense attorney to win sympathy for his client. The crocodile tears streaming down his face along with his melodramatic gestures are in stark contrast with the composure of the defendant. Yet her inscrutable smile suggests that she may not be quite as innocent as the lawyer pretends.

Cartoons have a long history of social commentary, consciousness raising, and political activism. We are all familiar with the children's books of Dr. Seuss, but few of us are aware of Theodor Seuss Geisel's political cartoons (Fig. **5-25**). For two years during World War II, Dr. Seuss was the chief editorial cartoonist for the New York tabloid newspaper *PM*. During that time, he drew more than 400 cartoons, many of which pertained to the war effort. It's fascinating to see Dr. Seuss's legendary, signature style (and creatures) called into service for an altogether different purpose.

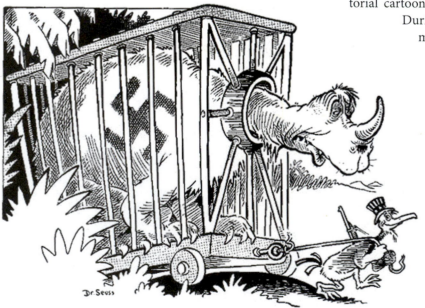

5-25 DR. SEUSS. *Cages Cost Money! Buy More U.S. Savings Bonds and Stamps!* From Dr. Seuss Collection, the Mandeville Special Collections Library, University of California, San Diego, CA.

NEW APPROACHES TO DRAWING

Drawings display endless versatility in terms of their intended purposes, their mediums, and their techniques. It is not unusual to find drawings that are not "drawn" at all on materials that are far removed from traditional paper. You'd be right to ask, "What *is* a drawing, after all?"

Chinese artist Cai Guo-Qiang is renowned for his works of ephemeral art, a contemporary genre in which works of art are transitory, impermanent, not intended to last (except in documentation) beyond the experience of a moment. His carefully calibrated fireworks displays (see Fig. 10-13) are among his most famous pieces, and Figure 5-26 is a drawing for one titled *Transient Rainbow*. The circular image emerges from a concentration of pinpoints of blackened paper, created through the discharge of gunpowder on two sheets of paper. As insubstantial as this work may first appear, it has more material substance—and potential longevity—than the monumental ephemeral work it inspired.

5-26 CAI GUO-QIANG. *Drawing for Transient Rainbow* (2003). Gunpowder on two sheets of paper. 179" × 159½" (overall).

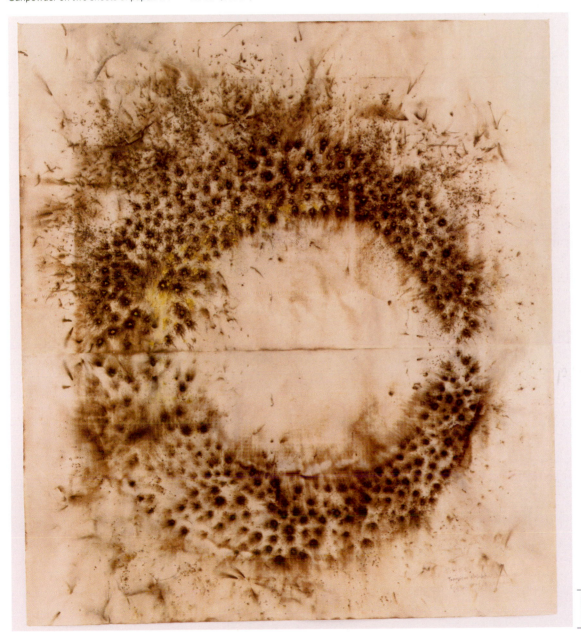

1 ft.

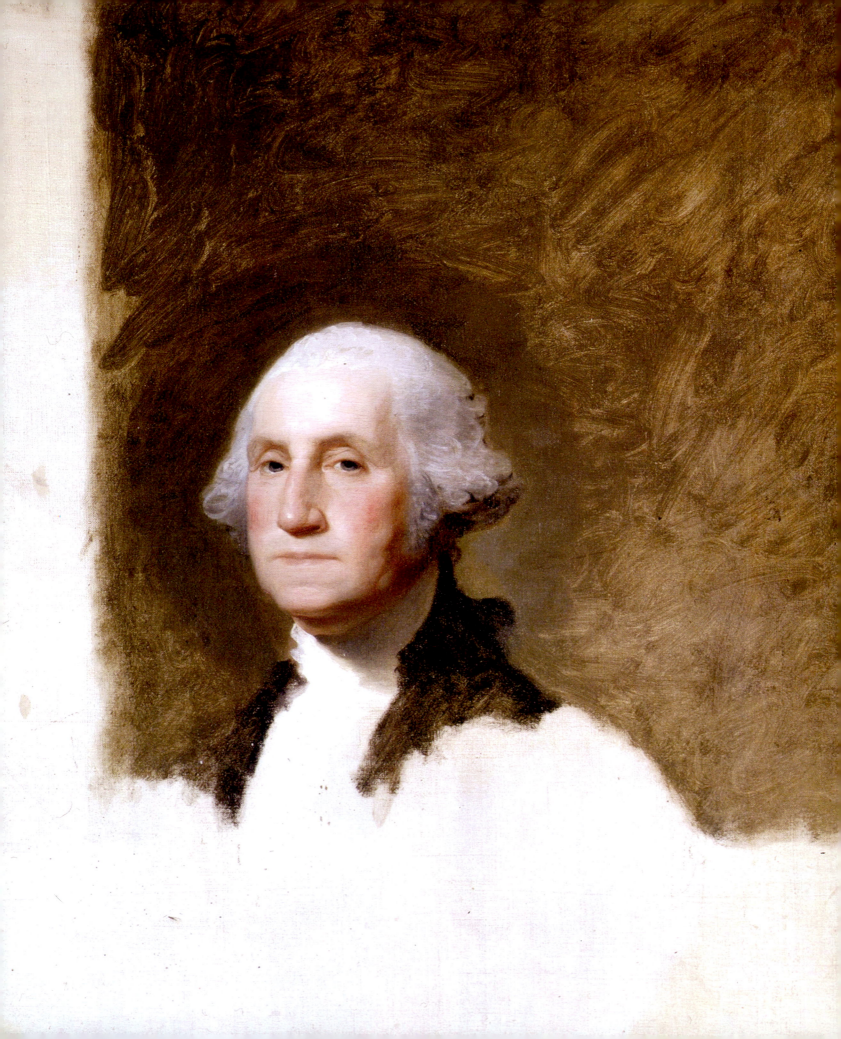

ch 5 book - 1st drawings done by accident
- drawing - implement running over surface + leaving trace
  - support - what drawing is done on
- monochromatic - one color
- linear - lines only
- basic to all visual arts
- categories: 1. record idea
              2. plan for other projects
              3. autonomous works
- dry mediums: 1. silverpoint - silver tipped implement over surface with ground
                  ground - bone or chalk mixed with gum, water, and pigment
               2. pencil - graphite (ground dust + clay)
                  harder p. - more clay, thin, light lines
               3. colored pencil
               4. charcoal - charred hardwood
                  sharpened with sand paper
                  good surface needed
               5. chalk + pastel (pigment + binder)
                  ocher - dark yellow from iron oxide
                  umber - red from manganese + iron
                  pastel - ground chalk + pigment + binder
               6. crayon - stick drawing material
                  conté" - compressed graphite or charcoal + wax or clay
- fluid mediums: 1. pen + ink
                    (1st - quills 2nd - nibs (metal)
                    created varied lines
                 2. brush + ink
                    size of brush
                 3. wash
- cartoons were originally any drawing on paper

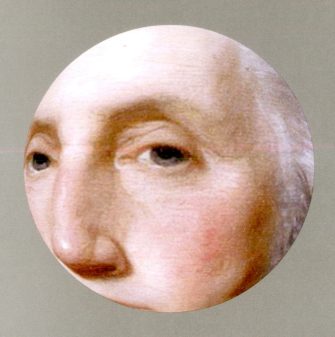

*Suddenly I realized that each brushstroke is a decision. . . .
In the end I realize that whatever meaning that picture has
is the accumulated meaning of ten thousand brushstrokes,
each one being decided as it was painted.*

—Robert Motherwell

PAINTING

6

A painting is a work in which the primary aspect is liquid material applied to a surface with an implement. By that definition, Michelangelo's *Sistine Ceiling* and the finger paintings on newsprint that you once brought home to hang on the refrigerator fall into the same category. Granted, the latter might not be defined as a work of fine art, but the technical components of your doodles remind us that the parameters of painting are indeed broad. In a traditional painting, the liquid material that is applied is pigment, the surface is two-dimensional, and the implement is a brush. More recently, the medium has come to include a wide variety of sometimes unorthodox materials (fabric dyes, synthetic polymers, glitter, resin, animal dung), tools (sticks, trowels, spray cans, and, yes, fingers), and surfaces (shaped canvas, cutout steel reliefs, ceramic slabs, Plexiglas, found objects).

As with drawing, there are almost no limits when it comes to the materials and processes that will constitute a painting. Nor is the use of paint, throughout art history, exclusive to what we would define as a painting per se. Paint has been used to decorate pottery, enhance sculpture, embellish architecture, and more.

GILBERT STUART. *George Washington* (1796). Oil on canvas. 39⅝" × 34½" (entire work).
National Portrait Gallery, Smithsonian Institution, Washington D.C.

PAINT

To most of us, paint is synonymous with color. The color in paint derives from its pigment. The pigment in powdered form is mixed with a binding agent, or **vehicle**, and a solvent, or **medium**, to form **paint**—the liquid material that imparts color to a surface. Pigments are available in a wide chromatic range. Their color is derived from chemicals and minerals found in plant and animal life, clay, soil, and sand.

Different vehicles are employed in different painting mediums. The main criterion for a successful vehicle is that it holds the pigments together. Lime plaster, wax, egg, oil, acrylic plastic, water, and gum arabic are commonly used vehicles. Unfortunately, most vehicles are subject to long-term problems, such as cracking, yellowing, or discoloration.

The task of a medium is to provide fluency to the paint so that the color may be readily dispersed over the surface. Water or turpentine is frequently used as a thinning agent for this purpose.

TYPES OF PAINTING

A variety of paints, surfaces, and tools have been used throughout the history of art to create paintings. In Chapter 13, you will see some of the first—Paleolithic paintings of animals on cave walls created with black pigment and red ocher that date back over 30,000 years. The ancient Egyptians painted on walls (**murals**), sheets of papyrus, and linen. The Greeks were renowned for their vase painting, which gives us an idea of what their other paintings must have looked like. Although no paintings on wood panels survive from ancient Greece, we know from writings that it was a highly developed art form associated with artists who were famous for their techniques. The historian Pliny the Elder, for example, remarked that the painter Zeuxis was so skilled that birds tried to eat the painted grapes in one of his works. Roman artists, who were very much influenced by the Greeks, nonetheless surpassed their predecessors in their painting innovations. Much of what we know about Roman painting comes from the ruins of the great sites of Pompeii and Herculaneum, preserved amid the ash of the historic eruption of Mount Vesuvius. Most medieval murals were destroyed, but brilliant painted (illuminated) manuscripts survive and offer stylistic parallels to other painting of the era.

Painting, as we typically define it, came into its own during the Renaissance—the so-called Golden Age of painting. Although artists continued to paint murals, paintings on wood panels and on canvas exploded in popularity, freeing the medium from its relationship to architecture. Paint-

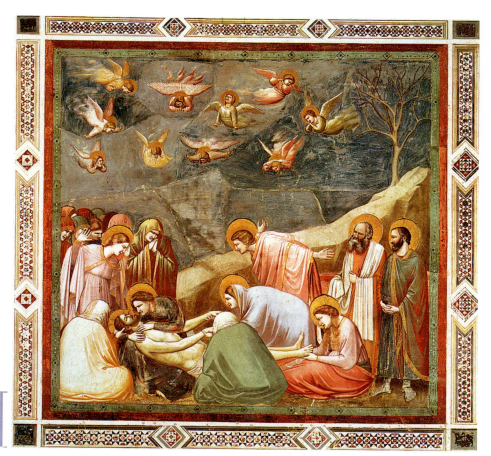

1 ft.

6-1 GIOTTO. *Lamentation* (c. 1305). Fresco. 7'7" × 7'9". Capella Scrovegni, Arena Chapel, Padua, Italy.

ch 6 book - painting - liquid applied to a surface
- pigment in paint : vehicle (binding agent) + medium (solvent)
- murals - painting on walls

ings could be hung anywhere and moved anywhere, were much less expensive and time-consuming to produce, and could be bought and sold to a wide variety of patrons and clients.

Fresco

Fresco is the art of painting on plaster. **Buon fresco**, or true fresco, is executed on damp, lime plaster; **fresco secco** is painting on dry plaster. In buon fresco, the pigments are mixed only with water, and the lime of the plaster wall acts as a binder. As the wall dries, the painted image on it becomes permanent. In fresco secco—a less permanent method—pigments are combined with a vehicle of glue that affixes the color to the dry wall.

Fresco painters encounter several challenges: Because in true fresco the paint must be applied to fresh, damp plaster, artists cannot bite off more than they can chew—or paint— in one day. For this reason, large fresco paintings are composed of small sections, each of which has been painted in a day. The artist tries to arrange the sections so that the joints will not be obvious, but sometimes it is not possible to do so. In a fourteenth-century fresco painting by the Italian master Giotto (Fig. **6-1**), these joints are clearly evident, particularly in the sky, where the artist was not able to complete the vast expanse of blue all at once. In spite of this limitation, or because of it, fresco painting is often noted for its freshness and directness of expression. The sixteenth-century art historian Giorgio Vasari wrote that of all the methods painters employ, fresco painting "is the most masterly and beautiful, because it consists in doing in a single day that which, in other methods, may be retouched day after day, over the work already done." Another challenge concerns chemistry. Although fresco paintings can be brilliant in color, some pigments will not form chemical bonds with lime. Thus, these pigments are not suitable for the medium. Artists in Giotto's era, for example, encountered a great deal of difficulty with the color blue. Such lime resistance limits the artist's palette and can make tonal transitions difficult.

Leonardo da Vinci, in his famous *The Last Supper* (see Fig. 16-17), attempted to meet these nuisances head-on, only to suffer disastrous consequences. The experimental materials and methods he employed to achieve superior results were unsuccessful. He lived to see his masterpiece disintegrate beyond repair, at least until modern conservation and restoration techniques preserved what remained by his hand.

Despite these problems, fresco painting enjoyed immense popularity from its origins until its full flowering in the Renaissance. Although it fell out of favor for several centuries thereafter, Mexican muralists revived the art of fresco after World War I.

Encaustic

One of the earliest methods of applying color to a surface was **encaustic**. It consists of pigment in a wax vehicle that has been heated to a liquid state. The ancient Egyptians and Greeks tinted their sculptures with encaustic to grant them a lifelike appearance. The Romans applied encaustic to walls, using hot irons. Often, as in the Egyptian mummy portrait of a priest of Serapis (Fig. **6-2**) dating back to the second century CE, the medium

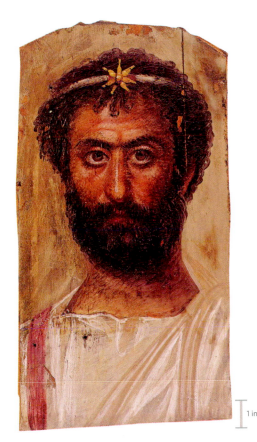

1 in.

6-2 Mummy portrait of a priest of Serapis, from Hawara, Egypt (c. 140–160 CE); Egypto-Roman, Faiyum (c. 160–179 CE). Encaustic on wood. 14" × 8". The British Museum, London, England.

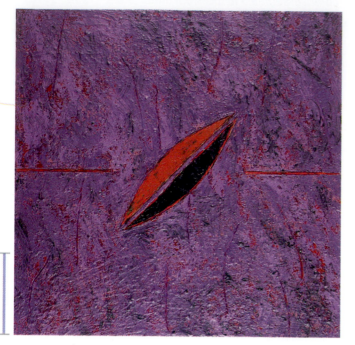

1 ft.

6-3 KAY WALKINGSTICK. *Solstice* (1982). Acrylic and wax on canvas. 48" × 48" × 3½". Collection of the artist.

6-4 GENTILE DA FABRIANO. *Adoration of the Magi* (1423). Tempera on wood panel. 9'10⅛" × 9'3". Galleria degli Uffizi, Florence, Italy.

was applied to small, portable wooden panels covered with cloth. As evidenced by the startling realism and freshness of the portrait, encaustic is an extremely durable medium whose colors remain vibrant and whose surface maintains a hard luster. But encaustic is a difficult medium to manipulate: one must keep the molten wax at a constant temperature. For this reason, it has been used by only a handful of contemporary artists.

Native American painter Kay Walkingstick derives a certain plasticity from her very different use of acrylic and wax on canvas (Fig. 6-3). In *Solstice*, two flattened arcs of sharply contrasting hues are about to merge in a viscous sea of mauve and purple. The canoelike image, although common to Native American symbolism, can also be viewed as an abstraction signifying the shifting of seasons from autumn to winter—a kind of quiet cosmological passage. Walkingstick builds her textural surface through successive layers of colored wax, gouging the field here and there with lines that reveal the palette of the lower layers. It is at once an image of power and of solitude.

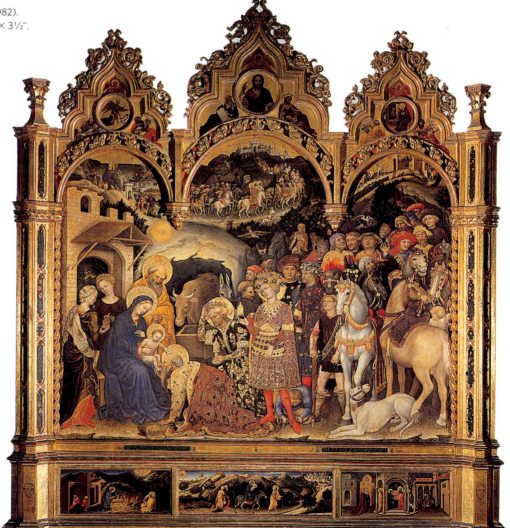

1 ft.

Tempera

Tempera, like encaustic, was popular for centuries, but its traditional composition—ground pigments mixed with a vehicle of egg yolk or whole eggs thinned with water—is rarely used today. Tempera now describes a medium in which pigment can be mixed with an emulsion of milk, different types of glues or gums, and even the juices and saps of plants and trees. The use of tempera dates back to the Greeks and Romans. Tempera was the exclusive painting medium of artists during the Middle Ages. Not until the invention of oil paint in northern Europe in the 1300s did tempera fall out of favor.

Tempera offered many advantages. It was an extremely durable medium if applied to a properly prepared surface. Pure and brilliant colors were attainable. Colors did not become compromised by gradual oxidation. Also, the consistency and fluidity of the mixture allowed for a great deal of precision. Tempera, unlike oil paint, however, dries quickly and is difficult to rework. Also, unlike oils, it cannot provide subtle gradations of tone.

Tempera can be applied to wood or canvas panels, although the latter did not come into wide use until the 1500s. Both types of supports were prepared by covering the surface with a ground. The ground was generally a combination of powdered chalk or plaster and animal glue called **gesso**. The gesso ground provided a smooth, glistening white surface on which to apply color.

All that is desirable in the tempera medium can be found in Figure **6-4**, the panel painting by the fifteenth-century Italian artist Gentile da Fabriano. Combined with the technique of **gilding**—the application of thinly hammered sheets of gold to the panel surface—the luminous reds and blues and pearly grays of the tempera paint provide a sumptuous display. The fine details of the ornate costumes testify to the precision made possible by **egg tempera**.

Several contemporary artists, such as the Swiss Photo-realist painter Franz Gertsch, have also been enticed by the exactness and intricacies made possible by tempera. Suited to a methodical and painstaking approach to painting, this medium of the old masters yields unparalleled displays of contrasting textures and sharp-focused realism, as shown in Gertsch's large-scale portrait of *Silvia* (Fig. **6-5**).

Oil

The transition from egg tempera to **oil paint** was gradual. For many years following the introduction of the oil medium, artists used it only to apply a finishing coat—a **glaze**—over a tempera painting. Glazes are thin, transparent or semitransparent layers of oil tinted with color that impart a warm atmosphere not possible with tempera alone. From the fifteenth century onward, the medium of oil painting became standard, and artists continued to use the glazing technique to create subtle tonal variations in their work. Venetian artists of the Renaissance, like Titian (Fig. 16-27), achieved a remarkable sense of realism in subtly modeled flesh made possible through glazing.

Oil paint consists of ground pigments combined with a linseed oil vehicle and turpentine medium or thinner. Oil paint is naturally slow drying, but this property can be accelerated by the addition of various agents to the basic mixture.

Oil painting's broad capability accounts for its popularity. Colors can be blended easily, offering a palette of almost limitless range. Slow drying facilitates the reworking of problem areas. It can be applied with any number of brushes or knives that yield different effects. When applied with smooth, fine-tipped brushes, oil paint can capture the most intricate detail and render a glasslike surface in which brushstrokes are barely evident (see Fig. 19-7). When considerably thinned and broadly brushed—or even poured (see Fig. 21-9) it can be used to create diaphanous fields of pulsating color.

1 ft.

6-5 FRANZ GERTSCH. *Silvia* (1998). Tempera on unprimed canvas. 9'6½" × 9'2¼". Museum Franz Gertsch, Burgdorf, Switzerland.

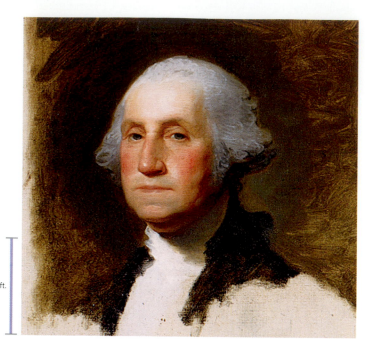

1 ft.

6-6 GILBERT STUART. *George Washington* (1796) (detail). Oil on canvas. 39⅝" × 34½" (entire work). National Portrait Gallery, Smithsonian Institution, Washington D.C.

imparted a sense of roundness to Stuart's figure is replaced by stylized shadows that sit flatly on the canvas. Lichtenstein forsakes the psychological portrait in favor of billboard advertising. Washington has been translated into a commodity. Unlike Stuart's Washington, the physical characteristics suggest nothing of the human being to whom they refer.

Oil paint, precisely handled, can be used to create implied texture. Stuart creates the illusion of soft ruddy flesh and wispy grey hair through carefully wrought strokes that do not have a dominant physical presence. Oil paint can also be used to create actual texture—a surface that has its own tangible property and, by contrast, a dominant physical presence. In a work like the *Head of St. Matthew* (Fig. **6-8**), the brushstrokes are thick and brusquely applied, as if the head had been modeled in clay with the artist's fingers. Glints of white and lighter tints of gold, red-orange, and brown visually pull the man out of the shadows and give him literal substance. The broken patches of pigment suggest movement and a departure from the typical "frozen moment." The artist does

It can be applied with a palette knife or square-tipped, rough-bristled brush in thick layers or strokes (**impasto**) that assert the physical aspect of the material as well as the physical process of the act of painting (see Fig. 6-8 and 21-2).

The versatility of oil paint is illustrated in portraits of George Washington by American artists who worked centuries apart. Gilbert Stuart's iconic eighteenth-century portrait (Fig. **6-6**)—the one on the U.S. dollar bill—is actually an unfinished work. Stuart created a realistic likeness through a fairly taut handling of the medium and the manipulation of light and shade to create a three-dimensional effect. His delicate treatment of Washington's pensive eyes and the firm outline of his determined jaw speak volumes about the personality traits of the wise and aging leader.

Roy Lichtenstein's contemporary portrait (Fig. **6-7**), by contrast, is an image of glamour and success. Lichtenstein capitalized on oil paint's clarity and precision, constructing the image from sharp contrasts of black and white and discrete lines and shapes. The only departure from the stark palette consists of occasional fields of gray with patterning that mimics the Ben-day dots found in comic strips. A younger, debonair Washington is presented as if on a campaign poster, or as a Marvel Comics hero with a chiseled profile akin to Dick Tracy's. His eyes are alert and enthralling; his chin is jaunty and confident. The mechanical quality of the portrait (no sense of the artist's touch in these brushstrokes) deprives it of any subtlety or atmosphere, and deliberately so. The rich modeling that

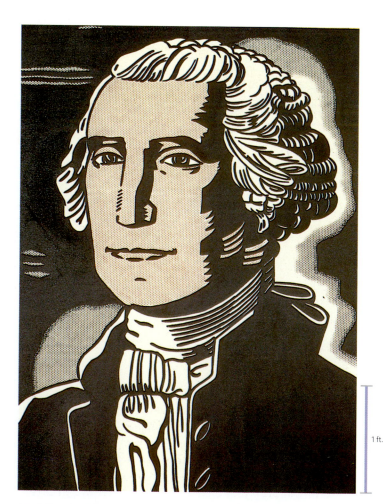

1 ft.

6-7 ROY LICHTENSTEIN. *George Washington* (1962). Oil on canvas. 51" × 38".

1 in.

not use his technique to create a grand illusion of reality but instead concentrates our attention on another reality—that of the painted surface.

The first oil paintings were done on wood panels, followed by a gradual shift to canvas supports. As for wood panels, the canvas surface is covered with a gesso ground prior to painting. The pliability of fabric stretched over a wooden frame renders the working surface more receptive to the pressure of the artist's implement. The lighter weight of canvas also allows for larger compositions than were possible on wooden panels.

Acrylic

Acrylic paint offers many of the advantages of oil paint, but "without the mess." Acrylic paint is a mixture of pigment and a plastic vehicle that can be thinned (and washed off brushes and hands) with water. Unlike linseed oil, the synthetic resin of the binder dries colorless and does not gradually compromise the brilliance of the colors. Also, unlike oil paint, acrylic can be used on a variety of surfaces that need no special preparation. Acrylic paint is flexible and fast drying, and, as it is water soluble, it requires no flammable substances for use or cleanup.

NOLAND'S *GRADED EXPOSURE* WITH DAVIE'S *BETWEEN MY EYE AND HEART*

OIL AND ACRYLIC PAINTS often mimic each other in effects, but their idiosyncratic properties account for why one material may be chosen over the other for a specific painting. Why did Kenneth Noland use acrylic for his *Graded Exposure* (Fig. **6-9**) and why did Karin Davie choose oil paint for *Between My Eye and Heart* (Fig. **6-10**)?

Oil painting produces rich colors, but the pigment often fades and cracks over time. The drying time for oil paint is much longer than that of acrylic paint, producing both advantages and disadvantages. A longer drying time means that artists can rework surfaces, blend colors, and apply glazes more smoothly. Also, even after oil paint is dry, it can be resuscitated with subsequent applications of turpentine mixtures. Acrylic, on the other hand, is a medium that dries quickly. The artist must work rapidly and, once the paint is dry, it cannot be resolubilized. Because of its drying time, acrylic is not conducive to color blending, but the upside is that sharply distinct zones of color can be created without the threat of colors blurring or running into each other.

Kenneth Noland was one of the pioneers of hard-edge Color Field painting in the 1960s. His *Graded Exposure* is composed of precisely delineated stripes or fields that represent abrupt transitions between variations on the color spectrum. Razor-sharp edges are achieved using tape lines and adjusting the acrylic medium so that each application dries quickly and will not leach into crevices between the tape and the canvas. The meticulous, glasslike, unbroken surface is free of gestural brushwork. The overall feeling is one of flatness, consistency, and control.

Karin Davie's oil-on-canvas painting, *Between My Eye and Heart*, appears the polar opposite of Noland's work. Lines loop around and over each other, nesting in the shallow pictorial space and pressing against the edges of the canvas. The artist's gesture is everywhere evident, though

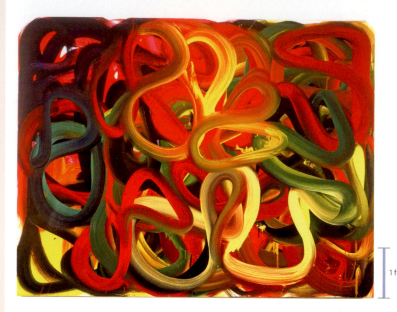

6-10 KARIN DAVIE. *Between My Eye and Heart No. 12* (2005). Oil on canvas. 5'6" × 7'. Margulies Warehouse Collection, Miami, FL.

also precise in its parameters. A single brush of a specific width is used to produce all of the lines and the palette is pretty much confined to red, yellow, and blue with some touches of white. The artist allows oil paint to do what it does best: blend. And it is the blending that adds dimension or volume to the lines. They aren't flat. They look more like tangled spaghetti. Variations in the overlapping hues also create a sense of space, with warm colors advancing and dark colors mostly receding.

Hard-edge painting can be done in oil and color-blending certainly is seen in acrylic works. But Noland and Davie offer us excellent case studies in the specific capabilities of each medium. ●

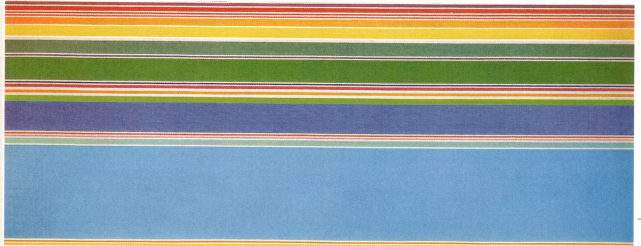

6-9 KENNETH NOLAND. *Graded Exposure* (1967). Acrylic on canvas. 7'4¾" × 19'1". Collection Mrs. Samuel G. Rautbord, Chicago, IL. Art © Estate of Kenneth Noland/Licensed by VAGA, NY.

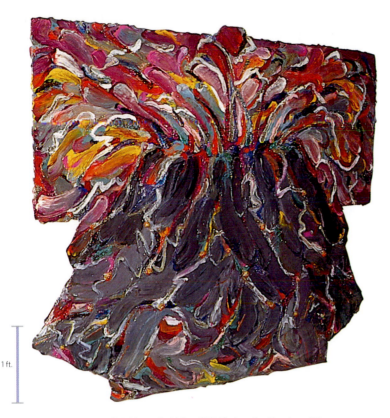

1 ft.

6-11 HELEN OJI. *Mount St. Helens* (1980). Acrylic, Rhoplex, glitter on paper. 60" × 72". Collection of Home Insurance Company, NY.

One of the few effects of oil paint that cannot be duplicated in acrylic is delicate nuance of colors. Like oil, however, acrylic paint can be used thinly or thickly; it can be applied in transparent films or opaque impastos, as in Helen Oji's *Mount St. Helens* (Fig. 6-11). The artist fills the shaped canvas with an explosion of color and texture that simulates the unbridled power of one of the world's few active volcanoes. This image, which gave rise to a whole series on these natural wonders, serves, from another perspective, as "textile" ornamentation for a Japanese kimono. Canvases shaped in this garment design first preoccupied Oji in an earlier series, and here the reference to her Japanese heritage (her parents were interned during World War II, while she grew up in California) and the volcano image may symbolize a convergence of cultures from both sides of the Pacific.

Watercolor

The term **watercolor** originally defined any painting medium that employed water as a solvent. Thus, fresco and egg tempera have been called watercolor processes. But today watercolor refers to a specific technique called **aquarelle**, in which transparent films of paint are applied to a white, absorbent surface. Contemporary watercolors are composed of pigments and a gum arabic vehicle, thinned, of course, with a medium of water.

Variations of the watercolor medium have been employed for centuries. Ancient Egyptian artists used a form of watercolor in their paintings. Watercolor was also used extensively for manuscript illumination during the Middle Ages, as we shall see in Chapter 15. **Gouache**, or watercolor mixed with a high concentration of vehicle and an opaque ingredient such as chalk, was the principal painting medium during the Byzantine and Romanesque eras of Christian art. This variation has enjoyed popularity across time and a myriad of styles and is used to great effect by many contemporary artists, such as David Hockney (Fig. 6-12).

Transparent watercolor, however, did not appear until the fifteenth century. It is a difficult medium to manipulate, despite its simple components. Tints are achieved by diluting the colors with various quantities of water. White, then, does not exist; white must be derived by allowing the white of the paper to "shine" through the color of the composition or by leaving areas of the paper exposed. To achieve the latter effect, all areas of whiteness must be mapped out with precision before the first stroke of color is applied.

With oil paint and acrylic, the artist sometimes overpaints areas of the canvas in order to make corrections or to blend colors. With transparent watercolors, overpainting obscures the underlying layers of color. For this reason, corrections are virtually impossible, so the artist must have the ability to

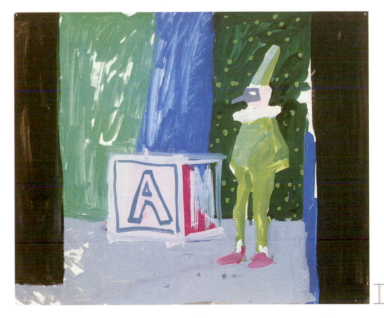

1 in.

6-12 DAVID HOCKNEY. *Punchinello with Block*, for "Parade Triple Bill" (1980). Gouache on paper. 14" × 17".

Types of Painting   **129**

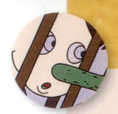

THE ACRYLIC PAINTINGS OF JAPANESE AMERICAN Roger Shimomura blend Western Pop Art with traditional Japanese imagery as found in *ukiyo-e* prints. As a child during World War II, Shimomura was interned with his parents and grandparents in Idaho. At the same time, ironically, his uncle served with the valiant 442nd division of Japanese Americans. Shimomura remembers statements made by white Americans about Japanese Americans during this deeply disturbing period. For example, Idaho's attorney general remarked, "We want to keep this a white man's country."

Shimomura's *Untitled* (Fig. **6-13**) is at first glance an amusing clash of American and Jap-anese pop cultures. American cartoon characters, Donald Duck, Pinocchio, Dick Tracy, and the combination Batman-Superman vie for space on the crowded canvas with Japanese samurai warriors and a contemporary Japanese portrait. The battle of East and West imagery may reflect the tensions within the artist regarding his ancestral roots and his chosen country. This is succinctly symbolized in the inclusion of Shimomura's self-portrait-as-Statue-of-Liberty in the extreme upper left. In this painting, conflicts between people and cultures are safely if not satirically played out among their stereotypes and myths. ●

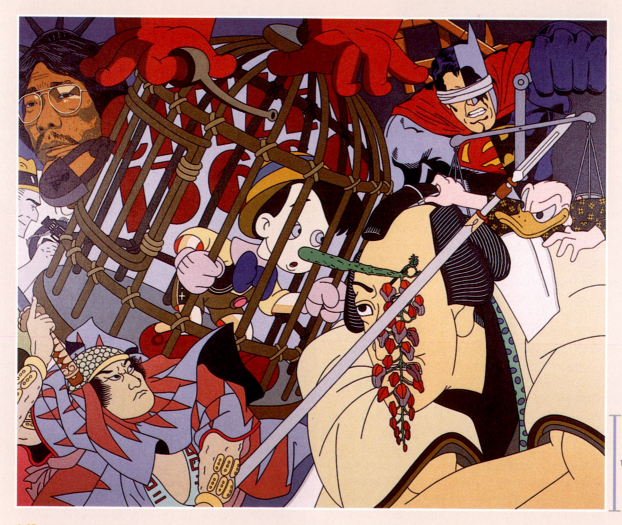

1 ft.

6-13 ROGER SHIMOMURA. *Untitled* (1984). Acrylic on canvas. 60" × 72".

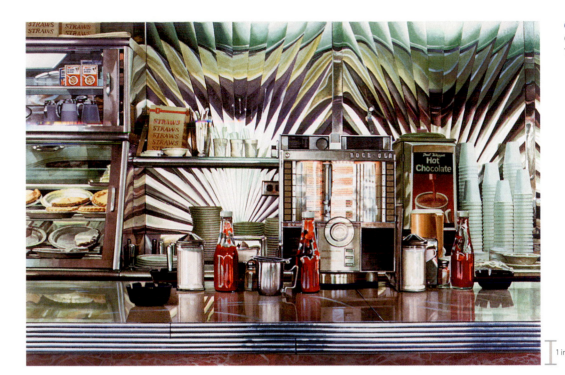

6-14 RALPH GOINGS. *Rock Ola* (1992). Watercolor on paper. 14" × 20¾".

plan ahead, as well as a sure hand and a stout heart. When used skillfully, watercolor has an unparalleled freshness and delicacy. The colors are pure and brilliant, and the range of effects surprisingly broad.

Contemporary painter Ralph Goings—one of the driving forces behind and consistent contributors to the school of **Photorealism**—uses transparent watercolor ingeniously. His virtuoso handling of the medium can be seen in works such as *Rock Ola* (Fig. **6-14**), which belie the difficulties of the medium. Confident strokes of color precisely define the gleaming "retro" chrome surfaces of a diner interior—the classic backdrop for the countertop jukebox and standard "still life with ketchup bottle and ashtray." Washes are kept to a minimum, as the painting emphasizes form over color, line over tonal patterns.

The broader appeal of watercolor, however, is not to be found in its capability of rendering meticulous detail. When the medium came into wide use during the sixteenth century, it was seen as having other, very different advantages. The fluidity of watercolor was conducive to rapid sketches and preparatory studies. Simple materials allowed for portability. Artists were able to cart their materials to any location, indoors or outdoors, and to register spontaneously their impressions of a host of subjects. Of course, watercolor is also used for paintings that stand as completed statements. German Expressionist Emil Nolde (Fig. **6-15**), who turned to watercolor when he was forbidden to paint by the Nazis during World War II (it doesn't smell like oil paint so

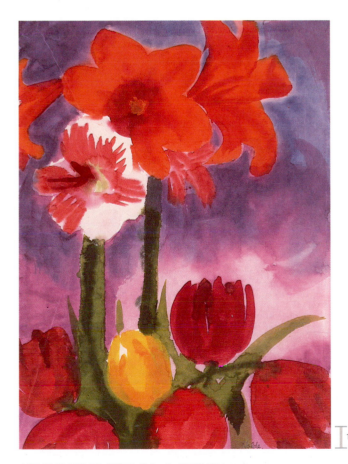

6-15 EMIL NOLDE. *Still Life, Tulips* (c. 1930). Watercolor on paper. 18½" × 13½". North Carolina Museum of Art, Raleigh, NC.

he could work in secrecy), was enticed by the transparency of tinted washes. Such washes permitted a delicate fusion of colors. As with the drawing medium of brush and wash, the effect is atmospheric. The edges of the forms are softened; they seem to diffuse into one another or the surrounding field. Nolde created his explosions of blossoms through delicately balanced patches of bold color and diaphanous washes. The composition is brightened by the white of the paper, which is brought forward to create forms as assertive as those in color.

Spray Paint

One can consider that spray painting has had a rather long history. The subtle coloration marking different species of animals on the walls of Paleolithic caves was probably achieved by blowing pigments onto a surface through

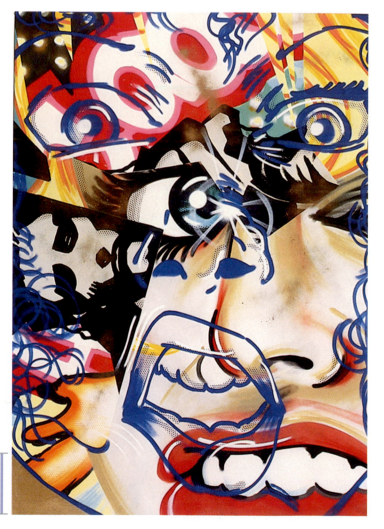

1 ft.

6-16 CRASH (JOHN MATOS). *Arcadia Revisited* (1988). Spray paint on canvas. 96¼" × 68".

hollowed-out reeds. Why are they there: decoration? ritual? history? Oddly enough, these questions can be asked of the contemporary graffiti artist and the thousands upon thousands of writings that range in definition from "tags" to "masterworks." Why do they do it? Is it art? urban ritual? Will it speak in history to the trials of inner-city living?

Everyone has seen graffiti, but the complexity of the work and the social atmosphere from which it is derived may not be common knowledge. Stylized signatures, or "tags," can be seen everywhere; it seems as though no urban surface—interior or exterior—is immune. Some are more likely to call this defacing public property than creating works of art, but how do we describe the elaborate urban "landscapes" that might cover the outside of an entire subway car, filling the space with a masterful composition of shapes, lines, textures, and colors? On the street, they are called masterworks, and their artists are indeed legendary.

Some graffiti writers have "ascended" to the art **gallery** scene, exchanging their steel "canvases" for some of fabric and their high-speed exhibition spaces for highbrow gallery walls. One such artist, Crash (or John Matos), created a parody of his own subway style in a complex canvas work called *Arcadia Revisited* (Fig. **6-16**). All of the tools and techniques of his trade—commercial cans of spray paint, the Benday dots of comic-strip fame, the sharp lines of the tag writer's logos, the diffuse spray technique that adds dimensionality to an array of otherwise flat objects—are used to describe a violent clash of cultural icons that are fragmented, superimposed, and barely contained within the confines of the canvas.

MIXED MEDIA

Contemporary painters have in many cases combined traditional painting techniques with other materials, or they have painted on nontraditional supports, stretching the definition of what has usually been considered painting. For example, in *The Bed* (see Fig. 21-11), Pop artist Robert Rauschenberg splashed and brushed paint onto a quilt and pillow, which he then hung on a wall like a canvas work and labeled a "combine painting." The Synthetic Cubists of the early twentieth century, Picasso and Braque, were the first to incorporate pieces of newsprint, wallpaper, labels from wine bottles, and oilcloth into their paintings. These works were called *papiers collés* and have come to be called **collages**.

The base mediums for Howardena Pindell's *Autobiography: Water / Ancestors, Middle Passage / Family Ghosts* (Fig. **6-17**) are tempera and acrylic, but the work, on sewn canvas, also incorporates an array of techniques and substances—markers, oil stick, paper, photo-transfer, and vinyl tape. The detail achieved is quite remarkable. The artist seems to float in a shimmering pool of shallow water, while all around her images and objects of memory seem to enter and exit her consciousness. Included among them are the prominent white shape of an African slave ship, a reference to Pindell's African ancestry, and the whitened face of the artist's portrait that may have been influenced by Michael Jackson's "Thriller" makeup. The work resembles as much a weaving as a painting, further reflecting the tapestry-like nature of human recollection.

Miriam Schapiro is best known for her paint and fabric constructions, which she has labeled "femmage," to express

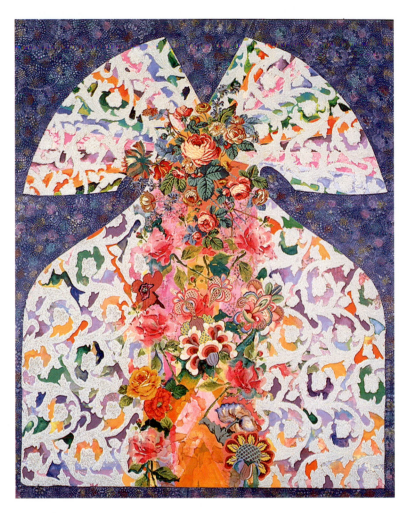

6-18 MIRIAM SCHAPIRO. *Maid of Honour* (1984). Acrylic and fabric on canvas. 60" × 50".

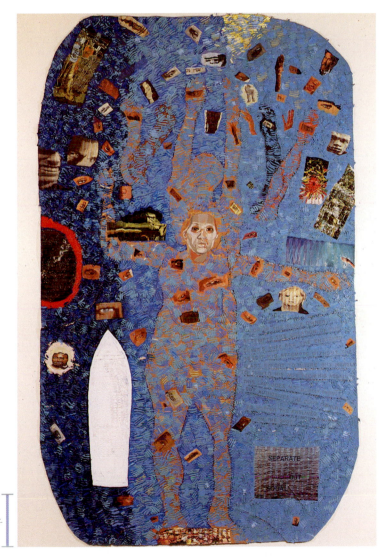

6-17 HOWARDENA PINDELL. *Autobiography: Water / Ancestors, Middle Passage / Family Ghosts* (1988). Acrylic, tempera, cattle markers, oil stick, paper, polymer photo-transfer, and vinyl tape on sewn canvas. 118" × 71". The Wadsworth Atheneum, Hartford, CT.

1 ft.

what she sees as their unification of feminine imagery and materials with the medium of collage. In *Maid of Honour* (Fig. 6-18), Schapiro combines bits of intricately patterned fabric with acrylic pigments on a traditional canvas support to construct a highly decorative garment that is presented as a work of art. The painting is a celebration of women's experiences with sewing, quilting, needlework, and decoration.

The two-dimensional mediums we have discussed in Chapter 5 and in this chapter, drawing and painting, create unique works whose availability to the general public is usually limited to photographic renditions in books such as this. Even the intrepid museumgoer usually visits only a small number of collections. So let us now turn our attention to the two-dimensional medium that has allowed millions of people to own original works by masters—printmaking.

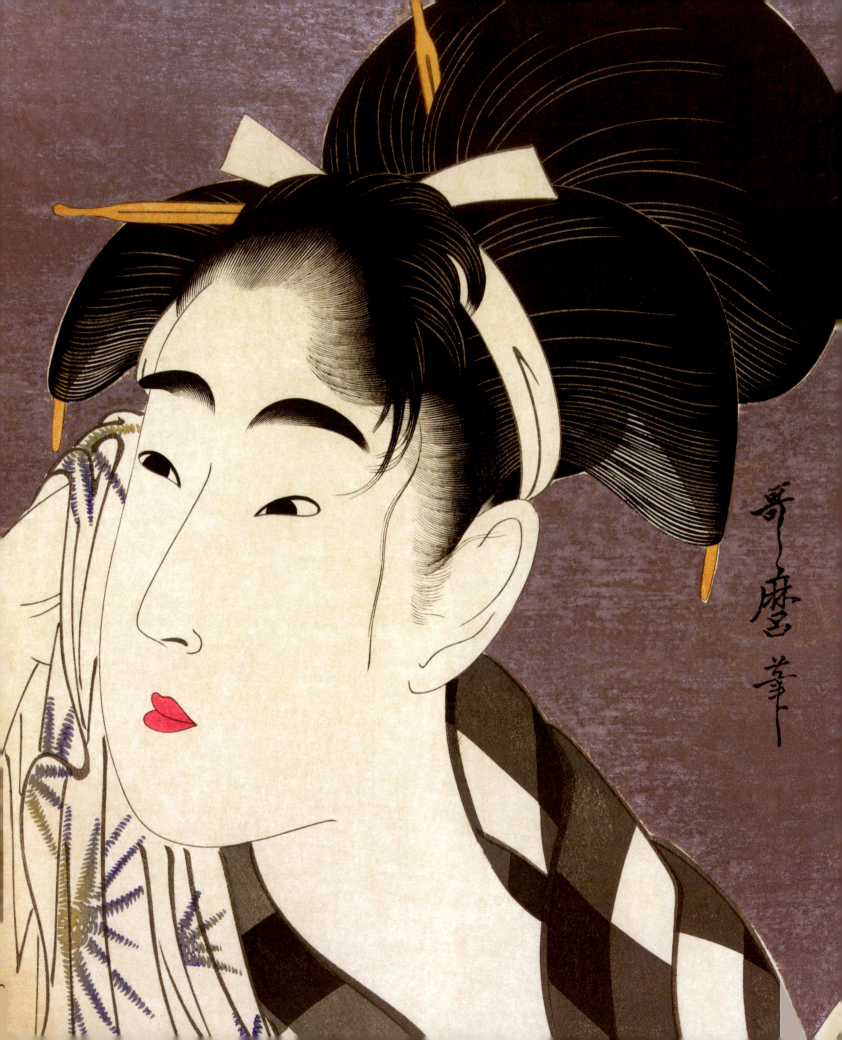

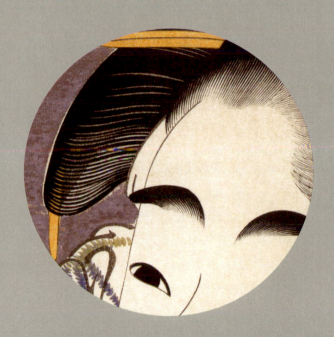

PRINTMAKING

7

The value of drawings and paintings lies, in part, in their uniqueness. Hours, weeks, sometimes years are expended in the creation of these one-of-a-kind works. Printmaking permits the reproduction of these coveted works as well as the production of multiple copies of original prints. Printmaking is an important artistic medium for at least two reasons. First, it allows people to study great works of art from a distance. Second, because prints are less expensive than unique works by the same artist, they make it possible for the general public, not just the wealthy few, to own original works. With prints, art has become accessible. Like some drawings, however, prints not only serve a functional purpose but may also be considered works of art in themselves.

Ukiyo-e color woodblock print (1798). Private collection.

METHODS OF PRINTMAKING

The printmaking process begins with a design or image made in or on a surface by hitting or pressing with a tool. The image is then transferred to paper or a similar material. The transferred image is called the **print**. The working surface, or **matrix**, varies according to the printmaking technique. Matrices include wood blocks, metal plates, stone slabs, and silkscreens. There are special tools for working with each kind of matrix, but the images in printmaking are usually rendered in ink.

Printmaking processes are divided into four major categories: relief, intaglio, lithography, and serigraphy (Fig. **7-1**). We shall examine a variety of techniques within each of these processes. Finally, we will consider the monotype and the combining of printmaking mediums with other mediums.

RELIEF

In **relief printing**, the matrix is carved with knives or gouges. Areas that are not meant to be printed are cut below the surface of the matrix (Fig. 7-1A), and areas that form the image and are meant to be printed are left raised. Ink is then applied to the raised surfaces, often from a roller. The matrix is pressed against a sheet of paper, and the image is transferred. The transferred image is the print. Relief printing includes woodcut and wood engraving.

Woodcut

Woodcut is the oldest form of printmaking. The ancient Chinese stamped patterns onto textiles and paper using carved wood blocks. The Romans used woodcuts to stamp symbols or letters on surfaces for purposes of identification. During the 1400s in Europe, woodcuts provided multiple copies of religious images for worshippers. After the invention of the printing press, woodcut assumed an important role in book illustration.

Woodcuts are made by cutting along the grain of the flat surface of a wooden board with a knife. Different types of wood and different gouging

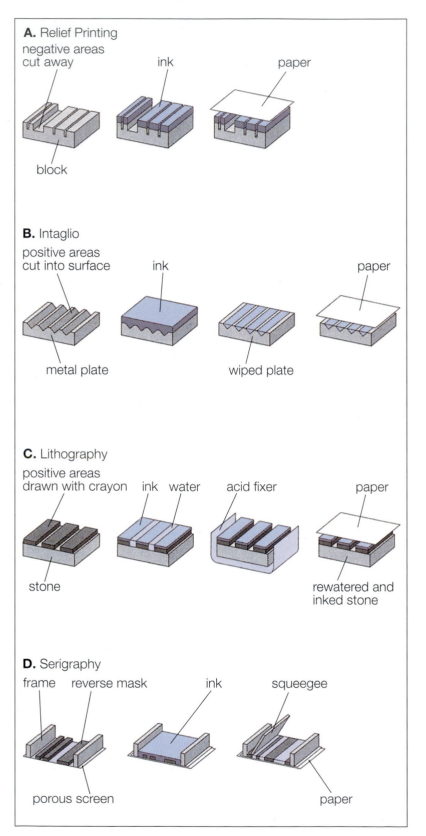

A. Relief Printing
negative areas cut away · ink · paper · block

B. Intaglio
positive areas cut into surface · ink · paper · metal plate · wiped plate

C. Lithography
positive areas drawn with crayon · ink · water · acid fixer · paper · stone · rewatered and inked stone

D. Serigraphy
frame · reverse mask · ink · squeegee · porous screen · paper

7-1 Printmaking technologies.

HIROSHIGE'S *RAIN SHOWER ON OHASHI BRIDGE* WITH XIAOMO'S *FAMILY BY THE LOTUS POND*

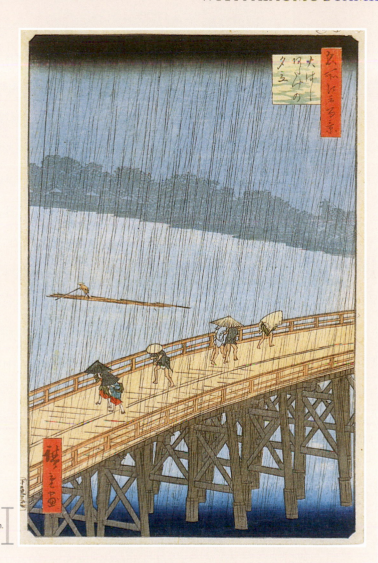

7-2 ANDO HIROSHIGE. *Sudden Rain at Atake and Ohashi* (1857). Color woodblock print. 13⅞" × 9⅛". The Cleveland Museum of Art, Cleveland, OH. Gift from J. H. Wade 1921.318.

ANDO HIROSHIGE, a nineteenth-century Japanese artist, achieved the finest detail in his works by choosing a close-grained wood and by tightly controlling the movement of his carving tools. Clean-cut, uniform lines define the steady rain and the individuals who tread huddled against

the downpour across a wooden footbridge (Fig. **7-2**). These fine lines provide a delicate counterpoint to bold shapes and broad areas of color and create the illusion of a drawing.

The meticulous process by which Hiroshige achieved his sharply defined images is used to a very different effect in Zhao Xiaomo's *Family by the Lotus Pond* (Fig. **7-3**). This contemporary Chinese printmaker uses a range of wood-block techniques to create complex, energetic compositions that often simulate oil paintings. Inspired by Chinese peasant paintings, as they are not bound by "academic rules," Xiaomo creates mosaic-like surfaces with bold, two-dimensional patterns.

How does the visual impact of these two works differ? Consider the use of line, shape, and color. ●

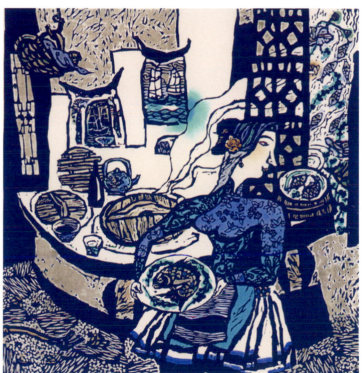

7-3 ZHAO XIAOMO. *Family by the Lotus Pond* (1998). Multiblock woodcut printed with water-soluble ink. 16¾" × 16½". The Art Institute of Chicago, Chicago, IL.

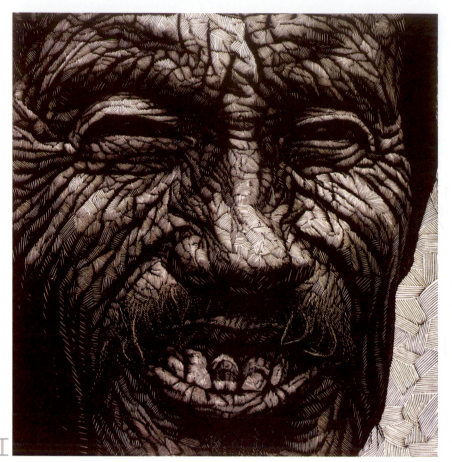

7-4 CHEN XUHAI. *Golden Autumn* (1998). Woodcut, printed with oil-based ink. 25¼" × 24". The Art Institute of Chicago, Chicago, IL.

1 in.

The razor-sharp tips of engraving implements and the hardness of the end-grain blocks make possible the exacting precision found in wood engravings such as that by Paul Landacre (Fig. **7-6**), a well-known twentieth-century American printmaker. Tight, threadlike, parallel, and cross-hatched lines compose the tonal areas that define the form. The rhythmic, flowing lines of the seedling's unfurling leaves contrast dramatically with the fine, prickly lines that emanate like rays from the young corn plant. The print is a display of technical prowess in a most demanding and painstaking medium.

tools yield various effects. *Golden Autumn* (Fig. **7-4**) by Chen Xuhai is a masterfully complex woodcut in which pockets of short lines of varying direction combine with long, velvet black crevices to create the signature landscape of an aging face.

Wood Engraving

The technique of **wood engraving** and its effects differ significantly from those of woodcuts. Whereas in woodcuts the flat surface of boards is used, in wood engraving many thin layers of wood are **laminated**. Then the ends of these sections are planed flat, yielding a hard, nondirectional surface. In contrast to the softer matrix used for the woodcut, the matrix for the wood engraving makes it relatively easy to work lines in varying directions. These lines are **incised** or engraved with tools such as a **burin** or **graver** (Fig. **7-5**), instead of being cut with knives and gouges. The lines can be extremely fine and are often used in close alignment to give the illusion of tonal gradations. This process was used to illustrate newspapers, such as *Harper's Weekly*, during the nineteenth century.

INTAGLIO

The popularity of relief printing declined with the introduction of the **intaglio** process. Intaglio prints are created by using metal plates into which lines have been incised. The plates are covered with ink, which is forced into the linear depressions, and then the surface is carefully wiped. The cut depressions retain the ink, whereas the flat surfaces are clean. Paper is laid atop the plate, and then paper and plate are passed through a printing press, forcing the paper into the incised lines to pick up the ink, thereby accepting the image. In a reversal of the

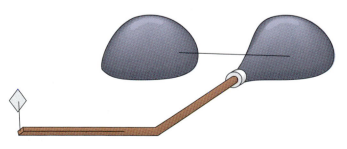

7-5 Burin.

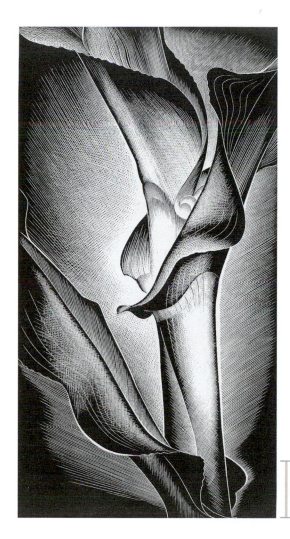

1 in.

7-6 PAUL LANDACRE. *Growing Corn* (1940). Wood engraving. 8½" × 4¼".

relief process, then, intaglio prints are derived from designs or images that lie *below* the surface of the matrix (Fig. 7-1B).

Intaglio printing encompasses many different mediums, the most common of which are engraving, drypoint, etching, and mezzotint and aquatint. Some artists have used these techniques recently in interesting variations or combinations and have pioneered approaches using modern equipment such as the camera and computer.

Engraving

Although **engraving** has been used to decorate metal surfaces such as bronze mirrors or gold and silver drinking vessels since ancient times, the earliest engravings printed on paper did not appear until the fifteenth century. In engraving, the artist creates clean-cut lines on a plate of copper, zinc, or steel, forcing the sharpened point of a burin across the surface with the heel of the hand. Because the lines are transferred to paper under very high pressure, they not only reveal the ink from the grooves but have a ridgelike texture that can be felt by running a finger across the print.

An early, famous engraving came from the hand of the fifteenth-century Italian painter Antonio Pollaiuolo (Fig. **7-7**). Deep lines that hold a greater amount of ink define the contours of the ten fighting figures. As Landacre did, Pollaiuolo used parallel groupings of thinner and thus lighter lines to render the tonal gradations that define the exaggerated musculature. The detail of the print is described with the utmost precision, revealing the artist's painstaking mastery of the burin.

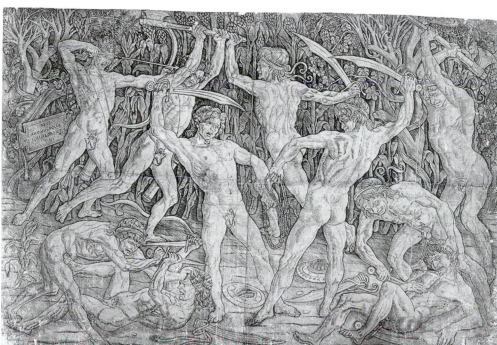

1 in.

7-7 ANTONIO POLLAIUOLO. *Battle of Ten Naked Men* (c. 1465–1470). Engraving. 15½" × 23³⁄₁₆". The Metropolitan Museum of Art, NY.

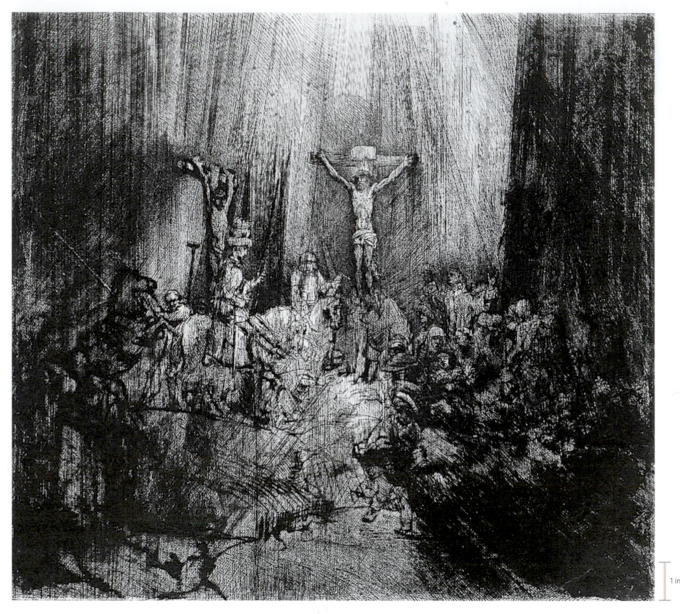

1 in.

7-8 REMBRANDT VAN RIJN. *Christ Crucified between the Two Thieves* (1653). Drypoint, 4th state. 15" × 17½". Museum of Fine Arts, Boston, MA.

Drypoint

Drypoint is engraving with a simple twist. In drypoint, a needle is dragged across the surface, and a metal burr, or rough edge, is left in its wake to one side of the furrow. The burr retains particles of ink, creating a softened rather than crisp line when printed. The burr sits above the surface of the matrix and therefore is fragile. After many printings, it will break down, resulting in a line that simply looks engraved.

The characteristic velvety appearance of drypoint lines is seen in Rembrandt's *Christ Crucified between the Two Thieves* (Fig. **7-8**). The more distinct lines were rendered with a burin, whereas the softer lines were created with a drypoint needle. Rembrandt used the blurriness of the drypoint line to enhance the sense of chaos attending the Crucifixion and the darkness of the encroaching storm. Lines fall like black curtains enshrouding the crowd, and rays of bright light illuminate the figure of Jesus and splash down onto the spectators.

Etching

Although they are both intaglio processes, **etching** differs from engraving in the way the lines are cut into the matrix. With engraving, the depth of the line corresponds to the amount of force used to push or draw an implement over the surface. With etching, minimal pressure is exerted to determine the depth of line. A chemical process does the work.

In etching, the metal plate is covered with a liquid, acid-resistant ground consisting of wax or resin. When the ground has hardened, the image is drawn upon it with a fine needle. Little pressure is exerted to expose the ground; the plate itself is not scratched. When the drawing is completed, the matrix is slipped into an acid bath, which immediately begins to eat away, or etch, the exposed areas of the plate. This etching process yields the sunken line that holds the ink. The artist leaves the plate in the acid solution just long enough to achieve the desired depth of line. If a variety of tones is desired, the artist may pull the plate out of the acid solution after a while, cover lines of sufficient depth with the acid-resistant ground, and replace the plate in the bath for further etching of the remaining exposed lines. The longer the plate remains in the

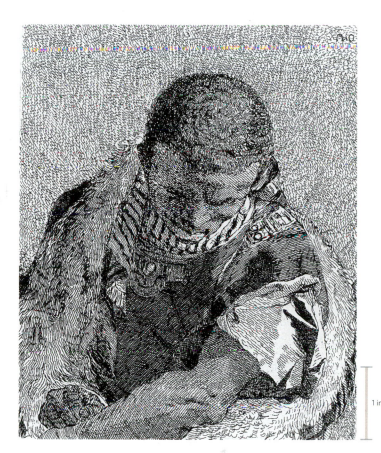

7-10 GIOVANNI DOMENICO TIEPOLO. *A Negro* (1770). Etching, 2nd state. 5⅝" × 4⁹⁄₁₆". Museum of Fine Arts, Boston, MA.

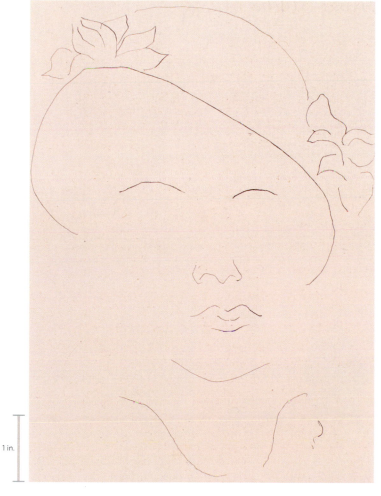

7-9 HENRI MATISSE. *Loulou Distracted* (1914). Etching, printed in black. 7¹⁄₁₆" × 5". Archives Matisse, Paris, France. © 2011 Succession H. Matisse/ Artists Rights Society (ARS), NY.

acid solution, the deeper the etching. Deeper crevices hold more ink, and for this reason they print darker lines.

Etching is a versatile medium, capable of many types of lines and effects. The modern French painter Henri Matisse used but a few dozen uniformly etched lines to describe the essential features of a woman, *Loulou Distracted* (Fig. **7-9**). The extraordinarily simple yet complete image attests to the delicacy that can be achieved with etching.

Whereas Matisse's figure takes shape through the careful placement of line, the subject of the etching by Giovanni Domenico Tiepolo (who was the son of Giovanni Battista Tiepolo) exists by virtue of textural and tonal contrasts (Fig. **7-10**). This eighteenth-century Italian artist used a variety of wavy and curving lines to differentiate skin from cloth, fur from hair, figure from ground. Lines are spaced to provide a range of tones from the sharp white of the paper to the rich black of the man's clothing. The overall texture creates a hazy atmosphere that caresses the pensive figure.

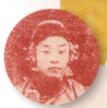

IN MANY WAYS, HUNG LIU epitomizes the concerns and preoccupations of the Chinese artist whose life experiences during that country's Cultural Revolution have shaped their art—indeed, their very existence. In 1984, Hung Liu arrived in the United States. In her words, with her "Five-thousand-year-old culture on my back. Late-twentieth-century world in my face. . . . My Alien number is 28333359." For four years in her country of origin, she was forced to work in the fields. In her chosen country, she is now a professor at Mills College and has had one-woman shows in New York, San Francisco, Texas, and Miami. Her art focuses on what she has called "the peculiar ironies which result when ancient Chinese images are 'reprocessed' within contemporary Western materials, processes, and modes of display."

Figure 7-11 shows an untitled mixed-media print, whose main image consists of a photo-etching onto which are affixed small rectangular wooden blocks—mahjong pieces—bearing the "high-fashion" portraits of Chinese women. The inspiration for this print, and full oil paintings on the same theme, came from a series of photographs of Chinese prostitutes from the early 1900s that Hung Liu discovered on a recent return trip to China. When the Communist revolution took hold and all able-bodied individuals were forced into labor, these women were forced into prostitution because the tradition of oppression that led to the practice of binding their feet made them unfit for physical toil. They could barely walk.

Hung Liu feels the need to make known the pain, suffering, and degradation of generations of women before her:

Although I do not have bound feet, the invisible spiritual burdens fall heavy on me. . . . I communicate with the characters in my paintings, prostitutes—these completely subjugated people—with reverence, sympathy, and awe. They had no real names. Probably no children. I want to make up stories for them. Who were they? Did they leave any trace in history?

In Hung Liu's work, we come to understand a piece of history. We are challenged to reflect, as she does, upon human rights and freedoms, spiritual and physical oppression, political expression, and silenced voices. ●

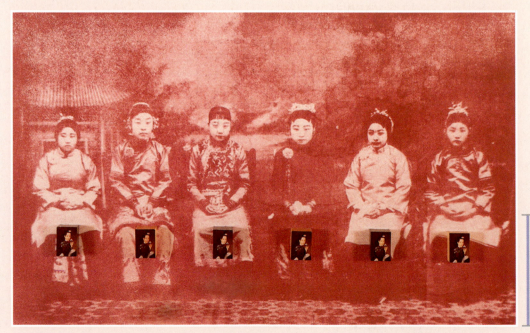

7-11 HUNG LIU. *Untitled* (1992). Photo-etching, mixed media. 33" × 22½".

1 ft.

The artist is a receptacle for the emotions that come from all over the place: from the sky, from the earth, from a scrap of paper, from a passing shape, from a spider's web.
—Pablo Picasso

Mezzotint and Aquatint

Engraving, drypoint, and etching are essentially linear mediums. With these techniques, designs or images are created by cutting lines into a plate. The illusion of tonal gradations is achieved by altering the number and concentration of lines. Sometime in the midseventeenth century, the Dutchman Ludwig von Siegen developed a technique whereby broad tonal areas could be achieved by nonlinear engraving, that is, engraving that does *not* depend on line. The medium was called **mezzotint**, from the Italian word meaning "half tint."

With mezzotint engraving, the entire metal plate is worked over with a curved, multitoothed implement called a **hatcher**. The hatcher is "rocked" back and forth over the surface, producing thousands of tiny pits that will hold ink. If printed at this point, the plate would yield an allover consistent, velvety black print. But the mezzotint engraver uses this evenly pitted surface as a point of departure. The artist creates an image by gradually scraping and burnishing the areas of the plate that are meant to be lighter. These areas will hold less ink and therefore will produce lighter tones. The more persistent the scraping, the shallower the pits and the lighter the tone. A broad range of tones is achieved as the artist works from the rich black of the rocked surface to the highly polished pitless areas that will yield bright whites. Mezzotint is a rarely used, painstaking, and time-consuming procedure.

The subtle tonal gradations achieved by the mezzotint process can be duplicated with a much easier and quicker etching technique called **aquatint**. In aquatint, a metal plate is evenly covered with a fine powder of acid-resistant resin. The plate is then heated, causing the resin to melt and adhere to the surface. As in line etching, the matrix is placed in an acid bath, where its uncovered surfaces are eaten away by the solution. The depth of tone is controlled by removing the plate from the acid and covering the pits that have been sufficiently etched.

Aquatint is often used in conjunction with line etching and is frequently manipulated to resemble tones produced by wash drawings. In *The Painter and His Model* (Fig. **7-12**), Pablo Picasso brought the forms out of void space by defining their limits with dynamic patches of aquatint. These tonal areas resemble swaths of ink typical of wash drawings. Descriptive details of the figures are rendered in fine or ragged lines, etched to varying depths.

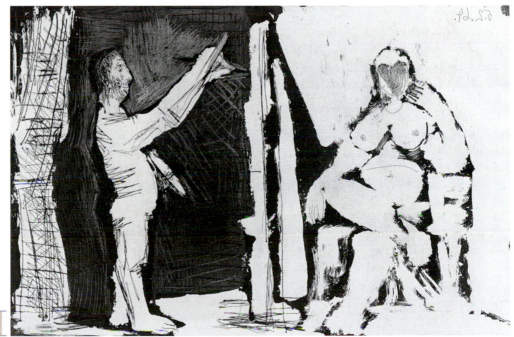

7-12 PABLO PICASSO. *The Painter and His Model* (1964). Etching and aquatint. 12⅝" × 18½". Museum of Fine Arts, Boston, MA. © 2011 Estate of Pablo Picasso/Artists Rights Society (ARS), NY.

1 in.

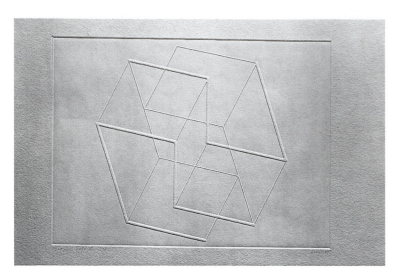

Solo V, the geometric image shown in Figure **7-13**, by etching the lines of his design to two different depths. Furrows in the plate appear as raised surfaces when printed. We seem to feel the image with our eyes, as light plays across the surface of the paper to enhance its legibility. Perceptual shifts occur as the viewer focuses now on the thick, now on the thin lines. In trying to puzzle out the logic of the form, the viewer soon discovers that Albers has offered a frustrating illustration of "impossible perspective."

LITHOGRAPHY

Lithography was invented at the dawn of the nineteenth century by the German playwright Aloys Senefelder. Unlike relief and intaglio printing, which rely on cuts in a matrix surface to produce an image, the lithography matrix is flat.

Other Etching Techniques

Different effects may also be achieved in etching by using grounds of different substances. **Soft-ground etching**, for example, employs a ground of softened wax and can be used to render the effects of crayon or pencil drawings. In a technique called **lift-ground**, the artist creates the illusion of a brush-and-ink drawing by actually brushing a solution of sugar and water onto a resin-coated plate. When the plate is slipped into the acid bath, the sugar dissolves, lifting the brushed image off the plate to expose the metal beneath. As in all etching mediums, these exposed areas accept the ink.

Given that the printing process implies the use of ink to produce an image, can we have prints without ink? The answer is yes—with the medium called **gauffrage**, or inkless intaglio. Josef Albers, a twentieth-century American abstract artist, created

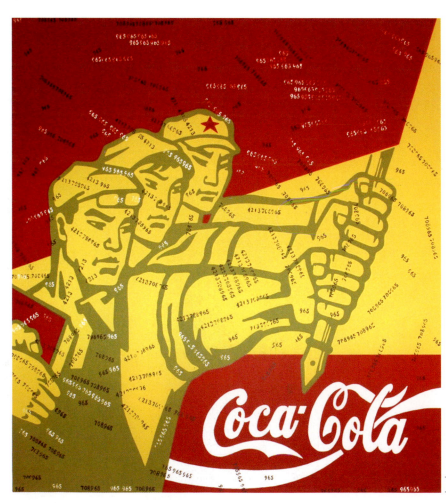

1 in.

Lithography is a surface or **planographic printing** process (Fig. 7-1C).

In lithography, the artist draws an image with a greasy crayon directly on a flat stone slab. Bavarian limestone is considered the best material for the slab. Sometimes a specially sensitized metal plate is used, but a metal surface will not produce the often-desired grainy appearance in the print. Small particles of crayon adhere to the granular texture of the stone matrix. After the design is complete, a solution of nitric acid is applied as a fixative. The entire surface of the matrix is then dampened with water. The untouched areas of the surface accept the water, but the waxy crayon marks repel it.

A roller is then used to cover the stone with an oily ink. This ink adheres to the crayon drawing but repels the water. When paper is pressed to the stone surface, the ink on the crayon is transferred to the paper, revealing the image. Different lithographic methods yield different results. Black crayon on grainy stone can look quite like the crayon drawing it is. On the other hand, lithographs with large blocks of colored ink can emphasize the commercial quality of the printmaking process.

Wang Guangyi's *Great Criticism: Coca-Cola* (Fig. **7-14**) reads like an anti-American propaganda poster, the kind that you could imagine seeing glued in multiples to plywood in an urban landscape. It features bold lines and a sharp definition of color and shape. The power of the image and its message are enhanced by the work's simplicity and directness, as well as our visual recognition of stereotypes—in this case the faces of Asian men, their standard laborer's overalls, and the Coca-Cola logo.

The impact of Käthe Kollwitz's lithograph *The Mothers* (Fig. **7-15**), which highlights the plight of lower-class German mothers left alone to fend for their children after World War I, could not be further removed from that of *Great Criticism: Coca-Cola*. The high contrast of the black and white and the coarse quality of the wax crayon yield a sense of desperation suggestive of a newspaper documentary photograph. All the imagery is thrust toward the picture plane, as in high relief. The harsh contours of protective shoulders, arms, and hands contrast with the more delicately rendered faces and heads of the children—all contributing to the poignancy of the work.

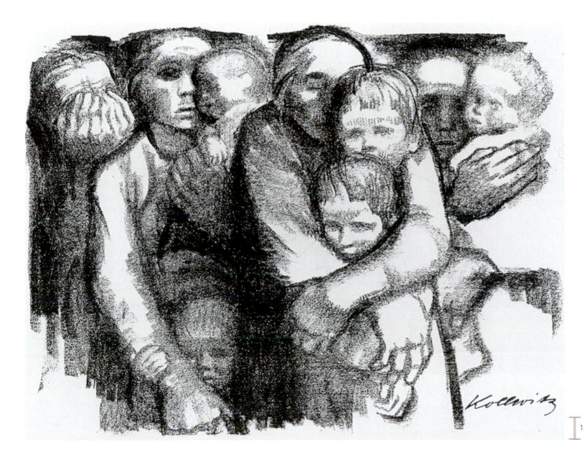

7-15 KÄTHE KOLLWITZ. *The Mothers* (1919). Lithograph. 17¾" × 23". The Philadelphia Museum of Art, Philadelphia, PA. © 2011 Artists Rights Society (ARS), NY/VG Bild-Kunst, Bonn.

1 in.

I think it was colors and weights and pushes and pulls and how to make a surface.
—Alex Katz, when asked what he learned from Matisse

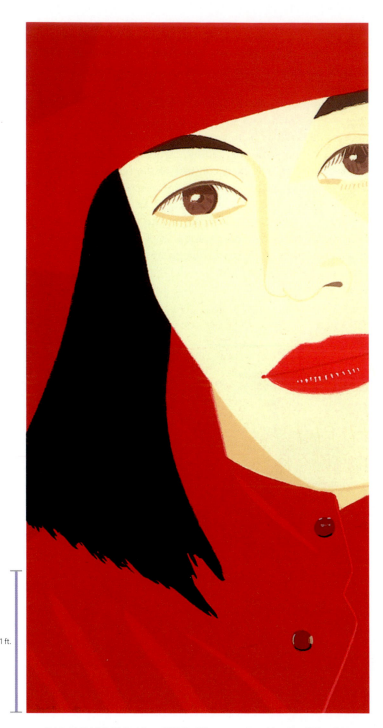

1 ft.

7-16 ALEX KATZ. *Red Coat* (1983). Silkscreen, printed in color. 58" × 29". The Museum of Modern Art, NY. John B. Turner Fund. Art © Alex Katz/ Licensed by VAGA, NY.

SERIGRAPHY

In **serigraphy**—also known as **silkscreen printing**—stencils are used to create the design or image. Unlike the case with other graphic processes, these images can be rendered in paint as well as ink.

One serigraphic process begins with a screen constructed of a piece of silk, nylon, or fine metal mesh stretched on a frame. A stencil with a cutout design is then affixed to the screen, and paper or canvas is placed beneath (Fig. 7-1D). The artist forces paint or ink through the open areas of the stencil with a flat, rubber-bladed implement called a **squeegee**, similar to those used in washing windows. The image on the support corresponds to the shape cut out of the stencil. Several stencils may be used to apply different colors to the same print.

Images can also be "painted" on a screen with use of a varnishlike substance that prevents paint or ink from passing through the mesh. This technique allows for more gestural images than cutout stencils would provide. Recently, a serigraphic process called **photo silkscreen** has been developed; it allows the artist to create photographic images on a screen covered with a light-sensitive gel.

Serigraphy was first developed as a commercial medium and is still used as such to create such things as posters and labels on cans of food. The American Pop artist Andy Warhol raised the commercial aspects of serigraphy to the level of fine art in many of his silkscreen prints of the 1960s, such as *Four Marilyns* (see Fig. 1-9). These faithful renditions of celebrities and everyday items satirize the mass media's bombardment of the consumer with advertising. They also have their amusing side.

Alex Katz defines his forms with razor-sharp edges, fixing his subjects in an exact time and place by the details of their clothing and hairstyles. At the same time, he transcends their temporal and spatial limits by simplifying and transforming their figures into something akin to icons. For example, the subject's intense red lips in his silkscreen *Red Coat* (Fig. **7-16**) serve as a symbol of contemporary glamour. *Red Coat* looks something like a photograph transported into another medium. The individual shapes seem carved into a single plane like sawed jigsaw puzzle pieces. As in a photo, the edges of the silkscreen crop off parts of the image. The woman looks like a supermodel, with her features exaggerated as they might be in a cover girl image.

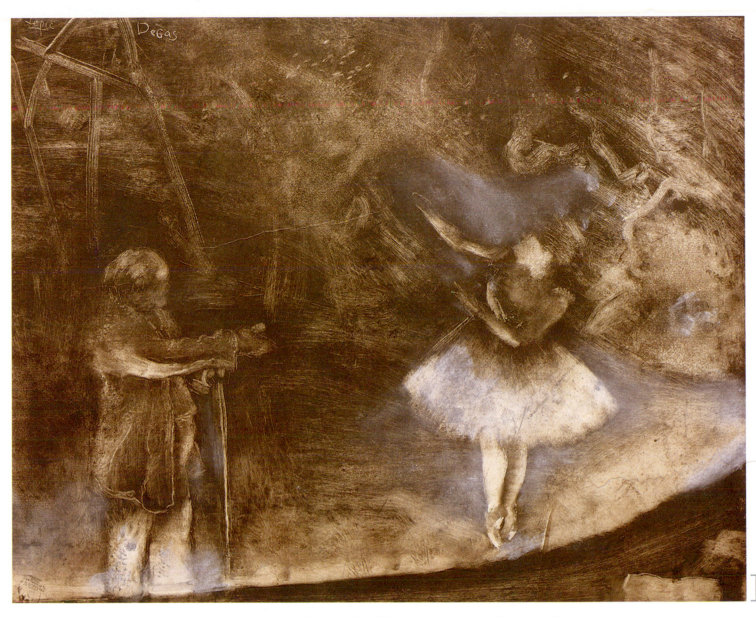

1 in.

7-17 EDGAR DEGAS. *The Ballet Master* (c. 1874). Monotype in black ink. 22" × 27½". National Gallery of Art, Washington, D.C.

MONOTYPE

Monotype is a printmaking process, but it overlaps the other two-dimensional mediums of drawing and painting. Like drawing and printmaking, monotype yields but a single image, and like them, therefore, it is a unique work of art.

In monotype, drawing or painting is created with oil paint or watercolor on a nonabsorbent surface of any material.

Brushes are used, but sometimes fine detail is rendered by scratching paint off the plate with sharp implements. A piece of paper is then laid on the surface, and the image is transferred by hand rubbing the back of the paper or passing the matrix and paper through a press. The result, as can be seen in a monotype by Edgar Degas (Fig. **7-17**), has all the spontaneity of a drawing and the lushness of a painting.

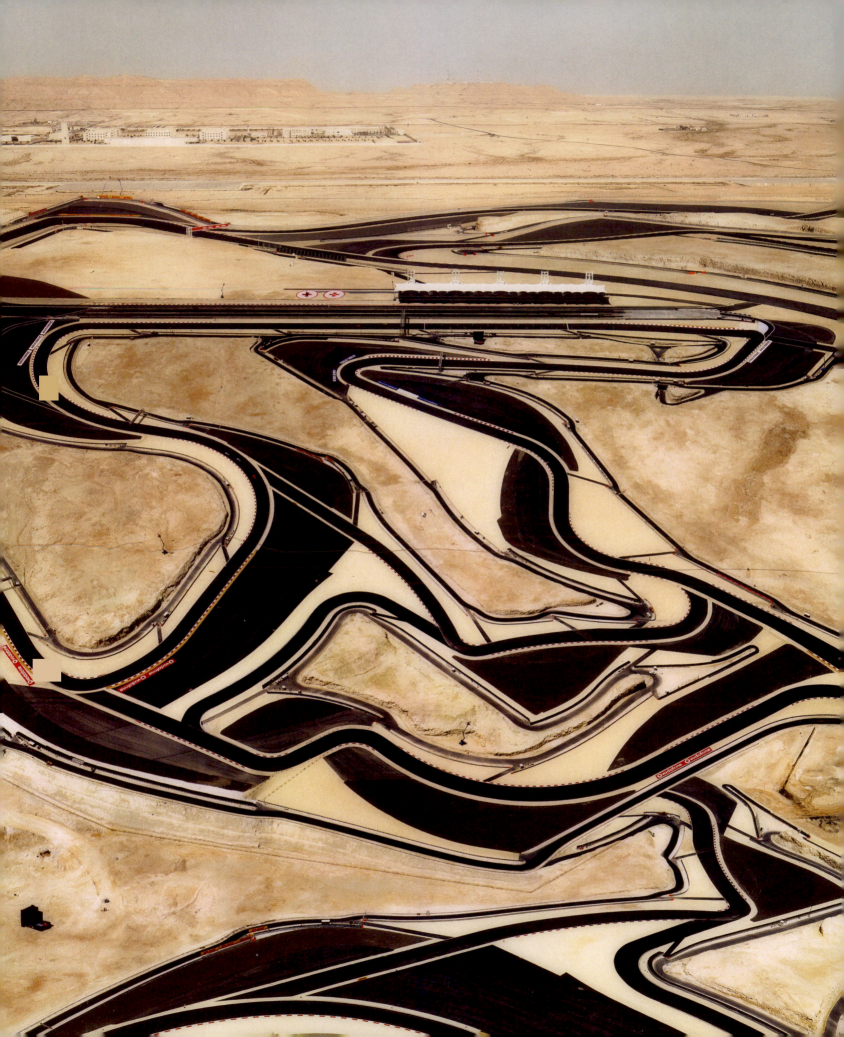

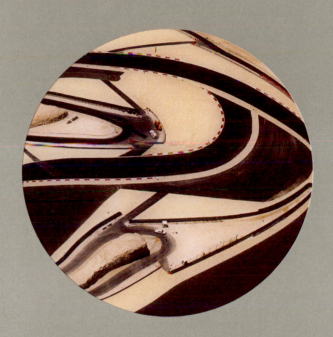

IMAGING: PHOTOGRAPHY, FILM, VIDEO, AND DIGITAL ARTS

8

Technology has revolutionized the visual arts. For thousands of years, one of the central goals of art was to imitate nature as exactly as possible. Today, any one of us can point a camera at a person or an object and capture a realistic image. Point-and-shoot cameras no longer even require that we place the subject in proper focus or that we regulate the amount of light so as not to overexpose or underexpose the subject. Technology can do all of these things for us.

Similarly, the art of the stage was once available only to those who lived in the great urban centers. Now and then a traveling troupe of actors might come by, or local groups might put on a show of sorts, but most people had little or no idea of the ways in which drama, opera, dance, and other performing arts could affect their lives. The advent of motion pictures, or cinematography, suddenly brought a flood of new imagery into new local theaters, and a new form of communal activity was born. People from every station of life could flock to the movie theater on the weekend. Over time, cinematography evolved into an art form independent of its beginnings as a mirror of the stage.

More recently, television has brought this imagery into the home, where people can watch everything from the performing arts to sporting events in privacy and from the multiple vantage points that several cameras, rather than a single set of eyes, can provide. Fine artists have also appropriated television—or, more precisely, the technology that makes television possible—to produce **video art**. Technology has also given rise to the computer as a creative video-mediated tool. With the aid of artificial intelligence, we can instantly view models of objects from all sides. We can be led to feel as though we are sweeping in on our solar system from the black reaches of space, then flying down to the surface of our planet and landing where the programmer would set us down.

Millions of children spend hours playing video games, such as Tetris, which challenges them to rotate plummeting polygons to construct a solid wall, or Mario Brothers and Tomb Raider, which require them to evade or blast a host of enemies before their computer-drawn heroes and heroines plunge into an abyss. Computer technology and computer-generated images have likewise been appropriated by fine artists in the creation of **digital art**. In illustrations of blue jeans that rocket through space, snappy graphics that headline sporting events, and the web design that greets us every time we go online, computer-generated images punctuate our daily lives. DVDs, multimedia computers, and software that can blend or distort one shape or face into another are bringing a "virtual reality" into our lives that is in some ways more alluring than, well, "real reality."

In this chapter, we discuss photography, film (cinematography), video, and digital arts. These mediums have given rise to unique possibilities for artistic expression.

PHOTOGRAPHY

Photography is a science and an art. The word *photography* is derived from Greek roots meaning "to write with light." The scientific aspects of photography concern the ways in which images of objects are made on a **photosensitive** surface, such as film, by light that passes through a **lens**. Chemical changes occur in the film so that the images are recorded. This much of the process—the creation of an objective image of the light that has passed through the lens—is mechanical.

It would be grossly inaccurate, however, to think of the *art* of photography as mechanical. Photographers make artistic choices, from the most mundane to the most sophisticated. They decide which films and lenses to use, and which photographs they will retain or discard. They manipulate lighting conditions or printing processes to achieve dazzling or dreamy effects. Always, they are in search of subjects—ordinary, extraordinary, universal, personal.

Photography is truly an art of the hand, head, and heart. Before the advent of digital photography, the photographer had to understand films and grasp skills related to developing **prints**. The photographer must also have the intellect and the passion to search for and to see what is important in things—what is beautiful, harmonious, universal, and worth recording.

Photography is a matter of selection and interpretation. Similar subjects seen through the eyes of different photographers will yield wildly different results. In Ansel Adams's *Moon and Half Dome*, *Yosemite National Park*, *California* (Fig. **8-1**), majestic cliffs leap into a deep, cold sky. From our earthbound vantage point, the perfect order of the desolate, spherical moon contrasts with the coarseness of the living rock. Yet we know that its geometric polish is an illusion wrought by distance—the moon's surface is just as rough and chaotic. Adams's composition is as much about design elements (shape, texture, value) as it is a visual document of the California landscape. Distance and scale come sharply into focus: This is a story of humans dwarfed by nature and nature dwarfed by the stars.

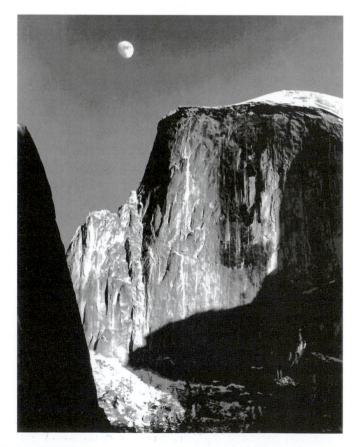

8-1 ANSEL ADAMS. *Moon and Half Dome, Yosemite National Park, California* (1960).

Photography records the gamut of feelings written on the human face, the beauty of the earth and skies that man has inherited and the wealth and confusion man has created.
—Edward Steichen

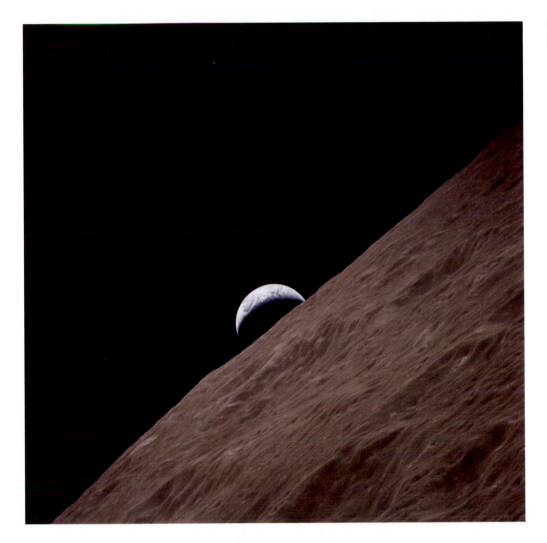

8-2 Crescent Earth, seen by Apollo 17.

In the early nineteenth century, when photography was invented, the technology that made Figure **8-2** possible would have been only fantasy. In this NASA photograph, taken during the first manned mission to the moon in July 1969, the crescent shape of sunlight blanketing a distant Earth is silhouetted against a velvet black sky. Its perfect geometry is a dramatic counterpoint to the irregular textured surface of the moon. Although only a sliver of Earth's blue color is evident at the point where light turns abruptly to shadow, it is enough to suggest a sense of life in contrast to the barren, unforgiving lunar landscape.

Both the Adams photograph and the one taken from space have artful compositions, even though the NASA photograph was not taken by an artist. Adams chose a specific

moment, when shadows were deep, the sky was clear, and the position of the sun exaggerated the textures of the rock. The black shadows and the uniform steel gray sky have such precise contours that they read as flat puzzle pieces. The NASA photograph is striking for two reasons. First, the "composition" is dramatically simple: a field bisected into two zones by the sharp diagonal created by the contour of the moon. Second, the perspective is intriguing: we sense the fluid glide of the ship through the stillness of space.

The aesthetic aspect of both photographs is not all they have in common. The history of photography is full of evidence of the artist-photographer boldly going where no man (or woman) has gone before or challenging the viewer to see anew the familiar and ubiquitous. The mood, stylistic inclinations, cultural biases, and technical preferences influence the nature of the creative product. As observers, we are as enriched by the diversity of this medium as much as any other in the visual arts.

Cameras

Cameras may look very different from one another and boast a variety of equipment, but they all possess certain basic features. As you can see in Figure **8-3**, the camera is similar to the human eye. In both cases, light enters a narrow opening and is projected onto a photosensitive surface.

The amount of light that enters the eye is determined by the size of the *pupil*, which is an opening in the muscle called the *iris*; the size of the pupil responds automatically to the amount of light that strikes the eye. The amount of light that enters a camera is determined by the size of the opening, or **aperture**, in the **shutter**. The aperture opening can be adjusted manually or, in advanced cameras, automatically. The size of the aperture, or opening, is the so-called **F-stop**. The smaller the F-stop, the larger the opening. The shutter can also be made to remain open to light for various amounts of time, ranging from a few thousandths of a second—in which case **candid** shots of fast action may be taken—to a second or more.

When the light enters the eye, the *lens* keeps it in focus by responding automatically to its distance from the object. The light is then projected onto the retina, which consists of cells that are sensitive to light and dark and to color. Nerves transmit visual sensations of objects from the retina to the brain.

retina (photosensitive surface)

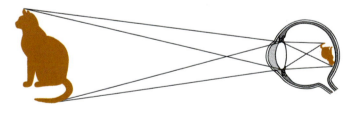

film (photosensitive surface)

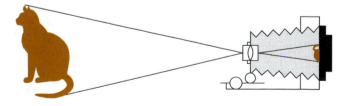

8-3 The camera and the human eye compared.

In the same way, the camera lens focuses light onto a photosensitive surface such as **film**. A camera lens can be focused manually or automatically. Many photographers purposely take pictures that are out of focus, for their soft, blurred effects. **Telephoto lenses** magnify faraway objects and tend to collapse the spaces between distant objects that recede from us. **Wide-angle lenses** allow a broad view of objects within a confined area.

In their early days, cameras tended to be large and were placed on mounts. Today's cameras are usually small and held by hand. *The Steerage* (see Fig. 1-27) was shot with an early handheld camera. Many contemporary cameras contain angled mirrors that allow the photographer to see directly through the lens and thereby to be precisely aware of the image that is being projected onto the film.

Film

When an image is "shot," it is recorded on a device such as film or an electronic memory device such as a disk or memory stick. Contemporary black-and-white films are very thin, yet they contain several layers, most of which form a protective coating and backing for the photosensitive layer. The active layer contains an **emulsion** of small particles of a photosensitive silver salt (usually silver halide) suspended in gelatin.

After the film is exposed to light and treated chemically, it becomes a **negative**, in which metallic silver is formed from the crystals of silver halide. In this negative, areas of dark and light are reversed. Because the negatives are transparent, light passes through them to a print surface, which becomes the final photograph, or print. Here the areas of light and dark are reversed again, now matching the shading of the original subject. Prints are also usually made significantly larger than the negative.

Black-and-white films differ in color sensitivity (the ability to show colors such as red and green as different shades), in contrast (the tendency to show gradations of gray as well as black and white), in graininess (the textural quality, as reflective of the size of the silver halide crystals), and in speed (the amount of exposure time necessary to record an image). Photographers select films that will heighten the effects they seek to portray.

Color film is more complex than black-and-white film, but similar in principle. Color film also contains several layers, some of which are protective and provide backing. There are two basic kinds of color film: **color reversal film** and **color negative film**. Both types of color film contain three light-sensitive layers.

Prints are made directly from *color reversal film*. Therefore, each of the photosensitive layers corresponds to one of the primary colors in additive color mixtures: blue, green, or red. When color reversal film is exposed to light and treated chemically, mixtures of the primary colors emerge, yielding a full-color image of the photographic subject.

Negatives are made from *color negative film*. Therefore, each photosensitive layer corresponds to the complement of the primary color it represents. (Additive color mixtures and primary and complementary colors are explained in Chapter 2.)

Color films, like black-and-white films, differ in color sensitivity, contrast, graininess, and speed. But color films also differ in their appropriateness for natural (daylight) or artificial (indoor) lighting conditions.

Digital Photography

Today, **digital photography** abounds. Digital cameras translate the visual images that pass through the lens into bits of digital information, which are recorded onto an electronic storage device such as a disk, not on film. High-quality (translation: extremely expensive) digital cameras take photos whose **resolution**—that is, sharpness—rivals that of images recorded on film. The stored information can then be displayed on a computer monitor. Rather than have several prints made, the photographer can "back up" the information repeatedly. It can also be sent over the Internet in digital form. Printed images can also be scanned, which converts them into digital formats, and then stored on computer hard drives or sent over the Internet.

Digital photography has some advantages. One is that the photographer need not deal with film—loading and unloading it and having it developed. The images can be displayed immediately on a display built into the camera or on a computer monitor. Software then permits you to manipulate the images as desired. You can also print them out as you would print out any other image or text.

The disadvantages are that (most) digital images do not have the sharpness of film images. Images take up a tremendous amount of storage space (several megabytes each!) on your hard drive. Also, your printer may not print images that approach the quality of film images, even if you have stored enough information to do so. To get professional-quality prints, you may have to invest in professional equipment or take your disk elsewhere, just as you have to take film to a lab or processor to be developed. But the price of this equipment is falling steadily, and we seem to be arriving at a point at which nearly anyone will be able to afford digital equipment that rivals the resolution of more traditional photography.

History of Photography

The cameras and films described previously are rather recent inventions. Photography has a long and fascinating history. Although true photography does not appear much before the mid-nineteenth century, some of its principles can be traced back another 300 years, to the camera obscura.

THE CAMERA OBSCURA The **camera obscura**—literally, the covered-over or darkened room—was used by Renaissance artists to help them accurately portray depth, or perspective, on two-dimensional surfaces. The camera obscura could be a box, as shown in Figure **8-4**, or an actual room with a small hole that admits light through one wall. The beam of light projects the outside scene upside down on a surface within the box. The artist then simply traces the scene, as shown, to achieve a proper perspective—to truly imitate nature.

DEVELOPMENT OF PHOTOSENSITIVE SURFACES The camera obscura could only temporarily focus an image on a surface while a person labored to copy it by tracing. The next developments in photography concerned the search for photosensitive surfaces that could permanently affix images. These developments came by bits and pieces.

In 1727, the German physicist Heinrich Schulze discovered that silver salts had light-sensitive qualities, but he never tried to record natural images. In 1802, Thomas Wedgwood, son of the well-known English potter, reported his discovery that paper soaked in silver nitrate did take on projected images as a chemical reaction to light. However, the images were not permanent.

HELIOGRAPHY In 1826, the Frenchman Joseph-Nicéphore Niepce invented **heliography**. **Bitumen**, or asphalt residue, was placed on a pewter plate to create a photosensitive surface. The bitumen was soluble in **lavender oil** if kept in the dark, but insoluble if struck by light. Niepce used a kind

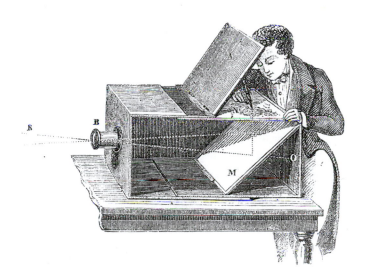

8-4 The camera obscura.

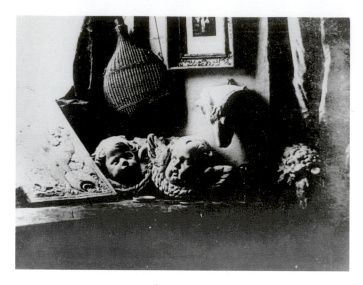

8-5 LOUIS-JACQUES-MANDÉ DAGUERRE. *The Artist's Studio* (1837).

of camera obscura to expose the plate for several hours, and then he washed the plate in lavender oil. The pewter showed through where there had been little or no light, creating the image of the darker areas of the scene. The bitumen remained where the light had struck, however, leaving lighter values.

THE DAGUERREOTYPE   The **daguerreotype** resulted from a partnership formed in 1829 between Niepce and another Frenchman, Louis-Jacques-Mandé Daguerre. The daguerreotype used a thin sheet of silver-plated copper. The plate was chemically treated, placed in a camera obscura, and exposed to a narrow beam of light. After exposure, the plate was treated chemically once more.

Figure **8-5** shows the first successful daguerreotype, taken in 1837. Remarkably clear images could be recorded by this process. In this work, called *The Artist's Studio*, Daguerre, a landscape painter, sensitively assembled deeply textured objects and sculptures. The contrasting light and dark values help create an illusion of depth.

There were drawbacks to the daguerreotype. It had to be exposed from 5 to 40 minutes, requiring long sittings. The recorded image was reversed, left to right, and was so delicate that it had to be sealed behind glass to remain fixed. Also, the plate that was exposed to light became the actual daguerreotype. There was no negative, and consequently, copies could not be made. However, some refinements of the process did come rapidly. Within 10 years, the exposure time had been reduced to about 30 to 60 seconds, and the process had become so inexpensive that families could purchase two portraits for a quarter. Daguerreotype studios opened

all across Europe and the United States, and families began to collect the rigid, stylized pictures that now seem to reflect days gone by.

THE NEGATIVE   The negative was invented in 1839 by British scientist William Henry Fox Talbot. Talbot found that sensitized paper, coated with emulsions, could be substituted for the copper plate of the daguerreotype. He would place an object, such as a sprig of a plant, on the paper and expose the arrangement to light. The paper was darkened by the exposure in all areas except those covered by the object. Translucent areas, allowing some passage of light, resulted in a range of grays. Talbot's first so-called photogenic drawings (Fig. **8-6**), created by this process, seem eerie, though lyrically beautiful. The delicacy of the image underscores the impracticality of the process: How on earth would you "photograph" an elephant?

As with the daguerreotype, this process produced completed photographs in which the left and right of the image were reversed. In Talbot's photogenic drawings, the light and dark values of the image were also inverted. Talbot improved

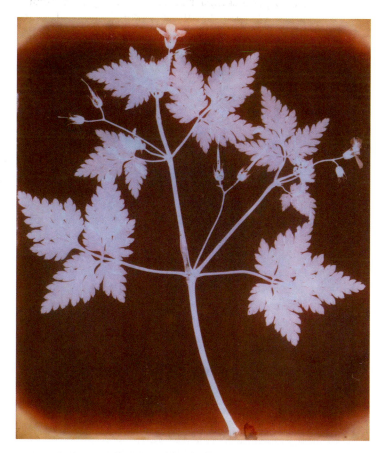

8-6 WILLIAM HENRY FOX TALBOT. *Botanical Specimen* (1839).
Photogenic drawing.

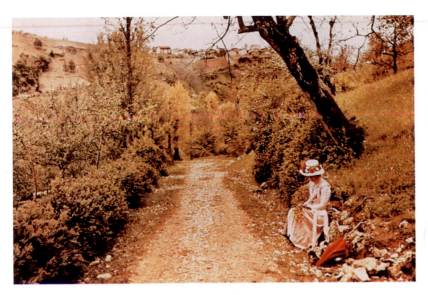

8-7 UNKNOWN (ATTR. LOUIS LUMIÈRE). *Young Lady with an Umbrella* (1906–1910). Autochrome. Institut Lumière, Lyon, France.

a burgeoning business in portrait photography. Having a likeness of oneself was formerly reserved for the wealthy, who could afford to commission painters. Photography became the democratic equalizer. The rich, the famous, and average bourgeois citizens could now become memorable, could now make their presence known long after their flesh had rejoined the elements from which it was composed.

Photographic studios spread like wildfire, and many photographers, such as Julia Margaret Cameron and Gaspard Felix Tournachon—called "Nadar"—vied for famous clientele. Cameron's impressive portfolio included portraits of Charles Dickens; Alfred, Lord Tennyson; and Henry Wadsworth Longfellow. Nadar's 1859 portrait of the actress Sarah Bernhardt (Fig. **8-8**) was printed from a glass plate, which could be used several times to create sharp copies. Early portrait photographers such as Nadar imitated both nature and the arts, using costumes and props that recalled Romantic paintings or sculpted busts caressed by flowing drapery. The photograph is soft and smoothly textured, with middle-range values predominating; Bernhardt is sensitively portrayed as pensive, intelligent, and delicate.

on his early experiments with his development of the **contact print**. He placed the negative in contact with a second sheet of sensitized paper and exposed them both to light. The resultant print was a "positive," with left and right, and light and dark, again as in the original subject. Many prints could be made from the negative. Unfortunately, the prints were not as sharp as daguerreotypes, because they incorporated the texture of the paper on which they were captured. Subsequent advances led to methods in which pictures with the clarity of daguerreotypes could be printed from black-and-white as well as color negatives.

Photography improved rapidly for the next 50 or 60 years—faster emulsions, glass-plate negatives, better camera lenses—and photographs became increasingly more available to the general public. The next major step in the history of photography came with the introduction by Louis Lumière of the autochrome color process in 1907. Autochromes were glass plates coated with a layer of tiny potato starch grains dyed in three different colors. A layer of silver bromide emulsion covered the starch. When the autochrome was developed, it yielded a positive color transparency. Due to the technical limitations of the process Autochrome Lumière photographs, such as *Young Lady with an Umbrella* (Fig. **8-7**), evoke late nineteenth-century French paintings in subject, palette, and texture. Autochrome technology was not replaced until 1932, when Kodak began to produce color film that applied the same principles to more advanced materials.

PORTRAITS By the 1850s, photographic technology and the demands of a growing middle class in the wake of the American and French revolutions came together to create

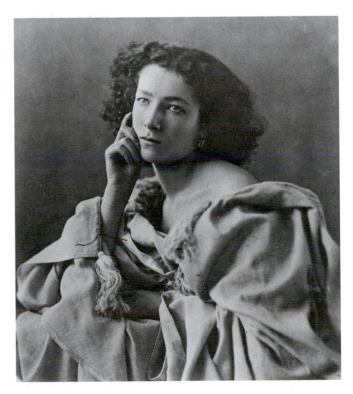

8-8 NADAR. *Sarah Bernhardt* (1859). Bibliothèque Nationale, Paris, France.

The American photographer Alfred Stieglitz (Fig. 1-27) expressed the view that portraits ought to be taken over the course of the subject's lifetime because that was only way to reveal the personality. Over a period of two decades, he photographed Georgia O'Keeffe (see Fig. 20-14) extensively; this body of work contains some 500 negatives. Contemporary photographer Nicholas Nixon began his documentary-portrait series *The Brown Sisters* (Fig. 8-9) in 1975 and has taken one black and white photograph of the group each year since. The format never changes—the sisters are always in the same position from left to right—but the locations do. More than family snapshots, although not unlike them, the series reads like a private diary of sibling relationships and the subtlety of the aging process.

PHOTOJOURNALISM Prior to the nineteenth century, there were few illustrations in newspapers and magazines. Those that did appear were usually in the form of engravings or drawings. Photography revolutionized the capacity of the news media to bring realistic representations of important events before the eyes of the public. Pioneers such as Mathew Brady and Alexander Gardner first used the camera to record major historical events such as the U.S. Civil War. The photographers and their crews trudged down the roads alongside the soldiers, horses drawing their equipment behind them in wagons referred to by the soldiers as "Whatsits."

Equipment available to Brady and Gardner did not allow them to capture candid scenes, so there is no direct record of the bloody to-and-fro of the battle lines, no photographic

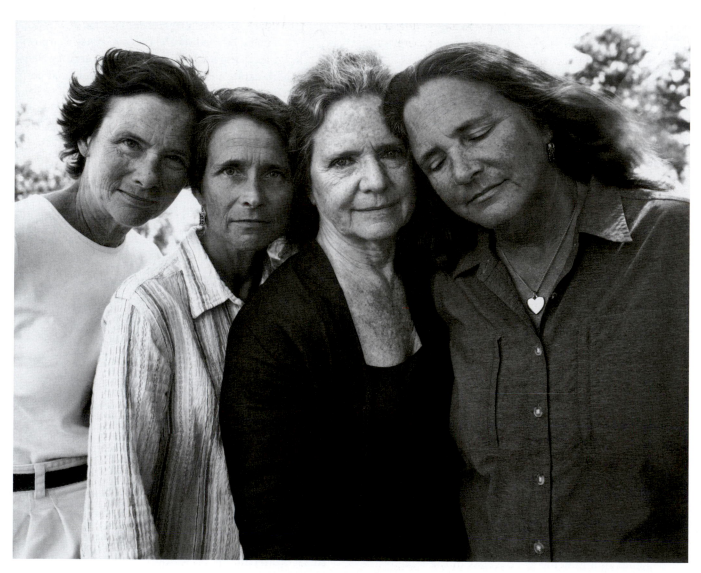

8-9 NICHOLAS NIXON. *The Brown Sisters* (2010). Gelatin silver print. 7 11/16" × 9½". The Museum of Modern Art, NY. The Family of Man Fund.

Documentary photography records the social scene of our time. It mirrors the present and documents [it] for the future. Its focus is man in his relation to mankind. It records his customs at work, at war, at play. . . . It portrays his institutions. . . . It shows not merely their facades, but seeks to reveal the manner in which they function, absorb the life, hold the loyalty, and influence the behavior of human beings.

—Dorothea Lange

record of each lunge and parry. Instead, they brought home photographs of officers and of life in the camps along the lines. Although battle scenes would not hold still for Gardner's cameras, the litter of death and devastation caused by the war and pictured in Gardner's *Home of a Rebel Sharpshooter, Gettysburg* (Fig. **8-10**) most certainly did. Despite their novelty and their accuracy, not many works of such graphic nature were sold. There are at least three reasons for this tempered success. First, the state of the art of photography made the photographs high priced. Second, methods for reproducing photographs on newsprint were not invented until about 1900; therefore, the works of the photojournalists were usually rendered as drawings, and the drawings translated into woodcuts before they appeared in the papers. Third, the American public might not have been ready to face the brutal realities they portrayed. In a similar vein, social commentators have suggested that the will of many Americans to persist in the Vietnam War was sapped by the incessant barrage of televised war imagery.

During the Great Depression of the 1930s, the conscience of the nation was stirred by the work of many photographers hired by the Farm Security Administration. Dorothea Lange

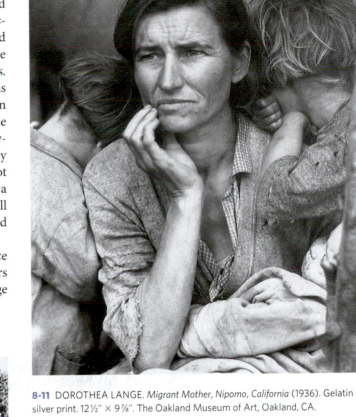

8-11 DOROTHEA LANGE. *Migrant Mother, Nipomo, California* (1936). Gelatin silver print. 12½" × 9⅞". The Oakland Museum of Art, Oakland, CA.

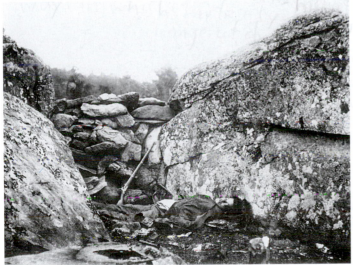

8-10 ALEXANDER GARDNER. *Home of a Rebel Sharpshooter, Gettysburg* (July 1863). Wet-plate photograph. Chicago History Museum, Chicago, IL.

and Walker Evans, among others, portrayed the lifestyles of migrant farmworkers and sharecroppers. Lange's *Migrant Mother* (Fig. **8-11**) is a heartrending record of a 32-year-old woman who is out of work but cannot move on because the tires have been sold from the family car to purchase food for her seven children. The etching in her forehead is an eloquent expression of a mother's thoughts; the lines at the outer edges of her eyes tell the story of a woman who has aged beyond her years. Lange crops her photograph close to her subjects; they fill the print from edge to edge, forcing us to confront them rather than allowing us to seek comfort in a corner of the print not consigned to such an overt display of human misery. The migrant mother and her children, who turn away from the camera and heighten the futility of their plight, are as much constrained by the camera's viewfinder as they are by their circumstances.

In the very year that Lange photographed the migrant mother, Robert Capa's fearless coverage of the Spanish Civil War resulted in such incredible photographs as *Death of a Loyalist Soldier* (see Fig. 3-17). During the early 1940s, photographers such as Margaret Bourke-White carried their hand-held cameras into combat and captured tragic images of the butchery in Europe and in the Pacific. In 1929, Bourke-White became a staff photographer for *Fortune*, a new magazine published by Henry Luce. When Luce founded *Life* in 1936, Bourke-White became one of its original staff photographers. Like Dorothea Lange, she recorded the poverty of the Great Depression, but in the 1940s, she traveled abroad to become one of the first female war photojournalists. As World War II was drawing to an end in Europe, Bourke-White arrived at the Nazi concentration camp of Buchenwald in time for its liberation by Gen. George S. Patton. Her photograph *The Living Dead of Buchenwald* (Fig. 8-12), published in *Life* in 1945, has become a classic image of the Holocaust, the Nazi effort to annihilate the Jewish people. The indifferent countenance of each survivor expresses, paradoxically, all that he has witnessed and endured. In her book *Dear Fatherland, Rest Quietly*, Bourke-White put into words her own reactions to Buchenwald. In doing so, she showed how artistic creation, an intensely emotional experience, can also have the effect of objectifying the subject of creation:

> I kept telling myself that I would believe the indescribably horrible sight in the courtyard before me only when I had a chance to look at my own photographs. Using the camera

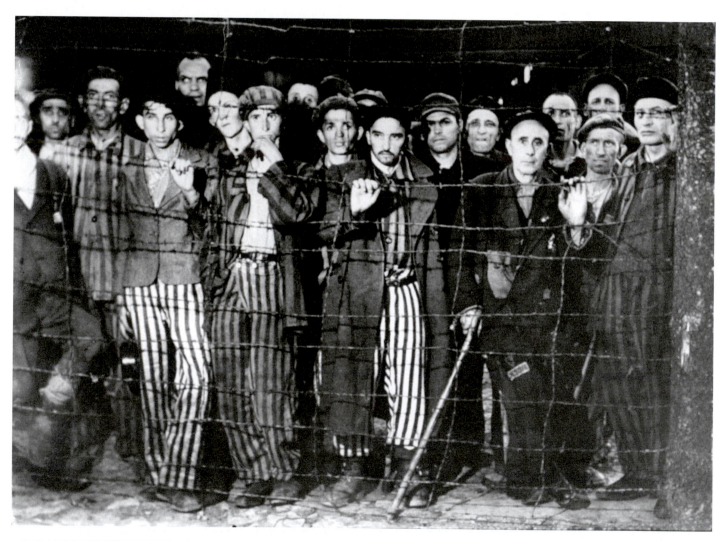

8-12 MARGARET BOURKE-WHITE. *The Living Dead of Buchenwald, April 1945* (1945).

It gradually began to dawn on me that something must be wrong with the art of painting as practiced at that time. With my camera I could procure the same results as those attained by painters. . . . I could express the same moods. Artists who saw my earlier photographs began to tell me that they envied me; that they felt my photographs were superior to their paintings, but that, unfortunately, photography was not an art. . . . There and then I started my fight— or rather my conscious struggle for the recognition of photography as a new medium of expression, to be respected in its own right, on the same basis as any other art form.

—Alfred Stieglitz

was almost a relief; it interposed a slight barrier between myself and the white horror in front of me . . . it made me ashamed to be a member of the human race.[1]

Dorothea Lange traveled rural America to photograph the effects of the Depression, and Margaret Bourke-White followed the U.S. troops abroad during World War II. As Bourke-White discovered, one of the keys to photojournalism is being in the presence of history in the making. On September 11, 2001, when terrorists hijacked commercial aircraft and flew them into the World Trade Center towers, Ron Berard was living on an upper floor of an apartment directly across from the devastation. His photograph (Fig. **8-13**) captures the hellish and almost surreal nature of the event in which almost 3,000 people lost their lives—the shard of the curtain wall that remained, the pile of rubble, the charred facade of a still-standing neighbor. The eerie smoke that rose from the pit would continue to rise for two months.

Another of Berard's photographs—an American flag flying, flapping, snapping against the grim background of the devastation of the World Trade Center site—was published by *Time* magazine. Yet perhaps the best-known photo from the tragedy of September 11 is the one taken a day later by Thomas E. Franklin, a staff photographer for *The Record*, a local New Jersey newspaper. That image of firefighters raising the flag amidst the rubble—a symbol of survival, heroism, and pride—was commemorated in a U.S. postage stamp. Its content, design, and emotional impact have been compared with the equally famous photograph of U.S. Marines raising the flag on the Pacific island of Iwo Jima during World War II.

PHOTOGRAPHY AS AN ART FORM Photographers became aware of the potential of their medium as an art form more than 100 years ago. Edward Weston (see Fig. 2-3), Paul Strand, Edward Steichen, and others argued that photographers must not attempt to imitate painting (as Lumière had) but must find modes of expression that are truer to

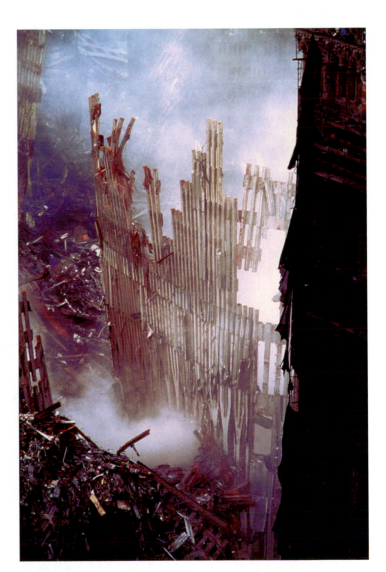

8-13 RON BERARD. *Untitled* (2001).

their medium. Synergistically, painters moved toward abstraction because the obligation to faithfully record nature was now assumed by the photographer. Why, after all, do what a camera can do better? In 1902, Alfred Stieglitz founded the Photo-Secession, a group dedicated to

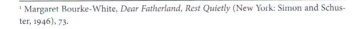

[1] Margaret Bourke-White, *Dear Fatherland, Rest Quietly* (New York: Simon and Schuster, 1946), 73.

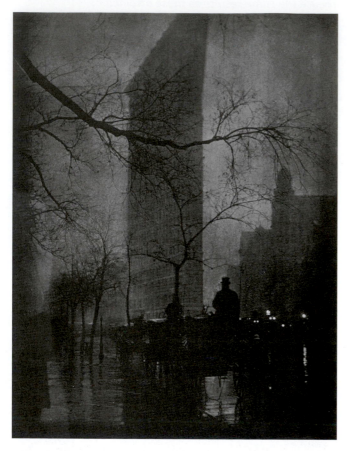

8-14 EDWARD STEICHEN. *The Flatiron Building—Evening* (1906).

cannot readily see, there is nothing gloomy or frightening about the scene. Rather, it seems pregnant with wonderful things that will happen as the rain stops and the twentieth century progresses.

It was not long before artists began to manipulate their medium so that they, too, could venture beyond imitation. The first steps were tentative, building on the familiar and the readily acceptable. Some portrait photographers, for example, experimented with double-exposed images and tableaus—elaborate painted backdrops against which people and objects were thoughtfully and deliberately arranged. The tableau form is also seen in the works of contemporary artists.

Sandy Skoglund's *Radioactive Cats* (Fig. **8-15**) portrays a phlegmatic elderly couple live out their colorless lives amidst an invasion of neon green cats. Skoglund sculpted the plaster cats herself and painted the room gray, controlling every aspect of the set before she photographed the scene.

Artist-photographer William Wegman happened upon his most famous subject when his Weimaraner puppy virtually insisted on performing before his lights. Man Ray, named by Wegman after the Surrealist photographer, posed willingly in hundreds of staged sets that range from the credible to the farcical. *Blue Period* (Fig. **8-16**) is a riff on Pablo Picasso's painting *The Old Guitarist* (see Fig. 20-5), enframed in a souvenir-sized reproduction in the left lower foreground. In both works, a guitar cuts diagonally across the composition, adding the only contrasting color to the otherwise mono-

advancing photography as a separate art form. Stieglitz enjoyed taking pictures under adverse weather conditions and at odd times of day to show the versatility of his medium and the potential for expressiveness.

Edward Steichen's *The Flatiron Building—Evening* (Fig. **8-14**), photographed a century ago, is among the foremost early examples of the photograph as a work of art. It is an exquisitely sensitive nocturne of haunting shapes looming in a rain-soaked atmosphere. The branch in the foreground provides the viewer with a psychological vantage point as it cuts across the composition like a bolt of lightning or an artery pulsing with life. The values are predominantly middle grays, although here and there, beacon-like, streetlamps sparkle in the distance. The infinite gradations of gray in the cast-iron sky-scraper after which the picture is named, and in the surrounding structures, yield an immeasur-able softness. Although much is present that we

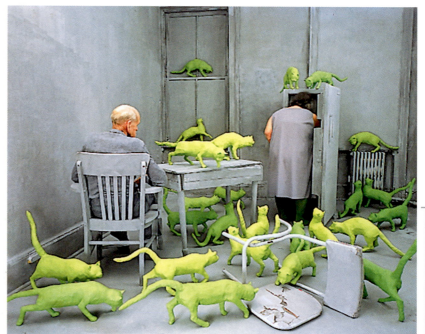

1 ft.

8-15 SANDY SKOGLUND. *Radioactive Cats* (1980). Cibachrome. 30" × 40".

view of the fashion industry. Sherman appears as a disheveled model with a troubling expression. Something here is very wrong. Regimented stripes go awry as the fabric of her dress is stretched taut across her thighs and knees. Her hands rest oddly in her lap, fingertips red with what seems to be blood. And then there is the smile—an unsettling leer implying madness.

Iranian American photographer and video artist Shirin Neshat came to the United States as a teenager, before the shah, or monarch, was removed from power in 1979, and returned in 1990 to witness a nation transformed by the rule of Islamic clergy. She was particularly concerned about how life had changed for Iranian women, who now had limited opportunities outside the home and were veiled behind black

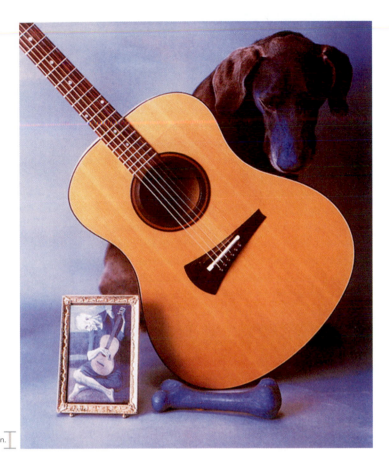

1 in.

8-16 WILLIAM WEGMAN. *Blue Period* (1981). Color Polaroid photograph. 24" × 22".

chromatic blue background. The heads of the old man and of Man Ray hang, melancholy, over the soulful instrument. As Picasso gave the old man's flesh a bluish cast, so did Wegman tint the Weimaraner's muzzle. In Wegman's photograph, however, we find the pièce de résistance—an object laden with profound meaning for the guitarist's stand-in: a blue rubber bone.

Cindy Sherman is her own exclusive subject, adopting diverse personae for her photographs. Sherman recalls a mundane, early inspiration for her approach: "I had all this makeup. I just wanted to see how transformed I could look. It was like painting in a way."[2] Soon she set herself before elaborate backdrops, costumed in a limitless wardrobe. Dress designers began to ask her to use their haute couture in her photographs, and works such as *Untitled* (Fig. **8-17**) were actually shot as part of an advertising assignment for French *Vogue*. The result is less a sales device than a harsh

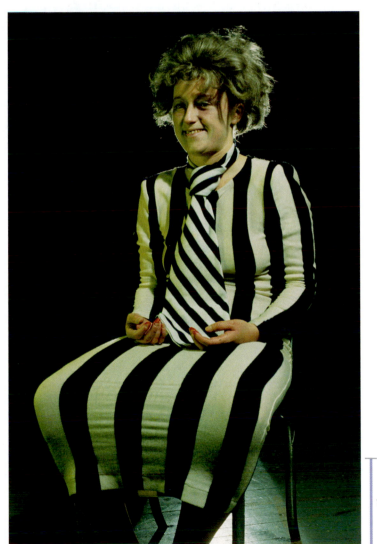

1 ft.

---

[2] Cindy Sherman, in Gerald Marzorati, "Imitation of Life," *Artnews* 82 (September 1983): 84–85.

8-17 CINDY SHERMAN. *Untitled* (1984). Color photograph. 71" × 48½".

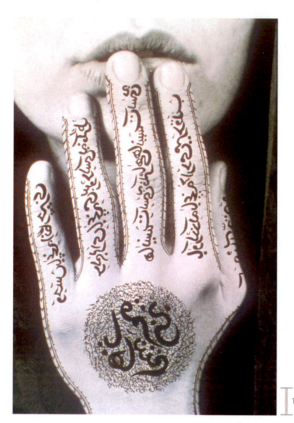

8-18 SHIRIN NESHAT. *Untitled (Women of Allah)* (1994).
Gelatin silver print, ink. 14⅛" × 11".

tured an aerial view of a racetrack in the sprawling desert. Thick lines and shapes of black asphalt crisscross the sand, resembling the broad strokes of an abstract painting. The allusion to works on canvas is underscored by sheer size of his prints: *Bahrain I* is almost 10 feet high.

Evolving technology has made it possible for photographers to achieve dazzling images such as the one in Harold Edgerton's *Milk Drop Coronet* (Fig. **8-20**), featured in the Museum of Modern Art's first exhibition of photography in 1937. Edgerton, called the father of high-speed and stop-action photography, was an electrical engineer at MIT who pioneered the use of the stroboscope—a device that emits brief and brilliant flashes of light that seem to slow or stop the

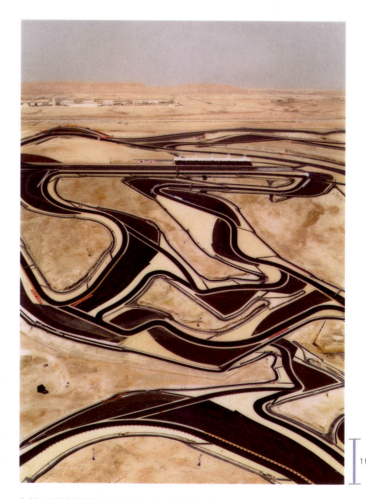

8-19 ANDREAS GURSKY. *Bahrain I* (2005). Chromogenic color print. 9' 10⅞" × 7' 2½". © 2011 Andreas Gursky/Artists Rights Society (ARS), NY/VG Bild-Kunst, Bonn.

chadors. Figure **8-18** is one of a series called *Women of Allah*, in which guns or flowers are frequently juxtaposed with vulnerable though rebellious faces and hands that emerge from beneath the veil. The exposed flesh is overwritten with sensual or political texts by Iranian women in the native tongue of Farsi. To a non-Arabic-speaking Westerner, the calligraphic writing may first appear to be little more than a mélange of elegant and mysterious patterns and designs. Yet there is no mistaking its purpose as one of resistance. The photos are unlikely to be seen and "decoded" by the eyes of Iranians living in Iran, but the message of the artist to the world outside is clear.

In contrast to Skoglund, Wegman, and Neshat, who stage their artistic photographs, Andreas Gursky infers the artistic from existing circumstances, often relying on the absence of context to focus the viewer's attention on lines, patterns, or textures rather than on subject. *Bahrain I* (Fig. **8-19**) is titled after the Middle Eastern island country in which Gursky cap-

action of people or objects in motion—for photography. He would synchronize the flashes with the movements of objects and capture them with an open shutter at many flashes per second. Edgerton applied the technology to capture ordinary and extraordinary events—water coming out of a faucet, a simple drop of milk splashing into a pool of the liquid, bullets penetrating helium balloons, and athletes in motion.

Edgerton's process was the opposite of what photographer Eadweard Muybridge aimed to do in his early experiments in filmmaking. Edgerton froze each and every fraction of actual motion in a single image. Muybridge combined numerous individual photographs of a moving object into a sequence that, if viewed in rapid succession, gave the illusion of actual motion. The door to cinema was open.

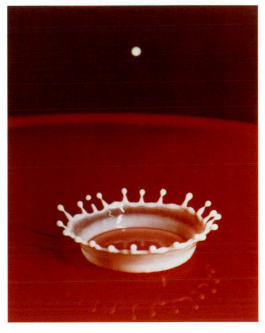

8-20 HAROLD EDGERTON. *Milk Drop Coronet* (1957, printed later). Silver gelatin print. 16" × 20".

FILM

Eadweard Muybridge's *Galloping Horse* (Fig. **8-21**) sequence was shot in 1878 by 24 cameras placed alongside a racetrack and was made possible by new fast-acting photosensitive plates. (If these plates had been developed 15 years earlier, Brady could have bequeathed us a photographic record of Civil War battle scenes.) Muybridge had been commissioned to settle a bet as to whether racehorses ever had all four hooves off the ground at once. He found that they did, but also that they never assumed the rocking-horse position in which the front and back legs are simultaneously extended.

Muybridge is generally credited with performing the first successful experiments in making motion pictures. He fashioned a device that could photograph a rapid sequence of images, and he invented the **Zoopraxiscope**, which projected these images onto a screen.

The birth of cinema was the result, then, of specific inventions. In 1889, Henry Reichenbach, working as an inventor for George Eastman's Kodak company, created film: images printed on celluloid and cut into strips. Two years later,

8-21 EADWEARD MUYBRIDGE. *Galloping Horse* (1878). George Eastman House, International Museum of Photography, Rochester, NY.

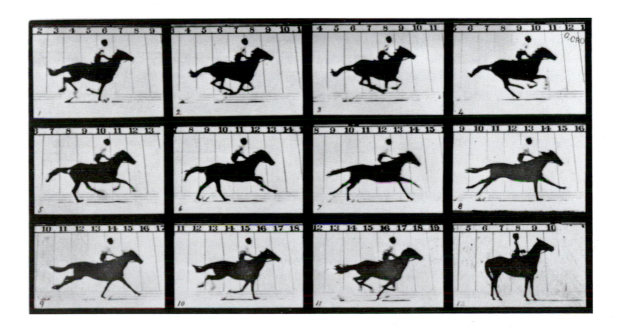

Thomas Alva Edison (who had met Muybridge in 1888) patented the **Kineto-scope**, a motion-picture viewing device. A sequence of images on film (something like Muybridge's galloping horse) was passed over a lamp, the light from which was broken into quick flashes by a revolving shutter placed between the film and the lamp. The light flashes illuminated each frame, and the rapidity of the progression of the frames, along with the phenomenon of persistence of vision, created the illusion of motion.

Edison's Kinetoscope was a box into which a viewer would peer to see a moving picture. The next step in the evolution of cinema was projection of the moving picture; this happened with the Cinematographe, a camera and projector in one piece of equipment, patented by the brothers August and Louis Lumière in France in 1895. Their first public motion-picture projection took place the same year, a 20-minute program of 10 short films. Among them was *The Demolition of a Wall*, a film that is known as the first to feature special effects: Lumière reversed the film to suggest that the wall was going up rather than going down. Soon after, the appearance of trick photography became the staple of Georges Melies, who used stop-motion and superimposed images to create true special effects in films that included adaptations of two novels by Jules Verne—*A Trip to the Moon* and *Twenty Thousand Leagues under the Sea*.

Within a few short years of these inventions, commercial movie houses sprang up in France and in the United States and motion pictures were distributed for public viewing. These were silent films accompanied by live orchestral music and stage shows. The next big step in movie making occurred with the first feature film incorporating sound—*The Jazz Singer* (1927). From then on, sound on film recording shaped the future of cinema.

CINEMATOGRAPHY

Cinematography is the art of making motion pictures by manipulating the technology and processes to achieve desired effects. As in any other medium, cinematography involves artistic choices. The specific cameras and lenses, lighting, "in camera" (multiple exposures, time lapse, or a dissolve or fade-to-black, for example) and postproduction effects, and the film stock that directors and cinematographers use will determine the character of a film. In *Under the Table* (Fig. 8-22),

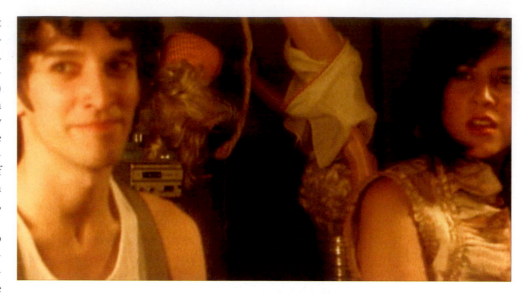

8-22 JORDAN RATHUS. Film still from *Under the Table* (2005). 16mm film. 11 min, 10 sec.

which posits the lives and intimate interactions of a family of four holed up in a post-apocalyptic shelter, filmmaker Jordan Rathus used Kodak Vision2 500T stock to obtain a grainy feel that would match the family's environment—what she describes as "a claustrophobic and long-forgotten bunker filled with retro objects and stale relationships." This film stock also enabled the use of fewer and smaller lights to fill in shadows. Additional methods were employed to "pump up the saturation" of color and achieve a warm look.

Varieties of Cinematographic Techniques

Motion pictures, then, begin with the creation of the illusion of movement; this is accomplished via stroboscopic motion or the presentation of a rapid progression of images of stationary objects. An audience is shown 16 to 24 pictures or frames per second, and each picture or frame differs slightly from the one preceding it. At a rate of 22 or 24 frames per second, the motion in a film seems smooth and natural. But what if a cinematographer wants to tweak that aspect and create the illusion of **slow motion**? It is not a matter of slowing down the rate of frames per second because at fewer than 16 or so the movement will seem choppy. Rather, slow motion is achieved by shooting 100 or more frames per second. When the films are played back at 22 or 24 frames per second, movement appears to be very slow yet smooth and natural. This is one example of the ways in which directors and cinematographers manipulate the materials and processes of the film medium for artistic purposes.

FIXED CAMERAS AND STAGED PRODUCTIONS With a stage play, the audience is fixed and observes the action from a single vantage point. Similarly, many early motion

8-23 BUSBY BERKELEY. Tutti Frutti number from *Dames* (1934).

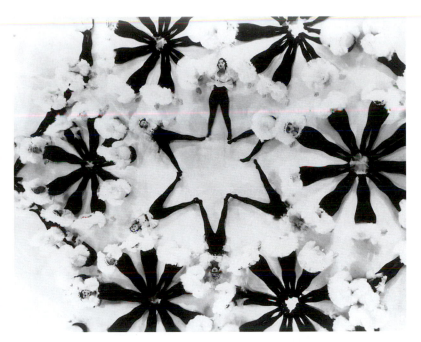

pictures used a single camera that was more or less fixed in place. The first film that the Lumière brothers shot used a fixed camera to record workers, animals, and a man on a bicycle leaving the Lumière Factory (1895). In other early films, actors entered and exited a stage before a fixed camera, much as they do in plays.

For the most part, the Busby Berkeley musicals of the 1930s (Fig. 8-23) were shot on indoor stages that pretended to be nothing but stages. The motion picture had not yet broken free from the stage that had preceded it. Many directors used cinematography to bring the stages of the great urban centers to small cities and rural towns. We can note that the musicals of the 1930s were everything that the photographs of Dorothea Lange and the other Depression photographers were not: they were bubbly, frivolous, light, even saucy. Perhaps they helped Americans make it through these difficult times. Some musicals of the 1930s showed apple-cheeked kids getting their break on the Great White Way. Others portrayed the imaginary shenanigans of the wealthy few in an innocent era when Hollywood believed that they would offer amusement and inspiration to destitute audiences rather than stir feelings of social conflict through depiction of conspicuous consumption and frivolity.

THE MOBILE CAMERA Film critics usually argue that motion pictures should tell their stories in ways that are inimitable through any other medium. One way is through the mobile camera. Film pioneer D. W. Griffith is credited with making the camera mobile. He attached motion-picture cameras to rapidly moving vehicles and used them to **pan** across expanses of scenery and action, as in the battle scenes in his *Birth of a Nation* (Fig. 8-24). Today it is not unusual for cameras to be placed aboard rapidly moving vehicles and also to **zoom** in on and away from their targets.

EDITING Griffith is also credited with making many advances in film editing. **Editing** is the separating and assembling, sometimes called "patching

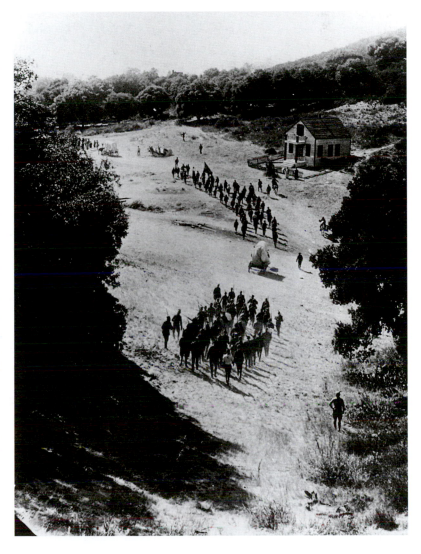

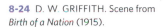
8-24 D. W. GRIFFITH. Scene from *Birth of a Nation* (1915).

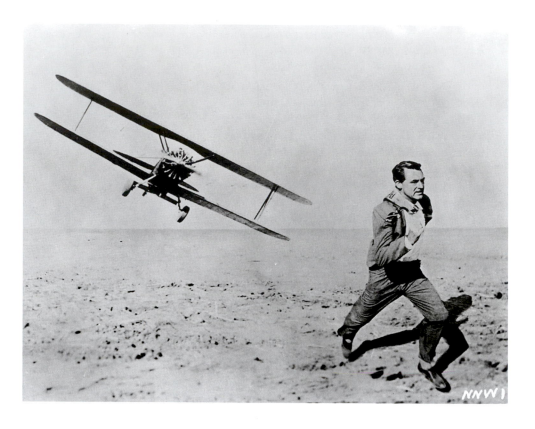

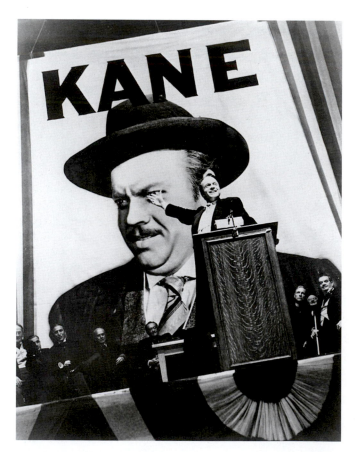

8-26 ORSON WELLES. Film still from *Citizen Kane* (1941).

and pasting," of sequences of film. Editing helps make stories coherent and heightens dramatic impact.

In **narrative editing**, multiple cameras are used during the progress of the same scene or story location. Then shots are selected from various vantage points and projected in sequence. Close-ups may be interspersed with **longshots**, providing the audience with abundant perspectives on the action while advancing the story. Close-ups usually better communicate the emotional responses of the actors, whereas longshots describe the setting, as in Alfred Hitchcock's thriller *North by Northwest* (Fig. **8-25**).

In **parallel editing**, the story shifts back and forth from one event or scene to another. Scenes of one segment of a battlefield may be interspersed with events taking place at another location or back home, collapsing space. Time may also be collapsed through parallel editing, with the cinematographer shifting back and forth between past, present, and future.

In the **flashback**, one form of parallel editing, the story line is interrupted by the portrayal or narration of an earlier episode, often through the implied fantasies of a principal character. Orson Welles's *Citizen Kane* (Fig. **8-26**) innovated the use of the flashback, which usually gives current action more meaning. In the **flash-forward**, editing permits the audience to see glimpses of the future. The flash-forward is frequently used at the beginning of dramatic television shows to capture the interest of the viewer who may be switching channels.

Motion pictures may proceed from one scene to another by means of **fading**. The current scene becomes gradually dimmer, or *fades out*. The subsequent scene then grows progressively brighter, or *fades in*. In the more rapid, current technique of the **dissolve**, the subsequent scene becomes brighter and the current scene fades out so that the first scene seems to dissolve into the second.

In **montage**, a sequence of abruptly alternating images or scenes conveys associated ideas or the passage of time. Images can suddenly flash into focus or whirl about for impact, as in a series of newspaper headlines meant to show the progress of the actors over time.

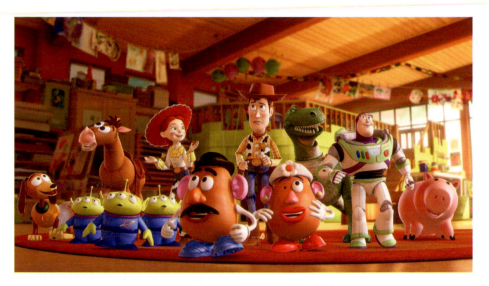

8-28 Film still from *Toy Story 3* (2010).

COLOR Color came into use in the 1930s. One early color film, *The Wizard of Oz*, depicted the farm world of Kansas in black and white and the imaginary Oz in glorious, often expressionistic color. Madonna sort of reverses the pattern in *Truth or Dare*, where her stage performances (fantasy?) are in color and her (real?) backstage life is in black and white. Yet interestingly, this pattern is now frequently reversed in music videos, where fantasy is often portrayed in black and white and reality in (everyday, natural?) color.

The screen version of Margaret Mitchell's *Gone with the Wind* (Fig. **8-27**) was one of the first color epics, or "spectaculars." It remains one of the highest-grossing works of all film eras. In addition to the sweeping **panoramas** of the Civil War battlefield wounded and the burning of Atlanta, *Gone with the Wind* included close-ups of the passion and fire communicated by Clark Gable as Rhett Butler and Vivien Leigh as Scarlett O'Hara.

ANIMATION **Animation** is the creation of a motion picture by photographing a series of drawings, each of which shows a stage of movement that differs slightly from the one preceding it. As a result, projecting the frames in rapid sequence creates the illusion of movement. The first cartoons were in black and white and employed a great deal of repetition.

During the 1930s, Walt Disney's studios began to produce full-color stories and images that have become part of our collective unconscious mind. Disney characters such as Mickey Mouse, Donald Duck, Bambi, Snow White, and Pinocchio are national treasures. In recent years, Disney has collaborated with Pixar Animation Studios to create a new generation of computer-animated films, including *Toy Story*; *Finding Nemo*; *Monsters, Inc.*; *The Incredibles*; *Up* (winner of two Academy Awards in 2010); and *Toy Story 3* (also winner of two Academy Awards, in 2011) (Fig. **8-28**). These films represent a dramatic technological departure from earlier animated features: they are created using computer graphics, more specifically three-dimensional computer-generated imagery (CGI). *Toy Story 3* was also the first animated film to be released in theatres with 7.1 surround sound, a system of eight speakers placed throughout the theater carrying eight channels of sound.

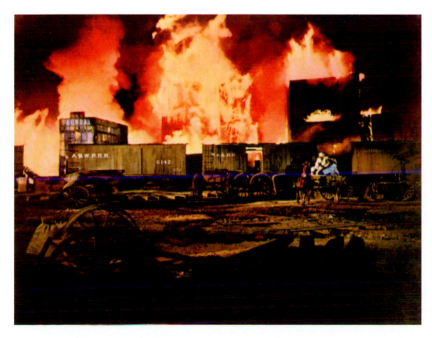

8-27 VICTOR FLEMING. "The Burning of Atlanta," film still from *Gone with the Wind* (1939).

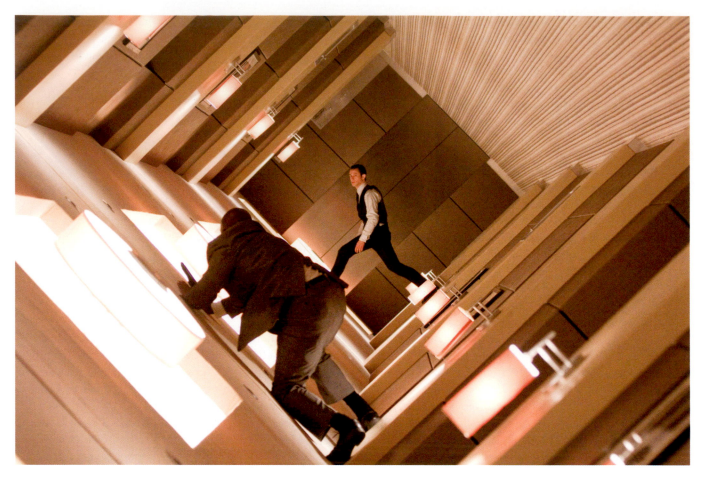

8-29 CHRISTOPHER NOLAN. Film still from *Inception* (2010).

SPECIAL EFFECTS In a turn-of-the-century example of special effects, George Melies made a film in which a music master removes his own head, soon to be replaced by a succession of heads that he persistently takes off one after the other. He tosses the heads onto a telegraph wire, each of which forms a musical note. Over the years, filmmakers have raised the technical bar for special effects in their action movies. The industry has come a long way, from Melies's trick photography and tiny exploding capsules planted in the ground to simulate gunfire to the extravaganzas of effects in films such as *Avatar* (2009) and *Inception* (2010; winner of 2011 Academy Award for special effects) (Fig. 8-29). Complex motorized sets and remote-controlled models as well as extensive computer graphics combine to create an extreme illusion of the director's reality. Notable scenes in *Inception* (the hotel corridor and the outdoor Paris café) feature complex movable sets, location explosions, sophisticated camera work, and postproduction enhancements using digital technology.

Varieties of Cinematographic Experience

No discussion of cinematography can hope to recount adequately the richness of the motion-picture experience. Broadly speaking, motion pictures are visual experiences that entertain or move us. For example, as in novels, we identify with characters and become wrapped up in plots. Like other artists, cinematographers make us laugh (consider the great films of the Marx brothers and Laurel and Hardy); create propaganda, satire, social commentary, fantasy, and symbolism; express artistic theories; and reflect artistic styles. Let us consider some of these more closely.

PROPAGANDA Although there are some early (and choppy) film records of World War I, cinematography was ready for World War II. In fact, while many American actors were embattled in Europe and the Pacific, former president Ronald Reagan was making films for the United States that depicted the valor of the Allied soldiers and the malevolence of the enemy.

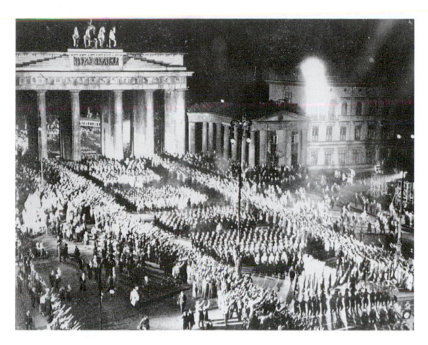

8-30 LENI RIEFENSTAHL. Film still from *Triumph of the Will* (1936).

tage of people, monuments, and flag-bedecked buildings unified flesh and stone into a hymn to Nazism. The United States, England, Canada, and some other nations paid a backhanded compliment to the power of *Triumph of the Will* by banning it.

SATIRE Satire is the flip side of propaganda. Although Riefenstahl glorified national socialism in Germany, American filmmakers derided it. In one cartoon, for example, Daffy Duck clubs a realistic-looking, speechifying Adolf Hitler over the head with a mallet. Hitler dissolves into tears and calls for his mommy. British American filmmaker Charlie Chaplin added to the derision of the Führer in *The Great Dictator* (Fig. 8-31). The film and television series *M*A*S*H* was set during the Korean War, but it satirized authoritarianism through the ages.

Our adversaries were active as well. Before the war, in fact, German director Leni Riefenstahl made what is considered one of the greatest (though also most pernicious) propaganda films of all time, *Triumph of the Will* (Fig. 8-30). Riefenstahl transformed the people and events of an historic event, the 1935 Nuremberg Congress, into abstract, symbolic patterns through the juxtaposition of longshots and close-ups, and aerial and ground-level views. Her mon-

SOCIAL COMMENTARY Filmmakers, like documentary photographers, have made their social comments. *The Grapes of Wrath* (Fig. 8-32), based on the John Steinbeck novel, depicts one family's struggle for survival during the Great Depression, when the banks failed and the Midwest farm basket of the United States turned into the Dust Bowl. Like a Dorothea Lange photograph, the camera comes in to record hopelessness and despair. Cinematographers have commented on subjects as varied as *Divorce, American Style*; *The Killing Fields* of Southeast Asia; and the excesses of *Wall Street*.

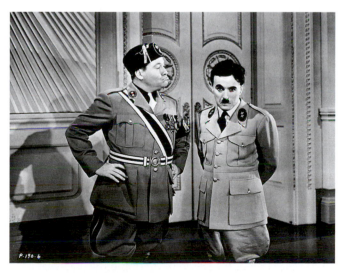

8-31 CHARLES CHAPLIN. Film still from *The Great Dictator* (1940).

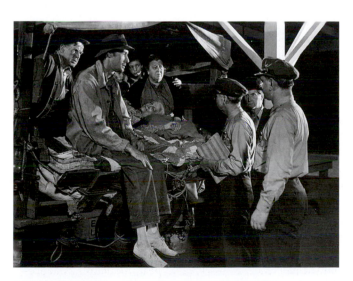

8-32 JOHN FORD. Film still from *The Grapes of Wrath* (1940).

Cinematography **169**

I can make an audience laugh, scream with terror, smile, believe in legends, become indignant, take offense, become enthusiastic, lower itself or yawn with boredom. I am, then, either a deceiver or—when the audience is aware of the fraud—an illusionist. I am able to mystify, and I have at my disposal the most precious and the most astounding device [the motion-picture camera] that has ever, since history began, been put into the hands of the juggler.

—Ingmar Bergman

FANTASY Fantasy and flights of fancy are not limited to paintings, drawings, and the written word. In the experimental films of Robert Wiene and Salvador Dalí and Luis Buñuel, events are not confined to the material world as it is; they occupy and express the innermost images of the cinematographer. The sets for Wiene's *The Cabinet of Dr. Caligari* (Fig. **8-33**) were created by three painters who employed Expressionist devices such as angular, distorted planes and sheer perspectives. The hallucinatory backdrop removes the protagonist, a carnival hypnotist who causes a sleepwalker to murder people who displease him, from the realm of reality. The muddy line between the authentic and the fantastic is further obscured by the film's ending, in which the hypnotist becomes a mental patient telling an imaginary tale. (It is akin to the ravings of the mad Salieri, who, through flashbacks, recounts his actual and fantasized interactions with Mozart in the film *Amadeus*.)

Caligari has a story, albeit an unusual one, but Dalí and Buñuel's surrealistic *Un Chien Andalou* (Fig. **8-34**) has a script (if you can call it a script) without order or meaning in the traditional sense. In the shocking opening scene, normal vision is annulled by the slicing of an eyeball. The audience is then propelled through a series of disconnected, dreamlike scenes.

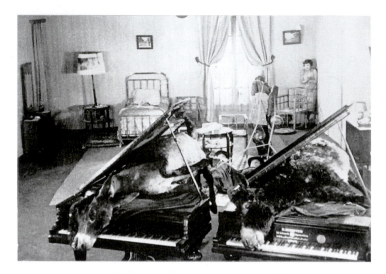

8-34 SALVADOR DALÍ AND LUIS BUÑUEL. Film still from *Un Chien Andalou* (1928). © Salvador Dalí, Fundació Gala-Salvador Dalí/Artists Rights Society (ARS), NY, 2011.

SYMBOLISM In writing about *Un Chien Andalou*, Buñuel claimed that his aims were to evoke instinctive reactions of attraction and repulsion in the audience, but that nothing in the film *symbolized* anything.[3] Fantastic cinematographers often portray their depths of mind literally. They create on the screen the images that dwell deep within their minds. Other cinematographers, such as Ingmar Bergman, frequently express aspects of their inner world through symbols.

Since the 1950s, filmgoers have been struck by Bergman's mostly black-and-white films (Fig. **8-35**). As in so much other art, nature serves as counterpoint to the vicissitudes of the human spirit in Bergman's films. The Swedish summers are short and precious. The bleak winters seem, to Bergman, to be the enduring fact of life. Against their backdrop, he portrays modern alienation from comforting religion and tradition. Bergman's films have ranged from jocular comedies to unrelieved dark dramas, and his bewitching screen images have brought together Nordic mythology and themes of love, death, and ultimate aloneness.

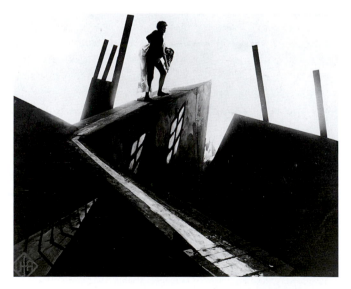

8-33 ROBERT WIENE. Film still from *The Cabinet of Dr. Caligari* (1919).

[3] Luis Buñuel, "Notes on the Making of *Un Chien Andalou*," in Art in Cinema, a symposium held at the San Francisco Museum of Art (repr., New York: Arno Press, 1968).

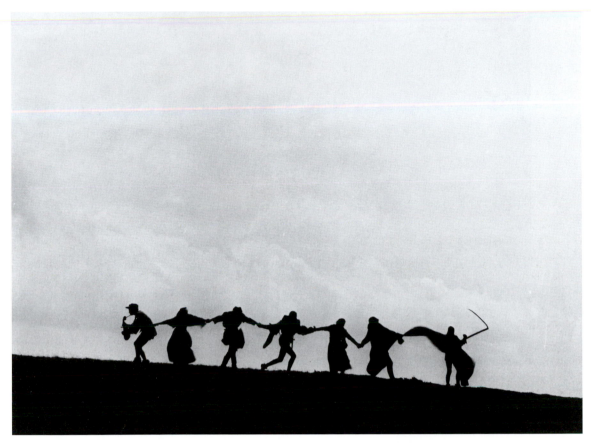

8-35 INGMAR BERGMAN. Film still from *The Seventh Seal* (1956).

VIDEO

Video technology was invented for television, which debuted to the masses in 1939 at the New York World's Fair in Flushing Meadows, Queens. As with film, video cameras capture and record a series of still images that are then reconstructed into a moving picture. With video, sights and sounds are transformed into electronic messages in the form of lengthy codes (a pattern of ones and zeros). Video also differs from film in the format of its storage systems. Today, analog video formats (VHS and Betamax, for example) have been largely replaced by digital formats (including DVD, Blu-Ray, QuickTime, and MPEG-4). Digital information can also be transmitted wirelessly or by cable; the television set then reconstructs the digital information into visual images and sounds.

Over about 60 years, television has radically altered American life and placed the American lifestyle before the world. Commercial television broadcasts many of the images that reflect and create our common contemporary culture—from reality programming like MTV's *Jersey Shore*, Bravo's *Real Housewives of* (fill in your favorite location), and Fox Network's *So You Think You Can Dance* to original program-

ming like HBO's *Sopranos*, *The Wire*, and *True Blood*; AMC's *Mad Men*, or ABC's cult classic *Lost*. Children spend as many hours in front of a TV set as they do in school, as congressional committees debate potential effects such as childhood obesity and the impact of televised violence.

"Live" TV coverage enabled hundreds of millions of viewers to witness Neil Armstrong's first steps on the moon in 1969. Millions watched in horror the live assassination of John F. Kennedy in 1963 and the explosion of the space shuttle *Challenger* in 1986. Viewers who came to be called "gulf potatoes" seemed to be addicted to the televising of the Gulf War, the nation's first real video war—which began with CNN's live description of fighter-bombers over Baghdad in 1991. In 2001, viewers watched the destruction of the World Trade Center live—whether from the suburbs of New York or from Chicago or Los Angeles—and in January 2011, the world witnessed the peaceful protests leading to revolution in the country of Egypt. Viewers become, so to speak, a single community connected by wireless broadcasting and by cable.

Commercial television programming, broadcast in the United States by privately owned media corporations, offers a wide variety of options to viewers, including news and

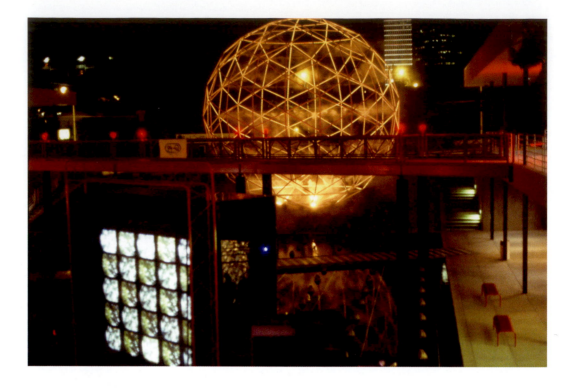

8-36 DARA BIRNBAUM. *Rio Videowall* (1989). Installation view of videowall in the public plaza of the Rio Shopping/ Entertainment Complex, Atlanta, GA.

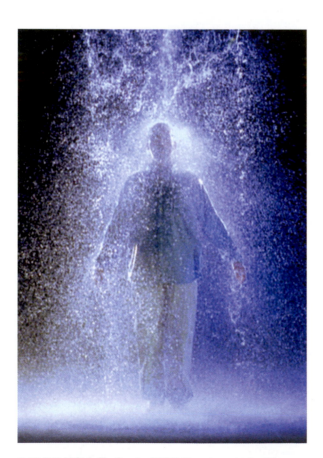

8-37 BILL VIOLA. *The Crossing* (1996). Two-channel color video and stereo-sound installation, continuous loop. 192" × 330" × 684". Solomon R. Guggenheim Museum, NY.

commentary, sporting events, situation comedies, reality programming, and films.

Video as a medium, distinguished from the commercial efforts of the television establishment, was introduced in the 1960s. Almost 30 years later, Dara Birnbaum addressed the relationship between television and video art, between the media and its mass-culture consumerism on the one hand and the discourse of contemporary art on the other. *Rio Videowall* (Fig. 8-36), an interactive public work of art commissioned by the developers of the Rio Shopping/Entertainment Complex in Atlanta, Georgia, consists of 25 monitors arranged in a five-by-five grid, in which individual moving images are unified into a single, although shifting composition. Movement of the shoppers triggers a change of imagery on the screens that includes snippets of live news feeds juxtaposed with an almost nostalgic reflection on nature at its most pristine—the land before the onslaught of the shopping mall.

Just as the Lumière brothers used film primarily as a documentary medium, artists first used video to record and document performances that were site specific and of limited duration. And just as Melies favored fantasy over reality in his early artistic films, generations of contemporary artists have appropriated video as their medium in the creation of works of art—video art.

Fantasy and documentary continue to be approaches to video art. Consider the works of Bill Viola and Gillian Wearing. Bill Viola's *The Crossing* (Fig. 8-37) is a video/sound installation that engulfs the senses and aims to transport the viewer into a spiritual realm. In this piece, the artist simultaneously projects two video channels onto separate 16-foot-high screens or on the back and front of the same screen. In each video, a man enveloped in darkness appears and approaches until he fills the screen. On one channel, a fire breaks out at his feet and grows until the man is apparently consumed in flames (the content is not what we would call graphic or disturbing, however). On the other channel, the one shown here, drops of water fall onto the man's head, develop into rivulets, and then inundate him. The sound tracks accompany the screenings with audio of torrential rain and of a raging inferno. The dual videos wash over the viewer with their contrasts of cool and hot colors and their encompassing sound. Critics speak about the spiritual nature of Viola's work, but it is also about the here-and-now reality of the viewer's sensory experience elicited by the encounter with the work.

By contrast, Gillian Wearing often incorporates a documentary style in her video art. In the multiscreen *Family History* (Fig. **8-38**), she juxtaposes footage from a 1974 BBC documentary series called *The Family* with a present-day interview with one of the original cast/family members, and a staged narrative in which someone posing as a young Gillian Wearing is watching the old TV show. The work invites reflection on the definition of reality and the limitations of the documentary genre. It also penetrates the relationship between the private and public realms, of intimate family dynamics with spectatorship.

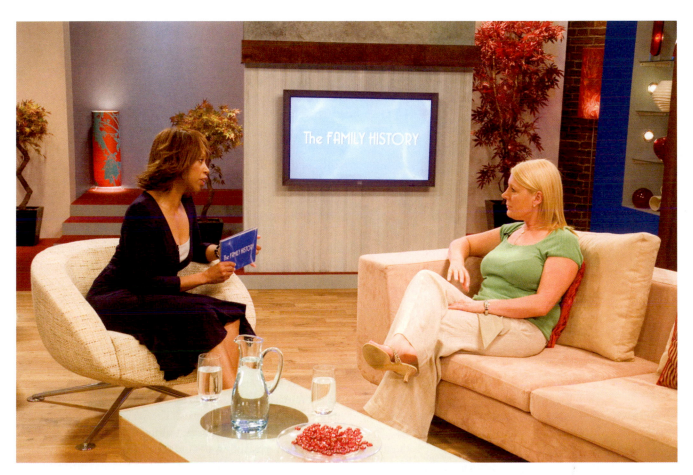

8-38 GILLIAN WEARING. *Family History* (2006). Shown at Brindley House, Newhall Street, Birmingham, England.

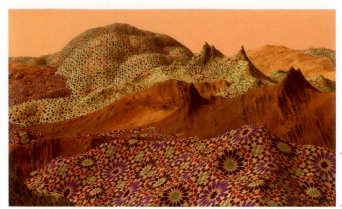

8-40 YAEL KANAREK. *Copy: Potentially Endless A* (2007). Lambda print. 44½" × 70". Edition of 3.

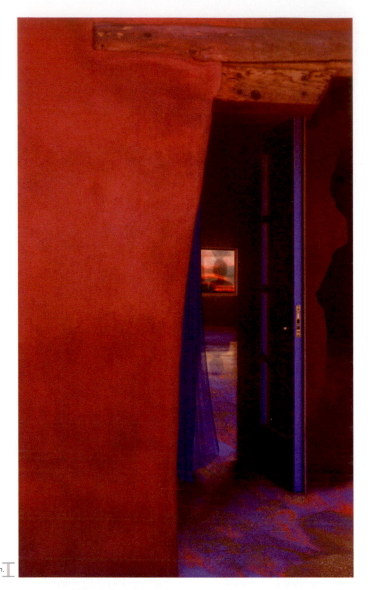

8-39 RUANE MILLER. *Blue Door* (2008). Archival limited edition digital print. 38" × 22¾".

DIGITAL ART

Most readers undoubtedly have toyed with computer programs such as Microsoft's Paint or Paintbrush or Apple's iPhoto or iMovie. Software such as this, typically part of the computer manufacturer's standard package, enables the user—artistic or otherwise—to create illustrations by manipulating stock shapes, drawing "freehand," "spray painting" color fields, or enhancing the images with a variety of textural patterns—all of which are selected by directing the mouse to a menu of techniques and design elements. The resultant shapes or drawings can be flipped and rotated or stretched in any direction. Even word-processing programs can be used to distort and otherwise play with images. Other

programs enable one to manipulate digital photographs and edit videos. In today's computer-tech-savvy environment, it is no longer unusual for the average teenager to be familiar with Adobe Photoshop software. Artistic results are only a point-and-click away.

Today computer graphics software programs offer palettes of tens of millions of colors, which can be selected and produced on the monitor almost instantaneously. Compositions can be recolored in seconds. Effects of light and shade and simulated textured surfaces can be produced with the point and click of a mouse. Software programs enable artists to create three-dimensional representations with such astounding realism that they cannot be distinguished from photos or films of real objects in space. They can be viewed from any vantage point and in any perspective. Images can be saved or stored in any stage of their development, be brought back into the computer's memory at will, and modified as desired, without touching the original image. It is difficult to believe that these images are stored in computers as series of zeroes and ones, and not as pictures, but they are.

Broadly speaking, digital art is the production of images by artists with the assistance of the computer. Ruane Miller's *Blue Door* (Fig. 8-39) begins with a photograph taken by the artist that is then altered using Photoshop painterly manipulations and compositing techniques. She is "interested in creating a coherent image with a convincing reality, though, after all . . . a virtual reality." Describing her work, Miller notes "Harmony, tension, complexity and counterbalance in the use of color, detail, and form are basic to the structure of [her] images."

Yael Kanarek's digital landscape in *Copy: Potentially Endless A* (Fig. 8-40) is a screenshot of an interactive digital journal containing entries by a virtual character whose gender and ethnicity remain hidden to us. The viewer finds love letters and travel logs that have been written by the character in the course of an expedition to find treasure in a fantastic desert landscape. The work is constructed of networked interfaces featuring text, photography, sculpture, and performance.

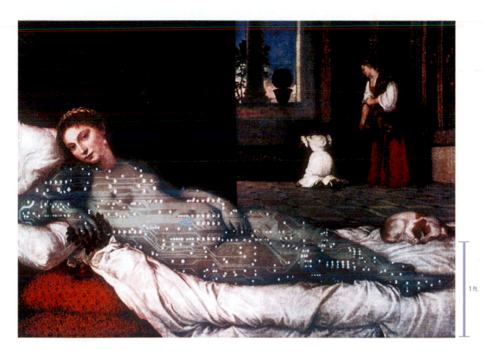

8-41 LYNN HERSHMAN. *Digital Venus* (1996). Iris print. 40⅛" × 59¾".

ums that narrow the gap, as it were, between them and the rest of us who are just seeking to express ourselves in some way. Portuguese-born artist, Jorge Colombo, creates his so-called "finger paintings" (Fig. **8-42**) on an Apple iPad using an "app" called Brushes. Because of the responsiveness of the app to quick, loose drawing, Colombo has used his device, on location, as an electronic sketchbook and diary of his impressions of New York City. Some of these drawings, which have garnered much attention and recognition as covers for *The New Yorker* magazine, are printed with special programs that allow for high-resolution large-format images.

Artists not only appropriate the technology of the day, but they also appropriate images that have special meaning within a culture. Lynn Hershman's *Digital Venus* (Fig. **8-41**) starts with Titian's well-known Renaissance painting *Venus of Urbino* (see Fig. 16-27) and substitutes digital imagery for the sumptuous glazes that defined the body. Many of Hershman's works comment on the voyeurism we find in the video medium, and *Digital Venus* is a way of showing how frequently the images that affect us are composed of pixels—microscopically small bits of digital information that fool our senses into believing we are somehow connecting with a corporeal reality. And like the work of Dara Birnbaum, *Digital Venus* addresses feminist issues pertaining to the male gaze and the exploitation of women.

Artists are now only scratching the surface of digital art as a medium. Art courses in digital arts and interactive multimedia have never been more in demand. Just as photography was once termed a "democratizer" in the visual arts—enabling anyone with a camera to capture anything— so has the ubiquitousness of the digital camera and computer opened the door to limitless experimentation among artists and outsiders alike.

The relative accessibility to non-artists of technology and software that will yield "artistic results" has spawned any number of manipulated digital photographs and videos appearing on social media sites. Apple's iPhoto, for example, allows you to take a picture of yourself and then transform it with options such as "Color Pencil," "Comic Book," or even "Pop Art"—which renders a single image into multiples in a grid that is a throwback to Andy Warhol. It is no surprise, then, that contemporary artists are creating works in medi-

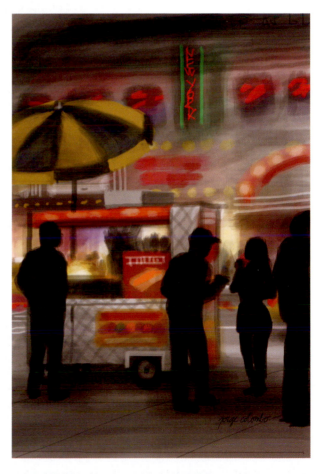

8-42 JORGE COLOMBO. *42nd Street* (2009). Finger painting (using Brushes on Apple iPad). Pixel dimensions: 1024 × 768 (7.75 × 5.82 inches). Originally published as the June 2009 cover image in *The New Yorker*.

Digital Art **175**

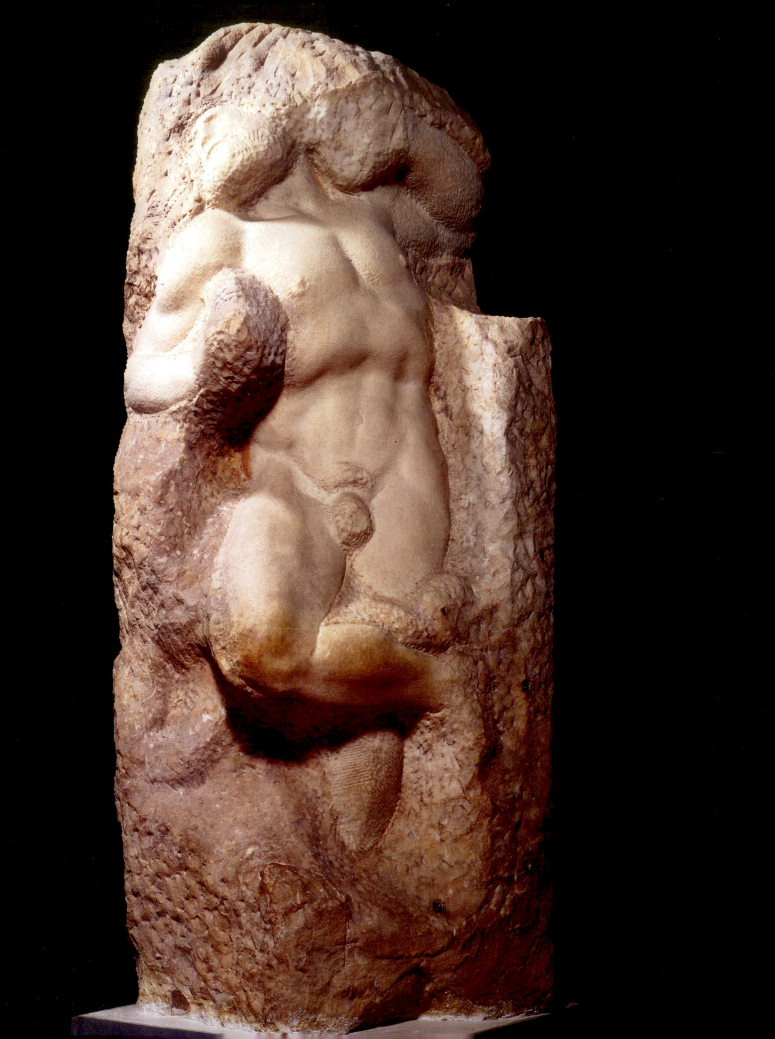

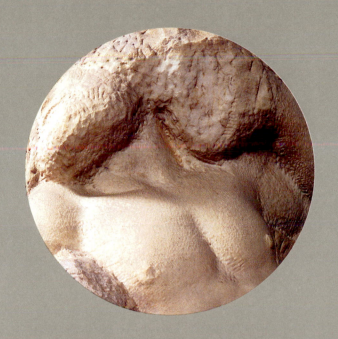

SCULPTURE

9

In *Metamorphosis*, Ovid's poetic narrative of the creation of the world, we meet a young Cypriot sculptor named Pygmalion. Now Pygmalion is pretty cynical about love. He vows never to marry, instead devoting his life to the perfection of his craft. Never say never. Pygmalion outdoes himself in carving a sculpture of a beautiful woman in ivory—so stunning, so lifelike, that he falls in love with his statue (Fig. 9-1). He makes a wish that his idol be brought to life and Venus hears his plea—the sculpture becomes flesh and Pygmalion finds his bride.

The myth of Pygmalion has been depicted in many versions and mediums, a subject that has suggested both the technical prowess of sculptors and the power to create the illusion of reality in spite of the harsh, seemingly unforgiving materials with which they work: marble, stone, bronze. Seeing Bernini's *Apollo and Daphne* (Fig. 2-72) in the flesh dispels any doubt that his skill was nothing short of transformative. The brain can hardly register as marble that which the eye sees.

Realism is, of course, only one stylistic dimension of sculpture, and marble, bronze, and wood are only a few examples of the wealth of materials that sculptors use. This chapter considers the definitions, materials, and techniques of sculpture—the carving, modeling, casting, constructing, and assembling of materials and objects into (primarily) three-dimensional works of art.

MICHELANGELO. The Cross-Legged Captive (c. 1530–1534). Marble. H: 7'6½". Galleria dell'Accademia, Florence, Italy.

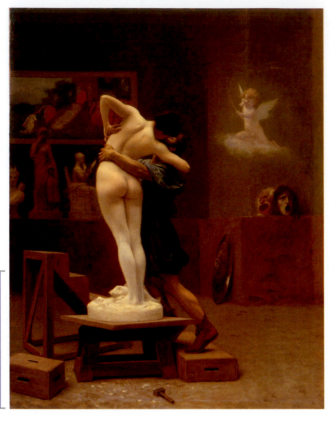

9-1 JEAN-LÉON GÉRÔME. *Pygmalion and Galatea* (c. 1890). Oil on canvas. 35" × 27". The Metropolitan Museum of Art, NY.

1 ft.

SCULPTURE

A viewer's relationship to a sculpture is often much more complex than it is to a drawing or painting. Two-dimensional works generally are viewed from a single, optimal perspective—head-on. Sculpture, on the other hand, exhibited—as it often is—in the open space of a gallery, museum, or the great outdoors, beckons the viewer to participate in the revelation of its form by walking around the work and observing it from multiple viewpoints.

Not all sculpture is three-dimensional, nor is all of it intended to be viewed from more than one vantage point. Sculpture is broadly categorized into two types: **relief sculpture** and **free-standing sculpture**, or **sculpture-in-the-round**. In a relief, figures or images project to varying degrees from a two-dimensional plane (a plank of wood or a slab of marble, for example). If the imagery does not project significantly from the surface, we refer to the technique as **low or bas-relief**. In **high relief**, by contrast, figures project dramatically from the plane of the relief, so much so that they barely seem attached to the background. It is not uncommon to see a combination of high, middle, and bas-relief in a single sculpture (see Fig. 16-9) and reliefs can be created in any material, including

bronze. As with two-dimensional works of art, though, reliefs are intended to be viewed primarily from one perspective. It is true that some freestanding sculpture or sculpture-in-the-round is meant to be seen head-on, from an optimal vantage point, or is installed in such a way that a viewer cannot walk completely around it (Fig. 17-7). But sculpture-in-the-round is not connected to a two-dimensional surface and, importantly, it is carved or cast or assembled in three dimensions.

Sculpture is also described, in the broadest of terms, by the basic process used to create it: subtractive or additive. With a **subtractive process**, such as carving, material is removed from the original, raw mass in order to define a figure or an image. With an **additive process**, such as modeling, material is added or built up to reach a desired form. These processes are linked to a wide variety of sculptural techniques.

Carving

In **carving**, a subtractive process, the sculptor begins with a block of material and chips or cuts portions of it away until the desired result takes shape. Carving is a demanding technique that requires intense physical labor. The idiosyncrasies of materials—stone, wood, ivory—influence the mechanics of the carving process, the sculptor's choice of tools, and the overall effect of the final product.

Michelangelo carved all of his sculptures from single blocks of marble, leading a fellow artist to say that "You could roll them down a mountain and no piece would come off." Sure and confident in his skill, Michelangelo said that he was simply "liberating the figure from the marble that imprisons it." This description of his technique is clearly illustrated in *The Cross-Legged Captive* (Fig. **9-2**), one of a series of unfinished sculptures intended for the tomb of his patron Pope Julius II. Because so much of the marble block remains around the partially embedded figure, we can see that Michelangelo worked from front-to-back; it is as if the figure is materializing from the stone before our eyes or wrestling to break free of it. The contrast between the gouged surfaces of the marble block and the supple flesh and smooth planes of muscle reveals a clash of raw energy and meticulous attention to realistic detail. There is a tension in *The Cross-Legged Captive*—movement balanced by restraint—that creates a sense of anticipation in the work. We seem to await the liberation of a slave from bondage, the emergence of perfection from the imperfect.

Carving, by its very nature, is subtractive. But this does not mean that all carved works of sculpture that you will view have necessarily been hewn from a single block of material. Although Michelangelo is renowned for having worked exclusively (and almost flawlessly) with single blocks of marble, other sculptors were known to cover up mistakes in carving by adding pieces of marble to their compositions. Too much subtraction sometimes resulted in addition.

No painter ought to think less of sculpture than of painting
and no sculptor less of painting than of sculpture.
—Michelangelo

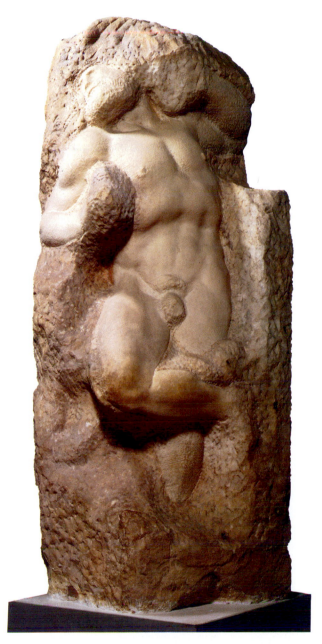

1 ft.

9-2 MICHELANGELO. *The Cross-Legged Captive* (c. 1530–1534). Marble. H: 7′6½″. Galleria dell'Accademia, Florence, Italy.

Modeling

In **modeling**, a pliable material such as clay or wax is built up, added, and shaped into a three-dimensional form. The artist may manipulate the material by hand and use a variety of tools. Unlike carving, which offers less of a margin for error or redirection, modeling enables the artist to work and rework the material until desired forms begin to emerge. The tactile nature of modeling leaves evidence of the artist's fingerprints as the soft material is pushed and gouged. Materials used in modeling are soft and, in the case of wax or unbaked clay, impermanent. Modeling is often the first step in the concept or creation of a sculpture in a more permanent medium such as bronze. Small **maquettes** are sometimes fashioned in clay by sculptors as a "first draft" of their final project.

Casting

The relationship between modeling and **casting** can be seen in Louise Bourgeois's *Portrait of Robert* (Fig. **9-3**). The artist began by modeling a pliable material and then converted the work to bronze through a casting process. The white patina Bourgeois applied to the surface curiously subverts

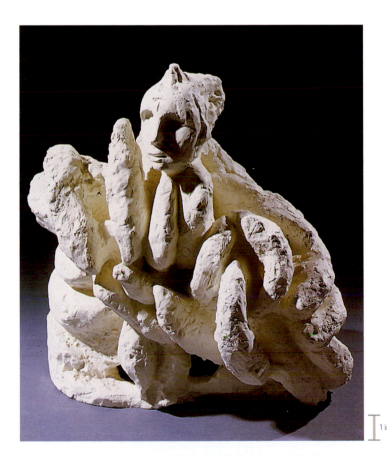

1 in.

9-3 LOUISE BOURGEOIS. *Portrait of Robert* (1969). Bronze, painted white. 13″ × 12½″ × 10″. Art © Louise Bourgeois Trust/Licensed by VAGA, NY.

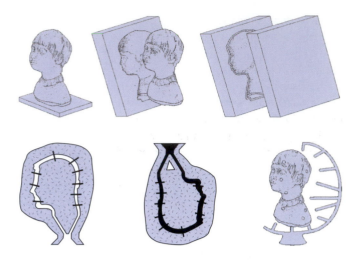

9-4 The lost-wax technique.

the shape of the mold. Once it cools, the mold is removed, leaving the cast piece, a more permanent version of the original object used to make the mold. Any liquid material that hardens can be used to in casting—molten metal, plaster, liquid plastics, paper pulp, clay diluted with water, and more. Once a mold has been made, the casting process may be duplicated, resulting in multiple casts of a single work.

THE LOST-WAX TECHNIQUE Pouring molten bronze into a mold results in a solid bronze cast. This is fine for small objects, like *Robert*, but what if the artist is creating a larger-than-life-size piece? The weight and expense, even the availability of bronze for a large sculpture, makes simple casting as previously described untenable. A hollow-casting technique was developed to create large-scale works in bronze and smaller works of precious metals like gold. It is seen in sculpture from ancient Greece and Rome and in Asian and Southeast Asian art, as well as in pre-Columbian and African art. In hollow casting, works of sculpture consist of thin shells of metal.

The process used for hollow casting, **lost-wax** or *cire perdu* ("lost wax" in French; Fig. **9-4**), has changed little over the centuries. This method, like casting, begins with a full-sized model, in this case usually sculpted in clay. A mold, also of clay, is made around the model. The mold is removed, in pieces, from the model, and molten wax is applied to the inside, negative surfaces of the mold. These individual pieces will eventually be reassembled to form the entire, completed work. When the molten wax is hard, the mold is removed and what remains

the typical look of bronze and imparts, instead, a claylike appearance, referencing the very material with which she began the piece.

In casting, a **mold** is first made by pressing a softish material around the wax or clay object that will record the impressions—in a kind of negative—of the surface of the object. This soft material becomes an inner mold, which is then surrounded by a more rigid material like plaster. The object is removed and liquid material is then poured into the hollow form of the mold. The liquid hardens into

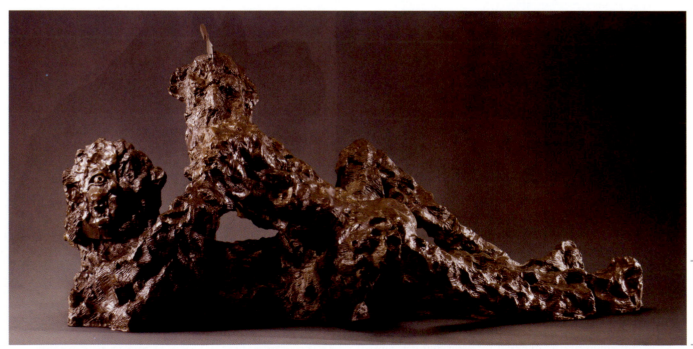

9-5 GEORGE CONDO. *The Butcher and His Wife* (2008–2009). Bronze. 43" × 48" × 85". Collection of the Artist. Shown at Whitney Biennial (2010).

1 ft.

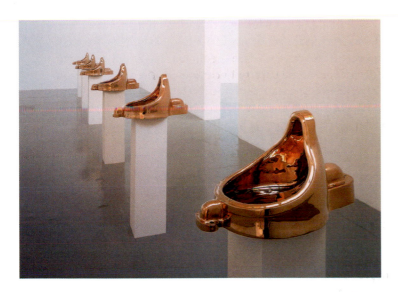

9-6 SHERRIE LEVINE. *Fountains after Duchamp* (1991). Bronze. Installation view at Sherrie Levine Exhibition in the Zürich Kunsthalle (February 11, 1991—March 1, 1992). Zürich, Switzerland.

is a hollow wax model that reflects the shape of the original clay model. The wax model will bear the marks and textures of the original clay sculpture, but the surface is malleable enough to be reworked with finer detail. The metal shell of the final product, let us note and keep in mind, will be equivalent in thickness to that of the hollow, molten wax model.

There are two next steps. One is to turn the hollow wax model upside down and fill it with liquid clay, allowing it to harden. The other is to create a clay mold, called an **investment**, around the hollow wax model. The investment and the clay core are separated, then, by the thin layer of the wax model and connected to each other with metal pins. The whole thing is heated so that the wax melts out (or is lost), leaving a space between the clay core and the investment—a space into which a molten metal such as bronze or gold can be poured. The metal hardens, the investment (mold) is removed, and the clay core is broken up and mostly extracted. The individual parts of the sculpture, now replicated in bronze, are rejoined with molten metal used to fill the gaps. The surface is then smoothed, polished, or treated with chemicals that yield a particular finish.

The appearance of cast bronze sculpture, reflecting the nature of the processes used to create it, is anything but consistent or predictable. Consider the visual contrast of works by contemporary artists George Condo and Sherrie Levine. *The Butcher and His Wife* (Fig. **9-5**) preserves the aggressively worked surface of the clay from which the work was cast, so much so that the technique dominates the overall appearance of the sculpture and obscures the legibility of the figures. Levine's *Fountains after Duchamp* (Fig. **9-6**) creates a completely different impression. The gleaming, flawless surfaces of her row of bronze urinals have the look of

factory-tooled, mass-produced utilitarian objects. Whereas the tactile quality of Condo's work conveys the immediacy of the artist's expressive gestures and close contact with his material—his signature, so to speak—Levine's work seems almost absent an author. She takes advantage of that quality to great effect. The urinals pay homage to Marcel Duchamp's infamous Dada work, a found object that he titled *Fountain* (see Fig. 1-36). Levine's "fountains" represent what lies at the heart of her artistic concept and strategy: the critical appropriation of objects and images that already exist in the visual lexicon of high art and mass culture. If Duchamp invested his readymades with a new *idea*—the reconsideration of ordinary objects in the artist's self-defined and self-imposed context of fine art—Levine's objects and reproductions are invested with a reconsideration of issues such as authorship and originality in relation to art making.

CASTING OF HUMAN MODELS *Three Figures and Four Benches* (Fig. **9-7**) by George Segal features an intriguing variation on the casting process. Segal produced ghostlike replicas of human beings by means of plaster casts. Live models were covered in plaster-soaked cloth, which was molded and kneaded by the artist's hands. When the plaster was dry, the cast was removed in sections and then reassembled into whole figures that consist of a hollow plaster shells. The plaster sculptures, with their rough surface textures of strips of gauze bandaging, were hauntingly juxtaposed with found objects—buses, gas stations, diners, and other settings, creating a kind of limbo of contemporary urban life. His work suggests an unimaginable aloneness. His figures do not seem to speak to one another or interact in any way. They are at once connected and disconnected, sharing a place and time and yet lost in their inner worlds.

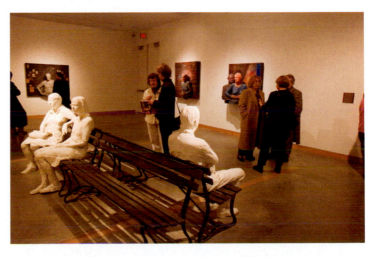

9-7 GEORGE SEGAL. *Three Figures and Four Benches* (1979). Painted bronze. 52" × 144" × 58". Theo Anderson, Allentown, PA. Art © The George and Helen Segal Foundation/Licensed by VAGA, NY.

TYPES OF MATERIALS

Sculpture as a medium is approached through any number of materials. Historically, wood, clay, stone, and metal are most typical. But the list of materials sculptors can employ and have employed is limitless and anything but typical—fiberglass, fluorescent tubes, high-heeled shoes, even human blood in the form of ice sculpture. The raw materials, possibilities, and products are endless in variety, appearance, and effect.

Stone

Stone is an extremely hard, earthen material that can be carved, scraped, drilled, and polished. The durability that makes stone, or rock—in all of its myriad aggregates including granite, marble, limestone, jade, and basalt—so appropriate for monuments and statues meant to outlive generations

1 ft.

9-8 LOUISE BOURGEOIS. *Eyes* (1982). Marble. 74¾" × 54" × 45¾". The Metropolitan Museum of Art, NY. Art © Louise Bourgeois Trust/Licensed by VAGA, NY.

is also what makes working with it a tedious process. The harshness of the granite used by ancient Egyptians—mostly quarried near Aswan—made it almost impossible to render fine detail, one reason that their figures were simplified and stay close to the shape of quarried blocks. Marble, by contrast, is a relatively soft stone and more conducive to carving and delicate detail. The Greeks, who manipulated marble with great facility, acquired most of their material from islands in the Aegean.

The hand tools used to carve stone—such as the chisel, mallet, and **rasp**—have not changed much over the centuries. Contemporary sculptors have the advantage of specialized power tools that enable them to remove large areas of unwanted material with relative ease and to polish a finished piece to a high gloss.

Carving in stone goes back to the Stone Age and small limestone figurines such as the *Venus of Willendorf* (see Fig. 13-2). In spite of the primitive nature of the sculptor's flint tools, an impressive amount of detail delineates arms, a torso, and a rounded head covered with either curly hair or a woven cap. The roundness of the sculpture suggests that its overall shape was determined by—and stays close to—the shape of the stone from which it was carved. *Venus* is just a bit over four inches high.

It is a dramatic leap from the *Venus of Willendorf* to, say, Bernini's *Apollo and Daphne* (see Fig. 2-72), a work that illustrates the potential of marble as a sculptural material. In the hands of an artist with breathtaking skill, marble can suggest a gamut of textures—the softness and sensuousness of flesh, the silky textures of hair, smooth-skinned leaves, and rugged, splintered bark. Imagine the intricacy of cutting away the obstinate stone to reveal the delicate leaves sprouting from Daphne's fingertips and locks of hair. Bernini portrays the exact moment from classical mythology when the nymph, Daphne, pursued by an adoring Apollo, beseeches her father, a river god, to change her form so that Apollo will not capture her. Just as Apollo reaches Daphne and puts his arm around her waist, she is transformed into a laurel tree. The fright and disbelief on the faces of the characters pushes the illusion of realism to its absolute limit.

Marble continues to be a favored material for contemporary sculptors. *Eyes* (Fig. **9-8**), by Louise Bourgeois, features two precisely tooled spheres perched atop a marble cube, some of which has been chiseled to create hollows and irregularities. Two deeply carved circular openings in the spheres suggest the penetrating pupils of eyes, a commonly used symbol among Surrealist artists

ch 9 book - sculpture has multiple viewpoints
- relief + free-standing sculpture - project to varying degrees from 2D surface
  - low or high relief
- sculpture in the round
- subtractive process - remove from mass
- additive " - material built up
- carving - cut portions of block away
- modeling - pliable material shaped into 3D form
  - margin for error
  - maquette - first draft
- casting - clay-like
- mold - material pressed around surface of obj.
  - liquid poured in + hardens to shape of mold
    - may be duplicated
- lost wax
- Segall - human models
- materials: 1. stone - life, difficult to work with
- power tool use
        2. wood - lower tensile strength than stone
- grain + type (hard or soft)

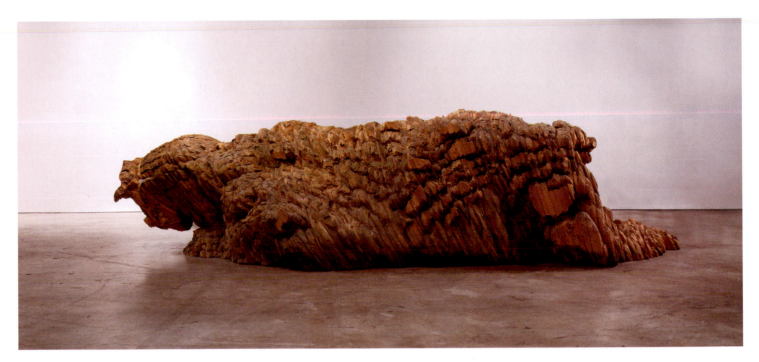

9-9 URSULA VON RYDINGSVARD. *Droga* (2009).

(see Chapter 20). Although Bourgeois's technique results in a finished work that remains close to the quarried marble block, the perfectly round eyes, the polish of the surfaces, and the carved interruptions create a striking contrast between a deliberate absence and an assertive presence of the artist's hand.

Wood

Wood, like stone, may be carved using a variety of tools and, like stone, possesses different degrees of hardness that affect its workability and durability. Sculptors carve works from solid blocks of wood or, in the case of very large works, laminate pieces of wood together using adhesive, heat, and pressure. Wood's **tensile strength** exceeds that of stone, so parts of a wood sculpture that protrude are less likely than their stone counterparts to break off. On the other hand, stone is less impervious to disintegration over time.

Sculptors working in wood take into consideration types of wood (hard or soft), their grain patterns (straight or wavy), and their color. Tools for carving and finishing wood blocks include gouges, saws, knives, chisels, planes, mallets, sanders, and polishers. In carving wood, artists particularly study the direction of the grain, as the strength of the wood is connected to its grain.

Plywood, a familiar building material, is also used for sculpture. Sheets of plywood are made by stacking and glu-ing thin strips of wood (veneers), laid in such a way that the grain of each individual sheet is at a right angle to the ones below and above it. The process yields a strong product that is resistant to warping, twisting, shrinking, or cracking. Under heat, plywood can be bent into any shape, making it a very flexible material.

Wood is a versatile material that yields dramatically different results depending on its type and the tools used to manipulate it. Barbara Hepworth's *Two Figures* (see Fig. 4-8), carved from elm wood, are highly polished and smooth to the touch. The natural wood grain of the outer "shells" imparts warmth to the surface that contrasts with the pure white, marblelike finish of the concavities. The shapes possess an organic roundness and sense of lightness that are enhanced by this color contrast. The hollowed-out, void spaces complete a composition that is has pleasing balance of positive and negative shapes.

The smoothness, sensuousness, and apparent suppleness of *Two Figures* could not be more sharply different from the aggressively worked surface of Ursula von Rydingsvard's *Droga* (Fig. **9-9**). Beginning by taking a chainsaw to commercially milled cedar beams, the artist then cut, gouged, glued, and assembled pieces into a sprawling, faceted, monumental whole (it is 10 feet high and 18 feet long). *Droga* may resemble strata of the earth's crust or a sci-fi monster taking shape from the mud and rock of a creepy underworld, but, more simply, in *Droga*, the audience never loses sight of the tactile aspects of wood as a raw material.

the medium, such as fingerprints and handprints, as we saw in works by Bourgeois and Condo in the section on casting earlier in this chapter. Compared to stone or wood, clay has little strength, and it is not typically considered a permanent material—unless it is exposed to heat, as in ceramics. Sculptors have always used clay to make three-dimensional sketches, or models, for works that are then cast in more durable materials such as bronze.

Clay can be fired in a kiln at high temperatures so that it becomes hard and nonporous, making the material more suitable to sculpture and ceramics. Before firing, clay can be coated with glazes that can be manipulated to create different designs and surface textures. Michael Doolan's *A Cautionary Tale Continuum* (*Yellow*) (Fig. 9-11) is created through a process that begins with hand-modeling and hand-building techniques to create a hollow stoneware figure. The figures are then often completed out of the studio by factory professionals with expertise in surface finishes such as automotive

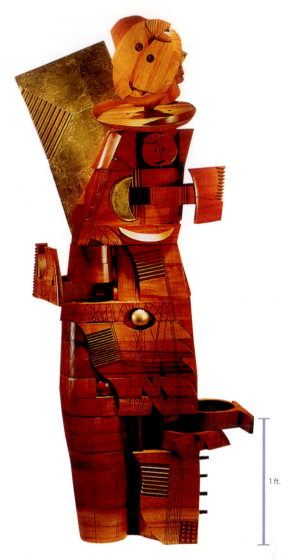

1 ft.

9-10 PO SHUN LEONG. *Figure* (1993). Mahogany with hidden drawers. H: 50".

Carving, gouging, cutting, assembling, and polishing are used to a very different effect by Po Shun Leong in his *Figure* (Fig. 9-10). The rich mahogany surfaces have a complexity, delicacy, and intricacy. There is a restlessness to the patterns and the myriad angles at which the pieces are set in relation one another. Coupled with the punctuation of hidden drawers that can be opened or closed, the handling of the surfaces creates a feeling of constant motion.

Clay

Clay is a naturally occurring material that is more pliable than stone or wood. Works in clay often preserve the evidence of the artist's direct handling of

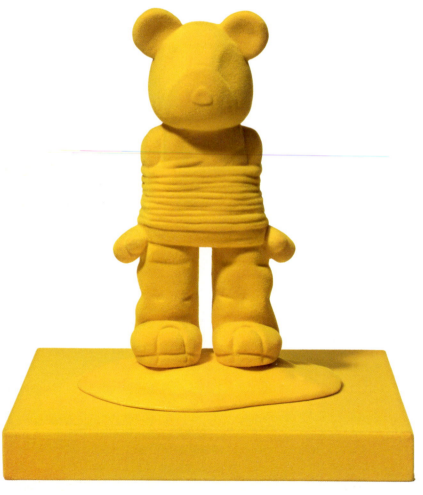

9-11 MICHAEL DOOLAN. *A Cautionary Tale Continuum* (*Yellow*) (2010). Hand-modeled earthenware, adhered automotive nylon.

nylon and metallic lusters. Doolan's earthenware sculptures have a *Toy Story* quality to them—familiar images of children's play objects caught in circumstances in which things seem to have gone terribly wrong. We shall consider ceramics further in our discussion in Chapter 12, Craft and Design.

Metal

The process of casting metals such as bronze, gold, silver, or iron has changed little over the centuries. Sculptors use any number of techniques including **extruding**, **forging**, **stamping**, **drilling**, **filing**, and **burnishing** to manipulate the material, mark it, and polish it. Contemporary artists have also assembled **direct-metal sculptures**, often of steel, by welding, riveting, and soldering. Modern adhesives have also made it possible to glue sections of metal together into three-dimensional constructions.

Different metals have different properties. Bronze, an alloy of copper, has been the most popular casting material because of its surface and color characteristics. A bronze finish can be dull or glossy, and chemical treatments can pro-duce colors ranging from greenish blacks to golden or deep browns. Because of oxidation, bronze and copper surfaces age to a rich green or greenish blue **patinas**.

For decades, Richard Serra has worked with steel, an alloy of iron, to create minimalist sculpture that expresses the physical properties and capabilities of his material. Like the installation at the Guggenheim Museum in Bilbao, Spain (Fig. **9-12**), many of his works have been monumental in scale and site-specific. Serra's steel surfaces grow more richly textured over time and with oxidation so that subsequent encounters with the same work reveals new visual dimensions. Serra's sculpture is intended to be experienced and not simply viewed, to be walked into, around, and through. Serra has said that one of his goals as an artist is the "opening up of the continuum of space." In some works, sheets of steel alternately enclose the visitor in a protected, almost private space and lead that same visitor, by way of an undulating path, to a more public, socially interactive space. The mass is solid and the texture is palpable, but the concept seems to reflect a nonmaterial realm—a gateway to something other within the real worlds we traverse every day.

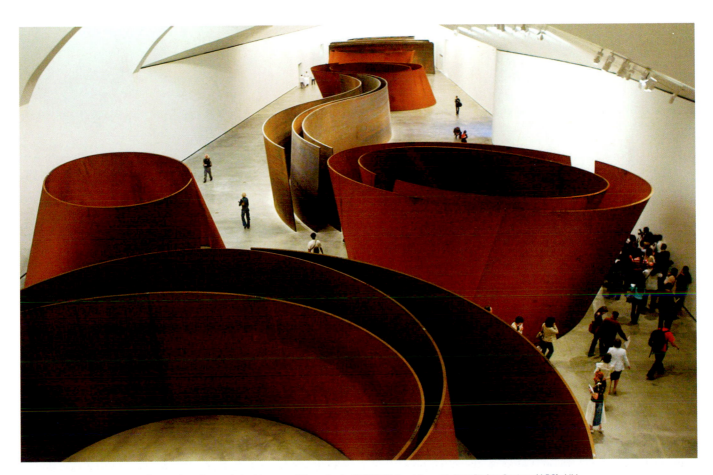

9-12 RICHARD SERRA. Installation view, Guggenheim Museum, Bilbao, Spain. © 2011 Richard Serra/Artists Rights Society (ARS), NY.

MODERN AND CONTEMPORARY MATERIALS AND METHODS

During the past century, technological changes have overleaped themselves, giving rise to new materials, such as plastics and fluorescent lights, and to new ways of working with traditional materials. Experimentation has led to new approaches to sculpture and to redefinitions.

Until the early years of the twentieth century, sculpture was defined by a handful of techniques and processes—all of which we have encountered in this chapter: carving, modeling, and casting. Pablo Picasso expanded that technical vocabulary when he introduced constructed sculpture, built up of scraps of wood and found objects, in his Cubist works. Sculpture would never be the same. Assemblage,

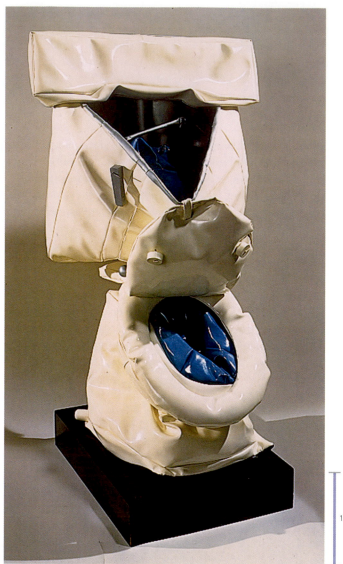

9-14 CLAES OLDENBURG. *Soft Toilet* (1966). Vinyl filled with kapok painted with Liquitex, and wood. 57 1/16" × 27 5/8" × 28 1/16". Whitney Museum of American Art, NY.

readymades, mixed-media installations, light sculpture, and kinetic sculpture are a sampling of contemporary approaches that followed. The list is by no means exhaustive.

Constructed Sculpture

Constructed sculpture is built or constructed from an assortment of materials—pieces of wood, sheet metal, wire, plastic, cardboard, found objects, just about anything. Picasso inspired experimentation with relief sculptures such as his 1913 *Mandolin and Clarinet* (Fig. **9-13**). As critic Robert Hughes remarked, such works were "everything that statues

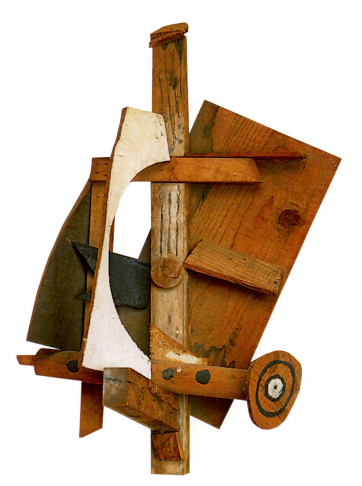

9-13 PABLO PICASSO. *Mandolin and Clarinet* (1913). Wood construction and paint. Musée Picasso, Paris, France. © 2011 Estate of Pablo Picasso/ Artists Rights Society (ARS), NY.

I began using found objects. I had all this wood lying around and I began to move it around,
I began to compose.
—Louise Nevelson

had not been: not monolithic, but open, not cast or carved, but assembled from flat planes."[1] In spirit and style, reliefs from this era were very close to Picasso's paintings. But the unorthodox materials challenged all traditions in art making.

A Russian visitor to Picasso's Paris studio, Vladimir Tatlin, is credited with having realized the three-dimensional potential of constructed sculpture, which was then further developed in Russia by the brothers Antoine Pevsner and Naum Gabo. Naum Gabo's *Column* (see Fig. 20-16) epitomizes a characteristic of many constructed works: the ascendance of shape and volume over sculptural mass. Gabo's translucent planes of plastic and glass encircle, frame, and slice into the surrounding space.

The precision of Gabo's *Column*, its simultaneously architectural and ethereal qualities—its overall look of perfection—

could not be more unlike the technique and sensibility that drove Pop artist Claes Oldenburg's construction *Soft Toilet* (Fig. 9-14). Stitched of vinyl and stuffed with kapok, a silky natural fiber, a familiar object that we know to be hard, cold, and unmovable is rendered soft, supple, and pliable. Our senses are utterly subverted.

Assemblage

Assemblage is a form of constructed sculpture in which pre-existing, or found objects, recognizable in shape, are integrated and combined in novel combinations that take on meaning of their own—meaning separate from their constituent parts. Louise Nevelson's *Royal Tide IV* (Fig. 9-15) is a compartmentalized assemblage of rough-cut geometric shapes and lathed wooden pieces including posts and finials, barrel staves, and chair slats—the pieces of a personal or collective

---

[1] Robert Hughes, "The Liberty of Thought Itself," *Time*, September 1, 1986, 87.

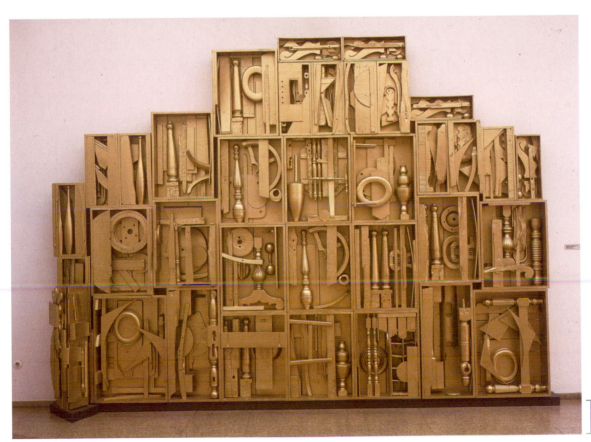

9-15 LOUISE NEVELSON. *Royal Tide IV* (1960). Wood, with gold-spray technique. 127" × 175½" × 21½".

1 ft.

past, of lonely introspective journeys amid the cobwebs of Victorian attics. Even though some of the objects are familiar and recognizable, Nevelson's unifying coat of paint deemphasizes their distinct identities. The whole—an exercise in variety within unity—is greater than the sum of the parts.

Willie Cole's assemblages show us the degree to which discreet, familiar, found objects can lose themselves utterly in their second lives as works of fine art. In *House Pet* (Fig. 9-16), brightly colored and wildly patterned women's high-heeled shoes are stacked, squashed, and nestled into an overall shape that resembles an adorable—if completely weird—crouching animal. Cole's early assemblages were built of vintage and modern clothes irons, and he has used shoes and multiple versions of other objects in his works as well. He challenges himself to find new resolutions by identifying and adhering to a constant—a particular object—and producing visually complex variations on it.

Found objects are at the root of these assemblages by Nevelson and Cole, but they are built on the concept of the **readymade** as art introduced by Marcel Duchamp during the **Dada** movement—"an ordinary object elevated to the dignity of a work of art by the mere choice of an artist." Duchamp created an uproar in 1917 when he submitted *Fountain* (Fig. 1-36), a porcelain urinal turned on its side and signed "R. Mutt," to an exhibition of the Society of Independent Artists. After a debate on the justification of the readymade as a valid work of art, the board decided not to show it. For Duchamp, the dimension of taste, good or bad, was irrelevant. Art could be defined by an idea, and the very action of choosing an object and creating a new context for it invested it with new meaning.

Mixed Media

Mixed media is a catchall category that describes constructions and assemblages in which artists use a combination of **mediums** and materials, sometimes in combination with found objects. Picasso's *Mandolin and Clarinet*, Miriam Schapiro's *Wonderland* (Fig. 1-35), Robert Rauschenberg's *Bed* (Fig. 21-11), Judy Pfaff's *Dragon* (Fig. 21-30), and Hew Locke's *El Dorado* (Fig. 22-5) are only a few examples of mixed-media works that you will find in your textbook. Note that not all mixed-media works are classified as sculpture; they can be two or three dimensional, reliefs, freestanding works, or installations. Ann Sperry's series *My Piano: The Fragmen-*

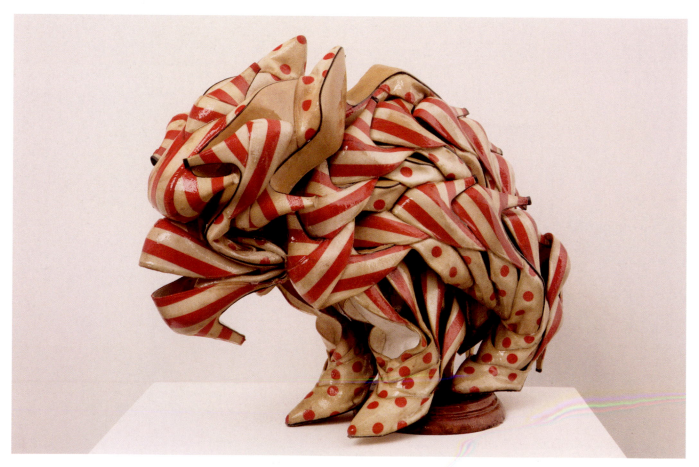

9-16 WILLIE COLE. *House Pet* (2010). Canvas, high-heeled shoes, resin.

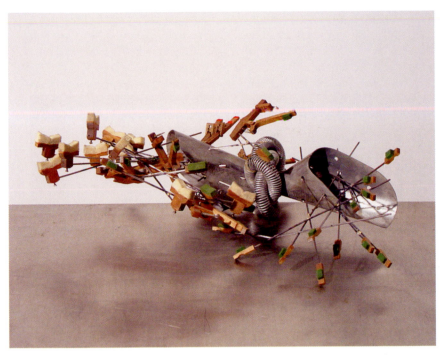

9-17 ANN SPERRY. *My Piano: The Fragmentation of Memory* (2002). Galvanized metal, piano parts. 7½" × 21" × 15½".

Light Sculpture

Sculptors, regardless of their techniques, are aware of the ways in which light influences the nature and perception of their work. Alternating between deep and shallow carving will yield gradations of tone from dark to light, as in Michelangelo's *Cross-Legged Captive*. Light plays an integral part in the perception of Helene Brandt's *Mondrian Variations* (Fig. 2-13). Lines of steel project from the surface of the wall, intersecting to form a three-dimensional grid. Under a spotlight, the grid creates a shadow that reads as the ghostly presence of the Dutch painter Piet Mondrian—the muse, as it were, who inspired Brandt's series of works based on his renowned grid paintings.

It is only in the past century that sculptors began to experiment with the use of artificial light as a material, taking advantage of its physical properties, psychological effects, and potential to create visual illusions. Dan Flavin worked principally with fluorescent tubes, exploring the

tation of Memory (Fig. **9-17**), features sculptures assembled from piano parts, sheets of galvanized metal, steel, and brass. One work in the series even incorporates **monoprints** (see Chapter 7, Printmaking, Fig. 7-17). Critic Rebecca Fenton said of the series that "Ann Sperry seeks to manipulate her materials away from their previous uses and, therefore, our preconceived expectations. Still, she relates new artwork to 'past life,' the associations and memories of her materials."

Kinetic Sculpture

Sculptors have always been concerned with the portrayal of movement, but **kinetic sculptures** incorporate actual movement caused by the wind, magnetic fields, jets of water, electric motors, variations in the intensity of light, or the active manipulation of the audience. During the 1930s, the American sculptor Alexander Calder introduced motion as a basic element—like line, shape, or color—into the compositions he called **mobiles** (see Fig. 2-71). Carefully balanced weights are suspended on wires such that the gentlest current of air sets them moving in prescribed orbits.

George Rickey's name has become synonymous with contemporary kinetic sculpture. The stainless steel shapes of his *Five Open Squares Gyratory* (Fig. **9-18**) are weighed and balanced to move silently and effortlessly with the slightest bit of breeze. As they rise, fall, and twirl, the squares frame shifting bits of the surrounding landscape, evoking the feeling of snapshots that capture the fleeting aspects of nature.

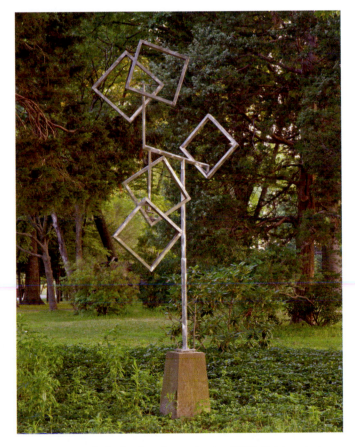

9-18 GEORGE RICKEY. *Five Open Squares Gyratory* (1981). Stainless steel. 9'4" × 6' × 42". Art © Estate of George Rickey/Licensed by VAGA, NY.

*The body is our common denominator for our pleasures and our sorrows.
I want to express through it who we are, how we live and die.*
—Kiki Smith

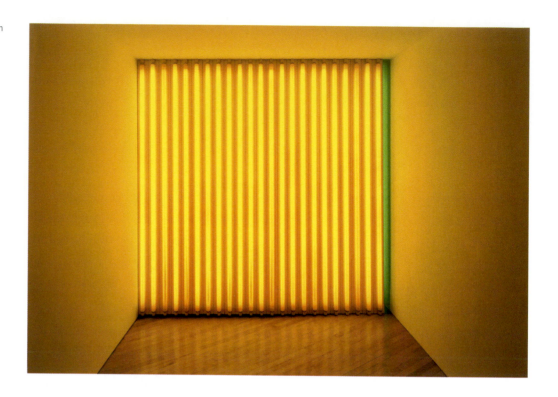

resonance of color and its ability to define space. In his untitled piece seen in Figure **9-19**, the installation room seems to dead-end with a screen of yellow light tubes placed back-to-back with a matching screen of green tubes (which you cannot see from this side). Because the sculpture blocked passage from one part of the room to another, only a glimpse of the light filling the space on the other side of the screen could be seen through the narrow spaces on either side of the piece. The result was an intriguing juxtaposition of regimented tubes of yellow and the unfettered glow of green light. The opposite effect was observed in viewing the work from the other side.

Other Materials

The trajectory of sculpture as a medium in the twentieth and twenty-first centuries has been dramatic and dynamic with new definitions of art and the artist's use of unconventional materials. This section considers a scant few examples of unexpected materials and techniques.

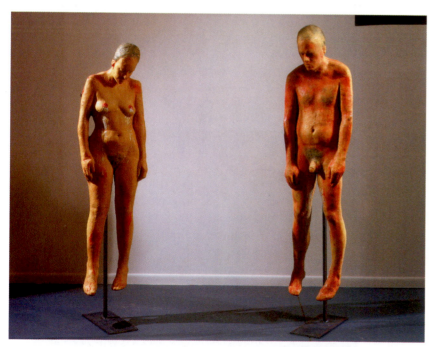

9-20 KIKI SMITH. *Untitled* (1990). Beeswax and microcrystalline wax figures on metal stands; female figure installed height 6'1½"; male figure installed height 6'4 15/16". Whitney Museum of American Art, NY.

The figures in Kiki Smith's *Untitled* (Fig. **9-20**) were constructed of beeswax and microcrystalline wax. The artist's realism is, in a sense, more realistic than realism has ever been—even when compared to the technical skills of a Bernini or the illusionism of a sculptor like Duane Hanson (see Fig. 21-26). The realism in Kiki Smith's couple is almost too painful to observe, too close to the realities of our own physical selves. Smith has written that as "Most of the functions of the body are hidden . . . from society," she aims to bring them out into the open, focusing on body parts and body byproducts. In their state of deterioration, the effigies in Smith's untitled work have lost control over their bodily functions. The woman's figure is stained with, or drained of, milk that drips from her nipples. Semen drips down the man's leg. They are suspended in space, isolated in their loss of control, sharing the frailties of the human condition.

Sylvie Fleury constructed her *Dog Toy 4 (Gnome)* (Fig. **9-21**) from Styropor, little balls of polystyrene that expand and stick together when heated. Styropor is commonly used for packaging and insulation because it can be shaped and molded and is almost weightless. Chances are, the last time you purchased

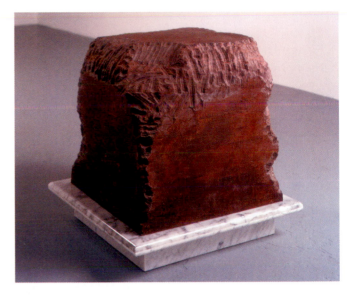

9-22 JANINE ANTONI. *Gnaw* (1992). Detail: (installation) 600 lb. lard, gnawed by the artist; 600 lb. collapsed lard, gnawed by the artist; 45 heart-shaped packages for chocolate made from chewed chocolate removed from the chocolate cube and 400 lipsticks made with pigment, beeswax, and chewed lard removed from the lard cube. The Museum of Modern Art, NY.

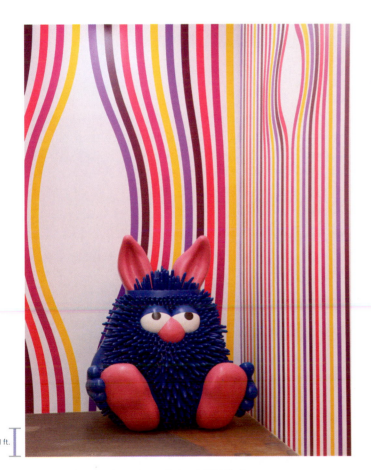

1 ft.

9-21 SYLVIE FLEURY. *Dog Toy 4 (Gnome)* (2000). Styropor. 78¾" × 74⅞" × 59¹⁄₁₆".

a flat-screen TV or other electronics, they were surrounded by protective panels of the same material. Fleury's point of departure was a familiar, nonthreatening, squeaky animal toy, blown up to the same nightmarish proportions that turned the smiling marshmallow man in the film *Ghostbusters* into a menacing monster crushing everything in its wake. In the tradition of Andy Warhol and the Pop artists, who had in turn been influenced by the found objects of the Dada artists before them, Fleury elevates consumer products of a "disposable society" to the level of fine art.

Janine Antoni's *Gnaw* (Fig. **9-22**) may pay tongue-in-cheek homage to a **minimalist** geometric sculpture, but it holds some sensory surprises: Antoni's material is chocolate and her "carving" tools consist of what nature has endowed her with—a strong set of teeth. The surface texture of the piece records the process, what Antoni has characterized as the most important element of her art. *Gnaw* was one of two companion pieces—the other was a cube of lard—which she bit and chewed, refashioning gnawed chunks into small objects such as lipstick tubes and chocolate boxes.

Perhaps because we are surrounded in our daily lives by monuments, we are accustomed to thinking of sculpture as a permanent and enduring. *Gnaw* is a work in which the notion of permanence is insignificant. Chocolate will melt in your mouth or, with a bit of heat, into a nondescript and gooey pool. Permanence is not necessarily a concern of some artists in particular works. In the next chapter, we will consider site-specific art, much of which exists in the moment.

THE STORM KING ART CENTER in Mountainville, New York, is a sculpture garden located about one hour north of Manhattan. But this sculpture garden consists of 500 acres of landscaped lawns and fields, hills, and woodlands, including views of the mountains of the lower Hudson Valley. There are permanent installations of works by sculptors including Isamu Noguchi, Alexander Calder, Henry Moore, Magdalena Abakanowicz, Mark di Suvero, Roy Lichtenstein, and Louise Nevelson. Works by Andy Goldsworthy and Richard Serra were commissioned for their sites. The Goldsworthy wall winds its way across more than 2,200 feet, dipping into ponds and climbing out. The four partially buried Serra shards of steel, *Schunnemunk Fork*, named after nearby Schunnemunk Mountain, occupy 10 acres. Whereas the Goldsworthy and Serra sculptures seem to have the permanence of the ages, the huge di Suvero sculptures, of steel but also airy, look as though they might without notice decide to pick themselves up and search out different prospects in the fields.

All this was founded by Ralph E. Ogden in 1960 as a museum for Hudson Valley painters. The landscape was wrecked from careless farming, and hundreds of truckloads of soil were brought in; grasses were planted. Fortunately, some woodlands with hills and boulders were in place. Ponds were dug and filled with water. A 1935 Normandy-style house was renovated, and it houses offices, temporary exhibitions, and a museum store. Early on, works were acquired

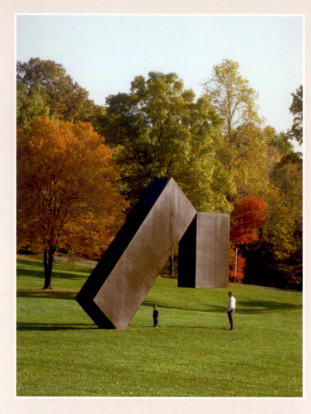

9-23 MENASHE KADISHMAN. *Suspended* (1977). Weathering steel. 276" × 396" × 48".

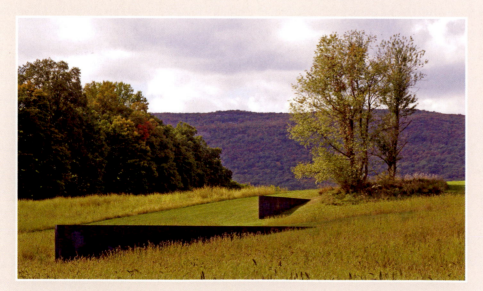

9-24 RICHARD SERRA. *Schunnemunk Fork* (1990–1991). Weathering steel. © 2011 Richard Serra/Artists Rights Society (ARS), NY.

A 96" × 589" × 2½".

B 96" × 421" × 2½".

C 96" × 460" × 2½".

D 96" × 652" × 2½".

Among sculpture parks of the world, Storm King is King.
—J. Carter Brown

from the estate of the sculptor David Smith, and these alone became a magnet for visitors.

The place is like no other: Visit once and you are ensnared. Visit twice and you are mesmerized, because no two visits are alike. The times of the day cast their own shadows, changing patterns of cloud cover dim or brighten sunlight, and the changing seasons bring a distinctive palette to grasses and leaves. What lay in shade may suddenly gush into radiance with a burst of sunlight. There is no good weather or bad weather for this art—only different weather with variable, sometimes capricious, degrees of illumination. Come and observe the play of the sky across the fields, as did the artists of the Hudson River School two centuries ago .●

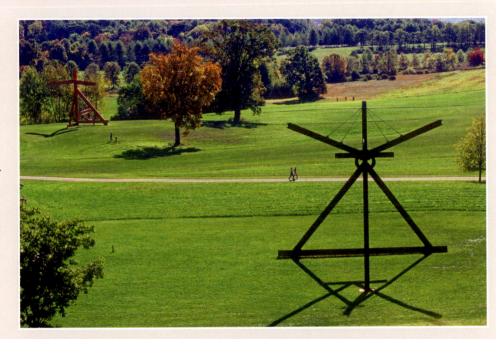

9-25 Mark di Suvero sculptures at Storm King Art Center.

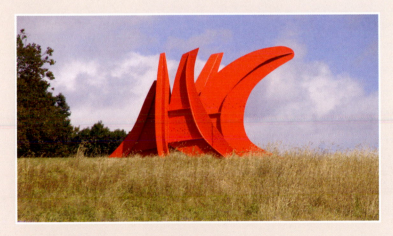

9-26 ALEXANDER CALDER. *Five Swords* (1976). Sheet metal, bolts, and paint. 213" × 264" × 348". © 2011 Calder Foundation, NY/Artists Rights Society (ARS), NY.

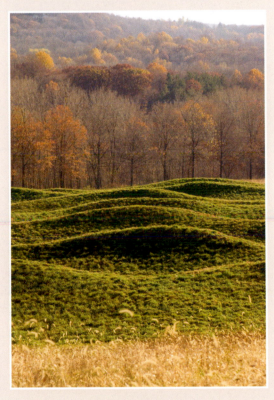

9-27 MAYA LIN. *Storm King Wavefield* (2007–2008).

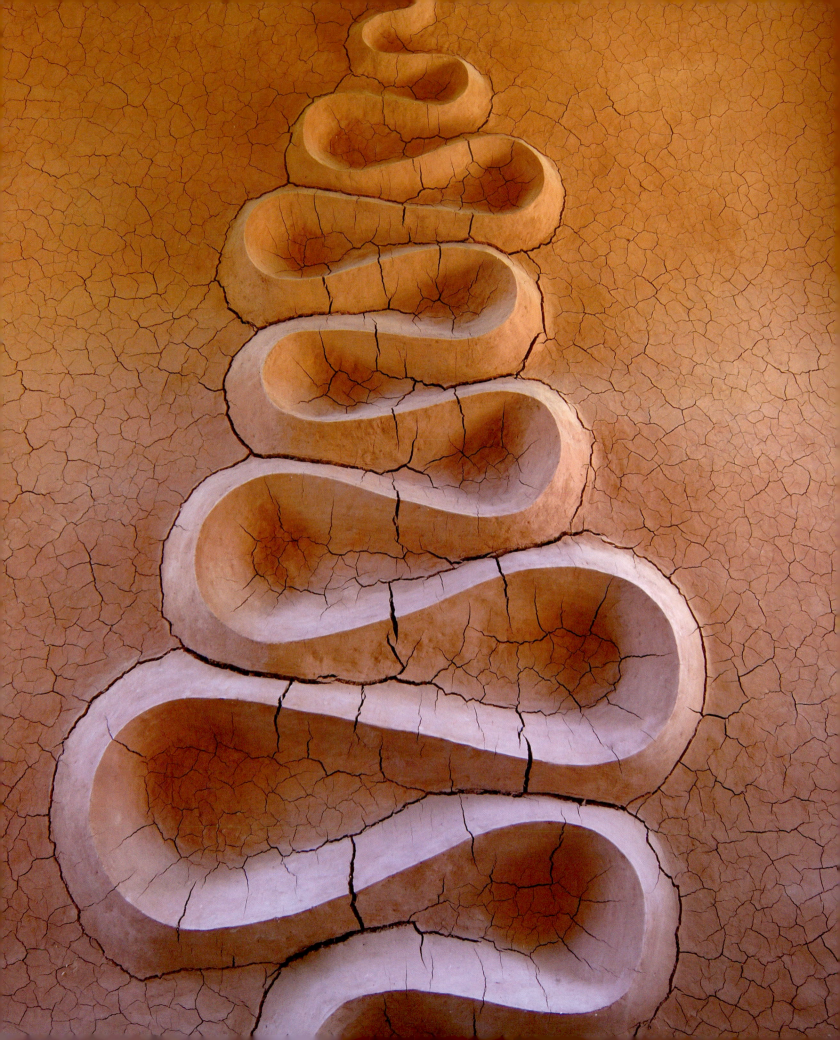

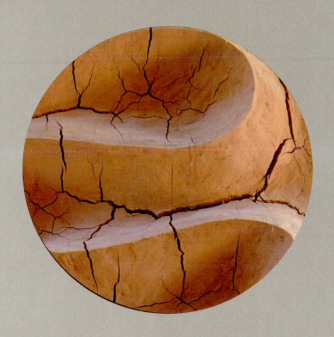

Give me a place to light and I will invent an installation that will bring it out.

—Dan Flavin

SITE-SPECIFIC ART

10

Site-specific works are distinguished from other artworks that are typically created in a studio with no particular spatial context in mind. Site-specific art is produced in or for one location and—in theory, at least—is not to be relocated. The work is in and of its site, and often the content and meaning of the work is inextricably bound to it. By this description, the history of art is full of examples of site-specific art, ranging from the sculptural decoration on the Parthenon (Fig. 14-10) and Michelangelo's Sistine Chapel ceiling (Figs. 16-21 to 16-22) to a mural by Orozco commissioned for Dartmouth College (Fig 1-39), or Kozloff's mosaic for a Philadelphia train station (Fig. 1-37). But the term *site-specific* came into use in the 1960s and 1970s as a blanket category for art that was created for or in a specific location. That location might be a museum or gallery, a public space, or a site in the natural landscape.

ANDY GOLDSWORTHY. Detail of a 2005 installation. One of a series of "refuges d'art" accessible by hiking trails in Provence, France.

As coincidence would have it, nearly all of these possibilities were met in *Big Bambú: You Can't, You Don't, and You Won't Stop* (Fig. 10-1), a temporary, site-specific work for the B. Gerald Cantor Roof Garden at the Metropolitan Museum of Art by twin-brother artists Mike and Doug Starn. Seasonal installations on the Met's rooftop have become a warm-weather must-see for New Yorkers for years. But repeated visits over the six months in 2010 when *Big Bambú* was in town offered unique rewards. It would never look the same twice. The installation, which ultimately rose 50 feet off the terrace floor and sprawled more than 100 feet, was a work in progress from start to finish. The artists and their team of collaborators—rock climbers—continually constructed the piece from bamboo poles and stalks that were meticulously knotted together with brightly colored lengths of nylon rope. The effect, according to the artists, was one of "chaos" and "interdependence," an "ever-changing living organism" that morphed and grew on its perch above Central Park—a dramatic counterpoint to the stone facades of the Met and the New York City skyline.

The junglelike environment offered another irresistible element: visitors were allowed to climb up into the work. A central concept of *Big Bambú* was audience participation. Guided tours brought the intrepid up bamboo ramps to lookout platforms and across a bridge that spanned a 25-foot gap in the network of poles. Viewing the work and understanding it was to experience it, to be a physical part of it. Six months after construction began, *Big Bambú* was gone, recorded in documentary photographs and films and imprinted on the minds of those who were there.

Site-specific art consists of many types, goals, and styles, including land and environmental art, ephemeral art, public art, and monuments.

LAND ART

Land art is site-specific work that is created or marked by an artist within natural surroundings. Sometimes large amounts of earth or land are shaped into sculptural forms, as in the earthworks of the 1960s and 1970s. These works could be temporary or permanent and included great trenches and drawings in the desert, bulldozed configurations of earth and rock, and delicately constructed compositions of ice, twigs, and leaves. What such works have in common is the artist's use of local materials to create pieces that are unified with or contrapuntal to the landscape.

Robert Smithson's *Spiral Jetty* (Fig. 10-2) is composed of basalt and earth bulldozed into a spiral formation in Utah's Great Salt Lake. The spiral shape of the jetty was inspired by a whirlpool, as well as the configuration of salt deposits that

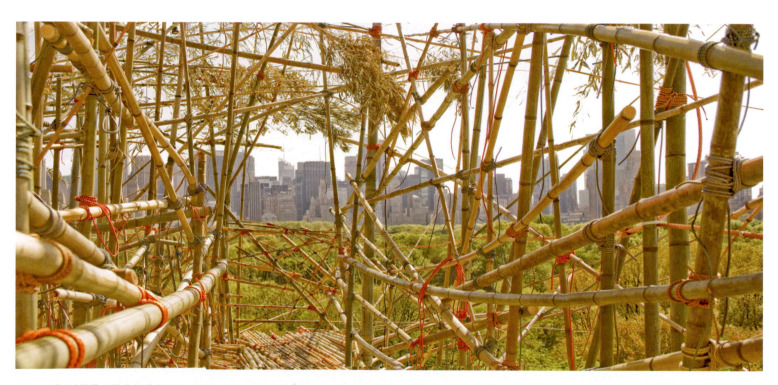

10-1 MIKE AND DOUG STARN. *Big Bambú: You Can't, You Don't, and You Won't Stop* (2010). Approx. 5,000 interlocking 30- and 40-foot-long fresh-cut bamboo poles, lashed together with 50 miles of nylon rope. Approx. 100' long, 50' wide, and 40' high. The Iris and B. Gerald Cantor Roof Garden, The Metropolitan Museum of Art, NY

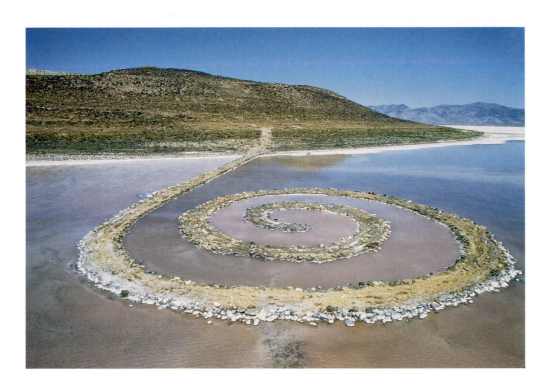

10-2 ROBERT SMITHSON. *Spiral Jetty* (1970). Black rocks, salt, earth, water, and algae. L: 1,500'; W: 15'. Great Salt Lake, UT. Art © Estate of Robert Smithson/Licensed by VAGA, NY.

10-3 ANDY GOLDSWORTHY. *Ice Star* (12 January 1987). Cibachrome photograph. 30" × 30". Scaur water, Penpoint, Dumfriesshire, Scotland.

accumulate on rocks bordering the lake. After its creation, the jetty lay submerged underwater for many years. With a prolonged drought, the spiral began to reemerge in 1999 and, depending on the water levels of the lake, now "comes and goes."

The delicacy of many of Andy Goldsworthy's constructions stands in marked contrast with Smithson's bulldozed mounds of earth. They communicate, from another perspective, the fragility and changeability of nature. Goldsworthy works with materials he finds on site—leaves, sticks, stones, ice fragments—manipulating them with a soft, controlled touch or even, as with *Ice Star*, his breath (Fig. 10-3). The following documentary narrative accompanied the piece:

thick ends dipped in snow then water
held until frozen together
occasionally using forked sticks as
support until stuck
a tense moment when taking them
away
breathing on the stick first to release it

Goldsworthy explores both the transitory and the timeless in his varied works. *Storm King*

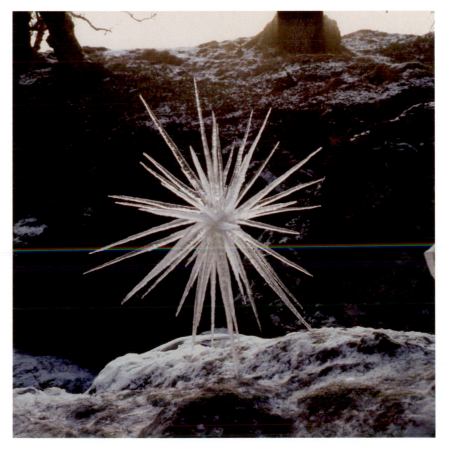

Land Art   **197**

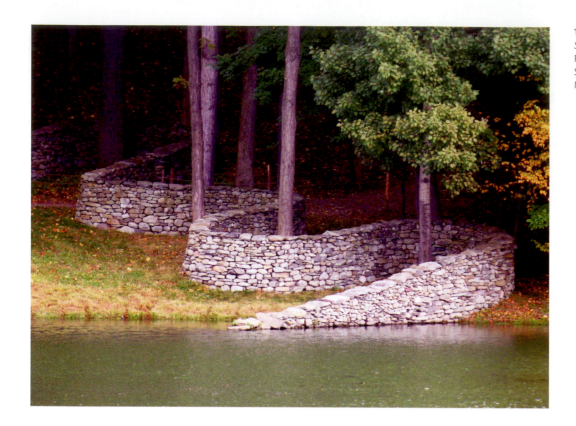

10-4 ANDY GOLDSWORTHY.
Storm King Wall (1997–1998).
Field stone. 5' × 2,278' overall.
Storm King Art Center,
Mountainville, NY.

10-5 MARCO EVARISTTI.
The Ice Cube Project (2004).
Red dye and seawater,
Greenland coast.

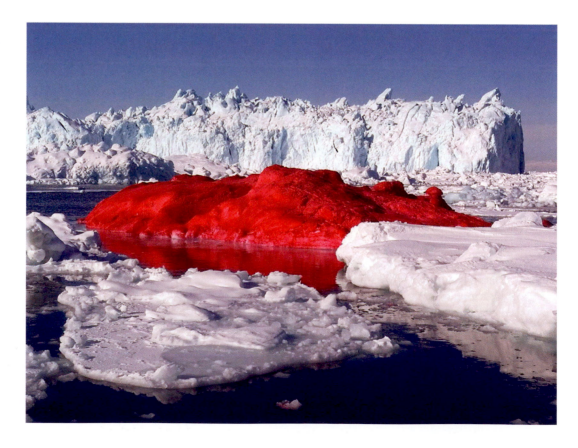

Wall (Fig. **10-4**) incorporates the remains of a dilapidated farm fence found on the site of the Storm King Art Center into a 2,278-foot-long fieldstone wall. The work snakes through fields and around trees, at one point dipping into a pond and reappearing at the other side to continue its march along the landscape. As with many of Goldsworthy's pieces, the viewer experiences a quiet human presence—sometimes fleeting, sometimes enduring—in the midst of the natural world.

Art that "makes marks" in nature is often temporary. In March 2004, Danish artist Marco Evaristti set sail in two icebreakers to find the perfect "frozen canvas" among the icebergs off the coast of Greenland. For two hours, a crew of 20 sprayed 780 gallons of red dye onto an almost 10,000-square-foot iceberg (Fig. **10-5**). The dye, diluted with seawater, was the same that is used for tinting meat. Evaristti's work can be found—for the time being, at least—near Ilullissat (which means "icebergs" in the Greenlandic language), a town of 4,000 that is popular among tourists for its spectacular and *artistic* scenery.

Another approach to land art can be seen in the works of Robert Smithson and Nancy Holt (see Fig. 2-24). Rather than creating works from natural materials present on the site, these artists interrupt the landscape with objects consisting of man-made materials. In so doing, the viewer is encouraged to consider the relationship between the environment and human activity. Holt's placement of gargantuan concrete cylinders on a desert floor is designed to enframe and focus the sun's light. In Smithson's *Yucatan Mirror Displacements* (Fig. **10-6**), topographic shifts, like vignettes, became the context for the placement of clusters of mirrors as the artist traveled through the landscape. The interactivity between nature and technology is clear. The mirrors transform the environment by interrupting the natural setting, and the environment in turn transforms them. The anonymity of the mirror surfaces is lost as they reflect the shapes, colors, and textures of their host environment.

One of the most spectacular examples of land art that combines nature and man-made materials is Walter de Maria's *The Lightning Field* (Fig. **10-7**). The field is constructed of 400 stainless steel poles (lightning rods) anchored in a 1-by-0.62-mile plot of earth. As with Holt's *Sun Tunnels*, nature's

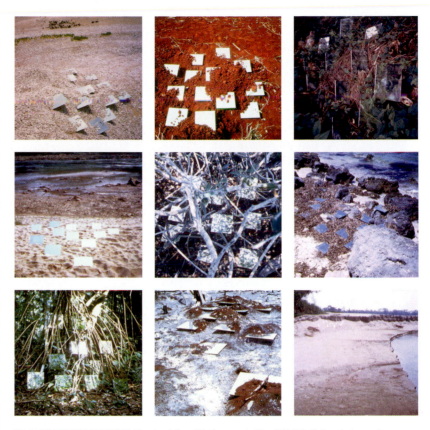

10-6 ROBERT SMITHSON. *Yucatan Mirror Displacements* (April 1969). Color photographs. Nine parts, 10½" × 10½" each. Solomon R. Guggenheim Museum, NY. Art © Estate of Robert Smithson/Licensed by VAGA, NY.

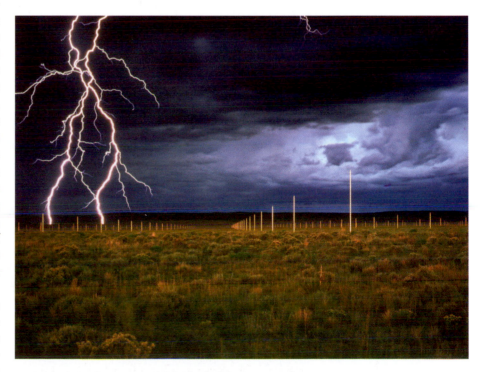

10-7 WALTER DE MARIA. *The Lightning Field* (1977). 400 polished stainless steel poles installed in a grid array measuring 1 mile × 1 km. The poles—2" in diameter and averaging 20'7½" in height—are spaced 220' apart and have solid pointed tips that define a horizontal plane. Quemado, NM.

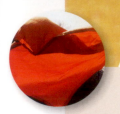

AS IF INTENTIONALLY TIMED TO SHAKE New York City out of its winter doldrums, 7,503 sensuous saffron panels were gradually released from the tops of 16-foot-tall gates along 23 miles of footpaths throughout Central Park. It was the morning of February 12, 2005—a date that marked the end of artists Christo and Jeanne-Claude's 26-year odyssey to bring a major project to their adopted city. For a brief 16 days, the billowy nylon fabric fluttered and snapped and obscured and enframed our favorite park perspectives (Fig. 10-8). The park's majestic plan of ups and downs, of lazy loops and serpentine curves (as originally designed by Frederick Law Olmsted and Calvert Vaux), was being seen or reseen for the first time as we—the participants—wove our walks according to the patterns of the gates. The artists have said that "the temporary quality of their projects is an aesthetic decision," that it "endows the works of art with a feeling of urgency to be seen." For a brief 16 days, it was clear from the crowds in a winter park, from the constant cluster of buses at the 72nd Street entrance, and from the rubbernecking traffic on the streets and avenues bordering the park that the urgency of which Christo and Jeanne-Claude speak was very real.

As with all of Christo and Jeanne-Claude's works of environmental art, every aspect of the *Gates* project was financed and fought for by the artists. They developed the concept for *The Gates* in 1979, but their first proposal to the city in 1981 was rejected. Mayor Michael R. Bloomberg granted permission for the 2005 version of the project on January 22, 2003. The vital statistics of *The Gates, Central Park, New York City, 1979–2005* are staggering. Placed at 12- to 15-foot intervals, 7,503 vinyl gates, 16 feet high, varying in width from 5 feet 6 inches to 18 feet, covered 23 miles of footpaths (Fig. 10-9). The free-hanging, saffron-colored fabric panels dropped from the top of each rectangular vinyl gate to 7 feet above the ground—just low enough for small children on their father's

shoulders to sneak a touch. The project required more than 1 million square feet of vinyl and 5,300 tons of steel. Hundreds of paid volunteers assembled, installed, maintained, and removed the work, and most of the materials were to be recycled. The estimated cost of the project—borne by the artists alone—was $20 million.

The artists finance their environmental sculptures, which have included Wrapped Reichstag, Berlin, 1971–1995; Surrounded Islands, Biscayne Bay, Greater Miami, Florida, 1980–1983; Running Fence, Sonoma and Marin Counties, California, 1972–1976; and others, by selling preparatory drawings and early works by Christo. Much of the funds thus accumulated have been used to cover the cost of the materials used in the project, to pay workers, and, when necessary, for legal fees to combat suits brought by concerned environmentalists (as was the case with the *Running Fence* project).

The environmental art projects of artists Christo and Jeanne-Claude have been seen by

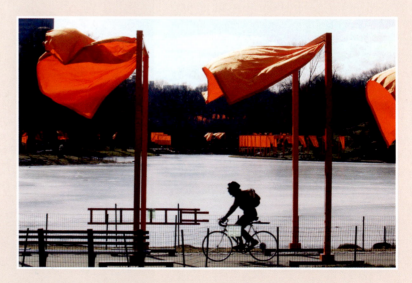

10-8 CHRISTO AND JEANNE CLAUDE. *The Gates, Central Park, New York City (1979-2005).*

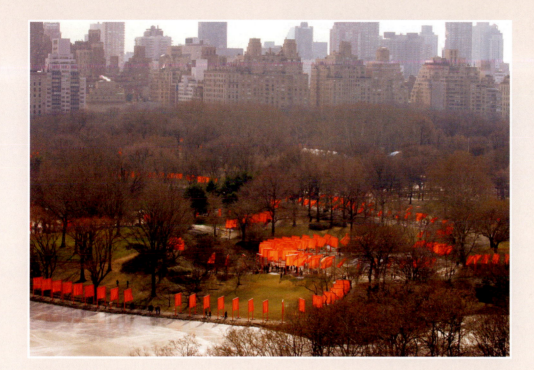

10-9 Aerial view of *The Gates* in Central Park with Manhattan skyline.

millions, who have been enticed to experience their familiar surroundings with a heightened sensibility. Like the artists, I, too, live in New York City. I walked *The Gates* many times over 16 days, each time with a group of family members and friends who made the pilgrimage. When asked why it was so important to realize this work in Central Park, Christo responded, "When our son was a little boy, we used to take him to Central Park every day—he loved to climb the beautiful rocks. Central Park was a part of our life." I think of my own daughter, whose school held gym class on the park's Great Lawn. The Central Park that she will remember as a part of her life growing up in New York will forever include the 16 days when, in clear and in cold and a glorious snowfall, a "golden river" snaked through a barren winter scene, lighting the landscape with flashes of color. ●

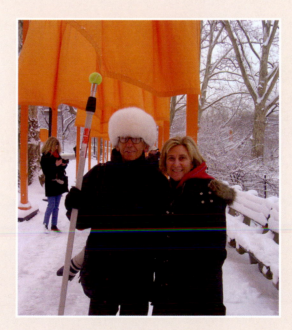

10-10 Christo with your author in Central Park on the day after *The Gates* officially closed.

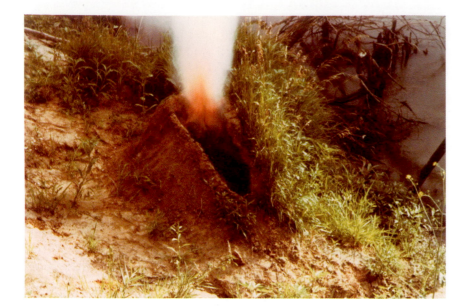

10-11 ANA MENDIETA. Untitled from the "Volcano" Series (1979). Performance, earth, gunpowder. Life size. Old Man's Creek, Iowa City, IA.

"behavior" in the grandest sense gives shape and meaning to the work. The enduring as well as transitory aspects of nature are woven into the varied experience of land art.

The intimate physical relationship between the individual artist and the environment forms the basis of the work of yet another group of land artists. Ana Mendieta's series of self-portraits (Fig. **10-11**) consisted of marking the presence of her body in the landscape using materials and methods such as impressions in the snow and mud and hollowed-out, body-shaped depressions filled with gunpowder and lit afire.

In a work that evokes the literary character Gulliver and his encounter with the tiny Lilliputians, Charles Simonds used his body as a building site for the miniature dwellings of an imagined civilization of little people (Fig. **10-12**). The artist lay

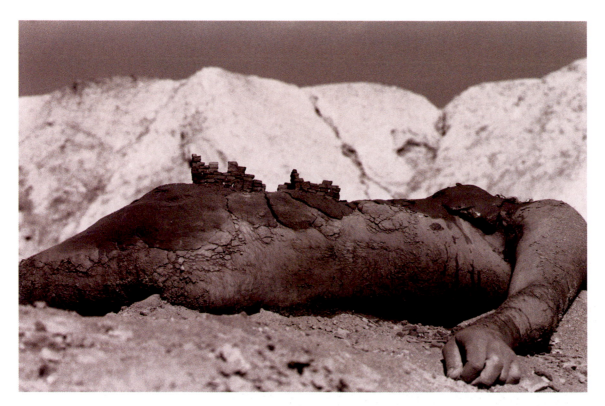

10-12 CHARLES SIMONDS. *Landscape–Body–Dwelling* (1971). Artist's body, clay. Life size.
© 2011 Charles Simonds/Artists Rights Society (ARS), NY.

down on the earth and covered himself with clay, providing a convoluted landscape setting for the diminutive structures. Simonds's work can also be seen in an inconspicuous corner of a ledge in the stairwell of New York's Whitney Museum of American Art.

EPHEMERAL ART

Hippocrates' oft-quoted words were intended to laud the significance of art, attributable in part to its longevity and survival across generations. Is its sentiment outdated? Consider much of the work we have discussed so far in this chapter, which did not last long beyond its creation. Goldsworthy's *Ice Piece* remained frozen just long enough for him to document it with his camera. Many artists work with ephemeral materials—in other words, materials that do not endure.

The term **ephemeral art** is used specifically to describe works that have a temporal immediacy or are built with the recognition that they will disintegrate. You see them one minute and the next they're gone. Most of this work is viewed only in photographs after the fact, unless one happens to be lucky enough to be present when the piece is crafted or performed. How does such work differ from land art? Sometimes it doesn't. Goldsworthy's *Ice Piece* comes under the cat-

egory of land art that is ephemeral, but his *Storm King Wall*, made of stone, is intended to endure.

Cai Guo Qiang's fireworks pieces (Fig. **10-13**) are classic examples of ephemeral art. *Transient Rainbow*, commissioned by the Museum of Modern Art (undergoing renovation at the time) was planned to coincide with the opening of its temporary space in Queens—across the East River from Manhattan. As Cai wrote:

In my hometown every significant social occasion of any kind, good or bad—weddings, funerals, the birth of a baby, a new home—is marked by the explosion of fireworks. They even use fireworks when they elect Communist party officials, or after someone delivers a speech. Fireworks are like the town crier, announcing whatever's going on in town.

The project was a masterpiece of coordination in conception, creation, and documentation. After several iterations, shaped by the concerns of the New York City Fire Department, Transit Authority, Coast Guard, and Federal Aviation Administration, Qiang's piece came and went, in some 15 seconds, on June 29, 2002. The fireworks display consisted of 1,000 shells that were launched in sequence from the Manhattan side of the river, ascending and descending in an arc toward Queens, on the opposite side. The brilliant color palette unfolded so that, for a moment, a transient moment, the fireworks rainbow spanned the river.

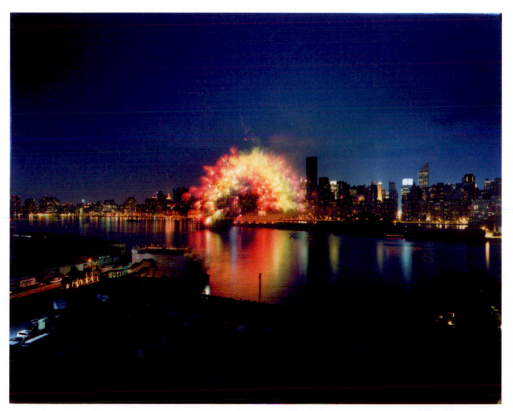

Anyone who has tried to capture a fireworks display with a camera knows that it's a tough thing to do. The vibrancy and shimmer that send "oooooos" through the crowd never seem to measure up in our photographic record. With a work that is literally there one minute and gone the next, its documentation becomes extremely important. Qiang hired 20 photographers in all—three of whom were specialized fireworks photographers from Japan—to capture *Transient Rainbow*. The video document and still photographs have become an essential part of the work: tangible records of an ephemeral art performance.

10-13 CAI GUO QIANG. *Transient Rainbow* over East River, New York City (2002).

HEIZER'S *RIFT* WITH LIBESKIND'S JEWISH MUSEUM

IN 1967, MICHAEL HEIZER took to the bottom of a dry lakebed for *Rift* (Fig. **10-14**), one piece in his land art series called *Nine Nevada Depressions*. Almost three decades later,

Daniel Libeskind used a startlingly similar shape for his extension of the Berlin Museum dedicated to the Holocaust and Jewish art and life (Fig. **10-15**). Libeskind's zigzag design was derived mathematically by plotting the Berlin addresses of Jewish writers, artists, and composers who were killed during the Holocaust. The building's jagged shape reads as a painful rift in the continuity of the neighborhood in which it stands; it is punctuated by voids that symbolize the absence of Jewish people and culture in Berlin.

Heizer's *Rift* consists of a displacement of local materials such that the normalcy of the landscape is interrupted. For Heizer, the process is perhaps less about symbolism than it is about artistic elements. His depressions play with the relative scale of humans and nature; he is as much interested in the disintegration of his piece by natural processes over time as he is with the initial creative act. Heizer's jagged "scar" on the earth faded over time and then disappeared. How did Libeskind use this shape to try to ensure that the story of the Jews of Berlin would not fade or disappear? Is there something inherent in these shapes in contrast to their surroundings that suggests a certain symbolism or elicits a certain emotional response? How much do content and context influence our analysis of works with such visual congruities? ●

10-14 MICHAEL HEIZER. *Rift* (deteriorated). First of *Nine Nevada Depressions* (1968). 1.5-ton displacement on the bottom of a dry lake bed. 6220½" × 177³/₁₆" × 118⅛". Massacre Dry Lake, NV.

10-15 DANIEL LIBESKIND. Extension of the Berlin Museum (1989–1996). Berlin, Germany.

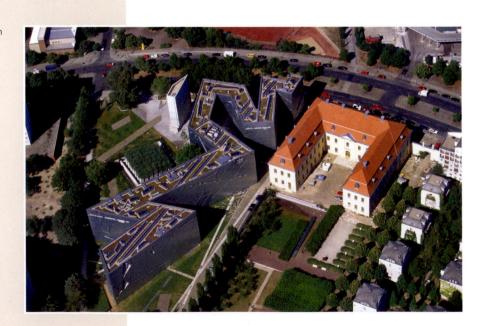

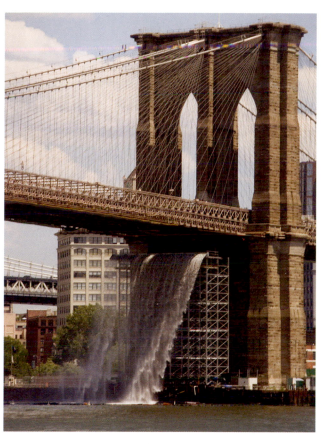

10-16 OLAFUR ELIASSON. *The New York City Waterfalls*, Brooklyn Bridge, NY (2008).

PUBLIC ART

The history of art is also full of works created for public spaces. Michelangelo's *David* (Fig. 16-25), even though it now has sanctuary in the Galleria dell'Accademia in Florence, was installed as a public work of art for the Piazza della Signoria, just outside the building that served as the political center of the city. A bit farther south, in Rome, one can see some of the most famous, most elaborate fountains in the world. They were created for the pleasure of the public (though often too for the glory of a pope). It is common also today for institutions (including the U.S. federal government) to allot a percentage of the overall cost of their building programs for works of art destined for the public spaces in and around buildings. You are probably familiar with works of public art in your own cities and towns, some dating back decades and some installed for a particular occasion or just for the season, as was Olafur Eliasson's *New York City Waterfalls* (Fig. **10-16**). Constructed under the Brooklyn Bridge in the summer of 2008, it was one of four sites featuring freestanding waterfalls funded by New York's Public Art Fund.

New York's Central Park forms the geographic and spiritual heart of that city and serves as the backdrop for one of its most beloved public sculptures. *Angel of the Waters* (Fig. **10-17**) (also known as Bethesda Fountain), by Emma Stebbins, towers above a circular brick plaza bordering a large lake. Warm weather brings sunbathers, break-dancers, newlyweds, and

10-17 EMMA STEBBINS. *Angel of the Waters* (Bethesda Fountain) (1873). Central Park, NY.

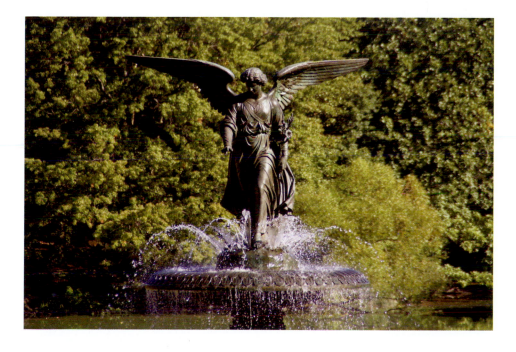

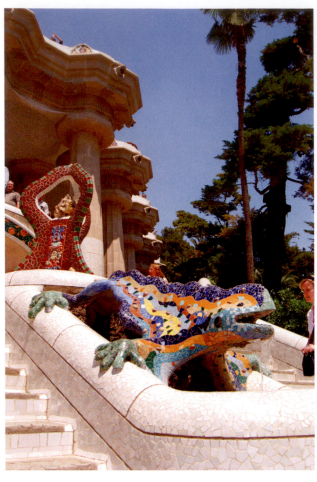

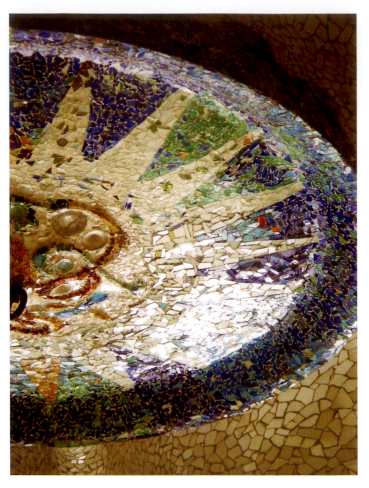

10-18 ANTONI GAUDÍ. *Serpent/Salamander* (1900–1914). *Parc Güell*, Barcelona, Spain.

10-19 ANTONI GAUDÍ. Detail of mosaic sunburst in ceiling of hypostyle hall (1900–1914). *Parc Güell*, Barcelona, Spain.

10-20 ANTONI GAUDÍ. Detail of mosaic serpentine bench, which sits in plaza above hypostyle hall (1900–1914). *Parc Güell*, Barcelona, Spain.

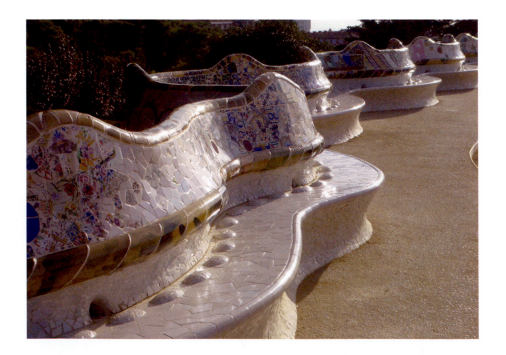

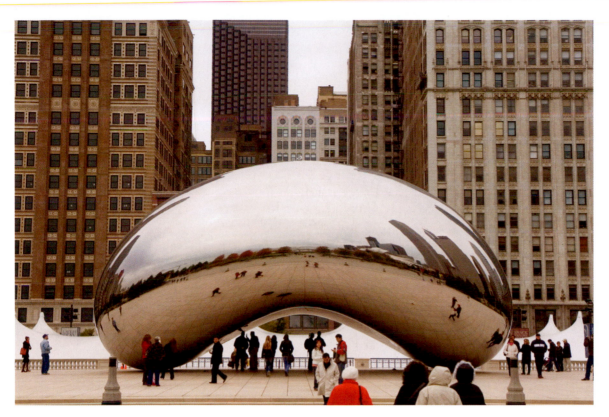

10-21 ANISH KAPOOR. *Cloud Gate* (2004–2006). *Cloud Gate*'s exterior consists of 168 highly polished stainless steel plates. It is 33' × 66' × 42' tall. Millennium Park, Chicago, IL.

splashing dogs to this public gathering space that seems to sit protectively beneath the outspread wings of an angel.

At the beginning of the twentieth century in Barcelona, one of its most famous native sons—Antoni Gaudí—was asked by his patron, Eusebi Güell, to create a gardenlike suburb for the very rich overlooking the city. The project was abandoned, but not before completion of what is now one of Barcelona's most treasured public sites, *Parc Güell*. A lively mosaic serpent (Fig. **10-18**) stands at the entrance of the park and has become one of the recognizable symbols of the city. Flights of steps lead to a variation on a hypostyle hall, with a forest of columns ornamented with lavish mosaic bases. The undulating ceiling is punctuated with mosaic discs called sunbursts (Fig. **10-19**). This space was originally intended to serve as a public market. Resting on top of the columned hall is an esplanade, the perimeter of which is lined with its serpentine, mosaic-clad stone bench (Fig. **10-20**). Gaudí was known for his playful, organic forms (see also his *Casa Mila*, Fig. 19-39) that helped define the Modernista style in Catalunya (or Catalonia), Spain.

Chicago's Millennium Park has its own very popular and very new gathering space, the focal point of which is Anish Kapoor's *Cloud Gate* (Fig. **10-21**). Nicknamed "the bean" because of its elliptical, beanlike shape, the work consists of highly polished, mirrorlike stainless steel plates that reflect the people, places, and things surrounding it, both permanent and transient. Kapoor has called his piece "a gate to Chicago, a poetic idea about the city it reflects." The work inspired a new jazz composition (*Fanfare for Cloud Gate*) by Orbert Davis, performed in Millennium Park on the occasion of the dedication of Kapoor's sculpture.

A bit of controversy surrounding *Cloud Gate* proves interesting with regard to the nature of land and environmental art, including commissioned public works of art. Kapoor owns the rights to the piece, and therefore photographs of it cannot be reproduced commercially (as in this book) without his permission. One particular photographer learned this the hard way, when he was not permitted to photograph "the bean" without a prepaid permit. The public response to limits on publishing personal photographs of this public work of art was strong; photographs began to appear all over the Internet (you can find them on Google Images or Flickr, a photo-sharing website). If public art is public (and sometimes supported in real dollars by the public), where, in your opinion, should the artist's rights end and the public's begin?

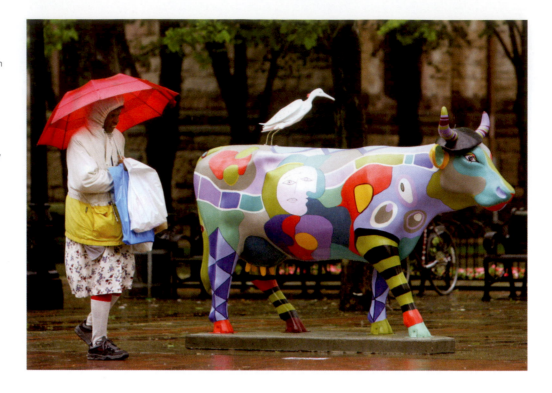

The Bethesda Fountain and *Cloud Gate* have become icons of their respective cities; there are permanent installations of comparable works of art in public spaces all over the globe. Public art can also be temporary, like the pandemic *Cow Parades*—installations of fiberglass cows painted in every conceivable style, on every imaginable theme, turning up in almost too many cities to mention: New York, Chicago, London, Brussels, Sydney, Stockholm, Athens, Sao Paolo, and Moscow, to name some on the list (Fig. **10-22**). In all, it is estimated that Cow Parade has been seen by more than 100 million people worldwide. Some of the cows have been purchased after exhibition, raising money for charities. *Waga-Moo-Moo*, one of the Dublin *Cow Parade*, fetched $148,000 for a good cause. The cow craze has spawned many imitators, with different creatures popping up in cities everywhere.

MONUMENTS

The few examples of site-specific public art that we have looked at were designed or installed to enhance a particular open, public space. Their main purpose is or was aesthetic—to create beauty or to enhance the environment. Monuments comprise another category of site-specific public art. Their purpose is to preserve the memory of a person or an event.

The category of monuments is so broad that the few works we are able to concentrate on here represent an absurdly small percentage of what we live with in our communities. Equestrian monuments—men on horseback—seem almost ubiquitous in cities and towns, even though the identities of those memorialized are often forgotten. One of the purposes of monuments is to institutionalize memory. Monuments serve as expressions of the need or desire of a city, a country, or perhaps of a generation to "never forget."

The Oklahoma City National Memorial and Museum was created to remember the victims, survivors, and rescuers of the 1995 bombing of the Alfred P. Murrah Federal Building in that city. It is a multipart memorial site that incorporates various symbolic elements, the most arresting of which is the *Field of Empty Chairs* (Fig. **10-23**). One hundred sixty-eight chairs representing the individual victims were placed in nine rows corresponding to the floors they inhabited. The chairs are crafted of stone and bronze on a glass base, each etched with a victim's name. The field of chairs overlooks a reflecting pool that is adjacent to a Rescuer's Orchard honoring those who risked their lives and rushed to the scene to help. The focal point of the orchard is the Survivor Tree, an elm that withstood the blast of the explosion and now honors the survivors of the attack. The memorial site, which occupies the footprint of the Murrah building, also includes a museum. The memorial was designed to touch everyone who experienced the event, reflecting the impact of the violence on the community. It is an interactive type of monument, a place where one comes to witness history and to remember the dead and the living. The grief and the mourning are col-

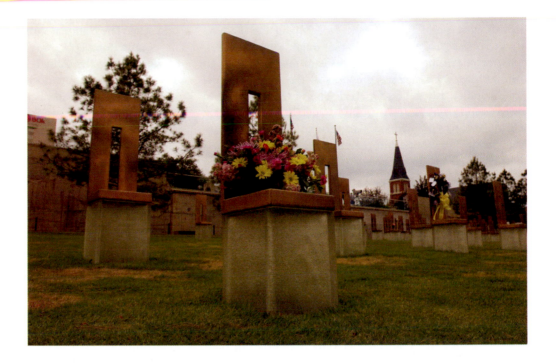

10-23 The Field of Empty Chairs (2000). Oklahoma City National Memorial and Museum, Oklahoma City, OK.

lective, but the relationship to the victims—through the symbol of the chair—is personal. The empty chair represents loss and literal absence—a father or mother or friend who is no longer at the table, no longer sharing in life's moments.

This sense of loss and absence is central to Peter Eisenman's Holocaust Memorial in Berlin (Fig. **10-24**), erected in memory of the European Jews murdered by the Nazis. Within view of the Brandenburg Gate and the Reichstag—

two architectural monuments associated with Adolf Hitler and Nazism—Eisenman placed 2,711 gray, concrete **stelae** side by side in claustrophobic rows. The stelae are the same length and width but vary in height and are placed on slabs that are tilted in different directions. The paths between the slabs slope up and then down so that the journey among these stones shifts and changes. The concentration of stelae is greatest at the center of the monument, creating a

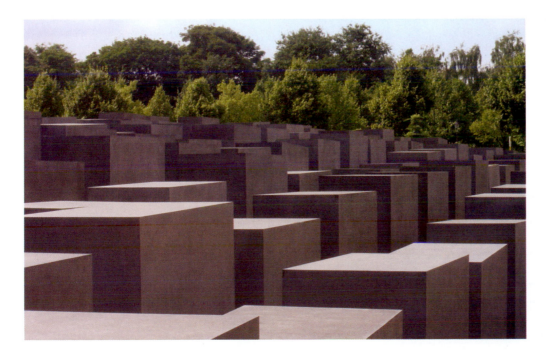

10-24 PETER EISENMAN. Holocaust Memorial (2004). Berlin, Germany.

disturbing sense of confinement. In sunlight, the shadows are sharp and harsh; shady areas that ought to provide welcome respite from the sun are, instead, menacing. On an overcast day, the relentless grayness of the stones and the sky is somber, ashen, and funereal. The site is also home to an exhibition space, underground beneath the stelae, that is dedicated to the historical background of the Holocaust. The feeling is cryptlike, but there are no bodies, no objects that belonged to the deceased, and therein lies a point of the memorial. The Nazis planned to annihilate the Jews of Europe and any memory of them.

As the competitions ensued for the commission of Berlin's Holocaust Memorial, questions were raised about the relevance of a modern, abstract design. Would it be understood? Would it have meaning? The same questions haunted Maya Lin's proposal for the Vietnam Veterans Memorial in Washington, D.C., decades earlier (see A Closer Look: The Vietnam Veterans Memorial—A Woman's Perspective).

The Oklahoma City Memorial, the Berlin Holocaust Memorial, and the Vietnam Veterans Memorial all have a very different feeling from traditional triumphal monuments. Rather than looking at stylized images of heroic figures, we are called upon to reflect quietly and intimately on acts of human courage in the face of death. Although an antitriumphal approach represents a significant trend in contemporary monument design, it is not by any means

universal. The National World War II Memorial (Fig. **10-25**) in Washington, D.C., was dedicated in 2004, more than 50 years after the Allied victories in Europe and Japan. The design for the memorial, with its pavilions and pillars, stirred a different kind of controversy in that its traditional, classical forms were reminiscent, to one journalist, of the pompous style embraced by the Fascist regimes of the 1930s, the very regimes that the Allies fought to defeat. One critic went so far as to refer to the memorial as a "monument on steroids—vainglorious, demanding of attention and full of trite imagery."[1]

The reception of the National World War II Memorial was not all negative, although the controversy raises an interesting question about the ways in which people relate to memorials and critics evaluate them. Many contemporary artists have gravitated toward designs that are interactive, educational, and reflective. Artists working in a more traditional mode emphasize the larger-than-human, the heroic. Reactions to memorials are highly personal, and the way memory is institutionalized is a very sensitive topic. Critics can find themselves in a situation in which their criticism is viewed, at best, as politically incorrect or, at worst, as unpatriotic.

---

[1] Thomas M. Keane Jr., *Boston Herald*, 2004.

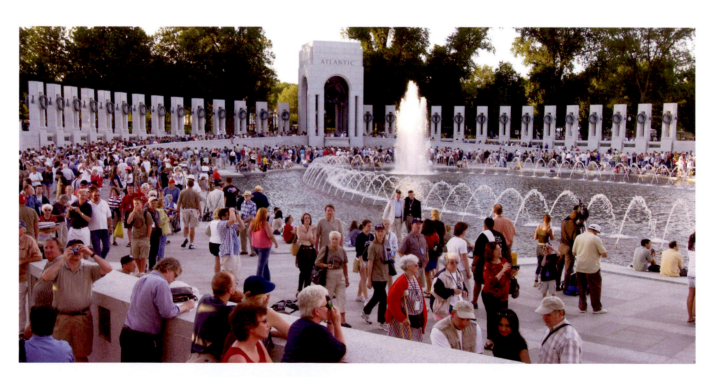

10-25 FRIEDRICH ST. FLORIAN. National World War II Memorial (2004). Washington, D.C.

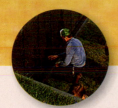

A CLOSER LOOK   THE VIETNAM VETERANS
MEMORIAL—A WOMAN'S PERSPECTIVE

WHEN WE VIEW THE EXPANSES of the Washington Mall, we are awed by the grand obelisk that is the Washington Monument. We are comforted by the stately columns and familiar shapes of the Lincoln and Jefferson memorials. But many of us do not know how to respond to the two 200-foot-long black granite walls that form a V as they recede into the ground. There is no label—only the names of 58,000 victims chiseled into the silent walls:

> As we descend along the path that hugs the harsh black granite, we enter the very earth that, in another place, has accepted the bodies of our sons and daughters. Each name is carved not only in the stone, but by virtue of its highly polished surface, in our own reflection, in our physical substance. We are not observers, we are participants. We touch, we write [letters to our loved ones], we leave parts of ourselves behind. This is a woman's vision—to commune, to interact, to collaborate with the piece to fulfill its expressive potential. . . .

> Maya Ying Lin has foregone the [format of the triumphal monument]. She has given us [the earth mother] Gaea, who, pierced by the ebony scar of suffering death, takes back her children, as she has done since the dawn of humanity.*

This is Maya Ying Lin's Vietnam Veterans Memorial (Fig. 10-26), completed in 1982 on a two-acre site on the Mall. In order to read the names, we must descend gradually into the earth, and then just as gradually work our way back up. This progress is perhaps symbolic of the nation's involvement in Vietnam. The eloquently simple design of the memorial also stirs controversy, as did the war it commemorates.

This dignified understatement in stone has offended many who would have preferred a more traditional memorial. One conservative magazine branded the design a conspiracy to dishonor the dead. Architecture critic Paul Gapp of the *Chicago Tribune* argued, "The so-called memorial is bizarre . . . neither a building nor sculpture." One Vietnam veteran had called for a statue of an officer offering a fallen soldier to heaven. The public expects a certain heroic quality in its monuments to commemorate those fallen in battle. Lin's work is antiheroic and antitriumphal. Whereas most war monuments speak of giving up our loved ones to a cause, her monument speaks only of giving up our loved ones.

How did the Vietnam Memorial come to be so uniquely designed? It was chosen from 1,421 entries in a national competition. The designer, Maya Ying Lin, is a Chinese American woman who was all of 22 years old at the time she submitted her entry. A native of Ohio, Lin had just graduated from Yale University, where she majored in architecture. Lin recognized that a monumental sculpture or another grand building would have been intrusive in the heart of Washington. Her design meets the competition criteria of being "neither too commanding nor too deferential" and is yet another expression of the versatility of stone. ●

It terrified me to have an idea that was solely mine to be no longer a part of my mind, but totally public.

—Maya Ying Lin, on her design for the Vietnam Veterans Memorial in Washington, D.C.

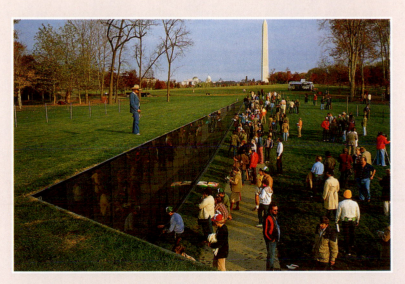

10-26 MAYA YING LIN. Vietnam Veterans Memorial (1982). Polished black granite. L: 492'. Washington, D.C.

---

* Lois Fichner-Rathus, "A Woman's Vision of the War," *New York Times*, August 18, 1991, H6.

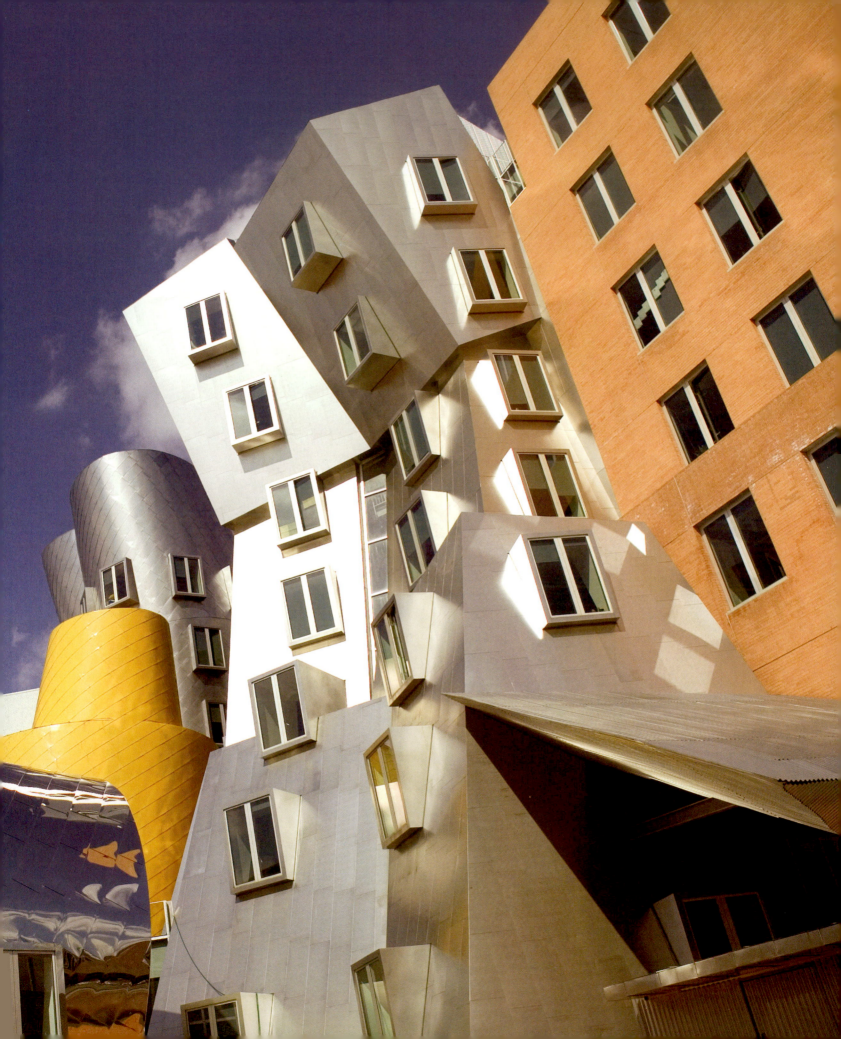

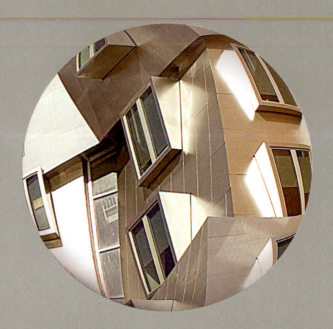

ARCHITECTURE

11

The earliest humans found shelter in nature's protective cocoons—the mouth of a yawning cave, the underside of a rocky ledge, the dense canopy of an overspreading tree. But the construction of dwellings goes back to the Stone Age. In the words of author Howard Bloom, "first came the mammoth, then came architecture." Before we became capable of transporting bulky materials over vast distances, we had to rely on local possibilities. Ice Age humans dragged the skeletal pieces of woolly mammoths to a protective spot and piled them into domelike structures (Fig. 11-1). Native Americans carved complex communities into the sides of mesa cliffs (Fig. 11-2). Later, they built huts from sticks and bark and conical teepees from wood poles sheathed in animal skins. African villagers wove sticks and grass into cylindrical walls, plastered them with mud, and capped them with geometrically pure cone roofs. Desert inhabitants fashioned sun-baked clay into bricks, and the Inuit stacked blocks of ice with precision to create igloos.

Architecture is the art and science of designing buildings, bridges, and other structures. Of all the arts, architecture probably has the greatest impact on our daily lives. It shapes the immediate environments in which we live, work, or entertain ourselves. And, as the history of architecture reveals, it reflects and symbolizes our concept of self and the societies in which we live, past and present.

FRANK GEHRY. Ray and Maria Stata Center for Computer, Information, and Intelligence Sciences at MIT (2005). Cambridge, MA.

Architects work within the limits of their materials and the technology of the day. Although architects are visionaries and designers with artistic skills, they also possess technical knowledge necessary to determine how materials may be used to span and enclose vast spaces efficiently and safely. Architects are collaborators. They work with other professionals—engineers, contractors and builders, tradespeople, and interior designers.

Architects are also compromisers. The architect mediates between a client and civic planning boards and build-

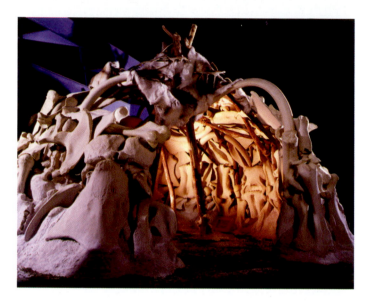

11-1 This house was built of hundreds of mammoth bones by hunters on windswept, treeless plains in Ukraine, about 15,000 years ago. Working as a team, hut builders needed only a few days to haul together hundreds of massive mammoth bones, then stack them into a snug home.

ing departments, historic preservation committees, and, of course, the properties and aesthetic possibilities of the site itself. Today's technology may make possible the erection of a 20-story-high, 20-foot-wide "sliver skyscraper" on an expensive, narrow urban site, but with what aesthetic impact on a neighborhood? Since the 1930s, architects in New York City have had to comply with the so-called setback law and step back or contour their high-rises from the street in order to let the sun shine in on an environment that seemed in danger of devolving into a maze of blackened canyons. For an architect, negotiation is part of the job description. Climate, site specifics, materials, building codes, **service systems**, funding, and human personalities are just some of the variables that the architect encounters in an attempt to create a functional and aesthetically interesting structure.

In this section, we will explore ways in which architects have come to terms with these variables. We will survey the use of building materials and methods including stone, wood, cast iron, steel, concrete, and new technologies.

STONE ARCHITECTURE

As a building material, stone is massive and virtually indestructible. Contemporary wood-frame homes frequently sport stone fireplaces, perhaps as a symbol of permanence and strength as well as of warmth. The Native American cliff dwellings at Mesa Verde, Colorado (Fig. **11-2**), could be considered something of an "earthwork high relief." The cliff itself becomes the back wall or "support" of more than 100 rect-

11-2 Cliff dwellings, Mesa Verde, CO.

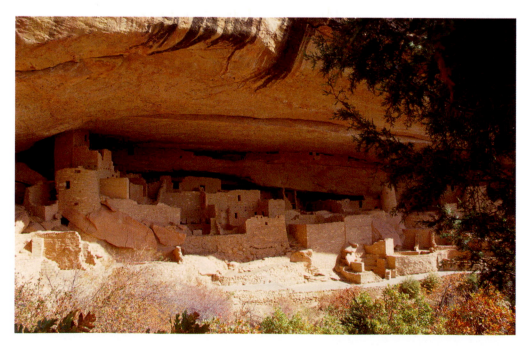

11book - first dwellings in Stone Age
   - architecture - art + sci. of designing structures

angular apartments. Circular, underground **kivas** served as community centers. Construction with stone, **adobe**, and timber creates a mixed-media functional fantasy. Early humans also assembled stone temples and memorials.

Post-and-Lintel Construction

The prehistoric Stonehenge (see Fig. 13-3) probably served religious or astronomical purposes. Its orientation toward the sun and its layout in concentric circles are suggestive of the amphitheaters and temples to follow. Stonehenge is an early example of **post-and-lintel construction** (Fig. **11-3A**). Two stones were set upright as supports, and a third was placed across them, creating an opening beneath. How the massive

blocks of Stonehenge were transported and erected remains a mystery.

Early stone structures were erected without benefit of mortar. Their dry **masonry** relied on masterly carving of blocks, strategic placement, and sheer weight for durability. Consider the imposing ruin of the fortress of Machu Picchu, perched high above the Urubamba River in the Peruvian Andes. Its beautiful granite walls (Fig. **11-4**), constructed by the Incas, are pieced together so perfectly that not even a knife blade can pass between the blocks. The faces of the Great Pyramids of Egypt (see Fig. 13-12) are assembled as miraculously, perhaps even more so considering the greater mass of the blocks.

Stone became the favored material for the public buildings of the Egyptians and the Greeks. The Egyptian Temple of

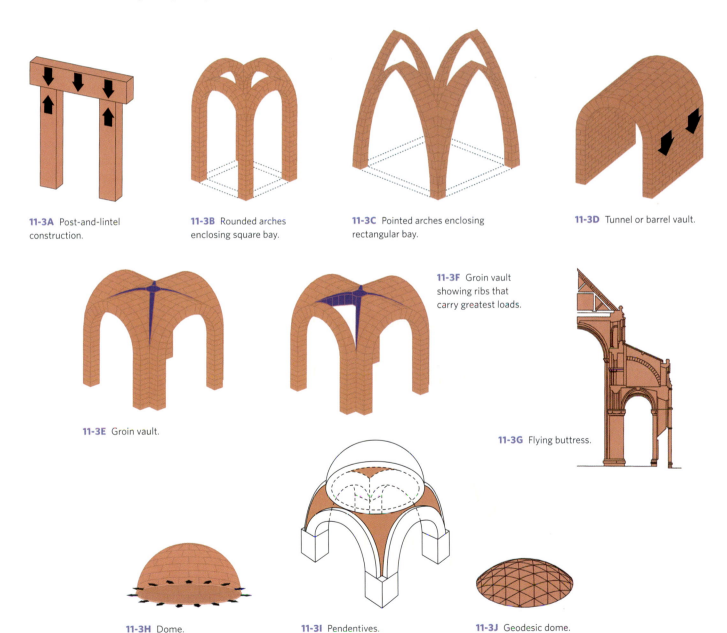

11-3A Post-and-lintel construction.

11-3B Rounded arches enclosing square bay.

11-3C Pointed arches enclosing rectangular bay.

11-3D Tunnel or barrel vault.

11-3E Groin vault.

11-3F Groin vault showing ribs that carry greatest loads.

11-3G Flying buttress.

11-3H Dome.

11-3I Pendentives.

11-3J Geodesic dome.

11-4 Walls of Fortress of Machu Picchu, Urubamba Valley, Peru. (1490–1530).

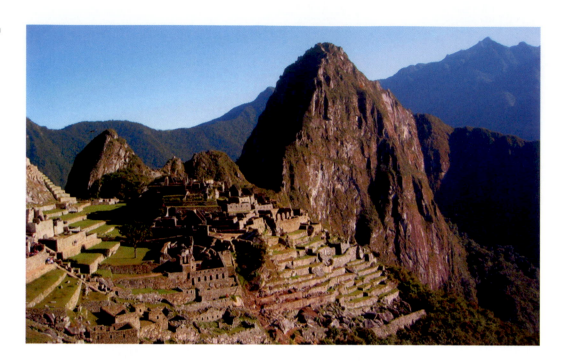

11-5 Hypostyle Hall, Temple of Amen-Re (1570-1342 BCE). Karnak, Egypt.

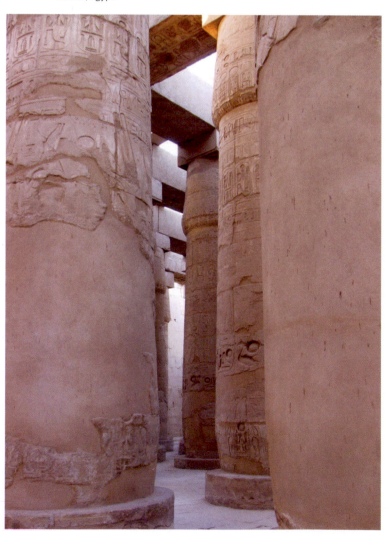

Amen-Re at Karnak (Figs. **11-5** and **11-6**) and the Parthenon (see Fig. 14-10) of the Classical period of Greece begin to speak of the elegance as well as the massiveness that can be fashioned from stone. The Temple of Amen-Re is of post-and-lintel construction, but the paintings, relief sculptures, and overall smoothness of the columns belie their function as bearers of stress. The virtual forest of columns was a structural necessity because of the weight of the massive stone lintels. The Parthenon is also of post-and-lintel construction. Consistent with the Greeks' emphasis on the functional purpose of columns, the surfaces of the marble shafts are free from ornamentation. The Parthenon, which may be the most studied and surveyed building in the world, is discussed at length in Chapter 14.

Arches

Architects of stone also use **arches** to span distances (Figs. **11-3B** and **11-3C**). Arches have many functions, including supporting other structures, such as roofs, and serving as actual and symbolic gateways. An Arch of Triumph, as in the city of Paris, provides a visual focus for the return of the conquering hero. Eero Saarinen's Gateway Arch (Fig. **11-7**), completed in St. Louis in 1966, stands 630 feet tall at the center and commemorates the westward push of the United States after the Louisiana Purchase of 1803. The Pont du Gard (see Fig. 14-22) near Nîmes, France, employs the arch in a bridge that is part of an aqueduct system. It is a marvel of Roman engineering. Early masonry arches were fashioned from **bricks**; each limestone block of the Pont du Gard weighs up to two tons, and they were assembled without benefit of mortar. The bridge stands and functions today, two millennia after its creation.

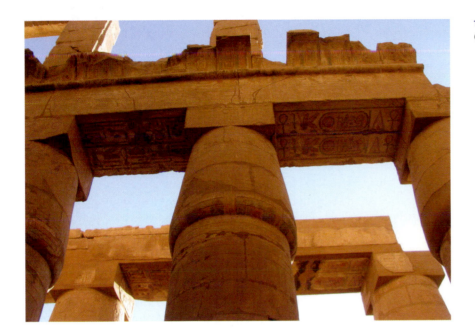

11-6 Hypostyle Hall, Temple of Amen-Re (1570-1342 BCE). Karnak, Egypt.

11-7 EERO SAARINEN. Jefferson National Expansion Memorial, Gateway Arch (1966). St. Louis, MO.

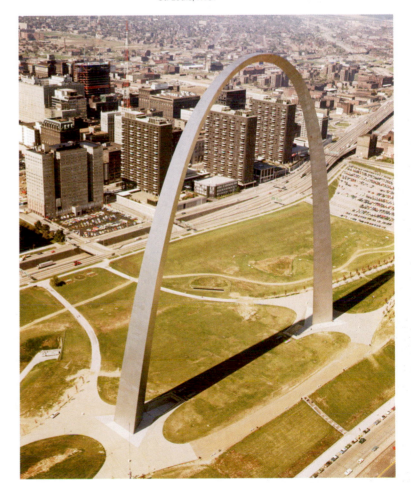

In most arches, wedge-shaped blocks of stone, called **voussoirs**, are gradually placed in position ascending a wooden scaffold called a **centering**. When the center, or **keystone**, is set in place, the weight of the blocks is all at once transmitted in an arc laterally and downward, and the centering can be removed. The pull of gravity on each block serves as "cement"; that is, the blocks fall into one another so that the very weight that had made their erection a marvel now prevents them from budging. The **compressive strength** of stone allows the builder to place additional weight above the arch. The Pont du Gard consists of three **tiers** of arches, 161 feet high.

Vaults

An extended arch is called a **vault**. A tunnel or **barrel vault** (Fig. **11-3D**) simply places arches behind one another until a desired depth is reached. In this way, impressive spaces may be roofed, and tunnels may be constructed. Unfortunately, the spaces enclosed by barrel vaults are dark, because piercing them to let in natural light would compromise their strength. The communication of stresses from one arch to another also requires that the centering for each arch be kept in place until the entire vault is completed.

Roman engineers are credited with the creation of the **groin vault**, which overcame limitations of the barrel vault, as early as the third century CE. Groin vaults are constructed by placing barrel vaults at right angles to cover a square space (Fig. **11-3E**). In this way the load of the intersecting vaults

Stone Architecture **217**

is transmitted to the corners, necessitating **buttressing** at these points but allowing the sides of the square to be open. The square space enclosed by the groin vault is called a **bay**. Architects could now construct huge buildings by assembling any number of bays. Because the stresses from one groin vault are not transmitted to a large degree to its neighbors, the centering used for one vault can be removed and reused while the building is under construction.

The greatest loads in the groin vault are thrust onto the four arches that compose the sides and the two arches that run diagonally across them. If the capacity of these diagonals is increased to carry a load, by means of **ribs** added to the vault (Fig. 11-3F), then the remainder of the roof can be fashioned from stone **webbing** or other materials much lighter in weight. A true stone skeleton is created.

Note in Figure 11-3B that rounded arches can enclose only square bays. One could not use rounded arches in rectangular bays because the longer walls would have higher arches. Architects over the centuries solved the rectangular bay problem in several ingenious ways. The most important of these is found in **Gothic** architecture, discussed in Chapter 15, which uses ribbed vaults and **pointed arches**. Pointed arches can be constructed to uniform heights even when the sides of the enclosed space are unequal (Fig. 11-3C). Gothic architecture also employed the so-called flying buttress (Fig. 11-3G), a masonry strut that transmits part of the load of a vault to a buttress positioned outside a building.

Most of the great cathedrals of Europe achieve their vast, open interiors through the use of vaults. Massive stone rests benignly above the heads of worshippers and tourists alike, transmitting its brute load laterally and downward. The **Ottonian** St. Michael's (see Fig. 15-19), built in Germany between 1001 and 1031 CE, uses barrel vaulting. Its bays are square, and its walls are blank and massive. The **Romanesque** St. Sernin (see Fig. 15-21), built in France between about 1080 and 1120, uses round arches and square bays. The walls are heavy and blunt, with the main masses subdivided by buttresses. St. Étienne (see Fig. 15-23), completed between 1115 and 1120, has high, rising vaults—some of the earliest to show true ribs—that permit light to enter through a **clerestory**. Stone became a fully elegant structural skeleton in the great Gothic cathedrals, such as those at Laon (see Figs. 15-28 and 15-29) and Chartres (see Fig. 15-31) and in the Notre-Dame of Paris (see Fig. 15-30). Lacy buttressing and ample **fenestration** lend these massive buildings an airy lightness that seems consonant with their mission of directing upward the focus of human awareness.

Domes

Domes are hemispherical forms that are rounded when viewed from beneath (see Figs. 11-3H and 11-3J). Like vaults, domes are extensions of the principle of the arch and are capable of enclosing vast reaches of space. (Buckminster Fuller, who designed the United States Pavilion [Fig. 11-25] for the 1967 World's Fair in Montreal, proposed that the center of Manhattan should be enclosed in a weather-controlled transparent dome two miles in diameter.) Stresses from the top of the dome are transmitted in all directions to the points at which the circular base meets the foundation, walls, or other structures beneath.

The dome of the Buddhist temple or Stupa of Sanchi, India, completed in the first century CE, rises 50 feet above the ground and causes the worshipper to contemplate the dwelling place of the gods (see Fig. 18-26). It was constructed from stones placed in gradually diminishing concentric circles. Visitors find the domed interior of the Pantheon of Rome (see Fig. 14-29), completed during the second century CE, breathtaking. Like the dome of the Stupa, the rounded inner surface of the Pantheon, 144 feet in diameter, symbolizes the heavens.

11-8 ANTHEMIUS OF TRALLES AND ISODORUS OF MILETUS. Interior of Hagia Sophia (532–537 CE). Istanbul, Turkey.

The dome of the vast Hagia Sophia (see Fig. **11-8**) in Constantinople is 108 feet in diameter. Its architects, building during the sixth century CE, used four triangular surfaces called **pendentives** (Fig. **11-3l**) to support the dome on a square base. Pendentives transfer the load from the base of the dome to the **piers** at the corners of the square beneath.

Today, stone is rarely used as a structural material in developed nations. It is expensive to quarry and transport, and it is too massive to handle readily at the site. Metals are lighter and have greater tensile strength, so they are suitable as the skeletons or reinforcers for most of today's larger structures. Still, buildings with steel skeletons are frequently dressed with thin facades, or **veneers**, of costly marble, limestone, and other types of stone. Many tract homes are granted decorative patches of stone across the front facade, and slabs of slate are frequently used to provide minimum-care surfaces for entry halls or patios in private homes.

WOOD ARCHITECTURE

Wood is as beautiful and versatile a material for building as it is for sculpture. It is an abundant and, as many advertisements have proclaimed, renewable resource. It is relatively light in weight and is capable of being worked on at the site with readily portable hand tools. Its variety of colors and grains, as well as its capacity to accept paint or to weather charmingly when left in its natural state, make wood a ubiquitous material. Wood, like stone, can be used as a structural element or as a facade. In many structures, it is used as both.

Wood also has its drawbacks. It warps and cracks. It rots. It is also highly flammable and stirs the appetite of termites and other devouring insects. However, modern technology has enhanced the stability and strength of wood as a building material. Chemical treatments decrease wood's vulnerability to rotting from moisture. **Plywood**, which is built up from sheets of wood glued together, is unlikely to warp and is frequently used as an underlayer in the exterior walls of small buildings and homes. Laminated wood beams possess great strength and are also unlikely to become distorted in shape from exposure to changing temperatures and levels of humidity.

Architects, like artists and designers, use contrasting materials to create visual diversity and surface interest. They often reference textures found in nature in order to integrate a building with its site, or to create a dramatic counterpoint to it. The tree houses (Fig. **11-9**) designed by the German architect studio baumraum are extreme and playful examples of both. The designers refer to their endeavors as a blend of architecture, landscape design, and "arboriculture," aiming to integrate the structures into their forest surrounds and, at the same time, preserve the integrity of the host trees. In designing its lofty wood dwellings, baumraum—which literally means "tree space" in German—also takes into consideration

11-9 BAUMRAUM.

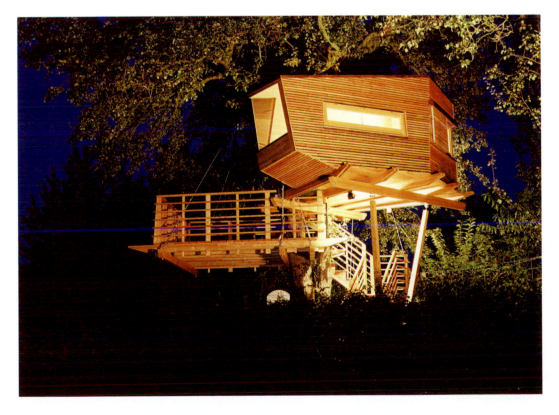

factors such as the species of a tree, its distance off the ground, and the amount of clear building space available in order to successfully suspend the structures. The result is a study in contrast and connection between humans and their natural surroundings.

Post-and-Beam Construction

Post-and-beam construction (Fig. **11-10A**) is similar to post-and-lintel construction. Vertical and horizontal timbers are cut and pieced together with wooden pegs. The beams span openings for windows, doors, and interior spaces, and they can also support posts for another story or roof trusses.

Trusses

Trusses are lengths of wood, iron, or steel pieced together in triangular shapes of the sort shown in Figure **11-10B** in order to expand the abilities of these materials to span distances. Trusses acquire their strength from the fact that the sides of a triangle, once joined, cannot be forced out of shape. In many buildings, roof trusses are exposed and become elements of the design.

Balloon Framing

Balloon framing (Fig. **11-10C**), a product of the industrial revolution, dates back to the beginning of the twentieth century. In balloon framing, factory-cut studs, including the familiar two-by-four, are mass-produced and assembled at the site using thousands of factory-produced metal nails. Several light, easily handled pieces of wood replace the heavy timber of post-and-beam construction. Entire walls are framed in place or on their sides and then raised into place by a crew of carpenters. The multiple pieces and geometric patterns of balloon framing give it a sturdiness that rivals that of the post and beam, permitting the support of slate or tile roofs. However, the term *balloon* was originally a derisive term: inveterate users of post and beam were skeptical that the frail-looking wooden pieces could provide a rugged building.

Balloon framing has now been used on millions of smaller buildings, not only homes. Sidings for balloon-framed homes include **clapboard**, asbestos shingle, brick and stone veneer, and aluminum. Roofs have included asphalt, cedar shingle, tile, and slate. These materials vary in cost, and each has certain aesthetic possibilities and practical advantages. Aluminum, for example, is lightweight, durable, and maintenance-free. However, when aluminum siding is shaped like clapboard and given a bogus grain, the intended trompe l'oeil effect usually fails and can create something of an aesthetic embarrassment.

Two other faces of wood are observable in American architect Richard Morris Hunt's J.N.A. Griswold House (Fig. **11-11**), built at Newport, Rhode Island, in 1862–1863 in the *Stick style*, and in the Cape Cod–style homes in Levittown, Long Island, a suburb of New York City (Fig. **11-12**). The Griswold House shows the fanciful possibilities in wood. The Stick style sports a skeletal treatment of exteriors that remind one of an assemblage of matchsticks, open interiors, and a curious interplay of voids and solids and horizontal and vertical lines. Shapes pro-

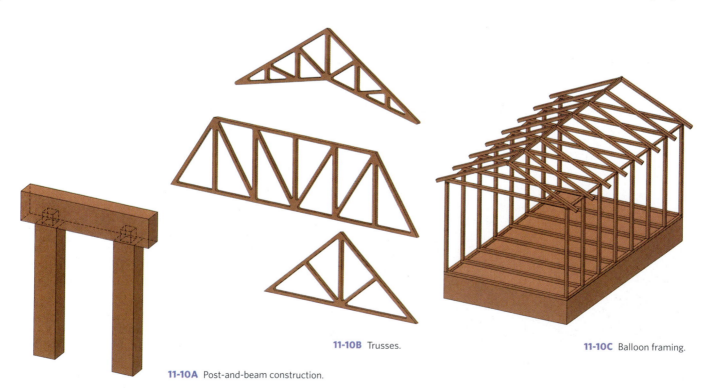

11-10B Trusses.

11-10C Balloon framing.

11-10A Post-and-beam construction.

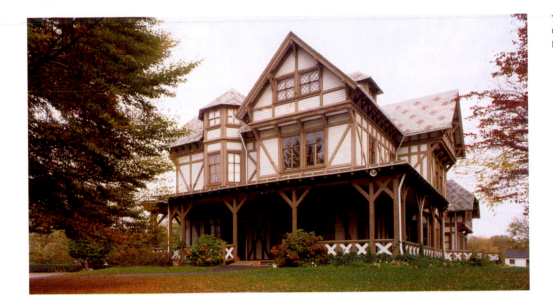

liferate in this short-lived movement. Turrets and gables and dormers poke the roof in every direction. Trellised porches reinforce a certain wooden laciness. One cannot imagine the Griswold House constructed in any material but wood.

The house at Levittown (Fig. 11-13) is more than a home; it is a socioaesthetic comment on the need for mass suburban housing that impacted so many metropolitan regions during the marriage and baby boom that followed World War II. This house and 17,000 others almost exactly like it were built, with few exceptions, on 60-foot by 100-foot lots that had been carved out from potato fields. In what was to become neighborhood after neighborhood, bulldozers smoothed already flat terrain and concrete slabs were poured. Balloon frames were erected, sided, and roofed. Trees were planted; grass was sown. The houses had an eat-in kitchen, living room, two tiny bedrooms, one bath on the first floor, and an expansion attic. Despite the tedium of the repetition, the original Levittown house achieved a sort of architectural integrity, providing living space, the pride of ownership, and an inoffensive facade for a modest price. Driving through Levittown today, it seems that every occupant thrust random additions in random directions as the family grew, despite the limitations of the lots. The trees only partly obscure the results.

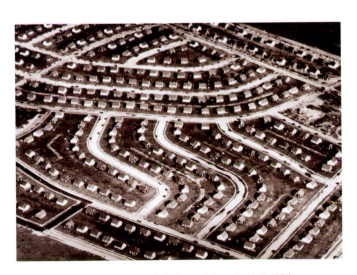

11-12 Cape Cod–style houses built by Levitt & Sons (c. 1947–1951). Levittown, NY.

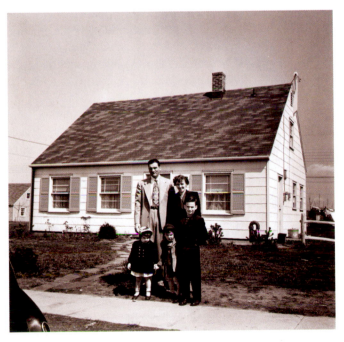

11-13 A family in front of their new Levitt home (1950).

No person who is not a great sculptor or painter can be an architect. . . . He can only be a builder.
—John Ruskin

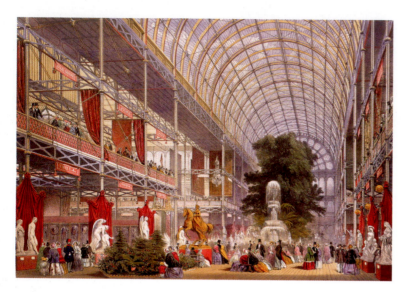

11-14 Engraving of Sir Joseph Paxton's Crystal Palace (1851). London, England.

CAST-IRON ARCHITECTURE

Nineteenth-century industrialization also introduced **cast iron** as a building material. It was one of several structural materials that would change the face of architecture. Cast iron was a welcome alternative to stone and wood. Like stone, iron has great strength, is heavy, and has a certain brittleness, yet it was the first material to allow the erection of tall buildings with relatively slender walls. Slender iron beams and bolted trusses are also capable of spanning vast interior spaces, freeing them from the forests of columns that are required in stone.

At the mid-nineteenth-century Great Exhibition held in Hyde Park, London, Sir Joseph Paxton's Crystal Palace (Fig. **11-14**) covered 17 acres. Like subsequent iron buildings, the Crystal Palace was **prefabricated**. Iron parts were cast at the factory, not the site. The new railroads facilitated their transportation, and it was a simple matter to bolt them together at the exhibition. It was also a relatively simple matter to dismantle the structure and reconstruct it at another site. The iron skeleton, with its myriad arches and trusses, was an integral part of the design. The huge plate-glass paneled walls bore no weight. Paxton asserted that "nature" had been his "engineer," explaining that he merely copied the system of longitudinal and transverse supports that one finds in a leaf. Earlier architects were also familiar with the structure of the leaf, but they did not have the structural materials at

hand that would permit them to build, much less conceptualize, such an expression of natural design.

The Crystal Palace was moved after the exhibition, and until heavily damaged by fire, it served as a museum and concert hall. It was demolished in 1941 during World War II, after officials discovered that it was being used as a landmark by German pilots on bombing runs.

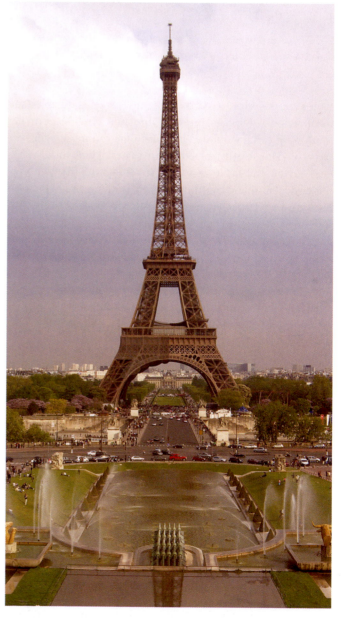

11-15 GUSTAVE EIFFEL. Eiffel Tower (1889). Paris, France.

The Eiffel Tower (Fig. **11-15**) was built in Paris in 1889 for another industrial exhibition. At the time, Gustave Eiffel was castigated by critics for building an open structure lacking the standard masonry facade. Today the Parisian symbol is so familiar that one cannot visualize Paris without the tower's magnificent exposed iron trusses. The pieces of the 1,000-foot-tall tower were prefabricated, and the tower was assembled at the site in 17 months by only 150 workers.

Structures such as these encouraged **steel-cage construction** and the development of the skyscraper.

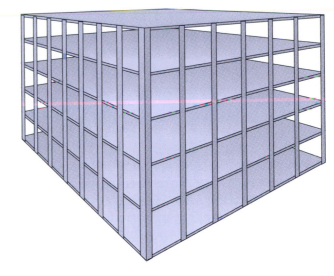

11-16 Steel-cage construction.

STEEL-CAGE ARCHITECTURE

Steel is a strong metal of iron alloyed with small amounts of carbon and a variety of other metals. Steel is harder than iron, and more rust and fire resistant. It is more expensive than other structural materials, but its great strength permits it to be used in relatively small quantities. Light, narrow, prefabricated I-beams have great tensile strength. They resist bending in any direction and are riveted or welded together into skeletal forms called **steel cages** at the site (Fig. **11-16**). Facades and inner walls are hung from the skeleton and frequently contribute more mass to the building than does the skeleton itself.

The Wainwright Building (Fig. **11-17**), erected in 1890, is an early example of steel-cage construction. Architect Louis Sullivan, one of the fathers of modern American architecture, emphasized the verticality of the structure by running **pilasters** between the windows through the upper stories. Many skyscrapers run pilasters up their entire facades. Sullivan also emphasized the horizontal features of the Wainwright Building. Ornamented horizontal bands separate most of the windows, and a severe decorated **cornice** crowns the structure. Sullivan's motto was "form follows function," and the rigid horizontal and vertical processions of the elements of the facade suggest the regularity of the rectangular spaces within. Sullivan's early "skyscraper"—in function, in structure, and in simplified form—was a precursor of the twentieth-century behemoths to follow.

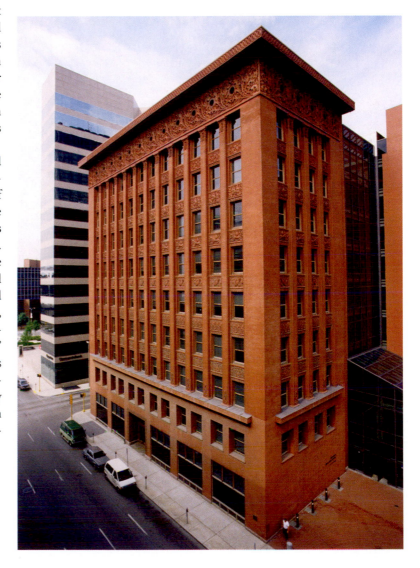

11-17 LOUIS SULLIVAN. Wainwright Building (1890-91). St. Louis, MO.

Less is more.
—Miës van der Rohe

With steel-cage construction, the weight of the building is borne by its structural core and not its walls, allowing for an expansive use of glass—called a *curtain wall*—on a building's elevations (Figure **11-18**). New York City's Lever House (Fig. **11-19**), designed by Gordon Bunshaft of Skidmore, Owings, and Merrill, is a landmark example of steel-cage construction using a curtain wall. Although the skyscraper, by contemporary standards, barely "scrapes the sky"—it is only 24 stories high—the austere, minimalist, rectangular profile of Lever House, with its uninterrupted wrap of glass, became the model for hundreds of buildings by the 1960s. Lever House is also credited with an innovation in urban planning—the integration of the office building with a public, open plaza on the ground floor, complete with gardens and walkways that enable pedestrians to cut across part of the city block on

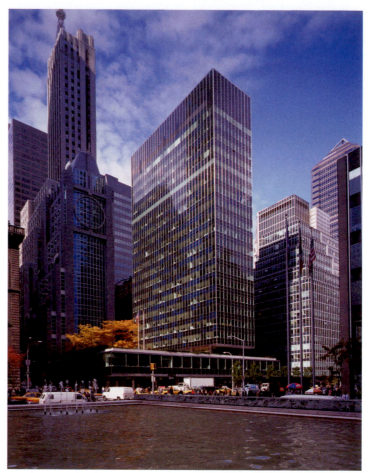

11-19 GORDON BUNSHAFT. Lever House (1951–1952). NY.

which the building sits. The plaza, covered by a flat roof only a couple of stories high, prevents the shaft of the office building from overwhelming its site. The evening light angles down across the plaza and illuminates the avenue beneath.

REINFORCED CONCRETE ARCHITECTURE

Although cement was first produced in the early 1800s, the use of **reinforced concrete** is said to have begun with a French gardener, Jacques Monier, who proposed strengthening concrete flower pots with a wire mesh in the 1860s. In reinforced concrete, or **ferroconcrete**, steel rods and/or steel mesh are inserted at the points of greatest stress into concrete

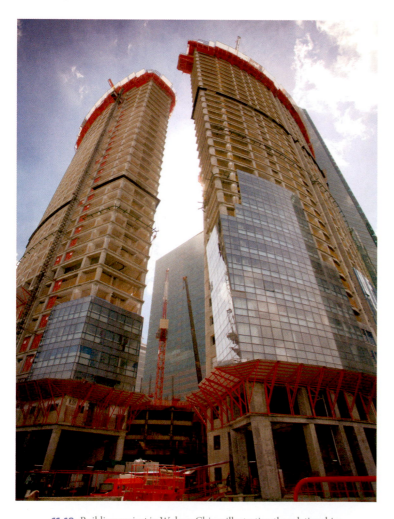

11-18 Building project in Wuhan, China, illustrating the relationship between the load bearing columns and the glass curtain exterior.

224   **Architecture**

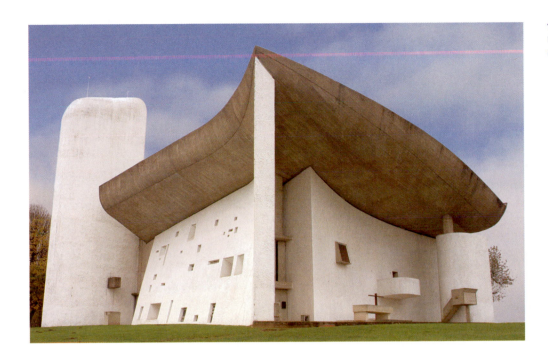

11-20 LE CORBUSIER. Chapel of Notre-Dame-du-Haut (1950–1954). Ronchamp, France.

slabs before they harden. In the resultant slab, stresses are shared by the materials.

Ferroconcrete has many of the advantages of stone and steel, without some of the disadvantages. The steel rods increase the tensile strength of concrete, making it less susceptible to tearing or pulling apart at stress points. The concrete, in turn, prevents the steel from rusting. Reinforced concrete can span greater distances than stone, and it supports more weight than steel. Perhaps the most dramatic advantage of reinforced concrete is its capacity to take on natural curved shapes that would be unthinkable in steel or concrete alone. Curved slabs take on the forms of eggshells, bubbles, seashells, and other organic shapes that are naturally engineered for the even spreading of stress throughout their surfaces and are, hence, enduring.

Reinforced concrete, more than other materials, has allowed the architect to think freely and sculpturally. There are limits to what ferroconcrete can do, however; initial spatial concepts are frequently somewhat refined by computer-aided calculations of marginally more efficient shapes for distributing stress. Still, it would not be far from the mark to say that buildings of almost any shape and reasonable size are possible today, if one is willing to pay for them. The architects of ferroconcrete have achieved buildings that would have astounded the ancient stone builders—and perhaps Joseph Paxton as well.

Le Corbusier's chapel of Notre-Dame-du-Haut (Figs. 11-20 and 11-21) is an example of what has been referred to as the "new brutalism," deriving from the French *brut*, meaning "rough, uncut, or raw." The steel web is spun, and the concrete is cast in place, leaving the marks of the wooden forms on its surface. The white walls, dark roof, and white towers are decorated only by the texture of the curving reinforced concrete slabs. In places the walls are incredibly thick. Windows of various shapes and sizes expand from small slits and rectangles to form mysterious light tunnels; they draw the

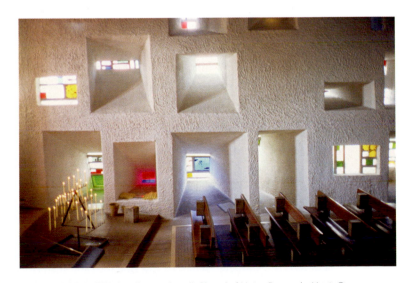

11-21 LE CORBUSIER. Interior, south wall, Chapel of Notre-Dame-du-Haut. © 2011 Artists Rights Society (ARS), NY/ADAGP, Paris/FLC.

Reinforced Concrete Architecture **225**

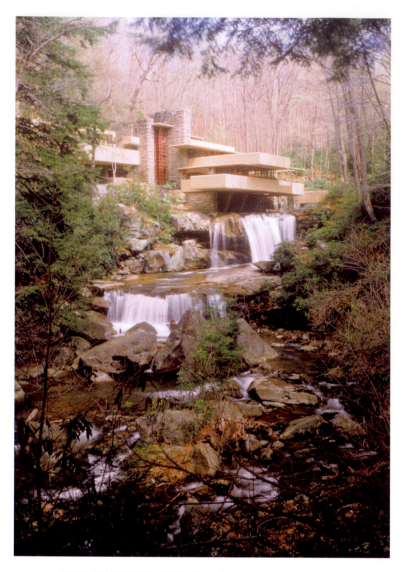

11-22 FRANK LLOYD WRIGHT. Kaufmann House ("Fallingwater") (1936). Bear Run, PA. © 2011 Frank Lloyd Wright Foundation/Artists Rights Society (ARS), NY.

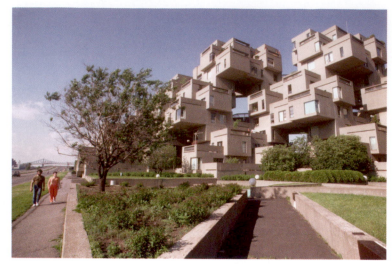

11-23 MOSHE SAFDIE. Habitat, Expo 67 (1967). Montreal, Québec, Canada.

broad white planes of a deck. The irregularity of the structural components—concrete, cut stone, natural stone, and machine-planed surfaces—complements the irregularity of the wooded site.

Israeli architect Moshe Safdie's Habitat (Fig. **11-23**) is another expression of the versatility of concrete. Habitat was erected for Expo 67 in Montreal as one solution to the housing problems of the future. Rugged, prefabricated units were stacked like blocks about a common utility core at the site, so that the roof of one unit would provide a private deck for another. Only a couple of Safdie-style "apartment houses" have been erected since, one in Israel and one in Puerto Rico, so today Safdie's beautiful sculptural assemblage evokes more nostalgia than hope for the future. Its unique brand of rugged, blocky excitement is rarely found in mass housing, and this is our loss.

STEEL-CABLE ARCHITECTURE

The notion of suspending bridges from cables is not new. Wood-and-rope suspension bridges have been built in Asia for thousands of years. Iron suspension bridges, such as the Menai Strait Bridge in Wales and the Clifton Bridge near Bristol, England, were erected during the early part of the nineteenth century. But in the Brooklyn Bridge (Fig. **11-24**), completed in 1883, John Roebling exploited the great tensile strength of steel to span New York's East River with **steel cable**. In such a cable, many parallel wires share the stress. Steel cable is also flexible, allowing the roadway beneath to sway, within limits, in response to changing weather and traffic conditions.

Roebling used massive vaulted piers of stone masonry to support parabolic webs of steel, which are rendered lacy by

observer outward more than they actually light the interior. The massive voids of the window apertures recall the huge stone blocks of prehistoric religious structures.

Frank Lloyd Wright's Kaufmann House (Fig. **11-22**), which has also become known as "Fallingwater," shows a very different application of reinforced concrete. Here cantilevered decks of reinforced concrete rush outward into the surrounding landscape from the building's central core, intersecting in strata that lie parallel to the natural rock formations. Wright's **naturalistic style** integrates his building with its site. In the Kaufmann House, reinforced concrete and stone walls complement the sturdy rock of the Pennsylvania countryside.

For Wright, modern materials did not warrant austerity; geometry did not preclude organic integration with the site. A small waterfall seems mysteriously to originate beneath the

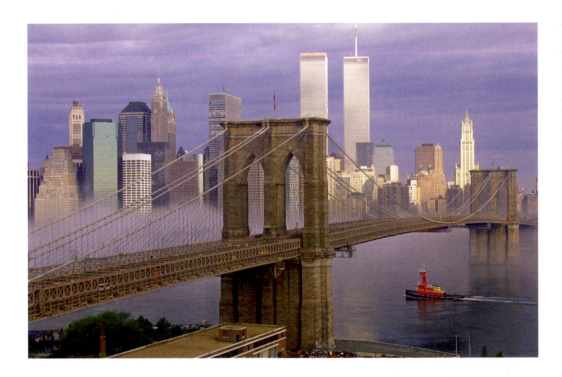

11-24 JOHN A. ROEBLING. Brooklyn Bridge (1869–1883), NY. There is another stirring aspect to the photograph of the Brooklyn Bridge. In the background, you can see the twin towers of the World Trade Center, which collapsed in the terrorist attack of September 11, 2001.

the juxtaposition. In many more recent suspension bridges, steel cable spans more than a mile, and in bridges such as the Golden Gate, the George Washington, and the Verrazano Narrows, the effect is aesthetically stirring.

SHELL ARCHITECTURE

Modern materials and methods of engineering have made it possible to enclose spaces with relatively inexpensive shell structures. Masonry domes have been replaced by lightweight shells, which are frequently flatter and certainly capable of spanning greater spaces. Shells have been constructed from reinforced concrete, wood, steel, aluminum, and even plastics and paper. The concept of shell architecture is as old as the canvas tent and as new as the geodesic dome (Fig. **11-25**), designed by Buckminster Fuller for the United States Pavilion at Expo 67 in Montreal. In many sports arenas, fabric roofs are held up by keeping the air pressure inside the building slightly greater than that outside. Like balloons, these roof structures are literally inflated.

Fuller's shell is an assemblage of lightweight metal trusses into a three-quarter sphere that is 250 feet in diameter. Looking more closely, one sees that the trusses compose six-sided units that give the organic impression of a honeycomb. Light

floods the climate-controlled enclosure, creating an environment for any variety of human activity—and any form of additional construction—within. Such domes can be covered with many sorts of weatherproofing, including lightweight metals and fabric and translucent and transparent plastics and glass. Here the engineering requirements clearly create the architectural design.

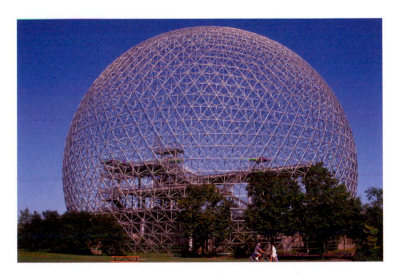

11-25 BUCKMINSTER FULLER. United States Pavilion, Expo 67 (1967). Montreal, Québec, Canada.

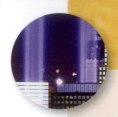

EVERY EVENING, FOR A MONTH IN THE SPRING OF 2002, twin towers of light, composed of 88 searchlights, rose toward the blackened sky from Ground Zero. The installation was mounted in memory of the victims of the terrorist attack on the World Trade Center on September 11, 2001, and the twin towers of glass and steel themselves. *New York Times* critic Herbert Muschamp* described the *Tribute in Light* (Fig. **11-26**) as "a moving piece of urban spectacle" whose "twin light towers . . . seemed to be looking for something." He praised the project for setting "a rhetorical tone worthy of emulation by those who [would] be shaping the future of Lower Manhattan" in the wake of the destruction. Intended to be a temporary installation, *Tribute in Light* shone yearly on September 11 until the tenth anniversary of the attacks in 2011.

*Herbert Muschamp, March 12, 2002. Copyright © 2002 by The New York Times Company.

In "My Lost City," the American novelist F. Scott Fitzgerald, writing in 1936 about the bygone New York he remembered as a younger man, lamented: ". . . I have lost my splendid mirage. Come back, come back, O glittering and white!" Construction is underway to do just that—to bring back the towers "glittering and white." Within months following September 11, dozens of architects and planners were submitting concepts to New York City for the rebuilding of the World Trade Center site, which included a memorial to those who had been killed in the attack and new buildings that might recapture the upward spirit of the city. Daniel Libeskind, for example, designed a light and airy steel and glass tower to replace the fallen ones. Even so, his design was to be significantly stronger than the original, taking into account the sobering realities of luring tenants into a super high-rise skyscraper in a post-9/11 world and the desire of most Americans to build high and build proud.

The final design of One World Trade Center (One WTC), however, is by the renowned architectural group

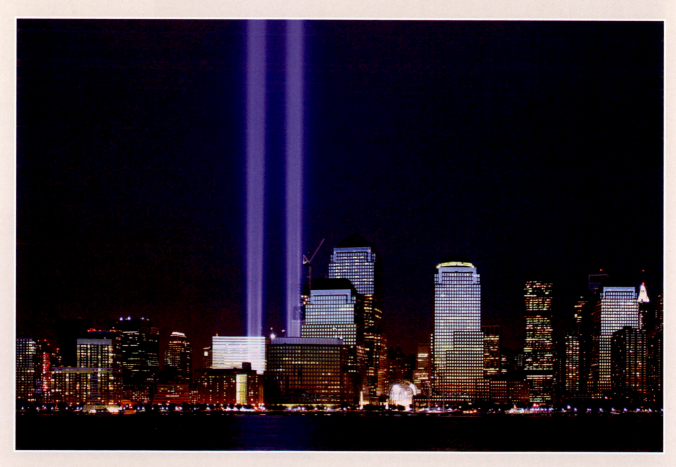

11-26 *Tribute in Light* (March–April 2002). NY.

the office tower with what will surely become a bustling plaza designed of textured granite cobblestones. In addition to a restaurant, there are zones for relaxation and spaces for memory and reflection. The building meets or exceeds construction standards for safety and security, but the overall impression is one of openness and accessibility—a careful balance that will facilitate the revival of urban life in a location that has extraordinary meaning to New Yorkers and the country (Figs. 11-27 and 11-28).

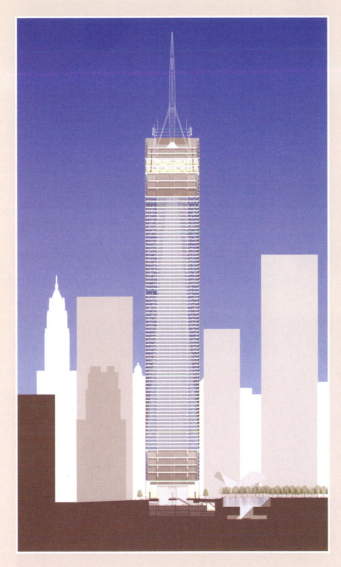

11-27 Cross-section of One World Trade Center (projected completion year: 2013). Height: 1776'. NY. © Skidmore, Owings & Merrill LLP.

of Skidmore, Owings, and Merrill, which pioneered midtwentieth century skyscraper architecture in buildings like Lever House (see Fig. 11-19). According to the firm, "the design solution is an innovative mix of architecture, structure, urban design, safety and sustainability." The tower, which is adjacent to the World Trade Center Memorial, rises a symbolic 1776 feet from a cubic base, supporting a structure with a prismatic glass curtain wall that captures refracted light in myriad ways, depending on the time of day and atmospheric conditions.

One WTC not only "recaptures" the lower Manhattan skyline, but also provides communal space that integrates

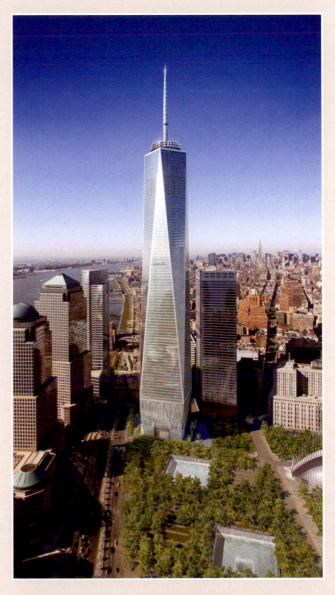

11-28 Rendering of the completed One World Trade Center, with the National September 11 Memorial in the foreground, sited on the footprints of the towers that were destroyed. © Skidmore, Owings & Merrill LLP.

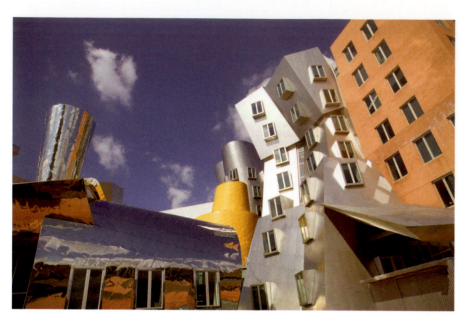

11-29 FRANK GEHRY. Ray and Maria Stata Center for Computer, Information, and Intelligence Sciences at MIT (2005). Cambridge, MA.

collaboration with materials manufacturers and to explore the potential of nascent technologies. Testa and his partner, Devyn Weiser, have designed a high-rise tower out of composite materials (Fig. 11-30). Their skyscraper would be held erect by a cross-hatched lattice made of carbon fiber—a material several times stronger than the traditional steel. The "woven building" would have an interior that is completely open (except for elevator shafts) and void of structural support.

Green Buildings

Green is the color associated with energy efficiency and environmental awareness. The clients of many architects seek the design of "green buildings" today to save money, to protect the environment, or, sometimes, to boost a corporate image. Green

NEW MATERIALS, NEW VISIONS

In architecture studios and schools, the saying goes, "Convention gets built; innovation gets published." But this adage is systematically being proven wrong as scientists and engineers have combined forces to turn architects' dreams into reality: "If you can think it, we can build it."

In 1997, Frank Gehry transformed architectural design with the use of titanium in the same way that reinforced concrete altered the look of the exterior "skin" of buildings in the 1950s and 1960s. His Guggenheim Museum in Bilbao, Spain (see Fig. 2-18), set a new artistic course for Gehry in terms of his own style and nurtured the adaptation of high-tech metals by architects worldwide. Gehry's Ray and Maria Stata Center (Fig. 11-29), which opened in 2005 on the Massachusetts Institute of Technology campus, stands as a visual summation of his most recent designs, materials, and theories of spatial relationships. The 730,000-square-foot complex will be a hub for research in the fields of computer science, linguistics, and philosophy. The assertive clashing of shapes signifies the disparate disciplines that will be housed in the structure, while communal lounges and shared interior spaces encourage interaction, collaboration, and the cross-fertilization of ideas. Gehry said of the Stata Center: "It reflects the different groups, the collision of ideas, the energy of people and ideas. . . . That's what will lead to the breakthroughs and the positive results."

Architect Peter Testa's view is that there is a "need to rethink how we assemble buildings" and that it is time to design in

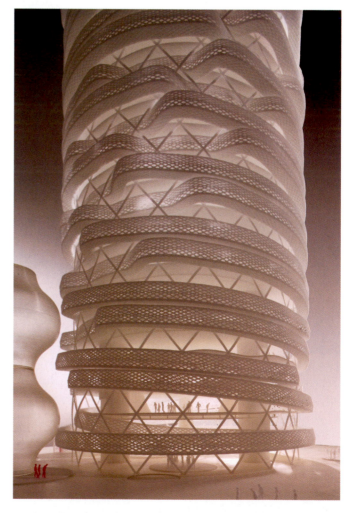

11-30 PETER TESTA AND DEVYN WEISER, TESTA ARCHITECTURE AND DESIGN. Carbon Tower.

buildings are efficient in terms of energy, water, and materials. They are constructed with attention to the quality of the indoor air as well as the building's emissions that could prove harmful to the environment. When possible, recycled materials—such as steel, woods, and plastics—are incorporated into design and construction. Converting to "green" is also sometimes facilitated by the location of a building. If residents and employees can access buildings by public transportation, they are less likely to drive to and from home or work, using fossil fuels that contribute to air pollution and greenhouse gases.

Architects employ simple energy conservation measures, such as well-sealed and insulated glass windows. Light-colored roofs reflect heat from the sun in warm climates; dark-covered roofs trap heat from the sun in cold climates. Pine trees can be planted along the north side of a building to protect against icy winds. Along the south side, deciduous trees will provide leafy shade and natural cooling in summer and, in winter, when their branches are bare, admit light and provide warmth. Digging a well to water the lawn or fill the swimming pool conserves water in reservoirs and aquifers. Using appliances with Energy Star ratings decreases the fossil fuels required to make them run. Rooftop solar panels are costly to install but save on electrical costs year after year.

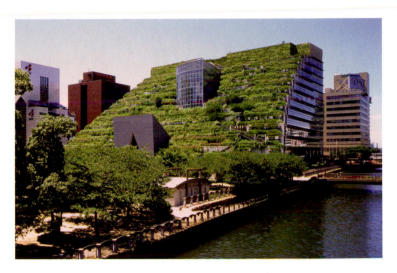

11-32 EMILIO AMBASZ & ASSOCIATES. Fukuoka Prefectural International Hall (1994). Fukuoka, Japan.

Green buildings are not necessarily recognizable as such from the exterior. The Hearst Tower (Fig. **11-31**), designed by Sir Norman Foster, began by preserving the façade of the 1928 stone structure upon which it was built. It is credited with being Manhattan's first green office skyscraper. Walls are coated with vapor-free paint. Floors are made of wood from sustainable forests. About 85 percent of the steel in the building was recycled. Rain is collected on the roof and stored in a basement tank, used in the building's cooling system and to water plants in the ten-story atrium. The triangular planes of glass on the tower's exterior are made of *low-E* glass, which minimizes the loss of heat during winter and the admission of heat during summer. Sensors determine the amount of natural light entering the building and adjust the lighting fixtures accordingly. The building uses 26 percent less energy than the amount deemed desirable by the city and was certified by the LEED (Leadership in Energy and Environmental Design) program of the U.S. Green Building Council.

Some green buildings are decidedly green. The Fukuoka Prefectural International Hall (Fig. **11-32**) was constructed on the last remaining green space in the city center of Fukuoka in Japan. Architects Emilio Ambrasz & Associates managed to keep it green even as they added 600,000 square feet of private and government office space, an exhibition hall, a museum, a 2,000-seat theater, conference facilities, retail shops, and underground parking. One side has the appearance of a conventional steel-and-glass office tower. The other consists of a dramatically descending terraced roof, covered with some 35,000 plants, that culminates in a public park. The literal green roof reduces the building's energy consumption by insulating it from the elements and capturing rainwater for use in the building. The lush terrace has also become home to more than 70 species of birds. Now that's green.

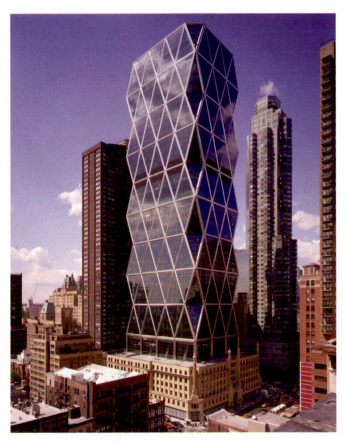

11-31 SIR NORMAN FOSTER. Hearst Tower (2004). NY.

ART TOUR DALLAS/FORT WORTH

ONE HUNDRED YEARS AGO, Will Rogers said, "Fort Worth is where the West begins and Dallas is where the East peters out." His description remains on the money even today. Although the city of Dallas conveys a certain formality and self-conscious sophistication, Fort Worth revels in its "Cowtown" image.

Both cities can claim their skyscrapers, but the creation of an impressive Dallas-type skyline seems not to have been a temptation to the developers of Fort Worth. There things lie closer to the horizon, as shown in the downtown cobbled streets. It is as if the connection with the land wants to be emphasized, or will not be shaken. Dallas and Fort Worth, then, cannot be called twin cities, but one thing they have in common is that they have both lured world-class architects to grace their avenues and their vistas. Although they may be thousands of miles from the coasts and from classic civilizations, civilization has clearly found its way to the Southwest.

Dallas and Fort Worth lie only 33 miles apart. Along with their suburbs, they make up "the Metroplex." If you are visiting them, chances are you drove in on one of the interstates or flew into Dallas/Fort Worth (DFW) International Airport, which sits halfway between the two cities. Although the airport is one of the largest in the world

RENZO PIANO. NASHER SCULPTURE CENTER, VIEW OF THE GARDEN. DALLAS, TX.

and entertaining in and of itself, this is Texas, and "big" is where you start.

Downtown Dallas is easy to navigate by subway or on foot, unless you're braving the heat of summer. Most museums and cultural sites can be found within reasonable proximity to one another. I say, get a big-brimmed hat and a bottle of water and "cowboy it up"! You can walk from one end of downtown to the other in an hour.

The Dallas Arts District is 60 acres of museums, a performing arts center, and outdoor sculptures. Its centerpiece is the Dallas Museum of Art—a space that stretches more than 250,000 square feet. The museum's vastness stretches not only over its site but also across continents and eras. It features works from the Americas, Africa, Asia, the Pacific, and Europe. You will find paintings by Frida Kahlo and Frederic Edwin Church, and more Mondrians than in any other museum in the country. The famous Wendy and Emery Reves collection is installed in a setting that recreates the owner-donors' home on the French Riviera. Among the collection's stars are van Gogh, Monet, and Renoir.

Before you get too far, stroll in the Nasher Sculpture Garden (still have your hat on?) adjacent to the Dallas Art Museum. This 2.4-acre site was designed by Renzo Piano, architect of the famed Centre Pompidou in Paris (see the Paris Art Tour), and displays work by artists such as Alexander Calder, Willem de Kooning, Barbara Hepworth, Joan Miró, Richard Serra, and Auguste Rodin.

In the same neck of the woods, you'll find something very different—the Trammel Crow Museum. Once a private collection, it has grown into one of the largest collections of Asian art in the American Southwest. More than 300 objects and works of art from India, Japan, and China (including deities, shrines, scrolls, and vases) are amassed in a 12,000-square-foot space.

As you walk south toward the center of downtown Dallas—finally in dire need of a water break—you will happily come upon Fountain Palace. The fountain, one of Dallas's most popular sites, bears a famous signature; it was designed by I. M. Pei, who created the pyramidal entrance to the Louvre. More than a million gallons of water leap and dance in rhythm, while 172 bubbler fountains shoot water high into the air. Cool. Actually, very cool.

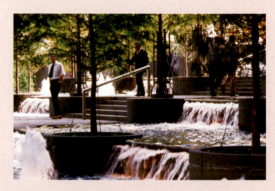

I. M. PEI. FOUNTAIN PALACE. DALLAS, TX.

Elsewhere in Dallas, you'll find quirky and not-so-quirky museums, collections, and sites, including the American Museum of Miniature Arts (fantastic dollhouses, tiny toy soldiers, itty-bitty trains and cars); the African American Museum of Art, History, and Culture (the only one in the Southwest and the largest in the nation); the Meadows Museum (nicknamed "The Prado on the Prairie" with one of the major collections of Spanish art outside Spain); and the Women's Museum: An Institute for the Future (an exhibit that focuses on contributions of women throughout American history). Speaking of the very near future, Dallas will soon be home to the cubic Dee and Charles Wyly Theater, designed by the pioneering Dutch architect Rem Koolhaas.

Pioneer Plaza—the setting for 70 six-foot-tall bronze longhorn steers being driven across a stream by a team of cowboys—is probably the largest bronze monument in the world. Speaking of longhorns, the Long-horn Trolley will steer you (pun intended) toward any of the three main districts that make up the metropolitan area of Fort Worth—the Cultural District, downtown/Sundance Square, and the Fort Worth Stockyards National Historic District.

Some of the country's best small museums are lined up like ducks in a row in Fort Worth's Cultural District—the Kimbell Art Museum, the Amon Carter Museum, and the Modern Art Museum. The Kimbell has, in fact, been called "America's best small museum." The initial funding was provided in the will of the industrialist Kay Kimbell, who called for a first-class museum in his name. In the 30 years since it opened its doors, the museum has amassed a diverse collection of art from antiquity to the modern, from Asia to Mesoamerica to Africa. It is best known, however, for its stunning examples of European painting and sculpture from the Renaissance through the twentieth century. You will see works by Caravaggio, El Greco, Vigée-Lebrun, Delacroix, Monet, Renoir, Cézanne, Leger, Miró, and more—wrapped in the extraordinary architecture of Louis I. Kahn, one of the significant modern architects of the twentieth century.

The Amon Carter Museum opened in 1961 as a niche collection of Western art that belonged to the Fort Worth publisher and philanthropist Amon G. Carter. The original 400 paintings have grown to more than 300,000 works of art, and curators have cast a wide aesthetic net to include all styles of American paintings, drawings, prints, photographs, and sculptures.

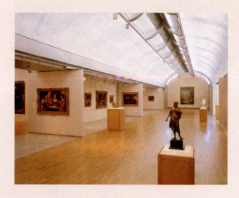

LOUIS I. KAHN. KIMBELL MUSEUM. FORT WORTH, TX.

More recently, the Carter expanded (tripled!) its exhibition space to do what some museums cannot afford to do—bring their treasures out of storage and into public view.

The nearby Modern Art Museum of Fort Worth amplifies the city's modern and American collections with its mission of collecting and presenting post–World War II art. The roster of artists in its permanent collection reads like a *Who's Who* in European and American art at midcentury and beyond: Pablo Picasso and Hans Hofmann; Jackson Pollock and Willem de Kooning; Agnes Martin and Dan Flavin; Andy Warhol and Jean-Michel Basquiat; Bill Viola and Tony Oursler; and the list goes on and on—at least 2,800 objects in all. But the permanent collection represents only a part of what the museum has to offer. Its vast interior (150,000 square feet) also provides ample space for changing installations of contemporary work in all mediums.

The Fort Worth Stockyards and downtown Fort Worth offer two distinct clusters of tourist sites. As the name suggests, the Stockyards have a long

THE DEE AND CHARLES WYLY THEATER.

and distinct history. If you are in the mood for a close-up look at how "Cowtown" got its name—including Cattleman's Walk, the Fort Worth Livestock Exchange, and the Cowtown (rodeo) Coliseum—this is your destination.

If, on the other hand, the symphony or ballet or opera is your game, blaze your trail to downtown/Sundance Square and visit the Bass Performance Hall. Nancy Lee and Perry R. Bass donated the land for this remarkable space, and it was built by private donations to the tune of $67.5 million. Cowtown architecture it is not. The structure is modeled after the great opera houses of old Europe, complete with an 80-foot-diameter dome and two 48-foot angels flanking a bank of tall, arched windows on the facade. In a bow to pride and tradition, this neo–Beaux Arts design is rendered in homegrown Texas limestone.

Dallas and Fort Worth offer a study in contrasts, but they also share common ground. Both cities, their traditions and their cultural aspirations, aim to preserve their unique identities and balance those identities with awareness of the world and their place in the world—and, of course, in Texas.

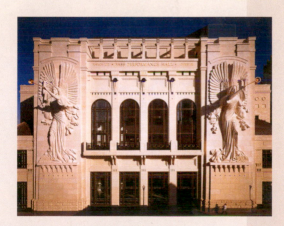

BASS PERFORMANCE HALL, SHOWING THE 48-FOOT ANGELS. FORT WORTH, TX.

WWW TO CONTINUE YOUR TOUR and learn more about Dallas/Fort Worth, go to CourseMate.

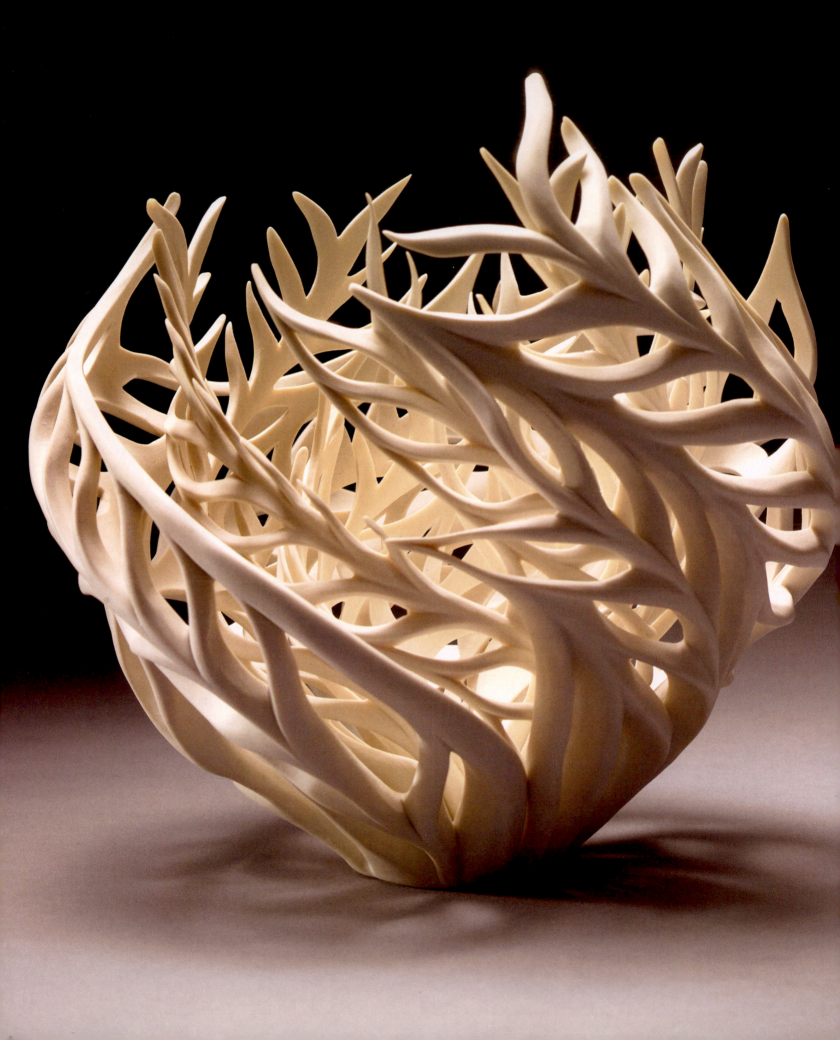

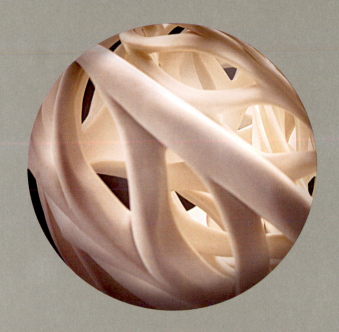

CRAFT AND DESIGN

12

Consider this story concerning one of the Metropolitan Museum of Art's most precious acquisitions, as retold by art critic Arthur C. Danto.[1] According to Thomas Hoving, the director of the museum at the time of the purchase, the vase in Figure 12-1 is "the single most perfect work of art I ever encountered . . . an object of total adoration." In his memoirs, Hoving further described his feelings upon his first encounter with the piece: "The first thought that came to mind was that I was gazing not at a vase, but at a painting." The director was obviously swept off his feet by this masterpiece of Greek art—a terra-cotta vessel painted with the scene of the *Dead Sarpedon Carried by Thanatos and Hypnos* and signed by both the potter and the painter. But why did Hoving diminish the significance of the potter's craft by essentially dismissing the pot as a mere vehicle for the work of an extraordinary painter? Danto suggests that Hoving's reaction is indicative of an art-world prejudice of sorts—one that attaches less importance to functional and decorative objects of any kind. He warns that "the painting [on the vase] is there to decorate an object of conspicuous utility" and cannot be considered without reference to the vase itself. In fact, doing so precludes any real understanding of the work in the historical and artistic context in which it was created.

---

[1] Arthur C. Danto, "Fine Art and the Functional Object," *Glass*, no. 51 (Spring 1993): 24–29.

JENNIFER McCURDY. *Coral Nest* (2009). Porcelain. H: 9".

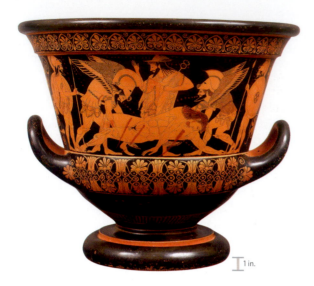

12-1 EUPHRONIOS AND EUXITHEOS. *Calyx Krater* (1st quarter of 5th century BCE). Ceramic. H: 18"; D: 21¹¹⁄₁₆". Villa Giulia, Rome, Italy.

What purpose does this argument have for us who, as students, are trying to understand art? Simply this: The distinction between fine art and functional object is linked to the historical and cultural context in which a work was created. As Danto pointed out, the Greek philosophers placed craftsmen somewhere between artists and philosophers, artists occupying the lowest rung. Danto paraphrases Plato in *The Republic*: "The carpenter knows how to fashion in real life what the painter can merely imitate; therefore . . . artists have no real knowledge at all, trafficking only in the outward appearance of things."[2] More than 2,000 years later, a French philosopher would declare, "Only what serves no purpose is truly beautiful,"[3] suggesting a sure separation between fine art and craft. The mediums of paint and bronze might be used to create works of art in which, to paraphrase Puryear, the idea transcends craft and function. But those materials closest to the artisan—clay, glass, and fiber, metal—these materials were the purview of craft art that prioritized technical skill and utility over the "idea." Today, such lines are often blurred. Miriam Schapiro's *Wonderland* (see Fig. 1-35), according to this distinction, would most certainly be labeled a work of fine art. Yet the composition is a conglomeration of bits and pieces of time-honored craft techniques: quiltmaking, needlework, and crochet. The work does not have a utilitarian function, but it does cast a spotlight on some of the functional objects that provided outlets for artistic expression by women for whom access to the world of fine art was the equivalent of intergalactic travel. As we have seen in Chapter 9, ceramic

artists are creating works of sculpture, and sculptors are finding innovative ways to manipulate clay, wood, and metal. Glassmaking has reached new heights of experimentation while employing centuries-old techniques. Some artists view the distinction between art and craft as artificial, limiting, and even denigrating. Others embrace that distinction, which has, after all, a pedigree going back to Plato.

In this chapter, we take a close look at the functional and artistic aspects of craftmaking and materials traditional to craft—clay, glass, fiber, metal, and wood. We also examine the ubiquity of design in our daily lives through examples of graphic design, industrial design, web design, and urban design. In design, as with craft, the distinction between art for art's sake and art for utility's sake is also sometimes blurred.

CERAMICS

Ceramics are objects made of clay. In the singular, ceramic refers to materials and processes that are used to produce a range of products including familiar **pottery** pots and bowls, clay sculptures, baked bricks, and the tiles that protect the outer surfaces of space shuttles from the intense heat of atmospheric reentry.

Methods of Working with Clay

Ceramics was a highly refined craft in the ancient Middle East and China, but its roots go back further than that. For thousands of years, people have worked wet clay with their

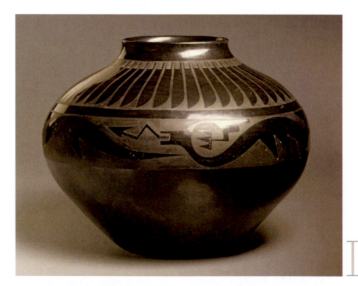

12-2 MARIA MARTINEZ AND JULIAN MARTINEZ. Bowl with plumed serpent (1920–30). Coiled and burnished earthenware. 6" × 9½". Gift of Amelia Elizabeth White, 1937. Newark Museum, Newark, NJ.

---

[2] Ibid.
[3] Théophile Gautier, Preface to his novel *Mademoiselle de Maupin*, 1835.

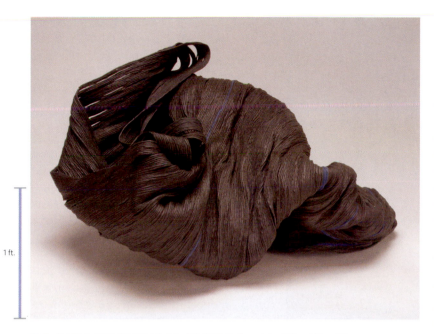

1 ft.

12-3 CHERYL ANN THOMAS. *Relic 130* (2008). Porcelain. 22" × 16" × 10".

created by smoothing the ridges of the stacked coils into flat, thin walls that belie the process. The surface effect of etched glass was achieved through a complex interplay of burnishing, glazing, and firing techniques. In Cheryl Ann Thomas's work (Fig. **12-3**), by contrast, individual coils retain their shape identity rather than being smoothed together. They are nestled next to one another and then folded and molded into trompe l'oeil objects resembling woven cloth. For Thomas, creating the delicate ropes of clay through the rhythmic movements of her hands forges an intimate connection with her material.

The Potter's Wheel

The potter's wheel (Fig. **12-4**) was first used in the Middle East around 4000 BCE and seems to have come into common use a thousand years later. A pot can be **thrown** quite rapidly and effortlessly on a wheel once the techniques have been mastered, in contrast to the more laborious and time-consuming process of building a pot by coiling. The walls of a wheel-thrown pot tend to be thinner and more uniform in thickness than those of coiled pots, and the outer and inner surfaces are smoother. As we saw in the work of Martinez, however, hand-built pots can be as thin walled and symmetrical as their wheel-thrown counterparts.

Anyone who has been a student of ceramics appreciates the difficulty of getting the rhythm of the potter's wheel. The

hands to create functional vessels for such basic things as carrying water or storing grain. Clay was patted and pinched and rolled, well before the invention of the potter's wheel, and these basic hand-built techniques continued (and still do) alongside wheel-thrown pottery. Shaping clay is only part of the process. To achieve hard, durable, and waterproof vessels, clay must be exposed to heat or fire.

Ancient cultures, such as Mesopotamia and Egypt, dried or baked clay and mud bricks in the broiling desert sun. Early ceramics were also hardened by fire in stone pits covered with flammable natural materials such as dried grasses, branches, perhaps even coal. Insulated **kilns**, or ovens, were developed to control temperature and regulate the firing process. Facility with firing techniques—and a growing knowledge of varieties of clay composition and ways to manipulate surface coatings, or **glazes**—culminated in magnificent, complex objects, valued as much for their artistic as utilitarian importance.

The earliest hand-built ceramics are described by their simple techniques. Pinch pots were created by shaping a lump of clay into a small cuplike container, slab pots by seaming together five flat slabs (four for the sides, one for the bottom). Coil pots are built from ropes of clay (you probably remember making snakes in preschool in exactly the same way) that are stacked on one another or coiled like a beehive. After the ropes are stacked, tools can be used to smooth them together, inside and out, or they might be left as is to reveal the coiling process.

These different effects can be seen in two examples of coiling. The perfect contours of the black-on-black, coil-built vessel of Native American potter Maria Martinez (Fig. **12-2**) were

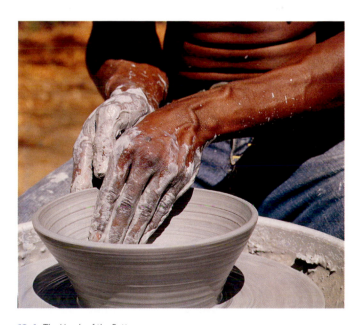

12-4 *The Hands of the Potter.*
Conrad Knowles forming a tray and a bowl for his collection of artful pottery.

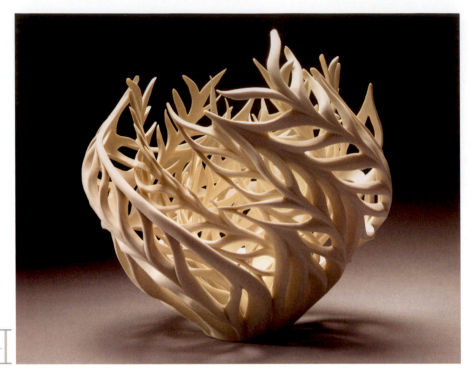

1 in.

tury BCE, ancient Babylonians constructed the Ishtar Gate from glazed bricks in a similar blue-green palette. By the first centuries and millennium CE, glazed ceramics was an accomplished art form across cultures from China and Japan to the Middle East, Southeast Asia, and more.

The surface characteristics of glazed pottery can be glossy or matte, smooth or textured, monochromatic or polychromatic, and simple or complex in pattern or decoration. All of these variations depend on the composition of the glaze, the temperature of the kiln, and sometimes multiple firings.

Glazes usually contain silica, found in sand or quartz, ground metals that facilitate the melting of silica into glass in the presence of heat, and other chemical compounds that produce a range of specific colors. Dry glazes can be rubbed onto clay, and liquid glazes—chemicals combined with ground minerals and liquid—can be brushed, sprayed,

speed of the wheel, placement of the clay, downward pressure of the hands, and force (or delicate touch) of the fingers are an exercise in extreme coordination. The goal, generally, is to achieve perfect symmetry and a smooth contour. How ironic, then, is the work of Jennifer McCurdy (Fig. **12-5**), who begins by throwing on the wheel and then quickly shapes, folds, and slices into her clay with an X-Acto knife. Two firings produce rock-hard porcelain objects that, in the potter's words, "are so durable that they should last 10,000 years." The result subverts the wheel-thrown technique and typically utilitarian function of a clay vessel and blur the boundaries between sculpture and ceramics, fine art and craft.

Glazing

Pottery is glazed for functional and artistic reasons. Without a glaze, a clay pot would remain porous and therefore useless for carrying liquids. Even the simplest glaze—a glassy coating applied to the surface of a vessel—will make it impervious to water. But the variety of glazing techniques and effects devised by potters for aesthetic purposes is rich, diverse, and connected to strong cultural traditions.

Glazing appears on clay bricks that date back to a thirteenth-century-BCE temple in Iran, and both the ancient Egyptian and Mesopotamian river cultures offer sophisticated examples of glazing. The earliest known glaze in Egypt—characteristically blue-green in hue—was found on a nonclay tile from the tomb of the Egyptian pharaoh Menes and dates from about 3000 BCE. In the sixth cen-

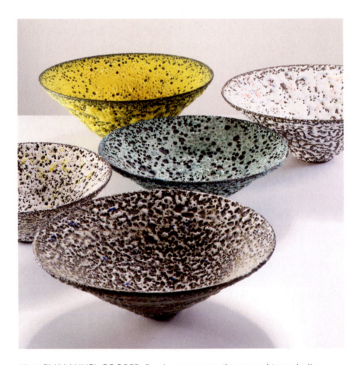

12-6 EMMANUEL COOPER. Bowls, stoneware, thrown and turned, slip, multiple glaze, 12¼" max.

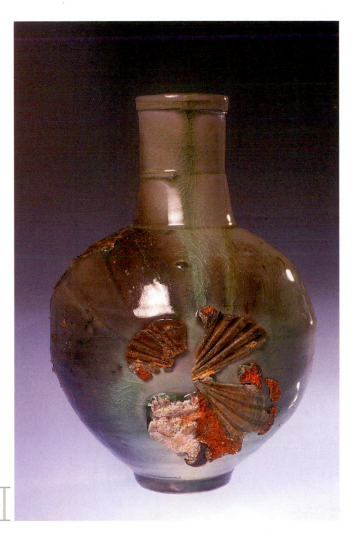

12-7 CHESTER NEALIE. *Bottle* (2000). Celadon glaze. H: 11¾".

scale drip compositions (see Chapter 21). Arneson's Pollock looks as if he stepped out of his Hamptons studio, his face an accidental and unsuspecting "canvas" for his signature drips, whips, and spatters. Arneson's glazed ceramics are purposefully purposefully unrefined and intentionally flawed, mirroring his view of human nature as imperfect.

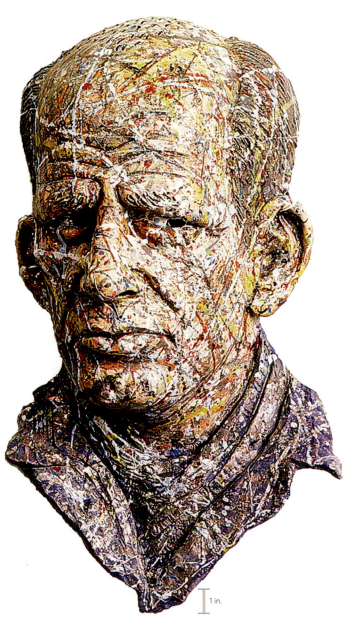

poured, or spattered onto the surface. A potter might also dip an object into a bath, so to speak, of liquid glaze.

Contrast the rough textured surfaces of Emmanuel Cooper's earthenware bowls (Fig. **12-6**) with the stunning glass-like finish of Chester Nealie's *Bottle* (Fig. **12-7**). The glaze on Cooper's bowls is reminiscent of volcanic rock or the cratered surface of the moon, while Nealie's pearlescent glaze enhances the sensual, graceful contours of what looks like a fragile glass vessel. These represent only two examples of the degree to which glazing affects the substance and sensibility of a piece, or, as in Robert Arneson's ceramic sculpture, its very meaning. *Jackson Pollock* (Fig. **12-8**) was an Abstract Expressionist painter who shook the art world with his large-

12-8 ROBERT ARNESON. *Jackson Pollock* (1983). Glazed ceramic. 23" × 13" × 7". Collection of Dr. Paul and Stacy Polydoran. Art © Estate of Robert Arneson/Licensed by VAGA, NY.

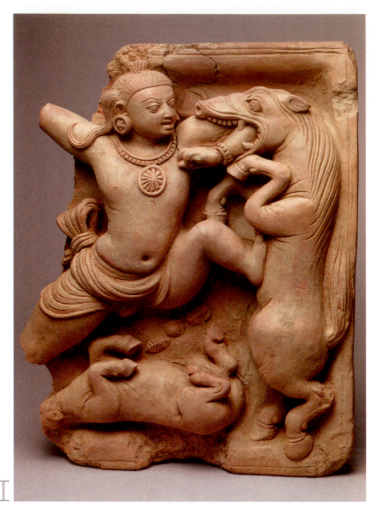

1 in.

12-9 *Krishna Killing the Horse Demon Keshi.* Gupta period (ca. 321–500), 5th century India (Uttar Pradesh). Terra-cotta. H: 21". The Metropolitan Museum of Art, NY.

Types of Ceramics

Ceramics are classified by their clay composition and by the temperature at which they are fired. **Earthenware** is pottery made from slightly porous clay that has been fired at relatively low kiln temperatures (1,000 to 2,000 degrees Fahrenheit). **Terra-cotta**, hard-baked red clay that has been fired at higher temperatures (2,070 to 2,320 degrees Fahrenheit), is used to create pottery, sculpture, building bricks, tile roofs, and architectural ornamentation with a characteristic reddish-brown hue. Utilitarian terra-cotta vessels are common finds in ancient archaeological sites, but the material was also used for sophisticated and large-scale works. The intricately carved and graphically realistic terra-cotta relief (Fig. **12-9**) from India's Gupta period illustrates Krishna, one of the avatars of the god Vishnu, battling and killing a

demon in the guise of a horse. Reliefs such as this one provided sculptural ornamentation on the exterior of stone and brick temples. Other terra-cotta works in your text include a carved sarcophagus from the Etruscan civilization (see Fig. 14-18), the renowned terra-cotta warriors from China's Han Dynasty (see Fig. 1-12), and several examples of pottery in Chapter 14.

Earthenware and terra-cotta span centuries and cultures, and contemporary potters continue to produce works from the same materials. Betty Woodman is described as one of the most important ceramic artists working today, blurring the boundaries between art and craft and conjoining cultural influences—East and West—in her painted vases. Works like *Aztec Vase #06-1* (Fig. **12-10**) belie functionality in their sculptural sensibility even though they are actual vessels. Her glazes and hand-painted decoration show a wide range of artistic references gleaned from her global voyages and

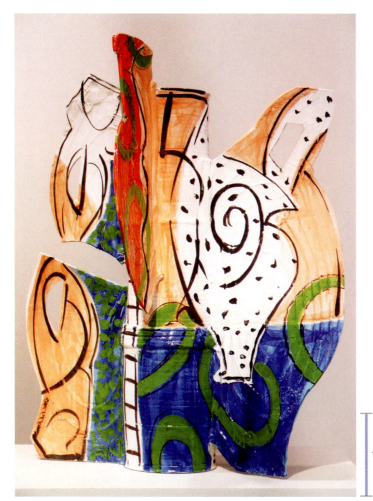

1 ft.

12-10 BETTY WOODMAN. *Aztec Vase #06-1* (2006). Glazed earthenware, epoxy resin, lacquer, and paint. 62" × 42" × 9".

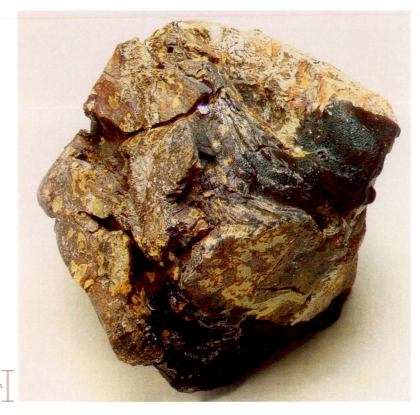

1 in.

12-11 CLAUDI CASANOVAS. *Block #43* (2001). 11¾" × 11¾" × 10¼".

fine, white kaolin clay and contains other minerals such as feldspar, quartz, and flint in various proportions. It is usually fired at 2,400 to 2,500 degrees Fahrenheit, and it is used for fine dinnerware. Chinese porcelain, or **china**, is white and fired at low temperatures. It is vitreous and nonporous, and it may be translucent. It makes a characteristic ringing sound when struck with a fingernail. Porcelain has been used by various cultures for vases and dinnerware for thousands of years, as well as for ceramic sculpture.

Harumi Nakashima's *Porcelain Form* (Fig. **12-12**), with its slippery-smooth surface and meticulously rounded shapes, stands in sharp contrast to the coarse textures often given center stage in other types of ceramics. The repetition in the polka-dotted glaze complements the rhythms found in the budding, biomorphic protuberances. Whereas the colors and textures of Casanovas's *Block* suggest the essence of tactile reality, Nakashima's bulging, morphing, amoeba-like sculpture seems surreal—outside or beyond conscious experience.

One of the fascinating features of clay is its versatility. It is said that one test of the integrity of a work is its truth to its material. In the case

the history of art. Woodman freely adopts shapes and colors from styles she is most drawn to, sometimes mixing and matching them on opposite sides of a vase. Her work is marked by an eclecticism and pluralism that energize her pieces and pay homage to a host of diverse styles.

Stoneware is usually gray or brown—owing to impurities in its clay—and vitreous or semivitreous (glasslike). It is very strong and durable and is therefore commonly used for cookware, dinnerware, and much ceramic sculpture. Claudi Casanovas's *Block #43* (Fig. **12-11**) is a hollow, cubic-form, stoneware sculpture that simulates the crude textures of hardened clay found in nature. The palette of glazes—black, brown, beige, and a hint of gold—deep fissures, and irregular contours combine to create the effect of a naturally occurring rock that has been worn away by time and the elements.

Porcelain is hard, nonporous, and usually white or gray in color. It is made from

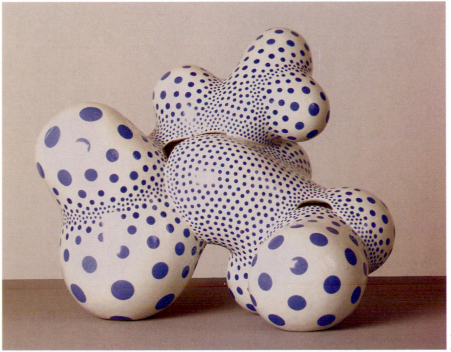

1 in.

12-12 HARUMI NAKASHIMA. *Porcelain Form* (2001). Porcelain. Inlaid decoration. 19¾" × 17¾" × 15¾". Den Bosch, Netherlands.

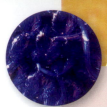

*They're going to think we're nuts over there, and of course
we are a little nuts, but we'll get this thing built.*
—Dale Chihuly, about the Icicle Creek chandelier

"A LITTLE BIT NUTS." Artists, and even the
rest of us, may have felt this way or been characterized this way at some point or another,
especially when we were seeing things in an
unconventional way. Glass artist Dale Chihuly
has redefined the conventional definition and
function of *chandelier* by designing works
he describes by this name for public spaces
from Venice to Jerusalem, from the world's
great museums to the wilderness of the great
outdoors. Although many chandeliers, in the
traditional sense, are ornamental, they are also
functional objects used, with candles or electricity, to illuminate an environment. But Chihuly's chandeliers are a different species. They
do not emit light of their own. Rather, they
reflect and transform ambient light—batteries
not included.

Chihuly's extraordinary glassworks capture, amplify, and channel light. In their
unusual stylistic juxtaposition with their surroundings, his chandeliers compel passersby
to take another look at the context in which
they are set—whether the Byzantine architecture and canals we find in Venice (Fig. **12-13**),
the ancient ruins in Jerusalem, or in the wilderness, the literal natural state of affairs.

Chihuly designed the chandelier shown in
Figure **12-14** for the Sleeping Lady mountain
retreat at Icicle Creek in the state of Washington. He erected it on an ancient granite
boulder among the grand pines of a primeval
setting, surrounded by a river and a profusion of wildlife. The chandelier reflects and
amplifies the frosted serenity of the site in
winter. It enriches visitors' relationships with
the area surrounding the retreat and with
nature as a whole. The chandelier also adds
Chihuly's—and humankind's—personal stamp
to a pristine wooded site. It also says some-

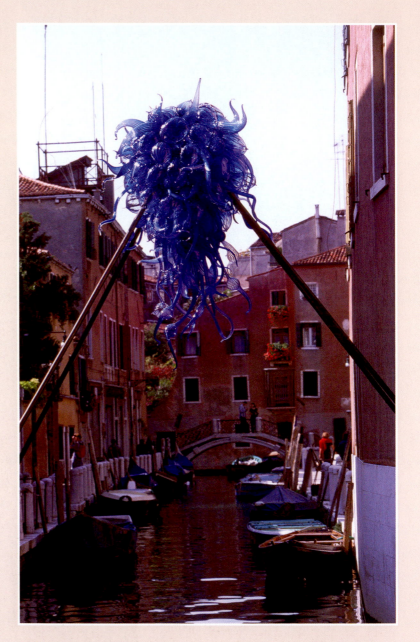

12-13 DALE CHIHULY. *Rio delle Torreselle Chandelier* (1996). A chandelier installation
in the Rio delle Torreselle, part of the *Chihuly over Venice* project, Venezia Aperto Vetro.
Venice, Italy.

Chihuly is a luminist. He uses glass as a literal and metaphorical prism through which he projects both ambient and intense theatrical light to produce sublime, luminous effects. This connects him to the long history of art in which light is cherished, "otherworldly," and implies divine presence.

—Jack Cowart

thing about the vision and the passion of the artist—unique in this case to Dale Chihuly, though made visual by a team of glassblowers and technicians. Does the work have deeper symbolic meanings—meanings that connect it with the history of art and civilization, meanings that connect it with contemporary technology and modes of expression? Much of the answer to that question lies in you. Perhaps you would like to consider these lines from Wallace Stevens's poem "Anecdote of the Jar":

I placed a jar in Tennessee,
And round it was, upon a hill.
It made the slovenly wilderness
Surround that hill.
The wilderness rose up to it,
And sprawled around, no longer wild.* ●

* From *The Collected Poems of Wallace Stevens* by Wallace Stevens, © 1945 by Wallace Stevens and renewed 1982 by Holly Stevens. Used by permission of Alfred A. Knopf, a division of Random House, Inc.

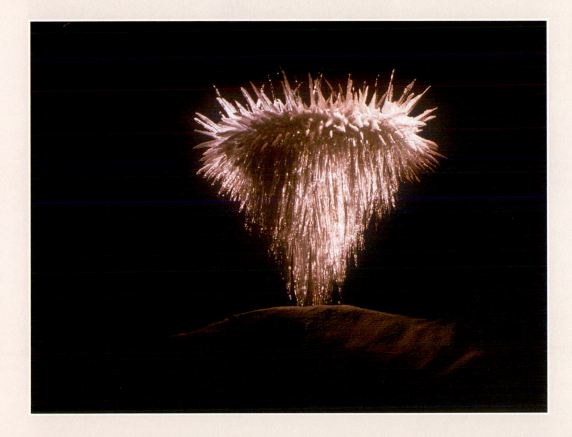

12-14 DALE CHIHULY. *Icicle Creek Chandelier* (1996). Sleeping Lady Conference Retreat, Leavenworth, WA.

of ceramics, however, one would be hard pressed to point to any one of the products of clay as representative of its "true" face.

GLASS

Glass, like ceramics, has had a long and multifarious history. The Roman historian Pliny the Elder traced the origins of glassmaking to an accidental discovery and an account of Phoenician sailors preparing a meal on a beach. They set their pots on lumps of *natron* (an alkali they had on deck to embalm the dead) and lit a fire, and when the hot natron mixed with the sand of the beach, molten glass flowed. In actual fact, glass predates the Phoenicians and the Romans (earliest examples date back to the civilizations of Mesopotamia and Old Kingdom Egypt), and Pliny's tale is certainly anecdotal and embellished. But the truth is that the recipe for glass is quite simple. Researchers have recreated the Phoenicians' scenario and have come to this conclusion: It could happen.[4] The result may not have been that wondrous substance—transparent or translucent—that has the power to transform light into an ephemeral, jewel-like palette, but it was surely glass. Glass is generally made from molten sand, or **silica**, mixed with minerals such as lead, potash, soda, and lime. Rich hues in glass are achieved by adding metal oxides with distinct color properties to molten silica: copper oxide produces green, and cobalt renders a deep blue.

Methods of Working with Glass

Glassblowing was discovered around 50 BCE, and with that the history of glassmaking was transformed. Earlier techniques included cold-working, in which room-temperature lumps of glass were scratched, ground, or delicately chipped to form objects, and casting, in which molten glass was poured into heat-resistant molds. Like ceramics, glass is a versatile medium. Molten glass can be modeled, pressed, rolled into sheets as it cools, and even spun into threads, as it is for **fiberglass**. Fine filaments can be woven into textiles, used in woolly masses for insulation, or molded into a material that is tough enough to be used for the body of an automobile.

Historically speaking, glassblowing was the game changer. Developed by the Romans, the technique enabled the creation of glass vessels of all shapes, sizes, functions, and colors. Glassblowing begins with a hollow tube or blowpipe that is dipped into molten glass and removed. Air is blown through the tube, causing the hot glass to expand to form a spherical bubble whose contours are shaped through rolling and pulling with various tools.

The *Portland Vase* (Fig. **12-15**), one of the earliest and best-known pieces of Roman glassware, was created in three steps: the body of the vessel was blown from dark blue glass; a coating of semi-opaque white glass was added to the surface of the basic blue vase; and the figures and vegetation that circumscribe the vase were carved in bas-relief on the white glass in subtle gradations of depth. Where the white glass is thinnest and therefore most translucent, the blue of the vase glows through and provides shading to the images. Imagine the

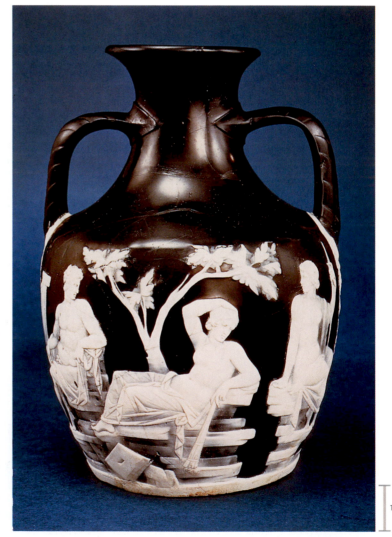

1 in.

12-15 *Portland Vase* (Roman, 3rd century). Cameo-cut glass. H: 9½"; D: 7". British Museum, London, England.

[4] William S. Ellis, "Glass: Capturing the Dance of Light," *National Geographic* 184, no. 6 (December 1993): 37–69.

delicacy of the handling—glass chipped away from glass, leaving unscratched the brittle blue surface that serves as background for the figures. Roman glassmaking skills were renowned in the ancient world, and cultures that had contact with the Romans—such as the Hindu kingdoms of India and the Arab world—adopted their techniques.

Different world centers became renowned for glassmaking in different eras. During the Middle Ages, stained-glass windows achieved their peak of perfection in French (see Fig. 15-30) and German cathedrals, while in Venice, luxury glass was prized for its lightness and delicacy. In the eighteenth century, on the other side of the Atlantic Ocean in Pennsylvania, Stiegel glass was known for a special hardness and brilliance attributed to the use of flint (lead oxide). **Flint glass** was used to create lenses for optical instruments and for fine crystal. Nineteenth-century Sandwich glass—from the town of Sandwich, Massachusetts—replicated the appearance of carved glass, but its patterns were created by pressing molten glass into molds. Ornamental Sandwich glass pieces in the shapes of cats, dogs, hens, and ducks became common home decorations.

During the second half of the nineteenth century, the name of Louis Comfort Tiffany became synonymous with expert handling of glass as a medium. His studios produced vases whose graceful, attenuated botanical forms married simplicity and exotic refinement, but the real treasures of Tiffany's oeuvre are his stained-glass windows. Large in scale, complex in imagery, and endlessly nuanced in palette, windows such as *Magnolias and Irises* (Fig. **12-16**) exhibit some of the particular material characteristics of much of Tiffany's work. Inspired by ancient glassware and the saturated colors of medieval stained glass, Tiffany sought to create recipes for glassmaking that produced rich color, yes, but also texture, opacity, and surface shimmer. In 1880, he patented **Favrile glass**, a technique of mixing together different colors of hot glass that yielded an iridescent finish. Tiffany described the result: "Favrile glass is distinguished by brilliant or deeply toned colors, usually iridescent like the wings of certain American butterflies, the necks of pigeons and peacocks, the wing covers of various beetles."

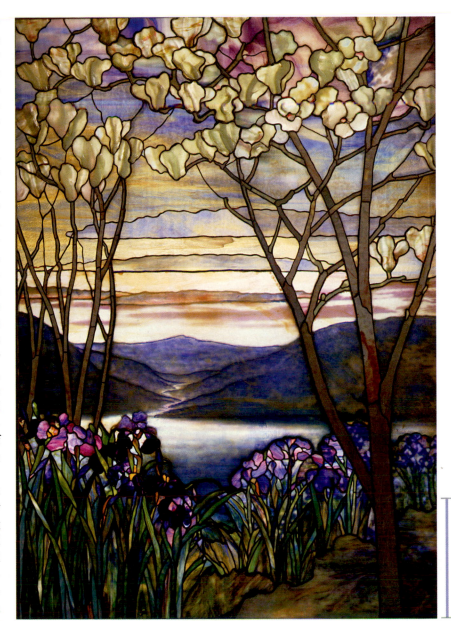

12-16 LOUIS COMFORT TIFFANY. *Magnolias and Irises* (c. 1908). Leaded Favrile glass. 60¼" × 42". Anonymous Gift, in memory of Mr. and Mrs. A. B. Frank, 1981 (1981.159). The Metropolitan Museum of Art, NY. Image copyright © The Metropolitan Museum of Art / Art Resource, NY.

TEXTILE ARTS

Textile arts are arts and crafts in which **fibers** are used to make functional or decorative objects or works of art. **Fibers** are slender, threadlike structures that are derived from animals (for example, wool or silk), plants (cotton, hemp, flax, or jute), or synthetic materials (rayon, nylon, or fiberglass). Textile techniques include, but are not limited to, weaving, embroidery, crochet, and macramé.

Weaving

Weaving was well known to the ancient Egyptians and Mesopotamians, although some examples date back to the Stone Age. Weaving was a staple craft in ancient and traditional cultures, including Native Americans of the desert Southwest and South Americans of the Amazon region. Textile art reached a degree of unparalleled accomplishment in Medieval Europe and in Islamic countries, where technological innovations contributed to the development of the craft.

The **weaving** of textiles is accomplished by interlacing horizontal and vertical threads—threads that are on a right angle to each other. The lengthwise fibers are called the **warp**, and the crosswise threads are called the **weft** or **woof**. The particular fiber and weave determine the weight and quality of the cloth. Wool, for example, makes soft, resilient cloth that is easy to dye. Nylon is strong, more durable than wool, mothproof, resistant to mildew and mold, nonallergenic, and also easy to dye.

There are many types of weave structures. The **plain weave** found in burlap, muslin, and cotton broadcloth is the strongest and simplest: the woof thread passes above one warp fiber and beneath the next. In the **satin weave**, woof threads pass above and beneath several warp threads. Warp and woof form broken diagonal patterns in the **twill weave**. In **pile weaving**, which is found in carpeting and in velvet, loops or knots are tied; when the knotting is complete, the ends are cut or sheared to create an even surface. In sixteenth-century Persia, where carpet weaving reached an artistic peak, pile patterns often had as many as 1,000 knots to the square inch.

The *Ardabil Carpet* (Figure **12-17**), completed in 1539–1540, is the oldest *dated* carpet in the history of art, although weaving has been an integral part of Persian culture since ancient times. Persian carpets are refined in technique, ambitious in size, and dazzling in color and complexity. They are classified according to design, pattern, and motif, in traditional and innovative combinations and variations. The *Ardabil Carpet* was woven of short pieces of wool that were knotted onto silk warps and wefts. As each row was completed, it was packed down and the pile trimmed to an even height after the entire rug was finished. The pattern consists of 10 colors. A large field with interlacing flowers and vines provides a backdrop for a central medallion surrounded by 16 pointed ovals. Hanging from the ovals—at 12 o'clock and 6 o'clock—are two lamps, the pointed bottoms of which face in opposite directions. The field is surrounded by four parallel bands of different widths filled with intricate patterns. The carpet, commissioned by an Iranian ruler for the shrine of an ancestor, had as many as 10 weavers working on it at the same time.

The *Ardabil Carpet* was created on a loom. During the Islamic Golden Age, foot pedals were introduced to operate looms, thus facilitating the weaving process. The Alaskan Chilkat robe (Fig. **12-18**), however, was created by Native American weaver Dorica Jackson without a loom. Chilkat women traditionally achieved a very fine texture with a thread

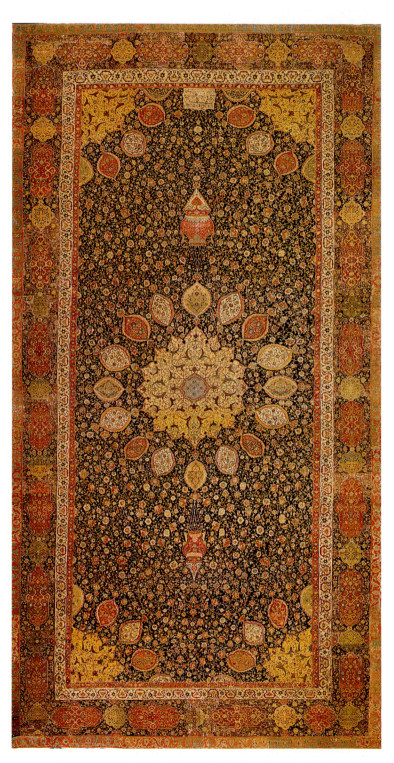

12-17 Ardabil Carpet, Iran (1539–1540). Woolen pile. 34" × 17½". Victoria and Albert Museum, London, England.

made from a core of a strand of cedar bark covered with the wool from a mountain goat. Clan members used robes such as these on important occasions to show off the family crest. Here a strikingly stylized, winged animal occupies the center of a field of eyes, heads, and mysterious symbols.

Traditional weaving techniques may surface in innovative ways in the hands of contemporary artists. Ed Rossbach's wall hanging (Fig. **12-19**), which, in overall shape, is not unlike the Chilkat robe, is worlds apart in its choice of materials and strong political message. Rossbach plaits construction paper in such a manner that his image emerges subtly from an overall mottled background.

The surfaces of fabrics can be enhanced by printing, embroidery, tie-dyeing, or batik. Hand printing has been known since ancient times, and Oriental traders brought the practice to Europe. A design was stamped on a fabric with a carved wooden block that had been inked. Contemporary machine printing uses inked rollers in the place of blocks, and fabrics can be printed at astonishingly rapid rates. In **embroidery**, the design is made by needlework.

Tie-dyeing and batik both involve dyeing fabrics. In **tie-dyeing**, designs are created by sewing or tying folds in the cloth to prevent the dye from coloring certain sections of fabric (Figs. 12-22 and 12-23). In **batik**, applications of wax prevent the dye from coloring sections of fabric that are to be kept light or white. A series of dye baths and waxings can be used to create subtly deeper colors.

Basket Weaving

In **basket weaving**, or basketry, animal or vegetable fibers (such as twigs, grasses, straw, and animal hair) are woven into baskets or other containers. Basket weaving is, like ceramics and textiles, an ancient craft, but because natural materials disintegrate, there is little physical evidence of such early basketry. Yet imprints of the woven patterns of baskets to decorate the surface of clay pots give us a sense of what the craft must have been. As with the other crafts we have considered, basket making crosses time and culture.

Pomo gift baskets, created by Native Americans from Northern California, are woven from materials such as grass, glass beads, shells and feathers (Fig. **12-20**). The Pomo have been described as the finest basket weavers in the world. Baskets such as the one illustrated were not woven for utilitarian purposes but rather served as gifts and treasures.

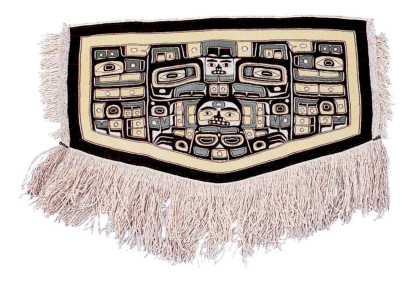

12-18 DORICA JACKSON. Chilkat robe (1976). Cedar bark warp; sheep's wool wefts. W: 60".

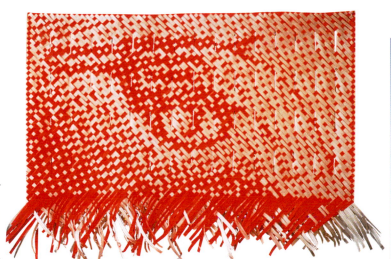

1 ft.

12-19 ED ROSSBACH. *Handgun* (1975). Plaited construction paper. 40" × 54". Craft Alliance, St. Louis, MO.

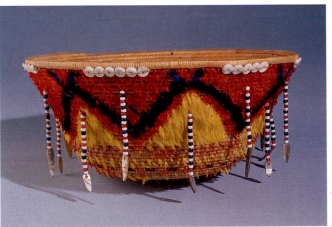

1 in.

12-20 Ceremonial feathered basket with bead and shell pendants. Pomo, CA (1900). H: 3½". Phoebe A. Hearst Museum of Anthropology, University of California, Berkeley, CA.

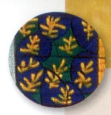

FAITH RINGGOLD WAS BORN in Harlem in 1930 and educated in the public schools of New York City. Raised with a social conscience, she painted murals and other works inspired by the civil rights movement in the 1960s and, a decade later, took to feminist themes after her exclusion from an all-male exhibition at New York's School of Visual Arts. Ringgold's mother, a fashion designer, was always sewing, the artist recalls, and at this time the artist turned to sewing and related techniques—needlepoint, beading, braided ribbon, and sewn fabric—to produce soft sculptures such as those in *Mama Jones, Andrew, Barbara, and Faith* (Fig. **12-21**), from her series *The Family of Women*. African garments inspired the clothing of these family members, and the faces are reminiscent of African masks.

More recently, Ringgold is most well known for her narrative quilts, such as the highly acclaimed *Tar Beach* (see Fig. 1-28), which combine traditions common to African Americans and women—storytelling and quilting. *Matisse's Chapel* (Fig. **12-22**) is from Ringgold's *French Collection*, which inserts contemporary American artists, other colleagues, and family members into French settings. In one quilt, *Dancing at the Louvre*, friends, including the children of one, are shown in high spirits before the *Mona Lisa*. In *Picasso's Studio*, the famed Spanish artist (literally) draws inspiration for *Les Demoiselles d'Avignon* from a black model. In an ironic twist on Manet's *Luncheon on the Grass* (see Fig. 19-12), a nude Picasso sits on the grass in the company of clothed women. *Matisse's Chapel* places a wedding party composed of the artist's family in the chapel made famous by dint of Matisse's contributions.

Crown Heights Children's Story Quilt (Fig. **12-23**) is on permanent display at a Brooklyn public school. The quilt pictures 12 folktales of peoples who have contributed to the life of New York, including Jamaicans and West Africans (the top three on the left), the Dutch (upper right), two Native American peoples, Asians, Puerto Ricans, Italian Americans, and Jewish Americans. True to the genre of quilting, the artist uses her skills to patch together the myths and stories of different peoples in a nation composed of diverse ethnic groups.

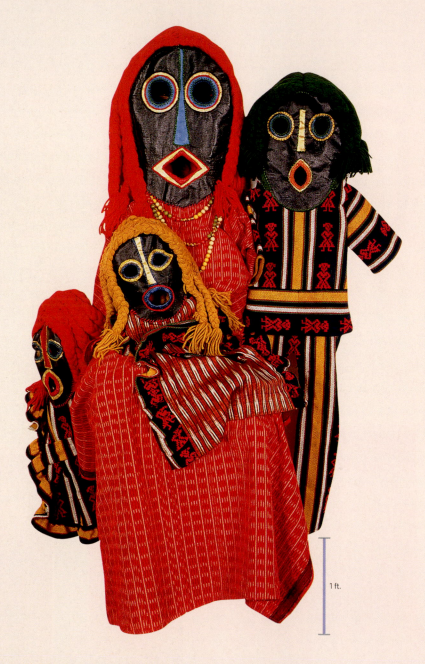

12-21 FAITH RINGGOLD. *Mama Jones, Andrew, Barbara, and Faith* (1973). Embroidery and sewn fabric. 74" × 69".

12-22 FAITH RINGGOLD. *Matisse's Chapel* (1991). Acrylic on canvas; tie-dyed, pieced fabric border. 74" × 79½". From *The French Collection* series, Part I, #6.

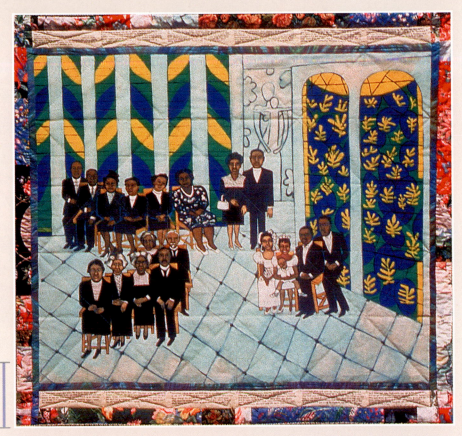

1 ft.

12-23 FAITH RINGGOLD. *Crown Heights Children's Story Quilt* (1994). Painted and pieced fabric. 108" × 144".

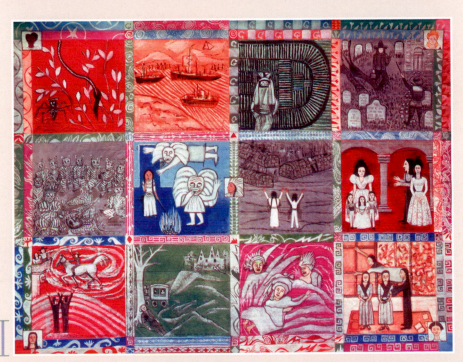

1 ft.

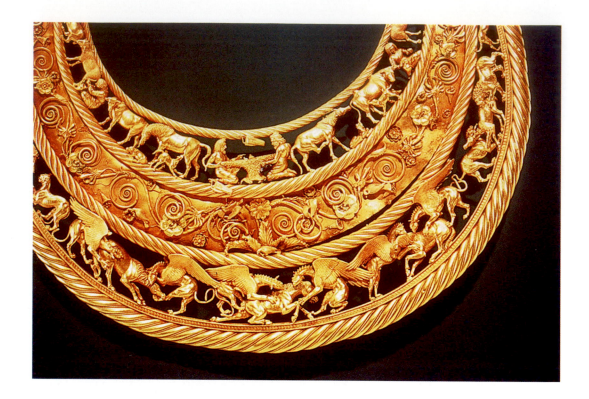

12-24 Pectoral piece from Ordzhonikidze, Russia (4th century BCE). Gold. D: 12". Historical Museum, Kiev, Ukraine.

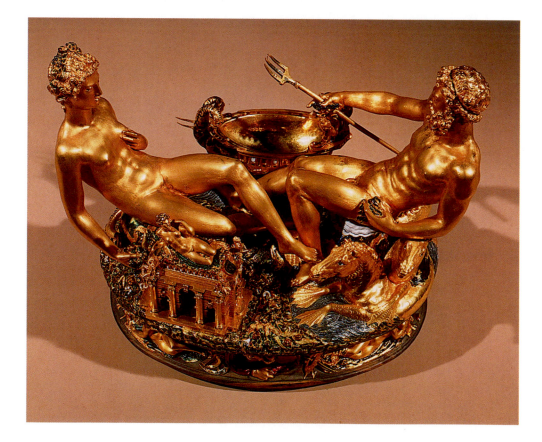

12-25 BENVENUTO CELLINI. *Saltcellar of Francis I* (1539–1543). Gold and enamel. H: 10"; L: 13 1/16". Kunsthistorisches Museum, Vienna, Austria.

METALWORK AND JEWELRY

The process of refining and working with metals is called **metalwork**, a word that encompasses a range of diverse objects and projects from the industrial world to the jeweler's workshop. **Iron** and its alloys were used, in the Iron Age, for arrowheads and, in the Industrial Age, for skyscrapers. **Stainless steel** is used in common kitchen utensils but was also used for the uncommon pinnacle of New York City's Chrysler Building and by postwar American sculptors such as David Smith (see Fig. 21-28). Lightweight **aluminum** is used in cookware and in aircraft; **bronze** has been used for coins, weaponry, farm tools, and sculptural monuments.

Silver and gold have been prized for millennia for their rarity and their appealing colors and textures. They are used in jewelry, fine tableware, ritual vessels, and sacred objects. In jewelry, these precious metals often serve as settings for equally precious gems or polished stones, or their surfaces can be **enameled** by melting powdered glass on them. These metals even find use as currency; in times of political chaos, gold and silver are sought even as the value of paper money drops off to nothing. Threads of gold and silver find their way onto precious china and into the garments and vestments of clergy and kings. Gold leaf adorns books, paintings, and picture frames.

Metals can be hammered, **embossed** with raised designs, and cast using the same techniques described in the section on bronze sculpture in Chapter 9. Each method for working metal has its own tradition and its advantages and disadvantages.

The pectoral piece shown in Figure 12-24 was meant to be worn across the breast of a nomadic chieftain from southern Russia and probably to be buried with him. People and animals are depicted with a realism that renders the fanciful **griffins** in the lower register as believable as the horses, dogs, and grasshoppers found elsewhere in the piece. The open work of the figures is contrasted by the refined gold-on-gold scrollwork in the central register; all are bordered by magnificent, twisted coils.

The Renaissance sculptor and goldsmith Benvenuto Cellini created a gold and enamel saltcellar (Fig. 12-25) for the French king Francis I that shows the refinement of his art. Its allegorical significance is merely an excuse for displaying the skill of Cellini's craft. Salt, drawn from the sea, is housed in a boat-shaped salt container and watched over by a figure of Neptune. The pepper, drawn from the earth, is contained in a miniature triumphal arch and guarded by a female personification of Earth. Figures on the base represent the seasons and the segments of the day—all on a pedestal only 13 inches in diameter. Unfortunately, the saltcellar is Cellini's sole major work in gold that survives.

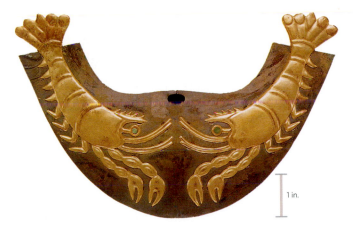

12-26 Nose ornament, crayfish, Peru (Loma Negra, 3rd century CE). Gold, silver, turquoise inlay. H: 4¾". The Metropolitan Museum of Art, NY.

Body ornament, ever growing in popularity to this day, spans history and geography. Consider the nose ornament from Peru in Figure 12-26. The piece is fashioned of gold, silver, and turquoise inlay and is a characteristic example of the ancient Peruvian facility in handling complex metal techniques. Much of the jewelry available for us to see today has been unearthed from tombs of the very wealthy among Peruvian society. The images and their symbolism remain mostly undeciphered, but archeologists have nonetheless constructed a view of these people from such artifacts.

Kiff Slemmons's *Transport* (Fig. 12-27) is a miniature sculpture that again bridges the supposed gulf between fine art and the functional object. It was constructed for the *Artworks for*

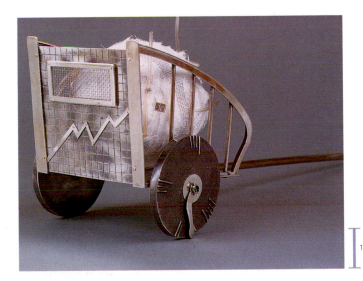

12-27 KIFF SLEMMONS. *Transport* (1990). Sterling silver, aluminum, gauze, mesh, tape, tubing, pearls. 5" × 14" × 4½".

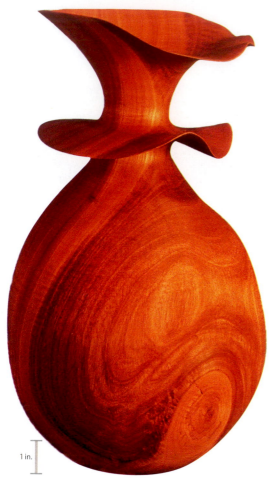

AIDS exhibition that was held in Seattle in 1990. It is a miniature two-wheeled cart that refers to the history of mass deaths. Throughout the ages, such carts have been used in cities to truck away the victims of epidemics. The wheels of the cart are clocks with human hands, seeming to tick away as the number of deaths due to AIDS mounts. Hospital waste and a stylized "progress" chart with an alarming indicator of the rising toll of the epidemic complete the political message.

WOOD

Some relatively sophisticated technology is required to convert glass, metal, and clay into something of use. Wood, however, has only to be cut and carved to form a functional object. Two wood vases hint at the versatility of the medium. The soft, flowing contours of Melvyn Firmager's vase (Fig. **12-28**) highlight the swirling grain patterns of the wood, which almost take on the character of glazing on a ceramic vase. The simple roundness, highly polished surface, and inherent grain patterns in David Ellsworth's vase (Fig. **12-29**) create the illusion of stone.

DESIGN

Design has a multiplicity of meanings. As a discipline or profession, it includes experts in industrial design (objects), fashion design (clothing), graphic design (communication),

12-28 MELVYN FIRMAGER. *Untitled* (1993). Destroyed in 1994 Los Angeles earthquake. Eucalyptus gunnii. H: 13½"; D: 8".

12-29 DAVID ELLSWORTH. *Vessel* (1992). Norway maple burl. H: 4"; D: 7".

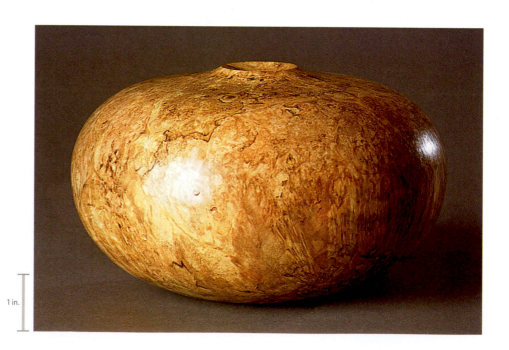

and web design (the Internet), to name a few. As a process, it involves the act of designing or creating a concept and product for consumption, communication, or interaction. We refer to the finished product as a design.

Industrial Design: The Object

Objects are three-dimensional products designed for consumer use by industrial designers, also known as product designers. They run the gamut from utilitarian designs (form follows function) to those in which aesthetics override usability (form over function). There are good and bad designs, and then there are objects for which the question "Good or bad?" seems moot. Consider the common houseware item—the citrus juicer—in Figures **12-30** to **12-32**. The first juicer seems to have been designed foremost with utility in mind. The user halves an orange, inverts it onto a conical plastic piece that has pronounced ribs or ridges, and twists it one way or another to release the juice from the orange. The juice flows down the cone between the ridges and into a plastic collection bowl in a quick and tidy fashion. The second juicer is also based on a thoughtful concept. The user presses the orange half onto a ridged cone, twists it back and forth, and the juice is collected in a flat bowl with a spout on one end for pouring. A row of plastic teeth is placed forward of the spout to hold back seeds and unwanted pulp. The only problem is that these teeth are placed exactly where the user's knuckles hit when twisting the orange to extract the juice—a great design

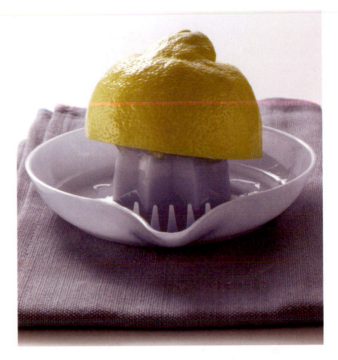

12-31 *Juicer.*

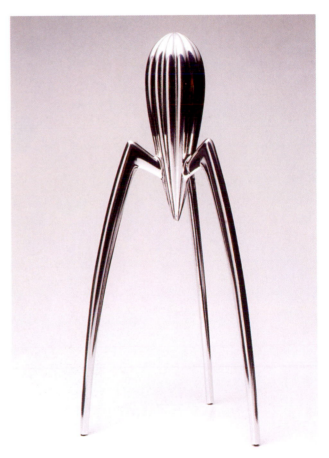

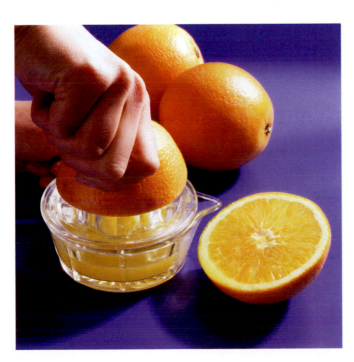

12-30 *Citrus Express.*

12-32 PHILIPPE STARCK. *Juicy Salif.*

in theory, but certainly not in practice. Now take a look at famed French designer Philippe Starck's citrus squeezer titled *Juicy Salif*, purportedly conceived during a meal in which he was squeezing lemon over a squid. A clear example of "form over function," Starck's juicer has become an icon of 1990s design, not because it works well, but because it looks great. In fact, *Juicy Salif*'s manufacturer, Alessi, recommends it for display and not for use.

Although few of us looking for a juicer would actually opt for Starck's product, consumers often make choices based as much on product design and cache as usability. Apple's iPhone (Fig. **12-33**) is a case in point. In terms of function, the iPhone is the electronic equivalent of a Swiss Army knife. You can surf the web; send texts and e-mails; navigate using GPS; record notes; set an alarm to wake up in the morning; take, save, and send photos; and download and play music. You can also make phone calls. However, there are many "smartphones" on the market, and a fair number of them compete in terms of function and are more economically priced than the iPhone. Even so, sales of the Apple product have swept the globe. In choosing an iPhone, consumers are not only buying a product but also buying into a lifestyle.

FORM AND FUNCTION IN PRODUCT DESIGN A great deal of contemporary product design embraces the philosophy of "form follows function" put forth by the architect Louis Sullivan, whose Wainwright Building we studied in Chapter 11 (see Fig. 11-17). Three of a multitude of examples come from the design collection of the Museum of Modern Art. Rody Graumans's *85 Lamps Lighting Fixture* (Fig. **12-34**) is an unadulterated cluster of naked lightbulbs and wiring that fans out into a more classic chandelier profile as a result of the spherical shapes of the touching bulbs. The "truth in art" that Sullivan sought through his philosophy seems also

12-33 iPhone. Apple, Inc.

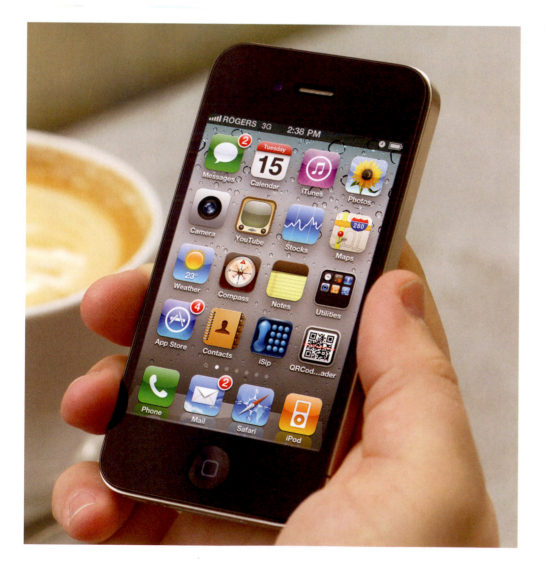

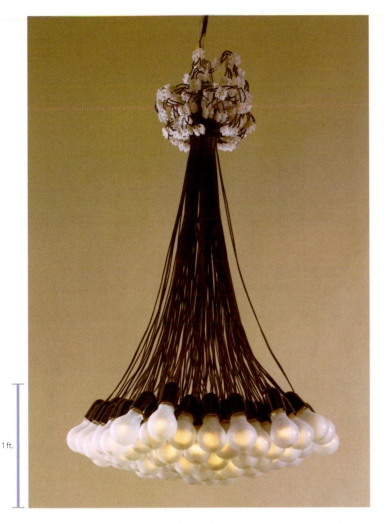

1 ft.

12-34 RODY GRAUMANS. *85 Lamps Lighting Fixture* (1992). Light bulbs, cords, and sockets. H: 39" (100 cm); D: 39" (100 cm). The Museum of Modern Art, NY.

Museum of Modern Art. The metal frame and mesh seat and back fully adjust to accommodate bodies of any shape, height, and weight. A tilt mechanism in the chair "floats" users with support no matter which position they are sitting in, and the mesh suspension system distributes weight equally. The quirky appearance of the Aeron Chair, a by-product of its adherence to ergonomic design, has achieved a sort of cult status among trendy office workers. One television commercial advertisement even shows 20-something-year-olds playing office hockey while cruising in their Aeron Chairs.

Graphic Design: Communication

Graphic design is an artistic process used to communicate information and ideas through writing, images, and symbols that are connected to contemporary human experience. Since the beginning of modern history, advances in technology—beginning with the printing press in the early 1400s—have enabled the global dissemination of graphic design products. Components of the graphic design include typography, page layout and book design, and corporate identity. Graphic design

to have inspired Graumans's lighting fixture design: the whole truth and nothing but the truth, in fact.

Many objects of contemporary industrial design take **ergonomics**—the applied science of equipment design intended to minimize discomfort and therefore maximize performance of the user—into account. If your shoulders, neck, elbows, or wrists hurt from the physical stress of prolonged work at your computer, you can purchase an ergonomically designed keyboard that will keep your wrists at a proper angle and a mouse that will support the weight of your arm while mousing. These designs are based on the physiognomy of the human body and typical product use.

The Aeron Chair (Fig. **12-35**), ergonomically designed by Bill Stumpf and Don Chadwick, has emerged as the Porsche of office chairs and is also part of the design collection at the

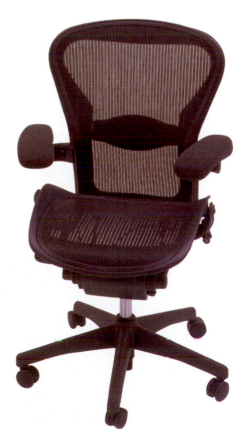

12-35 BILL STUMPF AND DON CHADWICK. Aeron Chair. The Museum of Modern Art, NY.

mediums include photography, printmaking, computer-aided design, and digital design. The history of graphic design can be traced back to marks made by humans on the walls of caves and the earliest forms of writing. In this section, we will consider contemporary examples of graphic design as it is the most ubiquitous of art forms, entering our consciousness and our lives in a steady stream on a daily basis.

TYPOGRAPHY **Typography** is the technical term for designing and composing letterforms. Until the digital age, printing was done with movable pieces of metal (or wood) cast or carved with letters raised above the surface of the piece. These pieces were put together into strings of words and lines by typesetters. Today typesetting is done on computers, as is type design. Designers can choose from hundreds of typefaces and can manipulate things like scale, color, perspective, and the overlapping of letters and other images. A designer will use type to communicate with optimal clarity—a variant of form follows function—or with expressiveness. It is an eye-opener to realize that any and all type that we come into contact with as consumers originated with a graphic designer who was skilled in typography.

The clearest, most utilitarian form of typography is probably the pictogram, which is widely used in signage. From the simplified shapes of a woman in a dress and man in trousers, we can figure out which restroom is intended for whom, even if we find ourselves in a foreign country where we don't speak the language (Fig. **12-36**). So-called barrier-free communication is also seen in the now-familiar graphic design of a red circle with a line drawn through it signifying "NO!"—whatever *no* may apply to. The pictogram in Figure **12-37** consists of simple, easily understood symbols designating areas in which smoking is forbidden.

LAYOUT A **layout** is a way of organizing the design elements in a printed work such as a poster, book, or magazine. Layouts typically consist of visual elements, including type and pictures, which may be drawings and photographs. The layout of children's books may also contain buttons to press, a variety of textures to feel, and speakers that make sounds.

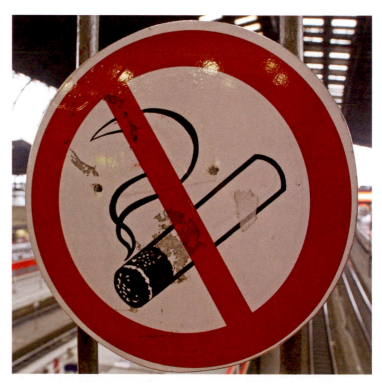

12-36 Signage for women's and men's restrooms.

12-37 Signage for nonsmoking and smoking areas.

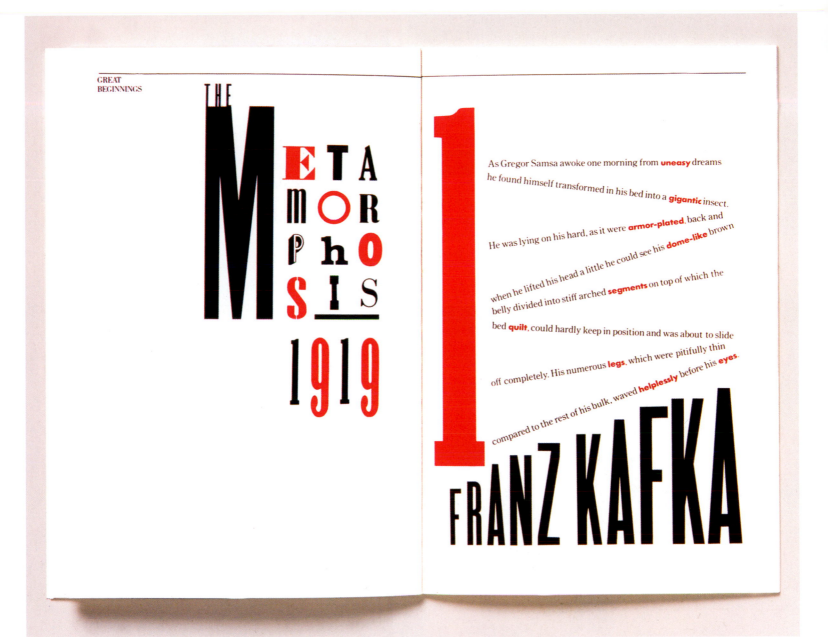

THE METAMORPHOSIS 1919

As Gregor Samsa awoke one morning from **uneasy** dreams he found himself transformed in his bed into a **gigantic** insect.

He was lying on his hard, as it were **armor-plated**, back and when he lifted his head a little he could see his **dome-like** brown belly divided into stiff arched **segments** on top of which the bed **quilt**, could hardly keep in position and was about to slide off completely. His numerous **legs**, which were pitifully thin compared to the rest of his bulk, waved **helplessly** before his **eyes**.

1 FRANZ KAFKA

12-38 PAULA SCHER. "Great Beginnings" spread for Koppel & Scher promotional booklet (1984).

The design of this book generally includes two columns of text which are "justified" (vertically aligned on both left and right). Photographs and drawings are interspersed throughout in various locations in an effort to provide aesthetic appeal and to have works of art displayed on the same page on which they are discussed. "Running feet" display the page numbers, the names of the chapters (on the left) and the names of the sections (on the right). Major and minor heads are distinguished both by color and size. Boxed features, such as "A Closer Look" and "Compare + Contrast," are placed on what are called *screens* or *tint panels* to help set them apart from the main text. You are not expected to be thinking about all this as you read, but the layout is intended to be stimulating yet refined, to complement the subject matter, and to assist the reader in navigating the material.

Figure **12-38** shows the layout for a spread for a promotional booklet, "Great Beginnings," by Paula Scher. Because of a tight budget, she limited her palette to three colors: black, red, and a putty color. She turned to rarely used typefaces and to features of Art Deco and Russian Constructivism (see Chapters 19 and 20) three to four generations after their passing. Put more simply, her typefaces went from thick to thin; her colors, like her subject, alternated; she worked her key letters and numbers like columns; and her horizontal lines of text ramped uphill then down, but always left to right, requiring dizzying backward leaps. Even the red and the black work like shocking figures against the calming putty-colored background. The layout is all "metamorphosis," or change, as is the title of the work.

Gitte Kath's poster for the Sydney Paralympics (Fig. 12-39) required her to collect materials such as the athletic shoe, glove, and feathers, post them on a worn, discolored wall in her home, paint and photograph them, then apply the graph-

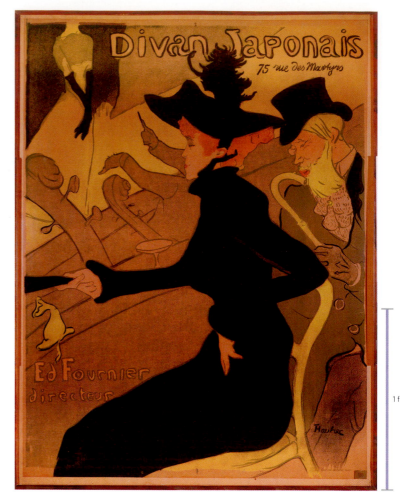

12-40 HENRI DE TOULOUSE-LAUTREC. *Le Divan Japonais* (1892). Color lithograph. 31⅝" × 23⅞". Musée Toulouse-Lautrec, Albi, France.

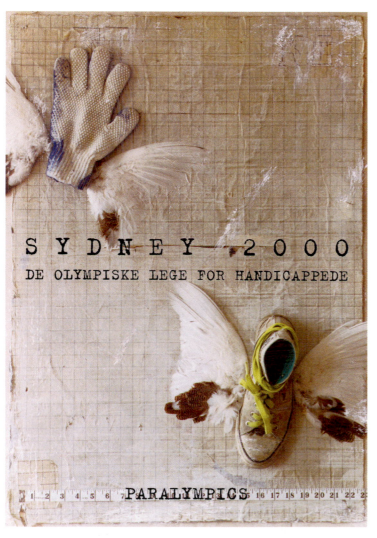

12-39 GITTE KATH. Poster for the Sydney 2000 Paralympics.

ics. The condition of the elements in the poster suggest the poignancy of the transitory nature of living things. There is nothing heroic about this poster; there is only the suggestion of loss and caring. The colors are muted, the positioning of the objects and the graphics are balanced, and the allover grid and decay provide unity.

Henri de Toulouse-Lautrec, a late-nineteenth-century French artist, is seen by some as the father of the color lithograph poster. Toulouse-Lautrec dwelled in nighttime Paris—its cafés, music halls, nightclubs, and brothels. The posters that he designed for concerts and other performances are among the most well known in the history of art. His designs (Fig. 12-40) are successful because they capture, in a single image, the spirit and personality of the establishment and the performer. Areas of unmodulated color and high-contrast values in the poster design evoke theater lighting and costuming. The lyrical

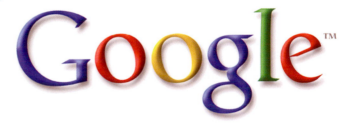

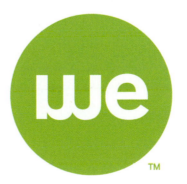

market research. When former vice president and Nobel Prize recipient Al Gore sought to promote his nonprofit advocacy group for the prevention of global warming (Alliance for Climate Protection), he hired a wellknown advertising firm to design an ad campaign, including a logo. The result was a simple green circle inscribed with white letters forming the word we (Fig. **12-43**). Answering questions about the concept, lead designer Brian Collins explained that the bright green color best expresses the idea of *green*—a word used to describe efforts to conserve and restore energy and the planet's environment and resources. The color is symbolic, but also uplifting and optimistic. The typeface used for the word *we*, turned upside down, reads *me* backward, and was created by typographer Chester Jenkins specifically for the Gore alliance's logo. The *we-me* inversion is intended to signify human cooperation to achieve a solution to the climate crisis. Finally, according to Collins, the circular shape of the logo symbolizes the earth and draws attention to the fact that the climate crisis affects all of its inhabitants.

12-42 Google Logo. http://www.google.com.

shapes and undulating lines, coupled with an oblique perspective and bold patterns influenced by Japanese prints, combine to catch the eye and draw the patron to the party.

Logos

A **logo** is an emblematic design used to identify and advertise a company or an organization. The most successful corporate identity designs—like Apple's instantly recognizable apple minus a single bite (Fig. **12-41**)—are inseparable from the entities they represent. The logo for the Internet search engine Google (Fig. **12-42**) features broadly spaced letters of intense—mostly primary—colors. The simplicity of the design and the straightforwardness of the color scheme suggest an ease of use (even a child can do it) that the company would want to promote.

Logos are well conceived and deliberately designed symbols that are decided upon after much consideration and

12-43 Alliance for Climate Protection logo. Courtesy Alliance for Climate Protection.

Web Design

Websites are an inextricable part of the information super-highway. Any of us cyberspace surfers can go online, access the website of a popular consumer magazine, and get the latest reviews on the new car we're drooling over. We can research without books, order DVDs, make reservations, or bid on a special reserve wine. And a big part of what keeps us attached to our PC's mouse at the end of an electronic umbilical cord is the visual feedback we get when we click. The better the design of the website, the more tantalizing the product or service—a clear fact not lost on the thousands of businesses, organizations, agencies, and individuals for whom the website is the new face and first face to the consumer in the age of electronics.

Web design consists of multiple tasks. One is technical and involves programming—how users click their way around a web page, how links to other pages and sites are established, and how to insert still images or animated clips and sound. Other tasks concern aesthetics and marketing,

where the main priority is designing a home page that will have the greatest visual impact, and thus entice the user to discover more by digging deeper into the site, or to buy whatever it is that is being sold.

As you surf the web, you have no doubt been struck by the endless variety, quality, and quantity of web design. I, like you, come across interesting websites almost every day, so it was hard to settle on just one or two to highlight in this chapter. Some current favorites include the website for the Alvin Ailey American Dance Theater in New York City (known for its brilliant mind- and body-stretching choreography) (Fig. 12-44). Another is the site for Squared Design Lab (Fig. 12-45). These, like other websites, feature icons or zones that the user can click on to navigate the site for more images or related web pages and information.

Squared Design Lab is a multidisciplinary design studio working with two- and three-dimensional animation, photomontage, graphic design, and other services. They are

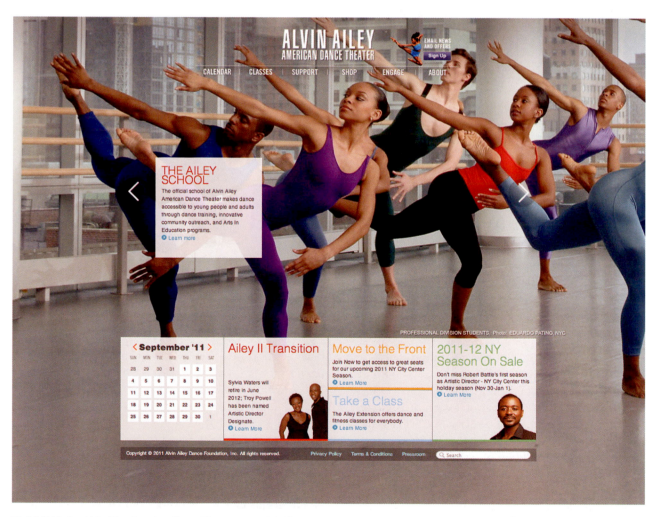

12-44 Website: Alvin Ailey American Dance Theater. www.alvinailey.org.

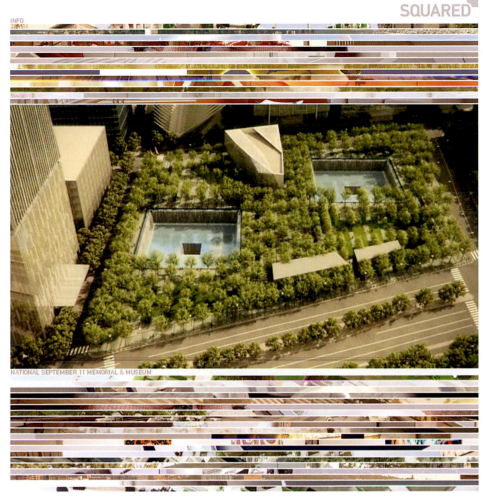

also known for their 3D digital visualization, as seen in this screen shot from their website; they have used a variety of techniques to create a visualization of a completed National September 11 Memorial and Museum at Ground Zero in Manhattan (also see Fig. 11-28 on page 229) as it was under construction. Run your mouse over the narrow bands that bracket the central image; as you do, each multicolored band converts to a white one that features the name of a site or a project. Click on one and the center screen will switch to a photograph, a bit of animation, or, in this case, a 3D visualization of that project. Click elsewhere and you will find an animation depicting the construction of a futuristic apartment building, or a rendering of gas-sipping minicars.

Art museums are also among the untold number of organizations that can be accessed through websites. In fact, you can engage in virtual museum visits by clicking your way through the world's most renowned collections: the Louvre in Paris, the Vatican Collection in Rome, the State Hermitage museum in St. Petersburg, Russia, or—closer to home—The Metropolitan Museum of Art in New York or any one of the collections featured in the Art Tours in your textbook.

Website design is a burgeoning business, but the ability to create sites does not reside exclusively among professionals. Students take courses that feature web design, software and templates for websites are widely available, and online tutorials give detailed information on how to "create your own." Like much related to the Internet, access is becoming universal.

Fashion Design

It has become routine for me to enter a classroom on any given day to overhear a play-by-play analysis of a previous night's episode of the Lifetime network's *Project Runway*. A reality TV program that pits established and up-and-coming fashion designers against one another in a series of challenges leading to a single winner, *Project Runway* has engendered a near cult-like following. So wide-ranging and popular is its appeal that in the wake of an early 2008 season of the show, *Saturday Night Live* writers created a skit around the winning designer Christian Siriano (Fig. **12-46**), who, along with his skinny jeans and signature hair-sprayed coif, brought the words *fierce* and *hot mess* into contemporary parlance. *Project Runway* has raised the consciousness of the realities of the world of fashion design from initial design sketches through the construction of a garment to a completed piece. It has also introduced terms like *haute couture*, *ready-to-wear*, and *mass-market apparel*.

Haute couture is the French term for "high fashion." Haute couture designs are technically made-to-measure for individual customers from expensive materials combined with meticulous stitching, detail work, and finishing. Runway shows feature many haute couture designs that are impressive for their innovation and aesthetics as artforms (Fig. **12-47**).

On the opposite end of the spectrum from haute couture is mass-market apparel, designed for ordinary consumers to be more universal in style and more affordable in price. Fabrics are generally of a lesser grade in terms of quality, and detailed hand-stitching is replaced by machine work that both expedites the execution and thus makes large quantities of an item possible. Designs for mass-market fashion often follow in the footsteps of couture designs, and it is not uncommon to find high-end designers creating product lines that are more accessible to department store shoppers. Ready-to-wear is a fashion category that straddles haute couture and mass-market fashion. Fabrics used for ready-to-wear are of high quality, and the workmanship is careful and often complex. Because apparel is created in smaller quantities, price tags are high. Ready-to-wear lines of the couture industry appear in major European and American cities during Fashion Week runway exhibits.

Fashion design has always reflected the culture and society of its time as much as it has contributed toward contemporary

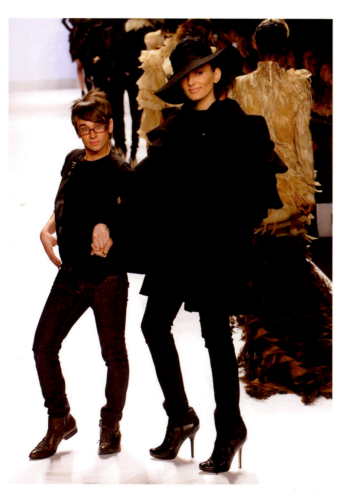

12-46 Christian Siriano, left, stands with a model on the runway during the Christian Siriano Fall 2008 Collection, part of Bravo Network's *Project Runway* final show during Mercedes-Benz Fall 2008 Fashion Week, in New York.

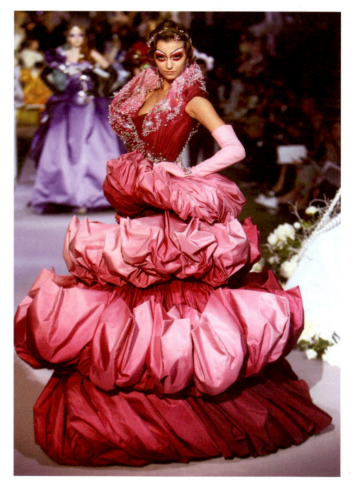

12-47 Haute couture design, Christian Dior, Autumn/Winter 2007–2008.

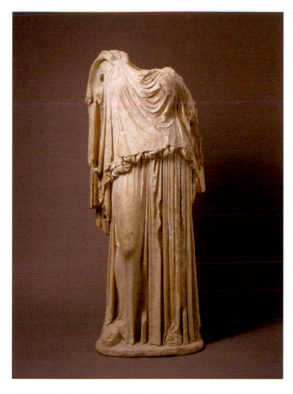

12-48 *Himation. Eirene, Daughter of Zeus and Themis.* Roman copy of a Greek original of the 4th century BCE. The Metropolitan Museum of Art, NY.

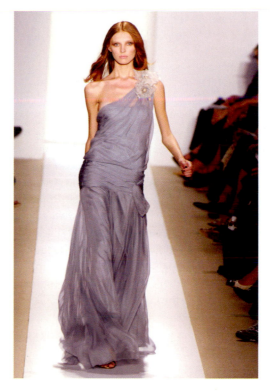

12-49 J MENDEL. A model walks the runway during the J Mendel Spring 2008 Fashion Show at The Promenade in Bryant Park during Mercedes-Benz Fashion Week on September 7, 2007, in New York City.

taste. And fashion has been inspired by history as much as it has anticipated the look of the future. One particular style that has been characterized by a remarkable longevity is one inspired by ancient Greece. The *chiton* (a loose-fitting gown pinned at the shoulders), *himation* (a mantle that was draped over one shoulder and sometimes wrapped around the body; see Fig. **12-48**), and *peplos* (a gown pinned at the shoulders and cinched at the waist; see Fig. 14-8) have been mimicked and interpreted by costume and fashion designers stretching back to the Napoleonic era in France forward to today (Fig. **12-49**).

On the opposite end of the chronological and fashion spectrum, consider the Hyper Space Couture Design Contest held in Tokyo in 2006. Participating designers focused on a couture line of personal fashions for space travel and habitation (Fig. **12-50**).

Urban Design: The Realm of the "Space in-Between"

Perhaps it is in urban design that our desire for order and harmony achieves its most majestic expression. Throughout history, most towns and cities have more or less sprung up. They have pushed back the countryside in all directions, as necessary, with little evidence of an overall guiding concept.

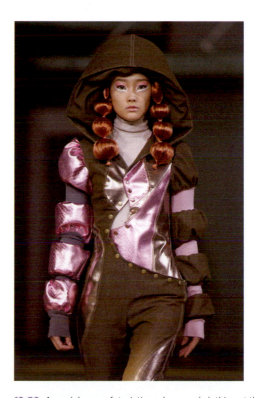

12-50 A model wears futuristic makeup and clothing at the Hyper Space Couture Design Contest held at Tokyo University on November 2, 2006.

Urban planners and designers "are the 'city builders' whose realm is 'the space in between,' 'in between' the buildings that are the province of architecture, and 'in between' the neighborhoods, cities and regions, the planning for which plays an often-under-appreciated role in the healthy development of our urban centers."
—Skidmore, Owings and Merrill

As a result, cities around the globe have experienced "the pollution of vital land, air, and water resources, shortages of food, energy, and potable water, inadequate housing, killing commutes, impersonal highrise districts, and aesthetically mind-numbing residential wastelands."[5] The Rome of the early Republic, for example, was an impoverished seat of empire, little more than a disordered assemblage of seven villages on seven hills. Later, the downtown area was a jumble of narrow streets winding through mud-brick buildings. Not until the first century BCE were the major building programs undertaken by Sulla and then the Caesars.

The new towns of the Roman Empire were laid out largely on a rectangular grid. This pattern was common among centrist states, where bits of land were parceled out to the subjects of mighty rulers. The gridiron was also found to be a useful basis for design throughout history—from the ancient Greeks to the colonial Americans. Many cities of the Near and Middle East, such as Baghdad, have a circular tradition in urban design, which may reflect the belief that they were the hubs of the universe. The throne room of the palace in eighth-century Baghdad was at the center of the circle. The palace—including attendant buildings, a game preserve, and pavilions set in perfumed gardens—was more than a mile in diameter, and the remainder of the population occupied a relatively narrow ring around the palace.

WASHINGTON, D.C. Few urban designs are as simple and rich as Pierre-Charles L'Enfant's plan for Washington, D.C. (Fig. **12-51**). The city is cradled between two branches of the Potomac River, yielding an uneven, overall diamond shape.

---

[5] Skidmore, Owings and Merrill. http://www.som.com/content.cfm/services_urban_design_and_planning (accessed March 18, 2011).

12-51 PIERRE-CHARLES L'ENFANT. Plan for Washington, D.C. (1792).

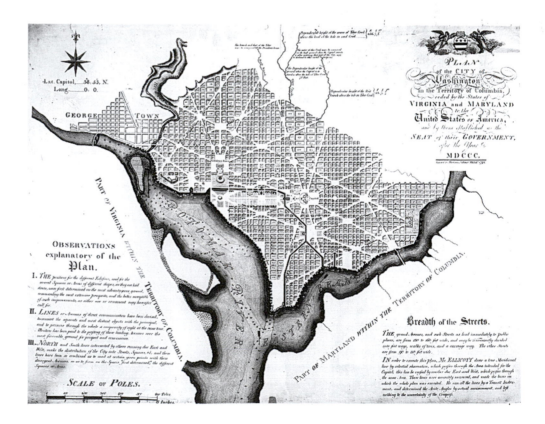

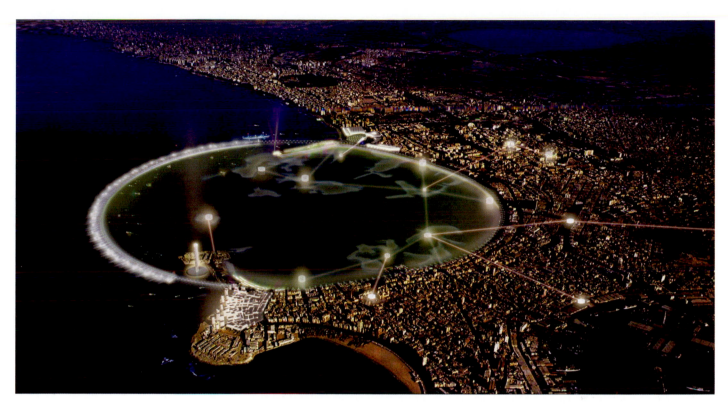

12-52 Rendering of the framework plan for Alexandria, Egypt, to complete the historic Eastern Harbor.

Within the diamond, a rectangular grid of streets that run east-west and north-south was laid down. Near the center of the diamond, with its west edge at the river, an enormous Mall or green space was set aside. At the east end of the Mall is the Capitol Building. To the north, at its west end, is the president's house (which is now the White House). Broad boulevards radiate from the Capitol and from the White House, cutting across the gridiron. One radiating boulevard runs directly between the Capitol and the White House, and other boulevards parallel it.

The design is a composition in which the masses of the Capitol Building and White House balance one another, and the rhythms of the gridiron pattern and intersecting diagonal boulevards create contrast and unity. The Mall provides an open central gathering place that is as much a part of American culture as it is respite from the congestion of the city. We see more of Washington, D.C., in the Art Tour at the end of the chapter.

ALEXANDRIA, EGYPT Alexandria, the ancient center of the Western cultural world, is now a city of 4 million. It was founded around 331 BCE by Alexander the Great. Its lighthouse, a hallowed beacon on the Mediterranean Sea, now gone, was one of the Seven Wonders of the Ancient World. Its library, built by the Greeks and accidentally burned down by Julius Caesar in 48 BCE, was the largest in the world. Alexandria was also a major center of shipping because of its overland proximity to the Red Sea, but with the building of the Suez Canal, completed in 1869, the city's importance as a transportation hub was diminished. The historic library has been replaced with the Bibliotheca Alexandrina, completed in 2002 at a cost of $220 million, but the once-beautiful harbor itself has remained underused and somewhat in decay.

The Master Plan by Skidmore, Owings and Merrill (Fig. **12-52**) is intended to bring new life to the Eastern Harbor and to help re-establish the city as a leading cultural center. New museums, cultural facilities, and hotels are intended to serve as magnets for the tourism industry. The design connects the harbor to various city districts via new rail lines and green pedestrian walkways, while sidewalks and tunnels lead to underwater archeological sites. In the plan, beaches are expanded and passenger boat terminals will be constructed. One of the design's most striking elements—a new breakwater—will improve the quality of the water in the city. What time and history have torn away, urban design can perhaps create anew.

ART TOUR WASHINGTON, D.C.

ON JULY 14, 1789, in what became the defining symbolic moment of the French Revolution, the Bastille prison was stormed by revolutionaries who freed a grand total of seven prisoners. Four years later, with the founding of a new Republic, the doors of the Louvre Museum (containing about 200 works that had belonged to the king) opened to the public.

The point to this story lies in its contrast with the next: In 1936, Andrew Mellon (an American statesman and financier) gave his art collection to the United States of America and built the National Gallery of Art in Washington, D.C., to house it. In subsequent years, other collectors followed suit until the "nation's collection" outgrew its space. Unlike many of the world's great art museums, such as the Louvre, the museums you will see in Washington, D.C., did not begin as private royal collections made accessible to the public only after revolution and democratization. The core of Washington's holdings came from entrepreneurs who willingly, even affectionately, gave their art to their fellow citizens. Much of what you will see in Washington, D.C., is yours by virtue of your U.S. citizenship. And seeing just about all of it costs you nothing.

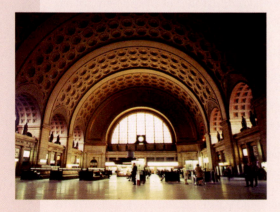

UNION STATION.

If you're coming to Washington by train, come hungry. You will arrive, most likely, at Union Station—a fine example of the Beaux Arts architectural style. From the three main archways that define the entry (based on the Arch of Constantine in Rome!) to the magnificent gilded barrel-vaulted ceiling, Union Station is not simply a transit center to move through—linger and look. It opened in 1907, and for more than 50 years this station was the largest in the world. After careful and costly restoration in 1988, this is now the second most visited site in Washington, D.C. Union Station is home to one of the most fantastic food courts you will ever come upon, with selections to entice every palate. Take a spin around the stalls before you commit to that Maryland crab-cake sandwich.

Union Station is a well-situated starting point for your art tour of the capital. From there, a short stroll along Delaware or Louisiana Avenue will bring you to the U.S. Capitol and the Mall, the site of many museums and memorials. Here you will experience the feeling of the nation's capital—its Classical architecture (inspired, as was the new democratic government, by Greek and Roman ideals), expanses of tree-lined grassy lawn, reflecting pools, and marble and granite monuments. The Capitol Building (see Fig. 3-9) is at the "top"—or eastern end—of the Mall and has much to offer to the art seeker. The dome, designed by Thomas U. Walter, is one of the largest in the world. The rotunda (the large, circular space in the interior beneath the dome) contains many paintings and sculptures and is capped by Constantino Brumidi's mural depicting the Apotheosis of Washington (bring your binoculars and your sense of humor).

Outside the Capitol, the Mall is arrayed before the visitor, offering a perspective toward the Washington Monument on the west end and all that lies between. The Mall was designed by the French architect Pierre L'Enfant, who imported many of his

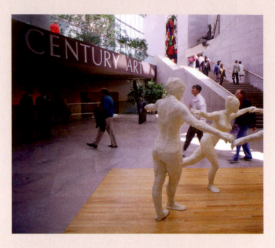

ENTRANCE LOBBY OF THE NATIONAL GALLERY OF ART, WASHINGTON, D.C., WITH SCULPTURE OF CHILDREN HOLDING HANDS.

elements of city planning (grand boulevards, elegant residences, well-situated monuments) from Paris. The first museum on your tour is the National Gallery of Art. The collection is divided between two buildings—East and West. The West (Neoclassical) Building is the earlier museum—the one financed by Andrew Mellon and designed by John Russell Pope. Here the visitor will find Western art spanning the thirteenth through the nineteenth centuries, featuring stellar examples of works by such artists as Giotto, Botticelli, Leonardo da Vinci, Raphael (*The Alba Madonna*), Rembrandt, Rubens (*Daniel in the Lion's Den*), El Greco, Monet (*Woman with a Parasol—Mme Monet and Her Son*), Cassatt, Cézanne, Toulouse-Lautrec (*Quadrille at the Moulin Rouge*), Homer (*Breezing Up*), and Whistler (*Symphony in White, No. 1: The White Girl*), among many, many others of fame and note. And that's just the west wing. The entire East Building, designed by I. M. Pei and one of the few Modernist works of architecture in the city, houses the country's collection of twentieth-century art. A dramatic, soaring atrium, featuring an enormous mobile by by Alexander Calder (see Fig. 2-70) and works by Henry Moore, Joan Miró, and Andrew Goldsworthy, is flanked by balconies and galleries in which one will find works from the permanent collection as well as traveling exhibitions. Both museums (connected underground) have wonderful restaurants and bookshops.

One of the highlights of the Mall is the Sculpture Garden of the National Gallery of Art, poised between the West Building and the National Museum of Natural History. Works of modern sculpture pepper the sections of lawn surrounding a refreshing fountain in summer and delightful skating rink in winter. Viewers can walk among and around pieces by Claes Oldenberg,

Roy Lichtenstein, Louise Bourgeois, Joan Miró, and others. And from these fun-filled, art-filled surroundings, one can cross over a broad expanse of lawn to another collection of outdoor sculpture belonging to the Hirshhorn Museum, a private-turned-public collection displayed in a cylindrical building affectionately referred to as "the doughnut." Rodin's *The Burghers of Calais* (see Fig. 19-36) finds itself in equally prestigious company in this collection.

The Mall contains a staggering number of museums, galleries, and monuments. The old Smithsonian Castle, the building that once housed works that are now found in other sites along the Mall (don't miss wandering through its splendid gardens); the spectacular National Air and Space Museum; and such small jewels as the Arthur M. Sackler Gallery of Asian Art, the National Museum of African Art, and the United States Holocaust Memorial Museum just beyond the Washington Monument merely scratch the surface of what one might discover on an art tour of the capital. And to these we must add artistic memorials such as the Vietnam Veterans Memorial (see "A Closer Look," page 211), the Korean War Vet-

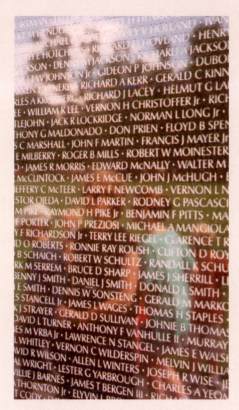

MAYA YING LIN. VIETNAM VETERANS MEMORIAL. NAMES AND REFLECTIONS ON THE WALL.

erans Memorial, and the Franklin D. Roosevelt Memorial, all of which have altered the very concept of meaningful memorials for Washington, D.C., and the country.

For many students in the United States, "the family trip to Washington" was viewed as essential to child rearing. For others, "the school trip to Washington" was the first independent trip away from home—traveling on a rowdy bus with one's peers to take in the sights and watch history come alive. Memories of these experiences traverse generations. We have always understood the importance of symbols to American history. Our own art tours of the nation's capital enable us to understand the importance of art to American people.

 TO CONTINUE YOUR TOUR and learn more about Washington, D.C., go to CourseMate.

SMITHSONIAN CASTLE.

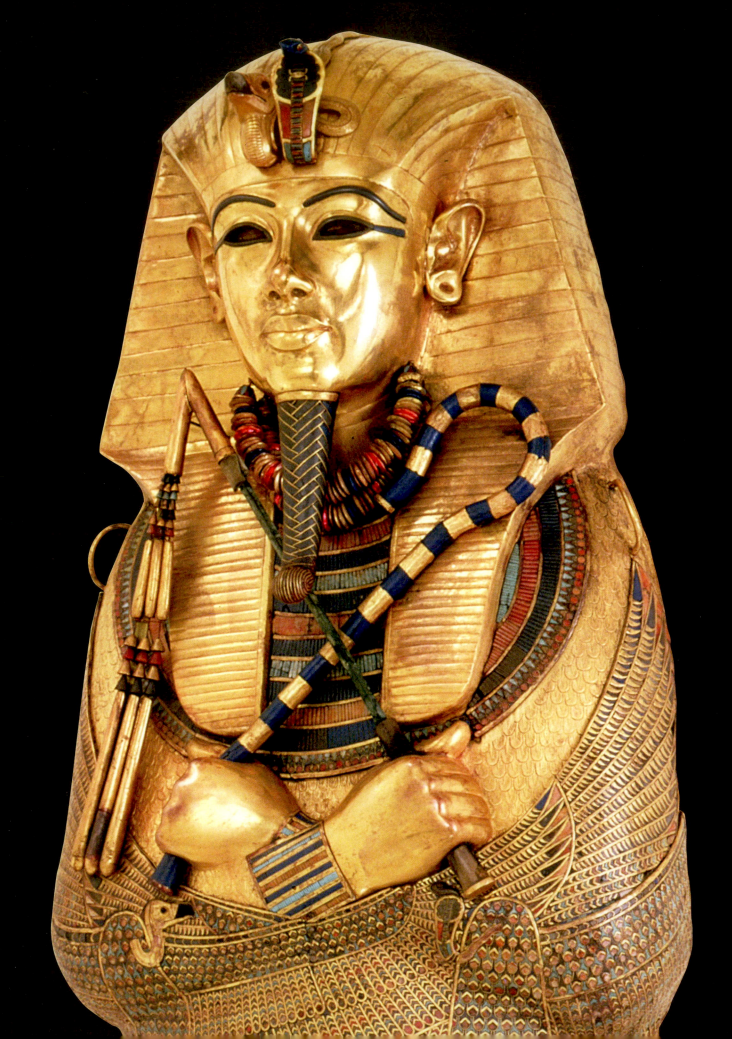

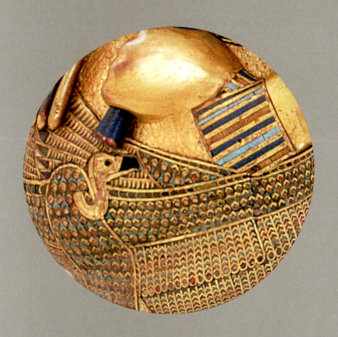

THE ART OF THE ANCIENTS

13

The term *Stone Age* often conjures an image of men and women dressed in skins, huddling before a fire in a cave, while the world around them—the elements and the animals—threatens their survival. We do not generally envision prehistoric humankind as intelligent and reflective; as having needs beyond food, shelter, and reproduction; as performing religious rituals; or as creating art objects. Yet these aspects of life were perhaps as essential to their survival as warmth, nourishment, and progeny.

As the Stone Age progressed from the Paleolithic to the Neolithic periods, humans began to lead more stable lives. They settled in villages and shifted from hunting wild animals and gathering food to herding domesticated animals and farming. They also fashioned tools of stone and bone and created pottery and woven textiles. Most important for our purposes, they became image makers, capturing forms and figures on cave walls with the use of primitive artistic implements.

The innermost coffin of the king, from the Tomb of Tutankhamen (c.1370–1352 BCE). Gold inlaid with semi-precious stones. Egyptian Museum, Cairo, Egypt.

Archeological exploration of Stone Age sites in France and Spain reveals the existence of shelters, tools, and an impressive array of sculptures and paintings in which humans and animals are represented. The sheer quantity of these art objects, although they are not works of art by the usual definition, would suggest a principal role for images and symbols in the struggle for human survival. As with much ancient art, we cannot know for certain what the reasons were for creating these works. But evidence suggests that Stone Age people forged links between religion and life, life and art, and art and religion. They faced intimidating and unknown forces in their confrontation with nature. Perhaps their "art" was an attempt to record and to control.

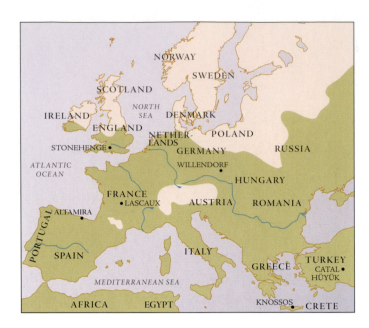

MAP 13-1 Prehistoric Europe.

PREHISTORIC ART

Prehistoric art is divided into three phases that correspond to the periods of Stone Age culture: **Paleolithic** (the late years of the Old Stone Age), **Mesolithic** (Middle Stone Age), and **Neolithic** (New Stone Age). These periods span roughly the years 14,000 to 2000 BCE.

Works of art from the Stone Age include cave paintings, reliefs, and sculpture of stone, ivory, and bone. The subjects consist mainly of animals, although some abstract human figures have been found. There is no surviving architecture as such. Many Stone Age dwellings consisted of caves and rock shelters. Some impressive monuments such as Stonehenge exist, but their functions remain a mystery.

Paleolithic Art

Paleolithic art is the art of the last Ice Age, during which time glaciers covered large areas of northern Europe and North America. As the climate got colder, people retreated into the protective warmth of caves, and it is here that we find their first attempts at artistic creation.

The great cave paintings of the Stone Age were discovered by accident in northern Spain and southwestern France. At Lascaux, France (Map **13-1**), two boys whose dog chased a ball into a hole followed the animal and discovered beautiful paintings of bison, horses, and cattle that are estimated to be more than 15,000 years old. At first, because of the crispness and realistic detail of the paintings, they were thought to be forgeries. But in time, geological methods proved their authenticity.

One of the most splendid examples of Stone Age painting, the so-called Hall of Bulls (Fig. **13-1**), is found in a cave at Lascaux. Here, superimposed upon one another, are realistic images of horses, bulls, and reindeer that appear to be stampeding in all directions. With one glance, we can understand

the early skepticism concerning their authenticity. So fresh, lively, and purely sketched are the forms that they seem to have been rendered yesterday.

In their attempt at **naturalism**, the artists captured the images of the beasts by first confidently outlining the contours of their bodies. They then filled in these dark outlines with details and colored them with shades of ocher and red. The artists seem to have used a variety of techniques ranging from drawing with chunks of raw pigment to applying pigment with fingers and sticks. They also seem to have used an early "spray painting" technique in which dried, ground pigments were blown through a hollowed-out bone or reed. Although the tools were primitive, the techniques and results were not. They used **foreshortening** and contrasts of light and shadow to create the illusion of three-dimensional forms. They strove to achieve a most convincing likeness of the animal.

Why did prehistoric people sketch these forms? Did they create these murals out of a desire to delight the eye, or did they have other reasons? We cannot know for certain. However, it is unlikely that the paintings were merely ornamental, because they were confined to the deepest recesses of the cave, far from the areas that were inhabited, and were not easily reached. Also, new figures were painted over earlier ones with no apparent regard for composition. It is believed that successive artists added to the drawings, respecting the sacredness of the figures that already existed. It is further believed that the paintings covered the walls and ceilings of a kind of inner sanctuary where religious rituals concerning

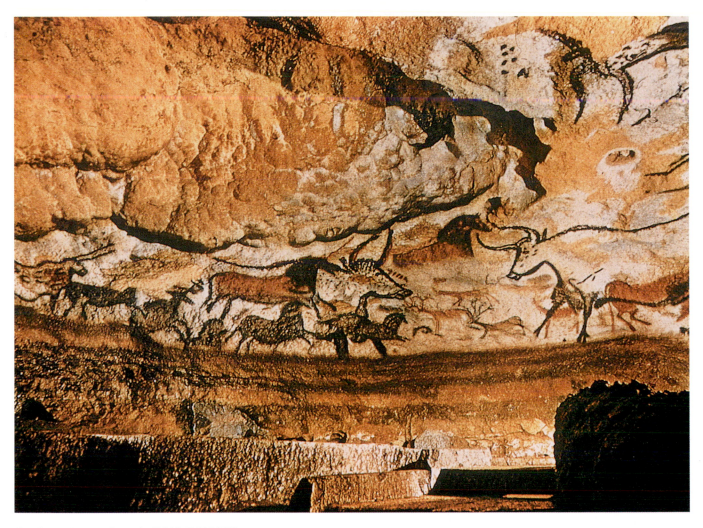

13-1 Cave at Lascaux, France (c. 15,000-13,000 BCE).

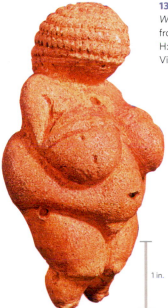

13-2 Nude Woman (*Venus of Willendorf*) (c. 28,000-25,000 BCE), from Willendorf, Austria. Limestone. H: 4⅜". Naturhistorisches Museum, Vienna, Austria.

the capture of prey were performed. Some have suggested that by "capturing" these animals in art, Stone Age hunters believed that they would be guaranteed success in capturing them in life. This theory, and others, is unproven.

Prehistoric artists also created sculptures, called **Venuses** by the archeologists who first found them. The most famous is the Venus of Willendorf (Fig. **13-2**), named after the site at which she was unearthed. The tiny figurine is carved of stone and is just over four inches high. As with all sculptures of this type, the female form is highly abstracted, and the emphasis is placed on the anatomical parts associated with fertility: the oversized breasts, round abdomen, and enlarged hips. Other parts of the body, like the thin arms resting on the breasts, are subordinated to those related to reproduction. Does this suggest a concern for survival of the species? Or was this figure of a fertile woman created and carried around

1 in.

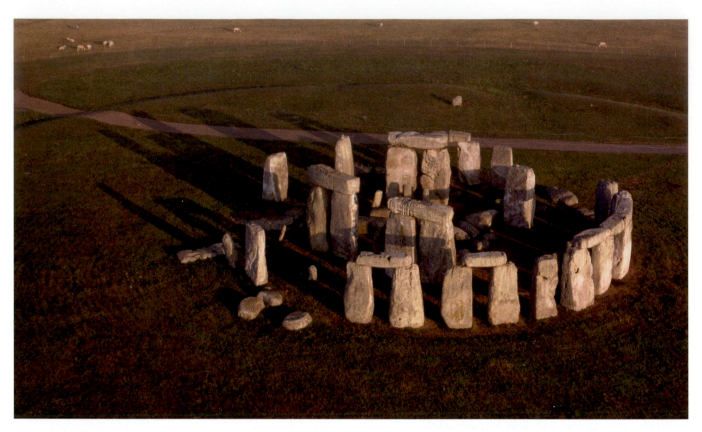

13-3 Stonehenge, Salisbury Plain (c. 1800–1400 BCE). Diameter of circle: 97'. Height of stones above ground: approx. 24'. Wiltshire, England.

as a talisman for fertility of the earth itself—abundance in the food supply? In either or any other case, people created their images, and perhaps their religion, as a way of coping with these concerns.

Neolithic Art

During the New Stone Age, life became more stable and predictable. People domesticated plants and animals, and food production took the place of food gathering. Toward the end of the Neolithic period in some areas, crops such as maize, squash, and beans were cultivated, metal implements were fashioned, and writing appeared. About 4000 BCE, significant architectural monuments were erected.

The most famous of these monuments is Stonehenge (Fig. **13-3**) in southern England. It consists of two concentric rings of stones surrounding others placed in a horseshoe shape. Some of these **megaliths** (from the Greek, meaning "large stones") weigh several tons. The purpose of Stonehenge remains a mystery. At one time it was believed to have been a druid temple, or the work of Merlin, King Arthur's magician. Lately, some astronomers have suggested that the monument served as a complex calendar that charted the movements of the sun and moon, as well as eclipses. What-

ever the meaning or function, the fact that it was undertaken at all is perhaps its most fascinating aspect.

The Neolithic period probably began about 8000 BCE and spread throughout the world's major river valleys between 6000 and 2000 BCE—the Nile in Egypt, the Tigris and Euphrates in Mesopotamia, the Indus in India, and the Yellow in China. In the next section, we examine the birth of the great Mesopotamian civilizations.

ART OF THE ANCIENT NEAR EAST

Historic (as opposed to prehistoric) societies are marked by a written language, advanced social organization, and developments in the areas of government, science, and art. They are also often linked with the development of agriculture. Historic civilizations began toward the end of the Neolithic period. In this section, we will discuss the art of the Mesopotamian civilizations of Sumer, Akkad, Babylonia, Assyria, and Persia. We will begin with Sumer, which flourished in the river valley of the Tigris and Euphrates about 3000 BCE.

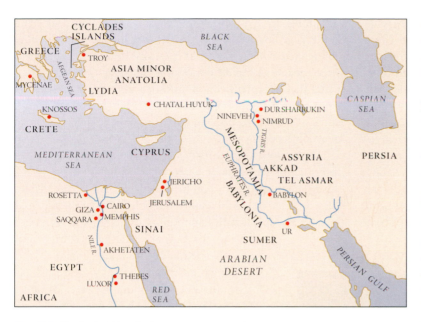

MAP 13-2 The Ancient Near East.

of later years. The ziggurat was the focal point of the Sumerian city, towering high above the fields and dwellings. Typically, the ziggurat was a multilevel structure consisting of a core of sunbaked mud bricks faced with fired brick, sometimes of bright colors. Access to the **temple**, on the uppermost level of the ziggurat, was gained by stairs or a series of ramps leading from one level to the next, or in some instances, by a spiral ramp that rose continuously from ground to summit.

The White Temple at Uruk (Fig. **13-4A** and Fig. **13-4B**) and ziggurat, so called because of its white-washed walls, are among the earliest and best preserved in the region. The ziggurat, the corners of which are oriented toward the compass points, is some 40 feet high but pales in comparison to the scale of later ziggurats. The ziggurat known to the Hebrews as the Tower of Babel, a symbol of mortal pride, was some 270 feet high.

The Sumerian gods were primarily deifications of nature. Anu was the god of the sky, Nannu the god of the moon, and Abu the god of vegetation. Votive sculptures found beneath

Sumer

The Tigris and Euphrates rivers flow through what is now Syria and Iraq, join in their southernmost section, and empty into the Persian Gulf (Map **13-2**). The major civilizations of ancient Mesopotamia lay along one or the other of these rivers, and the first to rise to prominence was Sumer.

Sumer was located in the Euphrates River Valley in southern Mesopotamia. The origin of its people is unknown, although they may have come from Iran or India. The earliest Sumerian villages date back to prehistoric times. By about 3000 BCE, however, there was a thriving agricultural civilization in Sumer. The Sumerians constructed sophisticated irrigation systems, controlled river flooding, and worked with metals such as copper, silver, and gold. They had a government based on independently ruled city-states, and they developed a system of writing called **cuneiform**, from the Latin *cuneus*, meaning "wedge"; the characters in cuneiform writing are wedge shaped.

Excavations at major Sumerian cities have revealed sculpture, craft art, and monumental architecture that seems to have been created for worship. Thus, the Sumerian people may have been among the first to establish a formal religion.

One of the most impressive testimonies to the Sumerians' religion-based society is the **ziggurat**, a monumental platform for a temple also seen in the Babylonian and Assyrian civilizations

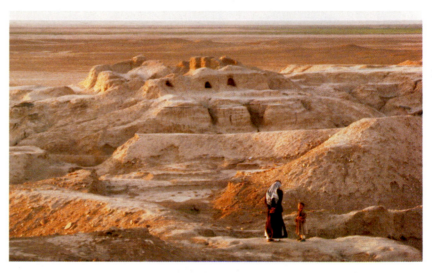

13-4A White Temple and ziggurat (c. 3200-3000 BCE). Uruk (modern Warka), Iraq.

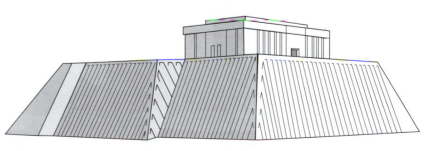

13-4B Reconstruction of White Temple and ziggurat.

the floor of a temple to Abu in Tell Asmar (Fig. **13-5**) reinforce the essential role of religion in Sumerian society. These works functioned as stand-ins, as it were, for donor-worshippers who, in their absence, wished to continue to offer prayers to a specific deity. They range in height from less than 12" to more than 30" and are carved from gypsum with alert inlaid eyes of shell and black limestone. The figures are cylindrical, and all stand erect with hands clasped at their chests around now-missing flasks. Distinctions are made between males and females. The men have long, stylized beards and hair and wear knee-length skirts decorated with incised lines describing fringe at the hem. The women wear dresses with one shoulder bared and the other draped with a shawl. These

sculptures are gypsum, a soft mineral found in rock. The Sumerians, however, worked primarily in clay because of its abundance. They were expert ceramists and, as we have seen, were capable of building monumental structures with brick while their Egyptian contemporaries were using stone. It is believed that the Sumerians traded crops for metal, wood, and stone and used these materials to enlarge their repertory of art objects.

The Sumerian repertory of subjects included fantastic creatures such as music-making animals, bearded bulls, and composite man-beasts with bull heads or scorpion bodies. These were depicted in lavishly decorated objects of hammered gold inlaid with **lapis lazuli**. Found among the remains of Sumerian royal tombs, they are believed by some scholars to have been linked to funerary rituals.

For a long time, the Sumerians were the principal force in Mesopotamia, but they were not alone. Semitic peoples to the north became increasingly strong, and eventually they established an empire that ruled all of Mesopotamia and assimilated the Sumerian culture.

Akkad

Akkad, located north of Sumer, centered around the valley of the Tigris River. Its government, too, was based on independent city-states, which, along with those of Sumer, eventually came under the influence of the Akkadian ruler Sargon. Under Sargon and his successors, the civilization of Akkad flourished.

Akkadian art exhibits distinct differences from that of Sumer. It commemorates rulers and warriors instead of offering homage to the gods. It is an art of violence instead of prayer. Also, although artistic conventions are present, they are coupled with a naturalism that was absent from Sumerian art.

Of the little extant Akkadian art, the Victory Stele of Naram Sin (Fig. **13-6**) shines as one of the most significant works. This relief sculpture commemorates the military exploits of Sargon's grandson and successor, Naram Sin. The king, represented somewhat larger in scale than the other figures, ascends a mountain, trampling his enemies underfoot. He is accompanied by a group of marching soldiers, spears erect, whose positions contrast strongly with those of the fallen enemy. One wrestles to pull a spear out of his neck, another pleads for mercy, and another falls headfirst off the mountain. The chaos on the right side of the composition is opposed by the rigid advancement on the left. All takes place under the watchful celestial bodies of Ishtar and Shamash, the gods of fertility and justice.

1 ft.

13-5 Two gypsum statuettes with folded hands (c. 2700 BCE), from Tell Asmar, Iraq. Gypsum. Male figure: 28⅜". Female figure: 23¼". Iraq Museum, Baghdad, Iraq.

has led to the theory that it was not human violence that put an end to Akkadian supremacy but rather a severe and unrelenting drought that gripped the region for 300 years. With the end of the drought, the Sumerians regained power for a while with a Neo-Sumerian state ruled by the kings of Ur, but they, too, were eventually overtaken by fierce warring tribes. Mesopotamia remained in a state of chaos until the rise of Babylon under the great lawmaker and ruler, Hammurabi.

Babylonia

During the eighteenth century BCE, the Babylonian Empire, under Hammurabi, rose to power and dominated Mesopotamia. Hammurabi's major contribution to civilization was the codification of Mesopotamian laws. Laws had become cloudy and conflicting after the division of Mesopotamia into independent cities.

This code of law was inscribed on the Stele of Hammurabi (Fig. **13-7**), a relief sculpture of **basalt** over seven feet high. The lower portion of the stele is inscribed with the code itself, written in the Akkadian language with cuneiform characters. Above the code is a relief depicting Hammurabi and the sun

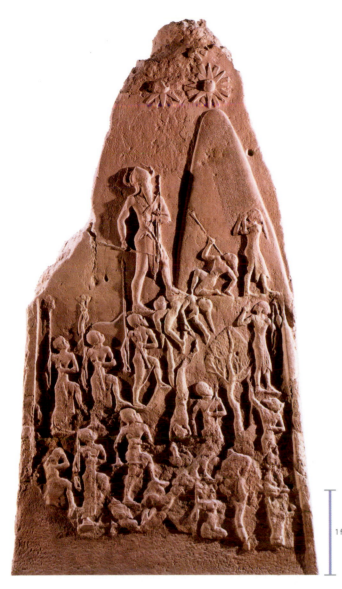

13-6 Victory Stele of Naram Sin (c. 2300–2200 BCE). Stone. H: 6'6". Louvre, Paris, France.

The king and his men are represented in a conceptual manner. That is, the artist rendered the human body in all of its parts as they are known to be, not as they appear at any given moment to the human eye. This method resulted in figures that are a combination of frontal and profile views. Naturalism was reserved for the enemy, whose figures fall in a variety of contorted positions. It may be that the convention of conceptual representation was maintained as a sign of respect. On the other hand, the conceptual manner complements the upright positions of the victorious, whereas the naturalism echoes the disintegration of the enemy camp.

The Akkadian Empire eventually declined, for reasons that are not clear. Historians have traditionally attributed its collapse to invading tribes. However, recent archeological research

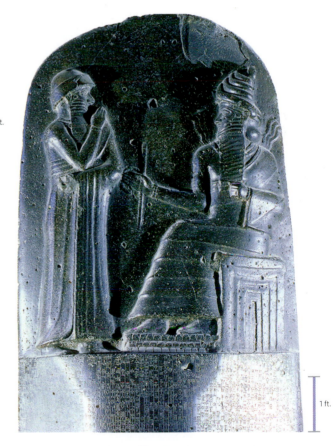

13-7 Stele (upper portion) inscribed with the Law Code of Hammurabi (c. 1760 BCE), from Susa. Diorite. H: 7'4". Louvre, Paris, France.

god Shamash. Hammurabi gestures in respect and Shamash reciprocates by handing over to him a rod and ring, symbols of authority. The observer is led to believe, through this interaction, that Hammurabi's authority is god-given and thus not to be challenged. The sculptor of the stele engaged in some conventions for representation, combining frontal and profile views as we have already seen in the Stele of Naram Sin. However, in the Hammurabi stele, there are some new attempts at naturalism. The artist has turned the figure of Shamash toward the viewer a bit and has rendered the lines in his beard as diagonals (rather than strict horizontals, as in the Sumerian votive figures), suggesting an experiment in foreshortening.

After the death of Hammurabi, Mesopotamia was torn apart by invasions. It eventually came under the influence of the Assyrians, a warring people to the north who had had their eyes on the region for hundreds of years.

Assyria

The ancient empire of Assyria developed along the upper Tigris River. For centuries, the Assyrians fought with their neighbors, earning a deserved reputation as a fierce, bloodthirsty people. They eventually overtook the Babylonians, and from about 900 to 600 BCE, they controlled all of Mesopotamia.

The Assyrians were influenced by Babylonian art, culture, and religion. But unlike Babylonia, Assyria was an empire built on military conquests and campaigns. Their obsession with war eventually depleted their resources, overtook their economy, and undermined their social structure. The Assyrian rulers ignored agricultural development, forcing the society to import most of its food. Their preoccupation with violence and power rather than stability and production eventually led to their demise.

Assyrian architecture consists of sprawling palaces and fortified citadels, and its extensive sculptural decoration—rendered in relief— reflects the power and might of the kings. The two most common subjects of these relief sculptures are the king's military exploits and brutal hunts that were staged and tightly controlled to safely showcase the strength of the ruler. One of the most touching and sensitive works of ancient art records a scene from one of King Ashurbanipal's hunting expeditions. The Dying Lioness (Fig. **13-8**) is a limestone relief that depicts carnage for the

sake of royal sport. A lioness, bleeding profusely from arrow wounds, seems to emit a pathetic, helpless roar as she drags her hindquarters, paralyzed in the assault. Her musculature is clearly defined, and the incised details are painfully realistic. The naturalism in this relief differs significantly from the way in which kings and members of their entourage were depicted. Artists adhered to rigid and stylized conventions for human forms.

Assyria waged almost constant warfare to protect its sovereignty in the area. Ashurbanipal's successors eventually lost control of the empire to Neo-Babylonian kings, the most famous of whom was the biblical King Nebuchadnezzar. They remained in power until the conquest of the Persians.

Persia

As Persia, led by King Cyrus, marched toward empire, Babylon was but one on a growing list of casualties. By the sixth century BCE, the Persians had conquered Egypt and, less than a century later, were poised to subsume Greece into their far-reaching realm. The Persian Empire stretched

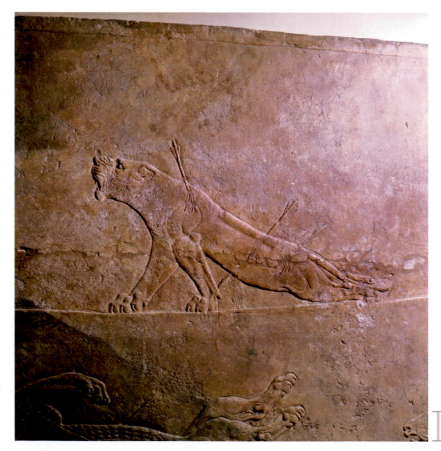

13-8 The Dying Lioness (660 BCE), from Nineveh. Limestone. H: 13¾". British Museum, London, England.

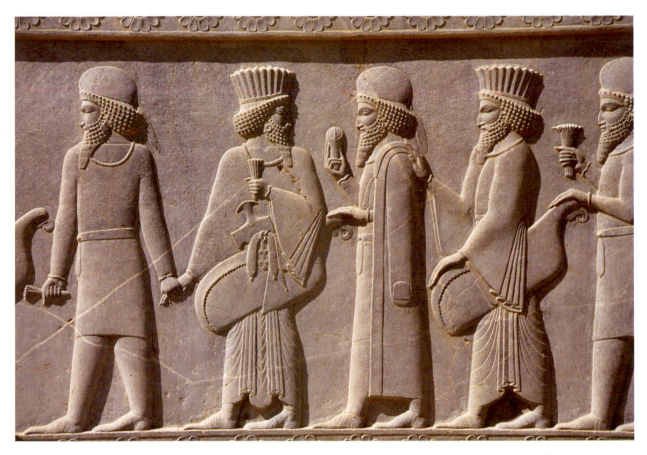

13-9 Processional frieze (detail) from the royal audience hall (c. 521–465 BCE). Persepolis, Iran.

from southern Asia to northeastern Europe and would have included southeastern Europe had the Greeks not been victorious over the Persians in a decisive battle at Salamis in 480 BCE. Cyrus's successors grew the empire until the defeat of Darius II by Alexander the Great in 330 BCE.

The citadel at Persepolis, the capital of the ancient Persian Empire, was a sprawling complex of palatial dwellings, government buildings, grand stairways, and columned halls whose architectural surfaces were richly adorned with relief sculpture. A processional frieze from the royal audience hall (Fig. **13-9**) illustrates a technique that is notably different from Assyrian predecessors such as The Dying Lioness. The Persian relief is more deeply carved; that is, the figures stand out more against the background. They are fleshier, more well-rounded. The artist has paid particular attention to detail, distinguishing the costumes of the participants, who include Persian nobles and guards and visiting dignitaries from nations under Persian rule. Although the procession is regimented, some figures twist and turn in space, alleviating the visual monotony. Persian

art is also characterized by fanciful animal forms and stylized floral decoration.

In 525 BCE, Persia conquered the kingdom of Egypt, but civilization in Egypt had begun some 3,000 years earlier.

EGYPTIAN ART

The lush land that lay between the Tigris and Euphrates rivers, providing sustenance for the Mesopotamian civilizations, is called the **Fertile Crescent**. Its counterpart in Egypt, called the **Fertile Ribbon**, hugs the banks of the Nile River, which flows north from Africa and empties into the Mediterranean Sea (Map 13-2). Like the rivers of the Fertile Crescent, the Nile was an indispensable part of Egyptian life. Without it, Egyptian life would not have existed. For this reason, it also had spiritual significance; the Nile was perceived as a god.

Like Sumerian art, Egyptian art was religious. There are three aspects of Egyptian art and life that stand as unique:

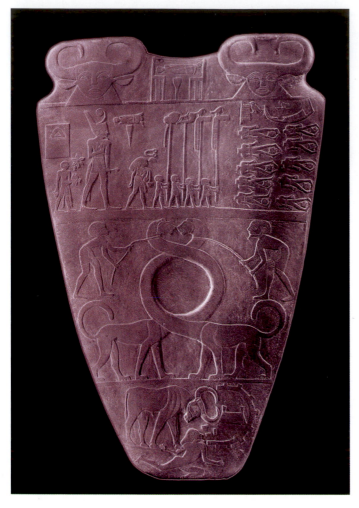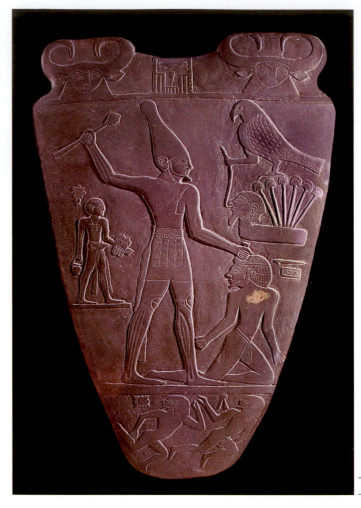

1 in.

13-10 Narmer Palette (c. 3200 BCE). Front (left) and back (right) views. Slate. H: 25". Egyptian Museum, Cairo, Egypt.

their link to religion, their link to death, and their ongoing use of strict conventionalism in the arts that affords a sense of permanence.

The art and culture of Egypt are divided into three periods: The Old Kingdom dates from 2680 to 2258 BCE, the Middle Kingdom from 2000 to 1786 BCE, and the New Kingdom from 1570 to 1342 BCE. Art styles proceed from the Old to the New Kingdom with very few variations.

A break in this pattern occurred between 1372 and 1350 BCE, during the Amarna Revolution under the unorthodox leadership of the pharaoh Akhenaton. After his death, Egypt retreated to the old order.

Old Kingdom

Egyptian religion was bound closely to the afterlife. Happiness in the afterlife was believed to be ensured through the continuation of certain aspects of earthly life. Thus, tombs were decorated with everyday objects and scenes depicting

common earthly activities. Sculptures of the deceased were placed in the tombs, along with likenesses of the people who surrounded them in life.

In the years prior to the dawn of the Old Kingdom, art consisted of funerary offerings of one type or another, including small, sculpted figures, ivory carvings, pottery, and slate palettes used to mix eye makeup. Toward the end of this period, called the Predynastic period, Egyptian stonecutters began to create the large limestone works for which Egypt became famous.

SCULPTURE Old Kingdom artists initiated a manner of representation that lasted thousands of years, a conceptual approach to the rendering of the human figure that we also encountered in Mesopotamian relief sculpture. In Egyptian reliefs, the head, pelvis, and legs are presented in profile, whereas the upper torso and eye are shown from a frontal view. The figures tend to be flat, and they are situated in a shallow space with no use of foreshortening. No attempt was made to give the illusion of forms that exist in three-dimensional space. Wall decoration was carved in very low relief with a great deal of **incised** detail. Sculpture in the round closely adhered to the block form. Color was applied at times but was not used widely because of the relative impermanence of the material. These basic characteristics were duplicated, with few exceptions, by artists during all periods of Egyptian art. There are instances in which a certain naturalism was sought, but the artist rarely strayed from the inherited stylistic conventions.

Art historian Erwin Panofsky stated that this Egyptian method of working clearly reflected their artistic intention, "directed not toward the variable, but toward the constant, not toward the symbolization of the vital present, but toward the realization of a timeless eternity."

One of the most important sculptures from the Old Kingdom period, the Narmer Palette (Fig. **13-10**), illustrates these conventions. The Narmer Palette is an example of a type of **cosmetic palette** found in Egypt (Egyptians applied dark colors around their eyes to deflect the sun's glare as football players do today), but its symbolism supersedes its function. The Narmer Palette commemorates the unification of Upper Egypt and Lower Egypt, an event that Egyptians marked as the beginning of their civilization.

The back of the palette depicts King Narmer in the crown of Upper Egypt (a bowling pin shape) slaying an enemy. Beneath his feet, on the lowest part of the palette, lie two more dead enemy warriors. To the right, a falcon—the god Horus—is perched on a cluster of papyrus stalks that sprout from an object with a man's head. The papyrus is a symbol for Lower Egypt, and Horus's placement would appear to sanction Narmer's takeover of that territory. The top of the palette is sculpted on both sides with two bull-shaped heads with human features. They represent the goddess Hathor, who traditionally symbolized love and joy.

The king is rendered in the typical conventional manner. He is larger than the people surrounding him, symbolizing his royal status. His head, hips, and legs are carved in low relief and in profile, and his eye and upper torso are shown in full frontal view. The musculature is defined with incised lines that appear more as stylized patterns than realistic details. The artist has chosen convention over naturalism and, in the process, created a timeless image, at least as far as Egyptian history is concerned.

The front of the palette is divided into horizontal segments, or **registers**, that are crowded with figures. A hollowed-out well in the center of the palette held eye paint, and it is emphasized by the long, entwined necks of lion-like figures tamed by two men with leashes. The top register depicts King Narmer once again, reviewing the captured and deceased enemy. He is now shown wearing the crown of Lower Egypt and holding instruments that symbolize his power. To his right are stacks of decapitated bodies. This is not the first time that we have seen such a monument to a royal conquest, complete with gory details. We witnessed it in the Akkadian Victory Stele of Naram Sin (Fig. 13-6). In both works, the kings are shown in commanding positions, larger than the surrounding figures, but in the Narmer Palette, the king is also depicted as a god. This concept of the ruler of Egypt, along with the strict conventions of his representation, would last some 3,000 years.

Egyptian tomb sculpture included large-scale figures carved in the round, usually from very hard materials that were likely to endure. Permanence was essential, as sculptures like Khafre (Fig. **13-11**) were created to house the *ka*, or soul, if the mummified remains of the deceased disintegrated. *Ka* sculptures were not portraits. The artists used stylistic conventions, including idealism. Regardless of the age of the deceased, the *ka* figure emblemized the individual in the prime of life. The statue of Khafre,

13-11 Statue of Khafre (c. 2500 BCE), from Gizeh. Diorite. H: 66". Egyptian Museum, Cairo, Egypt.

an Old Kingdom pharaoh, is typical. Carved in diorite, a gray green rock, it shows the pharaoh seated on a throne ornamented with the lotus blossoms and papyrus that symbolize Upper and Lower Egypt. He sits rigidly, and his frontal gaze is reminiscent of the staring eyes of the Mesopotamian votive figures. Khafre is shown with the conventional attributes of the pharaoh: a finely pleated kilt, a linen headdress gracing the shoulders, and a long, thin beard (present on the carved faces of both male and female pharaohs), part of which has broken off.

The sun god **Horus**, represented again as a falcon, sits behind the pharaoh's head and spreads his wings protectively around it. The artist confined his figure to the block of stone from which it was carved instead of allowing it to stand freely in space. The legs and torso appear molded to the throne, and the arms and fists are attached to the body. The sense of the solidity of the uncarved block is maintained and, with that, a certain confidence that the sculpture would remain intact. Few, if any, pieces were likely to break off. Khafre was rendered according to a specific **canon of proportions** relating different anatomical parts to one another. The forms rely on predetermined rules and not on optical fact. Naturalism was intermittent in Egyptian art, and more evident in the Middle Kingdom and the Amarna period.

ARCHITECTURE The most spectacular remains of Old Kingdom Egypt, and the most famous, are the Great Pyramids at Gizeh (Fig. **13-12**). Constructed as tombs, they provided a resting place for the pharaoh, underscored his status as a deity, and lived after him as a monument to his accomplishments. They stand today as haunting images of a civilization long gone, isolated as coarse jewels in an arid wasteland.

The pyramids are massive. The largest has a base that is about 775 feet on a side and is 450 feet high. It is constructed of 2,300,000 limestone blocks that weigh about 2½ tons each. The stone for the pyramids was quarried from a nearby plateau and moved by workers to the site using wooden rollers and sledlike apparatuses. Stonecutters on the site carved the blocks more finely, after which they were stacked on top of one another in rows, using systems of ropes and pulleys. Artisans finished the surfaces of the pyramid with fine limestone, creating a flawless, smooth, and gleaming sheath.

13-12 An aerial view of the Gizeh, Kheops, and Khepren and Mykerinos Pyramids (c. 2570-2500 BCE). Gizeh, Egypt.

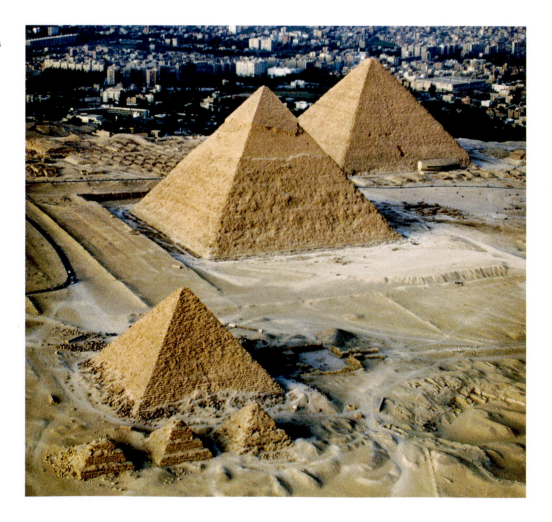

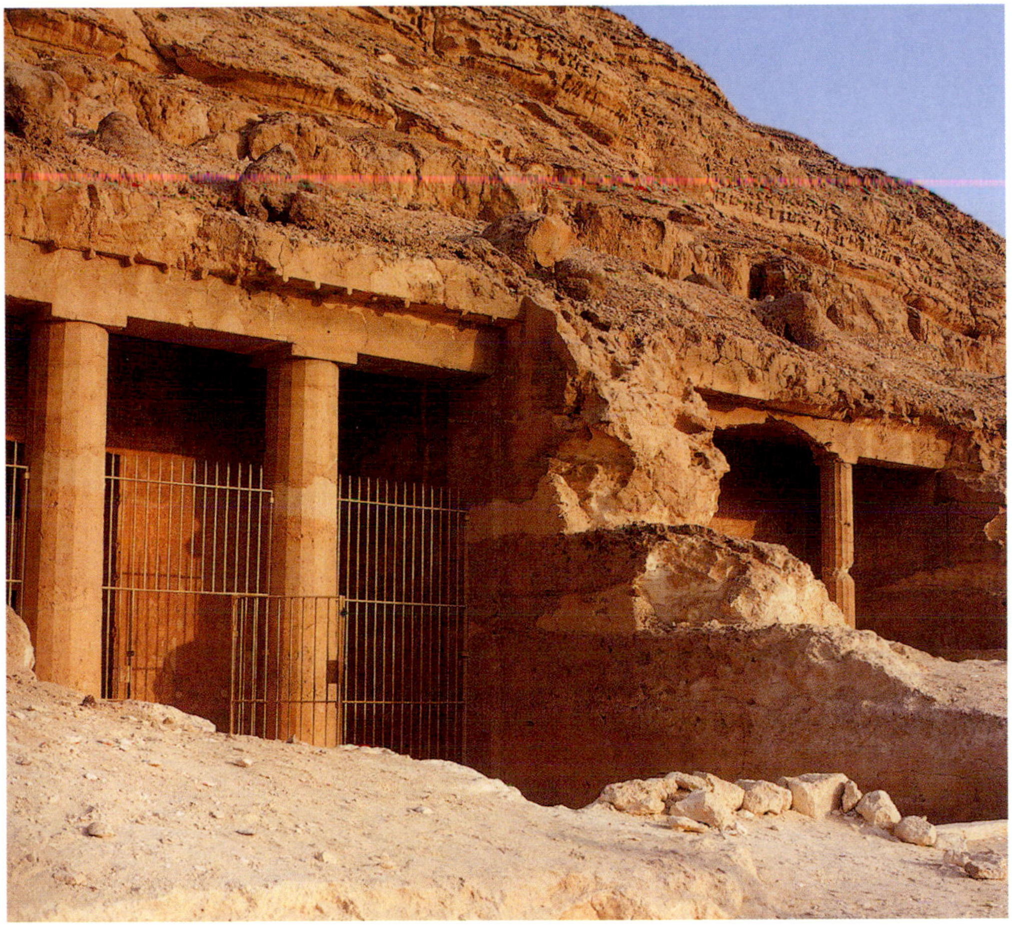

The interiors of the pyramids consist of a network of chambers, galleries, and air shafts. Ostentatious and conspicuous as the pyramids were, thieves wasted no time in plundering them. During the Middle Kingdom, Egyptians designed less easily penetrated dwelling places for their spirits.

Middle Kingdom

The Middle Kingdom witnessed a change in the political hierarchy of Egypt, as the power of the pharaohs was threatened by powerful landowners. During the early years of the Middle Kingdom, the development of art was stunted by internal strife. Egypt was finally brought back on track, reorganized, and reunited under King Mentuhotep, and art flourished once again.

Middle Kingdom art carried the Old Kingdom style forward, although there was some experimentation outside the mainstream of strict conventionalism. We find this experimentation in sensitive portrait sculptures and freely drawn fresco paintings.

A striking aspect of Middle Kingdom architecture was the rock-cut tombs (Fig. 13-13), which may have been designed to prevent robberies. They were carved out of the **living rock**, and their entranceways were marked by columned **porticoes** of post-and-lintel construction. These porticoes led to a columned entrance hall, followed by a chamber along the same axis. The walls of the hall and tomb chamber were richly decorated with relief sculpture and painting, much of which had a sense of liveliness not found in Old Kingdom art.

New Kingdom

The Middle Kingdom also collapsed, and Egypt fell under the rule of an Asiatic tribe called the Hyskos. They introduced Bronze Age weapons to Egypt, as well as the horse. Eventually, the Egyptians overthrew them, and the New Kingdom was launched. It proved to be one of the most vital periods in Egyptian history, marked by expansionism, increased wealth, and economic and political stability.

The art of the New Kingdom combined characteristics of the Old and Middle Kingdom periods. The monumental forms of the earliest centuries were coupled with the freedom of expression of the Middle Kingdom years. A certain vitality appeared in two-dimensional works such as painting and relief

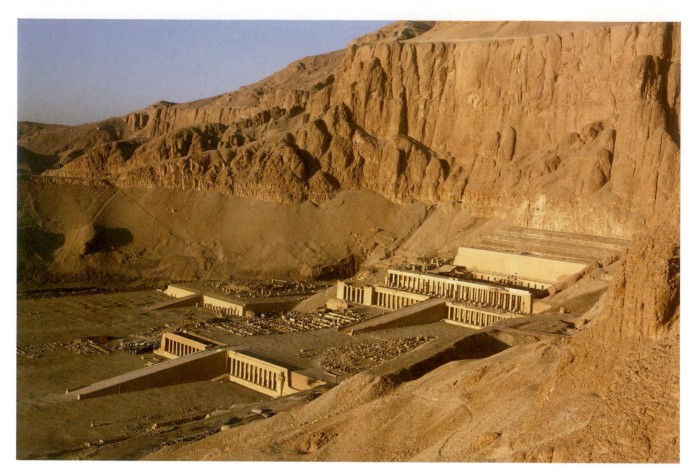

13-14 Mortuary Temple of Queen Hatshepsut (c. 1480 BCE). Thebes, Egypt.

sculpture, although sculpture in the round retained its concentration on solidity and permanence with few stylistic changes.

Egyptian society embraced a death cult, and some of its most significant monuments continued to be linked with death or worship of the dead. During the New Kingdom period, a new architectural form was created—the **mortuary temple**. Mortuary temples were carved out of the living rock, as were the rock-cut tombs of the Middle Kingdom, but their function was quite different. They did not house the mummified remains of the pharaohs, but rather served as their place for worship during life, and a place at which they could be worshipped after death.

One of the most impressive mortuary temples of the New Kingdom is that of a female pharaoh, Queen Hatshepsut (Fig. **13-14**). The temple backs into imposing cliffs and is divided into three terraces, which are approached by long ramps that rise from the floor of the valley to the top of pillared **colonnades**. Although the terraces are now as barren as the surrounding country, during Hatshepsut's time they were covered with exotic vegetation. The interior of the temple was just as lavishly decorated, with some 200 large sculptures as well as painted relief carvings.

As the civilization of Egypt became more advanced and powerful, there was a tendency to build and sculpt on a monumental scale. Statues and temples reached gigantic proportions. The delicacy and refinement of earlier Egyptian art fell by the wayside in favor of works that reflected the inflated Egyptian ego. Throughout the New Kingdom period, conventionalism was, for the most part, maintained. During the reign of Akhenaton, however, Egypt was offered a brief respite from stylistic rigidity.

The Amarna Revolution: The Reign of Akhenaton and Nefertiti

During the fourteenth century BCE, a king by the name of Amenhotep IV rose to power. His reign marked a revolution in both religion and the arts. Amenhotep IV, named for the god Amen, changed his name to Akhenaton in honor of the sun god, Aton, and he declared that Aton was the only god. In his monotheistic fury, Akhenaton spent his life tearing down monuments to the old gods and erecting new ones to Aton.

The art of Akhenaton's reign, or that of the Amarna period (so named because the pharaoh moved the capital of Egypt

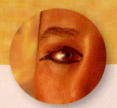
THE VALLEY OF THE KINGS, Luxor, Egypt; January 5, 2005. Nearly 3,300 years after his death, the leathery mummy of the legendary "boy king" was ever so delicately removed from its tomb and guided into a portable CT—computed tomography, or what we call "cat"—scanner. It was not the first time that modern technology was employed to feed the curiosity of scientists, archeologists, and museum officials over the mysteries surrounding the reign and death of Tut. More than three decades earlier, the mummy was X-rayed twice, in part to try to solve the mystery of the young pharaoh's death; Tutankhamen was crowned at age eight and died only 10 years later. These early X-rays revealed a hole at the base of Tut's cranium, leading to the suspicion that he was murdered. This time around, the focus—and the conclusions—changed. Dr. Zahi Hawass, secretary general of the Supreme Council of Antiquities in Cairo, said, "No one hit Tut on the back of the head." Scientists instead concluded that the damage noted in earlier X-rays was probably due to the rough removal of the golden burial mask by the tomb's discoverers. But they found something else: a puncture in Tut's skin over a severe break in the youth's left thigh. As it is known that this accident took place just days before his death, some experts on the scanning team conjectured that this break, and the puncture caused by it, may have led to a serious infection and Tut's consequent death. Otherwise, the young pharaoh was the picture of health—no signs of malnutrition or disease, with strong bones and teeth, and probably five and a half feet tall.

In all, scientists (including experts in anatomy, pathology, and radiology) spent two months analyzing more than 1,700 three-dimensional, high-resolution images taken with CT scans. Then artists and scholars took a turn. Three independent teams, one each from Egypt, France, and the United States, came up with their own versions of what Tut might very well have looked like in life: a bit of an elongated skull (normal, they say), large lips, a receding chin, and a pronounced overbite that seems to have run in the family (Fig. **13-15**). It was the first time—but certainly not the last—that CT scans would be used to reconstruct the faces of the Egyptian celebrity dead.

Although the price tag on this endeavor was most certainly steep, the Egyptian government stood to gain financially from the images. Their release was timed to coincide with the launch of the world-traveling exhibition "Tutankhamen and the Golden Age of the Pharaohs." Along with the scans and reconstruction images, the exhibit would feature King Tut's diamond crown and gold coffin, along with a total of almost 200 objects from his and various other noteworthy tombs. If history were any predictor of the insatiable thirst for things Egyptian, this, like the original exhibition of treasures from Tut's tomb, would attract millions of visitors. This time, however, it was hoped that the $10 million rental fee for each museum venue would bring in desperately needed funding for a museum being planned beside the pyramids in Gizeh. As in many parts of the world, antiquities are crumbling. "There are no free meals anymore," Hawass said. "We have a task. These monuments will be gone in 100 years if we don't raise the money to restore them." ●

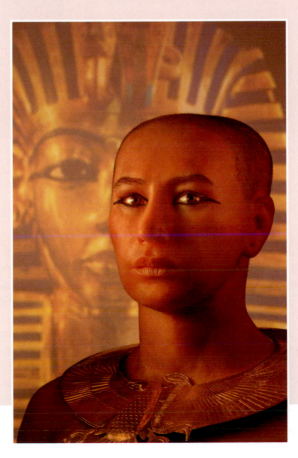

13-15 Reconstruction of face of King Tut.

to Tell el-Amarna), was as revolutionary as his approach to religion. The wedge-shaped stylizations that stood as a rigid canon for the representations of the human body were replaced by curving lines and full-bodied forms. The statue of Akhenaton (Fig. **13-16**) could not differ more from its precedents in the Old and Middle Kingdoms. The fluid contours of the body contrast strongly with those in earlier sculptures of pharaohs, as do the elongated jaw, thick lips, and thick-lidded eyes. These characteristics suggest that the artist was attempting to create a naturalistic likeness of the pharaoh, "warts and all," as the saying goes.

Aside from being at odds stylistically with other Egyptian sculptures, the very concept of the work is different. Throughout the previous centuries, adherence to a stylistic formality had been maintained, especially in the sculptures of revered pharaohs. If naturalism was present at all, it was reserved for lesser works depicting lesser figures. During the Amarna period, naturalism was used in monumental statues depicting members of the royal family as well.

One of the most beautiful works of art from this period is the bust of Akhenaton's wife, Queen Nefertiti (Fig. **13-17**). The classic profile reiterates the linear patterns found in the pharaoh's sculpture. An almost top-heavy crowned head extends gracefully on a long and sensuous neck. The realism of the portrait is enhanced by the paint that is applied to the limestone.

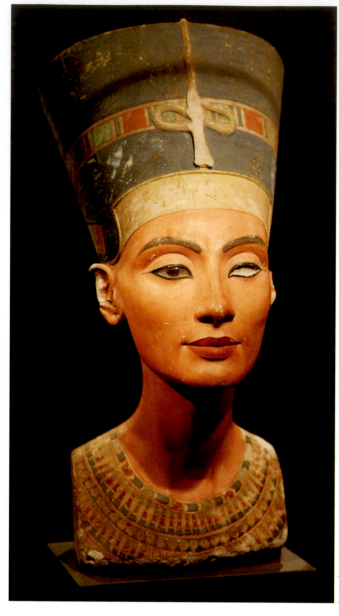

1 in.

13-17 Bust of Queen Nefertiti (c. 1344 BCE). Limestone. H: approx. 20". Ägyptisches Museum, Berlin, Germany.

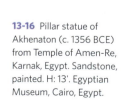

13-16 Pillar statue of Akhenaton (c. 1356 BCE) from Temple of Amen-Re, Karnak, Egypt. Sandstone, painted. H: 13'. Egyptian Museum, Cairo, Egypt.

The naturalism of the works of the Amarna period was short-lived. Subsequent pharaohs returned to the more rigid styles of the earlier dynasties. Just as Akhenaton destroyed the images and shrines of gods favored by earlier pharaohs, so did his successors destroy his temples to Aton. With Akhenaton's death came the death of amonotheism—for the time being. Some have suggested that Akhenaton's loyalty to a single god may have set a monotheistic example for other religions.

Akhenaton's immediate successor was Tutankhamen—the famed King Tut. Called "the boy king," Tut died at about age 18. His tomb was not discovered until 1922, when British archeologists led by Howard Carter unearthed a treasure trove of gold artworks, many inlaid with semiprecious stones. By far, the most spectacular find was the young pharaoh's coffin (Fig. **13-18**), made of solid gold and weighing almost 250 pounds. Within this, the last of three nesting coffins, lay the body of the king, wrapped in linen, his face covered with an astounding gold mask. The lid of the coffin was fashioned out of sheet gold, with eyes of aragonite (a semi-hard mineral) and obsidian (black volcanic glass) and eyebrows inlaid with lapis lazuli. The hands of Tut's effigy cross over the chest and clutch the royal symbols of the crook and the flail, encrusted in deep blue faience—a signature Egyptian opaque glazed earthenware.

Carter, upon viewing the revelation of the coffin, described the sense of marvel at the sight: "And as the last was removed a gasp of wonderment escaped our lips, so gorgeous was the sight that met our eye: a golden effigy of the young boy king, of most magnificent workmanship, filled the whole of the interior of the sarcophagus." Although Tut's coffin and mask are characteristically stylized, Carter observed an element of realism in the fashioning of the face. In fact, some residual stylistic effects of the Amarna period are evident in several works from Tut's reign—curvilinear forms not unlike those seen in the statue of Akhenaton, a certain naturalism and tenderness in representations of the boy and his queen.

After Akhenaton's death, Egypt returned to "normal." That is, the worship of Amen was resumed and art reverted to the rigid stylization of the earlier stages. The divergence that had taken place with Akhenaton and been carried forward briefly by his successor soon disappeared. Instead, the permanence that was so valued by this people endured for another 1,000 years virtually unchanged despite the kingdom's gradual decline.

AEGEAN ART

The Tigris and Euphrates valleys and the Nile River banks provided the climate and conditions for the survival of Mesopotamia and Egypt. Other ancient civilizations also flourished because of their geography. Those of the Aegean—Crete in particular—developed and thrived because of their island location. As maritime powers, they maintained contact with distant cultures with whom they traded, including those of Egypt and Asia Minor.

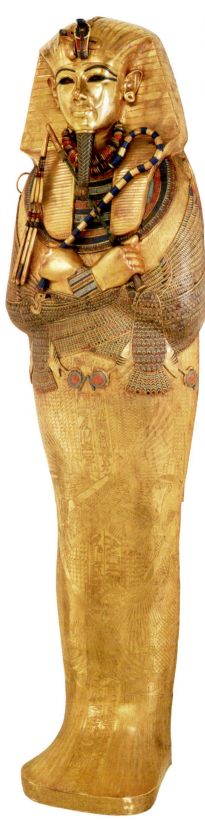

13-18 The innermost coffin of the king, from the Tomb of Tutankhamen (c.1370–1352 BCE). Gold inlaid with semiprecious stones. Egyptian Museum, Cairo, Egypt.

MAP 13-3 Greece (5th century BCE).

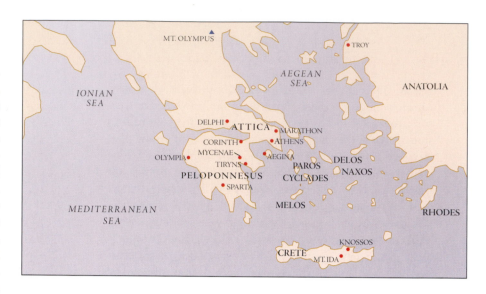

Until about 1870 CE, the Aegean civilizations that were sung by Greece's epic poet, Homer, in the *Iliad* and the *Odyssey* were viewed as fancy rather than fact. But during the last decades of the nineteenth century, the German archeologist Heinrich Schliemann followed the very words of Homer and unearthed some of the ancient sites, including Mycenae, on the Greek mainland (Map **13-3**). Following in Schliemann's footsteps, Sir Arthur Evans excavated on the island of Crete and uncovered remains of the Minoan civilization also cited by Homer. The Bronze Age civilizations of **pre-Hellenic** Greece comprised these cultures and that of the Cyclades Islands.

The Cyclades

The Cyclades Islands are part of an archipelago in the Aegean Sea off the southeastern coast of mainland Greece. They are six in number and include Melos, the site where the

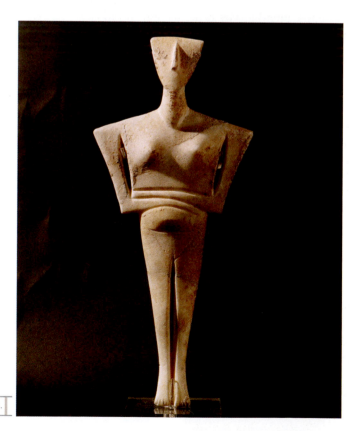

1 in.

13-19 Female idol (c. 2000 BCE), from Chalandriani, Isle of Syros, Greece. H: 18⅛". National Archeological Museum, Athens, Greece.

famed Venus de Milo (see Fig. 14-17) was found; and Paros, one of the chief quarries for marble used in ancient Greece. The Cycladic culture flourished on these six islands during the Early Bronze Age, from roughly 2500 to 2000 BCE.

The art that survives has been culled mostly from tombs and includes pottery and small marble figurines of women (Fig. **13-19**) and male musicians. It is not clear what purpose the small female figures served. Some say they represent goddesses, whereas others argue for a link to fertility. They are, in a way, pared-down, geometric versions of the Venus of Willendorf (Fig. 13-2); that is, the breasts, abdomen, and pubic area are more defined than the limbs and head. Because they were found in tombs, it would seem likely that they served a funerary function.

The figures range in height from a few inches to well over a foot, although some are life-size. They are essentially flat, with oval or wedge-shaped heads, squared torsos, and attenuated limbs. The smooth planes of the faces generally bear only one feature—a nose. Some traces of paint have been found. Male figures are typically seated and are playing stylized musical instruments. They were also found in tombs, and their function and identity are also open to speculation.

Crete

The civilization that developed on the island of Crete was one of the most remarkable in the ancient world, rich in painting, sculpture, and elaborate architecture. It also brought us names like King Minos (Crete's culture is known as Minoan, after the king) and creatures like the Minotaur. Homer spoke of youths sent to a Cretan labyrinth for sacrifice to the notorious man-beast, and of the hero Theseus, who slayed the Minotaur. Assuming that myths have some basis in fact, we might conclude that the extensive labyrinth that was part of the sprawling palace at Knossos—home to King Minos—inspired Homer's poetic narrative. Homeric descriptions of this island civilization were viewed as literary rather than historical. But as with Schliemann and Troy, the archeologist Sir Arthur Evan's excavations revealed Crete to have been an advanced and bustling civilization.

Evans divided the history of Minoan civilization into three parts: The Early Minoan period, known as the pre-Palace period, from which survive some small sculptures and pottery; the Middle Minoan period, or the period of the Old Palaces, which began around 2000 BCE and ended three centuries later with what was probably a devastating earthquake; and the Late Minoan period, when these palaces were reconstructed, which began during the sixteenth century BCE and ended probably in about 1400 BCE. At that time, the stronghold of Western civilization shifted from the Aegean to the Greek mainland.

During the Middle Minoan period, the great palaces, including the most famous one at Knossos, were constructed. A form of writing based on **pictographs**, called Linear A, was developed. Refined articles of ivory, metal, and pottery were also produced.

Unlike those of Mesopotamia and Egypt, Minoan architectural projects did not consist of tombs, mortuary temples, or shrines. Instead, the Minoans constructed lavish palaces for their kings and the royal entourage. Not much is known of the old palaces, except for those that were subsequently built on their ruins. Toward the end of the Middle Minoan period, the palace at Knossos was reduced to rubble either by an earthquake or by invaders. About a century after its destruction, however, it was rebuilt on a grander scale. Also during the Late Minoan period, a type of writing called Linear B was developed. This system, finally deciphered in 1953, turned out to be an early form of Greek. The script, found on clay tablets, perhaps indicates the presence of a Greek-speaking people—the Mycenaeans—on Crete during this period.

The most spectacular of the restored palaces on Crete is that at Knossos. It was so sprawling that one can easily understand how the myth of the Minotaur arose. The adjective *labyrinthine* certainly describes it. A variety of rooms were set off major corridors and arranged about a spacious central court. The rooms included the king's and queen's bedrooms, a throne room, reception rooms, servants' quarters, and many other spaces, including rows of **magazines**, or storage areas, where large vessels of grain and wine were embedded in the earth for safekeeping and natural cooling. The palace was three stories high, and the upper floors were reached by well-lit staircases. Beneath the palace were the makings of an impressive water-supply system of terra-cotta pipes that would have provided running water for bathrooms.

Some of the most interesting decorative aspects of the palace at Knossos—seen in the queen's bedroom (Fig. **13-20**)—are its unique columns and its vibrant fresco paintings. The columns, carved of stone, are narrower at the base than at the top. This proportion is the reverse of that of the standard columns found in Mesopotamia, Egypt, and later, in Greece. The columns are crowned by cushion-shaped capitals that loom large over the curious stem of the column shaft, often painted bright red or blue.

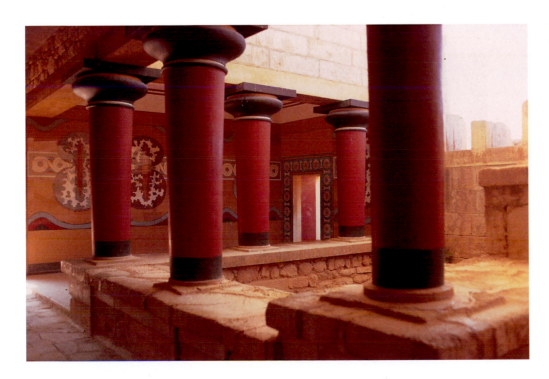

13-20 Queen's bedroom in Palace at Knossos (c. 1500 BCE). Knossos, Crete.

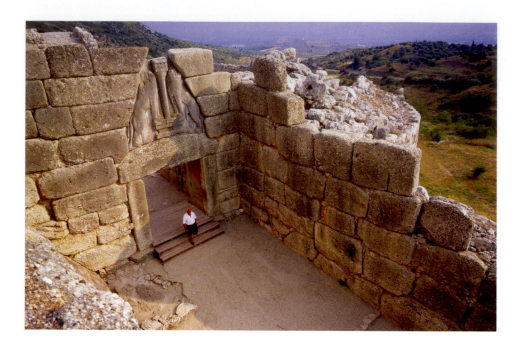

The rooms were also adorned with painted panels of plant and animal life. Stylized **rosettes** accent doorways, and delicately painted dolphins swim across the surface of the walls, giving one the impression of looking into a vast aquarium. This fascination with fish, sea mammals, and coastal plants in wall paintings and on pottery of the Late Minoan period reflects life on an island. The scale and complexity of the architecture reflects Crete as an impressive maritime power.

The palace at Knossos and all of the other palaces on Crete were again destroyed some time in the fifteenth cen-tury BCE. At this point, the Mycenaeans of the Greek main-land may have moved in and occupied the island. However, their stay was short-lived. Knossos, and the Minoan civiliza-tion, had been finally destroyed by the year 1200 BCE.

Mycenae

Although the origins of the Mycenaean people are uncertain, we know that they came to the Greek mainland as early as 2000 BCE. They were a Greek-speaking people, sophisti-

13-22 The Treasury of Atreus (c. 1300–1250 BCE). Mycenae, Greece.

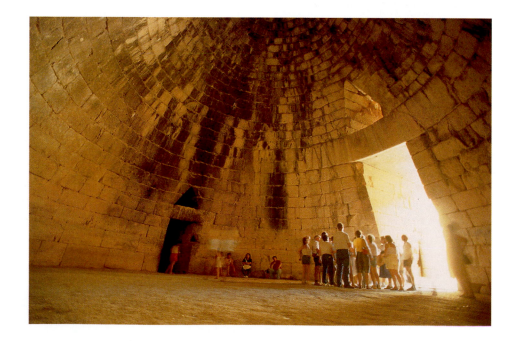

cated in forging bronze weaponry as well as versatile in the arts of ceramics, metalwork, and architecture. The Minoans clearly influenced their art and culture, even though by about 1600 BCE Mycenae was by far the more powerful of the two civilizations. Mycenaeans occupied Crete after the palaces were destroyed. The peak of Mycenaean supremacy lasted about two centuries, from 1400 to 1200 BCE. At the end of that period, invaders from the north—the fierce and undaunted Dorians—gained control of mainland Greece. They intermingled with the Mycenaeans to form the beginnings of the peoples of ancient Greece.

Lacking the natural defense of a surrounding sea that was to Crete's advantage, the Mycenaeans were constantly facing threats from land invaders. They met these threats with strong fortifications, such as the citadels in the major cities of Mycenae and Tiryns. Much of the architecture and art of the Mycenaean civilization reflects the preoccupation with defense.

ARCHITECTURE For the Mycenaeans, the need for impenetrable fortification did not preclude aesthetic solutions to architectural challenges. Even though the construction methods employed in palaces, tombs, and fortification walls are their most impressive attributes, citadels were embellished with frescoes and sculpture. One of the most famous carved pieces in Mycenae is the Lion Gate (Fig. 13-21), one of the entranceways to the citadel of that city. The actual gateway consists of a heavy **lintel** that rests on two massive vertical pillars—another example of post-and-lintel construction. Additional large stones were piled in rows, or courses, above the lintel and **beveled** to form an open triangle. A relief sculpture of two lions flanking a Minoan-style column fills the space. The heads of the beasts, now gone, were carved of separate pieces of stone and fitted into place. Although the animal figures are not intact, their prominent and realistic musculature, carved in high relief, is an awesome sight, one that signified to intruders the strength of the army within the walls.

Another contribution of the Mycenaean architect was the **tholos**, or beehive tomb. During the early phases of the Mycenaean civilization, members of the royal family were buried in so-called **shaft graves**. These were no more than pits in the ground, lined with stones, and marked by a **stele**, or headstone, set above the entrance to the grave. As time went on, however, tombs for the wealthy became more ambitious.

The Treasury of Atreus (Fig. 13-22), a tomb so named by Schliemann because he believed it to have been the tomb of the mythological ancient Greek king Atreus, is typical of such constructions. The Treasury consists of two parts: the *dromos*, or narrow passageway leading to the tomb proper; and the *tholos*, or beehive-shaped tomb chamber. The entire structure was covered by earth and has the appearance of a simple mound from the exterior. The interior walls were constructed of hundreds of stones laid on top of one another in concentric rings of diminishing size. The Treasury rose to a height of some 40 feet and enclosed a vast amount of space, an architectural feat not to be duplicated until the domed ceilings of ancient Rome were constructed.

GOLD WORK Homer's epithet for Mycenae was "rich in gold." Archeologists came to uphold that description with the discovery of extraordinary quantities of finely wrought gold objects in graves throughout Mycenae, although the tholos tombs, like the pyramids before them in Egypt, were plundered well before the modern excavations. Thieves found their way into the Treasury of Atreus, as they did other tombs, soon after its construction. Nevertheless, Schliemann unearthed a wealth of treasures just inside the Lion Gate, which were buried in more inconspicuous graves. Archeologists refer to the mound as Grave Circle A. The most impressive find was a gold mask, which Schliemann believed was that of Agamemnon himself (Fig. 13-23). Masks such as these were created from thin, hammered sheets of gold and placed over the faces of the deceased. Some aspects of the masks were stylized, such as the ears, eyebrows, and coffee-bean-shaped eyes, but the artists did endeavor to recreate specific characteristics that distinguished one portrait from another. Schliemann found other elaborate objects, including gold cups, bronze vessels, and daggers inlaid with silver and gold.

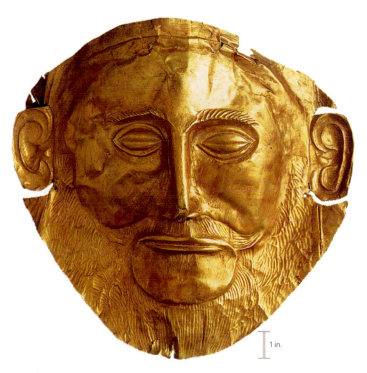

1 in.

13-23 Funerary mask, from Grave Circle A (c. 1600–1500 BCE), from Mycenae, Greece. Beaten gold. H: 12". National Archaeological Museum, Athens, Greece.

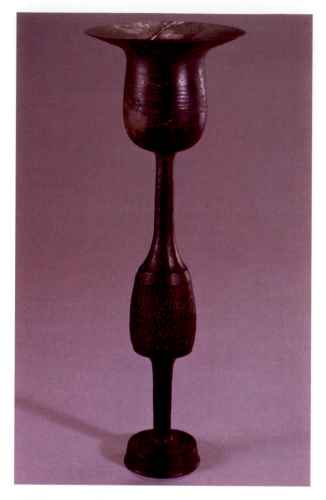

13-24 Black eggshell pottery, Longshan culture.

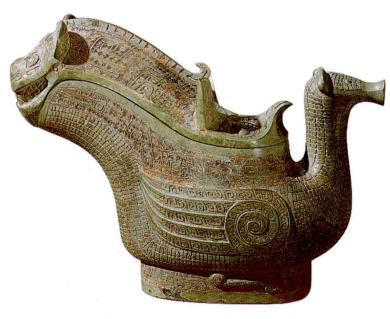

13-25 Ceremonial vessel (Guang) (12th century BCE), from a royal tomb at Anyang, Henan. Bronze. L: 12". Freer Gallery of Art, Smithsonian Institution, Washington, D.C.

The Cyclopean walls of the Mycenaean citadels did not ward off enemies for long. After roughly 1200 BCE, the Mycenaean civilization collapsed from internal warfare, the onslaught of the better-equipped Dorian warriors, or both. The period following the Dorian invasions produced no significant art, architecture, or writing. But the people who emerged from this "Dark Age" would sow the seeds of one of the world's most influential civilizations and enduring artistic legacies—that of ancient Greece.

ART OF ANCIENT CHINA AND INDIA

A glance at global history reveals the simultaneity of civilizations that developed around the world's great rivers: Mesopotamia in the Tigris and Euphrates Valley, Egypt on the Nile, South Asian cities in the Indus Valley, and China along the Yellow River.

Ancient China

Excavations in China have revealed numerous Neolithic settlements along with pictographic carvings that some scholars have tied to early written language. In the late Neolithic period, the Longshan culture developed along the Yellow River, overlapping chronologically with both the Egyptian Old Kingdom and the Sumerian civilization of Mesopotamia. As with other river civilizations we have discussed, the Longshan is marked by the establishment of cities. Of particular interest are examples of finely wrought pottery, some of which was wheel-thrown. The distinctive black pottery was thin walled (thus also called eggshell pottery), highly polished, and often decorated with elaborate patterns of incised line (Fig. **13-24**).

During the years that the Shang Dynasty (ca. 1520–1027 BCE) ruled China, Tutankhamen became pharaoh, the Mycenaeans lived in their fortified cities, and the Minoans decorated their elaborate palaces with brilliant frescos. The Shang Dynasty, too, was a Bronze Age urban civilization ruled by kings who, as in Egypt, inherited their positions and who, like the pharaohs, claimed their authority from the divine. The Shang culture is known for its accomplished metalwork, including bronze weaponry, fittings for chariots, and sophisticated ceremonial vessels such as the one in Figure **13-25**, which was discovered in a royal tomb. The two-headed fantastic animal is embellished with elaborate, stylized, linear detail that complements the curving shapes of vessel. The casting technique perfected by the Shang artisans consisted of pouring molten bronze into piece molds and, after casting,

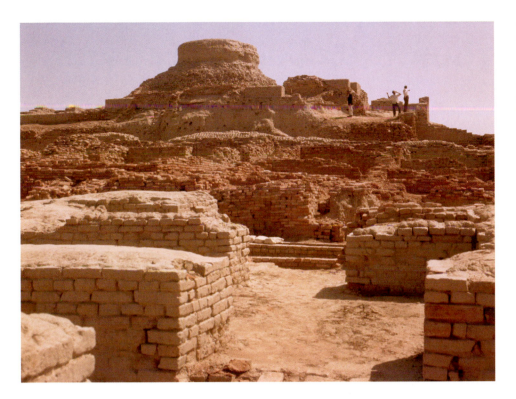

assembling the individual parts into a cohesively designed whole. The Shang royal tombs, as in Egypt and Mesopotamia, were filled with precious objects such as these.

Ancient India

The earliest South Asian cities developed in the Sindh region of the Indus River Valley, near the Arabian Sea in what is now Pakistan. Mohenjo-Daro was the largest and oldest of these urban centers, coinciding chronologically with the civilizations of Egypt, Mesopotamia, and Crete. The urban planning and engineering finesse of Mohenjo-Daro are impressive: a grid plan of streets with fire-brick rectilinear buildings, a central marketplace with a public well, a public bath waterproofed with bitumen, and a sewage system, to name but some of its features. The size of the city (at its peak it housed 35,000 inhabitants), its fortifications, and its variety of structures indicate that it was a city of great importance, perhaps the civilization's administrative center. Excavation of Mohenjo-Daro began in the 1920s, and today the ruins are designated as a UNESCO World Heritage Site (Fig. **13-26**).

The Sindh area of the Indus Valley gave birth to the words *India* and *Hindu*, and Mohenjo-Daro is considered one of India's earliest civilizations (India was partitioned in 1947, after which Pakistan and India became self-governing states). The Indus Valley civilization produced a written pictographic language and artisans who were highly skilled in bronze and stone sculpture. The *Bearded Man* (Fig. **13-27**)

from Mohenjo-Daro is carved from limestone with carefully crafted detail that seems to indicate the man's high status. His robe, draped over one shoulder, is delicately carved with a clover-leaf pattern, and he wears what appears to be jewelry around his exposed arm and head. The serene expression, enhanced by his placid lips and only slightly opened eyelids, perhaps indicates that he is a ruler or member of a priestly hierarchy.

Around the time of the New Kingdom in Egypt, Aryans invaded the Indus Valley, conquered the Sindh, and took them as slaves. The Aryans were light-skinned, seminomadic tribes who introduced the Sanskrit language and instituted the **caste system** that would persist in India until the modern era.

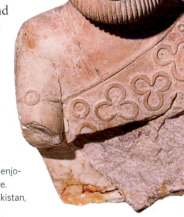

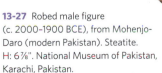

13-27 Robed male figure (c. 2000–1900 BCE), from Mohenjo-Daro (modern Pakistan). Steatite. H: 6⅞". National Museum of Pakistan, Karachi, Pakistan.

ART TOUR JERUSALEM

JERUSALEM—A CITY SET in history, a city beset by current events. Jerusalem—a city at once pluralistic and, more than once, intolerant. Jerusalem—spiritually, the home of three of the world's great religions and, emotionally, a house too often divided.

Over its 3,000-year history, Jerusalem and the Holy Land have been coveted territory. The ancient Egyptians battled the Canaanites in the coastal plains around the Dead Sea, bringing them under the rule of the pharaoh. And although the Hebrew tribes that coalesced into the entity known as Israel around 1200 to 1000 BCE came to dominate the region, they met continual violent struggles with such peoples as the Philistines, Assyrians, and Babylonians (who captured Jerusalem in 586 BCE, destroyed Solomon's Temple, and drove the Jews into exile). When the Jews returned to Jerusalem from Babylonian captivity, they built a new temple on the site of the old, ushering in the period of the "Second Temple." Yet even during this era, they were not self-governed; the Persians remained dominant over the region until they were conquered by Alexander the Great.

From that point forward, the Jewish nation met a series of enemies. None were more formidable than ancient Rome, whose legions first took the city of Jerusalem in 63 BCE. For almost 100 years, clashes between the Jews and the Romans were constant, and this, according to the

Christian Bible, was the state of affairs into which Jesus was born. Bloody skirmishes led to full-scale war in 66 CE. After four years, the Romans were finally victorious, capturing Jerusalem and destroying the city and the Second Temple. But the subjugation of the Jewish people did not occur until three years later, after a test of wills and military might at the fortress of Masada. It was a subjugation that would not last. A second war was fought from 132 to 135 CE, with Rome victorious once again. This time the Jews were driven from the city of Jerusalem, scattering in what is known as the Diaspora.

Other religions entered the region as watershed historical events took place. When the Roman emperor Constantine converted to Christianity and granted freedom of worship to early Christians in the year 313 CE, the doors to the Holy Land were opened to pilgrims of the new faith, who built churches on sites connected to events in the life of Christ. By the late fourth century, Christianity became the official religion of the Holy Land. A little more than three centuries later, Muslims—followers of Islam and its prophet, Muhammad—became the new rulers of the Holy Land. Muslims maintain, as do Jews and Christians, that Jerusalem is holy to their religion; they believe that Muhammad ascended into heaven from the same rock in Jerusalem on which, according to the Hebrew Bible, Abraham was about to sacrifice his son Isaac. The Dome of the Rock stands over this site, on which the Jews had originally built their temples. The coming and going of pilgrims to the Holy Land continued for some time, until Jerusalem fell to the Turks in 1071 and Christians were forbidden access to their religious sites. This event led to the Crusades, the military effort to take back the Holy City of Jerusalem and biblical sites.

It is against this historical backdrop that we can make sense of the present-day composition of the Old City of Jerusalem

and the nature of its historic sites. Within the walls are four delineated sections: the Christian quarter, the Jewish quarter, the Muslim quarter, and the Armenian quarter. Just outside the fortress walls are the Mount of Olives (on which can be found the Garden of Gethsemane, where the apostle Judas was said to have betrayed Jesus to the Roman authorities) and Mount Zion (the place where it was believed the Last Supper took place.)

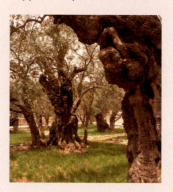

THE GARDEN OF GETHSEMANE.

The Muslim quarter is the largest and most densely populated of the sections of the Old City and is physically dominated by one of the most extraordinary works of Islamic architecture in the world—the Dome of the Rock. Built in 688–691 CE, the mosque-shrine represents the epitome of Islamic architectural design, from the mathematical relationships of the individual parts to the building as a whole to the supremely ornamented tiles and mosaics of its interior.

Because the Islamic faith traditionally proscribed the rendering of the human figure, the walls and dome contain complex, decorative organic and abstract patterns, sometimes interlaced with Qur'anic verses and other inscriptions rendered in Arabic calligraphy. The Muslim quarter also includes the El-Aqsa Mosque, several well-known gates to the Old City (such as the Damascus Gate and Herod's Gate), a museum of Islamic art, and the Central

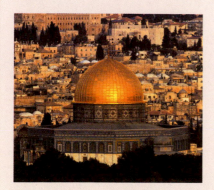

THE DOME OF THE ROCK.

Souk, a covered marketplace selling spices, clothes, and souvenirs. The Muslim quarter is also the site of the Via Dolorosa, venerated as the route taken by Jesus on the way to his Crucifixion.

The spiritual heart of the Jewish quarter of the Old City is the Western Wall—a section of the retaining wall of the Temple Mount that is the only part of the Second Temple complex that survives to this day. Since the sixteenth century, it has been Judaism's holiest site, having been reconstructed after Israel gained control of the Jewish quarter during the 1967 war. Jewish pilgrims from all over the world (non-Jews are also allowed to approach the wall) come to what is also known as the Wailing Wall to lament the destruction of the temple and to pray. Many leave prayers inscribed on the smallest bits of paper, tucked into the cracks between the huge stone blocks that make up the wall.

Today the Jewish quarter is a mixture of historic sites and contemporary places of business serving the local community as well as tourists. Here, as in the other quarters, souvenir shops abound. Several fascinating excavations have been undertaken in the Jewish quarter, including the Cardo—one of Jerusalem's oldest main thoroughfares. During the era of the Crusades, the

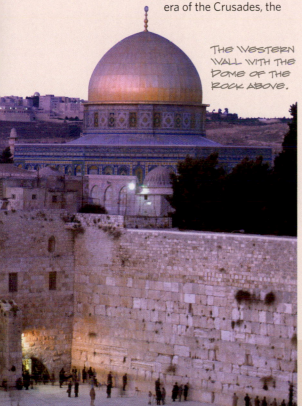

THE WESTERN WALL WITH THE DOME OF THE ROCK ABOVE.

Cardo became a covered marketplace; today it remains an exclusive shopping arcade, full of galleries and boutiques. The quarter has several synagogues and archeological museums, of which the Wohl Museum is perhaps best known. It is alive with bustling streets, such as Tiferet Yisrael Street, and squares that are the social centers of the contemporary Jewish quarter. Lovely homes built around courtyards are constructed—by decree of the British military governor in 1917—only of Jerusalem stone, a local material ranging from soft beige to pale rose in color.

Many of the common architectural elements and motifs of the three religious traditions are present even in these residential buildings, particularly the arch and the dome. The Christian quarter of Jerusalem took shape in the shadows of the domes of its most sacred site, the Church of the Holy Sepulchre. Within the walls of this vast structure are two of Christendom's most important monuments: Golgotha, or Calvary (the rock venerated as the site of Christ's Crucifixion), and Christ's tomb (a marble slab that covers the rock on which Jesus' body is believed to have been laid). Flanking the main entrance are a bell tower and many chapels that, together with many small churches, hospices, and souvenir shops, obscure the overall exterior plan of the church.

Over centuries, bitter disputes over who "owns" the church would arise until an Ottoman decree in 1852, known as the Status Quo, divided custody of the structure and its holy sites among the Roman Catholics, Copts, Armenians, Greeks, Ethiopians, and Syrians. Every day, a Muslim "key holder," a neutral intermediary, unlocks the doors of the church. Just within the walls of the Christian quarter, the Citadel of the Old City (most likely the place of Christ's trial and condemnation) now houses the Tower of David Museum of the History of Jerusalem. The museum contains specific routes that offer panoramic views of the city, a close look at archeological remains, and displays and dioramas focused on the three cultural-religious traditions of Jerusalem.

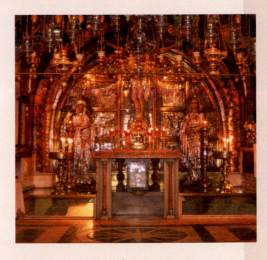

INTERIOR OF THE CHURCH OF THE HOLY SEPULCHRE, SHOWING CALVARY.

The story of the Armenians in Jerusalem begins in the time of Constantine (the kingdom of Armenia was the first to declare Christianity as its state religion after the emperor's edict of 313) and continues through the early twentieth century, when a large number of Armenian citizens fled to Jerusalem to escape the genocide being committed by the Turks. Although their numbers have dwindled significantly over the decades, the Armenian Church still maintains jurisdiction over such sites as the Church of the Holy Sepulchre, the Mosque of the Ascension, and the Tomb of the Virgin on the Temple Mount. Armenian works of ceramic, mosaic, and manuscript illumination can be seen in the library of St. James Cathedral and in the Mardigian Museum in the Armenian quarter.

Modern Jerusalem is as bustling and magnificent a city as one will ever lay eyes on—fashionable hotels, ornate synagogues and mosques, gardens, fountains, upscale shopping districts, colorful markets, important museums. One of the most poignant aspects of this art tour is the recognition that, for many, because of the continuing unrest, instability, and violence that grip the city, it is only what lies on these pages that will bring them to Jerusalem.

TO CONTINUE YOUR TOUR and learn more about Jerusalem, go to CourseMate.

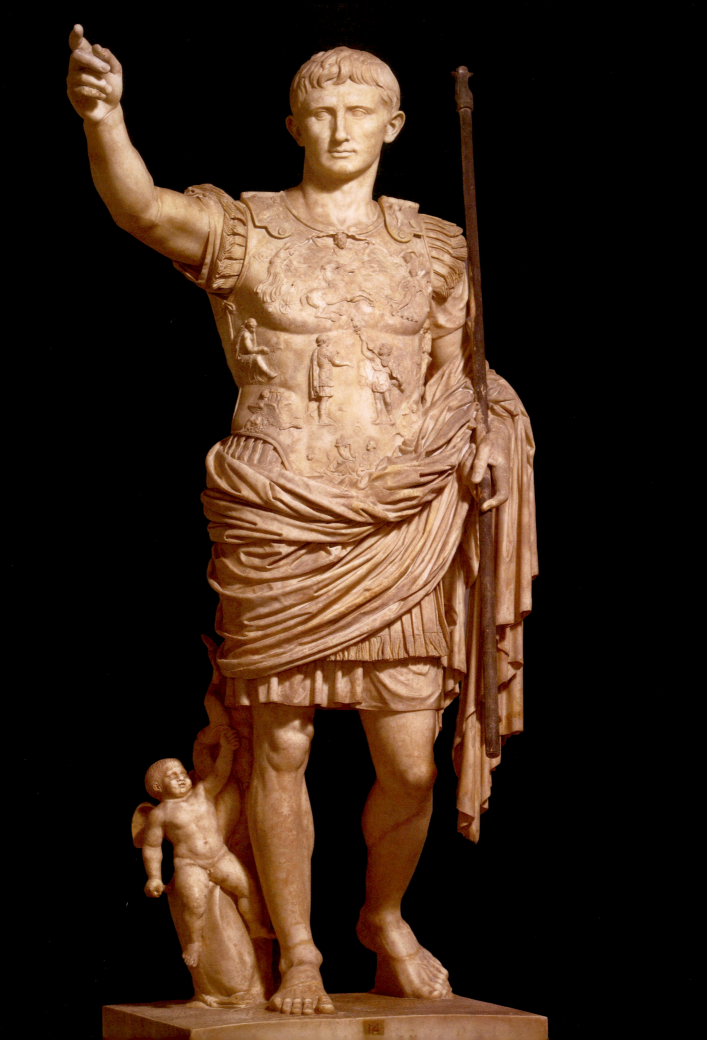

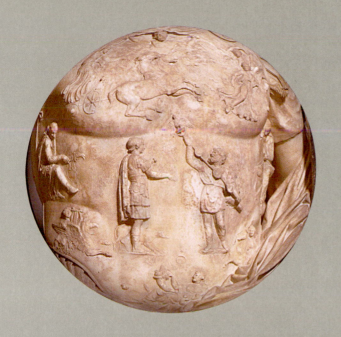

CLASSICAL ART: GREECE AND ROME 14

No other culture has had as far-reaching or lasting an influence on art and civilization as that of ancient Greece. It has been said that "nothing moves in the world which is not Greek in origin." To this day, the Greek influence can be felt in science, mathematics, law, politics, and art. Unlike some cultures that flourished, declined, and left barely an imprint on the pages of history, that of Greece has asserted itself time and again over the 3,000 years since its birth. During the fifteenth century, there was a revival of Greek art and culture called the Renaissance, and on the eve of the French Revolution of 1789, artists of the Neoclassical period again turned to the style and subjects of ancient Greece. Our founders looked to Greek architectural styles for the buildings of our nation's capital, and nearly every small town in America has a bank, post office, or library constructed in the Greek Revival style.

Despite its cultural and artistic achievements, ancient Greece was conquered and absorbed by Rome—one of history's strongest and largest empires. Although Greece's political power waned, its influence as a culture did not. It was assimilated by the admiring Romans. The spirit of **Hellenism** lived on in the glorious days of the Roman Empire.

Augustus of Primaporta (c. 20 BCE). Marble. H: 6'8". Vatican Museums, Rome, Italy.

In contrast to the Greeks' intellectual and creative achievements, Rome's cultural contributions lay in the areas of building, city planning, government, and law. Although sometimes thought of as uncultured and crude, the Romans civilized much of the ancient world following military campaigns that are still studied in military academies.

Despite its awesome might, the Roman Empire also fell. It was replaced by a force whose ideals differed greatly and whose kingdom was not of this world—Christianity. In this chapter, we shall examine the artistic legacy of Greece and Rome. This legacy—called **Classical art**—has influenced almost all of Western art, from Early Christian mosaics to contemporary Manhattan skyscrapers.

GREECE

Humanity, reason, and nature were central preoccupations of the Greek mind, together formulating their attitude toward life. The Greeks considered human beings the center of the universe—the "measure of all things." This concept is called **humanism**. The value the Greeks placed on the individual led to the development of democracy as a system of government among independent city-states throughout Greece and defined the character of Greek art, literature, and philosophy. To reach one's full potential, to be both physically and mentally fit, was an individual imperative. Perfection for the Greeks was the balance between elements: mind and body, emotion and intellect. Their love of reason and admiration for intellectual pursuits led to the development of **rationalism**, a philosophy in which knowledge is assumed to come from reason alone, without input from the senses.

The Greeks also had a passion and respect for nature and viewed human beings as a reflection of its perfect order. **Naturalism**, or truth to reality based on a keen observation of nature, guided the representation of the human figure. When what nature dispensed fell short of the Greek concept of perfection, **idealism** (the representation of forms according to an accepted standard of beauty) held sway. Humanism, rationalism, naturalism, idealism—these are the elements of Greek art and architecture.

From ancient Greece come the names of the dramatists Aeschylus, Aristophanes, and Sophocles; the poets Homer and Hesiod; the philosophers Aristotle, Socrates, and Plato; scientists like Archimedes and mathematicians like Euclid; and the historian Herodotus. It has given us gods like Zeus and Apollo, Athena and Aphrodite, and heroic figures named Achilles and Odysseus and Penelope. Even more astonishing, although Greek culture spans almost 1,000 years, its Golden

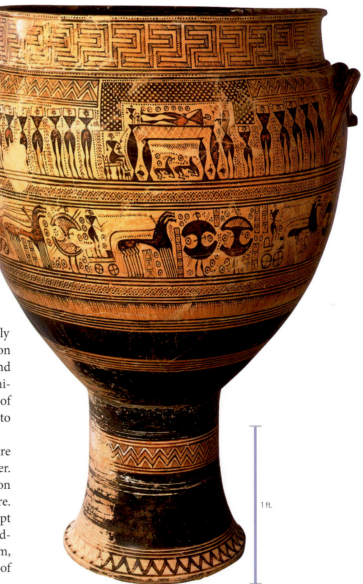

1 ft.

14-1 Geometric krater from the Dipylon cemetery, Athens, Greece (8th century BCE). Terra-cotta. H: 42⅝". The Metropolitan Museum of Art, NY.

Age, or period of greatest achievement, lasted no more than 80 years. As with many civilizations, the development of Greece occurred over a cycle of birth, maturation, perfection, and decline. These points in the cycle correspond to the four periods of Greek art that we will examine in this chapter: Geometric, Archaic, Classical, and Hellenistic.

Geometric Period

The **Geometric period** spanned approximately two centuries, from about 900 to 700 BCE. The period before is sometimes called the Dark Age of Greece because of a virtual collapse of civilization. Greece was gripped by chaos and poverty, the arts were lost, and its society was cut off from the outside world. During the eighth century, trade resumed, the economic situation improved, and with these, first steps were taken to regenerate the arts. The Geometric period is so called because of the predominance of geometric shapes and patterns in works of art. As in Egyptian art, the representation of the human figure was conceptual rather than optical, and usually reduced to a combination of geometric forms such as circles and triangles.

The Dipylon Vase (Fig. **14-1**), a large **krater** used as a grave marker and found in the Dipylon cemetery in Athens, is an early example of the Geometric style. Except for its base, most of the vessel is decorated with geometric motifs, some of which may have been inspired by the patterns of woven baskets. Two thicker bands around the body of the vase feature a funeral procession composed of stylized, geometric figures. Distinctions are made between males and females, but overall, they march along with the same rigidity of the geometric patterns. The figures are a familiar combination of frontal, wedge-shaped torsos, profile legs and arms, and a profile head with a frontal eye. In the center of one of the bands, the deceased rests on a bier. Below, figures of warriors with apple core–shaped shields and teams of chariots are in attendance. The deceased was likely a Greek soldier. These geometric elements can also be seen in small bronze sculptures of the period, but the stylistic development is most evident in the art of vase painting.

Archaic Period

The **Archaic period** spanned roughly the years from 660 to 480 BCE, but the change from the Geometric style to the Archaic style in art was gradual. As Greece expanded its trade with Eastern countries, it was influenced by their art. Flowing forms and fantastic animals inspired by Mesopotamian art appeared on Greek pottery. There was a growing emphasis on the human figure, which replaced Geometric motifs.

VASE PAINTING During the Archaic period, Eastern patterns and forms gradually disappeared. During the Geometric period, the human figure was subordinated to decorative motifs, but in the Archaic period, it became the preferred subject. In the François Vase (Fig. **14-2**), for example, geometric patterns are restricted to a few areas. The entire body of the vessel, a **volute krater**, is divided into six wide bands, or registers, featuring the exploits of Greek heroes and legends, including Achilles and Theseus. Even though the drawing is somewhat stilted, the figures of men and animals have substance, and an attempt at naturalistic gestures has been made. Unlike the figures of the Dipylon Vase, those of the François Vase are not static. In fact, the movement of the battling humans and the prancing horses is quite lively. This energetic mood is echoed in the curling shapes of the volute handles.

The François Vase is a masterpiece of Archaic vase painting. No doubt, the potter and painter were proud of their work, because the vessel is signed twice by each of them. The François Vase, named after the archeologist who found it, is an example of **black-figure painting**. The combination of black figures on a reddish background was achieved through a three-stage kiln-firing process. The figures were painted on a clay pot using a brush and a **slip**, a liquid of sifted clay, and then introduced to the kiln. The first stage of the firing

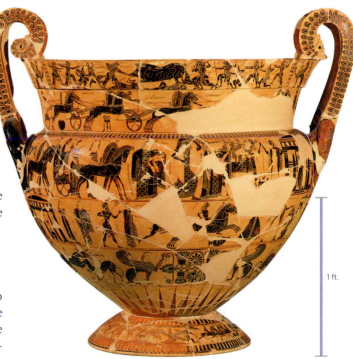

1 ft.

14-2 KLEITIAS AND ERGOTIMOS. *François Vase.* Attic volute krater (c. 570 BCE). Ceramic. H: 26". Museo Archeologico Nazionale, Florence, Italy.

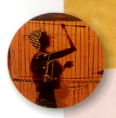

THE WOMEN WEAVERS OF ANCIENT GREECE

NO WORKS OF ART BY GREEK WOMEN have survived, and only a scant number of names have been recorded. Yet there is plenty of evidence that women did have outlets for creative expression, including ceramics, basketry, and particularly weaving. Noblewomen, commoners, and slaves wove as a pastime or to earn a living. Athena, the most important female god in the Greek pantheon, was best known as the goddess of war and wisdom, but she was also the patron goddess of potters and weavers.

Stories of women weaving come down to us from Homer in *The Iliad* and *The Odyssey*. In one scene in *The Iliad*, Helen of Sparta (now Helen of Troy) is visited by a goddess in disguise, who aims to rekindle her love for her abandoned husband, Menelaus:

> She found Helen in her room,
> weaving a large cloth, a double purple cloak,
> creating pictures of the many battle scenes
> between horse-taming Trojans and bronze-
>   clad Achaeans,
> wars they suffered for her sake at the hands
>   of Ares.

In *The Odyssey*, Penelope, the wife of the wily (and missing-in-action) Odysseus, wards off suitors on the promise that she will choose one of them after she finishes weaving a funeral shroud for her father-in-law. Unbeknownst to them, Penelope spends her days weaving and her nights tearing out her work.

> She set up a great loom in her palace, and set
>   to weaving
> a web of threads long and fine. Then she
>   said to us:
> "Young men, my suitors, now that great
>   Odysseus has perished,
> wait, though you are eager to marry me,
>   until I finish
> this web, so that my weaving will not be use-
>   less and wasted.
> This is a shroud for the hero Laertes, for
>   when the destructive
> doom of death which lays men low shall
>   take him, lest any
> Achaian woman in this neighbourhood hold
>   it against me

> that a man of many conquests lies with no
>   sheet to wind him."
> So she spoke, and the proud heart in us was
>   persuaded.
> Thereafter in the daytime she would weave
>   at her great loom,
> but in the night she would have torches set
>   by, and undo it.

The importance of women weavers is suggested in the subject of a black-figure vase attributed to the Amasis Painter (Fig. **14-3**). Its large central panel features a scene of women working on looms and engaged in other aspects of cloth production. Some scholars have posited the even more widespread influence of women's weaving by connecting the patterns of geometric vase painting (Fig. 14-1) with those of Dorian wool fabrics.

The connection of women to weaving continues throughout the centuries. In the Middle Ages, for example, noblewomen, nuns, and commoners were all taught the skills of weaving and embroidery, and the great tapestries of this era were most certainly created by women. In our time, artists such as Faith Ringgold (see Fig. 1-28) and Miriam Schapiro (see Fig. 1-35) have explored the expressive possibilities of traditional needlework. ●

14-3 AMASIS PAINTER. *Women Working Wool on a Loom* (c. 540 BCE). Terra-cotta. H: 6¾". The Metropolitan Museum of Art, NY.

1 in.

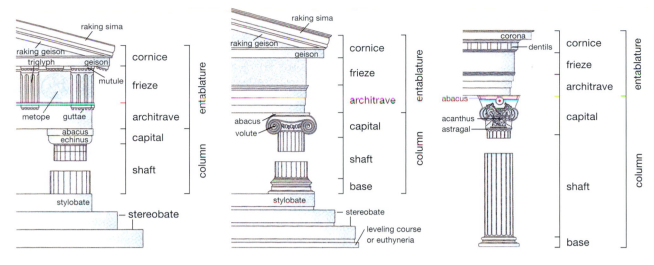

14-4 Left to right: Doric, Ionic, and Corinthian orders.

process was called the **oxidizing phase,** because oxygen was allowed into the kiln. Firing under these conditions turned both the pot and the painted slip decoration red.

In the second phase of firing, called the **reducing phase**, oxygen was eliminated from the kiln, and the vase and the slip both turned black. In the third and final phase, called the **reoxidizing phase**, oxygen was again introduced into the kiln. The coarser material of the pot turned red, and the fine clay of the slip remained black. The result was a vase with black figures silhouetted against a red ground. The finer details of the figures were incised with sharp instruments that scraped away portions of the black to expose the red clay underneath or highlighted with touches of red and purple pigment. Although this technique was fairly versatile, the black figures were ultimately too visually heavy for Greek artists. Around 530 BCE, a reversal of the black-figure process was developed, enabling painters to create lighter, more realistic red figures on a black ground.

ARCHITECTURE Some of the greatest accomplishments of the Greeks are witnessed in their architecture. Although their personal dwellings were simple, the temples for their gods were fantastic monuments. During the Archaic period, an architectural format was developed that provided the basis for temple architecture throughout the history and territories of ancient Greece. It consisted of a central room (derived in shape from the Mycenaean **megaron**) surrounded by a single or double row of columns. This room, called the **cella**, usually housed the cult statue of the god or goddess to whom the temple was dedicated. The overall shape of the temple was rectangular, and it had a pitched roof.

There were three styles, or orders, in Greek architecture: the **Doric**, **Ionic**, and **Corinthian**. The Doric order, which originated on the Greek mainland, was the earliest, simplest, and most commonly used. The more ornate Ionic order was introduced by architects from Asia Minor and was generally reserved for smaller temples. The Corinthian order, differentiated from the Ionic by its intricate column capital, was not used widely in Greece but became a favorite design of Roman architects, who adopted it in the second century BCE. Figure **14-4** compares the Doric, Ionic, and Corinthian orders and illustrates the basic parts of the temple facade.

The major weight-bearing elements of the temple are cylindrical columns composed of drums stacked on top of one another and fitted with dowels. They sit on either a platform (**stylobate**) or a base and helped support the roof. The main vertical body, or shaft, of the column is crowned by a **capital** that marks a transition from the shaft to a horizontal member (the **entablature**) that directly bears the weight of the roof. In the Doric order, the capital is simple and cushionlike. In the Ionic order, it consists of a scroll or volute similar to those seen on the François Vase (Fig. 14-2). The Corinthian capital is by far the most elaborate, consisting of an all-around carving of overlapping acanthus leaves. The columns directly support the entablature, which is divided into three parts: the **architrave**, **frieze**, and **cornice**. The architrave of the Doric order is a solid, undecorated horizontal band, whereas those of the Ionic and Corinthian orders are subdivided into three narrower horizontal bands. The frieze, which sits directly above the architrave, is typically carved with relief sculpture.

The Doric frieze is divided into sections called **triglyphs** and **metopes**. The triglyphs are carved panels consisting of three vertical elements. These alternate with panels that were filled with figurative sculpture carved in relief. The Ionic and Corinthian friezes, by contrast, were carved with a continuous band of figures or—particularly in the Corinthian order—repetitive, stylized motifs.

The Ionic order liberated sculptors from the constraints of the square spaces that defined the Doric frieze, allowing the figures and the narrative to flow more freely. The topmost element of the entablature is called a **cornice** and, together with the diagonals of the **raking cornice**, it forms a frame for the **pediment**. The triangular spaces of the pediments, formed by the slope of the roof lines at the short ends of the temple, was also decorated with figurative sculpture.

The Doric order originated in the Archaic period, but it attained perfection in the buildings of the Classical period. In some buildings, like the Parthenon, the Doric and Ionic orders are combined. The Corinthian order, although developed by the Greeks, was used more universally by the Romans.

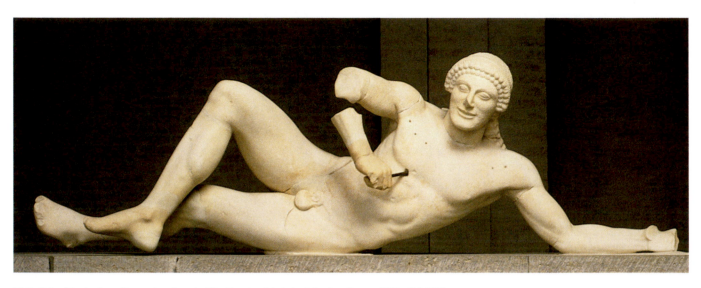

14-5 *Dying Warrior*, from the west pediment of the Temple of Aphaia at Aegina, Greece (500–490 BCE). Marble. Approx. 5'2½" long. Staatliche Antikensammlungen und Glyptothek, Munich, Germany.

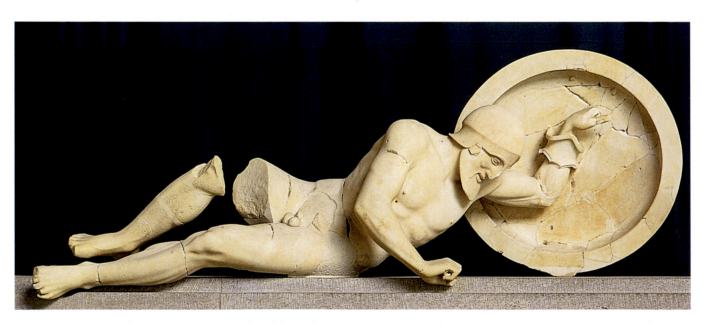

14-6 *Fallen Warrior*, from the east pediment of the Temple of Aphaia at Aegina, Greece (490–480 BCE). Marble. Approx. 6'1" long. Staatliche Antikensammlungen und Glyptothek, Munich, Germany.

SCULPTURE In the Archaic period, sculpture emerged as a principal art form. In addition to sculptural decoration for buildings, freestanding, life-size, and larger-than-life-size statues were created. Such monumental sculpture was probably inspired by Egyptian figures that Greek travelers would have seen during the early Archaic period.

In Greek temples, the nonstructural members of the building were often ornamented with sculpture. These included the frieze and pediment. Because early Archaic sculptors were forced to work within relatively tight spaces, the figures from this period are often cramped and cumbersome. However, toward the end of the Archaic period, artists compensated for the irregularity of the spaces by arranging figures in poses that corresponded to the peculiarities of the architectural element. For example, the *Dying Warrior* (Fig. **14-5**) from the Temple of Aphaia at Aegina was positioned to fit into one of the angles of its west pediment. The figure is based somewhat on the observation of nature, although conventions dominate—the thick-lidded eyes and stylized hair, overly defined lips that purse in an artificial "smile," and linear patterns that define musculature.

Building projects like the Temple of Aphaia took years to complete, and the hands of artists of different styles were involved. Compare the warrior from the west pediment with one from the east pediment of the same building (Fig. **14-6**). This warrior's feet would have been wedged into the left corner of the pediment; his body fans out toward the shield, corresponding to the dimensions of the angle. Some conventions remain, like the thick-lidded eyes, subtle "smile," and unnaturally pointed beard. The body may not be wholly realistic, but the patterns that play over the surface of the warrior in the west pediment have been virtually eliminated as the artist aims for a convincing representation of muscles, bones, and tendons. The work reveals a marvelous attention to detail, both physical and psychological. It is, after all, a pitiful sight. The warrior, wounded in battle, crashes down upon the field with his shield in hand. He struggles to lift himself with his right arm, but to no avail. The hopelessness of the situation is echoed in the helplessness of the left arm, which remains trapped in the grasp of the cumbersome shield. It hangs there useless, the band of the shield restricting its flow of blood. It is an emotionally wrenching scene, although (or perhaps because) the trauma is not revealed in the face of the warrior. It remains masklike, bound to the restraining conventions of the Archaic style.

The *Fallen Warrior* from Aegina was created during the last years of the Archaic period and represents a stylistic transition to the Classical era. The history of Archaic Greek sculpture, however, began more than a century earlier, about 600 BCE, with large, freestanding figures. Some of the earliest of these are called **kouros figures**, devotional or funerary statues of young men. Figure **14-7** is typical of these figures.

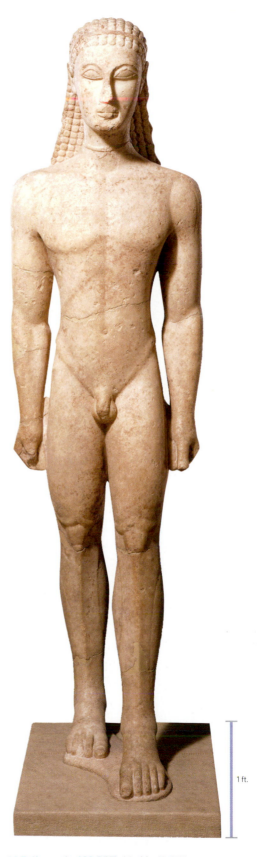

1 ft.

14-7 Kouros (c. 600 BCE). Marble. H: 6'4". The Metropolitan Museum of Art, NY.

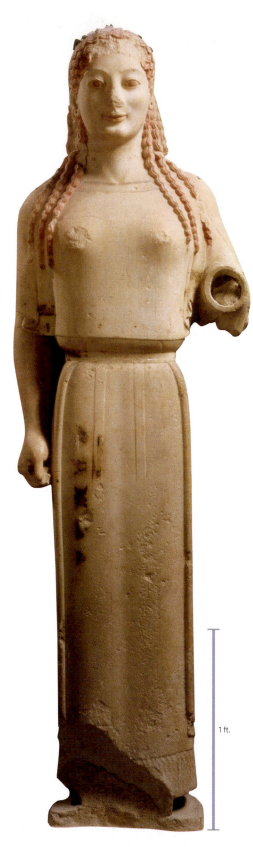

As in Egyptian sculptures, the arms lie close to the body, the fists are clenched, and one leg advances slightly. But the kouroi (plural) are different in a principal way: the stone was carved away from the body, releasing it from the block. These male figures are also depicted in the nude. The musculature is full and thick, and emphasized by harsh, patterned lines. The kneecaps, groin muscles, rib cage, and pectoral muscles are all flexed unrealistically. The head has also been treated according to the artistic conventions of the day. The hair is stylized and intricate in pattern. The eyes are thick-lidded and stare directly forward.

The youth has very high cheekbones and clearly defined lips that appear to curl upward in a smile. This facial expression, which we also saw on the warriors of the Temple of Aphaia, seems to have been an Archaic convention and thus is called an "Archaic smile." Kouroi were found in cemeteries, where they replaced large vases as grave markers. They were also used as votive sculptures (recall the votive figures of Tell Asmar, Fig. 13-5). In their stately repose and grand presence, these figures might impress us as gods rather than mortals. One is reminded of the oft-repeated statement, "The Greeks made their gods into men and their men into gods."

The female counterpart to the kouros is the **kore**. Unlike the kouros, the kore is clothed and often embellished with intricate carved detail. The *Peplos Kore* (Fig. **14-8**)—so named because the garment the model wears is a **peplos**, or heavy woolen wrap—is one of the most enchanting images in Greek art, partly because touches of paint remain on the sculpture, giving it a lifelike gaze and sensitive expression. We tend to think of Greek architecture and sculpture as pristine and glistening in their pure white surfaces, but most sculpture was painted with subtle colors. Architectural sculpture was embellished with red, blue, yellow, green, black, and sometimes gold pigments. None of this painted decoration remains on temple sculpture. However, statues and wooden panels were painted with encaustic, a more durable and permanent medium combining pigment and wax.

The beauty of the *Peplos Kore* lies in its simplicity. The woman's body is composed of graceful columnar lines echoed in the delicate play of the long braids that grace her shoulders. As with kouroi, she remains close to, but not strictly bound to, the marble block from which she was carved. Her right arm is attached to her side at the wrist, but the left arm, now missing, extended outward and probably held a symbolic offering. Although the function of the kore figures is uncertain, they have been interpreted as votive sculptures because many have been found among the ruins of temples. These architectural and freestanding sculptures were all made of marble. Although expensive, it was readily available, and some of the finest marble in the world came from quarries near Athens.

1 ft.

14-8 *Peplos Kore* (c. 530 BCE). Marble. H: 48". Acropolis Museum, Athens, Greece.

The late Archaic period produced significant works of art and architecture against the backdrop of brutal war with the Persians. We encountered the might of the Persian Empire in Chapter 13. By the late fifth century BCE, it appeared as if that empire would consume all of Greece. After horrible, violent losses, the Greeks defeated the Persians in a decisive battle on the plain of Marathon and captured a naval victory at Salamis. Greek pride surged and a Western identity was formed—one that stood in self-conscious opposition to the perceived barbarism of the Persians and their Asian civilization.

Early Classical Art

The change from the Archaic to the Classical period coincided with the Greek victory over the Persians at Salamis in 480 BCE. The Greek mood was elevated after this feat, and a new sense of unity among the city-states prevailed, propelling the country into its "Golden Age." Athens, which was sacked by the Persians, became the center for all important postwar activity and the revival of the arts. The style of Early Classical art is marked by a power and austerity that reflected what were seen as Greek traits responsible for the defeat of the Persians. Although Early Classical sculpture developed beyond Archaic stylizations, some of the rigidity of the earlier period remains. The Early Classical style is therefore sometimes referred to as the Severe style.

SCULPTURE The most significant development in Early Classical art was the introduction of implied movement in figurative sculpture. This went hand in hand with the artist's keener observation of nature. One of the most widely copied works of this period, which encompasses these new elements, is the *Diskobolos* (Fig. **14-9**), or Discus Thrower, by Myron. Like most Greek monumental sculpture, it survives only in a marble Roman copy after the bronze original. The life-size statue depicts an event from the Olympic Games—the discus throw. The athlete, a young man in his prime, is caught by the artist at the moment when the arm stops its swing backward and prepares to sling forward to release the discus. His muscles are tensed as he reaches for the strength to release the object. His torso intersects the arc of his extended arms, resembling an arrow pulled taut on a bow. It is

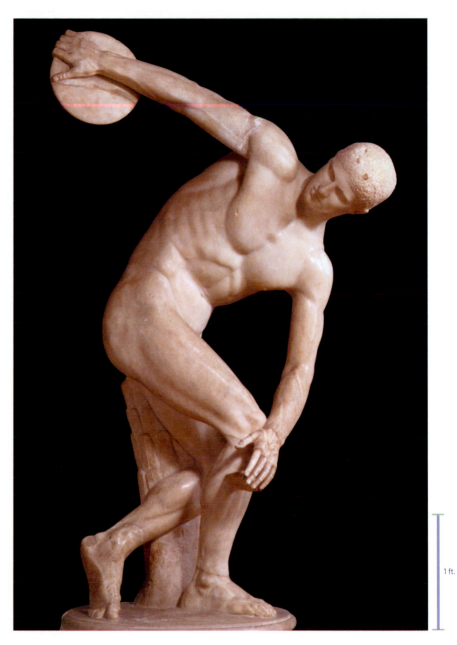

14-9 MYRON. *Diskobolos* (Discus Thrower) (c. 450 BCE). Roman marble copy after bronze original. H: 5'1". Palazzo Vecchio, Florence, Italy.

an image of pent-up energy at the moment before release. As in most of Greek Classical art, there is a balance between motion and stability, between emotion and restraint.

Classical Art

Greek sculpture and architecture reached their height of perfection during the Classical period. Greece embarked upon a period of peace—albeit short-lived—and turned its attention to rebuilding its monuments and advancing art, drama, and

Raphael is a great master. Velázquez is a great master. El Greco is a great master,
but the secret of plastic beauty is located at a greater distance:
in the Greeks at the time of Pericles.
—Pablo Picasso

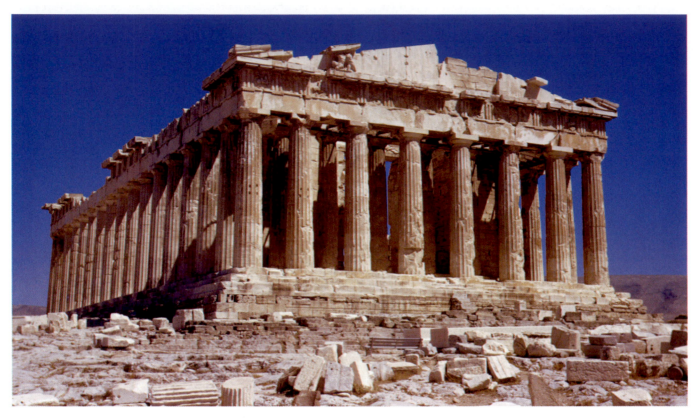

14-10 ICTINOS AND CALLICRATES. The Parthenon on the Acropolis, Athens, Greece (448–432 BCE).

music. The dominating force behind these accomplishments in Athens was the dynamic statesman Pericles. His reputation was recounted centuries after his death by the Greek historian Plutarch. On the one hand, Plutarch described the anger of the Greek city-states at Pericles' use of funds that had been set aside for mutual protection to pay for his ambitious Athenian building program. On the other hand, Plutarch wrote glowingly about postwar Athens: "in its beauty, each work was, even at that time, ancient, and yet, in its perfection, each looks even at the present time as if it were fresh and newly built. . . . It is as if some ever-flowering life and unaging spirit had been infused into the creation of these works."

ARCHITECTURE After the Persians destroyed the Acropolis, the Athenians refused to rebuild their shrines with the fallen stones that the enemy had desecrated. What followed was a massive building campaign under the direction of Pericles. Work began first on the temple that was sacred to the goddess **Athena**, protector of Athens. This temple, the

Parthenon (Fig. **14-10**), became one of the most influential buildings in the history of architecture.

Constructed by the architects Ictinos and Callicrates, the Parthenon stands as the most accomplished representative of the Doric order, although it does include some Ionic elements. A single row of Doric columns, now gracefully proportioned, surrounds a two-roomed cella that housed a treasury and a 40-foot-high statue of Athena made of ivory and gold. At first glance, the architecture appears austere, with its rigid progression of vertical elements crowned by the strong horizontal of its entablature. Yet few of the building's lines are strictly vertical or horizontal. For example, the stylobate, or top step of the platform from which the columns rise, is not straight, but curves downward toward the ends. This convex shape is echoed in the entablature. The columns are not exactly vertical, but rather tilt inward. They are not evenly spaced; the intervals between the corner columns are narrower. The shafts of the columns also differ from one another. The corner columns have a wider diameter, for example. In addition, the shaft of each column swells in diameter as it rises from the base, narrowing once again before reaching the capital. This swelling is called **entasis**.

The reasons for these variations are not known for certain, although there have been several hypotheses. Some art historians have suggested that the change from straight to curved lines is functional. A convex stylobate, for example, might make drainage easier. Others have suggested that the variations are meant to compensate for perceptual distortions on the part of the viewer that would make straight lines look curved from a distance. Regardless of the actual motive, we can assume that the designers of the Parthenon sought an integrated and organic look to their building. The wide base and relatively narrower roof give the appearance of a structure that is anchored firmly to the ground yet growing dramatically from it. Although it has a grandeur based on a kind of austerity, it also has a lively plasticity. It appears as if the Greeks conceived their architecture as large, freestanding sculpture.

The subsequent history of the Parthenon is interesting and shocking. It was used as a Byzantine church, a Roman Catholic church, and a mosque. The Parthenon survived more or less intact, although altered by these successive functions, until the seventeenth century, when the Turks used it as an ammunition dump in their war against the Venetians. Venetian rockets hit the bull's-eye, and the center portion of the temple was blown out in the explosion. The cella still lies in ruins, although fortunately the exterior columns and entablatures were not beyond repair.

SCULPTURE The sculptor Phidias was commissioned by Pericles to oversee the entire sculptural program of the Parthenon. Although he concentrated his own efforts on creating the ivory and gold statue of Athena, his assistants followed his style closely. The Phidian style is characterized by a lightness of touch, attention to realistic detail, contrast of textures, and fluidity and spontaneity of line and movement.

As on other Doric temples, the sculpted surfaces of the Parthenon were confined to the friezes and the pediments. The subjects of the Doric frieze were battles between the Lapiths and the Centaurs, the Greeks and the Amazons, and the gods and the giants. In addition, the Parthenon had a continuous, inner Ionic frieze. This was carved with scenes from the Panathenaic procession, an event that took place every four years when the peplos of the statue of Athena was changed. The pediments depicted the birth of Athena and the contest between Athena and Poseidon for the city of Athens.

The *Three Goddesses* (Fig. **14-11**), a figural group from the corner of the east pediment, is typical of the Phidian style. The bodies of the goddesses are weighty and well articulated, and their poses and gestures are naturalistic. The drapery falls over the bodies in realistic folds, and there is a marvelous contrast of textures between the heavier cloth that wraps around the legs and the more diaphanous fabric covering the upper torsos. The thinner drapery clings to the body as if wet, following the contours of the flesh. The intricate play of the linear folds renders a tactile quality not seen in art before this time. The lines both gently envelop the individual figures and integrate them in a dynamically flowing composition.

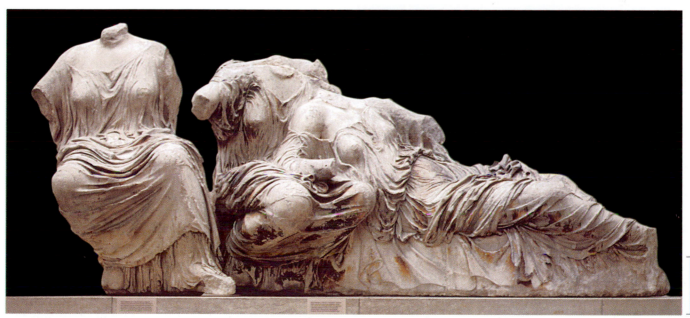

1 ft.

14-11 *The Three Goddesses*, from the east pediment of the Parthenon (c. 438–431 BCE). Marble. Height of center figure: 4'7".
British Museum, London, England.

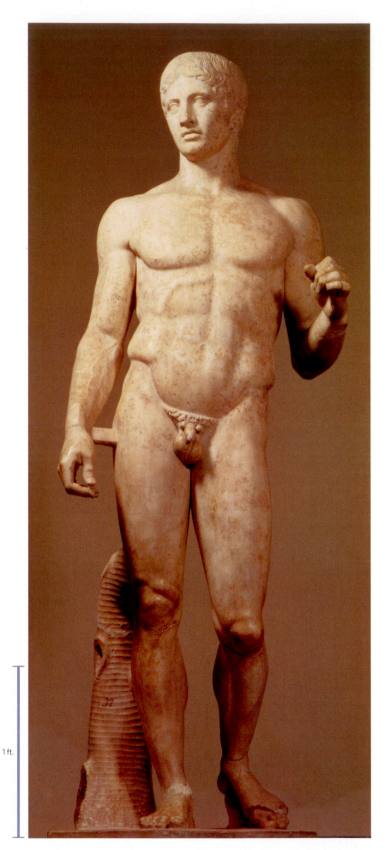

1 ft.

14-12 POLYKLEITOS. *Doryphoros* (Spear Bearer) (c. 450–440 BCE). Marble. Roman copy after Greek original. H: 6'6". Museo Archeologico Nazionale, Naples, Italy.

As mentioned previously, Greece had at one time come under Turkish rule. Some of the Parthenon sculptures were taken down by Lord Elgin between 1801 and 1803 while he was British ambassador to Constantinople. He sold them to the British government, who put them on display at the British Museum. Although there has been prolonged controversy concerning their return to Greece, there is no doubt that Lord Elgin saved the marbles from utter destruction.

Some of the greatest freestanding sculpture of the Classical period was created by a rival of Phidias named Polykleitos. His favorite medium was bronze, and his preferred subject was athletes. As with most Greek sculpture, we know his work primarily from marble Roman copies of the bronze originals. Polykleitos's work differed markedly from that of Phidias. Whereas the Parthenon sculptor emphasized the reality of appearances and aimed to delight the senses through textural contrasts, Polykleitos's statues were based on reason and intellect. Rather than mimic nature, he tried to perfect nature by developing a canon of proportions from which he would derive his "ideal" figures.

Polykleitos's most famous sculpture is the *Doryphoros* (Fig. **14-12**), or Spear Bearer. The artist has "idealized" the athletic figure—that is, made it more perfect and more beautiful—by imposing on it a set of laws relating part to part (for example, the entire body is equal in height to eight heads). Although some of Phidias's spontaneity is lost, the result is an almost godlike image of grandeur and strength. One of the most significant elements of Polykleitos's style is the **weight-shift principle**. The athlete rests his weight on the right leg, which is planted firmly on the ground. It forms a strong vertical that is echoed in the vertical of the relaxed arm. These are counterbalanced by a relaxed left leg bent at the knee and a tensed left arm bent at the elbow. Tension and relaxation of the limbs are balanced across the body *diagonally*. The relaxed arm opposes the relaxed leg, and the tensed arm is opposite the tensed, weight-bearing leg. The weight-shift principle lends naturalism to the figure. Rather than face forward in a rigid pose, as do the kouroi, the *Doryphoros* stands comfortably at rest. The ease and naturalism, however, were derived from a compulsive balancing of opposing parts.

VASE PAINTING The weight-shift principle and the naturalistic use of implied movement can also be seen in Classical vase painting such as the *Argonaut Krater* (Fig. **14-13**), a red-figure vase by the so-called Niobid Painter. In the Dipylon krater and the François Vase, the human figures were confined to registers (see Figs. 14-1 and 14-2). On later vases, these registers were eliminated, making the broad field of the vase available for the portrayal of the human figure in a variety of positions. Until the Classical period, though, the figures were placed in a friezelike arrangement. That is, all of the heads were pretty much on one level, and depth was limited.

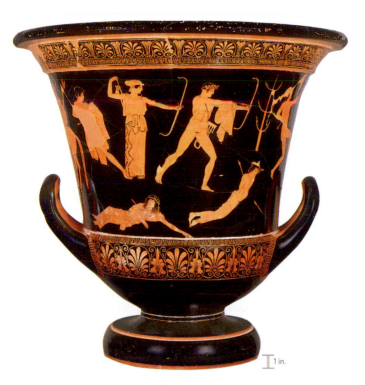

14-13 NIOBID PAINTER. *Argonaut Krater* (c. 460 BCE). Ceramic. H: 24¼".
Louvre, Paris, France.

The Niobid Painter, by contrast, attempted to create a sense of three-dimensional space by outlining a foreground, middle ground, and background. This was a noble attempt at realism, based on optical perception, but ultimately it fails because the artist did not shrink the sizes of the background figures to suggest distance. The ability to arrange figures in space convincingly came later with the development of perspective.

Vase painting was not the only two-dimensional art form in ancient Greece. There was also wall, or **mural painting**, none of which has survived. It is believed, however, that the Romans copied Greek wall painting, as they did sculpture, and it is thus possible to conjecture what Greek painting looked like by examining surviving Roman wall painting (Fig. 14-21).

Late Classical Art

SCULPTURE The Late Classical period brought a more humanistic and naturalistic style, with emphasis on the expression of emotion. The stocky muscularity of the Polykleitan ideal was replaced by a more languid sensuality and graceful proportions. One of the major proponents of this new style was Praxiteles. His works show a lively spirit that was lacking in some of the more austere sculptures of the Classical period.

The *Hermes and Dionysos* of Praxiteles (Fig. **14-14**), interestingly, is the only undisputed original work we have by the

Greek masters of the Classical era. Unlike most other sculptors who favored bronze, Praxiteles excelled in carving. His ability to translate harsh stone surfaces into subtly modeled flesh was unsurpassed. We need only compare his figural group with the *Doryphoros* to witness the changes that had taken place since the Classical period. Hermes is delicately carved, and his musculature is realistically depicted, suggesting the preference of nature as a model over adherence to a rigid, predefined canon. The messenger-god holds the infant Dionysos, the god of wine, in his left arm, which is propped

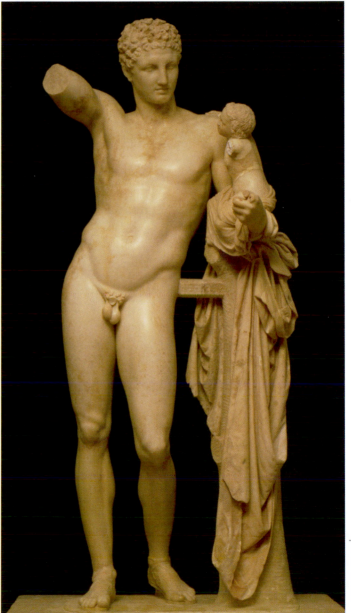

14-14 PRAXITELES. *Hermes and Dionysos* (c. 330–320 BCE). Marble. H: 7'1".
Archaeological Museum, Olympia, Greece.

up by a tree trunk covered with a drape. His right arm is broken above the elbow but reaches out in front of him. It has been suggested that Hermes once held a bunch of grapes toward which the infant was reaching.

Praxiteles' skill in depicting variations in texture was extraordinary. Note, for example, the differences between the solid, toned muscles of the man and the soft, cuddly flesh of the child; or rough, curly hair against the flawless, ivory skin; or the deeply carved, billowing drapery alongside the subtly modeled flesh. The easy grace of the sculpture comes from applying a double weight-shift principle. Hermes shifts his weight from the right leg to the left arm, resting it on the tree. This position causes a sway which is called an **S curve**, because the contours of the body form an S shape around an imaginary vertical axis.

Perhaps most remarkable is the emotional content of the sculpture. The aloof quality of Classical statuary is replaced with a touching scene between the two gods. Hermes' facial expression as he teases the child is one of pride and amusement. Dionysos, on the other hand, exhibits typical infant behavior—he is all hands and reaching impatiently for something to eat. There remains a certain restraint to the movement and to the expressiveness, but it is definitely on the wane. In the Hellenistic period, that classical balance will no longer pertain, and the emotion present in Praxiteles' sculpture will reach new peaks.

The most important and innovative sculptor to follow Praxiteles was Lysippos. He introduced a new canon of proportions that resulted in more slender and graceful figures, departing from the stockiness of Polykleitos and assuming the fluidity of Praxiteles. Most important, however, was his new concept of the motion of figure in space. All of the sculptures that we have seen so far have had a two-dimensional perspective. That is, the whole of the work can be viewed from a single point of view, standing in front of the sculpture. This is not the case in works such as the *Apoxyomenos* (Fig. **14-15**) by Lysippos. The figure's arms envelop the surrounding space. The athlete is scraping oil and grime from his body with a dull knifelike implement. This stance forces the viewer to walk around the sculpture to appreciate its details. Rather than adhere to a single plane, as even the S-curve figure of *Hermes* does, the *Apoxyomenos* seems to spiral around a vertical axis.

Lysippos's reputation was almost unsurpassed. In fact, his work was so widely admired that Alexander the Great, the Macedonian king who spread Greek culture throughout the Near East, chose him as his court sculptor. It is said that Lysippos was the only sculptor permitted to execute portraits of Alexander. Years after the *Apoxyomenos* was created, it was still seen as a magnificent work of art. Pliny, a Roman writer on the arts, recounted an amusing story about the sculpture:

> Lysippos made more statues than any other artist, being, as we said, very prolific in the art; among them was a youth scraping himself with a strigil, which Marcus Agrippa dedicated in front of his baths and which the Emperor Tiberius was astonishingly fond of. [Tiberius] was, in fact, unable to restrain himself in this case and had it moved to his own bedroom, substituting another statue in its place. When,

14-15 LYSIPPOS. *Apoxyomenos* (c. 330 BCE). Roman marble copy after a bronze original. H: 6'6¾". Musei Vaticani, Rome, Italy.

1 ft.

however, the indignation of the Roman people was so great that it demanded, by an uproar, that the Apoxyomenos be replaced, the Emperor, although he had fallen in love with it, put it back.[1]

Hellenistic Art

Greece entered the Hellenistic period under the reign of Alexander the Great. His father had conquered the democratic city-states, and Alexander had been raised amid the art and culture of Greece. When he ascended the throne, he conquered Persia, Egypt, and the entire Near East, bringing with him his beloved Greek culture, or Hellenism. With the vastness of Alexander's empire, the significance of the city of Athens as an artistic and cultural center waned.

Hellenistic art is characterized by excessive, almost theatrical emotion and the use of illusionistic effects to heighten realism. In three-dimensional art, the space surrounding the figures is treated as an extension of the viewer's space, at times narrowing the fine line between art and reality.

---

[1] J. J. Pollitt, *The Art of Greece 1400–31 BCE: Sources and Documents* (Englewood Cliffs, NJ: Prentice-Hall, 1965), 144.

SCULPTURE *The Dying Gaul* (Fig. **14-16**) illustrates the Hellenistic artist's preoccupation with high drama and unleashed passion. Unlike the *Fallen Warrior* (Fig. 14-6), in which the viewer has to extract the emotion by piecing together scattered realistic details that suggest a narrative, *The Dying Gaul* presents all of the elements that communicate the pathos of the work. Bleeding from a large wound in his side, the fallen "barbarian" attempts to sustain his weight on a weakened right arm. His head, rendered with coarse, disheveled hair, hangs down hopelessly. He has lost his battle and is now about to lose his life. Strength seems to drain out of his body and into the ground, even as we watch. Our perspective is that of a theatergoer; the Gaul seems to be sitting on a stage. Although the artist intended to evoke pity and emotion from the viewer, the figure's melodramatic pose and his placement on a stagelike platform detach the viewer from the event. We tend to see the scene as well-acted drama rather than cruel reality.

Hellenistic artists were often drawn to dramatic subjects. They did not focus on a balance between emotion and restraint but portrayed human excess. In the midst of this theatricality, however, another trend in Hellenistic art reflected the simplicity and idealism of the Classical period. The harsh realism and passionate emotion of the Hellenistic artist could not be further in spirit from the serene and

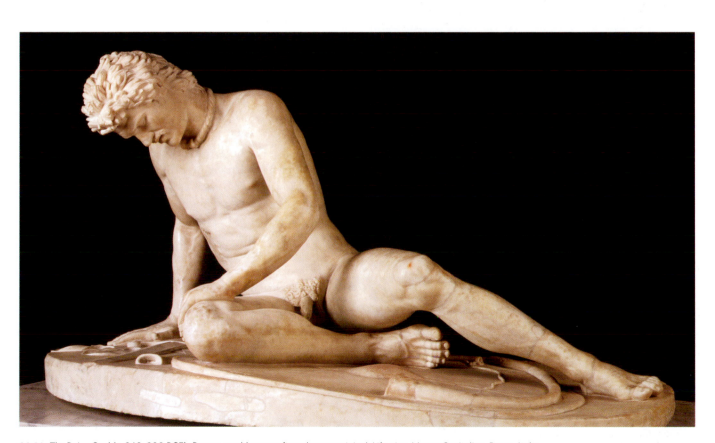

14-16 *The Dying Gaul* (c. 240–200 BCE). Roman marble copy after a bronze original. Life-size. Museo Capitolino, Rome, Italy.

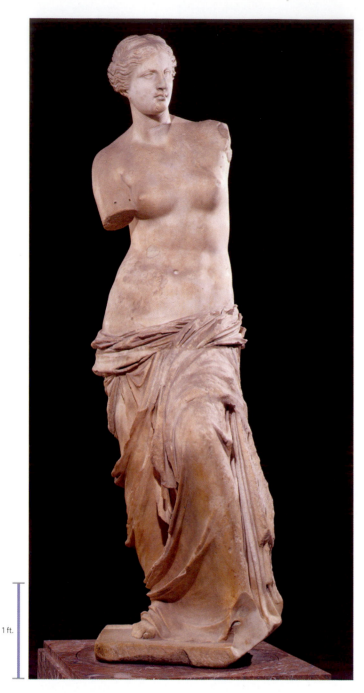

1 ft.

14-17 ALEXANDROS OF ANTIOCH-ON-THE-MEANDER. *Aphrodite* from Melos, Greece (*Venus de Milo*) (c. 150–125 BCE). Marble. H: 6'7". Louvre, Paris, France.

powerful and growing Roman state. It has been said that "all roads lead to Rome," and so will this chapter. First, however, let us examine the art of the Etruscans, a civilization on the Italian peninsula that predated that of the Romans.

THE ETRUSCANS

The center of power of the Roman state was the peninsula of Italy, but the Romans did not gain supremacy over this area until the fourth century BCE, when they began to conquer the Etruscans. The Italian peninsula was inhabited by many peoples, but the Etruscan civilization was the most significant one before that of ancient Rome. The Etruscans had a long and interesting history, dating back to around 700 BCE, the period of transition from the Geometric to the Archaic period in Greece. They were not an indigenous people but are believed to have come from Asia Minor. This link may explain some similarities between Etruscan art and culture and that of Eastern countries.

Etruria and Greece had some things in common. Both were great sea powers. Both were divided into independent city-states. The Etruscans even borrowed motifs and styles from the art of Greece. There is one more similarity between the two civilizations: Etruria also fell prey to the Romans. They were no match for Roman organization, especially because neighboring city-states never came to one another's aid in a time of crisis. By 88 BCE, the Romans had vanquished the last of the Etruscans.

Architecture

Although the Etruscans constructed temples, none survive beyond their foundations because they were constructed of impermanent materials such as wood and mud brick. Yet in what almost seems a throwback to ancient Egypt, underground tombs, carved out of bedrock, suggest the lives and habits of the Etruscan people. The interiors were constructed to resemble those of domestic dwellings. The walls were covered with hundreds of everyday items carved in low relief, including such things as kitchen utensils and weapons. Like the Egyptians, and unlike the Greeks, the Etruscans apparently wanted to duplicate their earthly environments in their funerary monuments.

Sculpture

Much sculpture of bronze and clay has survived from these Etruscan tombs, and we have learned a great deal about the Etruscan people from these finds. For example, even though no architecture survives, we know what the exterior of domestic dwellings looked like from the clay models of

idealized form of the *Aphrodite of Melos* (Fig. **14-17**), often called the *Venus de Milo*. This contradictory style owes more to the artistic legacy of Praxiteles than to the contemporary illusionism of the sculptor of *The Dying Gaul*.

In 146 BCE, the Romans sacked Corinth, a Greek city on the Peloponnesus, after which Greek power waned. Both the territory and the culture of Greece were assimilated by the

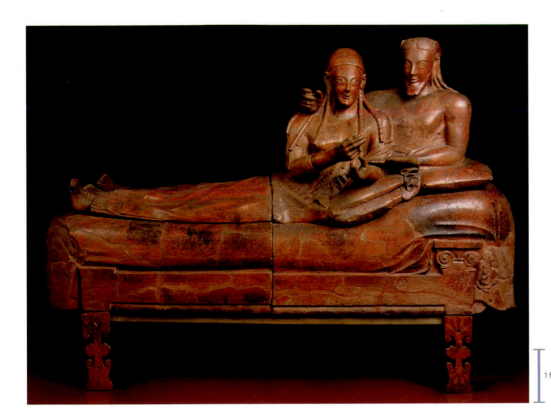

1 ft.

homes that served as **cinerary urns**. We have also been able to gain insight into the personalities of the Etruscan people through their figurative sculpture, particularly that found on the lids of their **sarcophagi**.

The Sarcophagus from Cerveteri (Fig. **14-18**) is a translation into terra-cotta of the banquet scenes of which the Etruscans were so fond. A man and wife are represented reclining on a lounge and appear to be enjoying the dinner entertainment. Their gestures are animated and naturalistic, even though their facial features and hair are rigidly stylized. These stylizations, especially the thick-lidded eyes, resemble Greek sculpture of the Archaic period and were most likely influenced by it. However, the serenity and severity of Archaic Greek art are absent. The Etruscans appear to be as relaxed, happy, and fun loving in death as they were in life.

ROME

In about 500 BCE, the Roman Republic was established, and it would last some four centuries. The Roman arm of strength reached into northern Italy, conquering the Etruscans, and eventually stretched in all directions, gaining supremacy over Greece, western Europe, northern Africa, and parts of the Near East (Map **14-1**). No longer was this the republican city of Rome flexing its muscles—this was the Roman Empire.

Roman art combined native talent, needs, and styles with other artistic sources, particularly those of Greece. The art that followed the absorption of Greece into the Roman

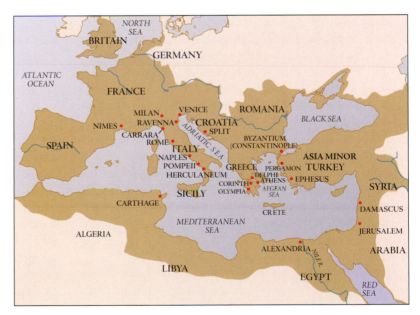

Map **14-1** The Roman Empire (2nd century CE).

Empire is thus often called Greco-Roman. It was fashionable for Romans to own—or at the very least, have copies of—Greek works of art. This tendency gave the Romans a reputation as mere imitators of Greek art, a simplistic view laid waste by scholars of Roman art history. A marvelous, unabashed eclecticism pervaded much of Roman art, resulting in vigorous and sometimes unpredictable combinations of motifs. The Romans were also fond of a harsh, almost trompe l'oeil, realism in their portrait sculpture, which had not been seen before their time. They were master builders (the inventors of concrete!), who created some of the grandest monuments in the history of architecture. Because of the vast expanse of the empire, these structures, or their remains, can be seen today almost everywhere.

The Republican Period

The ancient city of Rome was built on seven hills to the east of the Tiber River and served as the central Italian base from which the Romans would come to control most of the known world in the West. Their illustrious beginnings are traced to the **Republican period**, which followed upon the heels of their final victories over the Etruscans and lasted until the death of Julius Caesar in 44 BCE. The Roman system of government during this time was based on two parties, although the distribution of power was not equitable. The **patricians** ruled the country and could be likened to an aristocratic class. They came from important Roman families and later were characterized as nobility. The majority of the Roman population, however, belonged to the **plebeian class**. Members of this class were common folk and had less say in running the government. They were, however, permitted to elect their patrician representatives. During the Republican period, the famed Roman senate became the governing body of Rome. The rulings of the senate were responsible for the numerous Roman conquests that would expand its borders into a seemingly boundless empire.

By virtue of its construction, however, the republic was doomed to crumble. It was never a true democracy. The patricians became richer and more powerful as a result of the plundering of vanquished nations. The lower classes, on the other hand, demanded more and more privileges and resented the wealth and influence of the aristocracy.

After a series of successful military campaigns and the quelling of internal strife in the republic, Julius Caesar emerged as dictator of the Roman Empire. Under Caesar, important territories were accumulated, and Roman culture reached a peak of refinement. The language of Greece, its literature, and its religion were adopted along with its artistic styles.

On March 15 (the ides of March) in 44 BCE, Julius Caesar was assassinated by members of the senate. With his death came the absolute end of the Roman Republic and the beginnings of the Roman Empire under his successor, Augustus.

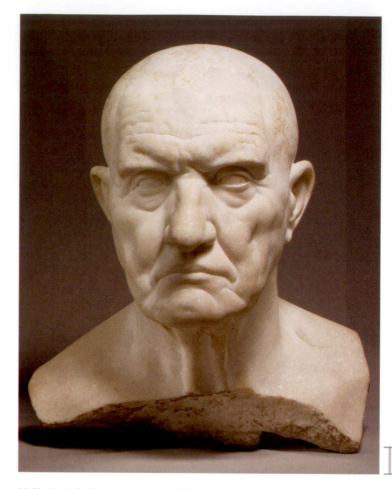

1 in.

14-19 *Head of a Roman* (1st century BCE). Marble. H: 14 ⅜". The Metropolitan Museum of Art, NY.

SCULPTURE Although much Roman art is derived in style from that of Greece, its portrait sculpture originated in a tradition that was wholly Italian. In this sculpture, we witness Rome's unique contribution to the arts—that of realism.

It was customary for Romans to make wax death masks of their loved ones and to keep them around the house, as we do photographs. At times, the wax masks were translated into a more permanent medium, such as bronze or terracotta. The process of making a death mask produced intricately detailed images that recorded every ripple and crevice of the face. Because these sculptures were made from the actual faces and heads of the subjects, their realism is unsurpassed. The *Head of a Roman* (Fig. **14-19**) records the facial features of an old man, from his bald head and protruding ears to his furrowed brow and almost cavernous cheeks. No attempt has been made by the artist to idealize the figure. Nor does one get the sense, on the other hand, that the artist emphasized the hideousness of the character. Rather, it serves more as an unimpassioned and uninvolved record of the existence of one man.

With the Greeks there's always an aesthetic element. I prefer the virile realism of Rome,
which doesn't embellish. The truthfulness of Roman art—it's like their buildings,
but all the more beautiful in their genuine simplicity.
—Pablo Picasso

ARCHITECTURE Rome's greatest contribution lay in architecture, although the most significant buildings, monuments, and civic structures were constructed during the Empire period. Architecture of the Republican period can be stylistically linked to both Greek and Etruscan precedents, as can be seen in the Temple of Fortuna Virilis (Fig. **14-20**). From the Greeks, the Romans adopted the Ionic order and post-and-lintel construction. From the Etruscans, they adopted the podium on which the temple stands, as well as the general plan of a wide cella extending to the side columns and a free portico in front. But there are Roman innovations as well. The column shafts, for example, are monolithic instead of being composed of drums stacked one on top of another. The columns along the sides of the temple are not freestanding but are engaged, or attached. Also, the frieze has no relief sculpture. The most marked difference between the temples of Greece and of Rome is the feeling that the Romans did not treat their buildings as sculpture. Instead, they designed them straightforwardly, emphasizing the relationship between form and function.

PAINTING The walls of Roman domestic dwellings were profusely decorated with frescoes and mosaics, some of which have survived the ravages of time. These murals are significant in themselves, but they also provide a missing stylistic link in the artistic remains of Greece. That country, you will recall, was prolific in mural painting, but none of it has survived. Roman wall painting passed through several phases, beginning in about 200 BCE and ending with the destruction of Pompeii by the eruption of Mount Vesuvius in 79 CE. The phases have been divided into four overlapping styles.

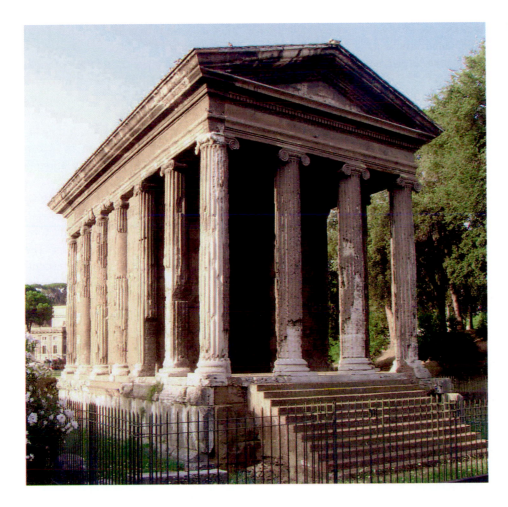

14-20 Temple of Fortuna Virilis, Rome, Italy (c. 75 BCE).

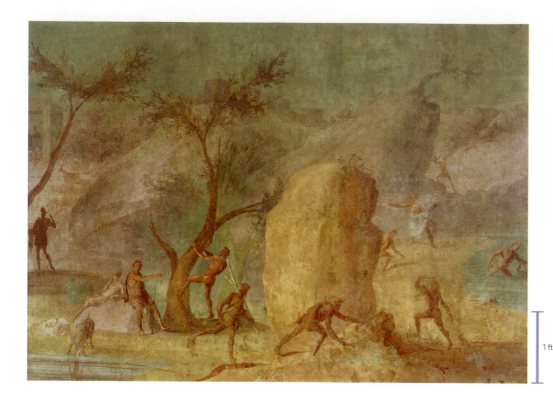

14-21 *Ulysses in the Land of the Lestrygonians*, from a Roman patrician house (50–40 BCE). Fresco. H: 60". Vatican Library, Rome, Italy.

1 ft.

Ulysses in the Land of the Lestrygonians (Fig. **14-21**) is an example of the **architectural style**, in which the illusion of retreating space is achieved through various pictorial devices. It is as if the viewer were looking through a window and into the distance. In a loosely sketched and liberally painted landscape, the artist recounts a scene from *The Odyssey*, in which Ulysses' men were devoured by a race of giant cannibals. The figures rush through the landscape in a variety of poses and gestures, their forms defined by contrasts of light and shade. They are portrayed convincingly in three-dimensional space through the use of **herringbone perspective**, a system whereby **orthogonals** vanish to a specific point along a vertical line that divides the canvas. It is believed that Greek wall painting was similar to the Roman architectural style.

With the death of Julius Caesar, a dictator, Rome entered its **Empire period** under the rule of Octavian Caesar—later called Augustus. This period marks the beginning of the Roman Empire, Roman rule by emperor, and the Pax Romana, a 200-year period of peace.

The Early Empire

With the birth of the empire, there emerged a desire to glorify the power of Rome by erecting splendid buildings and civic monuments. It was believed that art should be created in the service of the state. Although Roman expansionism left a wake of death and destruction, it was responsible for the construction of cities and the provision of basic human services in the conquered areas.

To their subject peoples, the Roman conquerors brought the benefits of urban planning, including apartment buildings, roads, and bridges. They also provided police and fire protection, water systems, sanitation, and food. They even built recreation facilities for the inhabitants, including gymnasiums, public baths, and theaters. Thus, even in defeat, many peoples reaped benefits because of the Roman desire to glorify the empire through visible contributions.

ARCHITECTURE Although the Romans adopted structural systems and certain motifs from Greek architecture, they introduced several innovations in building design. The most significant of these was the arch, and after the second century, the use of concrete to replace cut stone. The combination of these two elements resulted in domed and vaulted structures that were not part of the Greek repertory.

One of the most outstanding Roman civic projects is the **aqueduct**, which carried water over long distances. The Pont du Gard (Fig. **14-22**) in southern France carried water more than 30 miles and furnished each recipient with some 100 gallons of water per day. Constructed of three levels of arches, the largest of which spans about 82 feet, the aqueduct is some 900 feet long and 160 feet high. It had to slope down gradually over the long distance in order for gravity to carry the flow of water from the source.

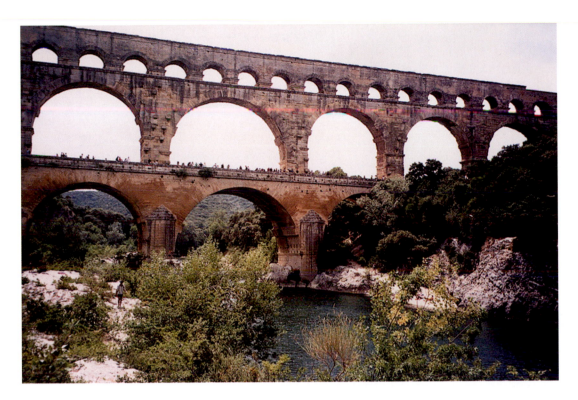

Although the aqueduct's reason for existence is purely functional, the Roman architect did not neglect design. The Pont du Gard has long been admired for both its simplicity and its grandeur. The two lower tiers of wide arches, for example, anchor the weighty structure to the earth, whereas the quickened pace of the smaller arches complements the rush of water along the top level. In works such as the Pont du Gard, form *follows* function.

One of the most impressive and famous monuments of ancient Rome is the Colosseum (see Fig. 14-24 in the Compare + Contrast feature). Dedicated in 80 CE, the structure consists of two back-to-back **amphitheaters** forming an oval arena, around which are tiers of marble bleachers.

Even in its present condition, having suffered years of pillaging and several earthquakes, the Colosseum is a spectacular sight. The structure is composed of three tiers of arches separated by engaged columns. (This combination of arch and column can also be seen in another type of Roman architectural monument—the triumphal arch (Fig. **14-23**). The Colosseum's lowest level, whose arches provided easy access and exit for the spectators, is punctuated by Doric columns. This order is the weightiest in appearance of the three

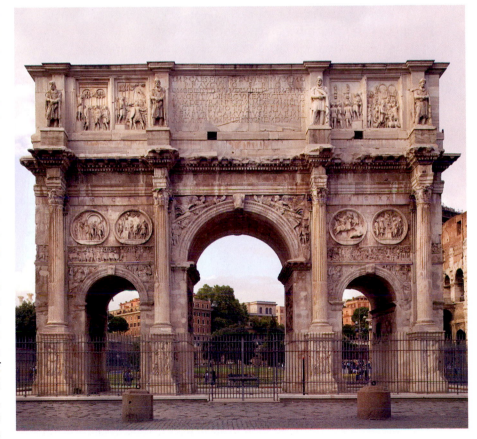

14-23 Arch of Constantine, Rome, Italy (312–315 CE).

STADIUM DESIGNS: THUMBS-UP OR THUMBS-DOWN?

THE SPORTS STADIUM HAS BECOME an inextricable part of our global landscape and our global culture. Just as diehard U.S. fans root for their football teams in the Louisiana Superdome, Olympic spectators half a world away cheer their country's athletes on to victory under a *super* dome likely erected just for the occasion. A city's bid for host of the Olympic Games can hinge entirely on the stadium it has to offer. These megastructures are not only functional—housing anticipated thousands—but they tend to become symbols of the cities, the teams, or now, the corporations who fund them. There's something about a space like this. The passion of friends and strangers and "fors and againsts" alike creates an odd sense of uniformity regardless of diversity. This observation has led some of history's political leaders to use—and abuse—the phenomenon of the stadium for their own propagandistic purposes.

The Colosseum (Fig. **14-24**) represented Rome at its best, but it also stood for Rome at its worst. A major feat of architectural engineering coupled with practical design, this vast stadium accommodated as many as 55,000 spectators who—thanks to 80 numbered entrances and stairways—could get from the street to their designated seats within 10 minutes. In rain or under blazing sun conditions, a gargantuan canvas could be hoisted from the arena up over the top of the stadium.

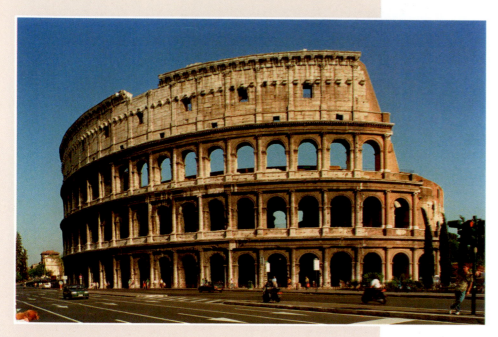

14-24 Colosseum, Rome, Italy (80 CE). Concrete.

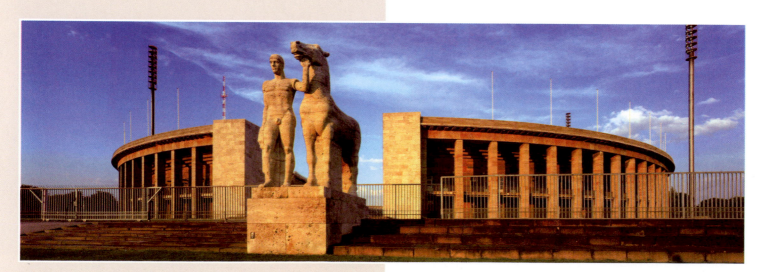

14-25 WERNER MARCH. Olympic Stadium, Berlin, Germany (1936).

Although the Colosseum was built for entertainment and festivals, its most notorious events ranged from sadistic contests between animals and men and grueling battles to the death between pairs of gladiators. If one combatant emerged alive but badly wounded, survival might depend on whether the emperor (or the crowd) gave the "thumbs-up" or the "thumbs-down."

As in much architecture, form can follow function and reflect and create meaning. In 1936, Adolf Hitler commissioned Germany's Olympic Stadium in Berlin (Fig. 14-25). Intended to showcase Aryan superiority (even though Jesse Owens, an African American, took four gold medals in track and field as Hitler watched), designer Werner March's stadium is the physical embodiment of Nazi ideals: order, authority, and the no-nonsense power of the state.

How different the message, noted critic Nicolai Ourussoff, when an architect uses design to cast off the shackles of "nationalist pretensions" and "notions of social conformity" in an effort to imbue the structure—and the country—with a sense of the future. Created in 1960 by Pier Luigi Nervi, the Palazzo dello Sport (Fig. 14-26) in Rome symbolized an emerging internationalism in the wake of World War II. The unadorned and unforgiving pillars of March's Berlin stadium seem of a distant and rejected past. Nervi's innovative, interlacing concrete roof beams define delicacy and seem to defy gravity.

In 2008, China hosted the Olympic Games in the city of Beijing. A doughnut-shaped shell crisscrossed with lines of steel as if it were a precious package wrapped in string, the stadium (Fig. 14-27) housed 100,000 spectators and came with a price tag in excess of $500 million. But beyond these staggering numbers, and like the Colosseum and the Berlin Stadium, it stands to symbolize the transformation of its city—and its country—into a major political and cultural force of its time. ●

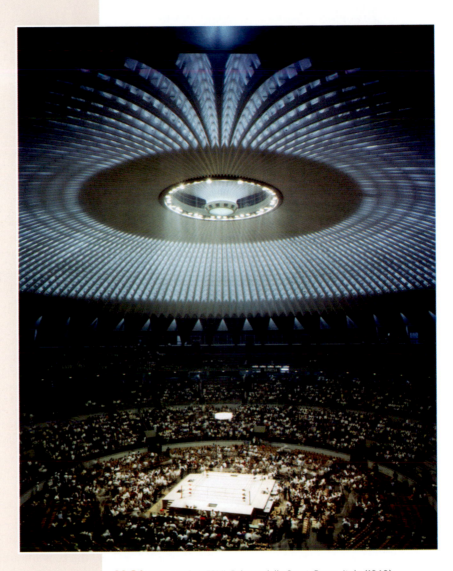

14-26 PIER LUIGI NERVI. Palazzo dello Sport, Rome, Italy (1960).

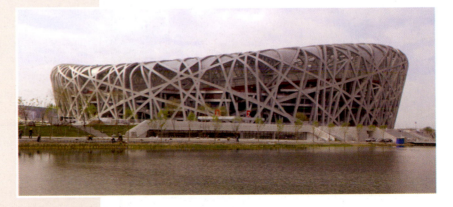

14-27 HERZOG AND DE MEURON. Beijing Stadium for the 2008 Olympic Games, Beijing, China (2005).

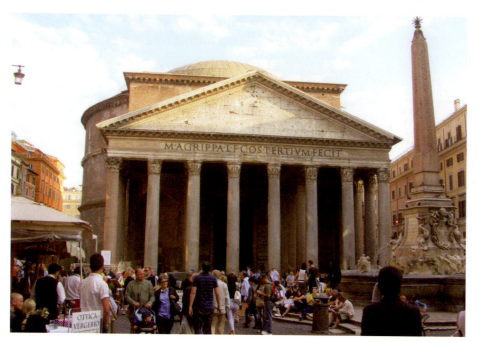

14-28 The Pantheon, Rome, Italy (117–125 CE).

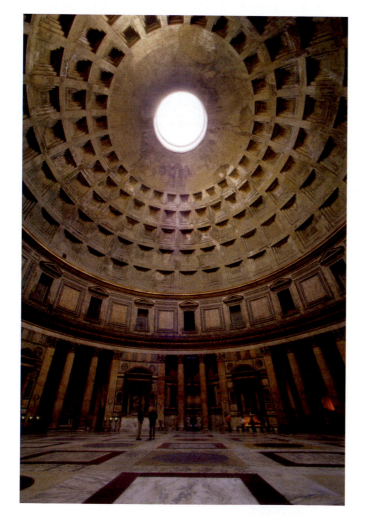

14-29 The Pantheon, Rome, Italy (117–125 CE). Interior view.

architectural styles and thus visually anchors the structure to the ground. The second level features the Ionic order, and the third level the Corinthian. This combination produces a sense of lightness as one's eye moves from the bottom to the top tier. Thick entablatures rest on top of the rings of columns, firmly delineating the stories. The uppermost level is almost all solid masonry, except for a few regularly spaced rectangular openings. It is ornamented with Corinthian pilasters and crowned by a heavy cornice.

The exterior of the Colosseum was composed of masonry blocks held in place by metal dowels. These dowels were removed over the years when metal became scarce, and thus gravity keeps the structure intact.

Roman engineering genius can be seen most clearly in the Pantheon (Figs. **14-28** and **14-29**), a brick and concrete structure originally erected to house sculptures of the Roman gods. Although the building no longer contains these statues, its function remains religious. Since the year 609 CE, it has been a Christian church.

The Pantheon's design combines the simple geometric elements of a circle and a rectangle. The entrance consists of a rectangular portico, complete with Corinthian columns and pediment. The main body of the building, to which the portico is attached, is circular. It is 144 feet in diameter and spanned by a dome equal in height to the diameter. Supporting the massive dome are 20-foot-thick walls pierced with deep niches, which in turn are vaulted in order to accept the downward thrust of the dome and distribute its weight to the solid wall. These deep niches alternate with shallow niches in which sculptures were placed.

The dome consists of a rather thin concrete shell that thickens toward the base. The interior of the dome is **coffered**, or carved with recessed squares that physically and visually lighten the structure. The ceiling was once painted blue, with a bronze rosette in the center of each square. The sole source of light in the Pantheon is the **oculus**, a circular opening in the top of the dome, 30 feet in diameter. The interior was lavishly decorated with marble slabs and granite columns that glistened in the spotlight of the sun as it filtered through the opening, moving its focus at different times of the day.

It has been said that Roman architecture differs from other ancient architecture in that it emphasizes space rather than form. In other words, rather than constructing buildings from the point of view of solid shapes, the Romans conceptualized a certain space and then proceeded to enframe it. Their methods of harnessing this space were unique in the ancient world and served as a vital precedent for future architecture.

SCULPTURE During the Empire period, Roman sculpture took on a different flavor. The pure realism of the Republican period portrait busts was joined to Greek idealism. The result, evident in *Augustus of Primaporta* (Fig. **14-30**), was often a curious juxtaposition of individualized heads with idealized, anatomically perfect bodies in Classical poses. The head of Augustus is somewhat idealized and serene, but his unique facial features are recognizable as those that appeared on empire coins. Augustus adopts an authoritative pose not unlike

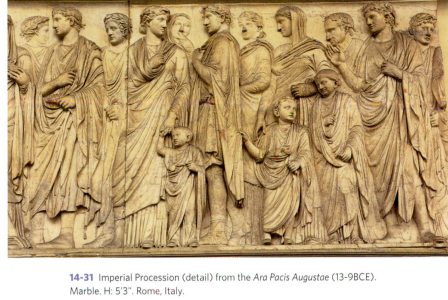

14-31 Imperial Procession (detail) from the *Ara Pacis Augustae* (13–9BCE). Marble. H: 5'3". Rome, Italy.

that of Polykleitos's *Doryphoros* (Fig. 14-12). Attired in military parade armor, he proclaims a diplomatic victory to the masses. His officer's cloak is draped about his hips, and his ceremonial armor is embellished with reliefs that portray both historic events and allegorical figures.

As the first emperor, Augustus was determined to construct monuments reflecting the glory, power, and influence of Rome on the Western world. One of the most famous of these monuments is the *Ara Pacis*, or Altar of Peace, created to celebrate the empire-wide peace that Augustus was able to achieve. The *Ara Pacis* is composed of four walls surrounding a sacrificial altar. These walls are adorned with relief sculptures of figures and delicately carved floral motifs.

Panels such as *The Imperial Procession* (Fig. **14-31**) exhibit, once again, a blend of Greek and Roman devices. The right-to-left procession of individuals, unified by the flowing lines of their drapery, clearly refers to the frieze sculptures of the Parthenon. Yet the sculpture differs from its Greek prototype in several respects: (1) the individuals are rendered in portrait likenesses; (2) the relief commemorates a specific event with specific people present; and (3) these figures are set within a shallow, though very convincing, three-dimensional space. By working in high and low relief, the artist creates the sense of a crowd; fully three rows of people are compressed into this space. They actively turn, gesture, and seem to converse. Despite a noble grandness that gives the panel an idealistic cast, the participants in the procession look and act like real people.

As time went on, the Roman desire to accurately record a person's features gave way to a more introspective portrayal of the personality of the sitter. Although portrait busts remained a favorite genre for Roman sculptors, their repertory also included relief sculpture, full-length statuary, and a new design—the **equestrian portrait**.

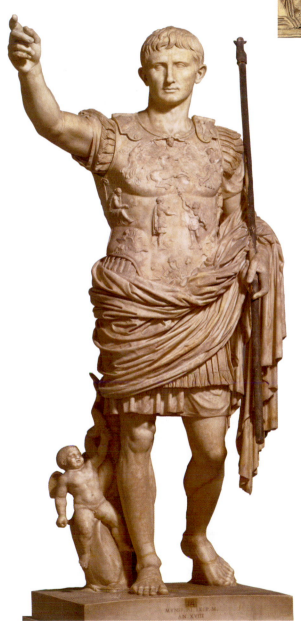

1 ft.

14-30 *Augustus of Primaporta* (c. 20 BCE). Marble. H: 6'8". Musei Vaticani, Rome, Italy.

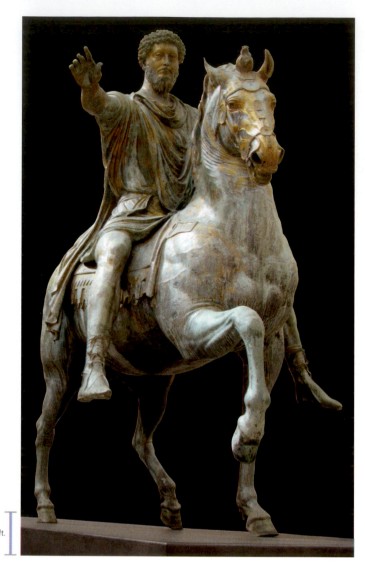

1 ft.

14-32 Equestrian Statue of Marcus Aurelius from Rome, Italy (c. 175 CE). Bronze. H: 11'6". Musei Capitolini, Rome, Italy.

The bronze sculpture of Marcus Aurelius (Fig. **14-32**) depicts the emperor on a sprightly horse, as if caught in the action of gesturing to his troops or recognizing the applause of his people. The sculpture combines the Roman love of realism with the later concern for psychologically penetrating portraits. The commanding presence of the horse is rendered through pronounced musculature, a confident and lively stride, and a vivacious head with snarling mouth, flared nostrils, and protruding veins. In contrast to this image of brute strength is a rather serene image of imperial authority. Marcus Aurelius, clothed in flowing robes, sits erectly on his horse and gestures rather passively. His facial expression is calm and reserved, reflecting his adherence to Stoic philosophy. **Stoicism** advocated an indifference to emotion and things of this world, maintaining that virtue was the most important goal in life.

The equestrian portrait of Marcus Aurelius survives because of a case of mistaken identity. During the Middle Ages, objects of all kinds were melted down because of a severe shortage of metals, and ancient sculptures that portrayed pagan idols were not spared. This statue of Marcus Aurelius was saved because it was mistakenly believed to be a portrait of Constantine, the first Roman emperor to recognize Christianity. The death of Marcus Aurelius brings us to the last years of the Empire period, which were riddled with internal strife. The days of the great Roman Empire were numbered.

The Late Empire

During its late years, the Roman Empire was torn from within. A series of emperors seized the reins of power only to meet violent deaths, some at the hands of their own soldiers. By the end of the third century, the situation was so unwieldy that the territory was divided into eastern and western empires, with separate rulers for each. When Constantine ascended the throne, he returned to the single-emperor model, but the damage had already been done—the empire had become divided against itself. Constantine then dealt the empire its final blow by dividing its territory among his sons and moving the capital to Constantinople (present-day Istanbul). Thus, imperial power was shifted to the eastern empire, leaving Rome and the western empire vulnerable. These were decisions from which the empire would never recover.

Some 300 years before Constantine's reign, however, a new force began to gnaw at the frayed edges of the Roman Empire—Christianity. The followers of Jesus of Nazareth were persecuted by the Romans for centuries until the emperor Constantine proclaimed tolerance for the faith in his Edict of Milan of 313, and accepted the mantle of Christianity himself.

ART AND RELIGION IN THE LATE EMPIRE In the Late Empire period, Rome continued to produce ambitious architectural monuments that glorified the empire, but sculpted portraits conveyed either an agitation in the sitter that reflected the upheaval of the times, or a curious lack of expression—as in the equestrian portrait of Marcus Aurelius—that seemed to suggest detachment. The beginning of the fourth century CE witnessed the emperor Constantine's prohibition of persecution of Christians, and his own stoic portrait, as we shall see, is a stylistic harbinger of the art of the Middle Ages. Yet it took some time for the Roman influence on art and architecture to dissipate. We should remember that Christians, Jews, and people of other beliefs and ethnicities lived under the aegis of the Roman Empire and it was Roman art that they looked to for inspiration.

The diversity and coexistence of religions in the Roman Empire of the third and fourth centuries are perhaps nowhere more apparent than in the Syrian town of Dura-Europos.

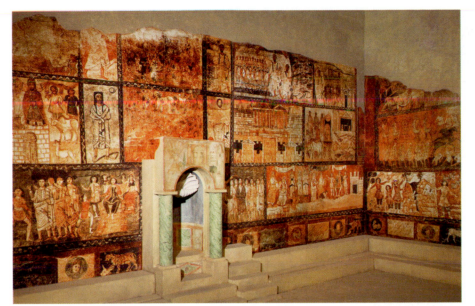

14-33 Interior of the synagogue, Dura-Europos, Syria, with wall paintings of Old Testament themes (c. 245–256 CE). Tempera on plaster. Reconstruction in National Museum, Damascus.

Commandments, did not create images associated with the worship of their God. The walls of the synagogue, divided into picturelike spaces, are covered with scenes from biblical stories and Jewish history. Stone benches line the walls of the meeting space, and, on one wall, there is a niche with a projecting arch and two columns that housed the Torah scroll.

In one fresco, the figure of Moses dominates a scene depicting the parting of the Red Sea and the Exodus from Egypt under the protective, outstretched arms of the Hebrew God (Fig. 14-34). Although God's face is never represented in the frescos, a guiding hand along the upper edge of a painting sometimes suggests his presence. In terms of style, Moses might look familiar to you. The frescoes of Dura-Europos owe much to Roman prototypes, both in terms the overall historical narrative and stylistic details. The emotionless expression on the face of Moses, for example, recalls the stoicism of Marcus Aurelius.

We also see reconciliation between Roman style and non-Roman beliefs in Early Christian art, that is, art created

From the perspectives of archeology and art history, it is a wonder that buildings from this era and this place survived at all, much less in such a well-preserved state. After an erratic history of shifting control of the town, the population of Dura-Europos left once and for all in 256 CE. It is as if they just closed the doors behind them and walked away. Among the collection of buildings: pagan temples and homes, one of which had been converted into an early Christian meeting house, and a synagogue replete with glorious frescoes.

The Synagogue in Dura-Europos (Fig. 14-33) belies the assumption that Jews, following the proscriptions of the Ten

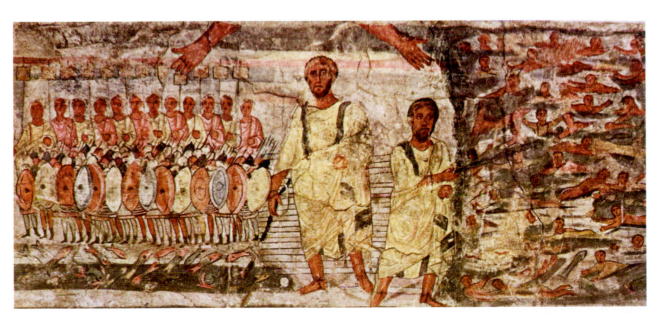

14-34 Fresco of Moses and the Exodus, from the Dura-Europos synagogue. Damascus, Syria.

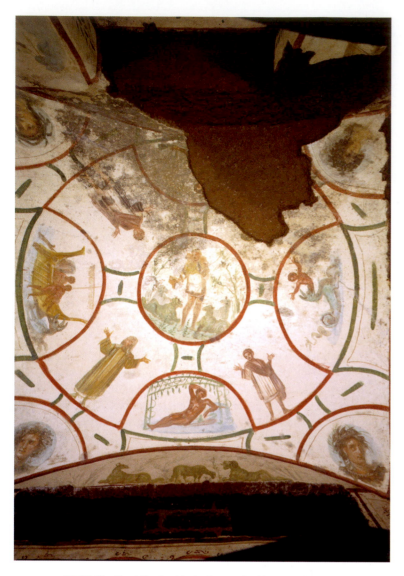

and style of the fresco illustrate a convergence of three traditions: Christian, Judaic, and Roman. The reference to Christ as a shepherd is traced to his own words, according to the Evangelist, John:

> I am the good shepherd; I know my sheep and my sheep know me—just as the Father knows me and I know the Father—and I lay down my life for the sheep. I have other sheep that are not of this sheep pen. I must bring them also. They too will listen to my voice, and there shall be one flock and one shepherd." (John 10:11–18).

For Christians, the image of the shepherd and his flock symbolized Jesus and his followers, his loyalty and sacrifice. The symbolism of Jonah provided an important connection between the Christian (New Testament) and Hebrew (Old Testament) Bibles: Early Christians saw the miracle of Jonah's deliverance, after three days, from the belly of the monster that swallowed him as a prefiguration of Christ's resurrection, three days after his crucifixion. And although the good shepherd image proved to be one of the most enduring in Christian iconography, it likely did not originate among Jesus's followers. It may be possible to draw a connection between sacrificial animals in Greek ritual and biblical references to a "Lamb of God" (the Messiah) who would be sacrificed to save humanity. In addition, the style of the figures in The Good Shepherd fresco is more generally reminiscent of that found in vase and wall paintings from Greece and Rome. The poses and proportions are realistic and the drapery falls over the body in naturalistic folds. Early Christians shared the art and culture of Rome, even if not its religion. There were bound to be similarities in style.

14-35 The Good Shepherd in the Catacomb of Saints Pietro and Marcellino, Rome, Italy (early 4th century CE).

during the third and fourth centuries. Consider a fresco depicting Christ as the Good Shepherd (Fig. **14-35**) found in the Catacomb of Saints Pietro and Marcellino outside Rome. Most Christian art from this period was found in **catacombs**—underground cemeteries carved out of bedrock and designed as an extensive network of galleries, burial chambers, and mortuary chapels in which secret worship took place. In the center of the painting, Christ stands within a perfect circle, represented as a young shepherd who carries one of his rescued sheep over his shoulders. Four "arms" in the shape of a cross extend outward from the circle, culminating in semicircular frames containing scenes from the Hebrew Bible story of Jonah and the whale. The meaning

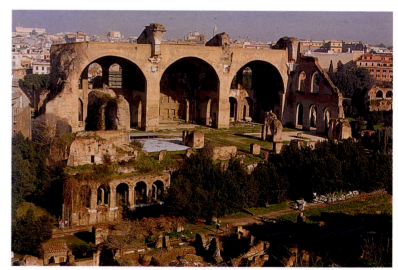

14-36 Basilica Nova, Rome, Italy (c. 310–320 CE).

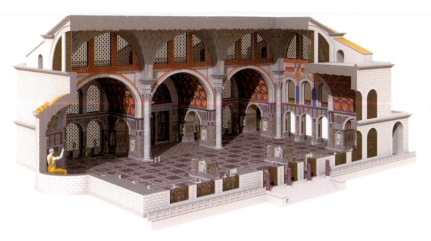

14-37 Reconstruction of Basilica Nova, Rome, Italy.

Constantine's face seems both resigned to the fall of his empire and reflective of the Christian emphasis on a kingdom that is not of this world.

Christianity spread among the ruins of the Roman Empire, even if it did not cause it to collapse. Over many centuries, Christianity also had its internal and external problems, but unlike the Roman Empire, it survived. In fact, the concept of survival is central to the understanding of Christianity and its art during the first centuries after the death of Jesus. To be a Christian before Constantine proclaimed religious tolerance, one had to endure persecution. Under the emperors Nero, Trajan, Domitian, and Diocletian, Christians were slain for their beliefs. Under Constantine, all that would change.

LATE EMPIRE ARCHITECTURE AND SCULPTURE

Although the empire was crumbling around him, Constantine continued to erect monuments to glorify it. In 312, he completed a basilica begun by his predecessor Maxentius (Fig. **14-36**), after Constantine defeated him in battle. In ancient Rome, basilicas were large public meeting halls that were usually built, like this one, in or around the **forums**. The Basilica of Maxentius and Constantine, also known as the Basilica Nova (Fig. **14-37**), was an enormous structure, measuring some 300 by 215 feet (as a point of reference, a football field measures 360 by 160 feet). The interior space was divided into a nave (or central aisle), flanked by two side aisles. The nave ceiling consisted of a coffered groin vault reaching a height of 114 feet and the interior was richly embellished with marble. Little remains of the basilica today, but it survived long enough to set a precedent for Christian church architecture. It would serve as the basic plan for basilicas and cathedrals for centuries to come.

The grandeur of the Basilica Nova seems to belie events in the empire at the time of its construction, more reflective of a Rome that was than the one that it had become. By contrast, the Head of Constantine (Fig. **14-38**)—part of a colossal sculpture of the seated emperor that was placed in the Basilica Nova—departs from the literalness and materialism of Roman art and life and gives way to a new spirituality and otherworldliness. The sculpture consisted of a wooden torso covered with bronze and a head and limbs of marble. The head is more than 8 feet high and weighs more than 8 tons. The realism and idealism that we witnessed in Roman sculpture were replaced by an almost archaic rendition of the emperor, complete with an austere expression and thick-lidded, wide-staring eyes. The artist elaborated the pensive, passive rigidity of form that we sensed in the portrait of Marcus Aurelius.

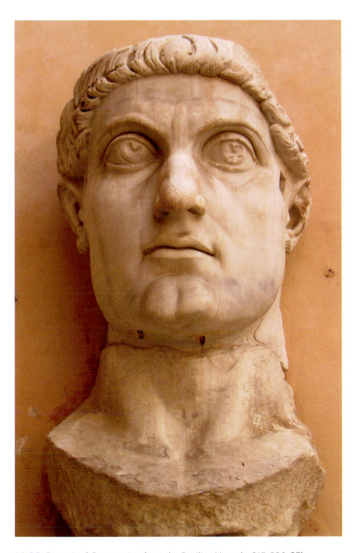

14-38 Portrait of Constantine from the Basilica Nova (c. 315-330 CE). Marble. H: 8'6". Musei Capitolini, Rome, Italy.

ART TOUR ROME

EVERYTHING ABOUT ROME is colossal—from the Colosseum (Rome's greatest amphitheater) (Fig. 14-24) to the colossal head of Constantine (Fig. 14-38), which is more than 8 feet high. As the center of two of the great powers of the Western world—the Roman Empire and the Catholic Church—the city is rife with symbols that trumpeted their status in the times of their glory. A week of travel to Rome would barely do justice to this treasure trove of art and architecture.

It was said that "all roads lead to Rome," and, in truth, any road the visitor might take would lead to something wonderful. Starting with the Capitol, or the southern summit of Capitoline Hill, you will be in what has been called the symbolic center of the Roman world—its citadel as well as the location of three of its most important temples, including the Temple of Jupiter, where triumphal processions giving thanks for victory reached

their climax. In the sixteenth century, Michelangelo, the Florentine artist otherwise famous for his sculpture of David (see Fig. 16-25) and murals for the ceiling of the Sistine Chapel (see Figs. 16-21 and 16-22), designed the geometric patterns of the elliptical plaza as well as the facades of the buildings that flank it on three sides. In the center stands a replica of the equestrian portrait of Emperor Marcus Aurelius (Fig. 14-32); the real thing can be found just steps away in one of the Capitoline museums, along with an extensive collection of painting and sculpture, including Caravaggio's unusual Baroque portrayal of St. John the Baptist, *The Dying Gaul*, and the excessively large head and assorted limbs from the statue of Constantine.

If you duck around the back of the museums, you'll come to a wonderful view of the Roman forum below. It's good to linger here awhile to get the "lay of the land" before descending to wander among the ruins (miraculously "restored" by way of computer-generated imagery for the film *Gladiator*). The forum was the religious, political, and commercial center of the ancient city—the site of temples, courts of law, and the Senate house, along with food stores and brothels teeming with customers. For the contemporary visitor, even the summer tourist crowds might pale in comparison to the hubbub of the forum at the height of the empire. Of particular interest are the central courtyard of the House of the Vestal Virgins (girls from noble families who served as priestesses tending an eternal flame in the Temple of Vesta), the triumphal arches of the emperors Septimius Severus and Titus, and the monumental barrel vaults that remain from the Basilica of Maxentius and Constantine. One of the most curious, composite structures along the Via Sacra (or sacred way) is the ancient Temple of Antoninus and Faustina, now incorporated into a Catholic church, San Lorenzo in Miranda.

Down in the area of the forum, where cats creep and sleep among the ruins, the visitor will also come upon the Arch of Constantine (a popular backdrop for wedding photos) as well as the spectacular and notorious Colosseum. Built during the reign of Emperor Vespasian in 72 CE, the amphitheater was the site of deadly clashes between gladiators and wild beasts staged as sport and theater for the Roman citizenry by the emperors and upper classes. Stadium seating accommodated up to 55,000 spectators, who, on opening day, witnessed the slaughter of more than 9,000 wild animals in addition to a mock naval battle. The tiers of the Colosseum, bearing columns in all three orders, or styles—Doric, Ionic, and Corinthian—served as inspiration for architects during the Renaissance. The artistic

THE TEMPLE OF ANTONINUS AND FAUSTINA IN THE FORUM.

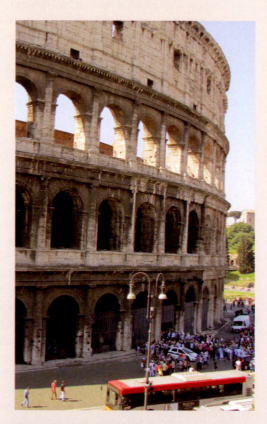

TOURISTS ENTERING THE COLOSSEUM.

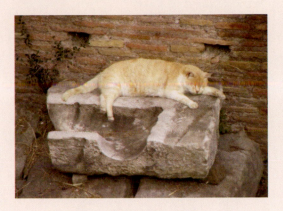

HUNDREDS OF CATS LIVE IN THE FORUM, THE COLOSSEUM, AND OTHER ANCIENT SITES. WOMEN VOLUNTEERS CALLED "LE GATTARE" FEED AND CARE FOR THEM.

and architectural sources for the rebirth of Classicism in Italy were not, as it happened, so far from home.

You can ride the 81 bus from the Colosseum to witness the influence of Roman architecture on the grandest cathedral in Christendom, the Basilica of St. Peter's. Its rhythmic colonnades, imposing temple-front facade, and expansive hemispherical dome epitomize the Renaissance relationship to antiquity. St. Peter's (see Fig. 17-2) is the emblem of Roman Catholicism and the centerpiece of the Vatican, the world's smallest sovereign state, nestled within the city of Rome and ruled by the pope. The current, commanding building is constructed on the ruins of an earlier basilica erected by Constantine, who believed the site to be that in which the apostle Peter was buried. In another part of town, Michelangelo's Moses—part of the tomb of Pope Julius II—overlooks the shackles

believed to have been used to imprison Peter before his execution.

Today St. Peter's is also the backdrop for magnificent works by Michelangelo (the Pietà—protected by glass since an attack on the sculpture in 1972—and the glorious dome over the main altar, the largest in the world) and by Gianlorenzo Bernini (the Baldacchino, or bronze canopy over the main altar, and several tombs and sculptures throughout the basilica, in addition to the design for the piazza and colonnades that grace the exterior). Visitors to St. Peter's should be aware that proper attire is required for entry to the cathedral; even in the oppressive heat of a Roman summer day, shorts and sleeveless shirts are forbidden.

The wealth of the popes is even more evident in the sublime collections and treasures of the Vatican Museums (the Hellenistic Belvedere Torso and Laocoön reside here) and the rooms of the Vatican Palace—including Michelangelo's paintings of the Sistine Chapel ceiling and Raphael's fresco for the Stanze della Segnatura (see Fig. 16-20) in the papal apartments. A grand boulevard—the Via della Conciliazone—leads the traveler from the steps of St. Peter's along the Tevere River toward the Castel Sant'Angelo. Constructed in 139 CE as a mausoleum for Emperor Hadrian, it went on to serve as a medieval citadel and prison, as well as a safe haven for popes (it was connected to the Vatican by an escape cor-

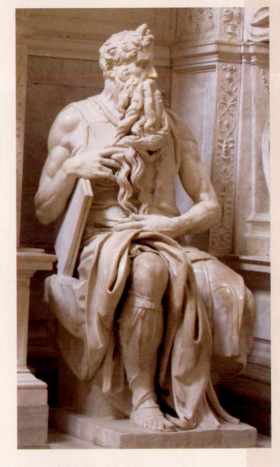

MICHELANGELO. Moses.

ridor). If you continue on foot along this broad avenue, you will eventually wind up in the area of the Roman Pantheon (Figs. 14-28 and 14-29), the great domed temple-turned-Christian-church, initially devoted to the gods and emperors of Rome. Raphael is buried here.

From its romantic fountains and lush gardens to its endless trattorias and pizzerias, museums and monuments, Rome is and has always been a cosmopolitan city on the go. It is a cacophonous mix of old and new (every youthful Roman seems to have a motor scooter and a cell phone), a vast city whose center is so small that a good map—and, even better, a pair of running shoes—will take you everywhere.

 TO CONTINUE YOUR TOUR and learn more about Rome, go to CourseMate.

CASTLE SANT'ANGELO.

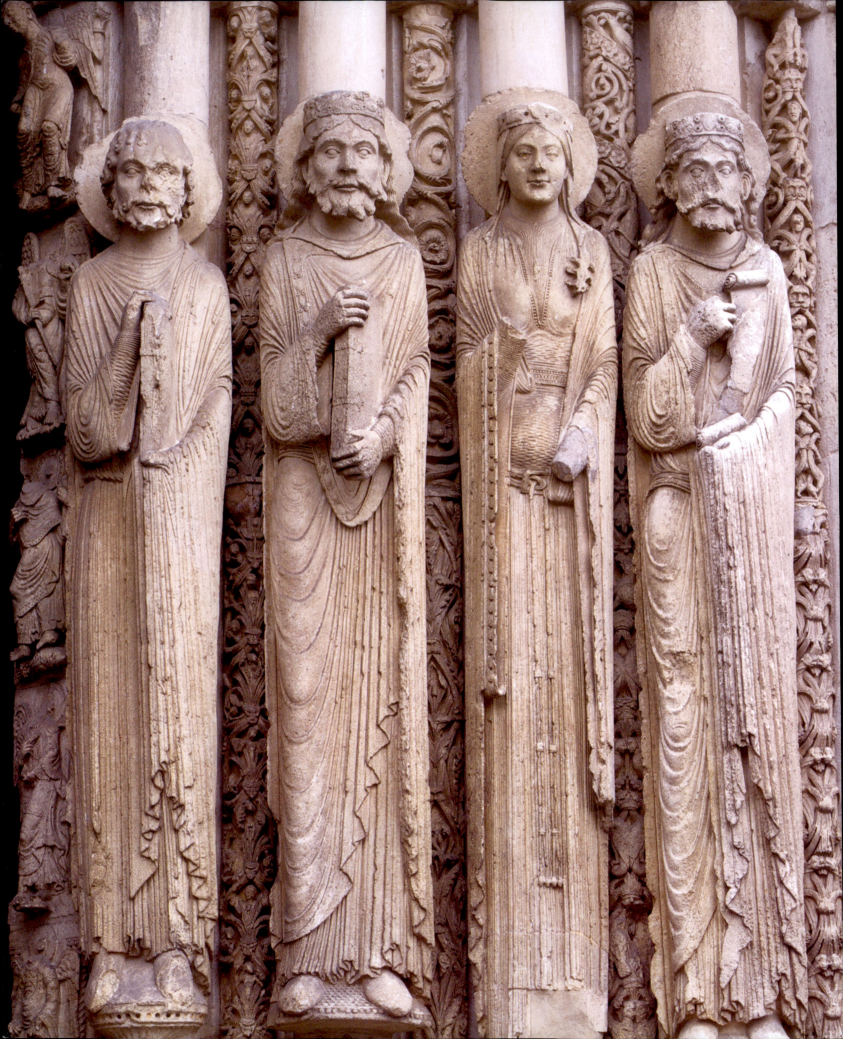

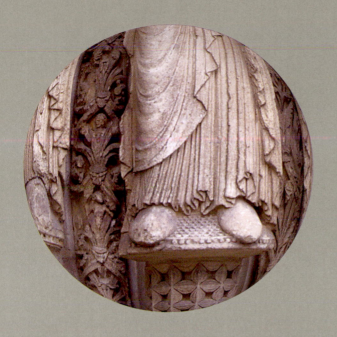

"The lamps are different, but the Light is the same: it comes from Beyond."

—from Jalal al-Din Rumi, "The One True Light"

THE AGE OF FAITH

15

When the Sufi mystic and poet Rumi was writing in the 1200s, Islam was in its Golden Age, Christianity was in the High Middle Ages, and it had been more than two millennia since the Hebrews drafted the tenets of their faith after, according to their belief, Moses received the Ten Commandments at Mount Sinai. Judaism, Christianity, and Islam—three "lamps" representing three of the world's most influential religions—have things in common: their "light" comes from a single God, and all are built on the belief in divine revelation from "beyond." Jews believe that God, whom the ancient Hebrews called Yahweh, spoke directly to Abraham and to Moses, establishing a covenant with their generations as his "chosen people." Christians believe that the same God spoke to Jesus at his baptism, calling him his "beloved son." And Muslims believe that the same God, whom they call Allah, revealed their holy book—the Qur'an—to the Prophet Muhammad. Rumi referred to a single God as "the kernel of Existence" but acknowledged the perspectives of many religions.

Jamb figures, west portals, Chartres Cathedral, Chartres, France (Gothic, c. 1140–1150 CE).

In the previous chapter, we discussed the pluralism of religious belief and practice in the waning years of the Roman Empire, examining Jewish and early Christian sites of worship in the far-flung garrison town of Dura-Europos, as well as other secret gathering spaces for ritual during the Christian period of persecution. This chapter begins with the emperor Constantine's commitment to Christianity and his construction of a grand basilica for worship in the city of Rome—the western capital of the Roman Empire. The first St. Peter's, begun in 319 CE, followed Constantine's own revelation, or more accurately, vision, that led to his own conversion to Christianity: Before he went into the Battle of the Milvian Bridge over the Tiber River against the emperor Maxentius in 312 CE, he said he saw a cross of light in the sky, along with the words, "by this, win." He ordered his soldiers to mark their shields with a Christian symbol and, indeed, the enemy was vanquished. Constantine believed he owed this victory to the Christian God. His gratitude would be expressed in riches and grandeur bestowed on the early Church.

CHRISTIANITY

Christianity (from the Greek *chrīstos*, meaning "messiah"), an Abrahamic religion as are Judaism and Islam, is monotheistic and based on the teachings of Jesus, as written in the New Testament, or Christian Bible. Christians believe that Jesus is the Son of God and the messiah who was prophesied in the Old Testament, or Hebrew Bible. At first a Jewish sect, Christianity flourished over its early centuries and became the dominant religion in the Roman Empire by the fourth century. Today there are some two billion Christians, almost one-third of the population of the world.

Christianity teaches that Jesus led a virtuous life, taught followers how to lead virtuous lives, and saved humankind from the consequences of original sin by his own suffering and death. Christians believe that Jesus was resurrected after his death and ascended into heaven. Most Christians believe that Jesus will return one day—on *Judgment Day*—to judge the dead and the living, and grant everlasting life to the deserving.

Theological councils in the fourth century affirmed the divinity of Jesus, putting him on an equal plane with God the Father. They also glorified the Holy Spirit. According to the gospels of Luke and Matthew, Jesus had been conceived by the Holy Spirit and was born by the Virgin Mary. These three divine "persons"—the Father, the Son, and the Holy Spirit—unified, are sometimes referred to as the Godhead. In the mid-fifth century, Jesus Christ was proclaimed to have both divine and human natures, to have had a human side subject to physical suffering, as are mortals. This duality would impact the ways in which Jesus was depicted in art, as

would details of the New Testament and Gospels describing his life from birth in a simple manger, through the performance of miracles and calling of his apostles, to his crucifixion and resurrection.

EARLY CHRISTIAN ARCHITECTURE

In Dura-Europos, Early Christians secretly worshiped in private community houses that had been renovated and adapted to accommodate their rituals and ceremonies. Persecution of Christians was officially forbidden by the Edict of Milan of 313 CE, which held "that it was proper that the Christians and all others should have liberty to follow that mode of religion which to each of them appeared best."[1] No longer compelled to hide their beliefs and practices—in catacombs or safe houses—Christians began to build churches, many of which were erected on the land on top of the catacombs where the martyrs for their faith had been buried. In terms of design, it is not surprising that they turned to what they already knew—Roman architecture. What may be surprising, on the other hand, is that the Roman emperor Constantine was one of their most generous supporters in this effort.

Old St. Peter's, Rome

Among the many churches Constantine helped to create in Rome and in Constantinople, the most significant was Old St. Peter's (Fig. **15-1**). Built on the site where St. Peter was believed to have been buried, the expansive basilican-plan church no longer exists. What stands in its place—at the heart of Vatican City in Rome—is the present-day St. Peter's Basilica (see Fig. 17-2), constructed during the Renaissance and Baroque periods.

The plan of Old St. Peter's looks to the past and to the future. The scale of the building, including many of its parts, reflects those of Roman basilicas. Both have wide, long, central **naves** flanked by two narrower side aisles, forming the main congregational space. Unlike many Roman basilicas, however, Old St. Peter's was entered from one of the short sides, through a kind of gateway into the large open courtyard or **atrium** called the **propylaeum**. Both the propylaeum and atrium appeared in subsequent cathedral designs, but not with any regularity. All of the other parts of the plan, however, became regular features. The worshiper gained access to the heart of the basilica through a series of portals, passing

---

[1] Lactantius, *De Mortibus Persecutorum*.

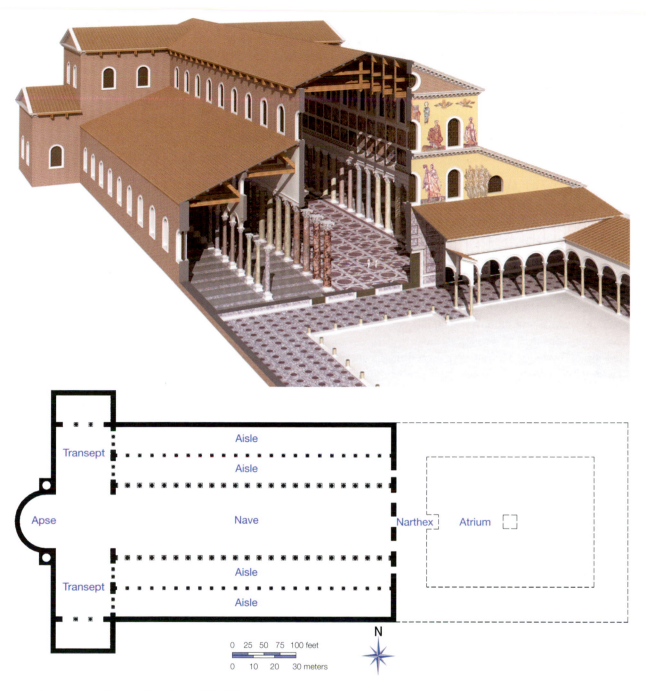

15-1 Restored cutaway view (top) and plan (bottom) of Old St. Peter's, Rome, Italy, begun ca. 319 CE (John Burge).

first through a vestibule called the **narthex**. On the opposite end of the 300-foot-long structure was the **transept**, an aisle that crossed over and was perpendicular to the nave and side aisles and that separated the congregational space from the altar. The transept often extended beyond the boundaries of the side aisles, resembling the arms of a cross. The altar, the focus of ritual and ceremony, was placed in a semicircular space called the **apse**, another holdover from Roman basilicas. This plan is called a **Latin Cross plan** or, because of the length of the nave and the orientation of the plan along a single dominant axis, a **longitudinal plan**. The Latin Cross plan was most prominent in western Europe, although smaller and more symmetrical plans—**central plans**—were more typical in eastern Empire cities such as Ravenna on the eastern coast of Italy. The central plan is characterized by a central (rather than longitudinal) focus.

Old St. Peter's was decorated lavishly with inlaid marble and mosaics, none of which survive. In fact, only one Early Christian church escaped destruction by fire, in large part because their ceilings were constructed of wood. The art of mosaic, much of it classical in style, was adopted from the Romans and comprised most of the ornamentation in Early Christian churches.

BYZANTINE ART

The term Byzantine comes from the town of ancient Byzantium, the site of Constantine's capital, Constantinople. The art called "Byzantine" was produced after the Early Christian era in Byzantium, but also in Ravenna, Venice, Sicily, Greece, Russia, and other Eastern countries. We may describe the difference between Early Christian and Byzantine art as a transfer from an earthbound realism to a more spiritual, otherworldly style. Byzantine figures appear to be weightless; they are placed in an undefined space. Byzantine art features a great deal of symbolism and is far more decorative in detail than Early Christian art.

San Vitale, Ravenna

The city of Ravenna, on the Adriatic coast of Italy, was initially settled by the ruler of the western Roman Empire, who was trying to escape invaders by moving his capital out of Rome. As it turned out, the move was timely; only eight years later, Rome was sacked. The early history of Ravenna was riddled with strife; its leadership changed hands often. It was not until the age of Emperor Justinian that Ravenna attained some stability and the arts truly flourished.

During Justinian's reign, the church of San Vitale (Fig. **15-2**), one of the most elaborate buildings decorated in the Byzantine style, was erected. San Vitale was designed as a central plan church, with an octagonal perimeter and a narthex set off axis to the apse. When you look at the plan, you can see that it is dominated by a central circle. This circle indicates a dome, which from the exterior appears as another octagon stacked wedding-cake fashion on the first. This circle is surrounded by eight massive piers, between which are semicircular niches that extend into a surrounding aisle, or ambulatory, like petals of a flower. The "stem" of this flower is a sanctuary that intersects the ambulatory and culminates in a multisided, or polygonal, apse. Unlike the rigid axial alignment of the Latin Cross churches that follow a basilican plan, San Vitale has an organic quality. Soft, curving forms press into the spaces of the church and are juxtaposed by geometric shapes that seem to complement their fluidity rather than restrain it. The space flows freely, and the disparate forms are unified. This vital, organic quality can also be seen in the details of the church interior. Columns are crowned by capitals carved with complex, interlacing designs. Decorative mosaic borders, inspired by plant life, comprise repetitive stylized patterns.

This stylized treatment of forms can also be seen in the representation of human figures in San Vitale's mosaics. *Justinian and Attendants* (Fig. **15-3**), an apse mosaic, represents the Byzantine style at its peak of perfection in this medium. The mosaic commemorates Justinian's victory over the Goths and proclaims him ruler of Ravenna and the western half of the Roman Empire. His authority is symbolized by the military and clerical representatives in his entourage. The figures form a strong, friezelike horizontal band that communicates unity. Although they are placed in groups, some slightly in front of others, the heads present as points in a single line.

Thickly lidded eyes stare outward. The heavily draped bodies have no evident substance, as if garments hang on invisible frames, and the physical gestures of the men are

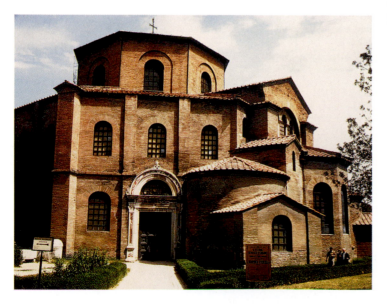

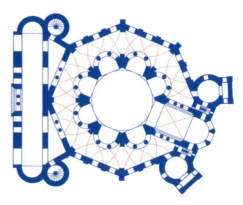

15-2 Church of San Vitale, Ravenna, Italy (Byzantine, 526–547 CE). Exterior and plan.

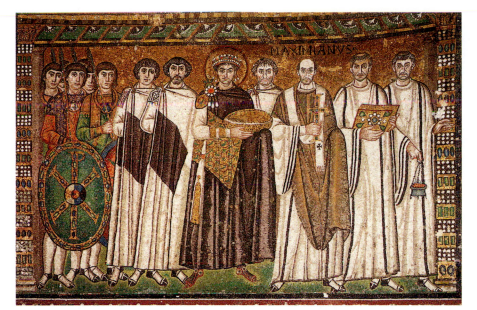

15-3 *Justinian and Attendants* (Byzantine, c. 547 CE). Mosaic. Church of San Vitale, Ravenna, Italy.

a manner of representation in which the corporeality of the body is less significant than the soul.

Hagia Sophia, Constantinople

Even though Ravenna was the capital of the western Empire, Justinian's most important public building was erected in Constantinople. Centuries earlier, Constantine had moved the capital of the Roman Empire to the ancient city of Byzantium and renamed it after himself. After his death, the empire was divided into eastern and western halves, and the eastern part remained in Constantinople. It is in this Turkish city—present-day Istanbul—that Justinian built his Church of the Holy Wisdom, or Hagia Sophia (Fig. **15-4**). It is a fantastic structure that has served at one time or other in its history as an Eastern Orthodox church, an Islamic mosque, and a museum. The most striking aspects of Hagia Sophia are its overall dimensions and the size of its

unnatural. Space is tentatively suggested by a grassy ground line, but the placement of the figures on this line and within this space is uncertain. Notice how the feet seem to hover rather than to support, like Colorforms stuck to a tableau background. These characteristics contrast strongly with the Classicism of Early Christian art and point the way toward

15-4A ANTHEMIUS OF TRALLES AND ISIDORUS OF MILETUS. Hagia Sophia, Constantinople (modern-day Istanbul), Turkey (532–537 CE). Exterior view. The four minarets were added following the Ottoman conquest of 1453, when the church was converted to an Islamic mosque.

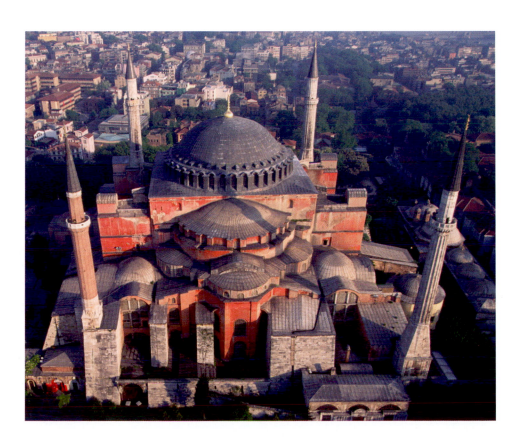

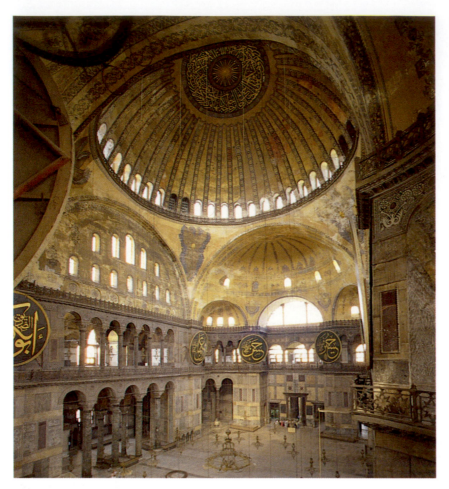

15-4B ANTHEMIUS OF TRALLES AND ISIDORUS OF MILETUS. Hagia Sophia, Constantinople (modern-day Istanbul), Turkey (532–537 CE). Interior view.

Later Byzantine Art

Byzantine church architecture continued to flourish until about the twelfth century, varying between central and longitudinal plans. One interesting variation of the central plan, called a **Greek cross plan**, was used in St. Mark's Cathedral in Venice (Fig. **15-5**). In this plan, the "arms" of the cross are of equal length, and the focus of the interior is a centrally placed dome that rises above the intersection of these elements. The interior of St. Mark's is likewise covered with gold and brightly colored mosaics.

ISLAM

Islam, like Judaism and Christianity, is a monotheistic religion in the Abrahamic tradition. It was founded by Muhammad, who was a native of Mecca in what is now Saudi Arabia. Muhammad was born around 570 CE and is seen by Muslims as the final prophet in the Abrahamic tradition. Muslims see Abraham, Moses, and Jesus as revelation prophets, but they view the revelations Muhammad received from God as corrections of previous distortions or misinterpretations of his divine message.

Muhammad's monotheism was rejected by the polytheistic majority in Mecca, forcing him and his followers to flee to a desert oasis—now called Medina ("City of the Prophet")—in 622 CE. Muhammad returned to Mecca in 630 CE, eight years later, with several thousand soldiers. He defeated the polytheists, converted the population to Islam, removed the idols of Arabian tribal gods housed in a small cubical building—called the *Kaaba* for "cube" in Arabic—and rededicated it as an Islamic house of worship. On pilgrimages to Mecca today, Muslims circle the Kaaba, which is the spiritual center of their world (Fig. **15-6**). From this beginning, Islam has grown to be the world's second largest religion, after Christianity, with nearly one and a half billion adherents. Islam today stretches from communities in Europe throughout North Africa, the Middle East, much of South Central Asia, and Indonesia. It once swept into and took control of the Iberian Peninsula, but was eventually pushed back by Christians. In the Middle Ages, Christians also fought Muslims to reclaim the "Holy Land," which is now Israel and the Palestinian Territories.

dome. Its floor plan is approximately 240 by 270 feet (Constantine's basilica in Rome was 300 by 215 feet). The dome is about 108 feet across and rises almost 180 feet above the church floor (the dome of the Pantheon, by contrast, is 144 feet high).

The grand proportions of Hagia Sophia put it on a par with the great architectural monuments of Roman times. Its architects, Anthemius of Tralles and Isidorus of Miletus, used four triangular surfaces called pendentives to support the dome on a square base. Pendentives transfer the load from the base of the dome to the piers at the corners of the square beneath. Although massive, the dome appears light and graceful due to the placement of a ring of arched windows at its base. The light filtering through these windows can create the impression that the dome is hovering above a ring of light, further emphasizing the building's spaciousness. Like most Byzantine churches, the relatively plain exterior of Hagia Sophia contrasts strongly with the interior wall surfaces, which are decorated lavishly with inlaid marble and mosaic.

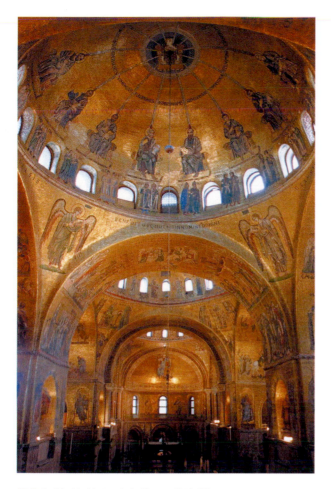

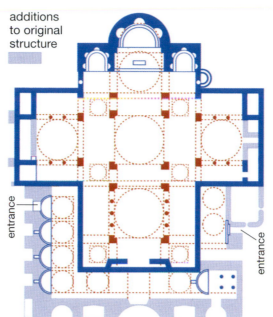

additions to original structure

Plan of St. Mark's, Venice, Italy (above).

15-5 St. Mark's, Venice, Italy (begun 1063 CE). Plan and interior view looking toward the apse.

The word *Islam* means to submit—to surrender the self to the will of Allah. A follower of Islam is called a Muslim, which is the past participle of Islam, meaning "one who has submitted to Allah." The holy book of Muslims is called the *Koran* or the *Qur'an*, and Muslims believe that it was revealed to Muhammad by the angel Gabriel. The Qur'an and Muhammad's own words and deeds—the *Sunnah*—constitute the

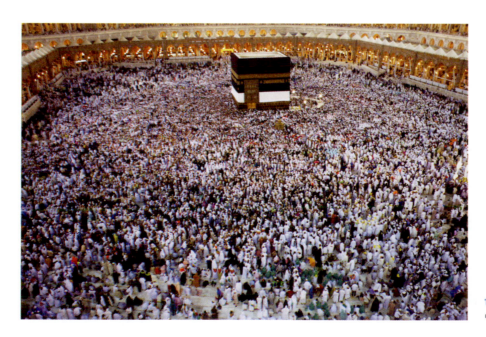

15-6 Muslim pilgrims walking around the Kaaba during a hajj (pilgrimage). Mecca, Saudi Arabia.

basic texts of Islam. Muslims worship God directly, without any hierarchy of rabbis, priests, pastors, or saints. In Islam, there is unity of church and state. The state is to be ruled by Islamic Law, or *Shariah*, as revealed in the basic texts. The proper ruler is both a religious and secular leader, a successor to Muhammad known as a *caliph*.

There are five duties or "Five Pillars" of Islam. These begin with the Shahadah, the basic tenet of submission: "I bear witness that there is none worthy of worship except Allah, the One, without any partner. And I bear witness that Muhammad is His servant and His Messenger." The Shahadah requires not only belief in Allah but also belief that Muhammad is the sole source of interpretation of the revelations of Allah. *Salat* is the requirement to pray five times a day, facing Mecca. *Zakah* is the giving of alms to the poor. *Sawin* is fasting during the holy month of Ramadan. During Ramadan, Muslims with the exception of children, old people, sick people, and women who are pregnant or breast-feeding abstain from food, drink, and sex—from dawn to dusk. Muslims are also obliged to make the *Hajj*—the pilgrimage to Mecca—at least once if they have the means to do so. They circle the Kaaba, which, according to the Qur'an, was built by Abraham, and is believed to be directly beneath the Gate of Heaven.

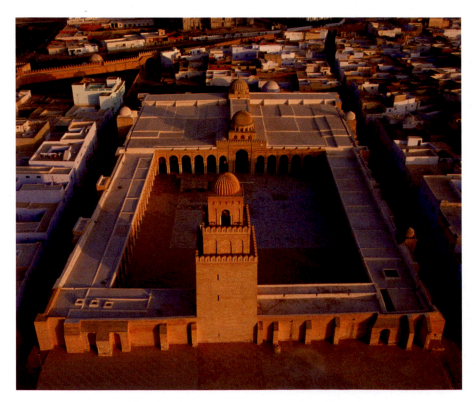

MAP 15-1 The extent of the Islamic world during the Umayyad Caliphate.

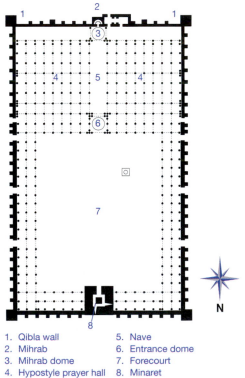

15-7 Aerial view (left) and plan (right) of the Great Mosque of Kairouan, Tunisia (c. 836–875 CE).

1. Qibla wall
2. Mihrab
3. Mihrab dome
4. Hypostyle prayer hall
5. Nave
6. Entrance dome
7. Forecourt
8. Minaret

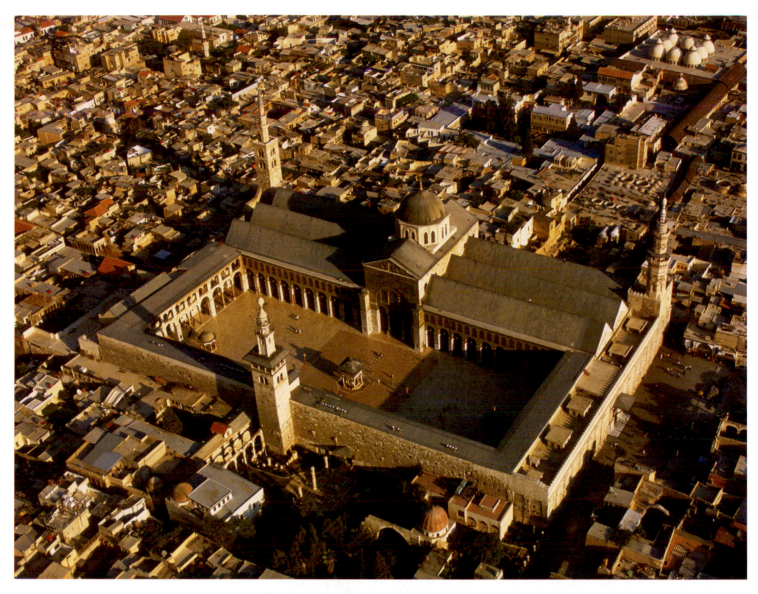

15-8 Aerial view of the Great Mosque, Damascus, Syria (706–715 CE).

The Umayyad Caliphate

Following the death of Muhammad in 632 CE, disputes arose over who would succeed him. A series of civil wars and assassinations eventually led to the founding of the Umayyad Caliphate (661 CE–750 CE). At its largest, the Umayyad Caliphate extended Islamic rule north into Persia, east into south-central Asia (modern-day Afghanistan, Pakistan, and adjacent regions), west across the north of Africa (to present-day Morocco), and, from there, across what is now the Strait of Gibraltar to the Iberian peninsula (now Portugal and Spain) and the south of present-day France (see Map **15.1**). The Umayyads were overthrown by the Abbasid Caliphate and moved into what is now Spain, where they founded the Caliphate of Córdoba, which they ruled until 1031.

One of the architectural achievements of the Umayyad Caliphate is the Great Mosque of Kairouan, built by General Uqba ibn Nafi in 670 CE in what is now the North African country of Tunisia. It has served as the model of mosques throughout the western reaches of Islam. It was replaced by the Great Mosque shown in Figure **15-7** two centuries later, about 836–875 CE. The mosque has a hypostyle prayer hall and a large square minaret. The immense marble courtyard was once used to collect rainwater in three underground tanks.

At about the same time, the Umayyad Mosque (or Great Mosque of Damascus, Fig. **15-8**) was being built in what is modern-day Syria and completed in 715 CE. Using stone, marble, tile, and mosaics, it was erected on the site of a Christian basilica dedicated to John the Baptist that had existed since the

15-9 The Shrine of St. John in the Umayyad Mosque, Damascus, Syria.

rule of the Roman emperor Constantine. Both Christians and Muslims honor John as a prophet, and there is a shrine of John the Baptist in the prayer hall of the mosque (Fig. **15-9**).

The most highly regarded architectural legacy of the Umayyad Caliphate is the Mezquita-Catedral (mosque-cathedral) in what is now the city of Córdoba in south cen-

tral Spain. The building originated as a church in about 600 CE. After the Islamic conquest of the region, the church was divided between Christians and Muslims. The Umayyad Prince Abd ar-Rahman I purchased the Christian half and began the development in 784 CE of what would become the Great Mosque of Córdoba upon completion in 987 CE. The interior of the mosque at Córdoba, Spain (Fig. **15-10**) shows the system of arches that spans the distances between columns in the hypostyle system. The hypostyle system enabled expansion in any direction as a congregation grew. By bowing toward Mecca in the same yard, worshipers were granted equal psychological access to Allah. A series of vaults, supported by heavier piers, overspreads the arches. There is no grand open space as in the Western cathedral; rather, air and light flow as through a forest of high-crowned trees. The interiors of mosques and other Islamic structures have traditionally been decorated with finely detailed mosaics, as seen

15-10 Sanctuary of the Mosque at Córdoba, Spain (786–987 CE). Interior view.

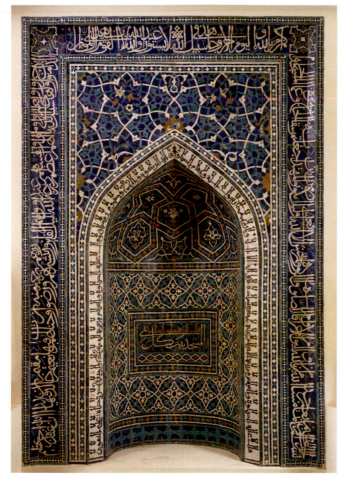

15-11 Mihrab from the Madrasa Imami, Isfahan, Iran (c. 1354 CE). Mosaic of monochrome-glaze tiles on composite body set on plaster to create floral and geometric patterns and inscriptions. 135¹⁄₁₆″ × 113¹¹⁄₁₆″. The Metropolitan Museum of Art, NY.

in the mihrab from the Madrasa Imami, from Isfahan, Iran (Fig. **15-11**). A **mihrab** is a niche in the wall facing Mecca that provides a focus of worship. There is no clerical hierarchy in Islam such as is found in many Christian religions. The leader of gatherings for worship, called the **imam**, stands on a pulpit in the mosque, near the wall that faces Mecca, the spiritual capital of Islam.

The Golden Age of Islam

The Abbasid Caliphate, which succeeded the Umayyads, has been called the Golden Age of Islam. It spanned five centuries, from 750 CE to 1258 CE (the time of the Mongol invasion and the sacking of Baghdad). During the Golden Age, citrus fruits were imported from China, and rice, cotton, and sugarcane were brought in from India and trained to grow in Muslim lands. A precursor of capitalism and free markets

were established. The scientific method was instituted, in which hypotheses are tested through experimentation. Muslim astronomers considered the possibility that the sun was the center of the solar system and that the earth spun on an axis. Algebra and trigonometry were invented. The concepts of inertia and momentum, later adopted by Newton, were discovered. The Mezquita was begun in Córdoba.

During the early part of the Golden Age, the Abbasid caliph Al-Mutawakkil commissioned the Great Mosque of Samarra in present-day Iraq in 848 CE and completed it in 851 CE. When built, it was the largest mosque in the world. From the vast spiraling structure for which the mosque is known—the Malwiya Minaret (Fig. **15-12**)—a crier known as a muezzin called followers to prayer at certain hours. *Malwiya* is Arabic for "snail shell." The photograph was taken before the top of the **minaret** was damaged by insurgents during the Iraqi war in 2006.

Mosques avoid symbols, and early mosques in particular do not show ornamentation. The mosque at Samarra was a simple building, 800 feet long and 520 feet wide, covered in part by a wooden roof, with a great open courtyard. The roof was supported by the hypostyle system of multiple rows of columns. Hundreds of years ago, the interior walls were paneled with resplendent dark blue glass mosaics.

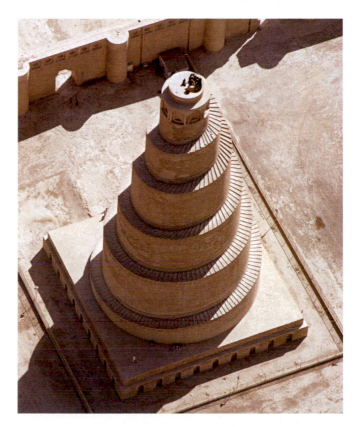

15-12 Great Mosque at Samarra, Iraq (848–852 CE).

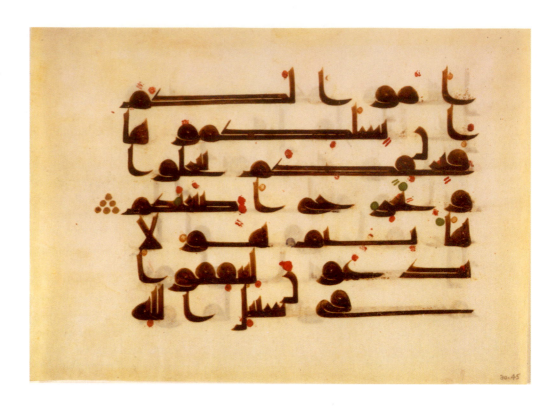

15-13 Leaf from a Qur'an manuscript, possibly from Syria (late 9th–10th century). Ink, gold, and colors on vellum. 13⅛" × 9⅜". The Metropolitan Museum of Art, NY.

15-14 Bowl, Iraq (10th century). Composite body, luster-painted. H: 2⁵⁄₁₆", diameter 9⁵⁄₁₆". The Metropolitan Museum of Art, NY.

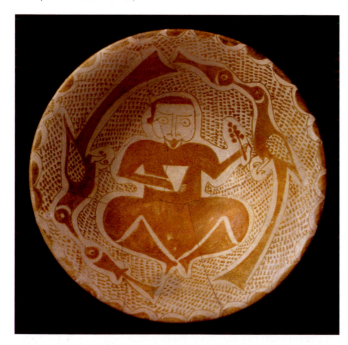

The stylized Arabic from a leaf of the Qur'an (Fig. **15-13**) was drawn around the middle of the Golden Age. Rounded letters serve as counterpoint to the angular script. The colored marks are aids that help the reader pronounce the script, but for those of us who are not readers of Arabic, the whole has something of a mysterious pictographic quality created by strong, measured strokes. The bowl from Iraq (Fig. **15-14**) was

made at about the same time, perhaps a bit later. It represents the monochromatic ceramic vessels of the time that commonly included stylized human figures. In this lively example, a seated man holds a beaker and a flowering branch. Two birds with fish in their beaks surround the vessel, but they look as if they could be kissing as well as eating their prey.

The Golden Age was brought to an end by the Mongol invasion, but the Mongols who remained in Islamic lands converted to Islam over the following century, as did Turks, who had also come in from the East. The Ottoman Empire emerged in the thirteenth and fourteenth centuries and was centered in present-day Turkey. The Hagia Sophia (see Fig. 15-4a and b) was the cathedral of Constantinople—renamed as Istanbul—from its dedication in 360 CE to the conquest by the Ottoman Turks in 1453, who had the building converted into a mosque. The cathedrals bells, altar, and religious figures were removed; a mihrab and the four minarets we see outside the structure today were installed. The Ottoman Empire was among the losers of World War I, in 1918; seventeen years later, in 1935, the Republic of Turkey made the Hagia Sophia into a museum—ending the Christian-Muslim conflict over the building.

The Alhambra (from the Arabic *Al-Hamra*, "the red one"), a fortress and palace, was built by Islamic Moorish rulers in Granada during the fourteenth century. It sits atop a hill on the edge of the city, in modern-day Spain. The Moors were expelled from Spain at about the same time as Columbus set sail on his western voyage, and today the Alhambra exhibits a combination of characteristic Islamic architectural elements

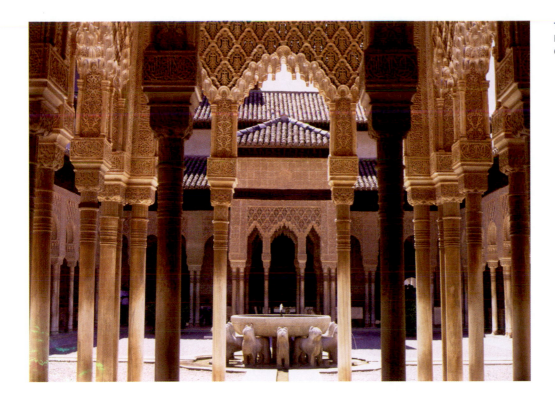

as well as a courtyard and fountain that seems reminiscent of those found in ancient Roman villas. Figure **15-15** shows a view of the Court of the Lions from a room of the palace. The mild Spanish winters make possible the full integration of the palace with its environment through a stately progression of intricately carved arched openings.

The Ardabil Carpet (see Fig. 12-17), discussed fully in the section on weaving in Chapter 12, was created during the Islamic Golden Age and is the oldest dated carpet in the history of art. It is not a religious work per se; the field of interlacing flowers and vines likely draws on references to paradise as a garden in the Qur'an.

The Islamic world moved as far to the East as China and what is now Indonesia. The Taj Mahal (Fig. **15-16**) at Agra, India, is a mausoleum that was built by Shah Jahan in the seventeenth century in memory of his wife. Tree-lined pools

15-16 Taj Mahal, Agra, India (1630–1648 CE).

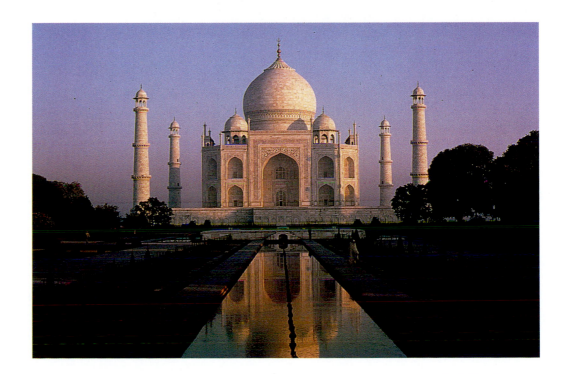

reflect a refined elegance. The three-quarters sphere of the dome is a stunning feat of engineering. Open archways, with their ever-changing play of light and shade, slender minarets, and spires give the marble structure a look of weightlessness. Creamy marble seems to melt in the perfect order.

EARLY MEDIEVAL EUROPE

As the power of the Roman Empire declined, non-Roman peoples (including the Huns, Vandals, Franks, Goths, and others once collectively called "barbarian tribes") gained con-

trol of parts of Europe. Over the centuries of tribal migrations across Eurasia, populations coalesced in what eventually would become the familiar countries of Europe—France, Italy, Scandinavia, Great Britain, and others.

Not much in the way of art and architecture remains of these migratory tribes, although finely wrought ornaments of gold, inlaid stones, and enamelware give us some indication of their artistic capabilities as well as the wealth and importance of their leaders. Two cemeteries excavated in Sutton Hoo, England, yielded a large number of ornaments and portable artifacts as well as an entire ship burial dating to the early seventh century CE. One such ornament, found in the ship, is a golden buckle intricately carved with intertwined serpents' and eagles' heads. Every last bit of the surface of the buckle is covered with interlaced decoration, a common stylistic characteristic that suggests the tangled world of mythic monsters in epics such as *Beowulf*.

Christian Art in the Early Middle Ages

Many works of Christian art from the Early Middle Ages combine characteristics of the small carvings and metalwork of these warrior tribes with symbols of the Christian faith. A carpet page from the *Lindisfarne Gospels*, so called for its resemblance to intricately patterned textiles (Fig. **15-17**), features a stylized cross inscribed with layers of intertwined, multicolored scrolls. The framed space surrounding the cross is similarly filled with repetitive linear patterns that can be decoded as snakes devouring themselves—an animal-interlace motif adapted from the decorative arts of non-Roman peoples.

Carolingian Art

The most important name linked to medieval art and culture during the period immediately following the migrations is that of Charlemagne (Charles the Great). This powerful ruler tried to unify the warring factions of Europe under the aegis of Christianity, and modeling his campaign on those of Roman emperors, he succeeded in doing so. In the year 800, Charlemagne was crowned Holy Roman Emperor by the pope, thus establishing a bond among the countries of western Europe that lasted more than a millennium (see Map **15-2**).

The period of Charlemagne's supremacy is called the **Carolingian period**. He established

15-17 Page from the *Lindisfarne Gospels* (Early Medieval, c. 700 CE). Illuminated manuscript. 13½" × 9¾".

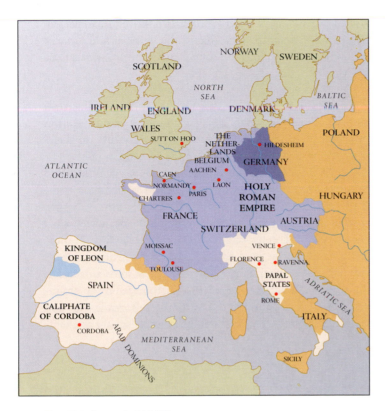

MAP 15-2 Europe (c. 800 CE).

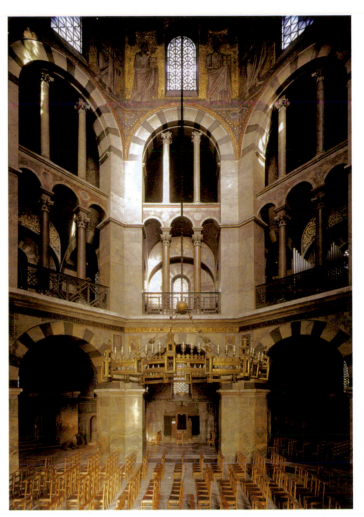

his court at Aachen, a western German city on the border of present-day Belgium, and imported the most significant intellectuals and artists of Europe and the Eastern countries.

THE PALATINE CHAPEL OF CHARLEMAGNE Charlemagne constructed his Palatine Chapel (palace chapel) with two architectural styles in mind (Fig. **15-18**). He sought to emulate Roman architecture but was probably also influenced by the central plan church of San Vitale, erected under Emperor Justinian. Like San Vitale, the Palatine Chapel is a central plan with an ambulatory and an octagonal dome. However, this is where the similarity ends. The perimeter of Charlemagne's chapel is polygonal, with almost sixteen facets instead of San Vitale's eight. There is also greater axial symmetry in the Palatine Chapel due to the more logical placement of the narthex.

The interior is also different from San Vitale. The semicircular niches that alternated with columns and pressed into the space of the Ravenna ambulatory have been eliminated at Aachen. There is more definition in the ambulatory between the central domed area and the building's perimeter. This clear articulation of parts is a hallmark of Roman design and stands in contrast to the fluid, organic character of some Byzantine architecture. The walls of the Palatine Chapel are divided into three distinct levels, and each level is divided by classically inspired archways or series of arches. Structural

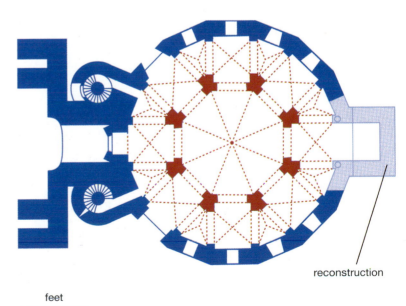

reconstruction

feet
0   20   40

15-18 Palatine Chapel of Charlemagne at Aachen, Germany (Carolingian, 792–805 CE). Interior and plan.

elements, architectural motifs, and a general blockiness of form point both backward and forward: to Roman architecture of the classical past and to the development of Romanesque architecture during the eleventh century.

MANUSCRIPT ILLUMINATION Charlemagne's court was an intellectual and artistic hub, and his love of knowledge and pursuit of truth helped keep the flame of scholarship flickering during the Early Middle Ages. His best-known project was the decipherment of the true biblical text, which, over decades, had suffered countless errors at the hands of careless scribes.

Ottonian Art

Following Charlemagne's death, internal and external strife threatened the existence of the Holy Roman Empire. It was torn apart on several occasions, only to be consolidated time and again under various rulers. The most significant of these were three German emperors, each named Otto, who suc-

ceeded one another in what is now called the Ottonian period. In many respects, their reigns symbolized an extension of Carolingian ideals, including the architectural and artistic styles that dominated Charlemagne's era.

ARCHITECTURE The most important architectural achievement of the Ottonian period was the construction of the abbey church of St. Michael in Hildesheim, Germany (Fig. 15-19).

St. Michael's offers us our first glimpse at a modified Roman basilican plan that will serve as a basis for Romanesque architecture.

The abbey church does not retain the propylaeum or atrium of Old St. Peter's, and it reverts to the lateral entrances of Roman basilicas. But all of the other elements of a typical Christian cathedral are present: narthex, nave, side aisles, transept, and a much enlarged apse surrounded by an ambulatory. Most significant for the future of Romanesque and Gothic architecture is the use of the crossing square as a tem-

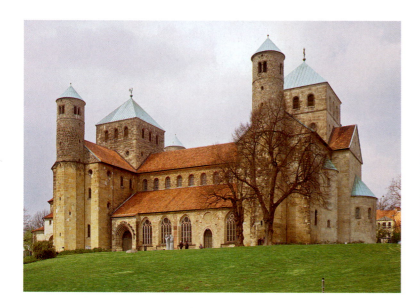

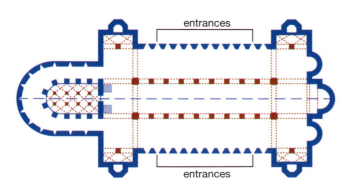

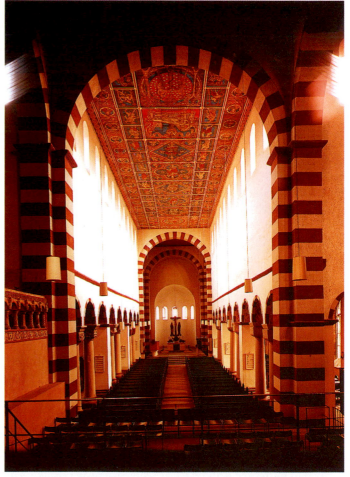

15-19 Abbey Church of St. Michael at Hildesheim, Germany (Ottonian, c. 1001–1031 CE). Restored. Exterior (above); interior (right); and plan (bottom).

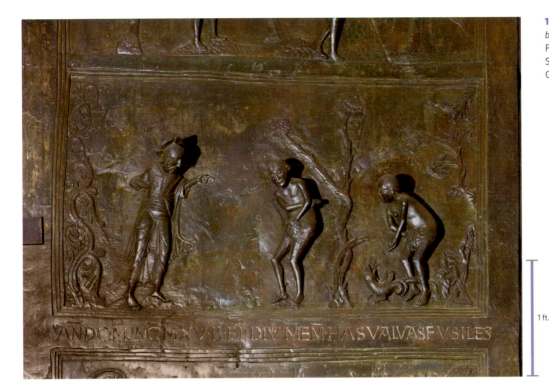

15-20 *Adam and Eve Reproached by the Lord* (Ottonian, 1015 CE). Panel of bronze doors. 23" × 43". St. Mary's Cathedral, Hildesheim, Germany.

1 ft.

plate for other spaces within the church. The crossing square is the area of overlap formed by the intersection of the nave and the transept. In the plan of St. Michael's, the nave consists of three consecutive modules that are equal in dimensions to the crossing square and marked off by square pillars. This design is an early example of square schematism, in which the crossing square (or a fraction or multiple thereof) determines the dimensions of the entire structure.

St. Michael's also uses an alternate support system in the walls of its nave. In such a system, alternating structural elements (in this case, pillars and columns) bear the weight of the walls and ultimately the load of the ceiling. The alternating elements in St. Michael's read as pillar-column-column-pillar; its alternate support system is then classified as a-b-b-a in terms of repetition of the supporting elements ("a" is assigned to a pillar and "b" is assigned to a column). An alternate support system of one kind or another will be a constant in Romanesque architecture.

As with Old St. Peter's, the exterior of St. Michael's reflects the character of its interior. Nave, side aisles, and other elements of the plan are clearly articulated in the blocky forms of the exterior. The exterior wall surfaces remain unadorned,

as were those of the Early Christian and Byzantine churches. However, the art of sculpture, which had not thrived since the fall of Rome, was reborn in St. Michael's.

SCULPTURE *Adam and Eve Reproached by the Lord* (Fig. **15-20**), a panel from the bronze doors of St. Mary's Cathedral in Hildesheim (originally commissioned for the Monastery of St. Michael by Bishop Bernward in the eleventh century), represents the first sculpture cast in one piece during the Middle Ages. In mood and style, the imagery closely resembles that seen in manuscript illumination of the period. It is an emotionally charged work, in which God points his finger accusingly at the pathetic figures of Adam and Eve. They, in turn, try to deflect the blame; Adam points to Eve and Eve gestures toward Satan, who is in the guise of a fantastic dragonlike animal crouched on the ground. These are not Classical figures who bear themselves proudly under stress. Rather, they are pitiful, wasted images that cower and try frantically to escape punishment. In this work, as well as in that of the Romanesque period, God is shown as a merciless judge, and human beings as quivering creatures who must beware of his wrath.

Early Medieval Europe　　**343**

ROMANESQUE ART

The Romanesque style appeared in the closing decades of the eleventh century among dramatic changes in all aspects of European life. Dynasties, such as those of the Carolingian and Ottonian periods, no longer existed. Individual monarchies ruled areas of Europe, rivaling one another for land and power. After the non-Roman peoples stopped invading and started settling, feudalism began to structure Europe, with monarchies at the head.

Feudalism was not the only force in medieval life of the Romanesque period. Monasticism also gained in importance. Monasteries during this time were structured communities that emphasized work and study, including manual labor (tending gardens, running bakeries, clearing tracts of wilderness, even building roads), reading and copying sacred texts, and memorizing music for chanting. Monasteries paved the way in education as monks became teachers. Salvation in the afterlife was a great preoccupation of the Middle Ages and served as the common denominator among classes. Nobility, clergy, and peasantry all directed their spiritual efforts toward this goal. Two phenomena reflect this obsession: the Crusades and the great pilgrimages.

The Crusades were holy wars waged in the name of recovering the Holy Land from the Muslims, who had taken it over in the seventh century. The pilgrimages were lengthy personal journeys undertaken to worship at sacred shrines or the tombs of saints. Participating in the Crusades and making pilgrimages were seen as holy acts that would help tip the scale in one's favor on Judgment Day. The pilgrims' need of a grand place to worship at journey's end gave impetus to church construction during the Romanesque period.

Architecture

In the Romanesque cathedral, there is a clear articulation of parts, with the exterior forms reflecting the interior spaces. The interiors consist of five major areas, with variations on this basic plan evident in different regions of Europe. We can add two Romanesque criteria to this basic format: spaciousness and fireproofing. The large crowds drawn by the pilgrimage fever required larger structures with interior spaces that would not restrict the flow of movement. After hostile invasions left churches in flames, it was also deemed necessary to fireproof the buildings by eliminating wooden roofs and covering the structures with cut stone.

ST. SERNIN The church of St. Sernin (Fig. **15-21**) in Toulouse, France, met all of the requirements for a Romanesque cathedral. An aerial view of the exterior shows the blocky forms that outline a nave, side aisles, the narthex to the west, a prominent transept crowned by a multilevel spire above the crossing square, and an apse at the eastern end from whose ambulatory extend five radiating chapels. In the plan

15-21 Church of St. Sernin, Toulouse, France (Romanesque, c. 1080–1120 CE).

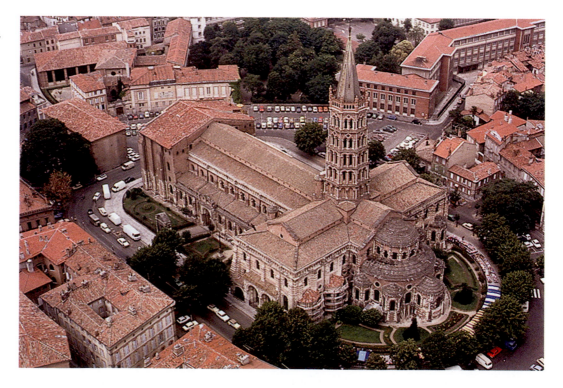

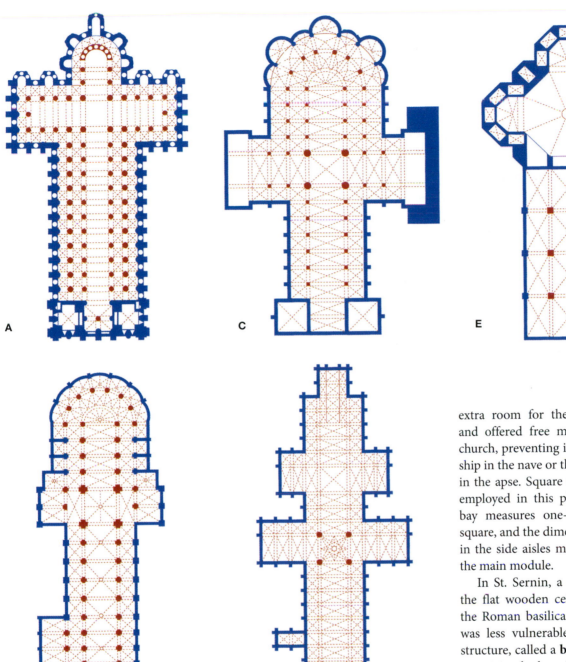

15-22 Basic differences among cathedral plans of the Romanesque and Gothic periods.

extra room for the crowds of pilgrims and offered free movement around the church, preventing interference with worship in the nave or the celebration of Mass in the apse. Square schematism has been employed in this plan; each rectangular bay measures one-half of the crossing square, and the dimensions of each square in the side aisles measures one-fourth of the main module.

In St. Sernin, a shift was made from the flat wooden ceiling characteristic of the Roman basilica to a stone vault that was less vulnerable to fire. The ceiling structure, called a **barrel vault**, resembles a semicircular barrel punctuated by arches that spring from engaged (attached) columns in the nave to define each bay. The massive weight of the vault is partially supported by the nave walls and partially by the side aisles that accept a share of the downward thrust. This is somewhat alleviated by the tribune gallery, which, in effect, reduces the drop-off from the barrel vault to the lower side aisles. The tribune gallery also provided extra space for worshipers.

Because the barrel vault rests directly on top of the tribune gallery, and because fenestration would weaken the structure

of St. Sernin (Fig. **15-22A**), the outermost side aisle continues around the outer borders of the transept arm and runs into the ambulatory around the apse. Along the eastern face of the transept, and around the ambulatory, a series of chapels radiate, or extend, from the aisle. These spaces provided

of the vault, there is little light in the interior of the cathedral. Lack of light was considered a major problem, and solving it would be the primary concern of future Romanesque architects. The history of Romanesque architecture can be written as the history of vaulting techniques, and the need for light provided the incentive for their development.

ST. ÉTIENNE The builders of the cathedral of St. Étienne in Normandy contributed significantly to the future of Romanesque and Gothic architecture in their design of its ceiling vault (Fig. **15-22B**). Instead of using a barrel vault that tunnels its way from narthex to apse, they divided the nave of St. Étienne into four distinct modules that reflect the shape of the crossing square. Each of these modules in turn is divided into six parts by ribs that spring from engaged columns and compound piers in the nave walls. Some of these ribs connect the midpoints of opposing sides of the squares; they are called transverse ribs. Other ribs intersect the space of the module diagonally, as seen in the plan; these are called diagonal ribs. An alternate a-b-a-b support system is used, with every other engaged column sending up a supporting rib that crosses the vault as a transverse arch. These engaged columns are distinguished from other nonsupporting members by their attachment to pilasters. The vault of St. Étienne is one of the first true rib vaults in that the combination of diagonal and transverse ribs functions as a skeleton that bears some of the weight of the ceiling. In later buildings, the role of ribs as support elements will be increased, and reliance on the massiveness of nave walls will be somewhat decreased.

Even though the nave walls of St. Étienne are still quite thick when compared with those of later Romanesque churches, the interior has a sense of lightness that does not exist in St. Sernin. The development of the rib vault made it possible to pierce the walls directly above the tribune gallery with windows. This series of windows that appears cut into the slightly domed modules of the ceiling is called a clerestory. The clerestory became a standard element of the Gothic cathedral plan. The facade of St. Étienne (Fig. **15-23**) also served as a model for Gothic architecture. It is divided vertically into three sections by thick buttresses, reflecting the nave and side aisles of the interior, and horizontally into three bands, pierced by portals on the entrance floor and arched windows on the upper levels. Two bell towers complete the facade, each of which is also divided into three parts (the spires were later additions). This two-tower, tripartite facade appeared repeatedly in Gothic structures, although the walls were pierced by more carving and fenestration and are thus lighter in appearance. The symmetry and predictability of the St. Étienne design, on the other hand, were maintained.

Sculpture

Although we occasionally find freestanding sculpture from the Romanesque and Gothic periods, it was far more common for sculpture to be restricted to archi-

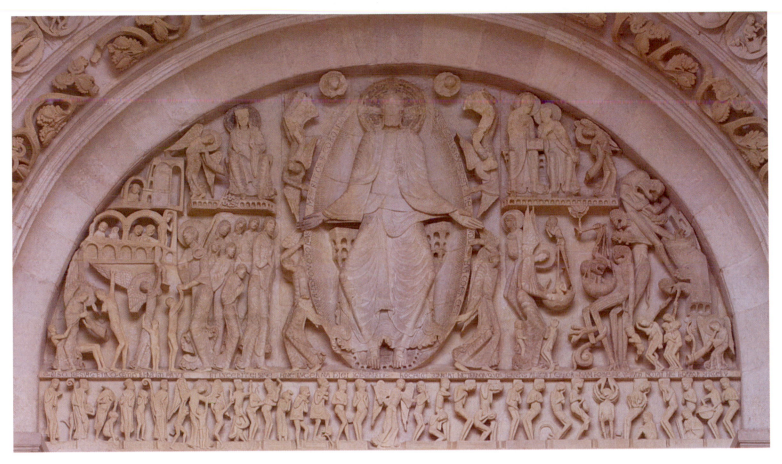

15-24 Cathedral of Saint-Lazare, Autun, France. West portal. Detail of Last Judgment tympanum.

tectural decoration around the portals. Some of the most important and elaborate sculptural decoration is found in the tympanum—a semicircular space above the doors to a cathedral—such as that of the cathedral at Autun in Burgundy (Fig. **15-24**). The carved portals of cathedrals bore scenes and symbols that acted as harsh reminders of fate in the afterlife. They were intended to communicate pictorially a profound message, if not direct warning, to the potential, primarily illiterate sinner that repentance through prayer and action was necessary for salvation.

At Autun, the scene depicted is that of the Last Judgment. The tympanum rests on a lintel carved with small figures representing the dead. The archangel Michael stands in the center, dividing the horizontal band of figures into two groups. The naked dead on the left gaze upward, hopeful of achieving eternal reward in heaven, while those to the right look downward in despair. Above the lintel, Jesus is depicted as an evenhanded judge. To his left, tall, thin figures representing the apostles observe the scene, while some angels lift bodies into heaven. To Jesus' right, by contrast, is a gruesome event. The dead are snatched up from their graves, and their souls

are being weighed on a scale by an angel on the left and a devil-serpent on the right. The devil cheats by adding a little weight, and some of his companions stand ready to grab the souls and fling them into hell. As in the bronze doors of St. Michael's, humankind is shown as a pitiful, defenseless race, no match for the wiles of Satan. The figures crouch in terror of their surroundings, in strong contrast to the serenity of their impartial judge.

The Romanesque sculptor sought stylistic inspiration in Roman works, the small carvings of the pre-Romanesque era, and especially manuscript illumination. In the early phase of Romanesque art, naturalism was not a concern. Artists turned to art rather than to nature for models, and thus their figures are at least twice, and perhaps a hundred times, removed from the original source. It is no wonder, then, that they appear as dolls or marionettes. The figure of Jesus is squashed within a large oval, and his limbs bend in sharp angles in order to fit the frame. Although his drapery seems to correspond broadly to the body beneath, the folds are reduced to stylized patterns of concentric arcs that play across a relatively flat surface. Realism is not the goal. The sculptor is focused on conveying his frightful message with the details and emotions that will have the most dramatic impact on the worshiper or penitent sinner.

Manuscript Illumination

The relationship between Romanesque sculpture and manuscript illumination can be seen in *The Annunciation to the Shepherds* (Fig. **15-25**), a page from the *Lectionary of Henry II*. As with the figure of Jesus in the Autun tympanum, the long and gangling limbs of the figures join their torsos at odd angles. Drapery falls at harsh, unnatural angles. Sent by God, the angel Gabriel alights on a hilltop to announce the birth of the Christ-child to shepherds tending their flocks. The angel towers over the rocky mound and appears to be almost twice the size of the shepherds. The shepherds, in turn, are portrayed as unnaturally large in relation to the animals. The animals along the bottom edge of the picture stand little more than ankle high. The use of hierarchical scaling implies that humans are less significant than celestial beings and that animals are lower than humans. The symbols in the scene take precedence over truth; reality fades in their wake.

Toward the end of the Romanesque period, there was a significant increase in naturalism. Drapery falls softly rather than in sharp angles, and the body begins to acquire more substance. The gestures are less frantic, and a balance between emotion and restraint begins to reappear. These elements reached their peak during the Gothic period and pointed to a full-scale revival of Classicism during the Renaissance of the fifteenth century.

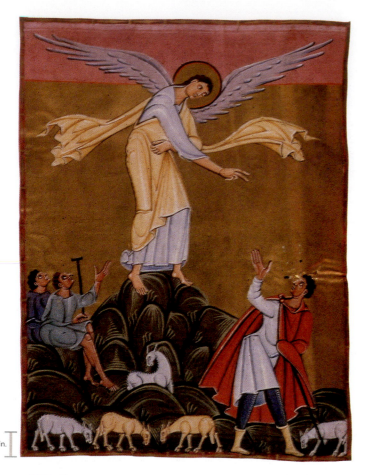

15-25 *The Annunciation to the Shepherds,* from the *Lectionary of Henry II* (1002–1014 CE). Approx. 17" × 13". Bayerische Staatsbibliothek, München, Germany.

1 in.

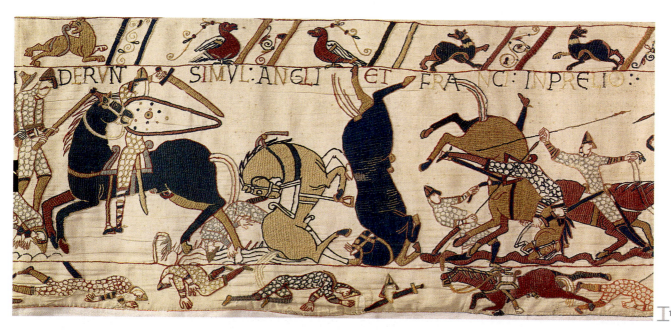

1 in.

15-26 Battle of Hastings, detail of the *Bayeux Tapestry,* from Bayeux Cathedral, Bayeux, France (c. 1070–1080 CE). Embroidered wool on linen. 1'8" high (entire length of fabric: 222'8"). Centre Guillaume le Conquérant, Bayeux, France.

Tapestry

Although the tasks of copying sacred texts and embellishing them with manuscript illuminations were sometimes assumed by women, the art form remained primarily a male preserve. Not so with the medium of tapestry. In the Middle Ages, weaving and embroidery were taught to women of all social classes and walks of life. Noblewomen and nuns would weave and decorate elaborate tapestries, clothing, and liturgical vestments, using the finest linens, wools, gold and silver thread, pearls, and other gems.

One of the most famous surviving tapestries, the *Bayeux Tapestry* (Fig. **15-26**), was almost certainly created by a team of women at the commission of Odo, the bishop of Bayeux. The tapestry describes the invasion of England by William the Conqueror in a continuous narrative. Although the tapestry is less than 2 feet in height, it originally measured in excess of 230 running feet and was meant to run clockwise around the entire nave of the Cathedral of Bayeux. In this way, the narrative functioned much in the same way as the continuous narrative of the Ionic frieze of the Parthenon.

GOTHIC ART

Art and architecture of the twelfth and thirteenth centuries in Europe is called Gothic. The term *Gothic* originated among historians who believed that the Goths were responsible for the style of this period. Because critics believed that the Gothic style only further buried the light of Classicism, and because the Goths were "barbarians," the term *Gothic* was used disparagingly. For many years, the most positive criticism of Gothic art was that it was a step forward from the Romanesque. *Gothic* is no longer a term of derision, and the Romanesque and Gothic styles are seen as distinct and as responsive to the unique tempers of their times.

Architecture

In the history of art, it is rare to be able to trace the development of a particular style to a single work, or the beginning of a movement to a specific date. However, it is generally agreed that the Gothic style of architecture began in 1140 with the construction of the choir of the church of St. Denis near Paris. The vaults of the choir consisted of weight-bearing ribs that formed the skeleton of the ceiling structure. The spaces between the ribs

were then filled in with cut stone. At St. Denis, the pointed arch is used in the structural skeleton rather than the rounded arches of the Romanesque style. This vault construction also permitted the use of larger areas of stained glass, dissolving the massiveness of the Romanesque wall.

LAON CATHEDRAL Although Laon Cathedral is considered an Early Gothic building, its plan resembles those of Romanesque churches. For example, the ceiling is a sexpartite rib vault supported by groups of columns in an alternate a-b-a-b rhythm (Fig. **15-27**). Yet there were important innovations at Laon. The interior displays a change in wall elevation from three to four levels. A series of arches, or triforium, was added above the tribune gallery to pierce further the solid surfaces of the nave walls. The obsession with

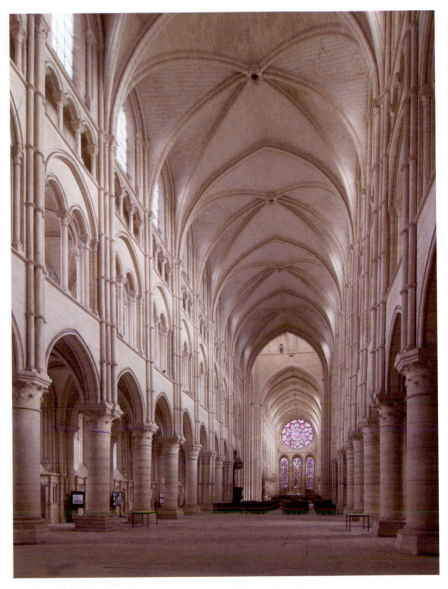

15-27 Interior of Laon Cathedral, view facing east, Laon, France (begun c. 1190 CE).

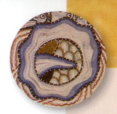

DURING THE MIDDLE AGES, the production and illustration of sacred books took place, for the most part, in the monastery and the abbey, with the greatest percentage of scribes and painters being men. Yet some upper-class women looking for an alternative to marriage and eager to follow these and other intellectual and aesthetic pursuits entered the contemplative life of the nunnery.

One such woman was the German abbess Hildegard of Bingen (1098–1179). Hildegard was a mystic whose visions of otherworldly phenomena began during childhood and led to a life of scholarship elucidating her extraordinary experiences. She wrote books on medicine and history, composed music, debated political and religious issues, and designed illustrations to accompany written records of her visions. Hildegard also devised a secret language. Her most valuable work is the *Liber Scivias*, a text built around images of light and darkness. Sun, stars, moon, and flaming orbs struggle against dragons, demons, and other denizens of darkness.

Figure **15-28** is a twelfth-century copy of Hildegard's *Vision of the Ball of Fire*, an illustration no doubt designed by the abbess and most likely executed by her nuns. An elaborately patterned orb floats in the center of a simpler rectangular frame. Its central symbols are surrounded by a field of star-flowers spreading outward toward a wreath of flames. Here and there one can spot demons spewing forth fire. The neatness of the execution bears similarity to the fine needlepoint and embroidery techniques characteristic of medieval tapestries. Here follows Hildegard's vision on which the painting was based:

Then I saw a huge image, round and shadowy. It was pointed at the top, like an egg. . . .

Its outermost layer was of bright fire. Within lay a dark membrane. Suspended in the bright flames was a burning ball of fire, so large that the entire image received its light. Three more lights burned in a row above it. They gave it support through their glow, so that the light would never be extinguished. ●

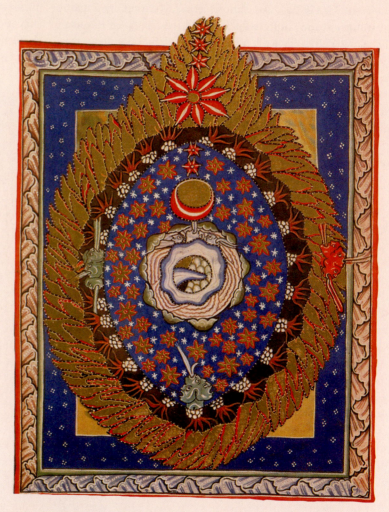

15-28 HILDEGARD OF BINGEN. *Vision of the Ball of Fire.* Illumination from the *Liber Scivias* (12th century CE). Rupertberg, Germany (original destroyed).

reducing the appearance of heaviness in the walls can also be seen on the exterior (Fig. **15-29**). If we compare the facade of St. Étienne with that of Laon, we see a change from a massive, fortresslike appearance to one that seems lighter and more organic. The facade of Laon Cathedral is divided into three levels, although there is less distinction between them than in a Romanesque facade. The portals jut forward from the plane of the facade, creating a tunnel-like entrance. The stone is pierced by arched windows, arcades, and a large **rose window** in the center, and the twin bell towers seem to be constructed of voids rather than solids.

As the Gothic period progressed, all efforts were directed toward the dissolution of stone surfaces. The walls were penetrated by greater expanses of glass, nave elevations rose to new heights, and carved details became more complex and delicate. There was a mystical quality to these buildings in the way they seemed exempt from the laws of gravity.

NOTRE-DAME One of the most famous buildings in the history of architecture is the Cathedral of Notre-Dame de Paris (Fig. **15-30**). Perched on the banks of the Seine, it has enchanted visitors ever since its construction. Notre-Dame is a curious mixture of old and new elements. It retains a sexpartite rib vault and was originally planned to have an Early Gothic four-level wall elevation. It was begun in 1163 and was not completed until almost a century later, undergoing extensive modifications between 1225 and 1250. Some of these

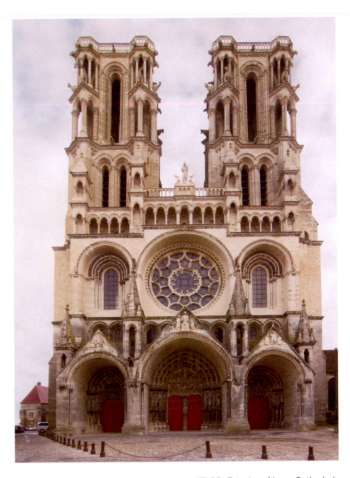

15-29 Exterior of Laon Cathedral, west facade, Laon, France (begun c. 1190 CE).

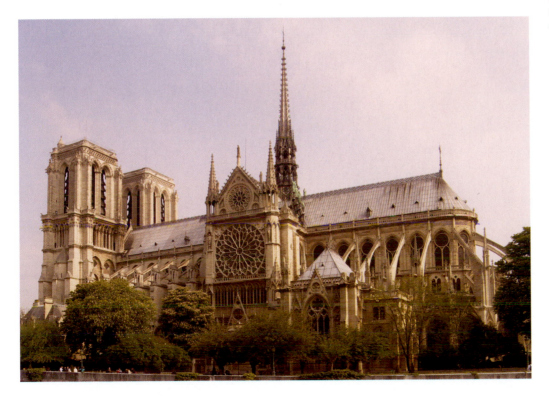

15-30 Cathedral of Notre-Dame de Paris, Paris, France. (Gothic, begun 1163 CE, completed 1250 CE).

changes reflected the development of the High Gothic style, including the elimination of the triforium and the use of flying buttresses to support the nave walls. The exterior of the building also reveals this combination of early and late styles. Although the facade is far more massive than that of Laon Cathedral, the north and south elevations look light and airy because of their fenestration and the lacy buttressing.

CHARTRES CATHEDRAL Chartres Cathedral is generally considered to be the first High Gothic church. Unlike Notre-Dame, Chartres was planned from the beginning to have a three-level wall elevation and flying buttresses. The three-part wall elevation allowed for larger windows in the clerestory, admitting more light into the interior (Fig. 15-31). The use of large windows in the clerestory was in turn made possible by the development of the flying buttress.

In the High Gothic period, there is a change from square schematism to a rectangular bay system (Fig. 15-22C). In the latter, each rectangular bay has its own cross rib vault, and only one side aisle square flanks each rectangular bay. Thus, the need for an alternate support system is eliminated. The interior of a High Gothic cathedral presents several dramatic vistas. There is a continuous sweep of space from the narthex to the apse along a nave that is uninterrupted by alternating supports.

There is also a strong vertical thrust from floor to vaults that is enhanced by the elimination of the triforium and the increased heights of the arches in the nave arcade and clerestory windows. The solid wall surfaces are further dissolved by quantities of stained glass that flood the interior with spectacular patterns of soft colored light. The architects directed all of their efforts toward creating a spiritual escape to another world. They did so by effectively defying the properties of matter: creating the illusion of weightlessness in stone and dissolving solid surfaces with mesmerizing streams of colored light.

GOTHIC ARCHITECTURE OUTSIDE FRANCE The cathedrals that we have examined thus far were built in France, where the Gothic style flourished. Variations on the French Gothic style can also be seen elsewhere in northern Europe, although in some English and German cathedrals the general "blockiness" of Romanesque architecture persisted. The plan of Salisbury Cathedral (Fig. 15-22D) in England illustrates some differences between English and French architecture of the Gothic period, as seen in the double transept and the unique square apse. The profile of Salisbury Cathedral also differs from that of a French church in that the bell towers on the western end are level with the rest of the facade, and a tall tower rises above the crossing square. Still,

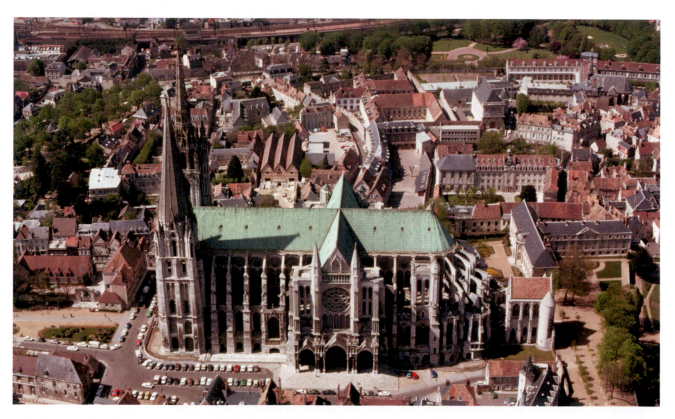

15-31 Aerial view from the northwest of Chartres Cathedral, Chartres, France (begun 1134 CE, rebuilt after 1194 CE).

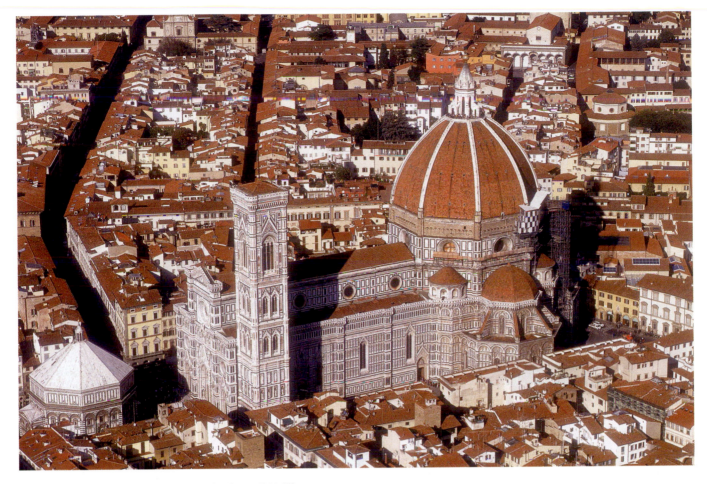

15-32 Florence Cathedral, Florence, Italy (Gothic, begun 1368 CE).

the remaining characteristics of the cathedral, including the rectangular bay system, bear close relationship to the French Gothic style. In Italy, on the other hand, the French style was not strictly adhered to, as is seen in the Florence Cathedral (Fig. **15-32**). The most striking features of its exterior are the sharp, geometric patterns of green and white marble and the horizontality, or earthbound quality, of its profile.

These contrast with the vertical lines of the French Gothic cathedral that seem to reach for heaven. The French were obsessed with the visual disintegration of massive stone walls. The Italians, on the other hand, preserved the mural quality of the structure. In the cathedral of Florence, there are no flying buttresses. The wall elevation has been reduced to two levels, with a minimum of fenestration.

The Florence Cathedral is also different in plan (Fig. **15-22E**) from French cathedrals. A huge octagonal dome overrides the structure. The nave consists of four large and clearly defined modules, flanked by rectangular bays in the side aisles. There is only one bell tower in the Italian cathedral, and it is detached from the facade.

Why would this Italian Gothic cathedral differ so markedly from those of the French? Given its strong roots in Classical Rome, it may be that Italy never succumbed wholeheartedly to Gothicism. Perhaps for this reason, Italy would be the birthplace of the revival of Classicism during the Renaissance. We shall discuss the Florence Cathedral further in the following chapter, because the designer of its dome was one of the principal architects of the Renaissance.

Sculpture

Sculpture during the Gothic period reveals a change in mood from that of the Romanesque. The iconography is one of redemption rather than damnation. The horrible scenes of Judgment Day that threatened the worshiper upon entering the cathedral were replaced by scenes from the life of Jesus or visions of the apocalypse. The Virgin Mary also assumed a primary role. Carved tympanums, whole sculptural programs, even cathedrals themselves (for example, Notre-Dame, which means "Our Lady") were dedicated to her.

Gothic sculpture was still pretty much confined to decoration of cathedral portals. Every square inch of the tympanums, lintels, and archivolts of most Gothic cathedrals was carved with a dazzling array of figures and ornamental motifs. However, some of the most advanced full-scale sculpture is to be found adorning the jambs, such as those flanking the portals of Chartres Cathedral (Fig. **15-33**). The figures are rigid in their poses, confined by the columns to which they are attached. The drapery falls in predictable stylized folds reminiscent of those seen in manuscript illumination.

Yet there is a certain weight to the bodies, and the "hinged" treatment of the limbs is eliminated, heralding change from the Romanesque. During the High Gothic period, these simple elements led to a naturalism that had not been witnessed since Classical times.

The jamb figures of Reims Cathedral (Fig. **15-34**) illustrate an interesting combination of styles. No doubt the individual figures were carved by different artists. The detail of the central portal of the facade illustrates two groups of figures. To the left is an Annunciation scene with the angel Gabriel and the Virgin Mary, and to the right is a Visitation scene depicting the Virgin Mary and St. Elizabeth. All of the figures are detached from columns and instead occupy the spaces between them. Although they have been carved for these specific niches and are perched on small pedestals, they suggest a freedom of movement that is not found in the jamb figures at Chartres.

The Virgin Mary of the Annunciation group is the least advanced in technique of the four figures. Her stance is the most rigid, and her gestures and facial expression are the most stylized. Yet her body has substance, and anatomical details are revealed beneath a drapery that responds realistically to the movement of her limbs. The figure of Gabriel contrasts strongly in style with that of the Virgin Mary. He seems relatively tall and lanky. His head is small and delicate, and his facial features are refined. His body has a subtle sway that is accented by the flowing lines of his drapery. Stateliness and sweetness characterize this courtly style; it will be carried forward into the Early Renaissance period in the **International Gothic style**.

Yet Classicism will be the major style of the Renaissance, and in the Visitation group of the Reims portals, we have a fascinating introduction to it. The weighty figures of Mary and Elizabeth are placed in a contrapposto stance. The folds of drapery articulate the movement of the bodies beneath with a realism that we have not seen

15-33 Jamb figures, west portals, Chartres Cathedral, Chartres, France (Gothic, c. 1140–1150 CE).

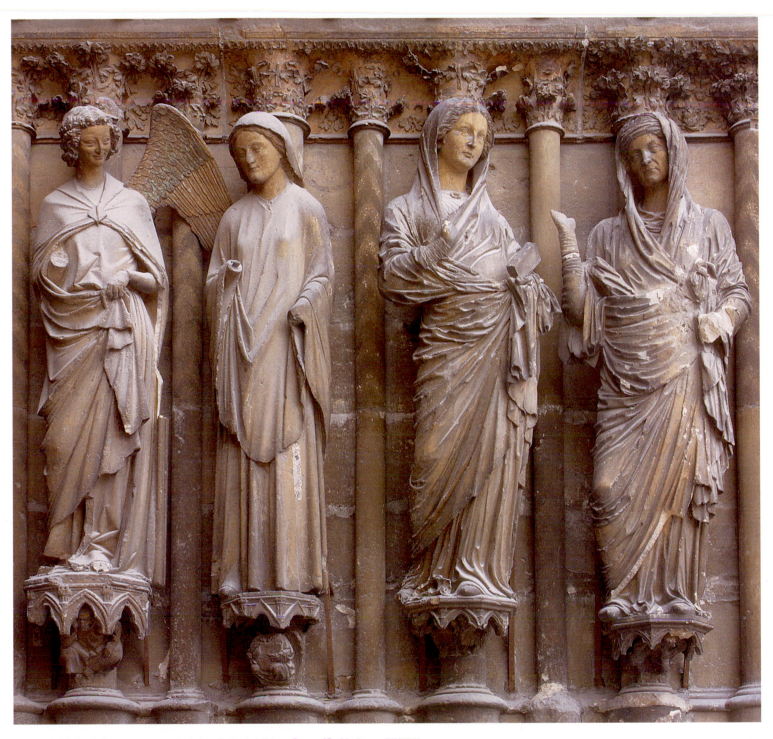

15-34 Jamb figures, west portals, Reims Cathedral, Reims, France (Gothic, begun 1210 CE).

since Classical times. Even the facial features and hairstyles are reminiscent of Greek and Roman sculpture. Although we have linked the reappearance of naturalism to the Gothic artist's increased awareness of nature, we must speculate that the sculptor of the Visitation group was looking directly to Classical statues for inspiration. The similarities are too strong to be coincidental. With his small and isolated attempt to revive Classicism, this unknown artist stands as a transitional figure between the spiritualism of the medieval world and the rationalism and humanism of the Renaissance.

Gothic Art   **355**

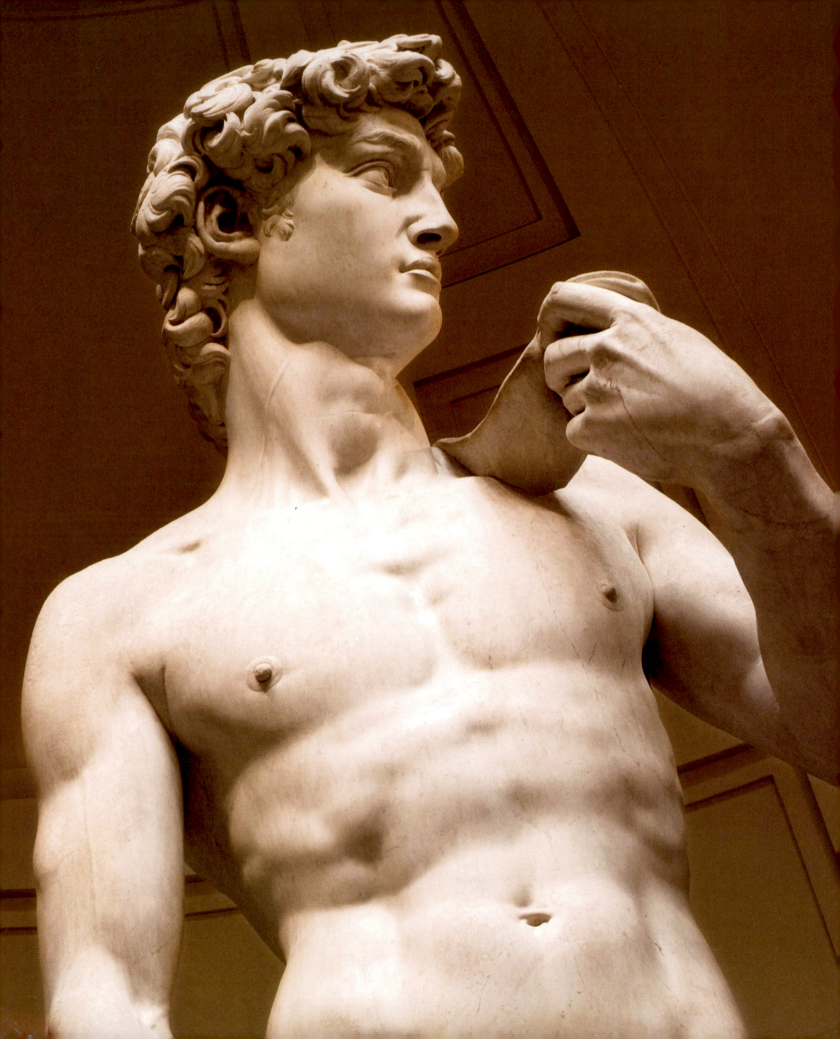

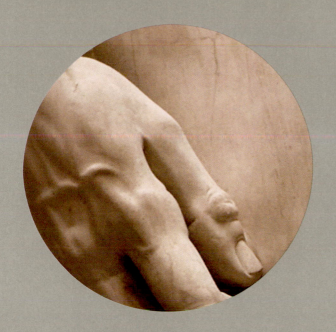

The fundamental principle will be that all steps of learning should be sought from Nature; the means of perfecting our art will be found in diligence, study, and application.

—Leon Battista Alberti

THE RENAISSANCE

16

While Columbus brought his ships to the New World in 1492, a 17-year-old Michelangelo Buonarroti was perfecting his skill at rendering human features from blocks of marble. In 1564, the year that Shakespeare was born, Michelangelo died. These are two of the marker dates of the **Renaissance**. *Renaissance* is a French word meaning "rebirth," and the Renaissance in Europe was a period of significant historical, social, and economic events. The old feudal system that had organized Europe during the Middle Ages fell to a system of government based on independent city-states with powerful kings and princes at their helms. The economic face of Europe changed, aided by an expansion of trade and commerce with Eastern countries. The cultural base of Europe shifted from Gothic France to Italy. A plague wiped out the populations of entire cities in Europe and Asia. Speculation on the world beyond, which had so preoccupied the medieval mind, was counterbalanced by a scientific observation of the world at hand. Although Copernicus proclaimed that the sun, and not the earth, was at the center of the solar system, humanity, and not heaven, became the center of all things.

MICHELANGELO. *David* (1501–1504). Marble. H: 13½'. Galleria dell'Accademia, Florence, Italy.

THE RENAISSANCE

The Renaissance spans roughly the fourteenth through the sixteenth centuries and is seen by some as the beginning of modern history. During this period, particularly in Italy, we witness a revival of Classical themes in art and literature, a return to the realistic depiction of nature through keen observation, and the revitalization of the Greek philosophy of humanism, in which human dignity, ideas, and capabilities are of central importance.

Changes, artistic and otherwise, took root all over Europe, but Italy and Flanders (present-day Belgium and the Netherlands) developed into world-class economic and cultural centers in the fifteenth century (see Map **16-1**). Given its Classical roots, Italy never quite succumbed to Gothicism and readily introduced elements of Greek and Roman art into its art and architecture. But Flanders was steeped in the medieval tradition of northern Europe and continued to concern itself with the spiritualism of the Gothic era, enriching it with a supreme realism. (It is worth noting that because the word *renaissance* generally refers to the artistic and cultural revival of Classical sources, some art historians no longer use it to describe northern art of this period.)

The difference in attitudes was summed up during the later Renaissance years by one of Italy's great artists, Michelangelo Buonarroti, not entirely without prejudice:

> Flemish painting will, generally speaking, please the devout better than any painting in Italy, which will never cause him to shed a tear, whereas that of Flanders will cause him to shed many. . . . In Flanders they paint with a view to external exactness or such things as may cheer you and of which you cannot speak ill, as for example saints and prophets. They paint stuffs and masonry, the green grass of the fields, the shadows of trees, and rivers and bridges.[1]

Thus, the subject matter of northern artists remained more consistently religious, although their manner of representation was that of an exact, trompe l'oeil rendition of things of this world. They used the "trick-the-eye" technique to portray mystical religious phenomena in a realistic manner. The exactness of representation of which Michelangelo spoke originated in **manuscript illumination**, where complicated imagery was reduced

to a minute scale. Because this imagery illustrated texts, it was often laden with symbolic meaning. Symbolism was carried into **panel paintings**, where it was fused with a keen observation of nature.

FIFTEENTH-CENTURY NORTHERN PAINTING

Flemish Painting: From Page to Panel

A certain degree of naturalism appeared in the work of the northern book illustrator during the Gothic period. The manuscript illuminator *illuminated* literary passages with visual imagery. As the art of manuscript illumination progressed, these thumbnail sketches were enlarged to fill greater portions of the manuscript page, eventually covering it entirely. As the text pages became less able to contain this imagery, the northern Renaissance artist shifted to painting in tempera on wood panels.

THE LIMBOURG BROTHERS One of the most dazzling texts available to illustrate this transfer from minute to more substantial imagery is *Les Très Riches Heures du Duc de Berry*, a Book of Hours illustrated by the Limbourg brothers (born after 1385, died by 1416) during the opening decades of the fifteenth century. Books of Hours were used by nobility as prayer books and included psalms and litanies to a variety of saints. As did most Books of Hours, *Les Très Riches Heures* contained calendar pages that illustrated domestic tasks and

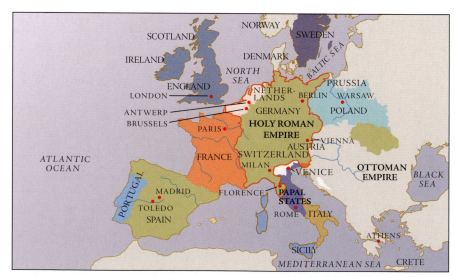

MAP **16-1** Renaissance Europe (c. 16th century).

---

[1] Robert Goldwater and Marco Treves, eds., *Artists on Art* (New York: Pantheon Books, 1972), 68.

social events of the 12 months of the year. In "May" (Fig. **16-1**), one of the calendar pages, we witness a parade of aristocratic gentlemen and ladies who have come in their bejeweled costumes of pastel hues to celebrate the first day of May. Complete with glittering regalia and festive song, the entourage romps through a woodland clearing on carousel-like horses. In the background looms a spectacular castle complex, the chateau of Riom.

The calendar pages of *Les Très Riches Heures* are rendered in the **International style**, a manner of painting common throughout Europe during the late fourteenth and early fifteenth centuries. This style is characterized by ornate costumes embellished with gold leaf and by subject matter literally fit for a king, including courtly scenes and splendid processions. The refinement of technique and attention to detail in these calendar pages recall earlier manuscript illumination. These qualities, and a keen observation of the human response to the environment—or in this case the merrymaking—bring to mind Michelangelo's assessment of northern painting as obsessed with representation of the real world through the painstaking rendition of its everyday objects and occurrences.

Although these calendar pages illustrated a holy book, the themes were secular. Fifteenth-century artists tried to reconcile religious subjects with scenes and objects from everyday life, and northern artists accomplished this by using symbolism. Artists would populate ordinary interiors with objects that might bear some spiritual significance. Many, if not most, of the commonplace items might be invested with a special religious meaning. You might ask how you, the casual observer, are supposed to decipher the cryptic meaning lurking behind an ordinary kettle. Chances are that you would be unable to do so without a specialized background. Yet you can enjoy the warm feeling of being invited into someone's home when you look at a northern Renaissance interior and be all the more enriched by the knowledge that there really is something more there than meets the eye.

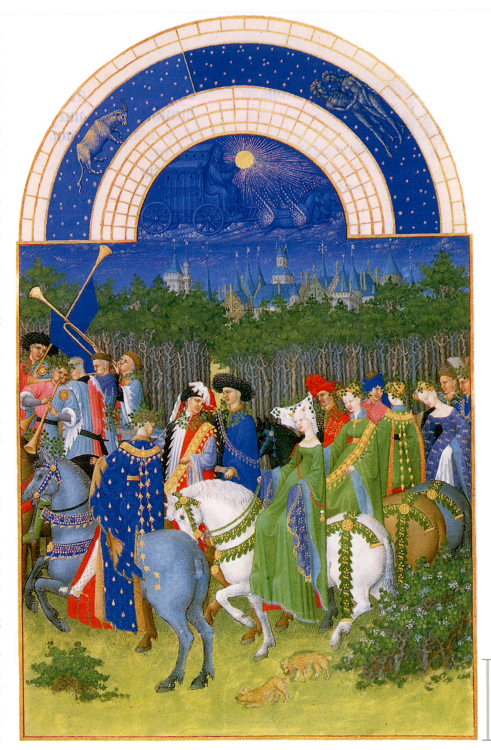

16-1 LIMBOURG BROTHERS. "May" from *Les Très Riches Heures du Duc de Berry* (1416). Ink on vellum. 8⅞" × 5⅜". Musée Conde, Chantilly, France.

ROBERT CAMPIN, THE MASTER OF FLÉMALLE Attention to detail and the use of commonplace settings were carried forward in the soberly realistic religious figures painted by Robert Campin, the Master of Flémalle (c. 1378–1444).

His *Merode Altarpiece* (Fig. **16-2**) is a triptych whose three panels, from left to right, contain the kneeling donors of the altarpiece; an Annunciation scene with the Virgin Mary and the angel Gabriel; and Joseph, the foster father of Jesus, at work in his carpentry shop. The architectural setting is a typical contemporary Flemish dwelling. The donors kneel by the doorstep in a garden thick with grass and wildflowers, each of which has special symbolic significance regarding the Virgin Mary. Although the door is ajar, it is not clear whether they are witnessing the event inside or whether Campin has used the open door as a compositional device to lead the spectator's eye into the central panel of the triptych.

In any event, we are visually and psychologically coaxed into viewing this most atypical Annunciation. Mary is depicted as a prim and proper middle-class Flemish woman surrounded by the trappings of a typical Flemish household, all rendered in exacting detail. Just as the closed outdoor garden symbolizes the holiness and purity of the Virgin Mary, the items within also possess symbolic meaning. For example, the bronze kettle hanging in the Gothic niche on the back wall symbolizes the Virgin's body—it will be the immaculate container of the redeemer of the Christian world. More obvious symbols of her purity include the spotless room and the vase of lilies on the table. In the upper left corner of the central panel, a small child can be seen, bearing a cross and riding streams of "divine light." The wooden table situated between Mary and Gabriel and the room divider between Mary and Joseph guarantee that the light accomplished the deed. Typically, Joseph is shown as a man too old to have been the biological father of Jesus, although Campin's depiction does not quite follow this tradition. He is gray, but by no means ancient. Jesus' earthly father is busy preparing mousetraps—one on the table and one on the windowsill—commonplace objects that symbolize the belief that Christ was the bait with which Satan would be trapped.

The symbolism in the altarpiece presents a fascinating web for the observer to untangle and interpret. Yet it does not overpower the hard-core realism of the ordinary people and objects. With the exceptions of the slight inconsistency of size and the tilting of planes toward the viewer, Campin offers us a continuous realism that sweeps the three panels. There is no distinction between saintly and common folk; the facial types of the heavenly beings are as individual as the portraits of the donors. Although fifteenth-century viewers would have been aware of the symbolism and the sacredness of the event, they would have also been permit-

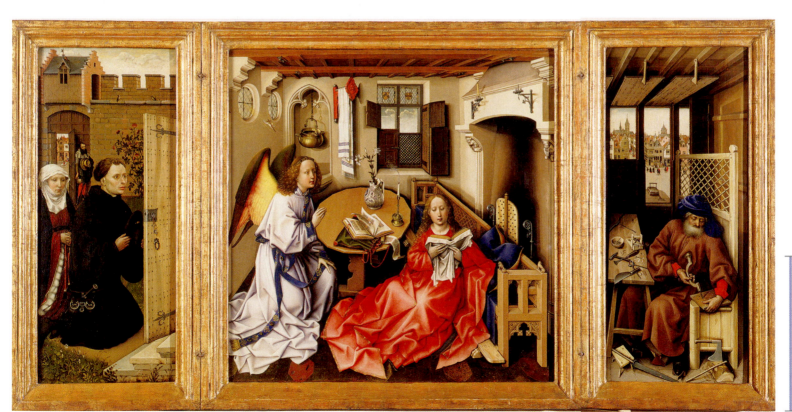

16-2 ROBERT CAMPIN. *Merode Altarpiece: The Annunciation with Donors and St. Joseph* (c. 1425–1428). Oil on wood. Center: 24¼" × 24⅞"; wings: each 25⅜" × 10⅞". The Metropolitan Museum of Art, NY (The Cloisters Collection).

ted to become "a part" of the scene, so to speak, and to react to it as if the people in the painting were their peers and just happened to find themselves in extraordinary circumstances.

JAN VAN EYCK We might say that Campin "humanized" his Mary and Joseph in the *Merode Altarpiece*. As religious subjects became more secular in nature and the figures became rendered as "human," an interest in ordinary, secular subject matter sprang up. During the fifteenth century in northern Europe, we have the development of what is known as **genre painting**, painting that depicts ordinary people engaged in run-of-the-mill activities. These paintings make little or no reference to religion; they exist almost as art for art's sake. Yet they are no less devoid of symbolism.

Giovanni Arnolfini and His Bride (Fig. **16-3**) was executed by one of the most prominent and significant Flemish painters of the fifteenth century, Jan van Eyck (c. 1395–1441). This unique double portrait was commissioned by an Italian businessman working in Bruges to serve as a kind of marriage contract, or record of the couple's taking of marriage vows in the presence of two witnesses. The significance of such a document—in this case a visual one—is emphasized by the art historian Erwin Panofsky: According to Catholic dogma, the sacrament of matrimony is "immediately accomplished by the mutual consent of the persons to be married when this consent is expressed by words and actions" in the presence of two or three witnesses. Records of the marriage were necessary to avoid lawsuits in which "the validity of the marriage could be neither proved nor disproved for want of reliable witnesses."[2]

Once again we see the northern artist's striking realism and fidelity to detail, offering us exact records of the facial features of the wedding couple. The figures of the two witnesses are reflected in the convex mirror behind the Arnolfinis. Believe it or not, they are Jan van Eyck and his wife, a fact corroborated by the inscription above the mirror: "Jan van Eyck was here." As in most Flemish paintings, the items scattered about are invested with symbolism relevant to the occasion. The furry dog in the foreground symbolizes fidelity, and the oranges on the windowsill may symbolize victory over death. Giovanni has kicked off his shoes out of respect for the holiness of the ground on which this sacrament takes place. Finally, the finial on the bedpost is an image of St. Margaret,

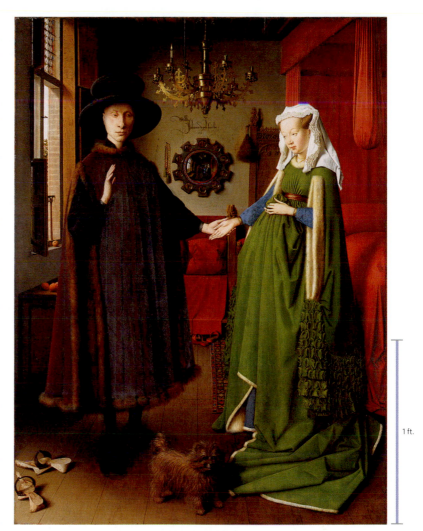

16-3 JAN VAN EYCK. *Giovanni Arnolfini and His Bride* (1434). Oil on wood. 33" × 22½". National Gallery, London, England.

the patroness of childbirth, and around her wooden waist is slung a small whisk broom, a symbol of domesticity. It would seem that Giovanni had his bride's career all mapped out. With Jan van Eyck, Flemish painting reached the height of symbolic realism in both religious and secular subject matter. No one ever quite followed in his footsteps.

German Art

Northern Renaissance painting is not confined to the region of Flanders, and some of the most emotionally striking work of this period was created by German artists. Their work contains less symbolism and less detail than that of Flemish artists, but their message is often more powerful.

---

[2] Erwin Panofsky, "Jan van Eyck's 'Arnolfini' Portrait," *Burlington Magazine* 64 (1934): 117–127.

MATTHIAS GRÜNEWALD These characteristics of German Renaissance art can clearly be seen in the *Isenheim Altarpiece* (Fig. **16-4**) by Matthias Grünewald (c. 1480–1528), painted more than three-quarters of a century after Jan van Eyck's Arnolfini portrait. The central panel of the German altarpiece is occupied by a tormented representation of the Crucifixion, one of the most dramatic in the history of art. The dead Christ is flanked by his mother, Mary, the apostle John, and Mary Magdalene to the left, and John the Baptist and a sacrificial lamb to the right. These figures exhibit a bodily tension in their arched backs, clenched hands, and rigidly pointing fingers, creating a melodramatic, anxious tone. The crucified Christ is shown with a deadly pallor. His skin appears cancerous, and his chest is sunken with his last breath. His gnarled hands reach painfully upward, stretching for salvation from the blackened sky. We do not find such impassioned portrayals outside Germany during the Renaissance.

ALBRECHT DÜRER We appropriately close our discussion of northern Renaissance art with the Italianate master Albrecht Dürer (1471–1528). His passion for the Classical in art stimulated extensive travel in Italy, where he copied the works of the Italian masters, who were also enthralled with the Classical style. The development of the printing press made it possible for him to disseminate the works of the Italian masters throughout northern Europe.

Dürer's *Adam and Eve* (Fig. **16-5**) conveys his admiration for the Classical style. In contrast to other German and Flemish artists who rendered figures, Dürer emphasized the idealized beauty of the human body. His Adam and Eve are not everyday figures of the sort Campin depicted in his Virgin Mary. Instead, the images arise from Greek and Roman prototypes. Adam's young, muscular body could have been drawn from a live model or from Classical statuary. Eve represents a standard of beauty different from that of other northern artists. The familiar slight build and refined facial features have given way to a more substantial and well-rounded woman. She is reminiscent of a fifth-century BCE Venus in her features and her pose. The symbols associated with the event—the Tree of Knowledge and the Serpent (Satan)—play a secondary role. In *Adam and Eve*, Dürer has chosen to emphasize the profound beauty of the human body. Instead of focusing on the consequences of the event preceding the taking of the fruit as an admonition against sin, we delight in the couple's beauty for its own sake. Indeed, this notion is central to the art of Renaissance Italy.

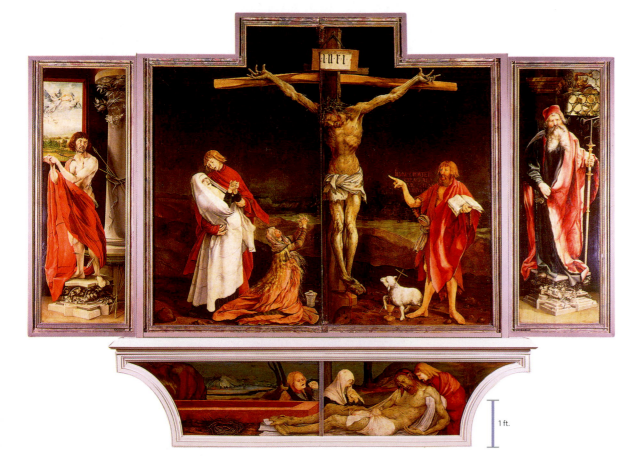

16-4 MATTHIAS GRÜNEWALD. *The Crucifixion*, center panel of *The Isenheim Altarpiece* (closed) (c. 1510-1515). Oil on panel. 8'10" × 10'1". Musée d'Unterlinden, Colmar, France.

1 ft.

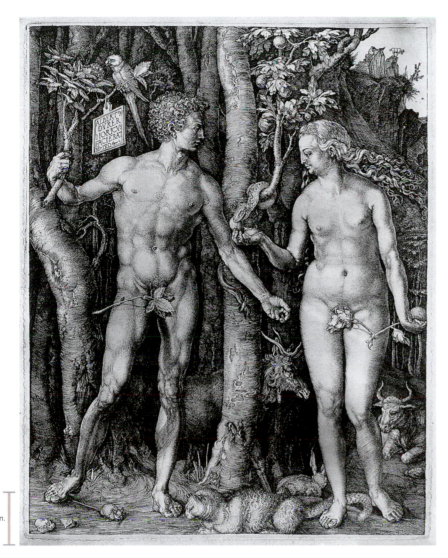

16-5 ALBRECHT DÜRER. *Adam and Eve* (1504). Engraving. 9⅞" × 7⅝". The Metropolitan Museum of Art, NY.

1 in.

THE RENAISSANCE IN ITALY

The Early Renaissance

Not only was there a marked difference between northern and Italian Renaissance art, but there were notable differences in the art of various sections of Italy. Florence and Rome witnessed a resurgence of Classicism as Roman ruins were excavated in ancient sites, hillsides, and people's backyards. In Siena, the International style lingered, and in Venice, a Byzantine influ-

ence remained strong. There may be several reasons for this diversity, but the most obvious is that of geography. For example, whereas the Roman artist's stylistic roads led to that ancient city, the trade routes in the northeast brought an Eastern influence to works of art and architecture. The Italian Renaissance took root and flourished most successfully in Florence. The development of this city's painting, sculpture, and architecture parallels that of the Renaissance in all of Italy. Throughout the Renaissance, as Florence went, so went the country.

Cimabue and Giotto

Some of the earliest changes from a medieval to a Classical style can be perceived in the painting of Florence during the late thirteenth and early fourteenth centuries, the prime exponents being Cimabue and Giotto. So significant were these artists that Dante Alighieri, the fourteenth-century poet, mentioned both of them in his *Purgatory* of *The Divine Comedy*:

> O gifted men, vainglorious for first place,
> how short a time the laurel crown stays green
> unless the age that follows lacks all grace!
> Once Cimabue thought to hold the field
> in painting, and now Giotto has the cry
> so that the other's fame, grown dim,
>   must yield.[3]

Who were these artists? Apparently they were rivals, although Cimabue (c. 1240–c. 1302) was older than Giotto (c. 1276–c. 1337) and probably had a formative influence on the latter, who would ultimately steal the limelight.

The similarities and differences between the works of Cimabue and Giotto can be seen in two tempera paintings on wood panels depicting the Madonna and Child enthroned. A curious combination of Late Gothic and Early Renaissance styles betrays Cimabue's composition as a transitional work

---

[3] From *The Divine Comedy* by Dante Alighieri, trans. John Ciardi. Copyright 1954, 1957, 1959, 1960, 1961, 1965, 1967, 1970 by the Ciardi Family Publishing Trust. Used by permission of W. W. Norton & Company, Inc.

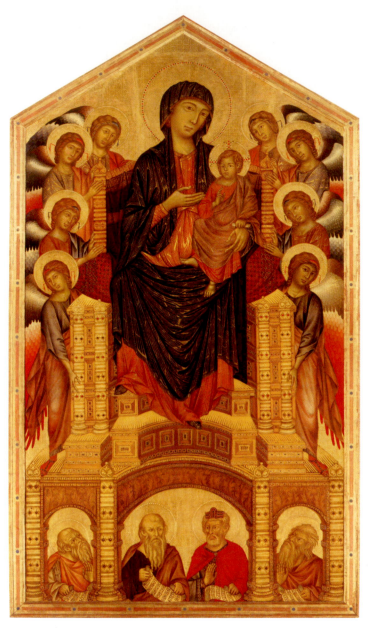

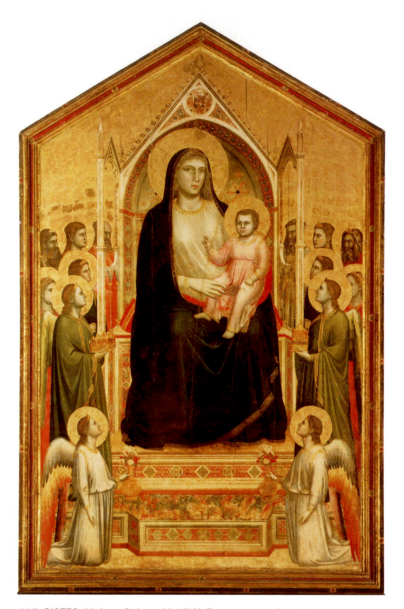

16-6 CIMABUE. *Madonna Enthroned* (c. 1280–1290). Tempera on wood panel. 12'7" × 7'4". Galleria degli Uffizi, Florence, Italy.

16-7 GIOTTO. *Madonna Enthroned* (c. 1310). Tempera on wood panel. 10'8" × 6'8". Galleria degli Uffizi, Florence, Italy.

(Fig. 16-6). The massive throne of the Madonna is Roman in inspiration, with column and arch forms embellished with **intarsia**. The Madonna has a corporeal presence that sets her apart from "floating" medieval figures, but the effect is compromised by the unsureness with which she is placed on the throne. She does not sit solidly; her limbs are not firmly planted. Rather, the legs resemble the hinged appendages of Romanesque figures. This characteristic placement of the knees causes the drapery to fall in predictable folds—concentric arcs reminiscent of a more stylized technique. The angels supporting the throne rise parallel to it, their glances forming an abstract zigzag pattern. The resultant lyrical ara-

besque, the flickering color patterns of the wings, and the lineup of unobstructed heads recall the Byzantine tradition, particularly the Ravenna mosaics (see Fig. 15-3).

Giotto's rendition of the same theme offers some dramatic differences (Fig. 16-7). The overall impression of the *Madonna Enthroned* is one of stability and corporeality instead of instability and weightlessness. Giotto's Madonna sits firmly on her throne, the outlines of her body and drapery forming a solid triangular shape. Although the throne is lighter in appearance than Cimabue's Roman throne—and is, in fact, Gothic, with pointed arches—it, too, seems more firmly planted on the earth. Giotto's genius is also evident in his conception of the forms in three-dimensional space. They not only have height and width, as do those of Cimabue, but they also have depth and mass. This is particularly noticeable in the treatment of the angels. Their location in space is from front to rear rather than atop one another as in Cimabue's composition. The halos of the foreground angels obscure the faces of the background attendants, because they have mass and occupy space.

The Renaissance Begins, and So Does the Competition

With Cimabue and Giotto, we witness strides toward an art that was very different from that of the Middle Ages. But artists, like all of us, must walk before they can run, and those strides that express such a stylistic advance from the "cutout dolls" of the Ravenna mosaics and the "hinged marionettes" of the Romanesque era will look primitive in another half century. Because the art of Cimabue and Giotto contains vestiges of Gothicism, their style is often termed *proto-Renaissance*. But at the dawn of the fifteenth century in Florence, the Early Renaissance began—with a competition.

Imagine workshops and artists abuzz with news of one of the hottest projects in memory up for grabs. Think of one of the most prestigious architectural sites in Florence. Savor the possibility of being known as *the* artist who had cast, in gleaming bronze, the massive doors of the Baptistery of Florence. This landmark competition was held in 1401. There were countless entries, but only two panels have come down to us. The artists had been given a scene from the Old Testament to translate into bronze—the sacrifice of Isaac by his father, Abraham. There were specifications, naturally, but the most obvious is the **quatrefoil** format. Within this space, a certain cast of characters was mandated, including Abraham, Isaac, an angel, and two "extras" who appear to have little or nothing to do with the scene. The event takes place out of doors, where God has commanded Abraham to take his only son and sacrifice him. When they arrive on the scene, Abraham, in loyalty to God, turns the blade to Isaac's throat. At this moment, God sends an angel to stop Abraham from completing the deed.

FILIPPO BRUNELLESCHI AND LORENZO GHIBERTI The two extant panels were executed by Filippo Brunelleschi (c. 1377–1446) and Lorenzo Ghiberti (1378–1455). The obligatory characters—bushes, animals, and altar—are present in both, but the placement of these elements, the artistic style, and the emotional energy within each work differ considerably. Brunelleschi's panel (Fig. 16-8) is divided into sections by strong vertical and horizontal elements, each section filled with objects and figures. In contrast to the rigidity of the format, a ferocious energy bordering on violence pervades the composition. Isaac's neck and body are distorted by his father's grasping fist, and Abraham lunges viciously toward his son's throat with a knife. With similar passion, an angel flies in from the left to grasp Abraham's arm. But

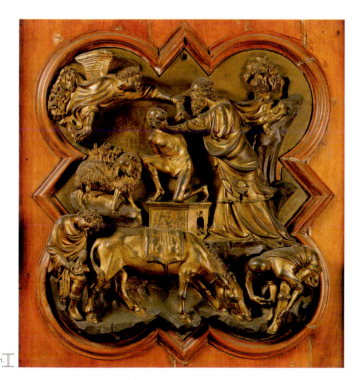

16-8 FILIPPO BRUNELLESCHI. *Sacrifice of Isaac* (1401–1402). Gilt bronze. 21" × 17½". Museo Nazionale del Bargello, Florence, Italy.

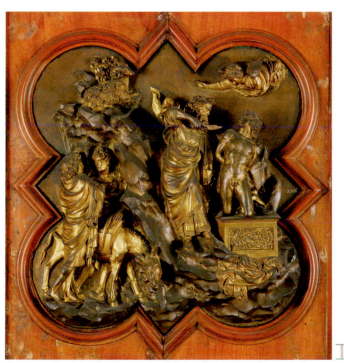

16-9 LORENZO GHIBERTI. *Sacrifice of Isaac* (1401–1402). Gilt bronze. 21" × 17½". Museo Nazionale del Bargello, Florence, Italy.

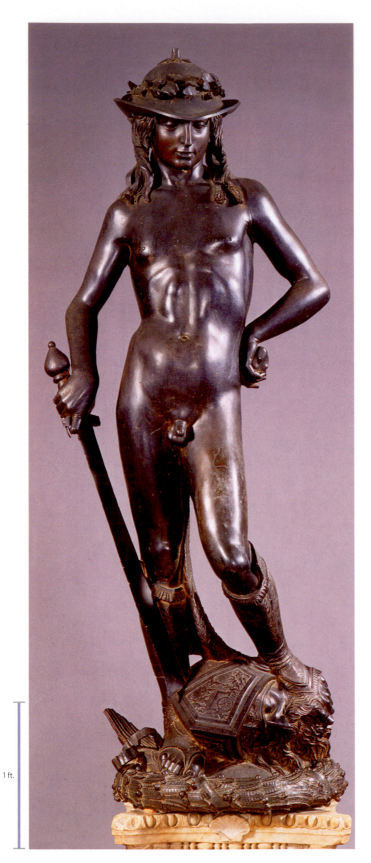

this intense drama and seemingly boundless energy are weakened by the introduction of ancillary figures that are given more prominence than the scene requires. The donkey, for example, detracts from Isaac's plight by being placed broadside and practically dead center. Also, one is struck by the staccato movement throughout. Although this choppiness complements the anxiety in the work, it compromises the successful flow of space and tires the eye.

In Lorenzo Ghiberti's panel (Fig. **16-9**), the space is divided along a diagonal rock formation that separates the main characters from the lesser ones. Space flows along this diagonal, exposing the figural group of Abraham and Isaac and embracing the shepherd boys and their donkey. The boys and donkey are appropriately subordinated to the main characters but not sidestepped stylistically. Abraham's lower body parallels the rock formation and then lunges expressively away from it in a dynamic counterthrust. Isaac, in turn, pulls firmly away from his father's forward motion. The forms move rhythmically together in a continuous flow of space. Although Ghiberti's emotion is not quite as intense as Brunelleschi's, and his portrayal of the sacrifice is not quite as graphic, the impact of Ghiberti's narrative is as strong.

It is interesting to note the inclusion of Classicizing elements in both panels. Brunelleschi, in one of his peasants, adapted the Classical sculpture of a boy removing a thorn from his foot, and Ghiberti rendered his Isaac in the manner of the fifth-century sculptor. Isaac's torso, in fact, may be the first nude in this style since Classical times.

Oh, yes—Ghiberti won the competition and Brunelleschi went home with his chisel. The latter never devoted himself to sculpture again but went on to become the first great Renaissance architect. Ghiberti was not particularly modest about his triumph:

> To me was conceded the palm of victory by all the experts and by all . . . who had competed with me. To me the honor was conceded universally and with no exception. To all it seemed that I had at that time surpassed the others without exception, as was recognized by a great council and an investigation of learned men . . . highly skilled from the painters and sculptors of gold, silver, and marble.[4]

DONATELLO If Brunelleschi and Ghiberti were among the last sculptors to harbor vestiges of the International style, Donatello (c. 1386–1466), the Florentine master, was surely among the first to create sculptures that combined Classicism with realism. In his *David* (Fig. **16-10**), the first life-size nude statue since Classical times, Donatello struck a balance between the two styles by presenting a very real image of an

1 ft.

16-10 DONATELLO. *David* (c. 1440–1460). Bronze. H: 5'2". Museo Nazionale del Bargello, Florence, Italy.

[4] E. G. Holt, ed., *Literary Sources of Art History* (Princeton, NJ: Princeton University Press, 1947), 87–88.

Italian peasant boy in the guise of a Classical nude figure. David, destined to be the second king of Israel, slew the Philistine giant Goliath with a stone and a sling. Even though Donatello was inspired by Classical statuary, notice that he did not choose a Greek youth in his prime as a prototype for his David. Instead, he chose a barely developed adolescent boy, his hair still unclipped and his arms flaccid for lack of manly musculature. After he has decapitated Goliath, whose head lies at David's feet, his sword rests at his side—almost too heavy for him to handle. Can such a youth have accomplished such a forbidding task? Herein lies the power of Donatello's statement. We are amazed, from the appearance of this young boy, that he could have done such a deed, much as David seems incredulous as he glances down toward his body. What David lacks in stature he has made up in intellect, faith, and courage. His fate was in his own hands—one of the ideals of the Renaissance man.

MASACCIO The Early Renaissance painters shared most of the stylistic concerns of the sculptors. However, included in their attempts at realism was the added difficulty of projecting a naturalistic sense of three-dimensional space on a two-dimensional surface. In addition to copying from nature and Classical models, these painters developed rules of perspective to depict images in the round on flat walls, panels, and canvases. One of the pioneers in developing systematic laws of one-point linear perspective was Brunelleschi, of Baptistery doors near-fame.

Masaccio's *Holy Trinity* (Fig. **16-11**) uses these laws of perspective. In this chapel fresco, Masaccio (1401–1428) creates the illusion of an extension of the architectural space of the church by painting a barrel-vaulted "chapel" housing a variety of holy and common figures. God the Father supports the cross that bears his crucified son while the Virgin Mary and the apostle John attend. Outside the columns and pilasters of the realistic, Roman-inspired chapel kneel the donors, who are invited to observe the scene. Aside from the trompe l'oeil rendition of the architecture, the realism in the fresco is enhanced by the donors, who are given importance equal to that of the "principal" characters, similar to Campin's treatment of the donors in the *Merode Altarpiece* (Fig. 16-2). The architecture appears to extend our physical space, and the donors appear as extensions of ourselves.

FILIPPO BRUNELLESCHI The revival of Classicism was even more marked in the architecture of the Renaissance. Some 20 years after Brunelleschi's unsuccessful bid for the

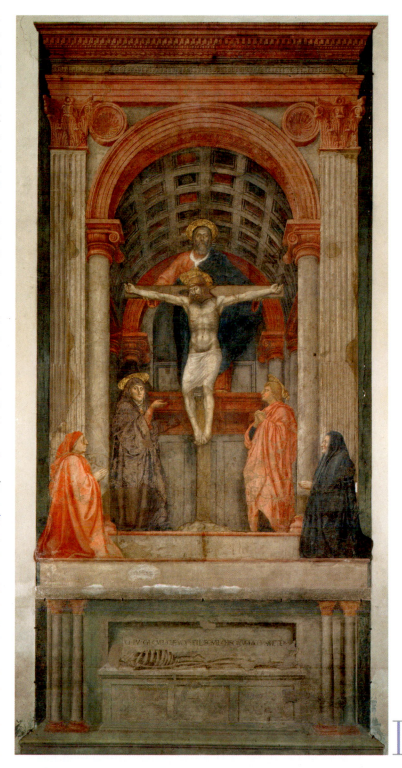

1 ft.

16-11 MASACCIO. *Holy Trinity* (c. 1428). Fresco. 21' × 10'5". Santa Maria Novella, Florence, Italy.

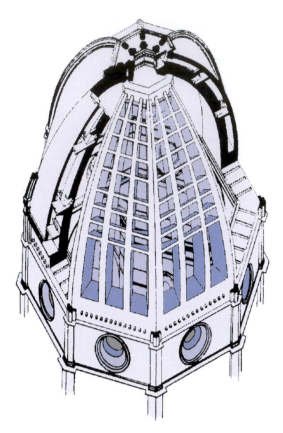

FILIPPO BRUNELLESCHI. Construction of the cathedral dome, Florence, Italy (1420–1436).

An extremely versatile artist who was trained as a goldsmith, Verrocchio ran an active shop that attracted many young artists, including Leonardo da Vinci. We see in Verrocchio's bronze *David* (Fig. 16-13), commissioned by the Medici family, a strong contrast to Donatello's handling of the same subject. The Medicis also owned the Donatello *David*, and Verrocchio probably wanted to outshine his predecessor. Although both artists chose to represent David as an adolescent, Verrocchio's hero appears somewhat older and exudes pride and self-confidence rather than a dreamy gaze of disbelief. Whereas Donatello reconciled realistic elements with an almost idealized, Classically inspired torso, Verroc-

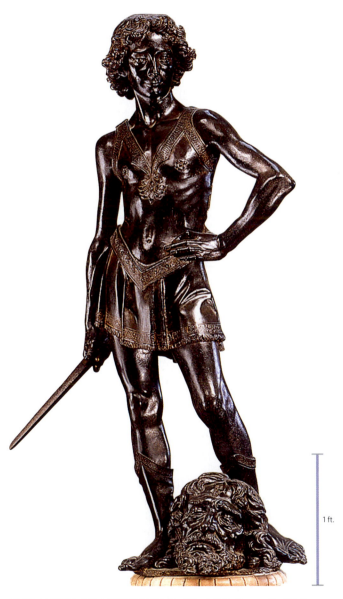

16-13 ANDREA DEL VERROCCHIO. *David* (c. 1470). Bronze. H: 49⅝". Museo Nazionale del Bargello, Florence, Italy.

Baptistery doors project in Florence, he was commissioned to cover the crossing square of the cathedral of Florence with a dome. Interestingly, Ghiberti worked with him at the outset but soon bowed out, and Brunelleschi was left to complete the work alone. It was quite an engineering feat, involving a double-shell dome constructed around 24 ribs (Fig. 16-12). Eight of these ribs rise upward to a crowning lantern on the exterior of the dome. You might wonder why Brunelleschi, whose architectural models were essentially Classical, would have constructed a somewhat pointed dome reminiscent of the Middle Ages. The fact is that the architect might have preferred a more rounded or hemispherical structure, but the engineering problem required an *ogival*, or pointed, section, which is inherently more stable. The dome was a compromise between a somewhat Classical style and traditional Gothic building principles.

Renaissance Art at Midcentury and Beyond

ANDREA DEL VERROCCHIO As we progress into the middle of the fifteenth century, the most important and innovative sculptor is Andrea del Verrocchio (1435–1488).

chio's goal was supreme realism in minute details, including orientalizing motifs on the boy's doublet that would have made him look like a Middle Easterner. The sculptures differ considerably also in terms of technique. Donatello's *David* is essentially a closed-form sculpture with objects and limbs centered around an **S-curve** stance; Verrocchio's sculpture is more open, as is evidenced by the bared sword and elbow jutting away from the central core. Donatello's graceful pose has been replaced, in the Verrocchio, by a jaunty **contrapposto** that enhances David's image of self-confidence.

PIERO DELLA FRANCESCA The artists of the Renaissance, along with the philosophers and scientists, tended to share the sense of the universe as an orderly place that was governed by natural law and capable of being expressed in mathematical and geometric terms. Piero della Francesca (c. 1420–1492) was trained in mathematics and geometry and is credited with writing the first theoretical treatise on the construction of systematic perspective in art. Piero's art, like his scientific thought, was based on an intensely rational construction of forms and space.

His *Resurrection* fresco (Fig. **16-14**) for the town hall of Borgo San Sepolcro reveals the artist's obsessions with order and geometry. Christ ascends vertical and triumphant, like a monumental column, above the "entablature" of his tomb, which serves visually as the pedestal of a statue. Christ and the other figures are constructed from the cones, cylinders, spheres, and rectangular solids that define the theoretical world of the artist. There is a tendency here toward the simplification of forms—not only of people, but also of natural fea-

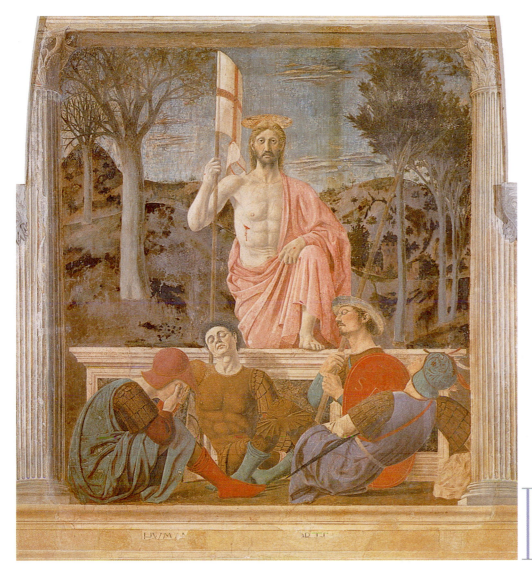

16-14 PIERO DELLA FRANCESCA. *Resurrection* (c. late 1450s). Fresco. 7'5" × 6'6½". Town Hall, Borgo San Sepolcro, Italy.

1 ft.

tures such as trees and hills. All of the figures in the painting are contained within a triangle—what would become a major compositional device in Renaissance painting—with Christ at the apex. The sleeping figures and the marble sarcophagus provide a strong and stable base for the upper two-thirds of the composition. Regimented trees rise in procession behind Christ, as they never do when nature asserts its random jests; Piero's trees are swept back by the rigid cultivation of scientific perspective. They crown, as ordered, just above the crests of rounded hills. The artist of the Renaissance not only was in awe of nature but also commanded it fully.

SANDRO BOTTICELLI During the latter years of the fifteenth century, we come upon an artistic personality whose style is somewhat in opposition to the prevailing trends. Since the time of Giotto, painters had relied on chiaroscuro, or the contrast of light and shade to create a sense

of roundness and mass in their figures and objects, in an effort to render a realistic impression of three-dimensional forms in space. Sandro Botticelli (c. 1444–1510), however, constructed his compositions with line instead of tonal contrasts. His art relied primarily on drawing. Yet when it came to subject matter, his heart lay with his Renaissance peers, for, above all else, he loved to paint mythological themes. Along with other artists and men of letters, his mania for these subjects was fed and perhaps cultivated by the Medici prince Lorenzo the Magnificent, who surrounded himself with Neoplatonists, or those who followed the philosophy of Plato.

One of Botticelli's most famous paintings is *The Birth of Venus* (Fig. **16-15**), or, as some art historians would have it, "Venus on the Half Shell." The model for this Venus was Simonetta Vespucci, a cousin of Amerigo Vespucci, the navigator and explorer after whom America was named. The

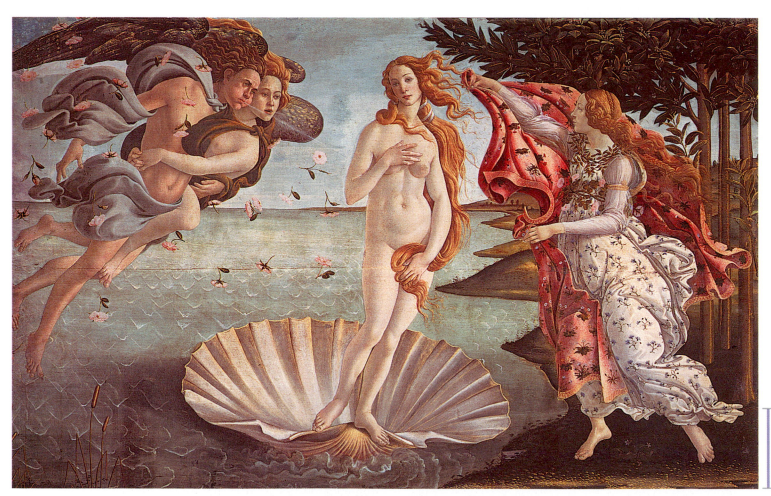

1 ft.

16-15 SANDRO BOTTICELLI. *The Birth of Venus* (c. 1486). Tempera on canvas. 5'8⅞" × 9'1⅞". Galleria degli Uffizi, Florence, Italy.

composition presents Venus, born of the foam of the sea, floating to the shores of her sacred island on a large scallop shell, aided in its drifting by the sweet breaths of entwined zephyrs. The nymph Pomona awaits her with an ornate mantle and is herself dressed in a billowing, flowered gown. Botticelli's interest in Classicism is evident also in his choice of models for the Venus. She is a direct adaptation of an antique sculpture of this goddess in the collection of the Medici family. Notice how the graceful movement in the composition is evoked through a combination of different lines. A firm horizon line and regimented verticals in the trees contrast with the subtle curves and vigorous arabesques that caress the mythological figures. The line moves from image to image and then doubles back to lead your eye once again. Shading is confined to areas within the harsh, linear, sculptural contours of the figures. Botticelli's genius lay in his ability to use the differing qualities of line to his advantage; with this formal element, he created the most delicate of compositions.

LEON BATTISTA ALBERTI You could never accuse Leon Battista Alberti (1404–1472) of false modesty, or of any modesty at all. Like so many other artists of the Renaissance, including Ghiberti, Michelangelo, and Leonardo—and unlike the anonymous European artists of the Middle Ages—he sought fame with conscious conviction.

Some of the purest examples of Renaissance Classicism lie in the buildings Alberti designed. Alberti was among the first to study treatises written by Roman architects, the most famous of whom was Vitruvius, and he combined his Classical knowledge with innovative ideas in his grand opus, *Ten Books on Architecture*. One of his most visually satisfying buildings in the great Classical tradition is the Palazzo Rucellai (Fig. **16-16**) in Florence. The building is divided by prominent horizontal string courses into three stories, crowned by a heavy cornice. Within each story are apertures enframed by pilasters of different orders. The first-floor pilasters are of the Tuscan order, which resembles the Doric order in its simplicity; the second story uses a composite capital of volutes and acanthus leaves, seen in the Ionic and Corinthian orders, respectively; and the top-floor pilasters are crowned by capitals of the Corinthian order. As in the Colosseum (see Fig. 14-24), this combination of orders gives an impression of increasing lightness

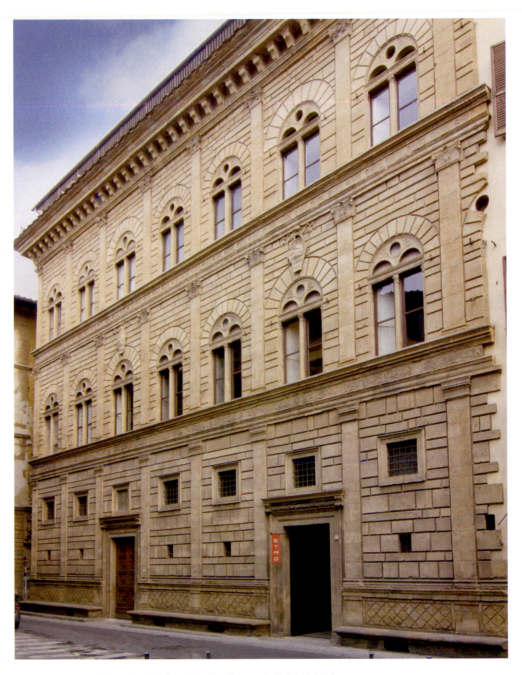

16-16 LEON BATTISTA ALBERTI. Palazzo Rucellai, Florence, Italy (1446–1451).

*I can make armored cars, safe and unassailable, which will enter the . . . ranks of the enemy
with their artillery, and there is no company of men-at-arms so great that they will not break it.
And behind these the infantry will be able to follow quite unharmed and without any
opposition. . . . If need shall arise, I can make cannon, mortars, and light ordnance,
of very beautiful and useful shapes, quite different from those in common use. . . .
Also I can execute sculpture in marble, bronze, and clay, and also painting, in which
my work will stand comparison with that of anyone else, who ever he may be.*
—Leonardo da Vinci (from a letter of application for a job)

as we rise from the lower to the upper stories. This effect is enhanced in Alberti's building by a variation in the masonry. Although the texture remains the same, the upper stories are faced with lighter-appearing smaller blocks in greater numbers. The palazzo's design, with its clear articulation of parts, overall balance of forms, and rhythmic placement of elements in horizontals across the facade, shows a clear understanding of Classical design adapted successfully to the contemporary nobleman's needs.

The High Renaissance

The High Renaissance ushered in a new era for some artists— one of respect, influence, fame, and, most important, the power to shape their circumstances. Here is an example: Sometime in 1542, Julius II and Michelangelo Buonarroti were in conflict, and the artist was feeling the brunt of the pope's behavior. As if backing out of his tomb commission and refusing to pay for materials were not enough, the pope laid the last straw by having Michelangelo removed from the Vatican when the artist sought to redress his grievances. Michelangelo let his outrage be known:

A man paints with his brains and not with his hands, and if he cannot have his brains clear he will come to grief. Therefore I shall be able to do nothing well until justice has been done me. . . . As soon as the Pope [carries] out his obligations towards me I (will) return, otherwise he need never expect to see me again.

All the disagreements that arose between Pope Julius and myself were due to the jealousy of Bramante and of Raffaello da Urbino; it was because of them that he did not proceed with the tomb, . . . and they brought this about in order that I might thereby be ruined. Yet Raffaello was quite right to be jealous of me, for all he knew of art he learned from me.[5]

Although this is only one side of the story (Michelangelo might also have been somewhat jealous of Raphael), this passage offers us a good look at the personality of an artist of the High Renaissance. He was independent yet indispensable— arrogant, aggressive, and competitive.

From the second half of the fifteenth century onward, a refinement of the stylistic principles and techniques associated with the Renaissance can be observed. Most of this significant, progressive work was being done in Florence, where the Medici family played an important role in supporting the arts. At the close of the decade, however, Rome was the place to be, as the popes began to assume the grand role of patron. The three artists who were in most demand—the great masters of the High Renaissance in Italy—were Leonardo da Vinci, a painter, scientist, inventor, and musician; Raphael, the Classical painter thought to have rivaled the works of the ancients; and Michelangelo, the painter, sculptor, architect, poet, and enfant terrible. Donato Bramante is deemed to have made the most significant architectural contributions of this period. These are the stars of the Renaissance, the artistic descendants of the Giottos, Donatellos, and Albertis, who, because of their earlier place in the historical sequence of artistic development, are sometimes portrayed as but stepping-stones to the greatness of the sixteenth-century artists rather than as masters in their own right.

LEONARDO DA VINCI If the Italians of the High Renaissance could have nominated a counterpart to the Classical Greek's "four-square man," it most assuredly would have been Leonardo da Vinci (1452–1519). His capabilities in engineering, the natural sciences, music, and the arts seemed unlimited, as he excelled in everything from solving drainage problems (a project he undertook in France just before his death), to designing prototypes for airplanes and submarines, to creating some of the most memorable Renaissance paintings.

The Last Supper (Fig. **16-17**), a fresco painting executed for the dining hall of a Milan monastery, stands as one of Leonardo's greatest works. The condition of the work is

---

[5] Robert Goldwater and Marco Treves, eds., *Artists on Art* (New York: Pantheon Books, 1972), 63.

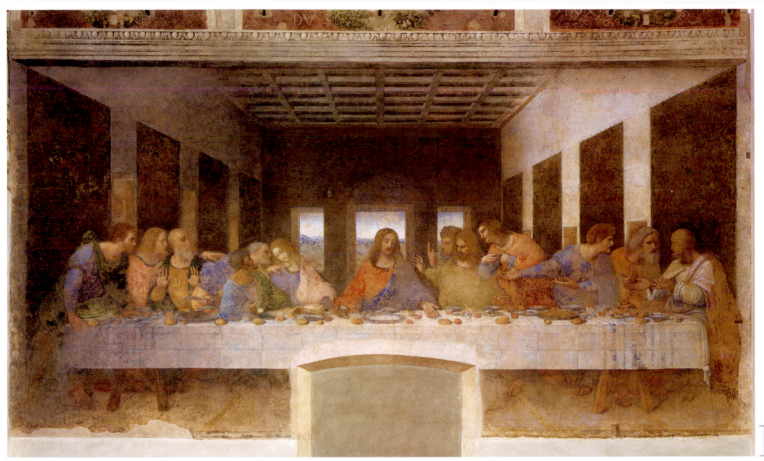

1 ft.

16-17 LEONARDO DA VINCI. *The Last Supper* (1495–1498). Oil and tempera on plaster. 13'9" × 29'10". Refectory, Santa Maria delle Grazie, Milan, Italy.

poor, because of Leonardo's experimental fresco technique—although the steaming of pasta for centuries on the other side of the wall may also have played a role. Nonetheless, we can still observe the Renaissance ideals of Classicism, humanism, and technical perfection, now coming to full fruition. The composition is organized through the use of one-point linear perspective. Solid volumes are constructed from a masterful contrast of light and shadow. A hairline balance is struck between emotion and restraint.

The viewer is first attracted to the central triangular form of Jesus sitting among his apostles by **orthogonals** that converge at his head. His figure is silhouetted against a triple window that symbolizes the Holy Trinity and pierces the otherwise dark back wall. One's attention is held at this center point by the Christ-figure's isolation that results from the leaning away of the apostles. Leonardo has chosen to depict the moment when Jesus says, "One of you will betray me." The apostles fall

back reflexively at this accusation; they gesture expressively, deny personal responsibility, and ask, "Who can this be?" The guilty one, of course, is Judas, who is shown clutching a bag of silver pieces at Jesus' left, with his elbow on the table. The two groups of apostles, who sweep dramatically away from Jesus along a horizontal line, are subdivided into four smaller groups of three that tend to moderate the rush of the eye out from the center. The viewer's eye is wafted outward and then coaxed back inward through the "parenthetic" poses of the apostles at either end. Leonardo's use of strict rules of perspective and his graceful balance of motion and restraint underscore the artistic philosophy and style of the Renaissance.

Although Leonardo does not allow excessive emotion in his *Last Supper*, the reactions of the apostles seem genuinely human. This spirit is also captured in *Madonna of the Rocks* (Fig. **16-18**). Mary is no longer portrayed as the queen of heaven, but as a mother. She is human; she is "real."

The soft, hazy atmosphere and dreamy landscape of *Madonna of the Rocks*, and the chiaroscuro that so realistically defines the form of the subtly smiling Virgin Mary, were still in Leonardo's pictorial repertory when he created what is arguably the most famous portrait in the history of art—the *Mona Lisa* (Fig. **16-19**). An air of mystery pervades the work—from her entrancing smile and intense gaze to her real identity and the location of the landscape behind her. With the *Mona Lisa*, Leonardo altered the nature of portrait

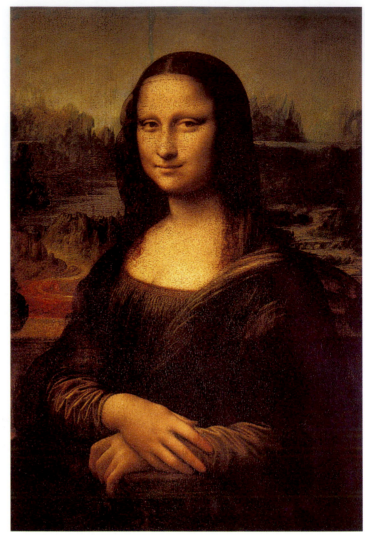

1 in.

16-19 LEONARDO DA VINCI. *Mona Lisa* (c. 1503–1505). Oil on wood. 30¼" × 21". Louvre, Paris, France.

painting for centuries, replacing the standard profile view of a sitter to one in which a visual dialogue could be established between the subject and the observer.

RAPHAEL SANZIO A younger artist who assimilated the lessons offered by Leonardo, especially on the humanistic portrayal of the Madonna, was Raphael Sanzio (1483–1520). As a matter of fact, Michelangelo was not far off base in his accusation that Raphael copied from him, for the younger artist freely adopted whatever suited his purposes. Raphael truly shone in his ability to combine the techniques of other masters with an almost instinctive feel for Classical art. He rendered countless canvases depicting the Madonna and Child along the lines of Leonardo's *Madonna of the Rocks.*

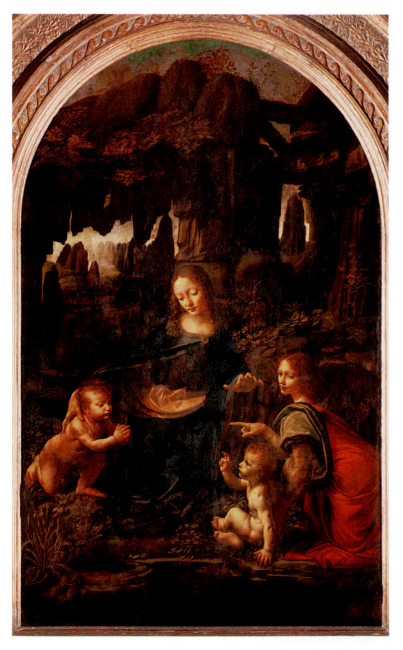

16-18 LEONARDO DA VINCI. *Madonna of the Rocks* (c. 1483). Oil on wood, transferred to canvas. 78½" × 48". Louvre, Paris, France.

Raphael was also sought after as a muralist. Some of his most impressive Classical compositions, in fact, were executed for the papal apartments in the Vatican.

The commission came from Pope Julius and, to add fuel to Michelangelo's fire, was executed at the same time Michelangelo was at work on the Sistine Chapel ceiling. For the Stanza della Segnatura, the room in which the highest papal tribunal was held, Raphael painted *The School of Athens* (Fig. **16-20**), one of four frescoes designed within a semicircular frame. In what could be a textbook exercise of one-point linear perspective, Raphael crowded a veritable *Who's Who* of Classical Greece convening beneath a series of barrel-vaulted archways. The figures symbolize philosophy, one of the four subjects deemed most valuable for a pope's education. (The others were law, theology, and poetry.) The members of the gathering are divided into two camps representing opposing philosophies and are led on the right by Aristotle and on the left by his mentor, Plato. Corresponding to these leaders are the Platonists, whose concerns are the more lofty realm of Ideas (notice Plato pointing upward), and the Aristotelians, who are more in touch with matters of the Earth, such as natural science. Some of the figures have been identified: Diogenes, the Cynic philosopher, sprawls out on the steps, and Herakleitos, a founder of Greek metaphysics, sits pensively just left of center. Of more interest is the fact that Raphael included a portrait of himself, staring out toward the viewer, in the far right foreground. He is shown in a group surrounding the geometrician Euclid. Raphael clearly saw himself as important enough to be commemorated in a Vatican mural as an ally of the Aristotelian camp.

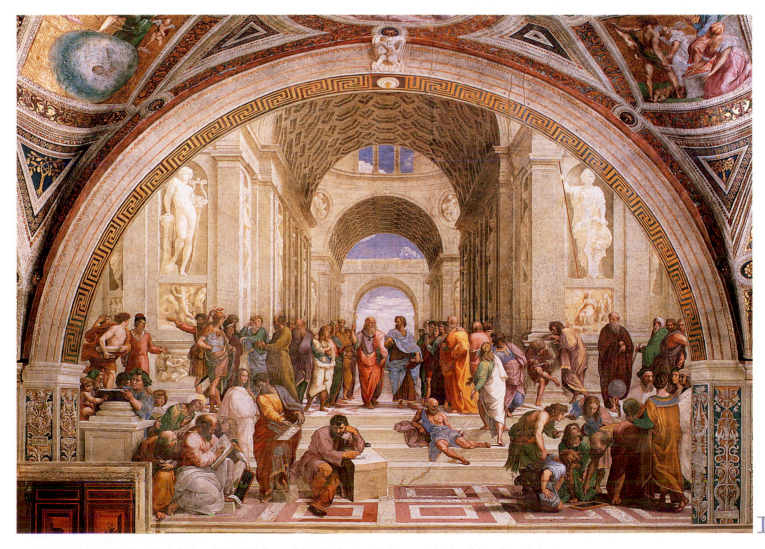

16-20 RAPHAEL. *The School of Athens* (1510–1511). Fresco. 26' × 18'. Stanza della Segnatura, Vatican Palace, Rome, Italy.

1 ft.

As in *The Last Supper* by Leonardo, our attention is drawn to the two main figures by orthogonals leading directly to where they are silhouetted against the sky breaking through the archways. The diagonals that lead toward a single horizon point are balanced by strong horizontals and verticals in the architecture and figural groupings, lending a feeling of Classical stability and predictability. Stylistically, as well as iconographically, Raphael has managed to balance opposites in a perfectly graceful and logical composition.

MICHELANGELO BUONARROTI Of the three great Renaissance masters, Michelangelo (1475–1564) is probably most familiar to us. During the 1964 World's Fair in New York City, hundreds of thousands of culture seekers and devout pilgrims were trucked along a conveyor belt for a brief glimpse of his *Pietà* at the Vatican Pavilion. A year later, actor Charlton Heston (who seems to bear a striking resemblance to the artist) reprised the tumultuous relationship between artist and patron and the traumatic physical experience surrounding the painting of the Sistine ceiling in the Hollywood film *The Agony and the Ecstasy*. These two works stand as symbols of the breadth and depth of Michelangelo's talents as an artist.

That famed ceiling is the vault of the chapel of Pope Sixtus IV, known as the Sistine Chapel. The ceiling is some 5,800 square feet and is almost 70 feet above the floor. The decorative fresco cycle was commissioned by Pope Julius II, but the iconographic scheme was Michelangelo's. The artist had agreed to the project in order to pacify the temperamental Julius in the hope that the pontiff would eventually allow him to

complete work on his mammoth tomb. For whatever reason, we are indeed fortunate to have this painted work from the sculptor's hand. After much anguish and early attempts to populate the vault with a variety of religious figures (eventually more than 300 in all), Michelangelo settled on a division of the ceiling into geometrical "frames" (Fig. **16-21**) housing biblical prophets, mythological soothsayers, and Old Testament scenes from Genesis to Noah's flood.

The most famous of these scenes is *The Creation of Adam* (Fig. **16-22**). As Leonardo had done in *The Last Supper*, Michelangelo chose to communicate the event's most dramatic moment. Adam lies on the earth, listless for lack of a

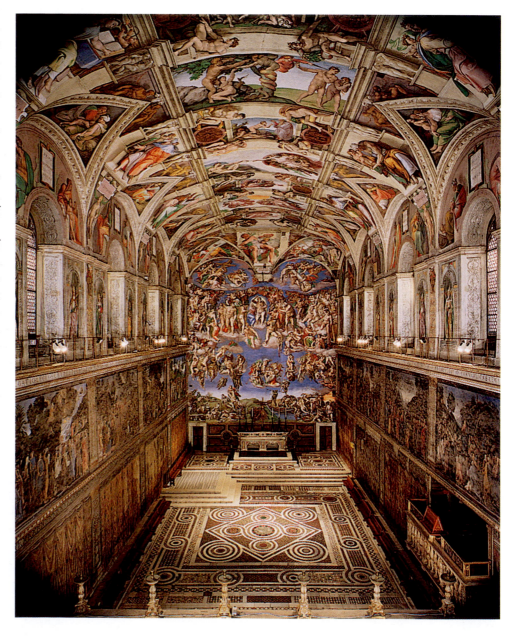

16-21 Interior of Sistine Chapel (constructed 1473). Vatican City, Rome, Italy.

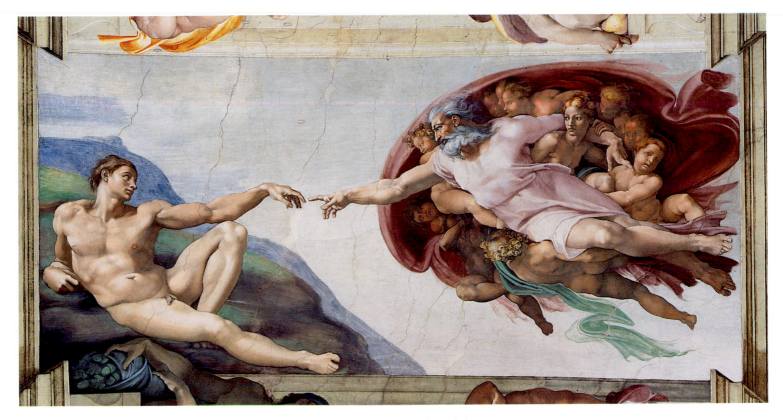

16-22 MICHELANGELO. *The Creation of Adam* (1508–1512). Sistine Chapel, Vatican City, Rome, Italy.

soul, while God the Father rushes toward him amidst a host of angels, who wrap him in a billowing cloak. The contrasting figures lean toward the left, separated by an illuminated diagonal that provides a backdrop for the Creation. Amidst an atmosphere of sheer electricity, the hand of God reaches out to spark spiritual life into Adam—but does not touch him! In some of the most dramatic negative space in the history of art, Michelangelo has left it to the spectator to complete the act. In terms of style, Michelangelo integrated chiaroscuro with Botticelli's extensive use of line. His figures are harshly drawn and muscular with almost marble-like flesh. In translating his sculptural techniques to a two-dimensional surface, the artist has conceived his figures in the round and has used the tightest, most expeditious line and modeling possible to render them in paint.

It is clear that Michelangelo saw himself more as a sculptor than as a painter. The "sculptural" drawing and modeling in *The Creation of Adam* attest to this. When Michelangelo painted the Sistine Chapel ceiling, he was all of 33 years old, but he began his career some 20 years earlier as an apprentice to the painter Domenico Ghirlandaio (1449–1494). His reputation as a sculptor, however, was established when, at age 27, he carved the 13 1/2-foot-high *David* (Fig. 16-25) from a single piece of almost unworkable marble. Unlike the Davids of Donatello and Verrocchio, Michelangelo's hero is not shown after conquering his foe. Rather, David is portrayed as a most beautiful animal preparing to kill—not by savagery and brute force but by intellect and skill. Upon close inspection, the tensed muscles and the furrowed brow negate the first impression that this is a figure at rest. David's sling is cast over his shoulder, and the stone is grasped in the right hand, the veins prominent in anticipation of the fight.

Michelangelo's *David* is part of the Classical tradition of the "ideal youth" who has just reached manhood and is capable of great physical and intellectual feats. Like Donatello's *David*, Michelangelo's sculpture is closed in form. All of the elements move tightly around a central axis. Michelangelo has been said to have sculpted by first conceptualizing the mass of the work and then carefully extracting all of the marble that was not part of the image. Indeed, in the *David*, it appears that he worked from front to back instead of from all four sides of the marble block, allowing the figure, as it were, to "step out of" the stone. The identification of the figure with the marble block provides a dynamic tension in Michelangelo's work, as the forms try at once to free themselves from and succumb to the binding dimensions.

THE *DAVID*S OF DONATELLO, VERROCCHIO, MICHELANGELO, AND BERNINI

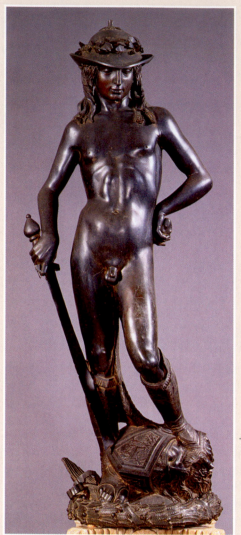

16-23 DONATELLO. *David* (c. 1440–1460). Bronze. H: 5'2". Museo Nazionale del Bargello, Florence, Italy.

umphing over the strong. The city of Florence triumphing over the aggressive dukes of Milan? *David* as a civic-public monument.

In the year 1469, Ser Piero from the Tuscan town of Vinci moved to Florence to become a notary. He rented a house on the Piazza San Firenze, not far from the Palazzo Vecchio. His son, who was a mere 17 years old upon their arrival, began an apprenticeship in the Florentine studio of the well-known artist Andrea del Verrocchio. At that time, Verrocchio was at work on a bronze sculpture of the young *David* (Fig. **16-24**). Might the head of this fine piece be a portrait of the young Leonardo da Vinci?

SOMETIME SOON AFTER THE YEAR 1430, a bronze statue of *David* (Fig. **16-23**) stood in the courtyard of the house of the Medicis. The work was commissioned of Donatello by Cosimo de' Medici himself, the founding father of the Republic of Florence. It was the first freestanding, life-size nude since Classical antiquity, poised in the same contrapposto stance as the victorious athletes of Greece and Rome. But soft, and somehow oddly unheroic. And the incongruity of the heads: David's boyish, expression-less face, framed by soft tendrils of hair and shaded by a laurel-crowned peasant's hat; Goliath's tragic, contorted expression, made sharper by the pentagonal helmet and coarse, disheveled beard. Innocence and evil. The weak tri-

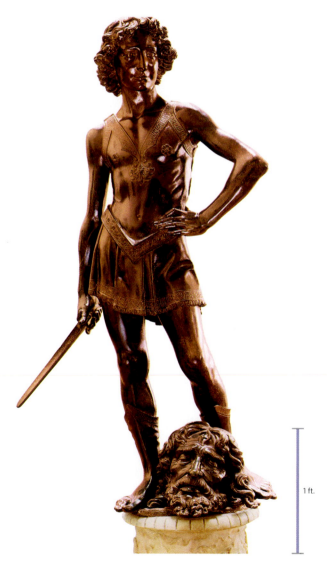

16-24 ANDREA DEL VERROCCHIO. *David* (c. 1470). Bronze. H: 49⅝". Museo Nazionale del Bargello, Florence, Italy.

For many years, a block of marble lay untouched, tossed aside as unusable, irretrievable evidence of a botched attempt to carve a human form. It was 18 feet high. A 26-year-old sculptor, riding high after the enormous success of his figure of the Virgin Mary holding the dead Christ, decided to ask for the piece. The wardens of the city in charge of such things let the artist have it. What did they have to lose? Getting anything out of it was better than nothing. So this young sculptor named Michelangelo measured and calculated. He made a wax model of David with a sling in his hand. And he worked on his *David* (Fig. **16-25**) continually for some three years until, a man named Vasari tells us, he brought it to perfect completion. Without letting anyone see it.

A century later, a 25-year-old sculptor stares into a mirror at his steeled jaw and determined brow. A contemporary source tells us that on this day, perhaps, the mirror

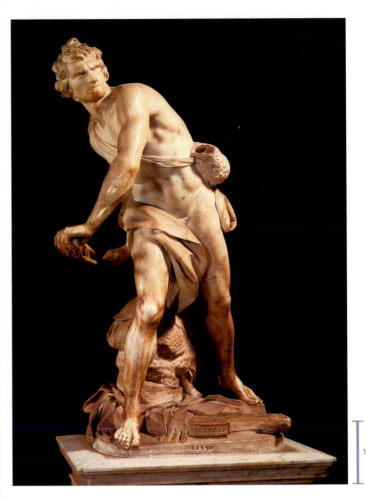

16-26 GIANLORENZO BERNINI. *David* (1623). Marble. H: 6'7". Galleria Borghese, Rome, Italy.

is being held by Cardinal Maffeo Barberini while Bernini transfers what he sees in himself to the face of his *David* (Fig. **16-26**). Gianlorenzo Bernini: sculptor and architect, painter, dramatist, composer. Bernini, who centuries later would be called the undisputed monarch of the Roman High Baroque, identifying with David, whose adversary is seen only by him.

The great transformation in style that occurred between the Early Renaissance and the Baroque can be followed in the evolution of David. Look at them: A boy of 12, perhaps, looking down incredulously at the physical self that felled an unconquerable enemy; a boy of 14 or 15, confident and reckless, with enough adrenaline pumping to take on an army; an adolescent on the brink of adulthood, captured at that moment when, the Greeks say, sound mind and sound body are one; and another full-grown youth at the threshold of his destiny as king. ●

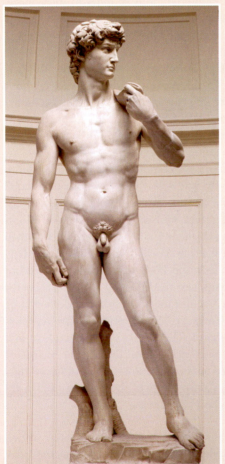

16-25 MICHELANGELO. *David* (1501–1504). Marble. H: 13½'. Galleria dell'Accademia, Florence, Italy.

High and Late Renaissance in Venice

The artists who lived and worked in the city of Venice were the first in Italy to perfect the medium of oil painting that we witnessed with van Eyck in Flanders. Perhaps influenced by the mosaics in St. Mark's Cathedral, perhaps intrigued by the dazzling colors of imports from Eastern countries into this maritime province, the Venetian artists sought the same clarity of hue and lushness of surface in their oil-on-canvas works. In the sixteenth century, Venice would come to figure as prominently in the arts as Florence had in the fifteenth.

TITIAN Although he died in 1576, almost a quarter century before the birth of the Baroque era, the Venetian master Tiziano Vecellio (b. 1477)—called Titian—had more in common with the artists who would follow him than with his Renaissance contemporaries in Florence and Rome. Titian's pictorial method differed from those of Leonardo, Raphael, and Michelangelo in that he was foremost a painter and colorist rather than a draftsman or sculptural artist. He constructed his compositions by means of colors and strokes of paint and layers of varnish rather than by line and chiaroscuro. A shift from painting on wood panels to painting on canvas occurred at this time, and with it a change from tempera to oil paint as the preferred medium. The versatility and lushness of oil painting served Titian well, with its vibrant, intense hues and its more subtle, semitransparent glazes.

Titian's *Venus of Urbino* (Fig. 16-27) is one of the most beautiful examples of the glazing technique. The composition was painted for the duke of Urbino, from which its title derives. Titian adopted the figure of the reclining Venus from his teacher Giorgione, and it has served as a model for many compositions since that time. In the foreground, a nude **Venus pudica** rests on voluptuous pillows and sumptuous sheets spread over a red brocade couch. Her golden hair, complemented by the delicate flowers she grasps loosely in her right hand, falls gently over her shoulder. A partial drape hangs in the middle ground, providing a backdrop for her upper torso and revealing a view of her boudoir. The background of the composition includes two women looking into a trunk—presumably handmaidens—and a more distant view of a sunset through a columned veranda. Rich, soft tapestries contrast with the harsh Classicism of the stone columns and inlaid marble floor.

Titian appears to have been interested in the interaction of colors and the contrast of textures. The creamy white sheet complements the radiant golden tones of the body of Venus, built up through countless applications of glazes over flesh-toned pigment. Her sumptuous roundness is created by extremely subtle gradations of tones in these glazes rather than the harshly sculptural chiaroscuro that Leonardo or Raphael might have used. The forms evolve from applications of color instead of line or shadow. Titian's virtuoso brushwork allows him to define different textures: the firm yet silken flesh, the delicate folds of drapery, the servant's heavy cloth dress, the dog's soft fur. The pictorial dominance of these colors and textures sets the work apart from so many examples of Florentine and Roman painting. It appeals primarily to the senses rather than to the intellect.

Titian's use of color as a compositional device is significant. We have already noted the drape, whose dark color forces our attention on the most important part of the composition—Venus's face and upper torso. It also blocks out the left background, encouraging viewers to narrow their focus on the vista in the right background. The forceful diagonal formed by the looming body of Venus is balanced by three elements opposite her: the little dog at her feet and the two handmaidens in the distance. They do not detract from her because they are engaged in activities that do not concern her or the spectator. The diagonal of her body is also balanced by an intersecting diagonal that can be visualized by integrating the red areas in the lower left and upper right corners. Titian thus subtly balances the composition in his placement of objects and color areas.

TINTORETTO Perhaps no other Venetian artist anticipated the Baroque style so strongly as Jacopo Robusti, called Tintoretto, or "little dyer," after the profession of his father.

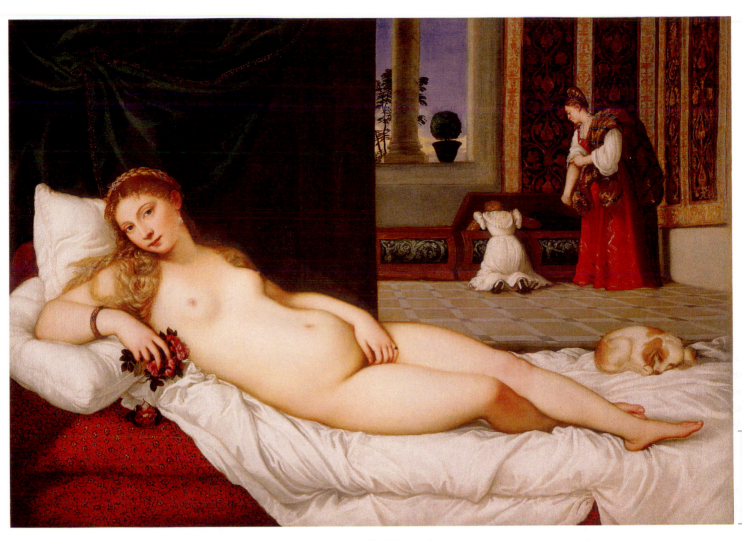

16-27 TITIAN. *Venus of Urbino* (1538). Oil on canvas. 65" × 47". Galleria degli Uffizi, Florence, Italy.

Supposedly a pupil of Titian, Tintoretto (1518–1594) emulated the master's love of color, although he combined it with a more linear approach to constructing forms. This interest in draftsmanship was culled from Michelangelo, but the younger artist's compositional devices went far beyond those of the Florentine and Venetian masters. His dynamic structure and passionate application of pigment provide a sweeping, almost frantic, energy within compositions of huge dimensions.

Tintoretto's painting technique was unique. He arranged doll-like figures on small stages and hung his flying figures by wires in order to copy them in correct perspective on sheets of paper. He then used a grid to transcribe the figures onto much larger canvases. Tintoretto primed the entire canvas with dark colors. Then he quickly painted in the lighter sec-

tions. Thus, many of his paintings appear very dark, except for bright patches of radiant light. The artist painted extremely quickly, using broad areas of loosely swathed paint. John Ruskin, a nineteenth-century art critic, is said to have suggested that Tintoretto painted with a broom.[6] Although this is unlikely, Tintoretto had certainly come a long way from the sculptural, at times marble-like, figures of the High Renaissance and the painstaking finish of Titian's glazed *Venus of Urbino*. This loose brushwork and dramatic white spotlighting on a dark ground anticipate the Baroque style.

---

[6] Frederick Hartt, *History of Italian Renaissance Art*, 2nd ed. (Englewood Cliffs, NJ: Prentice-Hall, 1979), 615.

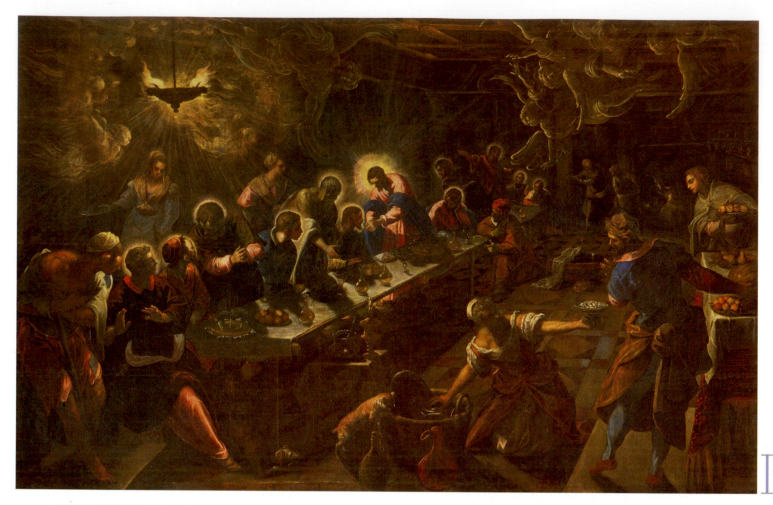

1 ft.

16-28 TINTORETTO. *The Last Supper* (1592–1594). Oil on canvas. 12' × 18'8". San Giorgio Maggiore, Venice, Italy.

The Last Supper (Fig. **16-28**) seals his relationship to the later period. A comparison of this composition with Leonardo's *The Last Supper* (Fig. 16-17) will illustrate the dramatic changes that had taken place in both art and the concept of art over almost a century. The interests in motion, space, and time; the dramatic use of light; and the theatrical presentation of subject matter are all present in Tintoretto's *The Last Supper*. We are first impressed by the movement. Everything and everyone are set into motion: people lean, rise up out of their seats, stretch, and walk. Angels fly and animals dig for food. The space, sliced by a sharp, rushing diagonal that goes from lower left toward upper right, seems barely able to contain all of this commotion, but this cluttered effect enhances the energy of the event.

Leonardo's obsession with symmetry, along with his balance between emotion and restraint, yields a composition that appears static in comparison to the asymmetry and over-powering emotion in Tintoretto's canvas. Leonardo's apostles seem posed for the occasion when contrasted with Tintoretto's spontaneously gesturing figures. A particular moment is captured. We feel that if we were to look away for a fraction of a second, the figures would have changed position by the time we looked back! The timelessness of Leonardo's figural poses has given way to a seemingly temporary placement of characters. The moment that Tintoretto has chosen to depict also differs from Leonardo's. The Renaissance master chose the point at which Jesus announced that one of his apostles would betray him. Tintoretto, on the other hand, chose the moment when Jesus shared bread, which symbolized his body as the wine stood for his blood. This moment is commemorated to this day during the celebration of Mass in the Roman Catholic faith. Leonardo chose a moment signifying death, Tintoretto a moment signifying life, depicted within an atmosphere that is teeming with life.

HIGH AND LATE RENAISSANCE OUTSIDE ITALY

El Greco

The Late Renaissance outside Italy brought us many different styles, and Spain is no exception. Spanish art polarized into two stylistic groups of religious painting: the mystical and the realistic. One painter was able to pull these opposing trends together in a unique pictorial method. El Greco (1541–1614), born Domeniko Theotokopoulos in Crete, integrated many styles into his work. As a young man, he traveled to Italy, where he encountered the works of the Florentine and Roman masters, and he was for a time affiliated with Titian's workshop. The colors that El Greco incorporated into his paintings suggest a Venetian influence, and the distortion of his figures and use of an ambiguous space speak for his interest in Mannerism, which is discussed later.

These pictorial elements can clearly be seen in one of El Greco's most famous works, *The Burial of Count Orgaz* (Fig. **16-29**). In this single work, El Greco combines mysticism and realism. The canvas is divided into two halves by a horizontal line of white-collared heads, separating "heaven" and "earth." The figures in the lower half of the composition are somewhat elongated, but well within the bounds of realism. The heavenly figures, by contrast, are extremely attenuated and seem to move under the influence of a sweeping, dynamic atmosphere. It has been suggested that the distorted figures in El Greco's paintings might have been the result of astigmatism in the artist's eyes, but there is no convincing proof of this.

For example, at times El Greco's figures appear no more distorted than those of other Mannerists. Heaven and earth are disconnected psychologically but joined convincingly in terms of composition. At the center of the rigid, horizontal row of heads that separates the two worlds, a man's upward glance creates a path for the viewer into the upper realm. This compositional device is complemented by a sweeping drape that rises into the upper half of the canvas from above his head, continuing to lead the eye between the two groups of figures, left and right, up toward the image of the resurrected Christ. El Greco's color scheme also complements the worldly and celestial habitats. The colors used in the costumes of the earthly figures are realistic and vibrantly Venetian, but the colors of the upper half of the composition are of discordant hues, highlighting the

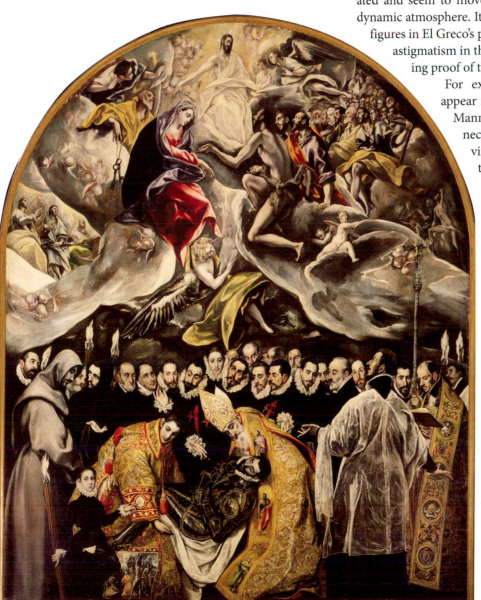

1 ft.

16-29 EL GRECO. *The Burial of Count Orgaz* (1586). Oil on canvas. 16' × 11'10". Santo Tome, Toledo, Spain.

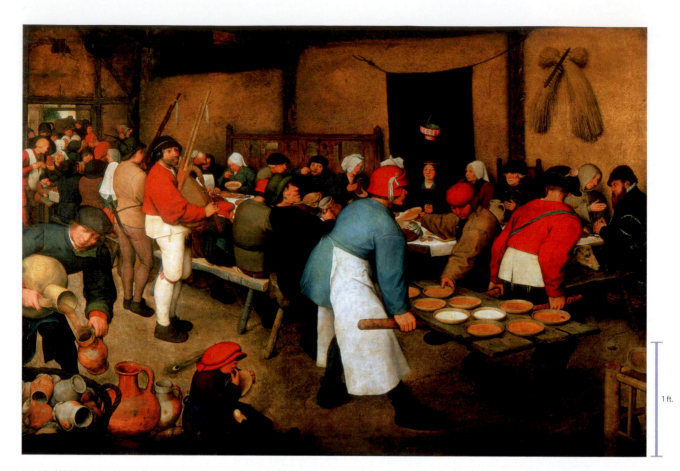

16-30 PIETER BRUEGEL THE ELDER. *The Peasant Wedding* (1568). Oil on wood. 45" × 64½". Kunsthistoriches Museum, Vienna, Austria.

Pieter Bruegel the Elder

During the second half of the sixteenth century in the Netherlands, changes in the subject matter of painting were taking place that would affect the themes of artists working in northern Europe during the Baroque period. Scenes of everyday life involving ordinary people were becoming more popular. One of the masters of this genre painting was Pieter Bruegel the Elder (c. 1520–1569), whose compositions focused on human beings in relation to nature and the life and times of plain Netherlandish folk. *The Peasant Wedding* (Fig. **16-30**) is a good example of Bruegel's slice-of-life canvases. The painting transports us to a boisterous hall, where food and drink flow in abundance, and music and merriment raise the rafters. The viewer's experience of this event relies on the degree to which the artist conveys the sense of noise, of laughter, of cel-

otherworldly nature of the upper canvas. The emotion is high-pitched and exaggerated by the tumultuous atmosphere. This emphasis on emotionalism links El Greco to the onset of the Baroque era. His work contains a dramatic, theatrical flair, one of the hallmarks of the seventeenth century.

ebration. The circular rims of soup bowls are echoed in the spherical caps of the peasants and the mouths of the stacked, earthenware pitchers. In a sea of confusion, this simple repetitive element provides visual unity and guides the path of the eye. There is no hidden message here, no religious fervor, no battle between mythological giants. Human activities are presented as sincere and viable subject matter. There are few examples of such painting before this time, but genre painting will play a principal role in the works of Netherlandish artists during the Baroque period.

MANNERISM

During the Renaissance, the rule of the day was to observe and emulate nature. Toward the end of the Renaissance and before the beginning of the seventeenth century, this rule was suspended for a while, during a period of art that historians have named Mannerism. Mannerist artists abandoned copying directly from nature and copied art instead. Works thus became "secondhand" views of nature. Line, volume, and color no longer duplicated what the eye saw but were derived instead from what other artists had already seen. Several characteristics separate **Mannerist art** from the art of the Renaissance and the Baroque periods: distortion and elongation of figures; flattened, almost two-dimensional space; lack of a defined focal point; and the use of discordant pastel hues.

JACOPO PONTORMO A representative of early Mannerism, Jacopo Pontormo (1494–1557) used most of its stylistic principles. In *Entombment* (Fig. **16-31**), we witness a strong shift in direction from High Renaissance art, even though the painting was executed during Michelangelo's lifetime. The weighty sculptural figures of Michelangelo, Leonardo, and Raphael have given way to less substantial, almost weightless, forms that balance on thin toes and ankles. The limbs are long and slender in proportion to the torsos, and the heads are dwarfed by billowing robes. There is a certain innocent beauty in the arched eyebrows of the haunted faces and in the nervous glances that dart this way and that past the boundaries of the canvas. The figures are pressed against the picture plane, moving within a very limited space. Their weight seems to be thrust outward toward the edges of the composition and away from the almost void center. The figures' robes are composed of odd hues, departing drastically in their soft pastel tones from the vibrant primary colors of the Renaissance masters.

The weightlessness, distortion, and ambiguity of space create an almost otherworldly feeling in the composition, a world in which objects and people do not come under an earthly gravitational force. The artist accepts this "strangeness" and makes no apologies for it to the viewer. The ambiguities are taken in stride. For example, note that the character in a turban behind the head of the dead Jesus does not appear to have a body—there is really no room for it in the composition. And even though a squatting figure in the center foreground appears to be balancing Christ's torso on his shoulders, having taken him down from the cross a moment before, there is no cross in sight! Pontormo seems to have been most interested in elegantly rendering the high-pitched emotion of the scene. Iconographic details and logical figural stances are irrelevant.

The artists from the second half of the sixteenth century through the beginning of the seventeenth century all broke away from the Renaissance tradition in one way or another. Some were opposed to the stylistic characteristics of the Renaissance and turned them around in an original but ultimately uninfluential style called Mannerism. Others, such as Titian and Tintoretto, emphasized the painting

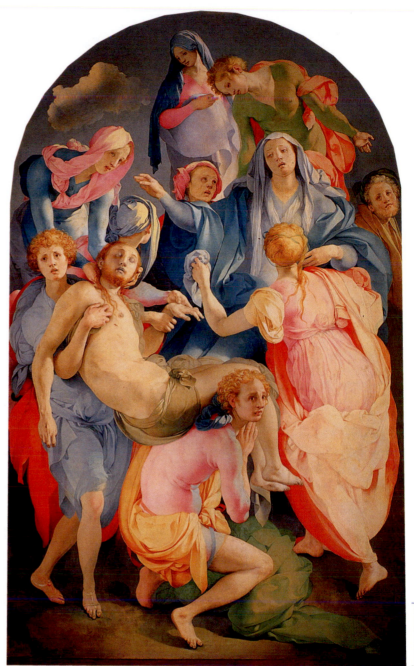

1 ft.

16-31 JACOPO PONTORMO. *Entombment* (1525–1528). Oil on wood. 10'3" × 6'4". Capponi Chapel, Santa Felicitá, Florence, Italy.

process, constructing their compositions by means of stroke and color rather than line and shadow. Still others combined an implied movement and sense of time in their compositions, foreshadowing some of the concerns of the artist in the Baroque period. The High and Late Renaissance witnessed artists of intense originality who provide a fascinating transition between the grand Renaissance and the dynamic Baroque.

ART TOUR *FLORENCE*

LEAF THROUGH THE pages of the chapter on Renaissance Art and survey the figure captions accompanying the illustrations of Italian Renaissance art and architecture. Surprised at how many are in Florence? The fact is, Florence commanded Europe in the fourteenth and fifteenth centuries—in the worlds of finance, patronage, arts, and culture. Dante Alighieri (author of *The Divine Comedy*); Michelangelo Buonarroti (sculptor of *David*, painter of the Sistine Chapel, architect of St. Peter's Basilica); Niccolo Machiavelli (political philosopher, advisor, and author of *The Prince*); Galileo Galilei (astronomer and mathematician, author of the heliocentric theory of the universe)—all were born in or lived in the city of Florence at this pivotal moment in history.

Florence began during Roman times when Julius Caesar passed a law providing land there for retired war veterans. The walls around the city were extended and fortified against the invasions of the Ostrogoths during the Byzantine era, but the territory was lost to the Lombards, along with all of Tuscany, by 570 CE. It was Charlemagne who "rescued" Florence from the "barbarians," incorporating the city into the Holy Roman Empire. From that point forward, it was ruled by princes and . . . the Medicis.

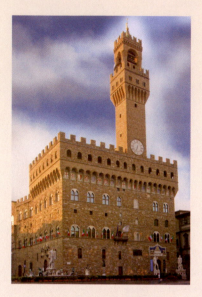

PIAZZA DELLA SIGNORIA WITH THE PALAZZO VECCHIO.

patronage. Evidence of their money and taste seems ubiquitous in Florence, as every building they owned or were somehow connected to bears their coat of arms (a shield with round balls—pills—that signify the family's trade as apothecaries). Works of art and architecture that were commissioned by the Medicis constitute the core of Florence's artistic legacy, bequeathed to the city by the last in the Medici family line—Anna Maria Luisa. The Galleria Degli Uffizi is home to many works from the Medici art collection, and the art institution that is a must-see for any traveler to Florence. (Make that every traveler to Florence.) Arrive early in the morning or a couple of hours before closing to avoid the outrageous lines, and start with this extraordinary monument to get a feel of the historic significance of the city.

It stands on one side of a public square—the Piazza della Signoria—which was the political center of Florence and site of things glorious and inglorious (Michelangelo's David once stood there; Savonarola, the would-be reformer-monk, was burned at the stake there). The piazza is also the

site of the Palazzo Vecchio, which has served as Florence's town hall since the fourteenth century and has a spectacular interior. While you are in the square, check out Florence's best source for postcards—the Sorbi newspaper kiosk—and sample what many rank as the best gelato (Italian ice cream) place in Florence—*Perché No!* ("Why not!")

Florence is an extremely walkable city, with an expansive pedestrian-only area that encompasses many of its highlights, including the Piazza della Signoria, the Duomo, the Ponte Vecchio, and Santa Croce.

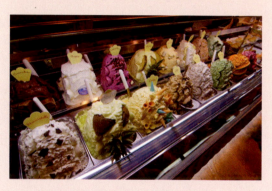

FLORENTINE GELATO.

If there is one symbol of Florence (like the Eiffel Tower in Paris or Big Ben in London), it is the Duomo. Literally the Italian word for "dome," the Duomo is the affectionate name for the cathedral of Santa Maria del Fiori. Looking at the skyline of the city, it is easy to understand its status as an icon. The dome, covered with reddish terracotta tiles and accented with eight white ribs, dominates its surroundings. It was constructed by Filippo Brunelleschi after he won a competition for the commission. Lorenzo Ghiberti, whose bronze reliefs for the doors of the nearby Baptistery are among Florence's greatest treasures, lost. Many tourists climb the 463 steps of the dome to the lantern on top to get an unsurpassed view of the city and surrounding hills. My advice is this: if

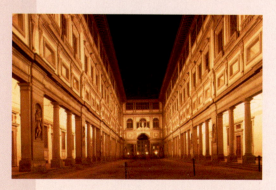

GALLERIA DEGLI UFFIZI

By far the dominant name associated with Renaissance Florence is Medici—a family renowned for their politics and

you want to climb, go up into the cathedral's bell tower (the Campanile) instead. You get not only a great view of Florence, but the best view of the dome to boot. And it's a mere 414 steps to the top. The cathedral, Baptistery, and bell tower are all faced with polychrome marble—white from Carrara, green from Prato, and pink from the Maremma area of southern Tuscany. The combination of light and dark marbles, in particular, characterize many of Florence's buildings, including the churches of Santa Maria Novella and Santa Croce.

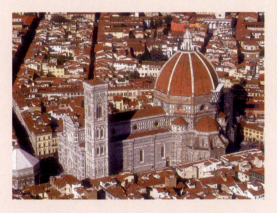

THE DUOMO AND CITY OF FLORENCE AS SEEN FROM THE CAMPANILE.

Santa Croce lies to the east of the Piazza della Signoria and is the burial place of Florence's famous—including Michelangelo, Machiavelli, Galileo, and the composer Gioacchino Rossini (*The Barber of Seville*). There is also a memorial to Dante, although he isn't buried there. Santa Croce is

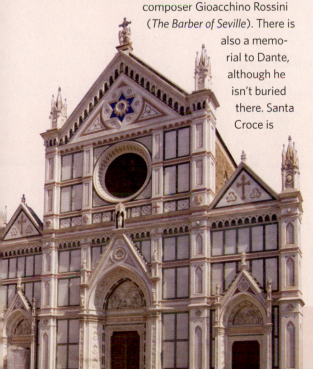

CHURCH OF SANTA CROCE.

filled with important frescoes by artists such as Taddeo Gaddi and Giotto and a relief sculpture by Donatello. While there, look for the tide mark on the pillars and walls—evidence of a devastating flood that gripped the city in 1966.

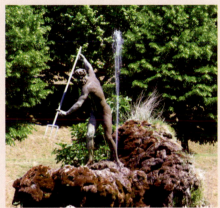

BOBOLI GARDENS.

Though many of the art and architectural treasures of Florence were imperiled by the flood, the Old Bridge, or Ponte Vecchio, somehow survived the onslaught of water and silt when the river Arno rose over its banks. It was not the first time that floodwaters threatened the bridge; it had to be rebuilt in the fourteenth century after a flood. The Ponte Vecchio has a long history. At one time it was the only bridge across the river, and it was the only bridge that the Germans did not destroy during World War II. The Ponte Vecchio looks a bit odd, with shops lining both sides of a walkway across the bridge and a corridor on top of the buildings on one side. The Medici family built the corridor so they could walk across the bridge and not have to run into any common people. The bridge was always—dating back to the thirteenth century, at least—a place to shop, and since 1593, exclusive home to goldsmiths and jewelers. You can purchase Florentine gold on the Ponte Vecchio, although the prices

can be significantly higher than in other shops around town. In addition to its gold (usually sold by weight), Florence is known for its leather goods, linens, ceramics, and marbled paper. You'll also find no shortage of plastic Davids and Duomos.

These highlights are clustered in the pedestrian area in the core of the city, but Florence has innumerable other sites within walking distance from one another: The Palazzos Pitti and Medici-Riccardi (Renaissance palaces that were at one time or another occupied by the Medici family); San Lorenzo (parish church and burial place of the Medici, and homage to their patronage of the arts); The Bargello (where all of the glorious sculpture is kept); the Galleria dell'Accademia (where Michelangelo's *David* now resides, along with the Slaves that the artist carved for the original design of the tomb of Pope Julius II); and the Boboli Gardens (an inner-city oasis of green behind the Palazzo Pitti to which travelers escape when they've had enough).

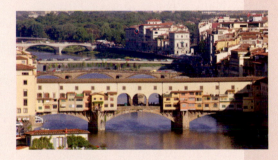

THE PONTE VECCHIO.

The Renaissance in Italy was a tale of two cities: Florence and Rome. The fourteenth and fifteenth centuries belonged to Florence. No other city in Europe had her impact on art and culture. During the High Renaissance, as the money moved, so did the artists—to papal Rome. At 15 million visitors per year, though, the city of Florence has never lost its premier place in the history of art.

 TO CONTINUE YOUR TOUR and learn more about Florence, go to CourseMate.

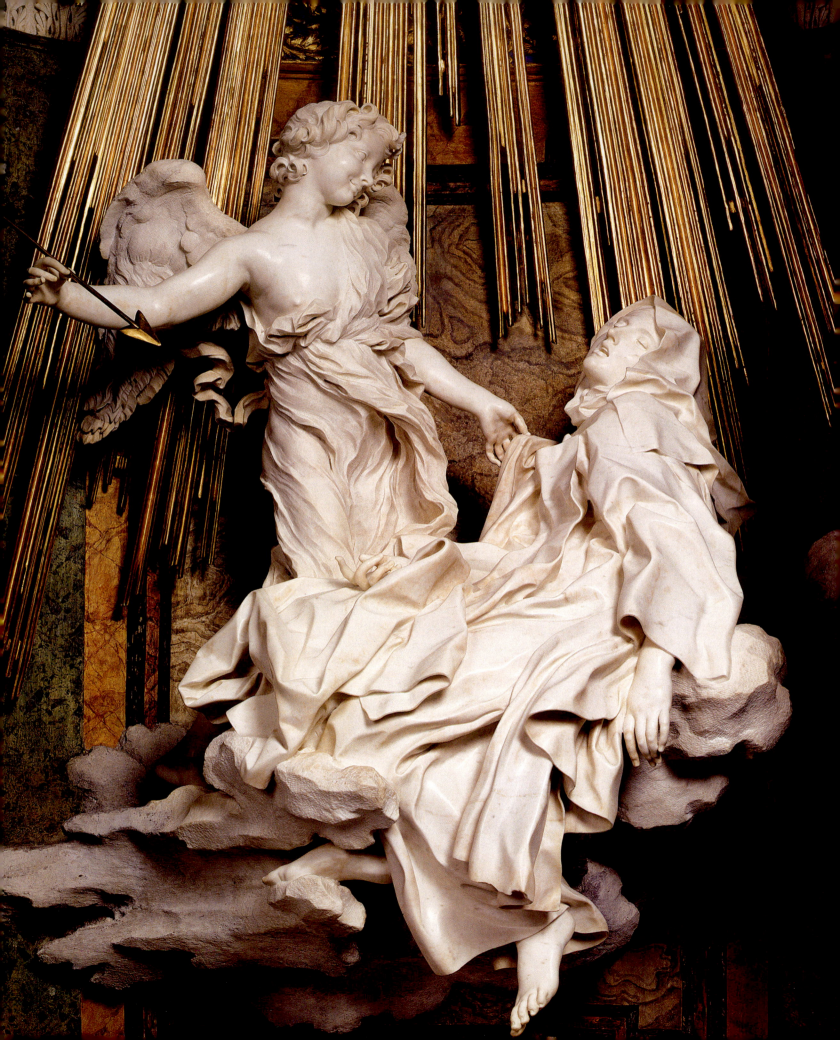

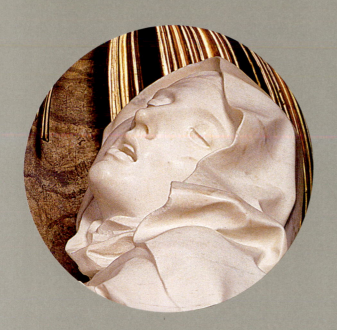

Nature, and Nature's laws lay hid in night.
God said: "Let Newton be!" and all was Light!

—Alexander Pope

THE AGE OF BAROQUE 17

The Baroque period spans roughly the years from 1600 to 1750. Like the Renaissance, which preceded it, the Baroque period was an age of genius in many fields of endeavor. Sir Isaac Newton derived laws of motion and of gravity that have only recently been modified by the discoveries of Einstein. The achievements of Galileo and Kepler in astronomy brought the vast expanses of outer space into sharper focus. The Pilgrims also showed an interest in motion when, in 1620, they put to sea and landed in what is now Massachusetts. Our founders had a certain concern for space as well—they wanted as much as possible between themselves and their English oppressors.

The Baroque period in Europe included a number of post-Renaissance styles that do not have all that much in common. On the one hand, there was a continuation of the Classicism and naturalism of the Renaissance. On the other hand, a far more colorful, ornate, painterly, and dynamic style was born. If one name had to be applied to describe these different directions, it is just as well that that name is **Baroque**—for the word is believed to derive from the Portuguese *barroco*, meaning "irregularly shaped pearl." The Baroque period was indeed irregular in its stylistic tendencies, and it also gave birth to some of the most treasured pearls of Western art.

Motion and space also preoccupied artists of the Baroque era. The concept of time, a dramatic use of light, and a passionate theatricality complete the list of the five most important characteristics of Baroque art, as we shall see throughout this chapter.

GIANLORENZO BERNINI. *The Ecstasy of St. Theresa* (1645–1652). Marble. Height of group: approx. 11'6". Cornaro Chapel, Santa Maria della Vittoria, Rome, Italy.

THE BAROQUE PERIOD IN ITALY

The Baroque era was born in Rome, some say in reaction to the spread of Protestantism resulting from the Reformation. Even though many areas of Europe were affected by the new post-Renaissance spirit (Map 17-1), it was more alive and well and influential in Italy than elsewhere—partly because of the strengthening of the papacy in religion, politics, and patronage of the arts. During the Renaissance, the principal patron of the arts was the infamous Pope Julius II. However, during the Baroque era, a series of powerful popes—Paul V, Urban VIII, Innocent X, and Alexander VII—assumed this role. The Baroque period has been called the Age of Expansion, following the Renaissance Age of Discovery, and this expansion is felt keenly in the arts.

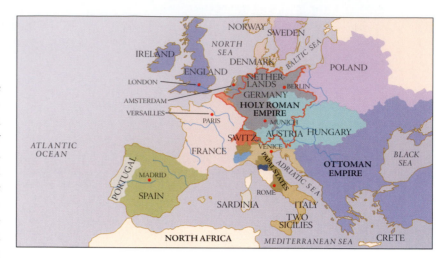

MAP 17-1 Europe (mid-18th century).

St. Peter's

The expansion and renovation of St. Peter's in Vatican City, Rome (Fig. 17-1) took place over a period that extended from the Renaissance into the Baroque, involved a number of artists and architects, and is the result of compromise and collaboration. Michelangelo designed the dome over the crossing square and the apse end of the basilica, Baroque architect Carlo Maderno finalized the facade, and Gianlorenzo Bernini—the acclaimed sculptor of the Baroque era—created the iconic piazza enveloped by dramatic colonnades.

Gianlorenzo Bernini

Gianlorenzo Bernini (1598–1680) made an extensive contribution to St. Peter's as we see it today, both to the exterior and the interior. In his design for the **piazza** of St. Peter's, visible in the aerial view (Fig. 17-2), Bernini had constructed two expansive arcades extending from the facade of the church and culminating in semicircular "arms" enclosing an oval space. This space, the piazza, was divided into trapezoidal "pie sections," in the center of which rises an Egyptian obelisk. The Classical arcades, true in detail to the arts that inspired them, stretch outward into the surrounding city, as if to welcome worshipers and cradle them in spiritual comfort. The curving arms, or arcades, are composed of two double rows of columns with a path between, ending in Classical pedimented "temple fronts." In the interior of the cathedral, beneath Michelangelo's great dome, Bernini designed a bronze canopy to cover the main altar. In the apse, Bernini combined architecture, sculpture, and stained glass in a brilliantly golden display for the Cathedra Petri, or Throne of St. Peter. Through his many other sculptural contributions to St. Peter's, commissioned by various popes, Bernini's reputation as a master is solidified.

Bernini's *David* (see Fig. 16-26) illustrates the dazzling characteristics of Baroque sculpture. This David is remarkably different from those of Donatello, Verrocchio, and Michelangelo. Three of the five characteristics of Baroque art are present in Bernini's sculpture: motion (in this case, implied),

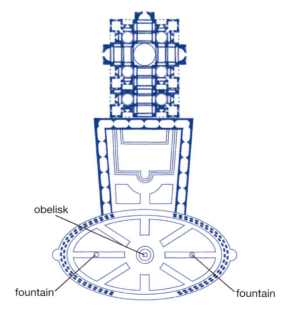

obelisk

fountain   fountain

17-1 Plan of St. Peter's Cathedral, Rome, Italy (1605–1613).

a different way of looking at space, and the introduction of the concept of time. The *Davids* by Donatello and Verrocchio were figures at rest after slaying their Goliaths. Michelangelo, by contrast, presented David before the encounter, with the tension and emotion evident in every vein and muscle, bound to the block of marble that had surrounded the figure. Bernini does not offer David before or after the fight, but instead in the process of the fight. He has introduced an element of time in his work. As in *The Last Supper* by Tintoretto (see Fig. 16-28), we sense that David would have used his weapon if we were to look away and then back. We, the viewers, are forced to complete the action that David has begun for us.

A new concept of space comes into play with David's positioning. The figure no longer remains still in a Classical contrapposto stance, but rather extends into the surrounding space away from a vertical axis. This movement outward from a central core forces the viewer to take into account both solids and voids—that is, both the form and the spaces between and surrounding the forms—in order to appreciate the complete composition. We must move around the work in order to understand it fully, and as we move, the views of the work change radically.

We may compare the difference between Michelangelo's *David* and Bernini's *David* to the difference between Classical and Hellenistic Greek sculpture. The movement out of Classical art into Hellenistic art was marked by an extension of the figure into the surrounding space, a sense of implied movement, and a large degree of theatricality. The time-honored balance between emotion and restraint coveted by the Classical Greek artist as well as the Renaissance master had given way in the Hellenistic and Baroque periods to unleashed passion.

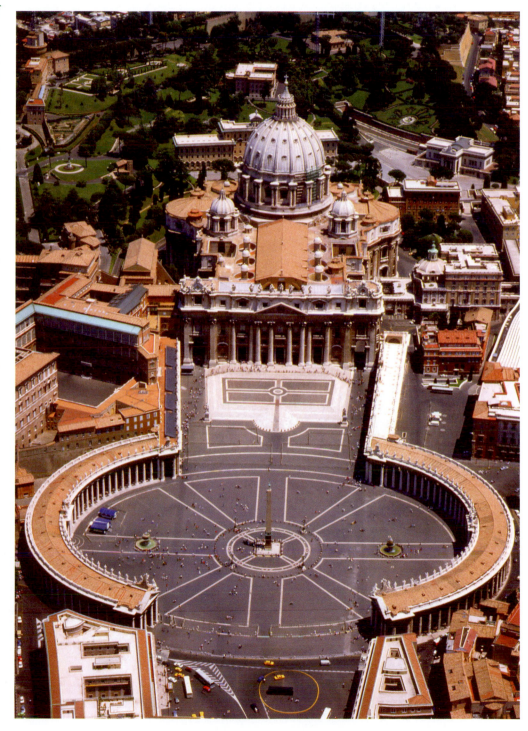

17-2 GIANLORENZO BERNINI. Piazza of St. Peter's (St. Peter's Square, Vatican State), Rome, Italy.

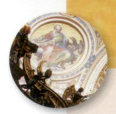

KAROL WOJTYLA DIED IN HIS Vatican apartment on April 2, 2005. He was 84 years old and had reigned over the Catholic Church as Pope John Paul II for 26 years—the second longest papacy in history. His death set into motion a series of rituals that had been fixed for centuries, from the destruction of his papal ring to the sequestering of the cardinals who would, in secrecy, elect his successor. The world bore witness to many, if not most, of these traditions as they unfolded before dignitaries, pilgrims, and the international media. And as an art appreciation and art history professor, I told all of my students, "Watch as much as you can." History was being made against the backdrop of the art and architecture they were studying—what *you* are studying in your Renaissance and Baroque chapters. For the most part, in our classes, we look at art outside its actual context, analyzing projected images that have the same dimensions regardless of the actual size of the art. We view photographs of works of architecture vast in scale with no sense whatsoever of what it might be like to *be* in those spaces. Regardless of one's religious beliefs, regardless of one's views on the teachings and actions of this particular pope, this meeting of history and art provided an opportunity to see—in context and on-site and in scale—some of the most spectacular treasures of Rome and the Vatican.

This brief portfolio of images was chosen to illustrate things that a student would not ordinarily see, even on a trip to Rome. We may study the design of Bernini's colonnades, extending from Maderno's facade and scooping around his elliptical piazza (Fig. **17-3**). But how much better did we grasp Bernini's concept of the arms of the church extending to embrace its fold when we saw throngs of pilgrims cradled in that space as they paid final respects to their beloved pope (Fig. **17-4**)? The elaborate frescoes of the Clementine Hall (Fig. **17-5**) became for us more than disembodied slides. What's

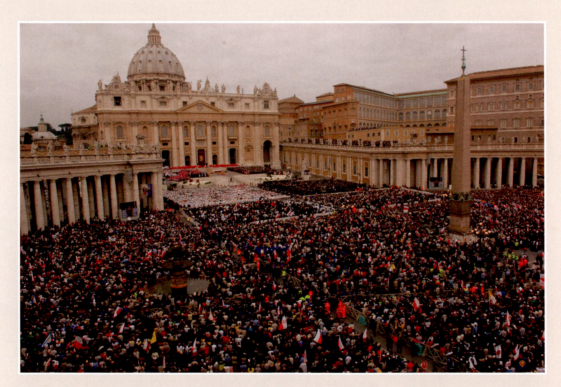

17-3 GIANLORENZO BERNINI. Piazza of St. Peter's Cathedral, Rome, Italy (1605–1613).
Bernini's piazza and colonnades of St. Peter's with crowds assembling for the funeral Mass for Pope John Paul II, April 8, 2005. Maderno's facade and Michelangelo's dome can also be seen.

more, they are works rarely, if ever, seen by the public, for the hall—part of the Papal Palace near St. Peter's Basilica—is used only by the pope for formal ceremonies and private receptions . . . and for the private viewing of his body in death before it is moved to St. Peter's.

And how to comprehend the vastness of the interior of St. Peter's Basilica itself? As we viewed the tens of thousands of diminutive mourners solemnly filing past the funeral bier at the foot of Bernini's colossal bronze canopy; as we looked upward to Michelangelo's expansive, enveloping dome and around the altar at the towering sculptures of saints standing watch (Fig. 17-6); as we took in the sweep of the seemingly endless nave—only then did we grasp the relationship between the magnitude of the event and the monumentality of the setting.

And as the reign of John Paul II ended and the election of his successor proceeded, the world's attention shifted to one of the Vatican's most beloved landmarks—the Sistine Chapel (see Fig. 16-21). The vastness of St. Peter's was supplanted by the intimacy of the Sistine. The College of Cardinals spent hours in prayer and reflection there as they elected the next pope through a series of secret ballots. Isolated from the outside world and surrounded by Michel-

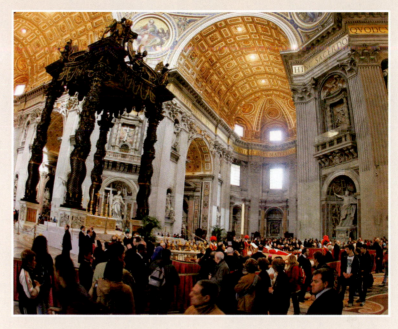

17-4 St. Peter's Basilica, Rome, Italy.
Pope John Paul II lying in state at the foot of Bernini's bronze canopy (left) in the transept of St. Peter's Basilica, April 6, 2005. Bernini's *St. Longinus* can be seen in the niche at right.

angelo's scenes from the Bible and his terrifying Last Judgment, it was within the walls of one of art history's most treasured monuments that these men judged who would be the next among them to make history (Fig. 17-6). ●

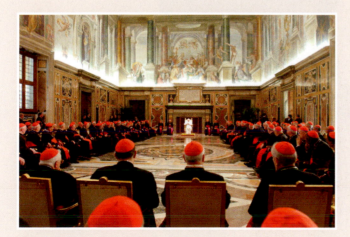

17-5 Clementine Hall, Papal Palace, Rome, Italy.
Pope Benedict XVI speaks during an audience with the cardinals in the Clementine Hall in the Vatican, April 22, 2005.

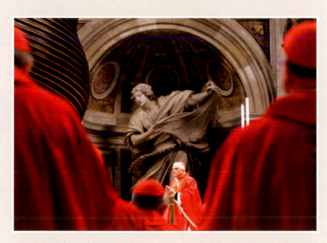

17-6 Cardinal Joseph Ratzinger leading Mass in the transept of St. Peter's Basilica. Mass held April 18, 2005, before cardinals sequestered themselves for their conclave. In the background is Francesco Mochi's sculpture *Saint Veronica* (1629).

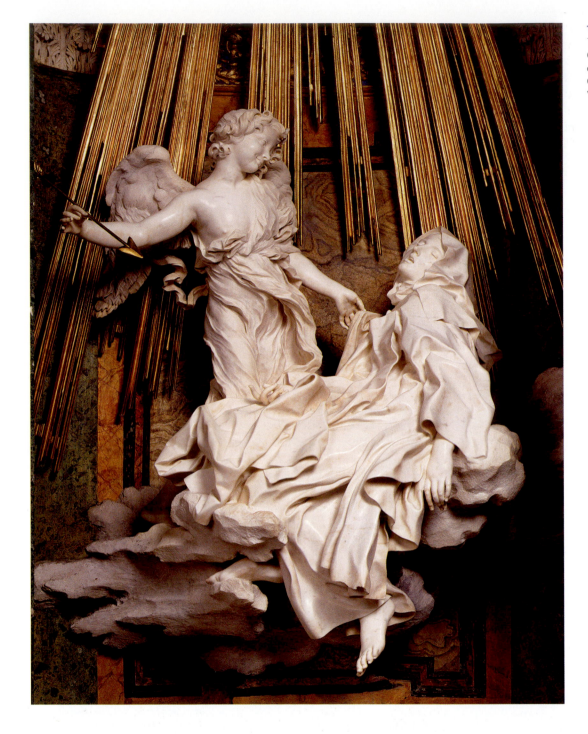

17-7 GIANLORENZO BERNINI. *The Ecstasy of St. Theresa* (1645–1652). Marble. Height of group: approx. 11'6". Cornaro Chapel, Santa Maria della Vittoria, Rome, Italy.

Uncontrollable passion and theatrical drama might best describe Bernini's *The Ecstasy of St. Theresa* (Fig. **17-7**), a sculptural group executed for the chapel of the Cornaro family in the church of Santa Maria della Vittoria in Rome. The sculpture commemorates a mystical event involving St. Theresa, a Carmelite nun who believed that a pain in her side was caused by an angel of God stabbing her repeatedly with a fire-tipped arrow. Her response combined pain and pleasure, as conveyed by the sculpture's submissive swoon and impas-

sioned facial expression. Bernini summoned all of his sculptural powers to execute these figures and combined the arts of architecture, sculpture, and painting to achieve his desired theatrical effect. Notice the way in which Bernini described vastly different textures with his sculptural tools: the roughly textured clouds, the heavy folds of St. Theresa's woolen garment, the diaphanous "wet-look" drapery of the angel. "Divine" rays of glimmering bronze—illuminated by a hidden window—shower down on the figures, as if emanating from the painted ceiling of the chapel. Bernini enhanced this self-conscious theatrical effect by including marble sculptures of the likenesses of members of the Cornaro family in theater boxes to the left and right. They observe, gesture, and discuss the scene animatedly as would theatergoers. The fine line between the rational and the spiritual that so interested the Baroque artist was presented by Bernini in a tactile yet illusionary masterpiece of sculpture.

Caravaggio

This theatrical drama and passion had its counterpart in Baroque painting, as can be seen in the work of Michelangelo de Merisi, called Caravaggio (1573–1610). Unlike Bernini's somewhat idealized facial and figural types, the models for Caravaggio came directly from those around him. Whereas Bernini could move in the company of popes and princes, Caravaggio was more comfortable with the outcasts of society. In a way he was one of them, having a police record for violent assaults. Caravaggio chose lower-class models for his shocking painting *The Conversion of St. Paul* (Fig. **17-8**). The artist marked the dramatic moment when Paul, persecuting Christians in the name of the Roman Empire, was confronted with his actions and, in response, changed the course of his life. Thrown from his horse and blinded by a bright light, Paul professed to have heard a voice asking why he engaged in murderous persecution. The voice, that of Jesus according to Paul, directed him to proceed to Damascus, where he was cured of his blindness and began to preach the tenets of Christianity. Very much in the Baroque spirit, Caravaggio chose to focus on the exact moment when Paul was thrown from his horse. He lies flat on his back, eyelids shut, arms groping in the darkness of his blindness. Paul looks as if he might be trampled by his horse, except for the rugged yet calming hands of a man nearby. A piercing light flashes upon the scene, spotlighting certain parts and casting others into the night, resulting in an exaggerated chiaroscuro called tenebrism.

Tenebrism, translated as "dark manner," is characterized by an often small and concentrated light source within the painting or what appears to be an external "spotlight" directed at specific points in the composition. The effect is harsh and theatrical, as if the events were playing out onstage and being lit from above. The lighting technique of tenebrism was used broadly by Italian Baroque painters but is seen throughout European painting at this time.

Artemisia Gentileschi

One of Caravaggio's foremost contemporaries was Artemisia Gentileschi (1593–c. 1652). Her father, the painter Orazio Gentileschi, who enjoyed much success in Rome, Genoa, and London, recognized and supported Artemisia's talents.

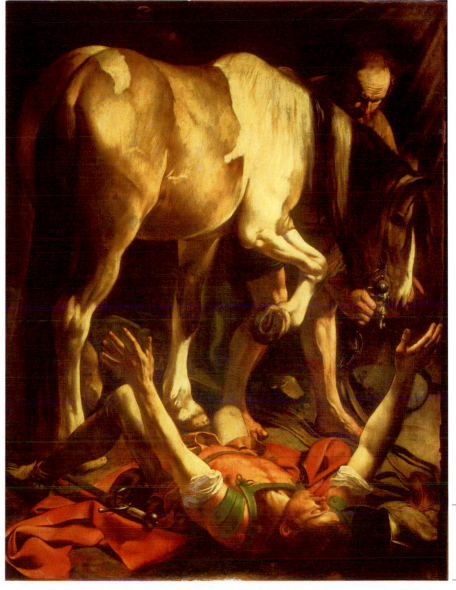

17-8 CARAVAGGIO. *The Conversion of St. Paul* (1600–1601). Oil on canvas. 90" × 69". Santa Maria del Popolo, Rome, Italy.

1 ft.

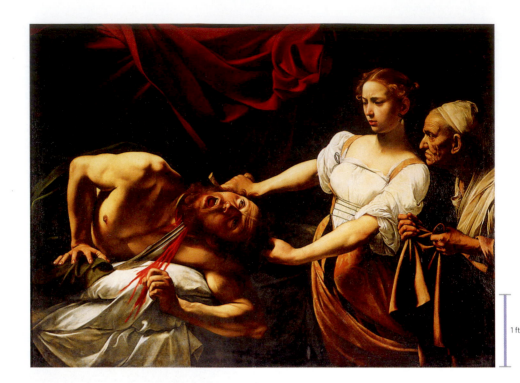

17-9 CARAVAGGIO. *Judith and Holofernes* (c. 1598). Oil on canvas. Approx. 56¾" × 76¾". Galleria Nazionale d'Arte Antica, Palazzo Barberini, Rome, Italy.

1 ft.

17-10 ARTEMISIA GENTILESCHI. *Judith Decapitating Holofernes* (c. 1620). Oil on canvas. 72½" × 55¾". Galleria degli Uffizi, Florence, Italy.

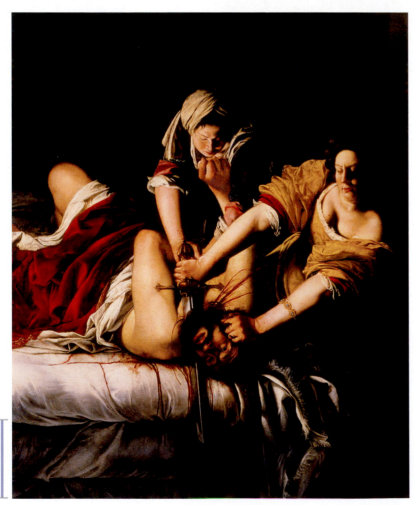

1 ft.

Although one of her father's choices for her ended in disaster—an apprenticeship with a man who ultimately raped her—Artemisia came to develop a personal, dramatic, and impassioned Baroque style. Her work bears similarities to that of Caravaggio, her own father, and others working in Italy at that moment, but it often stands apart in the emphatic rendering of its content or in its reconsideration and revision of subjects commonly represented by sixteenth- and seventeenth-century artists.

Consider, for example, the roughly contemporary paintings of *Judith and Holofernes* by Caravaggio (Fig. 17-9) and *Judith Decapitating Holofernes* by Gentileschi (Fig. 17-10). Both works reference a biblical story of the heroine Judith, who rescues her oppressed people by decapitating the tyrannical Assyrian general Holofernes. She steals into his tent under the cover of night and pretends to respond to his seductive overtures. When he is besotted, with her and with drink, she uses his own sword to cut off his head. Both paintings are prime examples of the Baroque style—vibrant palette, dramatic lighting, an impassioned subject heightened to excess by our coming face-to-terrified-face with a man at the precise moment of his bloody execution. But consider the differences: How would you compare Gentileschi's image of Judith with Caravaggio's? Look at the delicacy of Judith's demeanor and the disgust in her facial expression. Now observe Gentileschi's Judith—determined, strong, physically and emotionally committed to the task. In Caravaggio's painting, Holofernes is caught unaware and falls victim in his compromised, drunken state. Gentileschi's tyrant snaps out of his wine-induced stupor and struggles for his life. He pushes and fights and is ultimately overpowered by a righteous woman. What, if any, gender differences can you interpret in these renderings?

Gentileschi's *Judith Decapitating Holofernes* is one of her most studied and violent paintings. She returned to the subject repeatedly in many different versions, leading some historians to suggest that her seeming obsession with the story signified her personal struggle in the wake of her rape and subsequent trial of her accuser, during which she was tortured in an attempt to verify the truth of her testimony. Do you think that this context is essential to understanding Gentileschi's work?

Baroque Ceiling Decoration

The Baroque interest in combining the arts of painting, sculpture, and architecture found its home in the naves and domes of churches and cathedrals, as artists used the three mediums to create an unsurpassed illusionistic effect. Unlike Renaissance ceiling painting, as exemplified by Michelangelo's decoration for the Sistine Chapel, the space was not divided into "frames" with individual scenes. Rather, the Baroque artist created the illusion of a ceiling vault open to the heavens with figures flying freely in and out of the church. Baciccio's *Triumph of the Sacred Name of Jesus* (Fig. 17-11) is an energetic display of figures painted on plaster that spill out beyond the gilded frame of the ceiling's illusionistic opening. The trompe l'oeil effect is achieved by combining these painted figures with white stucco-modeled sculptures and a gilded stucco ceiling. Attention to detail is remarkable, from the blinding light of the heavens to the deep shadows that would be cast on the ceiling by the painted forms. Saints and angels fly upward toward the light, while sinners are banished from the heavens to the floor of the church. Artists like Baciccio and their patrons spared no illusionistic device to create a total, mystical atmosphere.

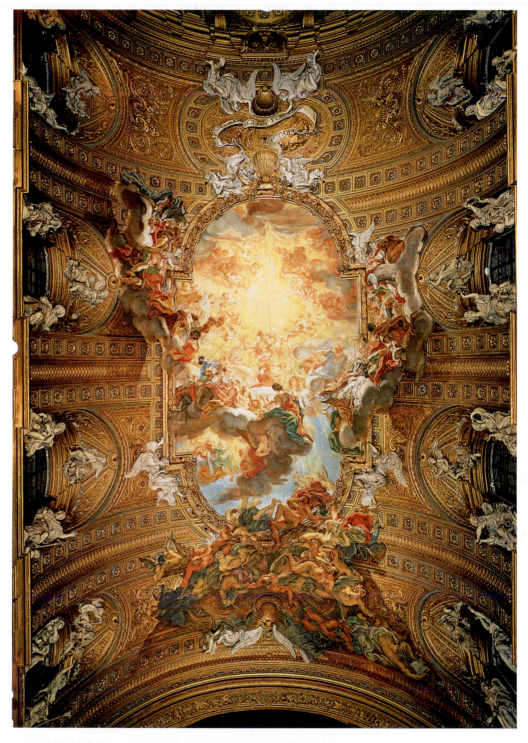

17-11 BACICCIO. *Triumph of the Sacred Name of Jesus* (1676–1679). Ceiling fresco. Il Gesù, Rome, Italy.

SUSANNAH AND THE ELDERS BY TINTORETTO AND GENTILESCHI

ARTEMISIA GENTILESCHI ONCE SAID, in reaction to being cheated out of a potentially lucrative commission, "If I were a man, I can't imagine it would have turned out this way." How particularly apt a statement to keep in mind as we consider these works on the subject of Susannah and the Elders.

The story of Susannah can be found in the book of Daniel in the Old Testament, or Hebrew Bible. Susannah was the wife of Joachim, a wealthy Babylonian Jew whose home was frequently visited by judges and elders of the community. Susannah was as pious as she was enchantingly beautiful, and when she rejected the sexual advances of two such elders, they accused her of committing adultery in order to retaliate. Susannah was put on trial for these fictitious accu-

sations, was found guilty, and would have been stoned to death were it not for the appearance in the court of Daniel. God had answered Susannah's prayers and sent her a lawyer of sorts. Daniel cross-examined the elders individually, poking holes in their contrived testimony. The tables turned: Susannah was saved, and the elders were put to death for bearing false witness.

With these details in mind, how would Tintoretto and Gentileschi tell this story pictorially? The choices they made are very different, and they are illuminating. Tintoretto's rendering of *Susannah* (Fig. **17-12**) befits her status. Her beauty and sensuality are enhanced by a show of precious possessions—perfume bottles, jewels and pearls, silken cloth. Bathing in the surrounds of a sumptuous, fertile

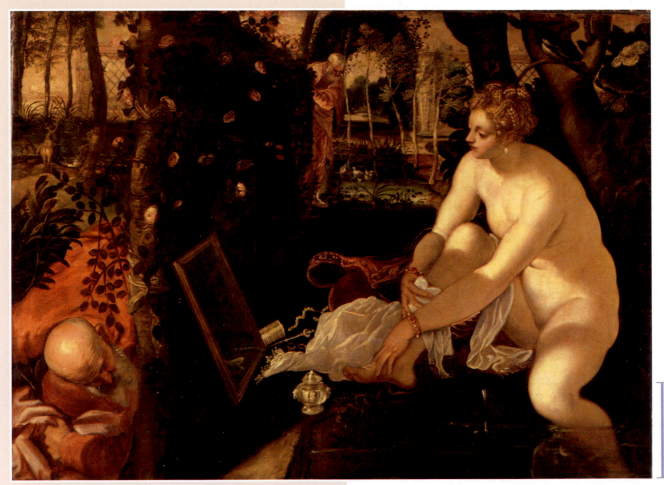

1 ft.

17-12 JACOPO TINTORETTO. *Susannah and the Elders* (1555–1556). Oil on canvas. 57¾" × 76¼". Kunsthistorisches Museum, Vienna, Austria.

garden, Susannah admires herself in a mirror propped up against a screen covered in vines and flowers. Our focus is entirely on her, as are the prying eyes of one of the elders whose bald head pokes around the screen in the lower left. Susannah, *pious*? Would we ever read that attribute in

Tintoretto's image? Is Tintoretto suggesting that Susannah played some role in her seduction? Is he turning us, the spectators, into voyeurs such as those who menaced her?

Gentileschi's *Susannah and the Elders* (Fig. **17-13**) tells the same story, but how? Tintoretto's deep, lush, garden setting, where Susannah lounges at her leisure, has been replaced by a compressed space in which she twists and turns her body to fend off the threatening, sleazy elders. There is nothing sensual about her contorted face and her nakedness against the harsh, cold stone. As one of the men gestures "Shhhhhh! You better not say a word!" Susannah finds herself trapped in a claustrophobic space— between her seducers, the stone, and us. If our eyes focus on Susannah, they focus on her anguish.

Faced with a narrative to be rendered, artists always make choices. Ask yourselves: What are those choices? Why, in my opinion, did the artist make them? Aside from the story, or *text* of the work of art, is the artist trying to convey some other message (that is, a *subtext*)? What do these choices say about the artist, or the patron, or the gender ideologies in place in the society that produced the work? ●

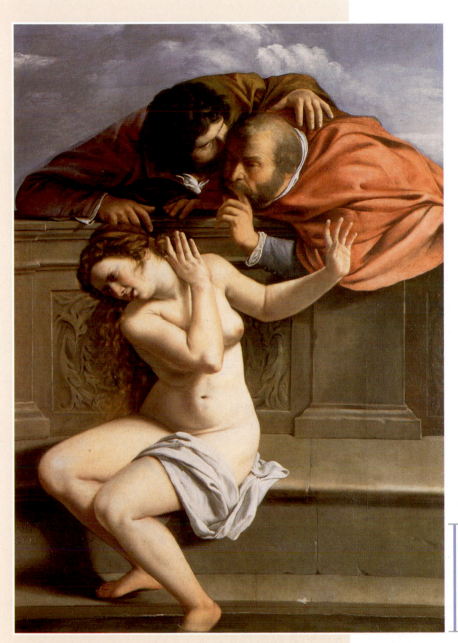

1 ft.

17-13 ARTEMISIA GENTILESCHI. *Susannah and the Elders* (1610). Oil on canvas. 66⅞" × 46⅞". Kunstsammlungen Graf von Schonborn, Wiesentheid, Germany.

Francesco Borromini

Although it is difficult to imagine an architect incorporating the Baroque elements of motion, space, and light in buildings, this was accomplished by the great seventeenth-century architect Francesco Borromini (1599–1667). His San Carlo alle Quattro Fontane (Fig. **17-14**) shows that the change from Renaissance to Baroque architecture was one from the static to the organic. Borromini's facade undulates in implied movement complemented by the concave entablatures of the bell towers on the roof. Light plays across the plane of the facade, bouncing off the engaged columns, while leaving the recessed areas in darkness. The stone seems to breathe because of the **plasticity** of the design and the innovative use of light and shadow. The interior is equally alive, consisting of a large oval space surrounded by rippling concave and convex walls. For the first time since we examined the Parthenon (see Fig. 14-10), we appreciate a building first as sculpture and only second as architecture.

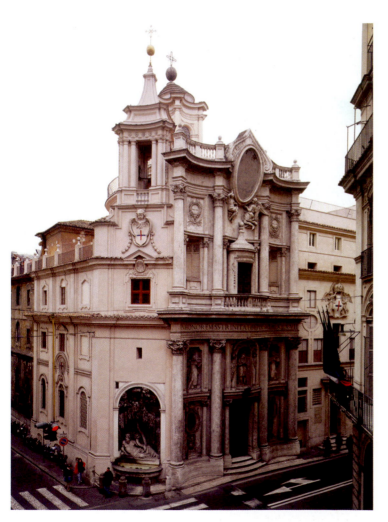

17-14 FRANCESCO BORROMINI. San Carlo alle Quattro Fontane, Rome, Italy (1665-1667).

THE BAROQUE PERIOD OUTSIDE ITALY

Baroque characteristics were also found in the art of other areas of Europe. Artists of Spain and Flanders adopted the Venetian love of color, and with their application of paint in loosely brushed swaths, they created an energetic motion in their compositions. Northern artists had always been interested in realism, and during the Baroque period, they carried this emphasis to an extreme and used innovative pictorial methods to that end. Paintings of everyday life and activities became the favorite subjects of Dutch artists, who followed in Bruegel's footsteps and perfected the art of genre painting. The Baroque movement also extended into France and England, but there it often manifested in a strict adherence to Classicism. The irregularity of styles suggested by the term *baroque* is again apparent.

Spain

Spain was one of the wealthiest countries in Europe during the Baroque era—partly because of the influx of riches from the New World—and the Spanish court was lavish in its support of the arts. Painters and sculptors were imported from different parts of Europe for royal commissions, and native talent was cultivated and treasured.

DIEGO VELÁZQUEZ Diego Velázquez (1599–1660) was born in Spain and rose to the position of court painter and confidant of King Philip IV. Although Velázquez relied on Baroque techniques in his use of Venetian colors, highly contrasting lights and darks, and a deep, illusionistic space, he had contempt for the idealized images that accompanied these elements in the Italian art of the period. Like Caravaggio, Velázquez preferred to use common folk as models to assert a harsh realism in his canvases. Velázquez brought many a mythological subject down to earth by portraying ordinary facial types and naturalistic attitudes in his principal characters. Nor did he restrict this preference to paintings of the masses. Velázquez adopted the same genre format in works involving the royal family, such as the famous *Las Meninas* (Fig. **17-15**). The huge canvas is crowded with figures engaged in different tasks. *Las meninas*, "the maids of honor," are attending the little princess Margarita, who seems dressed for a portrait-painting session. She is being entertained by the favorite members of her entourage, including two dwarfs and an oversized dog. We suspect that they are keeping her company while the artist, Velázquez, paints before his oversized canvas.

Is Velázquez, in fact, supposed to be painting exactly what we see before us? Some have interpreted the work in this way. Others have noted that Velázquez would not be standing behind the princess and her attendants if he were painting them. Moreover, on the back wall of his studio, we see the mirror images of the king and queen standing next to one another with a red drape falling behind. Because we do not actually see them in the flesh, we may assume that they are standing in the viewer's position, before the canvas and the artist. Is the princess being given a few finishing touches before joining her parents in a family portrait? We cannot know for sure. The reality of the scene has been left a mystery by Velázquez, just as has the identity of the gentleman observing the scene from an open door in the rear of the room. It is interesting to note the prominence of the artist in this painting of royalty. It makes us aware of his importance to the court and to the king in particular. Recall the portrait

of Raphael in *The School of Athens* (see Fig. 16-20). Raphael's persona is almost furtive by comparison.

Velázquez pursued realism in technique as well as in subject matter. Building upon the Venetian method of painting, Velázquez constructed his forms from a myriad of strokes that capture light exactly as it plays over a variety of surface textures. Upon close examination of his paintings, we find small distinct strokes that hover on the surface of the canvas, divorced from the very forms they are meant to describe. Yet from a few feet away, the myriad brushstrokes evoke an overall impression of silk or fur or flowers. Velázquez's method of dissolving forms into small, roughly textured brushstrokes that recreate the play of light over surfaces would be the

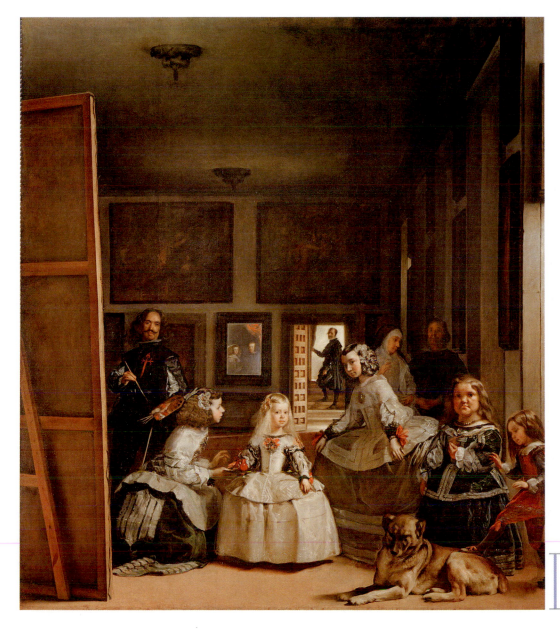

17-15 DIEGO VELÁZQUEZ. *Las Meninas* (*The Maids of Honor*) (1656). Oil on canvas. 10'5" × 9'¾". Prado Museum, Madrid, Spain.

1 ft.

foundation of a movement called Impressionism some two centuries later. In his pursuit of realism, Velázquez truly was an artist before his time.

Flanders

After the dust of Martin Luther's Reformation had settled, the region of Flanders was divided. The northern sections, now called the Dutch Republic (present-day Holland), accepted Protestantism, whereas the southern sections, still called Flanders (present-day Belgium), remained Catholic. This separation more or less dictated the subjects that artists rendered in their works. Dutch artists painted scenes of daily life, carrying forward the tradition of Bruegel, whereas Flemish artists continued painting the religious and mythological scenes already familiar to us from Italy and Spain.

PETER PAUL RUBENS Even the great power and prestige held by Velázquez were exceeded by the Flemish artist Peter Paul Rubens (1577–1640). One of the most sought-after artists of his time, Rubens was an ambassador, diplomat, and court painter to dukes and kings. He ran a bustling workshop with numerous assistants to help him complete commissions. Rubens's style combined the sculptural qualities of Michelangelo's figures with the painterliness and coloration of the Venetians. He also emulated the dramatic chiaroscuro and theatrical presentation of subject matter we found in the Italian Baroque masters. Much as had Dürer, Rubens admired and adopted from his southern colleagues. Although Rubens painted portraits, religious subjects, and mythological themes, as well as scenes of adventure, his canvases were always imbued with the dynamic energy and unleashed passion we link to the Baroque era.

17-16 PETER PAUL RUBENS. *The Rape of the Daughters of Leucippus* (1617). Oil on canvas. 7'3" × 6'10". Alte Pinakothek, Munich, Germany.

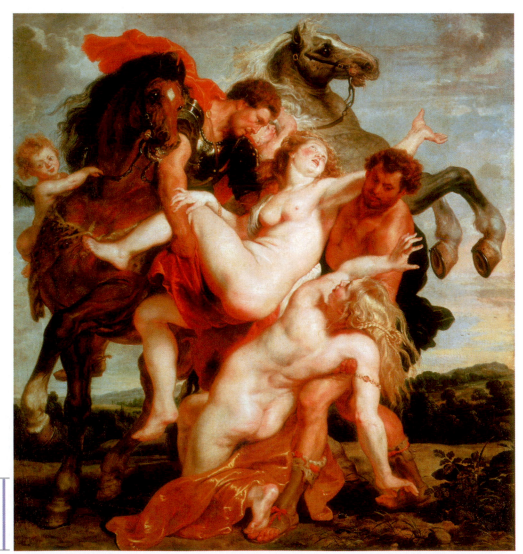

1 ft.

In *The Rape of the Daughters of Leucippus* (Fig. **17-16**), Rubens recounted a tale from Greek mythology in which two mortal women were seized by the twin sons of Zeus, Castor and Pollux. The action in the composition is described by the intersection of strong diagonals and verticals that stabilize the otherwise unstable composition. Capitalizing on the Baroque "stop-action" technique, which depicts a single moment in an event, Rubens placed his struggling, massive forms within a diamond-shaped structure that rests in the foreground on a single point—the toes of a single man and woman. Visually, we grasp that all this energy cannot be supported on a single point, so we infer continuous movement. The action has been pushed up to the picture plane, where the viewer is confronted with the intense emotion and brute strength of the scene. Along with these Baroque devices, Rubens used color and texture much in the way the Venetians used it. The virile suntanned arms of the abductors contrast strongly with the delicately colored flesh of the women. The soft blond braids that flow outward under the influence of all of this commotion correspond to the soft, flowing manes of the overpowering horses.

Holland

The grandiose compositional schemes and themes of action executed by Rubens could not have been further removed from the concerns and sensibilities of most seventeenth-century Dutch artists. Whereas mysticism and religious naturalism flourished in Italy, Flanders, and Spain amidst the rejection of Protestantism and the invigorated revival of Catholicism, artists of the Low Countries turned to secular art, abiding by the Protestant mandate that humans not create false idols. Not only did artists turn to scenes of everyday life, but the collectors of art were everyday folk. In the Dutch quest for the establishment of a middle class, aristocratic patronage was lost, and artists were forced to peddle their wares in the free market. Landscapes, still lifes, and genre paintings were the favored canvases, and *realism* was the word of the day. Although the subject matter of Dutch artists differed radically from that of their colleagues elsewhere in Europe, the spirit of the Baroque, with many, if not most, of its artistic characteristics, was present in their work.

REMBRANDT VAN RIJN The golden-toned, subtly lit canvases of Rembrandt van Rijn (1606–1669) possess a certain degree of timelessness. Rembrandt concentrates on the personality of the sitter or the psychology of a particular situation rather than on surface characteristics. This introspection is evident in all of Rembrandt's works, whether religious or secular in subject, landscapes or portraits, drawings, paintings, or prints.

Rembrandt painted many self-portraits that offer us an insight into his life and personality. In a self-portrait at age 46 (Fig. **17-17**), Rembrandt paints an image of himself as a self-confident, well-respected, and sought-after artist who stares almost impatiently out toward the viewer. It is as if he had been caught in the midst of working and has but a moment for us. It is a powerful image, with piercing eyes, thoughtful brow, and determined jaw that betray a productive man who is more than satisfied with his position in life. All of this may seem obvious, but notice how few clues he gives us to reach

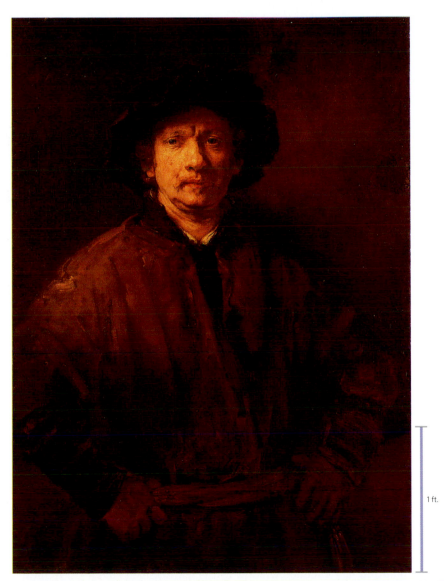

1 ft.

17-17 REMBRANDT VAN RIJN. *Self-Portrait* (1652). Oil on canvas. 45" × 32". Kunsthistorisches Museum, Vienna, Austria.

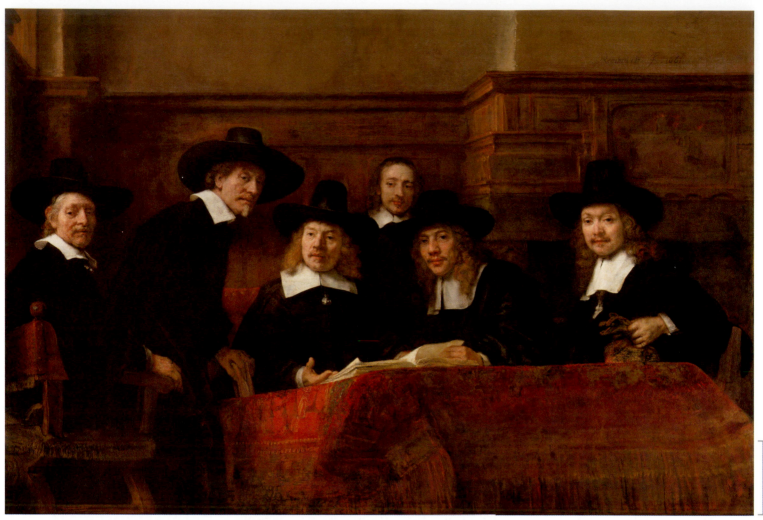

17-18 REMBRANDT VAN RIJN. *Syndics of the Drapers' Guild* (1661–1662). Oil on canvas. 72⅞" × 107⅛". Rijksmuseum, Amsterdam, Netherlands.

1 ft.

these conclusions about his personality. He stands in an undefined space with no props that reveal his identity. The figure is cast into darkness; we can hardly discern his torso and hands resting in the sash around his waist. The penetrating light in the canvas is reserved for just a portion of the artist's face. Rembrandt gives us a minute fragment with which he beckons us to complete the whole. It is at once a mysterious and revealing portrayal that relies on a mysterious and revealing light.

Rembrandt also painted large group portraits. In his *Syndics of the Drapers' Guild* (Fig. 17-18), which you may recognize from the cover of Dutch Masters cigar boxes, we, the viewers, become part of a scene involving Dutch businessmen. Bathed in the warm light of a fading sun that enters the room through a hidden window to the left, the men appear to be reacting to the entrance of another person. Some rise in acknowledgment. Others seem to smile. Still others gesture

to a ledger as if to explain that they are gathering to "go over the books." Even though the group operates as a whole, the portraits are highly individualized and in themselves complete. As in his self-portrait, Rembrandt concentrates his light on the heads of the sitters, from which we, the viewers, gain insight into their personalities. The haziness that surrounds Rembrandt's figures is born from his brushstrokes and his use of light. Rembrandt's strokes are heavily loaded with pigment and applied in thick impasto.

As we saw in the painterly technique of Velázquez, Rembrandt's images are more easily discerned from afar than from up close. As a matter of fact, Rembrandt is reputed to have warned viewers to keep their "nose" out of his painting because the smell of paint was bad for them. We can take this to mean that the technical devices Rembrandt used to create certain illusions of realism are all too evident from the perspective of a few inches. Above all, Rembrandt was capable of manipulating light. His is a light that alternately constructs and destructs, that alternately bathes and hides from view. It is a light that can be focused as unpredictably, and that shifts as subtly, as the light we find in nature. Although Rembrandt was sought after as an artist for a good many years and was granted many important commissions, he fell victim to the whims of the free market. The grand master of the Dutch Baroque died at age 63, out of fashion and penniless.

JAN VERMEER If there is a single artist who typifies the Dutch interest in painting scenes of daily life, the commonplace narratives of middle-class men and women, it is Jan Vermeer (1632–1675). Although he did not paint many pictures and never strayed from his native Delft, his precisely sketched and pleasantly colored compositions made him well respected and influential in later centuries.

Young Woman with a Water Jug (Fig. **17-19**) exemplifies Vermeer's subject matter and technique. In a tastefully underfurnished corner of a room in a typical middle-class household, a woman stands next to a rug-covered table, grasping a water jug with one hand and, with the other, opening a stained-glass window. A blue cloth has been thrown over a brass and leather chair, a curious metal box sits on the table, and a map adorns the wall. At once we are presented with opulence and simplicity. The elements in the composition are perfectly placed. One senses that their position could not be moved even a fraction of an inch without disturbing the composition. Pure colors and crisp lines grace the space in the painting rather than interrupt it. Every item in the painting is of a simple, almost timeless form and corresponds to the timeless serenity of the porcelain-like image of the woman. Her simple dress and starched collar and bonnet epitomize grace and serenity.

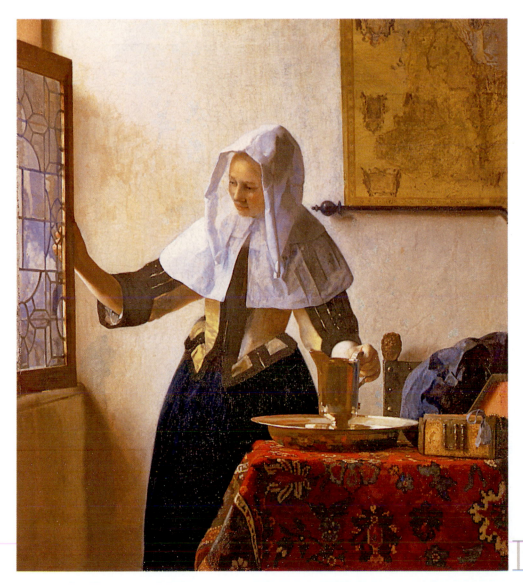

17-19 JAN VERMEER. *Young Woman with a Water Jug* (c. 1665). Oil on canvas. 18" × 16". The Metropolitan Museum of Art, NY.

1 in.

We might not see this as a Baroque composition if it were not for three things: a single source of light bathing the elements in the composition, the genre subject, and a bit of mystery surrounding the moment captured by Vermeer. What is the woman doing? She has opened the window and taken a jug into her hand at the same time, but we will never know for what purpose. Some have said that she may intend to water flowers at a window box. Perhaps she was in the midst of doing something else and paused to investigate a noise in the street. Vermeer gives us a curious combination of the momentary and the eternal in this almost photographic glimpse of everyday Dutch life.

France

During the Baroque period, France, under the reign of the "sun king," Louis XIV, began to replace Rome as the center of the art world. The king preferred Classicism. Thus did the country, and painters, sculptors, and architects alike created works in this vein. Louis XIV guaranteed adherence to Classicism by forming academies of art that perpetuated this style. These academies were art schools of sorts, run by the state, whose faculties were populated by leading proponents of the Classical style. When we examine European art during the Baroque period, we thus perceive a strong stylistic polarity. On the one hand, we have the exuberant painterliness and high drama of Rubens and Bernini, and on the other hand, a reserved Classicism that hearkens back to Raphael.

NICOLAS POUSSIN The principal exponent of the Classical style in French painting was Nicolas Poussin (1594–1665). Although he was born in France, Poussin spent much of his life in Rome, where he studied the works of the Italian masters, particularly Raphael and Titian. Although his *Rape of the Sabine Women* (Fig. **17-20**) was painted four years before he was summoned back to France by the king, it illustrates

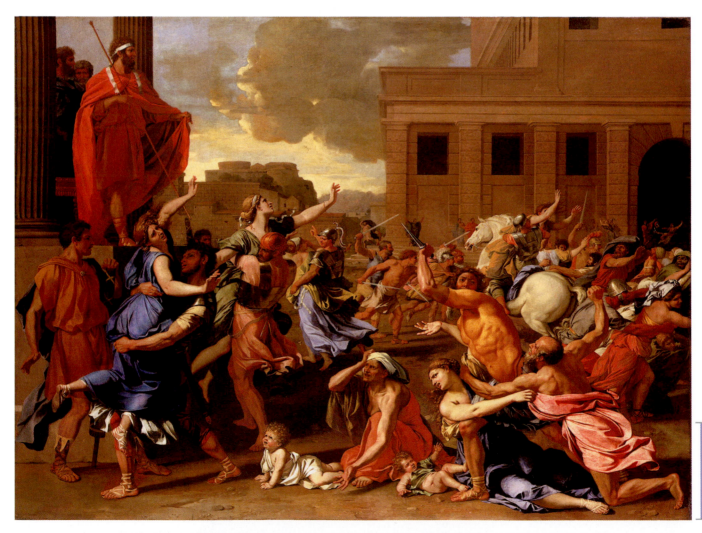

17-20 NICOLAS POUSSIN. *The Rape of the Sabine Women* (c. 1636–1637). Oil on canvas. 60⅞" × 82⅝". The Metropolitan Museum of Art, NY.

the Baroque Classicism that Poussin would bring to his native country. The flashy dynamism of Bernini and Rubens gives way to a more static, almost staged motion in the work of Poussin. Harshly sculptural, Raphaelesque figures thrust in various directions, forming a complex series of intersecting diagonals and verticals. The initial impression is one of chaos, of unrestrained movement and human anguish. But as was the case with the Classical Greek sculptors and Italian Renaissance artists, emotion is always balanced carefully with restraint. For example, the pitiful scene of the old woman in the foreground, flanked by crying children, forms part of the base of a compositional triangle that stabilizes the work and counters excessive emotion. If one draws a vertical line from the top of her head upward to the top border of the canvas, one encounters the apex of this triangle, formed by the swords of two Roman abductors. The sides of the triangle, then, are formed by the diagonally thrusting torso of the muscular Roman in the right foreground and the arms of the Sabine women on the left, reaching hopelessly into the sky. This compositional triangle, along with the Roman temple in the right background that prevents a radically receding space, are Renaissance techniques for structuring a balanced composition. Poussin used these, along with a stagelike, theatrical presentation of his subjects, to reconcile the divergent styles of the harsh Classical and the vibrant Baroque.

Polar opposites in style occur in other movements throughout the history of art. It will be important to remember this aspect of the Baroque, because in later centuries we will encounter the polarity again, among artists who divide themselves into the camps Poussiniste and Rubeniste.

VERSAILLES The king's taste for the Classical extended to architecture, as seen in the Palace of Versailles (Fig. 17-21). Originally the site of the king's hunting lodge, the palace and surrounding area just outside Paris were converted by a host of artists, architects, and landscape designers into one of the grandest monuments to the French Baroque. In their tribute to Classicism, the architects Louis Le Vau (1612–1670) and Jules Hardouin-Mansart (1646–1708) divided the horizontal sweep of the facades into three stories. The structure was then divided vertically into three major sections, and these were in turn subdivided into three additional sections. The windows march along the facade in a rhythmic beat, accompanied by rigid pilasters that are wedged between the strong horizontal bands that delineate the floors. A balustrade tops the palace, further emphasizing the horizontal sweep while restraining any upward movement suggested by the building's vertical members. The divisions into Classically balanced threes and the almost obsessive emphasis on the horizontal echo the buildings of Renaissance architects. The French had come a long way from the towering spires of their glorious Gothic cathedrals!

England

The Baroque in England had a different flavor from that in the European continent, in part because it was not dominated by an absolute monarchy as it was, for example, in France. Instead, England's Common Law and Parliament coexisted with a limited monarchy. Also, unlike other countries, England was also home to a variety of religious groups—including Anglicans and other Protestants, and Catholics. As in Holland, the Baroque era in England witnessed a burgeoning of trade, made possible by the nation's status as a maritime power.

England's most significant contribution to the arts in the seventeenth and early eighteenth centuries was in the realm of architecture. Two architects in particular—Inigo Jones (1573–1652) and Sir Christopher Wren (1632–1723)—were responsible

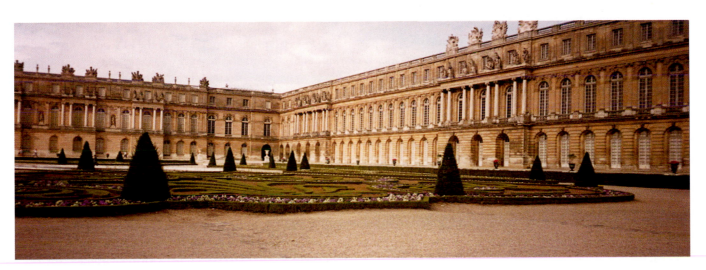

17-21 LOUIS LE VAU AND JULES HARDOUIN-MANSART. Palace of Versailles, as seen from the garden, Versailles, France (1669–1685).

for the architectural profile of London in its Baroque years. Both were heavily influenced by Italian Baroque architecture, which combined the regimentation and clarity of classical elements with occasional, unpredictable shapes or rhythms. Jones's Banqueting House at Whitehall (Fig. **17-22**) in London illustrates a certain symmetry and repetition of classical elements (for example, regularly spaced windows separated by engaged columns and an overall balance of horizontal and vertical lines). But the rigidity of the design scheme is subtly challenged by the use of pilasters in a different rhythm at the corners, and the mix-up of architectural orders—Ionic capitals on the lower floor and more ornate, Corinthian-style capitals on the second floor. The alternating pattern of vertical elements is not unlike that of the facade of St. Peter's in Rome.

Sir Christopher Wren began his career at age 25, although not as an architect. He was an engineer and professor of astronomy whose developing interest in mathematics led him to architecture. He was solicited by King Charles II to renovate St. Paul's Cathedral—a Gothic structure—and his plans for the project were in place when the devastating fire of London in 1666 consumed the old building. The new St. Paul's (Fig. **17-23**) stands as Wren's masterpiece and the most beloved structure in London. Influenced by Italian and French Baroque architecture, Wren reconciled the problematic relationship of the classical pedimented facade to hemispherical dome that we first encountered in the Baroque expansion of St. Peter's in Rome. He did this by placing tall bell towers on either side of the facade to soften the visual transition from the horizontal emphasis of the two-storied elevation to the vertical rise of the massive dome a nave's length away. Wren's

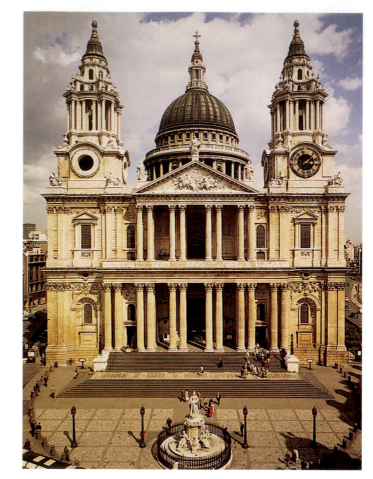

17-23 SIR CHRISTOPHER WREN. New St. Paul's Cathedral, London, England (1675-1710).

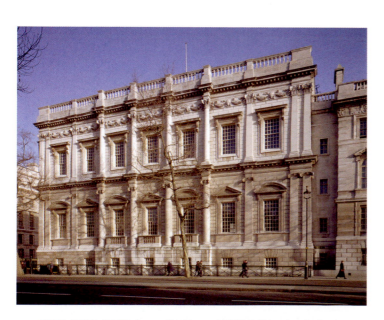

17-22 INIGO JONES. Banqueting House at Whitehall, London, England (1619-1622).

design stands midway between the organic, flowing designs of the Italian Baroque and the strict classicism of the French Baroque architects, integrating both in a reserved, but not rigid, composition. The double-columned, two-tiered portico is French Baroque in style (see the Palace of Versailles, Fig. 17-22), and the upper level of the bell towers (topped by pineapples—symbols of peace and prosperity) are similar to those found on Borromini's churches, such as San Carlo alle Quattro Fontane (see Fig. 17-14) in Rome.

The dome of St. Paul's is the world's second-highest at 361 feet (St. Peter's is higher). Inside the dome is the so-called Whispering Gallery; visitors who whisper against its walls can be heard on the opposite side of the dome. The interior is richly embellished with marble inlays, frescoes, mosaics, and wrought iron. Aside from its stature as an architectural masterpiece, St. Paul's holds a valuable place in British memory. Winston Churchill took extraordinary measures to protect the church from the Nazi bombing raids—the Blitz—of World War II. It survived amidst a virtually ruined city.

THE ROCOCO

We have roughly dated the Baroque period from 1600 to 1750. However, art historians have recognized a more distinct style within the Baroque that began shortly after the dawn of the eighteenth century. This **Rococo** style strayed further from Classical principles than did the Baroque. It is more ornate and characterized by sweetness, gaiety, and light. The courtly pomp and reserved Classicism of Louis XIV were replaced with a more delicate and sprightly representation of the leisure activities of the upper class.

The early Rococo style appears as a refinement of the painterly Baroque in which Classical subjects are often rendered in wispy brushstrokes that rely heavily on the Venetian or Rubenian palette of luscious golds and reds. The later Rococo period, following midcentury, is more frivolous in its choice of subjects (that of love among the very rich), palette (that of the softest pastel hues), and brushwork (the most delicate and painterly strokes).

Jean-Honoré Fragonard

Jean-Honoré Fragonard (1732–1806) is one of the finest representatives of the Rococo style, and his painting *Happy Accidents of the Swing* (Fig. **17-24**) is a prime example of the aims and accomplishments of the Rococo artist. In the midst of a lush green park, whose opulent foliage was no doubt inspired by the Baroque, we are offered a glimpse of the "love games" of the leisure class. A young, though not-so-innocent, maiden, with petticoats billowing beneath her sumptuous pink dress, is being swung by an unsuspecting bishop high over the head of her reclining gentleman friend, who seems delighted with the view. The subjects' diminutive forms and rosy cheeks make them doll-like, an image reinforced by the idyllic setting. This is eighteenth-century life at its finest—pampered by subtle hues, embraced by lush textures, and bathed by the softest of lights. Unfortunately, this was all a mask for life at its worst. As the ruling class continued to ignore the needs of the common people, the latter were preparing to rebel.

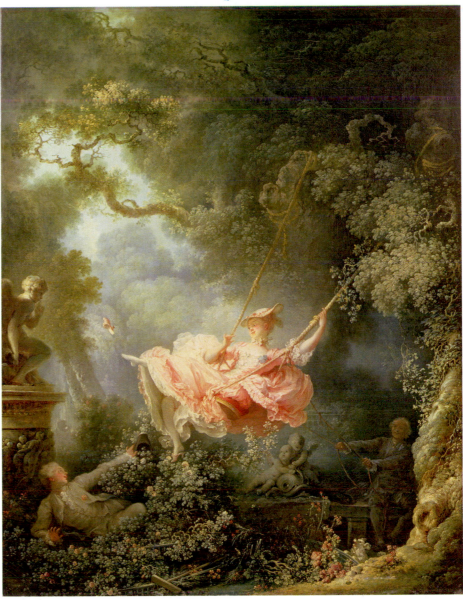

17-24 JEAN-HONORÉ FRAGONARD. *Happy Accidents of the Swing* (1767). Oil on canvas. 31⅞" × 25⅜". The Wallace Collection, London, England.

Élisabeth Vigée-Lebrun

Whereas Rembrandt epitomizes the artists who achieved recognition after death, Élisabeth Vigée-Lebrun (1755–1842) was a complete success during her lifetime. The daughter of a portrait painter, she received instruction and encouragement from her father and his colleagues from an early age. As a youngster she also studied paintings in the Louvre and was particularly drawn to the works of Rubens. By the time she reached her early twenties, she commanded high prices for her portraits and was made an official portrait painter for Marie

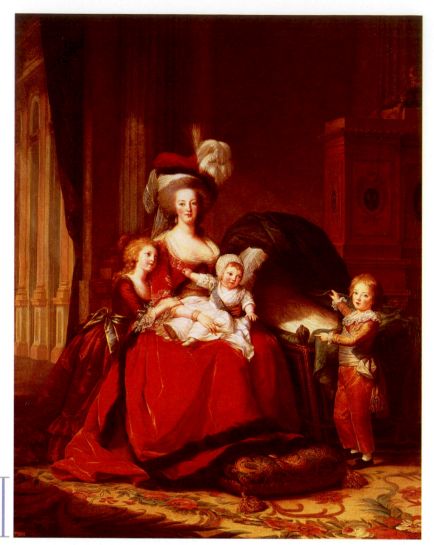

1 ft.

17-25 ÉLISABETH VIGÉE-LEBRUN. *Marie Antoinette and Her Children* (1781). Oil on canvas. 8'8" × 6'10". Palace of Versailles, Versailles, France.

images of the Madonna and Child (see Chapter 16), at once creating a sympathetic portrait of a mother and her children and, subliminally, asserting their divine right. Even amidst the opulence at Versailles, Marie Antoinette displays her children as her real jewels. The young dauphin to the right, set apart as the future king, points to an empty cradle that might have originally contained the queen's fourth child, an infant who died two months before the painting was scheduled for exhibition.

The French populace, of course, was not persuaded by this portrait or by other public relations efforts to paint the royal family as accessible and sympathetic. The artist, in fact, did not exhibit her painting as scheduled for fear that the public might destroy it. Two years after the painting was completed, the convulsions of the French Revolution shook Europe and the world. The royal family was imprisoned and then executed. More than the royal family had passed into history, and more than democracy was about to be born. Modern art was also to be ushered into this brave new world.

Enlightenment, Revolution, the Scientific, and the Natural

The aristocratic culture reflected in the Rococo style may symbolize the late eighteenth century in France, but it was not the only game in town. Enlightenment views and philosophies, which rejected the stranglehold of religion and superstition and promoted scientific inquiry and critical thinking about the world and the human condition, went hand in hand with revolutions in France and America. Many historical personalities are associated with the Enlightenment—France's René Descartes, England's Isaac Newton and John Locke, America's Benjamin Franklin and Thomas Jefferson. But the opposing viewpoints of the Enlightenment—the scientific versus the natural—are represented by, respectively, Voltaire (1694–1778) and Jean-Jacques Rousseau (1712–1778). Voltaire held that science and rationalism held the key to the improvement of the human condition, whereas Rousseau believed that feeling and emotions trumped reason and that the return to the natural, or the "primitive state," would lead to the salvation of humankind. Rousseau's philosophy was translated into the pictorial arts in England and America in works by painters such as Thomas Gainsborough (1727–1788) and John Singleton Copley (1738–1815). It also contributed to the demise of the Rococo, which represented an "artificial" rather than a "natural" state of being.

Gainsborough bridged the gap between the Rococo and the new naturalism as one of the most renowned portraitists

Antoinette, the Austrian wife of Louis XVI. Neither Marie Antoinette nor her husband survived the French Revolution, but Vigée-Lebrun's fame spread throughout Europe, and by the end of her career, she had created some 800 paintings.

Marie Antoinette and Her Children (Fig. **17-25**) was painted nearly a decade after Vigée-Lebrun had begun to paint the royal family. In this work, she was commissioned to counter the antimonarchist sentiments spreading throughout the land by portraying the queen as, first and foremost, a loving mother. True, the queen is set within the imposing Salon de la Paix at Versailles, with the famous Hall of Mirrors to the left and the royal crown atop the cabinet on the right. True, the queen's enormous hat and voluminous skirts create a richness and monumentality to which the common person could not reasonably aspire. But the triangular composition and the child on the lap are reminiscent of Renaissance

in eighteenth-century England. One of the initiators of so-called Grand Manner portraiture (see Fig. **17-26**), Gainsborough created an air of elegance and importance to his sitters by using several pictorial devices—a deep, lush landscape; relatively large-scale figure; simple pose; and dignified gaze. Soft, feathery strokes define both figure and background, and a pastel-colored light bathes the whole composition. These two characteristics are also seen in Rococo art.

Gainsborough's style was also seen in American art—particularly history paintings on a grand scale. But America offered a new twist in portraiture, perhaps best represented by John Singleton Copley of Massachusetts. Whereas Gainsborough combined naturalism with elements of French Rococo, Copley combined English naturalism with an American taste for realism and simplicity. His *Portrait of Paul Revere* (Fig. **17-27**), the silversmith-turned-revolutionary hero, has a directness of expression and unpretentious gaze that is markedly different from Gainsborough's sitter. *Mrs. Richard Brinsley Sheridan*'s dreamy, introspective air

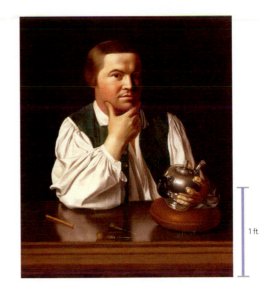

17-27 JOHN SINGLETON COPLEY. *Portrait of Paul Revere* (c. 1698–1770). Oil on canvas. 2'11⅛" × 2'4". Museum of Fine Arts, Boston, MA.

contrasts sharply with Revere's assertive, visual dialogue with the viewer. Tools at hand, he ponders the teapot on which he is working and raises his head momentarily from the task to acknowledge the visitor, the patron, the observer. Gainsborough's painterly touch contrasts with Copley's harsh linear style. The lighting is dramatic rather than subtle and the textures, softly blended in Gainsborough's portrait, are purposefully distinct and different from one another (the soft folds of Revere's shirtsleeves against his sculptural arms; the warm wood surface of his worktable against the gleaming metal of his teapot). It is tempting to read Copley's approach as one that reflects American values and sensibilities. Like some other American-born artists of his generation, however, he moved to London, where he adapted his style to the British taste.

Chapters 13 through 17 have focused on art and the Western heritage. Yet the West comprises but a fraction of the world's population and a particular historical, cultural, and aesthetic approach to art. Art beyond the West is not united by a common history or by common ideas as to what art is, who will produce it, or what place art will occupy in people's lives. The next chapter will bring us into contact with art that lies beyond the Western tradition, art that often requires a different critical vocabulary to be described, art that must be viewed in an altogether different context to be understood. For most Westerners, the art and culture of the non-West is "the other." In order to fully appreciate the meaning and function of art of cultures beyond the West, it is necessary, and immensely rewarding, to "think otherly"—to reframe your frame of reference to be something other than that which is familiar to you.

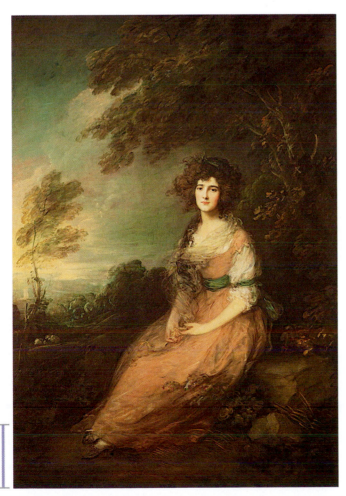

17-26 THOMAS GAINSBOROUGH. *Mrs. Richard Brinsley Sheridan* (1787). Oil on canvas. Approx. 7'2⅝" × 5'5⅝". National Gallery of Art, Washington, D.C.

ART TOUR LONDON

EUROPE'S LARGEST CITY cashes in big on tourism from the "colonies across the pond." There is a natural affinity between the United States and Britain for all sorts of reasons, including a common language, common political causes, and imports and exports such as Elvis and the Beatles. Even London's idiosyncratic phone booths have entered the popular culture with the Austin Powers movies. Because of the ease of travel (it takes no longer to jet from New York to London than it does to fly from New York to Los Angeles) and the ease of communicating, London is a natural first-trip-abroad destination for students. It also serves as a logical jumping-off point for other cities worldwide, many of which can be reached by booking discounted student and youth fares with local London travel agents. The center of London is easily explored on foot, and almost all of the city is accessible by an inexpensive and highly efficient subway system.

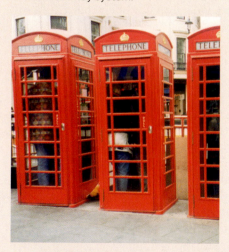

SIGNATURE LONDON TELEPHONE BOOTHS.

A good place to start is at the symbolic heart of the city of London—St. Paul's Cathedral. The building as you see it today is the reincarnation—in Classical dress—of the original medieval church that was brought to ruin during the Great Fire of London in 1666. No stranger itself to destruction, the St. Paul's of today was literally kept standing by the "Watch," a team of volunteers who kept nightly vigil over the cathedral during the Blitz—the Nazi bombing raids on London in 1940 and 1941 that caused devastation all over the city. The cathedral is viewed as the masterpiece of the architect Sir Christopher Wren, who borrowed porticoes and pediments from Greek temple architecture and whose Classical vision dominates some of the more medieval aspects of the cathedral plan, such as the cross shape of the nave and transept. The most spectacular feature of St. Paul's is the dome, whose inner and outer shells rival one another for beauty. It is the second-largest dome in the world, after St. Peter's in Rome (designed by Michelangelo).

It features an exterior, circular stone gallery, which offers the nonacrophobic a panoramic view of the city, and a pendant interior gallery—the so-called Whispering Gallery—from which you can hear whispers echoing from across the dome. St. Paul's is also a British monument that pays homage throughout to the United States for its unwavering devotion and support during World War II. The American visitor, while circling the apse, will come upon the American Memorial Chapel behind the high altar. St. Paul's has been the site of funerals (Sir Winston Churchill's) and weddings (Prince Charles and Lady Diana Spencer's) of the rich and famous and houses many memorials to popular heroes and historical figures including Lawrence of Arabia and Lord Nelson. Many more individuals who figure prominently in Britain's cultural history—such as Darwin and Chaucer—can be found entombed or enshrined in Westminster Abbey. But keep walking . . .

From St. Paul's, you can luxuriate in a walk down to the Thames, that long and serpentine body of water on which you can take a circular cruise to view some of London's most famous (and infamous) sights: the Houses of Parliament (with the bell tower, Big Ben); the Tower Bridge; and Traitors' Gate, the creepy river entrance to the Tower of London, used for prisoners fresh from their trials in Westminster Hall. If you've chosen not to take this detour, continue across the new Millennium Bridge directly to the sensational Tate Modern, one of the world's premier collections of twentieth-century art, now housed in the vast, old Bankside Power Station. Upon entering the building, visitors proceed down a ramp into an enormous hall that contained turbines in former days and is now brought to life with large-scale works of art. From this level, escalators lead up to three large suites of galleries arranged more or less chronologically to give some sense of a history of modern art. Interspersed among the many works by British artists in the museum are a large number of well-known international works, including Picasso's

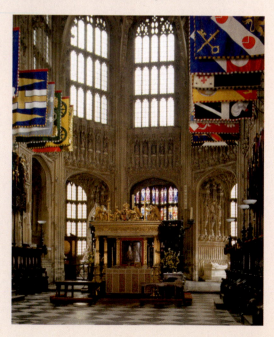

WESTMINSTER ABBEY.

Three Dancers and Warhol's *Marilyn Dip-tych.* The Tate Modern also offers some of the best views of the city from across the river in its glass-enclosed top floors, one of which includes a restaurant.

Continuing west along the river, the visitor will reach the world's tallest observation wheel, the British Airways London Eye, constructed to celebrate the new millennium. On a clear day, you can see forever (or maybe about 40 miles) from this overgrown Ferris wheel. As you can imagine, the lines are insufferably long, no matter the weather. Back across the river, a walk east and then north will bring you to the Covent Garden piazza and Central Market, where performers of all kinds command the square, and where you can eat just about anything cheaply. From here, find your way to Leicester Square and the half-price ticket booth, which offers theater tickets for same-day performances in legendary theaters such as the Palladium. When in London, do as the Londoners do—at least one play per visit in one of the city's famous theaters is a must.

You can ask directions (in English!) to the queen's "in-town" residence, Buckingham Palace, and try to catch the well-known changing of the guard. During the height of the tourist season, this event takes place at 11:30 a.m. daily; the rest of the year, it's every other day. Near the palace you can stroll through one of the most beautiful green spots in London, St. James Park. A route through the park will bring you eventually to Westminster Abbey, the site of the coronation chair, the wedding of Prince William and Kate Middleton, and the final resting place for the kings and queens

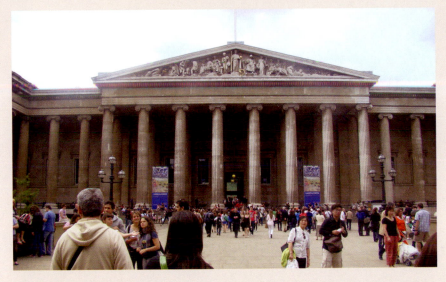

THE BRITISH MUSEUM.

of England for centuries. In contrast to the Classical perfection and serenity of St. Paul's, Westminster Abbey is one of the most glorious examples of medieval architecture in London, if not in all of Europe. From its splendid west front towers and the massive flying buttresses to the vaulted ceiling of the Lady Chapel and the magnificent tiles of the octagonal Chapter House, the abbey does not disappoint the dense throngs who visit this "half national church, half national museum." Negotiating the many transepts and chapels will reveal some of the abbey's finest memorials to musicians, poets, and artists.

Even if your trip to London is brief and much of your art tour seems to be taking place outdoors, you will not want to miss the extraordinary British Museum. Wandering amidst the world's

greatest collection of Mesopotamian, Egyptian, and Greek and Roman antiquities, even the most jaded or museum-fatigued among us will marvel at the Rosetta Stone—the slab we learned about in sixth grade, which unlocked the mysterious code of Egyptian hieroglyphs—or the Parthenon (see Fig. 14-10) marbles—removed from the temple by the British diplomat Lord Elgin between 1801 and 1804 and sold to the British nation in 1816. (In fact, Greece wants them back.)

Admission to the British Museum and other wonderful art places, such as the National Gallery and National Portrait Gallery in Trafalgar Square, the Tate Modern, and the Tate Britain, is free.

www. **TO CONTINUE YOUR TOUR** and learn more about London, go to CourseMate.

BIG BEN.

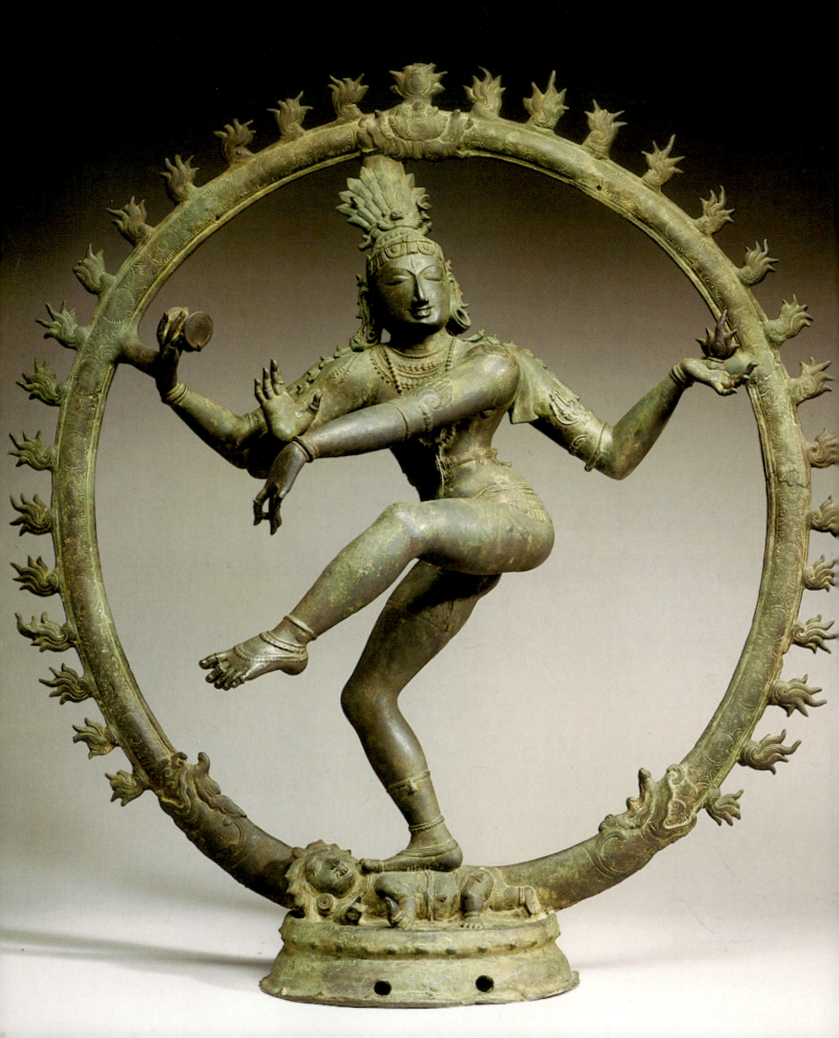

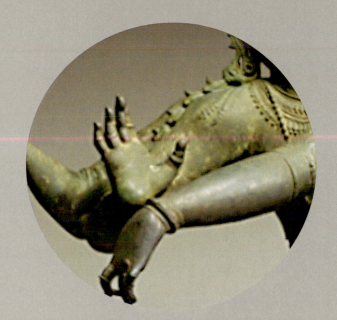

The map is open and connectable in all of its dimensions.

—Gilles Deleuze and Felix Guattari

NON-WESTERN PERSPECTIVES

18

The world is shrinking: the global village, the global stage, the era of globalization. As citizens of the world in the twenty-first century, we are connected to one another like never before. We travel to remote sites—across actual space (thanks to modern-day transportation) and cyberspace (thanks to the Internet). Money, goods, and services flow quickly from one part of the world to another. Information is more available to ordinary people, as access to modes of international communication has become the rule for the many rather than the exception for the few. Although *globalization* is a term most often linked to the current state of global business and politics, the concept has expanded to include historical and cultural studies. While investment bankers, corporate businesses, and entrepreneurs have developed mutually beneficial relationships with countries around the globe, which have only recently begun to tap into their rich economic potential, new groups of individuals—such as research academicians (sociologists, anthropologists, historians, political scientists)—have begun to investigate social, historical, cultural, and artistic phenomena of regions that are now within reach.

MAP 18-1 Art beyond the Western Tradition.

As citizens of the world, we also share an extensive and varied heritage. Western culture and the Western tradition in art—that which solidified in ancient Greece and developed in Western Europe and, later, the United States—may be more familiar to most of us than the art of other cultures and traditions that lie "beyond the West" (Map 18-1). But those non-Western perspectives are rich and varied and represent other ways of seeing and knowing that enable us to expand our understanding of ourselves in relation to the world.

Ancient African sculpture and the masquerade, intricately carved catamarans of the Oceanic islanders, colossal stone heads from pre-Columbian Mexico, the South American metropolises, Native American cliff palaces—these are but a handful of examples of art that embody ways of life that have developed along their own courses. They often reflect societal organizations based on the village or the tribe that are rural and self-sufficient and continue from generation to generation with little change. The art of such societies expresses the values and beliefs of a people and plays a pivotal role in the continuation of customs and traditions in societies that are dependent on oral rather than written history.

Europeans who colonized these territories between the sixteenth and twentieth centuries did not think much of the fetishes, idols, and other curiosities upon which they gazed. Today this art is avidly collected throughout the world, including the Western world. Islamic art or Chinese and Japanese art may be somewhat more familiar to the Western eye than the arts of Africa, Oceania, and Native America. As sacred spaces, the great mosques of the world of Islam, the cathedrals of Christian Europe, and synagogues around the world have some elements in common. Persian carpets are popular, and the Western eye need not be especially schooled to appreciate them. Some of the great works of the Indian subcontinent, such as the Taj Mahal (see Fig. 15-16), are also familiar, and the influence of China and Japan on Western art has been felt since the explorations and beginnings of trade, for many hun-

dreds of years. The refined ceramics of the Chinese, for example, were known to European potters, and the perspective techniques and delicacy of Japanese drawings and paintings influenced many modern artists of the nineteenth century.

In this chapter, we shall explore non-Western art. The breadth of the material precludes detailed discussion of the historical aspects of this work but need not preclude an appreciation for the widely diverse styles of these cultures and the significance of their art to their societies.

AFRICAN ART

African art is as varied as the cultures that have populated that continent. The earliest African art, like the earliest art of Europe and North America, consists of rock paintings and engravings that date to the Neolithic period. In tropical Africa—the central portion of the continent—the lost-wax technique was developed to cast small bronze sculptures as early as the ninth century.

The kingdom of Benin, which during the fourteenth through nineteenth centuries occupied what is now Nigeria, was rich in sculptures of many mediums, including iron, bronze, wood, ivory, and terra-cotta. Works such as the *Altar of the Hand* (Fig. 18-1) illustrate the skill with which the Benin manipulated bronze, as well as the importance of symbolism to their art. The many figures that are cast in relief around the circumference of this small work are meant to venerate the king and glorify his divine office. The king is the central figure both in the relief and in the freestanding figures on top of the altar. He holds the staffs of his office in his hands, and his head is larger than those of his attendants. This purposeful distortion signifies the head as the center of being and source of intelligence and power. The king's importance is further underscored by his placement within a triangular frame of sorts, his head at the apex. The entire altar is cast with symbolic forms or incised with decorative motifs, all arranged in a symmetrical pattern. The monumentality that this altar achieves in its mere 17 inches or so is remarkable and impressive.

This penchant for ornament can also be seen in more recent tribal art from Nigeria, such as that of the Yoruba. The carved wooden doors in Figure **18-2** depict scenes of tribal life and ritual. The figures are angular and stylized; as in the *Altar of the Hand*, the king, who is seated on a throne, is shown larger than his attendants. The work reads rather like a comic strip, with parts of the narrative confined to small compartments. In most sections, a geometric-patterned background adds a rich,

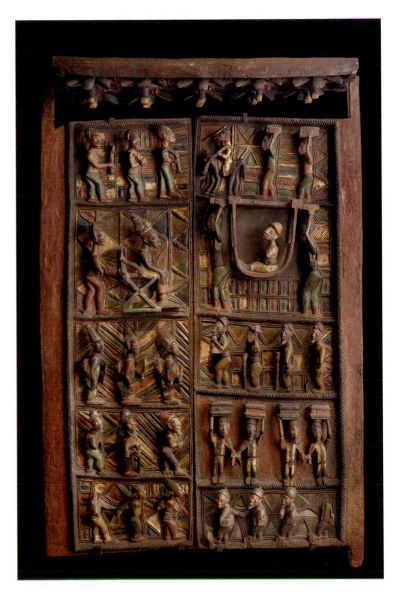

18-2 Door from Iderre, Nigeria (1910–1914). Wood. H: 6′. British Museum, London, England.

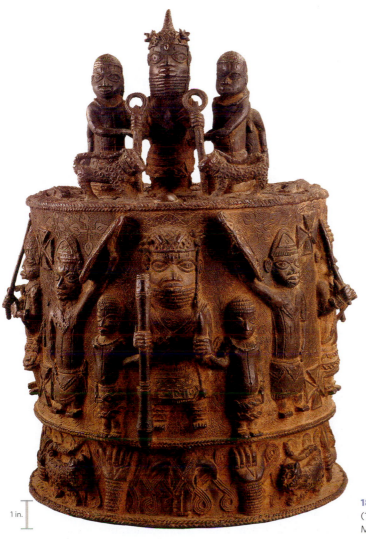

1 in.

18-1 *Altar of the Hand and Arm,* Benin, Nigeria (17th–18th centuries). Bronze. H: 17½″. British Museum, London, England.

beads covers the face, protecting onlookers from the power of the ruler's eyes. The height of the crown emphasizes the head as the center of power and often contains ritual medicines and potions to enhance that power.

Masks and headdresses are found in other regions of Africa as well, and their symbolism is as widely varied as their style. The simplest of these, such as the Etoumba mask (Fig. 18-5), have facial features resolved into abstract geometric shapes. They are also sometimes punched and slashed with markings intended to represent body scarification. More intricate pieces, such as the *mboom* helmet mask from the Kuba people of Zaire (Fig. **18-4**), might be embellished with brass, shells, beads, seeds, feathers, and furs. These contrasting textures, along with the protruding chin and prominent forehead, are symbols of royalty. The mask represents a primordial ancestor that oversees the passage of boys into adulthood.

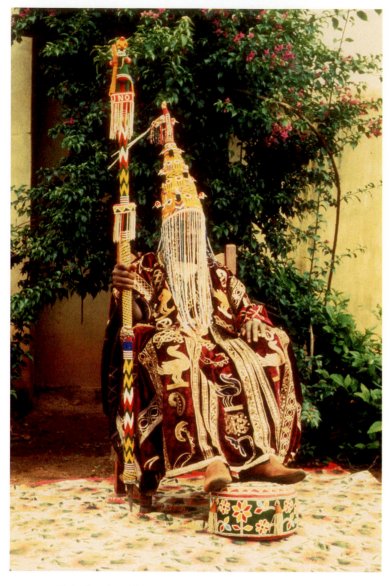

18-3 The ruler of Orangun-Ila, Airowayoye I, with a beaded scepter, crown, veil, and footstool. Nigeria (1977).

tapestry-like quality to the work. These doors continue artistic traditions that were established in much older works.

The Yoruba are famous for their mix of the old and the modern in fanciful objects crafted for ceremonial or ritualistic purposes. Masks and headdresses are used in performances called masquerades. They incorporate music, dance, and elaborate costuming in a combination of theater and ritual that often involves social criticism. The beadwork evident in headdresses similar to the crown that is worn by the royal Yoruba ruler in Figure **18-3** is created by a guild of artisans who pass their techniques down from generation to generation. In the ruler's costume, a veil composed of strands of

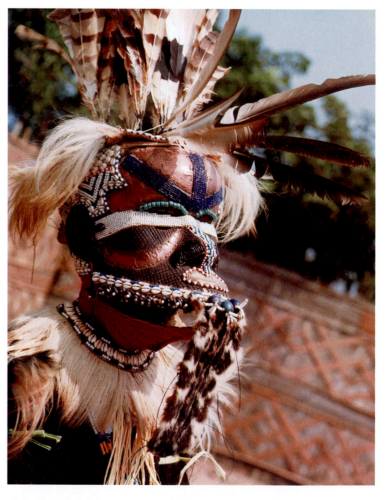

18-4 *Mboom* helmet mask, Zaire (19th–20th centuries). Wood, brass, cowrie shells, beads, seeds. H: 13". Royal Museum for Central Africa, Tervuren, Belgium.

PICASSO'S *NUDE WITH DRAPERY* AND AN ETOUMBA MASK

IN THE EARLY YEARS OF THE TWENTIETH CENTURY, painter Pablo Picasso saw two large exhibitions in Paris. One was of ancient sculpture from his native Spain, carved by the Iberians before their conquest by the Romans; the other was of the native art of African peoples. Both would have a lasting impression on his art.

Compare the facial features of Picasso's painting (Fig. **18-5**) with those of an African mask like the ones he may have seen at the Musée de l'Homme in Paris (Fig. **18-6**). What lines and shapes has Picasso adopted?

What other conventions or stylizations of African art has he used? How has the painter captured the simplicity and strength of the traditional mask in his painting?

Picasso was enamored of the aesthetic of African art. But as he came to understand more fully the importance of the sacred and mystical powers of that art to its society, he began to see his own art and perhaps art in general as "a form of magic designed to be a mediator between this strange, hostile world and us, a way of seizing the power by giving form to our terrors as well as our desires." ●

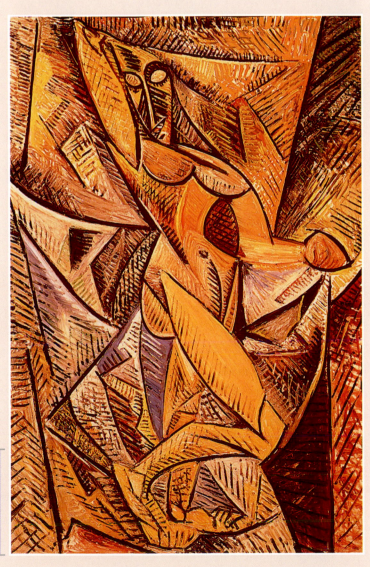

1 ft.

18-5 PABLO PICASSO. *Nude with Drapery* (1907). Oil on canvas. 59⅞" × 39¾". The State Hermitage Museum, St. Petersburg, Russia. © 2011 Estate of Pablo Picasso/Artists Rights Society (ARS), NY.

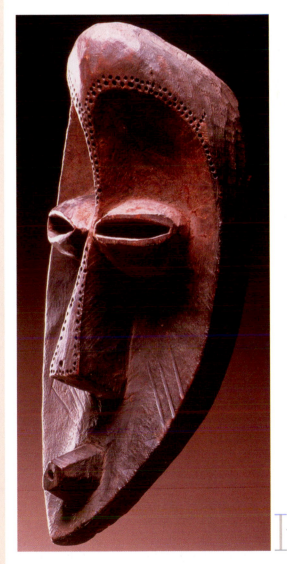

1 in.

18-6 Mask, Etoumba region, Republic of Congo. Wood. H: 14".

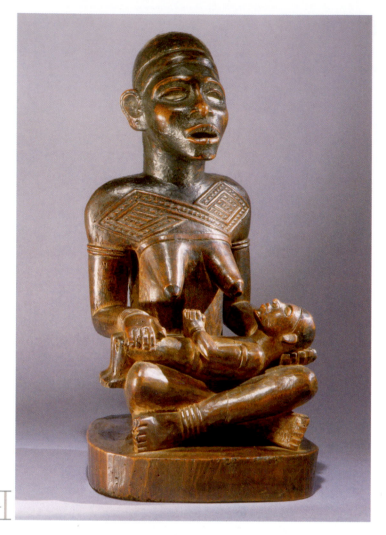

1 in.

18-7 Ancestral figure, Zaire (19th–20th centuries). Wood and brass. H: 16". Royal Museum for Central Africa, Tervuren, Belgium.

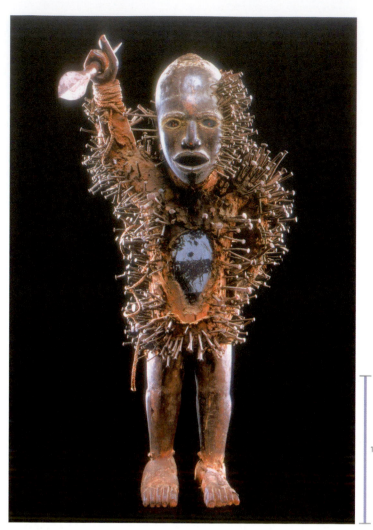

1 ft.

18-8 *Nkisi nkondi* (hunter figure), Democratic Republic of Congo (collected before 1905). Wood, nails, iron, fabric. H: 38³⁄₁₆".

Other work from Zaire is more conventional in form. A so-called ancestral or power image from the Kongo peoples (Fig. **18-7**) is a delicate wood carving of a mother and child, most likely intended as a repository of the soul of a deceased noblewoman (recall the *ka* figures of Old Kingdom Egypt). The function of the sculpture was probably to receive prayers for the woman's continuing guardianship and care of the community, but other such figures channeled ancestral powers from "medicines" placed within or on the sculptures to those in need—warriors in battle, farmers planting crops, or people trying to cure disease.

In many Western societies, Christians light votive candles to request favors from God, to seek the intervention of saints on their behalf, and to thank them for help. In many African soci-

eties, priests have hammered nails into carved wooden **fetish figures** (Fig. **18-8**) to seek help from the gods, to ward off evil, to vanquish enemies, or to solve problems in their villages. By driving nails into the figure, the villagers believe that wrongdoers will suffer pain. Once the social problem has been solved, the nails may be removed from the figure. Sometimes such fetish figures have human forms, but some are wild animals connected to ancestral spirits. In either case, these figures represent a vehicle for mediation between the living and the dead.

The seated primordial couple in Figure **18-9** are characteristic of another well-known style of African art—that of the Dogon people of Mali, in the western part of the continent. Although Dogon artists often worked in a more naturalistic style, here the artist has opted for a highly stylized, rigid, and elongated figure, incised with overall geometric patterns. This treatment removes the subjects from contemporary reality. The group represents the mythical ancestors of the human race, a kind of Adam and Eve of all of us.

Traders from North Africa brought Islam to Ghana in the eighth century CE, which, because of its wealth, became a vibrant center of Islamic culture. What emerged in terms of religious practice and art was a blend of both traditions. The plan of the Great Mosque at Djenne in Mali (Fig. **18-10**), like that of all early mosques, is based on the model of Muhammad's home in Medina. It has a walled courtyard in front of a wall that faces Mecca. Unlike the stone mosques of the Middle East, however, the mosque at Djenne is built of sun-dried bricks and puddled clay. Wooden poles jutting through the clay serve as a kind of scaffold support for workers who replaster the structure yearly to prevent complete erosion of the clay. They also provide a form of exterior ornamentation, an aspect of the highly decorative aesthetic of Muslim art and architecture.

OCEANIC ART

The peoples and art of Oceania are also varied. They span millions of square miles of ocean, ranging from the continent of Australia and large islands of New Guinea and New Zealand to small islands such as the Gilberts, Tahiti, and Easter Island. They are divided into the cultures of Polynesia, Melanesia, and Micronesia. We shall discuss works from Polynesia and Melanesia.

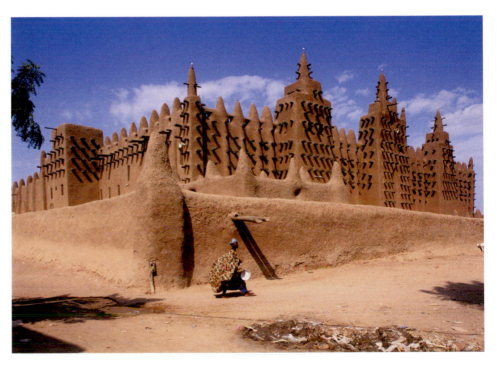

1 in.

18-9 Ancestral couple, Mali (Dogon). Wood. H: 28¾". The Metropolitan Museum of Art, NY.

18-10 The Great Mosque, Djenne, Mali (14th century CE). Puddled clay, adobe brick, and wooden poles.

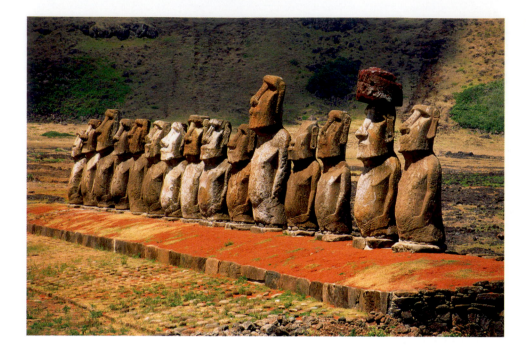

Polynesia

The Polynesian artists are known for their figural sculptures, such as the huge stone images of Easter Island (Fig. **18-11**). More than 600 of these heads and half-length figures survive, some of them 60 feet tall. Polynesian art is also known for its massiveness and compactness. Carved between the fifth and seventeenth centuries CE, their jutting, monolithic forms have the abstracted quality of African masks and ancestor figures. Figure after figure has the same angular sweep of nose and chin, the severe pursed lips, and the overbearing brow.

Archeologists have determined that these figures symbolize the power that chieftains were thought to derive from the gods and to retain in death through their own deification. Political power in Polynesia was believed to be a reflection of spiritual power. The images of the gods were thought to be combined with those of their descendants in the carvings and other artworks like those on Easter Island.

The Polynesian Maori of New Zealand are known for their wooden relief carvings. The plentiful nature of tough, durable pinewood allowed them to sculpt works with the curvilinear intricacy and vitality of the nearly six-foot-long canoe prow shown in Figure **18-12**. The figure at the front of the prow is intended to have an earthy phallic thrust.

The winding snake pattern on the mythic figure and scrollwork of the eighteenth-century canoe prow are like those found on the Maoris' tattooed bodies. Body painting and tattooing are governed by tradition and are believed to link the individual to the spirits of ancestors. Ancestor figures are intended to appear menacing to outsiders, but they are perceived as benevolent within the group. Other Maori carvings are found on assembly houses, storehouses, and stockades.

18-12 Canoe prow (pre-1935). Wood. 70⅞" × 29½". Musée d'Histoire Naturelle, Ethnographie et Prehistoire, Rouen, France.

Melanesia

Melanesian art is generally more colorful than that of Polynesia. The cloth masks of New Britain are woven with a certain flair, and the mixed-media ancestral

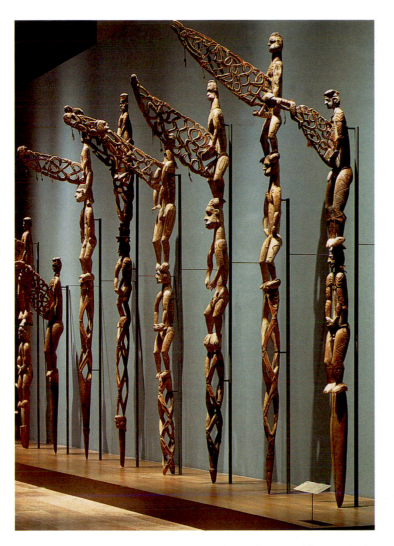

18-13 Ancestor poles, New Guinea (1960). Wood, paint, and fiber. Height of tallest pole: 17'11". The Metropolitan Museum of Art, NY.

the Pacific into the New World. Many historians and archeologists believe, in fact, that the Americas were first populated many thousands of years ago by migrations across the Pacific.

NATIVE ART OF THE AMERICAS

The art of the Americas was rich and varied before the arrival of European culture. We shall next explore the native arts of North America and Peru.

Native Arts of Mexico

Some of the earliest, and certainly the most massive, art of the Americas was produced by the Olmecs in southern Mexico long before the Golden Age of Greece. In addition to huge heads such as that in Figure **18-14**, the Olmecs produced small stone carvings, including reliefs.

poles of New Guinea (Fig. **18-13**) are painted in vivid hues. The intricate poles are carved from single pieces of wood and adorned with palm leaves and paint. Space flows around and through the ancestral poles as it could not pass through the figures at Easter Island. The expressionistically elongated and attenuated bodies again represent ancestors. The openwork banners are phallic symbols, intended to give courage to community men in ceremonies before combat with other tribes. Practical, ceremonial, and decorative uses of art swept across

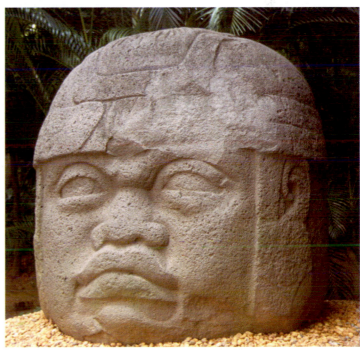

1 ft.

18-14 Colossal head, Villahermosa, Mexico (c. 500 BCE–200 CE). Basalt. H: 8'.

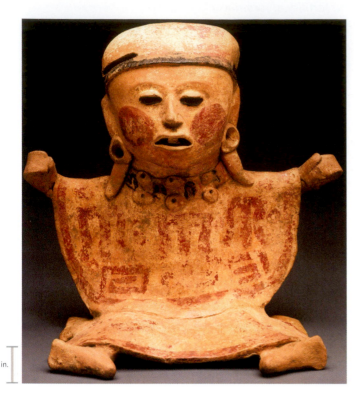

1 in.

18-15 Effigy vessel, girl on swing, from Remojadas region, Veracruz, Mexico (300–900 CE). Ceramic: 9¼". The Metropolitan Museum of Art, NY.

More than a dozen great heads up to 12 feet in height have been found at Olmec ceremonial centers. The hard basalt and jadeite from which they were carved had to be carted nearly 100 miles. The difficulty of working this material with primitive tools may to some degree account for the works' close adherence to the original monoliths. The heads share the same tight-fitting helmets, broad noses, full lips, and wide cheeks. Whether these colossal heads represent gods or earthly rulers is unknown, but there can be no doubting the power they project.

Henry Moore stated that Mexican sculpture is known for its massiveness, but contrast the Olmec heads with the sprightliness of the kinetic sculpture of the swinging girl (Fig. 18-15). This small piece is actually a whistle. The swinging girl was created hundreds of years after the Olmec heads and was found in the same region of southern Mexico. We can find a continuity of tradition in the oversized head, but note the delicacy of the curved body. The entire length of the body is nothing but a spread-eagled, draped abstraction.

The Mayans, whose civilization reached its height in the Yucatán region of Mexico and the highlands of Guatemala from about 300 to 600 CE, built many huge limestone structures with **corbelled** vaults. Mayan temples were highly ornamented with figural relief carvings that represent rulers and gods and with commemorative and allegorical murals. The

18-16 Detail: Mural from Mayan temple at Bonampak, Mexico (c. 6th century CE). Watercolor copy by Antonio Tejeda.

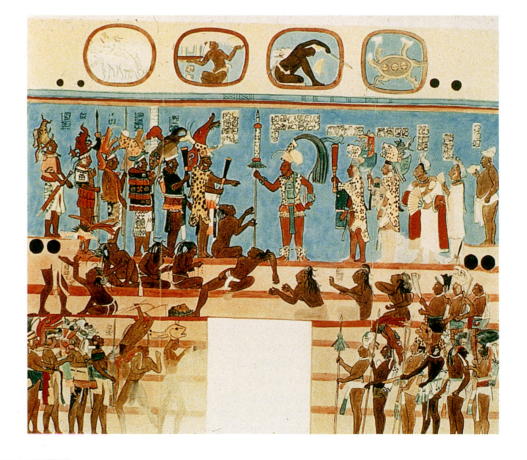

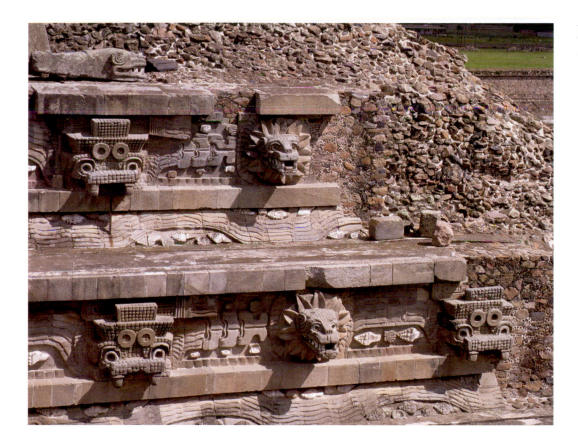

temple discovered at Bonampak in 1947 is decorated with murals of vivid hues, such as that in Figure 18-16, in which prisoners are being presented for sacrifice.

The placement of the reasonably realistic figures along the receding steps symbolizes the social hierarchy. At the bottom are the common people. On the upper platform are noblemen and priests in richly embellished headdresses, as well as their personal attendants, and symbols of the heavens. The prisoners sit and kneel on various levels, visually without a home, whereas the Mayans are rigidly erect in their ascendance. There is no perspective; the figures on the upper registers are not smaller, even though they are farther away. The eye is drawn upward to the center of the composition by the pyramidal shape formed by the scattered prisoners. The figures face the center of the composition, providing symmetry, and the rhythm of the steps provides unity. The subject of human sacrifice is repugnant to us, and well it should be. The composition of the mural, however, shows a classical refinement.

While the Mayans were reaching the height of their power in lower Mexico, the population of the agricultural civilization of Teotihuacán may have reached 100,000. The temples of Teotihuacán, harmoniously grouped in the fertile valley to the north of modern-day Mexico City, include the massive 250-foot-high Pyramid of the Sun and the smaller Temple of Quetzalcóatl (Fig. 18-17). The god Quetzalcóatl was believed to be a feathered serpent. The high-relief head of Quetzalcóatl projects repeatedly from the terraced sculptural panels of the temple, alternating with the square-brimmed geometric abstractions of Tlaloc, the rain god. Bas-reliefs of abstracted serpent scales and feathers follow sinuous paths on the panels in between.

The warlike Aztecs were a small group of poor nomads until they established their capital, Tenochtitlán, in about 1325 CE on the site of modern-day Mexico City. Once established in Tenochtitlán, the Aztecs made great advances in art and architecture, as well as in mathematics and engineering, but they also cruelly subjugated peoples from surrounding tribes. Prisoners of war were used for human sacrifice in order to compensate the sun god, who was believed to have sacrificed himself in the creation of the human race. It is not surprising that in the early part of the sixteenth century, the invading Spaniards found many neighbors of the Aztecs more than eager to help them in their conquest of Mexico. The Aztecs also helped seal their own fate by initially treating the Spaniards, who they believed were descended from Quetzalcóatl, with great hospitality. The Spaniards, needless to say, did not rush to disabuse their hosts of this notion and were thus able to creep into the hearts of the Aztecs within the Trojan horse of mistaken identity.

Coatlicue was the Aztec "Mother of Gods," associated with the earth and the cycle of birth, death, and rebirth. The

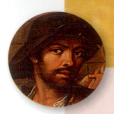

A CLOSER LOOK

IN THE YEAR 1492, the king and queen of Spain funded Columbus's trip to the New World. The day after he left Spain's shores, Jews were expelled from the country by decree. Some 27 years later, the Spaniard Hernán Cortez sailed to Mexico and conquered the Aztec Empire. His campaign was brilliant; the empire fell to only 500 Spanish soldiers. The Aztec capital was vanquished in a bloody siege, and much of the Native Mexican population eventually succumbed to smallpox, a virus that the Spaniards introduced and to which the Native Mexicans had not developed immunity. The picture of Spain in the sixteenth century is one of sharp contrasts. It was a country in its "Golden Age," marked by feats of exploration and cultural masterworks, and at the same time, marked by prejudice, savage domination, and the infliction of pain.

The culture of Mexico survived, albeit in a transformed state. And the works of art that emerged during the Spanish Colonial period in Mexico, Central America, and South America bear evidence as well of artistic transformation. These works were the subject of a 1993 exhibition at the Santa Barbara Museum of Art in California: "Cambios: The Spirit of Transformation in Spanish Colonial Art." Cultural clash almost always leaves in its wake fascinating artistic imagery; perhaps in no other encounter of peoples has the interaction and reconciliation of disparate motifs been more well defined than in the clash of the Spanish and Meso-American cultures.

The exhibition focused on how indigenous art forms, motifs, and techniques were integrated with European influences. In a review of the show in *Latin American Art*, Leslie West-brook noted that the exhibit illustrated the great diversity of design influences as well as the willingness of artists to combine vocabularies from different cultures and contexts to create a "new world order" on the palette, so to speak.[1] Some examples of motifs include the Meso-American jaguar, flower-filled jars, leaf patterns, and

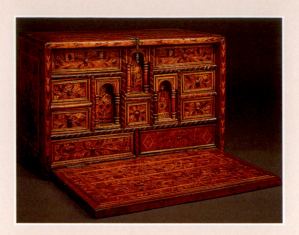

18-18 *Bargueño* (18th century). Inlaid wood. 17¼" × 28" × 16¼". Collection of Michael Haskell, Santa Barbara, CA.

elaborate borders (Fig. **18-18**) reconciled with the lion image, a European formal symmetry, and Christian subject matter. Of special interest is a newly attributed work by Miguel Cabrera entitled *Castas* (Depiction of Racial Mixtures) (Fig. **18-19**). It represents the *mestizo*—the child born of the union of a European and a Native American. These children bear the physical characteristics of the two peoples, and as such symbolize the marriage of two cultures.

The "Cambios" exhibition brought together remnants of a sometimes cruel history, where, as the reviewer remarked, one civilization superseded and dominated another. Yet nothing directly spoke of the cruel and devastating effects of Spanish domination. Instead, a freewheeling creativity—one of absorption, reconciliation, and ancestral legacy—dominated the show, a testimony to the resilience of the human spirit. ●

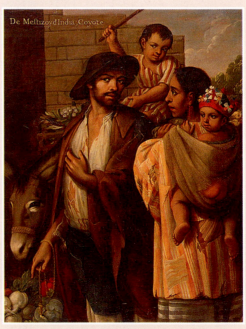

18-19 MIGUEL CABRERA. *Castas* (Depiction of Racial Mixtures) (1763). Oil on canvas. 52" × 40½". Private collection.

---

[1] Leslie A. Westbrook, "Cambios: The Spirit of Transformation in Spanish Colonial Art," *Latin American Art* 5, no. 1: 54–57.

their mother. The ferocity of the imagery, which is incised and carved in relief, though shocking, was typical of pre-Columbian societies.

Native Arts of Peru

The native arts of Peru include pyramid-shaped structures that form supports for temples, as in Mexico; stone carvings, mostly in the form of ornamental reliefs on ceremonial architecture; ceramic wares; and astounding feats of engineering.

The ceramic portrait jar shown in Figure **18-21** was created in about the fifth or sixth century CE by the Mochica culture along the Pacific coast of northern Peru. It has a typical flat bottom and stirrup-shaped spout. Other jars show entire human or animal figures, some of them caught in erotic poses.

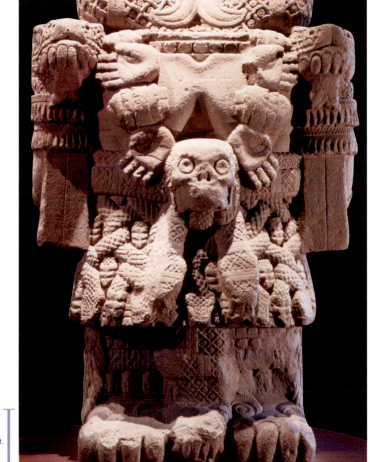

18-20 Statue of Coatlicue (15th century). Stone. H: 99". National Museum of Anthropology, Mexico City, Mexico.

compact, monumental stone effigy in Figure **18-20** depicts the goddess as symbol of creation and destruction (the earth gives but also takes away). She wears a skirt of carved serpents, representing fertility, and a necklace of severed hands, hearts, and skulls. Scholars offer different interpretations of the uppermost part of the sculpture. Some read it as Coatlicue's head, composed of the heads of two facing snakes, whose eyes and fangs become her own. Others have said that the sculpture portrays a decapitated Coatlicue in which snakes coil out of her severed neck. This interpretation more directly references one of two myths, in which one of Coatlicue's 400 children called upon her siblings to kill

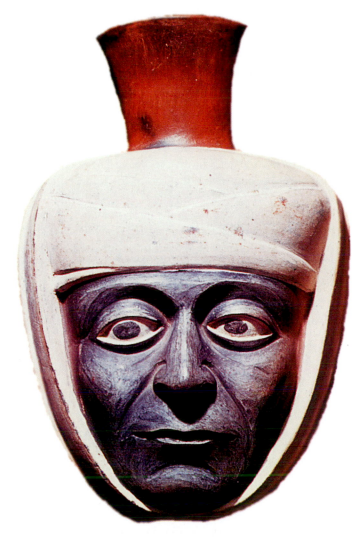

18-21 Ceramic portrait jar from Peru (c. 500 CE). Terra-cotta with paint.

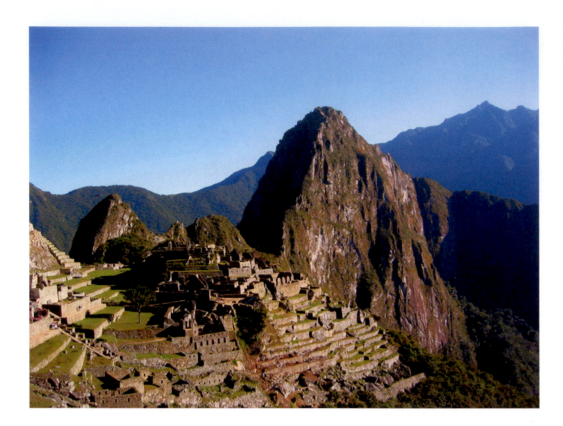

18-22 Fortress of Machu Picchu, Urubamba Valley, Peru (1490–1530).

Figure **18-22** shows the grand ruins of Machu Picchu, the fortress that straddled the Peruvian Andes. This structure, built by the Incas in about 1500 CE, shows an engineering genius that has been compared to the feats of the Romans. The tight fit of the dry masonry walls seems to reflect the tightness of the totalitarian fist with which the Incan nobility regulated the lives of their own masses and subjugated peoples from Ecuador and Chile. The conquering Spaniards were amazed by the great Incan "Royal Road of the Mountains." Thirty feet wide and walled for its entire 3,750 miles, it had no parallel in Europe.

Native Arts of the United States and Canada

Some native art objects in the United States and Canada date back nearly 12,000 years. As with African art, much of it is practical craft, much is ceremonial, and all is richly varied. Eskimo, or Inuit, sculpture exhibits a simplicity of form and elegant refinement in both its realistic and abstract designs. It can also be highly imaginative, as in a mask representing a moon goddess (Fig. **18-23**). Such masks, worn by shamans in ritual ceremonies, were carved of ivory or wood and often had movable parts that added to the drama and realism of the object.

Prehistoric sites in what is now the United States also have yielded many interesting works. One of the larger ceremonial sculptures to survive is an earthwork called the Serpent Mound, a snakelike form of molded earth that meanders

some 1,440 feet in the Ohio countryside. Pyramidal temple platforms reminiscent of those of Mexico and South America have also been unearthed.

Among Native Americans, the Navajos of the Southwest are particularly noted for their fiber artistry and stylized sand paintings that portray the gods and mythic figures. Some of these works are believed to be empowered to heal.

Peoples of the Northwest Coast have produced masks used by shamans in healing rituals; totem poles not unlike the ancestor poles of Oceania; and bowls, clothing, canoes, and houses that are embellished with carving and painted ornamentation. The wood and muslin of a four-foot-high Kwakiutl headdress from British Columbia (Fig. **18-24**) is vividly painted with abstracted human and animal forms. Like the Inuit moon goddess mask, it too has movable parts. When the string hanging from the inner mask is pulled, the two profiles to the sides are drawn together, forming another mask. The symbols represent the sun and other spirits. It is an extraordinary composition, balanced by the circular flow of fabric above the heads and by the bilateral symmetry in the placement of the shapes. As is often the case in ethnographic art, the embellishment of the work reflects traditional body decoration, such as painting, tattooing, or scarification.

The nomadic tribes of the Great Plains poured their artistic energies into embellishing portable items, such as garments and teepees. The muslin teepee lining of the Crow peoples of the Plains (Fig. **18-25**) is a multihued and fairly

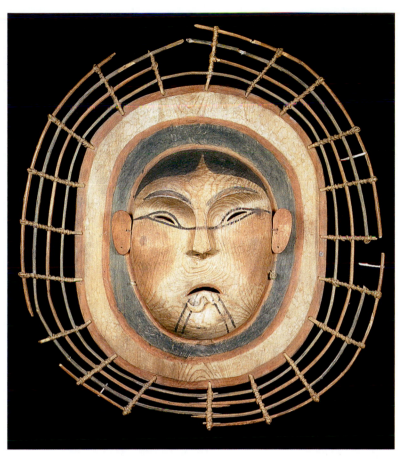

18-23 Eskimo mask representing a moon goddess (before 1900). Phoebe A. Hearst Museum of Anthropology. The University of California at Berkeley, Berkeley, CA..

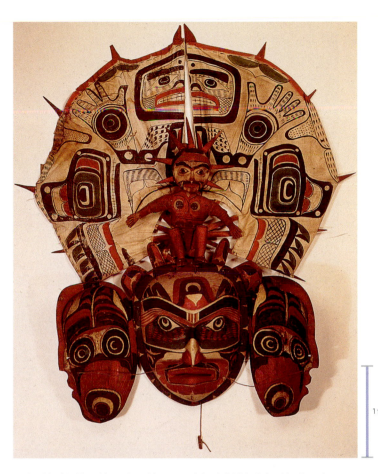

18-24 Kwakiutl headdress from Vancouver Island, British Columbia, Canada (c. 1895–1900). Wood and muslin. 52" × 46". National Museum of the American Indian, Smithsonian Institution, Washington, D.C.

1 ft.

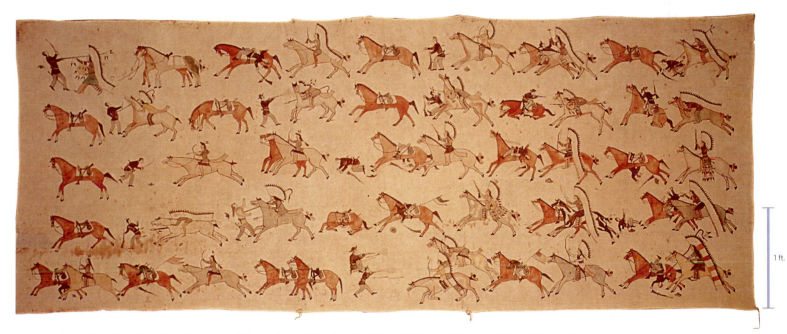

1 ft.

18-25 *Custer's Last Stand* (late 19th century). Teepee lining. Painted muslin. 35" × 85". National Museum of Natural History, Department of Anthropology, Smithsonian Institution, Washington, D.C.

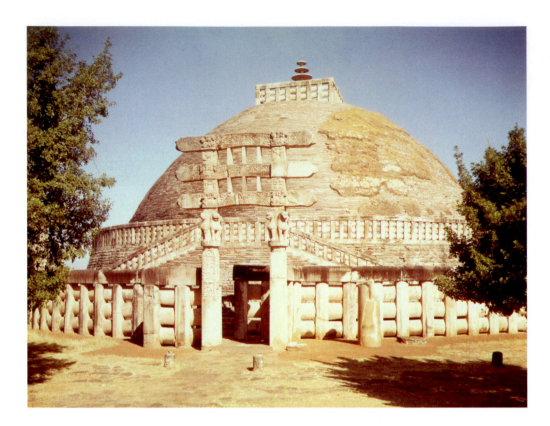

18-26 The Great Stupa, Sanchi, India (3rd century BCE–early 1st century CE). H: 65'.

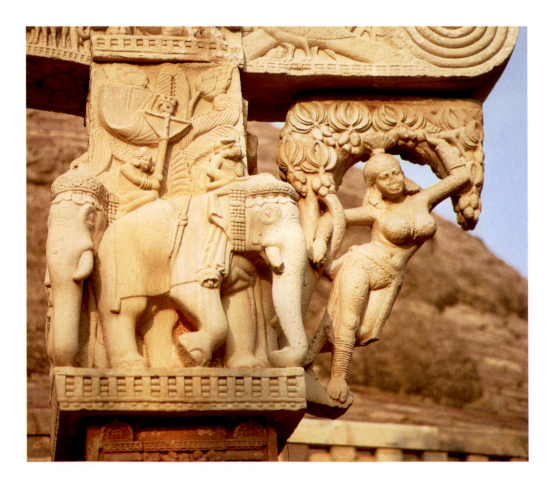

18-27 *Yakshi* sculpture on the East Torana at the Great Stupa of Sanchi, India.

realistic portrayal of nineteenth-century warfare with the U.S. cavalry. In this symbolic collection of events, Crow warriors advance rhythmically from the right. Many chieftains sport splendid feather headdresses. The cavalry is largely unhorsed and apparently unable to stop the implied momentum of the charge, which is very much like the sequence of frames in a motion picture.

INDIAN ART

Indian art, like that of the Americas, shows a history of thousands of years, and it too has been influenced by different cultures. Stone sculptures and **seals** that date to the second or third millennium BCE have been discovered. In low relief, the seals portray sensuous, rounded native animals and humanoid figures that presage the chief Hindu god, **Shiva**.

India once encompassed present-day Pakistan, Bangladesh, and the buffer states between modern India and China. Many religious traditions have conflicted and sometimes peacefully coexisted in India, among them the Vedic religion, Hinduism, Buddhism, and Islam. Today Islam is the dominant religion of Pakistan, and Hinduism predominates in India. Indian art, like Islamic art, is found in many parts of Asia where Indian cultural influence once reigned, as in Indochina.

Buddhism flowered from earlier Indian traditions in the sixth century BCE, largely as a result of the example set by a prince named Siddhartha. In his later years, Siddhartha renounced his birthright and earthly luxuries to become a Buddha, or enlightened being. Through meditation and self-denial, he is believed to have reached a comprehension of the universe that Buddhists call **nirvana**. After his death, Buddha's cremated remains were supposedly placed in **stupas** in eight different locations in India. These sites became places of worship and devotion for his followers. The Great Stupa at Sanchi (Fig. **18-26**) was completed in the first century CE. The stupa is crowned by a large dome that symbolizes the sky. The dome is visually separated from the base of the structure by a stone railing or fence—known as the *vedika*—echoing the separation of the heavenly and earthly spheres. Pilgrims circumnavigate the mound in a clockwise direction, as if tracing the path of the sun across the sky. The worshipers' relationship to the monument concentrates on the exterior rather than the interior as, for example, in the case of the Christian church.

The bracket figure (Fig. **18-27**) on a gateway to the Great Stupa is a *yakshia*, a pre-Buddhist goddess who was believed to embody the generative forces of nature. She appears to be nude, but a hemline reveals that she wears a diaphanous garment. Her ample breasts and sex organs symbolize the force of her productive powers. The voluptuousness of such figures

stands in contrast to the often ascetic figures we find in Western religious art.

For many hundreds of years, there were no images of the Buddha, but sculptures and other representations began to appear in the second century CE. Some sculpted Buddhas show a Western influence that can be traced to the conquest of northwestern India by Alexander the Great in 327 BCE. Others have a sensuous, rounded look that recalls the ancient seals and is decidedly Indian. The slender chlorite Buddha (Fig. **18-28**) shows delicate fingers and gauzelike, revealing drapery. The face exhibits a pleasant cast that is as inscrutable as the expression of La Gioconda in Leonardo's *Mona Lisa* (see Fig. 16-19).

Let us briefly travel west of India to view the colossal Buddha carved out of living rock at Bamiyan, Afghanistan

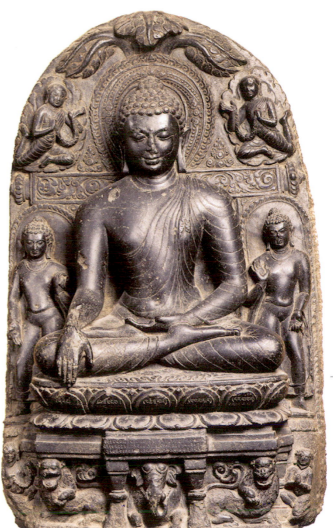

18-28 *Buddha Calling on Earth to Witness* (9th century CE), from India, Bengal, Bihar, Pala Period (750–1197 CE). Black chlorite. H: 39". The Cleveland Museum of Art, Cleveland, OH. © The Cleveland Museum of Art. Dudley P. Allen Fund 1935.146.

out of one's daily duties. Another reason for the popularity of Hinduism may be its frank appreciation of eroticism. Western religions impose a distinction between the body or flesh, on the one hand, and the soul or mind, on the other. As a consequence, sex is often seen as being at odds with religious purity. Hinduism considers sexual expression to be one legitimate path to virtue. Explicit sexual acts in high reliefs adorn temple walls and amaze Western visitors.

There are many Hindu gods, including Shiva, the Lord of Lords and god of creation and destruction, which, in Hindu philosophy, are one. Figure **18-30** shows Shiva as Nataraja, the King of Dance. With one foot on the Demon of Ignorance, this eleventh-century bronze figure dances within a symbolically splendid fiery aura. The limbs are sensuous, even erotic. The small figure to the right side of his head is Ganga, the river goddess. This periodic dance destroys the universe, which is then reborn. So, in Hindu belief, is the human spirit reborn after death, its new form reflecting the sum of the virtues of its previous existences.

Hindu temples are considered to be the dwelling places of the gods, not houses of worship. The proportions of the famous

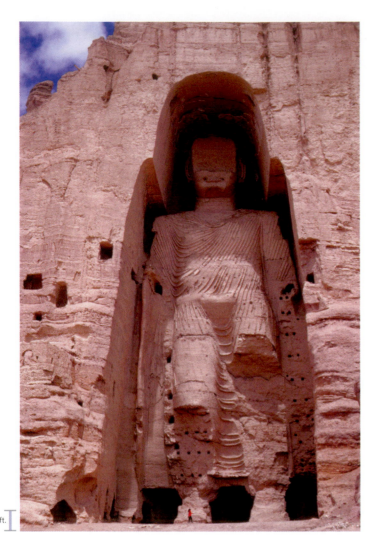

18-29 *Colossal Buddha*, Bamiyan, Afghanistan (2nd–5th centuries CE). Destroyed in 2001. Stone. H: 180'.

10 ft.

(Fig. **18-29**). The statue portrayed the eternal form of Buddha in the belief that his earthly form was purely transient. The concept of eternity is expressed in part through scale. This Buddha, 180 feet tall, and its somewhat smaller companion, 120 feet tall, commanded the surrounding landscape and was so well-known that tiny replicas were carved for visitors as souvenirs that they carried back to their home countries. Even though the photograph seems to suggest a rather rough-hewn rendering of Buddha, it is quite possible that it was gilded and had applications of plaster and pigment. The Taliban destroyed these figures in 2001 despite pleas by other nations, which offered to remove and preserve them at their own expense.

In the sixth and seventh centuries CE, Hinduism rose to prominence in India, perhaps because it permitted more paths for reaching nirvana, including the simple carrying

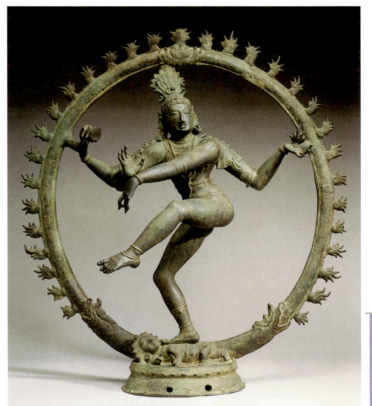

1 ft.

18-30 *Nataraja, Shiva as King of the Dance* (1000s CE), from South India, Chola period (900-13th century CE). Bronze. 43⅞" × 40". The Cleveland Museum of Art, Cleveland, OH. © The Cleveland Museum of Art. Purchase from the J. H. Wade Fund 1930.331.

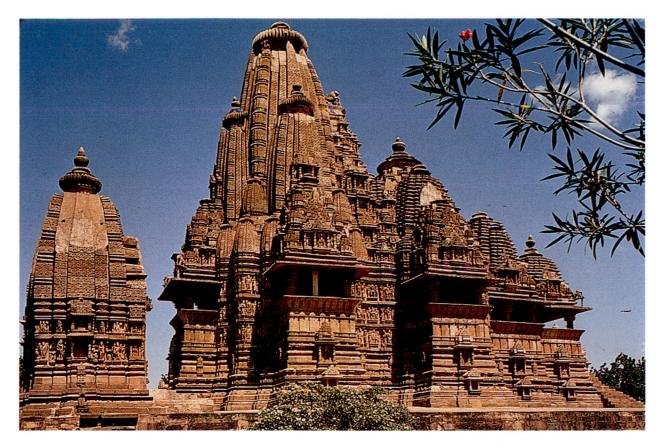

18-31 Kandariya Mahadeva Temple, Khajuraho, India (10th–11th centuries CE).

Kandariya Mahadeva Temple at Khajuraho (Fig. **18-31**) symbolize cosmic rhythms. The gradual unfolding of spaces within is highlighted by the sculptural procession of exterior forms. The organic, natural shapes of the multiple roofs are in most sections separated from the horizontal registers of the base by sweeping cornices. The main tower is an abstracted mountain peak, reached visually by ascending what appear to be architectural and natural hurdles. All of this can be seen as representing human paths to oneness with the universe. The registers of the base are populated by high reliefs of gods, allegorical scenes, and idealized men and women in erotic positions.

Other Hindu temples are even more intricate. Vast pyramidal bases contain forests of towers and spires, corniced at the edges as they ascend from level to fanciful level. They are thick with low and high reliefs. In the Buddhist temples of Indochina, the giant face of Buddha looms from the walls of imposing towers and gazes in many directions. Indian art, including Indian painting—of which little, sad to say, survives—teaches us again how different the content of the visual arts can be. Still, techniques such as that of stone carving and bronze casting, as well as elements of composition, seem to possess a universal validity.

CHINESE ART

China houses more than a billion people in a country not quite as large as the United States (compared to a U.S. population of approximately 309 million as of 2010). Nearly 4,000 years ago, inhabitants of China were producing primitive crafts. Beautiful bronze vessels embellished with stylized animal imagery were cast during the second millennium BCE, such as the one shown in Figure 13-25. During the feudal period of the Late Chou dynasty, which was contemporaneous with the Golden Age of Greece, royal metalworks were inlaid with gold, silver, and polished mirrors. Elegant carvings of fine jade were buried with their noble owners.

Confucianism ascended as the major Chinese way of life during the second century BCE. It is based on the moral principles of Confucius, which argue that social behavior must be derived from sympathy for one's fellows. Paintings and reliefs of this period show the **conceptual space** of Egyptian painting and create the illusion of depth by means of overlapping. Missionaries from India successfully introduced Buddhism to China during the second century CE, and many Chinese artists imitated Indian models for a few

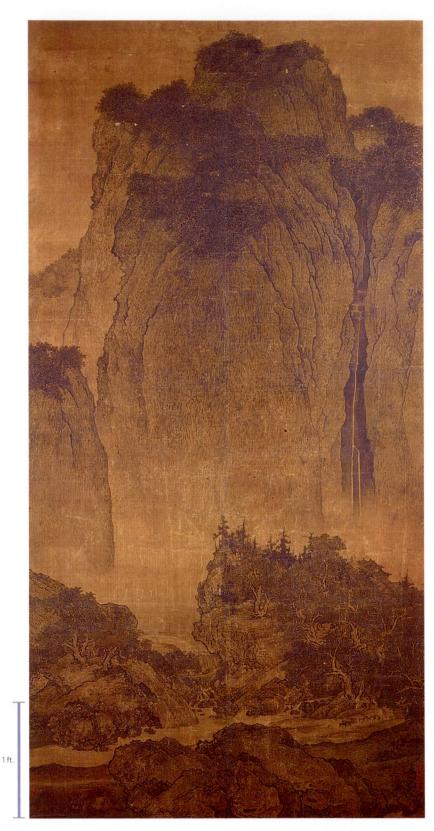

centuries afterward. But by the sixth century, Chinese art was again Chinese. Landscape paintings transported viewers to unfamiliar, magical realms. Many people believed that artist and work of art were united by a great moving spirit. Centuries after the introduction of Buddhism, Confucianism again emerged. The present-day People's Republic of China is officially atheistic, but many Chinese still follow the precepts of Confucius.

Fan K'uan's *Travelers among Mountains and Streams* (Fig. **18-32**) was painted on a silk scroll during the early part of the eleventh century. Years of political turmoil had reinforced the artistic escape into imaginary landscapes. It is executed in the so-called Monumental style. Rocks in the foreground create a visual barrier that prevents the viewer from being drawn suddenly into the painting. Rounded forms rise in orderly, rhythmic fashion from foreground through background. Sharp brushstrokes clearly delineate conifers, deciduous trees, and small temples on the cliff in the middle ground. The waterfall down the high cliffs to the right is balanced by the cleft to the left. A high contrast in values picks out the waterfall from the cliffs. Distant mountains dwarf human figures. In contrast to the perspective typical of Western landscapes, there is no single vanishing point or set of vanishing points. The perspective shifts, offering the viewer a freer journey back across the many paths and bridges.

The blue-and-white porcelain vase from the Ming dynasty (Fig. **18-33**) speaks eloquently of the refinement of Chinese ceramics. The crafting of vases such as these was a hereditary art, passed on from father to son over many generations. Labor was also frequently divided so that one craftsman made the vase and others glazed and decorated it. The vase has a blue underglaze decoration—that is, a decoration molded or incised beneath rather than on top of the glaze. Transparent glazing increases the brilliance of the piece. In many instances, the incising or molding was so subtle that it amounted to "secret" decoration.

Li K'an's fourteenth-century ink painting *Bamboo* (Fig. **18-34**) possesses an almost unbearable beauty. The entire composition consists of minor variations in line and tone. On one level, it is a realistic representation of bamboo leaves, with texture gradient providing a powerful illusion of depth. On another level, it is a nonobjective symphony of calligraphic brushstrokes. The mass of white paper

1 ft.

18-32 FAN K'UAN. *Travelers among Mountains and Streams* (c. 1000 CE). Hanging scroll, ink and colors on silk. H: 81¾". Collection of the National Palace Museum, Taipei, Taiwan, Republic of China.

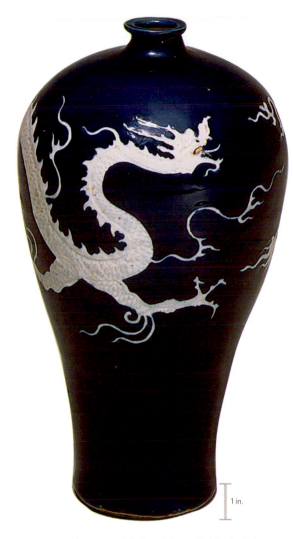

showing in the background is a symbolic statement of purity, not a realistic rendering of natural elements such as haze.

In much of Chinese art, there is a non-Western type of reverence for nature in which people are seen as integral parts of the order of nature, neither its rulers nor its victims. In moments of enlightenment, we understand how we create and are of this order, very much in the way Li K'an must have felt that his spirit had both created and been derived from these leaves of bamboo and the natural order that they represent.

How can we hope to have spoken meaningfully about the depth and beauty of Chinese philosophies and Chinese arts in but a few sentences? Our words are mean strokes, but perhaps they point in the right direction.

JAPANESE ART

Japan is an island country off the eastern coast of Asia, holding more than 120 million people in an area not quite as large as California (which holds approximately 36 million people). The islands were originally formed from porous volcanic rock, and thus they are devoid of hard stone suitable for sculpture and building. Therefore, Japan's sculpture tradition has focused on clay modeling and bronze casting, and its structures have been built from wood.

The Japanese tradition, like the Western tradition, has various periods and styles. In Japanese art, as in Western art, we find a developing technology, the effect of native materials, indigenous and foreign influences, a mix of religious traditions, and disagreement as to what art is intended to portray. Despite its vast differences from Western art, Japanese art

18-33 Vase (1368–1644 CE). Porcelain. 13¼". Musée Guimet, Paris, France.

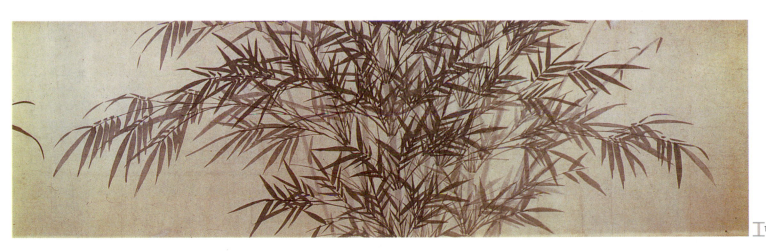

18-34 LI K'AN. *Bamboo* (1308 CE). Detail of 1st section. Hand scroll. Ink on paper. 14¾" × 93½". Nelson-Atkins Museum of Art, Kansas City, MO.

shows similar meanings and functions. Japanese artists also use the same elements of art, in their own fashion, to shape brilliant compositions.

Ceramic figures and vessels date to the fourth millennium BCE. Over the past 2,000 years, Japanese art has been intermittently influenced by the arts of nearby China and Korea. In the fifth and sixth centuries CE, the Japanese produced **haniwa**, hollow ceramic figures with tubular limbs modeled from slabs of clay. Haniwa were placed around burial plots, but their function is unknown.

By the beginning of the seventh century, Buddhism had been exported from China and established as the state religion in Japan. Many sculptors produced wooden and bronze effigies of the Buddha, and Buddhist temples reflected the Chinese style. Shinto, the native religion of Japan, teaches love of nature and the existence of many beneficent gods, who are never symbolized in art or any other visual form.

For nearly 2,000 years, wooden Shinto shrines, such as those shown in Figure 18-35, have been razed every 20 years and replaced by duplicates. The landscapes, portraits, and narrative scrolls produced by the Japanese during the Kamakura period, which spanned the late twelfth through the early fourteenth centuries CE, are highly original and Japanese in character. Some of them express the contemplative life of Buddhism, others express the active life of the warrior, and still others express the aesthetic life made possible by love of nature.

The Kumano Mandala (Fig. **18-35**), a scroll executed at the beginning of the fourteenth century, represents three **Shinto** shrines. These are actually several miles apart in mountainous terrain, but the artist collapsed the space between them to permit the viewer an easier visual pilgrimage. The scroll pays homage to the unique Japanese landscape in its vivid color and rich detail. The several small figures of the seated Buddha portrayed within testify to the Japanese reconciliation of disparate spiritual influences. The repetition of forms within the shrines and the procession of the shrines afford the composition a wonderful rhythm and unity. A **mandala** is a religious symbol of the design of the universe. It seems as though the universe of the shrines of the Kumano Mandala must carry on forever, as, indeed, it did in the minds of the Japanese.

Some periods of Japanese art have given rise to an extraordinary realism, as in the thirteenth-century wood sculpture of *The Sage Kuya Invoking the Amida*

1 ft.

18-35 The Three Sacred Shrines at Kumano: Kumano Mandala (c. 1300), from Japan, Kamakura period (1185–1333). Hanging scroll; ink and color on silk. 53¾" × 24⅜". The Cleveland Museum of Art, Cleveland, OH. John L. Severance Fund 1953.16.

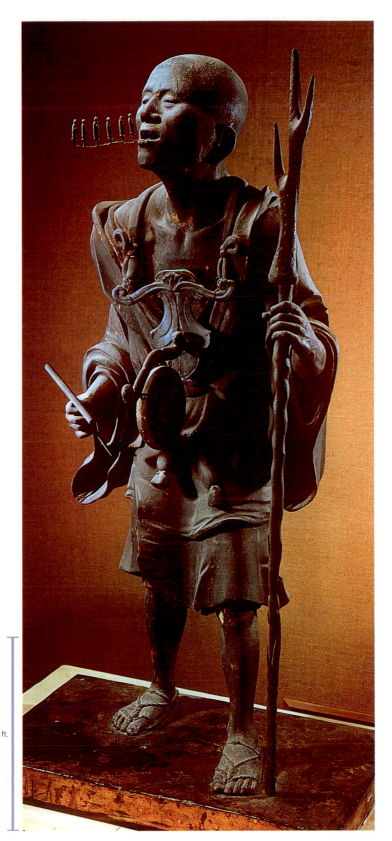

1 ft.

18-36 *The Sage Kuya Invoking the Amida Buddha* (13th century CE). Painted wood. H: approx. 46". Rokuhara Mitsu-ji Temple, Kyoto, Japan.

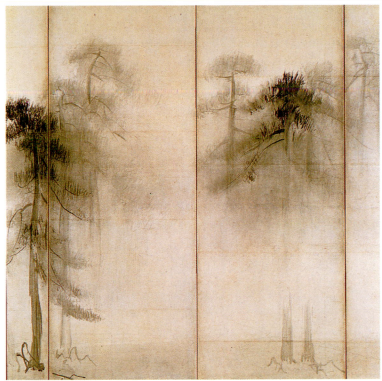

18-37 HASEGAWA TOHAKU. *Pine Wood* (1539–1610 CE). Detail from a pair of sixfold screens. Ink on paper. H: 61". Tokyo National Museum, Tokyo, Japan.

Buddha (Fig. **18-36**). From the stance of the figure and the keen observation of every drapery fold, to the crystal used to create the illusion of actual eyes, this sculptor's effort to reproduce reality knew no bounds. The artist even went as far as to attempt to render speech: Six tiny images of Buddha come forth from the sage's mouth, representing the syllables of a prayer that repeats the name of Buddha. A remarkable balance between the earthly and the spiritual is achieved through the use of extreme realism to portray a subject that refers to religion.

Some three centuries later, Hasegawa Tohaku painted his masterful *Pine Wood* (Fig. **18-37**) on a pair of screens. It is reminiscent of Li K'an's study of bamboo in that the plant life stands alone. No rocks or figures occupy the foreground. No mountains press the skies in the background. Like *Bamboo*, it is also monochromatic. The illusion of depth—and the illusion of dreamy mists—is evoked by subtle gradations in tone and texture. Overlapping and relative size also play their roles in the provision of perspective. Without foreground and background, there is no point of reference from which we can infer the scale of the trees. Their monumentality is implied by the power of the artist's brushstrokes. The groupings of trees to the left have a soft sculptural quality and the overall form of delicate ceramic wares. The groupings of trees within each screen balance one another, and the overall composition suggests the infinite directional strivings of nature to find form and express itself.

We noted that Picasso was strongly influenced by the art of Africa. Many Western artists of the nineteenth century were influenced by the art of the East, particularly prints from Japan, which were being imported to Paris and other Western cultural centers. The French Impressionist Edgar Degas, in fact, hung a print by Torii Kiyonaga in his bedroom. Modern artists were intrigued by the flatness of space, the decorative patterns, brilliant palette, and off-center compositions in Japanese woodcuts, such as Hiroshige's *Sudden*

Rain at Atake and Ohashi (Fig. **18-38**). Vincent van Gogh made an oil-on-canvas painting of this print, adding a decorative frame, complete with calligraphic patterns (Fig. **18-39**). The ordinariness of Japanese subjects also struck a chord among the Modernists, who were trying to escape the grip of mythological and historical painting.

The opening of trade between Japan and the West in the mid-nineteenth century revealed new artistic worlds to the painters in Western Europe. Van Gogh wasn't the only artist of his time to copy or reinterpret the masterworks of Japanese painters, printmakers, and porcelain artists. Copying, as we have seen, has always been a way to come to understand—and to know deeply—the process and the product of art. But according to art critic Lyle Rexer, for some self-taught, "outsider" artists (see Chapter 1), it has also been a way to experience times

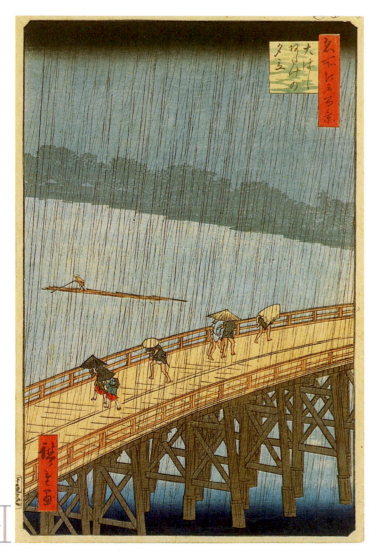

18-38 ANDO HIROSHIGE. *Sudden Rain at Atake and Ohashi* (1857). Color woodblock print. 13⅞" × 9⅛". The Cleveland Museum of Art, Cleveland, OH. Gift from J. H. Wade 1921.318.

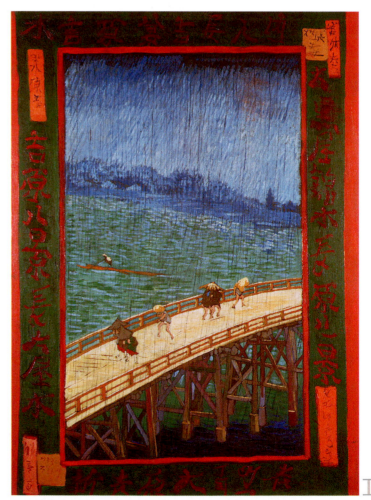

18-39 VINCENT VAN GOGH. *Bridge in the Rain*, copy after Ando Hiroshige (1887). Oil on canvas. 28¾" × 18¼". Van Gogh Museum, Amsterdam, Netherlands.

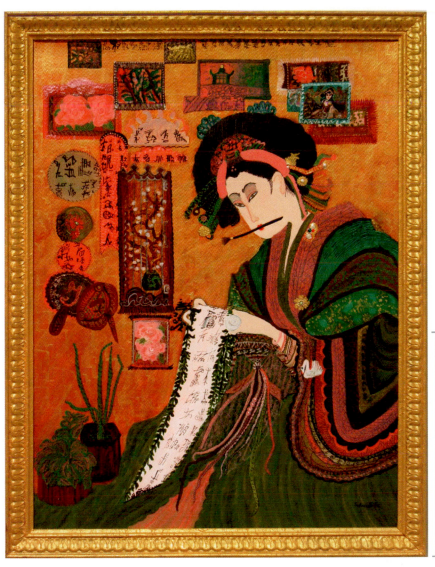

18-40 SILVIA REINSTEIN. *Untitled* (1980). Acrylic on paper with painted frame. 26" × 20". KS Art, NY.

1 ft.

and places that would otherwise remain unreachable. Although never intended to hang anywhere or appear in any compendium of art history, Silvia Reinstein's untitled acrylic work on paper, embellished by a painted gold frame (Fig. 18-40), bears the same hallmark of inspiration by Japanese prints as the works of her "insider," Impressionist predecessors.

The ability to represent nature with exacting realism was a goal that united most Western artists through the ages. There were occasional deviations, as among the Christian artists of the Middle Ages, for whom representing the physicality of the figure was unimportant. Their choice was not based on an inability to mirror nature, but on the belief that the soul—and not the body—was a more relevant and intimate part of God's celestial plan. During the Renaissance, Western artists—including those who portrayed religious subjects—devised perspective to master the illusion of reality. As humanism took hold, the figure in sculpture and painting also appeared "more human."

Mimesis—imitation in representation—was never as much a goal for artists beyond the West, not because of lack of skill but because their artistic goals were not the same. Once art entered the modern era in the West, and artists had reached the height of their ability to represent nature with utmost accuracy, some continued in the realistic tradition, but others found it meaningless. After all, early enough in the nineteenth century, the camera would be able to do that for them. It was when art no longer needed to be consonant with realism that art beyond the West spoke most cogently to these artists. It was the exploration of art beyond the West that steered Western modernism on a different course.

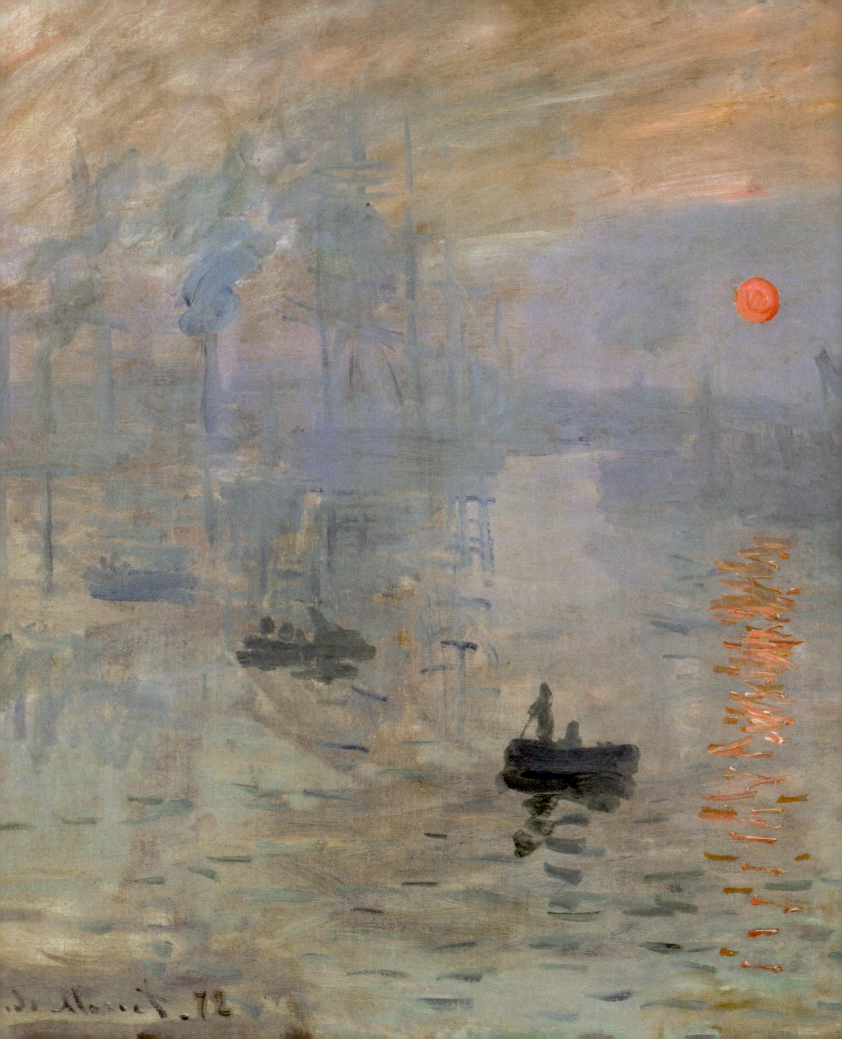

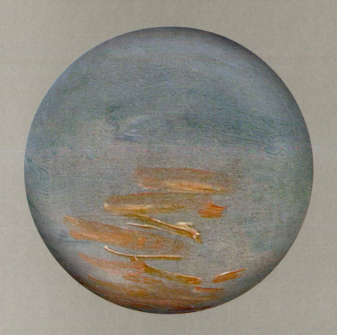

MODERN ART

19

Historians of modern art have repeatedly posed the question, "When did modern art begin?" Some link the beginnings of modern painting to the French Revolution in 1789. Others have chosen 1863, the year of a landmark exhibition of "modern" painting in Paris.

Another issue of interest has been "Just what is modern about modern art?" The artists of the mid-fifteenth century looked upon their art as modern. They chose new subjects, materials, and techniques that signaled a radical change from a medieval past. Their development of one-point linear perspective altered the face of painting completely. From our perspective, modern art begins with the changes in the representation of space as introduced by artists of the late eighteenth century. Unlike the Renaissance masters, who sought to open up endless vistas within the canvas, the artists of the latter 1700s thrust all of the imagery toward the **picture plane**. The flatness or two-dimensionality of the canvas surface was asserted by the use of **planar recession** rather than **linear recession**. Not all artists of the eighteenth and nineteenth centuries abided by this novel treatment of space, but with this innovation, the die was cast for the future of painting. In short, what was *modern* about the modern art of the eighteenth century in France was its concept of space. In a very real sense, the history of modern art is the history of two differing perceptions and renderings of that space.

CLAUDE MONET. *Impression: Sunrise* (1872). Oil on canvas. 19½" × 25½". Musée Marmottan, Paris, France.

The flattening of pictorial space begins in the late eighteenth century with Jacques-Louis David and *Neoclassicism*. **Romanticism** followed closely in its wake, at times displaying stylistic continuity with its predecessor and at times diametrically opposed to it. We shall discuss the survival of Academic painting in the nineteenth century and consider the relationship between art, politics, and social consciousness. In the mid-nineteenth century, change was everywhere. **Realist** artists rejected the content of Academic art and took to the subjects of life around them. The **Impressionists** rejected the isolation of the artist's studio and took to the outdoors to paint, recording the fleeting optical impressions of light and atmosphere. The new medium of photography experienced technical strides, and its growing familiarity had a marked influence on later-nineteenth-century painting. Paris had become the center of the art world.

NEOCLASSICISM

Modern art declared its opposition to the whimsy of the late Rococo style with Neoclassical art. The **Neoclassical style** is characterized by harsh sculptural lines, a subdued palette, and, for the most part, planar instead of linear recession into space. The subject matter of Neoclassicism was inspired by the French Revolution and designed to heighten moral standards. The new morality sought to replace the corruption and decadence of Louis XVI's France. The Roman Empire was often chosen as the model to emulate. For this reason, the artists of the Napoleonic era imitated the form and content of Classical works of art. This interest in antiquity was fueled by contemporaneous archeological finds at sites such as Pompeii, as well as by numerous excavations in Greece.

Neoclassical Painting

JACQUES-LOUIS DAVID The sterling proponent of the Neoclassical style and official painter of the French Revolution was Jacques-Louis David (1748–1825). David literally gave postrevolutionary France a new look. He designed items as varied as clothing and coiffures. David also set the course for modern art with a sudden and decisive break from the ornateness and frivolity of the Rococo.

In *The Oath of the Horatii* (Fig. 19-1), David portrayed a dramatic event from Roman history in order to heighten French patriotism and courage. Three brothers prepare to fight an enemy of Rome, swearing an oath to the empire on swords upheld by their father. To the right, their mother and other relatives collapse in despair. They weep for the men's safety but are also distraught because one of the enemy men is engaged to a sister of the Horatii. Family is pitted against family in a conflict that no one can win. Such a subject could descend into pathos, but David controlled any tendency toward sentimentality by

19-1 JACQUES-LOUIS DAVID. *The Oath of the Horatii* (1784). Oil on canvas. 14' × 11'. Louvre, Paris, France.

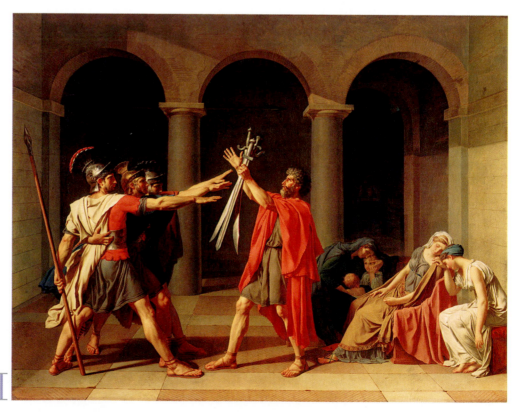

1 ft.

reviving the Classical balance of emotion and restraint. The emotionality of the theme is countered by David's cool rendition of forms. The elements of the composition further work to harness emotionalism. Harsh sculptural lines define the figures and setting. The palette is reduced to muted blues and grays, with an occasional splash of deep red. Emotional response is barely evident in the idealized Classical faces of the figures.

Several Classical devices in David's compositional format also function to balance emotion and restraint. The figural groups form a rough triangle. Their apex—the clasped swords of the Horatii—is the most important point of the composition. In the same way that Leonardo used three windows in his *Last Supper*, David silhouetted his dramatic moment against the central opening of three arches in the background. David further imitated Renaissance canvases by presenting cues for a linear perspective in the patterning of the floor. But unlike sixteenth-century artists, David led his **orthogonals** into a flattened space instead of a vanishing point on a horizon line. The closing off of this background space forces the viewer's eye to the front of the picture plane, where it encounters the action of the composition and the canvas surface. No longer does the artist desire to trick observers into believing they are looking through a window frame into the distance. Now the reality of the two-dimensionality of the canvas is asserted.

David was one of the leaders of the French Revolution, and his political life underwent curious turns. Although he painted *The Oath of the Horatii* for Louis XVI, he supported the faction that deposed him. Later he was to find himself painting a work commemorating the coronation of Napoleon. Having struggled against the French monarchy and then living to see it restored, David chose to spend his last years in exile in Brussels.

ANGELICA KAUFFMAN Angelica Kauffman (1741–1807) was another leading Neoclassical painter, an exact contemporary of David. Born in Switzerland and educated in the Neoclassical circles in Rome, Kauffman was responsible for the dissemination of the style in England. She is known for her portraiture, history painting, and narrative works such as *The Artist in the Character of Design Listening to the Inspiration of Poetry* (Fig. **19-2**). In this allegorical work, Kauffman paints her own features in the person of the muse of design, who is listening attentively with paper and pencil in hand to her companion, the muse of poetry. Poetry's idealized facial features, along with the severe architecture, classically rendered drapery, and rich palette, place the work firmly in the Neoclassical style.

JEAN-AUGUSTE-DOMINIQUE INGRES David abstracted space by using planar rather than linear recession. His most prodigious student, Jean-Auguste-Dominique Ingres (1780–1867), created sensuous, though pristinely Classical, compo-

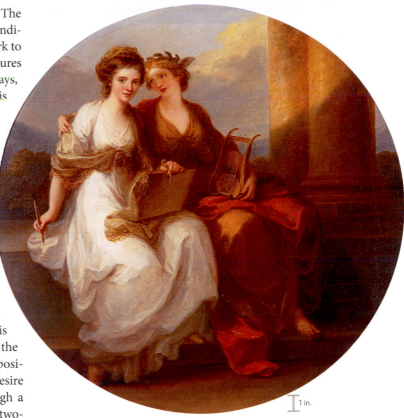

19-2 ANGELICA KAUFFMAN. *The Artist in the Character of Design Listening to the Inspiration of Poetry* (1782). Oil on canvas. D: 24". The Iveagh Bequest, Kenwood House, Hampstead, London, England.

sitions in which line functions as an abstract element. Above all else, Ingres was a magnificent draftsman.

Ingres's work is a combination of harsh linearity and sculptural smoothness on the one hand, and delicacy and sensuality on the other. His *Grande Odalisque* (Fig. 19-7 in the nearby Compare + Contrast feature) portrays a Turkish harem mistress in the tradition of the great reclining Venuses of the Venetian Renaissance. Yet how different it is, for example, from Titian's *Venus of Urbino*! (See the Compare + Contrast feature later in the chapter.) The elongation of her spine, her attenuated limbs, and the odd fullness of form recall the distortions and abstractions of Mannerist art. In the *Grande Odalisque*, Ingres also delights in the differing qualities of line. The articulation of heavy drapery contrasts markedly with the staccato treatment of the bed linens and the languid, sensual lines of the mistress's body. Like David's, Ingres's forms are smooth and sculptural, and his palette is muted. Ingres also flattens space in his composition by placing his imagery in the foreground, as in a relief.

Ingres's exotic nudes were a popular type of imagery in the late eighteenth century, but other artists often rendered such subjects quite differently. Popular style during this period was similar to that existing during the Baroque era.

On the one hand were artists such as David and Ingres, who represented the linear style. On the other hand were artists whose works were painterly. The foremost proponents of the painterly style were Géricault and Delacroix. The linear artists, called **Poussinistes**, followed in the footsteps of Classicism with their subdued palette and emphasis on draftsmanship and sculptural forms. The painterly artists, termed the **Rubenistes**, adopted the vibrant palette and aggressive brushstroke of the Baroque artist. The two factions argued vehemently about the merits and the shortcomings of their respective styles. No artists were more deeply entrenched in this feud than the leaders of the camps, Ingres and Delacroix.

Neoclassical Sculpture

The principles of Neoclassicism were embraced by sculptors working in France, England, and the United States. It was the style of choice for official portraits, relief sculptures, and monuments of all sorts. Antonio Canova (1757–1822), trained in Italy, wrote of having to "[sweat] day and night over the Greek models, imbibing their style, turning it into one's own blood." He became the sculptor to Napoleon Bonaparte and was responsible for numerous portraits of the emperor and members of his family, including his sister, Pauline Borghese (Fig. **19-3**). Just as Napoleon chose a Zeus-like pose for his coronation painting by Ingres, Pauline had herself portrayed as the goddess of love—Venus. The reclining figure clearly references classical Greek prototypes, although Ingres's approach combines realism and idealism. Pauline's face has the character of a portrait, however modified or improved, and the finely carved details of the elaborate lounge can almost be described as **trompe l'oeil**.

Neoclassical Architecture

In the late eighteenth and nineteenth centuries, Neoclassicism also dominated architectural design in France, England, and America. The architects and visionaries of the U.S. capital—Thomas Jefferson included—embraced classical models for their aesthetic beauty and simplicity. The reference to ancient Greece also befitted the young democracy. From Pierre L'Enfant's plan for Washington, D.C., with its radiating boulevards, geometric spaces, and vistas culminating in classical monuments, to Benjamin Latrobe's concepts for the U.S. Capitol building (see Fig. 3-9), the city was awash in the serenity and monumentality of columns, pediments, and pristine marble facades. Latrobe especially was a stickler for purity of Greek forms. He combined elements of the **Ionic order** for the Senate chamber and **Corinthian** capitals for the House of Representatives. Also of interest is Latrobe's contribution to the White House—an oval room with a columned portico that would come to symbolize the hub of presidential power.

ROMANTICISM

Both Neoclassicism and Romanticism reflected the revolutionary spirit of the times. Neoclassicism emphasized restraint of emotion, purity of form, and subjects that inspired morality, whereas Romantic art sought extremes of emotion enhanced by virtuoso brushwork and a brilliant palette. The two major proponents of the romantic style in France were Théodore Géricault and Eugène Delacroix.

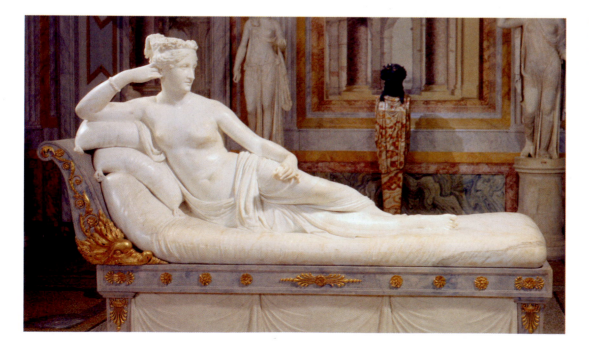

19-3 ANTONIO CANOVA. *Pauline Borghese as Venus* (1808). Marble. 6'7" long. Galleria Borghese, Rome, Italy.

Théodore Géricault

The depiction of nature as unpredictable and uncontrollable—in the words of the French philosopher Denis Diderot, as stunning the soul and imprinting feelings of terror—was a favorite theme of the romantic artist. Many French and British paintings of the period reveal a particular fascination with the destructive power of nature at sea, perhaps none as intensely as Théodore Géricault's *Raft of the Medusa* (Fig. **19-4**). Based on a shipwreck off the coast of West Africa in 1816, during which a makeshift raft laden with Algerian immigrants was set adrift by the captain and crew of the crippled French ship *Medusa*, the painting is viewed as Géricault's most controversial and political work.

Like many of his liberal contemporaries, Géricault (1791–1824) opposed the French monarchy and used the tragedy of the *Medusa* to call attention to the mismanagement and ineffectual policies of the French government, as well as the practice of slavery. The plight of the survivors and victims of the *Medusa* became a national scandal, and Géricault's authentic documentation—based on interviews with the rescued survivors and visits to the morgue—was intended as a direct attack on the government. The powerful composition is full of realistic detail and explores the full gamut of human emotion under extreme hardship and duress. Much of the drama of Géricault's composition occurs along a diagonal configuration of figures, from the corpse in the lower left that will soon slip into the dark abyss of the ocean, upward along a crescendo that culminates in the muscular torso of a black man waving a flag toward a rescue ship that is barely visible on the horizon. The fractured raft is tossed about mercilessly by the winds and waves; humans battle against nature, and their own, for sheer survival.

Eugène Delacroix

The most famous Rubeniste—and Ingres's archrival—was Eugène Delacroix (1798–1863). Whereas Ingres believed that a painting was nothing without drawing, Delacroix advocated the spontaneity of painting directly on a canvas without the tyranny of meticulous preparatory sketches. Ingres believed that color ought to be subordinated to line, but Delacroix maintained that compositions should be constructed of color.

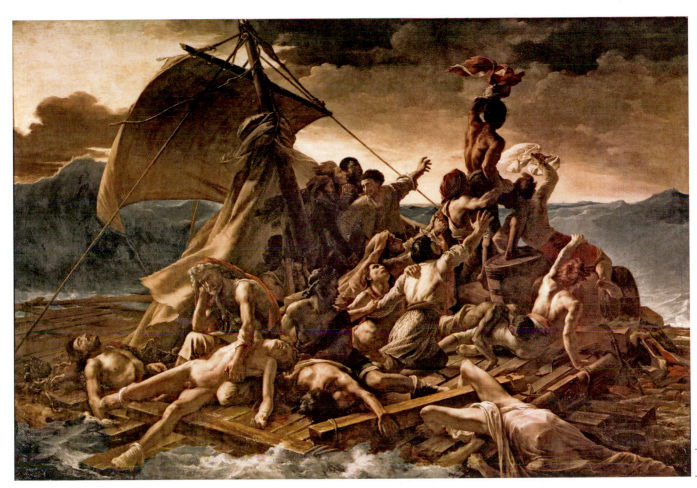

19-4 THÉODORE GÉRICAULT. *The Raft of the Medusa* (1818–1819). Oil on canvas. Approx. 16' × 23'. Louvre, Paris, France.

One of Delacroix's most dynamic statements of the Romantic style occurs in one of his many compositions devoted to the more exciting themes from literary history. *The Death of Sardanapalus* (Fig. **19-5**), inspired by a tragedy by Byron, depicts the murder-suicide of an Assyrian king who, rather than surrender to his attackers, set fire to himself and his entourage. All of the monarch's earthly possessions, including concubines, servants, and Arabian stallions, are heaped upon his lavish gold and velvet bed, now turned funeral pyre. The chaos and terror of the event are rendered by Delacroix with all the vigor and passion of a Baroque composition.

The explicit contrast between the voluptuous women and the brute strength of the king's executioners brings to mind *The Rape of the Daughters of Leucippus* by Rubens (see Fig. 17-16). Arms reach helplessly in all directions, and backs arch in hopeless defiance or pitiful submission before the passive Sardanapalus. Delacroix's unleashed energy and assaulting palette were strongly criticized by his contemporaries,

who felt that there was no excuse for such a blatant depiction of violence. But his use of bold colors and freely applied pigment, along with the observations on art and nature that he recorded in his journal, were an important influence on the young artists of the nineteenth century who were destined to transform artistic tradition.

Francisco Goya

Ironically, the man considered the greatest painter of the Neoclassical and Romantic periods belonged to neither artistic group. He never visited France, the center of the art world at the time, and he was virtually unknown to painters of the late eighteenth and early nineteenth centuries. Yet his paintings and prints foreshadowed the art of the nineteenth-century Impressionists. Francisco Goya (1746–1828) was born in Spain and, except for an academic excursion to Rome, spent his entire life there. He enjoyed a great reputation in his native country and

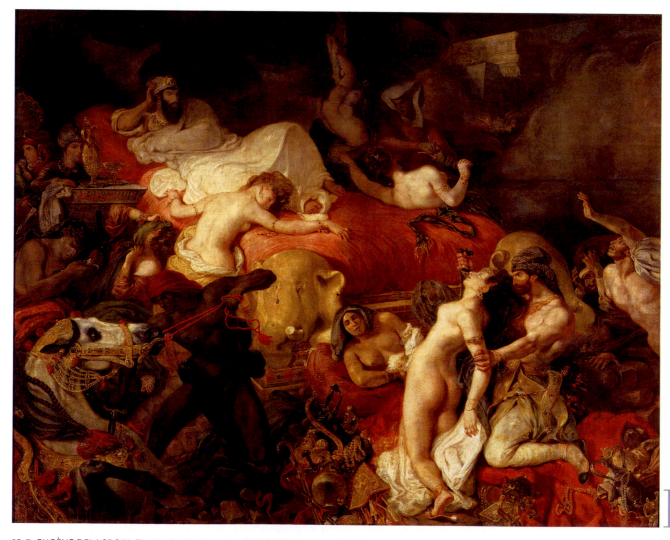

1 ft.

19-5 EUGÈNE DELACROIX. *The Death of Sardanapalus* (1826). Oil on canvas. 12'11½" × 16'3". Louvre, Paris, France.

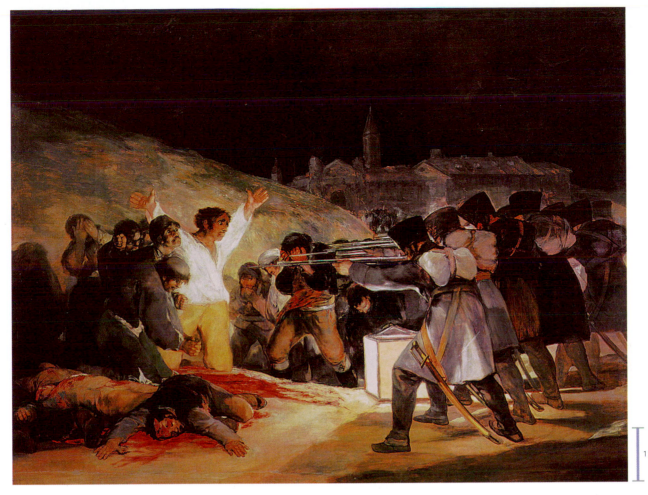

1 ft.

19-6 FRANCISCO GOYA. *The Third of May, 1808* (1814–1815). Oil on canvas. 8'9" × 13'4". Museo del Prado, Madrid, Spain.

was awarded many important commissions, including religious frescoes and portraits of Spanish royalty.

But Goya is best known for his works with political overtones, ranging from social satire to savage condemnation of the disasters of war. One of his most famous depictions of war is *The Third of May, 1808* (Fig. 19-6). The painting commemorates the massacre of the peasant-citizens of Madrid after the city fell to the French. Reflecting the procedures of Velásquez and Rembrandt—two Baroque masters whom Goya acknowledged as influential in the development of his style—Goya focuses the viewer's attention on a single moment in the violent episode. A Spaniard thrusts his arms upward in surrender to the bayonets of the faceless enemy. The brusqueness of the application of pigment corresponds to the harshness of the subject. The dutiful and regimented procedure of the executioners, dressed in long coats, contrasts visually and psychologically with the expressions of horror, fear, and helplessness on the faces of the ragtag peasants. The emotion is heightened by the use of acerbic tones and by a strong chiaroscuro that illuminates the pitiful victims while relegating all other details to darkness.

Goya devoted much of his life to the graphic representation of man's inhumanity to man. Toward the end of his life, he was afflicted with deafness and plagued with bitterness and depression over the atrocities he had witnessed. These feelings were manifested in macabre paintings and lithographs, which presaged the style of the great painters of the nineteenth century.

The Academy

Ingres's paintings spoke of a calm, though exotic, Classicism. Delacroix retrieved the dynamism of the Baroque. Goya swathed his canvases with the spirit of revolution. Ironically, the style of painting that had the least impact on the development of modern art was the most popular type of painting in its day. This was **Academic art**, so called because its style and subject matter were derived from conventions established by the Academie Royale de Peinture et de Sculpture in Paris. Established in 1648, the Academy had maintained a firm grip on artistic production for more than two centuries. Many artists steeped in this tradition were followers

INGRES'S *GRANDE ODALISQUE* AND SLEIGH'S *PHILIP GOLUB RECLINING*

COMPARE-AND-CONTRAST EXERCISES are often used to stimulate a student's powers of visual recognition and discrimination, to test the student's ability to characterize and categorize, and to force the student to think critically about the content and context of the work. If put together just right, they ought also to act as a springboard for discussion of issues that push beyond the discipline of art.

You can write paragraphs on the stylistic differences alone between the *Grande Odalisque* by Jean-Auguste-Dominique Ingres (Fig. 19-7) and Sylvia Sleigh's painting of *Philip Golub Reclining* (Fig. 19-8). Yet nineteenth-century art historian and feminist scholar Linda Nochlin has suggested that such paintings speak volumes about contemporary ideology and gender discourse:

> the ways in which representations of women in art are founded upon and serve to reproduce indisputably accepted assumptions held by society in general, artists in particular, and some artists more than others about men's power over, superiority to, difference from, and necessary control of women, assumptions which are manifested in the visual structures as well as the thematic choices of the pictures in question.

Among several that Nochlin lists are assumptions about women's weakness and passivity and sexual availability for men's needs.

The two works in this feature speak to the tradition of the reclining nude in Western art. In another Compare + Contrast feature in this chapter, you can see some other examples of this tradition and are asked for whose "gaze" you think they were intended. The concept of the "male gaze" has been central to feminist theory for the past decade. In a landmark article written in 1973, the filmmaker Laura Mulvey explained the roles of the viewer and the viewed in art, literature, and film this way: Men are in the position of looking, and women are "passive, powerless objects of their controlling gaze."

In *Grande Odalisque*, Ingres puts the viewer in the position of looking; his reclining female nude is the object of the male painter's scrutiny and our gaze. Sleigh reversed the power relationship in her painting. The artist is seen in the background, in mirror reflection, painting the nude torso of Philip Golub from the rear. Does the work raise questions such as "Is this also what women really want to paint?" or "Is this what women want to gaze upon?" Or do you think the purpose of this painting is to call our attention to a tradition in the arts of perpetuating ideological gender attitudes? ●

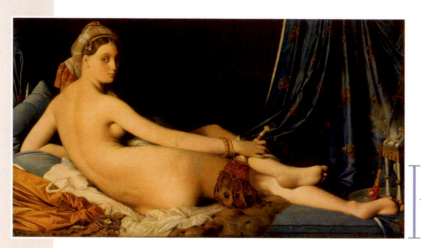

19-7 JEAN-AUGUSTE-DOMINIQUE INGRES. *Grande Odalisque* (1814). Oil on canvas. 35¼" × 63¾". Louvre, Paris, France.

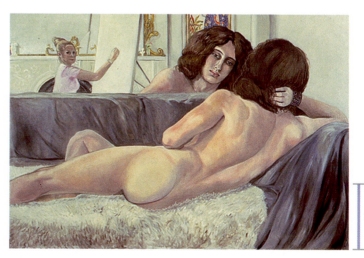

19-8 SYLVIA SLEIGH. *Philip Golub Reclining* (1971). Oil on canvas. 42" × 60".

rather than innovators, and the quality of their production left something to be desired. Some, however, like David and Ingres, worked within the confines of a style acceptable to the Academy but rose above the generally rampant mediocrity.

ADOLPHE WILLIAM BOUGUEREAU One of the more popular and accomplished Academic painters was Adolphe William Bouguereau (1825–1905). Included among his oeuvre are religious and historical paintings in a grand Classical manner, although he is most famous for his meticulously painted nudes and mythological subjects. *Nymphs and Satyr*

(Fig. 19-9) is nearly photographic in its refined technique and attention to detail. Four sprightly and sensuous wood nymphs corral a hesitant satyr and tug him into the water. Their innocent playfulness would have appealed to the Frenchman on the street, although the saccharine character of the subject matter and the extreme light-handedness with which the work was painted served only as a model against which the new wave of painters rebelled.

REALISM

The "modern" painters of the nineteenth century objected to Academic art on two levels: The subject matter did not represent life as it really was, and the manner in which the subjects were rendered did not reflect reality as it was observed by the naked eye.

The modern artists chose to depict subjects that were evident in everyday life. The way in which they rendered these subjects also differed from that of Academic painters. They attempted to render on canvas objects as they saw them (**optically**) rather than as they knew them to be (**conceptually**). In addition, they respected the reality of the medium they worked with. Instead of using pigment merely as a tool to provide an illusion of three-dimensional reality, they emphasized the two-dimensionality of the canvas and asserted the painting process itself. The physical properties of the pigments were highlighted. Artists who took these ideas to heart were known as the Realists. They include Honoré Daumier and two painters whose work stands on the threshold of the Impressionist movement: Gustave Courbet and Edouard Manet.

Honoré Daumier

Of all of the modern artists of the mid-nineteenth century, Honoré Daumier (1808–1879) was perhaps the most concerned with bringing to light the very real subject of the plight of the masses. Daumier worked as a caricaturist for Parisian journals, and he used his cartoons to convey his disgust with the monarchy and contemporary bourgeois society. His public ridicule of King Louis Philippe landed him in prison for six months.

Daumier is known primarily for his lithographs, which number some 4,000, although he was also an important painter. He brought to his works on canvas the technique and style of a caricaturist. Together, they make for a powerful rendition of his

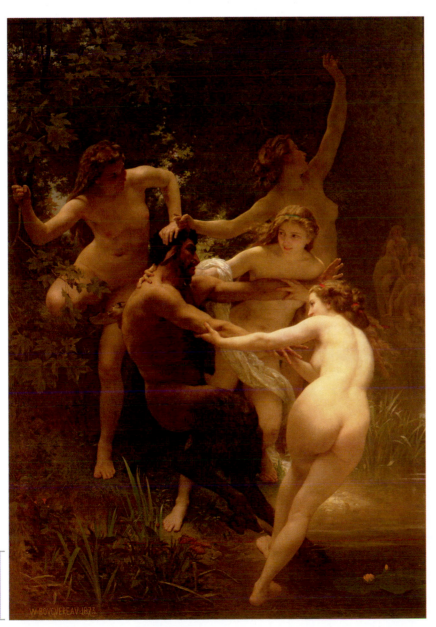

19-9 ADOLPHE WILLIAM BOUGUEREAU. *Nymphs and Satyr* (1873). Oil on canvas. 102⅜" × 70⅞". Sterling and Francine Clark Art Institute, Williamstown, MA.

1 ft.

realistic subjects. One of Daumier's most famous compositions is *The Third-Class Carriage* (Fig. **19-10**), an illustration of a crowded third-class compartment of a French train. His caricaturist style is evident in the flowing dark outlines and exaggerated features and gestures, but it also underscores the artist's concern for the working class by advertising their ill fortune. The peasants are crowded into the car, their clothing poor and rumpled, their faces wide and expressionless. They contrast markedly with bourgeois commuters, whose felt top hats tower above the kerchiefed heads. It is a candid-camera depiction of these people. Wrapped up in their own thoughts and disappointments, they live their quite ordinary lives from day to day, without significance and without notice.

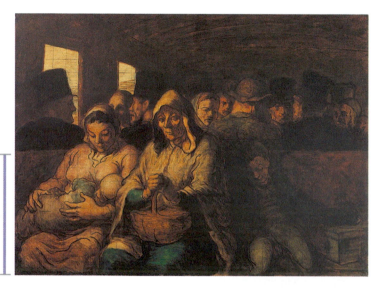

19-10 HONORÉ DAUMIER. *The Third-Class Carriage* (c. 1862). Oil on canvas. 25¾" × 35½". The Metropolitan Museum of Art, NY.

1 ft.

Gustave Courbet

The term *realist*, when it applies to art, is synonymous with Gustave Courbet (1819–1877). Considered to be the father of the Realist movement, Courbet used the term *realism* to describe his own work and even issued a manifesto on the subject. As was the case with many artists who broke the mold of the Academic style, Courbet's painting was shunned and decried by contemporary critics, but Courbet proceeded undaunted. After his paintings were rejected by the jurors of the 1855 Salon, he set up his own pavilion and exhibited some 40 of his own paintings. Such antics, as well as his commitment to realistic subjects and vigorous application of pigment, served as a strong model for the younger painters at midcentury who were also to rebel against the established Academic tradition in art.

Paintings such as *The Stone-Breakers* (Fig. **19-11**) were the objects of public derision. Courbet was moved to paint the work after seeing an old man and a young boy breaking stones on a roadside. So common a subject was naturally criticized by contemporary critics, who favored mythological or idealistic subjects. But Courbet, who was quoted as saying that he couldn't paint an angel because he had never seen one, continued in this vein despite the art world's rejection. It was not only the artist's subject matter, however, that the critics found offensive. They also spurned his painting technique. Although his choice of colors was fairly traditional—muted tones of brown and ocher—their quick application with a palette knife resulted in a coarsely textured surface that could not have been further removed from the glossy finish of an Academic painting. Curiously, although Courbet believed that this type of painting was more realistic than that of the salons, in fact the reverse is closer to the truth.

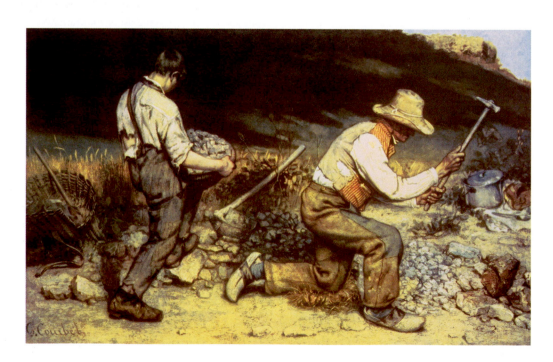

19-11 GUSTAVE COURBET. *The Stone-Breakers* (1849). Oil on canvas. 63" × 102". Formerly Staatliche Kunstsammlungen, Dresden (destroyed in World War II). Galerie Neue Meister, Dresden, Germany.

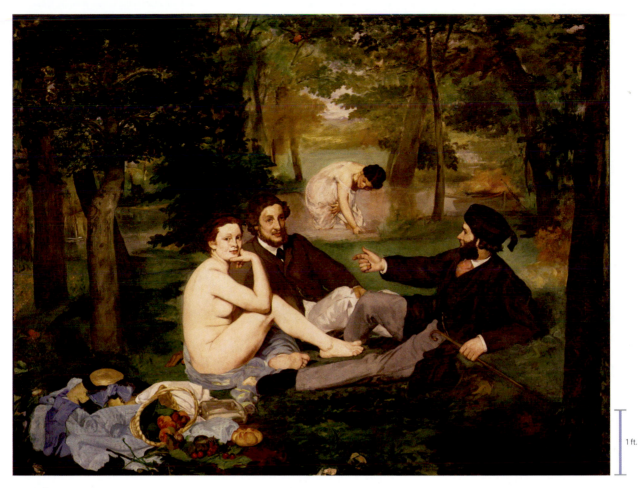

19-12 ÉDOUARD MANET. *Le Déjeuner sur l'Herbe* (*Luncheon on the Grass*) (1863). Oil on canvas. 7' × 8'1". Musée d'Orsay, Paris, France.

The Academic painter strove for what we would today consider to be an almost photographically exact representation of the figure, whereas Courbet attempted quickly to jot down his impressions of the scene in an often spontaneous flurry of strokes. (For this reason, Courbet can be said to have foreshadowed the Impressionist movement, which we discuss in the next section.) Despite Courbet's advocacy of hard-core realism, the observer of *The Stone-Breakers* is presented ultimately with the artist's subjective view of the world.

Édouard Manet

Courbet's painting may have laid the groundwork for Impressionism, but he was not to be a part of the new wave. His old age brought conservatism, and with it disapproval of the younger generation's painting techniques. One of the targets of Courbet's derision was Édouard Manet (1832–1883). According to some art historians, Manet is the artist most responsible for changing the course of the history of painting.

What was modern about Manet's painting was his technique. Instead of beginning with a dark underpainting and building up to bright highlights—a method used since the Renaissance—Manet began with a white surface and worked to build up dark tones. This approach lent a greater luminosity to the work, one that duplicated sunlight as closely as possible. Manet also did not model his figures with a traditional chiaroscuro. Instead, he applied his pigments flatly and broadly. With these techniques, he attempted to capture an impression of a fleeting moment, to duplicate on canvas what the eye would perceive within that collapsed time frame.

All too predictably, these innovations met with disapproval from critics and the public alike. Manet's subjects were found to be equally abrasive. One of his most shocking paintings, *Le Déjeuner sur l'Herbe* (*Luncheon on the Grass*) (Fig. **19-12**), stands as a pivotal work in the rise of the Impressionist movement. Manet's luncheon takes place in a lush woodland setting. Its guests are ordinary members of the French middle class. It is culled from a tradition of Venetian Renaissance pastoral scenes common to the masters Giorgione and Titian. The composition is rather traditional. The figural group forms a stable pyramidal structure that is set firmly in the middle ground of the canvas. In

TITIAN'S *VENUS OF URBINO,* MANET'S *OLYMPIA,* GAUGUIN'S *TE ARII VAHINE,* AND VALADON'S *THE BLUE ROOM*

"**WE NEVER ENCOUNTER** the body unmediated by the meanings that cultures give to it." Right out of the starting gate, can you challenge yourself to support or contest this statement with reference to the four works in this exercise? The words are Gayle Rubin's, and they can be found in her essay "Thinking Sex: Notes for a Radical Theory of the Politics of Sexuality." Which of these works, in your view, are about "thinking sex"? Which address the "politics of sexuality"?

Titian's reclining nude (Fig. **19-13**) was commissioned by the Duke of Urbino for his private quarters. There was a considerable market for erotic paintings in the sixteenth century. One point of view maintains that many of the "great nudes" of Western art were, in essence, created for the same purpose as the pinup. Yet there is also no doubt that this particular reclining nude has had an undisputed place in the canon of great art. And this much, at least, has been reaffirmed by the reinterpretations and revisions the work has inspired into contemporary times.

One of the first artists to use Titian's *Venus* as a point of departure for his own masterpiece was Édouard Manet. In his *Olympia* (Fig. **19-14**), Manet intentionally mimicked the Renaissance composition as a way of challenging the notion that modern art lacked credibility when brought face-to-face with the "old masters." In effect, Manet seemed to be saying, "You want a Venus? I'll give you a Venus." And just where do you find a Venus in nineteenth-century Paris? In the bordellos of the Parisian demimonde. What do these paintings have in common? Where

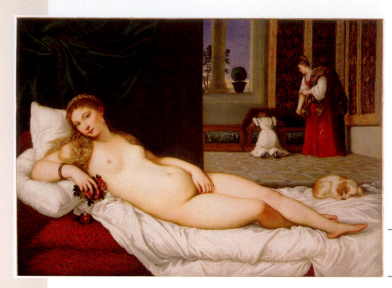

1 ft.

19-13 TITIAN. *Venus of Urbino* (1538). Oil on canvas. 65" × 47". Galleria degli Uffizi, Florence, Italy.

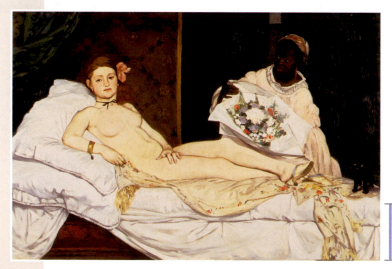

1 ft.

19-14 ÉDOUARD MANET. *Olympia* (1863–1865). Oil on canvas. 51⅜" × 74¾". Musée d'Orsay, Paris, France.

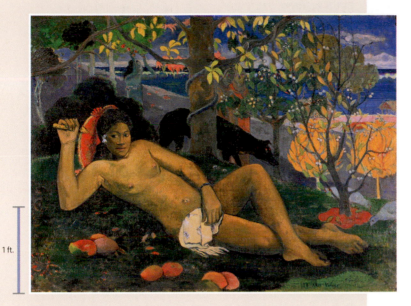

19-15 PAUL GAUGUIN. *Te Arii Vahine* (*The Noble Woman*) (1896). Oil on canvas. 38 3/16" × 51 3/16". Pushkin Museum, Moscow, Russia.

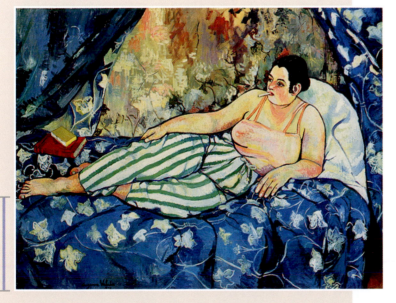

19-16 SUZANNE VALADON. *The Blue Room* (1923). Oil on canvas. 35 1/2" × 45 5/8". Musée National d'Art Moderne, Centre Georges Pompidou, Paris, France.

do they depart? What details does Titian use to create an air of innocence and vulnerability? What details does Manet use to do just the opposite?

Paul Gauguin, the nineteenth-century French painter who moved to Tahiti, was also inspired by the tradition of the Western reclining nude in the creation of *Te Arii Vahine* (*The Noble Woman*) (Fig. **19-15**). The artist certainly knew Manet's revision of the work; in fact, he had a photograph of *Olympia* tacked on the wall of his hut. How does this Tahitian Venus fit into the mix? All three of these works have a sense of self-display. In which do the women solicit our gaze? Refuse our gaze? How do the stylistic differences influence our interpretation of the women and our relationship to them? How is the flesh modeled in each work? What overall effects are provided by the different palettes? And the $64,000 question: Are these paintings intended for the "male gaze," "the female gaze," or both?

Suzanne Valadon would probably say that such an image is *not* one that appeals equally to men and women. More to the point, Valadon would argue that the painting of such subjects is not at all of interest to women artists. Perhaps this belief was the incentive behind her own revision of the reclining nude: *The Blue Room* (Fig. **19-16**). With this work, she seems to be informing the world that when women relax, they really *don't* look like the Venuses of Titian, or Manet, or Gauguin. Instead, they get into their loose-fitting clothes, curl up with a good book, and sometimes treat themselves to a bit of tobacco. ●

fact, the group is derived from an engraving by Marcantonio Raimondi after a painting by Raphael called *The Judgement of Paris*.

What was so alarming to the Parisian spectator, and remains so to this day, is that there is no explanation for the behavior of the picnickers. Why are the men clothed and the women undraped to varying degrees? Why are the men chatting between themselves, seemingly unaware of the women? The public was quite used to the painting of nudes, but they were not prepared to witness one of their fold—an ordinary citizen—displayed so shamefully on such a grand scale. The painting was further intolerable because the seated woman meets the viewer's stare, as if the viewer had intruded on their gathering in a voyeuristic fashion.

Viewers expecting another pastoral scene replete with nymphs and satyrs got, instead, portraits of Manet's model (Victorine Meurend), his brother, and a sculptor friend. In lieu of a highly polished Academic painting, they found a broadly brushed application of flat, barely modeled hues that sat squarely on the canvas with no regard for illusionism. With this shocking subject and unconventional technique, Modernism was on its way.

Manet submitted the work to the 1863 Salon, and it was categorically rejected. He and other artists whose works were rejected that year rebelled so vehemently that Napoleon III allowed them to exhibit their work in what was known as the *Salon des Réfusés*, or Salon of the Rejected Painters. It was

one of the most important gatherings of **avant-garde** painters in the century.

Although Manet was trying to deliver a message to the art world with his *Déjeuner*, it was not his wish to be ostracized. He was just as interested as the next painter in earning recognition and acceptance. Commissions went to artists whose style was sanctioned by the academics, and painting salon pictures was, after all, a livelihood. Fortunately, Manet had the private means by which he could continue painting in the manner he desired.

Manet was perhaps the most important influence on the French Impressionist painters, a group of artists who advocated the direct painting of optical impressions. *Déjeuner* began a decade of exploration of these new ideas that culminated in the first Impressionist exhibition of 1874. Although considered by his followers to be one of the Impressionists, Manet declined to exhibit with that avant-garde group. A quarter of a century later, only 17 years after his death, Manet's works were shown at the prestigious Louvre Museum.

Rosa Bonheur

Rosa Bonheur (1822–1899) was one of the most successful artists working in the second half of the nineteenth century. In terms of style, she is most closely related to Courbet and the other Realist painters, although for the most part she shunned human subjects in favor of animals—domesticated and wild. She was an artist who insisted on getting close to her subject;

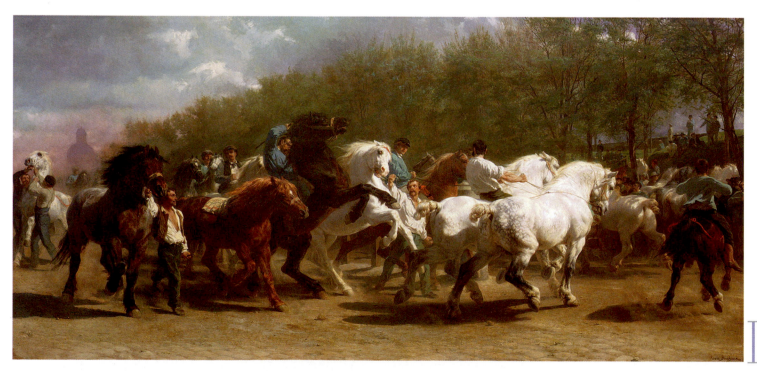

19-17 ROSA BONHEUR. *The Horse Fair* (1853). Oil on canvas. 96¼" × 199½". The Metropolitan Museum of Art, NY.

she reveled in working "in the trenches." Bonheur was seen in men's clothing and hip boots, plodding through the bloody floors of slaughterhouses in her struggle to understand the anatomy of her subjects.

The Horse Fair (Fig. 19-17) is a panoramic scene of extraordinary power, inspired by the Parthenon's horsemen frieze. The dimensions—more than twice as long as it is high—compel the viewer to perceive the work as just a small portion of a vast scene in which continuation of action beyond the left and right borders of the canvas is implied. The dramatic contrasts of light and dark underscore the struggle between man and beast, while the painterly brushwork heightens the emotional energy in the painting. *The Horse Fair* was an extremely popular work, which was bought widely in engraved reproductions, cementing Bonheur's fame and popularity.

IMPRESSIONISM

While Bonheur won quick acceptance by the Academy, a group of younger artists were banding together against the French art establishment. Suffering from lack of recognition and vicious criticism, many of them lived in abject poverty for lack of commissions. Yet they stand today as some of the most significant, and certainly among the most popular, artists in the history of art. They were called the *Impressionists*. The very name of their movement was coined by a hostile critic and intended to malign their work. The word *impressionism* suggests a lack of realism, and realistic representation was the standard of the day.

The Impressionist artists had common philosophies about painting, although their styles differed widely. They all reacted against the constraints of the Academic style and subject matter. They advocated painting out-of-doors and chose to render subjects found in nature.

They studied the dramatic effects of atmosphere and light on people and objects and, through a varied palette, attempted to duplicate these effects on canvas.

Through intensive investigation, they arrived at awareness of certain visual phenomena. When bathed in sunlight, objects are optically reduced to facets of pure color. The actual color—or local color—of these objects is altered by different lighting effects. Solids tend to dissolve into color fields. Shadows are not black or gray but a combination of colors.

Technical discoveries accompanied these revelations. The Impressionists duplicated the glimmering effect of light bouncing off the surface of an object by applying their pigments in short, choppy strokes. They juxtaposed complementary colors such as red and green to reproduce the optical vibrations perceived when one is looking at an object in full sunlight. Toward this end, they also juxtaposed primary colors such as red and yellow to produce, in the eye of the spectator, the secondary color orange. We shall discuss the work of the Impressionists Claude Monet, Pierre-Auguste Renoir, Berthe Morisot, and Edgar Degas.

Claude Monet

The most fervent follower of Impressionist techniques was the painter Claude Monet (1840–1926). His canvas *Impression: Sunrise* (Fig. 19-18) inspired the epithet *impressionist* when it

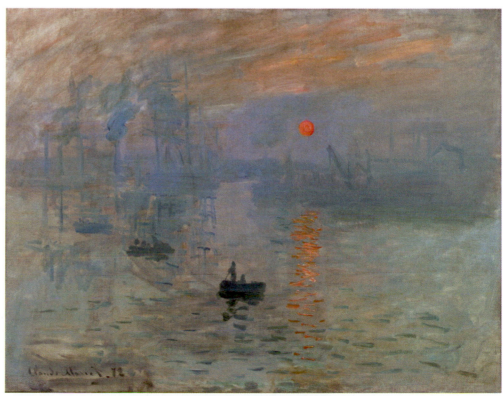

19-18 CLAUDE MONET. *Impression: Sunrise* (1872). Oil on canvas. 19½" × 25½". Musée Marmottan, Paris, France.

1 in.

was exhibited at the first Impressionist exhibition in 1874. Fishing vessels sail from the port of Le Havre toward the morning sun, which rises in a foggy sky to cast its copper beams on the choppy, pale blue water. The warm blanket of the atmosphere envelops the figures, their significance having paled in the wake of nature's beauty.

The dissolution of surfaces and the separation of light into its spectral components remain central to Monet's art. They are dramatically evident in a series of canvases depicting *Rouen Cathedral* (Fig. **19-19**) from a variety of angles, during different seasons and times of day. The harsh stone facade of the cathedral dissolves in a bath of sunlight, its finer details obscured by the bevy of brushstrokes crowding the surface. Dark shadows have been transformed into patches of bright blue and splashes of yellow and red. With these delicate touches, Monet has recorded for us the feeling of a single moment in time. He offers us his impressions as eyewitness to a set of circumstances that will never be duplicated.

Pierre-Auguste Renoir

Most Impressionists counted among their subject matter landscape scenes or members of the middle class enjoying leisure-time activities. Of all the Impressionists, however, Pierre-Auguste Renoir (1841–1919) was perhaps the most significant figure painter. Like his peers, Renoir was interested primarily in the effect of light as it played across the surface of objects. He illustrated his preoccupation in one of the most

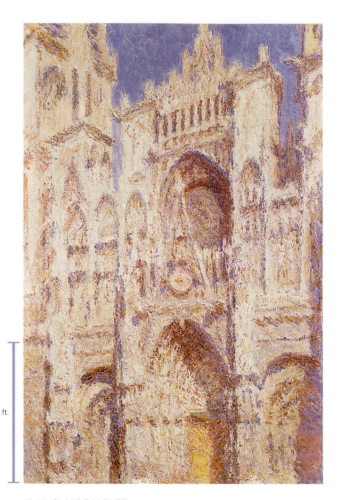

19-19 CLAUDE MONET. *Rouen Cathedral* (1894). Oil on canvas. 39¼" × 25⅞". The Metropolitan Museum of Art, NY.

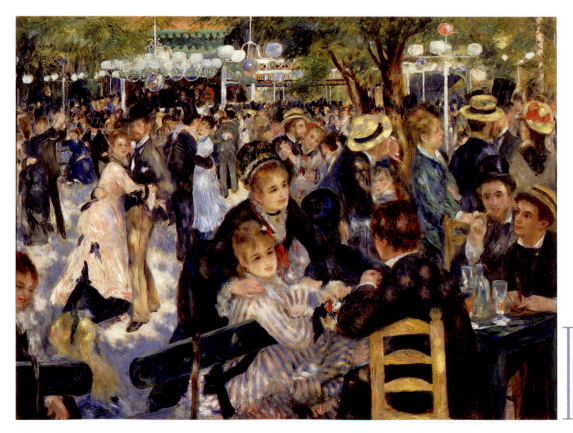

19-20 PIERRE-AUGUSTE RENOIR. *Le Moulin de la Galette* (1876). Oil on canvas. 51½" × 69". Musée d'Orsay, Paris, France.

wonderful paintings of the Impressionist period, *Le Moulin de la Galette* (Fig. **19-20**). With characteristic feathery strokes, Renoir communicated all of the charm and gaiety of an afternoon dance. Men and women caress and converse in frocks that are dappled with sunlight filtering through the trees. All of the spirit of the event is as fresh as if it were yesterday. From the billowing skirts and ruffled dresses to the rakish derbies, top hats, and skimmers, Renoir painted all of the details that imprint such a scene on the mind forever.

Berthe Morisot

Like other Impressionists, Berthe Morisot (1841–1895) exhibited at the Salon early in her career, but she surrendered the safe path as an expression of her allegiance to the new. Morisot was a granddaughter of the eighteenth-century painter Jean-Honoré Fragonard (see Chapter 17) and the sister-in-law of Edouard Manet. Manet painted her quite often. In fact, Morisot is the seated figure in his painting *The Balcony*.

In Morisot's *Young Girl by the Window* (Fig. **19-21**), surfaces dissolve into an array of loose brushstrokes, applied, it would seem, at a frantic pace. The vigor of these strokes contrasts markedly with the tranquility of the woman's face. The head is strongly modeled, and several structural lines, such as the back of the chair, the contour of her right arm, the blue parasol astride her lap, and the vertical edge of drapery to the right, anchor the figure in space. Yet in this, as in most of Morisot's works, we are most impressed by her ingenious ability to suggest complete forms through a few well-placed strokes of pigment.

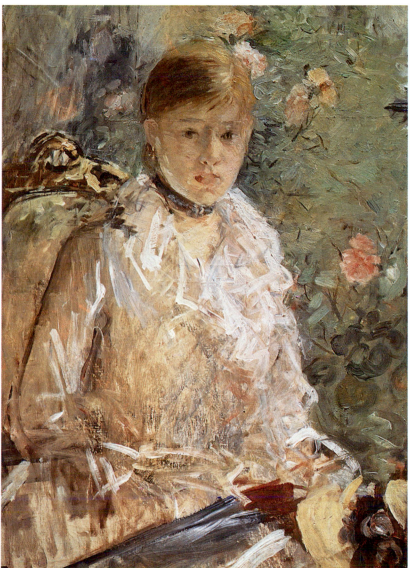

1 in.

19-21 BERTHE MORISOT. *Young Girl by the Window* (1878). Oil on canvas. 29¹⁵⁄₁₆" × 24". Musée Fabre, Montpellier, France.

Edgar Degas

We can see the vastness of the aegis of Impressionism when we look at the work of Edgar Degas (1834–1917), whose approach to painting differed considerably from that of his peers. Degas, like Morisot, had exhibited at the Salon for many years before joining the movement. He was a superb draftsman who studied under Ingres. While in Italy, he copied the Renaissance masters. He was also intrigued by Japanese prints and the new art of photography.

The Impressionists, beginning with Manet, were strongly influenced by Japanese woodcuts, which were becoming readily available in Europe, and oriental motifs appeared widely in their canvases. They also adopted certain techniques of spatial organization found in Japanese prints, including the use of line to direct the viewer's eye to different sections of the work and to divide areas of the essentially flattened space. They found that the patterning and flat forms of

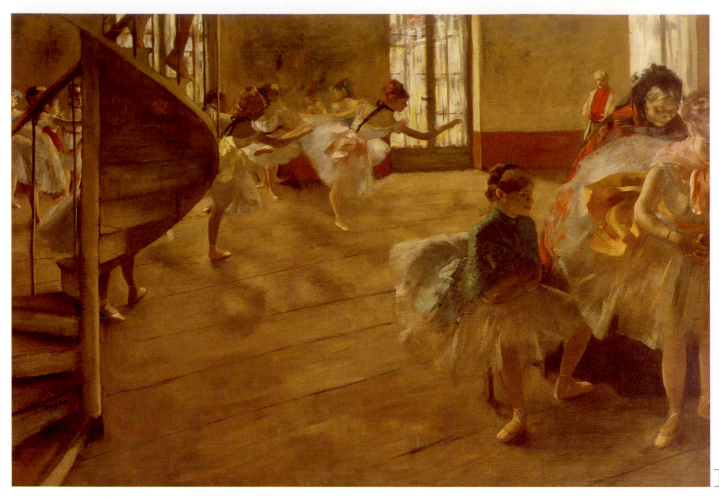

1 in.

19-22 EDGAR DEGAS. *The Rehearsal (Adagio)* (1877). Oil on canvas. 26" × 39⅜". The Burrell Collection, Culture and Sport Glasgow (Museums), Scotland.

Oriental woodcuts complemented similar concerns in their own painting. Throughout the Impressionist period, and even more so in the Postimpressionist period, the influence of Japanese artists remained strong.

Degas was also strongly influenced by the developing art of photography, and the camera's exclusive visual field served as a model for the way in which he framed his own paintings. *The Rehearsal (Adagio)* (Fig. **19-22**) contains elements both of photographs and of Japanese prints. Degas draws us into the composition with an unusual and vast off-center space that curves around from the viewer's space to the background of the canvas. The diagonals of the floorboards carry our eyes briskly from outside the canvas to the points at which the groups of dancers congregate. The imagery is placed at eye level so that we feel we are part of the scene. This feeling is enhanced by the fact that our "seats" at the rehearsal are less than adequate; a spiral staircase to the left blocks our view of the ballerinas. In characteristic camera fashion, the borders of the canvas slice off the forms and figures in a seemingly

arbitrary manner. Although it appears as if Degas has failed to frame his subject correctly or has accidentally cut off the more important parts of the scene, he carefully planned the placement of his imagery. These techniques are what render his asymmetrical compositions so dynamic and, in the spirit of Impressionism, so immediate.

POSTIMPRESSIONISM

The Impressionists were united in their rejection of many of the styles and subjects of the art that preceded them. These included Academic painting, the emotionalism of Romanticism, and even the depressing subject matter of some of the Realist artists. During the latter years of the nineteenth century, a group of artists who came to be called **Postimpressionists** were also united in their rebellion against that which came before them—in this case, Impressionism. The Postimpressionists were drawn together by their rebellion against what they considered an excessive concern for fleeting impressions and a disregard for traditional compositional elements.

Although they were united in their rejection of Impressionism, their individual styles differed considerably. Postimpressionists fell into two groups that in some ways parallel the stylistic polarities of the Baroque period as well as the Neoclassical–Romantic period. On the one hand, the work of Georges Seurat and Paul Cézanne had at its core a more systematic approach to compositional structure, brushwork, and color. On the other hand, the lavishly brushed canvases of Vincent van Gogh and Paul Gauguin coordinated line and color with symbolism and emotion.

Georges Seurat

At first glance, the paintings by Georges Seurat (1859–1891), such as *A Sunday Afternoon on the Island of La Grande Jatte* (Fig. **19-23**), have the feeling of Impressionism "tidied up."

The small brushstrokes are there, as are the juxtapositions of complementary colors. The subject matter is entirely acceptable within the framework of Impressionism. However, the spontaneity of direct painting found in Impressionism is relinquished in favor of a more tightly controlled, "scientific" approach to painting.

Seurat's technique has also been called **pointillism**, after his application of pigment in small dabs, or points, of pure color. Upon close inspection, the painting appears to be a collection of dots of vibrant hues—complementary colors abutting one another, primary colors placed side by side. These hues intensify or blend to form yet another color in the eye of the viewer who beholds the canvas from a distance.

Seurat's meticulous color application was derived from the color theories and studies of color contrasts by the scientists Hermann von Helmholtz and Michel-Eugène Chevreul. He used these theories to restore a more intellectual approach to painting that countered nearly two decades of works that focused wholly on optical effects.

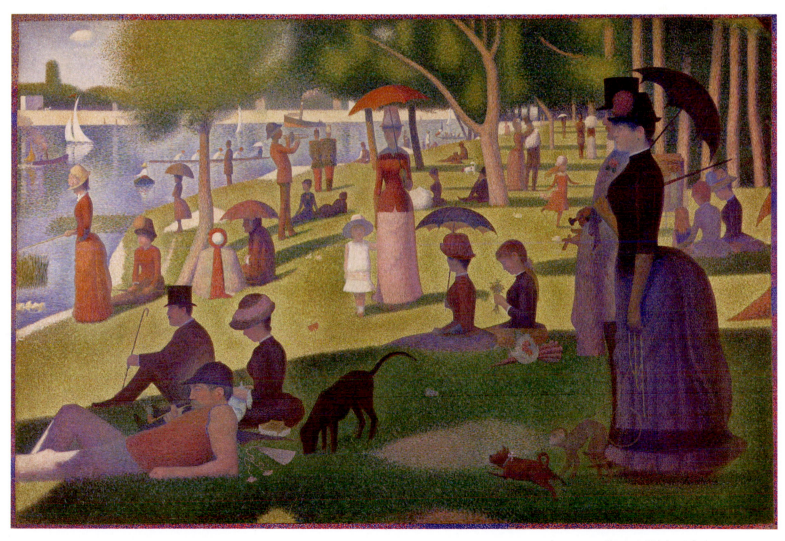

19-23 GEORGES SEURAT. *A Sunday Afternoon on the Island of La Grande Jatte* (1884–1886). Oil on canvas. 81" × 120⅜". The Art Institute of Chicago, Chicago, IL.

The same subject seen from a different angle gives a subject for study of the highest interest
and so varied that I think I could be occupied for months without changing my place,
simply bending a little more to the right or left.
—Paul Cézanne

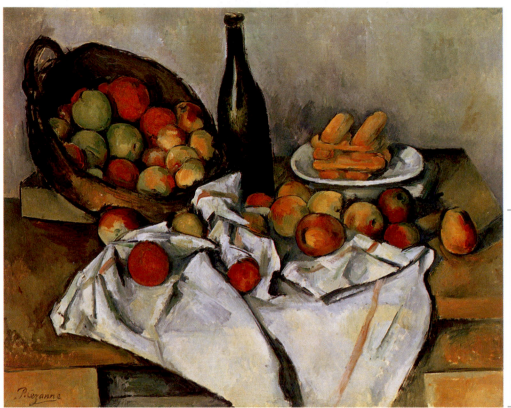

19-24 PAUL CÉZANNE. *Still Life with Basket of Apples* (c. 1895). Oil on canvas. 2'⅜" × 2'7". The Art Institute of Chicago, Chicago, IL.

1 ft.

Paul Cézanne

From the time of Manet, there was a movement away from a realistic representation of subjects toward one that was abstracted. Early methods of abstraction assumed different forms. Manet used a flatly painted form, Monet a disintegrating light, and Seurat a tightly painted and highly patterned composition. Paul Cézanne (1839–1906), a Postimpressionist who shared with Seurat an intellectual approach to painting, is credited with having led the revolution of abstraction in modern art from those first steps.

Cézanne's method for accomplishing this radical departure from tradition did not disregard the old masters. Although he allied himself originally with the Impressionists and accepted their palette and subject matter, he drew from old masters in the Louvre and desired somehow to reconcile their lessons with the thrust of Modernism, saying, "I want to make of Impressionism something solid and lasting like the art in the museums." Cézanne's innovations include a structural use of color and brushwork that appeals to the intellect, and a solidity of composition enhanced by a fluid application of pigment that delights the senses.

Cézanne's most significant stride toward Modernism, however, was a drastic collapsing of space, seen in works such as *Still Life with Basket of Apples* (Fig. **19-24**). All of the imagery is forced to the picture plane. The tabletop is tilted toward us, and we simultaneously view the basket, plate, and wine bottle from front and top angles. Cézanne did not paint the still-life arrangement from one vantage point either. He moved around his subject, painting not only the objects but also the relationship among them. He focused on solids as well as on the void spaces between two objects. If you run your finger along the tabletop in the background of the painting, you will see that it is not possible to trace a continuous line. This discontinuity follows from Cézanne's movement around his subject. Despite this spatial inconsistency, the overall feeling of the composition is one of completeness.

Cézanne's painting technique is also innovative. The sensuously rumpled fabric and lusciously round fruits are constructed of small patches of pigment crowded within dark outlines. The apples look as if they would roll off the table, were it not for the supportive facets of the tablecloth.

Cézanne can be seen as advancing the flatness of planar recession begun by David more than a century earlier. Cézanne asserted the flatness of the two-dimensional canvas by eliminating the distinction between foreground and background, and at times merging the two. This was perhaps his most significant contribution to future modern movements.

Vincent van Gogh

One of the most tragic and best-known figures in the history of art is the Dutch Postimpressionist Vincent van Gogh (1853–1890). We associate him with bizarre and painful acts, such as the mutilation of his ear and his suicide. With these events, as well as his tortured, eccentric painting, he typifies the impression of the mad, artistic talent. Van Gogh also epitomizes the cliché of the artist who achieves recognition only after death: just one of his paintings was sold during his lifetime.

"Vincent," as he signed his paintings, decided to become an artist only 10 years before his death. His most beloved canvases were created during his last 29 months. He began his career painting in the dark manner of the Dutch Baroque, only to adopt the Impressionist palette and brushstroke after he settled in Paris with his brother, Theo. Feeling that he was a constant burden on his brother, he left Paris for Arles, where he began to paint his most significant Postimpressionist works. Both his life and his compositions from this period were tortured, as Vincent suffered from what may have been bouts of epilepsy and mental illness. He was eventually hospitalized in an asylum at Saint-Rémy, where he painted the famous *Starry Night* (Fig. **19-25**).

In *Starry Night*, an ordinary painted record of a sleepy valley town is transformed into a cosmic display of swirling fireballs that assault the blackened sky and command the hills and cypresses to undulate to their sweeping rhythms. Vincent's palette is laden with vibrant yellows, blues, and greens. His brushstroke is at once restrained and dynamic. His characteristic long, thin strokes define the forms but also create the emotionalism in the work. He presents his subject not as we see it, but as he would like us to experience it. His is a feverish application of paint, an ecstatic kind of drawing, reflecting at the same time his joys, hopes, anxieties, and despair. Vincent wrote in a letter to his brother Theo, "I paint as a means to make life bearable. . . . Really we can speak only through our paintings."

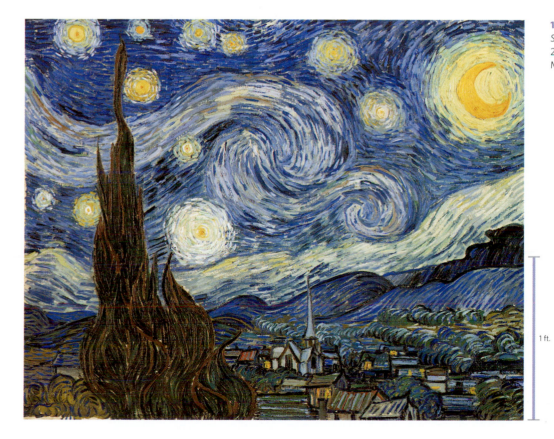

19-25 VINCENT VAN GOGH. *Starry Night* (1889). Oil on canvas. 29" × 36¼". The Museum of Modern Art, NY.

1 ft.

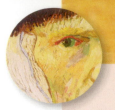

TWO DAYS BEFORE CHRISTMAS 1888, 35-year-old Vincent van Gogh cut off the lower half of his left ear (Fig. 19-26). He took the ear to a brothel, asked for a prostitute by the name of Rachel, and handed it to her. "Keep this object carefully," he said. How do we account for this extraordinary event? Over the years, many explanations have been advanced. Many of them are psychoanalytic in nature.* That is, they argue that van Gogh fell prey to unconscious primitive impulses.

As you consider the following suggestions, keep in mind that van Gogh's bizarre act occurred many years ago, and that we have no way today to determine which, if any, of them is accurate. Perhaps one of them cuts to the core of van Gogh's urgent needs; perhaps several of them contain a kernel of truth. But it could also be that all of them fly far from the mark. In any event, here are the explanations suggested in the *Journal of Personality and Social Psychology*:†

- Van Gogh was frustrated by his brother's engagement and his failure to establish a close relationship with Gauguin. The aggressive impulses stemming from the frustrations were turned inward and expressed in self-mutilation.
- Van Gogh was punishing himself for experiencing homosexual impulses toward Gauguin.
- Van Gogh identified with his father, toward whom he felt resentment and hatred, and cutting off his own ear was a symbolic punishment of his father.
- Van Gogh was influenced by the practice of awarding the bull's ear to the matador after a bullfight. In effect, he was presenting such an "award" to the lady of his choice.
- Van Gogh was influenced by newspaper accounts of Jack the Ripper, who mutilated prostitutes. Van Gogh was imitating the "ripper," but his self-hatred led him to mutilate himself rather than others.
- Van Gogh was seeking his brother's attention.
- Van Gogh was seeking to earn the sympathy of substitute parents. (The mother figure would have been a model he had recently painted rocking a cradle.)

- Van Gogh was expressing his sympathy for prostitutes, with whom he identified as social outcasts.
- Van Gogh was symbolically emasculating himself so that his mother would not perceive him as an unlikable "rough" boy. (Unconsciously, the prostitute was a substitute for his mother.)
- Van Gogh was troubled by auditory hallucinations (hearing things that were not there) as a result of his mental state. He cut off his ear to put an end to disturbing sounds.
- In his troubled mental state, Van Gogh may have been acting out a biblical scene he had been trying to paint. According to the New Testament, Simon Peter cut off the ear of the servant Malchus to protect Christ.
- Van Gogh was acting out the Crucifixion of Jesus, with himself as victim. ●

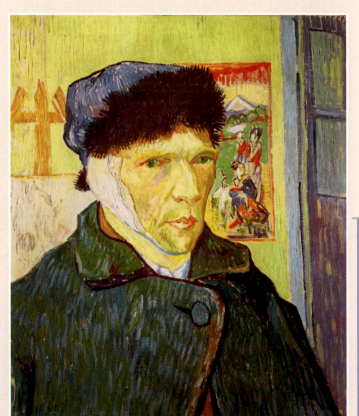

19-26 VINCENT VAN GOGH. *Self-Portrait with Bandaged Ear* (1889–1890). Oil on canvas. 23⅝" × 19¼". The Courtauld Gallery, London, England.

---

* William McKinley Runyan, *Journal of Personality and Social Psychology* (June 1981).
† Ibid.

Art is either plagiarism or revolution.
—Paul Gauguin

Paul Gauguin

Paul Gauguin (1848–1903) shared with van Gogh the desire to express his emotions on canvas. But whereas the Dutchman's brushstroke was the primary means to that end, Gauguin relied on broad areas of intense color to transpose his innermost feelings to canvas.

Gauguin, a stockbroker by profession, began his artistic career as a weekend painter. At age 35, he devoted himself full-time to his art, leaving his wife and five children to do so. Gauguin identified early with the Impressionists, adopting their techniques and participating in their exhibitions. But Gauguin was a restless soul. Soon he decided to leave France for Panama and Martinique, primitive places where he hoped to purge the civilization from his art and life. The years until his death were spent between France and the South Seas, where he finally died of syphilis five years after a failed attempt to take his own life.

Gauguin developed a theory of art called **Synthetism**, in which he advocated the use of broad areas of unnaturalistic color and primitive or symbolic subject matter. His *Vision after the Sermon* (*Jacob Wrestling with the Angel*) (Fig. **19-27**), one of the first canvases to illustrate his theory, combines reality with symbolism. After hearing a sermon on the subject, a group of Breton women believed they had a vision of Jacob, ancestor of the Hebrews, wrestling with an angel. In a daring composition that cancels pictorial depth by thrusting all elements to the front of the canvas, Gauguin presented all details of the event, actual and symbolic. An animal in the upper left portion of the canvas walks near a tree that interrupts a bright vermilion field with a slashing diagonal. The Bible tells us that Jacob had wrestled with an angel on the banks of the Jabbok River in Jordan. Caught, then, in a moment of religious fervor, the Breton women may have imagined the animal's four legs to have been those of the wrestling couple, and the tree trunk might have been visually analogous to the river.

Gauguin's contribution to the development of modern art lay largely in his use of color. Writing on the subject, he said, "How does that tree look to you? Green? All right, then use green, the greenest on your palette. And that shadow, a little bluish? Don't be afraid. Paint it as blue as you can." He intensified the colors he observed in nature to the point where they became unnatural. He exaggerated his lines and patterns until they became abstract. He learned these lessons from the primitive surroundings of which he was so fond. They were his legacy to art.

Henri de Toulouse-Lautrec

Henri de Toulouse-Lautrec (1864–1901), along with van Gogh, is one of the best-known nineteenth-century European artists—both for his art and for the troubled aspects of his personal life. Born into a noble French family, Toulouse-Lautrec broke his legs during adolescence, and they failed to develop correctly. This deformity resulted in alienation from his family. He turned to painting and took refuge in the demimonde of Paris, at one point taking up residence in a brothel. In this world of social outcasts, Toulouse-Lautrec, the dwarflike scion of a noble family, apparently felt at home.

He used his talents to portray life as it was in this cavalcade of cabarets, theaters, cafés, and bordellos—sort of

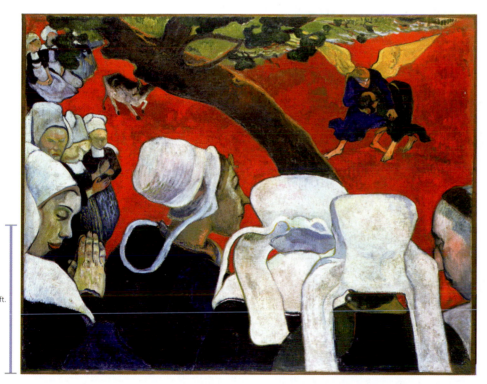

19-27 PAUL GAUGUIN. *Vision after the Sermon* (*Jacob Wrestling with the Angel*) (1888). Oil on canvas. 28¾" × 36½". National Gallery of Scotland, Edinburgh, Scotland.

seamy, but also vibrant and entertaining, and populated by "real" people. He made numerous posters to advertise cabaret acts and numerous paintings of his world of night and artificial light. In *At the Moulin Rouge* (Fig. **19-28**), we find something of the Japanese-inspired oblique perspective we found earlier in his poster work. The extension of the picture to include the balustrade on the bottom and the heavily powdered entertainer on the right is reminiscent of those "poorly cropped snapshots" of Degas, who had influenced Toulouse-Lautrec. The fabric of the entertainer's dress is constructed of fluid Impressionistic brushstrokes, as are the contents of the bottles, the lamps in the background, and the amorphous overall backdrop—lost suddenly in the unlit recesses of the Moulin Rouge. But the strong outlining, as in the entertainer's face, marks the work of a Postimpressionist.

The artist's palette is limited and muted, except for a few accents, as found in the hair of the woman in the center of the composition and the bright mouth of the entertainer. The entertainer's face is harshly sculpted by artificial light from beneath, rendering the shadows a grotesque but not ugly green. The green and red mouth clash, of course, as green and red are complementary colors, giving further intensity to the entertainer's masklike visage. But despite her powdered harshness, the entertainer remains human—certainly as human as her audience. Toulouse-Lautrec was accepting of all his creatures, just as he hoped that they would be accepting of him. The artist is portrayed within this work as well, his bearded profile facing left, toward the upper part of the composition, just left of center—a part of things, but not at the heart of things, certainly out of the glare of the spotlight. There, so to speak, the artist remained for many of his brief 37 years.

EXPRESSIONISM

A polarity existed in **Postimpressionism** that was like the polarity of the Neoclassical–Romantic period. On the one hand were artists who sought a more scientific or intellectual approach to painting. On the other were artists whose works were more emotional, expressive, and laden with symbolism. The latter trend was exemplified by van Gogh and particularly Gauguin. These artists used color and line to express their inner feelings. In their vibrant palettes and bravura brushwork, van Gogh and Gauguin foreshadowed Expressionism.

Edvard Munch

The expressionistic painting of Gauguin was adopted by the Norwegian Edvard Munch (1863–1944), who studied the Frenchman's works in Paris. Munch's early work was Impressionistic, but during the 1890s, he abandoned a light palette and lively subject matter in favor of a more somber style that reflected an anguished preoccupation with fear and death.

The Scream (Fig. **19-29**) is one of Munch's best-known works. It portrays the pain and isolation that became his central themes. A skeletal figure walks across a bridge toward the viewer, cupping his ears and screaming. Two figures in the background walk in the opposite direction, unaware of or uninterested in the sounds of desperation piercing the atmosphere. Munch transformed the placid landscape into one that echoes in waves the high-pitched tones that emanate from the sunken head. We are reminded of the swirling forms of van Gogh's *Starry Night*, but the intensity and horror pervading Munch's composition speak of his view of humanity as being consumed by an increasingly dehumanized society.

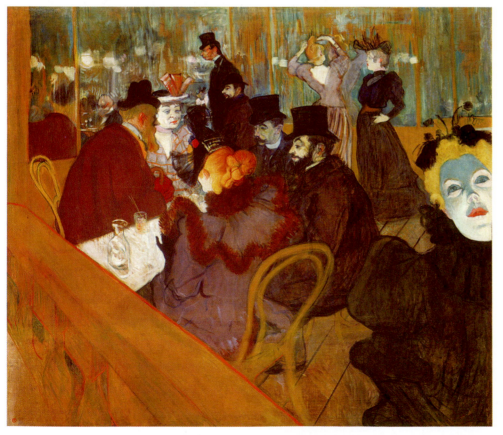

19-28 HENRI DE TOULOUSE-LAUTREC. *At the Moulin Rouge* (1892). Oil on canvas. 4' × 4'7". The Art Institute of Chicago, Chicago, IL.

The sky was suddenly blood-red—I stopped and leaned against the fence, dead tired. I saw the flaming clouds like blood and a sword—the bluish-black fjord and town—my friends walked on—I stood there, trembling with anxiety—and I felt as though Nature were convulsed by a great unending scream.
—Edvard Munch

Where do all the women who have watched so carefully over the lives of their beloved ones get the heroism to send them to face the cannon?
—Käthe Kollwitz

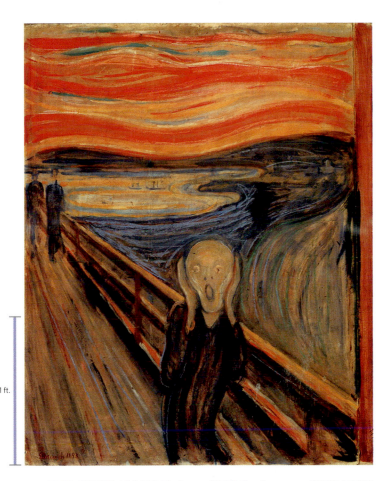

19-29 EDVARD MUNCH. *The Scream* (1893). Casein on paper. 35½" × 28⅔". National Gallery, Oslo, Norway. © 2011 The Munch Museum/The Munch-Ellingsen Group/Artists Rights Society (ARS), NY.

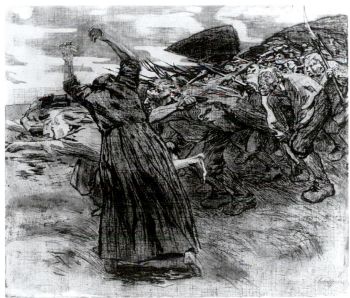

19-30 KÄTHE KOLLWITZ. *The Outbreak* (1903). Plate no. 5 from *The Peasants' War*. Etching, dry point, aquatint, and softground. 20³⁄₁₆" × 23⅛". Library of Congress, Washington, D.C. © 2011 Artists Rights Society (ARS), NY/VG Bild-Kunst, Bonn.

Käthe Kollwitz

It is not often in the history of art that we find two artists whose backgrounds are so similar that we can account for just about every variable except for personality when comparing their work. But such is the case with Edvard Munch and Käthe Kollwitz (1867–1945). They were born and died within a few years of each other. They both lived through two world wars; Kollwitz lost a son in World War I and a grand-

son in World War II. Both are Expressionist artists. Yet their choice of subjects speaks of their idiosyncratic concerns. Whereas Munch looked for symbols of isolation that would underscore his own sense of loneliness, or themes of violence and perverse sexuality that reflected his own psychological problems, Kollwitz sought universal symbols for inhumanity, injustice, and humankind's destruction of itself.

The Outbreak (Fig. **19-30**) is one of a series of seven prints by Kollwitz representing the sixteenth-century Peasants' War. In this print, Black Anna, a woman who led the laborers in their struggle against their oppressors, incites an angry throng of peasants to action. Her back is toward us, her head down, as she raises her gnarled hands in inspiration. The peasants rush forward in a torrent, bodies and weapons lunging at Anna's command. Although the work records a specific historical incident, it stands as an inspiration to all those who

I will not admit that a woman can draw so well.

—Edgar Degas, of Mary Cassatt

strive for freedom against the odds. There are few more forceful images in the history of art.

The styles of these early Expressionists would be adopted in the twentieth century by younger German artists who shared their view of the world. Many revived the woodcut medium to complement their expressive subjects. This younger generation of artists worked in various styles, but collectively were known as the Expressionists. We shall examine their work in Chapter 20.

AMERICAN EXPATRIATES

Until the twentieth century, art in the United States remained fairly provincial. Striving artists of the eighteenth and nineteenth centuries would go abroad for extended pilgrimages to study the old masters and mingle with the avant-garde. In some cases, they immigrated to Europe permanently. These artists, among them Mary Cassatt and James Abbott McNeill Whistler, are called the American Expatriates.

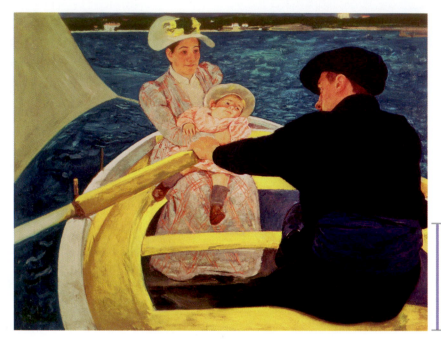

19-31 MARY CASSATT. *The Boating Party* (1893–1894). Oil on canvas. 35½" × 46⅛". National Gallery of Art, Washington, D.C.

1 ft.

Mary Cassatt

Mary Cassatt (1844–1926) was born in Pittsburgh but spent most of her life in France, where she was part of the inner circle of Impressionists. The artists Manet and Degas, photography, and Japanese prints influenced Cassatt's early career. She was a figure painter whose subjects centered on women and children.

A painting such as *The Boating Party* (Fig. **19-31**), with its flat planes, broad areas of color, and bold lines and shapes, illustrates Cassatt's interest and skill in merging French Impressionism with elements of Japanese art. Like many of her contemporaries in Paris, she became aware of Japanese prints and art objects after trade was established between Japan and Europe in the mid-nineteenth century. In their solidly constructed compositions and collapsed space, Cassatt's lithographs, in particular, stand out from the more ethereal images of other Impressionists.

James Abbott McNeill Whistler

In the same year that Monet painted his *Impression: Sunrise* and launched the movement of Impressionism, the American artist James Abbott McNeill Whistler (1834–1903) painted

one of the best-known compositions in the history of art. Who among us has not seen "Whistler's Mother," whether on posters, billboards, or television commercials? *Arrangement in Black and Gray: The Artist's Mother* (Fig. **19-32**) exhibits a combination of candid realism and abstraction that indicates two strong influences on Whistler's art: Courbet and Japanese prints. Whistler's mother is silhouetted against a quiet backdrop in the right portion of the composition. The strong contours of her black dress are balanced by an Oriental drape and a simple rectangular picture on the left. The subject is rendered in a harsh realism reminiscent of northern Renaissance portrait painting. However, the composition is seen first as a logical and pleasing arrangement of shapes in tones of black, gray, and white that work together in pure harmony.

AMERICANS IN AMERICA

While Whistler and Cassatt were working in Europe, several American artists of note remained at home working in the Realist tradition. This realism can be detected in figure painting and landscape painting, both of which were tinted with Romanticism.

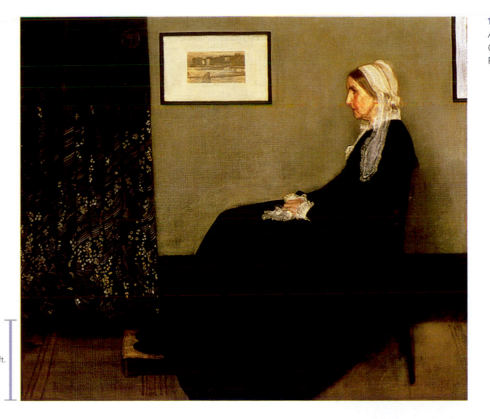

19-32 JAMES ABBOTT MCNEILL WHISTLER. *Arrangement in Black and Gray: The Artist's Mother* (1871). Oil on canvas. 57" × 64½". Louvre, Paris, France.

19-33 THOMAS EAKINS. *The Gross Clinic* (1875). Oil on canvas. 96" × 78". The Philadelphia Museum of Art, Philadelphia, PA.

Thomas Eakins

The most important American portrait painter of the nineteenth century was Thomas Eakins (1844–1916). Although his early artistic training took place in the United States, his study in Paris with painters who depicted historical events provided the major influence on his work. The penetrating realism of a work such as *The Gross Clinic* (Fig. 19-33) stems from Eakins's endeavors to become fully acquainted with human anatomy by working from live models and dissecting corpses. Eakins's dedication to these practices met with disapproval from his colleagues and ultimately forced his resignation from a teaching post at the Pennsylvania Academy of Art.

The Gross Clinic—no pun intended—depicts the surgeon Dr. Samuel Gross operating on a young boy at the Jefferson Medical College in Philadelphia. Eakins thrusts the brutal imagery to the foreground of the painting, spotlighting the surgical procedure and Dr. Gross's bloody scalpel, while casting the observing medical students in the background into darkness. The painting was deemed so shockingly realistic that it was rejected by the jury for an exhibition. Part of the impact of the work lies in the contrast between the matter-of-fact discourse of the surgeon and the torment of the boy's mother. She sits in the lower left corner of the painting, shielding

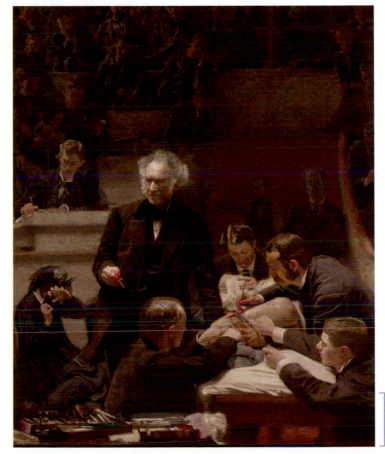

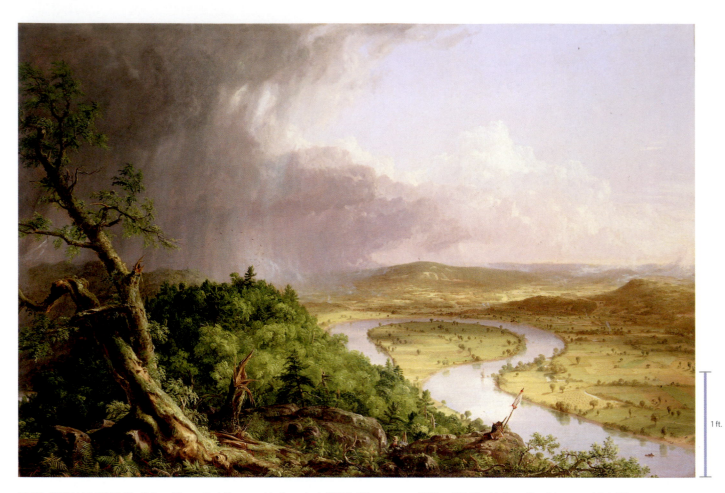

1 ft.

19-34 THOMAS COLE. *The Oxbow* (*Connecticut River near Northampton*) (1836). Oil on canvas. 51½" × 76". The Metropolitan Museum of Art, NY.

her eyes with whitened knuckles. In brush technique, Eakins is close to the fluidity of Courbet, although his compositional arrangement and dramatic lighting are surely indebted to Rembrandt.

Eakins devoted his career to increasingly realistic portraits. Their haunting veracity often disappointed sitters who would have preferred more flattering renditions. The artist's passion for realism led him to use photography extensively as a point of departure for his paintings as well as an art form in itself. Eakins's style and ideas influenced American artists of the early twentieth century who also worked in a Realist vein.

Thomas Cole

During the nineteenth century, American artists turned, for the first time, from the tradition of portraiture to landscape painting. Inspired by French landscape painting of the Baroque period, these artists fused this style with a pride in the beauty of their native United States and a Romantic vision that was embodied in the writings of James Fenimore Cooper.

One such artist was Thomas Cole (1801–1848), who was born in England and immigrated to the United States at age 17. Cole was always fond of landscape painting and settled in New York, where there was a ready audience for this genre. Cole became the leader of the **Hudson River School**—a group of artists whose favorite subjects included the scenery of the Hudson River Valley and the Catskill Mountains in New York State.

The Oxbow (Fig. **19-34**) is typical of such paintings. It records a natural oxbow formation in the Connecticut River Valley. Cole combines a vast, sun-drenched space with meticulously detailed foliage and farmland. There is a contrast in moods between the lazy movement of the river, which meanders diagonally into the distance, and the more vigorous diagonal of the gnarled tree trunk in the left foreground. Half of the canvas space is devoted to the sky, whose storm clouds roll back to reveal rays of intense light. These atmospheric effects, coupled with our "crow's-nest" vantage point, magnify the awesome grandeur of nature and force us to contemplate the relative insignificance of humans.

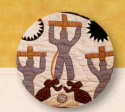

A CLOSER LOOK
WEAVING TOGETHER BIBLICAL AND PERSONAL STORIES

IN 1859, HARRIET BEECHER STOWE, renowned author of *Uncle Tom's Cabin*, described the quilting bee:

> The day was spent in friendly gossip as they rolled and talked and laughed. . . . One might have learned in that instructive assembly how best to keep moths out of blankets; how to make fritters of Indian corn undistinguishable from oysters; how to bring up babies by hand; how to mend a cracked teapot; how to take grease from a brocade; how to reconcile absolute decrees with free will; how to make five yards of cloth answer the purpose of six; and how to put down the Democratic party.*

Many years later, an author on quiltmaking quoted her great-grandmother: "My whole life is in that quilt. It scares me sometimes when I look at it. All my joys and all my sorrows are stitched into those little pieces."†

The art of quiltmaking was clearly not only an acceptable vehicle for women's artistic expression but also an arena for consciousness raising on the practical and political problems of the day. Beyond this, the object recorded family history, kept memory alive, and ensured the survival of the matriarch/quilter through that historical record.

Toward the end of the nineteenth century, African American quilter Harriet Powers created her *Bible Quilt*. Its 15 squares of cotton appliqué weave together stories from the Bible with significant events from the family and community of the artist (Fig. 19-35). For example, reading left to right, the fourth square is a symbolic depiction of Adam and Eve in the Garden of Eden. A serpent tempts Eve beneath God's all-seeing eye and benevolent hand. In the sixth square, Jonah is swallowed by a whale. The last square is a stylized depiction of the Crucifixion. Amidst

the religious subjects are records of meaningful days. For example, the eleventh square was described by Powers as "Cold Thursday," February 10, 1895. A woman is shown frozen at a gateway while at prayer. Icicles form from the breath of a mule. All bluebirds are killed. The thirteenth square includes an "independent" hog that was said to have run 500 miles from Georgia to Virginia, and the fourteenth square depicts the creation of animals in pairs.

Unity in the quilt is created by a subtle palette of complementary hues and by simple cutout shapes that define celestial orbs, biblical and familial characters, and biblical and local animals. The quilt has an arresting combination of widely known themes and private events known to the artist and her family. The juxtaposition establishes an equivalence between biblical and personal stories. The work personalizes the religious events and imbues the personal and provincial events with universal meaning.

Because of the hardness of the times, the artist sold the quilt for five dollars.‡ ●

‡ In Mirra Bank, *Anonymous Was a Woman* (New York: St. Martin's Press, 1979), 118.

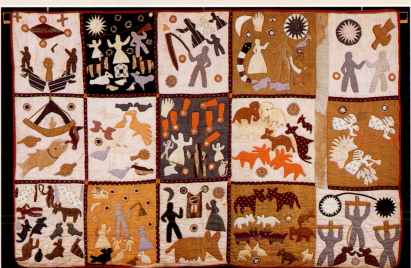

19-35 HARRIET POWERS. *Bible Quilt: The Creation of the Animals* (1895–1898). Pieced, appliquéd, and printed cotton embroidered with cotton and metallic yarn. 69" × 105". Museum of Fine Arts, Boston, MA.

1 ft.

* Harriet Beecher Stowe, *The Minister's Wooing* (New York: Derby and Jackson, 1859).
† Marguerite Ickis, *The Standard Book of Quiltmaking and Collecting* (New York: Dover, 1960).

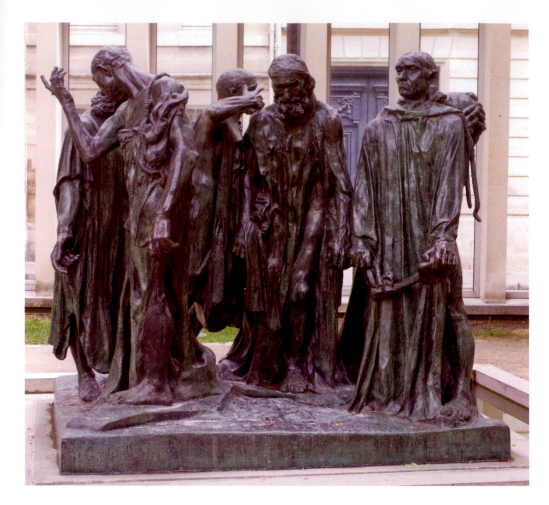

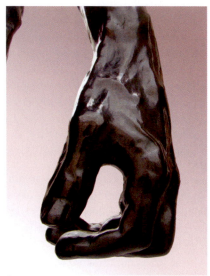

19-36 AUGUSTE RODIN. *The Burghers of Calais* (1884–1895). Bronze. 79⅜" × 80⅞" × 77⅛". Hirshhorn Museum and Sculpture Garden. Smithsonian Institution, Washington, D.C.

19-37 *The Burghers of Calais*, detail of hand.

THE BIRTH OF MODERN SCULPTURE

Some of the most notable characteristics of modern painting include a newfound realism of subject and technique; a more fluid, or impressionistic handling of the medium; and a new treatment of space. Nineteenth-century sculpture, for the most part, continued stylistic traditions that artists saw as complementing the inherent permanence of the medium with which they worked. It would seem that working on a large scale with materials such as marble or bronze was not well suited to the spontaneous technique that captured fleeting impressions. One nineteenth-century artist, however, changed the course of the history of sculpture by applying to his work the very principles on which modern painting was based, including Realism, Symbolism, and Impressionism—Auguste Rodin.

Auguste Rodin

Auguste Rodin (1840–1917) devoted his life almost solely to the representation of the human figure. His figures were imbued with a realism so startlingly intense that he was accused of casting the sculptures from live models. (It is interesting to note that casting of live models is used today without criticism.)

Rodin's *The Burghers of Calais* (Figs. 19-36 and 19-37) represents all of the innovations of Modernism thrust into three dimensions. The work commemorates a historical event in which six prominent citizens of Calais offered their lives to the conquering English so that their fellow townspeople might be spared. They present themselves in coarse robes with nooses around their necks. Their psychological states range from quiet defiance to frantic desperation. The reality of the scene is achieved in part by the odd placement of the figures. They are not a symmetrical or cohesive group. Rather, they are a scattered collection of individuals, who were meant to be seen at street level. Captured as they are, at a particular moment in time, Rodin ensured that spectators would partake of the tragic emotion of the scene for centuries to come.

Rodin preferred modeling soft materials to carving because they enabled him to achieve highly textured surfaces that captured the play of light, much as in an Impressionist painting. As his career progressed, Rodin's sculptures took on an abstract quality. Distinct features were abandoned in favor of solids and voids that, together with light, constructed the image of a human being. Such works were outrageous in their own day—audacious and quite new. Their abstracted features set the stage for yet newer and more audacious art forms that would rise with the dawn of the twentieth century.

ART NOUVEAU

In looking at examples of French, Norwegian, and American art of the nineteenth century, we witnessed a collection of disparate styles that reflected the artists' unique situations or personalities. Given the broad range of circumstances that give rise to a work of art, it would seem unlikely that a cross-cultural style could ever evolve. However, as the nineteenth century turned to the twentieth, there arose a style called **Art Nouveau** whose influence extended from Europe to the United States. Its idiosyncratic characteristics could be found in painting and sculpture, as well as architecture, furniture, jewelry, fashion, and glassware.

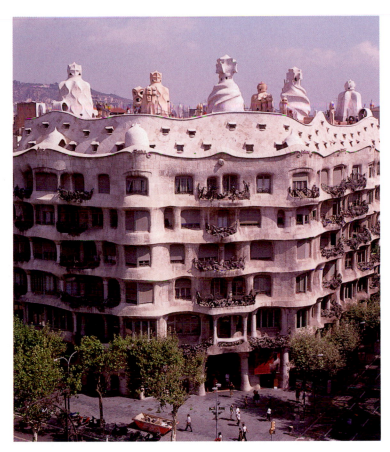

19-39 ANTONI GAUDÍ. Casa Mila Apartment House, Barcelona, Spain (1905–1907).

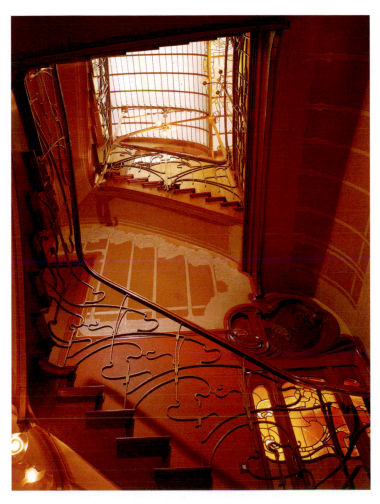

19-38 VICTOR HORTA. Interior of the Tassel House, Brussels, Belgium (1893).

Art Nouveau is marked by a lyrical linearity, the use of symbolism, and rich ornamentation. There is an overriding sense of the organic in all of the arts of this style, with many of the forms, such as those in Victor Horta's (1861–1947) foyer and staircase of the Tassel house (Fig. **19-38**), reminiscent of exotic plant life. Antoni Gaudí's (1852–1926) apartment house in Barcelona, Spain (Fig. **19-39**), shows an obsessive avoidance of straight lines and flat surfaces. The material looks as if it had grown in place or hardened in malleable wood forms, as would cement; in actuality, it is cut stone. The rhythmic roof is wavelike, and the chimneys seem dispensed like shaving cream or soft ice cream. Nor are any two rooms on a floor alike. This multistory organic hive is clearly the antithesis of the steel-cage construction that was coming into its own at the same time.

Art Nouveau originated in England. It was part of an arts-and-crafts movement that arose in rebellion against the pretentiousness of nineteenth-century art. Although it continued into the early years of the twentieth century, the style disappeared with the onset of World War I. At that time, art began to reflect the needs and fears of humanity faced with self-destruction.

ART TOUR PARIS

YOU COULD DEVOTE your entire life to the pursuit and still not see all of the visual delights of Paris. The city is one of the most beautiful in the world—a work of art in itself. Its origins, however, are far more humble. When the Romans conquered Paris in 55 BCE, it was a small fishing village on the north ("right") bank of the Seine River. Paris today has spread across the river to the Left Bank, and that tiny fishing village has expanded to hold more than 2 million people. It occupies the center of what is known as the Île-de-France, now home to one-fifth of France's 50 million people. The Île-de-France includes Versailles to the west (site of the glorious palace of King Louis XIV), Chartres with its famed Gothic cathedral (see Fig. 15-31) to the southwest, and numerous chateaus, such as Fontainebleau and—my favorite—Chantilly. Twenty miles and a short train or auto ride to the east is Disneyland Paris, and a ride northwest will get you to Giverny and Monet's famous gardens, where the famed Impressionist

painted water lilies, a Japanese footbridge, and many other outdoor delights. When in doubt, use the train. The Paris subway, called the Metro, is one of the best in the world, and the high-velocity trains out of town will move you around rapidly.

Take the Metro to the Trocadéro stop to visit the Eiffel Tower. Be captivated by the vista as you walk downhill between the museums on Chaillot Hill (Picasso might never have painted Les Demoiselles d'Avignon if he hadn't seen the African masks at the Musée de l'Homme) and across the Seine to the tower, which was built in 1889 for an industrial exhibition. At the time, the architect Gustave Eiffel was castigated by critics for building an open structure that lacked the standard masonry facade. The pieces of the 984-foot-tall tower were prefabricated, and the tower was assembled at the site in 17 months by only 150 workers. Napoleon's tomb and the Rodin Museum are a relatively short walk from the Tower.

Much of Paris is centered on the Place de la Concorde, from which one can look in any direction and find major monuments. This hub features a 3,200-year-old Egyptian obelisk that occupies the exact spot where, in the wake of the French Revolution (the Place de la Concorde was once the Place de la Revolution), a guillotine stood and the heads of more than 1,000 people rolled. To the west of the Concorde, along the Champs-Élysées—a wide boulevard where you can shop till you drop—is the Place de l'Étoile. The centerpiece of this star-shaped intersection is the Arc de Triomphe, built by Napoleon to celebrate his victorious military campaigns. It is one of the world's craziest rotaries; motorists enter it without looking anywhere but straight ahead. It is incumbent on the drivers already in the mess to do the watching out.

Just to the east of the Place de la Concorde—heading away from the Arc de

Triomphe—is the Jardin (garden) des Tuileries, with lovely paths for strolling, donkey rides, a carousel, and even a Ferris wheel. Along the north side of the Tuileries, you will find the Rue de Rivoli and some of the most expensive shopping in Paris.

Just past the Jardin des Tuileries is the Louvre Museum, which many art historians consider to have the foremost collection of art in the world. Here you will find Leonardo's *Mona Lisa* (see Fig. 16-19), David's *The Oath of the Horatii* (see Fig. 19-1), Géricault's *The Raft of the Medusa* (Fig. 19-4), *Aphrodite of Melos* (Venus de Milo, Fig. 14-17), Delacroix's *The Death of Sardanapalus* (Fig. 19-5), Manet's *Olympia* (Fig. 19-14), Whistler's *Arrangement in Black and Gray: The Artist's Mother* ("Whistler's Mother," Fig. 19-32), and many more famed works from around the world. But the museum has become a more noted work of art with I. M. Pei's controversial addition (the traditional first wing of the Palais du Louvre was built by François I in 1527).

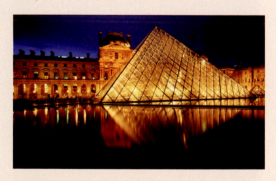

I. M. PEI. PYRAMID AT THE LOUVRE.

The south side of the Jardin des Tuileries runs along the Seine and is connected to the Left Bank by many bridges. Across from the Jardin, you will find the Musée d'Orsay. Before its opening as a museum in 1986, the building had been the old Gare d'Orsay, the grandest railway station in the city. In its new incarnation, the familiar floriated clock still tells time. Manets, Monets, Renoirs, Courbets, Rodins, and other beloved works

EIFFEL TOWER.

from the second half of the nineteenth century and the first decade of the twentieth populate byways where passengers once rushed. From its roof you can view the church of Sacré Coeur to the north, the Jardin des Tuileries just across the river, and the Louvre just to the right of the Jardin.

On the Right Bank in central Paris, you will find a very different museum, one of contemporary art: the Georges Pompidou National Center of Art and Culture, designed by Richard Rogers and Renzo Piano. It could not be more different from the Greek-inspired Classicism of the Louvre, given its trussed steel-cage structure, service ducts, huge escalator, and stacks that remind one of an ocean liner. While in the vicinity of the Pompidou Center, take in some of the street life in the large square in front of the building or relax by the Stravinsky Fountain with its huge red lips and other sculptures, thanks to the contemporary artistry of Niki de Saint Phalle. You will find numerous cafés around the fountain and the square. This is a great place to take a rest.

To the east of the Musée d'Orsay and the Louvre, the majestic cathedral of Notre-Dame rises on an island in the Seine—the Île de la Cité. With the stories of the hunchback of Notre-Dame, and with its perch on the banks of the river, the cathedral is one of the most famous buildings in the history of architecture. Notre-Dame is a curious mixture of old and new elements, begun in 1163 and not completed until almost a century later. While on the Île de la Cité, do not miss seeing

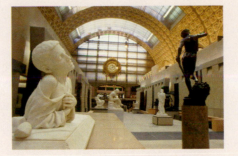

MUSÉE D'ORSAY.

Saint-Chapelle, which has been hailed as ethereal, magical, and one of the architectural wonders of the Western world. Multicolored light floods the upper chapel through 15 stained-glass windows.

Behind Notre-Dame—past the flying buttresses, a little park, and across a street usually populated by parked tourist buses—you'll find another park and then a surprising Deportation Memorial (Mémorial des Martyrs et de la Déportation), which is below ground level and against the river. You descend a narrow stairway onto a platform with bars that prevent you from reaching the water. No way out. A room off the platform names the Nazi death camps to which Jews and others were deported.

If you head south from the Île de la Cité along Boulevard St. Michel, you'll find outdoor cafés, including the Deux Magots, where Ernest Hemingway and F. Scott Fitzgerald drank and dined. Cross Boulevard Saint-Germain and you're in

University of Paris territory. Within a few blocks on the left, you'll see the Pantheon, which houses an interesting crypt where Madame Curie, among others, is interred. On the right side, you will come to the Luxembourg Gardens, with its hedged trees, palace, and sailboat pond.

Don't pass up Père Lachaise, which is the major cemetery in Paris. You will find graves and fascinating mausoleums for the Romantic painters Eugène Delacroix and Théodore Géricault, the Polish composer Frédéric Chopin, the British writer Oscar Wilde, the French actress Sarah Bernhardt, the French playwright Molière, the American Jim Morrison (lead singer of The Doors), and dozens of others whom you are likely to recognize.

No visit to Paris is complete without a trip to Versailles (see Fig. 17-22). This complex began as a hunting lodge and was rebuilt in 1668 by the Sun King (Louis XIV) into the grandest palace in Europe. The palace is well known for its magnificent Hall of Mirrors and its art collection, but you'll also want to spend time strolling in the gardens. When at Versailles, be sure to visit the Grand Trianon, one of the outbuildings of the complex, for its colonnade and sweeping vistas of hedged trees and human-made lakes. Take a boat ride or just wander among the greenery, as did Queen Marie Antoinette in her peasant-girl attire. Sometimes we all need to escape.

 TO CONTINUE YOUR TOUR and learn more about Paris, go to CourseMate.

NOTRE DAME CATHEDRAL, PARIS, FRANCE.

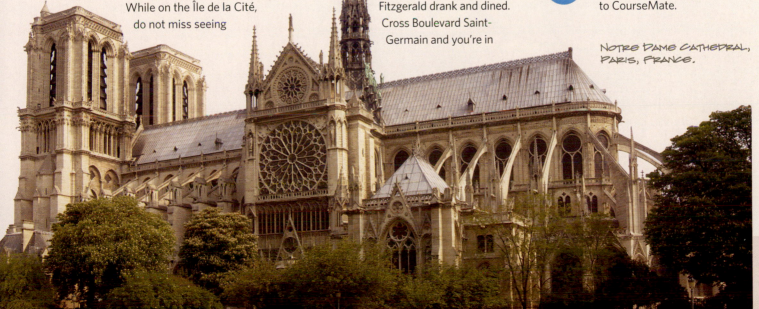

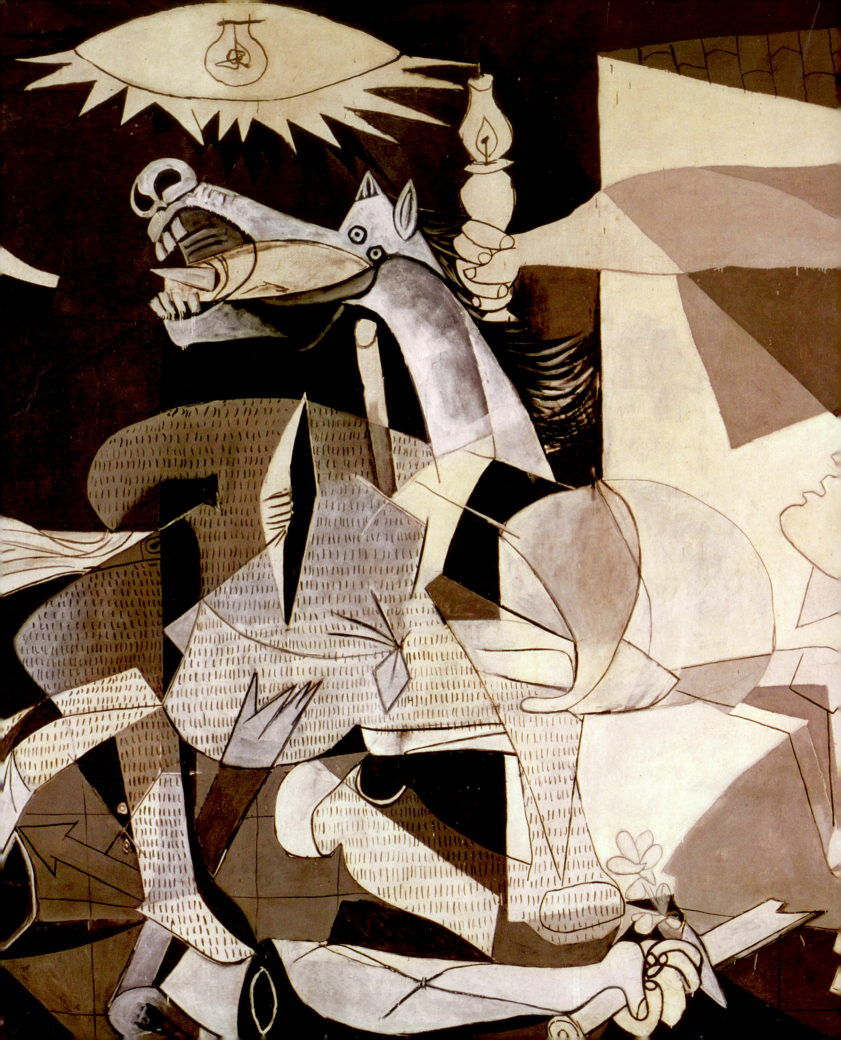

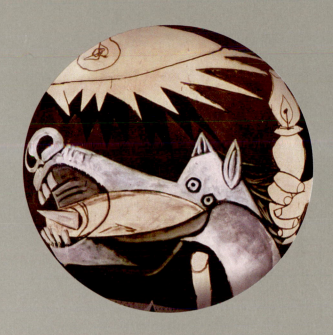

When people ask me to compare the 20th century to older civilizations, I always say the same thing: "The situation is normal."

—Will Durant

THE TWENTIETH CENTURY: THE EARLY YEARS

20

It could be said that the art world has been in a state of perpetual turmoil for the last hundred years. All of the important movements that were born during the late nineteenth and early twentieth centuries met with the hostile, antiseptic gloves of critical disdain. When Courbet's paintings were rejected by the 1855 Salon, he set up his own Pavilion of Realism and pushed the Realist movement on its way. Just eight years later, rejection by the Salon jury prompted the origin of the Salon des Réfusés, an exhibition of works including those of Manet. These ornery French artists went on to found the influential Impressionist movement. The very name—*Impressionism*—was coined by a hostile critic who degraded their work as mere "impressions," sort of quick and easy sketches of the painter's view of the world. Impressionism ran counter to the preferred illusionistic realism of Academic painting.

The opening years of the twentieth century saw no letup to these scandalous entrées into the world of modern art. In 1905, the Salon d'Automne—an independent exhibition so named to distinguish it from the Academic Salons that were traditionally held in the spring—brought together the works of an exuberant group of French avant-garde artists who assaulted the public with a bold palette and distorted forms. One art critic who peeked in on the show saw a Renaissance-type sculpture surrounded by these blasphemous forms. He was sufficiently unnerved by the juxtaposition to exclaim, "*Donatello au milieu des fauves!*" (that is, "Donatello among the wild beasts!"). With what pleasure, then, the artists adopted as their epithet "The Fauves." After all, it was a symbol of recognition.

THE FAUVES

In some respects, **Fauvism** was a logical successor to the painting of van Gogh and Gauguin. Like these Postimpressionists, the Fauvists also rejected the subdued palette and delicate brushwork of Impressionism. They chose their color and brushwork on the basis of their emotive qualities. Despite the aggressiveness of their method, however, their subject matter centered on traditional nudes, still lifes, and landscapes.

What set the Fauves apart from their nineteenth-century predecessors was their use of harsh, nondescriptive color; bold linear patterning; and a distorted form of perspective. They saw color as autonomous, a subject in and of itself, not merely an adjunct to nature. Their vigorous brushwork and emphatic line grew out of their desire for a direct form of expression, unencumbered by theory. Their skewed perspective and distorted forms were also inspired by the discovery of ethnographic works of art from Africa, Polynesia, and other ancient cultures.

ANDRÉ DERAIN One of the founders of the Fauvist movement was André Derain (1880–1954). In his *London Bridge* (Fig. 20-1), we find the convergence of elements of nineteenth-century styles and the new vision of Fauvism. The outdoor subject matter is reminiscent of Impressionism (Monet, in fact, painted many renditions of Waterloo Bridge in London), and the distinct zones of unnaturalistic color relate the work to Gauguin. But the forceful contrasts of primary colors and the delineation of forms by blocks of thickly applied pigment speak of something new.

Nineteenth-century artists emphasized natural light and created their shadows from color components. Derain and the Fauvists evoked light in their canvases solely with color

contrasts. Fauvists tended to negate shadow altogether. Whereas Gauguin used color areas primarily to express emotion, the Fauvist artists used color to construct forms and space. Although Derain used his bold palette and harsh line to render his emotional response to the scene, his bright blocks of pigment also function as building facades. Derain's oblong patches of color define both stone and water. His thickly laden brushstroke constructs the contour of a boat and the silhouette of a fisherman.

HENRI MATISSE Along with Derain, Henri Matisse (1869–1954) brought Fauvism to the forefront of critical recognition. Yet Matisse was one of the few major Fauvist artists whose reputation exceeded that of the movement. Matisse started law school at age 21, but when an illness interrupted his studies, he began to paint. Soon thereafter, he decided to devote himself totally to art. Matisse's early paintings revealed a strong and traditional compositional structure, which he gleaned from his first mentor, Adolphe William Bouguereau (see Fig. 19-9), and from copying old masters in the Louvre. His loose brushwork was reminiscent of Impressionism, and his palette was inspired by the color theories of the Postimpressionists. In 1905, he consolidated these influences and painted several Fauvist canvases in which, like Derain, he used primary color as a structural element. These canvases were exhibited with those of other Fauvists at the Salon d'Automne of that year.

In his post-Fauvist works, Matisse used color in a variety of other ways: structurally, decoratively, sensually, and expressively. In his *Red Room* (*Harmony in Red*) (Fig. 20-2), all of these qualities of color are present. A vibrant palette and curvilinear shapes create the gay mood of the canvas. The lush red of the wallpaper and tablecloth absorb the viewer in their brilliance. The arabesques of the vines create an enticing surface pattern.

A curious contest between flatness and three dimensions in *Red Room* characterizes much of Matisse's work. He crowds the table and wall with the same patterns. They seem to run together without distinction. This jumbling of patterns propels the background to the picture plane, asserting the flatness of the canvas. The two-dimensionality of the canvas is further underscored by the window in the upper left, which is rendered so flatly that it suggests a painting of a garden scene instead of an actual view of a distant landscape. Yet for all of these attempts to collapse space, Matisse counteracts the effect with a variety of perspective cues: the seat of the ladderback chair recedes into space, as does the table; and the dishes are somewhat foreshortened, combining frontal and bird's-eye views.

Matisse used line expressively, moving it rhythmically across the canvas to complement the pulsing

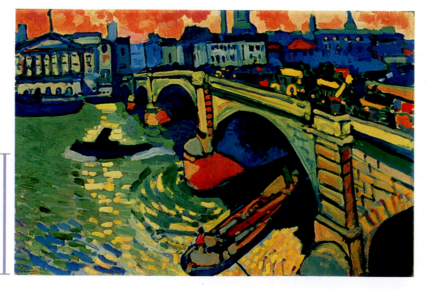

1 ft.

20-1 ANDRÉ DERAIN. *London Bridge* (1906). Oil on canvas. 26" × 39". The Museum of Modern Art, NY.

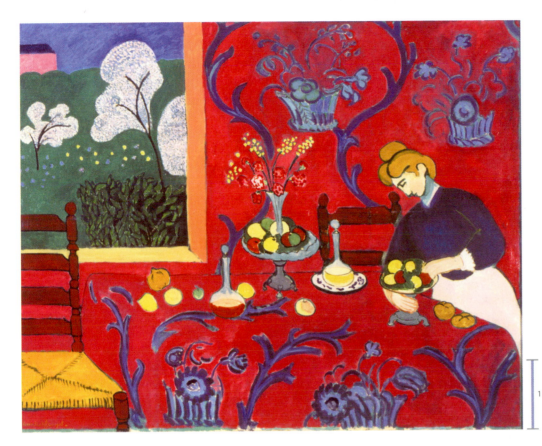

20-2 HENRI MATISSE. *Red Room* (*Harmony in Red*) (1908–1909). Oil on canvas. 69¾" × 85⅞". The Hermitage, St. Petersburg, Russia. © 2011 Succession H. Matisse/ Artists Rights Society (ARS), NY.

1 ft.

color. Although the structure of *Red Room* remains assertive, Matisse's foremost concern was to create a pleasing pattern. Matisse insisted that painting ought to be joyous. His choice of palette, his lyrical use of line, and his brightly painted shapes are all means toward that end. He even said of his work that it ought to be devoid of depressing subject matter, that his art ought to be "a mental soother, something like a good armchair in which to rest."[1]

Although the colors and forms of Fauvism burst explosively on the modern art scene, the movement did not last very long. For one thing, the styles of the Fauvist artists were very different from one another, so the members never formed a cohesive group. After about five years, the Fauvist qualities began to disappear from their works as they pursued other styles. Their disappearance was, in part, prompted by a

retrospective exhibition of Cézanne's paintings held in 1907, which revitalized an interest in this nineteenth-century artist's work. His principles of composition and constructive brush technique were at odds with the Fauvist manifesto.

While Fauvism was descending from its brief, colorful flourish in France, related art movements, termed *expressionistic*, were ascending in Germany.

EXPRESSIONISM

Expressionism is the distortion of nature—as opposed to the imitation of nature—in order to achieve a desired emotional effect or representation of inner feelings. According to this definition, we have already seen many examples of this type of painting. The work of van Gogh and Gauguin would be clearly expressionistic, as would the paintings of the Fauves. Even Matisse's *Red Room* distorts nature or reality in favor of

---

[1] Robert Goldwater and Marco Treves, eds., *Artists on Art* (New York: Pantheon Books, 1972), 413.

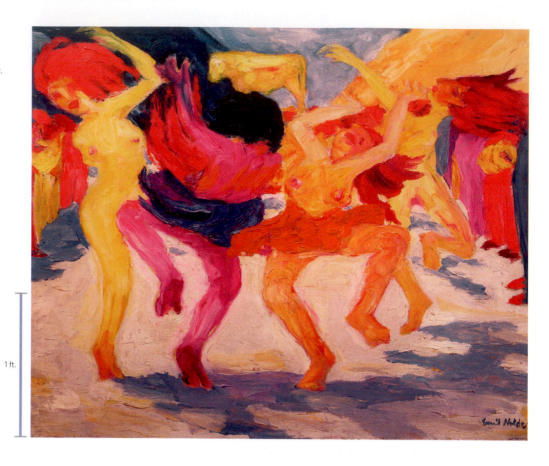

1 ft.

a more intimate portrayal of the artist's subject, colored, as it were, by his emotions. Edvard Munch and Käthe Kollwitz were expressionistic artists who used paintings and prints as vehicles to express anxieties, obsessions, and outrage.

Three other movements of the early twentieth century have been termed expressionistic: *Die Brücke*, *Der Blaue Reiter*, and The New Objectivity, or *Neue Sachlichkeit*. Although very different from one another in the forms they took, these movements were reactions against Impressionism and Realism. They also sought to communicate the inner feelings of the artist.

Die Brücke (The Bridge)

Die Brücke (The Bridge) was founded in Dresden, Germany, at the same time that Fauvism was afoot in France. The artists who began the movement chose the name *Die Brücke* because, in theory, they saw their movement as bridging several disparate styles. Die Brücke, like Fauvism, was short-lived because of the lack of cohesion among its proponents. Still, Die Brücke artists showed some common interests in techniques and subject matter that ranged from boldly colored landscapes and cityscapes to horrific and violent portraits. Their emotional upheaval may, in part, have reflected the mayhem of World War I.

EMIL NOLDE The supreme colorist of the Expressionist movement was Emil Nolde (1867–1956), who joined Die Brücke a year after it was founded. Canvases of his, such as *Dance around the Golden Calf* (Fig. **20-3**), are marked by a frenzied brush technique in which clashing colors are applied in lush strokes. The technique complements the nature of the subject—a biblical theme recounting the worshiping of an idol by the Israelites even as their liberator, Moses, was receiving the Ten Commandments on Mount Sinai. In Nolde's characteristic fashion, both ecstasy and anguish are brought to the same uncontrolled, high pitch. Nolde was also well known for his graphics. He used the idiosyncratic, splintered characteristics of the woodcut—a medium that had not been in vogue for centuries—to create ravaged, masklike portraits of pain and suffering.

Der Blaue Reiter (The Blue Rider)

Emotionally charged subject matter, often radically distorted, was the essence of Die Brücke art. **Der Blaue Reiter (The Blue Rider)** artists—who took their group name from a painting of that title by Wassily Kandinsky, a major proponent—depended less heavily on content to communicate feelings and evoke an emotional response from the viewer. Their work focused more on the contrasts and combinations of abstract forms and pure colors. In fact, the work of Der Blaue Reiter artists, at times, is completely without subject and can be described as nonobjective, or abstract. Whereas Die Brücke artists always used nature as a point of departure, Der Blaue Reiter art sought to free itself from the shackles of observable reality.

WASSILY KANDINSKY One of the founders of Der Blaue Reiter was Wassily Kandinsky (1866–1944), a Russian artist who left a career in law to become an influential abstract painter and art theorist. During numerous visits to Paris early in his career, Kandinsky was immersed in the works of Gauguin and the Fauves and was inspired to adopt the Fauvist idiom. The French experience opened his eyes to color's powerful capacity to communicate the artist's inmost psychological and spiritual concerns. In his seminal essay, "Concerning the Spiritual in Art," he examined this capability and discussed the psychological effects of color on the viewer. Kandinsky further analyzed the relationship between art and music in this study.

Early experiments with these theories can be seen in works such as *Sketch I for Composition VII* (Fig. **20-4**), in which bold colors, lines, and shapes tear dramatically across the canvas in no preconceived fashion. The pictorial elements flow freely and independently throughout the painting, reflecting, Kandinsky believed, the free flow of unconscious thought. *Sketch I for Composition VII* and other works of this series underscore the importance of Kandinsky's early Fauvist contacts in their vibrant palette, broad brushstrokes, and dynamic movement, and they also stand as harbingers of a new art unencumbered by referential subject matter.

For Kandinsky, color, line, and shape were subjects in themselves. They were often rendered with a spontaneity born of the psychological process of free association. At this time, free association was also being explored by the founder of psychoanalysis, Sigmund Freud, as a method of mapping the geography of the unconscious mind.

The New Objectivity (Neue Sachlichkeit)

As World War I drew to a close and World War II loomed on the horizon, different factions of German Expressionism could be observed. Some artists, such as Max Beckmann (1884–1950), calling themselves **The New Objectivity (Neue Sachlichkeit)**, reacted to the horrors and senselessness of wartime suffering with an art that commented bitterly on the bureaucracy and military with ghastly visions of human torture (see Fig. 1-19).

CUBISM

The history of art is colored by the tensions of stylistic polarities within given eras, particularly the polarity of an intellectual versus an emotional approach to painting. Fauvism and German Expressionism found their roots in Romanticism and the emotional expressionistic work of Gauguin and van Gogh. The second major art movement of the twentieth century, **Cubism**, can trace its heritage to Neoclassicism and the analytical and intellectual work of Cézanne.

Cubism is an offspring of Cézanne's geometrization of nature and his abandonment of scientific perspective, his rendering of multiple views, and his emphasis on the two-dimensional canvas surface. Picasso, the driving force behind the birth of Cubism, and perhaps the most significant artist of the twentieth century, combined the pictorial methods of Cézanne with formal elements from native African, Oceanic, and Iberian sculpture.

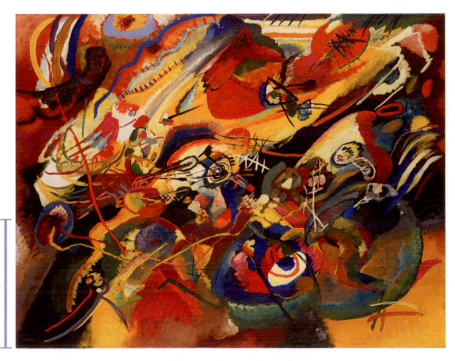

1 ft.

20-4 WASSILY KANDINSKY. *Sketch I for Composition VII* (1913). Oil on canvas. 30¾" × 39⅜". Private collection. © 2011 Artists Rights Society (ARS), NY/ADAGP, Paris.

PABLO PICASSO Pablo Ruiz y Picasso (1881–1973) was born in Spain, the son of an art teacher. As an adolescent, he enrolled in the Barcelona Academy of Art, where he quickly mastered the illusionistic techniques of the realistic Academic style. By age 19, Picasso was off to Paris, where he remained for more than 40 years—introducing, influencing, or reflecting the many styles of modern French art.

Picasso's first major artistic phase has been called his Blue Period. Spanning the years 1901 to 1904, this work is characterized by an overall blue tonality, a distortion of the human body through elongation reminiscent of El Greco

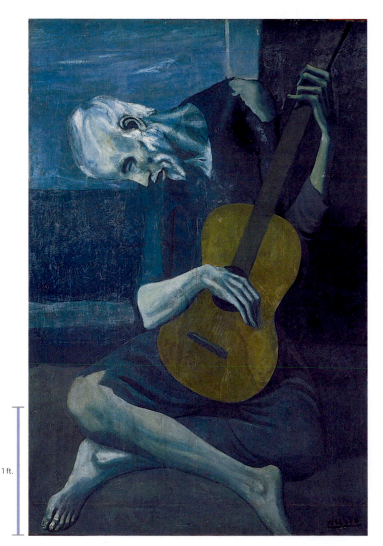

20-5 PABLO PICASSO. *The Old Guitarist* (1903). Oil on canvas. 47¾" × 32½". The Art Institute of Chicago, Chicago, IL. © 2011 Estate of Pablo Picasso/Artists Rights Society (ARS), NY.

1 ft.

and Toulouse-Lautrec, and melancholy subjects consisting of poor and downtrodden individuals engaged in menial tasks or isolated in their loneliness. *The Old Guitarist* (Fig. **20-5**) is but one of these haunting images. A contorted, white-haired man sits hunched over a guitar, consumed by the tones that emanate from what appears to be his only possession. The eyes are sunken in the skeletal head, and the bones and tendons of his hungry frame protrude. We are struck by the ordinariness of poverty, from the unfurnished room and barren window view (or is he on the curb outside?) to the uneventfulness of his activity and the insignificance of his plight. The monochromatic blue palette creates an unrelenting, somber mood. Tones of blue eerily echo the ghostlike features of the guitarist.

Picasso's Blue Period was followed by works that were lighter both in palette and in spirit. Subjects from this so-called Rose Period were drawn primarily from circus life and rendered in tones of pink. During this second period, which dates from 1905 to 1908, Picasso was inspired by two very different art styles. He, like many artists, viewed and was strongly influenced by the Cézanne retrospective exhibition held at the Salon d'Automne in 1907. At about that time, Picasso also became aware of the formal properties of ethnographic art from Africa, Oceania, and Iberia, which he viewed at the Musée de l'Homme. These two art forms, which at first glance might appear dissimilar, had in common a fragmentation, distortion, and abstraction of form that were adopted by Picasso in works such as *Les Demoiselles d'Avignon* (Fig. **20-6**).

This startling, innovative work, still primarily pink in tone, depicts five women from Barcelona's red-light district. They line up for selection by a possible suitor who stands, as it were, in the position of the spectator. The faces of three of the women are primitive masks. The facial features of the other two have been radically simplified by combining frontal and profile views. The thick-lidded eyes stare stage front, calling to mind some of the Mesopotamian votive sculptures we saw in Chapter 13.

The bodies of the women are fractured into geometric forms and set before a background of similarly splintered drapery. In treating the background and the foreground imagery in the same manner, Picasso collapses the space between the planes and asserts the two-dimensionality of the canvas surface in the manner of Cézanne. In some radical passages, such as the right leg of the leftmost figure, the limb takes on the qualities of drapery, masking the distinction between figure and ground. The extreme faceting of form, the use of multiple views, and the collapsing of space in

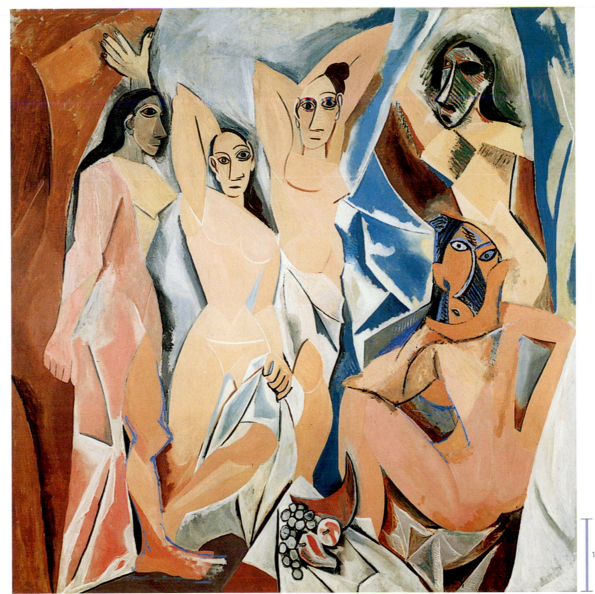

20-6 PABLO PICASSO. *Les Demoiselles d'Avignon* (1907). Oil on canvas. 8' × 7'8". The Museum of Modern Art, NY. © 2011 Estate of Pablo Picasso/ Artists Rights Society (ARS), NY.

1 ft.

Les Demoiselles together provided the springboard for **Analytic Cubism**, co-founded with the French painter Georges Braque in about 1910.

Analytic Cubism

The term *Cubism*, like so many others, was coined by a hostile critic. In this case, the critic was responding to the predominance of geometrical forms in the works of Picasso and Braque. *Cubism* is a limited term in that it does not adequately describe the appearance of Cubist paintings, and it minimizes the intensity with which Cubist artists analyzed their subject matter. It ignores their most significant contribution—a new treatment of pictorial space that

hinged upon the rendering of objects from multiple and radically different views.

The Cubist treatment of space differed significantly from that in use since the Renaissance. Instead of presenting an object from a single view, assumed to have been the complete view, the Cubists, like Cézanne, realized that our visual comprehension of objects consists of many views that we perceive almost at once. They tried to render this visual "information gathering" in their compositions. In their dissection and reconstruction of imagery, they reassessed the notion that painting should reproduce the appearance of reality. Now the very reality of appearances was being questioned. To Cubists, the most basic reality involved consolidating optical vignettes instead of reproducing fixed images with photographic accuracy.

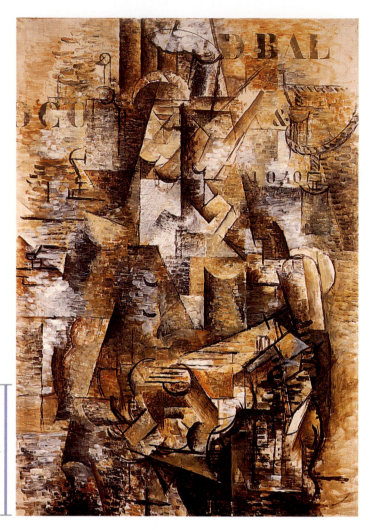

1 ft.

20-7 GEORGES BRAQUE. *The Portuguese* (1911). Oil on canvas. 45½" × 31½". Oeffentliche Kunstsammlung, Kunstmuseum, Basel, Germany. © 2011 Artists Rights Society (ARS), NY/ADAGP, Paris.

GEORGES BRAQUE During the analytic phase of Cubism, which spanned the years from 1909 to 1912, the works of Picasso and Braque were very similar. The early work of Georges Braque (1882–1963) graduated from Impressionism to Fauvism to more structural compositions based on Cézanne. He met Picasso in 1907, and from then until about 1914, the artists worked together toward the same artistic goals.

The theory of Analytic Cubism reached the peak of its expression in 1911 in works such as Braque's *The Portuguese* (Fig. **20-7**). Numerous planes intersect and congregate at the center of the canvas to form a barely perceptible triangular human figure, which is alternately constructed from and dissolved into the background. There are only a few concrete signs of its substance: dropped eyelids, a mustache, the circular opening of a stringed instrument. The multifaceted, abstracted form appears to shift position before our eyes, simulating the time lapse that would occur in the

visual assimilation of multiple views. The structural lines—sometimes called the *Cubist grid*—that define and fragment the figure are thick and dark. They contrast with the delicately modeled short, choppy brushstrokes of the remainder of the composition. The monochromatic palette, chosen so as not to interfere with the exploration of form, consists of browns, tans, and ochers.

Although the paintings of Picasso and Braque were almost identical at this time, Braque first began to insert words and numbers and to use **trompe l'oeil** effects in portions of his Analytic Cubist compositions. These realistic elements contrasted sharply with the abstraction of the major figures and reintroduced the nagging question, "What is reality and what is illusion in painting?"

Synthetic Cubism

Picasso and Braque did not stop with the inclusion of precisely printed words and numbers in their works. They began to add characters cut from newspapers and magazines, other

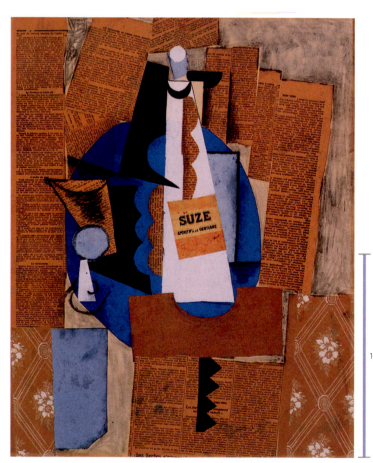

1 ft.

20-8 PABLO PICASSO. *La bouteille de Suze* (*Bottle of Suze*) (1912). Pasted paper, gouache, and charcoal. 25¾" × 19¾". Mildred Lane Kemper Art Museum, Washington University in St. Louis, St. Louis, MO. © 2011 Estate of Pablo Picasso/Artists Rights Society (ARS), NY.

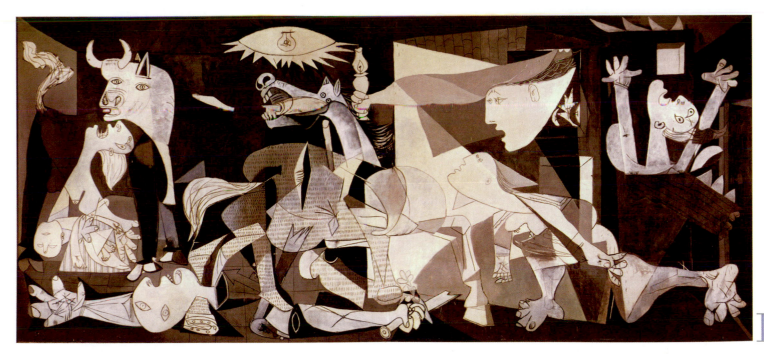

20-9 PABLO PICASSO. *Guernica* (1937). Oil on canvas. 11'6" × 25'8". Museo Nacional Centro de Arte Reina Sofia, Madrid, Spain.
© 2011 Estate of Pablo Picasso/Artists Rights Society (ARS), NY.

pieces of paper, and found objects such as labels from wine bottles, calling cards, theater tickets—even swatches of wallpaper and bits of rope. These items were pasted directly onto the canvas in a technique Picasso and Braque called *papier collé*—what we know as **collage**. The use of collage marked the beginning of the synthetic phase of Cubism.

Some **Synthetic Cubist** compositions, such as Picasso's *The Bottle of Suze* (Fig. **20-8**), are constructed entirely of found elements. In this work, newspaper clippings and opaque pieces of paper function as the shifting planes that hover around the aperitif label and define the bottle and glass. These planes are held together by a sparse linear structure much in the manner of Analytic Cubist works. In contrast to Analytic Cubism, however, the emphasis is on the form of the object and on constructing instead of disintegrating that form. Color reentered the compositions, and much emphasis was placed on texture, design, and movement.

After World War I, Picasso and Braque no longer worked together, and their styles, although often reflective of the Cubist experience they shared, came to differ markedly. Braque, who was severely wounded during the war, went on to create more delicate and lyrical still-life compositions, abandoning the austerity of the early phase of Cubism. Although many of Picasso's later works carried forward the Synthetic Cubist idiom, his artistic genius and versatility became evident after 1920, when he began to move in radically different directions. These new works were rendered in Classical, Expressionist, and Surrealist styles.

When civil war gripped Spain, Picasso protested its brutality and inhumanity through highly emotional works such as *Guernica* (Fig. **20-9**). This mammoth mural, painted for the Spanish Pavilion of the Paris International Exposition of 1937, broadcast to the world the carnage of the German bombing of civilians in the Basque town of Guernica. The painting captures the event in gruesome details, such as the frenzied cry of one woman trapped in rubble and fire and the pale fright of another woman who tries in vain to flee the conflagration. A terrorized horse rears over a dismembered body, while an anguished mother embraces her dead child and wails futilely. Innocent lives are shattered into Cubist planes that rush and intersect at myriad angles, distorting and fracturing the imagery. Confining himself to a palette of harsh blacks, grays, and whites, Picasso expressed, in his words, the "brutality and darkness" of the age.

Cubist Sculpture

Cubism was born as a two-dimensional art form. Cubist artists attempted to render on canvas the manifold aspects of their subjects as if they were walking around three-dimensional forms and recording every angle. The attempt was successful, in part, because they recorded these views with intersecting planes that allowed viewers to perceive the many sides of the figure.

Because Cubist artists were trying to communicate all of the visual information available about a particular form,

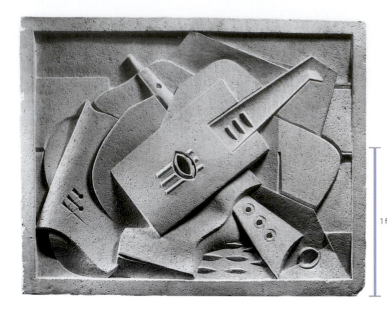

20-10 JACQUES LIPCHITZ. *Still Life with Musical Instruments* (1918). Stone relief. 22½" × 28". Marlborough Gallery, NY.

1 ft.

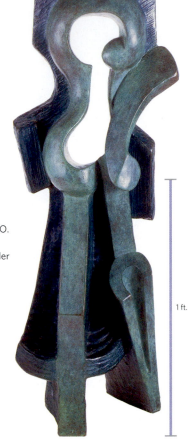

20-11 ALEXANDER ARCHIPENKO. *Walking Woman* (1912). Bronze. H: 26½". © 2011 Estate of Alexander Archipenko/Artists Rights Society (ARS), NY.

1 ft.

they were handicapped, so to speak, by the two-dimensional surface. In some ways, the medium of sculpture was more natural to Cubism, because a viewer could actually walk around a figure to assimilate its many facets. The "transparent" planes that provided a sense of intrigue in Analytical Cubist paintings were often translated as flat solids, as in Jacques Lipchitz's (1891–1964) *Still Life with Musical Instruments* (Fig. **20-10**).

ALEXANDER ARCHIPENKO One of the innovations in Cubist sculpture was the three-dimensional interpenetration of Cubist planes, as implied in Lipchitz's relief. Another was the use of void space as solid form, as seen in *Walking Woman* (Fig. **20-11**) by Alexander Archipenko (1887–1964). True to Cubist principles, the figure is fragmented; the contours are broken and dislocated. But what is new here are the open spaces of the torso and head, now as much a part of the whole as the solid forms of the composition. Although there is a good degree of abstract simplification in the figure, the overall impression of the forms prompts recognition of the humanity of the subject.

FUTURISM

Several years after the advent of Cubism, a new movement sprang up in Italy under the leadership of poet Filippo Marinetti (1876–1944). **Futurism** was introduced angrily by Marinetti in a 1909 manifesto that called for an art of "violence, energy, and boldness" free from the "tyranny of . . .

harmony and good taste."[2] In theory, Futurist painting and sculpture were to glorify the life of today, "unceasingly and violently transformed by victorious science." In practice, many of the works owed much to Cubism.

UMBERTO BOCCIONI An oft-repeated word in Futurist credo is **dynamism**, defined as the theory that force or energy is the basic principle of all phenomena. The principle of dynamism is illustrated in Umberto Boccioni's (1882–1916) *Dynamism of a Soccer Player*. Irregular, agitated lines communicate the energy of movement. The Futurist obsession with illustrating images in perpetual motion also found a

---

[2] F. T. Marinetti, "The Foundation and Manifesto of Futurism," in *Theories of Modern Art*, ed. Herschel B. Chipp, 284–288 (Berkeley: University of California Press, 1968).

Everything moves, everything runs, everything turns swiftly. The figure in front of us never is still, but ceaselessly appears and disappears. Owing to the persistence of images on the retina, objects in motion are multiplied, distorted, following one another like waves through space. Thus a galloping horse has not four legs; it has twenty.

—Umberto Boccioni

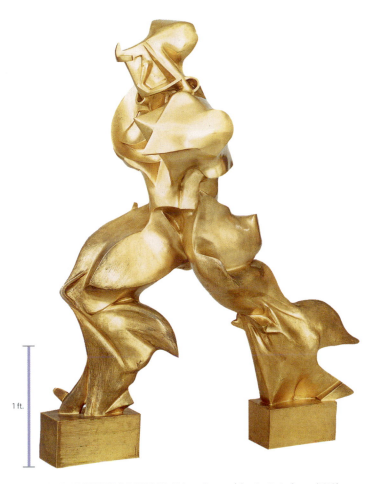

20-12 UMBERTO BOCCIONI. *Unique Forms of Continuity in Space* (1913). Bronze (cast 1931). 43⅞" × 34⅞" × 15¾". The Museum of Modern Art, NY.

manifests itself fully in Giacomo Balla's (1871–1958) pure Futurist painting, *Street Light* (Fig. **20-13**). The light of the lamp pierces the darkness in reverberating circles; V-shaped brushstrokes simultaneously fan outward from the source and point toward it, creating a sense of constant movement. The palette consists of complementary colors that forbid the eye to rest. All is movement; all is sensation.

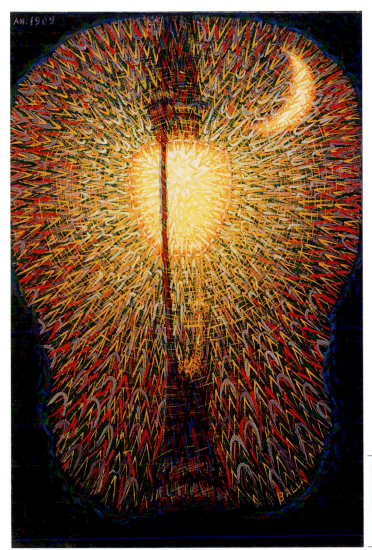

20-13 GIACOMO BALLA. *Street Light* (1909). Oil on canvas. 68¾" × 45¼". The Museum of Modern Art, NY.

perfect outlet in sculpture. In works such as *Unique Forms of Continuity in Space* (Fig. **20-12**), Boccioni, whose forte was sculpture, sought to convey the elusive surging energy that blurs an image in motion, leaving but an echo of its passage. Although it retains an overall figural silhouette, the sculpture is devoid of any representational details. The flamelike curving surfaces of the striding figure do not exist to define movement; instead, they are a consequence of it.

GIACOMO BALLA The Futurists also suggested that their subjects were less important than the portrayal of the "dynamic sensation" of the subjects. This declaration

I said to myself—I'll paint what I see—what the flower is to me but I'll paint it big and they will be surprised into taking the time to look at it—I will make even busy New Yorkers take time to see what I see of flowers.
—Georgia O'Keeffe

Cubist and Futurist works of art, regardless of how abstract they might appear, always contain vestiges of representation, whether they be unobtrusive details like an eyelid or mustache, or an object's recognizable contours. Yet with Cubism, the seeds of abstraction were planted. It was just a matter of time until they would find fruition in artists who, like Kandinsky, would seek pure form unencumbered by referential subject matter.

zoology. That is, her plants are animistic; they seem to grow because of will, not merely because of the blind interactions of the unfolding of the genetic code with water, sun, and minerals.

And although O'Keeffe denied any attempt to portray sexual imagery in these flowers (those who saw it, she said, were speaking about themselves and not her), the edges of the petals, in their folds and convolutions, are frequently reminiscent of parts of the female body. The sense of will and reaching renders these petals active rather than passive

EARLY TWENTIETH-CENTURY ABSTRACTION IN THE UNITED STATES

The Fauvists and German Expressionists had an impact on art in the United States as well as Europe. Although the years before World War I in America were marked by an adherence to Realism and subjects from everyday rural and urban life, a strong interest in European Modernism was brewing.

291 GALLERY The American photographer Alfred Stieglitz propounded and supported the development of abstract art in the United States by exhibiting modern European works, along with those of American artists who were influenced by the Parisian avant-garde—Picasso, Matisse, and others—in his 291 gallery (at 291 Fifth Avenue in New York). Georgia O'Keeffe was among the artists supported by Stieglitz.

GEORGIA O'KEEFFE Throughout her long career, Georgia O'Keeffe (1887–1986) painted many subjects, from flowers to city buildings to the skulls of animals baked white by the sun of the desert Southwest. In each case, she captured the essence of her subjects by simplifying their forms. In 1924, the year O'Keeffe married Stieglitz, she began to paint enlarged flower pictures such as *White Iris* (Fig. **20-14**). In these paintings, she magnified and abstracted the details of her botanical subjects, so that often a large canvas was filled with but a fragment of the intersection of petals. These flowers have a yearning, reaching, organic quality, and her botany seems to function as a metaphor for

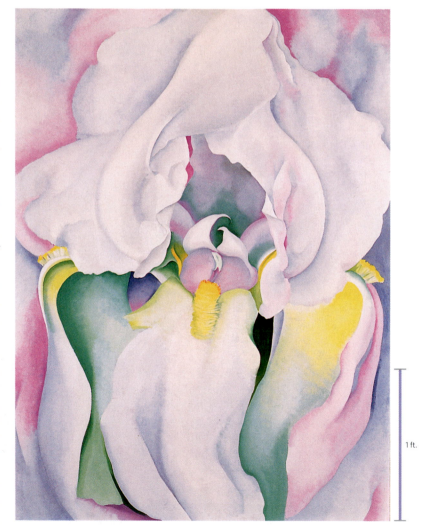

20-14 GEORGIA O'KEEFFE. *White Iris* (1930). Oil on canvas. 40" × 30". Virginia Museum of Fine Arts, Richmond, VA.

1 ft.

in their implied sexuality, so they seem symbolically to express a feminist polemic. This characteristic may be one of the reasons that O'Keeffe was "invited" to Judy Chicago's *Dinner Party* (see Fig. 1-10).

THE ARMORY SHOW Between 1908 and 1917, Stieglitz brought to 291—and thus to New York City—European Modernists, the likes of Toulouse-Lautrec, Cézanne, Matisse, Braque, and Brancusi. In 1913, the sensational Armory Show—the International Exhibition of Modern Art held at the 69th Regiment Armory in New York City—assembled works by leading American artists and an impressive array of Europeans including Goya, Delacroix, Manet and the Impressionists, van Gogh, Gauguin, Picasso, and Kandinsky. Many more American than European works were exhibited, but the latter dominated the show—raising the artistic consciousness of the Americans while raising some eyebrows. The most scandalous of the Parisian works, Marcel Duchamp's *Nude Descending a Staircase #2* (see Fig. 2-74), was dismissed as a "pile of kindling wood." But the message to American artists was clear: Europe was the center of the art world—for now.

CHARLES DEMUTH In the years following the Armory Show, American artists explored abstraction to new heights, finding ways to maintain a solid sense of subject matter in combination with geometric fragmentation and simplification. Charles Demuth (1883–1935) was one of a group of artists called "Cubo-Realists" or "Precisionists" who overlaid stylistic elements from Cubism and Futurism on authentic American imagery. *My Egypt* (Fig. 20-15) is a precise rendition of a grain elevator in Demuth's hometown of Lancaster, Pennsylvania. Diagonal lines—contradictory rays of light and shadow—sweep across the solid surfaces and lessen the intensity of the stonelike appearance of the masses. The shapes in *My Egypt* are reminiscent of limestone monoliths that form the gateways to ancient temple complexes such as that at Karnak in Egypt. The viewer cannot help being drawn to Demuth's title, which acknowledges the association of the architectural forms and, at the same time, asserts a sense of American pride and history in the possessive adjective *My*. It seems to reflect the desire on the part of the American artist to be conversant and current with European style while maintaining a bit of chauvinism about subjects that have meaning to their own time and place.

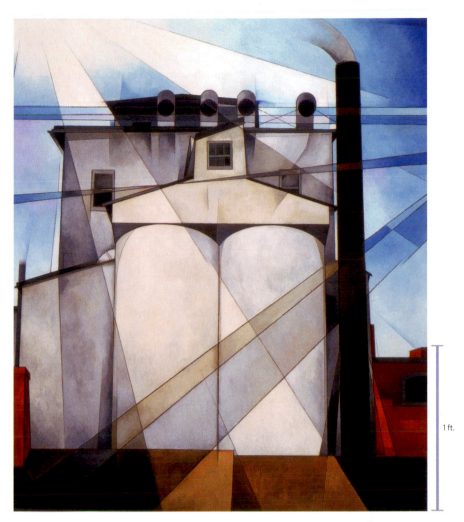

20-15 CHARLES DEMUTH. *My Egypt* (1927). Oil on composition board. 35¾" × 30". Whitney Museum of American Art, NY.

EARLY TWENTIETH-CENTURY ABSTRACTION IN EUROPE

The second decade of the twentieth century witnessed the rise of many dynamic schools of art in Russia and western Europe. Two of these—**Constructivism** and **De Stijl**, or **Neo-Plasticism**—were dedicated to pure abstraction, or nonobjective art. Nonobjective art differs from the abstraction of Cubism or Futurism in that it does not use nature as a point of departure and makes no reference to visible reality. Compositions by artists associated with Constructivism and De Stijl consist primarily of some combination of geometric shapes, mostly primary colors, and emphatic black lines. In nonobjective art, the earlier experiments in abstracting images by Cézanne and then by the Cubists reached their logical conclusion. Kandinsky is recognized as the first painter of pure abstraction, although several artists were creating nonobjective works at about the same time.

Constructivism

Born in Russia in the wake of the 1917 Communist revolution, Constructivists pushed the limits of geometric abstraction in painting. Three-dimensional work, which also features geometric shapes and planes, were constructed—or put together—from industrial materials such as plastic, metal, and glass. Constructivist sculptors thus challenged conventional materials and techniques such as carving, modeling, and casting that emphasized the manipulation of mass rather than space.

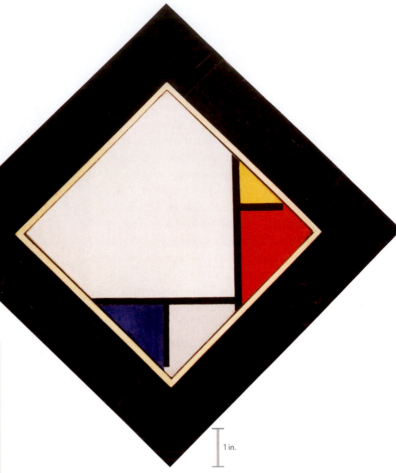

20-17 THEO VAN DOESBURG. *Composition* (1929). Oil on canvas. 11¹³⁄₁₆" × 11⅞". The Philadelphia Museum of Art, Philadelphia, PA.

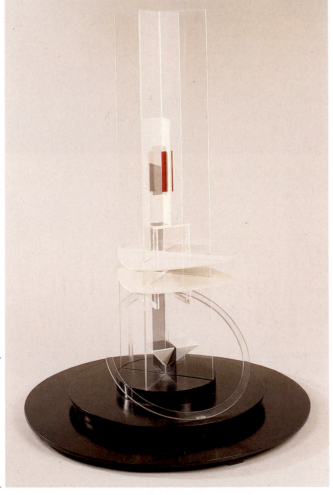

20-16 NAUM GABO. *Column* (c. 1923). Perspex, wood, metal, glass. 41½" × 29" × 29". Solomon R. Guggenheim Museum, NY.

NAUM GABO Naum Gabo (1890–1977) embraced the ascendance of space over mass in works like *Column* (Fig. 20-16), in which intersecting planes of metal, glass, and plastic penetrate, define, and frame the space in and around the sculpture. True to the Constructivist vision, that was, in a sense, Utopian, *Column* bridges the gap between fine art and industrial technologies. As such it symbolizes the Constructivist advocacy the utility of art. As the postrevolutionary years progressed, the work of the Russian Constructivists was censored by the Communist regime that found it elitist, in spite of everything that the art represented. Many of these artists left the country and contributed to a developing international Constructivist style.

DE STIJL OR NEO-PLASTICISM Theo van Doesburg (1883–1931), born in Holland just seven years before Vincent van Gogh's death, represents the Dutch answer to Russian Constructivism. Drawn to the purity and precision of geometric shapes and a complete abstraction of reality that would lead to nonobjective works, van Doesburg drew

*All painting is composed of line and color. Line and color are the essence of painting.
Hence they must be freed from their bondage to the imitation of nature
and allowed to exist for themselves.*

—Piet Mondrian

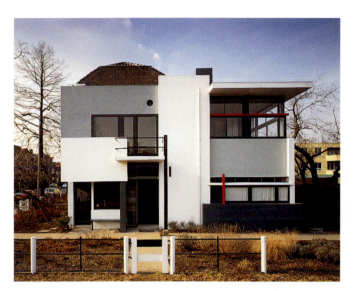

20-18 GERRIT RIETVELD. Schroeder House, Utrecht, Netherlands (1924).
© 2011 Artists Rights Society (ARS), NY/ c/o Pictoright Amsterdam.

together like-minded artists and played a principal role in the dissemination of their style and theories through the publication of a magazine called **De Stijl**. De Stijl, which translates as "the style," is also commonly referred to as Neo-Plasticism.

In van Doesburg's *Composition* (Fig. **20-17**), black gridlike lines intersect to create geometric zones filled with primary colors. As in Gabo's sculpture, the void space in the composition—the large white area, in van Doesburg's painting—becomes an active part of the work as a whole. Flatness was also a fundamental component of De Stijl movement paintings, as summarized by Piet Mondrian, an artist whose name is virtually synonymous with the style:

> Painting occupies a plane surface. The plane surface is integral with the physical and psychological being of the painting. Hence the plane surface must be respected, must be allowed to declare itself, must not be falsified by imitations of volume. Painting must be as flat as the surface it is painted on.[3]

If Mondrian's views had been a theory of architecture, perhaps they would have found expression in works such as Gerrit Rietveld's Schroeder House (Fig. **20-18**), which was built early in the twentieth century but continues to inspire architects today. Here there is an almost literal translation of geometry and color to architecture. Broad expanses of white

[3] Goldwater and Treves, 426.

concrete intersect to define the strictly rectilinear dwelling, or appear to float in superimposed planes. As in a van Doesburg or Mondrian painting, these planes are accented by black verticals and horizontals in supporting posts or window mullions. Like the paintings, the surfaces are clean and simple and only occasionally punctuated with color.

The De Stijl artists' obsessive respect for the two-dimensionality of the canvas surface may be viewed, in one sense, as the culmination of experiments with shallow, compressed pictorial space and the integration of figure and ground. In these works, canvas and painting, figure and ground are one.

CONSTANTIN BRANCUSI The universality sought by Mondrian through extreme simplification can also be seen in the sculpture of Constantin Brancusi (1876–1957). Yet unlike Mondrian's, Brancusi's works, however abstract they appear, are rooted in the figure. Brancusi was born in Romania 13 years after the Salon des Réfusés. After an apprenticeship as a cabinet-maker and studies at the Bucharest Academy of Fine Arts, he traveled to Paris to enroll in the famous École des Beaux-Arts. In 1907, Brancusi exhibited at the Salon d'Automne, leaving favorable impressions of his work.

Brancusi's work, heavily indebted to Rodin at this point, grew in a radically different direction. As early as 1909, he reduced the human head—a favorite theme he would draw upon for years—to an egg-shaped form with sparse indications of facial features. In this, and in other abstractions such as *Bird in Space* (Fig. **20-19**), he reached for the essence of the subject by offering the simplest contour that, along

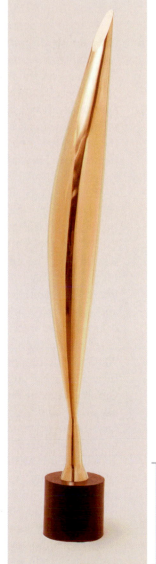

20-19 CONSTANTIN BRANCUSI. *Bird in Space* (c. 1928). Bronze (unique cast). H: 54". The Philadelphia Museum of Art, Philadelphia, PA. © 2011 Artists Rights Society (ARS), NY/ADAGP, Paris.

1 ft.

with a descriptive title, would fire recognition in the spectator. *Bird in Space* evolved from more representational versions into a refined symbol of the cleanness and solitude of flight.

FANTASY AND DADA

Throughout the history of art, most critics and patrons have seen the accurate representation of visual reality as a noble goal. Artists who have departed from this goal, who have chosen to depict their personal worlds of dreams or supernatural fantasies, have not had it easy. Before the twentieth century, only isolated examples of what we call **Fantastic art** could be found. The early 1900s, however, saw many artists exploring fanciful imagery and working in styles as varied as their imaginations.

How do we describe Fantastic art? The word *fantastic* derives from the Greek *phantastikos*, meaning "the ability to represent something to the mind" or "to create a mental image." *Fantasy* is further defined as "unreal, odd, seemingly impossible, and strange in appearance." Fantastic art, then, is the representation of incredible images from the artist's mind. At times the images are joyful reminiscences; at times, horrific nightmares. They may be capricious or grotesque.

PAUL KLEE One of the most whimsical yet subtly sardonic of the Fantastic artists is Paul Klee (1879–1940). Although influenced early in his career by nineteenth-century artists such as Goya, who touched upon fantasy, Klee received much of his stylistic inspiration from Cézanne. In 1911, he joined Der Blaue Reiter, where his theories about intuitive approaches to painting, growing abstraction, and love of color were well received.

A certain innocence pervades Klee's idiosyncratic style. After abandoning representational elements in his art, Klee turned to ethnographic and children's art, seeking a universality of expression in their extreme simplicity. Many of his works combine a charming naïveté with wry commentary. *Twittering Machine* (Fig. **20-20**), for example, offers a humorous contraption composed of four fantastic birds balanced precariously on a wire attached to a crank. The viewer who is motivated to piece together the possible function of this apparatus might assume that turning the crank would result in the twittering suggested by the title.

In this seemingly innocuous painting, Klee perhaps satirizes contemporary technology, in which machines may sometimes seem to do little more than express the whims

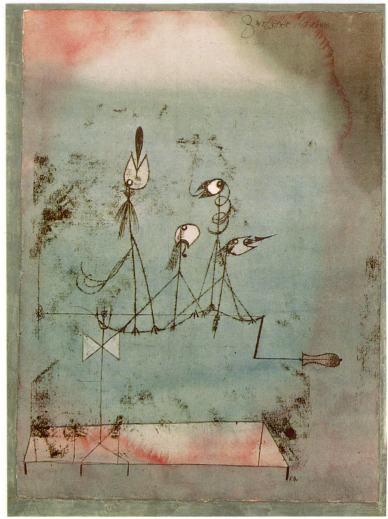

20-20 PAUL KLEE. *Twittering Machine* (1922). Watercolor, pen and ink. 25¼" × 19". The Museum of Modern Art, NY.

and ego of the inventor. But why a machine that twitters? Some have suggested a darker interpretation in which the mechanical birds are traps to lure real birds to a makeshift coffin beneath. Such gruesome doings might in turn symbolize the entrapment of humans by their own existence. In any event, it is evident that Klee's simple, cartoonlike subjects may carry a mysterious and rich iconography.

GIORGIO DE CHIRICO Equally mysterious are the odd juxtapositions of familiar objects found in the works of Giorgio de Chirico (1888–1978). Unlike Klee's figures, Chirico's are rendered in a realistic manner. Chirico attempted to make the irrational believable. His subjects are often derived from dreams, in which ordinary objects are found in extraordinary situations. The realistic technique tends to heighten the believability of these events and imparts a certain eeriness characteristic of dreams or nightmares. Part of the intrigue

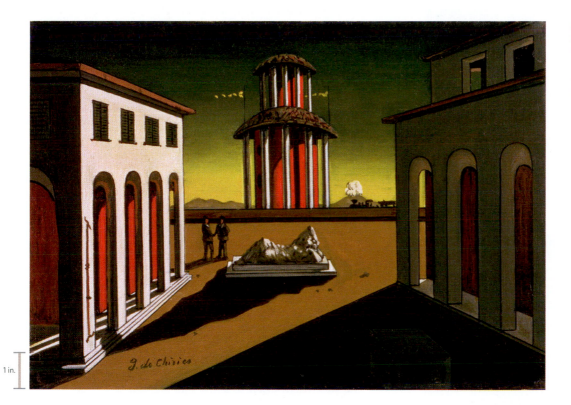

1 in.

20-21 GIORGIO DE CHIRICO. *Piazza d'Italia*. Oil on canvas. 9⅞" × 13⅞". Art Gallery of Ontario, Toronto, Ontario, Canada. © 2011 Artists Rights Society (ARS), NY/SIAE, Rome.

of Chirico's subjects lies in their ambiguity and in the uncertainty of the outcome. Often we do not know why we dream what we dream. We do not know how the strange juxtapositions occur, nor how the story will evolve. We may now and then "save" ourselves from danger by awakening.

The intrigues of the dream world are captured by de Chirico in works such as *Piazza d'Italia* (Fig. **20-12**). Some of his favorite images—icy arcades, deserted piazzas, a distant locomotive with a suspended puff of smoke rising from the engine car—provide a backdrop for an encounter between two figures at the far end of a diagonal zone of sunlight that connects them to the monumental sculpture resting in the square. We are drawn into a disturbing, dreamlike atmosphere that, in its juxtaposition of familiar shapes with unsettling presences, suggests a certain banality of danger. We perceive an overriding sense of doom for no apparent reason other than that we bring our own fears and superstitions to our interpretation of the painting.

Dada

In 1916, during World War I, an international movement arose that declared itself against art. Responding to the absurdity of war and the insanity of a world that gave rise to it, the Dadaists declared that art—a reflection of this sorry state of affairs—was stupid and must be destroyed. Yet in order to communicate their outrage, the Dadaists created works of art! This inherent contradiction spelled the eventual demise of their movement. Despite centers in Paris, Berlin, Cologne, Zürich, and New York City, Dada ended with a whimper in 1922.

The name **Dada** was supposedly chosen at random from a dictionary. It is an apt epithet. The nonsense term describes nonsense art—art that is meaningless, absurd, unpredictable. Although it is questionable whether this catchy label was in truth derived at random, the element of chance was important to the Dada art form. Dada poetry, for example, consisted of nonsense verses of random word combinations. Some works of art, such as the Dada collages, were constructed of materials found by chance and mounted randomly. Yet however meaningless or unpredictable the poets and artists intended their products to be, in reality they were not. In an era dominated by the doctrine of psychoanalysis, the choice of even nonsensical words spoke something at least of the poet. Works of art supposedly constructed in random fashion also frequently betrayed the mark of some design.

Fantasy and Dada **491**

LEONARDO'S *MONA LISA*, DUCHAMP'S *MONA LISA* (L.H.O.O.Q.), ODUTOKUN'S *DIALOGUE WITH MONA LISA*, AND LEE'S *BONA LISA*

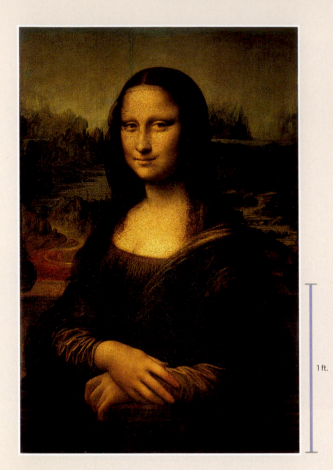

1 ft.

20-22 LEONARDO DA VINCI. *Mona Lisa* (c. 1503). Oil on panel. 30¼" × 21". Louvre, Paris, France.

IF YOU WERE ASKED to close your eyes and think of the most famous work of art in all of history, what would you say? Odds are that the first piece to come up on your memory screen would be none other than the lead-off work in this exercise. Her portrait has captivated poets and lyricists, museumgoers, and artists for centuries. Simply put, her face has been everywhere. Why and how did she attain this icon status? The *Mona Lisa* (Fig. **20-22**) is a portrait of a banker's wife, worked on by Leonardo for four years and, as was much of his work, left unfinished.

In its own day, though, it was quite an innovative composition. Among other things, Leonardo rejected the traditional profile portrait bust in favor of a three-quarter-turned, half-length figure. The inclusion of the hands in a natural position, for the most part uncharacteristic of earlier portraiture, was essential for Leonardo as a method of exploring and revealing the personality of the sitter: "A good

painter has two chief objects to paint, man and the intention of his soul; the former is easy, the latter hard, because he has to represent it by the attitudes and movements of the limbs." A new look at portrait painting, to be sure. But there is still the matter of that enigmatic smile. And those eyes, which many have vouched, follow the viewer's movements across a room. The *Mona Lisa* is a beautiful painting, but does that account for why a visitor in search of the masterpiece in Paris's Louvre Museum need only look for the one painting that cannot be viewed because of the crowd surrounding it?

The selection of images in this exercise represents but a sampling of work that attempts to come to terms with "Mona Lisa: The Icon." One of the earlier revisions of Leonardo's painting was assembled by the Dada artist, Marcel Duchamp (Fig. **20-23**). Using a reproduction of the original

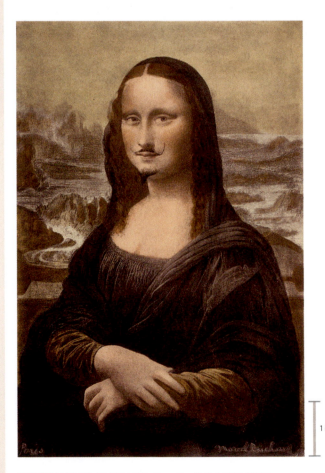

1 in.

20-23 MARCEL DUCHAMP. *Mona Lisa* (L.H.O.O.Q.) (1919). Rectified readymade; pencil on a reproduction. 7¾" × 4⅞". The Philadelphia Museum of Art, Philadelphia, PA. © 2011 Artists Rights Society (ARS), NY/ADAGP, Paris/Succession Marcel Duchamp.

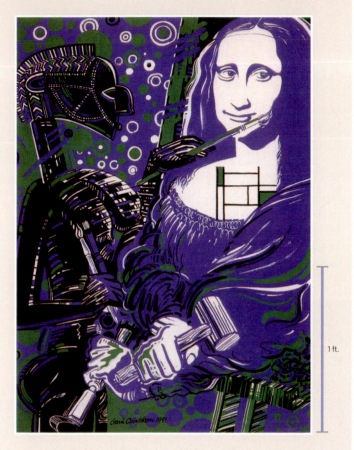

20-24 G. ODUTOKUN. *Dialogue with Mona Lisa* (1991). Gouache on paper. 30" × 22".

work, Duchamp modified the image—graffiti style—by penciling in a mustache and goatee. Beneath the image of the banker's wife is Duchamp's irreverent explanation of that enigmatic smile: If you read the letters aloud with their French pronunciation, using a slurred, legato style, the sound your ears will hear is *"elle a chaud au cul."* (Rough PG-13-rated translation: "She is hot in the pants.") Part of the underlying philosophy of the Dada movement was the notion that the museums of the world are filled with "dead art" that should be "destroyed." Why do you imagine Duchamp would have used the image of the *Mona Lisa* to convey something of this philosophy? Duchamp was certainly a capable enough draftsman to have rendered his own copy of the *Mona Lisa*. Do you think he used a reproduction simply to expedite completion of the work?

The gouache composition by G. Odutokun (Fig. **20-24**) is another clear illustration of the icon status of the *Mona Lisa*. In this work, cultural exchanges are explored through the interaction between images symbolic of Western and non-Western traditions. What do you think the artist aims to suggest through the title of the work? Look closely at the content of the piece. Who is painting whom; who is sculpting whom? Even though the artist seems to be portraying a cross-cultural encounter, would this work be as relevant to a contemporary European viewer as a contemporary African viewer? What does this composition say about standards of beauty that are culturally defined?

And is the standard of beauty that the *Mona Lisa* has represented for generations one that is gender biased as well as culturally biased? This question is posed in Sadie Lee's revision entitled *Bona Lisa* (Fig. **20-25**). At first glance, the portrait seems to be a male version of Leonardo's female sitter. In reality, Lee has represented the banker's wife as a lesbian with close-cropped hair and masculine attire. Edward Lucie-Smith has interpreted this work as an "ironic comment on the popular image of a 'butch' lesbian."

From politics and protest to the protest of political correctness, each of the artists we have here observed has understood the significance of attaching his or her message to Leonardo's masterwork. What are your impressions? ●

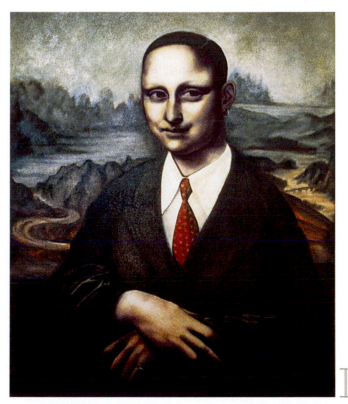

20-25 SADIE LEE. *Bona Lisa* (1992). Oil on board. 23" × 19".

MARCEL DUCHAMP In an effort to advertise their nihilistic views, the Dadaists assaulted the public with irreverence. Not only did they attempt to negate art, but they also advocated antisocial and amoral behavior. Marcel Duchamp offered for exhibition a urinal, turned on its back and titled *Fountain* (see Fig. 1-36). Later he summed up the Dada sensibility in works such as *Mona Lisa* (*L.H.O.O.Q.*) (see Fig. 20-23 in the nearby Compare + Contrast feature), in which he impudently defiled a color print of Leonardo da Vinci's masterpiece with a mustache and goatee. In *Nude Descending a Staircase #2* (see Fig. 2-74), Duchamp's simulation of the fourth dimension of time through a series of overlapping images added a new element to the experiments of Cubism.

Fortified by growing interest in psychoanalysis, Dada, with some modification, would provide the basis for a movement called Surrealism that began in the early 1920s. Like Max Ernst's Dada composition, *Two Children Are Threatened by a Nightingale* (Fig. 20-26), some Surrealist works offer irrational subjects

20-26 MAX ERNST. *Two Children Are Threatened by a Nightingale* (1924). Oil on wood with wood construction. 27½" × 22½" × 4½". The Museum of Modern Art, NY. © 2011 Artists Rights Society (ARS), NY/ADAGP, Paris.

and the chance juxtaposition of everyday objects. These often menacing paintings also incorporate the Realistic technique and the suggestion of dream imagery found in Fantastic art.

SURREALISM

Surrealism began as a literary movement after World War I. Its adherents based their writings on the nonrational, and thus they were naturally drawn to the Dadaists. Both literary groups engaged in **automatic writing**, in which the mind was to be purged of purposeful thought, and a series of free associations were then to be expressed with the pen. Words were not meant to denote their literal meanings but to symbolize the often seething contents of the unconscious mind. Eventually the Surrealist writers broke from the Dadaists, believing that the earlier movement was becoming too academic. Under the leadership of the poet André Breton, they defined their movement as follows in a 1924 manifesto:

> *Surrealism*, noun, masc., pure psychic automatism by which it is intended to express either verbally or in writing, the true function of thought. Thought dictated in the absence of all control exerted by reason, and outside all aesthetic or moral preoccupations.

> *Encycl. Philos.* Surrealism is based on the belief in the superior reality of certain forms of association heretofore neglected, in the omnipotence of the dream, and in the disinterested play of thought. It leads to the permanent destruction of all other psychic mechanisms and to its substitution for them in the solution of the principal problems of life.

From the beginning, Surrealism expounded two very different methods of working. **Illusionistic Surrealism**, exemplified by artists such as Salvador Dalí and Yves Tanguy, rendered the irrational content, absurd juxtapositions, and metamorphoses of the dream state in a highly illusionistic manner. The other, called **Automatist Surrealism**, was a direct outgrowth of automatic writing and was used to divulge mysteries of the unconscious through abstraction. The Automatist phase is typified by Joan Miró and André Masson.

SALVADOR DALÍ Modesty was not his strong suit. One of the few "household names" in the history of art belongs to a leading Surrealist figure,

1 in.

the Spaniard Salvador Dalí (1904–1986). His reputation for leading an unusual—one could say surrealistic—life would seem to precede his art, because many people not familiar with his canvases had seen Dalí's outrageous mustache and knew of his shenanigans. Once as a guest on the Ed Sullivan television show, he threw open cans of paint at a huge canvas.

Dalí began his painting career, however, in a somewhat more conservative manner, adopting, in turn, Impressionist, Pointillist, and Futurist styles. Following these forays into contemporary styles, he sought academic training at the Academy of Fine Arts in Madrid. This experience steeped him in a tradition of illusionistic realism that he never abandoned.

In what may be Dalí's most famous canvas, *The Persistence of Memory* (Fig. 20-27), the drama of the dreamlike imagery is enhanced by his trompe l'oeil technique. Here, in a barren landscape of incongruous forms, time, as all else, has expired. A watch is left crawling with insects like scavengers over carrion; three other watches hang limp and useless over a rectangular block, a dead tree, and a lifeless, amorphous creature that bears a curious resemblance to Dalí. The artist conveys the world of the dream, juxtaposing unrelated objects in an extraordinary situation. But a haunting sense of reality threatens the line between perception and imagination. Dalí's is, in the true definition of the term, a surreality—or reality above and beyond reality.

JOAN MIRÓ Not all of the Surrealists were interested in rendering their enigmatic personal dreams. Some found this highly introspective subject matter meaningless to the observer and sought a more universal form of expression.

The Automatist Surrealists believed that the unconscious held such universal imagery, and through spontaneous, or automatic, drawing, they attempted to reach it. Artists of this group, such as Joan Miró (1893–1983), sought to eliminate all thought from their minds and then trace their brushes across the surface of the canvas. The organic shapes derived from intersecting skeins of line were believed to be unadulterated by conscious thought and thus drawn from the unconscious. Once the basic designs had been outlined, a conscious period of work could follow in which the artist intentionally applied his or her craft to render them in their final form. But because no conscious control was to be exerted to determine the early course of the designs, the Automatist method was seen as spontaneous, as employing chance and accident. Needless to say, the works are abstract, although some shapes are amoebic.

Miró was born near Barcelona and spent his early years in local schools of art learning how to paint like the French Modernists. He practiced several styles ranging from Romanticism to Realism to Impressionism, but Cézanne and van Gogh seem to have influenced him most. In 1919, Miró moved to Paris, where he was receptive to different art styles. The work of Matisse and Picasso, along with the primitive innocence of Rousseau, found their way into his canvases. Coupled with a rich native iconography and an inclination toward fantasy, these different elements would shape Miró's unique style.

Miró's need for spontaneity in communicating his subjects was compatible with Automatist Surrealism, although the whimsical nature of most of his subjects often appears at odds with that of other members of the movement. In

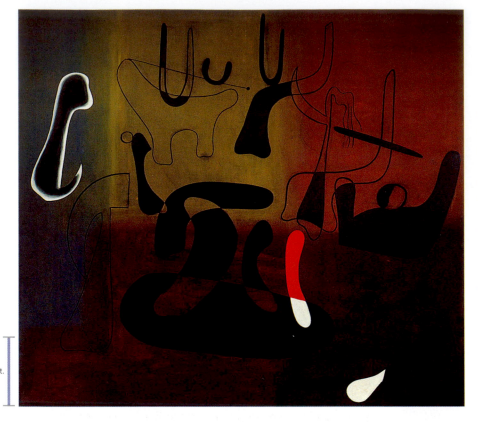

20-28 JOAN MIRÓ. *Painting* (1933). Oil on canvas. 68½" × 77¼". The Museum of Modern Art, NY.

1 ft.

this work, Miró applied Breton's principles of psychic automatism in an aesthetically pleasing, decorative manner.

By 1930, Surrealism had developed into an international movement, despite the divorce of many of the first members from the group. New adherents exhibiting radically different styles kept the movement alive.

THE BAUHAUS

The early part of the twentieth century also saw numerous innovations in architecture, including those of the American Frank Lloyd Wright, which were discussed in Chapter 11. The German architect Walter Gropius (1883–1969) and his followers brought several principles to modern architecture, amplifying the concepts that "form follows function" and "less is more." Gropius relied on basic forms, such as the rectangular solid, and diligently avoided ornamentation and embellishment. For Gropius, an overriding emphasis was on simplicity and on the economical use of space, time, materials, and money.

Painting (Fig. **20-28**), meandering lines join or intersect to form the contours of clusters of organic figures. Some of these shapes are left void to display a nondescript background of subtly colored squares. Others are filled in with sharply contrasting black, white, and bright red pigment. In

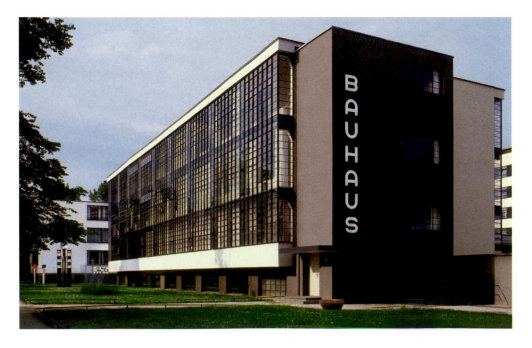

20-29 WALTER GROPIUS. Shop Block, The Bauhaus (1925–1926). Dessau, Germany. © 2011 Artists Rights Society (ARS), NY/VG Bild-Kunst, Bonn.

Miës chaired the architecture department of the school that would become the Illinois Institute of Technology. During its short life of 15 years, the Bauhaus gave birth to designers and designs that would shape much of the remaining two-thirds of the twentieth century.

In Chapter 21, we will see Miës's Farnsworth House (Fig. 21-43), a single-story residential design, although he also worked "tall." His visionary style can be seen in his model for a glass skyscraper that was never built (Fig. **20-30**). Miës's Seagram Building on New York's Park Avenue also has glass curtain walls, but is more compact, less soaring in appearance (see Fig. 21-44).

Marcel Breuer's (1902–1981) tubular steel chair (Fig. **20-31**) is an example of Bauhaus furniture. Gone are the overstuffed cushions. The sitter is suspended in midair on cloth or leather slings attached to steel tubing. The concept behind the chair is the use of simple shapes, but the result is actually quite complex. Bauhaus furniture, especially Breuer chairs of various kinds, remain popular to this day and are visible on many websites. Like Gropius, Breuer also moved to the United States and taught at Harvard University. Breuer would later design New York's Whitney Museum of American Art, which we see in the New York Art Tour following the next chapter.

As the decade of the 1930s evolved, Adolf Hitler rose to power, and war once again threatened Europe. Hitler's ascent drove not only architects but also refugee artists of the highest reputation to the shores of the United States. Among them were the leading figures of Abstraction and Surrealism, two divergent styles that would join to form the basis of an avant-garde American movement. The center of the art world had moved to New York.

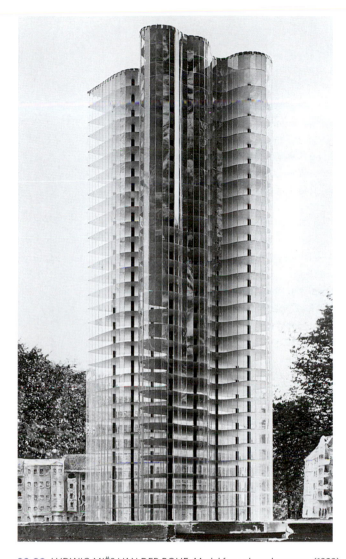

20-30 LUDWIG MIËS VAN DER ROHE. Model for a glass skyscraper (1922). The Museum of Modern Art, NY. © 2011 Artists Rights Society (ARS), NY/ VG Bild-Kunst, Bonn.

In 1919, Gropius became director of the Weimar School of Arts and Crafts. He renamed the school *Das Staatliche Bauhaus*, or "Building House of the State," referred to simply as The Bauhaus. Gropius believed that his vision was a doorway to the future of art and architecture, training architects, artists, designers, and craftspersons. Because of political conflicts, Gropius moved his school to Dessau in 1925 and designed its new home (Fig. **20-29**). Design and carpentry were integral to the Bauhaus curriculum, and Gropius had students and faculty create the furnishings for the building. Ludwig Miës van der Rohe (1886–1969) became director of the Bauhaus in 1928 and moved the school to Berlin.

The Nazis shut down the Bauhaus in 1933, and some of its faculty fled to the United States, Gropius and Miës van der Rohe among them. Gropius became chair of architecture at the Harvard University Graduate School of Design, and

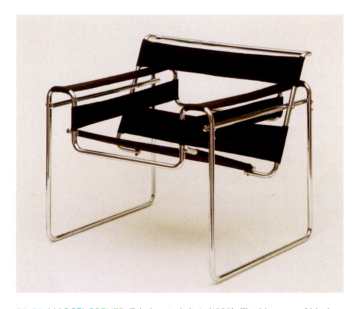

20-31 MARCEL BREUER. Tubular steel chair (1925). The Museum of Modern Art, NY.

ART TOUR *Chicago*

GO FOR THE LAKE and the miles of beaches. Go for the deep-dish pizza and hot dogs with the works. Go to cheer for the Chicago Cubs or the Bulls. But while you're in Chicago—for goodness' sake—make time in your day for the most magnificent art and architecture you can imagine.

Situated at the literal crossroads between the East and Midwest, Chicago grew rich on trade opportunities and began to take shape as a major commercial and cultural center in the nineteenth century. The Great Chicago Fire of 1871, however, destroyed most of the downtown buildings in a conflagration that lasted 36 hours. Out of this devastation, after which one-third of the city population was homeless, came one of the greatest building campaigns in U.S. history.

Experiencing Chicago starts with getting to know its neighborhoods—77 in all—and its unique topographic features—such as the Chicago River, which wends its way amidst skyscrapers, or Lake Michigan, which provides 15 miles of recreational beaches. At its heart is the Loop, but the long list contains neighborhoods such as the Magnificent Mile, River North, River West, the Gold Coast, Old Town, Lincoln Park, Wrigleyville, Lakeview, South Loop, and Chinatown.

We all know how good it feels to "be in the loop." But that expression couldn't have more meaning than when it's used to describe the city of Chicago. The Loop in this town refers to the very center of the downtown core and takes its name from the elevated train tracks that encircle the area.

The city of Chicago has always been synonymous with architectural innovation and world-class buildings. Balloon-frame construction (still one of the most common residential building types in the United States today, and so called because it was said to be as simple and easy as blowing up a balloon) originated in 1833 with a Chicago developer. Although most structures

of this kind went up in flames in the 1871 fire, you can still see a few of them in the North Side area of the city. After the fire, wood was banned as a building material and cast iron and terra-cotta took its place. Those materials—along with steel—made their most significant impact on the city's commercial architecture. It was here that the first skyscraper was built and the Chicago School of architecture—an internationally celebrated style—was born.

One of the weirder structures in the downtown core is the Monadnock Building, the two halves of which represent old-style and new-style architectural design and materials. One half—the northern half—was designed in 1891 by the firm of Burnham and Root. At 16 stories, it was the tallest masonry building ever to have been constructed. Two years later, the other, southern half was constructed, this time of a steel skeleton covered with a sheath of terra-cotta. This design, by the firm of Holabird and Roche, was pivotal for the future of the skyscraper. Many followed—the Rookery, the Reliance Building, and the Marquette Building, to name a few. All of these can be seen within the downtown core. Keep your eye out for the signature "Chicago windows" on some of these buildings. They were a stylistic by-product of the Chicago School's structural innovations and consist of a wide central glass pane that doesn't open flanked by two thinner windows that do.

Among the sentimental favorites of Chicago architecture are the Marshall Field and Company and the Carson Pirie Scott department stores. Marshall Field's began as a Renaissance-revival building that ultimately grew to accommodate 4,000,000 square feet of retail space; its southern atrium features a spectacular glass mosaic dome whose installation was supervised by Louis Comfort Tiffany himself. Louis Sullivan, one of the city's most prolific and beloved architects of the Chicago School,

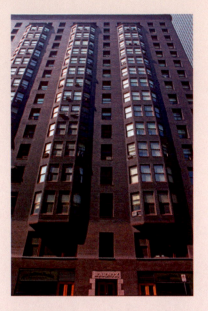

THE MONADNOCK BUILDING.
Robert Frerck/Odyssey.

finished the exterior of his steel-frame Carson Pirie Scott building with white terra-cotta and graced the first two stories of the entrance with ornamental cast-iron motifs consisting of organic and geometric forms. You can still pick out the initials *L.H.S.* above the entrance.

Surveying the architectural wonders of Chicago can keep a tourist busy. These historic examples are but the tip of the iceberg. Within the downtown core you'll find Beaux Arts–style gems such as the Chicago Theatre, Neoclassical monuments such as the Chicago Cultural Center and the Art Institute of Chicago (more later on this phenomenal collection), and on the opposite end of the style spectrum, the Sears Tower. Opened in 1974 after three years under construction, the building had, then lost, and then regained the title as the world's tallest building (thanks to the addition of one very tall antenna). Not surprisingly, its sky deck offers unparalleled views of the city, Lake Michigan, and beyond.

Extending your tour a bit north, you'll come to the Magnificent Mile. There

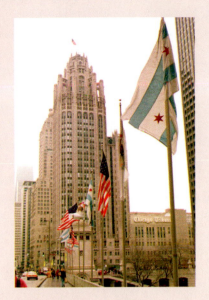

THE TRIBUNE TOWER.

you'll get a glimpse of the Wrigley Building (seat of the chewing gum empire), Marina City's corncob towers, Miës van der Rohe's exposed steel-frame IBM Building, and the Tribune Tower (home to one of the country's most influential newspapers). The Tribune Tower that you see was the winning design in a 1922 international competition calling upon architects to design the most beautiful office building in the world. The entrance features sculptures of figures from Aesop's fables, and gargoyles abound in the upper reaches of the facade. Most peculiar, perhaps, is the collection of stone fragments from the world's great architectural sites embedded in the outer walls of the building. You'll find pieces from London's Westminster Abbey, the Colosseum in Rome, and

FRANK GEHRY. PRITZKER PAVILION FOR MILLENNIUM PARK.

the Great Wall of China; a rock from Antarctica; and one from the moon. Believe it or not, most of these stones were pilfered by *Tribune* foreign correspondents at the behest (command?) of one of the paper's early publishers.

Among Chicago's newest additions to its architecture hall of fame is Frank Gehry's music pavilion for Millennium Park, an extension of Grant Park. Gehry's band shell, home to the Grant Park Symphony, is renowned for a sound system that reaches all of its 14,000 audience members.

Although architecture in Chicago has a way of monopolizing the spotlight, its art collections merit a significant piece of the action. For one thing, the Art Institute of Chicago, a venerable museum of art that was founded in 1879, has what some of us like to call "The Room." This term of endearment refers to a cluster of spaces featuring some of the best-known examples of Impressionist, Postimpressionist, and early twentieth-century art—Monet haystacks, Degas dancers, a van Gogh self-portrait; Cezanne's *Still Life with Basket of Apples* (Fig. 19-24), Picasso's *Old Guitarist* (Fig. 20-5), Hopper's *Nighthawks* (Fig. 1-29), Wood's *American Gothic* (Fig. 4-9), Toulouse-Lautrec's *At the Moulin Rouge* (Fig. 19-28), and one of Chicago's most prized possessions, Seurat's *A Sunday Afternoon on the Island of La Grand Jatte* (Fig. 19-23)—and more. Students remark that their textbooks unfold before their eyes as they wander these galleries.

Chicago's museums go far beyond the Institute. The Museum of Contemporary Art has an impressive permanent collection (Alexander Calder, Andy

Warhol, Cindy Sherman—to mention but a few artists featured in your textbook) mixed with cutting-edge rotating exhibitions by new and established contemporary artists. The Terra Museum of American Art, founded and funded by a man who invented fast-drying ink, is one of the few U.S. collections designed to feature exclusively works by American artists. It includes paintings of the Hudson River School, George Caleb Bingham, and Edward Hopper. The University of Chicago is also the site of both the Oriental Institute (specializing in Middle Eastern antiquities) and the Smart Museum (known for its old master prints, Asian paintings, and postwar Chicago artwork and craft). These museums, and the university, are in Chicago's South Side area, also the location of the famed Frank Lloyd Wright Robie House, designed for the bicycle manufacturer-magnate Frederick Robie. Wright's signature unity among all of the parts—exterior design, interior function, interior decoration—makes this one of the quintessential examples of Wright's Prairie style of architecture.

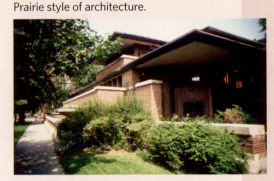

FRANK LLOYD WRIGHT. ROBIE HOUSE.
© 2011 Frank Lloyd Wright Foundation/Artists Rights Society (ARS), NY.

So grab a hot dog (which, in Chicago, has its own sort of architecture) with ketchup, mustard, relish, onions, and hot peppers and get yourself moving. You still have to meet Sue (the most complete *Tyrannosaurus rex* anywhere, on display at the Field Museum) before you catch the best jazz and blues in the world.

TO CONTINUE YOUR TOUR and learn more about Chicago, go to CourseMate.

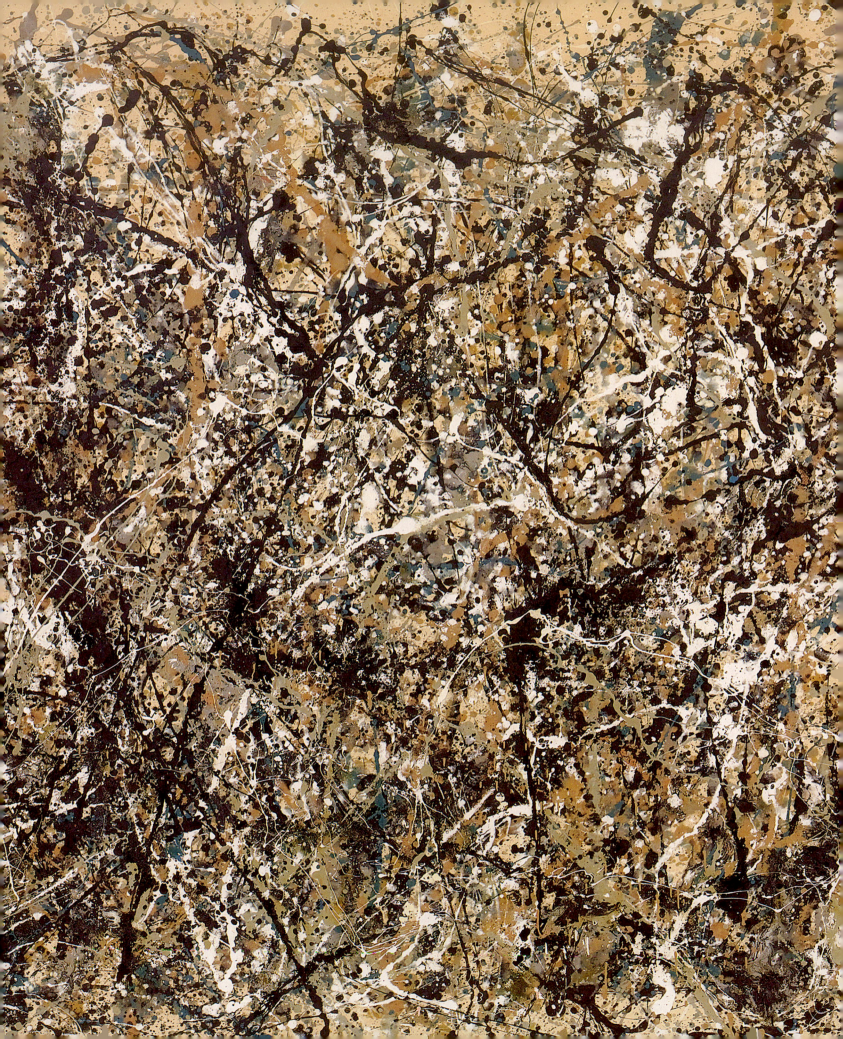

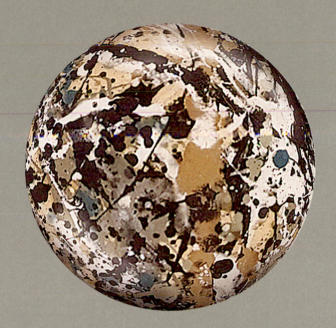

THE TWENTIETH CENTURY: POSTWAR TO POSTMODERN

21

There is a saying, once thought to be a Chinese curse, that reads, "May you live in interesting times." Whatever the origin, it captures the value of stimulation and novelty, even at the expense, perhaps, of tranquility. When it comes to contemporary art, we live in nothing if not interesting times. Louise Bourgeois, who was born in 1911 and continued to work avidly until her death at age 98, noted that "there are no settled ways"; there is "no fixed approach." Never before in history have artists experimented so freely with so many mediums, such different styles, such a wealth of content. Never before in history have works of art been so accessible to so many people. Go to Google Images, and the world of art and artists is a mouse click away.

In this chapter, we discuss painting, sculpture, architecture, and other works that have appeared since the end of World War II—the art of recent times and of today. After the war, the center of the art world shifted to New York following its long tenure in Paris, for several reasons. A wave of European immigrant artists, some of whom escaped the Nazis, had settled largely in New York. Among them were Marcel Duchamp, Fernand Léger, Josef Albers, and Hans Hofmann. The Federal Art Project of the Works Progress Administration (WPA), New Deal programs spearheaded by Franklin Delano Roosevelt, had also nourished the New York artist community during the Great Depression. Some of these artists, such as Jackson Pollock, Willem de Kooning, and Mark Rothko, constituted what became known as the first-generation New York School. Even the Mexican muralists Diego Rivera and

José Clemente Orozco sojourned and taught in the city. Just before the Great Depression began, Orozco had already argued that the artists of the New World should no longer look to Europe for their inspiration and their models.

In January 1929, he wrote: "If new races have appeared upon the lands of the New World, such races have the unavoidable duty to produce a New Art in a new spiritual and physical medium. Any other road is plain cowardice." Despite his devotion to the arts and culture of the Mexican Native Americans, Orozco added: "Already the architecture of Manhattan is a new value, something that has nothing to do with Egyptian pyramids, with the Paris Opera, with the Geralda of Seville, or with Saint Sofia, any more than it has to do with the Maya palaces of Chichen-Itzá or with the pueblos of Arizona."[1] New York City became the fertile ground for the experiments of the postwar generation of artists.

THE NEW YORK SCHOOL: THE FIRST GENERATION

At mid-twentieth century, the influences of earlier nonobjective painting, the colorful distortions of Expressionism, Cubism, the automatist processes of Surrealism, and a host of other factors—including interest in Zen Buddhism and Jungian psychoanalysis—converged in New York City. It was in this artistic melting pot that Abstract Expressionism flowered. Like other art movements that appeared radical, critics reacted to it with both intrigue and skepticism. Writing in *The New Yorker* in 1945, Robert M. Coates commented:

> [A] new school of painting is developing in this country. It is small as yet, no bigger than a baby's fist, but it is noticeable if you get around to the galleries much. It partakes a little of Surrealism and still more of Expressionism, and although its main current is still muddy and its direction obscure, one can make out bits of Hans Arp and Joan Miró floating in it, together with large chunks of Picasso and occasional fragments of [African American] sculptors. It is more emotional than logical in expression, and you may not like it (I don't either, entirely), but it can't escape attention.[2]

Spontaneity, gestural brushstrokes, nonobjective imagery, and fields of intense color characterize Abstract Expressionism. Many canvases are quite large which, at any proximity, seem to envelop the viewer in the artist's distinct pictorial world. Some lines and shapes seem to reference Far Eastern calligraphy (see Chapter 18) but their rendering is expansive and muscular compared with the gentle, circumscribed brushstrokes of Chinese and Japanese artists.

European Modernism in America

The Abstract Expressionists drew on several schools of European modernism, including nonobjective and surrealist art. Two European émigrés, Hans Hoffman and Arshile Gorky, were particularly influential on their work, although, more broadly speaking, the presence of a multitude of Europeans in New York City in the 1930s and 1940s had a significant impact on the developing aesthetic of the young Americans.

HANS HOFMANN Born in Bavaria, Hans Hofmann (1880–1966) studied in Paris early in the twentieth century. He witnessed at close hand the Fauvists' use of high-keyed colors and the Cubists' resolution of shapes into abstract planes. He immigrated to the United States from Germany in 1932 and established schools of fine art in New York City and in Provincetown, Massachusetts. With Hofmann as a mentor,

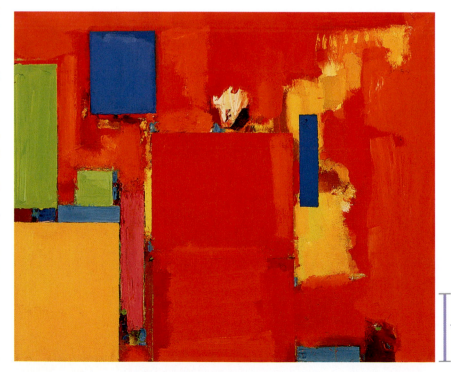

1 ft.

21-1 HANS HOFMANN. *The Golden Wall* (1961). Oil on canvas. 60" × 72½". The Art Institute of Chicago, Chicago, IL.

[1] Robert Goldwater and Marco Treves, eds., *Artists on Art* (New York: Pantheon Books, 1972), 479.
[2] Robert M. Coates, "The Art Galleries," *The New Yorker*, May 26, 1945, 68.

European modernist traditions were within the grasp of the new generation of American artists.

Hofmann's early works were figural and expressionistic, showing the influence of Henri Matisse. From the war years on, however, his paintings revealed a variety of abstract approaches to abstraction, from lyrical curving lines and freely applied color—influenced by Kandinsky—to more precisely defined geometric shapes and structured compositions that owed a debt to Cezanne and Cubism.

In *The Golden Wall* (Fig. **21-1**), intense fields of complementary and primary colors are pitted against one another in Fauvist fashion, but they compose abstract rectangular forms. The gestural brushstrokes in the color fields of paintings such as these would soon spread throughout the art world. Hofmann, the analyst and instructor of painting, knew very well that the cool blues and greens in *The Golden Wall* would normally recede and the warm reds and oranges would emerge; but sharp edges and interposition press the blue and green areas forward, creating tension between planes and flattening the canvas. Hofmann saw this tension as symbolic of the push and pull of nature, but the "tension" is purely technical, for the mood of *The Golden Wall*, as of most of his other works, is joyous and elevating.

ARSHILE GORKY Born in Armenia, Arshile Gorky (1905–1948) immigrated to the United States in 1920, and by 1942 the Museum of Modern Art had purchased one of his paintings. Some of his early still-life compositions show the influence of Cézanne, but later, more abstract works resolve familiar shapes of objects into sharp-edged planes that recall the so-called primitivist style of Picasso and Braque. Gorky's nonobjective paintings of the late 1940s show the influence of Expressionists such as Kandinsky and Surrealists such as Miró. *The Liver Is the Cock's Comb* (Fig. **21-2**) is six feet high and more than eight feet wide—a vast field of bold and saturated zones of color occasionally contained by coarsely sketched lines but more often than not, free of them. Vaguely organic but unrecognizable shapes move across the entirety of the surface—a brilliant panorama that stretches top to bottom, side to side. Here and there we pick out a few more defined bits of drawing that suggest razor-sharp feathers, spiky horns, or other allusions to primitive ancestral objects. These associations harken to surrealist images culled from remembrances of dream imagery.

Gorky was a pivotal figure in the connection between early twentieth-century abstraction and automatism and the gestural painting of the new Abstract Expressionism, particularly the works of Jackson Pollock and Willem de Kooning.

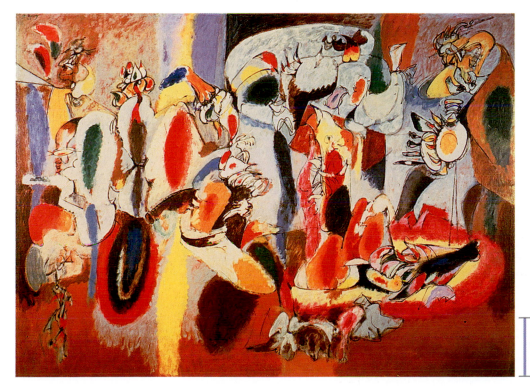

21-2 ARSHILE GORKY. *The Liver Is the Cock's Comb* (1944). Oil on canvas. 72" × 98". Albright-Knox Art Gallery, Buffalo, NY.

1 ft.

Focus on Gesture

For some Abstract Expressionists, such as Jackson Pollock and Willem de Kooning, the gestural application of paint seems to be the most important aspect of their work. For others, the structure of the color field seems to predominate.

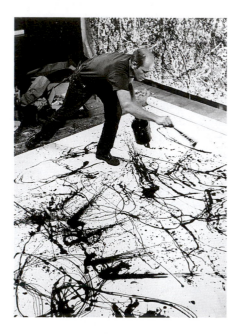

21-3 Jackson Pollock at work in his Long Island studio (1950).

JACKSON POLLOCK

Pollock's talent is volcanic. It has fire. It is unpredictable. It is undisciplined. It spills itself out in a mineral prodigality not yet crystallized. It is lavish, explosive, untidy. . . . What we need is more young men who paint from inner compulsion without an ear to what the critic or spectator may feel—painters who will risk spoiling a canvas to say something in their own way. Pollock is one.[3]

Jackson Pollock (1912–1956) is probably the best known of the Abstract Expressionists. Photographs or motion pictures of the artist energetically dripping and splashing paint across his huge canvases (Fig. **21-3**) are familiar to many people. Pollock would walk across the surface of the canvas as if controlled by primitive impulses and unconscious ideas. Accident became a prime compositional element in his painting. Art critic Harold Rosenberg coined the term **action painting** in 1951 to describe the outcome of such a process—a painting whose surface implied a strong sense of activity, as created by the signs of brushing, dripping, or splattering of paint.

Born in Cody, Wyoming, Pollock came to New York to study with Thomas Hart Benton at the Art Students League. The 1943 quote from Clement Greenberg shows the impact

[3] Clement Greenberg, quoted in Introduction to catalog of an exhibition, "Jackson Pollock," Art of This Century Gallery, New York, November 9–27, 1943.

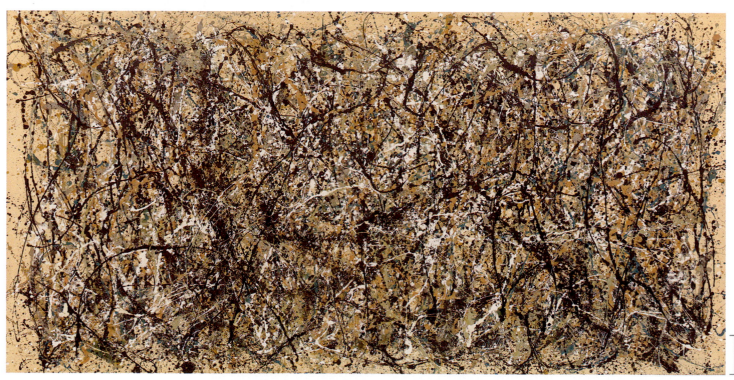

21-4 JACKSON POLLOCK. *One* (*Number 31, 1950*) (1950). Oil and enamel paint on canvas. 8'10" × 17'5⅝". The Museum of Modern Art, NY.
© 2011 Pollock-Krasner Foundation/Artists Rights Society (ARS), NY.

1 ft.

that Pollock made at an early exhibition of his work. His paintings of this era frequently depicted actual or implied figures that were reminiscent of the abstractions of Picasso and, at times, of Expressionists and Surrealists.

Aside from their own value as works of art, Pollock's drip paintings of the late 1940s and early 1950s made several innovations that would be mirrored and developed in the work of other Abstract Expressionists. Foremost among these was the use of an overall gestural pattern barely contained by the limits of the canvas. In *One* (Fig. 21-4), the surface is an unsectioned, unified field. Overlapping skeins of paint create dynamic webs that project from the picture plane, creating an illusion of infinite depth. In Pollock's best work, these webs seem to be composed of energy that pushes and pulls the monumental tracery of the surface like the architectural shapes of a Hofmann painting.

Pollock was in psychoanalysis when he executed his great drip paintings. He believed strongly in the role of the unconscious mind, of accident and spontaneity, in the creation of art. He was influenced not only by the intellectual impact of the Automatist Surrealists but also by what must have been his impression of walking hand in hand with his own unconscious forces through the realms of artistic expression. Before his untimely death in a car crash in 1956, Pollock had returned to figural paintings that were heavy in impasto and predominantly black. One wonders what might have emerged if the artist had lived a fuller span of years.

LEE KRASNER Lee Krasner (1908–1984) was one of relatively few women in the mainstream of Abstract Expressionism. Yet, despite her originality and strength as a painter, her work, until fairly recently, had taken a critical backseat to that of her famous husband—Jackson Pollock. She once noted:

> I was not the average woman married to the average painter. I was married to Jackson Pollock. The context is bigger and even if I was not personally dominated by Pollock, the whole art world was.[4]

Krasner had a burning desire to be a painter from the time she was a teenager and received academic training at some of

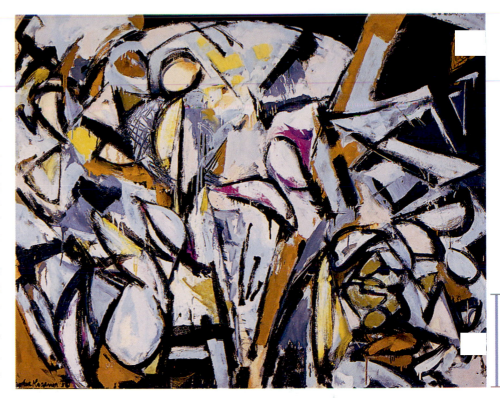

21-5 LEE KRASNER. *Easter Lilies* (1956). Oil on cotton duck. 48¼" × 60⅛". Private collection.
© 2011 Pollock-Krasner Foundation/Artists Rights Society (ARS), NY.

1 ft.

the best art schools in the country. She was influenced by artists of diverse styles, including Hofmann (under whom she studied), Picasso, Mondrian, and the Surrealists. Most important, like Pollock and the other members of the Abstract Expressionist school, she was exposed to the work of many European émigrés who came to New York in the 1930s and 1940s.

Both Pollock and Krasner experimented with allover compositions around 1945, but the latter's work was smaller in scale and exhibited much more control. Even after 1950, when Krasner's work became much freer and larger, the accidental nature of Pollock's style never took hold of her own. Rather, Krasner's compositions might be termed a synthesis of choice and chance.

Easter Lilies (Fig. 21-5) was painted in 1956, the year of Pollock's fatal automobile accident. The jagged shapes and bold black lines against the muddied greens and ochers render the composition dysphoric; yet in the midst of all that is harsh are the recognizable contours of lilies, whose bright whites offer a kind of hope in a sea of anxiety. Krasner once remarked of her work, "My painting is so autobiographical, if anyone can take the trouble to read it."[5]

4 Lee Krasner, in Roberta Brandes Gratz, "Daily Close-Up—After Pollock," *New York Post*, December 6, 1973.

5 Lee Krasner, in Cindy Nemser, "A Conversation with Lee Krasner," *Arts Magazine* 47 (April 1973): 48.

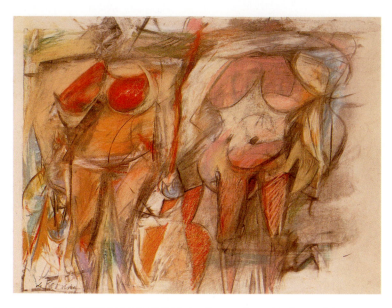

21-6 WILLEM DE KOONING. *Two Women's Torsos* (1952). Pastel drawing. 18⅞" × 24". The Art Institute of Chicago, Chicago, IL.

WILLEM DE KOONING Born in Rotterdam, Holland, Willem de Kooning (1904–1997) immigrated to the United States in 1926, where he joined the circle of Gorky and other forerunners of Abstract Expressionism. Until 1940, de Kooning painted figures and portraits. His first abstractions of the 1940s, like Gorky's, remind one of Picasso's paintings. As the 1940s progressed, de Kooning's compositions began to combine biomorphic, organic shapes with harsh, jagged lines. By the mid-twentieth century, his art had developed into a force in Abstract Expressionism.

De Kooning is best known for his series of paintings of women that began in 1950. In contrast to the appealing figurative works of an earlier day, many of his abstracted women are frankly overpowering and repellent. Faces are frequently resolved into skull-like native masks reminiscent of ancient fertility figures; they assault the viewer from a loosely brushed backdrop of tumultuous color. Perhaps they portray what was a major psychoanalytic dilemma during the 1950s—how women could be at once seductive, alluring, and castrating. In our own liberated times, this notion of woman or of eroticism as frightening seems sexist or out of joint. In any event, in some of his other paintings, abstracted women communicate an impression of being unnerved, even vulnerable.

The subjects of *Two Women's Torsos* (Fig. **21-6**) are among the more erotic of the series. Richly curved pastel breasts swell from a sea of spontaneous brushstrokes that here and there violently obscure the imagery. The result is

a free-floating eroticism. A primal urge has been cast loose in space, pushing and pulling against the picture plane. But de Kooning is one of the few Abstract Expressionists who never completely surrendered figurative painting.

De Kooning's work frequently seems obsessed with the violence and agitation of the "age of anxiety." The abstract backgrounds seem to mirror the rootlessness many of us experience as modern modes of travel and business call us to foreign towns and cities.

Focus on the Color Field

For some Abstract Expressionists, the creation of pulsating fields of color was more important than the gestural quality of the brushstroke. These canvases are so large that they seem to envelop the viewer with color, the subtle modulations of which create a vibrating or resonating effect. Artists who subscribed to this manner of painting, such as Mark Rothko and Barnett Newman, had in common the reworking of a theme in an extended series of paintings. Even though the imagery often remains constant, each canvas has a remarkably differ-

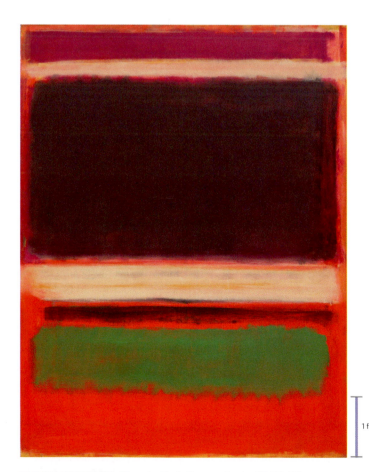

21-7 MARK ROTHKO. *Magenta, Black, Green on Orange* (1949). Oil on canvas. 7'1⅜" × 65".

ent effect as a result of often radical palette adjustments.

MARK ROTHKO Mark Rothko (1903–1970) painted lone figures in urban settings in the 1930s and biomorphic surrealistic canvases throughout the early 1940s. Later in that decade, he began to paint the large, floating, hazy-edged color fields for which he is renowned. During the 1950s, the color fields consistently assumed the form of rectangles floating above one another in an atmosphere defined by subtle variations in tone and brushwork. They alternately loom in front of and recede from the picture plane, as in *Magenta, Black, Green on Orange* (Fig. **21-7**). The large scale of these canvases absorbs the viewer in color, and the often-blurred edges of the rectangles have a vibratory effect on the eyes.

Early in his career, Rothko had favored a broad palette ranging from pale to vibrant and highly saturated colors. During the 1960s, however, his works grew somber. Reds that earlier had been intense, warm, and sensuous were now awash in deep blacks and browns and took on the appearance of worn cloth. Oranges and yellows were replaced by grays and black. Light that earlier had been reflected was now trapped in his canvases. Despite public acclaim, Rothko suffered from depression during his last years and his paintings of that period may reflect this.

FOCUS ON THE FIGURE

Although abstract and nonobjective styles dominated the American art scene in the 1940s and 1950s, these were not exclusive idioms. Some artists remained strong in their commitment to the figure, even as they integrated some aspects of the abstract expressionist style.

ROMARE BEARDEN Some critics have noted that Abstract Expressionism was essentially an exclusive group of white male artists. Few, if any, women artists or artists of color were counted among the household names associated with the movement. But others adopted the idiom of Abstract Expressionism, and scholars and curators have rediscovered their work.

African American artist Romare Bearden (1914–1988), like many in the New York School, began painting as a WPA artist and studied at the Art Students League. After mili-

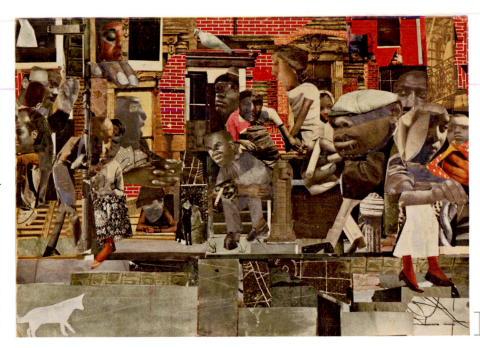

21-8 ROMARE BEARDEN. *The Dove* (1964). Cut-and-pasted paper, gouache, pencil, and colored pencil on cardboard. 13⅜" × 18¾". The Museum of Modern Art, NY.

tary service during World War II, he left for Paris to study philosophy on the GI Bill. During the late 1940s and 1950s, he swapped his social realist style for a version of Abstract Expressionism, but in the early 1960s he defined the signature artistic vocabulary, combining painting and collage, that would become characteristic of his mature style. Bearden's work began to include references to African life and culture that continued throughout his career (see Fig. 1-24).

A work such as *The Dove* (Fig. **21-8**) represents a synthesis of Cubism and Abstract Expressionism, constructed through the lens of African American experience. We are drawn into a Harlem street scene composed of clipped, irregularly shaped fragments of photographs—varying in scale and density—pasted onto a regimented backdrop that feels almost like a Cubist grid. The imagery spreads across the field uniformly, with no particular focal point—much the way Abstract Expressionists created their allover compositions. As in viewing a Pollock painting, we experience the tension between surface and depth: the overlapping lines in *One* (Fig. 21-4) draw us into the compressed space of the painting and then fix our eyes again on the surface. In *The Dove*, the clarity of some images in relation to others, and the shifts and subversions of scale, lead our eyes to believe that some figures are near and some are distant. Shape and scale shifting create a similar tension between surface and depth. Works like *The Dove* reflect Bearden's desire to capture flashes of memory that read like a scrapbook of consciousness and experience particular to his own life and times—from his childhood in North Carolina to his life and work in Harlem. The writer and literary critic Ralph Ellison wrote of Bearden's art:

> Bearden's meaning is identical with his method. His combination of technique is in itself eloquent of the sharp breaks, leaps in consciousness, distortions, paradoxes, reversals, telescoping of time and surreal blending of styles, values, hopes and dreams which characterize much of [African] American history.[6]

ALICE NEEL Alice Neel (1900–1984) was also employed by the WPA and in the 1930s was quite well known for her portraits of her fellow artists and intellectuals as well as neighbors, her friends, and their children. During and after World War II, when Abstract Expressionism dominated first the New York and then the international aesthetic, Neel's work fell by the critical wayside only to be rediscovered, so to speak, in the 1960s. From thereon, her reputation soared as she became an iconic figure—particularly for women artists who were trying to forge their own path in a male-dominated art world. In 1979 President Jimmy Carter awarded her a medal for outstanding artistic achievement. The designation "portraitist," however, in no way prepares the viewer for the radical nature of Neel's work. The drama, curiously, lies in the very *un*dramatic character of her work—stark, unflinching, realistic likenesses, simply rendered (see Fig. 3-33).

FRANCIS BACON Many of the figurative paintings of Francis Bacon (1909–1992) revisit works by art history's recognized masters such as Giotto, Rembrandt, Velasquez, and van Gogh. But Bacon's personalized interpretation of history is distorted by what seems a very raw response to the events of contemporary life.

Figure with Meat (Fig. 21-9) is one of a series of paintings from the 1950s in which Bacon reconstructed Velázquez's portrait of Pope Innocent X. The tormented, openmouthed figure is boxed in and partially obscured, as if seen through a curtain or veil. Bloody, graphically rendered slabs of beef, which stand like totems richly threaded with silver and gold, take the place of ornamental posts that rise from the back corners of the papal throne in the Velázquez portrait. Expressionistic conventions—including high drama and vigorous brushwork—are combined with references to unconscious dream (here, nightmarish) imagery.

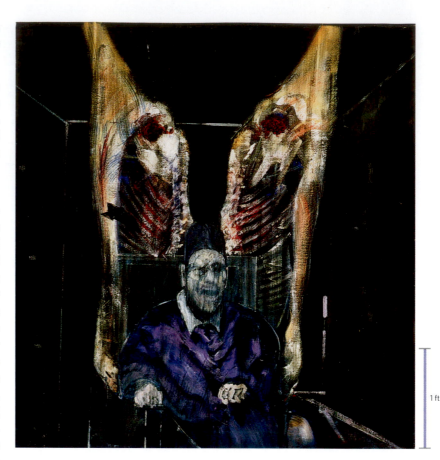

21-9 FRANCIS BACON. *Figure with Meat* (1954). Oil on canvas. 50⅞" × 48". The Art Institute of Chicago, Chicago, IL.

THE NEW YORK SCHOOL: THE SECOND GENERATION

Abstract Expressionism was a movement in part defined by its rogue nature, steeped in the intellectual and political discourse of the war years, heroic in scale, brash in its masculinity. The artists were in and of the city and symbolized, in many ways, the true grit required to make art in spite of poverty and to "make it" in the midst of an unforgiving urban universe. The second-generation New York artists, who inherited the mantle of Abstract Expressionism, were less likely to have been influenced by the community culture of Greenwich Village—its bars and hangouts—and more by the university or art academy experience in which they learned to paint—not to exorcise but to very self-consciously create works of art. Beyond a few common features, their styles were quite different. Some expanded on Abstract Expressionism's gestural approach, while others deemphasized it. Some pushed Pollock's experiments with staining unprimed canvas to a more radical conclusion—the **color-field painters**.

---

[6] Ralph Ellison, introduction to *Romare Bearden: Paintings and Projections* (The Art Gallery of the State University of New York at Albany: Albany, NY, 1968).

Others focused increasingly on clarity of line and crisp, hard edges of geometric shapes—the **hard-edge painters**.

Helen Frankenthaler (Fig. 2-23) and Kenneth Noland (Fig. 6-9), whose work we saw in previous chapters, were among the so-called Second Generation New York School. Frankenthaler, as we shall see, is considered a color-field painter. Noland's work featured fields or bands of color delineated by hard edges; he is known as a hard-edge painter. Several hard-edge artists also pioneered the shaped canvas, a deviation from the rectangular perimeter associated with conventional painting.

Color-Field Painting

HELEN FRANKENTHALER Kenneth Noland once said of Helen Frankenthaler (b. 1928): "She was a bridge between Pollock and what was possible." He claimed that Frankenthaler showed him and Morris Louis a way to push beyond Pollock, showed them "a way to think about and use, color."[7] *Lorelei* (Fig. **21-10**) pushes "beyond Pollock" toward a painting process that is less an extension of the inner world of the artist and more about creating sensuous, beautiful surfaces. *Lorelei*, in many ways, reconciles gesture and color-field Abstract Expressionism. The canvas is awash in color. Broad expanses of pigment—like translucent veils—seep into the fibers of the canvas, softening the edges of the colorful floating shapes; intermittent flowing lines, splotches and splatters of paint keep our eyes attuned to the decorative surface. With stain painting such as this, the image—open, billowing, abstract—and the canvas are now literally one.

THE 1960s: DIVERGENT TRENDS

The art of the 1960s could not appear more dichotomous. On the one hand, a group of artists emerged who, in the words of Robert Raschenberg, sought to work "in the gap between art and life." These **Pop** artists incorporated found objects (as did Marcel Duchamp and other Dada artists) and images of contemporary culture into their compositions, blurring the distinction between the fine art object and the stuff of everyday life. On the other hand were artists like Donald Judd, who focused on creating what he called "specific objects," which were typically geometric and which ranged from single, simple cubes to works consisting of a series of repeated, identical,

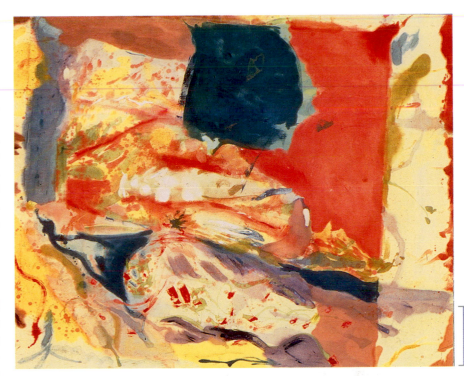

21-10 HELEN FRANKENTHALER. *Lorelei* (1957). Oil on canvas. 70¾" × 87". Brooklyn Museum, Brooklyn, NY. © 2011 Helen Frankenthaler/Artists Rights Society (ARS), NY.

industrial-looking forms arranged on the principle of "one thing after another" (see Fig. 21-14). Judd is associated with **Minimalism**. Though very different in style and in aims, Pop and Minimalism had at least one thing in common: the desire to eliminate the emotionalism, exclusivity, and egocentricity of Abstract Expressionism.

POP ART

If one were asked to choose the contemporary art movement that was most enticing, surprising, controversial, and also exasperating, one might select Pop Art. The term "Pop" was coined by English critic Lawrence Alloway in 1954 to refer to the universal images of "popular culture," such as movie posters, billboards, magazine and newspaper photographs, and advertisements. Pop Art, by its selection of commonplace and familiar subjects—subjects that are already too much with us—also challenges commonplace conceptions about the meaning of art.

Whereas many artists have strived to portray the beautiful, Pop Art intentionally depicts the mundane. Whereas many artists represent the noble, stirring, or monstrous, Pop Art renders the commonplace, the boring. Whereas other forms of art often elevate their subjects, Pop Art is often matter-of-fact. In fact, one tenet of Pop Art is that the work should be so objective

[7] Kenneth Noland, in James McC. Truitt, "Art-Arid D.C. Harbors Touted 'New' Painters," *Washington Post*, December 21, 1961, A20.

that it does not show the "personal signature" of the artist. This maxim contrasts starkly, for example, with the highly personalized gestural brushstroke found in Abstract Expressionism.

RICHARD HAMILTON Despite the widespread view that Pop Art is a purely American development, it originated during the 1950s in England. British artist Richard Hamilton (b. 1922), one of its creators, had been influenced by Marcel Duchamp's idea that the mission of art should be to destroy the normal meanings and functions of art.

Hamilton's tiny collage *Just What Is It That Makes Today's Homes So Different, So Appealing?* (see Fig. 1-30) is one of the earliest and most revealing Pop Art works. It is a collection of objects and emblems that form our environment. It is easy to read satire and irony into Hamilton's work, but his placement of these objects within the parameters of "art" encourages us to truly *see* them instead of just coexisting with them.

ROBERT RAUSCHENBERG American Pop artist Robert Rauschenberg (1925–2008) studied in Paris and then with Josef Albers and others at the famous Black Mountain College in North Carolina. Before developing his own Pop Art style, Rauschenberg experimented with loosely and broadly brushed Abstract Expressionist canvases. He is best known, however, for introducing a construction referred to as the **combine painting**, in which stuffed animals, bottles, articles of clothing and furniture, and scraps of photographs are attached to the canvas.

Rauschenberg's *The Bed* (Fig. 21-11) is a paint-splashed quilt and pillow, mounted upright on a wall as any painting might be. Here the artist toys with the traditional relationships between materials, forms, and content. The content

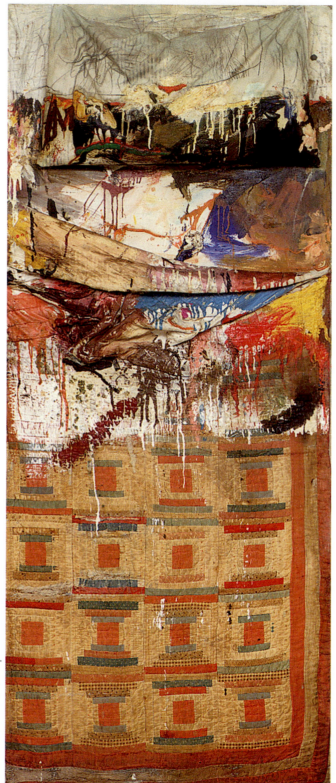

1 ft.

21-11 ROBERT RAUSCHENBERG. *The Bed* (1955). Combine painting: Oil and pencil on pillow, quilt, and sheet on wood supports. 75¼" × 31½" × 6½". The Museum of Modern Art, NY.

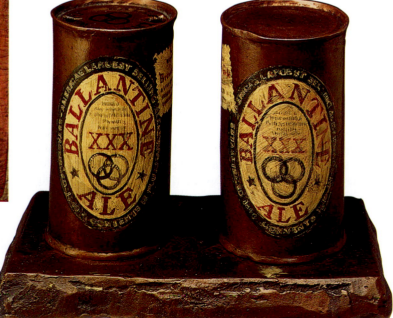

1 in.

21-12 JASPER JOHNS. *Painted Bronze* (*Ballatine Ale*) (1960). Painted bronze. 5½" × 8" × 4¾". Kunstmuseum, Basel, Switzerland.

of the work is actually its support; rather than a canvas on a stretcher, the quilt and pillow are the materials on which the painter drips and splashes his pigments. Perhaps even more outrageous is Rauschenberg's famous 1959 work *Monogram*, in which a stuffed ram—an automobile tire wrapped around its middle—is mounted on a horizontal base that consists of scraps of photos and prints and loose, gestural painting.

JASPER JOHNS Jasper Johns (b. 1930) was Rauschenberg's classmate at Black Mountain College, and their appearance on the New York art scene was simultaneous. His early work also integrated the overall gestural brushwork of the Abstract Expressionists with the use of found objects, but unlike Rauschenberg, Johns soon made the object central to his compositions. His works frequently portray familiar objects such as numbers, maps, color charts, targets, and flags integrated into a unified field by thick gestural brushwork.

One "tenet" of Pop Art is that imagery is to be presented objectively, that the personal signature of the artist is to be eliminated. That principle must be modified if we are to include as Pop the works of Rauschenberg, Johns, and others, for many of them immediately betray their devotion to expressionistic brushwork.

A work by Johns that adheres more to Pop Art dogma is his *Painted Bronze (Ale Cans)* (Fig. 21-12). In the tradition of Duchamp's readymades, Johns has bronzed two Ballantine beer cans and painted facsimile labels thereon. As with works such as the Dadaist's *Fountain* (see Fig. 1-36) or *Mona Lisa (L.H.O.O.Q.)* (see Fig. 20-23), questions concerning the definition of art are raised: Is it art because the artist chooses the object? because he or she manipulates it? or because the artist says it is art? One difference separates the Dada and Pop aesthetics, however: Whereas Duchamp believed that art should be destroyed, Johns firmly believes in the creative process of art. Whereas it was left for Duchamp to stop making art (he devoted his life to the game of chess), Johns remains first and foremost an artist.

ANDY WARHOL Andy Warhol (1930–1987) once earned a living designing packages and Christmas cards. Today he epitomizes the Pop artist in the public mind. Just as Campbell's soups represent bland, boring nourishment, Andy Warhol's appropriation of hackneyed portraits of celebrities, his Brillo boxes, and his Coca-Cola bottles (Fig. 21-13) elicit comments that contemporary art has become bland and boring and that there is nothing much to be said about it. Warhol also evoked contempt here and there for his underground movies, which have portrayed sleep and explicit eroticism (*Blue Movie*) with equal disinterest. Even his shooting (from which he recovered) by a disenchanted actress seemed to evoke yawns and a "What can you expect?" reaction from the public.

Warhol painted and printed much more than industrial products. During the 1960s, he reproduced multiple photographs of disasters from newspapers. He executed a series of portraits of public figures such as Marilyn Monroe and Jackie Kennedy in the 1960s, and he turned to portraits of political leaders such as Mao Zedong in the 1970s. Although his silkscreens have at least in their technique met the Pop Art objective of obscuring the personal signature of the artist, his compositions and his expressionistic brushing of areas of his paintings achieved an individual stamp.

It could be argued that other Pop artists owe some of their popularity to the inventiveness of Andy Warhol. Without Warhol, Pop Art might have remained a quiet movement, one that might have escaped the notice of the art historians of the new millennium. What, then, do we make of Pop Art? Is it a cynical gesture to place expensive but mundane objects in a gullible marketplace? Is it a searing commentary on consumerism? Is it, perhaps, the only contemporary art movement that is a reflection of its times? Is it an attempt to countermand the unreachable and esoteric in the art of the 1940s and 1950s and provide the public with an art to which it can relate on some level?

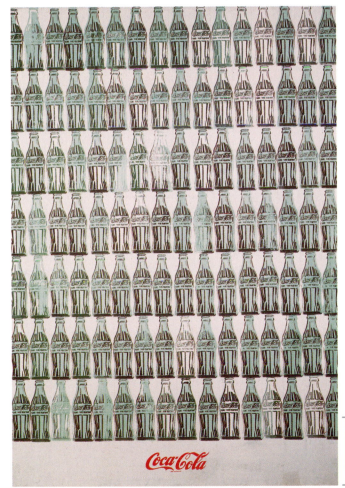

1 ft.

21-13 ANDY WARHOL. *Green Coca-Cola Bottles* (1962). Oil on canvas. 82¼" × 57". Whitney Museum of American Art, NY. © 2011 The Andy Warhol Foundation for the Visual Arts/Artists Rights Society (ARS), NY.

1 in.

21-15 AGNES MARTIN. *Untitled* (1989). Acrylic and graphite on canvas. 12" × 12". Pace Wildenstein Gallery, NY. © 2011 Agnes Martin/Artists Rights Society (ARS), NY.

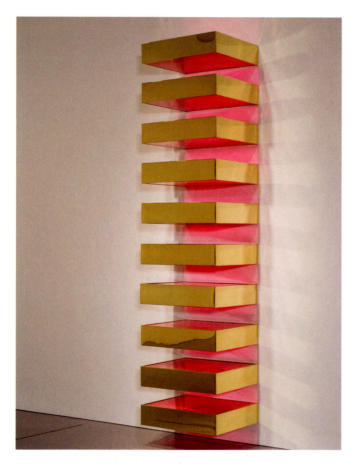

21-14 DONALD JUDD. *Untitled* (1969). Brass and red fluorescent Plexiglas (ten units, 6⅛" × 24" × 7" each with 6" intervals).

Minimal Art

With Minimalism, illusionism and the gestural qualities of expressionism were renounced in favor of shapes and materials that were pure and simple. Donald Judd's *Untitled* (Fig. **21-14**) reflects its characteristic style: it is nonobjective, fabricated in factories from industrial or nontraditional materials, austere, and composed of multiple, repetitive elements. Because skilled workers (and not the artist) created Minimalist works according to the artist's specifications, the traditional relationship between the idea of art and its literal creation is subverted.

Untitled (Fig. **21-15**) by Agnes Martin (1912–2004) is a quintessential example of Minimalist painting. A tiny 12-by-12-inch canvas provides a luminous backdrop for finely wrought bands of shimmering graphite. The absolute square of the canvas is deemphasized through the delicate, quiet handling of her medium. Martin said, "When I cover the square with rectangles, it lightens the weight of the square, destroys its power."

Op Art (Optical Painting)

If Agnes Martin's painting is measured by its quietude, the bold, vertiginous paintings of Bridget Riley (see Fig. 2-75) are measured by their visual potency. In **Op Art**, also called optical painting, the artist manipulates light or color fields, or repeats patterns of line, in order to produce visual illusions, as in Riley's *Gala*. Op art, as well as minimalism, was featured in an important exhibition at the Museum of Modern Art called "The Responsive Eye" (1964), in which attention was focused on contemporary artists whose work foregrounded the perceptual aspects of art. Although Op art was a short-lived style in painting, its aesthetic continued in the realm of popular culture and textile design. 1960s era mini-dresses with patterns based on optical illusions are still to be found in museum costume collections and thrift shops alike.

Conceptual Art

In conceptual art—also known as idea art—the artist's concept for a work takes priority over the methods and materials used to create it. Sol LeWitt (see Fig. 2-1) said, "In conceptual art the idea or concept is the most important aspect of the work. When an artist uses a conceptual form of art, it means that all of the planning and decisions are made beforehand and the execution is a perfunctory affair. The idea becomes a machine that makes the art."

Although conceptual art emerged in the 1960s, its origins can be traced to Dadaist works like Marcel Duchamp's *Fountain* (see Fig. 1-36) or *Mona Lisa (L.H.O.O.Q)* (see Fig. 20-23) or Robert Rauschenberg's erased de Kooning (a drawing by Willem de Kooning that Rauschenberg had fastidiously erased). Neither of Duchamp's works, nor Rauschenberg's, emphasized the material object per se; their art lay in their ideas. Contemporary conceptual artists work in a variety of styles, some of which are almost wholly based on communicating ideas or confronting beliefs by drawing attention to language. Likewise, their mediums are varied (LCD, typography, projections, performance, earth art [see Fig. 10-2], video, etc.). Some conceptual artists produce tangible artworks; others, such as Lawrence Weiner, have sold nothing but ideas, sometimes in the form of written texts, which may be instructions as to how to render a work (as in Weiner's "A two-inch wide, one-inch deep trench, cut across a standard one-car driveway").

Conceptual art of the 1960s and 1970s was not object-focused. It challenged the traditional view of artists as skilled artisans and masters of their mediums. Instead, conceptualism promoted the notion that the artist's thought process was more essential than the follow-through to some sort of concrete product.

PLURALISM: 1970S AND BEYOND

The 1970s witnessed a strong presence of realism in the visual arts that was, in part, a reaction against the introspective and subjective abstract tendencies that had gripped American art since World War II in one form or another. Although Minimalism and Conceptualism continued, what seemed, to some, to be lost was the act of painting itself. The period that followed was marked by a pluralism of artistic styles that reflected the growing pluralism in contemporary society in the wake of the civil rights and feminist movements.

Superrealism

Superrealism, or the rendering of subjects with sharp, photographic precision, is firmly rooted in the long, realistic tradition in the arts. But as a movement that first gained major recognition during the early 1970s, it also owes some of its impetus to the Pop artist's objective portrayal of familiar images.

Superrealism is also in part a reaction to the expressionistic and abstract movements of the twentieth century. That is, Superrealism permits artists to do something that is very new to the eye even while they are doing something very old.

AUDREY FLACK Audrey Flack (b. 1931) was born in New York and studied at the High School of Music and Art, at Cooper Union, and at Yale University's Graduate School. During the 1950s, she showed figure paintings that were largely ignored, in part because of the popularity of Abstract Expressionism, in part because women artists, in general, had not been privy to the critical attention that their male colleagues had received. Yet throughout these years, she persisted in a sharply realistic or trompe l'oeil style. Her illusionistically real canvases often result from a technique involving the projection of color slides onto her canvases, which she then sketches and paints in detail. Since the 1970s, Flack's focus has largely shifted away from the human figure to richly complex still-life arrangements.

One of Flack's best-known works from the 1970s is *World War II* (*Vanitas*) (Fig. **21-16**), a painting that combines Margaret Bourke-White's haunting photo *The Living Dead of*

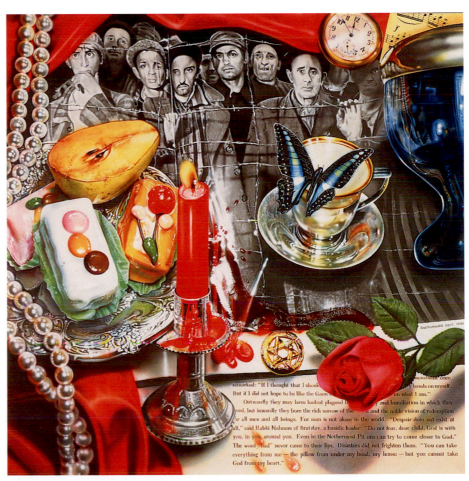

21-16 AUDREY FLACK. *World War II* (*Vanitas*) (1976–1977). Oil over acrylic on canvas. 96" × 96".

1 ft.

Buchenwald (see Fig. 8-12) with ordinary objects that teem with life—pastries, fruit, a teacup, a candle, a string of pearls. The subtitle of the work, *Vanitas*, refers to a type of still life frequently found in the sixteenth and seventeenth centuries. The content was selected specifically to encourage the viewer to meditate on death as the inescapable end to human life. Flack's items are all the more poignant in their juxtaposition because they suggest lives cut short—abruptly and drastically—by Hitler's Holocaust. The painting further functions as a memorial to those who perished at the hands of the Nazis and as a tribute to survivors. Flack is fascinated by the ways in which objects reflect light, and in this painting and others she uses an airbrush to create a surface that imitates the textures of these objects. She layers primary colors in transparent glazes to produce the desired hues without obvious brushstrokes. The resulting palette is harsh and highly saturated, and the sense of realism is stunning.

New Image Painting

The 1970s witnessed a strong presence of realism in the visual arts that was, in part, a virulent reaction against the introspective and subjective abstract tendencies that had gripped American painting since World War II.

Toward the end of that decade—in 1978—New York's Whitney Museum of American Art mounted a controversial, though significant, exhibition called "New Image Painting." The participants, including Jennifer Bartlett (b. 1941), Susan Rothenberg (b. 1945), and eight other artists, were doing

something very different. They were, in their own way, reconciling the disparate styles of abstraction and representation. The image was central to their compositions, much in the tradition of Realist artists. The images were often so simplified, however, that they conveyed the grandeur of abstract shapes. These images never dominated other aesthetic components of the work, such as color, texture, or even composition. Rather, they cohabited the work in elegant balance.

JENNIFER BARTLETT Jennifer Bartlett's *Spiral: An Ordinary Evening in New Haven* (Fig. **21-17**) combines a painted canvas and several sculptural objects in a virtual maelstrom of imagery that is alternately engulfed by flames and apparently spewed out by the turbulent blaze. In this work, Bartlett includes figurative imagery and explores the use of line and color. The title and the work invite the viewer's speculation as to exactly what has happened to cause the conflagration and how it can possibly represent an "ordinary evening" anywhere. This sort of interplay between the verbal and the visual is another hallmark of **New Image painting**. Bartlett combines narrative, conceptual art, representation, and some abstract process painting of the sort we find in Abstract Expressionism.

SUSAN ROTHENBERG Susan Rothenberg's *Diagonal* (Fig. **21-18**) also stands as an example of New Image painting in bringing together representational and abstract art. The highly simplified and sketchy contours of a horse in full gallop barely separate the animal from the lushly painted field. Although the subject is strong and inescapable, its reality is

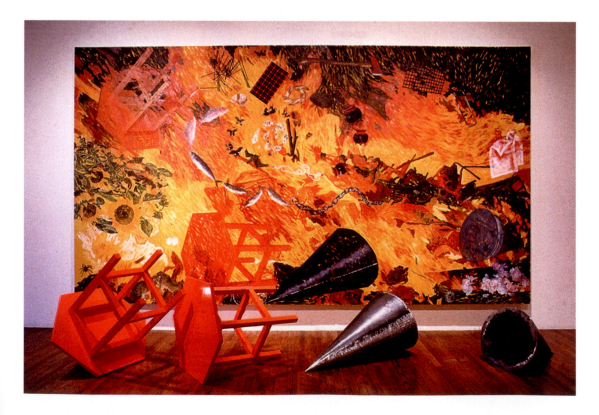

21-17 JENNIFER BARTLETT. *Spiral: An Ordinary Evening in New Haven* (1989). Painting: oil on canvas, 108" × 192"; tables: painted wood, 30½" × 32" × 35"; painted wood with steel base, 39½" × 41" × 35"; cones: welded steel, 20" × 30¼" × 21".

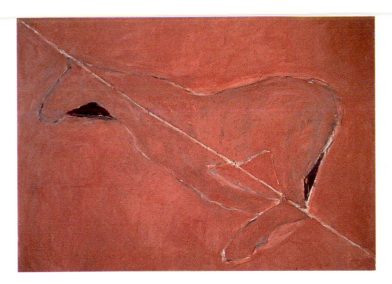

21-18 SUSAN ROTHENBERG. *Diagonal* (1975). Acrylic and tempera on canvas. 40" × 60". Private collection.

diminished by the unified palette, the bisecting diagonal line, and the structured composition with its repetitive triangles. Rothenberg favored the horse as image in the 1970s, although in the 1980s she turned to the human form. The artist has said of her earlier compositions, "The horse was a way of not doing people, yet it was a symbol of people, a self-portrait, really."[8]

The Shaped Canvas

The art of the 1980s was nothing if not pluralistic. Painters of extraordinary talent and innovation affirmed their love of the medium and put an end to the speculation of the late 1960s and 1970s that "painting was dead." Many artists, including Frank Stella, Judy Pfaff, and Elizabeth Murray, have obscured the lines between painting, sculpture, and installations by radically changing the shapes of their canvases.

ELIZABETH MURRAY In Elizabeth Murray (1940–2007), we find a painter who has affirmed a belief in abstraction as a viable style, in the midst of trends that find it sterile and unreachable. Coupling clear-cut, abstract shapes that nonetheless are suggestive of organic forms, or taking specific objects—such as a teacup or a table—and treating them as isolated abstract shapes, Murray has created an art form that is personal and reachable despite its emphasis on formal concerns. *Sail Baby* (Fig. 21-19) comprises three large shaped canvases. Although the somewhat repetitive shapes have strong, separate identities because of their prominent

contours, the entire work is unified by the painting of a teacup that traverses all three supports. Beyond the common imagery, Murray has explained that the painting functions as a narrative: "[It is] about my family. It's about myself and my brother and my sister, and I think, it is also about my own three children, even though Daisy [her youngest daughter] wasn't born yet."[9] The individual identities of the separate shapes may, in this context, represent the individuality of the siblings, whereas their interconnectedness is established by the image that overrides them as well as the snakelike green line (an umbilical cord?) that flows from the smallest shape and wends around to the right, behind the largest. Though essentially an abstract work, its references to human experience cannot be ignored or minimized. They are essential to our comprehension of the piece.

Neo-Expressionism

The center of the art world moved to New York in the 1940s for historical as well as artistic reasons. The first-generation Abstract Expressionists developed a style that was viewed worldwide as highly original and influential. They laid claim to the tenet that the *process* of painting was a viable alternative

---

[9] Elizabeth Murray: Paintings and Drawings, exhibition catalog organized by Sue Graze and Kathy Halbreich, essay by Roberta Smith (New York: Abrams, in association with the Dallas Museum of Art and the MIT Committee on the Visual Arts, 1987), 64.

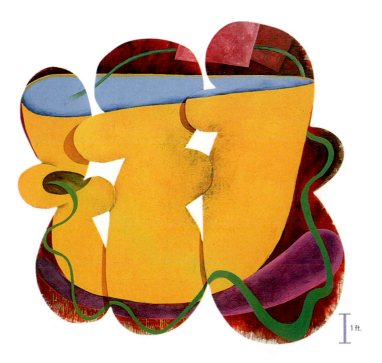

1 ft.

21-19 ELIZABETH MURRAY. *Sail Baby* (1983). Oil on canvas. 126" × 135". Walker Art Center, Minneapolis, MN. © 2011 The Murray-Holman Family Trust/Artists Rights Society (ARS), NY.

---

[8] Susan Rothenberg, in Grace Glueck, "Susan Rothenberg: New Outlook for a Visionary Artist," *New York Times Magazine*, July 22, 1984, 20.

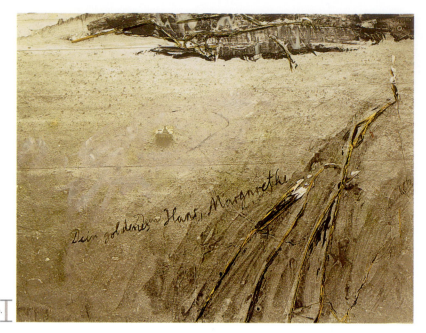

1 in.

21-20 ANSELM KIEFER. *Dein Goldenes Haar, Margarethe* (1981). Mixed media on paper.
14" × 18¾".

called **Neo-Expressionists**, detested painting "about nothing." Born as they were during the darkest years of postwar Europe, when Germany and Italy stood utterly defeated, these artists would mature to portray the bitter ironies and angst of their generation in emotionally fraught images that are rooted in history, literature, and expressionistic art.

ANSELM KIEFER Perhaps the most remarkable of these Neo-Expressionists is Anselm Kiefer (b. 1945). Kiefer has been able to synthesize an expressionistic painterly style with strong abstract elements in a narrative form of painting that makes multivalent references to German history and culture. The casual observer cannot hope to decipher Kiefer's paintings; they are highly intellectual, obscure, and idiosyncratic. But at the same time, they are overpowering in their scale, their larger-than-life subjects, and their textural, encrusted surfaces.

Kiefer's *Dein Goldenes Haar, Margarethe* (Fig. **21-20**) serves as an excellent example of the artist's formal and literary concerns. The title of the work, and others of this series, refers to a poem by Paul Celan titled "Your Golden Hair, Margarethe," which describes the destruction of European Jewry through the images of a golden-haired German woman named Margarethe and a dark-haired Jewish woman, Shulamith. Against a pale gray blue background, Kiefer uses actual straw to suggest the hair of the German woman, contrasting it with thick black paint that lies charred

to subject matter. In the early 1980s, a group of artists who were born during the Abstract Expressionist era—though on other shores—wholeheartedly revived the gestural manner and experimentation with materials that the Americans had devised four decades earlier, but with an added dimension. These young German and Italian artists, who came to be

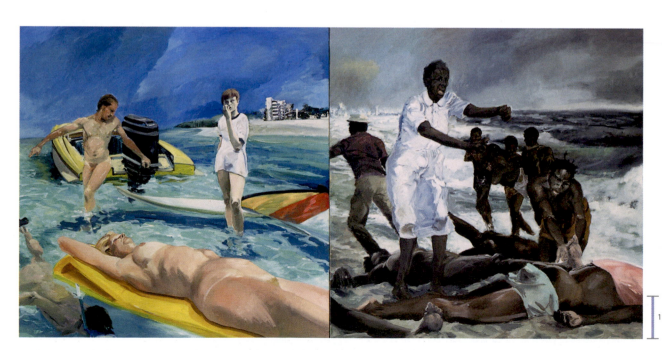

1 ft.

21-21 ERIC FISCHL. *A Visit To/A Visit From/The Island* (1983). Oil on canvas. Two panels; each panel: 84" × 84". Whitney Museum of American Art, NY.

on the upper canvas, to symbolize the hair of her unfortunate counterpart. Between them a German tank presides over this human destruction, isolated against a wasteland of its own creation. Kiefer here, as often, scrawls his titles or other words across the canvas surface, sometimes veiling them with his textured materials. The materials function as content; they become symbols to which we must emotionally and intellectually respond.

ERIC FISCHL Several American painters responded to European Neo-Expressionism with narrative works that have American references. For example, New York painter Eric Fischl (b. 1948) focused on middle-class life in the suburbs, including Levittown, Long Island. Fischl's *A Visit To/A Visit From/ The Island* (Fig. 21-21) shifts the locale from big-city suburbs to an island vacation setting. While his transported suburbanites blithely bob along in the turquoise waters of the Caribbean, oblivious to anything other than pleasure seeking, their counterparts—native islanders—are drowning in the surf. Fischl is underscoring the bipolar social structure we find in these vacation "paradises"—the affluent tourists versus the poverty-stricken workers. Although Fischl's style can be characterized as a lush realism, in some ways very different from that of the Europeans, he too embraces a narrative format.

JEAN-MICHEL BASQUIAT Jean-Michel Basquiat (1960–1988) was a Haitian-Hispanic artist who dropped out of school at 17, rose quickly to fame and fortune in his early twenties, and died at 27 of a drug overdose. He is now considered to have been one of the most talented artists of his generation, as well as a symbolic casualty of the cycle of work, success, and burnout that characterized the 1980s in the United States.

Basquiat's origins as an artist were not propitious. The themes, symbols, and strokes for which he is known first appeared on downtown New York City walls as graffiti. With Andy Warhol as a mentor, he brought his own complex form of collage to canvas, combining photocopies, drawing, and painting in intricate and overworked layers. In virtually all of Basquiat's art, there is a complex iconography at work. References to the black experience—from slavery and discrimination (Fig. 21-22) to hard-won successes of African Americans such as jazz musician Charlie Parker or athlete Jesse Owens—pour across the canvases in images, symbols, and strands of text. As Fischl and other artists of his generation looked back to the Expressionism of Jackson Pollock, Basquiat sought to emphasize the process of painting while never losing focus of the essential role of narrative.

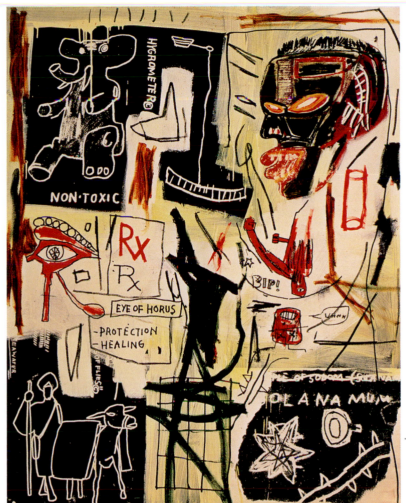

21-22 JEAN-MICHEL BASQUIAT. *Melting Point of Ice* (1984). Acrylic, oil paintstick, and silkscreen on canvas. 86" × 68". © 2011 Artists Rights Society (ARS), NY/ADAGP, Paris.

SCULPTURE

True experimentation in the medium of sculpture came with the advent of the twentieth century, and contemporary sculptors owe much to the trail-blazing predecessors who embraced unorthodox materials, techniques, and influences. Style, content, composition, materials, and, from midcentury onward, *scale* were completely up for grabs.

Sculpture at Mid-Twentieth Century

In the middle of the twentieth century, there were two major directions in sculpture: figurative and abstract. Sometimes they are divergent paths. Yet they seamlessly converge with the British artist Henry Moore, whose work encompasses both the figurative and the abstract and who, more than any other individual, epitomizes sculpture in the twentieth century.

21-23 HENRY MOORE. *Reclining Figure, Lincoln Center* (1963–1965). Bronze. H: 16'; W: 30'. Lincoln Center for the Performing Arts, NY. © 2011 Artists Rights Society (ARS), NY/DACS, London.

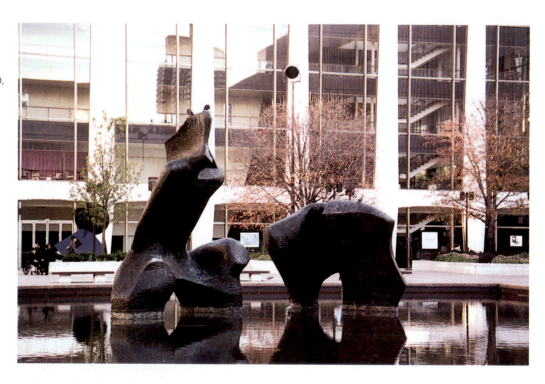

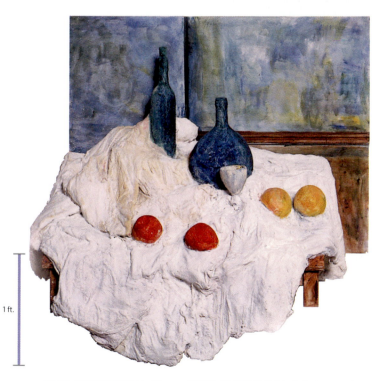

21-24 GEORGE SEGAL. *Cézanne Still Life #5* (1982). Painted plaster, wood, and metal. 37" × 36" × 29". Virginia Museum of Fine Arts, Richmond, VA.

HENRY MOORE Henry Moore (1898–1986) had a long and prolific career that spanned the seven decades since the 1920s, but we introduce him at this point because, despite his productivity, his influence was not generally felt until after World War II.

In the late 1920s, Moore was intrigued by the massiveness of stone. In an early effort to be true to his material, he executed blocky reclining figures reminiscent of the Native American art of Mexico. In the 1930s, Moore turned to bronze and wood and was also influenced by Picasso. His figures became abstracted and more fluid. Voids opened up, and air and space began to flow through his works.

At mid-twentieth century, Moore's works received the attention they deserve. He continued to produce figurative works, but he also executed a series of abstract bronzes in the tradition of his early reclining figures, such as the one at Lincoln Center for the Performing Arts in New York City (Fig. **21-23**). No longer as concerned about limiting the scope of his expression because of material, he could now let his bronzes assume the massiveness of his earlier stonework. However, his continued exploration of abstract biomorphic shapes and his separation and opening of forms created a lyricism that was lacking in his earlier sculptures.

Contemporary Figurative Sculpture

Figurative art continues to intrigue sculptors as well as painters. Some figurative works are utterly realistic. Others are highly abstract, such as the reclining figures of Henry Moore.

GEORGE SEGAL George Segal (1926–2000) was a student of Hans Hofmann and painted until 1958. During the 1960s, he achieved renown as a Pop Art sculptor. In many instances, he cast his figures in plaster from live models and then typically surrounded them with familiar objects—Coke machines, Formica and chrome tables, porcelain sinks and copper pipes, mirrors, neon signs, telephone booths, television sets, park benches. His figures evoke a mood of isolation and detachment, surrounded as they are by ordinary symbols of their day and age.

Segal also made sensuous reliefs of women and still lifes, as in *Cézanne Still Life #5* (Fig. **21-24**). The plaster of the drapery is modeled extensively by the sculptor's fingers in these reliefs, giving large areas an almost gestural quality. In many of his later works, Segal used primary colors, eliminating the ghostlike quality of his earlier works.

MARISOL Venezuelan artist Marisol Escobar (b. 1930), known to the world as Marisol, creates figurative assemblages from plaster, wood, fabric, paint, found objects, photographs, and other sources. As in *Women and Dog* (Fig. **21-25**), Marisol frequently repeats images of her own face and body in her work. She has also used these techniques to render satirical portraits of world leaders.

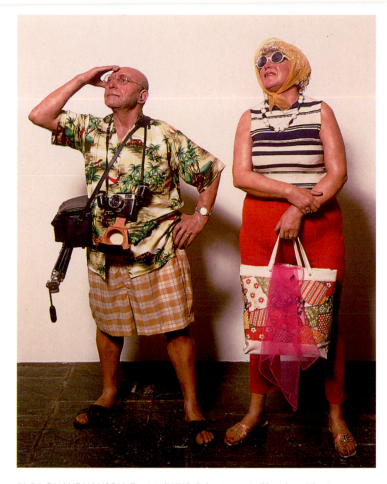

21-26 DUANE HANSON. *Tourists* (1970). Polyester resin/fiberglass. Life-size.

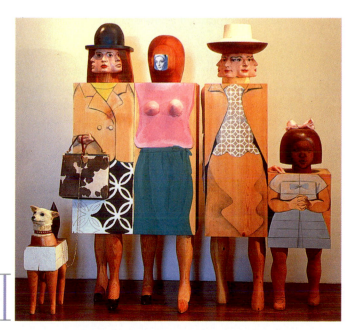

1 ft.

21-25 MARISOL. *Women and Dog* (1964). Fur, leather, plaster, synthetic polymer, and wood. 72" × 82" × 16".

DUANE HANSON Duane Hanson (1925–1996) was reared on a dairy farm in Minnesota. His *Tourists* (Fig. **21-26**) is characteristic of the work of several contemporary sculptors in that it uses synthetic substances such as liquid polyester resin to closely approximate the visual and tactile qualities of flesh. Such literal surfaces allow the artist no expression of personal signature. In the presence of a Hanson figure, or a John De Andrea nude, viewers watch for the rising and falling of the chest. They do not wish to stare too hard or to say something careless on the off chance that the sculpture is real. There is an electricity in gallery storerooms where these sculptures coexist in waiting. One tries to decipher which ones will get up and walk away.

Duane Hanson's liberal use of off-the-rack apparel and objects such as "stylish" sunglasses, photographic paraphernalia, and shopping bags gave these figures a caustic, satirical edge. But not all of Hanson's sculptures are lighthearted. Like Warhol, Hanson also portrayed disasters, such as death scenes from the conflict in Vietnam. In his later work, the artist focused more on the psychological content of his figures, as expressed by tense postures and grimaces.

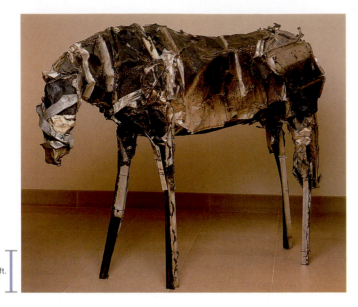

21-27 DEBORAH BUTTERFIELD. *Horse #6-82* (1982). Steel, sheet aluminum, wire, and tar. 76" × 108" × 41". Dallas Museum of Art, Dallas, TX.

1 ft.

DEBORAH BUTTERFIELD Montana sculptor Deborah Butterfield (b. 1949) has been interested in horses since her childhood in California. Horses are powerful creatures, and there is a history of equestrian sculptures that commemorate soldiers. Such horses are usually stallions that are vehicles of war, but Butterfield turns to mares. In this way, like Susan Rothenberg, she uses horses to create something of a symbolic self-portrait:

> I first used horse images as a metaphorical substitute for myself—it was a way of doing a self-portrait one step removed from the specificity of Deborah Butterfield. . . . The only horse sculpture I'd ever seen was very masculine. . . . No knight or soldier would ever be caught riding a mare into battle, it was just not done. . . . [What] I wanted to do [was] to make this small reference to the [Vietnam] war [with a] big sculpture that was very powerful and strong, and yet, very feminine and capable of procreation rather than just destruction.[10]

Horse #6-82 (Fig. **21-27**) is constructed from scrap metal derived from a crushed aluminum trailer. Ribbons of shiny metal wrap surfaces splattered with tar, giving form to the animal. Although her horses are figural, Butterfield notes that their meaning "isn't about horses at all."[11]

Contemporary Abstract Sculpture

Abstract sculpture remains vital, ever varied in form and substance. Contemporary abstract sculptures range from the site-specific works of Smithson and Christo to the mobiles of Alexander Calder (see Fig. 2-70), the mysterious wooden walls of Louise Nevelson, the machined surfaces of David Smith's cubes, and the anti-art machines of Jean Tinguely (Fig. 21-36).

DAVID SMITH American artist David Smith (1906–1965) moved away from figurative sculpture in the 1940s. His works of the 1950s were compositions of linear steel that crossed back and forth as they swept through space. Many sculptors of massive works create the designs but then farm out their execution to assistants or to foundries. Smith, however, took pride in constructing his own metal sculptures. Even though Smith's shapes are geometrically pure (Fig. **21-28**), his loving burnishing of their highly reflective surfaces grants them the overall gestural quality found in Abstract Expressionist paintings.

21-28 DAVID SMITH. *Cubi XVIII* (1964). Stainless steel. Art Resource, NY © Estate of David Smith/Licensed by VAGA, NY.

---

[10] Excerpts from Deborah Butterfield in *Deborah Butterfield* (Winston-Salem, NC: Southeastern Center for Contemporary Art, 1983; and Providence: Rhode Island School of Design Museum of Art, 1981).

[11] Deborah Butterfield, in Graham W. J. Beal, "Eight Horsepower," in *Viewpoints: Deborah Butterfield: Sculpture* (Minneapolis: Walker Art Center, 1982).

JACKIE FERRARA Jackie Ferrara's (b. 1929) works during the 1960s employed fetishistic materials such as feathers, fur, and rope, which were often suspended from the ceiling. In the 1970s, she began to deal with gravity from the other end, so to speak, and created pyramidal forms set firmly on the floor. *A207 Recall* (Fig. **21-29**) has something of the appearance of a Postmodern chimney and is constructed from pieces of pine that are glued together. Her concern with the interior as well as the exterior of the work is suggested by the series of patterns within that alternately complement the shape of the exterior and set it further awry. Although the wooden surface renders her work warm and the partial revelations make it mysterious, the sculpture was created with attention to precise mathematical relationships.

JUDY PFAFF Another contemporary sculpture form is the **installation**, in which materials from planks of wood to

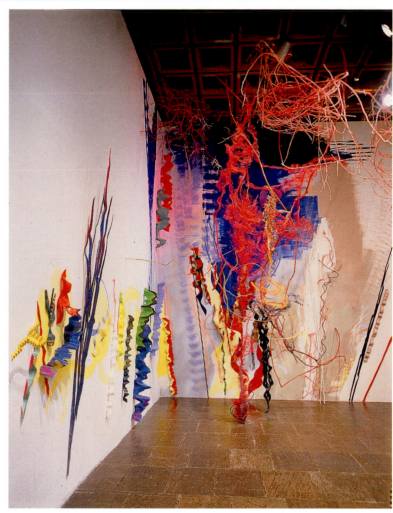

21-30 JUDY PFAFF. *Dragon* (January–April 1981). Installation view, Whitney Biennial, Whitney Museum of American Art, NY.

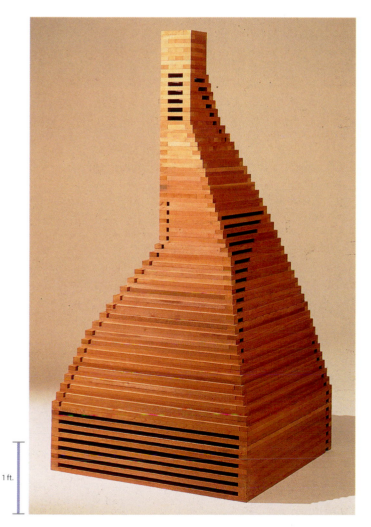

1 ft.

21-29 JACKIE FERRARA. *A207 Recall* (1980). Pine. 76½" × 37½" × 37½".

pieces of string and metal are assembled to fit within specific room-sized exhibition spaces. Installations are not necessarily intended to be permanent. In *Dragon* (Fig. **21-30**), by Judy Pfaff (b. 1946), the viewer roams around within the elements of the piece, an experience that can be pleasurable and overwhelming among the vibrant colors and assorted textures. Many of the elements of Pfaff's installations hang down around the viewer, creating an atmosphere reminiscent of foliage, sometimes of an underwater landscape.

NANCY GRAVES Nancy Graves (b. 1940) has worked both in figural and abstract styles and is comfortable with ignoring the traditional boundary between them. In addition to sculpture, she has also created drawings, prints, paintings, and films. When she was only 29 years old, the Whitney Museum exhibited her life-size, naturalistic camels.

DELACROIX'S *LIBERTY LEADING THE PEOPLE*, KOLLWITZ'S *OUTBREAK*, CATLETT'S *HARRIET*, AND GOYA'S *AND THEY ARE LIKE WILD BEASTS*

THE EVOLUTION OF FEMINIST ART finds its parallel in the evolution of feminist art history. The dust jacket of a text titled *Women, Art, and Power and Other Essays* by the nineteenth-century-art scholar Linda Nochlin, bears a detail of Eugène Delacroix's *Liberty Leading the People* (Fig. **21-31**). At its center is the allegory of Liberty—a fast-striding woman bearing the tricolor in one hand and a bayonet in the other—looking for all the world like an Amazon of ancient Greece. An archetypal figure set within an archetypal setting of an archetypal revolution. So, where's the rub?

Nochlin, who also explored the uncharted territory of feminist issues in art history and criticism, notes in her text:

> Delacroix's powerful figure of Liberty is, like almost all feminine embodiments of human virtue—Justice, Truth, Temperance, Victory—an allegory rather than a concrete historical woman, an example of what Simone de Beauvoir (French existential philosopher and author of *The Second Sex*) has called Woman-as-Other.

By contrast, the forceful figure who inspires courage and motivates action in Kollwitz's *The Outbreak* (Fig. **21-32**) is a historically documented leader of the sixteenth-century German Peasants' War. She was known as Black Anna. Delacroix's Liberty does not portray the role of women in the French Revolution, but rather embodies the intangible spirit that fueled the burning desire for freedom. Kollwitz's

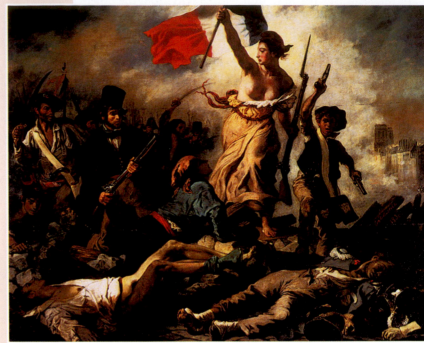

1 ft.

21-31 EUGÈNE DELACROIX. *Liberty Leading the People* (1830). Oil on canvas. 8'6" × 10'10". Louvre, Paris, France.

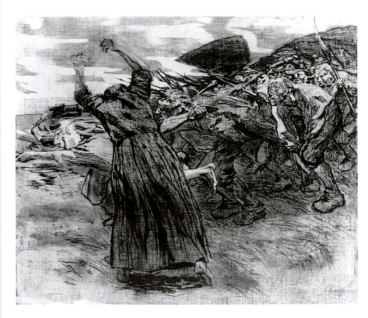

21-32 KÄTHE KOLLWITZ. *The Outbreak* (1903). Plate #5 from *The Peasants' War*. Etching and aquatint. © 2011 Artists Rights Society (ARS), NY/VG Bild-Kunst, Bonn.

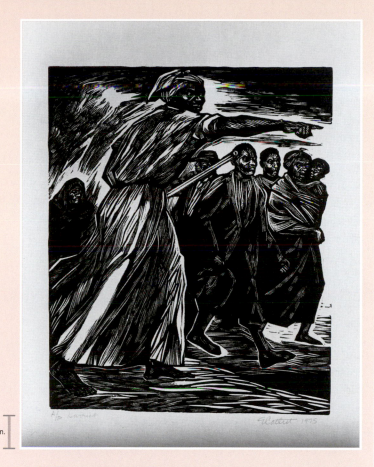

21-33 ELIZABETH CATLETT. *Harriet* (1975). Linoleum block print. 12½" × 10⅛".

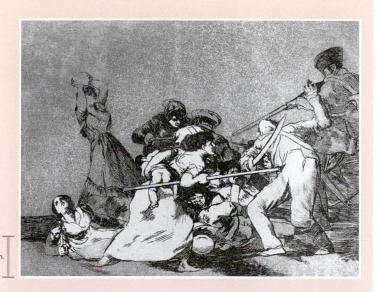

21-34 FRANCISCO GOYA Y LUCIENTES. *And They Are Like Wild Beasts* (*Y son Fieras*). From *Disasters of War* (1808–1820). Etching and aquatint. 6" × 7 15/16". Museum of Fine Arts, Boston, MA.

Anna is at the front. It is through her example—her indomitable spirit at the cost of her own life—that we experience, firsthand, the quest for justice.

A striking visual parallel can be seen in Elizabeth Catlett's *Harriet* (Fig. **21-33**), a linoleum block print that records the actions of Harriet Tubman, one of the "conductors" of the Underground Railroad, who led more than 300 slaves to freedom. Like Kollwitz's Anna, Harriet is a historic figure who loomed larger than life and is so depicted through her relative size.

The Spanish artist Francisco Goya also turned his attention to the subject of women and aggression (Fig. **21-34**) in one of a suite of prints titled *Disasters of War*. At first glance, we observe a group of women, one with an infant astride her hip, defending themselves with rocks and sticks against the swords and guns of male soldiers. Theirs is a valiant effort, inspired by raw courage and maternal instinct. And yet, if we note the title of the work, we come to understand that Goya equates this desperate attempt to protect themselves and their children with the animal instincts of "wild beasts."

In all four works, we witness the images of women astride or in the midst of chaos and destruction. How does each artist use vantage point in the composition (frontal, profile, rear) to involve the observer in the action of the scene? What is our relationship to the female figures, and to the action as a whole, in each of these works? Are we observers? participants? Stylistically, how does each artist use the medium to enhance the subject of the work? How do the use of perspective and compositional arrangement intensify the narrative? Can you speculate as to the gender ideologies reflected in or reaffirmed by the artists of each of these compositions? ●

The only stable thing is movement.
—Jean Tinguely

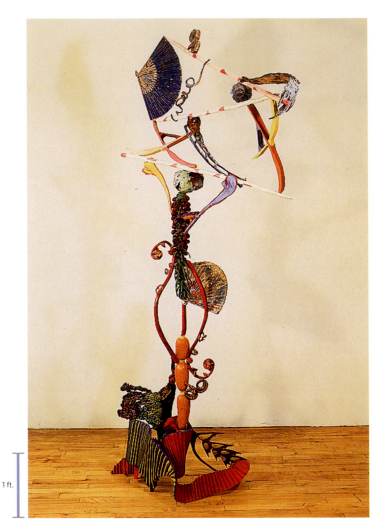

21-35 NANCY GRAVES. *Tarot* (1984). Bronze with polychrome patina and enamel. 88" × 49" × 20".

JEAN TINGUELY Swiss-born kinetic sculptor Jean Tinguely (1925–1991) was an able satirist of the machine age who shares the Dadaist view of art as anti-art. He is best known for his *Homage to New York* (Fig. **21-36**), a motorized, mixed-media construction that self-destructed (intentionally) in the garden of the Museum of Modern Art. But an unexpected fire within the machine necessitated the intervention of the New York Fire Department, which provided a spontaneous touch without charge. Tinguely's machines, more than those on which his work comments, frequently fail to perform precisely as intended.

As a further reflection of his philosophy of art, in the 1950s, Tinguely introduced kinetic sculptures that served as "painting machines." One of them produced thousands of "Abstract Expressionist" paintings—on whose quality, perhaps, we need not comment.

JACKIE WINSOR Canadian-born Jackie Winsor (b. 1941), like many of her contemporaries, is taken with the primal aesthetics of simple geometric forms. Yet unlike the machined smoothness employed by David Smith, her works are more likely to have a weathered organic, handmade look. Winsor's works are a while in the making, and though she has the

Tarot (Fig. **21-35**) is made of traditional bronze but is directly cast such that the original object is destroyed as it is reborn into the metal. In a sense, Graves redoes nature. Much of the innovation of the piece is derived from the juxtapositions and coloration. Graves has focused much of her attention on the development of polychrome (multicolored) patinas with poured acrylic and baked enamel. *Tarot* (the word refers to a set of allegorical cards used in fortune-telling) is an assemblage of sundry human-made and natural elements—strange flowers, lacy plants, noodles, dried fish, lampshades, tools and machinery, even packing materials. With this concoction—or perhaps this history—humankind is cast an eccentric fortune indeed.

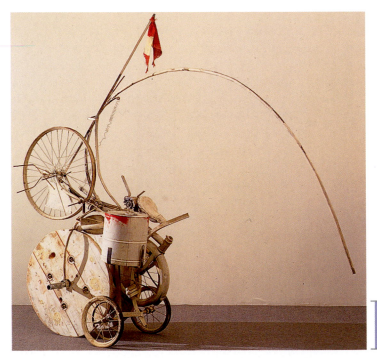

21-36 JEAN TINGUELY. Fragment from *Homage to New York* (1960). Painted metal. 6'8¼" × 29⅝" × 7'3⅞". The Museum of Modern Art, NY.

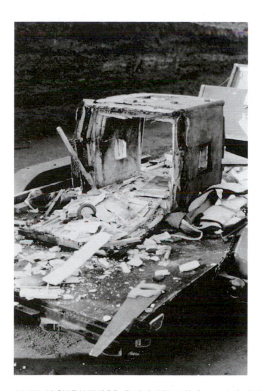
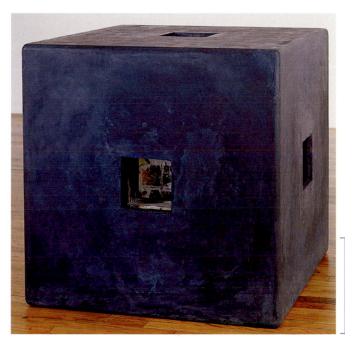

21-37 JACKIE WINSOR. *Exploded Piece* (*before and after*) (1980–1982). Wood, reinforced concrete, plaster, gold leaf, and explosive residue. 34½" × 34½" × 34½". Private collection.

resources to have others construct them from her design, hers is an art of the hand as well as of the heart and the mind.

Exploded Piece (Fig. **21-37**) is one of the sculptures that Winsor also sees as a performance piece. Winsor is not destructive in the mold of Tinguely. (In fact, the culmination of the "performance" was her reconstruction of the exploded parts into a perfect whole.) Rather, she seems preoccupied with the nature and the potentials of her materials. Another work, *Burnt Piece*, seemed to pose and answer the question, "What will happen to a half-concrete, half-wood cube when it is set afire?" *Exploded Piece*, similarly, explores the results of detonating an explosive charge within a cube made of wood, reinforced concrete, and other materials. It seems appropriate to leave the section on abstract sculpture with a bang.

FEMINIST ART

While on the East Coast, Pop Art was on the wane and Superrealism on the rise, happenings on the West Coast were about to change the course of women's art, history, and criticism forever.

In 1970, a Midwestern artist named Judy Gerowitz (b. 1939)—who would soon call herself Judy Chicago—initiated a feminist studio art course at Fresno State College in California. One year later, she collaborated with artist Miriam Schapiro (b. 1923) on a feminist art program at the California Institute of Arts in Valencia. Their interests and efforts culminated in another California project—a communal installation in Hollywood called *Womanhouse*.

Beyond being a milestone in the history of women's art, *Womanhouse* was a fantastic undertaking, a daring project. Teaming up with students from the University of California, Chicago and Schapiro refurbished each room of a dilapidated mansion in a theme built around women's experiences: The "Kitchen," by Robin Weltsch, was covered with breast-shaped eggs; a "Menstruation Bathroom," by Chicago, included the waste products of female menstruation cycles in a sterile white environment.

MIRIAM SCHAPIRO AND SHERRY BRODY Another room in *Womanhouse* housed a child-sized dollhouse, in which Miriam Schapiro and Sherry Brody juxtaposed mundane and frightening objects to effect a kind of black humor

Natalia Goncharov
Kate Greenaway
Barbara Hepworth
Eva Hesse
Hannah Hoch
Anna Huntingdon
May Howard Jackson
Frida Kahlo
Angelica Kauffmann
Hilma af Klimt

DURING THE 1980S, something of a backlash against inclusion of women and ethnic minorities in the arts could be observed.* For example, a 1981 London exhibition, *The New Spirit in Painting*, included no women artists. A 1982 Berlin exhibition, *Zeitgeist*, represented 40 artists, but only 1 was a woman. The 1984 inaugural exhibition of the Museum of Modern Art's remodeled galleries, *An International Survey of Recent Painting and Sculpture*, showed the works of 165 artists, only 14 of whom were

*Whitney Chadwick, *Women, Art, and Society* (London and New York: Thames and Hudson, 1990).

women. The New York exhibition *The Expressionist Image*: *American Art from Pollock to Now* included the works of 24 artists, only 2 of whom were women. And so it goes.

To combat this disturbing trend, an anonymous group of women artists banded together as the Guerrilla Girls. The group appeared in public with gorilla masks and proclaimed themselves to be the "conscience of the art world." They mounted posters on buildings in Manhattan's SoHo district, one of the most active centers in the art world today. They took out ads of protest.

Figure 21-38 shows one of the Guerrilla Girls' posters. This particular poster sardonically notes the "advantages" of being a woman artist in an art world that, despite the "liberating" trends of the postfeminist era, continues to be dominated by men. It also calls attention to the blatant injustice of the relative price tags on works by women and men. Note that at this writing, the inequity persists. A 1993 cover story for the *New York Times Magazine* pictures the "Art World All-Stars" of dealer Arnold Glimcher (Fig. 21-39). Women artists and artists of color are conspicuous by their absence. ●

THE ADVANTAGES OF BEING A WOMAN ARTIST:

Working without the pressure of success.
Not having to be in shows with men.
Having an escape from the art world in your 4 free-lance jobs.
Knowing your career might pick up after you're eighty.
Being reassured that whatever kind of art you make it will be labeled feminine.
Not being stuck in a tenured teaching position.
Seeing your ideas live on in the work of others.
Having the opportunity to choose between career and motherhood.
Not having to choke on those big cigars or paint in Italian suits.
Having more time to work after your mate dumps you for someone younger.
Being included in revised versions of art history.
Not having to undergo the embarrassment of being called a genius.
Getting your picture in the art magazines wearing a gorilla suit.

Please send $ and comments to:
Box 1056 Cooper Sta. NY, NY 10276 **GUERRILLA GIRLS** CONSCIENCE OF THE ART WORLD

WHEN RACISM & SEXISM ARE NO LONGER FASHIONABLE, WHAT WILL YOUR ART COLLECTION BE WORTH?

The art market won't bestow mega-buck prices on the work of a few white males forever. For the 17.7 million you just spent on a single Jasper Johns painting, you could have bought at least one work by all of these women and artists of color:

Berenice Abbott	Elaine de Kooning	Dorothea Lange	Sarah Peale
Anni Albers	Lavinia Fontana	Marie Laurencin	Ljubova Popova
Sofonisba Anguisolla	Meta Warwick Fuller	Edmonia Lewis	Olga Rosanova
Diane Arbus	Artemisia Gentileschi	Judith Leyster	Nellie Mae Rowe
Vanessa Bell	Marguérite Gérard	Barbara Longhi	Rachel Ruysch
Isabel Bishop	Natalia Goncharova	Dora Maar	Kay Sage
Rosa Bonheur	Kate Greenaway	Lee Miller	Augusta Savage
Margaret Bourke-White	Eva Hesse	Lisette Model	Varvara Stepanova
Romaine Brooks	Hannah Hoch	Paula Modersohn Becker	Florine Stettheimer
Julia Margaret Cameron	Anna Huntingdon	Tina Modotti	Sophie Taeuber-Arp
Emily Carr	May Howard Jackson	Berthe Morisot	Alma Thomas
Rosalba Carriera	Frida Kahlo	Grandma Moses	Marietta Robusti Tintoretto
Mary Cassatt	Angelica Kauffmann	Gabriele Münter	Suzanne Valadon
Constance Marie Charpentier	Hilma af Klimt	Alice Neel	Remedios Varo
Imogen Cunningham	Kathe Kollwitz	Louise Nevelson	Elizabeth Vigée Le Brun
Sonia Delaunay	Lee Krasner	Georgia O'Keeffe	Laura Wheeling Waring
		Meret Oppenheim	

Information courtesy of Christie's, Sotheby's, International Auction Records and Leonard's Annual Price Index of Auctions

Please send $ and comments to:
Box 1056 Cooper Sta. NY, NY 10276 **GUERRILLA GIRLS** CONSCIENCE OF THE ART WORLD

21-38 GUERRILLA GIRLS. Poster (c. 1987). www.guerillagirls.com.

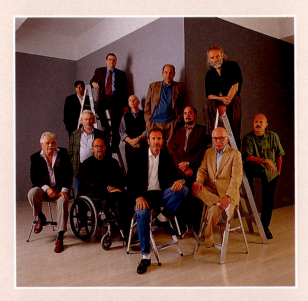

21-39 ARNOLD GLIMCHER AND HIS ART WORLD ALL-STARS. Used on the cover of *New York Times Magazine* (October 3, 1993).

(Fig. **21-40**). The now-famous installation became a much-needed hub for area women's groups and was the impetus for the founding a year later of the Los Angeles Women's Building, which is still active today.

Womanhouse called attention to women artists, their wants, their needs. In some ways, it was an expression of anger toward the injustice of art-world politics that many women artists experienced—lack of attention by critics, curators, and historians; pressure to work in canonical styles. It announced to the world, through shock and exaggeration, that men's subjects are not necessarily of interest to women; that women's experiences, although not heroic, are significant. And perhaps of most importance, particularly in light of the subsequent careers of its participants, the exhibition exalted women's ways of working.

We have already seen works by women that might be considered feminist (see Laurie Simmons's *Red Library #2*, Fig. 1-22; Suzanne Lacy and Leslie Labowitz's *In Mourning and in Rage*, Fig. 1-33; and Barbara Kruger's *Untitled* (*We Don't Need Another Hero*), Fig. 4-15); that highlight women's accomplishments (see Judy Chicago's *The Dinner Party*, Fig. 1-10); or that assimilate traditional women's craft (see Miriam Schapiro's *Wonderland*, Fig. 1-35; and Faith Ringgold's *Tar Beach*, Fig. 1-28). In this section, we shall examine other works by women artists. They, too, have been chosen because they make sharp feminist statements, speak directly to women's experiences, or raise materials and methods that have been employed by women for centuries to the level of fine arts.

ANA MENDIETA Much of the impact of *Arbol de la Vida* (*Tree of Life*), no. 294 (Fig. **21-41**) is related to the shock value of its extraordinary contrasts of texture. In this performance piece, feminist artist Ana Mendieta (1948–1985) presented her own body, draped in mud (an "earth–body sculpture"), against the craggy bark of a tree. Like some women artists, she shunned painting, especially abstract painting, as historically

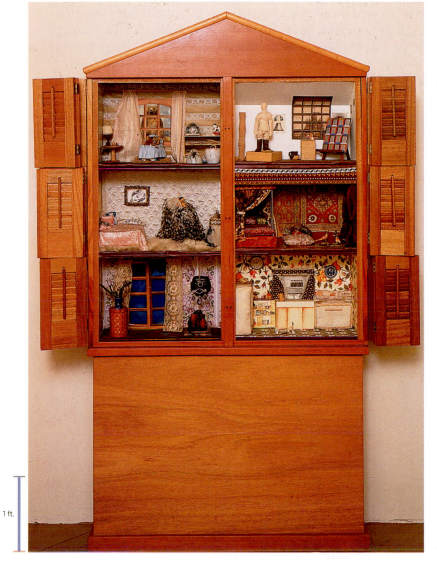

1 ft.

21-40 MIRIAM SCHAPIRO, IN COLLABORATION WITH SHERRY BRODY. *The Doll House* (1972). Mixed media. 84" × 40" × 41". Smithsonian American Art Museum, Washington, D.C.

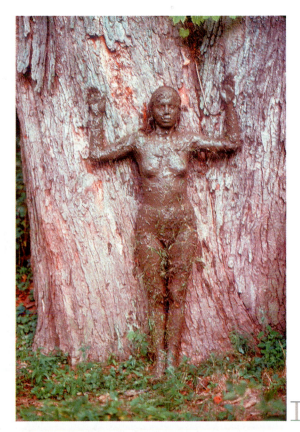

1 in.

21-41 ANA MENDIETA. *Arbol de la Vida, no. 294*, from the *Arbol de la Vida / Silueta* (*Tree of Life / Silhouette*) series (1977). Color photograph. 20" × 13¼". Documentation of earth–body sculpture with artist, tree trunk, and mud, at Old Man's Creek, Iowa City, IA.

inundated with male values. Mendieta tied her flesh and blood, instead, across time and cultures, to the ancient myths of the earth mother goddesses.

BARBARA KRUGER Many women artists have tried to call attention to stereotypes that influence the way women are perceived. Laurie Simmons's "Stepford Wife" in her *Red Library #2* shows a woman locked into the compulsive care of her home, to the exclusion of more worthwhile and rewarding activity. Barbara Kruger's (b. 1945) *Untitled* (*We Don't Need Another Hero*) (see Fig. 4-15) confronts her male and female viewers with stereotypical epithets for the "dominant sex," seeming to criticize females for feeding male expectations as much as males for having them.

Kruger's juxtaposition of images and text, tabloidlike in their visual attraction, cause the viewer to reconsider the ideological hold that words and pictures and familiar phrases

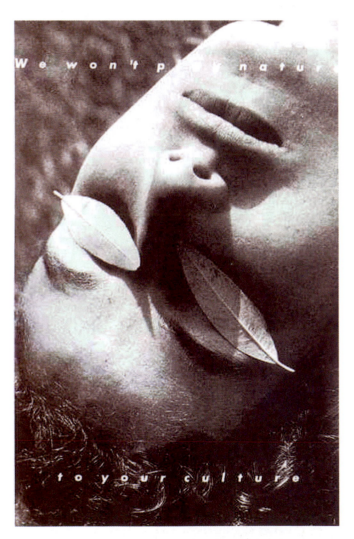

21-42 BARBARA KRUGER. *Untitled* (*We Won't Play Nature to Your Culture*). Photograph (1983). Ydessa Hendeles Art Foundation, Toronto, Ontario, Canada.

have on us. *We Won't Play Nature to Your Culture* (Fig. **21-42**) forces us to define those words and to come to terms with the way that women have been relegated to "nature" (motherhood, domesticity, the literal or figurative sequestering in the home), while men have had the privilege of participating in "culture" (the world of ideas, of thinking, talking, sharing, and acting). As in many of Kruger's works, her medium is the message—a call to action.

ARCHITECTURE

After World War II, architecture moved in many directions. Some of these were technological advances that allowed architects to literally achieve greater heights, as in the skyscraper, and to create more sculptural forms, as in Le Corbusier's Chapel of Notre-Dame-du-Haut (see Figs. 11-20 and 11-21). Millions of soldiers returned from Europe and the Pacific and established new families, giving birth not only to what we now call the baby boomers, but also to vast housing tracts like Levittown (see Fig. 11-12) that dotted suburbs that had earlier been farms, small towns, or wilderness. All these and more were examples of modern architecture.

Modern Architecture

Modern architecture rejected the ideals and principles of the classical tradition in favor of the experimental forms of expression that characterized many styles of art and literature from the 1860s to the 1970s. *Modernism* also refers to approaches that are ahead of their time. "Modern" suggests, in general, an approach that overturns the past and, by that definition, every era of artists doing something completely new can be considered modern in their time.

Modernism is a concept of art-making built on the urge to depict contemporary life and events rather than history. Modernism was a response to industrialization, urbanization, and the growth of capitalism and democracy. Modern architects, like modern artists, felt free to explore new styles inspired by technology and science, psychology, politics, economics, and social consciousness.

As we see in the differences among Le Corbusier's work, Levittown, Miës van der Rohe's Farnsworth House (Fig **21-43**) and his Seagram Building, designed in collaboration with Philip Johnson (Fig. **21-44**), modernism in architecture never comprised just one style. Rather, it serves as an umbrella term that encompasses the many architectural visions, including those of Frank Lloyd Wright (see Fig. 11-22), Le Corbusier, Miës van der Rohe, Gordon Bunshaft, and many others.

A rhythmic procession of white steel columns suspends Miës van der Rohe's Farnsworth House above the Illinois

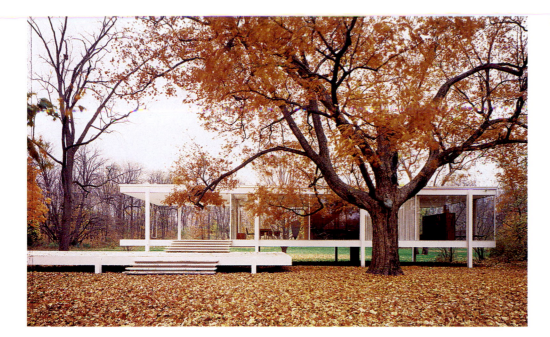

21-43 LUDWIG MIËS VAN DER ROHE. Farnsworth House, Fox River, Plano, IL (1950). © 2011 Artists Rights Society (ARS), NY/VG Bild-Kunst, Bonn.

21-44 LUDWIG MIËS VAN DER ROHE & PHILIP JOHNSON. Seagram Building, NY (1958).

countryside. In its perfect technological elegance, it is in many ways visually remote from its site. Why steel? Less expensive wood could have supported this house of one story and short spans, and wood might certainly have appeared more natural on this sylvan site. The architect's choices can be read as a symbol of our contemporary remoteness from our feral past. Perhaps the architect is suggesting that contemporary technology has freed humankind from victimization at the brutal hand of nature even as it allows humans to enjoy interaction with nature at an aesthetic level. The Farnsworth House is as beautiful as it is austere in ornamentation. It has platforms, steps, and a glass curtain wall that allows the environment to flow through. The steps and platforms provide access to a less well-ordered world below.

The Seagram Building, the American headquarters for the Canadian distiller Joseph E. Seagram's & Sons, was built across Park Avenue from its equally famous and equally modernist neighbor, Lever House (see Fig. 11-19). Designed by Miës van der Rohe and Philip Johnson, it is another signature example of the modernist credo "form follows function." There is no ornamentation. The vertical I-beams of bronze-coated steel form a perfectly regular pattern across the elevations of the structure and emphasize its upward reach. Miës, who abhorred irregularity, even specified that the window coverings for the building be uniform, so that from the outside, the windows would never look chaotic or messy. The sharp-edged columns at the entry-level plaza complement the stark grid of the building, but also define a softer, transitional space—with trees and fountains— between the chaos of the surrounding city and the austere serenity of the office interior.

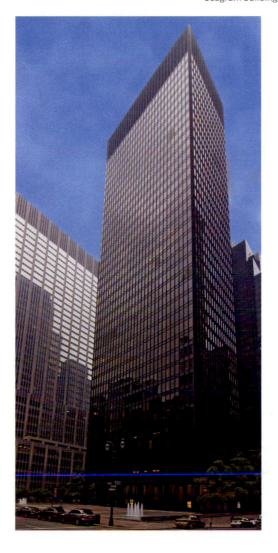

Postmodern Architecture

By the mid-1970s, the clean Modernist look of buildings such as the Seagram Building was overwhelming the cityscape. Architectural critics began to argue that a national proliferation of steel-cage rectangular solids was threatening to bury the nation's cities in boredom. Said John Perrault in 1979, "We are sick to death of cold plazas and 'curtain wall' skyscrapers."

In response—or in revolt—by the end of the 1970s, architects continued to create steel-cage structures but drew freely from past styles of ornamentation, including classical columns, pediments, friezes, and a variety of elements we might find in ancient Egypt, Greece, and Rome. The architectural movement was termed **Postmodernism**, and the idea was to once more "warm up" buildings, to link them to the architectural past, to a Main Street of the heart or mind—some sort of mass architectural nostalgia. Postmodernist structures rejected the formal simplicity and immacu-

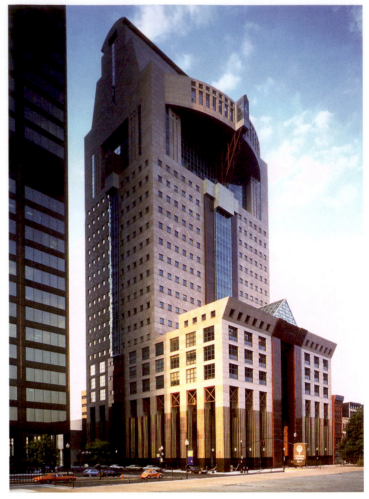

21-46 MICHAEL GRAVES. Humana Building, Louisville, KY (1986).

late finish of Modernist architecture in favor of whimsical shapes, colors, and patterns. Postmodern architects revived the concept of the decorative in architecture, a practice that was completely antithetical to the purity of modernism in the twentieth century.

One of the most interesting aspects of Postmodern architecture is its appropriation of historical motifs; Philip Johnson's and John Burgee's AT&T Building in New York City (subsequently sold to SONY) (Fig. **21-45**) is one of the earliest examples. The massive tower sits on a forest of columns, reminiscent—to Johnson—of an Egyptian **hypostyle hall**. Its pale pink facade is punctuated with fenestration, although the prominent stone grid lines regulate the pace of the upward sweep. The building is crowned with a broken roof pediment referencing the Chippendale style that originated with the eighteenth-century British cabinetmaker Thomas Chippendale. Beneath the ornamentation lies a steel-cage structure, now visually all but disguised.

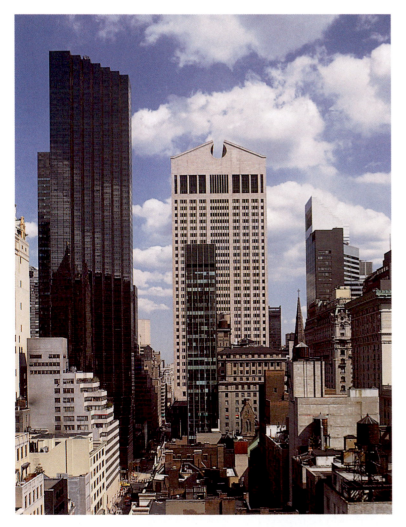

21-45 BURGEE ARCHITECTS WITH PHILIP JOHNSON. SONY Plaza (formerly AT&T Building), NY (1984).

If the SONY Building is a Postmodern steel-cage structure that draws on Chippendale furniture design for its signature pediment, Michael Graves's Humana Building (Fig. 21-46) looks to ancient Egypt for its particular historic reference. Tall, tightly arranged pillars (as in an Egyptian **hypostyle** hall) and a grid of square windows lighten the otherwise heavy rectangular solids, which seem to anchor the building firmly to the ground. The overall impression recalls the great pylons, or gateways, of Egyptian temple complexes such as the one at Karnak (see Figs. 11-5 and 11-6). The office building is set behind the entry in such a way that the overall contour mimics the blocklike seated body position in ancient statuary (see Fig. 13-11). The curved shape at the top of the front elevation, "adorned" with a projecting rectangle, recalls a pharaonic headdress.

Deconstructivist Architecture

What we have known as modern architecture is no longer modern, at least not in the sense of relating to the *present*. It's not even Postmodern, if we want to pigeonhole style. As we move forward in the third millennium, the world of architecture seems enmeshed in a movement called *Deconstructivism*.

The Deconstructivist movement originated in the 1960s with the ideas of the French philosopher Jacques Derrida. He argued, in part, that literary texts can be read in different ways and that it is absurd to believe that there can be only one proper interpretation. Similarly, in Deconstructivist architec-

tural design, the whole is less important than the parts. In fact, buildings are meant to be seen in bits and pieces. The familiar elements of traditional architecture are taken apart, discarded, or disguised so that what remains seems randomly assembled.

Deconstructivist architects deny the modern maxim that form should follow function. Instead, they tend to reduce their structures to purer geometric forms made possible by contemporary materials, and they make liberal use of color to express emotion. An early (1988) exhibition of Deconstructivist works at the Museum of Modern Art connected Deconstructivist architecture with Cubism and with the Constructivist Russian painting and sculpture of the 1920s (see Naum Gabo's *Column*, Fig. 20-16). American architect Philip Johnson contributed to that exhibition at age 82, and he was the only architect of note to have been a driving force in the Modern, Postmodern, and Deconstructivist movements.

FRANK GEHRY The Guggenheim Museums have always been on the cutting edge of design, beginning with Frank Lloyd Wright's unique spiral-shaped monument on New York City's Fifth Avenue (see the Art Tour at the end of this chapter). Frank Gehry designed the no-less-remarkable Guggenheim Museum Bilbao (see Fig. 2-18), which brings thousands of tourists to that industrial Spanish city each year. Gehry is now designing yet another Guggenheim Museum (Fig. 21-47) for Abu Dhabi in the United Arab Emirates—a 450,000-square-foot building sited on a peninsula adjacent to the city and surrounded on three sides by the Persian Gulf.

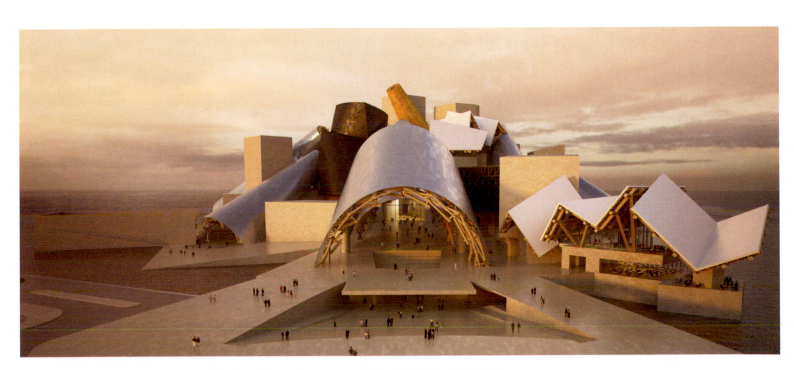

21-47 FRANK GEHRY. A rendering of the planned Guggenheim museum for Abu Dhabi, United Arab Emirates.

The void is one of the organizing features of the building. . . . It is the cut through German history, Jewish history. It is the extermination of Jews and the deportation of Jews not only from this city but from Germany and from Europe.

—Daniel Libeskind

It will be one of an untold number of architectural statements, including museums and arts centers by architects such as Zaha Hadid, Jean Nouvel, and Norman Foster. Gehry's deconstructivist design features fragmentation and nonrectilinear, sculptural shapes. Galleries will be connected by catwalks that encircle a covered courtyard and, like the building's exterior, will consist of a variety of shapes and materials. Part of the inspiration for the design was derived from traditional Middle Eastern wind towers that provide natural cooling and ventilation in the courtyards of buildings and sun-drenched village squares. Much of the new Guggenheim Museum will be devoted to the display of the works of well-known Middle Eastern artists, including Shirin Neshat (see Fig. 8-18) and Mona Hatoum. It will also have special exhibitions; a center for contemporary Arab, Islamic, and Middle-Eastern culture; a research facility; and a conservation laboratory.

DANIEL LIBESKIND Although Daniel Libeskind seems to have taken Deconstructivism as a point of departure in his design for the Jewish Museum Department of the Berlin Museum (Fig. 21-48), he invested its parts with profound symbolism. The addition is intended to communicate the vastness and also the legacy of things that are not completely visible. Contrary to public opinion, the flesh of architecture is not cladding, insulation, and structure, but the substance of the individual in society and history; a figuration of the inorganic, the body and the soul.

The zigzag, or lightning-bolt, shape of the building resembles a broken Star of David. It was derived mathematically by plotting the Berlin addresses of Jewish writers, artists, and composers who were killed during the Holocaust. The overall design is punctuated by voids that symbolize the absence of Jewish people and culture in Berlin. The zinc exterior of the museum is slashed by a linear pattern of windows that was determined by connecting the addresses of German and Jewish Berliners on a map of the museum's neighborhood. The visitor cannot help being struck by the overwhelming sense that every structural, design, and symbolic element—each of which attracts and holds interest—has been informed by the historic circumstances that gave rise to the building.

REM KOOLHAAS Herbert Muschamp, the architectural critic for the *New York Times*, said in his article on the Central Library (Fig. 21-49) in Seattle, Washington, that "there's never been a great building without a strong client in the history of the world, and Ms. [Deborah L.] Jacobs [Seattle's city librarian] is now up there with popes and princes as an instigator of fabulous cities." The accolades for the design of this extraordinary building go to Dutch architect Rem Koolhaas, but the laurels for making it happen go to Ms. Jacobs.

Koolhaas's name has become synonymous with Deconstructivist architecture. The library's exterior is faceted into folded planes of glass and steel supported by a diagonal grid of light blue metal. True to this aesthetic, the angles and shapes seem almost arbitrary, and the essential structure of the building is hard to decipher from the outside looking in. But within the building, Koolhaas's love of distinct parts and his tendency to subvert their traditional placement can be seen everywhere—from the bright red grand staircase and spiral ramp of book stacks to the "Mixing Chamber" at the heart of the building where librarians greet and help readers. Muschamp sees the Central Library as "a series of episodes in urban space." He also sees it as "where architecture is going."

SANTIAGO CALATRAVA Santiago Calatrava's architecture seems to be going up everywhere: a symphony center in Atlanta; 30 bridges including 3 that will span the Trinity River in Dallas; a $2 billion transportation hub for Ground Zero (the World Trade Center site); a residential tower composed of 12 cubes cantilevered from a con-

21-48 DANIEL LIBESKIND. Extension of the Berlin Museum (1989–1996). Berlin, Germany.

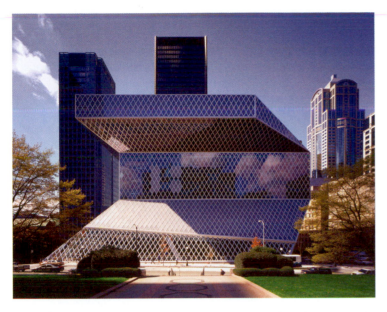

21-49 REM KOOLHAAS. Central Library, Seattle, WA (2004).

crete core overlooking the East River in New York City; a 2,000 feet tall residential tower in Chicago. *Time* magazine named Calatrava one of the 100 most influential people of 2005, and the American Institute of Architects awarded him their coveted gold medal in the same year.

Calatrava has erased the lines between architecture and sculpture. In his native city of Valencia, Spain, he designed a city-within-the-city to welcome the third millennium. The Hemesferic (Fig. **21-50**) was the first of several buildings completed for Valencia's "City of Arts and Sciences," which includes a planetarium (in the Hemesferic), an arts palace (with an opera house), an aquarium, and a science museum. The City of Arts and Sciences attracts millions of visitors each year, who visit the exhibits or, as Calatrava hoped, just stroll around the exteriors of the buildings to take in their sculptural forms. The Hemesferic, at once the simplest and perhaps the most astounding of the buildings in the complex, resembles a giant eyeball floating in a reflecting pool. A shutter made of steel and glass and operated by hydraulic lifts can be brought down over the sphere, resembling a blink of an eye.

Calatrava has said that he considers architecture "the greatest of all arts" because it embraces all of the others, including music, painting, and sculpture. Calatrava believes that he "couldn't be an architect without doing those things." His crossdisciplinary focus has yielded designs that seem sculptural, even painterly at times. His client for the transportation station called him "the da Vinci of our time . . . [an artist who] combined light and air and structural elegance with strength."[12]

---

[12] Robin Pogrebin, "An Artist Embraces New York." *New York Times*, April 23, 2005.

21-50 SANTIAGO CALATRAVA. Hemesferic, City of Arts and Sciences, Valencia, Spain (1998).

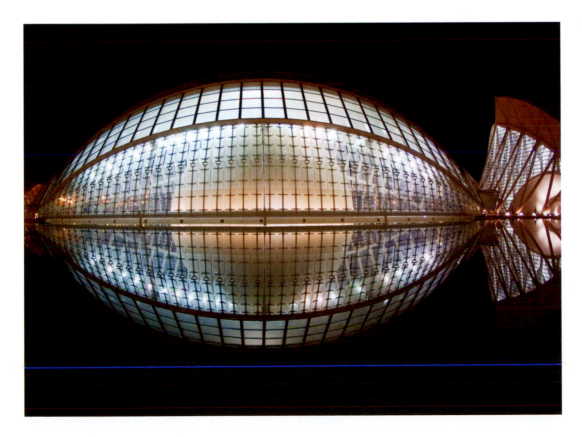

ART TOUR NEW YORK

WHEN WE LOOK AT NEW YORK and the arts, the Big Apple is the big show. For the performing arts—theater and music and dance—there's nothing like Broadway and Lincoln Center.

In terms of the visual arts, New York is renowned, and rightly so, for its museums and architecture, and for its public art, including Central Park and statues popping up everywhere. The Metropolitan Museum of Art houses one of the greatest and broadest collections in the world, including Egyptian, Greek and Roman, Asian, Islamic, Pacific Island, European, American, and contemporary art (which comes from anywhere and everywhere).

Even the most reluctant museumgoer will be charmed by the nineteenth-century European collection, which includes great paintings by the likes of Cézanne, Monet, Manet, Renoir, Degas, and van Gogh, and sculpture by Rodin. In the contemporary wing, you'll find paintings by Jackson Pollock, Georgia O'Keeffe, and Andy Warhol, for example. During the summer months, the roof of the Met is an outdoor sculpture garden. Take the elevator up for the art and for grand views of Central Park and the city. The main museum sits on Fifth Avenue, within Central Park, in the lower 80s. The Cloisters, which is part of the Met, is devoted to European medieval art and architecture and is located in northern Manhattan's Fort Tryon Park, which seems like a Manhattan island untouched by civilization.

Frank Lloyd Wright's Solomon R. Guggenheim Museum sits across Fifth Avenue from Central Park, about 10 blocks up from the Met, in New York's "Museum Mile." The main exhibition hall houses transient exhibitions. Marcel Breuer's Whitney Museum of American Art is found on Madison Avenue, which parallels Fifth Avenue, one block east, at 75th Street. The Whitney is devoted to American art, and its exhibitions include some of the edgiest and most controversial art in New York. My youngest daughter was captivated by Tony Oursler's Getaway #2, which was lying on the floor, repeatedly asking "Are you lookin' at me?" and cursing museumgoers. You can catch lunch in any of these museums.

The Museum of Modern Art (MOMA) has recently undergone a major renovation. The collection of the MOMA contains many familiar and beloved works that are not to be missed: van Gogh's *Starry Night* (see Fig. 19-25), Derain's *London Bridge* (see Fig. 20-1), Picasso's *Les Demoiselles d'Avignon* (see Fig. 20-6), Boccioni's *Unique Forms of Continuity in Space* (see Fig. 20-12), Balla's *Street Light* (see Fig. 20-13), Brancusi's *Bird in Space* (see Fig. 20-19), Ernst's *Two Children Are Threatened by a Nightingale* (see Fig. 20-26), Dalí's *The Persistence of Memory* (see Fig. 20-27), Pollocks, Monets, and . . . the list is, for all practical purposes, endless.

There are almost too many other museums and art galleries to mention. The Morgan Library on Madison Avenue in midtown contains one of the few remaining copies of the Gutenberg Bible (dated 1455). When visiting Harlem, check out the exhibitions at the Studio Museum on 125th Street. The Museo del Barrio is on Fifth Avenue in the 100s (don't forget

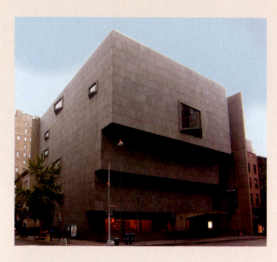

THE WHITNEY MUSEUM OF AMERICAN ART.

the charming garden within Central Park across from the Museo). As you're heading back down Fifth Avenue toward the 90s and the Museum Mile, you will find it worthwhile to visit the Jewish Museum and the Cooper-Hewitt National Design Museum. Down in the 70s, past the Met, you'll find the Frick Collection.

New York is also an architecture buff's dream. The Guggenheim and Whitney Museums are to be appreciated as works of art themselves, not just as houses for art. Some of the churches of the city are divine, including the Cathedral of St. John the Divine, on Amsterdam Avenue at 112th Street. This is the largest cathedral in the world (really), and St. Patrick's Cathedral, on Fifth Avenue at 50th Street, is the largest Catholic cathedral in the United States. The Cathedral of St. John the Divine was begun in 1892 and is still only about two-thirds finished.

When (and if) sufficient funds are raised, completion will require only about another half century. It is a very people- and environment-oriented cathedral, with chapels containing children's art and fish tanks that illustrate the ecology of the Hudson River.

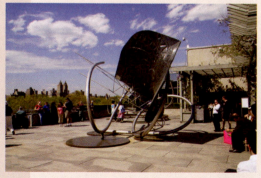

FRANK STELLA SCULPTURES ON THE ROOF OF THE MET, 2007.
© 2011 Frank Stella/Artists Rights Society (ARS), NY.

New York is looking up. That is, visitors to New York are always looking up. Look for the Art Deco stainless steel spire of the Chrysler Building (Lexington Avenue at 42nd Street), which resembles the grille of a car of the 1920s (its gargoyles resemble hood ornaments). It's worth a visit to check out the Art Deco doors of the elevators. The Empire State Building, at Fifth Avenue and 34th Street, provides wonderful views of the city. (King Kong enjoyed a visit to the top in 1933.) If you walk up Park Avenue from midtown, you'll come across the famed Waldorf Astoria Hotel; the Byzantine St. Bartholomew's Church (St. Bart's), with its wonderful ornate detail and gold dome; and prime examples of the steel-cage architecture of the 1950s, Lever House (see Fig. 11-19) and the Seagram Building (see Fig. 21-44).

Do not forget to spend time in Central Park, one of the city's greatest works of art, regardless of the time of year. It's never too hot to sunbathe or too cold to enjoy the Wollman Skating Rink or a horse-drawn carriage ride (there are blankets in the carriages). Designed by Frederick Law Olmsted, the park is a rectangular strip of grass, trees, hills, and lakes some 2½ miles long (running from 59th Street to 110th Street) and almost a mile wide (running from Fifth Avenue to Central Park West, which is the equivalent of Eighth Avenue). It forms the geographical and spiritual heart of Manhattan. Museums and other landmarks line its edges. Joggers circle the reservoir, young (and old) children guide miniature yachts in the sailboat pond, animals stretch and growl in the zoo, and lovers meander along its paths. New Yorkers pay a premium for apartments with a view of the park. Multiple roadways pass above and below one another so that through traffic, pedestrian walkways, and bridle paths all function simultaneously. Forty-six bridges and arches—all different—contribute to the harmonious functioning of the transportation system or simply provide decoration. Next to the lake (many blocks below the reservoir), you'll find Bethesda Fountain, where dozens of films have been shot and where you can experience acrobats, break-dancers, the beat of African drums, giant bubble blowers, and more. Spend a few extra dollars to eat at the Boathouse on the lake or just grab one

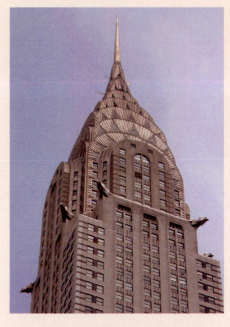

THE CHRYSLER BUILDING.

of New York's signature hotdogs from the ubiquitous vendors. After your urban interlude, a walk on a path around the lake can lead you to wooded areas that could just as easily be 100 miles upstate.

 TO CONTINUE YOUR TOUR and learn more about New York City, go to CourseMate.

FRANK LLOYD WRIGHT.
GUGGENHEIM MUSEUM.

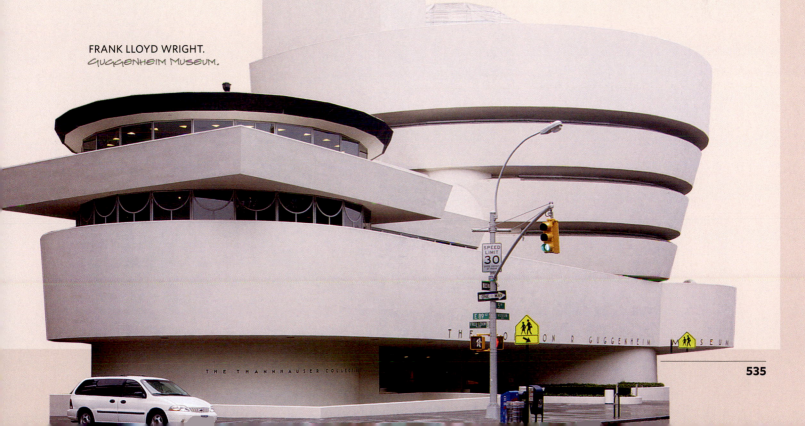

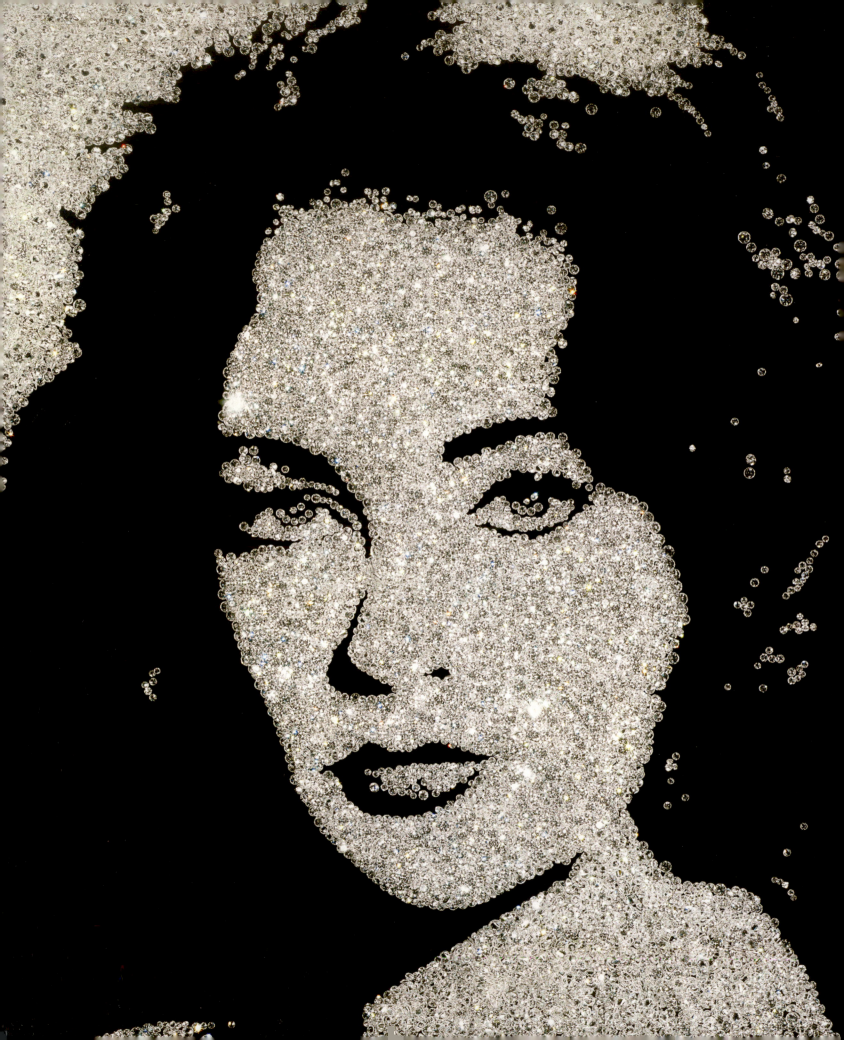

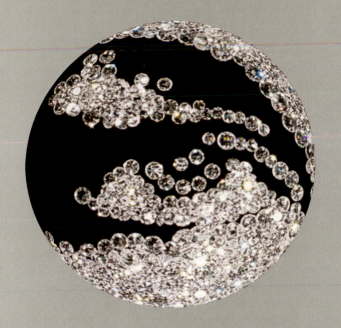

ART IN THE TWENTY-FIRST CENTURY: A GLOBAL PERSPECTIVE

22

When Holland Carter wrote these words for his introduction to an exhibition of Caribbean art at the Brooklyn Museum, he stated the facts as he observed them: that it seems no longer meaningful or even valid to be talking about a center of the art world, much less continuing to assign that center to the city of New York. Contemporary art has gone global—in venue, in subject, even in the raw economics of the art market—dovetailing with the phenomenon of globalization that characterizes spheres outside of the realm of culture. The word **globalization** has become ubiquitous in contemporary life, politics, economics, and art.

From this perspective, the 1929 Surrealist map of the world (Fig. 22-1) seems almost prophetic. The 48 United States and Western Europe are all but invisible, whereas territories out of the stream of Western culture—Russia, Labrador, Easter Island, and Alaska—are assigned more significance by their exaggerated scale. Although the imaginary map asserts a radical surrealist political and cultural view at a moment in time—with a good dose of humor—it does capture a specific point for us; namely, that boundaries in the art world are culturally constructed, changeable, and permeable. The map also suggests that the era of dominance and exclusivity of the old bastions of culture has passed.

---

[1] Holland Carter, "Caribbean Visions of Tropical Paradise and Protest," *New York Times*, August 31, 2007, F25, F27.

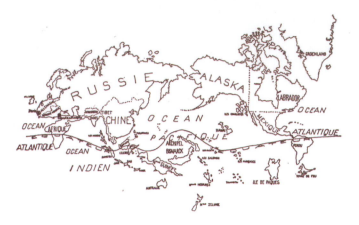

22-1 YVES TANGUY (probable artist). *Surrealist Map of the World* (1929). From a special issue of *Variétés*, titled "Le Surréalisme," June 1929 (p. 183).

The phenomenon of globalization has created a world in which cultures are no longer distant from one another, and people and places are no longer separate. Television and the Internet create an immediacy of communication of visual images as never before; a war around the globe finds its way into living rooms around the clock. "Distant" hurricanes, cyclones, and earthquakes happen everywhere at once. One stock market affects all stock markets. China's air pollution flows into California, and China's toys overflow in America's stockings at Christmastime. So too do visual images from various cultures invade the consciousness and the marketplace around the globe as never before. But familiarity and proximity do not necessarily beget understanding and tolerance. Much contemporary art on the global stage is directed toward awareness, understanding, and tolerance.

Art historians and critics have had to find new ways of analyzing and organizing material on the subject of multiculturalism and crossculturalism in contemporary art. The traditional vocabulary is insufficient. As we consider works of art in the twenty-first century, we will add to our critical rubric concepts such as *hybridity*, *appropriation*, *high art and low culture*, and *postcolonialism*.

Hybridity

In the visual arts, one of the effects of globalization is **hybridity**, or the mixing of the traditions of different cultures to create new blends and new connections. As an example of the ways in which globalization has led to an intermingling of the world's cultural icons, Takashi Murakami (b. 1962) has been dubbed Japan's Andy Warhol. Like the American Pop artist, Murakami draws on consumer culture for his imagery. And, like Warhol, Murakami is vigorously self-promotional, exhibiting his paintings and sculpture at major museums around the world while creating mass-market products ranging from T-shirts and key chains to mouse pads and upscale Louis Vuitton handbags.

As a boy, Murakami fantasized about illustrating Japanese graphic novels called *manga*, which are also hybrids. Though illustrated manuscripts have as long and distinguished a history in Japanese art as they do in Western art, their modern

22-2 TAKASHI MURAKAMI. *Tan Tan Bo* (2001). Acrylic on canvas mounted on board. 141¾" × 212⅝" × 2⅝".

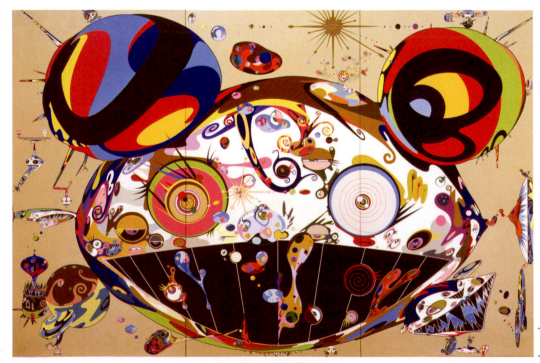

1 ft.

form is heavily influenced by American comic books, which infiltrated Japanese culture soon after the end of World War II, when Japan was occupied by the United States and American culture became popular.

As a student, Murakami experimented with the large-eyed cartoon figures in the popular *anime* style (a style of animation developed in Japan), but he was also trained in classical Japanese painting techniques. Consequently, his work often aims to reconcile "high art" and "low culture." *Tan Tan Bo* (Fig. **22-2**) is filled with cartoonlike imagery rendered in simple, dark outlines filled in with bright colors. The overall shape may resemble a fierce Mickey Mouse, but the artist has dubbed his signature character "Mr. DOB" and identified it as a monkey. Murakami has created a multimedia sensation of Mr. DOB in such objects as lithographs and inflatable balloons. In the tradition of "pure" pop, he makes no distinction between art and merchandise.

Appropriation

Appropriation became part of the lexicon of contemporary art with the advent of postmodernism in the 1980s. The concept, however, was not a new one, stretching back to early-twentieth-century art movements such as Cubism and Dada. Appropriation consisted then of borrowed elements. Picasso and Braque, for example, incorporated materials and techniques from the nonart world—newspaper, wallpaper, and wine labels—into their collages; Duchamp used ordinary or familiar objects for his readymades, including a urinal and a bicycle wheel. Appropriation in the postmodern era became a more refined idea, specifically referring to the use of another artist's work as a basis for one's own. Sometimes the new work built upon or changed the one appropriated, but at other times, the original image was left unaltered.

Brazilian artist Vik Muniz (b. 1961) has used just about anything to construct the imagery for his photographs— beans, dirt, pepper, caviar, chocolate, peanut butter, sand, and . . . junk. In fact, Muniz created an entire series called *Pictures of Junk* in which he and his assistants meticulously arranged garbage and debris into compositions based on Old Master paintings of mythological figures. Muniz refers to his appropriations as "the worst possible illusion." *Diamond Divas* is a series that subverts his earlier junk aesthetic with the most diametrically opposed material: diamonds. In *Diamond Divas*, Muniz arranged 500 carats of diamonds into the likenesses of film sirens such as Brigitte Bardot, Sophia Loren, and, Elizabeth Taylor. *Elizabeth Taylor* (Figure **22-3**) is a second-generation appropriation, based on a 1964 silkscreen by Pop artist Andy Warhol. Warhol based his own image on iconic photographs of the screen legend, taken at

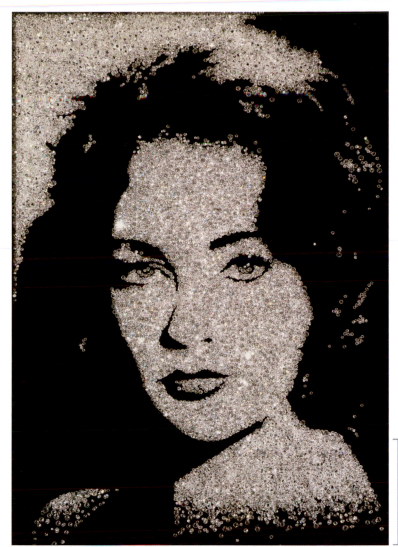

22-3 VIK MUNIZ. *Elizabeth Taylor* (*Diamond Divas*) (2004). Cibachrome print mounted on aluminum. 60¼" × 43". © Vik Muniz/Licensed by VAGA, NY.

the height of her fame after her starring role in *Cleopatra*. Taylor, especially, was known for her collection of lavish diamonds, including the famous "Taylor-Burton Diamond," a 69.42-carat pear-shaped stone given to her by her once-husband Richard Burton. The conspicuous value of the diamonds in the renderings suggests a connection between the actors and their monetary worth to producers in box office returns. *Elizabeth Taylor* shimmers in a palette of silvery black and white, further suggestive of the so-called silver screen of a bygone cinematic era.

High Art and Low Culture

High art and low culture were historically viewed as antithetical concepts. High art and high culture are associated with classical antiquity and perpetuated through the artistic traditions of the Renaissance. They include art of the Old Masters or compositions by Classical musicians or canonical works of literature, primarily from the West. These classics are associated with elitism; by contrast, low culture has been used derogatorily to describe popular or mass culture. Some contemporary art has focused particularly on the blurring of boundaries between high art and low culture, with artists appropriating images from low culture. Low art or low culture includes popular music, tattoo art, and **kitsch**—overly sentimental work that is viewed as tasteless decoration but that has its own sort of nostalgic charm.

Jeff Koons (b. 1955), like Andy Warhol, questions the separation of high art and low culture—and of merchandising and the museum—in his manipulation of ordinary, familiar, and cheaply produced objects. The common denominator of his content is kitsch. Koons has exhibited inflatable vinyl flowers and bunnies on mirrored pedestals and created assemblages of pool toys juxtaposed with mundane objects such as chairs and ladders. His mediums include painting, printmaking, found objects, and larger-than-life stainless steel replicas of vinyl toys and balloon animals.

Triple Hulk Elvis III (Fig. **22-4**) is based on The Hulk, a familiar Marvel Comics action figure. The subject is drawn from the well of images associated with low culture. At the same time, however, the work forces us to consider the nuanced relationship between high and low art: *Triple Hulk Elvis III* is a is self-consciously referential (and reverential)

homage to Andy Warhol's *Triple Elvis* silkscreen of 1963 which was based on a poster of Elvis Presley in the Hollywood western *Charro*.

Postcolonialism

Some aspects of globalization in the arts are a reaction to the retreat of the European empires that ruled much of the world throughout the middle of the twentieth century. The former colonies in the Americas, Africa, and Asia bear complex relationships with their former rulers—political, economic, ethnic, and, of course, cultural.

Trafalgar Square is a key tourist destination in London, named after the 1805 Battle of Trafalgar, in which Admiral Nelson defeated Napoleon's navy. A large column in the center of the square honors the admiral's efforts on behalf of the British Empire; four large plinths complement the column, serving as platforms for heroic sculpture. One of the plinths was never completed with a permanent monument but it has become a site for rotating contemporary art projects. London-based artist Hew Locke was raised in Guyana on the coast of South America. Like Canada, Australia, New Zealand, India, Pakistan, Egypt, and the original American colonies, Guyana was once part of the British Empire. Locke entered his equestrian statue *Sikandar* (Fig. **22-5**) as a potential occupant of "the fourth plinth." Sikandar is the Urdu name for Alexander the Great, and the overall form of the

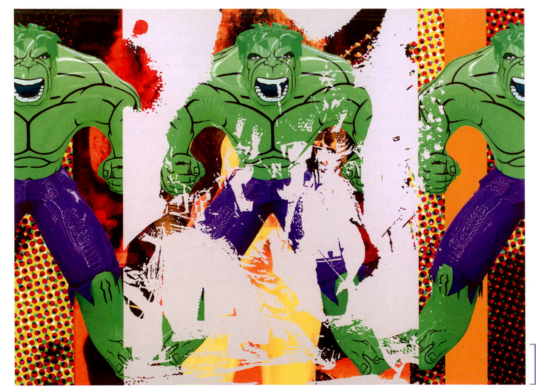

22-4 JEFF KOONS. *Triple Hulk Elvis III* (2005). Oil on canvas. 108" × 146".

1 ft.

gender and class can be traced to [the change from] "classic" European imperialism to a post-colonial condition.[2]

Some of the art we will look at in the next part of the chapter will be rooted in European artistic traditions or self-consciously use those traditions to communicate content that is at odds with them. We also note the early-twenty-first-century exhibition at London's Tate Gallery of works by contemporary artists from diverse geographic locations called "Century City." This installation can be seen as an an alogue for the process of globalization,[3] in that it focused on the avant-garde not only in art centers such as New York and Paris, but also in cities including Rio de Janeiro, Tokyo, and Mumbai. The rest of this chapter is organized along these lines—not around themes but around places.

LATIN AMERICA

The nations of the Caribbean and Latin America have a common history of colonialism, slavery, and interaction among racial and ethnic groups. Political instability and economic pressures have created migration northward to the United States and Canada, yet powerful cultural traditions and prejudices in new host countries have fostered unbreakable ties with Caribbean and Latin American homelands. Even as many natives attempt to leave, tourists from the north descend on the islands and the beaches of these southern paradises, especially in winter. Yet the tourist traps and resorts can be looked upon as "elaborate site-specific installations"[4] carved out of these postcolonial destinations. Tourists remain largely separated from native peoples during their visits, insulated from the harsh daily realties faced by most local people. The art produced by people of and from the Caribbean and Latin America tends to reflect these themes— the residue of colonialism, poverty, political conflict, the northward push, and what life means from day to day.

Cuba

Much of Cuban artist Alexandre Arrechea's work is a commentary on the irony that while his country builds its new socialist society, its jewels—like the capital city of Havana—

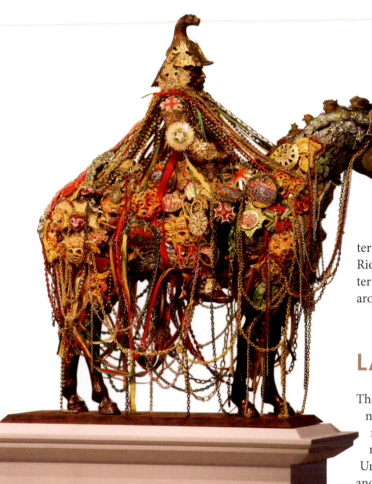

22-5 HEW LOCKE. *Sikandar* (2010). Height of maquette including plinth: approx. 31½". Mixed media maquette. © 2011 Artists Rights Society (ARS), NY/DACS, London.

statue is reminiscent of another British equestrian statue— that of Field Marshal, Sir George White, who commanded British armies in nineteenth century campaigns in the Middle East and South Central Asia, including modern-day Afghanistan. The empires of Alexander and Great Britain turned out to be ephemeral. Although they brought Western views of "civilization" to conquered peoples, they also plundered treasure and exacted other costs. Locke's *Sikandar* is no horseback hero of marble or bronze. Rather, it is embellished with charms, medals, sabres, votive offerings, jewels, Persian trinkets and Greek masks, encouraging viewers to ponder the interaction of cultures, and especially the meanings and endurance of conquest and colonialism.

Scholars have linked globalization to what they call the postcolonial condition:

> Many of the preoccupations and strategies of [postcolonial, global] art exhibit traces of continuity with earlier practice and theory exploring the legacy of European colonialism. . . . Many of the most intractable tensions between ethnicity,

[2] Niru Ratnam, "Art and Globalization," in *Themes in Contemporary Art*, Gill Perry and Paul Wood, eds. (New Haven, CT: Yale University Press, 2004), 277–313.
[3] Ibid.
[4] Annie Paul, "Visualizing Art in the Caribbean," in *Infinite Island*: *Contemporary Caribbean Art*, Tumelo Mosaka, ed. (New York: Brooklyn Museum in Association with Philip Wilson Publishers, 2007), 21–34.

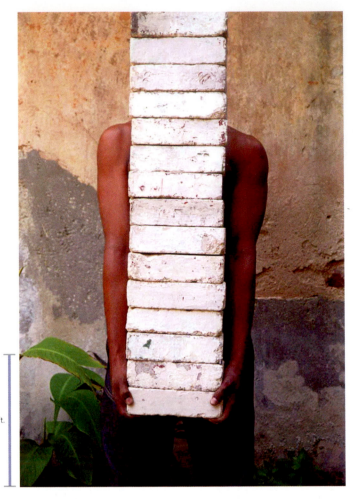

1 ft.

22-6 ALEXANDRE ARRECHEA. *Elementos Arquitectronicos* (2006). Chromogenic print. 43" × 31". Edition 2 of 4, 1AP.

22-7 JEAN-ULRICK DÉSERT. *The Burqa Project: On the Borders of My Dreams I Encountered My Double's Ghosts* (2001). Flag textiles, dye, lace. 63" × 118".

lie in disrepair. *Elementos Arquitectronicos* (Fig. **22-6**) is a stunning portrait of a laborer struggling to carry—or at least hold—a stack of whitewashed bricks that obscures his identity. Arrechea uses pictorial and symbolic devices—the hard fired clay of the brick against the man's flesh or the insinuation of the verdant plant life against the decaying stucco—to suggest the workers' struggle and chance at hope in a classless, collectivist society. The faceless man is locked into a task that seems to have no beginning or end; the image is one of quiet desperation.

There are also parallels to be found between Arrechea's work and the mid-nineteenth-century realists like Courbet (see Fig. 19-11), in which social issues were wrapped in the modernist aesthetic of the day. Arrechea's composition is constructed in a minimalist style, with sharp tonal contrasts and an overall starkness. The repetition of the whitewashed faces of the bricks piled on top of one another in a strict vertical pile is reminiscent of Donald Judd's minimalist sculptures (see Fig. 21-14). The artist's juxtaposition of a self-conscious modernity with the raw physicality of the laborer's life in a place that seems untouched by modernity raises questions about the relationships of art and life and social consciousness.

Haiti

Haitian artist Jean-Ulrick Désert has focused many of his projects on the relationship between immigrants and outsiders and their adopted or host countries, some of it growing out of his own experiences. *Negerhosen* is an ongoing work that began in 2000 after the artist was accosted in Berlin because of his race. It consists of a series of photographs

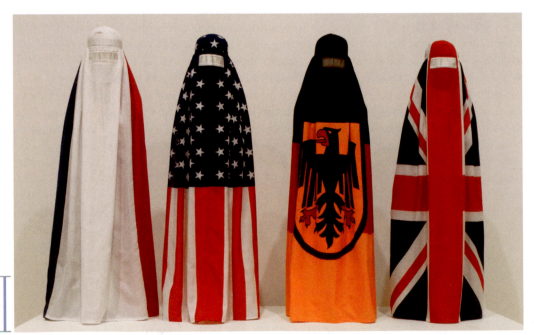

1 ft.

documenting the artist's encounters with locals and tourists while dressed in the traditional German folk costume of *lederhosen*, or leather shorts and knee socks. Lederhosen are particularly associated with the Bavarian area of Germany, where folk culture and national identity have been historically very strong. In this performance piece called *Negerhosen* (German for *black trousers*), Désert roams Germany, inviting Germans and others to walk with him and pose for photos. Many oblige with broad smiles, more engaged in the visual joke than aware of the artist's underlying message.

Cultural mixing and identity are also the concepts underlying *The Burqa Project* (Fig. 22-7), in which Désert stitched national flags into burqas and draped them on mannequins. *Burqas* are garments that Muslim women in some countries choose or are forced to wear for the sake of modesty. The flags used in *The Burqa Project* represent the Western countries of Germany, France, the United States, and the United Kingdom and seem to suggest the tensions between religious and national identity that occur when Western and non-Western cultures clash. Outward symbols of allegiance are often perceived as threatening to the homogeneity of nationalism and can lead to legislation (as it did in France) that forbids their use in state institutions (such as a public school). The burqa-clad mannequins in Désert's piece offer a tangible resolution to the dilemma of allegiance.

Puerto Rico

Puerto Rican artist Miguel Luciano focuses much of his work on the cultural and economic relationship between the Caribbean island of Puerto Rico and the United States. Puerto Rico is a self-governing commonwealth that was ceded to the United States in a treaty with Spain that ended the Spanish-American war at the end of the nineteenth century. Historically, both the United States and Puerto Rico have had wavering feelings about their relationship. In the postwar years, the U.S. Congress was not unanimous in its support of annexation, and even today Puerto Ricans continue to debate the island's political status, between options of statehood, independence, or the commonwealth status quo. Luciano's *Plántano Pride* (Fig. 22-8) shows a Puerto Rican adolescent boy in a universal white T-shirt and culture-specific bling. Sugar, tobacco, and plantains—a banana-like fruit—were once the island's cash crops. The boy poses for the camera with a cocky expression, wearing with pride a symbol associated with his country's national identity, but also with American materialism and rap culture. Luciano's work addresses political, economic, and cultural subjugation.

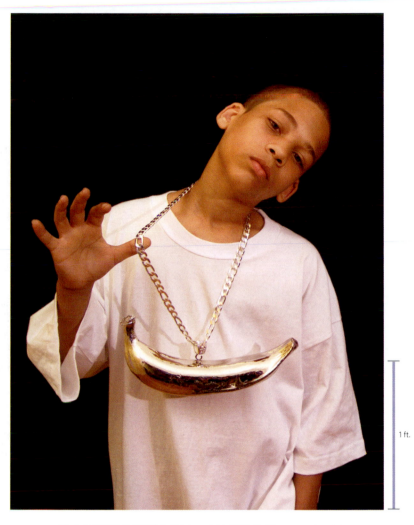

22-8 MIGUEL LUCIANO. *Plántano Pride* (2006). Chromogenic print (platinum plantain). 40" × 30".

Mexico

Enrique Chagoya's (b. 1953) paintings and prints chronicle cultural change and exchange, often suggesting alternative histories that better explain the realities of contemporary politics and social conditions. Chagoya, who was born in Mexico City, is known for his juxtapositions of historical and cultural references with images of pop culture, especially from the world of Disney. A suite of small pencil drawings, for example, consists of portraits of world figures cast in the roles of *Snow White and the Seven Dwarfs*: Condoleeza Rice, U.S. secretary of state under the George W. Bush administration, is portrayed as Snow White; Tony Blair, former British prime minister, is the Prince; Donald Rumsfeld, U.S. secretary of defense who led the invasion of Iraq, is Grumpy; President George W. Bush is Dopey; and Saddam Hussein is the Witch.

Chagoya most recently has turned his attention to immigration, a long-standing and unresolved issue between the United

States and Mexico. His print titled *Illegal Alien's Guide to Critical Theory* (Figs. **22-9** and **22-10**) is a satire on his own experience as an immigrant now leading an academic life at California's prestigious Stanford University. A detail of the work features Chagoya as a plucked chicken in a sombrero, pedaling a bicycle as fast as he can while spouting a "critically correct" phrase torn from the pages of literary or artistic theory. Playing on the common cardboard placard graphic "Works for food," a talk bubble next to the artist's head reads: "Works to suggest that the act finally distills into something dense and unknowable." Other details include visual references to pre-Columbian reliefs and wall paintings, particularly from the Mayan civilization (see Fig. 18-16). Chagoya says, "My artwork is a conceptual fusion of opposite cultural realities that I have experienced in my lifetime. I integrate diverse elements: from pre-Columbian mythology, western religious iconography, and American popular culture."

22-9 ENRIQUE CHAGOYA. *Illegal Alien's Guide to Critical Theory* (2007). Color lithograph. 24" × 40".

22-10 ENRIQUE CHAGOYA. Detail of *Illegal Alien's Guide to Critical Theory* (2007). Color lithograph. 24" × 40".

EUROPE

Europe was the center of the Western art world for hundreds of years, and remained so throughout the first half of the twentieth century. The focus shifted to New York following World War II, but Europeans may not necessarily agree. As in the United States, European art today takes many directions and is expressed through many mediums.

The United Kingdom

Damien Hirst (b. 1965) established his reputation as one of the "yBa" generation (young British artists) making conceptual and installation art that aimed to challenge traditional aesthetics, ethics, morality, and to some, plain good taste. He is perhaps best known for his infamous installation of a dismembered shark suspended in formaldehyde (*The Physical Impossibility of Death in the Mind of Someone Living*, 1991).

Hirst's diamond-encrusted skull fits with the artist's penchant for anatomy and sensation. *For the Love of God* (Fig. **22-11**), as he titled it after hearing his mother's response to his idea, is based on an eighteenth-century skull that Hirst found in a thrift shop. He commissioned London jewelers to copy the skull's proportions exactly in platinum and then cover it with 8,601 diamonds valued at more than $20 million. Hirst put it on the art auction block for $100 million. One critic noted that the result was the "most ambitious piece of British jewelry since the crown jewels."

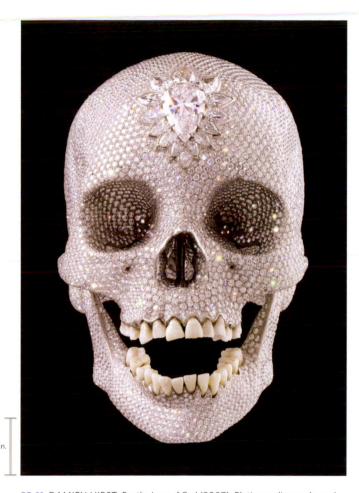

the transitory nature of life and the ultimate uselessness of material things.

British-born Tracey Emin (b. 1963), another yBa, has gained celebrity status and is often followed by paparazzi because of her controversial drawings, installations, and other works. A 1997 piece, *Everyone I Have Ever Slept With 1963–1995*, consisted of an ordinary camping tent, the inside walls of which were emblazoned with the first and last names of her paramours. Two years later, she exhibited the controversial *My Bed*, an installation that included her own mattress and bedding along with pantyhose, condoms, a half-drunk bottle of vodka, newspapers, slippers, and the ordinary stuff of bedroom clutter. The bed was sold to a gallery owner for close to a quarter of a million dollars and was shortlisted for the prestigious Turner Prize in 1999. Emin has made numerous sexually explicit drawings and performed in various states of undress. More recently, she has created neon wall pieces (Fig. **22-12**) featuring handwritten statements about love, sex, and self.

Edward Steichen wrote, "Every other artist begins [with] a blank canvas, a piece of paper . . . the photographer begins with the finished product." Implicit in Steichen's statement is the reality of the planning and selection that permits the instantaneous creation of an image to be a "finished product." The contemporary images of Sam Taylor-Wood (b. 1967), who lives and works in England, are created with extensive forethought and with knowledge of, and reverence for, the history of art.

Taylor-Wood has become known for her room-encompassing video installations and 360-degree photographic panoramas, accompanied by soundtracks that depict people in the midst of personal dramas and fantasies. Although the actors in her dramas may be visually attractive, something about them is awkward and vulnerable, out of place. Even though some are involved in sexual activity, they appear to be emotionally isolated. Some of Taylor-Wood's photographs are structured like multipaneled Renaissance altarpieces, replete with art-historical references. In her

1 in.

The skull is laden with references. In Christian iconography, it is a symbol of mortality. Shakespeare's *Hamlet* recites one of his most well-known soliloquies—a meditation on death—with a skull in hand. And, in the history of art, *vanitas* paintings often contain images of skulls. *Vanitas* is a Latin word that means "emptiness," and it is often used to suggest

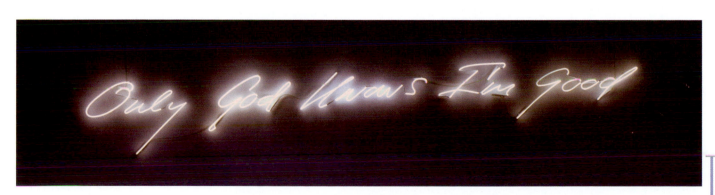

1 ft.

22-13 SAM TAYLOR-WOOD. *Bram Stoker's Chair II* (2005). C-print. 48" × 38". Edition of 6. White Cube Gallery, London, England.

22-14 ANSELM KIEFER. *Sonnenschiff* (2007). Concrete, earth, iron, lead, sunflowers.

Soliloquy III, for example, a reclining nude mimics the pose of Velázquez's *Rokeby Venus*, and her 35-mm film/DVD *Self-Pietà* evokes the renowned version of the Virgin Mary holding the dead Christ by Michelangelo in St. Peter's in Rome. Taylor-Wood's *Bram Stoker's Chair* series (Fig. **22-13**) appear to capture split-second, mid-air acrobatics, but for these photographs, the artist was suspended from the ceiling with meticulous trussing and constrictive harnesses, the evidence of which was removed with computer manipulation. What seems effortless and carefree in fact involved hours of physical stress and discomfort. They seem, altogether, to suggest a liberation of female sexuality from societal constraints. Bram Stoker was the author of *Dracula*. "His" chair, like a vampire, casts no shadow.

Germany

German artist Anselm Kiefer (b. 1945) became known in the 1970s and 1980s for his Neoexpressionist paintings (see Fig. 21-20) and lead sculptures that unearthed memories of the Holocaust and probed historic German myths. In more recent years, Kiefer has turned his attention to monumental sculpture, several examples of which he created to fill the vacuous space of Paris's Grand Palais for a solo exhibition. *Sonnenschiff* (*Sun Ship*) (Fig. **22-14**) comprises concrete, earth, iron and lead, and sunflowers—objects that frequently also find their ways in Kiefer's paintings. As in all of Kiefer's work, literary and historical references are woven throughout. Along with an enormity of scale, these references give the work a timeless, biblical quality. Kiefer has described himself as an individual who is in despair, who in order to survive creates illusions to escape melancholy and pessimism. Although he currently resides in rural France, his historical consciousness as a German continues to weigh heavily on him and his art.

The Netherlands

Kiefer's art is much about change—in his case from life to ruin to the process of rebuilding. Dutch photographer Rineke Dijkstra's (b. 1959) work also revolves around change, although on a much more personal scale. Her subjects, who have included a Bosnian girl in a home for refugees and young

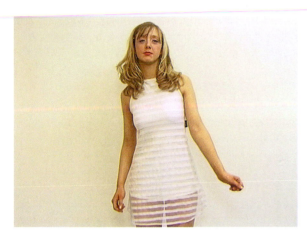

22-15 RINEKE DIJKSTRA. Still from *The Krazy House, Liverpool, UK* (*Megan, Simon, Nicky, Philip, Dee*), 2008–2009. 4-channel video HD installation. Color, sound, 32 minutes, loop. Marion Goodman Gallery, NY.

Israelis undertaking military service, are mostly adolescents whom we observe at a transitional moment in their development. Dijkstra's large-format color photographs range from bust-size to full-length portraits against backgrounds that range from specific to nondescript. Dijkstra also uses video as a medium. In *The Krazy House Liverpool, UK,* from which the still in Figure 22-15 is taken, the artist constructed a studio on the dance floor of a British nightclub and invited young dancers to come by on days when the club was closed and move to their favorite music. The dancers were captured against a stark white backdrop and, when exhibited, the video was projected on four different walls. Critic Mark Prince wrote that "the single dancer performing for the camera . . . is an ideal template from which to study the drama between self-assertion and self-doubt" (*Frieze*, April 2010).

Switzerland

Pipilotti Rist (b. 1962) is a video-performance artist whose most common subject is her own nude body afloat in an endless sea. Her work has been projected in venues as diverse as New York's Times Square and the baroque ceiling of an Italian church (the Chiesa di San Stae) during the 2005 Venice Biennale, an international art exhibition. The first artist to adapt a music-video aesthetic, her videos are saturated with psychedelic color and play against a soundtrack of her own music (she created the all-women band *Les Reines Prochaines*—The Next Queens). Rist's installations are sensuous and joyous, and according to one reviewer, the "walls liquefy and wash over the people like a psychic Jacuzzi, in order to set them afloat."[5] New York's Museum of Modern Art commissioned Rist to produce a site-specific installation that bathed several walls of the second-floor atrium of the museum in 25-foot-high images (Fig. 22-16). At any one time, scores of viewers could be seen walking through the space, sitting on the floor beneath the projections, or lounging on a cushioned island designed by the artist.

---

[5] Pipilotti Rist, in *Art Now*, Uta Grosenick, ed. (Cologne, Germany: Taschen, 2005), 442.

22-16 PIPILOTTI RIST. Still from *Pour Your Body Out* (*7354 Cubic Meters*) (2008). Multichannel video projection (color, sound), projector enclosures, circular seating element, carpet. The Donald B. and Catherine C. Marron Atrium, The Museum of Modern Art, NY.

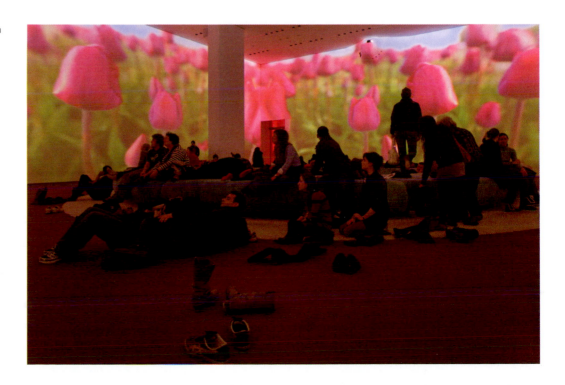

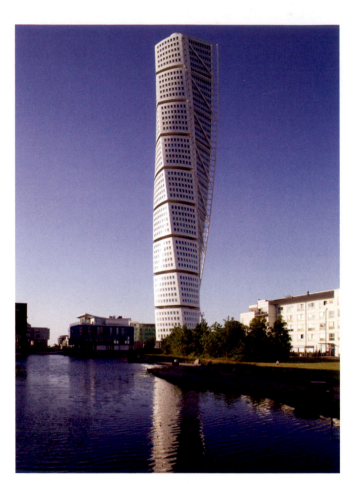

22-17 SANTIAGO CALATRAVA. *Turning Torso* (2005). Malmö, Sweden.

Spain

Spanish architect Santiago Calatrava is one of a few architects currently in demand all over the globe. He has designed the shell-like transportation hub under construction at Ground Zero in Manhattan and the Chicago Spire, which, with its broadcast antenna, will rise to 2,000 feet and make it, for now, the tallest structure in North America. At 54 stories, his *Turning Torso* (Fig. 22-17), completed in 2005, contains nine modules of five-story pentagons that turn as they rise, so that the highest module is twisted 90 degrees in relation to ground level. The building is supported by a concrete core that carries the weight of the whole structure. Wind resistance is provided by both a steel exoskeleton and the twisting of the tower, which shears off turbulence in multiple directions rather than allowing it to build up in a single force. Although the design seems to embody architect Louis Sullivan's maxim that "form

follows function," its overall effect is sculptural. It is not surprising that the building is based on a marble sculpture by Calatrava titled *Twisting Torso*.

AFRICA

Kenyan artist Wangechi Mutu (b. 1972) juxtaposes contemporary magazine models and African museum objects in politically charged collages that feature women's bodies surrounded by rich, explosive colors, animal prints, botanical elements, and abstract patterns that evoke traditional textiles. In *Mask* (Fig. 22-18) the model becomes an exotic temptress who invokes the sexualized stereotype of the dominatrix and overturns the traditional male-female power relationship.

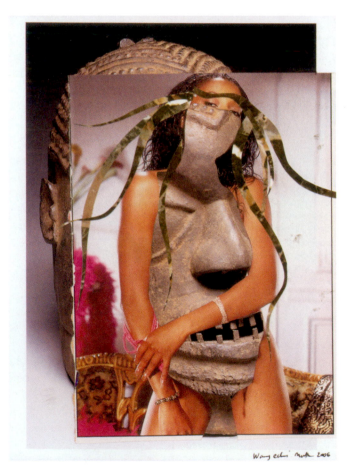

22-18 WANGECHI MUTU. *Mask* (2006). Mixed-media collage. Saatchi Gallery, London, England.

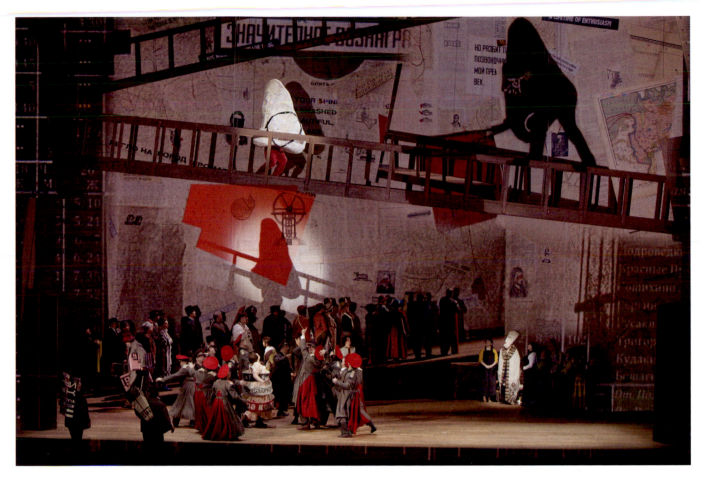

22-19 WILLIAM KENTRIDGE AND SABINE THEUNISSEN. The production set for *The Nose*, an opera by Dmitri Shostakovich based on the story by Nikolai Gogol (2010).

Many of Mutu's works illustrate twisted female anatomy and conditions of deterioration that draw attention to what she describes as the sexualization and neglect of African women by dominant men. Underneath the stereotype, women are suffering, and Mutu wants her viewers to challenge their assumptions about race, gender, and beauty.

South African artist William Kentridge (b. 1955) is a multimedia and performance artist who often wears the hats of musician, actor, and director. There is a German word that composers, architects, artists, and philosophers have used to describe their efforts to synthesize diverse mediums into a unifying whole that includes an element of theater or the theatrical: *gesamtkunstwerk*. Taken apart, *gesamt* can be defined as "total" and *kunstwerk* means "work of art." For early-twentieth-century composer Richard Wagner, this was the ideal; for Kentridge, it has become his most complex and intriguing form of expression.

Kentridge's stage sets for New York City's Metropolitan Opera 2010 debut of *The Nose* (Fig. **22-19**) is an illustration of contemporary *gesamtkunstwerk* at its best. The Dmitri Shosta-

kovich opera, based on a Nicolai Gogol's *The Nose*, follows the misadventures and bureaucratic run-ins of a man who wakes up one day to discover that his nose has left his face and that it is off leading a life as a renegade alter ego among St. Petersburg high society. Although Gogol's story was written before the Communist revolution in Russia, Kentridge's sets reference the Soviet era of the 1930s, when the Shostakovich opera premiered and when the country was awash in Communist propaganda. Print is everywhere. Oversized panels covered with collages of newspaper and magazine articles, encyclopedia entries, a map of St. Petersburg, and portraits with red or black shapes in place of noses form a backdrop for continuous video projections, still images, and stop-action animation. Even *The Nose*, worn by an actor in tights, is constructed from what looks like newsprint papier-mâché. Critic Maria Gough described Kentridge's ingenious integration and transformation of mediums, writing that "these projections helped to transpose much of the drama from the horizontal space of the stage floor onto the vertical plane of the screen, thereby transforming the Met into a hybrid opera-movie house."

THE MIDDLE EAST

The Middle East is rich in tradition, rich in oil, and often drenched in conflict. As described in the Art Tour on Jerusalem (see Chapter 13), the Middle East is the birthplace of the three Abrahamic religions: Judaism, Christianity, and Islam. Contemporary art by artists in or from this region often reflects on the tensions between the secular and the religious within and among societies, particularly as these tensions are interwoven with politics.

Iran

Shirin Neshat (b. 1957) was born in Iran of parents who led westernized lives before the Islamic revolution. She embraced feminism at an early age, encouraged by a father who insisted that his daughters have the same access as anyone else when it came to education, travel, and experiences. Neshat was in college in California when the revolution began, and she did not return to Iran until 1990. As a photographer, video artist, and filmmaker, she has devoted much of her work to issues concerning gender roles in postrevolutionary Islamic society. Her renowned photo-work series, *Women of Allah* (1993–1997), is a commentary on the ways in which social and political changes in Iran directly affected the lives of women, particularly in terms of oppression by men. Neshat is often the sitter in these photographs, dressed in the tradi-

tional *chador*—a black garment that is pulled over the head and wrapped around the body, covering the hair, arms, and legs. Although wearing the chador is not required by law in Iran, many women choose to wear it, and many others are forced to wear it by men. The garment, like the burqa, has become a symbol of female identity and oppression in the Muslim world.

Neshat's film *Passage* (Fig. 22-20), commissioned by the world-renowned composer Philip Glass, follows the ritual of passage from this world to the next as men carry a shrouded body, women prepare a grave with their bare hands, and a little girl sets a fire that comes to circumscribe the scene. During one of the film's most abstract and intensely visual passages, Glass's pulsating score juxtaposed with a close-up of the women's thrumming chadors creates a sense of oil bubbling from the desert ground. The ingredients are natural and elemental—sticks, stones, fire, smoke, sand, and dust— and the repetitive movements, chanting, and music form a circle of life, death, and perhaps, rebirth.

Palestinian Territories

Emily Jacir was born in Saudi Arabia in 1970 and currently divides her time between the Palestinian territory of the West Bank and New York. She has engaged in numerous activities to bring to light the hardships of the Palestinian people, such as secretly filming Palestinian workers being delayed as they try to pass Israeli checkpoints in the West Bank or using her own U.S. passport and free-movement status to facilitate communication and grant requests among Palestinians living in occupied territory who are denied access to their families. Addressing the nature of life under occupation, the hardships, and the almost Darwinian approach to survival, Jacir has placed bogus personal ads in New York's *Village Voice* publication purportedly by Palestinian women in search of Israeli husbands in order to get residency permits. One of her most literal works is a tent stitched with the names of Palestinian villages (Fig. 22-21) that have been depopulated by Israel over long years of conflict between the two peoples. Tents like these can be seen in refugee camps throughout Gaza.

22-20 SHIRIN NESHAT. Still from *Passage* (2001). Color video installation with sound, 00:11:40. Dimensions vary with installation. Edition 5 of 6. Solomon R. Guggenheim Museum, NY.

Israel

Adi Nes (b. 1966) is best known for his hyperstaged photographs of young male actors posing as Israeli soldiers. The artist has said that, as a gay man, he is interested in issues of masculinity and male identity, particularly in a society that prizes—almost mythologizes—physical strength. His single most

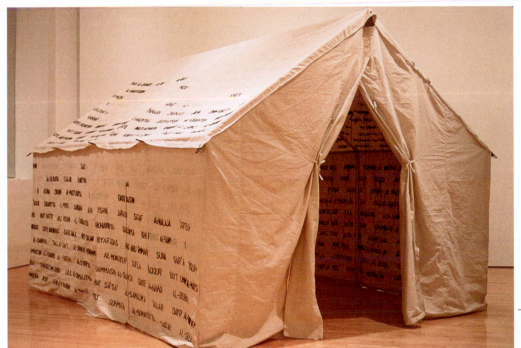

1 ft.

famous photograph recreates Leonardo da Vinci's fresco *The Last Supper* (see Fig. 16-17), substituting soldiers at a table in a mess hall for apostles. Aside from the visual pun, Nes draws our attention to the concrete place (Israel) where so many events of the Bible (Hebrew and Christian) are said to have occurred, and the links between the larger-than-life aspect of those events and the ordinary plight of individuals struggling to survive in his country today.

In Leonardo's version of *The Last Supper*, the apostles react to Jesus' announcement to them that one among them will betray him and that he will die. Despite the laughing and talking going on in Nes's version of the masterpiece, there is an implicit threat of danger and death embodied in the image of the soldier. In his *Abraham and Isaac* (Fig. **22-22**), a homeless man wheels his hapless son and his few belongings through the streets of Tel Aviv. The founder of the people of Israel—who was asked by God to sacrifice his son—is invoked to symbolize the sacrifices that people must make on a daily basis to survive. The lighting in the photo is intended to be reminiscent of the Baroque era, particularly the painting of Caravaggio. In Nes's role of artist as social critic, he uses his work to point out the discrepancy between the dream of Israel and certain social realities of contemporary Israel.

Iraq

Of all of the artistic disciplines, architecture perhaps has been the most difficult when it comes to women breaking through the proverbial glass ceiling. This, along with the reality that

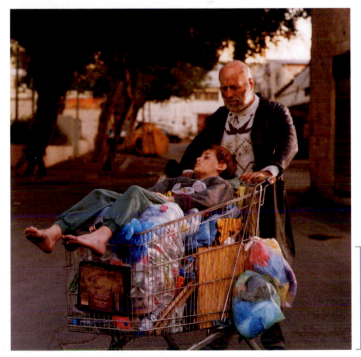

1 ft.

22-22 ADI NES. *Abraham and Isaac* (2005). Chromogenic print. 39⅜" × 39⅜".

traditional Islamic societies in the Middle East often restrict the social and professional roles that women can play, make Zaha Hadid's global position as an award-winning and highly sought architect especially notable. Hadid was born in Baghdad and educated in London, where she currently resides,

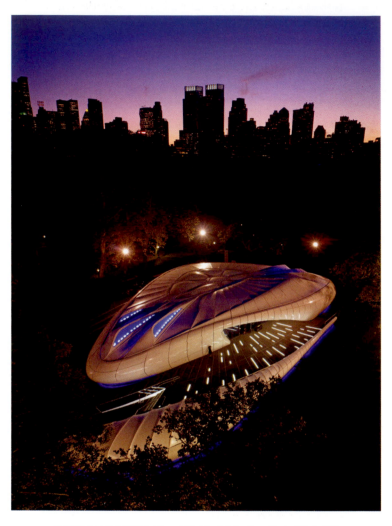

all the world, like an alien ship had landed. One critic wrote, "A rectangular patch of sand in Central Park may be the last place you'd expect to find a gleaming 'Star Trek'-style spacecraft."[6] The pavilion traveled from city to city, with a steel structure designed to be assembled in less than a week. Participating artists created commissioned works that evoked signature elements of the Chanel bag. Included among them were Sylvie Fleury (see her *Dog Toy 4* in Chapter 9), and Subodh Gupta (in this chapter). The pavilion was donated by Chanel to the Arab World Institute in Paris, where it took up permanent residence

---

[6] Carol Vogel, "A 7,500-Square-Foot Ad for Chanel, with an Artistic Mission." *New York Times*, July 24, 2008.

22-23 ZAHA HADID. Chanel Mobile Art Pavilion, Central Park, NY (October–November, 2008). Façade: Fiber-reinforced plastic roof: PVC, ETFE roof lights; Primary structure: Steel; 1752 different steel connections; Secondary structure: Aluminum extrusions. 128′ × 148′, a total of 7534 ft².

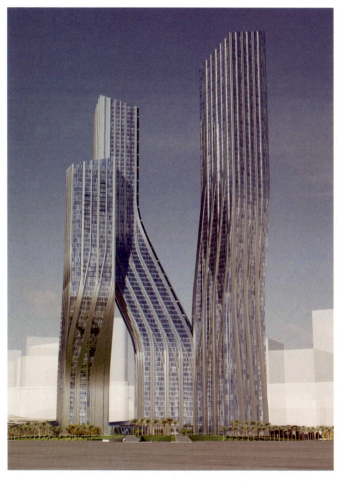

22-24 ZAHA HADID. Dancing Towers (2009). Dubai, United Arab Emirates.

but she has had several Middle Eastern commissions, including the Dancing Towers project in Dubai (Fig. **22-24**).

Hadid is a deconstructivist architect and, as such, works in the overall aesthetic of architects like Santiago Calatrava, Frank Ghery, Daniel Libeskind, and her teacher, Rem Koolhaas. Her design for the Chanel Mobile Art Pavilion (Fig. **22-23**) echoes the iconic quilted handbags of the haute couture house of Chanel, although the siting of the temporary exhibition space in the middle of New York City's Central Park in Fall 2008 looked, for

in a prominent entry courtyard and will feature works of art by artists from the Arab world.

The Dancing Towers in Dubai resemble a choreographed interlacing of abstract torsos. Three towers originate on a common base and then appear to "do their own thing," touching their companion towers here and there on certain levels where the functions of the individual towers overlap—offices, a hotel, residences, leisure facilities, and restaurants. The Dancing Towers evoke the fluidity of the oft-referenced image of the Three Graces in art history, in which a trio of beautiful women intertwine in dance, their collective positions combining to create a single, perfect form.

ASIA

The phenomenon of globalization is perhaps nowhere more evident than in the Eastern nations of India, China, and Japan. Phone calls for tech support when our electronics go awry, or for customer service when our credit cards go missing, are often fielded by teams across the planet in places such as Bangalore, India. Our basic life necessities—T-shirts, pet food, the Nintendo Wii—are met, or at least supplemented, with products from China and Japan. As their economies and standard of living have boomed, so too have their art markets. Years ago, Japanese investors had little competi-

tion in auction houses when it came to high-ticket works of art; today, American investors, among others, are scrambling to own works of art from their part of the world. Our familiarity with the work of Indian, Chinese, and Japanese artists is attributed certainly to the decentralization of the art world, with artists of all countries exhibiting all over the world, but also is tied into the accessibility of popular culture and imagery over the Internet.

The art of these Eastern nations exhibits the same diversity of style that characterizes contemporary art in general around the globe. Although art from India, China, and Japan is often grounded in techniques that are traditional to these cultures, content often reflects global trends. Hybridity flourishes; many of their works combine contemporary subjects and traditional fashion, or express ancient ideas in novel ways.

India

Subodh Gupta (b. 1964) was born in one of the poorest and most violent provinces in India and lives today in New Delhi, a city of economic extremes. His work includes painting, sculpture, photography, installations, and video art. It taps into sacred symbols and ancient cultural identity but is connected to contemporary life realities through its found objects. A work like *Silk Route* (Fig. **22-25**) is an example. Just as India was once a key component of the Silk Route or Silk Road—a web of ancient trade routes that ran some 5,000

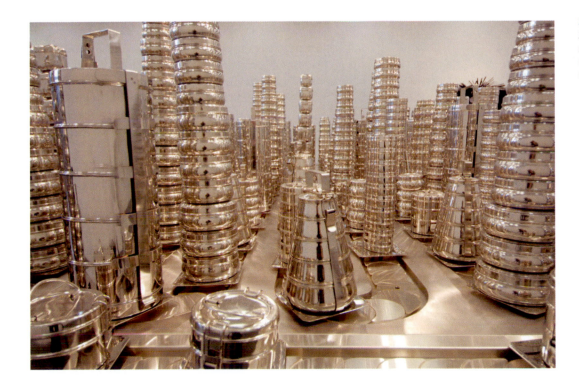

22-25 SUBODH GUPTA. *Silk Route* (2007). Stainless steel kitchen utensils. BALTIC Centre for Contemporary Art, Gateshead, UK.

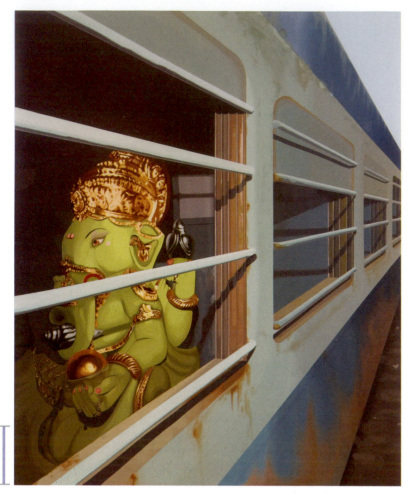

1 ft.

22-26 PRAJAKTA PALAV AHER. *Ganpati Series Untitled I* (2007). Acrylic on canvas. 96" × 72". Vadehra Art Gallery, New Delhi, India.

Ganpati), has the head of an elephant and is seen as a remover of obstacles. Perhaps the artist is suggesting in her ironic portrait of the noble elephant aboard the train that something has happened to the myths, the symbols, and the spiritual life of India—or to Ganesh. The remover of obstacles is now, perhaps, more of a road warrior with a briefcase and a quota. Or perhaps—in a true manifestation of globalization—he handles phone calls from the United States and books airline reservations or troubleshoots software glitches on computers, removing obstacles for travelers or office workers.

China

Chinese painter Fang Lijun (b. 1963) is a proponent of the so-called Cynical Realist school, which sprang up in reaction to the 1989 demonstration in Tiananmen Square, in which the Communist government cracked down on protestors who were demanding more freedom. In that same year, the government closed an exhibition of Chinese avant-garde art, leaving the new generation of contemporary artists disenfranchised and disillusioned. Lijun's work from the 1990s featured what became one of the most famous images in contemporary Chinese art: a group of uniformly dressed, bald-headed men symbolizing the "mindless, manipulated masses." These early images had a desperation and despondency about them, but his newer work addresses some of the same social and political concerns with a lighter hand. His painting *30th Mary* (Fig. **22-27**), for example, is a cynical adaptation of Western European baroque church ceilings wherein the ubiquitous cherubs are replaced by doll-like figures with Lijun portrait heads. The bald-headed figures, outfitted in pastel pinafores, seem to be sucked—smiling—into a cloud-lined vortex. The artist's commentary on disillusionment, individual identity, and government oppression may be intact, but it is delivered here with a dose of humor.

Wang Gongxin (b. 1960) is credited with being one of the first artists in China to transform video from a mere recording medium to an art medium. His works have largely focused on the anxieties experienced by ordinary Chinese people as their lives have been transformed by rapid industrialization—with its attendant pollution, relocations, and changes in traditional values. In recent years, China has experienced an unparalleled economic boom that has led to mushrooming growth of cities, mass migration from rural lands into these cities, and the projection of new economic and military power overseas.

miles through the Indian subcontinent and connected China to the Mediterranean Sea—so is it in today's era of globalization an important economic conduit. Gupta's piece, composed of simple, mundane kitchen utensils, is intended to illustrate the "current state of India's shifting society, migration, a sense of home and place, and the effects and frictions caused by a rapidly globalizing society."

Prajakta Palav Aher (b. 1979), who lives and works in Mumbai, is known for the photographic precision of her realist paintings. In the *Ganpati Series* (Fig. **22-26**), this realism lends a certain veracity to what otherwise appears to be a tall tale—a dressed-to-kill elephant riding on what appears to be a well-worn commuter train. In India, dreams of elephants are deemed messages of transformation and divine power—the emergence of one's Highest Self from the Collective Unconscious Mind. In Hinduism, the most widespread Indian religion, the deity, Ganesh (also known as

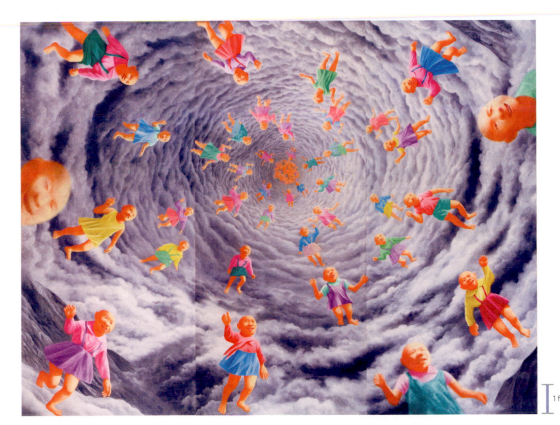

I 1 ft.

Our Sky Is Falling In! (Fig. 22-28) portrays an everyday family scene that is suddenly disrupted when the ceiling begins to collapse. The video tells a personal story but is also a commentary on the helplessness of the individual amidst the titanic forces of progress and modernization that are shaping the New China.

Shanghai artist Zhang Huan (b. 1965) grew up on a farm in rural China but received an advanced degree in traditional painting techniques from the Beijing Central Academy of Fine Arts. Soon after graduation, he and fellow students, who found their art education too limiting for the expression of their own concerns and themes, formed the East Village group and focused on time-based pieces. Huan's performance art has since been seen in China and Western Europe; he also appeared at the 2002 Whitney Museum Biennial dressed in a fat suit fashioned from raw meat and, in a Buddhist gesture of compassion, released a flock of caged doves. Although China is officially atheist, Huan has maintained his interest in his childhood religion, Buddhism. Travel to Tibet brought him into contact with

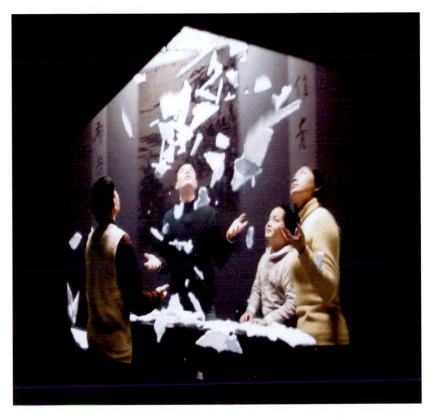

22-28 WANG GONGXIN. *Our Sky Is Falling In!* (2007). Video. The Tate Gallery, London, England.

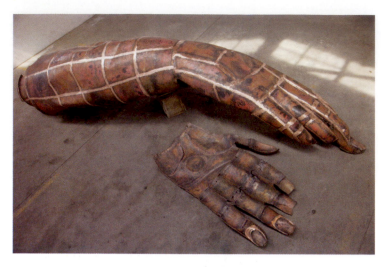

22-29 ZHANG HUAN. *Fresh Open Buddha Hand* (2007). Copper. 252" × 56" × 67"; 101" × 57" × 14".

large, broken figures that he has emulated in recent works, such as the copper hands we see in Figure **22-29**. He has also made ashlike sculptures and paintings to reflect Buddhist religious rituals.

Chinese cities have become boomtowns for contemporary architecture, although—at least for the time being—the principal architects involved in the designs for these cities are not Chinese, but European and American. Zaha Hadid has called China "an incredibly empty canvas for innovation." Anthony Fieldman, of the Hong Kong office of architects Skidmore, Owings & Merrill, has said that in China, "you're seeing things that no one in their right mind would build elsewhere." Looking at Shanghai's conglomerate Pudong New Area skyline (Fig. **22-30**), it's no wonder that Wang Lu of Beijing-based *World Architecture* magazine has said, "Architecture in China has become like a kung fu film, with all of these giants trying to vanquish each other."

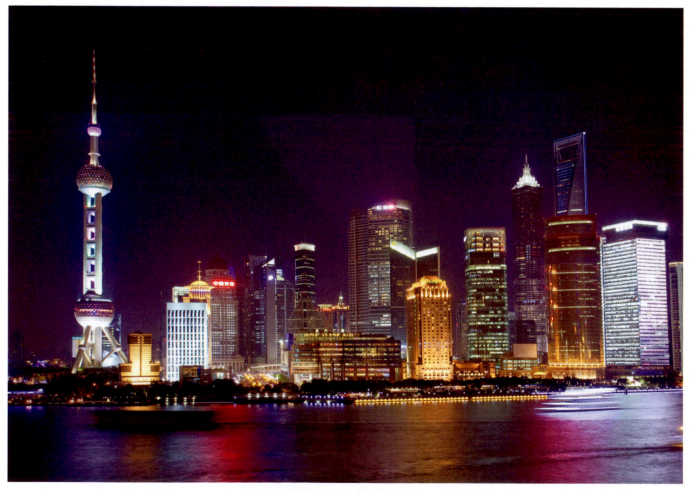

22-30 A night view of Shanghai's bustling Pudong New Area, across the Huangpu River from the older section of Shanghai. You can see the Oriental Pearl Broadcasting Tower on the left, its spherical components reminiscent of toys on a steel kabob. The Jin Mao Building and Shanghai World Financial Center are on the right. Three hundred office towers are planned for the Pudong New Area, which comprises most of the eastern part of Shanghai, between the river and the Pacific Ocean. It is China's financial hub. A Disney Theme Park is also under development in Pudong.

The Jin Mao Tower (Fig. **22-31**), an integral part of Shanghai's transmogrified skyline, was completed in 1999. A hybrid design by Skidmore, Owings & Merrill, it combines Chinese pagoda architecture with the steel-cage postmodern architecture frequently seen in the West. Constructed to withstand 200-kilometer-per-hour typhoon winds and earthquakes as strong as 7.0 on the Richter scale, the design also makes whimsical, persistent reference to the number "8," associated with prosperity in China. An eight-sided core concrete structure supports the building and is surrounded by eight composite columns and eight exterior steel columns.

A completely different aesthetic is to be seen across the street from the Jin Mao Tower in the Shanghai World Financial Center (Fig. **22-32**), designed by the international architectural firm Kohn Pedersen Fox (KPF). Their 101-story structure is the tallest skyscraper in the financial

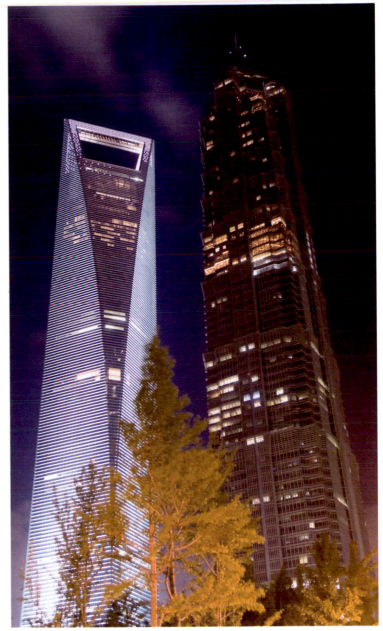

22-32 SHANGHAI KOHN PEDERSEN FOX ARCHITECTS. Shanghai World Financial Center (left) (2008). Shanghai, China.

district of Shanghai. The cutout near the building's apex is designed to alleviate wind pressure. The base of the cutout, at the 100th floor, is designed with an observation deck for the intrepid visitor.

Japan

Japanese artist Akira Yamaguchi (b. 1969) finds many of his sources in historic subject matter and styles, often mixing past and present, West and non-West. One work, painted

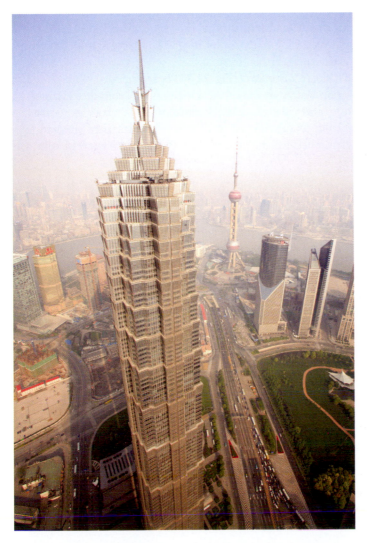

22-31 SKIDMORE, OWINGS & MERRILL, CHICAGO OFFICE. Jin Mao Building and View of Shanghai. (1999). Pudong New Area, Shanghai, China.

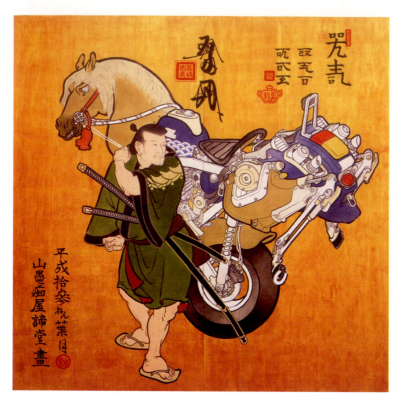

22-33 AKIRA YAMAGUCHI. *Votive Tablet of a Horse* (2001). Oil, varnish on plywood. 71⅞" × 72". Mizuma Art Gallery, Tokyo, Japan.

on a traditional scroll, pairs ancient customers and contemporary sales clerks in a department store. His *Votive Tablet of a Horse* (Fig. **22-33**) resembles wooden plaques with the image of a sacred white horse that were given as religious offerings to Japanese shrines and temples for many hundreds of years. The horses are believed to have symbolized purity, divine messages, and immortal poets. Yamaguchi replaces the horse's legs with a fantastical combination of motorcycle parts and robotics, as if to supercharge it into a more invincible machine. Yamaguchi's hybrid, alongside its sword-yielding samurai, raises the question: Would history have been different if its famed warriors had mounts like these?

Japanese photographer and video artist Mariko Mori (b. 1967), a self-described "daughter of Warhol and granddaughter of Duchamp," has been labeled a "cyberchick" and "a cross between a geisha girl and a gidget." As descriptive as these images are, they only scratch the surface of what defines her. Channeling her experience as a former model and fashion design student, Mori has created computer-manipulated self-portraits in futuristic cyber-couture. Her wide-eyed stare and plastic smile look a bit like a real-life version of Takashi Murakami's cartoon images.

Mori's *Wave UFO* (Fig. **22-34**) is a futuristic "vehicle" with a pop flair that mixes the mediums of sculpture, architecture, and video to create a transporting, sensory experience for the participant. We use the word "participant" instead of viewer because the imagery that appears on the screen within

22-34 MARIKO MORI. *Wave UFO* (2003). Brainwave interface, vision dome, projector, computer system, fiberglass, Technogel, acrylic carbon fiber, aluminum, magnesium. 194" × 446½" × 207⅞".

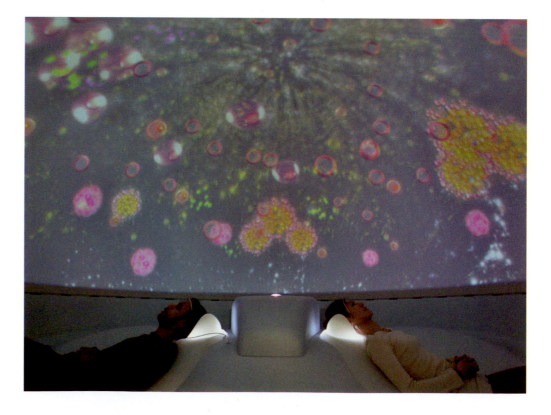

NORMAN ROCKWELL'S *FREEDOM FROM WANT* WITH JOHN CURRIN'S *THANKSGIVING*

THANKSGIVING CONJURES AN IMAGE of warm gatherings, a time when people travel long distances to share home and hearth and celebrate their blessings. It's about as wholesome a symbol of family ties as we can imagine. But we also know that holidays are stressful times during which people often become intensely aware of the discrepancies between their lives as they actually are and as they think they ought to be, especially when they compare them with the images of idealized families depicted in the media.

Norman Rockwell, the famed illustrator of the *Saturday Evening Post*, has created many a "default image" in our minds of Americans and their holidays, including Thanksgiving. His *Freedom from Want* (Fig. **22-35**), painted in 1943, is one of the artist's series of "Four Freedoms," inspired by a speech on these freedoms—including *Freedom from Fear*, *Freedom of Worship*, and *Freedom of Speech*—delivered by President Franklin Delano Roosevelt to Congress two years earlier. Rockwell depicted a traditional Thanksgiving dinner in which an aproned matriarch brings her main-course masterpiece to a well-set table filled with gleeful, fresh-faced children and grandchildren. The patriarch stands at

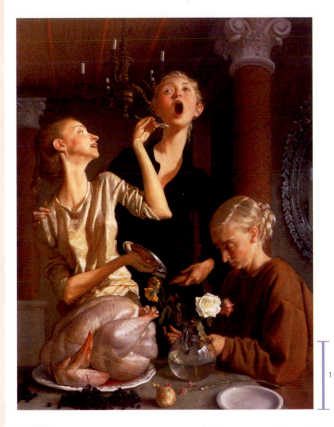

22-36 JOHN CURRIN. *Thanksgiving* (2003). Oil on canvas. 68" × 52".

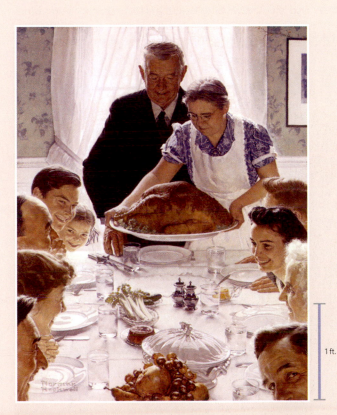

22-35 NORMAN ROCKWELL. *Freedom from Want* (1943). *The Saturday Evening Post*, March 6, 1943 (story illustration). Oil on canvas. 45¾" × 35½". Norman Rockwell Art Collection Trust, Norman Rockwell Museum, Stockbridge, MA.

the head, looking proudly at his wife's accomplishment and, perhaps, nostalgically at his family. Rockwell, as always, captures a slice of life and instills it with his particular brand of ideology—this time family values.

What a perversion, then, of this ideal is John Currin's *Thanksgiving* (Fig. **22-36**). Gone is the squeaky-clean, Midwestern, all-American family with their freckled faces and upturned noses. In their place, Currin has given us an eccentric gaggle of pasty-faced women whose skin tones echo those of their undercooked turkey. In an age of abstraction and new media, John Currin (b. 1962) focuses on the figure, typically young women wearing off-kilter expressions that denote psychological beings distorted by the modern age. Dressed in sexless and timeless clothing, his Thanksgiving celebrants appear to mimic cheer among some classic props.

Both Thanksgiving paintings are meticulous in detail, suggesting a photographic veracity, yet both are contrived in their own way. How? And how does each artist use extreme realism to convey truth, despite the unlikelihood that these scenes describe most real-life experience? Happy Thanksgiving—are you convinced? ●

the eye-shaped capsule is determined by connecting a participant's brainwaves to an interactive biofeedback loop. Mori, who has begun to integrate references to Japanese religion and culture into her recent work, alludes to the Buddhist vision of nirvana in *Wave UFO*. She has said that the experience of the piece reveals that "human beings as collective living beings shall unify and transcend cultural differences and national borders through positive and creative evolution."[7]

THE UNITED STATES AND CANADA

New York may no longer be the one center of the art world, but much that is vital continues to happen in this and other North American cities today. There is still a certain cachet in

[7] Bregrenz, Austria (March 23, 2003), "Wave UFO" by Mariko Mori in Kunsthaus Bregenz—A "Walk-in" Sculpture and Virtual Voyage in Space. http://swissart.ch/e/news/index.php3?gl_cont=%2Fe%2Fnews%2Farchive-article.php3%3Fmyeditid%3D308%261angindex%3Den.

exhibiting in galleries in New York City, Los Angeles, Chicago, and Toronto, and architects still compete for major projects in these places.

Stephen Holden, the *New York Times* film critic, considers Matthew Barney (b. 1967) to be "the most important American artist of his generation." His works encompass mediums including drawing, sculpture, performance, photography, video, film, and installation. Barney is perhaps best known for his *Cremaster* film series, in which androgynous nymphs, satyrs, and other legendary figures are, or are not, what they seem to be. The narratives are peppered with symbolic pagan pageantry, but they circle around various ritual masculine athletic challenges—a recurring theme of sorts in Barney's work. His *Drawing Restraint* series is based on his posited parallels between resistance training for athletes and physical encumbrance as a way of challenging an artist to produce work. Early videos in the series show Barney climbing around his studio, burdened by various physical restraints as he struggled to make drawings. In an excerpt from *Drawing Restraint 9* (Fig. 22-37), Barney transfers the physical aspect of restraint to a commentary on restrictions in Japanese rituals. In this particular scene, the artist and his real-life partner, musician-performer Björk—dressed in the attire of a bride

22-37 MATTHEW BARNEY. *Drawing Restraint 9* (2005). Production still.

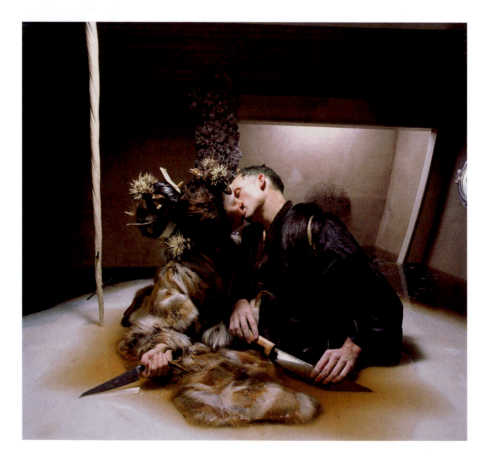

and groom in a traditional Shinto wedding—partake in the formalized tea ceremony ritual.

Elizabeth Peyton (b. 1965) is best known for small-scale but dazzling portraits of her friends, boyfriends, celebrities, and famed historical figures such as Napoleon, Marie Antoinette, and Queen Elizabeth—somewhat sanitized likenesses rendered in pastel hues and with a delicate touch. Recent work, such as the portrait of Matthew Barney (Fig. 22-38), features a more varied palette and a more forthright handling of paint. The broad, bold, gestural brushstrokes suggest a more concrete, unromanticized reality. Barney, with the circles beneath his eyes, staring into the distance or deep in thought, reads more like a "mortal" than a model or a star.

Photographer Andres Serrano (b. 1950) has generated more than his share of controversy with strangely beautiful images of what are often perceived as vulgar subjects. He has photographed KKK members, burn victims, and corpses in morgues and has included bodily substances such as semen,

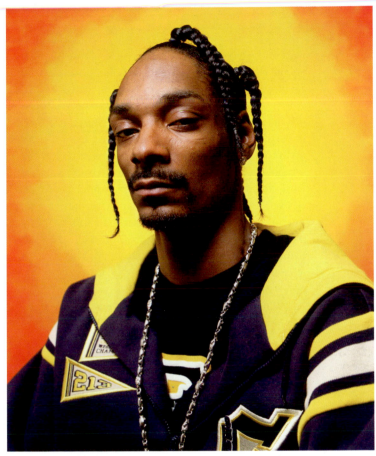

22-39 ANDRES SERRANO. *America* (*Snoop Dogg*) (2002). Cibachrome print, 45¼" × 37⅝". Brooklyn Museum, Brooklyn, NY.

menstrual blood, and human feces. One of his most notorious works is "Piss Christ," a photograph of a plastic crucifix submerged in a glass container of urine. One art critic remarked that his photos were "far more about being lurid than anything else."[8] Following the terrorist attack on the World Trade Center on September 11, 2001, Serrano began a series of portraits titled *America* with the goal of capturing the ethnic, racial, and socioeconomic diversity of the U.S. population—who we really are and how we live. A small sampling of what will constitute an eventual portfolio of 100 subjects includes a firefighter, a Boy Scout, a Playboy Bunny, a pimp, a migrant worker, a postal worker, a Holocaust survivor, and the entertainer Snoop Dogg (Fig. 22-39). The larger-than-life-size and straightforward simplicity of the backlit subjects gives them an iconic, heroic presence.

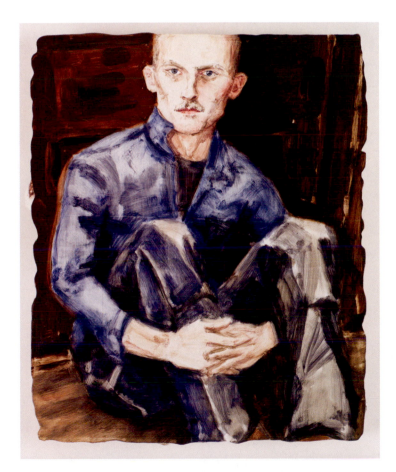

22-38 ELIZABETH PEYTON. *Matthew* (2008). Oil on board. 12½" × 9". At Gavin Brown.

---

[8] Adrian Searle, "Negative Energy," *The Guardian*, October 13, 2001.

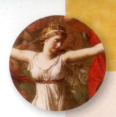

A CLOSER LOOK — JACQUES-LOUIS DAVID ON A BROOKLYN TENNIS COURT

JACQUES-LOUIS DAVID'S *Intervention of the Sabine Women* (Fig. 22-40), in all of its Classical idealization, patriotism, and heroism, hangs among other prized examples of Neoclassicism in a quiet, stately gallery in the Louvre Museum in Paris. But on a raw, wintry day in 2005, the myth that gave birth to one of David's most symbolic works was revisited—reenacted—on a tennis court in Brooklyn, New York. Video artist Eve Sussman was once again exploring the "pictorial evolution of a masterpiece." In Sussman's version, the men wore suits (in David's painting, they are in their birthday suits). The women were not in chic retro Roman attire; they wore vintage 1960s couture.

We have already studied Nicolas Poussin's *The Rape of the Sabine Women* (see Fig. 17-21), which recounts the subject of the Romans' abduction of their neighbors' (the Sabines') women for the dubious purpose of growing their city's population. David's painting is, in effect, a follow-up to the story. Three years after the attack by Romulus (Rome's founder) and his men, the Sabine men organized a counterat-

tack to reclaim their women. When they arrive, the Sabine-turned-Roman women intervene! For the first time in David's career as a history painter, he placed a woman at the center of the action. She is Hersilia, daughter of the Sabine Tatius and wife of Romulus. And she's not going back. Hersilia and other now-Roman women stand between the warriors and their children and, through their gestures, appeal for a peaceful solution to the crisis. As in most examples of the Neoclassical style, there is balance between action and restraint. The flailing arms and emotional expressions of the women contrast with the firmly planted stances of the fighting men. The movement seems controlled, even frozen, despite the overall sense of violence and chaos.

Enter Eve Sussman. Lights . . . camera . . . smoke machine. "Just walk around," her choreographer told the actors. "Okay, now find somebody in the group and lock eyes with them, like they are a magnet pulling you together. Now lean your body against theirs." From these first tentative movements, a full-scale battle scene ensued (Fig. 22-41). Clothes

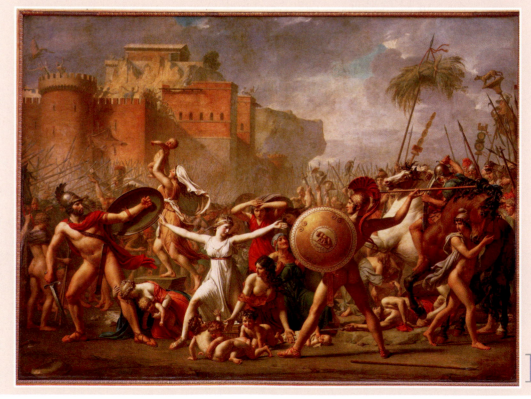

22-40 JACQUES-LOUIS DAVID. *The Intervention of the Sabine Women* (1799). Oil on canvas. 151½" × 205½". Louvre, Paris, France.

1 ft.

were ripped off; people bumped, grinded, and fell over one another. The women screamed, cried, and desperately held children up in the air. Figures moved through the mist stepping over the carnage, surveying the destruction. Cut.

The scene thus shot may or may not be used in Sussman's video-opera project, *The Raptus of the Sabine Women*, a piece in progress that is based on the myth of the Sabine women (*raptus*, in ancient Rome, meant "carrying off by force" and was a crime of property theft). It follows a similar successful work based on Diego Velázquez's *Las Meninas* (see Fig. 17-15) called *89 Seconds at Alcázar* (Fig. **22-42**). The video and film stills visualize imagined moments before and after the scene that Velázquez chose to represent. Sussman said of her thought process in generating the idea for *89 Seconds at Alcázar*: "[The painting] has the feeling of a snapshot . . . as if the Enfanta could walk out and come back again. And you think, if this is a film still, then there is a still that came before, and one that came after."

Unlike *89 Seconds at Alcázar*, which involved sets and elaborate costumes replicating the interior backdrop of Velázquez's famous portrait, *Raptus* is far more loosely based on the David prototype. The artist admits to making it up as she and the actors go along. Working with a loose outline rather than a complete script, the collaborators are coming up with their own version of the myth, based on interpretation, interaction, and reaction. "We know we want a fight involving the Sabine women, and other than that we don't have a clue." ●

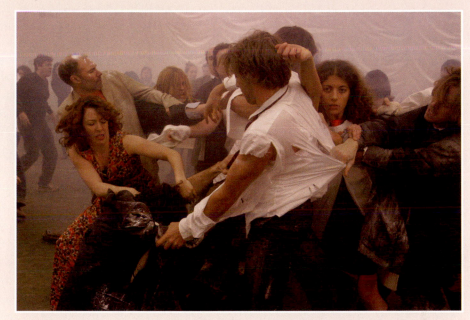

22-41 EVE SUSSMAN. Rehearsal footage for *The Raptus of the Sabine Women* (2005). Performance video.

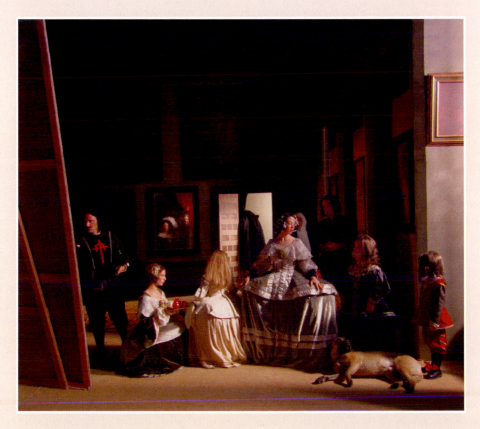

22-42 EVE SUSSMAN. *Her Back to the Camera* (2004). Screen grab from *89 Seconds at Alcázar*. Whitney Museum of American Art, NY.

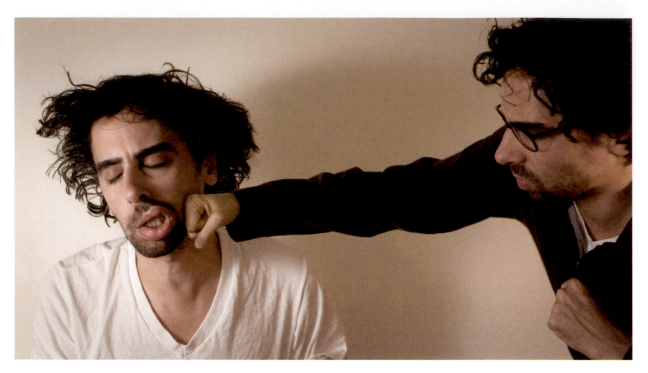

22-43 ANDREW ADOLPHUS. *Untitled* (2010). Digital photograph.

Canadian photographer and editor Andrew Adolphus is known for his eerie riffs on double portraits (Fig. 22-43). Using himself almost exclusively as subject, Adolphus constructs scenarios of emotional encounters (between himself and himself, of course) with computer manipulation. Although humorous and engaging in their trompe l'oeil effects, the portraits also conjure complex notions of the psychology of self, including inner conflict, self-criticism, and self-acceptance.

As an African American woman, Kara Walker (b. 1969) has experienced much of her life in terms of black and white and now produces much of her art in this dichotomous palette. She has worked in many mediums, but her life-size paper cutouts, which are used to silhouette her comments on the often brutal history of race relations in the United States, have captured the attention of the art world. Her figures are two-dimensional—often black figures pasted onto white gallery walls—and their flatness seems to echo the stereotyping that prevents people of one background from seeing people of other backgrounds in their full vitality and individualism.

Insurrection! (*Our Tools Were Rudimentary, Yet We Pressed On*) (Fig. 22-44) recounts some grisly events taken from the history of slavery in the United States. A nude slave is propositioned by a plantation owner. A woman with a baby barely escapes being lynched. Elsewhere a group tortures a victim. The piece fills the walls of a large room, where additional shapes are projected onto the walls, and visitors find their own shadows projected among them. Viewers are thus integrated into the haunting works, as if they share in culpabil-

ity or victimhood. Walker's installations are haunting in their disconnect between the lyrical shadow-puppet display and the dark content of the narrative.

Visitors to Architect Daniel Libeskind's (b. 1946) addition to the staid Royal Ontario Museum (Fig. 22-45) enter an atrium of interlocking spatial volumes from which they can glimpse exhibitions that epitomize the museum's two themes: nature and culture. The entire ground level is made into a seamless space that unifies what Libeskind refers to as the "inherited architecture" and the new construction. The crystal-like "explosion" of the addition draws attention to the fortresslike older building, as if asking the passerby to reconsider what is housed within and to evaluate it from a different perspective. The Royal Ontario Museum is just one of Libeskind's deconstructivist designs that marries traditional buildings with shockingly disparate additions.

All of the architecture in your textbook illustrates a significant historic monument, landmark building, or particularly good example of materials and construction methods. But architecture is one of those art forms that is ubiquitous in our lives and is just plain fun to watch out for. You will not be surprised to find "architecture" in a cathedral when you travel to Paris, France, but what about in a parking garage if you should happen to be in Miami, Florida? Parking garages are taken for granted. They are generally consigned to the basements of buildings or adjacent to shopping malls, usually unremarkable, simply functional, and sometimes outright tasteless. But Herzog & de Meuron, the architects of such acclaimed

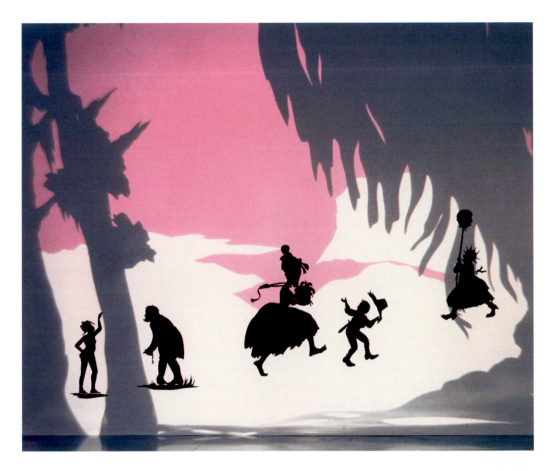

22-44 KARA WALKER. *Insurrection!* (*Our Tools Were Rudimentary, Yet We Pressed On*) (2000). Projection, cut paper, and adhesive on wall. Site-specific dimensions. Solomon R. Guggenheim Museum, NY.

22-45 DANIEL LIBESKIND. Addition, Royal Ontario Museum, Queen's Park and Bloor Street, Toronto (2007). Steel structure with aluminum cladding and glass facade. Toronto, Ontario, Canada.

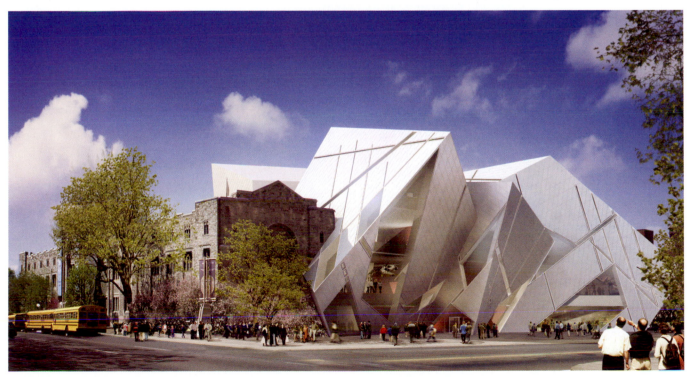

structures as the Olympic Stadium in Beijing (Fig. 14-27) and the Tate Modern Museum in London, brought the lowly parking garage to a new level at the top of the Lincoln Road pedestrian mall in South Beach (Fig. 22-46). The design is subversive in every respect, challenging our standard definition of functionality (in addition to housing cars, the garage space is rented for weddings and Bar Mitzvahs) and preconceived notions of what we typically need to feel safe (cars are kept from driving off the edges of open floors by industrial-strength cable and not concrete walls). Critics have hailed the garage as homage to the luxury car culture of Miami, and at least one Ferrari owner agrees. In spite of a tariff that is easily three or four times higher than local parking facilities, he exclaims: "I wouldn't even think of parking anyplace else when I'm downtown."

Social critics point out that the "post-9/11 wars," fought by volunteer troops, directly affect the lives of only about one percent of the American population. The rest of us come to know or to experience the violence and tragedy of war through mediated images—on television, in print, or in the historical fiction of high-budget film productions. Jon Kessler's *Palace at 4 a.m.* (Fig. 22-47) is a commentary on the constructions of reality by the media as well as a warning to media consumers to be suspicious of images—to consider how and why images are used, for what purpose and outcome. Kessler's mixed-media installation delivers images of destruction and symbols of unchecked authority in the pre-

ferred mode of the electronic era—a monitor. But his bytes and clips engulf us like a dark well of images that lurk in a perverse collective unconscious constructed in the wake of the terrorist attack. The title of Kessler's piece is identical to that of a work by Surrealist Alberto Giacometti that consists of a delicate wood structure—like a house of sticks without walls—in which evocative shapes entice us to divine their meaning. Created with his lover in mind, Giacometti said that they had "constructed a fantastical palace in the night—a very fragile palace of matches. At the least false movement a whole section would collapse. We always began it again." In his sculpture, a small bird skeleton seems to fly out a window; in Kessler's piece, toy bomber planes and GI Joe-style figures circle overhead, powered by infernal machinery that rattles and clangs. Here too, the whole of it (the world?) seems as though it might collapse.

Kessler has said that his work encapsulates rage, disappointment, and alienation. Shelly Silver's feature-length video *Suicide* (Fig. 22-48) follows the protagonist, Amanda (Silver herself), on her odyssey through the shopping malls, airports, and train stations of Asia, Europe, and Central America, in search for a reason to go on living. "Having it all"—the reliable and comforting patterns of life like a home, a husband, a family, even a career—is a goal that is disconnected from Amanda's "reality." Although her name means "worthy to be loved," Amanda plows alone through public spaces, like a tourist through life who is confronted and confronts. Because

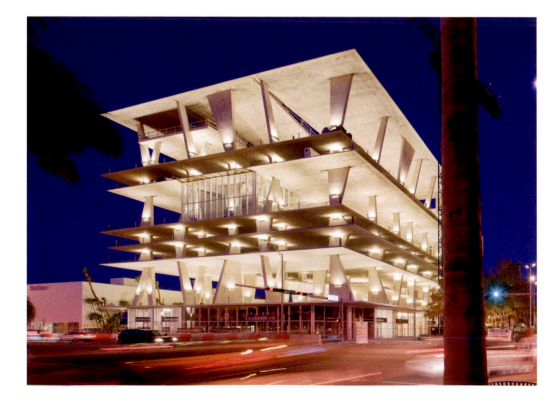

22-46 HERZOG & DE MEURON. 1111 Lincoln Road (2010). Miami Beach, FL.

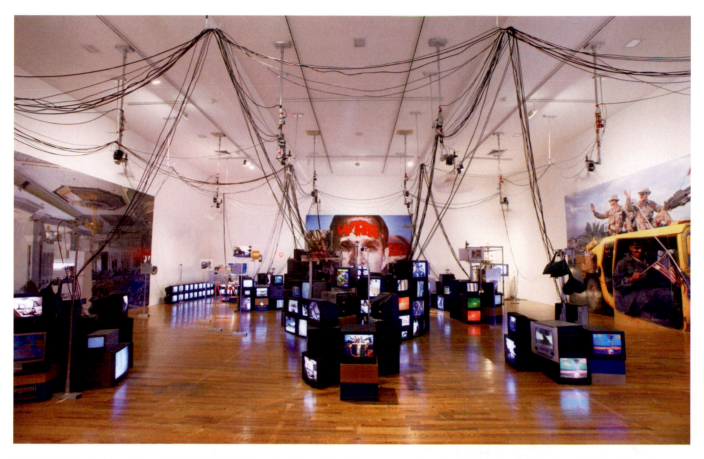

22-47 JON KESSLER. *The Palace at 4 A.M.* (2005). Mixed media with motors, video cameras and monitors. Dimensions variable. Phoenix Kulturstiftung/ Sammlung Falkenberg, Hamburg, Germany.

"normalcy" is not an option, her desires follow uncontrolled, unexpected, and sometimes fantastic courses—as does the video itself. In the absence of direction imposed from without or even within, life becomes characterized by anomie—a feeling of alienation, uncertainly, and normlessness that leads to drifting through time and space.

Artists throughout the world are informed by their cultural and national traditions and by their artistic training. Today, more than ever, they are also influenced by their knowledge of what is happening in the political world at large, and by their awareness of the art world all around them—past and present. Globalization has struck the world of art as it has struck our political, social, and economic lives. Yet even as their worldview has expanded, their perspectives have widened, and their choices have become many, artists have held fast to their individual and local ideas and ideals.

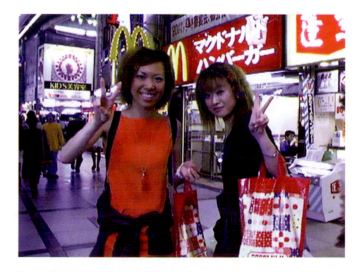

22-48 SHELLY SILVER. *Suicide* (2003). Feature-length video. 70 min.

ART TOUR LOS ANGELES

"Tip the world over on its side and everything loose will land in Los Angeles."
Frank Lloyd Wright

WHEN FRANK LLOYD WRIGHT MADE THIS REMARK the better part of a century ago, Los Angeles already had much of its present character. Along with the rest of California, Los Angeles was purchased by the United States in 1848, following the Mexican-American War. This Mexican past—and the current influence of a large Mexican-American population—is expressed in many ways, including the prevalent hacienda-style architecture, with its white or light-colored stucco walls and reddish tile roofs. Yet as part of the United States, Los Angeles has also imported architectural styles from the East Coast and the Midwest, so that many of Beverly Hills' palm-lined streets feature stately New England style colonial homes. Los Angeles' location on the Pacific Ocean also invites

cultural influences from the "Pacific Rim," as well as from China, Japan, and elsewhere across the ocean's broad waters.

Consider the kitschy pagoda-style architecture of Mann's Chinese Theatre, a fixture on Hollywood Boulevard since 1927, capped by a bronze roof and copper turrets. When we think of Los Angeles, we think of Hollywood, and this theatre boasts a court-yard of stars inlaid in the pavement—stars with the footprints of Hollywood's glitterati, including Marilyn Monroe, Tom Hanks, Brad Pitt, and Will Smith. The courtyard also has the "print" of the legs of famed World War II-era dancer and movie star, Betty Grable. Lotus-shaped fountains flank the courtyard. Two giant "heaven dogs" imported from China have guarded the theatre's entrance since its opening.

Also arriving in Los Angeles during the early twentieth century, by way of England and the East Coast, were Arts and Crafts style buildings, such as the Gamble House (1908–1909), built in the suburb of Pasadena. (Dorothy Parker described Los Angeles as "72 suburbs in search of a city.") Arts and Crafts houses are intended to be true to their materials, and the forms of the Gamble House are clearly defined by its wooden construction. The view from the front porch reveals a post-and-beam struc-ture (see Fig. 11-3A) influenced not only by the Eastern United States, but also by the Far Eastern architecture of Japan.

Los Angeles also boasts what is con-sidered to be the first modern steel frame house in the United States—the Lovell House built by architect Richard Neutra in 1927. The walls are made of gunite (sprayed-on concrete), which is com-monly used in swimming pools. One could say that the house landed in Los Angeles

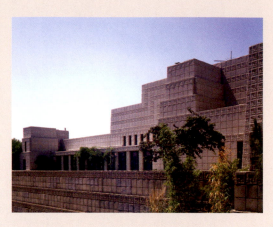

ENNIS HOUSE

from Chicago, where Neutra had become familiar with the use of steel frame con-struction in larger buildings. The Lovell House predates Philip Johnson's Glass House (New Canaan, Connecticut) and Mies van der Rohe's Farnsworth House (Plano, Illinois; see Fig. 21-43) by nearly a quarter of a century.

Frank Lloyd Wright's own Ennis House was built in 1923. Its stepped walls and textured concrete blocks ("textile blocks") are reminiscent of pre-Columbian (Mayan) Architecture—an influence from South America. The exterior of the house became well-known when it was used in the 1959 film, *House on Haunted Hill*. The house's interior has played a role in TV shows and films such as *Buffy the Vampire Slayer, Twin Peaks*, and *Blade Runner*. Wright's Free-man House, also in Los Angeles, was built in 1924 as an experimental prototype for mass-produced affordable housing. It also features the textile-block exterior of the Ennis House, and is the first house ever to use glass-to-glass corner windows. The photographer Edward Weston and the architects Philip Johnson and Richard

MANN'S CHINESE THEATRE

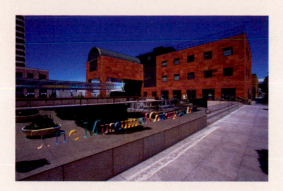

MUSEUM OF CONTEMPORARY ART
(MOCA), LOS ANGELES

complex overlooks the Pacific Ocean and downtown Los Angeles, and its galleries are illuminated by filtered natural light. The collection boasts Cezanne's *Still Life with Apples* (see Fig. 19-24), Van Gogh's *Irises*, and paintings by Titian and Rubens. (Try to find time to view the art as well as wander through the pools, fountains, and gardens.)

Downtown Los Angeles' Museum of Contemporary Art (MOCA) was designed by Japanese architect Arata Isozaki and was completed in 1986. Its post-modern design is composed of basic geometric solids and square windows. Its walls are made of natural reddish stone punctuated by transparent skylights. The entrance is defined by stone columns with a cylindrical barrel vault of glass-covered offices perched above. The MOCA has been home to a distinguished collection of art since 1940.

Frank Gehry's Disney Concert Hall, which was designed for downtown Los Angeles in 1991, opened in 2003. The Hall is home to the Los Angeles Philharmonic Orchestra and the Los Angeles Master Chorale, but has also housed the premiere of the film *The Matrix: Revolutions*, and has been featured in such films as *Iron Man*, *Get Smart*, and *The Soloist*, as well

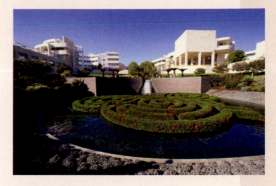

GETTY CENTER

as in many TV programs. Like Gehry's museum in Bilbao, Spain (see Fig. 2-18), the concert hall is a free-form collision of smoothly machined stainless steel forms. The exterior serves as a sort of testament to what technology allows us to do today, but the Hall's interior walls, ceiling, and floor are finished with a variety of woods for the sake of the acoustics. The musical director of the orchestra once remarked, "Everyone can now hear what the L.A. Phil is supposed to sound like."

 TO CONTINUE YOUR TOUR and learn more about Los Angeles, go to CourseMate.

Neutra all spent time at the house, which functioned as a meeting place for discussions about the future of the arts.

We think of Los Angeles as a leader in cultural and technological developments in the United States, so let's move up to contemporary times. The magnificent Getty Museum, designed by Richard Meier in the 1980s, hugs the Santa Monica Mountains on the Western edge of Los Angeles and has been likened to a modern Acropolis—the hill-top citadel and sanctuary that housed the Parthenon and other culturally significant structures in ancient Athens. The Getty

DISNEY CONCERT HALL

GLOSSARY

NOTE: Words in italics are also defined in the glossary. Figure numbers in blue illustrate the definition.

Abstract art A form of art characterized by simplified (abstracted) or distorted rendering of an object that has the essential form or nature of that object; a form of *nonobjective art* in which the forms make no reference to visible reality. (Fig. **4-6**)

Abstract Expressionism A style of painting and sculpture of the 1950s and 1960s in which artists expressionistically distorted abstract images with loose, gestural brushwork. Also see *expressionistic*. (Fig. **2-7**)

Academic art A neoclassical, nonexperimental style promoted by the Royal French Academy during the eighteenth and nineteenth centuries. (Fig. **19-9**)

Acropolis An elevated, fortified area of a Greek city and site of important temples; literally, "high city." (Fig. **14-10**)

Acrylic paint A paint in which pigments are combined with a synthetic plastic medium that is durable, water soluble, and quick drying. (Fig. **6-9**)

Action painting A contemporary method of painting characterized by *implied motion* in the brushstroke and splattered and dripped paint on the canvas. (Fig. **21-3**)

Actual balance Equal distribution of weight. Contrast with *pictorial balance*. (Fig. **3-7**)

Actual line The path made by a moving point; a connected and continuous series of points. Contrast with *implied line*. (Fig. **2-1**)

Actual mass The physical mass of an object as determined by its weight. Contrast with *implied mass*. (Fig. **2-15**)

Actual motion The passage of a body or an object from one place to another. Contrast with *implied motion*. (Fig. **2-71**)

Actual texture The texture of an object or picture, as determined by the sense of touch. Contrast with *visual texture*. (Fig. **2-49**)

Additive color system A system of mixing or overlapping different wavelengths of light, projected from different sources, to produce sensations of color and white light. Contrast with *subtractive color system*. (Fig. **2-41**)

Additive process In sculpture, adding material (as in modeling) or assembling materials (as in constructing) to create form. Contrast with *subtractive process*. (Fig. **9-10**)

Adobe Brick that has been dried in the sun rather than fired in a kiln.

Afterimage The lingering impression from a stimulus that has been removed. The afterimage of a color is its complement. Also see *complementary color*. (Fig. **2-76**)

Allegory A narrative in which people and events have been given consistent symbolic meanings; extended metaphor. (Fig. **4-16**)

Altar A raised platform or stand used for sacred ceremonial or ritual purposes.

Alternate a-b-a-b support system An architectural support system in which every other nave wall support sends up a supporting rib that crosses the vault as a transverse arch.

Alternate support system An architectural support system in which alternating structural elements bear the weight of the walls and the load of the ceiling.

Ambulatory In a church, a continuation of the side aisles of a *Latin cross plan* into a passageway that extends behind the choir and apse and allows traffic to flow to the chapels, which are often placed in this area (from *ambulare*, Latin for "to walk").

Amorphous Without clear shape or form. (Fig. **2-22**)

Amphitheater A round or oval open-air theater with an arena surrounded by rising tiers of seats. (Fig. **14-24**)

Analogous colors Colors that lie next to one another on the color wheel and share qualities of hue as a result of the mixture of adjacent hues; harmonious hues. (Fig. **2-43**)

Analytic Cubism The early phase of *Cubism* (1909–1912) during which objects were dissected or analyzed in a visual information-gathering process and then reconstructed on the canvas. (Fig. **20-7**)

Animation Creation of an animated *cartoon*; the photographing of a series of drawings, each of which shows a stage of movement that differs slightly from the previous one, so that figures appear to move when projected in rapid succession. (Fig. **8-29**)

Annunciation   The angel Gabriel's announcement to the Virgin Mary that she would give birth to Jesus.

Aperture   Opening.

Apocalypse   The ultimate triumph of good over evil foretold in Judeo-Christian writings.

Appropriation   (1) Borrowing elements from the non-art world such as newspapers and wine labels, as by Picasso and Braque. (2) The use of another artist's work as a basis for one's own. (Fig. 22-3)

Apse   A semicircular or polygonal projection of a building with a semicircular dome, especially on the east end of a church. (Fig. 15-1)

Aquarelle   A *watercolor* technique in which a transparent film of paint is applied to a white, absorbent surface.

Aquatint   An *etching* technique in which a metal plate is colored with acid-resistant resin and heated, causing the resin to melt. Before printing, areas of the plate are exposed by a needle, and the plate receives an acid bath. Aquatinting can be manipulated to resemble washes. (Fig. 7-12)

Aqueduct   A bridgelike structure that carries a canal or pipe of water across a river or valley (from Latin roots meaning "to carry water"). (Fig. 14-22)

Arch   A curved or pointed structure consisting of wedge-shaped blocks that span an open space and support the weight of material above by transferring the load outward and downward over two vertical supports, or piers. (**Figs. 11-3B** and **11-3C**)

Archaic period   A period of Greek art dating roughly 660–480 BCE. The term *archaic* means "old" and refers to the art created before the Classical period.

Architectural style   A style of Roman painting in which walls were given the illusion of opening onto a scene. (Fig. 14-21)

Architecture   The art and science of designing aesthetic buildings, bridges, and other structures to help people meet their personal and communal needs. (Fig. 11-22)

Architrave   In architecture, the lower part of an *entablature*, which may consist of one or more horizontal bands. (Fig. 14-4)

Archivolts   In architecture, concentric moldings that repeat the shape of an arch.

Armature   In sculpture, a framework for supporting plastic material.

Art Nouveau   A highly ornamental style of the 1890s characterized by floral patterns, rich colors, whiplash curves, and vertical attenuation (French for "new art"). (Fig. 19-38)

Assemblage   A work of art that is composed of (assembled from) found objects. Artists manipulate preexisting objects and sometimes incorporate them with other mediums, such as painting or printmaking. (Fig. 9-15)

Asymmetrical balance   Balance in which the right and left sides of a composition contain different shapes, colors, textures, or other elements and yet are arranged or "weighted" so that the overall impression is one of balance. Contrast with *symmetrical balance.* (Fig. 3-11)

Athena   The Greek goddess of wisdom, skills, and war.

Atmospheric perspective   An illusion of depth created through grades of texture and brightness, color saturation, and warm and cool colors. An indistinct or hazy effect produced by distance and the illusion of distance in visual art (the term derives from recognition that the atmosphere between the viewer and the distant objects would cause the effect).

Atrium   A hall or entrance court. (Fig. 15-1)

Automatic writing   Writing based on free association, practiced by Dadaists and Surrealists.

Automatist surrealism   An outgrowth of *automatic writing* in which the artist attempts to derive the outlines of images from the unconscious through free association. (Fig. 20-28)

Avant-garde   The leaders in new, unconventional movements; the vanguard (from French, "advance guard").

Balance   The distribution of the weight, mass, or other elements of a work of art so as to achieve harmony. (Fig. 3-7)

Balloon framing   In architecture, a wooden skeleton of a building constructed from prefabricated studs and nails. (Fig. 11-10C)

Baroque   A seventeenth-century European style characterized by ornamentation, curved lines, irregularity of form, dramatic lighting and color, and exaggerated gestures. (Fig. 17-11)

Barrel vault   A roofed-over space or tunnel constructed as an elongated arch. (Fig. 11-3D)

Basalt   A dark, tough volcanic rock. (Fig. 13-7)

Basket weaving   The process of weaving vegetable fibers (such as wood, grass, reeds, straw) into baskets. (Fig. 12-20)

Bas-relief   Sculpture that projects only slightly from its background (from *bas*, French for "low"). Contrast with *high relief.*

Batik   The process of making designs in cloth by waxing fabric to prevent dye from coloring certain areas; a cloth or design made in this way.

Bay   In architecture, the area or space spanned by a single unit of vaulting that may be marked off by piers or columns.

Bevel   To cut at an angle.

Bilateral symmetry   Mirror-type similarity between the sides of a composition. Also termed "pure" or "formal" symmetry. (Fig. 3-9)

Binder   A material that binds substances together.

Biomorphic   Having the form of a living organism. (Fig. 2-21)

Bisque firing   In ceramics, a preliminary firing that hardens the body of a ware.

Bitumen   Asphalt.

Black-figure painting   A three-stage firing process that gives vases black figures on a reddish ground. In the first, oxidizing phase of firing, oxygen in the kiln turns the vase and slip red. In the second, reducing phase, oxygen is eliminated from the kiln and the vase and slip turn black. In the third, reoxidizing phase, oxygen is reintroduced into the kiln, turning the vase red once more. (Fig. 14-2)

Brass   A yellowish alloy of copper and zinc.

Brick   A hard substance made from clay, fired in a kiln or baked in the sun, and used in construction. (Fig. 14-22)

Brightness gradient   The relative degree of intensity in the rendering of nearby and distant objects, used to create an illusion of depth in a two-dimensional work. (Fig. 2-69)

Bronze   A metal alloy consisting primarily of copper, with tin as the main additive.

Buddha   An enlightened being. (Fig. 18-28)

Buon fresco   True fresco, executed on damp lime plaster. Contrast with *fresco secco.*

Burin   A pointed cutting tool used by engravers. (Fig. 7-5)

Burnish   To make shiny by rubbing or polishing.

Buttress   To support or prop up construction with a projecting structure, usually built of brick or stone; a massive masonry structure on the exterior wall of a building that presses inward and upward to hold the stone blocks of arches in place. Also see *flying buttress*. (Fig. **11-3G**)

Byzantine   A style associated with Eastern Europe that arose after 300 CE, the year that Emperor Constantine moved the capital of his empire from Rome to Byzantium and renamed the city Constantinople (present-day Istanbul). The style was concurrent with the Early Christian style in Western Europe.

Calligraphy   Beautiful handwriting; penmanship; ornamental writing with a pen or brush.

Camera obscura   An early camera consisting of a large dark chamber with a lens opening through which an image is projected onto the opposite surface in its natural colors. (Fig. **8-4**)

Candid   In photography, unposed, informal.

Canon of proportions   A set of rules (or formula) governing what are considered to be the perfect proportions of the human body or correct proportions in architecture. (Fig. **3-7**)

Capital   In architecture, the area at the top of the shaft of a column that provides a solid base for the horizontal elements above. Capitals provide decorative transitions between the cylinder of the column and the rectilinear *architrave* above. (Fig. **14-4**)

Caricature   The gross exaggeration or distortion of natural features for the purpose of benign or malevolent satire. (Fig. **5-24**)

Carolingian Period   Referring to Charlemagne or his era. Charlemagne was emperor of the Holy Roman Empire from 800 to 814 CE.

Cartoon   Originally, a preparatory drawing made for a *fresco*, usually on paper and drawn to scale; a drawing that caricatures or satirizes an event or person of topical interest. Also see *animation*. (Fig. **5-23**)

Carving   In sculpture, the process of cutting away material, such as wood.

Cast iron   A hard alloy of iron containing silicon and carbon that is made by casting.

Casting   The process of creating a form by pouring a liquid material into a mold, allowing it to harden, and then removing the mold.

Catacomb   A vault or gallery in an underground burial place.

Cella   The small inner room of a Greek temple, used to house the statue of the god or goddess to whom the temple was dedicated. Located behind solid masonry walls, the cella was accessible only to the temple priests.

Centering   In architecture, a wooden scaffold used in the construction of an arch.

Central plan   A design for a church or a chapel with a primary central space surrounded by symmetrical areas around each side. Contrast with *longitudinal plan*. (Fig. **15-2**)

Ceramics   The art of creating baked clay objects, such as pottery and earthenware. (Fig. **12-1**)

Chalk   A form of soft limestone that is easily pulverized and can be used as a drawing implement. (Fig. **5-10**)

Charcoal   A form of carbon produced by partially burning wood or other organic matter; it can be used as a drawing implement. (Fig. **5-8**)

Chiaroscuro   An artistic technique in which subtle gradations of value create the illusion of rounded three-dimensional forms in space; also termed *modeling* (from Italian for "light-dark"). (Fig. **2-34**)

China   Whitish or grayish porcelain that rings when struck.

Cinematography   The photographic art of creating motion pictures.

Cinerary urn   A vessel used for keeping the ashes of the cremated dead.

Clapboard   In architecture, siding composed of thin, narrow boards placed in horizontal, overlapping layers.

Classical Art   Art of the Greek Classical period, spanning roughly 480–400 BCE; also known as Hellenic Art (from "Hellas," the Greek name for Greece).

Clerestory   In a *Latin cross plan*, the area above the *triforium* in the elevation of the nave, which contains windows to provide direct lighting for the nave. (**Figs. 15-28** and **15-29**)

Close-up   In cinematography or video, a "shot" made from very close range, providing intimate detail.

Coffer   A decorative sunken panel. (Fig. **14-29**)

Coiling   A pottery technique in which lengths of clay are wound in a spiral fashion.

Collage   An assemblage of two-dimensional objects to create an image; works of art in which materials such as paper, cloth, and wood are pasted to a two-dimensional surface, such as a wooden panel or canvas (from *coller*, French for "to paste"). (Fig. **20-8**)

Colonnade   A series of columns placed side by side to support a roof or a series of arches. (Fig. **13-14**)

Color negative film   Film from which color negatives are made.

Color reversal film   Film from which color prints ("positives") are made directly, without the intervening step of creating negatives.

Color-field painting   Painting that uses visual elements and principles of design to suggest that areas of color stretch beyond the canvas to infinity; figure and ground are given equal emphasis. (Fig. **21-10**)

Combine painting   A contemporary style of painting that attaches other media, such as found objects, to the canvas.

Complementary color   One of a specific pair of colors (e.g., red and green) that most enhance, or exaggerate, one another by virtue of their simultaneous contrast. Each pair of complementary colors contains one *primary color* plus the *secondary color* made by mixing the other two primaries. Because the complements do not share characteristics of hue and are as unlike as possible, the eye readily tells them apart. When complementary colors are placed next to one another, the effects are often jarring. (Fig. **2-44**)

Composition   The organization of the visual elements in a work of art.

Compound pier   In Gothic style, a complexly shaped vertical support to which a number of colonnettes (thin half columns) are often attached.

Compressive strength   The degree to which a material can withstand the pressure of being squeezed.

Computer art   The production of images with the assistance of the computer. Artists can use the computer to create art for its own sake or as a design tool, as in architecture and graphic design. (Fig. **8-40**)

Conceptual   Portrayed as a person or object is known or thought (conceptualized) to be; not copied from nature at any given moment. Conceptual figures tend to be stylized rather than realistic.

Conceptual art   An anticommercial movement begun in the 1960s in which works of art are conceived and executed in the mind of the artist. The commercial or communal aspect of the "work" is often a set of instructions for what exists in the artist's mind. (Fig. **1-20**)

Conceptual space   Space that is depicted as conceptualized by the artist rather than in realistic perspective. (Fig. **18-32**)

Conceptual unity   Unity in a work that is achieved through the relationship between the meaning and function of the images. (Fig. **3-5**)

Constructed sculpture   Sculpture in which forms are built up from such materials as wood, paper, string, sheet metal, and wire.

Constructivism   A sculptural outgrowth of *Cubist* collage in which artists attempt to use a minimum of mass to create volumes in space. (Fig. **20-16**)

Contact print   A photographic print that is made by placing a negative in contact with a sheet of photosensitive paper and exposing both to light so that the second sheet of paper acquires the image.

Conté crayon   A wax crayon with a hard texture. (Fig. **5-16**)

Content   All that is contained in a work of art: the visual elements, subject matter, and underlying meaning or themes.

Contour line   A perceived line that marks the edge of a figure as it curves back into space. (Fig. **2-3**)

Contrapposto   A position in which a figure is obliquely balanced around a central vertical axis. Also see *weight-shift principle*. (Fig. **16-13**)

Cool color   A color such as a blue, green, or violet that appears to be cool in temperature and tends to recede spatially behind warm colors.

Corbel   A supportive, bracket-shaped piece of metal, stone, or wood.

Corinthian order   The most ornate of the Greek architectural styles, characterized by slender, fluted columns and capitals with an acanthus leaf design. (Fig. **14-4**)

Cornice   In architecture, a horizontal molding that projects along the top of a wall or a building; the uppermost part of an *entablature*. (Fig. **14-4**)

Cosmetic palette   A palette for mixing cosmetics, such as eye makeup, with water. (Fig. **13-10**)

Crayon   A small stick of colored wax, chalk, or charcoal.

Cross-hatching   Intersecting sets of parallel lines used to shade a drawing. (Fig. **2-10**)

Crossing square   In architecture, the area that defines the right-angle intersection of the vaults of the nave and the transept of a church.

Cubism   A twentieth-century style developed by Picasso and Braque that emphasizes the two-dimensionality of the canvas, characterized by multiple views of an object and the reduction of form to cubelike essentials. (Fig. **20-6**)

Cuneiform   Wedge-shaped; descriptive of the characters used in ancient Akkadian,

Assyrian, Babylonian, and Persian alphabets.

Curvilinear   Consisting of a curved line or lines. (Fig. **2-18**)

Dada   A post–World War I movement that sought to use art to destroy art, thereby underscoring the paradoxes and absurdities of modern life. (Fig. **1-36**)

Daguerreotype   A photograph made from a silver-coated copper plate; named after Louis Daguerre, the innovator of the method. (Fig. **8-5**)

Deconstructivist architecture   A Postmodern approach to the design of buildings that disassembles and reassembles the basic elements of architecture. The focus is on the creation of forms that may appear abstract, disharmonious, and disconnected from the functions of the building. Deconstructivism challenges the view that there is one correct way to approach architecture.

Der Blaue Reiter (The Blue Rider)   A twentieth-century German Expressionist movement that focused on the contrasts between, and combinations of, abstract form and pure color. (Fig. **20-4**)

Design   The combination of the visual elements of art according to such principles as balance and unity.

De Stijl   An early twentieth-century movement that emphasized the use of basic forms, particularly cubes, horizontals, and verticals. (Fig. **20-17**)

Diagonal balance   The type of balance in which the elements on either side of a diagonally divided pictorial space seem to be about equal in weight, number, or emphasis. (Fig. **3-15**)

Diagonal rib   In architecture, a *rib* that connects the opposite corners of a groin vault.

Die Brücke (The Bridge)   A short-lived German Expressionist movement characterized by boldly colored landscapes and cityscapes and by violent portraits. (Fig. **20-3**)

Digital art   Art that makes use of—or is developed with the assistance of—electronic instruments, such as computers, that store and manipulate information through the use of series of zeros and ones (digits); including but not limited to web design, *graphic design*, and *digital photography.* (Fig. **8-41**)

Digital photography   Photography that stores visual information electronically rather than on film.

Direct-metal sculpture   Metal sculpture that is assembled by such techniques as

welding and riveting rather than *casting*. (Fig. **9-12**)

Dissolve   In cinematography and video, a fading technique in which the current scene grows dimmer as the subsequent scene grows brighter.

Dome   In architecture, a hemispherical structure that is round when viewed from beneath. (**Figs. 11-3H** and **11-3J**)

Doric order   The earliest and simplest of the Greek architectural styles, consisting of relatively short, squat columns, sometimes unfluted, and a simple, square-shaped capital. The Doric *frieze* is usually divided into *triglyphs* and *metopes*. (Fig. **14-4**)

Drawing   The art of running an implement that leaves a mark over a surface; a work of art created in this manner.

Dry masonry   Brick or stone construction without use of mortar.

Dry media   Drawing materials that do not involve the application of water or other liquids. Contrast with *fluid media*. (Fig. **5-4**)

Drypoint   A variation of engraving in which the surface of the matrix is cut with a needle to make rough edges. In printmaking, rough edges make soft rather than crisp lines. (Fig. **7-8**)

Dynamism   The Futurist view that force or energy is the basic principle that underlies all events, including everything we see. Objects are depicted as if in constant motion, appearing and disappearing before our eyes. (Fig. **20-12**)

Earthenware   Reddish tan, porous pottery fired at a relatively low temperature (below 2,000°F). (Fig. **12-10**)

Eastern Orthodox   A form of Christianity dominant in Eastern Europe, western Asia, and North Africa.

Editing   In cinematography and video, rearranging a film or video record to provide a more coherent or interesting narrative or presentation of the images.

Egg tempera   A painting medium in which ground pigments are bound with egg yolk. (Fig. **6-4**)

Emboss   To decorate with designs that are raised above a surface.

Embroidery   The art of ornamenting fabric with needlework. (Fig. **12-21**)

Emphasis   A design principle that focuses the viewer's attention on one or more parts of a composition by accentuating certain shapes, intensifying value or color, featuring directional lines, or strategically placing the objects and images. (Fig. **3-19**)

Empire period   The Roman period from about 27 BCE to 395 CE, when the empire was divided.

Emulsion   A suspension of a salt of silver in gelatin or collodion used to coat film and photographic plates.

Enamel   To apply a hard, glossy coating to a surface; a coating of this type. (Fig. **12-25**)

Encaustic   A method of painting in which the colors in a wax medium are burned into a surface with hot irons. (Fig. **6-2**)

Engraving   Cutting; in printmaking, an *intaglio* process in which plates of copper, zinc, or steel are cut with a *burin* and the ink image is pressed onto paper. (Fig. **7-7**)

Entablature   In architecture, a horizontal structure supported by columns, which, in turn, supports any other element, such as a pediment, that is placed above; from top to bottom, the entablature consists of a *cornice*, a *frieze*, and an *architrave*. (Fig. **14-4**)

Entasis   In architecture, a slight convex curvature of a column used to provide the illusion of continuity of thickness as the column rises.

Ephemeral art   Works that have a temporary immediacy or are built with the recognition that they will disintegrate. (Fig. **10-3**)

Equestrian portrait   A depiction of a figure on horseback. (Fig. **14-32**)

Ergonomics   The applied science of equipment design intended to minimize discomfort and therefore maximize performance to the user.

Etching   In printmaking, an *intaglio* process in which the matrix is first covered with an acid-resistant ground. The ground is removed from certain areas with a needle, and the matrix is dipped in acid, which eats away at the areas exposed by the needle. These areas become grooves that are inked and printed. (Fig. **7-10**)

Etruscan   From ancient Etruria, located along the northwestern shores of present-day Italy.

Expressionism   A modern school of art in which an emotional impact is achieved through agitated brushwork, intense coloration, and violent, hallucinatory imagery. (Fig. **20-3**)

Expressionistic   Art that aims to relay an artist's emotional response to a subject or event; art that reveals the inner feelings of an artist. Expressionistic art is typically associated with vivid color, vigorous brushwork, distortion or exaggeration

of imagery, or intimate subject matter. (Fig. **4-5**)

Extreme unity   Unification of all elements in a composition. (Fig. **3-1**)

Extrude   To force metal through a die or small holes to give it shape.

Facade   A French term for the face or front of a building. (Fig. **15-29**)

Fading   In cinematography and video, the gradual dimming or brightening of a scene, used as a transition between scenes.

Fantastic art   The representation of fanciful images, sometimes joyful and whimsical, sometimes horrific and grotesque. (Fig. **20-20**)

Fauvism   An early twentieth-century style of art characterized by the juxtaposition of areas of bright colors that are often unrelated to the objects they represent, and by distorted linear perspective (from French for "wild beast"). (Fig. **20-1**)

Favrile glass   A technique of mixing together different colors of hot glass to yield an iridescent finish. (Fig. **12-16**)

Fenestration   The arrangement of windows and doors in a structure, often used to create balance and rhythm as well as light, air, and access.

Ferroconcrete   Same as *reinforced concrete*. (Fig. **11-20**)

Fertile Crescent   The arable land lying between the Tigris and Euphrates rivers in ancient Mesopotamia.

Fertile Ribbon   The arable land lying along the Nile River in Egypt.

Fetish figure   An object believed to have magical powers. (Fig. **18-8**)

Fiber   A slender, threadlike structure or material that can be woven.

Fiberglass   Fine spun-glass filaments that can be woven into textiles.

Figurative art   Art that is derived from objects that can be seen in reality; also *representational art*.

Figure–ground relationship   The relationship between the primary subject (figure) and other parts of the composition (ground or background). (Fig. **2-23**)

Figure–ground reversal   A shift in a viewer's perception of a composition in which what at one moment appears to be the figure becomes the ground (or background), and vice versa. (Fig. **2-26**)

Filing   Metal or woodworking technique that removes material from the surface, often in an effort to achieve a smooth finish.

Film   A thin sheet of cellulose material coated with a photosensitive substance.

Flashback   In cinematography and video, an interruption of the story line with the portrayal of an earlier event.

Flash-forward   In cinematography and video, an interruption of the story line with the portrayal of a future event.

Flint glass   A hard, bright glass containing lead oxide.

Fluid media   Liquid-based drawing materials. Contrast with *dry media*. (Fig. **5-17**)

Flying buttress   A buttress that is exterior to a building but connected in a location that permits the buttress to support an interior vault. (Fig. **11-3G**)

Focal point   A specific part of a work of art that seizes and holds the viewer's interest. (Fig. **3-19**)

Foreshortening   Diminishing the size of the parts of an object that are represented as farthest from the viewer. Specifically, rendering parts of an object as receding from the viewer at angles oblique to the picture plane so that they appear proportionately shorter than parts of the object that are parallel to the picture plane.

Forge   To form or shape metal (usually heated) with blows from a hammer, press, or other implement or machine.

Form   The totality of what the viewer sees in a work of art; a product of the composition of visual elements.

Formalist criticism   An approach to art criticism that concentrates on the elements and design of works of art rather than on historical factors or the biography of the artist.

Forum   An open public space, particularly in ancient Rome, used as a market and a gathering place. (Fig. **14-36**)

Freestanding sculpture   Sculpture that is carved or cast in the round, unconnected to a wall, and thereby capable of being viewed in its entirety by walking around it. Freestanding sculpture can also be designed for a niche, which limits the visible portion of the sculpture.

Fresco   A type of painting in which pigments are applied to a fresh, wet plaster surface or wall and thereby become part of the surface or wall (from Italian for "fresh").

Fresco secco   Dry fresco; painting executed on dry plaster. Contrast with *buon fresco*.

Frieze   In architecture, a horizontal band between the *architrave* and the *cornice* that is often decorated with sculpture. (Fig. **6-1**)

Futurism   An early twentieth-century style that portrayed modern machines and the dynamic character of modern life and science. (Fig. **20-12**)

Gauffrage   An inkless *intaglio* process. (Fig. **7-13**)

Genre painting   A type of figurative painting that focuses on themes taken from everyday life.

Geometric period   A period of Greek art from about 900 to 700 BCE during which works of art emphasized geometric patterns. (Fig. **14-1**)

Geometric shape   A shape that is regular, easy to measure, and easy to describe, as distinguished from *organic* or *biomorphic shape*, which is irregular, difficult to measure, and difficult to describe. (Fig. **2-17**)

Gesamtkunstwerk   A German term widely used in aesthetics. Literally, "total work of art," it describes work that unifies a number of diverse mediums (painting, sculpture, architecture, stained glass) in a single work. (Fig. **17-11**).

Gesso   Plaster of Paris that is applied to a wooden or canvas support and used as a surface for painting or as the material for sculpture (from Italian for "gypsum").

Gild   To apply thin sheets of gold leaf or goldlike substance to a surface. (Fig. **6-4**)

Glassblowing   The art of shaping molten glass into glass objects by blowing air through a tube.

Glaze   In painting, a semitransparent coating on a painted surface that provides a glassy or glossy finish. In ceramics, a hard, glossy coating formed by applying a liquid suspension of powdered material to the surface of a ware, which is then dried and fired at a temperature that causes the ingredients to melt together. (Fig. **16-27**)

Globalization   In general, the mutual influence of cultures, economies, marketplaces, and current events that were once distant and separate. In art, more specifically the world-wide invasion of visual images and the art marketplace from various cultures into people's consciousness; multiculturalism and cross-culturalism in contemporary art.

Golden mean   The principle that a small part of a work should relate to a larger part of the work in proportion to the manner in which the larger part relates to the whole. (Fig. **3-33**)

Golden rectangle   A rectangle based on the *golden mean* and constructed so that its width is 1.618 times its height. (Fig. **3-34**)

Golden section   Developed in ancient Greece, a mathematical formula for determining the proportional relationship

of the parts of a work to the whole. (Fig. **3-33**)

Gothic   A Western European style developed between the twelfth and sixteenth centuries CE, characterized in architecture by ribbed vaults, *pointed arches*, *flying buttresses*, and steep roofs. (Fig. **15-28**)

Gouache   Watercolor paint that is made opaque by mixing pigments with a particular gum *binder*. (Fig. **6-12**)

Graphic design   Design for advertising and industry that includes design elements such as *typography* and images for communication purposes. (Fig. **12-38**)

Graphite   A soft black form of carbon used as a drawing implement (from *graphein*, Greek for "to write"). (Fig. **5-6**)

Graver   A cutting tool used by engravers and sculptors. (Fig. **7-5**)

Greek cross plan   A cross-shaped design, particularly of a church, in which the arms (nave and transept) are equal in length. (Fig. **15-5**)

Griffin   A mythical creature with the body and back legs of a lion, and the head, talons, and wings of an eagle.

Groin vault   In architecture, a vault that is constructed by placing *barrel vaults* at right angles so that a square is covered. (Fig. **11-3E**)

Ground   The surface on which a two-dimensional work of art is created; a coat of liquid material applied to a surface that serves as a base for drawing or painting. Also, the background in a composition. Also see *figure–ground relationship*.

Gum   A sticky substance found in many plants, used to bind pigments as found, for example, in silverpoint, chalk, and pastel drawings.

Gum arabic   A gum obtained from the African acacia plant.

Haniwa   A hollow ceramic figure placed at ancient Japanese burial plots.

Hard-edge painting   A contemporary style which emphasizes visual elements (line, shape, color) and de-emphasizes textural brushwork. Geometric forms are rendered with precision and smooth, glass-like finish. (Fig. **6-9**)

Hatcher   An engraving instrument that produces thousands of tiny pits that will hold ink.

Hatching   Fine parallel lines drawn or engraved to represent shading. (Fig. **2-10**)

Heliography   A photographic process in which *bitumen* is placed on a pewter plate to create a photosensitive surface that is

exposed to the sun (from *helios*, Greek for "sun").

Hellenism   The culture, thought, and ethical system of ancient Greece.

Herringbone perspective   A portrayal of space in which *orthogonals* vanish to a specific point along a vertical line that divides a canvas. (Fig. **14-21**)

Hierarchical scaling   The use of relative size to indicate the comparative importance of the depicted objects or people. (Fig. **3-28**)

High relief   Sculpture that projects from its background by at least half its natural depth. Contrast with *bas relief*. (Fig. **16-9**)

Horizon   In linear perspective, the imaginary line (frequently, where the earth seems to meet the sky) along which converging lines meet. Also see *vanishing point*.

Horizontal balance   Balance in which the elements on the left and right sides of the composition seem to be about equal in number or visual emphasis. (Fig. **3-13**)

Horus   The ancient Egyptian sun god.

Hudson River School   A group of nineteenth-century American artists whose favorite subjects included the scenery of the Hudson River Valley and the Catskill Mountains of New York State.

Hue   Color; the distinctive characteristics of a color that enable us to label it (as blue or green, for example) and to assign it a place in the visible spectrum.

Humanism   A system of belief in which humankind is viewed as the standard by which all things are measured.

Hybridity   In art, the mixing of the traditions of different cultures to create new blends and new connections. (Fig. **22-2**)

Hypostyle   In architecture, a structure with a roof supported by rows of piers or columns. (Fig. **21-46**)

Iconography   A set of conventional meanings attached to images; as an artistic approach, representation or illustration that uses the visual conventions and symbols of a culture. Also, the study of visual symbols and their meanings (often religious). (Fig. **4-16**)

Idealism   The representation of forms according to a concept of perfection.

Illumination   Illustration and decoration of a manuscript with pictures or designs. (Fig. **15-25**)

Illusionistic surrealism   A form of *surrealism* that renders the irrational content, absurd juxtapositions, and changing forms of dreams in a highly illusionistic manner that blurs the distinctions between the real and the imaginary. (Fig. **20-27**)

Imam   A prayer leader in a mosque; a religious and temporal ruler of a Muslim community or state.

Imbalance   A characteristic of works of art in which the areas of the composition are unequal in *actual weight* or *pictorial weight*. (Fig. **3-17**)

Impasto   Application of a medium such as oil or acrylic paint so that an actual texture is built up on a surface. (Fig. **2-47**)

Implied line   A line that is completed by the viewer; a discontinuous line that the viewer perceives as being continuous; a line suggested by series of points or dots or by the nearby end-points of series of lines; or a line evoked by the movements and glances of the figures in a composition. Contrast with *actual line*.

Implied mass   The apparent mass of a depicted object as determined, for example, by the use of forms or fields of color. Contrast with *actual mass*. (Fig. **2-16**)

Implied motion   An impression of movement created by the use of visual elements, composition, or content. Contrast with *actual motion*. (Fig. **2-72**)

Implied time   An impression of time's passage through the depiction of events that occur over a period of time. (Fig. **2-72**)

Impressionism   A late nineteenth-century style characterized by the attempt to capture the fleeting effects of light by painting in short strokes of pure color.

Incise   To cut into with a sharp tool.

Industrial design   The planning and artistic enhancement of industrial products. (Fig. **12-35**)

Installation   A work of art created for a specific gallery space or outdoor site. (Fig. **21-30**)

Intaglio   A printing process in which metal plates are incised, covered with ink, wiped, and pressed against paper. The print receives the image of the areas that are below the surface of the matrix. (Fig. **7-1B**)

Intarsia   A style of decorative mosaic inlay. (Fig. **16-6**)

International Gothic style   A refined style of painting in late fourteenth-century and early fifteenth-century Europe characterized by splendid processions and courtly scenes, ornate embellishment, and attention to detail.

Investiture   The fire-resistant mold used in metal casting.

Ionic order   A moderately ornate Greek architectural style introduced from Asia Minor and characterized by spiral scrolls (*volutes*) on capitals and a continuous *frieze*. (Fig. **14-4**)

Jamb   In architecture, the side post of a doorway, window frame, fireplace, etc.

Ka figure   According to ancient Egyptian belief, an image of a body in which the soul would dwell after death.

Keystone   In architecture, the wedge-shaped stone placed in the top center of an arch to prevent the arch from falling inward.

Kiln   An oven used for drying and firing ceramics.

Kinetic art   Art that moves, such as a mobile. (Fig. **2-70**)

Kinetic sculpture   Sculpture that actually moves (as opposed to providing the illusion of movement). (Fig. **2-70**)

Kinetoscope   An early motion picture device patented by Thomas Alva Edison with which films could be viewed by looking through the window of a cabinet housing equipment, including light and a high-speed shutter used to create the illusion of movement.

Kitsch   Overly sentimental work that is viewed as tasteless decoration but nevertheless has its own sort of nostalgic charm.

Kiva   A circular, subterranean structure built by Native Americans of the Southwest for community and ceremonial functions.

Kore figure   A clothed female figure of the Greek Archaic style, often adorned with intricate carved detail. A counterpart to the male kouros figure. (Fig. **14-8**)

Kouros figure   The male figure as represented in the sculpture of the geometric and Archaic styles (from Greek for "boy"). (Fig. **14-7**)

Krater   A wide-mouthed ceramic vessel used for mixing wine and water. (Fig. **12-1**)

Labyrinth   Maze.

Lamination   The process of building up by layers.

Land art   Site-specific work that is created or marked by an artist within natural surroundings. (Fig. **10-2**)

Lapis lazuli   An opaque blue, semiprecious stone.

Latin cross plan   A cross-shaped church design in which the nave is longer than the transept. (Fig. **15-1**)

Lavender oil   An aromatic oil derived from plants of the mint family.

Layout   A way of organizing design elements in printed material, such as a magazine or book page.

Lens   A transparent substance with at least one curved surface that causes the convergence or divergence of light rays passing through it. In the eye and the camera, lenses are used to focus images onto photosensitive surfaces.

Lift-ground etching   A technique in which a sugar solution is brushed onto a resin-coated plate, creating the illusion of a brush-and-ink drawing.

Light   The segment of the spectrum of electromagnetic energy that stimulates the eyes and produces visual sensations.

Linear   Determined or characterized by the use of line. (Fig. **5-19**)

Linear perspective   A system of organizing space in two-dimensional works of art in which lines that are, in reality, parallel and horizontal are represented as converging diagonals. The method is based on foreshortening, in which the space between the lines grows smaller until it disappears, just as objects appear to grow smaller as they become more distant. (**Figs. 2-61** to **2-67**)

Linear recession   Depth as perceived through the convergence of lines at specific points in the composition, such as the horizon line.

Lintel   In architecture, a horizontal member supported by posts. (Fig. **13-21**)

Lithography   A surface printing process in which an image is drawn onto a matrix with a greasy wax crayon. When dampened, the waxed areas repel water while the material of the matrix absorbs it. An oily ink is then applied, which adheres only to the waxed areas. When the matrix is pressed against paper, the paper receives the image of the crayon. (Fig. **7-1C**)

Living rock   Natural rock formations, as on a mountainside.

Local color   The hue of an object created by the colors its surface reflects under normal lighting conditions (contrast with *optical color*). Color that is natural rather than symbolic for the depicted objects.

Logo   A distinctive emblematic design or signature (short for "logogram" or "logotype") used to identify and advertise a company or an organization. (Fig. **2-42**)

Longitudinal plan   A church design in which the nave is longer than the transept and in which parts are symmetrical against an axis. Contrast with *central plan*. (Fig. **15-1**)

Longshot   In cinematography and video, an image or sequence made from a great distance, providing an overview of a scene.

Loom   A machine that weaves thread into yarn or cloth.

Lost-wax technique   A bronze-casting process in which an initial mold is made from a model (usually clay) and filled with molten wax. A second, fire-resistant mold is made from the wax, and molten bronze is cast in it. (Fig. **9-4**)

Lunette   A crescent-shaped space or opening (French for "little moon").

Magazine   In architecture, a large supply chamber.

Mandala   In Hindu and Buddhist traditions, a circular design symbolizing wholeness or unity.

Mannerist art   A sixteenth-century, post-Renaissance style characterized by artificial poses and gestures, vivid—sometimes harsh—color, and distorted, elongated figures. (Fig. **16-31**)

Manuscript illumination   Illustration or decoration of books and letters with pictures or designs. (Fig. **16-1**)

Masonry   Units of building material (such as brick, stone, concrete block, marble) laid in proximity and bound with mortar (a paste that hardens when set).

Mass   In painting, a large area of one form or color; in three-dimensional art, the bulk of an object. Also see *implied mass* and *actual mass*. (Fig. **2-15**)

Matrix   In printmaking, the working surface of the block, slab, or screen. In sculpture, a mold or hollow shape used to give form to a material that is inserted in a plastic or molten state.

Measure   Extent, dimensions, or capacity as determined by a standard.

Medium   The materials and methods used to create an image or object in drawing, painting, sculpture, and other arts (from Latin for "means").

Megalith   A huge stone, especially as used in prehistoric construction. (Fig. **13-3**)

Megaron   A rectangular room with a two-columned porch.

Mesolithic   Of the Middle Stone Age.

Metalwork   The process of refining and working with metals. (Fig. **12-24**)

Metope   In architecture, the panels containing *relief sculpture* that appear between the *triglyphs* of the *Doric frieze*. (Fig. **14-4**)

Mezzotint   A nonlinear engraving process in which the *matrix* is pitted with a *hatcher*.

Middle Ages   The thousand-year span (400–1400 CE) from the end of Roman Classical Art to the rebirth of Classical traditions in the Renaissance. Although this period is sometimes referred to as the Dark Ages, it was actually a time of important contributions to economics, science, and the arts.

Mihrab   A niche in the wall of a mosque that faces Mecca and thus provides a focus of worship. (Fig. **15-11**)

Mimesis   The practice of exact imitation in artistic representation.

Minaret   A tall, slender tower of a mosque from which Muslims are called to prayer. (Fig. **15-12**)

Minimalist art   Contemporary art that adheres to the philosophy and stylistic principles of Minimalism. (Fig. **21-14**)

Minimalism   A twentieth-century style of *non-objective art*, primarily seen in sculpture, in which visual elements are simplified and reduced to their essential properties. (Fig. **21-14**)

Mixed media   The use of two or more media to create a single image. (Fig. **1-35**)

Mobile   A type of *kinetic* sculpture that moves in response to air currents. (Fig. **2-70**)

Modeling   In two-dimensional works of art, the creation of the illusion of depth through the use of light and shade (*chiaroscuro*). In sculpture, the process of shaping a pliable material, such as clay or wax, into a three-dimensional form. (Fig. **2-10**)

Modernism   A contemporary style of architecture that deemphasizes ornamentation and uses recently developed materials of high strength.

Mold   A pattern or matrix for giving form to molten or plastic material; a frame on which something is modeled.

Monochromatic   Literally, "one-colored"; descriptive of images that are executed in a single color or with so little color contrast as to appear uniform in hue.

Monotype   In printmaking, a technique in which paint is brushed onto a matrix that is pressed against a sheet of paper, yielding a single print. (Fig. **7-17**)

Montage   In cinematography or video, the use of flashing, whirling, or abruptly alternating images to convey connected ideas, suggest the passage of time, or provide an emotional effect.

Monument   A type of site-specific public art that is intended to preserve the memory of a person or an event.

Mortuary temple   An Egyptian temple of the New Kingdom in which the pharaoh worshiped and was worshiped after death. (Fig. **13-14**)

Mosaic   A medium in which the ground is wet plaster on an architectural element, such as a wall, into which small pieces (tesserae) of colored tile, stone, or glass are assembled to create an image.

Muezzin   Crier who calls Muslims to prayer five times a day from a *minaret*.

Mummification   A process by which the skin and organs of a body are preserved by the removal of moisture or exposure to chemicals.

Mural   Image(s) painted directly on a wall or intended to cover a wall completely (from *muralis*, Latin for "of a wall"). (Fig. **6-1**)

Narrative editing   In cinematography or video, selecting from multiple images of the same subject to advance a story.

Narthex   A church vestibule that leads to the nave, constructed for use by the catechumens (individuals preparing to be baptized). (Fig. **15-1**)

Naturalism   Representation that strives to imitate nature rather than to express intellectual theory.

Naturalistic style   A style prevalent in Europe during the second half of the nineteenth century that depicted the details of ordinary life. (Fig. **11-22**)

Nave   The central aisle of a church, constructed for use by the congregation at large. (Fig. **15-1**)

Negative   In photography, an exposed and developed film or plate on which values—that is, light and dark—are the reverse of what they are in the actual scene and in the print, or *positive*.

Negative shape   Space that is empty or filled with imagery that is secondary to the main objects or figures depicted in the composition. Contrast with *positive shape*.

Neoclassical style   An eighteenth-century revival of Classical Greek and Roman art, characterized by simplicity and straight lines.

Neo-Expressionism   A violent, figurative style of the second half of the twentieth century that largely revived the German Expressionism of the early twentieth century. (Fig. **21-20**)

Neolithic   Of the New Stone Age.

New Image painting   An art style of the second half of the twentieth century that sought to reconcile abstraction and representation through the use of simplified images to convey the grandeur of abstract shapes without dominating visual elements such as color and texture. (Fig. **21-17**)

New Objectivity (Neue Sachlichkeit)   A post–World War I German art movement that rebelled against German Expressionism and focused on the detailed representation of objects and figures. (Fig. **1-19**)

Nib   The point of a pen; the split and sharpened end of a quill pen.

Nirvana   In Buddhist belief, a state of perfect blessedness in which the individual soul is absorbed into the supreme spirit.

Nonobjective art   Art that does not portray figures or objects; art without real models or subject matter. (Fig. **4-11**)

Nonporous   Not containing pores and thus not permitting the passage of fluids.

Ocher   A dark yellow color derived from an earthy clay.

Oculus   In architecture, a round window, particularly one placed at the apex of a dome (from Latin for "eye"). (Fig. **14-29**)

Oil paint   Paint in which pigments are combined with an oil medium. (Fig. **6-6**)

One-point perspective   Linear perspective in which a single vanishing point is placed on the horizon. (Fig. **2-60**)

Op Art   A style of art dating from the 1960s that creates the illusion of vibrations through afterimages, disorienting perspective, and the juxtaposition of contrasting colors. Also called "optical art" or "optical painting." (Fig. **2-76**)

Optical   Portrayal of objects as they are seen at the moment, especially depicting the play of light on surfaces. The painting of optical impressions is a hallmark of *Impressionism*.

Optical art   See *Op Art*. (Fig. **2-76**)

Optical color   The perception of the color of an object, which may vary markedly according to atmospheric conditions. Contrast with *local color*.

Oran   A praying figure.

Organic shape   A shape characteristic of living things and thus appearing soft, curvilinear, and irregular. Contrast with *geometric shape*. (Fig. **2-21**)

Orthogonal   Composed of right angles.

Ottonian   Of the period characterized by the consecutive reigns of German kings named Otto, beginning in 936 CE. (Fig. **15-19**)

Oxidizing phase   See *black-figure painting*.

Paint   A mixture of a pigment with a vehicle or medium.

Painting   The application of a pigment to a surface; a work of art created in this manner.

Palatine chapel   A chapel that is part of a palace.

Palette   A surface on which pigments are placed and prepared and from which the artist works; the artist's choice of colors as seen in a work of art.

Paleolithic   The "old" Stone Age during which the first sculptures and paintings were created.

Pan   To move a motion picture or video camera from side to side to capture a comprehensive or continuous view of a subject. (Fig. **8-25**)

Panel painting   A painting, usually in tempera but sometimes in oil, whose ground is a wooden panel. (Fig. **16-2**)

Panorama   An unlimited view in all directions.

Papyrus   A writing surface made from the papyrus plant.

Parallel editing   In cinematography or video, shifting back and forth from one event or story line to another.

Pastel   A drawing implement made by grinding coloring matter, mixing it with gum, and forming it into a crayon. (Fig. **5-11**)

Patina   A fine crust or film that forms on bronze or copper because of oxidation. It usually provides a desirable greenish or greenish blue tint to the metal.

Patrician   A member of the noble class in ancient Rome.

Pediment   In architecture, any triangular shape surrounded by *cornices*, especially one that surmounts the *entablature* of the *portico facade* of Greek temple. The Romans frequently placed pediments without support over windows and doorways.

Pencil   A rod-shaped drawing instrument with an inner shaft that is usually made of *graphite*. (Fig. **5-4**)

Pendentive   In architecture, a spherical triangle that fills the wall space between the four arches of a *groin vault* in order to provide a circular base on which a dome may rest. (Fig. **11-3l**)

Peplos   In Greek Classical Art, a heavy woolen wrap. (Fig. **14-8**)

Photography   The creation of images by exposure of a photosensitive surface to light. (Fig. **8-1**)

Photorealism   A movement dating from the 1960s in which subjects are rendered with hard, photographic precision.

Photosensitive   Descriptive of a surface that is sensitive to light and therefore capable of recording images. (Fig. **8-3**)

Photo silkscreen   A variation of *serigraphy*, or *silkscreen printing*, that allows the artist to create photographic images on a screen covered with a light-sensitive gel.

Piazza   An open public square or plaza. (Fig. **17-2**)

Pictograph   A simplified symbol of an object or action; for example, a schematized or abstract form of an ancestral image, animal, geometric form, anatomic part, or shape suggestive of a cosmic symbol or microscopic life.

Pictorial balance   The distribution of the apparent or *visual weight* of elements in two-dimensional works of art. Contrast with *actual balance*.

Picture plane   The flat, two-dimensional surface on which a picture is created. In much Western art, the picture plane is viewed as a window opening onto deep space.

Pier   In architecture, a columnlike support with a rectilinear rather than cylindrical profile. Piers generally support arches.

Pigment   Coloring matter that is usually mixed with water, oil, or other substances to make paint.

Pilaster   In architecture, a decorative element that recalls the shape of a structural *pier*. Pilasters are attached to the wall plane and project very little. They may have all the visual elements of piers, including base, shaft, *capital*, and *entablature* above. (Fig. **11-17**)

Pile weave   A weave in which knots are tied, then cut, forming an even surface. (Fig. **12-17**)

Plain weave   A weave in which the woof thread passes above one warp fiber and below the next.

Planar recession   Perspective in which the illusion of depth is created through parallel planes that appear to recede from the picture plane.

Planographic printing   Any method of printing from a flat surface, such as *lithography*. (Fig. **7-1C**)

Plastic elements   Those elements of a work of art, such as line, shape, color, and texture, that artists manipulate to achieve desired effects.

Plasticity   Capacity of a material to be molded or shaped. (Fig. **17-14**)

Plebeian class   In ancient Rome, the common people.

Plywood   Sheets of wood that resist warping because they are constructed of layers glued together with the grain oriented in different directions.

Pointed arch   An arch that comes to a point rather than curves at the top. (Fig. **11-3C**)

Pointillism   A systematic method of applying minute dots of unmixed pigment to the canvas; the dots are intended to be "mixed" by the eye when viewed. Also called "divisionism." (Fig. **19-23**)

Pop Art   An art style originating in the 1960s that uses commercial and popular images and themes as its subject matter. (Fig. **21-13**)

Porcelain   A hard, white, translucent, non-porous clay body. The *bisque* is fired at a relatively low temperature and the *glaze* at a high temperature. (Fig. **12-12**)

Portico   The entrance facade of a Greek temple, adapted for use with other buildings and consisting of a *colonnade*, *entablature*, and *pediment* (from Greek for "porch"). (Fig. **13-13**)

Positive shape   The spatial form defined by the objects or figures represented in works of art. Contrast with *negative shape*. (Fig. **2-24**)

Post-and-beam construction   Construction in which vertical elements (posts) and horizontal timbers (beams) are pieced together with wooden pegs. (Fig. **11-10A**)

Post-and-lintel construction   Construction in which vertical elements (posts) are used to support horizontal crosspieces (lintels). Also termed "trabeated structure." (Fig. **11-3A**)

Postimpressionism   A late nineteenth-century style that relies on the gains made by Impressionists in terms of the use of color and spontaneous brushwork but that employs these elements as expressive devices. The Postimpressionists, however, rejected the essentially decorative aspects of Impressionist subject matter. (Fig. **19-25**)

Postmodernism   A contemporary style that arose as a reaction to *Modernism* and that returns to ornamentation drawn from Classical and historical sources. (Fig. **21-45**)

Pottery   Pots, bowls, dishes, and similar wares made of clay and hardened by heat; a shop at which such objects are made. (Fig. **12-5**)

Poussiniste   Those Neoclassical artists who took Nicolas Poussin as their model. Contrast with *Rubeniste*.

Prefabricate   In architecture, to build beforehand at a factory rather than at the building site. (Fig. **11-15**)

Pre-Hellenic   Of ancient Greece before the eighth century BCE.

Primary color   A hue—red, blue, or yellow—that is not obtained by mixing other hues; all other colors are derived from primary colors.

Print   In printmaking, a picture or design made by pressing or hitting a surface with a plate or block; in photography, a photograph, especially one made from a *negative*. (Fig. **7-1**)

Prism   A transparent, polygonal body that breaks down white light into the colors of the visible spectrum.

Proportion   The relationship in size of the parts of the body, a building, or objects within a composition. (Fig. **3-7**)

Propylaeum   In architecture, a gateway building leading to an open court in front of a Greek or Roman temple; specifically, such a building on the *Acropolis*. (Fig. **15-1**)

Psychic automatism   A process of generating imagery through ideas received from the unconscious mind and expressed in an unrestrained manner. (Fig. **4-7**)

Psychological line   A connection between two points in a composition created by the action in a work, such as a figure pointing to an object or looking at another figure. Also referred to as a *compositional line*. (Fig. **2-7**)

Public art   Works created for public spaces. (Fig. **10-17**)

Quatrefoil   In architecture, a design made up of four converging arcs that are similar in appearance to a flower with four petals. (Fig. **16-8**)

Quill   A pen made from a large, stiff feather.

Radial balance   Balance in which the design elements radiate from a center point. (Fig. **3-16**)

Radiating chapel   An apse-shaped chapel, several of which generally radiate from the *ambulatory* in a *Latin cross plan*.

Raking cornice   The cornice, or frame, on the sloping sides of the pediments of classical temples.

Rasp   A rough file that has raised points instead of ridges.

Rationalism   The belief that ethical conduct is determined by reason; in philosophy, the theory that knowledge is derived from the intellect, without the aid of the senses.

Readymade   Found objects that are exhibited as works of art, frequently after being placed in a new context with a new title. (Fig. **1-36**)

Realism   A style characterized by accurate and truthful portrayal of subject matter; a nineteenth-century style that portrayed subject matter in this manner. (Fig. **4-9**)

Rectangular bay system   A church plan in which rectangular *bays* serve as the basis for the overall design. Contrast with *square schematism*.

Rectilinear   Characterized by straight lines. (Fig. **2-17**)

Reducing phase   See *black-figure painting*.

Reformation   A social and religious movement of sixteenth-century Europe in which various groups attempted to reform the Roman Catholic Church by establishing rival religions (Protestant sects).

Register   A horizontal segment of a structure or work of art.

Regular repetition   The systematic repetition of the visual elements in a work to create *rhythm*. (Fig. **3-24**)

Reinforced concrete   Concrete that is strengthened by steel rods or mesh. Same as *ferroconcrete*. (Fig. **11-20**)

Relative size   The size of an object or figure in relation to other objects or figures or the setting. See *scale*. (Fig. **2-57**)

Relief printing   Any printmaking technique in which the matrix is carved with knives so that the areas not meant to be printed (that is, not meant to leave an image) are below the surface of the matrix. (Fig. **7-1**)

Relief sculpture   Sculpture that is carved to ornament architecture or furniture, as opposed to *freestanding sculpture*. Also see *bas-relief* and *high relief*. (Fig. **16-9**)

Renaissance   A period spanning the fourteenth and fifteenth centuries CE in Europe. The Renaissance (French for "rebirth") rejected medieval art and philosophy; it first turned to Classical antiquity for inspiration and then developed patterns of art and philosophy that paved the way toward the modern world.

Reoxidizing phase   See *black-figure painting*.

Representational art   Art that presents natural objects in recognizable form. (Fig. **4-2**)

Republican period   The Roman period lasting from the victories over the Etruscans to the death of Julius Caesar (527–509 BCE).

Resolution   In video and digital photography, the sharpness of a picture as determined by the number of lines or pixels composing the picture.

Rhythm   The orderly repetition or progression of the visual elements in a work of art. (Fig. **3-24**)

Rib   In Gothic architecture, a structural member that reinforces the stress points of *groin vaults*. (Fig. **11-3F**)

Rococo   An eighteenth-century style during the Baroque era that is characterized by lighter colors, greater wit, playfulness, occasional eroticism, and yet more ornate decoration. (Fig. **17-25**)

Romanesque   A style of European architecture of the eleventh and twelfth centuries that is characterized by thick, massive walls, the *Latin cross plan*, the use of a *barrel vault* in the *nave*, round arches, and a twin-towered facade. (Fig. **15-21**)

Romanticism   A nineteenth-century movement that rebelled against academic *Neoclassicism* by seeking extremes of emotion as enhanced by virtuoso brushwork and a brilliant palette.

Root five rectangle   A rectangle whose length is 2.236 (the square root of 5) times its width that can be constructed by rotating the diagonal of a half square left and right. (Fig. **3-35**)

Rosette   A painted or sculpted circular ornament with petals and leaves radiating from the center. (Fig. **13-20**)

Rose window   A large circular window in a Gothic church, assembled in segments that resemble the petals of a flower, usually adorned with stained glass and plantlike ornamental work. (Fig. **15-29**)

Rubeniste   Those Romantic artists who took Peter Paul Rubens as their model. Contrast with *Poussiniste*.

Salon   An annual exhibition of the French Academy held in the spring during the eighteenth and nineteenth centuries.

Salon d'Automne   An independent exhibition of experimental art held in the autumn of 1905; named the "Salon of Autumn" to distinguish it from the Academic salons that were usually held in the spring.

Sanguine   Blood colored, ruddy; cheerful and confident (from Latin for "blood").

Sarcophagus   A coffin or tomb, especially one made of limestone. (Fig. **14-18**)

Satin weave   A weave in which the woof passes above and below several warp threads at a time.

Saturation   The degree of purity of hue measured by its intensity or brightness.

Scale   The relative size of an object compared to other objects, the setting, or people. (Fig. **3-26**)

Sculpture   The art of carving, casting, modeling, or assembling materials into three-dimensional figures or forms; a work of art made in such a manner.

S curve   Developed in the Classical style as a means of balancing the human form, consisting of the distribution of tensions so that tension and repose are passed back and forth from one side of the figure to the other, resulting in an S shape; *contrapposto*. (Fig. **14-14**)

Seal   A design or stamp placed on a document as a sign of authenticity.

Secondary color   A color that is derived from mixing pigments of *primary colors* in equal amounts. The secondary colors are orange (obtained by mixing red and yellow), violet (red and blue), and green (blue and yellow).

Serigraphy   A printmaking process in which stencils are applied to a screen of silk or similar material stretched on a frame. Paint or ink is forced through the open areas of the stencil onto paper beneath. Also termed *silkscreen printing*. (Fig. **7-1D**)

Service systems   In architecture, mechanical systems that provide structures with transportation, heat, electricity, waste removal, and other services.

Shade   The degree of darkness of a color determined by the extent of its mixture with black.

Shaft grave   A vertical hole in the ground in which one or more bodies are buried.

Shape   An area within a composition that has boundaries that separate it from its surroundings. (Fig. **2-12**)

Shaped canvas   A canvas that departs from the traditional rectangle and often extends the work into three-dimensional space, thus challenging the traditional orientation of a painting. (Fig. **21-19**)

Shinto   A major religion of Japan that emphasizes nature and ancestor worship. (Fig. **18-35**)

Shiva   The Hindu god of destruction and regeneration. (Fig. **18-30**)

Shrine   A repository for sacred relics and art objects intended to arouse feelings of religious devotion. A small structure or area intended for private religious devotion; a site or structure used in religious devotion.

Shutter   In photography, a device for opening and closing the *aperture* of a *lens* so that the film is exposed to light.

Siding   In architecture, a covering for an exterior wall.

Silica   A hard, glossy mineral compound of silicon and oxygen.

Silkscreen printing   A printmaking process in which stencils are applied to a screen of silk or similar material stretched on a frame. Paint or ink is forced through the open areas of the stencil onto paper beneath. Also termed *serigraphy*. (Fig. **7-1D**)

Silverpoint   A drawing medium in which a silver-tipped instrument inscribes lines on a surface that has been coated with a *ground* or pigment. (Fig. **5-3**)

Site-specific art   Art that is produced in or for one location and is not intended to be relocated. (Fig. **10-1**)

Slip   In ceramics, clay that is thinned to the consistency of cream for use in casting, decorating, or cementing.

Slow motion   A cinematographic process in which action is made to appear fluid but slower than actual motion by shooting a greater than usual number of frames per second and then projecting the film at the usual number of frames per second.

Soft-ground etching   An etching technique in which a ground of softened wax yields effects similar to those of pencil or crayon drawings.

Soundtrack   An area on the side of a strip of motion picture film that carries a record of the sound accompanying the visual information.

Square schematism   A church plan in which the crossing square serves as the basis for determining the overall dimensions of the building. Contrast with *rectangular bay system*.

Squeegee   A T-shaped tool with a rubber blade used to remove liquid from a surface.

Stainless steel   Steel that has been alloyed with chromium or other metals to make it virtually immune to corrosion. (Fig. **21-28**)

Stamp   To impress or imprint with a mark or design.

Steel   A hard, tough metal composed of iron, carbon, and other metals, such as nickel or chromium.

Steel cable   A strong cable composed of multiple intertwined steel wires. (Fig. **11-24**)

Steel-cage construction   A method of building that capitalizes on the strength of steel by piecing together slender steel beams to form the skeleton of a structure. (Fig. **11-16**)

Stele (or stela)   An engraved stone slab or pillar that serves as a grave marker.

Stippling   Drawing or painting small dots or dabs to create shading or a dappled effect. (Fig. **2-10**)

Stoicism   The philosophy that the universe is governed by natural laws and that people should follow virtue, as determined by reason, and remain indifferent to passion or emotion.

Stoneware   A ceramic that is fired at 2,300°F–2,700°F. The resulting object is usually gray but can be tan or reddish. Stoneware is *nonporous* or slightly porous and is used in dinnerware and ceramic sculpture. (Fig. **12-11**)

Stop   In photography, the *aperture* of a *lens*, which is typically adjustable; the "f-number."

Stopped time   In photography, an image that captures action in midmovement by exposing the film very briefly. (Fig. **2-71**)

Stroboscopic motion   The creation of the illusion of movement by the presentation of a rapid progression of stationary images, such as the frames of a motion picture.

Stupa   A dome-shaped Buddhist shrine.

Style   A characteristic manner or mode of artistic expression or design.

Stylobate   A continuous base or platform that supports a row of columns. (Fig. **14-4**)

Stylus   A pointed, needlelike tool used in drawing, printmaking, making impressions on electronic media, and so on.

Subtractive color   A system in which pigments are mixed, producing a color that is weaker, or reflects less light. Combining colors in paint (rather than light) produces gray or black. (Fig. **2-42**)

Subtractive process   In sculpture, the removal of material, as in carving. Contrast with *additive process.* (Fig. **9-2**)

Subversive texture   Texture that is chosen or created by artists to foil or undermine our ideas about the objects that they depict. (Fig. **2-55**)

Support   A surface on which a two-dimensional work of art is made.

Surrealism   A twentieth-century art style whose imagery is believed to stem from unconscious, irrational sources and that therefore takes on *fantastic* forms. Although the imagery is fantastic, it is often rendered with extraordinary realism. (Fig. **20-27**)

Symmetrical balance   Balance in which imagery on one side of a composition is mirrored on the other side. Symmetrical balance can be pure, or it can be *approximate*, in which case the whole of the work has a symmetrical feeling but with slight variations that provide more visual interest than would a mirror image. Contrast with *asymmetrical balance.* (Fig. **3-9**)

Symmetry   Similarity of form or arrangement on both sides of a dividing line.

Synthetic Cubism   The second phase of Cubism, which emphasized the form of the object and constructing rather than disintegrating that form. (Fig. **20-8**)

Synthetism   Gauguin's theory of art, which advocated the use of broad areas of unnatural color and primitive or symbolic subject matter. (Fig. **19-27**)

Telephoto lens   A lens that is shaped and distanced from the photosensitive surface so that it produces large images of distant objects.

Tempera   A kind of painting in which pigments are mixed with casein, size, or egg—particularly egg yolk—to create a dull finish. (Fig. **6-5**)

Tenebrism   A style of painting in which the artist goes rapidly from highlighting to deep shadow, using very little modeling.

Tensile strength   The degree to which a material can withstand being stretched.

Terra-cotta   A hard, reddish brown earthenware used in sculpture and pottery; usually left unglazed. (Fig. **12-9**)

Tertiary colors   Colors derived from mixing pigments or primary colors and the secondary colors that adjoin them on the color wheel.

Textile arts   Arts and crafts in which *fibers* are used to make functional or decorative objects or works of art.

Texture   The surface character of materials as experienced by the sense of touch. (**Figs. 2-47** and **2-48**)

Texture gradient   The relative roughness of nearby and distant objects in two-dimensional media; nearby objects are usually rendered with more detailed and rougher surfaces than distant objects. (Fig. **2-68**)

Tholos   In architecture, a beehive-shaped tomb. (Fig. **13-22**)

Throwing (a pot)   In ceramics, the process of shaping that takes place on the potter's wheel. (Fig. **12-4**)

Tie-dyeing   Making designs by sewing or tying folds in cloth to prevent a dye from reaching certain areas. (Fig. **12-22**)

Tier   A row or rank.

Tint   The lightness of a color as determined by the extent of its mixture with white.

Transept   The "arms" of a *Latin cross plan*, used by pilgrims and other visitors for access to the area behind the crossing square. (Fig. **15-1**)

Transverse rib   In architecture, a rib that connects the midpoints of a *groin vault.*

Tribune gallery   In architecture, the space between the *nave* arcade and the *clerestory* that is used for traffic above the side aisles on the second stage of the elevation.

Triforium   In a church, a gallery or arcade in the wall above the arches of the *nave*, *transept*, or *choir.*

Triglyph   In architecture, a panel incised with vertical grooves (usually three; hence, *tri*-glyph) that serve to divide the scenes in a *Doric frieze.* (Fig. **14-4**)

Trompe l'oeil   A painting or other art form that creates such a realistic image that the viewer may wonder whether it is real or an illusion (from French for "fool the eye"). (Fig. **2-52**)

Truss   A rigid, triangular frame used for supporting structures such as roofs and bridges. (Fig. **11-10B**)

Twill weave   A weave with broken diagonal patterns.

Two-point perspective   Linear perspective in which two *vanishing points* are placed on the horizon line. (**Figs. 2-61** and **2-67**)

Tympanum   Semicircular space above the doors of a cathedral.

Typography   The art of designing, arranging, and setting type for printing. (Fig. **12-36**)

Umber   A kind of earth that has a yellowish or reddish brown color.

Unity   The oneness or wholeness of a work of art. (Fig. **3-1**)

Value   The lightness or darkness of a color. (Fig. **2-30**)

Value contrast   The degrees of difference between shades of gray. (Fig. **2-32**)

Vanishing point   In linear perspective, a point on the horizon where parallel lines appear to converge. (Fig. **2-67**)

Vantage point   The actual or apparent spot from which a viewer observes an object or picture.

Vault   In architecture, any series of *arches* other than an *arcade* used to create space. See *barrel vault* and *groin vault.* (Fig. **11-3D**)

Vehicle   A liquid such as water or oil with which pigments are mixed for painting.

Veneer   In architecture, a thin layer of high-quality material used to enhance the appearance of the facade of a structure.

Venus The Roman goddess of beauty; a prehistoric fertility figure, such as the Nude Woman (*Venus of Willendorf*). (Fig. **13-2**)

Venus pudica A Venus with her hand held over her genitals for modesty. (Fig. **16-27**)

Vertical balance Balance in which the elements in the top and bottom of the composition are in balance. (Fig. **3-14**)

Video A catch-all term for several arts that use a video screen or monitor, including, but not limited to, commercial and public television, *video art*, and *computer graphics*.

Video art Works that feature moving images with recorded video or audio data that are, projected on objects or one or more screens or monitors. (Fig. **8-38**)

Visible light That segment of the spectrum of electromagnetic energy that excites the eyes and produces visual sensations.

Visitation In Roman Catholicism, the visit of the Virgin Mary to Elizabeth; a church feast commemorating the visit.

Visual elements Elements, such as line, shape, color, and texture, that are used by artists to create imagery. Also termed *plastic elements*.

Visual texture Simulated texture in a work of art; the use of line, color, and other visual elements to create the illusion of various textures in flat drawings and paintings. Contrast with *abstract texture*. (Fig. **2-50**)

Visual unity The unity in a work of art as created by use of visual elements. Contrast with *conceptual unity*. (Fig. **3-3**)

Vitrify To become hard, glassy, and nonporous.

Volume The mass or bulk of a three-dimensional work; the amount of space such a work contains. (Fig. **2-14**)

Volute In architecture, a spiral scroll ornamenting an Ionic or Corinthian capital.

Volute krater A wide-mouthed vessel (*krater*) with scroll-shaped handles. (Fig. **14-2**)

Voussoir A wedge-shaped stone block used in the construction of an arch.

Ware Pottery or porcelain; a good to be sold by a merchant. (Fig. **12-6**)

Warm color Colors—reds, oranges, and yellows—that appear to be warm and to advance toward the viewer. Contrast with *cool colors*.

Warp In weaving, the threads that run lengthwise in a loom and are crossed by the weft or woof.

Wash A thin, watery film of paint, especially watercolor, applied with even, sweeping movements of the brush.

Watercolor A paint with a water medium. Watercolors are usually made by mixing pigments with a gum binder and thinning the mixture with water. (Fig. **6-15**)

Weaving The making of fabrics by the interlacing of threads or fibers, as on a loom.

Webbing In architecture, a netlike structure that composes that part of a ribbed vault that lies between the ribs.

Weft In weaving, the yarns that are carried back and forth across the warp. Also called *woof*.

Weight-shift principle The situating of the human figure so that the legs and hips are turned in one direction and the chest and arms in another. This shifting of weight results in a diagonal balancing of tension and relaxation. See *contrapposto*. (Fig. **14-12**)

Wide-angle lens A lens that covers a wider angle of view than an ordinary lens.

Woodcut Relief printing in which the grain of a wooden matrix is carved with a knife. (Fig. **7-4**)

Wood engraving A type of relief printing in which a hard, laminated, nondirectional wood surface is used as the matrix. (Fig. **7-6**)

Woof See *weft*.

Zen A Buddhist sect that seeks inner harmony through introspection and meditation.

Ziggurat A temple tower in the form of a terraced pyramid, built by ancient Assyrians and Babylonians.

Zoogyroscope An early motion-picture projector.

Zoom To use a zoom lens, which can be adjusted to provide long shots or *close-ups* while keeping the image in focus.

CREDITS

CHAPTER 1: Page xviii Guild Hall East Hampton New York; **1-01** Réunion des Musées Nationaux/Art Resource, NY; **1-02** Jim Zuckerman/Flirt/Corbis; **1-03** 2009 Artists Rights Society (ARS), New York/ADAGP, Paris; **1-04** Scala/Art Resource, NY; **1-05** George Condo/Skarstedt Gallery; **1-06** Bildarchiv Preussischer Kulturbesitz/Art Resource, NY; **1-07** 2008 Banco de México Diego Rivera & Frida Kahlo Museums Trust. Av. Cinco de Mayo No. 2, Col. Centro, Del. Cuauhtémoc 06059, México, D.F; **1-08** Image courtesy of Michael Berger Gallery, Pittsburgh, PA; **1-09** The Andy Warhol Foundation, Inc./Art Resource, NY /©Copyright The Andy Warhol Foundation for the Visual Arts/ARS, NY; **1-10** 2009 Judy Chicago/Artists Rights Society (ARS), New York; **1-11** ©Corbis; **1-12** akg-images/Laurent Lecat; **1-13** ©The Metropolitan Museum of Art/Art Resource, NY; **1-14** The Carl Van Vechten Gallery of Fine Arts, Fisk University, Nashville, TN; **1-15** Bildarchiv Preussischer Kulturbesitz/Art Resource, NY; **1-16** Scala/Art Resource, NY; **1-17** CNAC/MNAM/Dist. Réunion des Musées Nationaux/Art Resource, NY; **1-18** The Museum of Modern Art/Licensed by SCALA/Art Resource, NY; **1-19** The Saint Louis Art Museum. Bequest of Morton D. May. 841:1983 ©2009 Artists Rights (ARS), New York/ VG Bild-Kunst, Bonn.; **1-20** Guild Hall East Hampton New York; **1-21** Kaz Chiba/Riser/Getty Images; **1-22** Courtesy of Sperone Westwater, NY; **1-23** The Museum of Modern Art/Licensed by SCALA/Art Resource, NY; **1-24** The Walter O. Evans Collection/SCAD Museum of Art.

Art ©Romare Bearden Foundation/Licensed by VAGA, New York, NY; **1-25** 2007 Jaune Quick-to-See Smith and Flomenhaft Gallery; **1-26** Purchased with funds from National Endowment for the Arts and Alliance for Contemporary Art, 1982.53. Photograph ©Denver Art Museum.; **1-27** NMeM/Royal Photographic Society Collection/SSPL/The Image Works; **1-28** Collection of the Solomon R. Guggenheim Museum, New York, Gift, Mr. and Mrs. Gus and Judith Lieber, 1988, 88.3620. ©Faith Ringgold 1988; **1-29** ©Francis G. Mayer/CORBIS; **1-30** Kunsthalle, Tubingen, Germany/©DACS /The Bridgeman Art Library; **1-31** Courtesy Zaha Hadid Architects; **1-32** Réunion des Musées Nationaux/Art Resource, NY; **1-33** Photograph courtesy of Suzanne Lacy and Leslie Labowitz; **1-34** Betye Saar (b.1926) The Liberation of Aunt Jemima, Collection of University of California, Berkeley Art Museum; purchased with the aid of funds from the National Endowment for the Arts (selected by The Committee for the Acquisition of Afro-American Art). Courtesy of Michael Rosenfeld Gallery, LLC, New York, NY; **1-35** Smithsonian American Art Museum, Washington, DC/Art Resource, NY; **1-36** 2009 Artists Rights Society (ARS), New York/ ADAGP, Paris/ Succession Marcel Duchamp; **1-37** Penn Center Suburban Station, Philadelphia. Courtesy of Henri Gross, Penn Associates, Philadelphia; **1-38** Courtesy of Dale Chihuly, Seattle, WA; **1-39** Commissioned by the Trustees of Dartmouth College, Hanover, New Hampshire. Hood Museum of Art. ©2009 Artists Rights Society

(ARS), New York/ SOMAAP, Mexico City; **1-40** Nik Wheeler/Encyclopedia/Corbis.

CHAPTER 2: Page 26 ©Iñaki Caperochipi/age fotostock/SuperStock; **2-01** Whitney Museum of American Art, purchase, with funds from the Gillman Foundation, Inc. (78.1.-4). ©2009 The LeWitt Estate/Artists Rights Society (ARS), New York; **2-02** Yale University Art Gallery/Art Resource, NY ©ARS, NY. Yale University Art Gallery/New Haven, CT/USA; **2-03** San Francisco Museum of Modern Art, San Francisco, CA. Alan M. Bender Collection. Bequest of Alan M. Bender. ©1981 Center for Creative Photography, Arizona Board of Regents; **2-05** Réunion des Musées Nationaux/Art Resource, NY; **2-06** Réunion des Musées Nationaux/Art Resource, NY; **2-07** Nameless and Friendless, 1857 (oil on canvas), Osborn, Emily Mary (1834-93)/Private Collection / The Bridgeman Art Library; **2-08** Copyright by the artists, www.gerlovin.com; **2-09** Hampton University Museum, Hampton, VA. Art ©Elizabeth Catlett./Licensed by VAGA, New York, NY; **2-10** Cengage Learning; **2-11** Scala/Art Resource, NY; **2-12** Hampton University Museum, Hampton, VA. ©2009 The Jacob and Gwendolyn Lawrence Foundation, Seattle/Artists Rights Society (ARS), New York; **2-13** Courtesy of the artist; **2-14** Image ©Jannes Linders. ©2009 Artists Rights Society (ARS), New York/ Pictoright, Amsterdam; **2-15** Herwig Prammer/Reuters/Corbis; **2-16** Mark Tansey. Courtesy Gagosian Gallery, New York; **2-17** Greenberg Van Doren Fine Art/ Artists Rights Society (ARS),

New York; **2-18** Eberhard Streichan/Bridge/ Corbis; **2-19** ©2011 Estate of Pablo Picasso/ Artists Rights Society (ARS), New York. Digital Image ©The Museum of Modern Art/Licensed by SCALA/Art Resource, NY; **2-20** Collection of Hanford Yang, New York, courtesy Phyllis Kind Gallery; **2-21** Elizabeth Murray, courtesy PaceWildenstein, New York; **2-22** 2008 Helen Frankenthaler; **2-23** Image ©CNAC/MNAM/ Reunion des Musees Nationaux/ Art Resource, NY. Courtesy Mary Boone Gallery; **2-24** Scott T. Smith/Documentary/Corbis; **2-25** Cengage Learning; **2-26** Digital Image ©The Museum of Modern Art/Licensed by SCALA/Art Resource, NY /© Jasper Johns/Licensed by VAGA, New York, NY; **2-27** Réunion des Musées Nationaux/Art Resource, NY; **2-28** Swim Ink 2, LLC/Corbis; **2-29** Ouwerkerk/ Redux; **2-30** Rheinisches Bildarchiv Köln. Courtesy of the artist; **2-31** Cengage Learning; **2-32** Cengage Learning; **2-33** © David Salle/ Licensed by VAGA, New York, NY. Courtesy of Mary Boone Gallery; **2-34** Bridgeman Art Library; **2-35** Museu Picasso, Barcelona. ©2009 Estate of Pablo Picasso/ Artists Rights Society (ARS), New York; **2-36** Courtesy of the Artist; **2-37** Digital Image ©The Museum of Modern Art/Licensed by SCALA/ Art Resource, NY; **2-38** The Solomon R. Guggenheim Museum, New York. Gift, The Mark Rothko Foundation, Inc., 1986. 86.3422 ©1998 Kate Rothko Prizel and Christopher Rothko/Artists Rights Society (ARS), New York; **2-39** Courtesy of Bausch & Lomb; **2-40** Cengage Learning; **2-41** Fritz Goro/Time & Life Pictures/Getty Images; **2-42** Fritz Goro/Time & Life Pictures/Getty Images; **2-43** Pezzimenti Photography, Courtesy of Norman and William Roth, Winter Haven, FL. Copyright Miriam Schapiro; **2-44** Courtesy Galerie Bruno Bischofberger, Zurich; **2-45** ©Audrey Flack, courtesy Louis K. Meisel Gallery; **2-47** Image ©the artist. Norton Museum of Art, West Palm Beach, Florida; Purchase, through the generosity of the Contemporary and Modern Art Council and the R. H. Norton Trust, 2006; **2-48** Credit: Portrait of Mrs. Peto No. 2, c.1972- 73 (oil on board), Kossoff, Leon (b.1926)/ Private Collection /The Bridgeman Art Library International; **2-49** City of Detroit Purchase, 28.99. Photograph ©1989 The Detroit Institute of Arts. ©2009 Artists Rights Society (ARS), New York/ADAGP, Paris; **2-50** Image copyright ©The Metropolitan Museum of Art/Art Resource, NY; **2-51** The Toledo Museum of Art, OH. Purchased with funds from the Libbey Endowment, Gift of

Edward Drummond Libbey, 1956.57; **2-52** Cheim & Read Gallery/© Lynda Benglis/ Licensed by VAGA, New York, NY; **2-53** Art ©James Rosenquist./Licensed by VAGA, New York, NY; **2-54** Erich Lessing/Art Resource, NY; **2-55** ©2007 Frank Stella/Artists Rights Society (ARS), NY; **2-56** ©2011 Artist's Right's Society (ARS), NY/ProLitteris, Zu_rich.. Digital Image ©The Museum of Modern Art/Licensed by SCALA/Art Resource, NY; **2-57** Cengage Learning; **2-58** Smithsonian American Art Museum, Washington, DC/Art Resource, NY; **2-59** Image copyright ©The Metropolitan Museum of Art/Art Resource, NY; **2-60** Cengage Learning; **2-61** Cengage Learning; **2-62** Cengage Learning; **2-63** Cengage Learning; **2-64** Cengage Learning; **2-65** Scala/Art Resource, NY; **2-66** Scala/Art Resource, NY; **2-67** Charles H. and Mary F. S. Worcester Collection, 1964.336, The Art Institute of Chicago. Photography ©The Art Institute of Chicago; **2-68** Charles H. and Mary F. S. Worcester Collection, 1964.336, The Art Institute of Chicago. Photography ©The Art Institute of Chicago; **2-69** Original purchase from the Mary Reynolds Babcock Foundation, Z. Smith Reynolds Foundation, ARCA Foundation, and Anne Cannon Forsyth, 1966.2.9. Reynolda House Museum of American Art, Winston-Salem, North Carolina; **2-70** Courtesy of Dallas Museum of Art, Dallas, TX; **2-71** University of Kentucky Art Museum. Bequest of George and Susan Prokauer 1992.17.55/ Copyright 2007 Estate of Alexander Calder/ Artists Rights Society (ARS), NY; **2-72** ©2004 Liz Magic Laser; **2-73** Galleria Borghese, Rome/Art Resource, NY; **2-75** Courtesy of The Metropolitan Museum of Art. Gift of Charles Bregler, 1941 (41.242.11). Copy photograph ©The Metropolitan Museum of Art, New York; **2-76** Photograph ©The Philadelphia Museum of Art. The Louise and Walter Arensberg Collection, 1950/Art Resource, NY. ©2011 Artists Rights Society (ARS), New York/ ADAGP, Paris/Succession Marcel Duchamp; **2-77** ©Bridget Riley 2011. All rights reserved, courtesy Karsten Schubert, London.

CHAPTER 3: Page 68 Chuck Close, courtesy of PaceWildenstein, New York; **3-01** Whitney Museum of American Art. Jointly owned by the Whitney Museum of American Art, New York, and the Metropolitan Museum of Art; Gift of Ethel Redner Scull 86.6 1a-jj. ©2009 Andy Warhol Foundation for the Visual Arts/Artists Rights Society (ARS), New York; **3-02** The Howard University Gallery of Art, Washington, D. C. Courtesy

Valerie Gerrard-Browne and Chicago History Museum; **3-03** The Nelson-Atkins Museum of Art, Kansas City, Missouri. Bequest of the artist, F75-21/2. /Licensed by VAGA, New York, NY; **3-04** Smithsonian American Art Museum, Washington, DC/ Art Resource, NY; **3-05** Courtesy of the artist and Flomenhaft Gallery; **3-06** New York State Office of General Services, Adam Clayton Powell, Jr.,State Office Building, New York, New York, USA; **3-07** Scala/Art Resource, NY; **3-09** Scala/Art Resource, NY; **3-10** Olga Bogatyrenko/Shutterstock; **3-11** Collection of Lois Fichner-Rathus. ©William Wegman; **3-12** Private Collection /The Bridgeman Art Library International; **3-13** 1990 Deborah Butterfield, Bozeman, Montana /© Deborah Butterfield/Licensed by VAGA, New York, NY; **3-14** NMPFT/Royal Photographic Society/SSPL/The Image Works; **3-15** Princeton University Art Museum. Gift of the Estate of Kay Sage Tanguy. y1964-162. Photo Credit: Bruce M. Whittey. ©Photo: Trustees of Princeton University; **3-16** Adil Jain Photography in perpetuity; **3-17** Victoria & Albert Museum, London/Art Resource, NY; **3-18** Magnum Photos, Inc./Robert Capa; **3-19** ©2011 Niki Charitable Art Foundation. All rights reserved/ARS, NY/ADAGP, Paris. Photograph: ©Whitney Museum of American Art, New York; **3-20** Chuck Close, courtesy of PaceWildenstein, New York; **3-21** Courtesy Ray Hughes Gallery, Sydney, Australia; **3-22** Chester Dale Collection, 1963.10.190. Image ©2007 Board of Trustees, National Gallery of Art, Washington, DC. ©2009 Estate of Pablo Picasso/Artists Rights Society (ARS), New York; **3-23** The Museum of Modern Art/Licensed by SCALA/Art Resource, NY; **3-24** The Metropolitan Museum of Art/Art Resource, NY; **3-25** ©Magdalena Abakanowicz. Courtesy of the Marlborough Gallery, New York; **3-26** Courtesy of Deitch Projects, New York and the Mary Boone Gallery; **3-27** NMPFT/RPS/SSPL/The Image Works; **3-28** ©2010 C. Herscovici, London/Artists Rights Society (ARS), New York. Location: Private Collection. Banque d'Images, ADAGP/Art Resource, NY; **3-29** Hirshhorn Museum and Sculpture Garden, Smithsonian Institution, Washington, DC. Gift of Rena Bransten, 1996, 96.39. Art ©Artists Legacy Foundation/Licensed by VAGA, New York, NY; **3-30** Bildarchiv Preussischer Kulturbesitz/Art Resource, NY; **3-31** Samuel H. Kress Collection, Image ©2006 National Gallery of Art, Washington, DC; **3-32** Albright-Knox Art Gallery, Buffalo, NY. Gift of Seymour H. Knox, 1964. Art

America, LLC/Alamy; **11-25** June Marie Sobrito/Shutterstock.com; **11-26** ©SOM/dbox; **11-27** ©SOM; **11-28** Lee Snider/The Image Works CSMO4362; **11-29** Jeff Titcomb/Alamy; **11-30** ©2005 Testa Architecture/Design, Los Angeles.; **11-31** Arcaid/Alamy; **11-32** Emilio Ambasz & Associates; **Page 232L** Photograph by Tom Jenkins, Courtesy Nasher Sculpture Center, Dallas, TX.; **Page 232R** Wes Thompson Photography/All residual rights reserved.; **Page 233B** Copyright REX/ OMA, Office for Metropolitan Architecture; **Page 233T** ©Kimbell Art Museum, Fort Worth, Texas/Art Resource, NY; **Page 233R** Hedrich-Blessing Ltd. Courtesy Bass Performance Hall, Fort Worth, TX.

CHAPTER 12: Page 234 Gary Mirando; **12-01** The Metropolitan Museum of Art. Bequest of Joseph H. Durkee. Gift of Darious Ogden Mills, and gift of C. Buxton Love. By exchange (1972.11.10). Photograph ©1999 The Metropolitan Museum of Art, New York. Courtesy Il Ministero per i Beni e le Attività Culturali of Italy; **12-02** Museum of Fine Arts, Houston, Texas, USA/Gift of Miss Ima Hogg/The Bridgeman Art Library International; **12-03** Thomas Cheryl Ann; **12-04** 2005 Fritz Henle Estate; **12-05** Photographed by Gary Mirando; **12-06** Emmanuel Cooper, photograph by Michael Harvey.; **12-07** Courtesy of the artist, Chester Nealie, woodfire potter.; **12-08** Courtesy of George Adams Gallery, New York. Art ©Estate of Robert Arneson/Licensed by VAGA, New York.; **12-09** The Metropolitan Museum of Art, NY.; **12-10** Photo by Eli Ping Weinberg. Image courtesy of the artist and Max Protetch Gallery, New York; **12-11** Claudi Casanovas. Photo courtesy of Lois Fichner-Rathus. Photo reproduced by kind permission of Galerie Besson.; **12-12** European Ceramic Work Centre, The Netherlands. Photograph by Corné Bastiaansen.; **12-13** Photography by Russell Johnson; **12-14** Photography by Terry Rishel; **12-15** Art Media/Heritage/The Image Works; **12-16** Image copyright ©The Metropolitan Museum of Art/Art Resource, NY; **12-17** Victoria & Albert Museum, London/Art Resource, NY; **12-18** Courtesy of the U.S. Department of the Interior. National Park Service. Sitka National Historical Park, Sitka, AK.; **12-19** The Collection of Craft Alliance.; **12-20** Phoebe A. Hearst Museum of Anthropology, University of California, Berkeley.; **12-21** Copyright ©1973 Faith Ringgold. Artist's collection.; **12-22** Copyright ©1991 Faith Ringgold.; **12-23** Copyright ©1994 Faith Ringgold/The New York City

Board of Education PS90, Brooklyn, NY; **12-24** Beniaminson/Art Resource, NY; **12-25** Erich Lessing/Art Resource, NY; **12-26** The Metropolitan Museum of Art, New York. The Michael C. Rockefeller Memorial Collection. Bequest of Nelson A. Rockefeller, 1979 (1979.206.1236) Photograph ©1998 The Metropolitan Museum of Art, New York.; **12-27** Courtesy of the artist. Photo by Rod Slemmons.; **12-28** Photo David Peters, courtesy of Del Mano Gallery, Los Angeles; **12-29** Courtesy of the artist.; **12-30** Teubner/StockFood Creative/Getty Images; **12-31** ©Foodcollection.com/Alamy; **12-32** PhotoLibrary; **12-33** Pixellover RM 3/Alamy; **12-34** Digital Image ©The Museum of Modern Art/Licensed by SCALA/Art Resource, NY; **12-35** Digital Image ©The Museum of Modern Art/Licensed by SCALA/Art Resource, NY; **12-36** ©graficart.net/Alamy; **12-37** AP Photo/Fabian Bimmer; **12-38** Courtesy of Pentagram Design; **12-39** Courtesy of the artist.; **12-40** Erich Lessing/Art Resource, NY; **12-41** Jerzy Dabrowski/dpa/Corbis; **12-42** Google Logo ©Google Inc. 2008, Reprinted with Permission.; **12-43** Courtesy Alliance for Climate Protection; **12-44** Alvin Ailey American Dance Theater; **12-45** www.squareddesignlab.com; **12-46** AP Photo/Jennifer Graylock; **12-47** ©Stephen Lock/The Daily Telegraph; **12-48** The Metropolitan Museum of Art, New York., Rogers Fund, 1906 (06.311) Photograph ©1997 The Metropolitan Museum of Art, New York.; **12-49** Karl Prouse/Catwalking/Getty Images; **12-50** REUTERS/Michael Caronna /Landov; **12-51** National Archives; **12-52** ©SOM; **Page 266L** Bettmann/CORBIS; **Page 266R** Bernard Annebicque/CORBIS SYGMA; **Page 267R** Photograph ©Spencer A. Rathus. All rights reserved.; **Page 267L** ©Stock Connection Blue/ Alamy.

CHAPTER 13: Page 268 Boltin Picture Library/ The Bridgeman Art Library; **13-01** Jean Vertut; **13-02** Erich Lessing/Art Resource, NY; **13-03** Adam Woolfitt/Corbis; **13-04A** Nik Wheeler/CORBIS; **13-04B** Cengage Learning; **13-05** Erich Lessing/Art Resource, NY; **13-06** Mesopotamian/Louvre, Paris, France /The Bridgeman Art Library; **13-07** Erich Lessing/Art Resource, NY; **13-08** Werner Forman/Topham /The Image Works; **13-09** David Poole/Robert Harding Picture Library; **13-10L** Werner Forman/Art Resource, NY; **13-10R** Erich Lessing/Art Resource, NY; **13-11** ©BeBa/Iberfoto/The Image Works; **13-12** Yann Arthus-Bertrand/CORBIS; **13-13** Marburg/Art Resource, NY; **13-14** De Agostini/

SuperStock; **13-15** Kenneth Garrett/National Geographic; **13-16** Scala/Art Resource, NY; **13-17** Sean Gallup/Getty Images; **13-18** Boltin Picture Library/ The Bridgeman Art Library; **13-19** Erich Lessing/Art Resource, NY; **13-20** ©Art Resource, NY; **13-21** ©SIME/eStock Photo; **13-22** Vanni/Art Resource, NY; **13-23** Nimatallah/Art Resource, NY; **13-24** Asian Art & Archaeology, Inc./CORBIS; **13-25** Freer Gallery of Art, Smithsonian Institution, Washington, DC.; **13-26** Paul Almasy/CORBIS; **13-27** ©John C. Huntington; **13-28** ©Alan Carey/Corbis; **13-29** Richard T. Nowitz/CORBIS; **13-30** Richard T. Nowitz/CORBIS; **13-31** Carmen Redondo/CORBIS.

CHAPTER 14: Page 294 Scala/Art Resource, NY; **14-01** Image copyright ©The Metropolitan Museum of Art/Art Resource, NY; **14-02** Canali Photobank; **14-03** The Metropolitan Museum of Art/Art Resource, NY; **14-04** Cengage Learning; **14-05** Courtesy of Saskia Ltd. ©Dr. Ron Wiedenhoeft; **14-06** SASKIA Ltd. Cultural Documentation. ©Dr. Ron Wiedenhoeft; **14-07** Image copyright ©The Metropolitan Museum of Art/Art Resource, NY; **14-08** Nimatallah/Art Resource, NY; **14-09** Scala/Art Resource, NY; **14-10** Herbert SA House-Lank/Superstock/Photolibrary; **14-11** ©Corbis; **14-12** Scala/Art Resource, NY; **14-13** Réunion des Musées Nationaux/Art Resource, NY; **14-14** The Bridgeman Art Library International; **14-15** Scala/Art Resource, NY; **14-16** Dying Gaul/Corbis Art/Corbis; **14-17** The Gallery Collection/Corbis; **14-18** Araldo de Luca/Corbis Art/Corbis; **14-19** Metropolitan Museum of Art, New York. Rogers Fund, 1912 (12.233). Photograph ©2003 The Metropolitan Museum of Art; **14-20** Canali Photobank; **14-21** Scala/Art Resource, NY; **14-22** Photograph ©Spencer A. Rathus. All rights reserved.; **14-23** akg/Bildarchiv Monheim/Achim Bed; **14-24** UPPA/Topham/The Image Works; **14-25** Harf Zimmermann/Focus/ Contact Press Images.; **14-26** ©David Lees/CORBIS; **14-27** LIU JIN/AFP/Getty Image; **14-28** Lois Fichner-Rathus; **14-29** Copyright: Photo Henri Stierlin, Geneve; **14-30** Scala/Art Resource, NY; **14-31** SASKIA Ltd. Cultural Documentation.; **14-32** copyright Spencer and Lois Fichner-Rathus; **14-33** Erich Lessing/Art Resource, NY; **14-34** ©Zev Radovan/ The Bridgeman Art Library; **14-35** foto Pontificia Commissione per l'Archeologia Sacra; **14-36** Canali Photobank; **14-37** John Burge/Cengage Learning, Originally published in A History of Roman Art by Fred S. Kleiner (Belmont, Calif.: Thomson Wadsworth, 2007;

Museum of Art/Art Resource, NY; **19-11** The Stone Breakers, 1849 (oil on canvas) (destroyed in 1945), Courbet, Gustave (1819-77)/Galerie Neue Meister, Dresden, Germany/©Staatliche Kunstsammlungen Dresden/The Bridgeman Art Library; **19-12** Erich Lessing/Art Resource, NY; **19-13** Alinari Archives/CORBIS; **19-14** Erich Lessing/ Art Resource, NY; **19-15** Erich Lessing/ Art Resource, NY; **19-16** CNAC/MNAM/ Dist. Réunion des Musées Nationaux/ Art Resource, NY; **19-17** Image copyright ©The Metropolitan Museum of Art/Art Resource, NY; **19-18** Erich Lessing/Art Resource, NY; **19-19** Image copyright ©The Metropolitan Museum of Art/Art Resource, NY; **19-20** Réunion des Musées Nationaux/ Art Resource, NY; **19-21** Giraudon/Art Resource, NY; **19-22** Glasgow Art Galleries and Museum; **19-23** Georges Seurat French, 1859-1891, A Sunday on La Grande Jatte -- 1884, 1884-86, Oil on canvas, 81 3/4 x 121 1/4 in. (207.5 x 308.1 cm), Helen Birch Bartlett Memorial Collection, 1926.224, The Art Institute of Chicago. Photography ©The Art Institute of Chicago; **19-24** The Art Institute of Chicago; **19-25** Art Resource/The Museum of Modern Art; **19-26** Self Portrait with Bandaged Ear, 1889 (oil on canvas), Gogh, Vincent van (1853-90)/©Samuel Courtauld Trust, The Courtauld Gallery, London, UK / The Bridgeman Art Library; **19-27** The Vision after the Sermon (Jacob wrestling with the Angel) 1888 (oil on canvas), Gauguin, Paul (1848-1903)/©National Gallery of Scotland, Edinburgh, Scotland /The Bridgeman Art Library; **19-28** The Art Institute of Chicago; **19-29** ©2011 The Munch Museum/The Munch-Ellingsen Group/Artists Rights Society (ARS), NY. Photo: ©Erich Lessing/Art Resource, NY; **19-30** Artists Rights Society; **19-31** The Boating Party, 1893-94 (oil on canvas), Cassatt, Mary Stevenson (1844-1926)/National Gallery of Art, Washington DC, USA/Index/The Bridgeman Art Library; **19-32** The Gallery Collection/ Corbis; **19-33** The Philadelphia Museum of Art/Art Resource, NY; **19-34** Image copyright ©The Metropolitan Museum of Art/Art Resource, NY; **19-35** Museum of Fine Arts, Boston; **19-36** Vanni/Art Resource, NY; **19-37** Fichner-Rathus Lois; **19-38** Erich Lessing/Art Resource, NY; **19-39** Art Resource, Inc.; **Page 472L** Jonathan Poore/Cengage Learning; **Page 472R** ©Pixtal/SuperStock; **Page 473** Sergio Gaudenti/Kipa/Corbis.

CHAPTER 20: **Page 474** ©2011 Estate of Pablo Picasso/Artists Rights Society (ARS), NY. Photo: ©Erich Lessing/Art Resource, NY; **20-01** Digital Image ©The Museum of Modern Art/Licensed by SCALA/Art Resource, NY; **20-02** Archives Matisse, France. ©2009 Succession H. Matisse, Paris/Artists Rights Society (ARS), New York.; **20-03** Dance Around the Golden Calf, 1910 (oil on canvas), Nolde, Emil (1867-1956)/Staatsgalerie Moderner Kunst, Munich, Germany /The Bridgeman Art Library; **20-04** Sotheby's Picture Library; **20-05** 2001 Estate of Pablo Picasso/Artists Rights Society (ARS), New York; **20-06** ©2011 Estate of Pablo Picasso/ Artists Rights Society (ARS), New York. Digital Image ©The Museum of Modern Art/Licensed by SCALA/Art Resource, NY; **20-07** ©2011 Artists Rights Society (ARS), NY/ADAGP, Paris. Photo: ©Bridgeman-Giraudon/Art Resource, NY; **20-08** Pablo Picasso, La bouteille de Suze (Bottle of Suze), 1912. Pasted papers, gouache, and charcoal, 25 3/4 x 19 3/4. Mildred Lane Kemper Art Museum, Washington University, St. Louis.; **20-09** ©2011 Estate of Pablo Picasso/Artists Rights Society (ARS), NY. Photo: ©Erich Lessing/Art Resource, NY; **20-10** ©The Estate of Jacques Lipchitz, courtesy Marlborough Gallery, New York; **20-11** ©2009 Estate of Alexander Archipenko/Artists Rights Society (ARS), New York.; **20-12** Digital Image ©The Museum of Modern Art/Licensed by SCALA/ Art Resource, NY; **20-13** The Museum of Modern Art/Licensed by SCALA/Art Resource, NY; **20-14** Virginia Museum of Fine Arts. Gift of Mr. and Mrs. Bruce Gotwald. Image ©Virginia Museum of Fine Arts. Photo by Katherine Wetzel. ©2009 The Georgia O'Keeffe Foundation/ Artists Rights Society (ARS), New York.; **20-15** ©2003 Whitney Museum of American Art; **20-16** The Work of Naum Gabo ©Nina & Graham Williams. Photograph by David Heald ©The Solomon R. Guggenheim Foundation, NY, 55.1429; **20-17** The Philadelphia Museum of Art/Art Resource, NY; **20-18** Artists Rights Society; **20-19** ©2011 Artists Rights Society (ARS), NY/ADAGP, Paris. ©Philadelphia Museum of Art/Corbis, 1950-134-14, 15.; **20-20** ©2011 Artists Rights Society (ARS), NY/VG-Bild Kunst, Bonn. Digital Image ©The Museum of Modern Art/Licensed by Scala/Art Resource, NY, 564.1939.; **20-21** Art Gallery of Ontario, Toronto, Canada/ Gift of Sam and Ayala Zacks, 1970/ The Bridgeman Art Library; **20-22** Réunion des Musées Nationaux/Art Resource, NY; **20-23** Artists Rights Society; **20-24** ©Gani Odutokun - 1991; **20-25** ©Visual Arts Library/Art Resource, NY; **20-26** ©2011 Artists Rights Society (ARS), NY/ADAGP, Paris. Digital Image ©The Museum of Modern Art/Licensed by Scala/Art Resource, NY, 00256.37; **20-27** Digital Image ©The Museum of Modern Art/Licensed by SCALA/ Art Resource, NY; **20-28** ©2011 Successió Miró/Artists Rights Society (ARS), NY/ ADAGP, Paris. Digital Image ©The Museum of Modern Art/Licensed by Scala/Art Resource, NY, 229.1937.; **20-29** ©2011 Artists Rights Society (ARS), NY/VG Bild-Kunst, Bonn. Photo ©Vanni/Art Resource, NY.; **20-30** ©2011 Artists Rights Society (ARS), NY/ VG Bild-Kunst, Bonn. Digital Image ©The Museum of Modern Art/Licensed by Scala/ Art Resource, NY.; **20-31** Digital Image ©The Museum of Modern Art/Licensed by Scala/ Art Resource, NY; **Page 498** Copyright ©2011 by Robert Frerck and Odyssey Productions, Inc.; **Page 499T** John Zich/zrImages/Corbis News/Corbis; **Page 499B** ©John Zich/Corbis; **Page 499R** Art Resource, NY ©ARS, NY.

CHAPTER 21: **Page 500** The Museum of Modern Art/Licensed by SCALA/Art Resource, NY; **21-01** The Art Institute of Chicago; **21-02** Albright Knox Art Gallery; **21-03** Center for Creative Photography, University of Arizona; **21-04** The Museum of Modern Art/Licensed by SCALA/Art Resource, NY; **21-05** Artists Rights Society; **21-06** The Art Institute of Chicago; **21-07** ©Fine Art Images/SuperStock; **21-08** Romare Bearden/Museum of Modern Art /© Romare Bearden Foundation/Licensed by VAGA, New York, NY; **21-09** The Art Institute of Chicago; **21-10** The Brooklyn Museum; **21-11** Art Resource; **21-12** Rheinisches Bildarchiv; **21-13** Collection of Whitney Museum of American Art, New York. Purchased with funds from the Friends of the Whitney Museum of American Art, 68.25. ©2009 Andy Warhol Foundation for the Visual Arts/Artists Rights Society (ARS), New York.; **21-14** Hirshhorn Museum and Sculpture Garden, Smithsonian Institution, Washington, DC. ©Donald Judd, licensed by VAGA, New York.; **21-15** Photograph courtesy of PaceWildenstein Gallery, New York. ©2009 Agnes Martin/ Artists Rights Society (ARS), New York; **21-16** incorporating a portion of Margaret Bourke White's photograph "Buchenwald, 1945." ©Time, Inc. Photograph courtesy of the Louis K. Meisel Gallery, New York.; **21-17** Courtesy of the artist. and The Pace Gallery; **21-18** Image courtesy Sperone Westwater, New York. ©Susan Rothenberg/Artists Rights Society (ARS), New York.; **21-19** Collection of the Walker Art Center, Minneapolis. Walker Special Purchase Fund, 1984.; **21-20** Courtesy of the Marian Goodman Gallery, New York.

INDEX